News Clippings from Delta,Utah
1861 - 1919

Including:
Abraham, Black Rock, Burtner, Deseret,
Hinckley, Leamington, Lynndyl, Oak City,
Oasis, South Tract, Sugarville, Sutherland,
Woodrow

Compiled from the Beaver County News (Utah), Deseret News (Utah), Deseret Evening News (Utah), Millard County Chronicle (Utah), Millard County Progress (Utah), Ogden Daily Enquirer (Utah), Provo Daily Enquirer (Utah), Salt Lake Herald (Utah), Salt Lake Telegram (Utah), Salt Lake Tribune (Utah), & contributions from other regional papers.

Often while working on family history (genealogy) I wonder about more than is listed on the pedigree sheets and am so grateful for their sacrifices and love for the generations to follow.

Some of the names include: Abbott, Abraham,Ackerman, Alldredge, Allen, Allison, Allred, Alory, Alva, Alvery, Anderson, Andrus, Ashby, Ashman, Badger, Band, Barben,Barnett, Barney, Basset, Beal, Beauregard, Beck, Beckstrand, Beeston, Bell, Bennett, Billings, Bishop, Black, Blake, Bliss, Booth, Bowman, Braddus, Brees, Brooks, Brower, Browen, Brunson, Buckanan, Bucknell, Bunker, Burke, Bushnell, Cahoon, Callister, Carey, Carlson, Chestnut, Chidester, Christensen, Clark, Clove, Coles, Conkling, Connelly, Cooper, Copening, Cottrell, Cox, Craig, Crane, Croft, Cronholm, Cropper, Damron, Davis, Day, Dennam, Dennison, Dixon, Dorrity, Draper, Dryden, DuBois, Durrins, Duston, Dutson, Eccles, Ednay, Ellison, Elmer, Felix, Finlinson, Fisher, Folsom, Foot, Forest, Fox, Freckleton, Fredericks, Freese, Fullmer, Funk, Furrer, Gardner, George, Giles, Greathouse, Green, Greener, Greenwood, Gronning, Gull, Hales, Hall, Hamilton, Hansen, Harnes, Harsh, Hawes, Hawkins, Hawley, Henry, Herrick, Hickman, Higgins, Hilliard, Hilton, Hogan, Holdridge, Hollenbeck, Hook, Houser, Huff, Hulda, Hultz, Humphries, Hunt, Hunter, Hutchingson, Ide, Iverson, Jackson, Jacob, Jacobson, Jarvis, Jeffrey, Jeffries, Jenkins, Jensen, Johns, Johnson, Jones, Keller, Kelly, Knight, Koch, Lackyard, Lake, Lambert, Langston, Larsen, Law, Leigh, Lewis, Leuthaeuser, Lippetts, Littlewood, Locke, Lovelers, Lovell, Lundahl, Lyman, Lyon, Mace, Mahew, Mahoney, Mansfield, Marshall, Martin, Maxfield, McClain, McClay, McCosh, McCullough, McLellan, McMahon, McPherson, Mead, Mecham, Melville, Memmott, Michelprang, Moffitts, Moody, Moulton, Murphy, Nazman, Nelson, Neutsch, Nielson, Nott, Olsen, Ottley, Overson, Pace, Pack, Parker, Partridge, Paswaters, Patton, Pay, Pederson, Peterson, Petty, Pierce, Pierson, Plimer, Pocock, Poecart, Porter, Pratt, Prows, Radford, Rawlinson, Ray, Reeve, Richards, Ridings, Rigby, Robison, rogers, Roper, Runyon, Russell, Rutherford, Reid, Ryan, Salmon, Sampson, Sandercock, Scannell, Schwartz, Searle, Shepherd, Sheriff, Sherrick, Shipley, Simkins, Simonson, Sinclair, Skeems, Slaughter, Smith, Snow, Sorenson, Stanworth, Stark, Sparksman, Spendlove, Steele, Steffenson, Stephenson, Stevens, Stewart, Strange, Strickley, Stringam, Stockham, Stott, Stout, Styler, Talbot, Taylor, Terry, Theobald, Thompson, Thurston, Tozer, Tracy, Turner, Tyler, Underhill, Volhart, Vorwaller, Walker, Wallace, Ward, Watts, Webb, Welch, Western, Whicker, Whitehead, Wilkins, Willets, Wind, Winn, Winterrose, Wood, Woodward, Workman, Wright, Young, and many, many more.

Some of the articles are easier to read than others, please consider that they are 100 years or more old.

ISBN-13: 978-1537710778

ISBN-10: 153771077X

THE NEW SETTLEMENT ON THE SEVIER.

FILLMORE CITY, May 26th, 1861.

BR. ELIAS:—Having returned from the new settlement on the Sevier, or rather from Deseret City, I thought a short account of that place might be interesting to you and to the readers of the News.

The settlement was commenced there one year ago last spring, and is situated on a natural canal, or an old bed of the river three miles from where it now runs. At the head of this canal there has been a substantial dam made in the river. The canal is large enough to contain all the water running in the stream and continues in a curve on high ground some twenty miles and comes back again into the river. From this natural canal a large tract of land, say fifteen thousand acres can be watered.

The men in that new settlement have done a great amount of hard work since they went there, for, in addition to making the dam in the river, they have made two dams in the canal, also many large water ditches, and from the work already done by making some smaller ditches, this vast tract of land can be watered. I can say with safety that if all the wealth of Millard county had been spent in making dams, canals and ditches, for irrigating purposes, none could have been constructed that would compare with the natural facilities that exist, for watering this tract of land.

The early sown grain there looked well.

CHILDREN DROWNED.—On the first instant Elias, only son of Hiram B. and Martha S. Bennett, aged about two years and four months, was drowned at Meadow Creek, near Fillmore. The child had not been absent from the house but a few minutes when his body was found in a small stream near by. All efforts made to resuscitate it were unavailing. On the 3d instant a daughter of Mr. Stephen Duggins, of Deseret city, Millard county, aged eight years, was drowned in Oak Creek, near that place. Particulars not reported.

FROM MILLARD COUNTY.

By letter from Bishop Callister, at Fillmore, under date of July 20th, we are informed that things in general throughout all the settlements in Millard county, were in a most prosperous condition. The high waters there, as in nearly every county in the State, did considerable damage, the carrying away of the dam in the Sevier river, at Deseret city, not being the least in the catalogue of losses, and it was feared that it would prove disastrous to the farming operations there, as all the farming lands in that vicinity were irrigated by the waters taken out by means of that dam which had been constructed at great expense and could not easily be rebuilt. The copious showers of rain with which the country has been visited since the first of June, had, however, rendered artificial irrigation measurably unnecessary, and the wheat crop there had matured, and the harvest had commenced with a fair prospect of an abundant yield—a blessing which the people duly appreciated. The crops in all parts of the county are represented as being unusually promising, but somewhat late.

It has been, heretofore, believed by many, that fruit could not be successfully cultivated in that part of the State, but Bishop Callister states that at Fillmore, the fruit trees, although young, are loaded with fruit, and that peaches, apples, apricots, plums, pears and grapes bid fair to do well, notwithstanding all that has been said about the unsuitableness of the location for successful orcharding.

The grain fields of the Indians, on Corn Creek, are represented as being inferior to none in that county. They have labored very industriously this season to provide for themselves the necessaries of life, and the prospects are, that their exertions will be crowned with complete success.

Deseret News
October 22, 1862

FROM MILLARD COUNTY.

FILLMORE CITY, Oct. 12th, 1862.

BR. ELIAS:

I resume my pen to give you a few items of news from Fillmore. Millard county has not seceded, but stands firm to the stars and stripes. We have beautiful weather this fall; crops of all kinds are abundant, especially potatoes; they exceed any I ever witnessed for size and quantity. I saw one to-day weighing 3lbs. 7oz., raised by Gabriel Huntsman.

At Deseret city, crops of all kinds have done well, notwithstanding they were not watered after the first days of June, the dam in the river having been taken away about that time. Preparations are now being made to put in another this fall. The cry in that place is not "Give us room that we may dwell," but they say to the Saints who wish to live by farming, that there is a good chance to get a good home there, and extend to as many as wish an invitation to come and dwell with them.

Our men and teams, that went to the States last spring to assist in bringing home the poor Saints, arrived home last Monday, the cattle looking remarkably well, evincing great care and good management on the plains. A company of Danish Saints came with the teams, most of them destined for Deseret. The people of Fillmore cheered their hearts on their arrival with the fruits of the earth in abundance, for which they felt truly thankful. Although they could not speak but little English, they showed by the tears of gratitude that rolled down their cheeks how they appreciated the reception. They held meeting this afternoon, speaking in their own tongue, and felt joyous that they had got home.

THOMAS CALLISTER

FROM MILLARD COUNTY.

FILLMORE CITY, }
Feb. 22d, 1863. }

ED. DESERET NEWS:

Dear Sir:—I again resume the pen to give you a few items about Millard County, having visited all the settlements since my return from the Legislature.

The people of *Deseret City* have been laboring faithfully during the winter, to replace the dam in the river, which was taken away by the high waters last summer. Much credit is due to their perseverance and zeal in this matter. They have already got the water into the canal, and from present appearances there is nothing to retard the progress of that great farming district.

The health of the people in the various settlements in this county, is in general very good. Some few have been afflicted with putrid sore throat, and at Corn Creek two children died lately very suddenly of that disease— one the daughter of W. E. Bridges, aged 10, and the other the daughter of Thomas Charlesworth, aged 12 years. We have found the following an effectual cure for the disease, viz.,—one teaspoonful of burnt alum, half a teaspoonful of saltpetre, to half a gill of honey or molasses well mixed, half a teaspoonful taken and well gurgled in the throat, to be repeated at short intervals until the cure is effected.

The winter so far has been very severe, and more snow has fallen than during any previous winter since the country was settled. Very few cattle have died to date, but should the winter continue much longer as severe as it has been many of them must perish.

The long winter evenings have passed off very agreeably and profitably to the young people of this place, by the establishing of an evening school, which was commenced last fall under the supervision of Benjamin Robison, and has been taught successfully by him, assisted by other qualified teachers, who have given their time and talent gratuitously to this valuable institution.

The scholars have made great proficiency in the following branches, viz.—reading, writing, arithmetic, English grammar, history and geography. There has quite an interest been manifested in the school by both old and young, and it bids fair to result in much good.

There is also an evening school for the instruction of the Danish Saints in the English language, taught by Dr. O. H. Speed, in which those concerned are very much interested. The Danes residing here were all rebaptized yesterday. We had a very interesting meeting at four o'clock, when they were confirmed. They enjoy themselves, and feel well in being permitted to gather in these latter days.

I Remain very respectfully,
Your Brother in the Gospel,
THOMAS CALLISTER.

Died: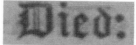

At Deseret city, Millard co., April 15th, GEORGE HENRY, son of George and Martha Lovell, aged 6 months and 4 days, of whooping cough and inflamation of the lungs.

PROCLAMATION

By James Duane Doty, Governor of Utah Territory.

EXECUTIVE OFFICE, G. S. L. CITY,
October 29th, 1863.

To all whom it may concern:—

At the General Election held in each precinct in the several counties of the Territory of Utah, on the first Monday in August, A. D. 1863, the following named persons received the highest number of votes in each of the Council Districts, for members of the Council, according to the returns received at the office of the Secretary of the Territory, from the several County Clerks, to wit:

Washington county—Erastus Snow,

Iron and Beaver counties — George A. Smith.

Millard and Juab counties—Amasa Lyman.

Sanpete county—O. Hyde,

Utah and Wasatch counties—L. E. Harrington, Aaron Johnston.

Great Salt Lake, Tooele, Summit and Green river counties—Daniel H. Wells, Wilford Woodruff, Albert Carrington, Daniel Spencer.

Davis and Morgan counties—Charles C. Rich.

Weber and Box Elder counties—Lorenzo Snow.

Cache county—Ezra T. Benson.

I do, therefore, declare the said persons duly elected members of the Council of the Legislative Assembly of Utah from their respective districts.

And also that at the same election, the following named persons received the highest number of votes in each Representative District for members of the House of Representatives, according to said returns, to wit:

Washington county—Orson Pratt, sen.

Iron county—Henry Lunt.

Beaver county—C. W. Wandell.

Millard county—Thomas Callister.

Juab county—Samuel Pitchforth.

Sanpete county—John Patten, R. N. Allred.

Utah county—A. K. Thurber, David Cluff, jr., Joseph E. Johnson.

Wasatch county—William M. Wall.

Summit and Green river counties—Ira Eldredge.

Great Salt Lake county—John Taylor, Edwin D. Woolley, A. P. Rockwood, John V. Long, F. D. Richards, John Van Cott.

Tooele county—John Rowberry.

Davis and Morgan counties—Wm. R. Smith, John Stoker.

Weber county—Jefferson Hunt, Lorin Farr.

Box Elder county—J. C. Wright.

Cache county—Peter Maughan, William B. Preston.

And I do therefore declare the said persons duly elected members of the House of Representatives of the Legislative Assembly of Utah from their respective districts.

JAMES DUANE DOTY.

Attest: AMOS REED, Secretary of Utah Territory.

Deseret News
November 18, 1863

Died:

At Deseret City, Millard county, Nov. 2, 1863, ROBERT C. EGBERT, aged 42 years, 5 months and 20 days.

Deceased was born in Green county, Indiana, May 12, 1821; was bapt'zed into the church by Elder David W. Patten, in the year 1833, was a member of the Mormon Battalion, a faithful Saint, and highly respected by all who knew him. He has left a widow and seven children to mourn their loss

At Petersburg, Millard county, Oct. 12, 1863, of consumption, CHARLES HOPKINS, aged 54 years 7 months and 22 days.

Deceased was born in the State of New Jersey, Feb. 20, 1803, was bapt'zed in 1844, went to Nauvoo in 1842, and in 1846, left for the western wilderness. He served in the Mormon Battalion, and returned to his family at Council Bluffs in 1849, he brought his family to this Tertory in 1853, he went to Iron county, where he resided till 1859, when he departed for Fillmore. He died firm in the faith of those principles revealed from the heavens in these last days, and which had governed and sustained him for upwards of twenty years.—[COM.

Deseret News
August 24, 1864

FROM MILLARD COUNTY.

FILLMORE CITY, Aug. 17, 1864.

EDITOR DESERET NEWS:

DEAR BROTHER:—Presuming a few items from Millard county might not be entirely uninteresting to your readers, I take the liberty to drop you a line.

Our citizens are now busy in the harvest field. A few early pieces of wheat were cut some weeks ago, but the crop in general is now being reaped, and, so far as I have learned, promises a rich reward to the husbandman.

No very great amount of grain is raised in and around Fillmore city, but the lack will be in a great measure, if not altogether, supplied the present season by the excellent crops raised at Deseret city, a fine grain growing region on the Sevier river, about thirty miles to the northwest. Of sugar cane there will probably be an average crop raised in Fillmore; how it is in other parts of the county I am not advised.

Fillmore promises to be a fine fruit growing district. It is really gratifying to behold so many fine orchards where, a few years ago, there was nothing to be seen but sage brush. Peaches will be very plentiful, and there will be quite a quantity of a fine assortment of choice apples and plums. Yesterday, br. Starley and myself had had the pleasure of visiting a few of the orchards here, and we saw some as fine looking apples and plums as one need wish to look upon. To name the proprietors of the various orchards we visited, and to enumerate the many varieties of fruit growing therein, would perhaps trespass upon your valuable time and space; but to give you an idea of the size of the apples, I cannot forbear mentioning that we found one in br. Stokes' garden that measured 11 5-16 inches in circumference; one in A. Henry's 11 1-2 inches; and one in br. Wm. Stott's 12 inches. We also saw some fine looking pears in br. A. Russell's orchard. One curiosity I saw in br. Starley's garden was a yearling plum tree bearing quite a quantity of fruit. I may also mention that I noticed in br. Starley's orchard some of the finest black and white mountain currants (seedling) I had ever before seen, some of which measured 2 11-16 inches in circumference.

Hoping you will excuse this, perhaps too lengthy scrawl, I subscribe myself your's very respectfully,　　　　JOHN KELLY.

ELECTION.—At the late Annual Election, the people of Millard county voted for the following gentlemen.

Territorial Officers.

Commissioners to locate University Lands:—Ira Eldredge, Chester Loveland, Vincent Shirtleff.

Representative:—Thomas Callister.

County Officers

Selectman:—Daniel Thompson.
Sheriff:—Byron Warner.
County Surveyor:—Thomas E. King
Treasurer:—Jno. W. Dutson
Superintendent of Common Schools:—Jno. Kelly.

Yours very Respectfully,
JNO. KELLY, County Clerk.

Correspondence.

DESERET CITY, Millard County,
December, 15, 1864.

EDITOR DESERET NEWS:

DEAR SIR:—Believing that you welcome with a degree of pleasure, favorable reports from the various settlements, I embrace the present opportunity to pen a few words in behalf of our young thriving settlement. Undoubtedly you have been favored with communications from abler pens than mine, concerning the past experience of the people here, together with the natural advantages of the surrounding country. I will endeavor to confine myself to present facts and future prospects.

The past season, on the whole, has been to us most favorable, and the amount of grain, &c., raised has been very considerable, taking into consideration the circumstances of the people last spring, in connection with the fact that they had almost entirely lost their crops for three successive years, and by that means been so reduced in circumstances as to be unable to procure the necessary amount of seed grain requisite for 1864. But, by the blessings of God, together with the united efforts of the people, ably assisted by the Fillmore brethren, we have been enabled to put in a dam across the Sevier river, which, whilst it supplys us with a sufficiency of water for all purposes, stands as a monument of the unity of purpose in the people of this county, and the good influence exercised over them by their leaders. Though the people here in the past have had cause to feel a little cast down, they now feel glad that they have stood by the rack, and feel that in their bins full of the staff of life they have an ample reward for previous disappointments.

In the past there has been but a few families here, but during the present fall we have received quite an immigration, and the cry is still they come; so that with the additional assistance thus obtained we calculate to make a permanent finish of the dam, a good foundation of which was laid last fall. In our eagerness after other matters public improvements are not forgotten, and, though through ill fortune we are now somewhat behind the older settlements, still the feeling is to improve upon the example set by the most enterprising of them. Neither is the training of our children forgotten, we have a good school, and trust to be able to progress in the elements of knowledge, as well as in other matters.

Deseret in the past has had its troubles and trials, but it would seem that better days are dawning. We have a good place here, one that bids fair to become one of the fairest and most blooming settlements in our mountain home. We have land in abundance, of good quality, and the water to irrigate it, and the general feeling is, together with past experience proving, that most all the things necessary for the comfort and enjoyment of the people can be produced in abundance with energy and industry.

But I have already tresspassed long enough upon your time. Praying for the prosperity of Deseret together with all the cities of the Saints,

I am yours ever,
THOMAS MEMMOTT.

Died:

At Round Valley, Millard co., Jan. 1, of inflammation, HARRIET ELIZABETH, infant daughter of Benjamin H. and Mary Jane Johnson, aged 13 days.

At Deseret City, Millard co., Jan. 6, 1865, PHEBE PIERCE, relict of the late Isaac W. Pierce, and daughter of Aaron M. and Julia Baldwin, aged 61 years, 10 months and 4 days.

She was baptized into the Church of Jesus Christ of Latter-day Saints, in the fall of 1833, in Chautauque co., New York, moved to Far West, Mo., in 1838, she endured with the rest of the Saints in Missouri, the persecutions peculiar to that time, and, finally, expulsion from the State, under the exterminating order of Gov. Boggs. She resided mostly in Illinois, until after the exodus of the Saints; she arrived in these valleys in 1852, where she enjoyed, until her decease, the blessings and privileges of the Saints.—COM.

DESERET CITY, Millard County,
April 21, 1867.

EDITOR DESERET NEWS:—

As a general thing we enjoy good health and are prospering, though our location is somewhat isolated and, as a consequence, we labor under some disadvantages.

We feel grateful to the Legislative Assembly for its liberal appropriations to make Mud Lake passable in all seasons.

The project of bridging the Sevier and getting the "Dixie" travel to pass through here is a good deal talked of. It seems that this route would have many advantages over the old one, principally in being so much shorter and, on the whole, a better road. If these improvements were made and the railroad through, we would feel ourselves in closer proximity to "the rest of mankind."

Our soil is rich, fertile and well adapted to the production of the various cereals, and we have water in abundance. This region has been justly called the granary of the south.

Br. William H. Walker has built a saw mill at Oak Creek and opened a road to the timber, and has now completed an excellent grist mill. It is one of Straud's patent, and is driven by a suction wheel. The work was superintended by Jonathan Smith.

It is said that br. Croft's mill makes as good an article of flour as any in the Territory.

Above all things we try to live our religion and enjoy the Spirit of it.

Yours,
JOHN FRECKLETON.

DESERET CITY, Millard Co.,
June 16, 1867.

EDITOR DESERET NEWS:

Our enterprising citizens have concluded to bridge the Sevier river at this place, and for this purpose have formed a company with br. Charles Robinson at the head, assisted by brs. Paul and Littlewood. Active opperations have already commenced; part of the timber is on the ground, and a party of men just returned from the mountains report that the timber is all cut, ready for hauling. The company anticipate having the bridge completed by the twenty-fourth of July.

It will be situated about sixty miles below the old bridge; and the route will be on a straight line due north and south, through Rush and Tooele Valleys; good road all the way, convenient watering places and plenty of grass.

On the 9th inst. we were favored with a visit from Bishop Callister and br. M. F. Lyman, when much valuable instruction was imparted. Among other good things we were counseled to take care of our sheep and improve them. The Bishop also established a Sunday school.

Our crops look very promising; there was a beautiful rain yesterday, that did our irrigating for us. We have completed a commodious Bowery. Our worthy President, br. Robinson, is a go-a-head man.

Yours truly,
JOHN FRECKLETON.

DESERET CITY, Millard Co.,
July 25th, 1867.

EDITOR DESERET NEWS:

Dear Brother:—The citizens of this place endeavored to keep the 24th in a manner befitting the occasion; and if good feelings, smiling faces and amply expressed satisfaction are to be the criteria judged by they evidently succeeded.

The order of the day was as follows:—Unfurling of the "Stars and Stripes" at sunrise, saluted by firing of cannon and musketry by Lieut. Thomas Cropper's company. At 9 a.m. the people assemblen under our spacious bowery, where speeches were made by Elders Thomas Memmott, B. H. Robinson, Henry Roper and M. Littlewood, intermixed with numerous songs, toasts, recitations, &c.

In the afternoon a large number assembled and partook of a plentiful dinner; after which songs, toasts, recitations, &c., were freely offered.

In the evening at 7 p.m. the company assembled together and enjoyed themselves in the dance until the "wee sma hours," when all dispersed to their several homes, well pleased with the movements of the day.

Marshal of the day, Wm. Hawley; Orator, Thomas Memmott; Chaplain, John Ellett; Committee of Arrangements, M. Littlewood, Thos. Memmott and Wm. Layton.

Our crops are ripening fast and all are preparing for the harvest; many already have begun, and we anticipate a bountiful harvest.

Praying that prosperity may attend Zion in all her movements,

I am yours,

E. C.

DESERET, MILLARD Co.,
July 24, 1868.

Editor Deseret News:—Dear Brother:—Although our dam has been washed away by the high waters, and we are left high and dry; and for this and other causes it has been considered expedient to leave this location for higher ground, our people determined to enjoy themselves upon the 24th, and throw, at least for that day, all care away. And if one might judge by their looks and actions they were remarkably successful, for probably in our most prosperous days no holiday time was ever spent with greater zest and enjoyment.

The programme of the day was as follows: the stars and stripes unfurled at daybreak; salute of musketry by Capt. Peter Lovell's company; at 8 o'clock the school pupils left their school-house and promenaded the city, visiting as many of our citizens as convenient, and entertaining them with songs, &c., for which they were very hospitably entertained by some of the brethren.

At 10 o'clock meeting in the school-house. After prayer and singing, an oration was delivered by Elder Martin Littlewood, the orator of the day, which was followed by a number of volunteer speeches, songs, toasts, &c.

At 2 o'clock the juveniles met and enjoyed themselves in the dance, and in the evening the adults passed a pleasant time in the social dance until a late hour.

Committee of arrangements—H. Roper, G. Lovell and H. Anderson.

Marshal of the day, J. McMahon.

The people of Deseret have really toiled and suffered to build up this place. It is now nine years since the first attempt to settle here; during that time the dam has washed out three times, the last time was on the 15th of this month, just when the people felt that the dam, at least, was safe, whatever else was unsafe. It is now considered wise to make a general move to Oak Creek, some twenty miles east from here, on the benches, which is probably one of the finest locations for a settlement in the mountains.

Yours respectfully,

T. MEMMOTT.

OAK CREEK, MILLARD CO.,
July 26, 1868.

Editor Deseret News:—I have thought proper to pen a few words for your disposal, concerning the city and citizens of Deseret. This place was settled in 1860, when the people by a united exertion succeeded in completing a dam across the Sevier river, which was carried away by high water in 1862. In 1862 it was commenced to be rebuilt, but most of it was again carried away before completion. The few then concerned became discouraged, but through the kindness of Bishop Callister a general call was made in the county to assist, and by this means we were enabled to accomplish the work.

The citizens of Deseret have anticipated great rewards for their hard labors in the past, but about two weeks ago the dam was washed out again, and the inhabitants felt like abandoning the place, when Bishop Callister came and located and caused this place to be surveyed, which he thinks capable of supporting fifty or a hundred families. This place as yet has no name given. It is situated about twenty miles east of Deseret city. It is surrounded with an abundance of good cedars and a good range for stock.

One saw mill is in operation and one grist mill is being removed from Deseret, and the people feel encouraged to go ahead and put out orchards and try to ornament the place, and make it such as President Young would like to visit and cheer us up and bless us.

Before closing I will say, the few here had the "Stars and Stripes" unfurled to the breeze on the 24th, and enjoyed themselves in social amusements; and had a sumptuous dinner graced with sweet mountain trout.

Yours truly,
J. W. RADFORD.

PRESIDING

ELDERS AND BISHOPS

Of the Church of Jesus Christ of Latter-day Saints, in Utah Territory and adjacent Settlements.

MILLARD COUNTY.

THOMAS CALLISTER, Presiding Bishop.

Scipio, Daniel Thompson.
Cedar Springs, alias Holden, David Stephens.
*Fillmore, Thomas Callister.
Meadow Creek, W. H. Stott.
Oak Creek, P. D. Lyman.
Kanosh, Culbert King.

FATAL ACCIDENT.—The following account of a fatal accident at Oak Creek came to hand this morning:

"A very serious accident occurred on Saturday, Sept. 27th, at Oak Creek, Millard county, under the following circumstances, causing the death of a little girl, named Albertine Pearson, aged four years, daughter of Per Pearson.

"She went to the field with her father and mother, riding on a wagon with a rack on it. When they got to the field the parents commenced cutting corn, and left the little girl playing around the wagon. In about half an hour after they found her suspended by her neck, between the side of the rack and a piece of wood, quite dead.

"The same evening George Finlinson, justice of the peace, and a jury held an inquest, and the following was the verdict:

"Territory of Utah,
"Oak Creek Precinct,
"Millard County.

"An inquisition holden at Oak Creek Precinct, on the 27th day of September, A.D. 1873, at 7 o'clock p.m., at the residence of Per Pearson, upon the body of Albertine Pearson, there lying dead, before George Finlinson, justice of the peace of the above precinct, by the jurors whose names are hereunto subscribed. Said jurors upon their oath do say, that she came by her death through accidental strangulation.

"JOHN LOVELL,
"HENRY ROPER,
"PETER ANDERSON.
"GEORGE FINLINSON,
"Justice of the Peace."

DARING STAGE ROBBERY IN MILLARD COUNTY.

The following special to the News was received to-day—

Fillmore, May 31st.

The coach coming from the north was robbed, by two masked men, between 10 and 11 o'clock last night, about three miles north of Sevier River. Only one lady passenger and the driver were on the stage. One of the robbers held a gun at the head of the driver, while the other went through Wells, Fargo's treasure box and the register sack, etc. They cut three mail sacks to pieces and smashed the treasure box and also took some express packages. The driver's name is Daniel Whitbeck. G. Huntsman, Gilmer & Salisbury's agent, goes to the place where the robbery was committed, to find out all he can concerning the matter. He takes Whitbeck with him.

DIED.

At Oak City, Millard County, Oct. 3, 1876, of inflammation of the bowels, after an illness of two days, CHRISTIAN ANDERSON.

Deceased was born February 19, 1853, in Vemlov, Co., Denmark; was respected by all who knew him as a strictly honest, upright man; and died in full faith of the gospel. He leaves a wife and two children and a large circle of friends to mourn his loss.

Correspondence.

**The Lower Sevier — Dam — Crops—
Plenty of Land, Water and Timber
—More Settlers Wanted.**

DESERET, Millard Co.,
Nov. 25, 1876.

Editor Deseret News:

Deseret is situated about twenty-five miles northwest from Fillmore City in Millard County. It is watered by the Sevier River. A dam was constructed by G. Webb in the spring of 1875. It is built mostly of rock and willows, the willows being bound in bundles and sunk with large rocks until it was raised to the surface of the water. Sills being laid, four cribs were built of logs, thirty feet long and sixteen wide, leaving a space between each crib of sixteen feet, which was divided into four parts by upright posts, morticed into a sill, gates being put into each space so that the water can be raised and lowered as wanted. The cribs are built up to high water mark, and filled with large rocks. The first summer the dam leaked, and we did not have sufficient water. We then made a fill in front, which tightened the dam, so that we could raise the water as needed. The river was very low, as it was drained at Richfield, about one hundred miles above here. We had surplus water for thousands of acres of land. We have raised this year about twenty thousand bushels of small grain, and some corn. The soil is very good and easily cultivated. All kinds of vegetables grow well. The climate is mild, good for fruit. Timber i- plenty, within thirty miles. Lumber, twenty-five miles, at from $2,50 to $4,00 per hundred, according to quality. Good adobie clay is in abundance. Wood in abundance, about twelve miles, and thousands of acres of unimproved land inviting the husbandman. We have a large tract of meadow land unoccupied. A townsite has been surveyed. At present we live on our farms. We want more settlers, and to the industrious farmers that want to make homes, we say come. The land cannot be excelled in Utah, and the water we think is sure.

We have no mail yet, but hope soon to have. We get our mail from Fillmore.

Yours very respectfully,
JOSEPH S. BLACK.

Postoffices Established.

Postoffices have been established in this territory as follows: Deseret, Millard county, Marcellus H. Webb, postmaster; Joseph, Sevier county, Alonzo L. Farnsworth, postmaster; Koosharem, Sevier county, F. Peter Petersen, postmaster; Mayfield, San Pete county, John Williams, postmaster.

DIED.

At Oak Creek, Millard County, Jan. 10, 1877, of inflammation of the bowels, PLATTE DE ALTON, only son of Platte De Alton and Adelia Lyman, aged 4 years and 5 months.

DIED.

At Deseret, Millard Co., Utah, May 26th, 1877, of inflammation of the lungs, in the thirtieth year of his age, REUBEN SAMUEL WESTERN.

Deceased was born December 17th, 1847, at Tiverton, Devonshire, England; was baptized at eight years of age in Birmingham, England; emigrated to Utah in 1868; was a firm believer in the Gospel, and died in the hope of a resurrection with the faithful. He leaves a wife and four children to mourn his death, and a large circle of relatives.

Millennial Star, please copy.

On Saturday, May 19th, 1877, at 15 minutes past 9 in the evening, of lung disease, after 21 days' illness, ANN WINSBROW, wife of Samuel R. Western.

Deceased was born October 6th, 1814, at Tiverton, Devonshire; first embraced the Gospel March 8th, 1852, in Livery Street, Birmingham, England; emigrated to Utah in 1868; was the mother of thirteen children, ten of them living; was a firm believer in the Gospel, and died in full faith of a glorious resurrection. She prayed for death, and her last words were, "I am going to be happy," and she quietly sank to rest. She leaves a husband and a large family and relatives to mourn her loss.

Millennial Star, please copy.

DESERET, Millard Co.,
August, 27, 1877.

Editors Deseret News:

We are now about half done harvesting our grain, every one seems to be well satisfied with the yield of crops and some think it cannot be beat in the Territory.

We have a very extensive farming country here, considerable vacant land yet to be taken up, and as we have generally taken up 160 acres each, land can be purchased at reasonable figures near our city location. Persons wishing a home will do well to visit Deseret before locating elsewhere. We have good land, a good climate, and plenty of water for irrigation without attention of nights and Sundays.

The dam at present is owned by individuals and we are paying one dollar per acre for the land we farm, with the understanding that the tax is to be reduced as fast as the county becomes developed so as to only make a reasonable per centage on the means invested.

We have a church organization, with Joseph S. Black for bishop, and I should judge by the way he takes hold he means business.

We had fifty one rebaptisms into the united order on the 18th inst., and expect more next fast day. The school trustees are busily engaged getting the material together to build a school house. We have organized a co-operative mercantile company, and the board of directors are making arrangements to build a house and start a store this fall.

Our greatest inconvenience is the want of a good grist mill; we would be glad if some good citizen would come here and build one, there would be plenty of work.

We have a Sunday school with good attendance. We have a very interesting literary paper published once a month called the *Deseret Advocate*.

I remain, fraternally,
WM. W. DAMRON.

MILLARD STAKE CONFERENCE.

The second quarterly conference of the Millard Stake, was held at Fillmore on the 23d and 24th insts.

On the stand were President Ira N. Hinckley and Counselors Edward Partridge and Jos. V. Robison; also Bishops from seven wards out of the eight in the Stake; with leading members from all of the wards. After singing and prayer, President Hinckley offered a few introductory remarks.

Elder C. Anderson spoke at considerable length on the necessity of starting such enterprises as will make us self-sustaining.

President Hinckley spoke upon the importance of putting the tannery into running order, so that leather might be made and boots, shoes, saddles, etc., be manufactured. We wanted, at this conference, to consider the enforcement of the no-fence law.

Elder E. Partridge showed the necessity of those called to preside living faithfully that they may have wisdom to work for the interests of the people; also the obligations that heads of families were under to their families. He referred to co-operation and said the co-operative store in this county had paid out as dividend about $2.80 on every dollar in seven years.

Singing and benediction.

1 p.m.

Singing and prayer.

After which Brother L. Holbrook read the statistical report of the Stake.

The bishops of the various wards then gave a verbal report of their different wards which were very favorable, showing marked improvement since their last report.

President Hinckley said that the graded school that had been recently started in the State house was doing well and it was for the benefit of any that wished to attend; he felt anxious to make this school one of the leading schools of the Territory.

Conference adjourned to the State House till Sunday at 10 a.m.

Sunday, 10 a.m.

Singing and prayer.

The Bishops of the Scipio Ward, Elder Geo. Finlinson of Oak Creek Ward and Bishop Jos. S. Black of Deseret Ward, each addressed the congregation stating the condition of their respective wards and showing their willingness to assist in starting home industries.

Elder J. V. Robison followed with a very interesting discourse upon the duties of the Saints and our future condition if we do not take hold of manufacturing and stop importation.

Singing and benediction.

2 p.m.

Singing and prayer.

The sacrament was administered.

Elder E. Partridge presented the general authorities, also the Stake authorities, who were unanimously sustained.

President Hinckley gave some valuable instructions to the Bishops and the acting Priesthood.

Elder N. Pratt followed with some very spirited remarks, showing that the co-operative store, of which he was superintendent, was in a prosperous condition.

A Priesthood meeting was held Saturday evening at which meeting the enforcement of the no-fence law was the principal subject discussed. It was resolved that the no-fence law be enforced after the first of March, 1875.

L. Holbrook, Clerk.

CORRESPONDENCE.

FILLMORE, June 11th, 1878.

Editors Deseret News:

I herewith send you a notice of the death of Mother Partridge, who departed this life at seven o'clock p. m., on the 9th inst., at Oak City, in Millard County, and was interred at Fillmore on the 11th. She was sick all last summer, but when the weather became cooler, got better, so that she was able to be around and perform light work. As the warm weather set in again she was again prostrated and suffered a great deal until she died. Her maiden name was Lydia Clisbee—parents, Joseph Clisbee and Merriam Howe. She was born in Marlboro, Middlesex County, Mass. While she was very young, they moved to New Hampshire, her mother dying when she was about 22; she and her sister Eliza and Brother Lewis went to Ohio, where she became acquainted with Edward Partridge, to whom she was married in the year 1819. They lived in Painesville several years and became identified with a religious organization effected by Sidney Rigdon, professing the doctrines taught by Alexander Campbell. Her husband was a hatter by trade and carried on quite a business in that line and was in prosperous circumstances when the gospel found them. The first "Mormon" Elders who visited them were P P Pratt, O. Cowdery, Peter Whitmer and Ziba Peterson. She was baptized by Parley P. Pratt in 1830, her husband joining the church soon after, and being called by revelation to be a bishop, and to go to Missouri and locate. Sister Partridge was left with the care of a sick family, and afterwards performed the journey with her children to that land, which, in those days, without the protecting care of her husband, was no small undertaking, she had $500 in money when starting from Painesville, but it was thought unsafe for a woman to carry so such money, therefore, she gave it into the care of another person for safe keeping. She never received one dollar of it back again. The bishop was required to devote his time to the duties of his office, and his property being used up or sold for little or nothing, they were many times brought into straightened circumstances, and suffered in common with the rest of the Saints the hardships and persecutions endured by them, which have become matter of history, and briefly to relate a few of them would require more space than wisdom would dictate. Sister Partridge was again compelled to make a journey without her husband, and having the care of six children, arriving at Quincy, Ills. they were well received by the citizens of that place. In Nauvoo she lost her husband and one daughter, those only who passed through the early settling of Nauvoo can realize the sickness and suffering of the saints in those days. She was married to Father William Huntington, whose wife had likewise died. They left Nauvoo with the first companies, in Feb., 1846, crossing the river on the ice with their teams and wagons. At Mount Pisgah Father Huntington was appointed to preside over those who were left there to raise a crop, and come on the next season, but he was taken sick and died. In the spring of '47 Mother Partridge and family were moved to Winter Quarters, on the Missouri River, by teams sent by President Brigham Young, and arrived in the Salt Lake Valley with the companies of saints, in 1848.

Although their property was sacrificed in becoming identified with the "Mormons," and her husband had labored for the people and worn himself out in the cause, yet Mother Partridge was always loth to ask for assistance, and labored diligently to support herself and family, and was always found earning something. She was exemplary in her daily life, and never was known to be aught else than a true and faithful Latter-day Saint, and it is not known that she ever had a personal enemy. In disposition she was quiet and unassuming, and her good works were performed without ostentation but from an innate love of the right, and the natural kindness of her heart. Having been identified with the Church almost from the commencement, she was intimately acquainted with a great many of the Latter-day Saints, who will ever think of her with kindly and pleasing remembrance.

EDWARD PARTRIDGE.

Deseret as a Farming District.

FILLMORE, Millard County,
August 1st, 1878.

Editors Deseret News:

Deseret is distant from Fillmore, in a northwesterly direction, about 30 miles. The principal part of the land now being farmed lies on the south side of the Sevier River. The "canal," which is an old bed of the Sevier, starts from the river in a southerly direction and describes a semi-circle of several miles diameter and, after supplying numerous irrigating ditches, empties its waters into the river several miles below the dam or head of the "canal." The soil varies from a sand and vegetable loam to a heavy clay, all of it being more or less impregnated with "mineral," *i.e.,* salt and alkali.

On the untilled land a heavy growth of "greasewood" covers the soil; and on the tilled land sunflowers, milkweed, pigweed and bitterweed are fighting for the victory, as a general thing with grain in the minority, sadly hiding its modest heads in shame for the shiftlessness or ignorance of the cultivator. The cause of this state of things is found in the fact that there is an abundance of water at Deseret, and as it costs one dollar per acre for it, the people, with the true instinct of the Chinaman, when buying his boots, want to get all they can for *their money,* and they pour on the water in season and out of season, when it needs it and when it don't need it, and usually the latter.

The land is very level, and the water settles in the lowest places, which causes - the "mineral" to raise, and morning finds the grain as effectually cut off as if an army of grasshoppers had visited it. A large breadth of land was sown last spring, and not over one-third, or at least one-half of a crop, will be raised. In fact, the crops are not nearly as good as those of last season.

Residents of Deseret, men of good judgment, told me that the best grain is that which has had the least water, and those men are the most successful farmers. They assert that early irrigation stunts the grain and *starts* the weeds, and too much water raises the "mineral," which causes an almost irreparable injury to the land. Those that have farmed in a judicious manner are gradually improving their surroundings, and *vice versa.* And they unanimously agree that a radical and thorough change in the method of farming must follow or the district hopelessly ruined. For instance a man that is this season farming in a slovenly manner, say 40 acres, must reduce the area of grain 20 acres, cultivate well and carefully, and when the weeds on the uncultivated 20 get a good start, in the latter part of June or first of July, go to with his plow and turn them under, then the following season sow to grain, and serve the other in the same manner, thus reducing his water tax one-half, and getting as much off the 20 acres as he now gets off the 40.

However, the farmers on the north side and a few on the south side of the river, have grown very fine grain, giving promise of what *can be done* with a little admixture of brains with the "elbow grease."

The appearance of the "survey," as it is called, is anything but inviting, being an almost interminable stretch of greasewood; an occasional sand ridge, with here and there a house, completes the exilerating landscape.

The townsite is the best that could be found in that locality, and shows considerable enterprise, as they have a tidy school house, store, etc.

A small outlay of labor only, would soon make Deseret a pleasant and inviting place. Lombardy poplars, mulberrys, etc., grow rapidly from cuttings. Let them and other kinds be planted on section and 40 acre lines, and in a few years the metamaphorsis will be complete.

Deseret possesses all the elements of substantial wealth, if they are but judiciously used.

With many kind wishes for the prosperity of the Desereters, I remain their friend.

Respectfully,
JUNIUS.

Deseret News
October 23, 1878

DIED.

In Deseret City, Millard County, O t. 14, 1878, DENOVA B, daughter of Rosalie and Samuel Henry Alexander, aged 11 months and 4 days.

Deseret News
February 26, 1879

DESERET, Millard Co.,
Feb. 9th, 1879.

Editors Deseret News:

We have had a very open winter, and everything looks promising for an early spring. We have built a good bridge across the Sevier River at this place. Our people are feeling well in the principles of the Gospel of Jesus Christ, our meetings are well attended, and our worthy Bishop Bro. Jos. S. Black and his counsel are energetic in their endeavors to unite the hearts of the people together. We have a Female Relief Society organized, with Sister Eliza Whicker as President, and Sisters Cinthia and Victoria Black as Counselors. The ladies of this place held a mass meeting, on the 13th of January, to enter protest against the anti-polygamy crusade, and unanimously sustained the proceedings of the general mass meeting held in the Theatre, Salt Lake City. We have also a Y.M.I. Association, with Bro. S. W. Western as President, and L. R Cropper and Daniel Hunter, Counselors, G. [Mills, Secretary, Robert Canham, Treasurer; also a Y. L. I. Association. We have an excellent Sunday School, with about one hundred scholars, and two day schools, well attended. The health of the people is good, and we are feeling well in the principles of the Gospel, there is a great improvement in our young folks, who have a desire to learn of the principles of truth. There is plenty of room for honest workers of the soil, and we invite all such to come and see for themselves.

Your Brother in the Gospel Covenant.   JAMES BENNETT.

Deseret News
June 11, 1879

At Oak Creek, Millard County, March 29, 1879, of dropsy and puerperal fever, CARLIE B. CALLISTER, wife of Thomas Callister and daughter of Amasa M. and Eliza M. Lyman, aged 27 years, 7 months and 19 days.

She left a baby 12 days old, also a mother and numerous brothers and sisters to mourn her loss; she was an exemplary member of the Church, and died in full faith and the hope of a glorious resurrection.—COM.

Salt Lake Herald
October 25, 1879

Cattle Thieves Captured.

Sheriff Peter Huntsman, of Millard County, arrived in Provo on Friday with a couple of cattle thieves. He had captured the birds on the Sevier River, in Millard County, and took them to Provo for safe keeping. Their names are Newell Green and Press Newcom, better known, however, as Press Parker.

Correspondence.

DESERET, Millard Co., Utah,
May 18th, 1880.

Editors Deseret News:

We have good health and prosperity. The weather in general has been quite cold this spring; grass slow in starting, vegetation and small grain, etc., all seem to be late. However, it is pleasant weather now. Farmers just commencing to irrigate. We have mines of some kind situated some 35 miles west, which are said to be quite satisfactory to those who are working them.

Last Friday, the 14th, was held as a May holiday by our Sunday School, Jas. Hutchinson, Joshua Bennett and J. C. Webb acting committee; R. Canham, marshal, and Joseph Damron, chaplain. At about 10 o'clock a. m. the whole school formed in procession at the house of Bishop Joseph S. Black. "Our Own Sunday School" was sung by Elder J. Nield and his juvenile choir; then proceeded to the new house of Prest. E. Partridge, now in course of erection; singing on the march and also when we arrived at the building; from the scaffold of the same Bro. Partridge addressed the school, thanking them for the visit, etc., said he hardly felt to be settled in the place as yet, but would in the future try to take a part in all such celebrations. Proceeded to the meeting-house and spent two hours in listening to songs, recitations from teachers and scholars, and a cheering address from our worthy Bishop.

In the afternoon the juveniles went forth in the dance in a crowded house, and seemed to enjoy themselves very much; amongst other things, Miss Florence Warren was duly crowned as Queen of the May, by her young companions. In the evening a dance for the adults; all passed off well and peacefully, all concerned feeling that we had contributed to the pleasure of our children, and done no harm to any one.

Deseret is a big-little town, covering an area of some twelve miles, nevertheless our meetings are uncommonly well attended. The ward teachers on their rounds to visit the Saints sometimes have to travel on horseback, still they seem to get around regularly. In fact, for the six months I have been here I have been visited oftener than I ever was in any other place in double the time.

Our day school is in better condition than ever in this place, and is now nearing its second quarter for present term; will then have vacation long enough to fix up the house and then go on again. The NEWS is always a welcome visitor. Yours respectfully, J. NIELD.

THE CENSUS.

We publish below the census returns by counties, as shown by the official schedules in possession of Supervisor Thomas. We also give the population by counties of the census of 1870:

COUNTIES	1880.	1870.
Beaver	3,915	2,007
Box Elder	6,780	4,855
Cache	12,620	8,229
Davis	5,350	4,459
Emery	460	*
Iron	4,020	2,277
Juab	3,510	2,034
Kane	3,090	1,513
Millard	3,740	2,753
Morgan	1,780	1,972
Piute	1,230	82
Rich	1,270	1,955
Rio Virgen	‡	450
Salt Lake	31,700	18,337
San Juan	210	*
Sanpete	11,700	6,786
Sevier	4,475	19
Summit	4,940	2,512
Tooele	4,530	2,177
Uintah	810	*
Utah	18,000	12,203
Wasatch	2,940	1,344
Washington	4,240	3,064
Weber	12,380	7,858
	143,690	86,786

Increase in ten years 56,904.
* Not organized.
‡ Incorporated in Kane and Washington Counties.

Utah's Population.

The following list gives the corrected census returns for Utah, by counties:

Beaver county	3 915
Box Elder county	6,780
Cache county	12 650
Davis county	5 850
Emery county	460
Iron county	4 020
Juab county	3 810
Kane county	3 090
Millard county	3 710
Morgan county	1 780
Piute county	1 230
Rich county	1 270
Salt Lake county	31 700
San Juan county	210
San Pete county	11 700
Sevier county	4 175
Summit county	4 910
Tooele county	4 530
Uintah county	810
Utah county	18 010
Wasatch county	2 910
Washington county	4 210
Weber coun y	12 280
	143,690

Deseret News
September 8, 1880

GENERAL CONFERENCE OF MILLARD STAKE OF ZION,

Held in State House, Fillmore, August 21st, 1880.

Present on the stand: Of the Apostles, Albert Carrington; Prest. Geo. Teasdale, of Juab Stake; Prest. Hinckley and counselors and Bishops of this Stake.

Meeting opened as usual.

Bishops J. D. Smith, of Fillmore, A. A. Kimball, of Kanosh, Daniel Thompson, of Scipio, D. R. Stevens, of Holden, and J. S. Black, of Deseret, each reported their respective wards as being in good condition and the people generally trying to live their religion; all spoke of the good being done by the Mutual Improvement Associations, Relief Societies also alive to their duties.

Elder Fisher reported the Meadow Ward as doing as well as possible under the circumstances.

Apostle Carrington said where the head of the Church is, there also will the powers of Satan be operating with the greatest force. This opposition should not discourage, but invite the saints to renewed action.

2 p.m.

After singing and prayer, Brother Teasdale, in a spirited discourse, showed the people the blessings they enjoyed as saints of the latter days; advised them to be prompt in paying their tithing and obeying the gospel, that they might lay up treasures in Heaven and be blessed while upon the earth.

Sunday, 10 a.m.

After opening exercises, Brother Teasdale showed the happiness to be gained in obeying the principles of our religion, and exhorted the Saints to apply themselves in studying the Church works; explained the results which would arise from allowing the reins of government to slip from our hands.

Apostle Carrington rejoiced in the good spirit apparent in the remarks he had heard.

2 p.m.

Counselor Ed. Partridge presented the Church and local authorities to be sustained by the people.

A. H. Kimball then read the statistical reports of the Stake.

Home missionaries appointed.

Apostle Carrington, in an instructive discourse, showed the benefits accruing from living our religion. Spoke at some length upon the back tithing and indebtedness of the P. E. Fund; advised the Saints who were in debt to live within their means, get out of debt and be free and independent.

Counselor Partridge felt glad that he had been present to enjoy the spiritual feast all present had heard.

Singing; benediction by President Hinckley.

A. H. KIMBALL,
J. L. ROBINSON,
Clerks.

DIED.

At his residence in Oak Creek, Millard Co., Utah, Saturday, November 6th, 1880, after an illness of about three months, SOREN CHRISTIANSEN, aged 36 years and 6 days; buried on Monday, November 8th.

Deceased was born in Denmark and came to Utah with his parents many years ago Brother Christiansen embraced the gospel when very young; has resided at Oak Creek for over nine years, during which time he has acted as a teacher in the ward and also as a teacher in the Sunday school. He leaves wife and many relatives and friends to mourn his loss. He died with an assurance of coming forth in the morning of the first resurrection.—[Com.

THE CENSUS.

The following statement exhibits the results of the first count of population in Utah, according to the schedules returned to the census office by the enumerators of the several districts concerned.

The statement of the population in relation to any township, town, city, or county is still subject to possible corrections by reason of the discovery of omissions or duplications of names in the lists of inhabitants returned:

COUNTIES.	Total.	Male.	Female.	Native	Foreign	White	Col'd
The Territory	143,907	74,471	69,436	99,974	43,933	142,381	1,526
Beaver	3,918	2,372	1,546	2,820	1,098	3,828	90
Box Elder	6,761	3,585	3,176	4,714	2,047	6,357	404
Cache	12,561	6,271	6,290	8,363	4,198	12,543	18
Davis	5,026	2,529	2,497	3,716	1,310	5,019	7
Emery	556	313	243	427	129	555	1
Iron	4,013	2,031	1,982	3,206	807	3,948	65
Juab	3,473	1,809	1,664	2,469	1,004	3,467	6
Kane	3,085	1,594	1,491	2,708	377	3,079	6
Millard	3,727	1,910	1,817	2,794	933	3,721	6
Morgan	1,783	962	821	1,263	520	1,766	17
Piute	1,651	893	758	1,339	312	1,529	122
Rich	1,263	665	598	934	329	1,262	1
Salt Lake	31,978	16,099	15,879	20,291	11,687	31,697	281
San Juan	204	104	100	171	33	204	—
Sanpete	11,557	5,773	5,784	7,439	4,118	11,485	72
Sevier	5,138	2,700	2,438	3,599	1,539	5,109	29
Summit	4,240	2,458	1,782	2,819	1,421	4,191	49
Tooele	4,497	2,500	1,997	3,196	1,301	4,331	166
Uintah	799	479	320	708	91	780	19
Utah	17,918	8,974	8,944	12,949	4,969	17,891	27
Wasatch	2,927	1,555	1,372	2,134	793	2,919	8
Washington	4,235	2,356	1,879	3,205	1,030	4,156	79
Weber	12,597	6,539	6,058	6,710	5,887	12,544	53

Colored includes in the Territory, 501 Chinese, 804 Indians and half-breeds, and 17 East Indians and half-breeds; in Beaver County, 28 Chinese, 45 Indians and half-breeds, and 17 East Indians and half-breeds; in Box Elder, 159 Chinese and 237 Indians; in Cache, 9 Indians; in Davis, 7 Indians and half-breeds; in Iron, 55 Indians and half-breeds; in Juab, 4 Indians; in Kane, 6 Indians; in Millard, 1 Chinese and 4 Indians and half-breeds; in Morgan, 17 Chinese; in Pi-Ute 120 Indians and half-breeds; in Rich, 1 Indian; in Salt Lake, 131 Chinese and 19 Indians and half-breeds; in Sanpete, 71 Indians and half-breeds; in Sevier, 24 Chinese and 4 Indians and half-breeds; in Summit, 43 Chinese; in Tooele, 10 Chinese and 152 Indians; in Uintah, 18 Indians and half-breeds; in Utah, 25 Indians and half-breeds; in Wasatch, 2 Chinese and 6 Indians and half-breeds, in Washington; 53 Chinese and 25 Indians; in Weber, 33 Chinese and 3 Indians.

Sad Hearts in Deseret.

The *Deseret News* learns of the following lamentable event:

Wednesday morning the settlement of Deseret, Millard County was visited by a great disaster.

The south winds broke up the ice in the Sevier River, and it swept down in such huge masses that it carried away the Deseret dam and bridge.

So great was the power of the moving piles of ice, that persons standing on the bank, a couple of rods from the stream, could feel the ground vibrate under their feet.

The settlement is damaged to the extent of nearly $50,000, causing many sad hearts, the people in many instances feeling homeless, as it is too late in the season to put in another dam in time to raise a crop, this year. The general feeling is that the settlers will live as best they can, and get a dam constructed for next year.

Changes of Registrars. — Yesterday the Commission made the following changes of appointments for county registrars: Millard, Alvin Robison in place of John Kelly; Kane, John Stewart in place of John Steele; Morgan, Anthony Peterson instead of L. P. Edholm.

BISHOP. — At Deseret, Millard County, Sunday, October 21st, 1882, Mary Lydia Naish, wife of George Bishop, and daughter of Thomas and Harriet Naish, aged 34 years and 3 months. Deceased was born June 26th, 1848, at Pontypool, Monmouthshire, Wales; was the mother of seven children, the oldest thirteen years old, the youngest three weeks. Sister Bishop was a true and faithful Latter-day Saint, and a useful member and teacher in the Relief Society. She died with full hope of coming forth in the morning of the first resurrection.

Funeral services were held in the Schoolhouse, at which the people generally attended, when discourses were delivered by Bros. M. M. Bishop, Joshua Bennett and Sister Eliza Whicker, President of the Relief Society.

Killed by a Mule.

The *Deseret News* of Wednesday learns the following particulars of a violent death:

At Deseret, Millard County, on the 9th inst., while Chris. Christianson was carrying feed to one of his mules, which was blind, the brute kicked him violently in the stomach. The most distressing symptoms immediately ensued, including vomiting, continuing for three days and nights, till the 12th, when the unfortunate man expired.

Deceased was a good faithful Latter-day Saint, well respected among the people. His funeral was largely attended.

MILLARD STAKE CONFERENCE.

The regular quarterly conference of Millard Stake of Zion was held at Scipio, Saturday and Sunday, Nov. 25th and 26th, 1882. Present, Apostle F. M. Lyman, the Presidency of the Stake and all the Bishops and other leading Elders of the Stake.

Saturday, 10 a.m.

After singing and prayer, President I. N. Hinckley said he had nothing but good to report about the condition of the Stake and the feelings existing between himself and his brethren who were laboring with him; had visited all the wards in the Stake since last conference, and found the Saints willing, as a general thing, to hearken to the counsels of the Priesthood.

Bishop Joseph D. Smith, of Fillmore Ward; Bishop A. A. Kimball, of Kanosh Ward, and Bishop Jos. S. Black, of Deseret Ward, gave encouraging reports of their wards, after which Elder John Cooper delivered a spirited discourse, touching upon many points of vital importance to the people.

2 p.m.

After singing and prayer, Bishop M. B. Bennett, of Meadow Ward; Bishop D. R. Stevens, of Holden Ward; Bishop Peter Anderson, of Oak Creek Ward, and Bishop Thos. Yates, of Scipio Ward, reported their wards in a prosperous condition. After which, Elder J. L. Robison addressed the meeting in an interesting manner, on the first principles of the Gospel, and also spoke about the two opposing powers of good and evil which he saw would soon be made manifest as they never have before.

Apostle F. M. Lyman delivered a discourse replete with philosophical reasoning on what the Gospel will do for the human family if they will obey its teachings.

Sunday, 10 a.m.

After singing and prayer, President Daniel Thompson spoke about the power of God which had been made manifest in behalf of His people and would be again; also of the necessity of being united that we may have strength with the Lord

President Joseph V. Robison said the first important thing for us to learn is that this is the work of God, then we need have no fear or doubt about the outcome. Spoke about the harmony existing between our religion and true science.

L. Brunson, President of the High Priests, spoke on the duties of the brethren bearing the High Priesthood.

Apostle F. M. Lyman then presented the general authorities of the Church and the presidency of this Stake.

C. C. Anderson presented the rest of the local authorities, and all were unanimously sustained, including the filling of vacancies as follows: Samuel W. Western, second counselor to Bishop Black, of Deseret, in place of Hyrum Dewsnup, who is on a mission; J. L. Robison, president of the Elders in Millard Stake, with N. S. Bishop as his first and P. E. Olson as his second counselor; F. A. Robison, superintendent of the Y. M. M. I. Associations, with Joshua Greenwood as his first and J. L. Robison as his second assistant; Delilah Olson, president of the Primary Associations.

Apostle F. M. Lyman then referred to the many and varied organizations in this Church and how they should work harmoniously. Explained how the different quorums of the Lesser Priesthood should be organized and each quorum presided over by a president and two counselors of their own number, and all be presided over by the Bishop and his counselors in their respective wards. The Bishop of a ward presides over every member in that ward, and no authority is exempt from his jurisdiction; and when the Bishop or his counselors visits the meetings of the various associations in their ward, they should be res-

pected; and the same should be the case with the higher authorities when they visit the Bishops' meetings. No presiding officer should be exposed or sat down on in public, but should be told of his errors in private, and then let him correct them himself. We should have proper regard for each other's feelings.

Sunday, 2 p.m.

After singing and prayer the sacrament was administered.

Elder C. Anderson spoke on the necessity of obeying all the principles of the Gospel, commencing with faith and repentance and continuing onward and upward, they are all revealed for the salvation and exaltation of the human family.

Prest. I. N. Hinckley expressed his satisfaction with the many good things which he had heard during their conference, and hoped that we would all treasure them up and profit thereby, be united, live our religion and trust in the Lord.

Apostle F. M. Lyman read from the book of Doctrine and Covenants, Sec. 68, commencing with the 25th verse, and spoke with much earnestness about the duties of parents toward their children, etc. This people have been gathered from 25 different nationalities, and are of the most independant and determinate class of people, having embraced the Gospel, unpopular as it is, of their own free will and choice in the face of great opposition, and showed what kind of children can be expected of such parents. Conference adjourned for three months.

C. ANDERSON, Clerk.

Deseret News
March 28, 1883

A MYSTERIOUS FIND.

THE REMAINS OF A MAN ARE DISCOVERED ON THE GROUND NEAR CLEAR LAKE.

We learn from Dr. J. D. M. Crockwell, who is located at Clear Lake, Millard County, that while his son William, a lad of about ten years of age, was hunting stock in that locality last Wednesday, he discovered a portion of the remains of a man lying upon the ground. When the boy returned home and reported to his father, the latter with the lad and Mr. Peter Wolsey, proceeded to the spot where the bones lay. With them were portions of a snuff colored fustian box coat, with side pockets. None of the other clothing could be identified so far as color was concerned. There were also found near the spot a silver watch, brass chain and six dollars in money. Dr. Crockwell at once sent a messenger to Fillmore, to notify the coroner.

MILLARD COUNTY CONVENTION.

The loyal citizens of Millard County (the members of the People's party) held their primary meetings in the various precincts on the 13th inst., for the purpose of taking initiatory steps for the coming August election.

In this precinct the officers nominated were two justices—C. P. Beaureguard and W. H. King—and one constable—C. C. Beaureguard; and the delegates elected to the convention were Messrs. Beaureguard, Melville, Gull, Huntsman and King.

On the 14th inst. the convention of Millard County convened in Fillmore City, Joseph S. Giles was chosen chairman and W. H. King secretary. By ballot the following named gentlemen were elected to fill the offices appended: Joseph V. Robison, Member to the Legislature; Thos. C. Callister, Supt. District Schools; George Crane, Selectman (full term); Hyrum Mace (unexpired term) Probate Judge; W. H. King, County Clerk; Thos. C. Callister, Assessor and Collector; Joseph Holbrook, Sheriff; James McMahon, Coroner; Joseph S. Giles, Prosecuting Attorney; Joseph S. Giles, Surveyor; David Stevens (unexpired term) Selectman.

After the completion of the election of officers the convention considered the advisability of changing the headquarters of the Central Committee of the People's Party from Fillmore to some other place in the county. Deseret was determined upon as a fit place, and Jos. S. Black was elected chairman and L. R. Cropper and W. C. Moody (with the chairman) the executive body of the committee. The members of the committee representing the various precincts are, W. H. King, Fillmore; Joseph Fisher, Meadow; Ben. Goddard, Kanosh; B. J. Stringham, Holden; Thomas Memmott, Scipio; Peter Anderson, Oak Creek; Christian Overson, Leamington. Unanimity prevailed in Convention.

W. H. KING, Sec'y.

DIED.

BECKSTRAND—At Oak City, Millard County, Dec. 7th, 1883, after a few days' illness Carl J. Beckstrand, born June 28th, 1820, in Sweden; embraced the Gospel in Denmark in 1852; performed a mission in Seland, Denmark in 1860 Emigrated to Utah in 1861, was ordained a Seventy in the year 1862, and belonged to the Sixty-fifth Quorum. He leaves a wife and two sons to mourn his death.

DEATHS.

BENNETT.—February 4th, 1884, at Deseret, Millard County, of pneumonia, Sarah Elizabeth, daughter of John and Isabella Jane Bennett; born November 15th, 1883.

WESTERN.—At Deseret, Millard County, February 8th, 1884, of pneumonia, Earnest, son of Samuel W. and Sarah Ann Weston; born July 21st, 1882.

Deseret News
March 5, 1884

DEATHS.

DEWSNUP.—In Fillmore, Feb. 26th, and interred at Deseret, Millard County. Jemima, wife of John Dewsnup, deceased. She was a faithful member of the Church, having passed through many privations for the Gospel's sake and never wavered from her honest convictions to the truth to her last moments of life. She died in full faith of a glorious resurrection. She leaves a number of children, grandchildren and friends to mourn her loss.

Deseret News
April 23, 1884

MARRIAGES.

HORNUNG-WEBB. — At Oasis, Millard county, Utah, April 15th, 1884, by Elder Joseph Horne, John Henry Hornung, son of Henry and Josephine Hornung, of Philadelphia, Pa., to Elizabeth Lorena Webb, daughter of Edward M. and Elizabeth A. Webb, of Oasis, Utah, and granddaughter of Joseph and M. Isabella Horne, of Salt Lake City.

Salt Lake Herald

MILLARD COUNTY.

After leaving Juab, the first town of importance on the line of the railroad is Deseret. For many miles north and south of Deseret a few ranches, farms and section houses are about all that greet the traveler. Deseret, I believe, is more scattered than any place in Utah. It is Deseret a long while before you get there and the same after you leave. But for all that it is destined to become a place of considerable importance. Even at this time it has the best commercial facilities of any place in Millard county. Tanning is the principal industry of the inhabitants —and a very fair market for the farm products is found in Eastern Nevada and on the line of the Utah Central railway. The soil in this vicinity, although variable, is well adapted to raising grain and hay, and live stock appear to do well. A dam in the Sevier river, above the town, will cause an abundance of water to be had for this season's irrigation. The Deseret Store, kept J. B. Black, supplies the people with all the necessaries; as do also Mr A. Ray and W. V. Black & Co., who carry a full line of general merchandise. Mr. E. Webb provides for the wants of the weary traveler. A good grist mill will soon be in operation here, and is expected to be kept busy this season. A new meeting-house is in course of erection, which is calculated to be as neat, substantial and commodious as any in the county.

THE SAVAGE SEVIER.

Damage and Destruction by Water.

DESERET, MILLARD COUNTY, UTAH, May 30'h, 1884.

Editors Herald:

Thinking probably a few items from here will not be uninteresting to your readers I send you a little information regarding the effect of high water. When this state of affairs is so prevalent we expect our full share and we have it. The Sevier River at this place is the highest it has been for many years. We have been busy day and night for some time past trying to save our dam which we have so far been successful in doing and think we can stand two or three feet more rise in the river. The low lands are all under water and several families have been compelled to leave their homes. The river is now rising about three inches per day. We have been obliged to cut our main north canal to carry water off, and we have also constructed a new canal on the south side to reduce the pressure.

The water is now all cut off from our farming lands, but all hands that can be spared from the dam are busy making a new ditch, which will be completed in a few days. I am proud to say the people are working in unison for the best good of the settlement, and I think by the blessing of the Lord that we shall be able to save all our grain, as our agricultural prospects have never been so good since we settled this place.

Yours truly,
Jos. S. BLACK.

LIST OF PASSENGERS

Sailing from Liverpool per S. S. Arizona, May 17th, 1884. Ephraim H. Williams in charge.

DESERET.

Henry, Emma and Amelia Plimer.

CORRESPONDENCE.

OASIS—ITS OBSTACLES AND ADVANTAGES.

OASIS, Utah, July 27, 1884.

Editor Deseret News:

Frequently hearing the question asked "Where is this place designated Oasis?" it would, perhaps, be of some interest to your many many readers to learn something about it, especially geographically, for our embryo city, though not boasting of many thousand inhabitants, nevertheless covers no mean number of square acres, or rather miles I might consistently add, and if only the area would be considered to entitle us to a place on the scale, in proportion, undoubtedly, we would occupy a position near to Philadelphia or Boston.

Our boundary, though not precisely defined yet, may be said to include more or less the greater portion of that part of Zion lying between the third and fourth standard parallels south and 112 and 113 longitude west, but of course, if this appears to be a "stretch" I can deduct a few miles from the sides. We are in the large and spacious county of Millard, on the line of the Utah Central Railway; our postoffice is Oasis, while our station bears the misnomer "Deseret," so also does our telegraph office. The indispensible store flourishes. We have also a hotel and restaurant, and since the grateful change of time on the U. C. opportunities of seeing and inspecting our situation and facilities are given passengers who may feel so inclined; for it is now a breakfast station, with a generous allowance of 25 minutes in which to enjoy both the comfort and luxury of a nice, warm breakfast (for to the traveler it seems indeed a luxury when he has plenty of time to comfortably swallow his meal) at the table of our genial caterer Brother Edward Webb.

Our prospects for becoming a large and wealthy settlement and eventually a city, are beyond a doubt excellent, and any one who closely examines the facilities of the place cannot fail to discern the same bright future, for firstly, we have plenty of land, miles and miles of it: secondly, there is an abundance of water, which needs only the labor combined with good management (common sense) to bring it upon the land. The only drawback is the distance to fuel and timber, the former is 15 to 20 miles away, and the latter 25 or 30 miles, yet even this disadvantage is slight, for coal can be obtained by the car-load at $8 per ton, and may be lower next fall, while two or three together could easily purchase a car of coal, which with a load or two of wood, would last all winter. Then again, our winters are very mild, there are few days but what the south side of the house is actually hot. Our summers are long and dry, and if Dr. Koch's theory is correct then indeed we have no morbi-fied soil, for the dreaded cholera microbe could not live or flourish in this arid spot, and not a healthier place exists in the land as all who visit us or reside here can prove.

The unusual high water has caused us a great deal of damage, labor and expense; for the third time has the angry Sevier overcome us and cut a new channel; but through the mercy and assistance of Him who has promised to be with his Saints in their labors to build up Zion, we know we shall finally succeed, and this fall when the river is low, en masse, we will secure all breaks and dangerous places, and tighten and strengthen the dam (Deseret dam), until we feel satisfied that the next Spring's freshet will have no effect, unless it be to triple our supply of water.

We cordially invite settlers. Come and see us before you go to Arizona, or Colorado, or New Mexico if you are intending to leave or change your residence: our bonanza is sure.

With the best of wishes for the NEWS which comes regularly to hand,

I remain sincerely,

J. H. H.

Ogden Herald
August 25, 1884

Fearful Fatal Fight.

On Wednesday night last, a most unprovoked and fatal case of stabbing took place at Lemington, in Millard County. Two men named Joseph Curtis and Martin Rasmussen quarreled over a trivial matter which ended in the killing of the latter. Both were in the employ of a storekeeper named Geo. Morrison, and, on Wednesday night, Curtis was told to ask Rasmussen to come in to supper. He did so in a playful manner, and, catching hold of Rasmussen's coat pulled him rather rudely, which so irritated him, that he dealt Curtis a blow on the side of the head. Curtis resented by pulling out his pocket knife and stabbing Rasmussen, once in the left side and once in the right, making a fearful gash about two inches or more long, from which the bowels protruded in a horrible manner. A surgeon was immediately telegraphed for who, on his arrival, next morning, pronounced the wound fatal.

Rasmussen died at 10:15, Friday morning, and, Saturday night, Curtis was brought to Provo by the Constable of Lemington and lodged in the County jail to await the action of the Grand Jury which will convene, early next month.—

Salt Lake Herald
October 12, 1884

HORSETHIEVES CAPTURED.

Arrest of Two Nevada Jail Breakers in Utah.

[Special telegram.]

OASIS, Utah, October 11.—After a long and desperate chase of 300 miles, United States Deputy Marshal Nuckols, and a posse from Nevada, succeeded in capturing, in the mountains a few miles east of Scipio, Millard County, Abe Fonsaco and Frank Hopper, two horse thieves, who escaped from the Eureka, Nevada, jail some three days ago. The marshal, with his prisoners, leaves here this afternoon, en route for home.

Deseret News
December 31, 1884

ALLRED—On December 16, 1884, at Deseret, Millard County, Sister Lucy Ann Butler Allred, from the effects of a congestive chill. She was born Dec. 6, 1814, in Simpson County, Kentucky, and was therefore 70 years, 4 months and 10 days old. She was a faithful Latter-day Saint.

Deseret News
March 11, 1885

MILLARD STAKE CONFERENCE.

The regular quarterly Conference of Millard Stake was held in Fillmore City, Saturday and Sunday, February 21st and 22nd, 1885.

All the wards were represented by their Bishops or Counselors, and reported in a very favorable condition.

A number of changes were made in the local authorities as follows: Bishop J. D. Smith, who had been called to go on a mission to England, resigned his position as Bishop of Fillmore Ward, and Thomas C. Callister was selected to fill the vacancy, who chose Alma Greenwood for his first and James A. Melville for his second counselor.

Bishop Callister was then released from his position as a member of the High Council, as first counselor to the President of the High Priests and as Superintendent of the Sunday Schools, and Ira Noble Hinckley was chosen to fill the vacancy in the High Council, Alexander Melville was chosen as first counselor to the President of the High Priests, and Joseph L. Robison as Superintendent of the Sunday Schools, with F. A. Robison and Ira Noble Hinckley as his assistants.

Reuben McBride, 82 years of age, and infirm, resigned his position as a member of the High Council, and Christian Anderson was chosen to fill the vacancy.

Joshua Greenwood, who had been called to go on a mission to England, resigned his position as a member of the High Council, and Platte D. Lyman was chosen to fill that vacancy.

The visiting brethren, and also several of the local brethren, spoke with much freedom, and many valuable instructions were given, which will long be remembered and be of lasting benefit to many. Many remarks of approval of what had been done, and expressions of satisfaction with what had been said were also heard among the Saints, and harmony, confidence and good feelings seem to exist in the various departments of the laboring Priesthood.

C. ANDERSON, Stake Clerk.

Deseret News
July 8, 1885

JUDGES OF ELECTION.

The following is the list of election judges appointed yesterday to act at the August Election:

MILLARD COUNTY.

Burbank—Wm. Atkinson, Charles Rowland, Brigham Young.

Fillmore.—A. C. Robinson, E. Bartholomew, Jas. A. Melville.

Holden—Jos. S. Gyles, Thos. Evans, Enoch Dodge.

Scipio—Saml. Rowley, Peter Neilson, Hans Marquarson.

Oak Creek—Maxwell Webb, Ole Jacobson, Simms Walker.

Leamington—Judge Wilson, Christian Overson, Louis Stout.

Deseret—Edward Webb, Thos. W. Cropper, Willard Rogers.

Meadow—Jos. Adams, Jno. Stredder, Abraham Greenhalgh.

Kanosh—Peter Robison, Geo. Crane, Richard Hatton,

DEATHS.

HUTCHINSON—In Deseret, Millard County, September 3rd, 1885, of typhoid fever, Sarah Ellen, daughter of James and Ellen Hutchinson; born October 12th, 1869. She was a loving and obedient girl, greatly endeared to all who knew her, and lived and died a true Saint.

Deseret News
September 23, 1885

EVENTS AND PROSPECTS AT OASIS.

Oasis, Millard County, Utah,
September 12, 1885.

Editor Deseret News:

As it has been some time since I noticed anything from this part of the country in your valuable paper, I deem it my duty to inform your readers and all who feel interested in the welfare of our "Deseret," and in the conversion of its still remaining alkaline soil into fertile farms and gardens, that the good work is progressing.

Many are still in ignorance of

THE WHEREABOUTS OF OASIS,

and our people complain that when they are away from home it becomes obvious that many of the brethren are not acquainted with our location, therefore, to inform the people in general I will, if you can allow me space, give a brief description of our situation, our advance and our hopes.

We are located upon the Utah Central Railway, 52 miles southwest from Juab Station, and but two miles or so from the town of Deseret. The main portion of our town is clustered around the Utah Central station (which is still known as Deseret) and extends east and south towards Holden and Fillmore. At present we draw our water supply from the Deseret dam, but contemplate the digging of a canal, starting some eight or nine miles above; which, besides furnishing our present limits, will also irrigate a fine plateau of some 100,000 acres, lying north and east of us. Several estimates of different routes show that the venture would be highly satisfactory considering the benefit that would arise from its completion. Many hundreds of farms and homes would cover the present grease-wood slope and the promised

CITY OF THE DESERT

would Phœnix-like arise. The work would commence at once, but we need a few more hands; we are too few in number yet and our funds are insufficient for the undertaking. We need a few more young and hardy settlers, who are not afraid to put their "shoulders to the wheel" and overcome the difficulties that faced their fathers in days gone by; a dozen or two such sturdy and determined workers could in a few years secure that independence and comfort without which there can be no true human happiness.

If there are any whom this meets who feel "crowded," and who feel like striking out in the world for an atmosphere of more freedom let them come and inspect our facilities and reflect over the opportunities that are here. All honest men are cordially invited.

This has been a year of success: the most sanguine expectations have been realized. Nature seems to have attempted to outdo even her own usual generosity, and the poorest among us smile with that happiness and contentment a bountiful harvest alone brings and there cannot be one of us but thanks the star that led him to the

OASIS IN THE DESERT.

Every cereal can be raised here and I think all of the hardy fruits, though very few orchards have been set out. One objection to tender vegetation is the early and late frosts. This will be somewhat removed when we have shade trees and fences.

Besides the Railway station, we have the Deseret Telegraph and Pacific Express offices under the same roof, two stores a little way from the depot, one, a co-operative concern (Oasis Co-op,) does a flourishing business, both in town and up and down the track. In connection with the other store is the Oasis restaurant and hotel, which formerly did very well, but since the late disagreeable arrangements, much to the annoyance and disgust of passengers, the trains do not pretend to give them time enough to get a hot breakfast, which lessens the restaurants, usefulness somewhat, as far as that part is concerned. By the way we noticed Hon. John T. Caine among the disappointed ones the other morning, but hope he had a pleasant journey otherwise.

There has been considerable stir lately over the

DUCKING OF A BRIDEGROOM,

on Saturday, Sept. 5th, by a number of Deseret boys who waited on him to learn the reason why he would not give the customary dance, and a satisfactory excuse not being made they deemed it their duty to throw him into the canal; three times they threw him in, and at the third time one of his assailants fell in with him. The boys laughed and the bridegroom cried; but before "His Honor" yesterday the groom laughed and the boys—well felt pretty sick; $15 apiece, could not be found every day, and thus the laugh and cry were reversed.

THE RABBITS

are very plentiful this season and have become a pest, destroying much grain and lucern; where they are few and far between, it is sport to hunt them, but where it takes but a few minutes to get a dozen it becomes tedious work, as a certain gentleman from Detroit, Mich., (Mr. John Baker), who is out here on business, discovered this afternoon. He is a mighty hunter (among the squirrels) at home; but a load of jack rabbits in 50 minutes proved too much for his conscience, and he mournfully said, "Let us go home."

A meeting of railroad employes occurred last evening at Oasis, for the purpose of organizing a

"RAILROAD EMPLOYES CO-OPERATIVE SHEEP COMPANY."

We suppose they want to help the road out in the way of wool shipments. Sheep are more certain than mines! The company was organized with the following officers: Jas. Latimer, road master, president; John H. Kinder, foreman sec. 34, vice-president; John H. Horning, agent Deseret station, secretary; Robert L. Scott, foreman sec. 35, treasurer; David N. Purdie, C. B. McGregor, Henry McCardell, C. S. Higgins, James Garrett, B. P. Textorious and James Kelly, foremen of various sections, directors.

As will be seen, the road from Juab to Frisco was well represented. The company is to continue for 25 years; capital $40,000, one-fourth of which is already subscribed, and it is the purpose of the company to purchase a herd and commence operations immediately. The range is in the vicinity of the railroad through Juab, Millard and Beaver Counties. The principal place of business and headquarters will be at Oasis, Millard County. J. H. H.

Salt Lake Democrat
December 29, 1885

From the Hospital to the Pen.

Deputy Smith arrested Jack Watkins this morning at the Hospital of the Holy Cross on a warrant issued from the First District, charging him with grand larceny. Watkins was brought to the hospital some months ago from Deseret, Millard county, Utah, with a wound in the leg from an accidental gunshot, requiring amputation of the limb just below the knee joint. He was placed in confinement at the Penitentiary to await his trial.

DEATH OF A GOOD WOMAN

SISTER ELIZA M. LYMAN, A FORMER WIFE OF THE PROPHET JOSEPH SMITH, PASSES FROM THIS LIFE.

Provo, March 8, 1886.

Editor Deseret News:

Many of your readers will be pained to learn of the death of Sister Eliza M. Lyman, who departed this life on the morning of the 2d inst., at Oak City, Millard County, U. T. She was the eldest daughter of Edward and Lydia Partridge and was born April 20th, 1820, at Painesville, Geauga County, Ohio. Her parents joined the Church of Jesus Christ of Latter-day Saints when she was quite young. This action changed the prospects of her whole life. From having been in easy circumstances before, her subsequent life was to be one of privation and self-sacrifice. Becoming identified with the Saints in her youth, she was early imbued with a love for the principles of the Gospel and a reverence for truth and honesty. Having to suffer the privations incident to the persecutions endured by the Saints in Missouri and Illinois, she was deprived of those advantages of education generally considered necessary to qualify a young woman to appear to advantage in company; at the same time her inherent qualities of modesty and good sense, coupled with a studious disposition, enabled her to surmount obstacles and gain sufficient book learning to become a teacher, and she was able to appear to advantage in the best society. With no ostentation she was generally self-possessed under all circumstances.

Although having filled honorable positions in connection with the benevolent institutions among the Saints, her life labor has been most appreciated by her intimate friends and relatives.

She was one of the first to receive the doctrine of celestial marriage being taught that principle by the Prophet Joseph Smith, to whom she was married in 1843 by Apostle Heber C. Kimball. In those days it required considerable self-sacrifice as well as faith to enter into that order. After the death of the Prophet Sister Eliza was married to Apostle Amasa Lyman by whom she had five children; three of them are now living. Her son Platte D. Lyman was born in a wagon on the Platte River, near Fort Laramie, while journeying to the valleys of the mountains, the parents having been driven out by mob violence with the rest of the Saints from Nauvoo.

She accompanied her son P. D. Lyman to San Juan, where he was sent to take charge of a company of settlers, having to make a road through an almost impassable country in the winter time. The suffering and anxiety consequent upon that journey, and the residence in the San Juan country where her son Joseph A. was shot in the knee by a horse thief and lay helpless between life and death for about a year; being surrounded by Indians, Utes on the one side and Navajos on the other; no doubt served to break down a constitution by no means robust.

Upon the release of her son from the Presidency of the San Juan Stake, she returned to her old home in Oak City, where she appeared to feel unusually contented. Although enjoying the society of the Saints and always rejoicing in the principles of the Gospel, her lot in life has not been an easy one; but it has been one of self-sacrifice almost from infancy, and she was never happier than when ministering to the comforts of others.

If honesty of purpose and integrity to the principles of the Gospel will insure a crown of celestial glory, Sister Eliza will certainly receive one.

EDWARD PARTRIDGE.

Successful Examination.—On Saturday afternoon, April 3d, the annual commencement exercises of Dr. Ellis R. Shipp's school in midwifery were held at her office, No. 18 Main Street. The examining board of physicians were Drs. Richards, Bower and Harrison.

Very successful and creditable examinations were passed by the following named ladies: Paulina Lyman, Parowan, Iron County; Anna E. Lyman, Oak City, Millard County; M. E. Clark, Farmington, Davis County; Rebecca R. Hillyard, Smithfield, Cache County; Amanda Harmon, Mill Creek, Salt Lake County, Theresa Pearson, Salt Lake City.

It is gratifying to know that some of our sisters are being awakened to the great advantage of having the towns and villages of the Territory well supplied with skilful nurses and accoucheurs, and we think great credit is due the Relief Societies which have interested themselves in this direction, and would recommend other organizations to follow the example.

Mrs. Shipp expects to open a class within a few weeks for the instruction of mothers in the duties of maternity, and not specially for practitioners in midwifery, but next October will organize another class in obstetrics similar to that whose studies have just closed.

Deseret News
May 5, 1886

Deputy Registrars. — The Utah Commission appointed the following deputy registration officers.

Millard County—Alvin L. Robinson, Fillmore precinct; John Streddler, Meadow precinct; Geo. Chesley, Kanosh precinct; Wm. Atkinson, Snake Valley precinct; Nicholas Paul, Holden precinct; Geo. Monroe, Scipio precinct; Wm. A. Ray, Deseret precinct; John Wilson, Leamington precinct; Geo. Finlinson, Oak Creek precinct.

Ogden Herald
September 8, 1886

Sad Occurrence.

The following dispatch, received by a gentleman in this city, refers to a sad occurrence which took place at Oasis, Millard County, yesterday (Monday) morning:

John Webber has been accidentally killed. His body is every much bruised. Will bury him to-d unless his father wishes to see him.

No particulars of the accident have been received. The deceased was 14 years of age, and was in the employ of George Busby, near Deseret, Millard County. His father resides in the 11th Ward of this city, his mother being dead. Mr. Webber was not in town when the painful news arrived, and his son was probably buried to-day.—*Des-*

Deseret News
September 22, 1886

A BOY KILLED.

FATAL CASUALTY IN A QUARTZ MILL IN MILLARD COUNTY.

DESERET, Millard County,
September 6th, 1886.

Editor Deseret News:

A fatal accident occurred at Crafts & Co.'s quartz mill on Saturday evening last, the victim being a boy recently from Salt Lake City.

Mr. Geo. Busby furnishes the following particulars: The boy, named John Webber, who has a father and sister residing in Salt Lake City, was living with Mr. Busby at Lake Town (Ingersol) about 12 miles from here down the river.

Crafts & Co.'s mill is situated about 30 miles northwest of Lake Town. Mr. Busby having occasion to visit the mill took the lad, who is about 15 years old, along with him. On arriving

THE BOY WAS CAUTIONED

by Mrs. Busby about the danger of getting into the machinery, and Mr. Busby intended to take him into the mill and point out to him the dangerous places, and in the mean time requested him to go in to supper, while Mr. Busby assisted a friend to unharness the horses. The lad hastily swallowed a few mouthfuls and, unknown to Mr. Busby, went over to the mill. Mr. L. Crafts, the engineer, noticed the boy standing near the supply pump watching its movements, and turned to inspect the water gauge. A few feet from the pump the driving belt was running at a great speed, connecting the drive wheel of the engine with the battery. Mr. Crafts was startled by the instant stopping of the stamps, and thought the driving belt had broken and struck the steam pipe a few feet above the engine. Turning quickly he saw the boy lying on the floor a few feet from where he last saw him, in a

FEARFULLY MANGLED CONDITION.

It is surmised that the little fellow attempted to step over the belt, and got caught by the left leg below the knee, the belt carrying him under and partly around the drive wheel, and hurling him against the steam pipe overhead with such force as to crush the left side of his head. His left leg was also broken in two places. The lad was a favorite with Mr. and Mrs. Busby on account of his obedient and cheerful disposition.

His remains were brought to Deseret last evening and interred to-day. The people here did everything in their power to assist Mr. Busby in preparing the body for burial. The funeral service was conducted under the auspices of the ward authorities, and was followed to the grave by many whose eyes were moist with sorrow, for the fate of the little stranger, as also for the stricken parents and sister. Mr. Busby was very much affected while relating the incidents and especially so when he spoke of a letter the boy had received a day or two previous to his death from his sister younger than he, wherein she had counseled him to be a good, obedient boy and God would guide his footsteps.

Mr. Busby telegraphed a friend in Salt Lake City to

FIND THE FATHER

and apprise him of the fatality, as also to get his wishes with regard to the disposition of the body—whether to read to city or bury here. No answer being received, it was deemed best to inter the remains, as the body was rapidly advancing in decomposition.

Justice L. R. Cropper summoned Messrs. Louis Phillips, Albert Petty and T. W. Cropper, who held an inquest and rendered their decision in accordance with the facts set forth by

the evidence, and found that no one could be held blameable for the boy's accidental death.

The health of the people here is excellent, notwithstanding they are enduring, with praiseworthy fortitude, a severe attack of the flowing well fever.

Respectfully,

UNCLE SI.

Deseret News
September 29, 1886

DEATHS.

STARK—At Deseret, Millard County, September 10th, 1886, of paralysis, Elsie Stark, born June 22nd, 1827. Deceased embraced the Gospel in Sweden in 1857, and died in full faith.

HAWKINS.—At Deseret, Millard County, Utah, September 22, 1886, John S. Hawkins, aged 68 years.

Salt Lake Democrat
December 1, 1886

Postmaster Wm. A. Ray is up from Deseret, Millard county. He reports that the stockmen feel very much alarmed because there is so little feed for stock and the otherwise unfavorable indications of an unusually hard winter. This, together with the fact that the cereal crop this year was not so good as common, on account of the canal dam being washed out during the irrigating season, makes the people of that section feel far from being millionaires.

Deseret News
February 2, 1887

DEPUTIES AT DESERET.

Special to the DESERET NEWS.]

OASIS, Millard County, Utah,
January 28, 1887.

Deputy marshals raided Deseret this morning. They searched Bishop Black's house and subpœnaed two witnesses for the Harder case. No arrest.

DEATHS

DUTSON.—At Oak Creek, Millard County, May 6th, 1887, after a lingering illness of fifteen months, John W. Dutson; born September 28th, 1829, in Herefordshire, England; embraced the Gospel September 24th, 1840; emigrated in 1843, went through many of the trials and persecutions of the Saints in the days of Nauvoo; crossed the plains in 1857; moved to Fillmore and was called from there to Oak Creek in 1871. He held many prominent positions in the Church and at the time of his death was one of the seven Presidents of the Twenty-first Quorum of Seventies; was highly respected and was followed to the grave by a numerous and respected family and a large circle of friends and acquaintances.—[COM.

MILLARD STAKE CONFERENCE.

The Millard Stake Quarterly Conference was held at Fillmore City on the 21st and 22nd of May, 1887, President Ira N. Hinckley presiding.

We were favored with the presence of Apostle Lorenzo Snow, who spoke to the Conference Saturday and Sunday in the afternoon. His preaching was very encouraging and comforting and was highly appreciated by the Saints.

The reports of the temporal and spiritual condition of the wards were good, harmony and good feelings existing among the laboring priesthood, and an increase of diligence and faithfulness among the members.

The following local brethren addressed the Conference: Presidents Ira N. Hinckley and J. V. Robison, Elders J. D. Smith, D. P. Callister, Alma Greenwood, Joshua Greenwood and J. L. Robison.

The addresses of the speakers were wrought with the power of the Holy Spirit, and much freedom of expression characterized the teachings and exhortations of the servants of God who administered the word.

The general and local authorities of the Church were presented and unanimously sustained.

The local authorities now stand as follows: Ira N. Hinckley, President of Millard Stake, with Daniel Thompson first and J. V. Robison second Counselors.

Members of the High Council: Platte D. Lyman, James Abraham, Christian Anderson, Wm. Beeston, Christian Hanson, Allen Russell, C. P. Beauregard, B. J. Stringam, Jesse B. Martin, Ira N. Hinckley, J. C. Robison and W. H. Stott.

Alternate High Councilors—Joshua Greenwood, James McMahon, Alfred Gull, J. D. Smith, D. P. Callister, Niels M. Stewart, Geo. Crane, L. N. Hinckley, F. K. Lyman and George Badger.

Lewis Brunson, president of the High Priests' Quorum, with Alexander Melville as his first and William North as his second Counselor.

Abram A. Kimball, agent for Presiding Bishop.

Christian Anderson as Historian and Stake Clerk.

Richard Day as President of the First Quorum of Elders, with H. C. Jackson as his second Counselor.

Thomas C. Callister, Bishop of Fillmore Ward, with Alma Greenwood as his first and James A. Melville as his second Counselor.

Hiram B. Bennett, Bishop of Meadow Ward, with James Fisher as his first and James Duncan as his second Counselor.

A. A. Kimball, Bishop of Kanosh Ward, with C. W. Hopkins as his first and C. F. Christianson as his second Counselor.

Joseph S. Black, Bishop of Deseret Ward, with Robt. Hunter as his first and S. W. Western as his second Counselor.

Nelson Higgins, as Presiding Priest of Beaver Bottom Branch, under the presidency of the Bishop of Deseret.

Peter Anderson, Bishop of Oak Creek Ward, with Geo. Tinlinson as his first and C. H. Jenson as his second Counselor.

L. N. Christianson, Bishop of Leamington Ward, with B. P. Textarius his first and John Talbott as his second Counselor.

Thos. Yates Bishop of Scipio Ward, with Peter Nielson as his first and John A. Vance as his second Counselor.

David R. Stevens Bishop of Holden Ward, with A. P. Harmon as his first and Wm. Probert, Jr., as his second Counselor.

J. L. Robison, superintendent of the Sunday schools, with F. A. Robison as his first and Ira Noble Hinckley as his second assistant.

F. A. Robison, President of the Young Men's Mutual Improvement Association, with J. C. Robison and Joshua Greenwood as his Counselors.

Elizabeth Yates, President of the Relief Societies, with Lorinda Thompson first and Martha J. Robison second Counselor.

Isabel E. Robison, President of the Young Ladies' Mutual Improvement Associations, with Lizzie Henry first and Anna Stringam second Counselor.

Delilah Olson, President of the Primary Association, with Alice Callister as her second Counselor.

Home Missionaries—All the members of the High Council and all the alternate High Councilors and Levi Brunson, F. A. Robison, W. S. Ellison, Wm. Alldridge, Joseph Anderson, W. E. Robison, John Ashby and Jesse J. Martin, Jr.   C. ANDERSON, Stake Clerk.

Deseret News
October 19, 1887

DEATHS.

DUTSON—At Oak City, Millard County, Utah, September 30, 1887, of typhoid pneumonia, Joseph Willard, son of John W. and Caroline Jenkins Dutson; born January 9, 1862.

Southern Utonian
January 13, 1888

An Old Man Frozen to death.

At Deseret, Millard County, on Sunday night, an old man named Swenson was frozen to death. Parties up from that place to-day state that the unfortunate man was 87 years of age, and for some time past had been living at the homes of his children, first visiting one and then another. On Sunday it is alleged he was at his daughter's house at Deseret, and some words passed between them, in which the old gentleman was ordered away. Though the words were not intended to have the effect they did on the old gentleman, he was considerably offended, and went out and made his bed in the haystack, to which place he retired when evening came. During the night the thermometer went down to 23 degrees below zero, and on Monday morning his relatives, who had no idea but that he was safe at one of his children's houses, were horrified to find him frozen to death. Further particulars' or whether there is any different version of the causes which led Mr. Swenson to seek a sleeping place in the stack, were not obtainable this afternoon.—*Deseret News.*

Deseret News
April 18, 1888

Drowned.

On Saturday afternoon, at Deseret, Millard County, Lewis Bishop, a five year old son of M. M. Bishop, accidentally fell into the Sevier River, and was drowned. Efforts were made to recover the body, but the stream is deep and wide at the place where the child fell in, and it is uncertain whether or not he will be found. He was a bright child, and his death is a severe blow to his parents.

Fatality at Oasis.

In general the celebration of the Fourth in this vicinity was a complete success—the inhabitants of Oasis, Wyno' Ingersoll and Deseret joined hands and forces, irrespective of religious or political differences, and doing honor to the day of our national birth. But a sad accident which occurred at the schoolhouse and bowery at the latter place, marred the event. At about noon of that day, Moroni Bennett, a young man 16 years old, while riding on a horse behind another young man, was thrown off, receiving several bruises about the head. It was at first thought he would recover, for the extent of his internal injuries were not known. Dr. Miner, of Nephi, was duly summoned, and a though all was done that medical skill could suggest, the patient passed away during the evening of the 8th and was buried at 10 o'clock this morning. Deceased was a bright and promising son of Joshua and Isabel Bennett, who have the heartfelt sympathy of a wide circle of friends.

Oasis, Millard County, July 10, 1888.

AN ACCIDENTAL DEATH.

A Sad Affair—Impressive Funeral Ceremonies.

Brother Samuel W. Westein, writing from Deseret, Millard County, July 11, 1888, gives the following account of a fatal accident to a young man at that place, while the celebration of Independence Day was in progress:

"It was not long before our mirth was turned to sorrow. Two of our young men rode up town and were returning to their homes, both being on the same horse. When near their homes, on crossing a water ditch at full speed, the horse slipped and fell, throwing both riders headlong to the ground. Moroni Bennett, in his seventeenth year, alighted on his head, causing a fracture of the skull at the base. The other young man escaped with a severe fall. As soon as the latter young man, Juel Moody, gained his feet he saw his comrade lying insensible, and the blood gushing from his mouth. He with others picked him up and carried him into his father's house, that of Brother Joshua Bennett, which was close by. All was done for him that loving hands and hearts could do. Dr. Miner of Nephi was telegraphed for. He came and did all he could, but said there was no hope for the youth, who lingered until 3 o'clock Monday morning, the 9th inst., when his spirit peacefully passed away causing his parents and the community much sorrow.

The funeral services were held on the morning of the 10th in the school house. Bishop J. S. Black and Elder Wm. V. Black made some very consoling remarks and gave some excellent counsel to the young.

The remains were followed to the grave by about 300 of our citizens in 87 carriages and wagons, led by 12 young men with white shirts and black sashes; also one young man leading the horse of deceased, the saddle being covered with crape. Next followed 35 young ladies on foot, two and two, with white dresses and black sashes. Next came the hearse, carriages and wagons, containing relatives and friends.

This sad accident has caused a deep feeling of sorrow in this place, and much sympathy is felt for Brother and Sister Bennett and family, who are bowed down in sorrow. May God comfort them is the feeling of the Saints in this ward.

SAMUEL W. WESTERN.

FATAL SHOOTING AFFAIR.

Thomas Nookes, A Rancher, Killed at Warm Creek.

To the Editor of THE HERALD.

A bloody shooting affair occurred at Warm Creek, a small valley in Millard County, situated near the Nevada line on Friday last, in which Thomas Nookes was literally riddled with buckshot and instantly killed, while his partner, Isaac Preston, had a very narrow escape from the same fate. Information of the affair was brought here by George Bishop, who rode eighty-five miles without resting. He says the shooting took place in the night time, and that the deceased and his partner did not fire a shot except in self-defense.

Alexander Doutre, one of the participants, came in this morning and surrendered himself to the authorities. I am unable to give the names of all the parties who were engaged in the conflict, but from the recital of both sides it appears that ill feeling has existed between some of the prominent ranchers of that vicinity for some time past over a certain piece of land, but further than threats and hard words, nothing had occurred, when the rival claimants, each accompanied by one or more assistants, met on the ground with the result stated above. From Mr. Bishop it was learned that the deceased, besides having a full load of buckshot in his breast and another in the thigh; also received a bullet from a rifle. We refrain from further comment, preferring to wait until the examination, when the facts will be brought out.

J. H. H.

OASIS, MILLARD COUNTY, July 22d.

SEVIER LAKE

As it Was and Is, It being Nearly Extinct. — The Surrounding Scenery. — Description of the Spot Where Captain Gunnison and Party Were Massacred by Indians.

SALT LAKE CITY, Aug. 27, 1887.

Editor Deseret News:

Since my first arrival in Utah, 21 years ago, I have heard a great many conflicting stories about the Nicholet or Sevier Lake, situated in the great Pauvan Valley, Millard County. Some have described it as a beautiful fresh water lake with well defined shores, others as an immense salt marsh that could not be approached without imminent danger to the adventurer of sinking down his full length in mud, without any possible chance of extracting himself, and the Indians have told the most ridiculous stories about monsters and huge serpents inhabiting its briny waters, and even to this day shun it as a haunted place.

It is true the lake has been visited by a number of persons at various times. In 1852, we understand, the first party of white men (consisting of Albert Carrington, Joseph A. Young and others) visited its shores, and at that time found a lake with well defined shores about thirty miles long and from eight to fifteen miles wide, and having an average depth of some six or seven feet. But since the waters of the Sevier River (the only feeder the lake has) have been utilized for irrigation purposes, the lake has gradually dried up until the question of late years has arisen whether or not there were any water at all left in it. Having received an invitation from Bishop Jos. S. Black, of Deseret, to accompany him on a trip to the desert, I left Salt Lake City, by the Utah Central train on the afternoon of Aug. 21st and arrived in Deseret about midnight. The next morning, Aug. 22nd, Bishop Black, Dr. John E. Park and David K. Allen, of Salt Lake City, Joseph S. Black, Jr., of Deseret, and your correspondent, started from Deseret with two horse teams kindly furnished by the Bishop.

Byron Warner, a resident of Deseret, accompanied us down the river about six miles, to the spot where Capt. J. W. Gunnison and escort were killed by Pauvan Indians, early on the morning of September 26th, 1853. On that memorable day, just as the party were sitting down to breakfast they were surprised by a company of Indians, who killed Captain Gunnison, Mr. R. H. Kern, (topographer of the party) Mr. Creutzfeldt, (botanist) William Potter, of Manti, (guide) three soldiers (Liptrott, Caulfield and Merhteens) and one employe (John Bellows). The captain was killed a few hundred yards from camp, while attempting to reach the horses, and the others were killed at various points in and around the camp, and their bodies were subsequently found strung through the greasewood for a distance of about three quarters of a mile. Only four of the party escaped, leaving instruments, notes, animals, and all the baggage in possession of the Indians. Through the prompt action of Governor Brigham Young, who immediately upon hearing the sad news, dispatched D. B. Huntington, Indian interpreter, with a sufficient party, to the scene of disaster, most of the lost property was recovered and what remained of the bodies was gathered up and buried, Oct. 4th.

This party found that the flesh of the bodies had almost entirely been eaten by wolves, and the bones gnawed and widely scattered, but after a careful and patient search they succeeded in obtaining nearly the entire skeleton of Mr. Potter, some of the hair and thigh bone of Captain Gunnison and several bones of the balance of the party; the latter were all carefully buried on the spot, and the relics of Captain Gunnison and Mr. Potter were taken to Fillmore and interred.

This massacre was the direct result of the foolish and reckless conduct of a party of emigrants from the states on their way to California by the southern route, who killed a Pauvan Indian on Corn Creek and wounded two others a short time previous; hence followed the Indian rule of revenge on the next American party found on their grounds.

Byron Warner, our guide, being the only man in that part of the country who took part in the burial of the murdered men, and could tell the exact spot where the massacre took place, he found it without difficulty, and pointed out to us the spot where Gunnison's camp was located, where the camp fires were kindled, where the captain himself was killed and where the dead bodies were found and finally interred. Bishop Black had squared a large cedar post, which we brought along and dug in the ground on the identical spot where the bodies were buried. Strange enough this is the first monument of any kind that has ever been raised by friendly hands to mark the last resting places of these unfortunate men. And as there was not now the least trace to be found of the grave, we had entirely to rely on the good memory of our guide. It was with solemn feelings we listened to his recital of the incidents connected with the unpleasant task of burying the bodies, which had lain on top of the ground about two days before they were interred.

Leaving this memorable spot we drove about five miles further to the little settlement called Lake Town (also known as Ingersoll), consisting of about a dozen families living in a scattered condition along the river. After partaking of the hospitality of Elder Henry W. Hale, who presides over the few Saints there, we continued our journey over the desert in a southwesterly direction for nearly twenty miles further, and finally camped on the Sevier, near the upper end of the lake, but as the river is entirely dry except where there are standing pools of water, the lake is not fed by it at the present time. We camped when the sun was nearly two hours high, and the doctor struck out on foot westward, following the course of the river bed for several miles out into the lake bottom, where your correspondent crossed the river bed and proceeded southward over the desert to the northeast arm of the lake, but found no water. He walked through the mud for some distance until he reached a small salt island, from which, looking southward, he could see nothing but a salty, miry lake bottom, but far beyond the Frisco Mountains raise their lofty summits heavenward. On the west the "Saw-tooth" Mountains (a spur of the House range) obstructs the view; northward the desert—and a desert it truly is—stretches its dreary waste far away; eastward is the Cricket Mountains, a low range running in a northeasterly direction.

If any new arrivals or any of the "strangers within our gates" would like to see how Utah as a whole looked when the "Mormon" Pioneers first came here in 1847, I would advise them to take a trip to the lower end of the Pauvan Valley.

Early on the morning of the 23d we continued our journey and soon found ourselves passing along the lake shore, but no water in sight anywhere. After traveling about fifteen miles through one of the wildest and most forbidding countries I ever saw we nooned on the west shore of the lake without water, and made up our mind to return with the assurance that the Sevier lake was a thing of the past. The shores of the lake that once existed was marked very plainly by a gravelly beach some six feet above the present level of the lake bottom.

While the horses were feeding Dr. Park and the writer concluded to proceed on foot to a rocky prominence which appeared to be distant southward about a mile, but we found it more like five miles before we got to it. From the top of this prominence we had a fine view of the lake surface, but what was our surprise when we discovered, not far from shore, that which we so long had looked for in vain—water extending for miles north and south. Fearing that it might be a delusion—for we had previously been deceived by a number of beautiful mirages—it was decided that the writer should wade out from shore to the waters edge. This, however, was

found to be no easy task, for he had not proceeded far when he found himself breaking with his bare feet a crust of salt, about four inches thick, resting on top of stinking soft mud, which became deeper and deeper as he advanced from the shore. Finally, after working hard scooping away the salt with his hands and feet in order to make a passage, he reached the edge of the water, and thus established the fact that there is still water in the lake. After returning to the wagon Brother Allen, with much exertion, waded out through the salt and mud, a few miles north of the point previously named, and secured two bottles of the brine, and also some of the salt, for analytical purposes. We were now satisfied that the Sevier Lake, at the present time of low water, consists of an immense mud bottom, covered with from four to ten inches of salt, the top of which is covered some distance out from shore with a very little water, perhaps not exceeding six inches where it is the deepest.

Brother Allen having reached the shore in a somewhat exhausted condition, we started on our homeward journey after sundown, and after traveling for about five hours, most of the time without a road, we finally reached our camp ground of the previous night about midnight, all pretty tired, especially the horses who had been without water all day.

On Friday, August 24th, we returned to Deseret, where we arrived safe and well at 2 o'clock p. m., fully satisfied with our discoveries and adventures.

ANDREW JENSON.

Utah Enquirer
November 13, 1888

DIED.

CROFT.—At the residence of J. W. Turner, in this city, George Croft, of Deseret, Millard County, Utah. The deceased came to Provo for medical treatment about one week ago, and was examined by Dr. W. R. Pike, who informed him that he had cancer of the liver, and there were no hopes of his recovery. Brother Croft passed away quietly at 7:30 o'clock Saturday, November 10, 1888, and was conscious until a very short time before he died. He expressed his full faith in the Gospel of Jesus Christ till the last, referring to his mission to England and the satisfaction of having performed the same to the best of his ability. He leaves a wife and eight children to mourn his loss, as well as his aged father, upwards of 80 years.

Deseret News
November 28, 1888

DEATHS

TB.. OT.—At Leamington, Millard C., Oct. 7, 1888, Stephen Barton, son of Stephen B. and the late Roselletta G. Brownell Talbot, aged 1 year, 3 weeks and 1 day.

Surrendered Himself.

Today Treflle Doutre appeared before Commissioner Norrell and gave bail in the sum of $2500 to appear at the next term of the First District Court and stand trial on a charge of murder in the first degree, the grand jury at Provo having found an indictment against him for that offense. He is accused of having taken part in the killing of Mr. Nokes, in Millard County, a few months ago. Jerry Patnode and Alex. Doutre, the latter a brother of Treflle, are now in the penitentiary awaiting trial for the same deed. Treflle came from Nevada when he learned that he was indicted, to answer to the charge, of which he says he is innocent. He says that he was about a mile distant when Mr. Nokes was killed, having been shot by Alex Doutre. Patnode was with Alexander Doutre at the time of the homicide. Judge Powers defends Treflle Doutre.

Utah Enquirer
April 30, 1889

MURDER AT DESERET.

Jas. A. Wright Kills Soren Christensen

WHILE ON HIS WAY HOME FROM MEETING.

A Wife Compelled to Witness Her Own Husband's Murder.

(Special to the ENQUIRER.)

OASIS, Millard Co., Utah, April 29, 1889. Soren Christensen, of Deseret, was shot and instantly killed yesterday afternoon at 4:30 o'clock, about a mile below town, by James A. Wright. From facts learned after the shooting it appears that Christensen had in the forenoon called Wright a bad name, which Wright wanted him to retract. When they met, Christensen was returning from meeting in his wagon with his wife and nursing infant beside him. Wright was on foot, waiting for him. When Christensen came to where Wright was, he was covered with a shotgun, loaded with duck shot. Wright demanded a retraction, and after a few words pulled the trigger. The contents of the gun blew half of Christensen's head off, bespattering his brains and blood over his wife and babe. Wright is in custody. Christensen was over 50 years of age, and leaves a young wife and two children. Wright is about 50 years, and has a wife and large family in very poor circumstances.

Deseret Evening News
December 28, 1889

Millard Stake Conference.

The quarterly conference of this Stake was held at Fillmore, Nov. 24th and 25th. Present, Apostles F. M. Lyman and Abraham H. Cannon, of the local authorities, President Ira N. Hinckly, and most of the High Council. The attendance was large, and much valuable instruction was given by the speakers. Apostles F. M. Lyman and A. H. Cannon addressed the conference on the subjects of charity, and the education of our children in all stages—physically, mental, morally and religiously, and tithing, and the order of the Priesthood. The regular Priesthood meeting, was held on Sunday evening, with a good attendance. The general and local authorities were presented and unanimously sustained. The reports of the Bishops of the various wards showed a spirit of improvement among the people.

After the meeting on Monday afternoon, Apostles Lyman and Cannon, in company with the Stake presidency and others, went to Meadow Ward and assembled with the Saints.

On Tuesday morning, at 10 o'clock, meeting convened at Kanosh Ward, for the purpose of electing a Bishop, which was done by unanimous consent. Brother Jesse Hopkinson was the choice of the people.

At 2 o'clock a meeting was called of all the members of the ward. Brother Jesse Hopkinson was sustained as Bishop and Brother C. P. Christiansen as First and James Gardner as Second Counselor.

At 4 o'clock we left for Fillmore, and at 2 o'clock on Wednesday held a meeting at Deseret, when Vergie Kelly was presented as First Counselor to Bishop Jos. S. Black. Brother Kelly was unanimously sustained.

Some important questions were answered by Apostle F. M. Lyman upon the duties and callings of Presidents of Stakes, High Councilors, Bishops and other officers of the Priesthood.

Meeting adjourned at 4 p.m.

C. ANDERSON,
Stake Clerk.

Released From Prison.

December 27th, Bishop Joseph S. Black, of Deseret, Millard County, was released from the penitentiary, having served 75 days and paid his fine for unlawful cohabitation. He went south today.

PAHVANT VALLEY.

Developments at and Near the Town of Deseret.

"Elsmore and 'Neveraweat.'
'Suckertown' and Deseret.'

The name of the author of these lines, probably through his own modesty, is lost to everlasting fame! Some persons may fail on first reading to detect any sign of poetical genius in the couplet, but to those who fifteen years ago were acquainted with the towns above named will detect the sarcasm in the comparison drawn.

The history of Deseret, like that of scores of other "Mormon" settlements, has been a perpetual struggle with natural obstacles, consisting of extreme fluctuations in the volume of water in the Sevier River, a loose soil causing dam building to be not only expensive but uncertain and oft-times disastrous. From its first settlement until some four years ago Deseret has been an arena wherein the unflinching courage and perseverance of the average "Mormon" settlers have been pitted against great natural obstacles and forbidding surroundings. Twice deserted on account of bursted dams, its generous soil, with an abundance of water, has caused a return.

Four years ago, right on the heels of a most disastrous season, the settlers rallied, and with the assistance rendered by the now confiscated Church fund (which furnished bread to the toilers, who had but scant food and clothing in midwinter) built a canal twenty-four feet wide on the bottom, over four miles long, and nearly all in heavy cutting. They thus solved the water problem in a permanent manner, and gave a stability to the place which invites settlers to permanent homes.

That Deseret was not the third time deserted is chiefly due to the assistance of Church funds, which fact, with many other examples, stands as an enduring refutation against the allegation that the Church fund was being used for unworthy purposes, as also against the wilful perversity of those who have been chiefly instrumental in its confiscation.

Deseret is situated in the Pahvant Valley, midway between the east and west ranges of mountains, the nearest of which is about twenty miles distant. The surrounding country—which in the remote past was a small part of the slimy bed of Lake Bonneville—is flat and unbroken, save here and there where sand dunes and uplifted plateaus of volcanic rock relieve the monotony of the landscape. Imagine this wild plain covered with greasewood—a shrub generally conceded to be both useful and ornamental in the absence of any other vegetation—the Sevier River winding its way across the valley to the Dead Sea of Millard County, with occasionally a few patches of willows and meadow along the river bottom, and a good idea of Deseret scenery will have been obtained.

Making our unfinished meeting house, which stands near the north bank of the river, the initial point for description, it will be about one mile east to Oasis, a station on the O. S. & U. N. Railway. East of that point the farming land is taken for two or three miles. Three or four miles south and southwest are numerous ranches and stock farms. Following the course of the river towards the west, ranches and stock farms can be made for a distance of at least fifteen miles.

The principal part of the farming land, however, lies north and northwest, the northern limit being about three miles distant and marked by a branch of our canal. To the northwest a fine tract of land stretches out in an almost unbroken plain for a distance of from fifteen to twenty miles, and nearly all susceptible of profitable tillage.

Six miles north and three miles west we came upon a scene which, in its strange contrast with those of ninety days since, fills us with admiration for the pluck and enterprise which have, within so short a time, transformed one thousand acres of greasewood desert into a green stretch of growing grain, giving ample promise of an abundant return. It is known as the Co-op. farm, with Lehi Pratt, of your city, as its superintendent. The Co-op. farm is owned by the Salt Lake and Deseret Irrigation and Manufacturing Company. This company commenced work last fall on a canal eighteen feet wide on the bottom and upwards of twenty feet deep at its intersection with the upper portion of the Deseret Canal, and ran it several miles in a westerly direction to the surface, where, for many miles

west and north, the precious fluid can be spread and thousands of acres of choice land made to yield abundant crops of grain and alfalfa.

Last, but by no means least, are the enterprising efforts of Messrs. Crafts and Jensen at Laketown, or "Ingersoll," about twelve miles below here, on the river. Mr. Crafts, an old-time resident of Laketown, and several others last year located and improved several natural lakes, with a view of storing water for irrigation purposes. These lakes cover an area of from sixteen to twenty-four square miles of surface, which by a reasonable outlay of labor can be made to hold four feet of water available for irrigation. They are now well stocked with carp. Let any one interested figure out the importance of this enterprise. A canal from the lowest lake is nearly completed to a fine body of land lying north and west, where two hundred acres of oats and alfalfa are going in with a rush. This is merely a test; next year will witness a revolution for Laketown.

Those who saw the Sevier River dry below its numerous tributaries in the months of July and August may smile at the idea of such a large acreage being cultivated so far down the river; but it has been demonstrated that by seeding in November, flooding the land, and letting it freeze up during the winter, grain will be in advance of the drouth by the time the spring floods are over. This is usual with us from the 20th to the last of June, or later. There is a body of water at least sixty feet wide and twelve feet deep now flowing by here, with a four-mile current, and during many years' observation it has never been less than six or eight feet deep at this season. This wealth will be used in the immediate future sufficiently for domestic purposes.

We now number nearly 1500 souls. A good shoemaker could find steady employment and would be welcomed, and hundreds of those from the "boom" towns of Northern Utah, while finding rest here from real estate agents, may meet with prosperity if they will but "put their shoulder to the wheel," but they must not expect to move in the "upper crust" of Deseret society unless they are "rushers."

QUIN.

Deseret, June 4th, 1890.

Deseret Evening News
August 9, 1890

A SAD CASE.

Some Dreadful Inroads Made by Diphtheria.

On Wednesday, July 30th, a funeral cortege arrived in Fillmore from Deseret with the body of Thomas Croft, a lad who had died on his tenth birth day, from disease supposed to have been induced from too frequent bathing in the river. His mother, the widow of the late George Croft, wished to bury him by the side of his father, who is interred in the Fillmore cemetery. The funeral services, conducted by Bishop Callister, were held at the house of Brother Thomas Davis, the residence of the parents of Mrs. Croft. The lad had been treated for sore throat, but no idea of contagion was thought of. The day after the funeral of the boy Mrs. Croft was taken ill, alarming symptoms developed, and Dr. Hoxford from San Pete County being in town, he was summoned to the assistance of the sick woman. He instantly pronounced it a bad case of diph-theria. On the morning of August 2nd Brother Thomas Davis died, and on the evening of the same day Sister Croft also passed away, leaving seven young children orphans in our midst. The youngest, a little boy eighteen months old, was born on the day of his father's burial. This event has cast a gloom over our community. The city authorities, under the direction of the Mayor, have taken vigorous measures to prevent the further spread of the disease, and no further development of it has appeared. Brother Thomas Davis was born in England, April 7th, 1841, has resided in Fillmore since 1852, was a faithful member in the Church. Sister Lætilia Croft was born at St. Louis, Mo., November 21st, 1851, was a woman of faith, and great energy, devoted to the great responsibility of raising her fatherless children, and directing their course in the paths constantly walked in by their lamented father. There is no other case of diphtheria in our county, and we have turned it out here. G. C.

FILLMORE, Millard County, Utah, August 7th, 1890.

Salt Lake Herald
August 20, 1890

MILLARD COUNTY.

The canvass of Millard county was also completed yesterday, and the result is as follows:

Selectman—David R. Stevens 313; Wm. A. Rae 58.

County Clerk—T. C. Callister 315; A. L. Robinson 53.

Assessor and Collector—Joseph A. Lyman 315; William Mimmett 52.

County Prosecuting Attorney—Joseph S. Giles 312; D. C. Liddle 53; scattering 3.

Coroner—Byron Warner 315; George Greenway 53.

Recorder—T. C. Callister 315; A. L. Robinson 53.

Sheriff—A. T. Ashman 256; G. W. Cropper 112.

Deseret Evening News
February 2, 1891

Notes From Millard County.

A correspondent, signing himself "Occasional," writes from Oak City, Millard County, under date January 28th, as follows:

Sheriff Fowler, of Utah County, passed through here yesterday, having in charge two horse thieves. It appears that the prisoners had stolen the horses from a man for whom they had been working at Provo, and were attempting escape in this direction, but Sheriff Fowler pursued and overtook them at Deseret.

The much needed snow has come at last. The "beautiful" fell all Monday night and yesterday, and now we have sufficient to make our hearts rejoice.

Our little meeting-house was filled to overflowing last Monday evening to listen to the excellent address of Brother Hinkley, President of this Stake of Zion. Other prominent brethren also spoke on the occasion.

DOINGS AT DESERET.

We have been honored here by a visit of four of the Quorum of the Twelve Apostles, viz.: Elders Lyman, Smith, Cannon and Lund. A ward conference was held by previous notice from the Stake Presidency who were present, except Brother Daniel Thompson, first counselor to President Hinckley, who is very sick.

Brother Joseph S. Black, who has been our Bishop from the first organization of the ward, desired to resign that office, and by unanimous vote was honorably released therefrom. Elder Lyman and all associated with him, in view of the rapid growth of numbers and the large tract of country over which they were scattered, thought the time opportune for dividing the ward into three separate wards, which was done. The Central Ward is Deseret, and Milton Moody was chosen Bishop, with A. F. Warnock and Isaac Wicker for counselors. Oasis on the east. The depot being the central point will have for Bishop Brother John Styler, with Lars Hansen and Jacob Hawley for counselors. The new district on the north side of the river, which is fast filling up with good people, will be called the Hinckley Ward, and will be presided over by Brother William H. Pratt, with George A. Black and Thomas Davis for counselors. Full quorums of teachers were also unanimously sustained for each ward.

In the Hinckley district is a large tract of land owned by gentlemen of Salt Lake City, who have spent large sums of money in clearing the land and planting about 1000 acres last year, from which they have realized very little returns, owing to the loss of water during the irrigating season, from the dam being washed out. The same company also spent several thousand dollars putting in the river a very substantial dam, under the Superintending of Mr. Charles Haun. This enterprise was looked upon by some at first with a degree of suspicion, as a menace to vested rights. But the strength and permanency of the new dam has given a degree of confidence which make its projectors appear as benefactors to Millard County.

We have a vast area of splendid land in this valley, but for fifteen years the people have been heavily taxed to keep a rickety, shifty dam in the treacherous river, and were often left without water when they most needed it for irrigation. Now the future looks bright for water, and a unity of well directed muscle and brains will yet furnish happy homes for thousands of industrious people. We thank the boys of the Oasis Band for their pleasant serenade of the Apostles during their visit.

On Friday last some of the family of Mr. Thomas Cropper drove about 250 sheep to the river for water. The sheep got into the quicksand and water and could not get out. Mr. C. and his neighbors worked like Trojans to extricate the sheep, but so firmly were the sheep's legs embedded in the sand that it took the strength of a man to pull them out, one at a time. Twenty-one of the sheep were dead when taken out.

La grippe is getting in its work amongst us. Bishop Black being one of its victims. W. W. Black was unable to be out at the conference. Bishop Styler has been sick for some time and had to be taken home unable to remain at the meetings.

A. BIRD.

DESERET, March 23rd, 1891.

Returned Missionaries.

Elder Samuel W. Western, of Deseret, Millard County, called at our office yesterday, having returned September 2 from his mission to Great Britain. Brother Western left this city August 14th, 1889, and has labored principally in Birmingham conference, over which he presided for the last sixteen months. He has enjoyed, he says, his labors very much and has been well treated everywhere.

Elders Hans Eriksen, of Logan, and George Marshall, of Minersville, Beaver County, have also returned from their fields of labor.

DESERET DOINGS.

Not Booming But Prosperous, and Blessed With Marvelous Weather.

It is not often that we, of Deseret, trespass on the valuable columns of THE HERALD, but fearing that unless we speak out occasionally, we will become like our esteemed neighboring town of Fillmore, and become forced to have "Millard county" added to our mail matter in order to find us.

Although not a boom town, the wave of prosperity which is rolling over Utah has given us more of life and vigor, and the result is that substantial dwellings and business houses are springing up in every direction.

The almost unlimited resources of land, water, meadow and range, second to none south of Utah county, which this section affords, are attracting the attention of home-seekers in many parts of Utah, but more particularly in "our Dixie," where scores of families are contemplating a move to this place with the return of spring. They will not bring much cash, but what is better, the pluck, energy and frugality which have been the last potent factors in redeeming the southern part of Utah from sterility.

Notwithstanding, we are centrally located in a valley over sixty miles wide; the "everlasting hills" are adding largely to our general prosperity. Valuable finds of the precious metals are being made west of us in the House Range, and without doubt, the coming season will witness great activity in the mining industry all along that range of mountains from Fish Springs, south to Frisco, as there are ore croppings every few miles all along the entire range. The most important of the

RECENT DISCOVERIES

is that of a large vein of silver lead ore made by Messrs. Alexander and Palmer, of this place, in what is known as Morgan gap, an opening through the House range, about forty-five miles west.

About seven tons of ore is arriving daily from the Fish Springs district for shipment over the Union Pacific, and as the hauling is being almost entirely done by residents, it becomes a profitable source of revenue, besides making a lively demand for grain at good prices.

The present winter is verifying our claim that Deseret has the boss climate of Utah, and that while reaping our full share of the benefits derived from heavy deposits of snow in the mountains, we experience

THE MINIMUM OF DISCOMFORTS,

for, while the beautiful is being piled up for future use, and the residents of cities and towns contiguous to the mountains are slushing around in the snow and mud, we are in the enjoyment of sunny skies and dry ground. A sleighing party here would be a genuine curiosity, a fact which should be known by the implement dealers, who, every time it snows in Salt Lake city flood this section with bob-sled circulars.

Many of us are watching the natural gas developments near Salt Lake with a more than general interest, for, geologically speaking, the eastern and western ranges of mountains which bound this valley are nearly identical in formation with those that form the eastern and western boundaries of Salt Lake valley. In fact, ours is a prolongation of that valley to the south. And the western range represents the base of the lower silurian with a dip of about 150 towards the east, while our eastern range is of the upper silurian with about the same general dip and direction, proving almost beyond doubt that the Trenton formation lies directly under this valley, and at about the same depth as found in Salt Lake valley. And should the present gas finds prove permanent and profitable, a magnificent field of nearly 300 miles in length will be open for natural gas explorations.

AN ENCOURAGING INCIDENT

occurred here a short time since: a resident in driving a pipe for a flowing well struck a body of gas, the well ejecting gas and mud for some time. This is regarded as a pointer.

While on the subject of "formations," will it not be strange if the reported strike of coal on Antelope island should be correct, and thus prove that dame nature has been capable of sandwiching a slice of carboniferous between two formations infinitely older, and where least expected, thus placing the "fragment" theorists "on top" in the creation controversy. Perhaps!

Respectfully, IGNOT.
Deseret, Jan. 9.

Millard County Races.

OASIS, Utah, Jan. 18.—[Special to TRIBUNE.]—The Millard County Race Association opened up on a track midway between Oasis and Deseret to-day. The track was good, the weather fine, and there were entries from all parts of the county. Oasis and Deseret horses wear the blue ribbons. The races of note were as follows:

First race, quarter-mile dash—Two entries; a bay horse, owned by Harvey Watts of Kanosh, won by a close call.

Second race, quarter-mile dash—Two entries; a bay owned by Mr. Cropper of Deseret, and a gray owned by Mr. Maxfield of Oasis; won by the gray mare of Oasis in her own time.

Third race—Same entries as the second; won by the Maxfield mare.

Fourth race—Run by a mare owned by Lee Cropper of Deseret and a sorrel mare owned by Sims Hawley of Oasis; won by Hawley's mare.

Fifth race, one-half mile dash—Two entries, a horse owned by Childsworth of Kanosh and a horse owned by Moody of Deseret; won by the Moody horse.

Sixth race—Same entries as in the fifth race; won by the Moody horse. Good time was made on the new track.

A Murder in Millard County.

OASIS, Utah, Jan. 18.—[Special telegram to THE HERALD.]—Saturday, January 16, Treffley Deutrie shot and killed William Stephenson at Warm Creek near Smithville, Millard county, Utah. This is one of the brothers known as the French boys, who killed Tom Noakes three years ago last July. Then it was a dispute over land. This time it is a dispute over water. This is the same party whom Governor Thomas referred to in his message to Congress two years ago. Further particulars after the inquest. This information has just been received from George Bishop, who has just arrived from Smithville, who is a witness in the case.

Deseret Evening News
May 12, 1892

A NEW POSTOFFICE

Established at Hinkley, Millard County, and a Postmaster Appointed for Holliday! Salt Lake Co.

Information has been received from Hon. John T. Caine, Utah's delegate to Congress, of the establishment of a postoffice at Hinkley, Millard county, and the appointment of William Alldridge as postmaster, also the appointment of James Neilson as postmaster at Holliday, Salt Lake county.

For the present the Hinkley mail should be sent to Deseret.

Deseret Evening News
September 26, 1892

A Sad Bereavement.

The biggest funeral that Riverton ever witnessed since the ward was organized, was held at that place September 21st, 1892. This ward was called to mourn the death of one of our most esteemed and intelligent young ladies, Olive May Walker, the daughter and only child of Edwin A. and Lavina Walker, born in Deseret, Millard County, September 4th, 1877. The funeral services lasted about three hours. Many excellent remarks were made over her remains, which were laid away in a beautiful white brocaded plush casket.

So great was the respect for the deceased that not only Riverton but Herriman, Bluff Dale, and South Jordan wards, turned out to pay their last token of love to the deceased.

A fine composition of poetry, composed and written by Wm. H. Silock, for the occasion, a young man in the ward, was read at the services.

N. J. C.

Salt Lake Tribune
September 30, 1892

Obituary.

At his home in Burbank, Millard county, Utah, September 1st, 1892, Delbert I. Hockman died from catarrh of the stomach. The above few words have worlds of meaning to the bereaved mother, who suffers the loss of a dutiful son, and the sisters and brothers, who mourn for a devoted brother.

The deceased was the oldest son of Samuel and Jane E. Hockman, born on the Big Thompson, Weld county, Colorado, November 20, 1868; moved from Colorado to Utah with his parents in his early youth, where he grew into manhood and spent his last days, loved by many and respected by all. His genial face was ever welcomed by all who knew him, and his kind and loving heart made many friends, now disconsolate in a loss that can never be replaced.

May his sleep be peaceful.

Deseret Weekly
October 15, 1892

DEATHS

WALKER.—Of typhoid pneumonia, Olive May Walker, daughter and only child of Edwin A. and Lavine Walker, born in Deseret, Millard county, September 4th, 1877; died at Riverton, Salt Lake county, September 20th, 1892, at 5 o'clock a. m., aged 15 years and 16 days.

SMITH.—At Sandy, September 24, 1892, Annie Elvira, wife of Joseph Smith, after an illness of four days.

The deceased was the daughter of Lachoneus and Annie Hemmeaway. She was born at Corn Creek, Millard County, Utah, Oct 13th, 1870. She leaves a husband and a young babe. She was a faithful Latter-day Saint during her life.

Deseret Weekly
December 17, 1892

ITEMS FROM MILLARD.

Millard county with her vast area and genial climate, owing to her limited water supply has been considered slow, but there are signs that warrant the prediction that she is going to "get thar" all the same. Early settlements were only possible upon the small mountain streams on the east side of the county. Later several heroic efforts were made to dam the Sevier river, and plant the city of "Deseret," but time after time the treacherous quicksand in the river bed gave way, and the toil and hunger-planted dam went with the mighty stream, leaving scores of families without a prospect for bread, except as they scattered through the land among those who had not made the venture. This happened so often that the name of "Deseret" was whispered in derision of those who had once settled there. But undaunted men again went down to subdue the land, and with poverty and prayers they worked the woven willows in the water, checked the current, and watered their little farms, pointed with becoming pride to their labors, and felt safe in what they had accomplished. But the insidious enemy was again at work, and would have again wrought ruin, had not friends and capital come to the rescue

and scientifically put a substantial dam miles above the old location, necessitating an immense outlay of money and labor for canals and ditches, but giving security and future homes for thousands. Deseret with its neighboring settlements is there, and flourishing. We speak of them now with respect; they answer with a smile and hint at our absorption. We laughed at first, but now we stop to consider, for the developments of the last three years have sobered us with facts. About that time one of our citizens was wading through the wastes in search of ducks; his practical eye perceived a future for the slumbering land, which have materialized in the investment of hundreds of thousands of dollars and the great future for the Swan Lake country about eleven miles southwest from Deseret.

I have just fished out a few facts about another project or enterprise of this same citizen. Again it is a reservoir and the irrigation of one hundred thousand acres of land, land unsurpassed in fertility in all our Territory. The reservoir, a natural basin, will be four miles long by one mile

wide, of great depth, fed by an enormous living spring, affording a stream thirteen feet wide and six feet deep, with a fall of six feet to the mile. There are three other streams that will be poured into the reservoir, for from six to eight months of the year. The outlet will be through a tunnel in solid rock, about seventy-five feet long. There will be no trouble from wave action, the lake being almost entirely surrounded by hills, filled with saw timber and fire wood of the best kind.

I have gathered these facts mostly from parties well acquainted with the country and have not found one doubter of the feasibility and success of this great enterprise. From my own knowledge the land is covered with black sage and amongst the best that ever responded to the toil of husbandman. It lays in the western part of our country. The father of these great schemes of development, is our respected citizen, Mr. Jos. E. Ray, not a grasping speculator, but an easy-going fellow who seems to glide through the world with great and practical ideas and willing that those who work with him shall share in these profits. He has already secured rights from land owners, and done work on the scheme. The small amount of capital necessary will easily be found.

Yes, Millard is surely "getting thar" and "Joe" Ray's name will be written with honor in her history. A. BIRD.
FILLMORE, Dec. 6, 1892.

Deseret Evening News
May 24, 1893

In The British Mission.

The *Millennial Star* of May 15th announces the release of Elder Chas. W. Watts, of Millard county, from his labors as president of the Norwich conference of the British mission, to return home. Elder Watts has been absent from home nearly two years. Elder J. Campbell is appointed to succeed him as president of the Norwich conference.

Deseret Evening News
October 6, 1894

MILLARD HOTEL BURNED.

Fire Started From a Lamp Left by a Man Who Went Off to Play Cards.

Mr. H. W. Hales, of Deseret, arrived in this city today, bringing with him the information that the Millard hotel at Oasis was completely destroyed by fire on Thursday night.

It appears that a man left a lamp standing in a window in his room about 9 o'clock at night and went down to play a game of cards. By some means a short time afterward the flame of the lamp was communicated to the curtains and from there spread rapidly. The alarm was given by some young ladies who went upstairs to dress for a ball to be given in the neighborhood that night. A glance showed that the building, which was a two story frame structure, was doomed. By the hardest kind of work the furniture and clothing on the first floor was all saved, but everything above the first story was destroyed with the building. The loss was $4,000. The insurance amounted to $3,000.

A HAPPY FAMILY.

Mr. and Mrs. Ashman Celebrate Their Fiftieth Wedding Anniversary.

A PROGRESS reporter had the pleasure of an interview with Mr. John Ashman, of this city, from whom he elicited the following: To commence with, Mr. Ashman is a true type of an English gentleman. Having been born in England on the 7th day of February, 1823, at Salton Cottage, near Dover, County of Kent, he served his country in the Royal Horse Artillery for four years, and was engaged in suppressing the charter riots of 1842, which were widespread throughout Lancashire.

He became acquainted with Ann Wild in 1743, at Leeds, Yorkshire, whom he subsequently married at London, Nov. 18, 1844, at which place he resided until 1848. He removed to Leeds, where he embraced the gospel in 1851, in which his wife soon followed. During the remainder of Mr. Ashmans stay in England, he became a zealous and ardent worker in advocating the doctrine of the gospel of Christ, and at different times occupied important ecclesiastical positions, having presided over the consolidated branches of the Church at (Newton and Clayton) and being the founder of these branches. Mr. Ashman remained at Newton Heath, and presided over the Salford branch of the church until he emigrated to Utah in 1864, arriving in Fillmore Sept. 15th of the same year.

Commencing with nothing to help him except his energy and physical strength with the assistance of his amiable and preserving companion he has built up a home that "my lords" of the old realm might truely be proud of.

In 1856 he was called by Bishop Thos. C. Callister to preside over the Elders Quorum. The first organized in Millard county, and the lesser priesthood.

At present Mr. Ashman is filling the following ecclestical positions. Alternate high-council man, home missionary and preceptor of Deacons quorum.

Mr. Ashman holds a commission as company adjutant of Pan santo military district under the organization of the Nauvoo Legion. He has also held several municipal offices.

It can truly be said of Mr. Ashman that whether in public or private life he has used always that zeal and energy that but few men posess.

On Nov. 18. 1894, Mr. Ashman and wife celebrated the anniversary of their fiftieth wedding, the following church dignitaries being present: Apostle F. M. Lyman and President I. N. Hinckley. At 6 P. M. a royal repast was spread.

The branches of Mr. Ashman's family are as follows: Five children, forty-seven grand children, and nineteen great grand children. Mr. Ashman is seventy-two years of age, and his wife is sixty-seven, both being as hale and hearty as most people at the age of thirty five.

Mrs. Ashman has been a constant and prominent singer the Fillmore choir for thirty years, and bids fair to continue as such for twenty more. The PROGRESS wishes Mr. and Mrs. Ashman many happy returns of the day.

Oak City:

Oak City, January 18.

Success to Anderson & Knapp, the new managers of THE PRO-GRESS-REVIEW. May they prosper as publishers, and thereby give unto the people a paper that will contribute much to the growth and prosperity of Millard county.

Oak City and Oasis are now connected by a line of telephone poles. The wire is to be stretched at an early date.

Representative Walter C. Lyman spent Saturday and Sunday in this place. He is working faithfully with our own representatives, for the bill providing for the establishment of an experiment farm in Millard county and an appropriation to sustain it.

Mrs. Kate Summers, of Stockton, is visiting with her parents, Mr. and Mrs. Harry Roper,

Geo, E. Finlinson and John E. Lovell, representing the Young Men's Mutual, and Ida and Maggie Jacobson, of the Young Ladie's Mutual, attended the M. I. A. convention in Kanosh Sunday. They report a profitable time.

School is running with a full attendance, one hundred per cent of the school population being enrolled.

County Supt. Finlinson has apportioned the state school fund to the several districts, upon a basis of $3.60 per capita of the persons of school age of this county. The distribution is as follows: Fillmore $1,883.75, Meadow $898.52, Kanosh $701.79, Hatton $110.70, Deseret $487.08, Oak City $284.18, Leamington $280.17, Holden $594.00, Scipio $686.84, Oasis $806.27, Hinckley $603.72, Garrison $132.84. Abraham $191.88, Smithville $84.87, Black Rock $40.50, Hockman $73.80, Clear Lake $55.35; total $6,464.88 Millard county has a school population of 17 52

Hinckley

Hinckley, Feb. 12.

The dense fog still prevailes here. We have not seen the Sun for two weeks. The people will welcome the Sun when it appears again.

Mr. O. C. Glover will leave for California in a few days to make it his future home.

Our District Schools have put in a good winter this year, not having to stop on account of sickness, for which we feel greatfull.

Mrs W. F. Pratt is able to be in our midst again. Mrs E. M. Workman is very ill at the present time.

One day last week Henry Reeve met with a very painfull accident while working on a bailor having his foot mashed. which will lay him up for a while.

Hinckley

Hinckley, Feb. 19.

We are having fine weather now, most too fine to last long.

Farmers are begining spring work with happy hearts for the coming season.

School teachers have just returned from Nephi. Owing to the wreck 2½ miles this side of Lynn Junction, They did not get here in time for school Monday.

Mrs. Annie Peterson of Eureka is here visiting with her parents.

Quite a number of our people attended Conference at Holden.

Frank Whitehead Jr. and J. E. Pratt are at Provo taking Missionary courses.

The many friends of Clarence A. Pack are pleased to hear that he is recovering from his accident which occured at Eureka mine, and that the report was false of him being dead.

Mrs. E. M Workman is slowly improving

Mrs Clark has sold her residence to Wm. Reeve and will make Mercur her future home.

Bishop Frank Pratt has bought the residence of Mrs. Alfred Damron and will move there before long.

Hinckley

Hinckley, Feb. 27.

Dr. Robison made a hurry call to hinckey to attend Geo. Theabald who is very ill.

An interesting program was rendered on Washington's birthday.

We are having spring weather with rain, snow and wind.

Whooping cough is in our midst again.

Mrs. Ella Whitehead is down from Mercur visiting relatives and friends.

Mrs. Mary Stevenson is down from Cottonwood visiting father and family.

Mr. Bennet of Holden is visiting with his daughter Mrs. Heifer Bishop.

Hinckley

Hinckley, Mar. 5th

Grandma Martendale's brother of Pensylvania has been here visiting with her and Mr. N. B. Badger for a while but has left for his home again.

Bro Harmon of Holden was seen on our streets last week having just returned from a trip to California.

Geo. A. Black and wife are back from Mexico he reports every thing favorible down there and if he can dispose of his property in Utah he will go there to make it his future home.

Geo. Theobald is able to be up again.

Dr. Robison was in our midst last week on professional business.

Mrs. Geo Talbot has gone to Mercur to attend her sister Mrs Wm. Wright who is ill

Oak City

Oak City, Feb. 28
(late)

The unseasonable mild weather of the last month has dried the ground and placed it in a splendid condition to work. As a result many farmers are beginning their spring work of ploughing and sowing. This warm weather is also rapidly reducing the visible supply of snow in the mountains and foot hills.

Our schools gave a very enjoyable party last Thursday evening in memory of George Washington's birthday.

Samuel Dutson and family of Aurora spent a few days with relatives in Oak City last week. Samuel will run Mr. Mack Webbs farm in Deseret during the season.

More thoroughbred chickens. Simeon Walker has just received from the north a trio of fine Rhode Island Reds. These are the first of their kind to be brought into Oak City. They are beauties.

Stake Sunday School Board meetings were held in this place last Saturday and the following were present: Supt. John Reeve, Joseph Finlinson, Emma Wright, R. E. Robison, N. L Peterson and Millie Lyman also Wm. A. Morton of the General Sunday School Board. In the meetings plans for the future work in the Sunday Schools were made and forceable instructions given with reference to carrying them out. A public meeting was held in the evening at which Supt. Reeve, N. L. Peterson, R. E. Robison and W. A. Morton spoke. Their remarks were all seasoned with the proper spirit and interspersed with singing by the ward choir and a song by Emma Wright rendered in the Maori tongue.

Abraham

Abraham Mar. 12th.

Bro. Eric Hogan, who has been in Salt Lake having treatment for his eyes, has returned home. His eyes are somewhat improved.

Pres. A. A. Hinckley, from Hinckley was out visiting the people of Abraham, yesterday for the afternoon meeting A splendid sermon was delivered by him.

Miss Annie Hilton has just returned to Cedar City to re-sume her labors in school, which has been closed for the past four months on account of sickness.

Elder Wm. S Taylor, the first missionary from Abraham, expects to leave Salt Lake City, on the 4th of April for the Southern States.

A banquett, program and dance is being arranged to give the missionary an excellent send off.

Hinckley

Hinckley. Mar.15th

Mrs. Geo. Talbot has just returned from Mercur and reports the camp in a good prosperous condition.

We have had a beautiful fall of 10 inches of snow and it still looks as though we might have more before long.

Mr Joseph Talbot and family Pocotallo Idaho have come to make this their future home

Reports are that Jacob Langston has purchased the farm of Leroy Young. Brother Young will leave for the North in the near future.

Wm. Walker of Oak City has also bought him a home here of J. B. Pratt.

Mr. Joel Moody's family is quarantine having been exposed to small pox.

Another Pioneer called hence. It was this morning grandma Stalks was well and ate her breakfast after, she said she was never so sick in her life and expired in a few minutes. She is some where about her 87th year she leaves a large posterity to mourn her departure.

Hinckley

Hinckley, Apr. 10th

We had a hard rain here Friday last. It lasted all day and the roads are muddy, but the south wind is blowing and it is cloudy like it might storm again.

Born—to Mr. and Mrs. Edward Davis, a son. Mother and child doing well.

A nice young lady came to the home of N. B. Badger. and was welcomed by all, so she will stay with them All well.

The many friends of Miner Aldredge, who is at Mercur, will be pleased to hear that he is better, though not out of danger. He is at the hospital in Salt Lake City.

Norman Bliss is reported to be better.

Oak City

Oak City, Apr 1.
(late)

The month of March in and around Oak City has been an ideal one so far as storm is concerned Entering with a week of rain and snow the ground was well soaked. The middle and last decades of March brought copious rains and snows, which the absorbent soils of this section took into complete saturation. April was ushered in with a big snow storm and at the close of the first 24 hours the weather man measured up 1.25 inches of precipitation. This, together with the 3.6 inches of March precipitation, makes the water supply for the coming season decidedly favorable.

Wm H. Walker and family have moved to Hinckley. A few days prior to their departure their friends gave them a pleasant surprise party, at which singing, games and refreshments were enjoyed. Hinckley must certainly have some good, substantial inducements for settlers, as this makes the fifth family to move there from this place.

After a successful winter's work, the grammar grades of our district schools closed last Friday. Miss Millie Lyman, who has served as principal in our school, and over these leaves this week for Salt Lake, to do substitute teaching in the very satisfactory manner. She grades, executed her work in a Salt Lake City schools.

Mr. and Mrs. Antone Christenson must be holding a family reunion. We notice the return of their son, John A., from a 2½ years' mission to the Northern States, and Edward, who has been taking the winter's course at the B. Y. U. Also their daughter, Mrs. Mattie Talbot, who has been living in Idaho for the past six years.

Co. Surveyor Willard Rogers is doing business in Oak City. He has located a county road between this place and Lynn, and is now doing work for private individuals.

We now have seven incubators running night and day, hatching out thoroughbred chickens.

Charles Roper Jr. is in receipt of a fine pen of Buff Orpingtons, consisting of five pullets and one cockerel.

Samuel Greenwood was here Saturday and received orders from the district for school supplies.

Co. School Supt. Finlinson leaves Wednesday for Salt Lake, to attend the annual convention of city and county superintendents, to be held Apr. 5-6.

Leamington

Leamington, April. 18.

The Leamington primary grades close their work Friday, April 18th after a short, but not unsuccessful year, one thoroughly enjoyed by pupils and teachers and teachers. Although the enrolments are far from ideal yet with the intelligent corporation of the parents the children have made encouraging progress

The following promotions and retentions have been made: Promoted to the fourth grade, unconditionally; Marion Adams Benj. Dutson and Nola Greathouse. Conditionally,—Blake Robison, promoted to the third grade unconditionally:—Tho Dutson, Loreta Dutson, Leta Overson, and Sina Overson. Conditionally,—Ada Robinson and Wallace Nielson. Retained in the third grade, Lucretia Robison. Promoted to the second grade unconditionally—George Terry Jay Nelson, Vivian Dutson, Birdie Adams, and Manilla Overson. Conditionally Winnie Strange. Promoted to the first grade unconditionally—Earl Greathouse, Shelby Nielson, Orvis Robison, Leonard Dutson, Marvin Textorious, Marvin Textorious, May Dutson, Fern Dutson, Rhea Nelson, Eleanor Ashby, Edith Nelson and Myrtho Strange. Conditionally—Marion Terry, Mary McCardell, Erma Dutson. Retained in beginners grade—Selma Johnson, Alice Holman, Daniel Downing, Lorence Strange, Junior Overson, Will Overson.

In punctuality and regularity the record of little Rhea Nelson stands highest, having not been tardy absent nor unprepared during the entire school year. Closely following hers, and nearly perfect are the records of

Earl Greathouse. Nola Greathouse, Jay Nelson, Wallace Nelson, George Terry, Eleanor Ashby Beatrice Nielson, and Birdie Adams.

Jessie M. Johnson,
Teacher.

Hinckley

Hinckley, April 23d.

We are having wind, wind, wind for a change.

From the appearance around the homes of the people here, Arbor Day was observed by planting trees and shrubs which improves the homes.

Grandpa Terry who has been ill for sometime is reported to be some better.

Now is the time for our young men to get homes. Take a draw on the Melville Irrigation Co. land. There is none better in this section.

Bro. Robison who recently moved here, was the speaker Sunday, and he delivered a fine discourse.

Bro. Wm. Alldredge sen. is on the sick list and we have hopes for his speedy recovery.

Sister A. A. Hinckley is reported better. She is intending to go to Fillmore for the benefit of her health. We hope she will soon be able to be around again.

The farmers are all busy irrigating their farms.

Deseret, Apr. 18.

This place was blessed with a

slight shower last evening. Just the thing to make our early garden seeds spring up.

Some of our people are to be congratulated on the interest they have taken to improve the looks of their homes. Arbor Day was well spent by most of our citizens and if everything grows that was planted, there will be quite an improvement in the looks of this place in a few years.

Miss Carrie Black of this place is quite sick. It is hoped that She will soon be around again without having any serious disease to battle against.

In the Kimball piano word contest, Mrs J. W. Damron Jr. was awarded $78.00, and only spent two afternoons in collecting her words.

Quite a number of our citizens attended conference in Salt Lake City and reported a splendid time.

Millard County Progress
June 1, 1906

Hinckley

Hinckley, June 1.

We are having wind and rain which makes it very disagreeable

We are pleased to hear that the county has responded so well in turning out to try and save the reservoir dam which is in great danger yet. Bro. A. A Hinckley has just returned from there and reports the condition better tho not out of danger.

Our meeting last Sunday was well attended considering that most of the brethren were away.

Mr. F. T. Slaughter and bride have returned from Salt Lake.

We wish them peace and happiness thru life's journey.

Wallace and Joseph Wright have returned home from school. The former has been attending at Logan and the latter at Beaver.

The community was deeply grieved over the sad death of Bro Edward Lyman of Oak City. Our heartfelt sympathy is extended to the bereaved family.

Misses Elmira and Laura Walker and Hattie Theobald are with us again, after completing their winter's work at school.

The infant son of Mr. and Mrs Edward Davis is very ill.

Oak City

Oak City, May 29

A gloom has been cast over our whole community by the untimely death of Edward L. Lyman, who died May 22nd from an attack of pneumonia, which lasted about ten days.

On the 12th inst. Mr. Lyman was assisting with the funreal of Mr. Lovegreen an aged man of this place, in the necessary work of burying the dead, and little did any one think then that he would be the next over whom the sad rites would be performed. He went home that night and took sick, and gradually grew worse until the end came as stated above.

Notwithstanding everything was done that could be done for his relief, it was of no avail. Mr. Edward L. Lyman was the son of Amasa M. and Lydia Partridge Lyman, he was born in Salt La e City, Jan. 4th, 1857, was baptized into the Church of Jesus Christ of latter Day Saints Nov., 18th, 1865 by Daniel Thompson, and confirmed a member on the same date by Thomas Callister. At the age of seven he removed with his father's family to Fillmore and later to Oak City where he has spent the greater part of his life.

The deceased was a man of marked ability, of splendid virtue, wise, honest, honorable, whose word was sacred, and who never forsook a cause once espoused. He had his pinions and convictions, they were based upon his best deliberate judgement. He was wide awake and took the leadin all things that added to the welfare of this town. Indeed he had many manly qualities which should be recorded as a rich heritage to the youth of any community. He leaves six children and a devoted wife to mourn his departure. His children are, Leo, Millie, Lydia, Callis, Willie and Rich.

The funreal was held Wed. the 23rd, and was largely attended. Bishop Anderson, Coun. Geo. Finlinson, Elder Joseph Finlinson, and Pres. F. M. Lyman spoke in words of praise of the life and labors of the departed, and gave words of comfort to the bereaved frmily and friends

There were no public gatherings held in Oak City last Sunday due to the breaking out of small pox. All precautions against its further spread have been taken by our health officer O. H. Jacobson, and it is to be hoped the disease will be checked.

Jacob Nielson was taken to the hospital at Salt Lake City last week to be operated upon for urinary trouble. He left in a somewhat critical condition, but we trust that he has received permanent relief by this time.

Hinckley

Hinckley, July 1 t.

One week ago yesterday our town was thrown into sorrow by the sudden death of A. W. Wright. While at work mowing hay, Mrs. Robert Reeve, his wife's mother, saw him leave the machine and fall to the ground. He acted so strangely she called her daughter and they then summoned Charles Stratton, who came and took him to his home He had just got in the house when he sank down in Mr. Stratton's arms and expired. The cause of death was heart failure. The funeral services were held in the ward meeting house on Monday the 25th. The house was filled to overflowing. When all were seated Prof. Whitehead played a march and his Sunday school class marched around the casket, and each deposited a beautiful boquet of flowers on it. The speakers were Richard Parker, R. W. Reeve, D. A. Morris, Jacob Langston, A. A. Hinckley and Bishop W. F Pratt. His past life and labors were dwelt upon and consoling remarks were given to the bereaved. Mr. and Mrs Joseph Workman were down from Lehi. Mrs. Workman was a sister of the deceased. Mr. and Mrs. W. W. Right from Mercur were in attendance. Eleven years ago on the same day as his funeral was held, he left his home for a mission to the Southern States, where he remained almost three years. Four years ago on the same day he in company with his wife left for a mission to New Zealand, which they faithfully performed, returning a little over a year ago. He was 46 years of age. The bereaved wife and relatives have the sympathy of the community

A wedding dance was given by F. T Slaughter on Friday nig... The bride was elegantly arrayed in white silk and orar blossoms. Mr. Slaughter was dressed and wore a smiling countenance, as they marched through the hall. They were followed by Mr. Slaughter's two daughters, Rose and Effie, who bride's maids. They were dressed in white and looked very neat. Foster, Mr. Slaughter's son, and Jodie Black were best men. The hall was well filled and all had an enjoyable time, and no one went home disappointed.

The Fourth of July will be appropriately celebrated. A lively time was had over goddess of liberty between the married and single men. The cost of a vote was one cent. The married men voted for Mrs. Hally Young, and the single men for Miss Cora Robison. Mrs. Young was elected by forty votes, and $55 was taken in.

Oak City

Oak City, July 7th

The Fourth of July was enjoyably celebrated by the people of Oak City. At 10 o'clock a. m. an interesting program was rendered, consisting of songs, music and speeches. In the afternoon games and contests were indulged in and in the evening a pleasant dance was enjoyed.

Alvin, the eldest son of Mr and Mrs. William Lovell, while playing around was accidently kicked by a horse last Thursday. The hoof of the animal struck the boy on the right hip and lower rib, rendering a very painful bruise which appeared to be internal. Dr. Robison waited on the little fellow and at the present writing he appears to be getting along nicely.

The annual primary convention of the Millard stake was held here last Sunday. There was a good attendance of primary workers from most of the wards, also Presidents Hinckley and Callister. Sisters Bennion and Romney of the general board of primary workers were present and gave some wholesome instructions.

A young lady came to the home of Mr. and Mrs Joel Moody and was welcomed by all, so will make her future home there. All well.

The health of Bro. William Alldridge, Sr., is very poorly. Hopes are that he will have better health in the near future.

Mrs. H. F. Stout is very ill at present. Her son, Hosea, and wife are down from Eureka to spend a few days with her.

Oak City

Oak City, Aug. 14th

Arthur J. Lovell the eleven year old son of Brigham and Harriet T. Lovell died on the 10th inst., from dropsy. The funeral was held Friday afternoon at the residence and was well attended.

Henry Roper and Joseph Finlinson were the speakers and both offered words of comfort to the bereaved family. A number of the choir members furnished the singing which was very sweet and inspiring.

Mrs. Harry Roper who underwent an operation at the Cedar City hospital some few weeks ago, has returned and is improving nicely.

A number of our prominent citizens have engaged Albert Day of Fillmore to build and burn a kiln of brick. Work commenced on the same last Monday.

Our large grain crop will be threshed out this year with a new improved threshing machine. The purchasers are Charlie Roper, Wm. Lovell, Abel Roper. Lem Roper and Geo. Finlinson.

Mrs. Ida Lyman Sorenson of Salt Lake is visiting relatives in this place.

Our local game commissioner has found it necessary to apply to the state commissioner for ten thousand eastern brook trout to be placed in the Oak Creek canyon streams. This new supply is to supplant the scarcity which has been caused by numerous rusticators from this and neighboring settlements. Pres. A. A. Hinckley is still in the canyon Of late he has experienced some difficulty in getting sufficient fresh fish to supply the needs of himself and family. It appears that while in the canyon he must eat fish, fresh or otherwise and of course it has been necessary of late for him to place with our merchant an order or two for canned salmon.

Deseret

Funeral services were held here recently over the remains of John Warnick, younger son of the late A. P. Warnick. The young man was at work in Eureka in a mine and while thus engaged he was overcome with gas and in the attempt to reach the surface by way of the bucket used for hoisting he fell back and was dashed to death. He was one of the most promising young men of our town, had accepted a call for a mission to leave in October and was at work to obtain means to take him to his field of labor. The accident has caused a deep gloom to come over the whole neighborhood, for he was beloved by all who knew him. His aged mother and family have the heartfelt sympathy of the good people of Deseret All mourn the loss together.

The bishop's first counselor, W. R. Black has a new smile on his countenance and his step seems more elastic than before; he has again become the f—— of a bouncing baby boy.

Our people are mak—— preparations for harv——. Some grain is ripe and —— prospects for alfalfa seed a good in some localities.

Millard County Progress
September 28, 1906

Hinckley

Hinckley, Sept 23

The old people of Hinckley were honored last Saturday with a festive entertainment which was a complete success, the weather being most favorable. Three of our aged people have gone behind the veil since gathering a year ago—Bro. N. M. Peterson, Bro. Wm. Alldredge and Sister Mary Stokes.

Jack Frost has paid us a visit nipping some of the tender plants.

Mrs. Clark of Mercur who has been visiting with her sister Mrs. Nellie Blake and mother, was summoned home, her husband having a bad accident in one of the mines. He is now at the Hospital in Salt Lake City.

A number of our people attended the farewell party given at Abraham in honor of Bro. Geo. Nuttle who leaves for a mission in a few days, all present reported having had a good time.

The nine month old baby girl of Mr. and Mrs. C. C. Dutson passed away last Wednesday. Dr. J C. Robison has been treating the little one for two or three weeks, to no avail.

Millard County Progress
November 2, 1906

Hinckley

Hinckley, Nov 1

We are having fine weather for this time of the year.

Threshing is under good head way, there being three steam threshers in this locality. One of our young men had a pleasant smile after threshing his alfalfa seed, there being a little over 60 bushels, which is over the average this year.

Work has commenced on the new spill. We hope to put in a cement spill which will stand all high water.

A son was born to Mr. and Mrs. John M. Wright. All well

George Theobald is wearing a pleasant smile, over the arrival of a new daughter who has come to bless his home. Mother and child doing nicely

Mrs Lizzie Nelson while visiting her relatives, made herself a birthday present in the form of a daughter. She is staying with her sister, Mrs. Eddie Anderson.

Millard County Progress
November 30, 1906

Hinckley

Hinckley, Nov 27.

We are having a very cold period with wind and snow. It is quite clear tonight but snowed this morning.

Work is still in progress on the new spill contract.

Mr. Lyman receiving the sad news of his brothers death, left to be in attendance at the funeral; but will not return for some time on account of it freezing.

The Hinkley School played the White Lie, to a full house, last week. The play is fine, we wish them to appear again.

A fine reception was given in honor of Elder J. W. Blake, who has just returned from a mission. Also a farewell party given last Thursday to Elder L. R. Cropper Jr. who leaves to-night for a mission. We wish Brother Cropper every success.

A baby girl arrived at the home of Charles Theobald.

Born to Mrs. J. E. Wright a boy; mother and child doing nicely

Mr. Dixon is down from Payson visiting her daughter. Mrs. F. L. Hickman.

We are sorry to learn that Mrs. W. W. Wright is still in a very critical condition at Mercur. We hope that sister Wright will soon recover.

Mrs Robison is reported to be on the improve. She is afflicted with dropsy.

Leamington

Leamington, Nov. 27.

Elder H. O. Sorenson left Monday morning for a mission to Scandinavia.

Two new girls, one at the home of James Dutson, the other at Jeff Finlinson's, has caused many smiles of satisfaction in both ends of our town.

A very quiet wedding took place at the home of widow Stout on the 22nd inst. Her brother Hosea and Bishop Ashby and wife being present, Andrew Johnson formerly of Tintic being the groom and the widow is not now a widow. Bishop Ashby officiated.

Wm. Holman is home again from New Mexico where he has been the past year with Mr. Greathouse railroading.

Elder Joseph L. Anderson and wife visited relatives and friends here last Sunday. Monday Joseph left for a mission to the Southern States. His wife accompanying him as far as Provo, where she visited her sister Amanda who is there attending school.

The school gives a Thanksgiving program tomorrow night all are invited.

We are having a long siege of cold weather with frequent small snow storms. Many cattle are still on the range here and are doing well.

Millard County Progress
January 3, 1907

Petit Jurors Drawn For January Term of District Court

Name	Residence
James H Western	Deseret
Albert Hales	Deseret
Orson Wasden	Scipio
Ole H. Jacobson	Oak City
John B. Stephenson	Holden
Leslie George	Kanosh
John E. Lovell	Oak City
David R. Stevens	Holden
George W. Badger	Holden
Orson Johnson	Holden
E. B. Theobald	Hinckley
Anthony Paxton, Jr.	Kanosh
Hyrum Robison	Hatton
Charles Burke	Hinckley
Peter P. Brown	Scipio
E. F. Pack	Hinckley
James C. Peterson	Fillmore
Howard B. Bushnell	Meadow
William A. Reeve	Hinckley
Charles Iverson	Fillmore
Daniel Melville	Fillmore
Edward Bennett	Holden
Joseph Whitaker	Kanosh
F. A. Robison	Fillmore

Millard County Progress
January 11, 1907

Oak City

Oak City, Jan. 9

A family reunion of the late John W. Dutson of this place was held in the school house last Friday afternoon and evening. It was the first gathering of the kind that has been held by his posterity and proved in every way to be a successful social affair. In the afternoon a pleasing program, consisting of songs speeches and instrumental selections, was carried out. After which a sumptuous dinner was served. In the evening a free dance was enjoyed. Your correspondent is not prepared to say just how many Dutsons were gathered together on this occasion but suffice to say the numbers were large.

A big rabbit hunt took place last Saturday between sides selected by Eddie L. Dutson and John L. Anderson. The final count showed a victory for Dutsons side by a majority of 45 rabbits.

After enjoying the holiday vacation our students have returned to Provo to resume their school work.

Supt. Joseph Finlinson and Ellen Neilson have returned from Ogden where they have been in attendance at the State Teachers Convention.

Hans Bogh of Greyson, San Juan Co. is visiting with relatives of this place.

Pres. A. A. Hinckley and Stake Clerk Wm. A. Reve are in town auditing the ward tithing accounts.

Oak City

Oak City, Jan. 16

The Relief Society held a special session Jan. 8. in honor of the eightieth birthday of their ex president Sister Caroline E. Lyman. An interesting program was rendered and refreshments served. Some forty members participated.

Antone Christensen, who had expected to leave on the 12 inst. for a mission to Denmark has been honorably released.

Bishop Christensen of Aurora and Neils Christensen and family of Hinckley are visiting with their parents Mr. and Mrs. Antone Christensen.

Pres F. R. Lyman of the Melville Irrigation co. has gone to Hinckley to attend the annual meeting called for the election of officers.

Hinckley

Hinckley, Feb 3

Just as we were about to shed tears because no correspondence was coming in, we received this splendid, well written and interesting communication from Hinckley:

It is a noted fact that the people of Hinckley are a prosperous and a happy community. The hum of the Cream Separators the toot of our Creamry whistle, the blat of sheep and the sound of the carpenter's hammer makes one's heart glad.

Our citizens are beginning to see the good of centralizing, as there has been of late a number of very creditable cottages erected by the Hon. F. L. Hickman, our worthy merchant Thos. Pratt; Dan Rogers, Thos. Greener, James Blake, John E. Wright, Joseph Talbot, Arthur Talbot,

Geo. Theobald, R. E. Robinson, which is a credit to our city and county. Many others are making arrangements for the same good cause.

The I N. Hinckley lot has been purchased by the trustees for the erection of a $10,000 schoolhouse which will be built this coming season and all prepared for a high school next year. Also a site for a new meeting house has been selected and paid for. The dimensions of said building will be 65 by 80 ft.

We are fast populating our county from the spirit world as well as from adjacent towns. Our streets and sidewalks are well trodden on the Sabbath by

children and parents going to and from the house of worship

The great trouble at present is too much land and water. If the farmers of this community would dispose of at least one half of their realty, better results would be obtained in every particular. However it will yet be said of Hinckley that she is the leading town of Millard.

It was a pleasing scene today to note our worthy bishop with his band of obedient brethern paving the sidewalks with asphaltum, from the new meeting house site, which will be very much appreciated,

Leamington

Leamington, Mar. 7.

(Too late for last week)

Since last writing, four infant emigrants have arrived in our town, all boys, and have taken up contented and welcomed abode at the homes of Huff Strange, Joseph H. Neilson, August Neilson and Lewis Neilson. Dry farming has taken on a vigorous aspect here and these helpful little strangers seemed to know they would be needed.

Misses Hannah and Elverda Anderson are to run an outfit of workman cars in the near future, aided by their brother John and his wife. Their experience at cooking for large crowds will no doubt bring them success in their new enterprise.

Sunday Feb. 24, Frank L. Copening and wife of Lynn, ing gave a spirited and interest joined our ward. Bro. Copening talk on Religion Class work at sacrament meeting He is R. R. agent at Lynn. The same date Bros. Gardner and Blake of Hinckley, made a flying trip here in intrest of Religion Class, resulting in selecting B. P. Textorious as Supt. of that work, who with some of his members attended a meeting last night in Oak City, hold by Bro. Kelch.

In the near future our Dramatic Co. are to give us a rare treat with "Millie the Quadroon, Trust us that we will all turn out, as we know the company.

Mr. and Mrs. Wm. Holman, who moved here from Silver City a few years ago, have sold their place and are moving back to Silver. In the move we lose our Y. L. M. I. A. Pres. and a faithful S. S. teacher.

In passing the R. R. station tonight we saw 32 gal. of (34c butter fat) cream waiting for the express to convey it to Nephi and Elgen creameries, and this is no rare sight either.

If you think our town people are not united you should have seen them today out in mass hawling brick for our new meeting house from the old smelter smokestack. The frames for said house are almost completed and the work on same is to be finished as fast as means and time will allow.

Mr. Mc Intire shipped two cars of stock from Nevada to his ranch here a few days ago.

Jap instead of white labor is now employed on the R. R. here.

When the Leghorns here saw in the last issue of your paper what their brothers and sisters at Oak Creek were doing, they hung their heads in shame, then resolved to lay more eggs to buy more incubators, to hatch more chickens, to lay more eggs.

Our cows bawled tears of butter fat trying to see how their own kin could do so well.

County commissioner Nixon and Attorney Stout were in our town some time since at the earnest request of our citizens, to see how near we were completely closed in and we are confident that the good judgement of these two officials, will result in more good roads for our town and county.

Mr. and Mrs Wm. H. Ashby have been here for a week past visiting their two sons and families. The father while here has been making some improvments on the home of our Bishop.

Bishop Stephenson and wife visited their daughter and family Saturday and Sunday.

There has been considerable sickness here of late among the children and a peculiar disease it was in some cases seeming to approach near to pneumonia accompanied by a sharp pain which moved from one part of the body to another, with high fever, and in some cases leaving the person in a much swollen condition. We are glad to note that all are improving and that none of the cases have proven fatal.

A representative of the Utah Nursery did some business for his Co. here some time ago and our townsmen the last few years have taken some wise steps to improve and enlarge their orchards.

Millard County Progress
April 26, 1907

Hinckley

Hinckley, Apr. 2[?]

The health of the people is generally good.

High water has taken our reservoir. Water dashing down the Sevier River bursted what is known as the Cropper cut, but contract has been let to Mr. Parker of Abraham to put the water in the old canal and we are in hopes to be irrigating in about ten days.

We are pleased to report that the health of Sister Robison is improving. She been afflicted with dropsy for some time.

Storks have visited our little place and left a girl to Mr. and Mrs. Clarence Pack's, to Mr. and Mrs. Joseph Christenson s, a girl, to Mr. and Mrs. Jeffreys' a boy, and to Mr. and Mrs W. I. Alldredge a boy.

Mr. and Mrs. John Keate are here from Mexico, visiting her sister Mrs. Susie Theobald

Our District Schools closed Friday, the 19th. The children have made good progress this season and we are sorry to see school close.

Mr Hickman and Mr Gardner have put in a new brick plant and we expect to see several new buildings going up in the near future.

Mr. and Mrs. John Keate and Mrs. E. B. Theobald left last night for Ferron to visit their sister, Mrs. Dessy Johnson.

Oak City

Oak City, Apr 24

The recent fall of temperature, coming as it did after a spell of warm weather has had a serious effect on our orchards Prior to last week the outlook for the fruit grower was all that could be wished for but the frost of last Friday and Saturday nights brought a change. Fruit growers who have examined their orchards report a complete loss and considerable damage has been done to the grain, lucern and garden plants.

After spending thirty months in South Carolina doing missionary work Joshua Finlinson is again in our midst. Last Sunday afternoon in ward meeting he gave an interesting report of his labors during his absence.

A large real estate transaction has taken place in the south part of our town. It is reported that Collier Lovell of Hinckley and Wm. Lovell of this place have purchased for a handsome consideration the property belonging to Wm Huff.

Our school grounds present a very pleasing appearence. The lot has been cleaned and a considerable portion of it has been planted to trees.

Salt Lake Herald
May 11, 1907

POSTAL MATTERS.

(Special to The Herald.)

Washington, May 10.—Postoffices established:

Utah—Lynedyl, Millard county, Ida M. Edwards, postmaster.

Idaho—Cliffs, Owyhee county, Frank M. Lockett, postmaster.

Postmasters appointed:

Idaho—Irma Smith, Evers, Custer county, vice Terrence Masterson, resigned.

Wyoming—Oakley, Uinta county, George R. Symes, vice A. M. King, resigned; Pinedale, Fremont county, Helen Belknap, vice C. M. Brandon, resigned.

Hinckley

Hinckley, June 4

The weather is very changeable and threatening storm.

The crops are very backward. alfalfa is very short, and it will be some time before it will be ready to cut.

Decoration Day was observed and the cemetery was decorated with beautiful flowers. Some new tomb stones were erected fences placed, and native flags were planted.

The present amusement for our young men is base ball. They are doing very good playing.

Mrs. T. H Pratt is home again, after visiting her parents in Holden.

Mr. and Mrs. John Houston, who have been visiting relatives and friends, have returned to their home in American Fork.

Miss Lemira Walker has returned from Eureka, where she has been visiting her sister, Mrs. Alma Peterson.

Mrs. Mary E. Peterson is down from Provo, spending a few days with her daughters, Mrs. Charles Burke and Mrs. Frank Whitehead Jr.

The 18 year old daughter of Mrs. Steenie Johnson is suffering with typhoid fever and is very sick.

The little son of John Reeve, who had the misfortune to fall from a wagon, had the wheel pass over him, also a mower that was tied behind, cutting his head and bruising him up. He is progressing nicely.

Hinckley

Hinckley, June 16

The silver wedding of Mahonri and Janette Bishop was celebrated June 15th, at their residence in eastern Hinckley. There was a host of guests and it was a very successful affair all around. The bride's brothers, John, William, Frank and Peter, with their wives, also the mother and sister, Mesdames Smith and Hanson, came across the desert, bringing flowers and silver gifts. Mr. Bishop's children gave them a beautiful tea set and cabinet. Other silver tokens, cake stands and tea pots came from Bp. Cahoon, Merchant Damron and J. J. Bennott of Deseret. A sumptuous supper was served under a large awning on the lawn, and the roast chicken, strawberries, oranges and bananas disappeared with much gusto. The music was furnished by Miss Walker and the Bishop boys, with the exception of a few selections from the guests. "Dixie" was sung by Bro. Langston and "Come Where the Lilies Bloom" by Mr. and Mrs. J. W. Damron and Mrs. Nellie Moody. Following is a poem written for the occasion by Mr. Bishop's daughter, Mrs. Nellie Moody:

Twenty-five years ago today,
Two barks were launched in a sacred way
Upon life's stormy ocean.
Down the stream they never faltered
While gathering stars for a crown immortal
Until they nine have numbered
Bright and precious were the spirits given
Paying in full for all thou hast striven
To bless you in after years.
We, your friends and children today
Congratulate and together say:
"Sail on through every weather
Nor cease thy vigilance and care.
Thou art soon past the dangers everywhere,
To a calm and smoother sailing.
The little rocks that first were hit
Were reminders that thou couldst not sit
But arise and work the harder.
You have labored up stream day by day
Against strong currents all the way,
But an unseen hand assisted.
Weary and worn almost to despair
When thy barks would clash then and there
A bolder effort was gathered.

And when the fierce storms overtook
Thy noble hearts ne'er once forsook,
But clung to each the tighter
Until by unity that strength was gained
That brought the barks through sleet and rain
To an isle within the voyage.
This isle of twenty-five years is a resting place
Where new strength is gathered once more to face
The storms that may arise
But may thy steerage be as true
May the same courage bring you through
Safely to the other shore.
May the high places be made low
May thy sailing always smooth-er go
And bring you sweet content
May thy children ever cling about
Following the way thou hast marked out
And meet they all together
On the Golden Shore of life
There to rest, from toil and strife
Never more to sever.

Hinckley

Hinckley, July 29

We are having changeable weather with nice showers which make the air fresh and pleasant.

The first crop of alfalfa is now in the stacks, but the crop is light

Grain is looking well and weeds away up.

Several of our Sunday School workers attended Sunday School Conference at Oak City. They reported having a pleasant spiritual feast.

Mrs. Julia Spiers is down from the North visiting her mother Mrs. Stena Johnson.

Pioneer Day was celebrated in grand style all having an enjoyable time.

One day last week the base ball teams of Hinkly and Deseret had a friendly game. Tallies were 14 to 3 in favor of Hinkley.

Mr. and Mrs. Atkins and daughter are up from St. George visiting Mrs. Atkins' brothers Joseph and James Blake.

Mr. and Mrs. F. T. Slaughter spent Pioneer Day with his mother and chatting with his old friends. Come again.

Oak City

Oak City, July 29

The Millard Stake Sunday School Conference convened in Oak City last Sunday beginning at 10 A.M. Elder J. W. Summerhays and Reynolds of the general board were in attendance, also the Stake S. S. Superentendency. Stake Presidency and a large representation of Sunday School officers and teachers from all the wards.

The program formulated by the General Board was carried out in detail. The principal parts in the morning session were the consideration of the twenty one vital points by Elder Summerhays and the superintendents, and the dicussion of paper read by Joseph Finlinson on "How to increase our attendance and promote a livelier interest in our Union Meetings.

The afternoon program consisted of a report of the Stake Supt., and address by N. B. Badger on "The spirit of the S. S. work," and addresses by the visiting brethren also a class demonstration given by the 2nd Int. department of the Oak City school. The program throughout was of interest especially the earnest heartfelt remarks made that were made in so fervent a manner by the visiting brethren.

Our hall facilities were altogether too small to accomadate the large crowd present so the meetings were held under the large locust trees in front of the school building. This innovation (made necessary by circumstances) we heartily recommend, especially in warm weather.

The arrival of a pair of fine boys at the home of Jense Anderson accounts for the smiling face and active walk which have characterized him of late. Mother and babies are doing fine.

Our young people are nearly all in the canyon this week rusticating.

Oasis

Oasis, July 25

We're one of the busiest towns just now, brushing flies and mosquitoes.

We had a lively time on the 24th from 10 o'clock a. m. till 6 o'clock p. m.

The Batallion boys kept the air ringing with their saluting. Then the pioneer drill, the speeches and the singing was all full of the spirit of the day.

The baby show was a success The prize (a cassimere dress) given to the Jenson baby. Its fair face, large blue eyes and sweet timidity won its way.

The Relief Society sold 13 gal. of ice cream, and still the demand was greater than the supply, no one wanted berries while the cream was in sight

Our night agent, Mr. Bartles, is released, and Mr. Mornham has taken his place.

Something about the atmosphere or water doesn't agree with night agents; they change so often.

Mrs. Campbell is visiting her sister Mrs. A. J. Henry; also Mr and Mrs. Smoot of Provo are here on the same business.

Bp. Styler and J. W. Reid have gone south west prospecting. It is hoped they will find a fortune.

The Stake officers of the Y. L. M. I. A. will hold a meeting Sat. at 3 o'clock p. m., all are invited.

Millard County Progress
August 30, 1907

Hinckley

Hinckley, Aug. 26

The new bridge over the Sevier river at M. M. Bishop's is now completed.

Prof. Richard R. Lyman and his brother John C., have a force of men and teams at work on the concrete spillway. We will all be glad to see it finished.

Farmers are all busy putting up their second cutting of hay; an excellent crop is reported. Prospects are very good for some seed.

They will have an excellent crop of oats at Abraham.

Miss Nancy Stanworth is very sick with typhoid fever.

The Millard champion base ballists returned from Kanosh last evening. The boys say they run 17 tallies. Kanosh only got 3, and they run them after the Hinckley boys had given out and quit. The champion boys report having a royal good time at the dance with the Kanosh boys best girls. They would have us think that the boys had taken to the woods.

Girls don't you believe all those Hinckley boys told you, because they were nearly all married men and not quite responsible for all they say and do when away from home.

Capt. Hickman says they are ready to meet any team in Millard Co., but owing to the busy time, he will insist on them comming to Hinckley to play.

Mercur

Mercur, Sept. 22, 1907.

(Delayed in transit)

The weather still continues cool, with frost at night.

The Union Merk Co. has purchased the A. Swenson Co.'s Store and Bakery shop We under stand the price paid was $15,000.

The Roaster department in the Con Mercur Mill is again in running order.

Born to Mr. and Mrs. Geo. Edwards a girl. Also to Mr. and Mrs. Will Bacon a boy.

Mrs. Wm A. Reeve of Hinckley and Mrs. J. N. Workman of Lehi were visiting at their Bros. Mr. W. W. Wright last week.

Miss Katie Coffey is home after a summers absence.

The L. D S. Primary will give a concert on Wed, next.

Mr. Minor Alldredge in trying to catch his team which became frightened was thrown violently to the ground but no bones were broken, yet was bruised quite bad.

Burtner

March. 8, 1908

Burtner still grows.

Jan. 18, 1908, a postoffice was presented to Melville, by name of Burtner with Levi H. McCullough as the first post-master. The first phone line reached Burtner on the night of Jan. 19, 1908, by the hand of Thos C. Callister and son. And the same was placed in the home of Burtner's first Bishop, a two story house of eight rooms affording good accommodations for the weary traveler and tourist. A commodious lumber yard also finds a home there. And a grocery store is now begun in the post-office, which we hope can furnish supplies for the laborers close at hand. New houses are gradually appearing in the greese woods one by one And land is being cleared and ploughed at the rate of 40 acres to the clatter.

The large canals are completed There remains unfinished a few small ones going to individuals land The dam and spillway at head are gradually towering towards the top While the excessive high water is retarding the work somewhat and holding us from putting a dam in the old channel turning water through new one by side of concrete spill. Nevertheless we feel assured that water will be on Melville land some time this spring. The first days of winter have just set in and more snow and rain has fallen than we've had during the season yet we hope this winter will be short and that spring will soon come with days of cheerfulness and sunshine We now feel that Melville or Burtner (as it has so been called) is finding favor in the eyes of the representatives of the county, and we are soon to be granted a civil district with river as western boundry. Hinckley as southern running east 8 miles In which a road supervisor, constable, and justice of the peace are to be selected by the citizens in the district and appointed by the county court. While those favors are greatly appreciated we yet look forward to a day in the near future, when a school district will be granted the town of Burtner, which will necessitate the erection of a building where in our children may develop in educational lines with the rest of the world.

Hinckley

Hinckley, March. 22.

Thinking a short piece from here would be of interest to the County paper I send you the following items:

Farmers are working their land and getting ready for spring crops.

Mrs. John Terry, who has been seriously ill, is reported on the improve.

Mr. Charles Stratton is wearing a pleasant smile over the arrival of a new baby. All well.

Robert Slaughter and wife have just returned from Deep Creek, having made a hurried trip there and back.

We are having fine weather after a cold breeze from the north for two days, and hope spring will soon be here.

The Relief Society gave a fine program and lunch last Friday night for the benefit of their new Relief hall, which is nearly completed

The Home Dramatic Company will appear on the stage next Tuesday night. They have gave some very interesting plays this winter. We wish them success.

March. 28, 1908.

"BURTNER'S FIRST WEDDING."

At the home of Walter M. Gardner on the eve of March 21st were gathered a group of relatives and friends to celebrate the wedding of his daughter Maude and Luther Buchanan, who were married in the Manti Temple on the 11th inst.

A sumptuous dinner was served, everything being the very best, after which an informal program was rendered. The young couple are apparently very elaborate in their affections. May they continue thus on the sea of matrimony is the wish of their many friends.

A GREATER MILLARD COUNTY

Down in Millard county, at a point near Riverside, on the San Pedro Los Angeles and Salt Lake Railroad, there is being constructed by the Oasis Land and Irrigation Company and the Melville Irrigation Company, one of the largest diverting dams in the State of Utah. This dam is part of the largest irrigation system in the State and is supplied directly by the waters stored in the Sevier Reservoir, located in Juab and San Pete counties and having a capacity of 90,000 acrefeet. The waters diverted at the Riverside dam will serve the arid lands lying in the Pahvant Valley, of which 43,000 acres have been recently withdrawn from entry at the United States

Land Office in Salt Lake, in accordance with an application made under the Carey Act by the Oasis Land and Irrigation Company. It will also serve about 15,000 acres which have been located under the desert and homestead acts by the members of the Melville Irrigation Company. It is expected that the Department of the Interior will take action on the application made by the Oasis Land and Irrigation Company, some time in May, when a drawing will be held and the lands thrown open for entry in accordance with the Carey Act.

Millard County has the largest tract of arable land in the State. It has a deep alluvial soil, formed by a delta deposit of the Sevier River, which has the largest drainage area of any river in Utah. The latent possibilities of this territory are beginning to attract the engineer, capitalist and homeseeker. In addition to having a rich and exhaustless soil, this valley has ideal conditions for irrigation and drainage, the latter being most essential for the best results in an irrigation system The productiveness of this region is further enhanced by long periods of sunshine in each year and a beneficent climate that gives abundant yield of crops and vigor to the home-builder.

The Riverside dam is, roughly, 800 feet long on the crest, 170 feet wide on the bottom and 35 feet above the bed of the river. It has a reinforced concrete spillway, a concrete tunnel, 200 feet long, 4 feet wide and 8 feet high through the center of the dam, in which is set the steel gates—one 8 feet high and 4 feet wide, and two gates serving a three and four foot pipe, respectively, that are used in connec-tion with the electric power plant, which will be constructed at this point. Approximately 500 electrical horse power will be generated. This will be trans mitted to the towns of Burtner, Oasis, Deseret, Hinckley, Abra ham and other points where it may be needed. Four sets of large steel gates are being in-stalled in the dam at the Sevier Bridge Reservoir, and while this work is going forward, the con-struction will be completed, at the Riverside or Melville dam in closing off the river, installing floodgates in the canals, etc. About fifteen miles of main canals have been completed, leading from this diverting dam, and upwards of 15,000 acres will be served by the system during the present year. The dam proper will be fully completed by May 1st.

Millard County is beginning an era of progression, and the po tential desert is being trans-formed into the garden of Utah.—Deseret News.

Millard County Progress
April 24, 1908

Oak City

Oak City, April 20, 1908.

Mrs. Levi McCullough of Burt ner spent Thursday and Friday with her sister Mrs. Mary M. Lyman of this place.

At this writing the eight grade students of the Oak Creek dis trict school are busy with the state uniform examination

Lars Nielson of Lemington is visiting with relatives of this place. He was the main speaker at the Sunday afternoon meeting

Unless some bounteous spring rains come to replenish our wat er supply the indications at pres ent for a prosperous water year are somewhat discouraging.

Supt. Joseph Finlinson was in Lynn last Thursday looking after school matters. He reports that the growth of the place in popu lation is such as to entitle them to school next winter.

The entertainment last Friday in honor of the old-folks was en-tirely successful. A delicious dinner was served, afthe which a pleasing program was render ed. The committee in charge is to be commented.

The attendence at Sunday School and afternoon meeting Sunday was better than is usual on Easter Sunday. This is due to the fact that Saturday was utilized to a great extent by our people for taking their Easter outing.

Millard County Progress
May 8, 1908

Oak City

Oak City, May 4, 1908.

Miss Ely Amderson came down from Salt Lake Sunday morning and will remain for some time.

During the past week Mrs. Carolina E. Lyman has been suf fering from a severe attack of pneumonia. The fact that she is passed eighty years of age, and is in a frail physical con dition makes her chance for re covery somewhat slim. At this date she is very weak.

Supt. Joseph Finlinson left Monday for Salt Lake City. Mr. Finlinson is a member of the State Text Book Committee which commences Wednesday on the important work of selecting text books to be used in the public schools during the coming five years.

President Francis M. Lyman met with the people of Oak City in meeting Monday afternoon. He delivered an interesting dis cussion on temperance and kindred subjects.

Oak City fruit crop is not all killed. From the information available at this time the crop in the northeast part of town which lies in the canyon wind belt will be at least 70 per cent.

Oasis, April 27 1908

We thought it was time you should hear a word from us. We have made rapid strides in many directions; We have a city all built in our minds and part of the land purchased in reality.

Yes the "Oasis Land and Irrigation Co." are going to transform our little town if what we hear is true. Mr. Reed put up a meat market which flourished for a time and now we hope some one will open it again soon.

Mr. Stevens sold all his property to the new company, and we are grieved to loose such good citizens, but our loss is Holden's gain as they are going back to their old home.

Mrs. Harty sold her place to Mr. Rogers, and went north.

The alfalfa is looking fine so is the new Relief Hall, which is almost completed. The plasterer is at work and We expect to have it ready for a grand opening in a couple of weeks. The Relief officers are deserving a great deal of praise for their pluck, as they started it with only about $400. to build a $2000. house. The brethern assisted in the labor part to about a thousand dollars and the sisters have raised the balance almost entirely and will only be indebeted a few hundred. We will ask the people of the near by towns to be on the lookout for the date of the House Warning as we want them to come and assist in raising funds to seat the same, and we will give them full value received in a rousing time.

We still prove our loyalty to the first great commandment, as a boy come to the home of Mr. and Mrs. Charles Thompson Mr. and Mrs. William Huff, and Mr. and Mrs. Milton Moody, all are doing well.

Mrs. Ellen Ayers has returned to her home after a siege of sickness, all winter in the City. Her son in law Peter Kroman also came with her for his health, but only lived a week. The funeral services were held here. He leaves a wife and two children to mourn his departure as well as many other relatives and friends.

Leamington

LEMINGTON, April 26, 1908.

It having been some length of time since you had any news from here allow a few items that may be of some interest.

Our new phone line between Oak City via. Lemington to Lynn has proved to be so good a one that it has spoiled the people or trying to talk over the other system in our county in its truly bad condition, we hope it can be improved in the very near future; as it would save much lung power and patience which will be scarce commodities along that line if not soon put out of commission. Talk already has a line north from here as an outlet to the county and one from Oak City to Holden as these three towns are getting quite related and we hope the end is not yet, to the phone line nor the relationship.

Arbor day though some time past, was observed in a truly loyal manner this year A plot of ground immediately back of our meeting house site was leveled and one hundred trees, Box Elder and Carolina popular, having been secured from a Utah Nursery were planted while this work was on, the women Folks were loading tables in the school house till they fairly tottered, with more good food than some of our farming appetites could master. A dance in the afternoon for the children and one in the evening for adults Ice cream and program interspersed closed the most enjoyed and successful Arbor day ever spent by our people here.

Jack Frost more active than the season of year would seem to warrant, visited us last night and although fought by many of our citizens, with smoke and flames. he succeeded in capturing every orchard in our town, at daybreak worn and dust stained those who had tried so hard to save the promising fruit store. crestfallen, defeated but not conquered, left the field for morning Sabbath School with hope for the future and faith and song such as "The Lord will provide."

The grain and hay crops look fine except where now and then a stalk bowed to the frost king.

Studebakers agent from Nephi Mr small. raided our town and left in his wake four fine buggies last week. The next agent on similar business here must prepare to take in exchange second hand rigs or not sell, as there are few families here now not riding a good buggy.

John Anderson has just completed a new residence on his dry farm on Fool Creek flat. And the Anderson sisters shipped their kitchen outfit again preparitory for a season feeding R. R. men Elvira Stout, accompanied them as aid She just returned from Salt Lake City.

Benjamin Lovell who returned lately from the mission field, returned from Salt Lake a few days ago with a young wife, who was Miss Millie McArdell till he made this last trip to the City. Ben has charge of the section at Parley five miles east of here, and it would be just like Millie to go up there and live with him, as she is a better house keeper than Ben.

Mrs. Overson who met with a serious accident in Salt Lake City, Conference time, is again home and her broken arm is knitting nicely

Millard County Progress
May 22, 1908

Hinckley

HINCKLEY, May 17, 1908

We have been visited by several showers of late and the weather cold which makes every thing backward this spring

The work is being pushed on the new school house. We are in hopes of having a good school this year as we have had the past two winters

Mrs. Geo. Talbert has recently returned home after spending a week with her sister Mrs. W W. Wright who is seriously ill at Mercur. We hope to soon hear that Mrs. Wright is on the improve.

The ladies of the Relief Society gave a grand ball with lunch and ice cream Friday night

Miss Berta Reave went to Kanosh last week but is seen on our streets again to-day

Mr. and Mrs. William Reeve are rejoicing over the new arrival at their residence this is their eleventh child. Mother and child doing nicely

Millard County Progress
June 5, 1908

Hinckley

HINCKLEY June 1, 1908,

We are having a stormy period it rained most all day Sunday but our meeting was very well attended and reports given by the B. Y. U. students,

The primary will celebrate the 1st of June, a program will be rendered and a dance for the children in the afternoon, with a dance at night for adults.

The work on the new school house is progressing very fast and looks like we are going to have a good accomodation for both teachers and children next winter.

John M. Wrights new residence is going up very fast.

Wedding bells are beginning to sound in our little town a couple are going to be married, and others are chiming for the near future.

The following young folks have returned from the Academy: Joseph Blake, Jacob Felix, Samuel Knights, Dora Blake, Miss Knights and others will return later.

Mr. and Mrs. Edward Davis have welcomed the arrival of a son at their residence, all well.

Millard County Progress
June 12, 1908

Deseret

DESERET, June 8, 1908.

It begins to look as if haying will be posponed until July. The weather continues cold and frosty at night.

Our Sunday School has just been reorganized with Marion Black as Superintendent and H. S Cahoon Sr as first asst. and D. H. Palmer as second asst Joseph W. Damron was honorably released as superintendent, as he had recently been called as bishop. With the good choice of new officers, we believe the Sunday School will continue to do the good work it has done in the past

News has just been received from Mexico stating that Geo. A. Black, formerly of Deseret, had been shot and killed by a young Mexican. Bro. Black was always an energetic worker in the various wards where he lived The sad news cast a gloom over the entire community. We extend our sympathy to the breft.

Mr. and Mrs. Damron just returned from Idaho, where they have been visiting their children They report having had a very nice visit. It rained every day they were there. And on account of not being used to so much "wet" they both returned with bad colds.

The mutual will give a dance and refreshments in Petty's Hall to-night. The purpose of which is to raise means to send delegates to the mutual conference at Salt Lake.

Relief Society will surprise Mrs. Blythe Tuesday. it being her eighty fourth birthday.

Abraham and Deseret will play a social game of ball this afternoon.

The following has been dictated by the leaders of the Deseret Base Ball Team.

There seems to be a misunderstanding in some of the towns as to whom the Championship Club of Millard Co., belongs. There has been but one club made by Millard Co.. that is acknowledged as the champion club and it was first held by Fillmore and afterwards by Kanosh, from whom Deseret won it about 15 years ago, and have held it ever since, and is now at the home of Mr. Wm R. Black. It is true that Deseret has been defeated in ball games since, but never when playing for the championship. Last year after having defeated Deseret in a game, for a dollar to the man. Hinckley had a club made and printed as the Championship club of Millard County. It was one of their own design and not of the county, as the one held by Deseret.

Hinckley challenged the county through the Progress Review. They had no need of doing so, as they knew who held the championship. We claim the championship of Millard County and claim that we have never been defeated, when playing for it during the last fifteen years.

We have sent a challenge to Hinckley for five dollars to the man, or for as much more as they desire, but so far have been unable to obtain a definate reply.

We make the above statement so the county may know our claims as to the Championship Base Ball Club of Millard County."

JUNE 9.—Deseret is happy to welcome home her students who have been attending school. They are Mary Cropper of the B. Y. U., John Oahoon, Ray Justensen, George Cahoon, and Jerold Bennett of the A. C. C.

Mr. and Mrs. Robert Ashby of Alpine have been visiting here with relatives and friends.

There was a base ball game pulled off yesterday between the base ball fans of Deseret and Abraham, the former being victorious.

G. A. Damrons new house is nearing completion.

Hinckley

HINCKLEY, JUNE 8, 1908.

The weather seems to have moderated some since our last writing and alfalfa is looking better.

The many friends of George A. Black, feel the greatest sympthy for his loved ones over his sad demise. Bro. Black labored for some years as counseler to bishop W. H. Pratt here in the Hinckley ward he was a good man, we also feel for his aged parents Wm. Black and wife in Deseret. Bro. Black met his death by being shot by a treacherous mexican.

Missis Arettia Webb, Maddie Wright and Johnie Wright are home from school.

The wedding dance given by Mr. and Mrs. Ernest Nelson was a grand affair Mrs. Nelson is the youngest daughter of Charles Talbot and wife we wish them much joy in their matriominal venture.

A game of base ball was played between the stiffs and limbers of Hinckley which ended in favor of the stiffs for a dance and ice cream.

Millard County Progress
June 26, 1908

Burtner

BURTNER, June, 18, 1908.

A distructive hail storm visited Burtner yesterday afternoon destroying cow pastures and all grown crops, and proving beyond doubt that tent roofed houses are good sprinkling cans.

At the close of this distructive storm "Burtner's First Daughter" arrived at the home of Mr and Mrs. Irvine E. Jeffery, causing a mid night chase to Holden for Sister Stringham on one of the darkest nights seldom ever experienced; bewildering three teamsters and causing many roads to be made back and forth between here and Holden. The chase covering the space of 6 hrs and 30 minutes. The new comer had been in this sphere of life in the neighborhood of 6 hrs when the wild chase came to an end. By the moon shedding forth its beautiful light to guide them to its birthplace. The delay caused some suffering on the part of the mother but when help arrived all was well.

Hinckley

HINCKLEY, June 18, 1908

Yesterday at about 3 p. m., a severe hail storm passed through here doing hundreds of dollars worth of damage Stripping the alfalfa leaving it standing like straws, and gardens are completely out of sight. The ground under the trees and some distance around looks like a green carpet of leaves. It is the worst hail storm ever witnessed here, it seemed as though it passed in one streak, there is a few farmers it did not damage much.

J. H. Langston and wife are home again they have been visiting in the Dixie Land.

Mrs. Mary Stevens of S L. C. is visiting with her brother Ray Slaughter and family.

The wedding reception of Mr. and Mrs. Don Bishop was celebrated at the residence of the brides parents, Mr. and Mrs. Robert Slaughter June 17. We wish the young people happiness through life.

The old folks party was a grand affair, all had an enjoyable time, we wish them many more rush days.

OASIS

OASIS, July 28 1908.

We joined with Deseret in celebrating the 24th of July. We met at the Oasis Relief Hall and formed in a grand parade to the Deseret meeting house. After the program in the morning we returned to Oasis in afternoon for sports; basket ball being the chief attraction.

Our boys went over to Abraham with a heavy heart, to play a game of base ball, but came back with the big head for they stood 24 to 30 and one innings in their favor.

A base ball craze has struck the West,
Each one confident their the best. —

And place large stakes as boot,
The people gather rain or shine
Just as anxious as the nine,
That their side be the gainers.
Strange how wild the people go
~~River an unsolont ~~~~~~~~~~
For talleys they were numerous.

Hinckley was the first to beat Deseret,
Which put then all in an awful sweat
To have another trial,
Then Deseret did two games take,
And Hinckley's turn to stand and wait
For a chance to now get even.

Not long ago young Abraham
Got left with Deseret's second nine
At Hinckley too the same.
Now Oasis couldn't watch all the time

So scratched around and found a nine
Who'd tackle Abraham.
And left their homes with shaking knees
Heart sick at the dust as it flew with the breeze,
But struck their ball with vengence.
And now the bighead they've got,
And no telling when the thing will stop,
And Oak City better practice.
For I'm sure another dose it'll take,
And maybe a tour of the Co. make
For their spirits are gradually rising.
So be on the look out for the

Oasis team,
And don't be caught in a sleepy dream
For they'll wake you up if they hit you.

Lemington

LEMINGTON, July 20, 1908

Surveyors representing Livingston, Melvell, and others are and have been here for the past six weeks working out a canal route from the south side of the river eight miles east of here, to irrigate a large tract of good land south of here and west of Oak City.

They are all eastern boys and a jolly set as is evidenced by the way they splash the river waters each night at sunset while bathing and then keep the piano ringing accompanied with song and laughter till train time which brings them all promptly for their mail at the post office.

The woods in these parts seem full of returning missionaries, as four of them have left the train here for their homes in the past five days, Richard Wixon and wife of Holden, Edgar Nielson of Oak City and Fred Nielson who lives here all have smiles of satisfaction, either because of the good labers performed or because they are home again or both. The last named gave us an interesting talk Sunday.

Frank L. Copening and wife and Emma Peterson of Lyn who are members of this ward were here visiting friends and attending services Sunday.

Last Thursday Mrs. I. B. Robison and Mrs. Adeline Smith of the Stake Presidency of the Relief Society were here and effected a reorganization in the ward officers, placing as president Emma Nielson with J. M. Ashby and Martha Dutson as counslors, after meeting ice cream was served at the Bishop's and a good social time was had.

Joseph D. Smith and wife were here Sunday night.

The Anderson sisters who have lately built their mother a fine home, returned last night from a short visit to Salt Lake City.

First crop hay, which was good and heavy is in the stacks and another is making rapid growth, being more than two feet high.

Anna Eider is recovering very slowly from poisoning by aconite and turpentine which she had taken for medicine, and all but cost her life. Dr. Damron made two trips here in attendence.

· OASIS

OASIS, Aug. 10 1908.

About six years ago the legislature appropriated about $800 for the purpose of building the Sevier River bridge directly west of Oasis which is the depot for Hinckley, Abraham, and Deseret, also for White Pine Co. Nevada and consequently the most important point in Millard County.

Individuals owning the land along this road granted to the County a six rod street, fencing the same at their own expense thus making the only ingress and egress to the R. R. Station at that time, outside of the R.R. right of way, and a sort of trail which travelers had made over private land without the consent of the owners.

Through a political pull the contract was let to a party who was without experience, never having built a bridge and had no interest whatever in this part of the country, and as results have proven, slighted the work, as a consequence of which one of the approaches was washed away, and although the county had accepted the road it was allowed to remain in this condition until it was entirely washed out by the bursting of the reservoir a year or so ago when at a small expense it might have been saved. The material from this bridge which was furnished by the state, and private parties lodged at the Deseret bridge and was appropriated by the county commissioners and has been used in constructing other bridges and the people of Oasis are without any means of egress to the west, other than a round about way which necessitates the traveling of two miles when one would do with the bridge.

Your correspondent wishes to know if there is any hope of relief from the present commissioners who he is informed are residents of Deseret and Hinckley and are perfectly satisfied with the present arrangment, or whether we are to look to the state for relief.   Sincerely
M. M. Johnson

Being unaquainted with the situation complained of in the above communication, we offer no comment, but suggest that the matter be presented properly before the county commissioners, whom we know as men always studying the public welfare.   Ed.

Hinckley

HINCKLEY Aug. 10 1908

We are having warm days with an occasional shower to freshen the air.

The new Relief Society hall is completed and was dedicated on the 30th of July. Pres. Joseph F. Smith offering the dedicatory prayer.

The Relief Society president Mrs. N.R. Theobald being honorably released from office, Sister Pheobe Mechan was chosen in her place, with Sisters Lucinda Greener and Josephine Christenson as councilors. Sisters Katheren Allred and Jane Pratt were chosen as sec. and treas. respectively.

Conference at Fillmore was well attended by our people.

Bro. Joseph E. Spendlove will leave shortly to fulfill a mission in his native land England.

Another of our prominent young men has the matrimonial fever; this time it is Joseph Blake his bride is a young lady from the south; the couple were married in June. We wish them happiness.

A number of our young folks have been rusticating in Oak Creek Canyon; they report having had a good time.

There has been a new arrival in the family of Mr. and Mrs. Richard T. Cropper, a little boy; mother and child are both doing well.

Burtner.

BURTNER SEPT. 17, 1908

The Stake Superintendent of Sunday Schools, John Reeve, with W.E. Robinson and J. Fill nason and Leo Lyman, stake leader of parent's class, met with the people of Burtner last Sunday and organized a Sunday School. W.E. Bunker was chosen, Superintendent with L H. McCullough as first and Jos. P. Callister as second assistant, Miss McCullough as sec. & treas. Sister W.E. Bunker as organist H. Peterson Chorister, E.W. Jeffery & H. McCullough parent class teachers D.P. Callister as second intermediate teacher and Clara E. Jeffery as primary teacher. The sum of $10 was given to the treasurer with which to buy record book etc. A new blacksmith shop has also been started here and the new buildings are coming along nicely.

Oasis.

OASIS SEPT. 17, 1908.

A movement is on foot here to put a new bridge across the river on the county road west of the R.R. station, at the same point where a miserable make-shift was thrown across some years ago and about $1000 worse than wasted.

This time, plans will be furnished by competent engineers and an estimate of costs will be submitted and bids advertised for, as is usual in public works in other parts of the state.

Oasis is now on the eve of a great boom. All the land, contiguous to the depot is being surveyed and cut up into town lots. 43,000 acres will be thrown open for actual settlement, in tracts of from 40 to 160 acres, at a cost, to the settler, of $4.50 an acre.

A company of local capitalists have organized a bank, which will be open for business on the 28; inst., in a hastily constructed room, which must serve as its temporary quarters until their permanent home is built, which is now being planned. It is to be of cream pressed brick, a home product, many thousand of which are being made and used in this neck of the woods, in the construction of modern cottages, and of which the beautiful new schoolhouse at Hinckley is built.

The canals are all full of water, an unusual state of affairs for this time of the year and due to the immense new reservoir at the Sevier bridge, which conserves the water that formerly ran to waste and now contains sufficient water to irrigate all the land now under cultivation after the irrigation season over, notwithstanding the fact that it was emptied early in the summer, while the steel and concrete head gates were being put in, and has been drawn on during the summer and furnished more water than the farmers could use.

New life is being injected into the whole country and no wonder at last the country at large is being enlightened as to the great possibilities of this vast empire of unoccupied land and being made to sit up and take notice. The wonder is that it has not been done before.

On the 28th inst., a drawing will take place here; 43,000 acres of Carey Act land will be frittered away by the State at $5.50 an acre. Everybody should come preparations are being made to accomadate 2500 people, but to make sure of sleeping accomodatious, it would be wisdom to bring a blanket.

Millard County Progress
October 16, 1908

Hinckley.

Clouds seem to hang around to remind us winter is approaching.

Threshing has commenced with the farmers having fairly good crops.

Many of our people attended Conference in S. L. C and had a good time although the weather was very disagreeable

Elders John Hutchingson and Fred Park have just returned from the mission field. We welcome them home.

Elder Berry Robison will leave Monday for a mission in the Northern States.

Miss Effie Slaughter is here visiting her brother Ray.

Matrimony has again struck here, this being Jacob Felix and Amelia Greener, Walter Funk and Ellen Draper. Our best wishes are for their future happiness.

Our schools have started with a determination for a good season. The new school house is near completion, and all schools will be running there in the near future. We believe we have a good selection of teachers this year, all it lacks is for the parents to stay with the teachers. Principal F. L. Hickman has 8th and 9th grades, Mr. Rasmusson Miss Olsen Miss Brunson and Miss Monroe the other grades.

Millard County Progress
November 13, 1908

Hinckley.

We are having very nice weather once more, and threshing is in order with very fair crops. Miss Effie Slaughter is here visiting her brother Ray and family.

Mr. and Mrs. George Talbot have just returned from Layton having been there to attend the the Talbot family Reunion, they report having an excellent time.

The new school house is completed and school is being held there

Pres'ent A. A. Hinckley and family have returned home bringing with them a new daughter.

Mr. Simon Webb has recently moved in the A. J. Talbot residence on Main street.

Miss Ethel Curtis is visiting her sister Mrs. Joseph Christenson.

Deseret Evening News
December 19, 1908

POSTMASTER FOR LYNNDYL.

(Special to the "News.")

Washington, D. C. Dec. 21.—Orlando T. Meade has been appointed postmaster at Lynndyl, Millard county, Utah, vice I. M. Edwards, resigned.

Millard County Progress

List of Jurors Drawn For The Year 1909

Walter Maycock	Fillmore Ut.
Ova Peterson	" "
Rufus Day	" "
Almon Robison	" "
James Anderson	" "
Brigham Tomkinson	" "
P. L. Brunson	" "
Wm. N. McBride	" "
John Carling	" "
Albert Day	" "
James A. Kelly	" "
Frank Cooper	" "
Wm. P. Payne	" "
Lewis Smith	" "
O. C. Holbrook	" "
F. C. Melville	" "
A. Q. Robison	" "
James Swallow	" "
Arthur Brunson	" "
John Starley	" "
Samuel F. Wade	" "
Frank Cummings	" "
C. W. Lambert	" "
Lewis L. Brunson	" "
Thomas Phelps	" "
George Rogers	" "
Roy Dame	" "
J. W. Payne	" "
Milo D. Warner	" "
R. H. Seguine	" "
G. E. Littlewood	Meadow Ut.
J. S. Dame	" "
J. B. Bushnell	" "
P. L. Greenhalgh	" "
J. A. Beckstrand	" "
J. M. Stewart	" "
E. Stott Jr.	" "
J. H. Fisher	" "
A. Paxton Jr.	Kanosh Ut.
F. Penney	" "
G. A. George	" "
G. Day	" "
L. Barnes	" "
A. Christensen	" "
J. M. Robison	" "
J. Hopkins	" "
B. J. Roberts	" "
Wm. H. Robison	Hinton Ut.
Noah Stow	" "
J. W. Damron	Deseret Ut.
Virgil Kelly	" "
J. M. Moody	" "
D. S. Cahoon	" "
D. J. Black	" "
J. R. Bennet	" "
S. W. Western	" "
J. Rogers	" "
F. R. Lyman	Oak City Ut.
A. M. Roper	" "
A. Christensen	" "
S. Walker	" "
J. S. Anderson	" "
A. Nielson	Leamington Ut.
Ben. Lovell	" "
Nath. Ashby	" "
H. O. Sorenson	" "
J. E. Hunter	Holden Ut.
P. Stephenson	" "
Ben. Kenny	" "
A. E. Stephenson	" "
G. W. Nixon Jr.	" "
M. A. Harmon	" "
Ed. Wood	" "
Hyrum Johnson	" "
L. M. Stevens	" "
A. W. Memmott	Scipio Ut.
S. Memmott	" "
J. P. Brown	" "
B. H. Johnson Jr.	" "
Adolph Hanseen	" "
J. Stone	" "
Samuel Probert	" "
F. M. Fisher	" "
J. B. Martin	" "
C. A. Memmott	" "
W. I. Hatch	" "
T. C. Robins	" "
Andreas Peterson	" "
Henry Huff	Oasis, Ut.
Sims M. Hawley	" "
Thomas J. Wade	" "
Wm. F. Pratt	Hinckley Ut.
A. A. Hinckley	" "
Herbert L. Bishop	" "
W. E. Robison	" "
N. S. Bishop	Burtner, Ut.
J. H. McCullough	" "
Edgar W. Jeffery	" "
John Reeve	Hinckley Ut.
Ray Slaughter	" "
C. N. Ashman	Garrison Ut.
G. C. Richardson	Burbank Ut.
Isaac Robison	Smithville Ut.
E. R. Smyth	Black Rock Ut.
Joseph L. Wade	Clear Lake Ut.

Utah's Greatest Irrigation System.

COVERING CAREY ACT IRRIGATED LANDS TEN YEAR PAYMENTS,

ONE hundred and thirty-five miles southwest of Salt Lake City on the main line of the Salt Lake Route there has recently been set aside by the state twenty thousand acres of the best bench land in Utah to be reclaimed under the "Carey Act." This land is located in the valley of the Sevier River, near the new town of Burtner, in Millard County, Utah.

Already a large number of home-seekers have taken advantage of this opportunity of securing good lands at a nominal cost, and it is a fair prediction that during the next three months hundreds of others will flock to this country to share in the reclamation of this land.

All of the land under this segregation is being irrigated by water which is stored in the largest reservoir in the State of Utah, known as the Sevier Bridge Reservoir, situated in Sanpete and Juab Counties. At this point a mammoth dam has been constructed at an expenditure of a large sum of money. This dam was completed during the past summer and is now storing an immense quantity of water. The construction of this dam is of the most modern type and character, being built under the supervision of eminent engineers to insure its safety and permanency. The height of this structure is 66 feet, being 764 feet wide on the west and 236 feet in width at the bottom. It is so situated that it can easily be raised and the capacity greatly increased. The present capacity of the reservoir approximately 90,000 acre feet, having an area of 2,790 acres and a drainage area of 3,856 square miles. The provisions made for the discharge tunnel and spillway by the engineers in designing and constructing the dam will permit of the washing out of all

SPILLWAY 120 FOOT CONCRETE SPILLWAY OF RIVERSIDE DIVERTING DAM

the reservoirs on the stream without in any way endangering the safety or efficiency of the Sevier Bridge Dam. The overflow spillway was cut in solid rock, its depth in this material being six feet on one side and about twenty on the other, and having a width of 120 feet. This wasteway will carry six feet in depth of water.

A discharge tunnel 8 feet high, 13 feet wide and about 425 feet long was cut in solid rock on a level with the bed of the stream for the purpose of drawing water from the reservoir during the irrigating season. The gates controlling the flow of the water are located near the middle of the tunnel. They are raised and lowered by hoisting apparatus that operates in a gate well. There are three of these gates, each being 4½ feet wide by 8 feet in height, and having a total weight of 12 tons. They are set in concrete and are in charge of a keeper.

The water, after being drawn through the discharge tunnel, follows the old channel of the river to a point near Burtner in Millard County, which is near the lands being reclaimed. At this point another large dam has been constructed for the purpose of diverting the water and raising it to the level of these bench lands. The diverting dam is 300 feet long on the east side and has a

maximum height of 36 feet above the river bed. A concrete gate well has also been provided at this point, and steel gates have been put in plan to control the water.

From this point the water is brought through what is known as the Main Convey Canal, from which smaller canals distribute the water to the various parts of the land.

The climate in this section of the country is suitable for most any sort of agriculture, fruits, and grains of all kinds, flourishing most abundantly.

The Burtner Irrigated Lands Company with offices at 623 Judge Building, Salt Lake City, Utah, are selling agents for these lands which are sold for $40.50 per acre, including perpetual water right.

Under the provisions of the Carey Act the settler is allowed ten years in which to pay for the land, which must be considered a very favorable time limit.

Great activity is already apparent in this locality and thriving farms can be seen throughout the surrounding country.

The Burtner Irrigated Lands Company have arranged for an excursion round trip rate of $5.75 from Salt Lake City to Burtner, Utah every Tuesday and Friday evening, of which hundreds have taken advantage and viewed this vast tract of bench land.

UP-STREAM FALL OF SEVIER BRIDGE DAM, FORMING THE LARGEST RESERVOIR IN UTAH.

Hinckley.

An excellent drama entitled "A Woman's Honor" was presented to a large audience here Dec. 17th by the Hinckley school teachers and others, the proceeds of which are to be used in fitting up the new school house library.

Prof. Hickman of the Murdock academy gave a fine talk to the literary society of the school Dec. 18th his subject was "The Progress of Science."

Babies have arrived at the homes of Charles Theobald and John Talbot.

Ward conference was held here Sat. night Dec. 19th. Bros Wooley and Cannon of Salt Lake were here in the interests of the new priesthood movement and gave the saints some good advice all wards were represented except two.

An interesting program was given by the Sunday School Dec. 20th in honor of the prophet's birthday.

It has been bitter cold weather the thermometer registering as low as 24 degrees below zero; but it has begun to moderate and the snow is almost gone now.

The students from the church schools have been home for the holidays among them were Miss Dora Blake, Miss Mabel Stout, Mr. Samuel Knight and David Jennings.

Christmas was celebrated by the rendering of an excellent program in the Sunday School at 11 A.M., a basket ball game and a young folk's dance in the afternoon and a tag dance in the evening. Everyone enjoyed themselves immensely.

A Leap Year party will be held next Monday evening in the old meeting house, which has been remodeled and converted into a fine ball room. The music stand is now located in the middle of the north side; a beautiful piano has been purchased and the music is better than ever before.

Mr. and Earl Bishop have moved into their new home on Main St.

Mrs. Edith Stout, wife of Ho—— F. Stout, has returned from Salt Lake, where she has been taking a course of study in nursing.

HINCKLEY.

Ex Bishop of Desert Bro. Frank Hinckley delivered a splendid talk on prohibition Sunday afternoon.

Born to Mr. and Mrs. F. H. Pratt a baby boy on the 3rd inst.

Miss Mary Wright has had the misfortune to break one of her wrists that was set by the Dr. at Burtner and is improving nicely.

Oweing to a slip of the pen the word Jr was omitted from the name of H. F. Stout in our last correspondence Bro. Stout has received many congratulations and much merriment has been caused but we hope that it will not have the effect to cause him to lose the smiles and friendship of some of the fairer sex and we would like to announce the same story for Bro Stout sen. in the near future if he will give us the chance. What about it Bro. Stout.

Nearly every Sunday certificates of membership are read in meeting. Many new settlers are arriving and every house and hut in town is occupied and many homes have two families in them. More new homes are being built and the people are prospering.

Miss Clara Walker has returned home after a visit of two months with relatives and friend in Sunny Dixie.

Bro. and Sister Scott who recently sold out here to John Terry, have been home again for some days visiting friends and relatives.

Some are trying to talk up a central telephone so that more phones can be installed in the homes of people. We hope they will succeed.

Many were wondering a few days ago what Bro. J. B. Pratt was going to Salt Lake City for but we understand now that Miss Myra Knight is to accompany him. Bro. Pratt and Miss Knight are among the most respected citizens of our ward and will receive the hearty wishes and congratulations of all.

Sunshine bright and clear has come again and every body seems free and happy at least it is so in the homes of two families where baby girls made their appearance and want to stay. One came to the home of John R. Terry and the other in the home of Geo. A. Webb. Dr. Theobald was the attending Dr. at the former and Dr. McClaren of Oasis the latter. It is needless to tell how intently George gazed at the firmament above us this is the first visit of Mistress Stork at his home.

BURTNER.

The people of Burtner were surprised with a snow storm after this was over a genuine blizzard came; the way the wind made cotton fly was amazing. And now they are comfortably situated each one well supplied with mud.

The annual stockholders meeting of the Melville Irrigation Co. was held Jan. 11, 1909, at the Burtner school house.

General business was attended to and the following officers elected:

Fredric R. Lyman, President.
Hiet E. Maxfield, Vice President
Edgar W. Jeffery, Sect. & Treas.
D. R. Stevens, member of board.
Wm E. Bunker, " " "

After all was over for the day a pleasant surprise was tendered Wm E. Bunker at his home. A spicy program, games and lunch were the enjoyment of the evening.

The first wedding took place in Burtner about one year ago. Now the young couple have been visited by the stork. A bouncing baby boy being the treasure the stork bestowed.

Miss Virgie Searles came home for the holidays and still remains

OASIS.

We have taken a fresh start all around at the beginning of this New Year. Not only with renewed efforts financially and morally. But Ecclesiastically we are plunging ahead. Our new Bp., Marcus Skeem is as active as a new broom in sweeping everything clean, and to add to his many accomplishments he has taken a wife, Miss Betsy Jensen, being the lucky girl. They were married in the Salt Lake Temple the 7inst. He has new hall chairs to make his congregation more comfortable, which is a great improvement over a backless bench.

We have a new primary School teacher for the balance of this year, Miss Erma Turner of Holden is the young lady employed. We have a new salesman in the lumber company, Andrew Skeem is at present holding forth in a new room joining the bank.

A baby boy arrived at the home of Mr. and Mrs. Samuel Rutherford, all doing well. Our flourishing meat market is quite new. The proprietor Mr. Frank, and his genial wife is gaining favor every day.

But there's one thing that isn't new. It's old time mud, that's with us at the present time, especially around the station. Why don't we pave? They will take that up at the next meeting of the Bank Co.

We were sadly disappointed at the result of our petition to close the saloon, but we are living in great hope that when our petition with the others reach the Legislature; they will do something for us.

I forgot to mention a new procedure in school punishment; for nearly every offense the child is sent home; its very pleasant to some of them as they like the road better than the room. Its unpleasant to parents who would like them kept in the school.

DESERET.

Considering the very inclement weather the dance of last week given under the auspices of the Sunday School was highly successful.

The annual meeting of the Indian War Veterans of this side was held Saturday 23rd. Veterans from Hinckley and Oasis were in attendance.

The veterans of the Deseret Post, on Monday afternoon, visit for the day was laid aside and the visitors and pupils, led by principal Robt. McOrmie and teachers, repaired to the meeting house where a most enjoyable program was rendered.

T. H. Church. who has carried the mail for the last sixteen years from Oasis to Abraham Via Deseret and Hinckley celebrated his eighty-fifth birthday on the 20th. The date was made the occasion for a family reunion, Major. Robert and John, sons of Mr. Church, were down from Eureka.

At a recent meeting of Deseret farmers, the possibility of draining a large tract of land north and west of the river, was considered. The belief that much benefit will be gained by adopting this plan is evidenced by the immediate action taken by those interested. An early day this week surveys were made and men are already turning the ground for the proposed drain-ditch.

MERCUR.

On the night of the 22nd we were visited by a great blizzard which piled the snow in drifts and made travel difficult until trails were broken but the last two days the sun has shown his smiling face and the world looks pure and white.

While returning home from school Miss Emma Dykiman, one of the teachers, fell breaking a blood vessel and is reported quite ill

During the past week fifty miners have been laid off.

A baby boy has arrived at the home of Mr. and Mrs. T. Royce.

Three men were injured in the mines last week, one receiving a broken leg the other two being injured in the head

DESERET.

T.B. Allred Sr. is to be around again after a painful illness.

Dr. M. E. Damron, who has been confined to her bed for several weeks, is improving but slowly.

County commissioner H.S. Cahoon and J.R. Bennett health officer, have been to Lynn to investigate a reported case of small pox.

Virgil Kelly Sr. made a hurried run to Salt Lake Tuesday.

The Hinckley M. I. A. very creditably presented the drama "Strife", Thursday afternoon and evening to appreciative audiences.

Mr. Virgil Kelly contractor,

and force of men finished up a half mile on the Burtner ditch this week.

The Agricultural College train reached Oasis Friday.

Among the well paid visitors to the Stake Conference at Holden were Bp. J.W. Damron, H.W Hales Miss Kelly and R. L. Whicker who extended his visit to Fillmore.

A special feature of the program for the meeting of the mutuals next Sunday evening will be the singing by a male quartett, consisting of the following young men; Edgar Petty and Marion Western, tenors, Geo. Kelly and Lorenzo Black, basses.

Mrs. May Oroft and Mrs. Ella Webb entertained a large party at Petty's Monday evening.

After several months spent with relatives Miss Helen Smoot left Thursday for her home in Antimony.

OASIS.

Mrs. Nancy Hawley is in town visiting her son; she recently returned from Seattle where she visited a son and daughter.

The town turned out to surprise Mrs. Elmira Stuyler in honor of her long and faithful services as Pres. of the relief society The sisters presented with a photograph album.

HINCKLEY.

Many of the saints from here attended Conference at Holden; all report having had a good conference.

Notice was given at church Sunday that the apostles and Elder Hart would hold a meeting in Abraham Tuesday at 1 o'clock for the purpose of organizing that branch into a ward again. They will also hold meeting here the same day at 7 P.M.

The snow and mud are gone and the roads are as slick as glass

Town Marshal G. H. Walker and Town Clerk J.B. Pratt have been busy collecting dog taxes this week.

Babies are about the best crop that comes to bless the people of Hinckley two more having arrived last week at the homes of F. Wilkins and Norman Bliss.

Strife is the title of the drama that was presented to a large audience by the Hinckley Dramatic troop last week

The parts were well rendered, we have heard of no one but

what thinks they got their money's worth from this play as the house was roaring all the time so that some of the speeches were not heard. Two more dramas will be given in the near future.

Additional rooms are being built to the homes of Pres. A.A. Hinckley and O. Theobalds.

The little son of Bro. and Sist. Workmans died Jan. 28th of pneumonia. The funeral services were held at their residence and interment was in the Hinckley graveyard.

OASIS.

More snow bespeaks more mud our roads were only just dry, when another storm came; but we console ourselves with the fact that we are not alone.

A meeting of the board of directors of the D. I. Co. was held at the Pres. residence, the 19th inst. They considered the building of cement headgates, repairing of flume and long dyke, on the Gunnison bend Reservoir, also the commencing of work on the canal for power purposes in the Leamington canyon; arrangements are also made for the raising of the Sevier Bridge Reservoir.

Mr. Thomas Church, the mail carrier, while coming home from Abraham, went into Pratt Bros. Store for a dose of cough medicine, and through a mistake took a dose of formaldehyde; Dr. Hamilton was immediatly summoned, and they are very anxious over the outcome.

The town ladies have decided to join with Deseret in their Home Economics, and a class will be organized March 1st. in Deseret Relief Hall at 3 P. M. It is hoped a good turn out will be had.

DESERET.

Vera Cropper, the 11 year old daughter of Mr. and Mrs. Lloyd Cropper, died early Wednesday the 18th. The little girl had been in declining health for several months but her condition was not thought serious until a few weeks ago when she was stricken with partial paralysis and an affection of the spine which resulted in her death. Funeral services were held at 2 P.M. Thursday from the ward meeting house Bp. Damron officiating. Condoling remarks were made by Virgil Kelly and Jos. Damron. Jesus Lover of my Soul and Some glad sweet day, were sung by the choir. Much sympathy was expressed for the sorrowing family in the loss of one, who, in the home circle and elsewhere, was loved so well for her gentle disposition.

In a runaway which occured Saturday morning, Lorin Black, son of Mr. and Mrs. P. T. Black, was terribly and fatally injured. The wagon on which he rode was overturned dragging him some distance. When help arrived the boy was found tightly wedged in the forks of an old tree which had been left lying in the road. He was tenderly carried to the home of his parents, where upon investigation he was found to have sustained several broken bones, severe bruises and internal injuries. Every thing that loving and skilfull hands could do was done but nothing allayed his intense suffering until death came to his relief at 9.30 Sunday evening. Lorin would have been 15 years old April next. In school he stood with the best in his class and would have graduated this year. With his friends he was a favorite and to all was known as a manly, noblehearted boy.

Impressive funeral services held Wednesday were largely attended. The floral offerings were beautiful.

A number of ladies of Deseret and Oasis will in the near future organize a club for the purpose of taking up the studies offered by the A. O. College Institute. A meeting has been called for Monday, March 1st at 3 P. M. and will be held in the Deseret Relief Hall. All are requested to be present.

Dr. M.E. Damron, accompanied by her husband and son, was removed to the Groves L. D. S. hospital last week. On Monday she was successfully operated on for gall stones and other troubles.

A company of young people from Oak City played "Uncle Rueben" to a fair sized house Saturday night. Mr. Rawlinson in the title role proved himself capable of much good work and worthy of the splendid support which he had.

As a respite from the strenuous labors of the past few weeks Dr. Hamilton made a short visit to Salt Lake City, returning last Thursday.

HINCKLEY.

The 11th inst the Hinckley ward choir gave a social dance and picnic in the amusement hall, a very enjoyable time was had.

Lincoln's birthday was fittingly celebrated by the schools. A

programe was given at 10 A. M. and a childrens dance at 2 P. M. the day closing with a large dance for the adults in the evening in the assembly room of the new school building.

The golden wedding of Bro. Alfred Spendlove and wife was celebrated by the married people of the ward under the direction of the Relief Society officers on the 13th inst. About 120 people were seated at the tables and partook of a bounteous feast A short program was rendered and toasts were given, H.F. Stout being toast master. Bro. Spendlove is 71 years old and Sister Spendlove 68. The reception was given as a mark of appreciation for the kindness shown the Mormon Elders in the mission-field in England. Bishop Pratt being one that has visited them and partook of their hospitality before they emigrated to Zion.

Their son J. E. Spendlove is now on a mission in his old home country.

Word was received last week of the death of sister Lizzie Scott wife of G. R. Scott. She was a noble woman and to know her was to love her for she possessed one of the sweetest and most lovely dispositions it has been our lot to meet. She died of cancer of the stomach at the L. D. S. hospital and was buried in Salt Lake City.

The Sunflower club of Oak City very creditably presented the drama "Uncle Rub," to a large and appreciative audience Fri. 19th. Come again Sunflowers.

Our merchant G. A. Robison is so happy that he has a chore boy at his home. He has such a broad smile on his face that we are afraid he will never get straight again. Mother and baby are doing well but Bert is kept quite busy managing the store and son too.

Babies have also arrived at the homes of Robert Slaughter, John Reeve, and Frank Webb.

Sunday services were not as well attended owing to a severe snow storm all day. Three visiting brethren from Twinfalls Idaho and Murry Utah, who are here seeking a home, were the speakers at the afternoon services.

Co. Chairman of the Republican party, J.H. Langston was unanimously chosen by the Hinckley Republicans to represent them at the State Republican Convention to be held in Salt Lake City this week for the purpose of refuting the charges made by the Inter Mountain Republican. 90 per cent plus 1 per cent of the people of Hinckley are in favor of State wide prohibition, and the people are watching with pride the hearty endeavor our County Representative to the legislature is working for the passage of the Cannon Bill.

HINCKLEY.

Yes March came in like a lamb but a lion must be running after the lamb and has just got this far.

Mrs. Kate Hutchinson has gone to the City to study millinery for about two weeks and will then establish a millinery shop at her residence on Main Street.

Mrs. Elizabeth Walker has returned from California after a months visit with sisters and friends. She reports having had the best time in her life.

Mrs. Ellen Funk has been taken to a hospital in the City, she is in a very critical condition, it is thought she has a bad case of leakage of the heart.

Born to Mr. and Mrs. Don A. Bishop a baby girl all concerned doing nicely.

Bro. John R. Terry met with a very painful accident last Wednesday the 3rd. He was on the platform of his windmill when the vane turned almost knocking him off, and to keep from falling he grabbed hold of the mill and his fingers were caught in the cogs and held him from falling the long distance to the ground. His fingers were badly crushed and his middle finger was pulled entirely out just hanging by a slender piece of skin, but he was obliged to stand there untill the vane turned again before he could get out. Dr. Hamilton of Deseret was sent for post haste, but Bro. Terry was very weak from the loss of blood and has been confined to his bed since, but is improving.

We suppose Bro. J. M. Wright will be pleased if that Bill before the legislature pertaining to the paying of rewards to familys of 12 children and over, passes as the 13th baby appeared at his home last week.

We're from Missouri and you'll have to show us if any one can show us a better place for the Church High School than the nice plot selected. It has been cleared and plowed and a nice race track has been made and more work is being done on it every day. Everybody come and see the place.

What is the matter with the County Commissioners, and what has become of those petitions sent in to them. Will they please let the people know where they stand on the subject of prohibition.

A Character Ball will be given in the Amusment Hall Friday next for the benefit of the Ward choir.

What Hinckley needs most now is a good large hotel.

HINCKLEY.

There are quite a few cases of sickness in town at present.

Mrs. Daniel A. Morris is very low with pnuemonia but is improving the last few days.

The little infant of Bro. Neils Christenson is very sick with pnuemonia, also the baby of Bro Ray Slaughter.

The yellow flag is up at the residence of Charles Strattons for scarlet fever but the children are not sick at least they can run around out doors and play, and it is thought by some to be chicken poxus there are several cases of that disease in town.

The Literary society of the school gave a very interesting program last Friday. Miss Rasmusson of Fillmore came down from Payson and gave several nice pieces, one being the Ben Hur Chariot race. She is one of the best elocutionists it has been our privilege to hear.

Miss Eliza Stout has returned home from Provo but is quite ill.

Samuel Knight has just arrived home having completed his winter semester at the B. Y. U.

Bro. Geo. A. Cole is in town again. It is said he has purchased the home and farm of Bro. Terrys.

At Sunday afternoon services the speakers were Bro. Rieve of Kannarra who is here in quest of a home, and Bro. Frank Hinckley.

We hope, now that the prohibition bill is killed, that our Co. Commissioners will take up the question and let us see what can be done toward making Millard Co. dry.

The remark was heard the other day that Senator Hyde's hide was tanned for him now. It seems strange how quick some men will sell their honor and future prospects for a paltry sum of money. But those Senators that did do so will find out that although they have delayed State wide prohibition for a little while Utah will yet appear white on the U. S. Maps.

Work is opening up and wages are good.

OAK CITY.

Mr. Arthur Talbot will soon move into his fine new residence which adds another to the rapidly increasing list of fine dwellings erected lately in Oak City.

The weather is getting milder and spring work has began. Prospects for fruit are better than usual as the trees are being kept back by the cold weather which has prevailed.

The Sun Flower Basket Ball Club is practising every afternoon at the Park. Prof. Soren Rollinson is giving them a course of training. The club is composed of young ladies and they are doing very well.

Mr. Colyer Lovell and John Neilson are recovering from the effect of getting hurt with team runaways.

A birthday dinner was given in honor of T. B. Talbot's seventy-first birthday. All of their children were present; their names are George Talbot and Mrs. and Lyda Theabald of Hinckley, Mrs. Harriet T. Lovell Mr Thomas G. Talbot all of Oak City Twenty-one grand-children were present, and an enjoyable time was had.

DESERET.

Mr. Frank Hinckley of Provo, is in town in the interest of the Hinckley Bros. Moapa Valley farm lands.

Miss Gladys Western who has been very ill for some time is greatly improved.

We are pleased to report among those who have recently come here to reside, Mr. and Mrs Glen Trimble of Fillmore, Mr. Clayton and family of Newhouse and Mr. Geo. Whitehead and family of Eureka.

A dance for the benefit of the Mutuals athletic club was held at Pettys Hall Tuesday night.

Some good work is being done by the boys and girls who expect to meet in the contest at Fillmore.

It is reported that the Y. L. M. I. A. basket ball team of Hinckley has challenged the team of Deseret. The challenge will probably be accepted in the near future.

Mrs. Nellie Jensen made for herself a place in the hearts of the young folks, by tendering them recently grounds south of residence, for basket ball and tennis. No pleasanter place could be found, and this kindness is much appreciated.

Girl babies have recently arrived at the homes of Mr. W. R. Black, Mr. and Mrs. Jno. Cook, Mr. and Mrs. Orson Cahoon, at the home of Mr. and Mrs. V. Kelly Jr. a boy.

Millard County Progress
April 30, 1909

OASIS.

The Bank officers are very proud to talk of their new equipment in the business. They have two new fireproof safes, one six feet high and weighs twenty hundred pounds for books and papers only.

Another with a double time lock and automatic bolt work, with another chest in lower part with combination lock, and is positively burglar proof. There being no openings of any discription for any burglar to work upon. It is one solid box of steel and weighs forty five hundred lbs, the money is absolutely safe within.

Miss Hulda Peterson and Surn Anderson of Oak City were married in the Salt Lake temple. They gave their wedding dance and reception, last Tuesday. We are sorry to lose Miss Peterson and only wish they would settle down here and row their little bark among us. At any rate we wish them a smooth and pleasant journey.

Milton Moody is making rather a lengthy stay in Los Angeles. In his absence Mrs. Moody has opened a land office in Burtner with Miss Laura Penny of Kanosh as assistant house keeper.

The primary school closed this week with a lawn party and a program. Miss Erma Turner who has worked so faithfully with the children will return to her home in Holden and another dear face will be missing.

morning this time left a boy at the home of Benjamin Sampson.

Crops are being sown, men are busy watering.

BURTNER.

Pres. Francis M. Lyman of the quorum of the apostles, Pres. A. A. Hinckley, councilor Fredric R. Lyman and Stake clerk Wm. A. Reeve meet with the Burtner Branch last Tuesday night Apr. 20. There were present 102 persons. An enjoyable time was had the instructions from Apostle Lyman were along the lines most needed now.

Tuesday the male citizens meet in mass meeting to appoint a water master.

The Stork came again this

HINCKLEY.

School is out and the children are busy helping with the spring work. Mrs. Pack and Miss Brunson closed their school work last Thursday and gave a very enjoyable program. We are very sorry Miss Brunson cannot be with us another winter for she has been a very excellent teacher and a great help in the ward. Your correspondent visited her department and was very agreeably surprised at the rapid progress of the children under her teaching, many of the beginners were as good writers as many in the higher grades and they were excellent in their other studies as well.

Mr. Rasmussen and Miss Monroe gave their program Friday night which told of the high and noble work they have accomplished in their department and we are sorry they can not be with us the coming winter.

The 8th and 9th grades gave their program the following Tuesday night. The students rendered their parts very creditably and the trustees spoke very highly of the energetic work of our principal.

Prof. Hickman announced that the school had challenged the town young people for base ball basket ball and other games which have been excepted and would play Thursday and that Saturday the Hinckley school would play Fillmore school all kinds of games on the high school campus.

The death of Bro. William Taylor occured last week caused by being kicked twice in the stomach. He was buried in the Hinckley grave yard but which is also used by the people of Abraham which place he resided in.

It is said that the Deseret basket ball team refused the challenge of this town and say their basket ball season is over, so which rightfully holds the championship?

Mr. Small, the umpire at the Fillmore meet was in attendance at the ball given Friday night he told more than one of the girls while dancing that the decision given between the Deseret girls and Hinckley girls was unfair and that rightfully the game belonged to the Hinckley team, but of course we will have to consider the circumstances a man's word is not always to be relied on when he will decide on one side at one time and on another at another time which can you believe he means. But there is more than one team that was there which says Hinckley won the game fair and square.

A baby girl was born to Mr. and Mrs. Earnest Nielson who are here from Leamington.

A nice gentle rain has come to lay the dust and fix the roads nice for conference.

Mrs. Thomas Greener has gone to Kanosh to the bedside of her mother in law who is reported to be in a dying condition.

HINCKLEY.

Bro. E. F. Pack and family have moved to Provo to make their future home.

One of the most pleasing features that has occured of late was the wedding reception of Bro. H. F. Stout Sen. which was held the 7th of May. He has succeeded in capturing a beautiful lady from Sunny Tenn. and they were married in the Salt Lake temple, May 5th, he going that far to meet his bride, Miss Martha Sherrill. They are at present residing at Burtner, where he is building a house for G. A. Robison.

Miss Clara Walker has gone to Salt Lake to attend the summer school.

T. H. Pratt is having more rooms added to his neat little home.

The infant babe of Bro. and Neils Christensons is very sick again.

Mrs. Amanda Johnson of Leamington has been here visiting friends and relatives, she came to attend the reception of Bro. H. F. Stout. His daughter Miss Mabel Stout also arrived in time to attend it, coming from Provo, where she has been attending the B. Y. U. She was acompanied by Mr. Heber Sornson of Leamington, and it is thought by some that there is a likelyhood of another wedding in the Stout family before long.

A good program was rendered at the Peace meeting Sunday afternoon. Bro. Willie E. Robison gave a short sketch of the Hague conference. Sisters Jennie Robinson and Myrtle Langston sang "The Angel of Peace" and Mrs. Laura Webb rendered the beautiful song, "The Flag with out a stain." Miss Cora Robinson gave a piano solo, there were also skecches, and a resolution was read and unanimously voted on. May the time soon come when there will be peace on earth and good will to all men.

Mr. Vincent Knight has come from Idaho to visit his parents Bro. and sister James V. Knight He may decide to make Hinckley his future home, which we hope he will.

Word came from Burtner Sunday that our dear old friend J. P. Knight has had a stroke, it is hoped he may recover soon.

OAK CITY.

Mr. Sheriff is building a fine residence on south main street, a good number of builders and carpenters are working there, and when completed will add another to the fine buildings erected at Oak City lately.

Miss Nellie Broadhead has accepted a position as clerk in Jacobson & Co. store.

Mr. Willis Lyman and Miss Silvia Lovell have returned from Salt Lake City where they have been going to school.

Mr. Peter Anderson is making some extensive improvements in his home.

O. W. Rollinson has returned from Burtner where he has been engaged in building.

Mrs. Retta Peterson of Eureka who has been visiting her parents Mr. and Mrs. Brigham Lovell of Oak city, returned to her home last Wednesday.

Mrs. Margaret Talbot who took treatment at a hospital at Salt Lake city, for a bad hand, is recovering slowly.

Eastern Utah Advocate
June 3, 1909

Mrs. O. T. Mead of Lynndyl arrived in Price, her former home, last Sunday to visit with friends and relatives. Her husband, "Doc" Mead, is in business there and is doing nicely.

Millard County Progress
June 4, 1909

HINCKLEY.

The cold backward weather has delayed the hay crop considerable here, and as hay is not to be got for love or money it has been a hard spring for the farmers, for their teams are in such a poor condition to do hard work.

May 27th a very enjoyable surprise party was given sister Katherine Allred, by the Relief Society sisters in the Relief Hall.

Elizabeth Walker had a very serious accident the other night. She was walking from one room to another up stairs, and owing to the deep darkness was unable to see where she was going and stepped of the top step of the stairs. She fell the entire distance before she touched anything but the door at the foot, which was closed but not fastened and busted the bottom pannel all to pieces.

The first she realized was when she found herself laying on the kitchen floor and felt blood running down her back from cuts in her head. She was living all alone and so had to crawl until she could get to her cupbard to obtain something to stop the flow of blood. She is better and able to work around but has a severe pain in her shoulders yet.

Born to Mr. and Mrs. Jacob Felix a baby boy.

Bro. Samuel Knight of Santa Clara, oldest son of Knewell K. Knight, is a guest at sister Walkers. He has come to visit his brother James P. Knight, whose illness was reported last week. Sister Walker worked for him when she was 12 years old.

Don Bishop and family have moved to Burtner where they have built them a home.

More people have come to buy homes amongst us. Bro. Talbot now of Oak City, has sold his farm here to a Mr. Stapley and Bro. Hallaoak of Idaho has bought him a home here.

The Primary association gave a program on the 1st of June, consisting of drills, dialogues, songs speeches and song of Brigham Young and a cantata entitled "The Little Gipsy."

Sister Susie Theobald has tendered her resignation as president of the primary association.

Profs. Cummings and Whitaker were here in the interest of the church school last week. Contractor G. G. Theobald now has the plans for building and it is expected that work will commence on the building before long.

BURTNER.

After an illness of one week Elizabeth Grundy Taylor departed this life on the afternoon of May 24, 1909. The cause of her death being pneumonia. She was the wife of Lorin I. Taylor, who moved here some 5 weeks ago. One little son is left in this world without a mother but three babies have preceded her. Her mother, Basheba Grundy came to her bedside some two hours previous to her death. After packing her body in ice, her loved ones left for Loa Wayne Co. where she will be buried beside her children. It is the first death here and so soon after their coming here. We all feel to sympathize with the bereaved. The news of her came like a thunder bolt to us all. She was a noble young woman energetic in the cause of truth, loved and respected by all who knew her.

Thos. C. Callister was in attendance at our ward meeting Sunday.

Millard County Progress
June 11, 1909

HINCKLEY.

The boys of this place accepted the challenge of the Burtner baseball team and a very good game was played at that place last Saturday the Burtner team winning the game; the score was 28 to 21. Some of Hinckley's best baseball boys have moved to Burtner which helps that team and cripples ours.

Mr. Camp, president of the Conference has bought the home of Bro. Lerrip which has been owned by Juel Moody for the past three months. It is said that it was sold for $4,000.

The parents class in Sunday school is increasing rapidly the attendance last Sunday was 98.

Five children were blest last Sunday and thirteen confirmed members of the church.

Dr. Henderson, a very good dentist, is located at Bro. Whiteheads and is having considerable work to do judgeing from the number of people one sees around with their mouths too empty or too full.

Mrs. Christina Johnson is having a room added to her home.

Town Marshal G. H. Walker has been having considerable work to do looking after strays. The other day while trying to drive a mare and colt into the stray pound, the mare whirled and kicked him in the stomach but owing to his presence of mind he saved himself from being hurt very badly for when he saw that he could not get away he threw himself backward and thus lessened the force. He is able to walk around but cannot work or eat but a very little.

R. E. Robinson lost his best cow last Sunday by bloating.

The farewell party of Elders Greener and Bishop will take place Monday the 18th as they are to leave Salt Lake City on the 17th for their missions.

Elder Charles Burke has been released from his call and will not go as reported.

OASIS.

Tuesday morning last saw the passing away of one of our most worthy veterans H. P. Skeem. He was eighty years old and has been suffering from dropsy for a number of weeks. His son Christian in Idaho and daughter Mrs. Thompson have been notified and services will be held Thursday the 10th and the remains taken to Deseret where others of the family have been lain.

The Oasis relief society are happy in the thought that they are soon to have the hall dedicated. The painters are ready to go to work and through the aid given by the tithing, the indebtedness will be lifted and we hope everything will be ready by the 18th as the county society officers are to pay us a visit.

Miss Emma Anderson of this place and Mr. Oda Day of Fillmore were married in the Salt Lake Temple on the 2nd inst. and gave a reception and dance the 9th. We are sorry to lose Emma as she was one of our real workers and Oasis needs all who can or will assist in a public way but she goes with the hearty good will of all.

The Sego Club gives the ball of the season on the 15th. It is termed an old fashioned hard time affair and we dress to suit the occasion and serve an old fashioned lunch of corn bread, hominy, baked beans, cake etc.

If you want a good cheap time don't miss this dance. Prizes will be given for the best representations of the times. Everybody invited, tickets 50 cents.

OAK CITY.

The Sevier River Land and Water Company have their surveying party located here although there is not anything definitely given out, we believe it means much to bring under cultivation thousands of rich sage brush soil in Fair Millards Wide Domain.

Mr. Wanda a Japanese Railroad Section laborer spent a day with us and showed some skill in horse back riding that was almost laughable.

Mr. Lee Anderson is just finishing a fine concrete granery and storage house and with its concrete cellars it makes a very good building.

Grain crops are looking very good, lucern is growing very rapidly and will soon be ready to cut, and rye cultivated without being watered is looking exceptionally good.

An epidemic of whooping cough is here and most all the children have it.

MERCUR.

We have had cold weather until the last few days when old Sol has sent his warming smile to earth and we realize that summer is here.

Mr. and Mrs. J. D. Brown have moved to Pleasant Grove where they will make their future home

Mrs. Minor Alldredge leaves for Deseret today to visit relatives.

Several weeks ago eight of the leaching tanks of the Con-Mercur Mill, caved in and what seems almost a mirical, until that morning the men had been working at that end of the mill, but that morning were taken from the other end, when the cavein came and no one was hurt

Mrs. Parley Pratt is visiting friends at Provo.

Mr. and Mrs. Harvey Dickbury have returned to make their home here.

Last evening a bundle shower was given for Miss Emma Dykeman whose wedding will take place June 9th.

Miss Nellie Spargo and Mr. Gilbert will be married at the home of the bride on Tuesday next.

The closing school exercises was a pleasure to those who attended. The cantata "Peggies Dream" was rendered very well, and great credit is due both teachers and students.

Mrs. James Spiers will visit her mother at Hinckley for the next two or three weeks.

Millard County Progress
June 18, 1909

OAK CITY.

Oak City will celebrate the 4th of July in a fitting manner, an excellent program was read in the ward meeting last Sunday.

Mr. and Mrs. Jens Anderson are rejoicing over the arrival of a fine baby boy.

The wedding dance given by Mr. and Mrs. Peter Neilson was the social event of the season a liberal supply of five lemonade was also in evidence.

George and Ernest Theobald and Ed. Wright are doing some carpenter work and finishing the new A. J. Talbot residence.

The loud whistle of the William Aldridge saw mill engine is evidence that the mill has started again.

Millard County Progress
June 25, 1909

HINCKLEY.

The main topic of the day is the damages from the water that flooded over the county when the Burtner dam washed out.

Word was not sent to any one here when it was found that the dam was going and the head watermaster here did not know about it until he made his morning trip to the reservoir just above here and then he saw the water was raising and he opened the headgates to the canals and worked as hard as he could to get the spill gates open but oweing to the vast amount of water pressing against them he was unable to get but a few hoards out. The water raised so fast that it soon washed over the banks around the reservoir and when it had wet and loosened the dirt at the cropper cut it all slid out at once letting the enormous volume out so quick it was impossible to save anything. The water swept over the field called Packs bottoms and carried some 30 head of horses and mules down but it was found that they all swam out except a $700. Jack belonging to Juel Moody. The Oasis flume was washed away and when it struck the bridge at M. M. Bishop it broke in two and it is said that they went down the river so fast that a horse could not have kept up with them. The homes of M. M. Bishop, Bro. Reeds, Alice Westerns, Bro. Kinders, Bro. Damrons, J. Bennetts, N. Palmers and the saloon at Deseret was washed against until they fell. It is not known if the people got their furniture out before their houses fell or not except Bro. Bishops where with the help of kind friends they were enabled to save most every thing except some 50 turkeys and some chickens. The brick yard suffered considerable Mr. Hickman places his damages near 7 or 8 hundred dollars. Teams are in demand to work on the reservoir and bridges now and it is expected that we will have the water in the canals in a week or so.

DESERET.

Mrs. Hanna Ashby, of Lehi, spent last week with her parents Mr. and Mrs. T. W. Cropper.

After an absence of four years Mrs. Ida Alldredge is again visiting with relatives of this place.

Mrs. Phoebe Reed and family of Mammoth will spend the summer here. Mrs. Reed has rooms in the post office building.

Mrs. Clare Warnick of Provo was among the old home visitors recently.

Miss Vernell Moody came home last week from Provo where she attended the B. Y. U. this winter.

Peter G. Peterson was a Salt Lake visitor last week.

Miss Emily Frampton of Oasis and Gilbert Black were married Wednesday at the home of the grooms parents, ex-sheriff and Mrs. Black. A reception following the ceremony was attended by many friends and relatives.

The Moody Hotel which was among the many buildings badly damaged by the flood has been repaired and Mr. and Mrs. Moody are again at home to their friends

Mr. and Mrs. Jas. H. Robison and party of Snake Valley who have been visiting in Salt Lake City, were delayed on their homeward journey several days, by by the going of the river bridge

Mrs. Gandy and Mrs. Lake of the Robison party returned via Newhouse.

An invitation has been extended to the citizens of Oasis to join us in celebrating Independence day. Many excellent numbers are on the program and a good time assured.

Mr. Geo. W. Cropper, for B. T. Sunders, last week brought in from the West about twelve hundred head of cattle, shipping them out on Monday for points in Wyoming.

Sunday evening traffic was again resumed over the Sevier river at the crossing point of the Deseret bridge which was cut out by the floods of the 16th. A substantial floating bridge was hurriedly constructed under the supervision of the county commissioners who were all on the ground..

Pres. F. R. Lyman and Mr. Copling of the Burtner Co. accompanied by the Millard Co _____ _____ government, the from Deseret visited the flood swept district Thursday 18th personally investigating the damages done homes and property. The method of adjusting a settlement between the damaging companies and damaged has not been given out but assurance is had that immediate action will be taken in behalf of those who have lost home and the work of many years. Work of filling in the Cropper cut is already under way, and the bridges and flumes will be replaced at as early a time as materials can be supplied.

Millard County Progress
July 23, 1909

DEPARTMENT OF THE INTERIOR

U. S. Land Office at Salt Lake City, Utah, July 16th, 1909. Notice is hereby given that James H. Craig, of Lynndyl, Utah, who on June 17th, 1907, made homestead entry No. 16881, Serial, No. 02603, for w¼nw¼; nw¼sw¼ Sec.13 se¼ne¼, Section 14, Township 15 south, Range 5 west, S. L. Meridian, has filed notice of intention to make final commutation proof, to establish claim to the land above described, before the Register and Receiver of the U. S. Land Office at Salt Lake City, Utah, on the 3rd. day of September, 1909. Claimant names as witnesses: Orlando T. Mead, Hugh J. Dixon and A. E. Brooks all of Lynndyl, and F. M. Baer, Salt Lake City, Utah.

E. D. R. Thompson
Register.

HINCKLEY.

The 24th passed off quite jolly here as the weather was ideal and every body well. The program started at 10 a. m. with the following floats parading up and down the street, Utah, The Sunday School with the primary and kindregarten classes seated on the wagon, Utah as it is to-day and Pratt Bros. & Co. who showed their generosity by throwing bags of candy and nuts by the dozens into the crowds lined on each side of the street. The services started at eleven o'clock at the school house D. E. Bishop being marshal of the day The choir sang Utah the Queen of the West.

Prayer Chaplin Nathan B. Badger

Singing Beautiful home

Oration Willis E. Robison

Song Brigham Young by Mrs. Laura Webb.

Song by "Utah" Miss Geneva Robison, "Utah We Love Thee Song Lymond Richards and wife

Singing Choir

This afternoon sports consisted of races, a basket ball game between the girls and a base ball game between the limbers and stiffs, the limbers winning the game. A baby show in which about 25 children under one year old were brought to the stand the

prize being awarded to Mrs. Edgar Jeffery's baby, of Burtner.

Mrs. Annie peterson is here visiting her mother Mrs E. Walker, Mrs. Mary E. Peterson is here visiting her daughters, Mrs. O. Burke and Frank Whitehead. Miss Clara Walker has returned from summer school.

Quite a number of people went to Holden to attend conference and report having had a good time.

M. M. Bishop has bought a lot from J. S. Blake, close to the church school campus and is hauling material there to build a home.

Gravel, rock and cement has been hauled to the campus ready to start on the church school building.

Last Thursday the Stiffs and Limbers played a game of ball to decide which side should clean the ball grounds, the Stiffs won so the boys turned out and cleaned them up in good shape.

The stork visited the homes of Mr. Joseph Christenson and Roy Webb and left them rejoicing over the present that was given to them.

OASIS.

We had a fine time on the 24th Sperry's string band from Nephi was with us, and everything went off lovely, even the ball game between Burtner and Deseret, while Deseret obtained so many tallies on the first two innings that Burtner never caught them, they did make fewer after the new pitcher was installed.

Its a true saying, "A bird never flutters till he's hit." And by the way that Kanosh crane flopped, he must have been fatally wounded. We are sorry our aim at Meadow glanced, for it leaves him no longer innocent. If he understood facts would never have thrust a blow at our fertility, true some of our land needs draining, and if we get the assistance from the government we have applied for it will not be long before we have a scientific drainage system, but while we are waiting and working the land is not idle except for want of laborers. We plead guilty to ignorance as to the number of years a piece of land should be used before renewing or resowing; as there are farms on the river that have produced alfalfa for 40 years, and never been resowed nor rested a single year. It

is true a certain man did move to Fillmore, but it is folly to hold him up as a sample of failure; while his sons are all here, and flourishing. We in turn can mention several who came from there over here and are growing wealthy in the land. Just so, the "Hon. Captain J. D." who so lately stood on the deck of his granery, will soon mount the summit of his sky scraper, and look back over the draggy days he spent in Kanosh. We are very pleased if the dry farm proposition has come to your rescue

for we are growing so rapidly that we will be able to consume all you can haul over, that is in wheat (if the miller can use it) for he says if he gets any good wheat he has to send to idaho for it. When we get our water system perfected he wont have to make such statements. Now again as to our "fertility" I will give you a few facts, real facts about what this alkali spot can produce and the ignorant take notice. Twenty years ago John Iverson planted barley and alfalfa together, the first year he got 92½ bushels of barley and 1½ tons of hay from one acre. The next

year he cut 9 tons of alfalfa from one acre. That same land is still producing 5 and 6 tons to the acre, and last year he raised 30 tons of beets from less than ½ acre, 95 bu. of alfalfa seed from 10 acres, 15 bu. of artichokes on 8 rows, 8 rods long, and a patch of wheat that grew 6 ft before it headed. The wind topped it over and it grew up again 5 ft. and made quite good grain that had to be cut with the mower as the binder could not get through it, now this is not exaggerating he has actually grown cabbage a single head weighed over 20lbs. and have had new potatoes this year since the 26 of June, The agricultural men told us we had the strongest and best land for sugar beets in the state. And we are proud of our pure lithia water that isn't like yours after a storm so thick you can cut it. Now Kanosh again you are mistaken about the poor jack that went down in the flood. He was worth more money, and as to his ever having been rode, we have a more modern means of travel and if you doubt it, come over and witness the automobile sailing around our streets daily and if your "minds eye" will look a little farther you will see a more beautiful panorama than floating bridges and braying donkey, for instance you might see electric lights, street cars, and a sugar factory where you can bring over your grain and take back a load of sugar, and a picture of this kind would show a larger vision and a more extensive brain.

Millard County Progress
October 8, 1909

OASIS.

"No great loss without some small gain," is demonstrated in our case, by living in the desert we escape the heavy rainfalls. Our crops were all gathered in without any delay from bad weather.

John Styler and others are at Conference. Bro. Styler expects to have his arm examined and the heavy case removed we hope that it will be all O.K. this time.

The Mexicans have been very troublesome coming in after pay day and spending their money in the saloon.

There has been a photographer through here takeing shots at some of our FERTILE spots, but the frost has left only beets and artichokes. John Iverson's patch will make a swell picture, they stand 12ft high and are in full bloom. Then the large seed stacks fat cattle and some of the orchards. If they had come 3 weeks ago they would have seen one of the finest cucumber patches that Millard produces, the owner Mr. Williams from a 20 by 75 foot patch gathered 50 gallon at one picking and the ground is still covered.

Moody Bros. have just received a car load of young jacks and jannettes from Missouri.

Sims Hawley's little daughter Lorain just returned from Mammoth where she contracted scarlet fever, one other of the family has since taken it and we hope the rest as well as the public will escape.

Miss Jennie Kemp of Hinckley will sing in our meeting Sunday afternoon. Miss Kemp is a graduate in vocal as also Miss Dora Henry in instrumental, who will accompany her. Miss Henry is our town girl and it is reported she will teach music in our public schools this winter.

A missionary dance was given for the benefit of Samuel Rutherford who leaves some time this week for a mission to the Western States.

CORRESPONDENCE.

HINCKLEY.

We are having such lovely weather, such pleasant days and cool nights. The thrashers are busy trying to get all they can done before it storms again.

Many of our people attended conference at Salt Lake City.

Samuel Knight has received a call from Box B. He will leave some time this month or next for the Northwestern State Mission.

Prof. Plumb of Lincoln Neb. who is teaching school here this winter has organized a band and has some 30 members at present. He is a very competent teacher and we are indeed pleased that we have him in our midst to help us in our musical lines.

Jacob Felix lost a valuable mare last week. She was jumping and running just for the fun of it when her foot caught on a hay knife in such a manner as to cut sever the foot from the leg just above the ankle, all that could be done was done to save her but she took sick from laying on the ground and straining while they were sewing the foot on again and died from colic.

Two deaths have occured since our last correspondence was written. The first was Howard Draper, age 14 years. He was thrown from a horse and knocked unconcious on the 13th of Sept., he lived until the 17th when he passed away with out gaining conciousness. The sympathy of the entire people went out to the bereaved family as it had only been six months since their oldest child, Mrs. Ellen Funk had died. The second death occured the 7t of October, the loved one that was taken was Miss Eliza Stout, daughter of H. F. Stout Sen., aged 21 years 4 months, cause of death being blood poison caused from appendicitus. She took very sick Tuesday Sept. 28th, Dr. Hamilton of Deseret was called and pronounced it a bad case of appendicitus and recommended her taken at once to the hospital but hopes was held out that she might get better with out her being taken while she was so bad and she was not taken until the 1st of October, when she was taken to the L. D. S. Hospital where Drs. Allen and Middleton made an examination but found it was too late as the appendix had broken, but all that skill and loving hands could do for her was done but she passed away at the hospital the 6th of October and was brought home the 9th and interred in the Hinckley graveyard. Many beautiful flowers were spread over her coffin by friends and members of the Y. L. M. of which she was a faithful worker. Bishop W. F. Pratt, R. E. Robison, John Reeve and Bishop Damron of Deseret were the speakers at funeral and all spoke of the noble pure, sweet life she had lived.

Mrs G. H. Walker has been to the city to take her little daughter to the Dr. under whose care she has been for the last 3 years for treatment of dislocation of the hips. They are happy to report that she is getting along fine and is able to walk again a little and the Dr. says that by rubbing and working the muscles for a time she will be alright now. Dr. Baldwin is the Dr. that has been treating her and he has the reputation of being the best Dr. in the west for deformed people.

Friday the 1st Mr. and Mrs. Jacob Langston gave an excellent dinner in honor of their Silver wedding, many friends and relatives were present and many beautiful presents were given.

LYNN JUNCTION.

Last week Mr. D. W. Scannell coupled his cars that has been standing in the yards all summer and proceeded to Lund to take charge of the concrete work putting in Arch Piers for Bridges.

Mr. Thos. Buckley is donning the badge as foreman of the B. & B. department of Lynn and improvements are steadily progressing.

Mr. O. S. Gilbert special agent from Los Angeles gave us a call in the interest of detective department. Supervisor Biglow gave us his regular weekly call

On the 8th inst Mr. Huge Dixons saloon was entered through a back window by a Mexican, while the proprietor was out to dinner. On his return he found an intruder behind the bar filling up on fire water, and on examination found the cash register had been robbed of its contents. Dixon proceeded at once to justice Craig for a warrant, in the mean time Deputy Sheriff Hunter was notified and followed Mr. Mexican to the store where he was jerking a slot machine hunting money. He was quickly taken a prisoner and disarmed and the shinning bracelets placed on his wrists. He was held a prisoner until the arrival of county attorney King, examination was held on the 11th and he entered a plea of guilty and was bound over to the custody of the constable to be delivered to the Sheriff of Millard County for safe keeping for his appearance before the District court. What is much needed here is a jail as it is a very difficult job to hold men three or four days, guarding night and day, besides it is a very expensive proposition.

BURTNER.

Our dam is nearing completion and our people will all move into town soon.

On Oct. 9th we begin our mutual work for the winter. The young mens association was organized in September with Anthony E. Stephenson as Pres. Lewis R. Humphries as first and Emery Peterson as 2nd councellor Wilford McClellan secretary, Duglass Lisonbe, Treasurer, Orson McClellan chorister and Delbert Searles librarian. A successful year's work is anticipated.

A misfit party will be given Friday night for the benefit of the Sunday school at which picnic will be served.

Pres. Francis M. Lyman and Stake Presidency will meet with us tomorrow evening.

The Astle Bros. are planning to leave us for an indefinate time

School is running with a large attendance under the able tutorship of Mr. and Mrs. Avery Bishop.

At our sacrament meeting Sunday Mrs. Anthony Stephenson was congratulated over the beautiful baby girl in her possession. Our choir rendered some very beautiful selections Sunday thanks to our chorister, Bro. Eccles and his co-laborers.

E. W. Jeffery is suffering a bruised ankle, being stepped on by his horse early Friday morning.

Mr. Delbert Searles has sold 40 acres of his land to Cotreal the Engineer. He will plow same for above party.

BURTNER.

Pres. Francis M. Lyman met with us according to appointment also Stake Pres. A. A. Hinckley, Counselor F. R. Lyman and Stake Tithing Clerk Wm. A. Reeve. At this meeting Hiet E. Maxfield was set apart as bishop of Burtner with Edgar W. Jeffery as his first and Wm. Bunker as his second councelor and Irvin E. Jeffery as Ward Clerk.

Our dam is finished and water is again running in our canals.

The people are all in town now. Wednesday Oct. 27 we will have a Ward Jubilee or reunion. Base ball game and races in forenoon, meeting and program at two thirty, general supper at five and a old time dance in the evening.

The infant son of Emery Peterson has been seriously ill for a few days, we hope he is on the mend now.

Mr. Willoughby is poorly, having hurt himself lifting.

Our misfit party was a success, the prize being awarded to Mr. Lawrence Abott and Miss Workman.

Mrs. Wm E. Bunker is visiting in Dixie.

HINCKLEY.

Thanksgiving passed off here very nicely, father, mother, sister, brother, grandmother, grand father and relatives gathered at their old homes for a thanksgiving dinner, and a spirit of union and peace seemed to prevail throughout the ward. At 8 o'clock the people asembled at the school house for the program which was all rendered very creditable. The choir rendered four selections and the quartett given by Prof. Hickman, Jennie Camp, Elmer Stout and Silvia Stout called forth a deafning encore. All the pieces are of worthy mention especially the selections rendered by the Bross Band. Prof Plumb told the audience that the band had only had two practices on piece work but hoped they would over look the mistakes but, after they had played one selection the astonishment of the people could be plainly seen they did so well.

The ball at night was attended by old and young and all seemed to enjoy themselves fine.

Mistress Stork has been busy again and has left a boy at the home of E. M. Workman, a girl at George E. Talbots and if you want to see two proud happy people just take a peep into the home of Joseph and Delta Blake my but they do smile when you take a look at that pretty black haired miss and exclaim "O is'nt she a pretty baby, just like her mother."

Bro. Reeves is very low, he has had two strokes now and is in a helpless condition.

The last thrasher has just been pulled into the yards to be silent for another year.

The flour mill is running day and night and flour is selling at $3.00 a hundred and $2.75 by the ton.

Work is being pushed on the Church high school teams are being called to haul the brick.

Bro John Hilton of Abraham has bought a lot by the side of John Wright and is rushing a brick house up as fast as possible

Bro. Holyoke has his home near completion and M. M. Bishop has moved in his new home.

A number of our people and the most of the eighth grade students have gone to Fillmore to attend the farmers school.

Millard County Progress
December 24, 1909

BURTNER.

Arrived baby girls at the homes of Levi H. McCullough and Irvin E. Jeffery. All concerned doing well.

A dance will be given next Friday night for which the Burtner Orchestra will furnish the music.

The ward bishopric is visiting the families of the ward.

A nice program has been arranged for Xmas.

At our Sabbath meeting Sunday Bro. John Reeves and W. E. Robison of the Stake Presidency of the Sunday School was present. A reorganization was effected. Bro. Wm E. Bunker and Asst. Levi H. McCullough and Jos Callister were released with a vote of thanks and Lewis R. Humphries chosen superintendent with Abram Workman as 1st and Ezra Bunker as 2nd Asst.

Come to our meetings enjoy our singing under the able management of Bro. Stewart Eccles, may his work not be burdensome to him. He is certainly very energetic.

Millard County Progress
December 31, 1909

Jury List For The Year 1910.

List of names from which the Grand and Petit Jurors will be drawn to serve in the District Court in and for Millard County, State of Utah.

FILLMORE.

Nels Bearegard, Frank Robison, Dan Melville, Heber Jackson, Arthur Cooper, John Cawar James C. Peterson, Hans Peterson, Heber J. Mitchel, Martin Hanson, Frank Partridge, Almon D Robison, Peter Beauregard, Willard Rogers, John J. Starley, Wm. Cummings, Peter Shields, Joseph Seguine, Wm. Swallow, James Swallow, John H. Davis, John Scottern.

MEADOW.

Peter Pearson, Howard Bush-

nei, John Labrum, Nephi Stewart, Joseph Beckstrand, John Stewart.

HATTON.

Hyrum Robison, George Whitaker.

KANOSH.

George D. Hunter, Joseph Christensen, James Gardner, John Roberts, Wm. Staples, D Rogers, Leslie George, George Crane, Orson Whitaker, William Penny.

DESERET.

B. P. Craft, John Bennett, A. Allred, George Hales, John H. Western, Peter Hanson.

OAK CITY.

George Finluson, Joseph Anderson, Ole H. Jacobson, John Lovell, John C. Lovell, Edwin Dutson.

LEAMINGTON.

Lewis Nielson, Chris. Overson Rodney Ashby, Richard Dutson, William J. Finlinson.

HOLDEN.

Richard Nixon, A. Stephenson G. Badger, A. J. Poulson, Orson Johnson, Edward Bennett, Ed. Stevens, Joseph Hunter.

SCIPIO.

Thomas Memmott, William Memmott, Wm. R. Thompson, Wm. McArthur, James Ivie, T.

R. Wasden, John Strange, Orson Wasden, Sam Rowley, Thomas W. Memmott, Wm. Bradfield, Wm. J. Rallins, Marion Monroe, John Hanseen.

OASIS.

Marcus Skeem, John Styler, Alfred Johnson, Milton Moody.

HINCKLEY.

J. C. Webb, J. H. Langston, J. M. Wright, J. S. Blake, T. G. Theobald, O. C. Draper, G. Walker, N. B Badger, N. Christensen.

BURTNER.

H. Maxfield, Wm. Bunker

ABRAHAM.

John Hilton, Donald Hogan.

BLACK ROCK; W. James.

CLEAR LAKE: Al. Warner,

HOCKMAN: J. F. Christoferson.

SMITHVILLE: J.H. Robison

GARRISON: D. A. Gonder.

OAK CITY

The many friends of Mrs. Annie L. Anderson will be pleased to learn she is recovering after an illness of three weeks.

A large number of Oak City people attended the quarterly conference at Deseret.

Our enterprising citizen Mr. William Aldridge who has recently moved here from Hinckley has just completed a dwelling house on North Main Street and expects to move into it in the near future. We are glad to see people move in here and build up our town which is growing fast.

A large force of workmen including masons, brick carriers and teams ect. have been working on the Amusement Hall the past week. The white brick walls in this building look fine and our enerjetic bishop who has charge of construction said the work would now go forward.

HINCKLEY.

The health of the people is better than it has been for the last two months. The funeral of Bro. Alfred Spendlove was held Jan. 9th at the Ward Chapel Bishop Pratt conducting the services. The speakers were Jas. S. Blake, B. H. Peterson and Bishop Pratt. Very good reports were given of his life labors in England before he emigrated to this place; how he had worked for forty years for one company and was only late once, showing how punctual he was in all his work, also how he has boarded and fed many many Elders some of whom have almost lived at his home while they were on their missons he emigrated four of his children to Utah and then saved enough to bring himself, aged wife and an adopted daugther who has stayed by them to help and comfort them in their old age and to much can not be said of the tender devotion she has bestowed on them. Sister Spendlove is quite sick and feeble but is recovering a little. Her son Joseph E. is in England on a mission.

The Walter Stock Company gave us three nights of very entertaining dramatic play. The acting of Messers Christensen McDougal and Corrine LaVaunt were exceedingly good.

Mrs. Elizabeth Walker has gone to Salt Lake to visit her daugther Mrs. Elma Peterson. She also expects to go to California for a few months visit with her sister and friends.

Born to Mr. and Mrs. Carson C. Draper and Mr. and Mrs. Jos. Talbot baby boys. All doing well.

The Hinckley Dramatic Co. presented the drama "The Dead Witness" to a large audience on the 19th also played in Deseret the 25th.

The baby of Mrs. Phoebe Meacham has been very sick with phenemonia but is recovering now.

The Primary Officers gave a basket ball last Friday for the purpose of getting money enough to buy some books and papers for that assocation. Bids were quite slow and low for a while but finally run up to $1.00 and $2.00 a basket, so the officers are quite encourged over their success.

Has every body seen the comet that appears in the west every night?

PLANS FOR LYNNDYL.

Alex McPherson Tells of Big Opening Under Sevier River.

The announcement recently made of the land opening at Lynndyl on April 11, by the Sevier River Land & Water company, under the provisions of the Carey act, has aroused considerable interest. Alex McPherson, manager of the project in this city, said this morning that 629,000 acre feet of water went to waste from the Sevier river last year, and the company hopes to prevent this in future.

"We have purchased from people holding old rights on the river, reservoir sites and 160,000 acre feet of water, sufficient to irrigate 75,000 acres of land," said Mr. McPherson. "The company has also filed on 2,000 second feet, or the entire floodtide flow of the river, and this amounts at Lemington to 629,000 acre feet, which went to waste last year. A townsite is to be opened at Lynndyl, or Lynn Junction, together with acreage tracts surrounding it. Plans have been drawn for a $40,000 hotel, and this will be constructed at Lynndyl the coming season. The same company which developed the Twin Falls section in Idaho is back of this project, and it is bound to be a great success."

LEAMINGTON.

After the continuous cold weather we have had so long, everybody seems to be pleased with the occasional outbursts of warm sunshine in between cold north west winds and sleets of hail and snow, also the merry chatter of blackbirds proclaiming the approach of spring, and we have seen one robin.

The frost which has had so tight grasp on the soil, is fast releasing hold and the farmer is beginning to see if the plow and harrow are in shape for use.

Our genial townsman Jos. H. Neilson is making an addition on his residence and his brother Louis has walled in his large hay barn.

We are soon to have a new store and a young merchant in our town, as Alma Harder is building and intends taking over the stock of merchandise now owned by the L. W. Harder Bros. We feel sure he will be successful.

Geo. W. Nixon was in our town last week on a return trip from S. L. C.

The two Mrs. Ashby's are here visiting relatives in Holden this week and will attend annual conference there.

Eddie Dutson of Oak City comes to our town once each week to practice our choir and give music lessons, and our choir leader Joseph Dutson is being trained for his work by him, an awakening along these lines have materially increased our attendance at ward meeting.

The Hinckley Dramatic Co. played here on the 19th to a crowded house The Irishmans music was much enjoyed as our people are training themselves to love high minded pleasures.

We greatly enjoyed ourselves last Friday afternoon and evening the occasion being a debate between the Oak City and Leamington schools in the afternoon and a basket ball game and dance in the evening, attending each the People packed the halls a goodly number were over from Oak City. The debaters did creditable work on the foreign immigration question and were enthusiastically applauded. The honors of the contest were equally divided by the judges. The basket ball game scored 35 to 27 in favor of the Leamington school.

We are sure much good comes of these contests if carried on in a friendly manner and with a view of physical, social and mental developement and hope many such meets will be engaged in.

We enjoyed the rare sight of the comet which appeared some time ago in the west and are waiting with much intrest the appearence of Halley's.

The graveling of the walks on the school grounds last Saturday by the men and boys was neatly done and will be appreciated by every body.

All are invited to attend the Relief Society bazar March 17th.

Millard County Progress
March 11, 1910

HINCKLEY.

It has been some time since there was any correspondence from here in our county paper our correspondent seems to have the spring fever and enjoys being out in the warm sunshine, rather than writing up items and, who doesn't after such a cold hard winter.

Our little town has had its share of sickness and death of late.

Sister Allred more generally known as "Aunt Kate" took a severe fall some three or four weeks ago and broke her hip joint. Dr. Hamilton of Deseret was called in after some two days of suffering and examined her, finding her as stated above. He came next day and put a cast on her and she is getting along just fine.

Sister Nellie Badger has returned from the hospital where she has been under medical treatment and is reported getting along well.

Aunt Nemia Theobald has been very sick and is under the treatment of Dr Hamilton. T. G. Theobald the carpenter is bed fast and had to undergo an operation for a very bad sore gathering on the leg. Dr Ham-

ilton preformed the operation cutting the flesh open and extracting some few pieces of bones and scraping others. He has been bothered with this sore for years but it has grown worse of late.

Feb. 27th Sister Selenia Dutson wife of Columbus Dutson died after a very severe spell of sickness of some few weeks, she had been having very severe pains in her head for some months but of late they became so bad that she went into convulsions. Dr. Hamilton pronounced it a bursted blood vessel in the head. She was unconcious for days before death, having convulsions from every 15 to 35 minutes and those that helped to wait on her and saw her say they never witnessed anything as horrible and bad. Her funeral was held on March 1st and as her body was being taken past the door of her brother, Jos. Talbot his baby boy's spirit passed away, its funeral being held the next day at their home. Sister Dutson leaves a husband and four children their ages ranging from 2 to 14 years, four children having preceeded her to the great beyond.

On Friday a missionary dance was given in the ward hall un-

der the direction of the Relief Society, a lunch and a chance on a quilt was sold for 25 cents There was some $34.00 taken in which will be divided and sent to each of our missionary men in the field, which is five in number.

Bro. T. R. Greener was called home from his mission owing to the illness of his son Ray, who was very low with brights disease, but is able to be out now and getting better, but his mother is now very sick with gall-stones or inflamation of the gall.

Work is being rushed as fast as possible on the Church School building, load after load of lumber has been hauled from the depot and brick from the brick yard.

The school boys and teachers turned out en mass last Saturday and fixed up the grounds around the old meeting house for a ball ground and basket ball grounds also a race track Saturday a large crowd was out running races and playing ball.

Another event that has transpired during the past month is the marriage of Miss Mable Stout daughter of Hosea F. Stout, and Mr. Heber Sorenson of Leamington, a wedding dinner was given at the home of the bride's brother H. F. Stout about 60 of the bride's relatives being seated at the tables.

Mr. Lyman Ricards has purchased a lot from Mr. Carson Draper and will move on it immediatly and commence to build a home.

John Reeve has erected a barn of the latest type and is now

building a large house which will be used for renting purposes so report has it.

Mr. Norman the painter and Mr. Taylor both of which have recently moved here are busy building their homes on main street.

New Millard Tract

SCENE AT LEAMINGTON, UTAH,
Showing fruit orchards and irrigated lands in new tract of Sevier valley.

AN event that means much to the Sevier valley is the opening of 50,000 acres of land at Lynndyl, Millard county, April 11, under the provisions of the Carey act. The great tract of land that is to be reclaimed comprises some of the most fertile bench lands in central Utah. The company back of the new reclamation project is the Sevier River Land & Water company.

The principal townsite on the big tract is Lynndyl, formerly known as Lynn Junction, a division point on the Salt Lake Route. It is about 114 miles south of Salt Lake. Two hundred acres have been set aside for the new town, and already many prospective settlers in that part of the state have made purchases of lots.

The altitude of the lands to be reclaimed is about 4,700 feet. The winters are mild and open, comparatively free from snow in the valley. It is claimed for this section that there are 300 days of sunshine during the year.

Provision has been made by the Sevier River Land & Water company for large storage reservoirs, and water in plenty will be available for the 50,000 acres. Sevier river, from which the water supply will be obtained, is one of the largest streams in central Utah, and its drainage area of 5,500 square miles includes several mountain ranges where a heavy snowfall occurs.

Surrounding the tract some land has already been reclaimed, which demonstrates the fact that there is no experiment about the raising of crops in that section of the state.

Census Enumerators For Millard County.

Salt Lake City, Utah, March 28, 1910.

The following named persons have been appointed enumerators for Millard County by Hugh A. McMillin Supervisor of Census for the District of Utah. Before entering upon the active duties of the office, each person must subscribe to an oath, after which Supervisor McMillin will mail each appointee his or her badge, necessary instructions, schedules, etc.

District No. 62, Hosea F. Stout of Hinckley, for Abraham precient, Burtner precient and Hinckley precient including Hinckley town and Lynn precient.

District No. 68, Wm. H. Bennett of Meadow, for Black Rock precient Kanosh precient including Kanosh town and Meadow precient including Meadow town including Fillmore National Reserve, part of District No. 64, Geo. T. Smith of Garrison for Burbank precient, Garrison precient and Smithville precient.

District No. 65, Wm. Memmott of Scipio for Clear Lake precient, Holden precient and Scipio precient including Scipio town including Fillmore and Nebo National Forest Reserve (part of). District No. 67, Alonzo Huntsman of Fillmore for Fillmore precient and Fillmore City and Fillmore National Forest Reserve (part of).

District No. 68, John L. Nielson of Oak City for Leamington precient and Oak Creek precient including Fillmore and Nebo National Forest Reserve (part of).

Mercur.

Owing to the continued illness of your correspondent here, have neglected to write to your valuable paper.

We are always pleased to read the Millard paper as we get the home news, and it is generally appreciated.

There were a couple of Italians engaged in a fight last night one stabbing the other the assailant is under arrest.

Mrs. W. W. Wright is an inmate of the L. D. S. Hospital where she has undergone two very serious operations, she is now improving very nicely.

We are having winter again the snow being about 2 or 3 inches deep.

Mr. Ivan Wells is moving down on his farm near Payson, where he intends to make his future home.

Mrs. McCormick of Salt Lake City is here visiting with her daughter Mrs. Frevenna for a few days.

The health of the people here is generally pretty good.

SALT LAKE MAN IS WINNER AT DRAWING FOR LYNNDYL LANDS

W. M. Ratzier Has First Choice on Sevier Land and Water Project.

(Special to The Telegram.)

LYNNDYL, Utah, April 11.—The attendance at the Lynndyl land drawing today was over 540, with a registration of 202. The first number drawn from the box by T. C. Callister, former secretary of the state land board, was No. 31, being William M. Ratzier of Salt Lake City. The rest of the drawing was done by Elsie Talbott, the twelve-year-old daughter of Arthur J. Talbott of Oak City, Utah. The winners in order are:

70, Jennie J. Hulbert, Morrison, Ill.
110, William Hamill, Salt Lake.
3, H. P. Taylor, Los Angeles.
202, John Y. Smith, Lehi.
98, Bessie H. Fitting, Salt Lake.
105, Frank K. Nelson, Salt Lake.
123, Alma Gibby, Roy, Utah.
6, Joseph Y. Stewart, Malad, Ida.

The greater part of the registrations are for 160 acres each.

HINCKLEY.

The old adage that "if March begins like a lamb it will go out like a lion", did not prove true here this year, for we had lovely weather both at the begining and end of the month, but there was some pretty tough days between and the last three days of this month has been cold and stormy.

Work is being pushed through pretty fast on the Church School building. The masons are "making the brick fly" as the old saying is.

Aunt Kate Allred is getting along fine with her broken hip but is not able to get out of bed.

Miss Elsie Spendlove went to Pleasant Grove last week and was joined there by Ira Draper formerly of this place and together they took a trip to Salt Lake where they were married in the temple. We wish them a happy journey through life.

We hope the fruit in the neighboring towns is not killed by the frosts of the last few nights and the people here would greatly appreciate it, if some one would bring in a few wagon loads of apples now.

Mistress stork has been busy here again. A baby boy was brought to the home of J. S. Blake. Dr. Dammorn attending A bouncing boy to Mr. and Mrs. H. F. Stout Sr. the 18th Dr. Lee A girl to Mr. and Mrs. S. T. Webb, but it only lived 3 hours. A 12lb boy to Mr. and Mrs. Geo. H. Walker the 29th. Dr. Theobald attending the last two named. All are getting along well.

OAK CITY

This valley seems to be especially adapted to fruit growing. All the hardy kinds. such as apples, peaches, pears, plums, cherries and grapes of all kinds thrive. Four year old apple trees yielded on an average of one bushel to each tree last year. The peach crop of this valley is a sure crop three years out of four and if fire pots were used for heating the orchards three or four nights in the early spring it would never fail to yield bounteous harvest. Grapes have been grown here for years and never fail, as the vines need but little water. The grape is a most profitable crop, it brings the top price in the local market.

Messrs. Collis Lyman, John E. Lovell and Lafe Oleson are building new homes.

Mr. John Nielson has been appointed Census Enumerator for Oak City and Leamington.

The Finlinson Bros will erect an up to date barn on east main street.

Mr. Edgar Nielson and Twissie Roper were married last week and the best wishes of the people of Oak City go with them.

OAK CITY

The Hinckley Brass Band was here last week and paraded the streets and gave a band concert and dance, they made a fine apearance in their band uniforms and their music was just fine.

Born to Mr. and Mrs. Peter Nielson a boy. Mother and child doing well.

A surveying party is here surveying for a higher line, it will cover an immense amount of land in this valley Mr. E. E. Forslmy is the engineer.

Mr. Eddie Dutson has just planted eight acres of apple trees they are a good selection of all choice varities and also Mr. Clarence Nielson.

The silver loving cup given at the Mutual Track Meet was won by the Oak City boys at Holden and we are pleased with honor, Hurrah for Oak City!

Mrs. Nettie White of Beaver City formely of Oak City is visiting her parents Mr. and Mrs. Harry Roper and expects to stay all summer.

Millard County Progress
May 13, 1910

HINCKLEY.

A number of saints attended conference at Scipio and report having the best time and one of the best conferences they ever attended. Sister Loyd one of the visitors at conference will lecture to the women of the west side in Deseret next Wednesday at 2 and 7 P. M.

Those who attended the county meet at Holden say they think it was a grand success, they say the Holden people certainly know how to entertain a large crowd and make them feel at home and give them a royal time. Pres. T. H. Pratt of the Y. M. M. I. A. recieved a request from the Era for the photos of the Jr. B. B.

team. We hope next year to be able to enter in all the sports.

T. H. Pratt is in Salt Lake attending the federal grand jury.

Born to Mr. and Mrs. J. P. Mecham a baby girl, on the 3rd Dr. Lee attending.

The Relief Society on the 4th of this month gave a childrens dance and 16 young girls and boys braided the may pole and at night the queen Miss Sobrina Cropper was crowned and a ball was given in the amusement hall Ice cream was served and the Relief Society recieved $32 and all expenses paid. This is to go towards paying for an organ for the Relief Hall.

Bro. Wm. Camp has bought the barn of Peter Nielsons just south of the old meeting house, and is engaged in painting it now.

John Reeve has his hotel ready for the plasterers and J. W. Blake is getting material on the ground for his hotel so those that have been afraid that there would not be any places for students of the church school to rent rooms may rest a little easier now.

James Faust of Salt Lake City and F. T. Slaughter were the speakers at the Sunday meeting.

An old folks party will be given next Friday afternoon and night all over 45 are invited.

Salt Lake Herald
June 12, 1910

JOSEPH JEFFRIES HURT.

Eureka, June 11.—Joseph Jeffries, master mechanic of the San Pedro shops at Lynndyl, was taken to Salt Lake today, after being injured by a heavy piece of machinery falling on him. Dr. Harvielle, the company surgeon, accompanied him. It is understood that Jeffries' injuries are not fatal.

Millard County Progress
June 17, 1910

HINCKLEY.

Continued from last week.

Bro. M. M. Bishop has been quite ill the last few days his son Edwin who is on a mission has been sent for.

Elder Alma Langston who has been on a mission for nearly 3 years has been released to return home, he will sail from Liverpool the 18th of this month.

Nearly all the students who have been off to school have returned also Miss Clara Walker who has been teaching in "Utah's Dixie."

Born to Mrs. Charles Burke a baby boy also Mrs. Alvin Jenson a boy. Dr. Lee attending both.

Quite a number of our people are helping to get the water out again for the Burtner people. It is hoped that the grain crops may be saved for the people feel rather discouraged.

The church school is nearing the completion of the second story. Another kiln of brick and a car of lumber has been hauled during the past week.

Mrs. Laura Webb has gone to Salt Lake City to attend the primary conference.

The flag that was placed at home of Geo. Talbots for whoop-

ing cough has been taken down. No more cases have developed.

Hinckley seems to be dead this year as far as base ball is concerned. We'd like to have some of our county teams challenge our's to see if it would not wake them up even if they did get beat.

Two Simpkins familys from Wayne Co. have moved here and are renting rooms from Mrs. J. V. Knight and Margot Richards.

Mrs. Elsie Draper formerly Miss Spendlove who was married this spring has come down to take her mother to live with her at her home in Pleasant Grove. Sister Spendlove has been alone since her husband died in January and her daughter married.

Millard County Progress
July 15, 1910

NOTICE.

Department of the Interior U. S. Land Office at Salt Lake City, Utah, June 20, 1910.

Notice is hereby given that Susannah T. Robison, of Hinckley, Utah, for the heirs of Benjamin H. Robison, deceased on Sept. 25, 1908 made Desert Land Entry No.5065 Serial No. 0639, for S2 SE4 Sec. 6, E2 NE4, & E2 SE4 Sec. 7; & w2 NW4, Sec. 8, Township 17 S; Range 6 west, Salt Lake Meridian, has filed notice of intention to make final Proof, to establish claim to the land above described, before the Clerk of the District Court at Fillmore, Utah, on the 30th day of July, 1910.

Claimant names as witnesses:
G. W. Black and Edward Trimble of Fillmore, Utah. John Jarvis of Hinckley Utah, and H.L. Fisher of Burtner, Utah. E. D. R. Thompson Register.
July 1, July 29.

Millard County Progress
September 16, 1910

Judges of Election Appointed.

Kanosh, D. S. Dorrity, James Gardner, A. T. Rapplye.

Meadow, Jesse J. Bennett, John Bushnell, Allison A. Stott.

Fillmore, No. 1 Richard T. Ashby, Mish Day, Proctor H. Robison, Fillmore, No. 2 Daniel Melville Chas. Christopherson, Joseph Carling.

Holden, Lorenzo Stevens, John Alma Stevens, Edward Wood.

Scipio, W. J. Robins, D. F. Olson, Erwin Brown.

Oak Creek, Joshua Finlinson, Joseph S. Anderson, Simeon Walker.

Leamington, Joseph Overson, Rodney B. Ashby, Richard Dutson.

Lynn, O. M. Moorley, J. S. Black, Lewis B. Noble.

Burtner, Levi H. McCullough Emory Peterson, H. E. Maxfield.

Abraham, Donald Hogan, Wm. S. Taylor, Sherman Talbot.

Hinckley, H. F. Stout, Alma Langston, John B. Pratt.

Deseret, John H. Western, Orson Cahoon, Joseph W. Damron Jr.

Oasis, John Styler, John W. Reed, A. C. Christensen.

Clear Lake, Frank Cummings, James Thompson, George H. Davis.

Black Rock, Albert G. James, Jack Travers, Walter James.

Garrison, Thomas Deardon, E. M. Smith, Joseph H. Dearden.

Smithville. Albert J. Bishop, Lorenzo Miller. Byron Foote.

Burbank, Brich Hockman, Lafe Christopherson, Chas. Fillmore.

Millard County Progress
October 28, 1910

Two Sad Deaths Last Sunday.

The death of Marcellas Warner at Fillmore, and of William A. Reeve at Hinckley, about the same hour last Sunday, brought sorrow to two families and two communities.

Marcellas Orange Warner was the son of Dorus B. and Cordilia Webb Warner, and was born at Fillmore Mar. 28, 1867, about twenty years ago he married Alvarette McMahon and she with their three sons, Lawrence 19 years; Orvel, 16 years and Evan 12 years old, are left to mourn the seemingly untimely death of a loving and kind husband and father. The accident which cost his life happened Friday evening, when he and Nephi Anderson were engaged in sorting over some furs of coyotes which had been bountied, and while Mr. Warner was cutting off the feet of a hide, his knife slipped and entered his left arm, making a slit clear to the bone, severing a number of veins starting the blood in a stream. As the wounded man staggered, Anderson caught him in his arms and hurriedly with a handkerchief bandaged the arm above the wound and marched him to Dr. Steven's office, and while the Dr. was dressing the wound, Mr. Anderson went for a conveyance and brought him home. On Sunday the blood started again, and before the Doctor's arrival the loss of blood proved too much, and he expired about 3 o'clock on Sunday afternoon.

Funeral services were held in the Chapel on Tuesday, when Nephi A. Anderson, James A. Kelly, Joseph V. Robison, Thos. C. Callister and Francis M. Lyman all spoke words of comfort and condolence to the bereaved family. Beautiful and appropriate singing was rendered by the ward choir. The floral offerings were profuse and the audience quite large, and a long cordage followed the remains to the "City of the Dead," where the dedicatory prayer was offered by Nephi Anderson.

The whole community sympathize deeply with the sorrowing family.

The demise of William A. Reeve occurred about the same hour as that of Mr. Warner, so we have been informed. Mr. Reeve had been suffering with a bad leg for a number of years, which lately kept growing worse necessitating the amputation of the limb below the knee, after blood poisn followed, resulting fata...

BU____R.

Albert P. W____, Chronicle
Repres____tive.

Dr. Dryden made a trip to Meadow last week to examine applicants for life insurance. He examined thirteen while there.

The stork visited Burtner on November 29, leaving a boy at the home of J. E. Steele, and a girl at Geo. R. Scotts. All doing well.

Ord E. Scott of Salt Lake was a Burtner visitor last week.

N. S. Bishop made a business trip to Salt Lake City last week.

Milando Pratt of Salt Lake is visiting here with his son Orson M.

Our west side merchant S. W. Eccles has transferred his store over to his lot on Clark street and opened up for business in his new location on Monday.

Miss Minnie Clark and her brothers, Mitchell and Richard, have returned to their former home at Santa Ana, California, to spend the winter. They will return to Burtner in the spring.

Dr. and Mrs. Dryden are shipping their household goods to Modena where they will spend the winter. The doctor will work for the Gold Spring Mining Co.

Miss E. S. Marshall was called to the bedside of her brother, Mr. Kelly at Mills, Juab Co., on account of his serious illness.

Everybody attend the Relief Society dance in Burtner next Friday, December 16. Hinckley Orchestra will furnish the music and an oyster supper will be served in the basement.

L. D. West of Colorado has been in Burtner for several days looking over this section with a view to buying some land. He owns land in Colorado and Idaho and says Burtner looks good to him.

JURORS SELECTED FOR 1911.

The jury commissioners named by Judge Greenwood last month, have just completed their work for Millard County for 1911. The following named persons were drawn to serve as jurors the coming year:

Fillmore.

Edwin Bartholomew, Thomas Phelps, Antone Sorenson Frank Cooper, Chas. Christopherson, Walter Maycock, Almon Robison, C. Anderson, Albert Day, Peter L. Brunson, E. L. Velte, John Carling, Richard T. Ashby, William Jackson, Milo D. Warner, Ova Peterson, Simeon Nichols, James Woodard, N. E. Lewis, John Y. Speaksman, Eugene Colegrove.

Meadow.

Hyrum Adams, George E. Littlewood, John Bushnell, Erastus Iverson, Joseph L. Stott, James M. Stewart, H. G. Labrum, Jesse J. Bennett.

Kanosh.

Arthur Howlet, James Cortesen, C. W. Hopkins, George Day, James Charlesworth, Frank Christianson, Noah Avery, A. A. Kimball, Edward L. Black, B. J. Roberts.

Hatton.

William Robison, Joseph C. Whitaker.

Deseret.

Virgil Kelly, Daniel Black, S. W. Western, William Justeson, Albert Hales, Lee R. Cropper.

Oak City.

Alvin Roper, Peter Anderson, Jos. Finlinson, Joseph W. Lovell.

Leamington.

August Neilson, Nathaniel Ashby, Joseph Overson.

Holden.

Thomas R. Evans, G. W. Nixon, Charles Wood Jr., James Stephenson, Hyrum Johnson, David R. Stevens, John Crossland, Samuel Bennett.

Scipio.

Charles E. Peterson, Peter [Bro.......] Benjamin H J.......erson, Edson Robison, F. Lewden, William Bradfield, Alfred ...mott, James Sorenson, John P. Olson, George Monroe.

Oasis.

John Iverson, Jacob C. Hawley, A. C. Christiansen.

Hinckley.

John Reeves, William H. Walker, George Terry, J. E. Spendlove, J. R. Pratt, John W. Hutchinson, John E. Wright, Ernest Theobald, D. E. Bishop, E. M. Workman, John Jarvis.

Hoakman.

George C. Richardson.

Smithville.

Albert J. Bishop.

Garrison.

Rufus Pack.

Burtner.

Jeffrey Irvin, J. H. Peterson, J. M. Rigby, Levi McCollough, Alonzo Billings.

Abraham.

B. Roy Young, Charles Hogan.

Black Rock.

William W. Jingles, Peter S. Martin, Erastus Bone.

Following are the dates set for holding court at the Fifth Judicial District Court for the year 1911:

In Millard County the first term of court shall be held, commencing at the hour of 10 a. m. on Feb. 15, 1911.

The second term of court shall be held, commencing at the hour of 10 a. m. on the 17th day of May, 1911.

The third term of court shall be held, commencing at the hour of 10 a. m. October the 11th, 1911.

BURTNER.

Albert P. Wallace, Chronicle Representative.

George Day and sisters spent part of the holidays in Fillmore.

Tuesday a dance was given by Chas. Sampson, the late bridegroom.

The bow and weight dance given Saturday was a perfect success.

Miss Lily Bryan of Lyman, Wayne County, is visiting old friends in Burtner.

Mrs. Janet Bishop of Hinckley was visiting in Burtner the latter part of the week.

The stork paid a Christmas visit to the home of Ezra Bunker and left a fine boy.

Mrs. Mae McCullough has been ill with an attack of lagrippe and rheumatism.

Mr. Wm. Hannah, the government land inspector, was doing business in Burtner this week.

Mr. and Mrs. Fred Lyman spent the fore part of the holidays at their old home in Oak City.

One of our enterprising citizens, Mr. Cass Lewis, has started in the livery business. Watch for his ad next week.

Dr. Murphy left he fore part of the week for Western Millard and Eastern Nevada. He goes on insurance business.

Mr. Lorenzo Brunson of Fillmore was in town last week. He left Thursday in company with Levi McCullough for Garfield County.

Dr. and Mrs. Ernest Underhill left Monday for Modena for a short visit.

LIQUOR SEIZURE AT LYNNDYL.

It has been pretty generally known for a long time that liquor was being illegally sold at Lynndyl. Millard is a prohibition county and one can't possibly get drunk on the pure lithia water of Millard county. But Sheriff Black has never been able to find any liquor there or catch any one selling it. He has made repeated efforts but he can't leave Oasis for any point without word being sent to Lynn of his movements and all evidence of booze except some strong breaths had been put out of sight by the time he got there. Last week he got a search warrant from Justice Pierson at Oasis and went up to Lynn determined to run down the illicit traffic if possible. He made a thorough search of two suspected places, one on the east and one on the west side of the track. There was every evidence that liquor had been dispensed in both places, but no liquor could be found at first in either place. Finally a cache was found in the cellar back under the floor, the opening to which was cunningly hidden by some ties. Here two barrels of bottled beer and a lot of other liquor was found. At the other building a quantity of liquor was found buried in the ground beside the building. An account book was also found containing the sales of liquor to different parties. The original entries had evidently been changed so as to show the liquor to have been pop, root beer, and other prohibition drinks, but the prices of 75 cents and $1.25 would indicate pretty stiff prices for these cheap and harmless beverages.

Warrants were issued and Dell Steel and Orin McDermott were arrested for selling liquor illegally. At first they plead not guilty, but when they saw that Sheriff Black meant business and that he held convincing proof of their guilt they changed their plea to guilty. On their solemn promise that they would quit the business Justice Neville imposed a minimum fine of $100 each.

Sheriff Black had locked the seized liquor in an adjoining cellar and when he went to get it the next morning he found that the cellar had been broken into and a large quantity of the liquor had been stolen. As snow had fallen since the theft all efforts to locate the stolen liquor were fruitless. It is generally believed that the owners of the buildings were the chief beneficiaries of the business, but as the traffic was broken up no efforts were made to convict them.

The people of Lynn profess themselves as very glad to have the business stopped, but the sheriff has had no aid whatever from any one there in his efforts to suppress it. It seems as if those who want liquor are more active to protect it than the others are to suppress it. Sheriff Black is determined to break it up in this county and he ought to have the support of every law abiding citizen to do so.

Liquor selling is no good to any community, the citizens of the county are overwhelmingly opposed to it, every man who engages in it knows this to be the case. It is only a question of time when the illegal trafficker will be caught, and the next one caught will be cinched so hard that all his illegal profits will be wiped out and he will be taught that the business is the most unprofitable one he could engage in.

LYNNDYL IS ON THE MAP

Our New Correspondent Sends News of the Junction City

Leta Morris, Chronicle Representative.

Mr. A. Mead has returned to his home at Levan on account of serious illness.

Mr. J. C. Jeffers has just returned from Iowa, where he has been spending Christmas holidays with his relatives and friends.

A number of the Lynndyl young people attended the dance at Leamington Friday night and all reported having an enjoyable time.

Mr. Bill Fancher, E. Hudlsen and Vaughn Morris spent Christmas holidays in Salt Lake. They have now returned and resumed their labors again.

The work train with the ditcher left for Oasis on the first to do some much needed filling in around the depot and other low places in the yards at that place.

Mrs. A. V. Morris has purchased the old store building of O. T. Mead, and is having some improvements added to it. When completed she will put in a first class restaurant.

Mrs. C. Gothrup is visiting in Pasadena with friends and relatives. Her husband who was severely burnt while burning rubbish is much improved and will join her at that place.

Miss Clara Morris was to return to Salt Lake to school on the first, but owing to a slight case of throat trouble, thought it best to stay under the care of her mother until an improvement is noticeable.

The big machine shops at Los Vegas, Nevada, are now finished and all the old-time machinists and boiler-makers of Lynndyl, who wish to accept, have been given a chance to go there and _____ At least five are going to take _____ of the chance, as the climate there is much milder in the winter than it is here.

Mr. O. T. Mead has installed a new cash register, the best the National people make, costing in the neighborhood of six hundred dollars; also a pair of counter scales that catch the eyes of everyone coming into the store. When the finishing touches are applied to this store it will be the handsomest and most up-to-date trading establishment in this part of the country.

Booze got the best of a stranger the other night while waiting for his train. While it had him down, someone helped themselves to the contents of his pocket, while someone else borrowed his suit case, which was the next day located in Caliente through the efforts of N. M. Miller, our always wide-awake deputy sheriff, in the possession of a Mexican. Much to the displeasure of everyone, the thief was let loose unpunished.

Millard County Chronicle
January 12, 1911

DEPUTIES NAMED.

The following are the deputies that have been appointed by the various county officers and confirmed by the county commissioners:

Deputy Assessors—W. Y. Rappleye and James A. George.

Deputy Sheriff—Wm. C. Payne, Fillmore; N. M. Miller, Lynndyl.

Deputy County Clerks—Christian Anderson and Mrs. Dora Anderson.

All the old registrars of vital statistics were reappointed.

LYNNDYL.

Leta Morris, Chronicle Representative.

Mr. Fred Blake went to Salt Lake Monday on important business.

S. D. Atkins of Milford has opened up a store in Lynndyl.

Miss Delma Talbot returned to her home at Leamington on account of serious illness.

O. M. Morley has returned from Los Angeles where he has been for some time with friends and relatives.

W. F. Hunter has been added to O. T. Mead's clerking force.

A. E. Brooks is going into the dog business again. Brooks says dogs are dogs these days. Look out for your dogs.

The grader has been here for a few days grading the streets, which has made a great improvement in the appearance of the town.

H. E. Van Housen, general superintendent of the Salt Lake division, was in town Sunday on his regular inspecting trip. He always leaves some of our people feeling better than others.

Joe Kinney who had charge of the switch engine at Caliente for the past few months, has been given a run out of Lynndyl. There's a reason.

The new two hundred ton wrecker that has been expected for so long has at last arrived, and is being equipped for immediate service. The old one which is of a much smaller capacity will be sent down the line to do service at some less important division.

D. W. Scannell, the bridge and building man, is in town with blue prints for a number of material buildings which are to be erected here. One is for an oil house, one a lumber shed and the other is a carpenter and paint shed, 24x50, two stories. When this is completed a great deal of the work now being done by different Salt Lake cabinet makers, can be done here and at a great saving to the company.

THE NEWS FROM BURTNER

Albert P. Wallace, Chronicle Representative.

County Assessor Leslie George, of Kanosh, has been in Burtner the last week looking up assessable property, and from the bunch of papers he was carrying around with Burtner written on them, it looks as if everybody in Burtner had obtained a deed to their property.

Manager T. Clark Callister of the Millard County Telephone Co., has been busy installing a switchboard at the Riding Photo Studio, and also private phones. Burtner has four private phones installed, and within the next few weeks there will be several more. The new subscribers are W. E. Bunker, R. J. Law, N. S. Bishop and H. P. Wallace.

Mrs. Cora Willoughby has been quite ill for the past week, but is up and about again.

Messrs Jas. A. Melville and Geo. A. Snow, of Salt Lake City, were transacting business in Burtner last Wednesday and Thursday.

Charles H. McClain, of Salt Lake City, was in town the last week looking after some of his interests here.

Mr. S. H. Vowles, who is at the present time running the Deseret Roller Mills, gave us a very pleasant call last Sunday afternoon. Mr. Vowles was the first editor of the Lehi Banner.

We were very glad to see such an old friend of the press and to see him trying to help out our country. He is doing all he can to advertise our country and to get the people to go and see the exhibition train from the State Agricultural College that will be in Oasis on February 6th, 1911. We hope he will give us many such cars, as such men as he is are the kind we need in this country to keep building it up.

Everybody should visit the exhibition train at Oasis and hear the many good lectures that will be given. Ladies are invited as well as men, as lectures are given for them in domestic science and cooking. Read all about it in this issue and see some of the photos of some of the professors who will accompany this train.

Our box car railroad station was somewhat enlarged this last week, another car being added. The end of the car that was used as a living room was cleared out and is now used as a waiting room. The car just put in will be used as living rooms for the agent.

FOR SALE.—One thoroughbred S. C. White Leghorn Cockrel. Apply A. P. Wallace.

LYNNDYL.

Leta Morris, Chronicle Representative.

Geo. Vittetoe and Victor Pederson have gone to Caliente to work.

Lew Stout of Leamington made a business trip to Lynndyl last week.

W. N. Fancher has been spending a few days with his family at Salt Lake.

J. B. Beeson and wife have returned from Denver where they have been for the past few months.

Mrs. Geo. Buck went to Salt Lake this week on important business.

Mrs. T. R. Wagner went to Los Angeles where she will spend a few weeks taking in the sight of that city.

Mrs. A. V. Morris' new restaurant is about completed and she is expecting to start up business early next month.

Through the efforts of Maurice Seiburg Nathan Goodman secured a position in Lynndyl.

Tilford Johnson from Scipio has secured a position here and has moved his family to Lynndyl for the remainder of the winter.

H. J. Thomas has resigned his position as boiler-maker for the San Pedro and has accepted a position on one of the other railroads.

LYNNDYL.

Leta Morris, Chronicle Representative.

J. E. Donald has gone to Salt Lake on important business.

W. Taylor has arrived in town after spending a few weeks at Milford.

Mrs. O. T. Mead is visiting with friends and relatives in Price, Utah.

Mrs. W. J. Starten has been visiting in Murray, Utah, with friends and relatives.

O. T. Mead has been sick for several days, his chief trouble being neuralgia.

Mr. Scannell left Lynndyl last week to take charge of some work at Island. Mr. King takes his place until his return.

The round house is equipped with an efficient force of mechanics and up-to-date workmen. A number of engines have recently been overhauled and made practically as good as new.

Fred Blake intends building two new residences which will be an important addition to the town.

Mr. Newheart was in town Sunday inspecting the round house work.

Dr. J. E. Christie was in town for a few days, being located at the Mead Hotel.

The force in the round house and yards has been cut down to eight hours a day on account of the wash out.

W. Dudson and son Joseph of Leamington made a business trip to Lynndyl this week.

Mr. Harry Johnson's speeder became uncontrollable down the grade and the brake did not work until the flat at Leamington was reached.

N. M. Miller, deputy sheriff for the railroad company between here and Salt Lake, was notified by Mr. Jenson at Juab, that a fancy quilt had been taken from his clothes line. At ten P. M. a freight train pulled into the yards at Lynndyl and the quilt was found in the possession of three young men while jumping the box car. But was taken promptly into custody, and the quilt was returned to the owner.

On January 24th, Mrs. Edward Whicker presented her husband with a bouncing baby boy. All concerned doing well.

The infant babe of Ezra Bunkers has been very ill the past week, but at this writing it is reported much better.

Our merchant, Mr. Eccles, is stocking the confectionery store of R. E. Robinson at Hinckley with a stock of goods.

We understand that the Stake Quarterly Conference has been changed from Hinckley to Deseret. All persons who will attend the conference must go to Deseret.

Last Sunday evening at 6 p. m. the infant babe of Mr. and Mrs. Charles Patten died of bronchitis. It had only been ailing about three or four days. It is only just a year ago that they lost another child of about the same age, and in same way. The funeral services were held at the residence of James M. Rigby at 4 p. m. Monday evening. The speakers were Bishop H. E. Maxfield, W. L. Bishop and Jas. M. Rigby. Interment took place in the Burtner cemetery.

Mrs. Martha Ashby returned home last Saturday morning from Salt Lake City, where she had been called to the bedside of her brother.

The Burtner Commercial Club was organized last Tuesday night with the following men as officers: Andrew C. Sorenson, president; Hyrum A. Knight, vice-president; John E. Steel, secretary; Nelson P. Bishop, treasurer, with H. E. Maxfield, Cass Lewis and John A. Bishop as members of the board.

Obituary.

Fredric Rich Lyman, who departed this life at Oak City Feb. 4, 1911, the son of Amasa Mason Lyman and Caroline Ely (Partridge) Lyman, was born at Salt Lake City, October 12th 1827. He was a grandson of Edward Partridge, the first bishop of the church of Jesus Christ of Latter day Saints.

With his parents and others of his fathers family he removed to Fillmore in the early 60's he was baptised Nov. 18, 1865 by Daniel Thompson and confirmed on the same day by Thomas Callister. About the year 1871 in connection with his brothers Platte D., Edward L., Joseph A Walter C. and George Finlinson John W. Dutson and others, he was called by Pres. Thomas Callister to settle in Oak City for the purpose of strengthening the small colony which was then located at that place and then began the eventful career which characterized his lif's labors.

On the 6th day of December 1875 at Salt Lake City he married Ann Elizabeth Lovell, daughter of John and Ann (Jorgensen) Lovell. She was born in Fillmore Dec. 13, 1859 their only child Edith Alzina Lyman was born at Oak City Aug. 4th 1879. She is now the wife of Bp. Joseph Finlinson of the Oak Creek Ward in the Millard Stake of Zion. About the year 1886 he filled a mission to the Southern States and shortly after his return he was called to labor in the Bishopric of the Oak Creek ward as a counselor to Bp. Peter Anderson in which capacity he labored for about 20 years.

In 1907 he was called to labor in the Millard Stake of Zion as first counselor to Pres. Alonzo A Hinckley in which capacity he labored during the remainder of his life, and in the same year he became connected with the settlement of the Burtner Ward of the Millard Stake and was President of its Irrigation Co. from its inception. In all these labors he endeared himself to the hearts of the people among whom he labored, as few men could do. He was an intense lover of nature and could see its beauties in all its creation, he was a leading spirit in all public improvements and his hard work may be seen in all the public improvements of his home town and of the town of Burtner the growth of which he watched with such fatherly care. He spared no pains to make his home surroundings attractive and beautiful and his is one of the finest homes in Oak City. His taking away closes the mutual career of one of the Lords noble men a kind and affectionate husband and father a friend of the needy a stay and strength to the weak, a benefactor to his race and a latter-day saint in every deed.

His demise occured 34 years to a day after that of his father, and has cast a gloom over the entire stake of Zion and wherever he was known. Two hundered and sixty-five relatives and friends attended the funeral services which were held at Oak City Feb. 6th 1911 the opening prayer was offered by Willis E. Robison, beautiful and appropriate music was rendered by the Oak Creek ward choir under the direction of chorister Eddie Q. Dutson and the casket was covered with beautiful and fragrant floral offerings. Many eulogies and comforting remarks were made by elders Thomas C. Callister, Bp. Peter Anderson, Richard R. Lyman, David R. Stevens, Ernest D. Partridge, Bp. H. E. Maxfield of Burtner, Pres. Orvil L. Thompson, Pres. Alonzo A. Hinckley, Apostal George F. Richards and Pres. Francis M. Lyman. The benidiction was pronounced by Bp. Wm. R. Thompson of Scipio and Elder Egdar W. Jeffery of Burtner offered the dedicatory prayer at the grave.

Peace be unto the dead and may the Lord bless and comfort the loving.

"Through deepening trials throng thy way, Press on, press on ye saints of God, Ere long the resurection day, will spread its light and mirth abroad."

Yours very Truly,
Thomas Callister.

THE NEWS FROM BURTNER

Albert P. Wallace, Chronicle Representative.

Don C. Wixon, Verne Bartholomew, Charles Iverson and Edward Trimble of Fillmore were recent visitors in Burtner.

Mr. John A. Coles, our railroad agent, has got a change of working hours. Since the railroad has been washed out his hours are from 9 p. m. to 10 a. m.

Mr. D. P. Callister moved his blacksmith shop back from the east side and is prepared to do all kinds of blacksmithing now at his old stand.

J. W. Vandervanter has begun the erection of a cement block store building on his lot on Clark street.

H. E. Maxfield, E. W. Jeffrey, A. Billings and John E. Steel made a trip to Salt Lake City last week to meet the men who are taking over the Oasis project. They returned Sunday morning, and prospects are reported very encouraging.

Mrs. Ella Bassit of American Fork is visiting relatives in Burtner.

Last Saturday night a series of three basket ball games were played here, two with Deseret and one with Oasis. The district school team of Deseret played the school boys of Burtner. The score was 13 to 29 in favor of Burtner. The Junior team of Deseret played the Junior team of Burtner. Score 15 to 19 in favor of Burtner. The Senior team of Oasis and the Senior team of Burtner played a hotly contested game with the visiting team winning out with a score of 29 to 25 in favor of our visitors. After the games dancing was indulged in and everything went off very pleasantly. We think our visitors had a very good time, and we extend them a hearty welcome at any time.

Current Events last Sunday evening. Mutual Mildred McClellan as a report of the Saturday night and Burtner in playing basket ball the night before.

Mrs. N. L. Bishop has been quite ill the past week.

Arthur Gull of Meadow has been in Burtner this last week selling the world-renowned Watkins Remedies and Extracts.

The Burtner Commercial Club was the only one represented from Millard County, according to the city papers. Andrew Sorenson and H. A. Knight were the representatives.

Stewart Eccles and son have opened a branch store at Hinckley and are making a special sale on shoes. Read his new ad and see the attractive offers he makes.

N. S. Bishop went over to Hinckley last Saturday to attend the funeral of his nephew, the infant son of Daniel Earl Bishop.

THE NEWS FROM BURTNER

Burtner Also Plays Ball--Relief Society Anniversary Entertainment

Albert P. Wallace, Chronicle Representative.

T. Clark Callister of Fillmore was in town on business last week.

H. E. Maxfield made a business trip to Salt Lake City last week.

A good team of work horses wanted. Apply to A. P. Wallace, Burtner.

Delbert Serio is the new partner of Will Jenkins in the butcher shop here, he having purchased the interests of Rob Jenkins.

FOR SALE—Purebred Light Bramah Chickens, also eggs for hatching. Apply to H. Willoughby, Burtner.

A non-resident desires to have 80 acres of land in West Burtner cultivated on shares. If you want the job tell A. P. Wallace all about it.

Things are quite lively around here now, active work having begun on the new spill way. Quite a number of men are employed there, they are blasting off the dirt and making the cut wider to put the concrete in.

Attorney McInnich was down from Salt Lake City this week in the interest of the farmers that he is representing in the damage suits against the Oasis Land and Irrigation Co.

D. A. Bunker of Salt Lake has been in town for the past week, helping to get things straightened out in the new warehouse of the Hub Company.

David R. Stevens of Holden made a trip to Burtner last week.

Copening and McClain were down from Salt Lake City last week gathering up their things that they had here in connection with the O. L. & I. Co., as that company is a thing of the past now. They still own something like

In a few weeks we expect it will be Delta instead of Burtner. The Delta Irrigation Company want that name, the railway people have no objections, and we expect the post office department will be satisfied with it. We have given it that name on the new map we are publishing for the special edition.

Mrs. John A. Coles, wife of our local agent, returned to Burtner last week from an extended visit to California, their former home; she has been housed up since her return, as it was too disagreeable to get out, and coming from a nice summer country to a place where the snow was about 4 inches deep is enough to house up most anybody.

The Hinckley basket ball teams came up last Saturday night and beat the home team at the local sport. The junior team beat by a score of 13 to 26 in favor of the visitors. The lineup was as follows:

Hinckley		Burtner
L. Whitehead	C.	G. Billings
W. Wilkins	R. F.	N. Gardner
G. Talbot	L. F.	O. Mahew
F. Theobald	L. G.	A. Humphries
W. Robison	R. G.	T. Brower

The game was played swift and fast till the beginning of the second half when Whitehead got struck in the eye by Billings elbow, that delayed the game for about ten minutes, but the boys went after them and beat the home team by a big score.

The game between the seniors was a more closely contested one, the visiting team beating by two points. One minute before the time was up the home boys made a field throw and brought the score up to a tie, but the time-keeper let them play about a half minute over-time, and the visitors made a field score which beat us 26 to 24 in their favor. The lineup was as follows:

Hinckley		Burtner
Hilton	C	Lyman
Blake	R. F.	Pace
E. Bishop	L. F.	C. Billings
Wright	L. G.	W. Gardner
Langston	R. G.	A. Bishop

G. E. Billings, Referee.

March 17th is the anniversary of the Relief Society, and we all want to turn out and help them celebrate in great style. The following program will be given in the hall to begin at 1 o'clock p. m. sharp:

Oh! Blest was the Day, etc., by the choir.

Prayer—Mrs. J. H. Peterson.

Quartette—Mary Olson and Co.

Song—Malissa Callister.

Address of welcome—President, Annie Bishop

Song—(Guitar accompaniment)—May Peterson.

Instrumental Music—Wilford McLellan

Recitation—Ida Patten.

Song—Ruth Serle.

Comic Reading—H. E. Maxfield.

Instrumental Music—Fred S. Lyman and Co.

History of Relief Society—Clara Jeffrey.

Duet—Emma Bunker and Co.

Stump Speech—Abram Workman, Sr.

Quartette—J. H. Peterson and Co.

Harmonica Music—Levi McCullough.

Song—Cordelia Knight.

Recitation—Eliza Hook.

Instrumental Music—L. R. Humphries and Son.

Song—"Come, Come, Ye Saints."—Congregation.

Benediction—Sarah J. Rigby.

Refreshments will be served immediately after the program, then a children's dance will be given, after which the amusements will be adjourned till 8 o'clock sharp, when all the ward will meet for an old time calico dance, in which old time dances will be indulged in, and all the ladies will be expected to wear calico dresses. Everybody invited.

Millard County Chronicle
March 16, 1911

BURTNER.

Albert P. Wallace, Chronicle Representative.

Vice-President and Manager Geo. Snow of the new Delta Land and Water Company, has been in Burtner this week seeing about the improvements that are under way for their irrigation system. The new company evidently intends to put everything in good shape and have the money to do it with. Owners of land on the west side are beginning to arrive and a large acreage will be planted this season.

Mr. F. C. Callister is in town this week working on the telephone lines. Burtner now has ten phones and the list is growing.

A non-resident desires to have 80 acres of land in West Burtner cultivated on shares. If you want the job tell A. P. Wallace all about it.

FOR SALE—Purebred Light Bramah Chickens, also eggs for hatching. Apply to H. Willoughby, Burtner.

Burtner played basket ball last Friday with Oak City, and we are sorry to say that we were beaten again. One explanation we wish to offer is that our team has never had anyone to show them how to play the game, and that is a great disadvantage to the players.

Mr. Charles Ashby and family were visiting relatives in Holden last week.

Mr. E. W. Cottrell, one of the O. L. & I. Co.'s engineers, came back to Burtner last Monday morning to assist Mr. Strain in the work across the river.

Mr. Frank Woods of Holden is building a nice residence on East Clark street.

OAK CITY.

Mrs. Maggie Lovell of Oak City died last Wednesday evening, of appoplexy, she was only ill about fifteen minutes, and had been recovering well, and was in excellent health from her recent confinment of two week's ago, until the evening of her death.

In last week's issue we stated that death was due to blood poison, this was a false report given to us and the statement should have read appoplexy instead of blood poison,

The funeral was held last Friday at Oak City, a large circle of relatives and friends were in attendance.

Bp. Finlinson, a brother of the deceased officiated at the services, which was held in the meeting house. Pres. Hinckley, By. Ashby and Brothers Roper, Christensen, and Lyman were the principal speakers.

The ward choir furnished some very appropriate singing which was much appreciated.

BURTNER.

A. O. SORENSON, REPRESENTATIVE

The Commercial Club of Burtner, met last Saturday evening, and passed a resolution, setting aside Saturday 18, as quimp or squirrel day. The club is buying poison and wheat and will allot a certain amount to each farmer on the two Irrigation projects here at Burtner.

Last Saturday while playing basket ball a couple of Burtner's young bloods got in a dispute as to who was the best scrapper, some few blows were struck, the boys came in and paid their fine and have come to the conclusion that fighting doesn't pay. No! Never again!

We are having some lovely sunshine days here the ground is nice and dry and the farmers are busy plowing and putting in their crops. It is estimated that between fifteen and twenty thousand acres of land will be put into crops here this season.

On March 11th Sorenson & Day started two four horse loads of produce for Black Horse Nev.

Mr. Frank Wood is erecting a nice dwelling house on Clark St. J. W. Hall has the contract.

Mr. Thos. Patten is building a nice dwelling house on State St.

Mr. Benjaman Oluff formerly of Provo has moved his family to Burtner, he intends to make his home here. We all join in extending him a hearty welcome.

Mr. Abbott, ex-sheriff of Sevier Co. has moved to Burtner, he is largely interested here and expects to make his future home here. Welcome to Burtner Brother Abbott.

Marriage Licenses Issued.

Marriage license was issued on Wednesday to Mr. Miles Greener of Hinckley and Miss Lillie Adams of Meadow.

Marriage license was issued Wednesday to Peter M. Anderson and Miss Tora Jenson both of Oasis.

The last named couple were married the same day at the court house. Elder N. A. Anderson officiating.

The Newest Town in Millard

The Past History and Future Prospects of Burtner or Delta

Burtner's Past.

A number of the leading citizens of Millard County met together in the early part of 1906 and organized the Melville Irrigation Company. This new company bought from the Deseret Irrigation Company a half interest in the Sevier Bridge reservoir, which was then only partially constructed. The tract to be watered by this company comprised about 12,000 acres of choice level land located along the S. P., L. A. & S. L. Ry., about five miles north of Oasis. The lands were surveyed, a diversion dam was built across the river to raise the water into the ditches and a town site was laid out one mile by a mile and a quarter size.

Work was begun on the ditch October 28, 1906, and water was turned on to the land in the fall of 1908. Every person purchasing 40 shares of water of the company was given a lot in the townsite at cost. The first family to move into the neighborhood was Walter Gardner, in the spring of 1907. N. S. Bishop built the first house on the townsite in April, 1907, and moved his family into it the following month.

In January, 1908, a postoffice was established with H. J. McCullough as postmaster.

The Oasis Land & Irrigation Company purchased a half interest in the Sevier River reservoir and laid out a tract of about 43,000 acres of land under the Carey Act on the west side of the Sevier river, adjoining Burtner. They began work on their ditches in January, 1909, and opened up the tract for settlement. A new era dawned for Burtner. Land selling excursions were conducted weekly, the new town was filled with strangers, while thousands of dollars were invested in town lots and farming lands. The farmers on both the Melville and Oasis tracts prepared their land for cultivation, and sowed for their first harvest. Everything was propitious and it looked as if Burtner would be a town of 1,000 population by 1910. But in June, 1909, their hopes were dashed by the failure of the diversion dam just above Burtner, which raised the water of the river into the head canal of the Melville and Oasis Irrigation Companies' ditches.

The hope of a harvest that season was destroyed, but the people set to work and rebuilt the dam during the summer. The spring of 1910 found them again preparing their land for harvest.

Thousands of acres of land had been sold during the winter and spring and a larger acreage than ever was under cultivation. But disaster overtook them once more. In May, 1910, the dam again went out and the farmers were left to face another year without a harvest. This time instead of attempting to rebuild the dam a canal was extended up the river several miles and the water taken out from a ten-foot dam instead of a 30-foot dam, as was the old one. It is also built on a solid clay foundation, with a spillway and headgates of concrete cut through a high ridge of solid formation. There is no possibility of the farmers again being left without water.

As a result of these misfortunes Burtner instead of being a town of 1,000 or 2,000 people, has only about 500. Many people have had to go away for the winter to make a living for their families. But nobody is selling out or leaving permanently who can possibly help it. Everyone has confidence in the town and adjoining country. 100,000 acres of the finest land adjoins the town and we know that these now desert lands will in a year or two be converted into prosperous farms. Our crops of grain, vegetables, alfalfa and alfalfa seed are not surpassed by any locality in Utah. Our domestic water supply is a pure lithia water, a sure cure for kidney troubles and bright's disease. Our climate is equal to any in Utah, while no section is more favorably located as to markets.

During the year 1910 the farmers within a radius of six miles of Burtner realized about $160,000 from alfalfa seed, besides large amounts for

hay, grain, vegetables, dairy products
and stock. The soil is also specially
adapted for sugar beets.

With this outlook and the certainty
that one harvest will put everybody
on their feet the people of Burtner
are hanging on without any doubt
whatever that their town will in a very
few years be the metropolis of Millard
county.

NELSON S. BISHOP

O. T. MEAD.

One of the boosters for Lynndyle is O. T. Mead, who opened up the first store in that place four years ago. He has seen the town grow to an important railway center and has always been ready to invest his money and boom his town and any enter-prise that will advance the interests of his section. As a proof of his confi-dence he has just erected and moved into an $8,000 stone store building, one of the finest in the county. His stock is worthy of his new building, as it comprises $9,000 worth of general mer-chandise and $1,000 in farm imple-ments and machinery. His store is equipped with all modern improve-ments and enjoys a large and growing trade. Mr. Mead is also the post-master of Lynndyle.

The Old Town of Deseret

Its Past Vicissitudes and Present Prosperity
Prospects for the Future

This was the first settlement along the Sevier river. The first dam and canal was built in 1886. The first years of the settlement were full of hardship and misfortune. The dams on the treacherous Sevier were frequently carried out and the farmers often suffered the loss of their crops. But since the construction of the concrete headgates and spillway they have had no trouble and the water supply has been uninterrupted. Last summer a new concrete apron was built at the spillway which will prevent any possibility of future accidents.

Deseret has a fine new school house, an excellent meeting house and a large amusement hall, where dances and other entertainments are held. It is surrounded by splendid farms, where great quantities of grain, hay and vegetables are raised. It is especially adapted for the growing of vegetables, and a pickle factory and canning factory are proposed to take care of these products. Sugar beets are grown here to perfection and it is probable that considerable land will be put out to this profitable crop the coming season.

DESERET NEWS NOTES.

Miss Roan Kelly has recently returned from a long visit in Salt Lake. Deseret is always a bit brighter and more interesting when Miss Kelly is here.

Mrs. John Dewsnup has been ill, but is around again and feeling somewhat better.

Dr. Mary E. Damron, who has served this community for so many years, has been ill most of the winter, due to adhesions formed after an operation for gallstones some time ago. Finally she yielded to the urgent advice of Dr. Broaddus to seek surgical aid in Salt Lake. Dr. A. A. Kerr recently performed a very serious operation for her, and we are glad to hear that she rallied splendidly from the operation and is improving with remarkable rapidity.

Basketball practice in Petty's hall makes it a merry, noisy place these spring evenings.

Damron & Hawley have just received a stock of new ladies' goods for Easter. The Chronicle will tell you all about it next week.

On St. Patrick's day the Relief Society here celebrated the sixty-ninth anniversary of its organization in Nauvoo. An interesting program by the young people was given in the Relief Hall in the afternoon and sketches of the original organization and of the early days of the Deseret Relief Society were given by the president, Mrs. H. S. Cahoon and Mrs. Cropper. In the evening a picnic supper and dance were enjoyed.

No doubt our small houses, small stoves and our fear of open windows and plenty of fresh air are responsible for much of this winter's sickness. The sunny spring days are sending us out of doors and banishing much sickness. Dr. Broaddus has been very busy all winter. In the fall, Deseret had several very serious cases; during the winter, Hinckley, with its smallpox, measles, pneumonia and typhoid, claimed most of the doctor's time, and lately Oasis and Burtner (or Delta, rather!) have demanded their share.

Mr. William Justensen and family are talking of moving to California. We can't afford to lose them, for Mr. Justensen is one of the most energetic and successful farmers in Millard county. He has also made a fine success at vegetable gardening and is one of those who know that all this land needs is work.

PIONEER.

MRS. J. D. BLACK.

Has been established in business at Deseret for about eight years. She deals chiefly in dress goods, ladies' and childrens' underwear and suits and millinery. She has just received a fine stock of spring sample hats and shapes which she can furnish trimmed or can trim to suit the taste of her customers. She has a great variety of the latest things in trimmings and with her experience and taste can satisfy the most fastidious customer. She makes a specialty of ladies' suits and has a great variety of patterns to choose from. Mrs. Black also carries a line of groceries, fruit and candy, and is doing a nice and growing trade.

DAMRON & HAWLEY.

The business carried on by this firm at Deseret was established in 1880 by Bishop Partridge. It was afterward sold to Wm. Ray, who retired from the business in 1899 after making a competency out of it. Mace & Damron and afterward J. W. Damron Jr. leased it for a few years. In August, 1902, J. W. Damron and J. C. Hawley purchased the business and have run it ever since, Mr. Damron being in charge. The building, a good illustration of which is given above, is a large structure 25 x 50 feet, well stocked with a large line of general merchandise. It has been the leading stand for Western Millard County from its establishment to the present time, and the headquarters for the sheep men on the western desert. The management has catered specially to this trade by providing corrals, tents, artesian well and the most commodious grainary in the county. The firm deal in hay, grain and farm products, beside farm implements, wagons, etc. They have recently received a carload of seed oats from Idaho and the farmer who wants a clean, first-class grain should secure some of these oats.

Deseret Meeting House.

THE NEWS FROM BURTNER

Albert P. Wallace, Chronicle
Representative.

Last Tuesday night a surprise party was given in the Hall in honor of Bishop Maxfield's 52nd birthday, quite a large crowd greeted him there. He was presented with a very beautiful 18 size, 21 jeweled Elgin watch with his initials, H. E. M., engraved on the back. L. I. Taylor went to his place and told him the boys were having a big fight in the hall over the basket ball, and were breaking things up in general, and wanted him to come over and help him quell the disturbance. The story worked like a charm. He was willingly led over to stop a fight and when he arrived in the door he found everybody, ready to shout surprise.

Last week Mr. J. B. Heydt, former vice-president of the Oasis Land and Irrigation Co. of Saint Louis, was in Burtner, and told his foreman, Mr. H. Munster, to proceed with the work of putting in their crops. They own the entire section, No. 14, north of Burtner.

Fred Barben, of Midway, Utah, one of our old-timers, was in Burtner last week. He only stayed a couple of days, said he had to go back and bring his things down here and live, that this country was far ahead of any he had seen yet, and he was coming back to stay.

Monday night and Tuesday of last week the heaviest snow storms of this winter made its appearance, it snowed about 7 inches on the level, and since then we have had some very severe weather. One of our ambitious citizens, Mr. D. P. Callister, got out and made trails all over town to the special satisfaction of the women.

At the Hall last Wednesday night a number of the young ladies entertained our basket ball team, serving

Basket ball and dancing completed the rest of the program for the evening.

Mrs. Bert Johnson is reported on the sick list.

Millard County Progress
March 24, 1911

OAK CITY.

S. J. RAWLINSON, REPRESENTATIVE

The members of our orchestra returned from Holden yesterday, having played for two dances on Friday and Saturday evenings. They report the trip as one profitable to them.

On Friday last the school basket ball team went to Hinckley inorder that they might measure their own strength.

They were weighed in the balance and were found wanting by six points. The score being 17 to 11. Come to our town Hinckley and we'll weigh you on our scales.

Mr. Claud Huff, of Meadow, has given us two calls recently.

His object is to buy beef. Claud was born and raised here, and is always welcome in his home town.

The girls basket ball team has been on the grounds the past few evenings, they are promising good form. Miss Geneva Lundahl is making a high jump each practice game and will undoubtly make what our ladie's team has always wished for, a 'center' Some think that her reach will be surpassed by none, save Mr. Childs from Holden.

The track has been put into shape and the boys are working out with a determined interest. The M. I. A. meet at Hinckley will no doubt peer all others held in our county. We are glad to learn of other towns taking up this phase of development with renewed vigor.

New men will spring surprises from unexpected places which always makes these meets so interesting.

The Oak City debators club gave an interesting debate on Sunday evening March 19, 1911. The debators were as follows: Winslow R. Walker, S. J. Rawlinson and Joshua Finlinson for the affirmative.

The negative side was defended by Willis J. Lyman, Joseph Finlinson and Edgar Nielson.

The question being "Resolved that the U. S. Senators be elected by the direct vote of the people." It required some hard thinking. The score was six and one half points in favor of the negative.

The judges were as follows: Leo Lyman, Joseph L. Anderson and Charles Roper. The next time we wish our affirmatives success.

A debating committee will be organized and next Friday will go to Scipio where they will oppose the above question.

BURTNER.

A, O. SORENSON, REPRESENTATIVE

The Delta Land and water Co. at Burtner has in the neighborhood of fifty teams at work, excavating for the new spillway. It will take about six weeks to complete the new spill.

The Delta land and water Co. has a force of men at work building cement drops, widening and strengthing canals. It is their intention to put two steel flumes across the Sevier River one flume will be built this spring and the other will be built after the irrigation season is over.

On March 18th the people of Burtner turned out for the purpose of destroying quimps and squirrels, a considerable amount of rolled barley was saturated with strychnine solution. Every man and boy in town was allowed as much of the poisoned grain as they could properly distribute on their farms. It is estimated of the pests were exterminated It was through a call by the Commerical Club that a war was declared on these pests, and it is the club's intention to have another quimp day in the near future.

Mr, Charley Clawson who has been doing assessment work on his mining claims at Black Horse, Nevada, returned to Burtner a few days ago. Mr. Clawson has some very valuable mining property at Black Horse for which he was offered $35,000 which he refused.

On March 31, the Burtner Commercial Club will give a grand ball in the Burtner Amusement Hall, the club extends an invitation to all the neighboring towns to come and join with us in making this the grandest affair that was ever pulled off at Burtner. It is the clubs intention to import a first class orchchestra for this occasion.

The calico bow and dress ball given by the Relief Society on Mar. 17th was a grand success, nearly every lady wore a new calico dress, adainty lunch was served.

Mr. Fred Barten has returned to Burtner, he is quite heavily interested here.

On March 19th the stork visited the home of Wilfred McClelland and left the prettiest little girl in the county. All concerned doing nicely.

Mr. Lewis Smith Z. C. M. I. shoe man was visiting the merchants of Burtner this week, Mr. Smith is quite positive that the Z. C. M. I. carries the best line of shoes made.

Mr. R. J. Law one of Burtner's enterprising merchants is building an addition to his residence on Clark St.

Mr. John E. Steele who has for some time been housed up, with a bad case of quinsy, is again able to be around and attend to his work at the Hub.

Deseret.

Last Tuesday, A. J. Ashman, County School Superintendent visited our school. At 5 o'clock a basket ball game was played between the grade teams of Burtner and Deseret the score was about 12 to 25 in favor of Deseret.

At 7 P. M. a banquet given in honor of Mr. Ashman by the 8th grade, was spread in the Relief hall, about sixty persons received invitations. The trustees and their wives were present.

After partaking of a fine repast, the floor was cleared and everyone enjoyed the fine dance and program that was given.

Last Thursday the Deseret basket ball team went to Hinckley to play, the score was 12 to 24 in favor of Deseret.

Mrs. Susie Bennett went to Fillmore last Wednesday to visit with her relatives.

Robison House Notes

Mr. and Mrs. Moore, and Mr. and Mrs. Huber, Mr. Dobson and Mr. Shubert all of Hinckley stopped here last week.

Two gentlemen named Gilbert from Salt Lake came in Saturday left Wednesday.

Mr. Earnest Herbert of Scipio range rider came in Sunday left Wednesday.

Mr. Henry Robison of Richfield came in Monday afternoon.

Mr. Owen and son Z. C. M. I. traveling men came in Tuesday left Wednesday.

Miss McDonald left Wednesday for Meadow and Kanosh.

HAPPENINGS AT HINCKLEY

We are all glad to see the special issue of the Chronicle, and it is up to all we have expected, and we can see why it has been delayed so long. We note that the editor had an accident the other day, and we wish him speedy recovery.

Our Jap was in town the other day trying to secure about 200 acres of land which he could lease for the cultivation of sugar beets. Prospects are very favorable that he will secure the required amount and the sugar factory man will be down in the near future to sign up with land owners and the Japs.

Spring, it seems, has come at last, and the farmers are beginning to prepare and sow their crops. Every one is very busy, taking advantage of the little spell of good weather.

The Mutual Improvement Association of Hinckley and Deseret met in debate last evening at the latter town where the question, "Resolved, That United States Senators should be elected by popular vote," was discussed, and the Deseret talkers got off with the most points. William Stapley and John Reeve defended the negative for Hinckley and William N. Gardner and Neils Peterson were on the affirmative for Deseret Both sides had very good arguments and showed that they had considerable information on the subject. A large crowd was in attendance and much spirit and enthusiasm manifested.

The townspeople and students of the academy are busy preparing the circular track on the High School grounds for the coming Mutual Improvement track and field meet, which will be held at Hinckley in the early part of May.

The Domestic Science Department, under the supervision of Miss Edith Homer, banqueted the basket ball team and members of the board last Friday evening. A good feed, interspersed with musical numbers from the music department of the school and toasts from the guests were very much enjoyed by all, after which all attended a very good ball in the gymnasium.

H. H. Cummings, superintendent of Church Schools, spent the first part of last week visiting at the Millard Stake Academy. He was well pleased with the work done at the academy this year.

T. Geo. Theobald has a new advertisement this week. If you need money, a new home, see what he has today and investigate personally.

The Cockle Burr Click of Leamington appeared on the academy stage in the thrilling little comedy entitled "The Old New Hampshire Home." The company did exceptionally well, and we invite them to come again, and we will try and patronize them fully as well as this time. The house was packed to its limit, although more might have been crowded in by standing a few of the up along the wall.

The Hinckley Dramatic Company is preparing the exciting little comedy drama, "Because I Love You," and will present it about May 1. Keep your "hearers" susceptible and watch the columns of the Chrinocle for the announcement.

Mr. Joseph Pederson eloped last night with one of the young ladies from the neighboring town—Delta. It is presumed that he took the fair Miss Mayhew to Salt Lake. We would suggest that the county clerk look out for him and issue them a license on application.

In the last issue of this paper we note that Oak City claims the county championship in baseball this season. Last fall, during the Bazaar, Hinckley played an exhibition game with Linndyl and Oak City, for the benefit of the Millard Stake Academy. August 27 Hinckley played an exhibition game at Oak City with the local team, assisted by four good players from Linndyl. The proceeds were for the Oak City Sunday School. On September 19 two exhibition games were played at Hinckley with Linndyl and Oak City, for the benefit of the Millard Stake Academy. The first game was won by the visitors by a score of 4 to 2, and the local team took off the laurels in the second game by a score of 14 to 5. We fail to see how Oak City's team can claim any honor unless they bought the laurels from Linndyl players. To our knowledge the championship was not even mentioned and as to the challenge sent out to the entire county, it was kept mighty quiet as this was the first our manager had ever heard of it. We admire the nerve of the Oak City captain to claim honors won by Linndyl with the assistance of a few men from his own team.

Since Hinckley won the championship at Fillmore during Indian War Veterans encampment, they have expected a challenge and held themselves in readiness for the occasion, and are still ready to cross bats with any one town team. NOW DON'T ALL SPEAK AT ONCE!

Mr. Ves Neilson of Kimberly, Ida., is in town visiting with his parents, Mr. and Mrs. Neilson. He is somewhat surprised at the outlook for this part of the state and will probably make his home here.

Mr. and Mrs. C. L. Tripp of Calla, Nev., are visiting with Mrs. Tripp's parents, Mr. and Mrs. F. W. Wilkins.

Fred Wilkins has returned from Black Horse, where he has been working in the mines the past winter.

Ingolf Norman left for Provo Monday night. He has sold his home here and is going to try city life.

LATE DOINGS AT DESERRT

Joshua Bennett, Chronicle Representative

We are having very nice weather at present and the farmers are all busy putting in crops. Lucerne is showing green. Irrigation is commencing.

The Utah Mine at Fish Springs continues to make their regular shipments of ore, keeping four, eight and ten horse teams steady at work.

Mr. L. R. Cropper administrator of the estate of Mrs. Margaret M. Blythe, deceased, is offering at private sale all of the cattle and horses belonging to the estate.

The daughter of Mr. and Mrs. Joseph V. Black is improving, but is very weak yet from the effects of typhoid fever.

About a week ago the Deseret Senior Basket Ball Team met with the Hinckley team in the M. S. A. gym. Score, 23 to 12 in favor of Deseret. The Hinckley boys promised to give a return game in the Petty Hall last Saturday night, but for some unexplained reason did not show up. What's the matter with Deseret? Boys, are you afraid of her, what's the matter?

Deseret Junior team and Oasis team played last Saturday night with honors largely in favor of the home boys, as also the Junior team with Burtner team, also in favor of Deseret. One of the Burtner boys, although possibly not intentionally, played very roughly and had to be warned by the umpire. Oasis and Burtner also played with honors in favor of Oasis, one of the Deseret boys assisting Oasis. Deseret may not enter into the Stake meet owing to the restrictions agreed upon, but would not refuse to play any team in the county if challenged to play in Deseret.

On Sunday evening the appointed debate, subject, "Resolved that the United States Senators should be ███████████ Mr. N. L. Peterson and Wm. Gardner taking the affirmative for Deseret and Wm. Stapley and John Reeve of Hinckley, the negative. Judges Eugene Hilton of Hinckley, Jos. W. Damron Jr. of Deseret, and Milton Moody of Salt Lake City, who rendered a secret decision, Hilton in favor of the negative and Damron and Moody for the affirmative. Good reasons were given for and against the question.

ABRAHAM.

Donald Hogan, Representative.

Work is progressing nicely on the canal improvements and it is expected to be ready for the water in about two weeks. Mr. Reed is overseeing the work.

On account of the poor condition of the cattle range the framers are selling their surplus stock. About thirty head were sold last week by Messrs. Hogan Bros. and Richard Parker.

Mr. Franklin who got kicked by a horse is able to be about again.

Mr. Chas. Tyng, secretary of the Abraham Irrigation Company, was in town last week and met with the directors Saturday.

Our debating team is having a hard time getting to meet the other towns. They were booked to meet Burtner Friday night last, but received word that they were not prepared to meet them. Then they matched Hinckley for Sunday night, but when they got over there they found that they had all flown to Deseret. We are hoping that Leamington will not get "cold feet" next Friday evening.

Mr. Rigby and family of Burtner visited us at Sabbath school and meeting Sunday. Mr. Rigby is a member of the high council of the Stake, also a member of the Sunday School Union Board. He gave us some very good talks at meeting. Misses Sidwell and Sperry accompanied them and all were entertained at dinner by Mr. and Mrs. Donald Hogan.

Mrs. Larke has returned from Salt Lake.

With the opening of the fine weather there is evidence of farming on every hand. All the farmers are plowing and putting in grain. From the present outlook there will be several thousand acres cropped this year.

Work commenced Monday, March 20 on the canals, cleaning and repairing. The wages are $5 for man and team.

Mr. Franklin was kicked by a horse last week and had his leg badly fractured.

More Deseret.

This has been an exciting week for the Eighth Graders. Mr. Ashman, county superintendent, missed stage connections that would have brought him to Deseret on Monday; so the banquet and dance planned for him and the Burtner team had to be postponed until Tuesday evening. All day Monday and Tuesday the boys and girls of the eighth grade were busy transforming the Relief Society building into a banquet hall, carrying furniture, dishes, potted plants, cleaning chickens and making lemonade punch.

Tuesday Mr. Ashman visited the grade school and in the evening a delightful banquet and dance were enjoyed by Mr. Ashman, the Burtner ball team just defeated by Deseret, the teacher, the eighth grade students and their friends, Mr. Gardner the principal and the trustees with their wives. After interesting toasts and a short program the hall was cleared for the dance.

Wednesday, while Mr. Ashman visited Hinckley and Abraham, the eighth graders were busy cleaning up the debris, and in the evening they furnished a program of songs and recitations for the parents' meeting at the school house. Mr. Ashman talked to the parents urging the necessity of their co-operating with the teachers in order to make a success of the Millard County schools. He plead for co-operation especially in these matters: home help only by suggestion and not by doing the children's work for them; willingness to have the teachers put pupils in the grades where they could do their best work; special training in character by lessons in economy, honesty, diligence, and the fullest development of all talents. He expressed deep appreciation of the cordial hospitality of the Deseret people.

Who says Deseret is dead? Cupid doesn't think so, for he has been very lively about here and he knows that where there is love there is life. He is proud to announce that next week two Deseret couples will make a memorable pilgrimage to Salt Lake.

Miss Ruby Webb and Lorenzo Black, and Miss Eliza Whicker and Orson Ericson, the latter couple to be married in the temple. Mr. Ericson has recently returned from a mission in Tennessee. We wonder what Damron's store will do without Miss Whicker.

Saturday night about twenty-five young people, most of them from Deseret, surprised Miss Eliza Whicker with a bundle shower at the home of Miss Roan Kelly. First they attended the basket ball games in Petty's Hall, where many of the boys of the party were playing and then at about ten o'clock returned to Miss Kelly's home where the rest of the evening and a few of Sunday's wee hours were spent in games, refreshments and in the fun of watching Miss Whicker open all her bundles of house-keeping necessities.

The basket ball games with Oasis and Burtner last Saturday night were such overwhelming victories for Deseret as to be almost uninteresting. It takes more evenly matched teams to make a really exciting game.

It is understood that the Athletic Club of Deseret plans to elect new officers soon and effect a complete re-organization.

The entire time of the Sunday evening meting of the M. I. A. was devoted to a preliminary debate, Resolved: "That popular election of United States Senators is preferable to the present method of election by the state legislatures," between John Reeve and William Stapeley of Hinckley and William Gardner and Nels Peterson of Deseret. Although some of the speakers were not fully prepared, the debate proved very interesting and the majority decision of the judges, Milton Moody, Bishop Damron and Mr. Hilton was in favor of the affirmative, represented by Deseret. Our team will meet the Fillmore debaters in the near future.

The rapid recovery of J. V. Black's little girl from typhoid fever is a fine example of what intelligent care on the part of the parents, good nursing and strict following of the doctor's orders can do in the treatment of that disease. Carelessness as to perfect cleanliness and disinfection, promiscuous feeding, confusion and the admission of visitors, lack of efficient nursing are sure to run up a needlessly large doctor's bill and prolong the illness.

The people of Deseret extend their sincere sympathy to Editor Dresser in his dreadful misfortune. We ought more than ever to appreciate his efforts in behalf of Millard County, for certainly no county in the state can boast of a better county paper.

Apparently a good many Deseret people are planning to go to Salt Lake during Conference. May Salt Lake be good enough to provide pleasant weather and send us all home more satisfied with Millard County and more determined to develop all its resources.

"PIONEER."

BURTNER.

A. O. SORENSON, REPRESENTATIVE

Last Saturday evening the infant baby of Mr. and Mrs. Wilford McClelland passed away, funeral services were held Sunday.

Mr. Simans, brother-in-law of H. A. Knight, has moved to Burtner. Mr. Simans thinks Burtner will be one of the best farming towns in Utah.

Mr. Rube Turner and family have moved to Burtner.

On account of the boys being busy working on the canals, the Burtner Commercial Club have decided to postpone the ball which they intended to give March 31st.

The ladies basket ball team of Burtner, challenges any team in the county, that is if they will come to Burtner to play.

Mr. J. Pederson of Hinckley, and Miss Luella Mayhow of Burtner left for Salt Lake, they were married in the Salt Lake Temple Wednesday.

Mr. Sam Wade of Fillmore, was in Burtner last Wed. Mr. Wade brought a load of phone poles over for T. O. Callister.

The Simkins boys have just returned from Black Horse Nev. They report that on account of bad weather every thing is quiet at that point.

Mr. Delial Knight who has been bed fast for several weeks with rheumatism is again able to be around.

Ti's the man with the shovel,
Not the man with hot air,
Who is shaping the destinies
Of Delta so fair,
Tis the man with the shovel
That you behold
Scraping the dirt off the ledges
of gold,
Tis the man with the shovel
That turns the stream
From its fountain source
To a paradise dream.
Where the orchards will bloom
And roses perfume the air,
Where beauty and plenty
You can see everywhere
He's not at all like the man
with hot air.
The man with the shovel
In Delta so fair
And the man with the shovel
In Delta will be blessed,
For the future to him,
If he does his best,
Is bright with the promise
Of plenty and rest.

Oasis

SAMUEL RUTHERFORD REPRESENTATIVE.

There has been some teams going through here to Burtner to work on the spill. We have word here that teams are wanted at Lund to work on the R. R Grade. Word came here last Monday that they could use all the teams and men we could furnish, teams and men at $4.50 per day. Men at $2.50 all should board and furnish themselves.

We are having beautiful spring weather here now and farmers are taking advantage of same.

The mutual will have a meet here soon, work hard boys let's see who are our best men for the coming Co. meet.

Mr. Frank Wozman has purchased a forty acre tract of land here and is building a new house now, it appears he has quit the railroad and is going to farming we believe this is a good move and encourage such with all our young people.

Mr. William Ward has been sick for some time and it is thought he may have to go to the hospital his case seems to baffle the Dr. some, but it is hoped he will soon change for the better.

Mrs. T. G. Reid who has been sick for some time is slowly improving.

Born to Mrs. Alfred Wozman a fine baby boy. mother and child doing well.

Mrs. Will Huff is reported on the sick list but at this time is very much improved.

OAK CITY.

S. J. RAWLINSON, REPRESENTATIVE

Mr. Lewis Sommers, recently from the state of Kansas, has purchased a building site from his father-in-law, Harry Roper, and has commenced the erection of a four room cottage. Mr. Sommers carries the spirit of industry. We welcome all such citizens into our community.

Joshua Finlinson is in wonderment concerning one of his milch cows which he has broken of late. The peculiar feature is that while he is milking her, she kicks viciously with her left foot. (He asserts that he always milks from the right side.) We offer the following explanation. Psychologists tell us that our right limbs have their nerve centers in the left brain and that our left side centers all its nerves of motion in the right brain. This explains why it is so difficult for the left handed person to use his right hand. We have also observed that a stunning blow dealt upon the right of the head paralizes the left limbs. Undoubtedly this applies to cows as well as man. And again, perhaps this cow's perceptive training has been neglected and thus she has no power to locate or place.

We do not hesitate in giving this advice; that if cows are determined to kick, teach them the above trick

Last Saturday evening the Hinckley school boys were compelled to give back the victory which they had taken from us one week ago on their own battle ground. A large crowd witnessed the game in our gymnasium. It was well contested resulting in a score of 40 to 20.

While it fell to our lot to meet defeat in our M. I. A. debate with Scipio last Friday evening, we express our appreciation of the fairness of encounter our opponents manifested and also the large and attentive audience that greeted us there.

BURTNER.

A. O. SORENSON, REPRESENTATIVE

Mr. Verne Bartholomew and Mr. Don Wixom of Fillmore passed through Burtner on their way north. Mr. Bartholomew went to Salt Lake on land business and Mr. Wixom went to Idaho to visit relatives and friends,

Mr. Geo. Day and his sisters Rose and Cora have gone to Fillmore to visit with relatives It is rumored that Mr. Geo Day will pay the county clerk a visit while at the county seat.

Monday 10th is the Delta Land Co. and the Melville Irrigation Co's pay day on this date there will be several thousand dollars put in circulation in Burtner.

Last week the Lehi Sugar Factory sent their expert beet man down to Burtner and neighboring towns for the purpose of interesting the farmers in this neighborhood in the sugar beet industry. Contracts were signed up at Hinckley for 100 acres of beets, owing to the fact that the land at Burtner hasn't been cultivated sufficiently, no contracts were signed at this point, but an agreement was made to purchase all the beets raised here at $4.25 per ton F. O. B. cars several of our farmers are going to put in a small piece of land to beets, for the purpose of determining whether or not the land will grow beets in large enough tonnage to make it a profitable crop.

Mr. Otto Roundy has returned to Burtner. Mr. Roundy owns land under the Delta Land Co.

Mr. Luther Buchanan and family has moved to Burtner

It is said that where there is a will there is a way the latest is the ladie's hat pin way.

A number of our people have gone to Salt Lake to attend conference.

Wanted at Burtner, a first class barber. an up-to date Drug Store, a Bank a depot, the best between Salt Lake and Los Angeles, a few thousand people to make their homes here and develop the many thousand of acres of undeveloped land in and adjourning Burtner. If interested write the secretary of the Burtner Commercial club.

OAK CITY.

S. J. RAWLINSON, REPRESENTATIVE

April 3, 1911

A refreshing shower of rain, preceded by a fast hail is visiting us this evening It is as wet as can be and the arid wheat fields are receiving it with open mouths and thankful hearts.

Not so with the peach and plum trees, they are not in high spirits tonight. They well remember that April showers deceived them one year ago, and notwithstanding the red fire is frequently illuminating the heavens, and apparently spreading warmth, yet they are half suspicious that it is the search light of their old, Jack Frost.

Many men turn their backs upon the old. They forget that in the accession the old was the new. Not so with John E. Lovell. He has turned his hands upon the old house, that has served him so faithfully and will carefully take it down and give it back to the elements. Let a few more of us get in line and have a general cleaning up of premises.

Peter Nelson and Lem Roper have ordered a (large capacity) car load of pressed brick, fresh from the Provo yards, and ere long will build two neat and handsome houses.

Leo Anderson's large overshot steel wheel is now at the mouth of the flume, awaiting the coming of the water, which will not be long if Leo keeps up the speed he now has on.

On April fool's day a few brave school boys determined to explore Devil's den, a peculiar hole near the mouth of the main canyon. They were quite positive that no other foot dare venture within several rods of it. How great would be their joy, should they succeed in this adventure, and per chance like Aladdin might find magical changes never known of before. I am convinced that some such thot must have dawned upon them, since they carried a lantern and pockets of matches. I can imagine their conversation as they sojourned to the cave. I see them cautiously approach it. They halt, light their lantern, keep plenty of matches near in case certain currents of air will extinguish their light, and leave them in darkness. but as they enter they see the end is near.

Alas! this cave feared and dreaded by man so long. extends into the mountain not more than six feet.

BURTNER.

Albert P. Wallace, Chronicle Representative.

Prof. R. R. Lyman was in town on business last Sunday looking over the work of the Delta Land & Water Company.

Mr. Fred H. Strain made a trip to Salt Lake City last Sunday.

N. S. Bishop was a conference visitor last week.

Mr. H. B. Prout, secretary and treasurer of the Delta Land & Water Company, was down from Salt Lake City last week with a party of land buyers

The Relief Society of this ward was reorganized last Thursday with Mrs Jennie Rigby as president, Mrs. Ida Patten as first, and Martha Ashby as second counselors. Lamira Bishop secretary, and Elizabeth Callister as treasurer.

The retiring officers were: Mrs Ann Bishop, president; Ruth Maxfield and Almeda Lewis, as counselors; Mrs Rigby, secretary; Mrs. J. H. Peterson treasurer. The new officers will give a party in the hall next Saturday night in honor of the retiring officers. Everybody in the ward over 18 years of age is invited.

Mr. Jas. A. Melville arrived here from Los Angeles, Calif., last Thursday morning with some land buyers. Although they think California very nice, they think that they will make this place their home.

Milanda M. Pratt was down from Salt Lake City last week on business.

The excavating for the new spillway is completed and when finished will be one of the finest spillways in the country. It will have a solid clay formation, which is next best to solid rock.

Quite a number of trees have been received here within the last week, mostly from local nurseries.

DESERET.

Joshua Bennett, Chronicle Representative.

A very nice rain fell on Sunday night, which will be a great benefit to crops just coming through the ground. Irrigation has commenced and farmers are busy with their spring work. We have had quite a lot of frost lately.

Contractor V. Kelly has quite a number of teams doing ditch work for the Delta Land & Water Company.

From all reports a number of acres of mangel wurtzel and beets will be put in this spring, as farmers are learning the valuable feeding qualities of these crops.

George Western, son of Samuel W. Western, Jr., was held in the sum of $500 bail to appear before the District court for burglary in the second degree.

A number of those who attended the conference in Salt Lake City have returned, also those who went and contracted to live together through life; all return with broad smiles upon their faces, and no doubt feel that they have bettered life's conditions.

Miss Rose Kelly left last week to visit with rer sister, Mrs. Maggie Ryan of Salt Lake City.

Great claims are being made as to which is the champion baseball team of Millard county, but we have yet to learn when Deseret, that had carried that honor for a number of years, lost it to another club.

Sheriff Peter T. Black, wife and two children, are in Salt Lake City. Mr. Black expects to attend the meeting of all the state sheriffs while there.

Sunday meeting was very poorly attended owing to the fact that many were out of town, and it was a very windy day.

A number of head of cattle have died from bloat, having been let to pasture on the lucern crops. Experience is the great teacher.

HAPPENINGS AT HINCKLE[Y]

Geo. E. Billings, Chronicle Representative.

Bishop Pratt and A. Billings walke[d] from Oasis depot this morning returning from conference. They had a ver[y] slippery path, as it rained a good portion of the night. T. Geo. Theobald[,] Prof. John D. Spiers, Willis E. Robison[,] John Reeve and some others also returned from spending a few days sigh[t] seeing in Salt Lake.

We understand that Mr. E. Fre[d] Pack has been engaged as principal o[f] the District School here next year. Applications are being received all the time for grade teachers, but we are no[t] yet informed who will be the corp[s] with Mr. Pack, but it is expected tha[t] a good bunch of boosters will be engaged.

A. L. Simons and family of Salt Lak[e] moved into Hinckley a few weeks ag[o.] Mr. Simmons has purchased som[e] farming land in our district and w[e] welcome him to our town.

William H. Denison and Georg[e] Whitehead are building on the ne[w] street to be opened by H. F. Wright'[s] home. Mr. Denison sold his forme[r] home to Richard Parker of Abraham[,] who intends to erect a fine home thi[s] coming summer. The plasterer is no[t] by any means asleep—he looks out fo[r] a job himself and makes way for ne[w] buildings in Hinckley.

George Cushman is placing a cemen[t] walk around the home of Thos. W[.] Cropper, who is changing the corne[r] lot south of the District School building, from a delapidated waste to one o[f] the most attractive homes in Hinckley[.] We need a few more such persons t[o] set an example for the rising generation.

Mr. F. L. Hickman, a former residen[t] of Hinckley, was in town a few day[s] ago. He leased his brick yard t[o] Hosea Stout, Jr., and George Cushman[,] who will start work there in the nea[r] future.

The Chronicle representative o[f] Oak City must have got a tip just before sending in his correspondence last week. He would lead the reader to think that every one in Hinckley was a liar so far as a base-ball stor[y] goes. Our baseball club did not think he would make such a fuss and story just to get a little honor as a baseball county champion. His story was exaggerated from start to finish, so we feel it is useless to waste more printers' ink to discuss the matter and apologize to the public for using so much lather to shave an ass.

Mr. Walter Carlson and family are moving back to Oak City, where they expect to spend the summer. They have been living in the home of Mr. Miles Greener; but since he has returned from the east side of the county with his new cook it is necessary for Carlson to vacate.

"Academy Notes" have not appeared for several issues of the Chronicle. No reason has been offered, but it is suspected that "Moody Notes" require most of the reporter's extra time.

Hinckley Co-op has a fine new line of men's and boys' clothing. Call in and let them fit you up with that new suit for Easter.

Mr. W. L. Apgood, traveling salesman for the U. S. Cream Separator, was in town Tuesday looking up the separator business.

T. H. Pratt, manager of Pratt Bros. Co., went to the City Friday on business.

Mr. L. R. Cropper, Jr., distributed a carload of tree and shrubs from the Provo nurseries in the three towns along the mail route from Oasis and has sent in a great many orders to be delivered later. We are pretty sure of having some good shade trees in a few years.

OASIS.

Mrs. Mina Jackson, Chronicle Repre-

This section was again visited by a nice little rain Sunday night, which brings smiles to the face of the farmers. It makes everything look green and inviting.

A few of the brethren came out and assisted President Almira Styler and Counselor Phoebe Henry to plant 24 trees around the Relief hall Monday morning, which improves its appearance, and will greatly add to its shade in the hot summer days.

Among the conference visitors this week at Salt Lake were Bishop Marcus Skeens and H. L. Jackson and wife. They have just returned, also William Bennett.

William Huff, one of the Oasis merchants, went to Salt Lake on Saturday night on business.

The stork has again visited us, this time at the home of Stanley Robison of Snake Valley, Utah, who came here to stay for a short time. Mother and the little infant son are doing fine.

Mr. Jim Thompson formerly section foreman at Clear Lake, has just moved to the John Reid farm, which he purchased some time ago.

Mr. and Mrs. William Ward are still in Salt Lake City, where they went some ten days ago for Mr. Ward to consult a good physician. From all reports the doctor pronounced the case as being leakage of the heart. Mr. Ward has been in rather a critical condition for a month past.

Mrs. T. G. Reid is still unable to be around on account of the swelling that is troubling her lower limbs.

Mr. Earl Huff has just moved over here from Scipio, and expects to make his home here for a season. Report that Mr. Huff has leased the Washington Rogers farm, the Chambers ranch and his father's. This will no doubt keep him busy.

Mr. Orvell Jackson is here from Fillmore. He came after his father, Heber Jackson.

RESPECTED WOMAN PASSES; FORMERLY OF SUNNYSIDE

WINTER QUARTERS, Utah, April 14.—A gloom was cast over Winter Quarters on the 23d inst. by the death of Mrs Emma Jane Petersson She was born at Sunderland, Durham county, Eng, on the 23d of October, 1886, being the fourth child of John C and Emma J Preston Her parents belonged to the Church of Jesus Christ of Latter day Saints and she was baptized when 8 years old in the North Sea When she was young her parents moved to Wallsend, Northumberland county, and there she was a member of the Latter-day Saints Sunday school She married Nicholas P. Petersson on the 26th of August, 1905, at Sunderland, and emigrated to this country in October, 1907 She first lived in Sunnyside, after coming to this land, and took great interest in the Sunday school of that ward, and went to Lynndyl, where she belonged to the Leamington ward, and while at Lynndyl she walked to Leamington, which was five miles away, many a time to attend the meetings there She then moved to Salt Lake City and belonged to the Fifteenth ward for a few months, and moved to Winter Quarters in February, 1910

Wherever she went she took a great interest in Sunday school work and was a very active member of the parents' class here She also became a member of the relief society. It is sad that one so active in the faith she believed in should be taken away while yet so young, only 25 years of age. The remains were interred in the Scofield cemetery on Sunday, March 26th, the funeral services being held in the Pleasant Valley ward meeting house, Winter Quarters, at which S W. Golding, school principal at Winter Quarters Bishop George Ruff of Scofield ward, and Bishop T. J. Parmley of the Pleasant Valley ward, were the speakers

She leaves a husband and three children to mourn her loss, as well as her parents, four brothers and four sisters, and a host of friends

THE NEWS FROM BURTNER

Albert P. Wallace, Chronicle Representative.

Last week the hustling correspondent at Scipio was over and had trees planted around his lots in Burtner. He is the sort of land owner we like to have—one who believes in improving his property.

The Ladies' Basket Ball team of Hinckley beat the Burtner team last Saturday evening. The Burtner boys evened it up by beating their Hinckley opponents the same evening.

The Hinckley orchestra will play for the dance here next Friday evening.

Mr. Bloomquist, foreman of the concrete gang at the spillway made a trip to the city last week.

Mrs. Fred Lyman of Oak City was a visitor in Burtner last week.

H. L. Fisher, who went to California last winter with his family has returned. He says Burtner is good enough for him.

We hear a great deal of complaint of the way the Melville Co. is keeping up the ditches in town. The water is allowed to break out and spread all over the streets in many places, much to the annoyance of pedestrians.

Mrs. Kate Hatton of Fillmore passed through Burtner last Monday on her way home from an extended visit in Idaho with her daughter.

Loren A. Taylor is the new water master on the west side.

The Delta Company has a large force of men and teams on the west side putting in cement head gates, fixing ditches, etc. A large amount of work remains yet to be done before every one gets what water he needs. The company automobile is kept busy taking land buyers over the tract.

Richard Parker and wife of Abraham were visitors in Burtner last week.

The Chronicle editor and his brother have been busy the past two weeks putting up buildings on their land in west Burtner and planting crops.

A much needed public improvement is a bridge across the canal on the road between Burtner and Oasis. The banks are so steep and high that it is impassable with a load. The editor knows for he got badly stuck there last week.

Principal Moench is going to be an agriculturist as well as an educator. He has taken up 120 acres of land just east of the Deseret reservoir and is having it cultivated. It is excellent soil and well located and will make a splendid farm.

OCCURRENCES AT OAK CITY

W. R. Walker, Chronicle Representative.

Two wagon missionaries have been in our midst the past week. They visited all the people and held two public meetings.

Friday evening a welcome party was given in honor of Elder Wm. Jacobson. A very large crowd turned out and all enjoyed a good time.

Mr. Axel Johnson and Peter Johnson came over from Leamington to attend the dance.

The "First Spring Irrigation Company" sold out to the "Oak City Irrigation Company" last Friday.

The frost that struck Oak City two weeks ago did considerable damage to the early fruit crop, but the apples are unharmed, and a fair crop of peaches will be had.

We are pleased to state that Mrs. Edgar Nielson is much better, and will soon be able to be around again.

Mr. E. H. Roberts, general agent for the J. I. Case Threshing Machine Co., was in town Sunday in his auto. He showed some of the local threshing machine men a good time for a while, but all at once the automobile refused to go. Mr. Walker was called upon and with a horse landed him at the Walker hotel, where he is at this time.

Miss Corline Nielson of Gunnison, is here visiting her aunt, Mrs. Corline Rawlinson.

Mr. F. S. Lyman of Burtner was in town Saturday and Sunday.

Saturday a buggy load of Burtner women paid us a visit, and judging by the looks of their buggy upon leaving town one would think Burtner was going to raise small fruit by the car load lot.

With only two more weeks before the big track meet, Coach S. J. Rawlinson has his men rounded up. Of his old stars are back and are getting in first class condition. Besides these men, he has developed a number of new men who are making good. Not only has he developed new men, but he has brought some old 'has beens" back into good shape.

He has Bishop Finlinson, once L. D. S. U. star jumper, making his young men look to their laurels.

He has given instructions to his athletes to keep good hours, etc., and to hear him tell it, he is going to win.

OASIS.

Mrs. Mina Jackson, Chronicle Repre-

There has been a great number of home seekers here lately. They were taken to the East Side by Raymond Ray, who is here at this point on land business.

Mrs. Flora Goulter, her son John, and two daughters, are here visiting with relatives and friends.

Mr. David Day is erecting a summer kitchen at the rear of his building. Carpenter Andrew Skeems is doing the mechanical part.

A car load of shingles were unloaded at the Millard Company lumber yard yesterday.

Irrigation is now on. The roads are being watered as well as the farms.

Who says Oasis can't produce gardens. If you think not, call at Edmond Williams and you will see as fine a garden as any in the county, considering the backward spring.

T. G. Reid is doing some planting and plowing at Burtner for Mr. Sours of Salt Lake City.

Miss Margie Bradley of California was here for a few days and returned last week to her home.

There is a new operator here at present. This one has a wife to accompany him, so we are in hopes he has come to stay. The operator who has been here for the last six months left here Monday morning on a pleasure trip to California.

Mr. and Mrs. Wm. Ward returned recently from Salt Lake.

Mr. and Mrs. Milton Moody of Salt Lake, formerly of this place, were callers on Monday the 17th inst., as they were here for the funeral of Mrs. Moody's mother.

Easter Sunday was appropriately celebrated by services in the L. D. S. chapel, Miss Dora Henry, Jacob C. Hawley and John Styler being the speakers, who did honor to the occasion.

Mrs. Jacob C. Hawley of Provo has been spending a few days with her husband and friends.

ABRAHAM.

Donald Hogan, Representative.

Mrs. Rudy and daughter, Mrs. Fernstrom, arrived here from Salt Lake City, Saturday morning to spend a few days with Mr. Charles E. Hogan and family who have a sick baby. The child has been ailing since Christmas. Mrs. Hogan is Mrs. Rudy's daughter.

Miss Doritha Hansen is going to Deseret this week. She expects to stay all summer. We trust she may meet some nice young man over there who would like to accompany her home occasionally. It is to be re-

gretted there was not a larger attendance in the theological class at Sunday School last Sunday to have heard the lesson on the observance of the Sabbath day. No doubt we are all more or less slack in that respect.

We are pleased to note the great amount of work the Taylor Brothers have done on their land between here and Hinckley. They have it all planted to grain and are now irrigating.

Mr. Richard Parks went to Partner yesterday to see about letting the contract for the building of his new house at Hinckley.

Millard County Progress
April 28, 1911

Oasis

SAMUEL RUTHERFORD REPRESENTATIVE.

Some time ago during a very short electric storm Mr. Peter Skeems had three milk cows struck by lightning and all killed, this is unusual for this part of the country but such things occur some times.

Mrs. Mary Helebrant of Idaho, who was very ill came to Hinckley for a visit and passed away at the home of Mrs. Lula Cropper (her daughter) last Sunday morning at 6 o'clock, the body was sent to Idaho for burial. The

deceased leaves a husband and eight children but the children are all grown and nearly all are married. They have our deepest sympathy.

Very cold weather has almost stopped the alfalfa from any progress, but we hope Mr. Cold will soon go home to the north or die from suffocation or heat.

Mr. T. H. Church is somewhat under the weather but we hope to see him around soon he is the oldest person in Oasis and we think lots of him. He is now 87 years old and has been very strong. He drives the stage

from here to Abraham, which he has done for years.

William Ward who went to the hospital returned much improved and is now able to be around again.

Mrs. T. G. Reed is still improving but her improvement seems to be very slow.

We see Wm. Huff has his wind mill up and also a nice water tank, thus giving him a private waterworks all his own so we expect a nice garden this year also a real lawn in front. We would encourage more of the same so we can beautify our homes.

BURTNER.

A. O. SORENSON, REPRESENTATIVE

Last week the Delta Land and Water Co. shipped in about fifty men to work on the new Cement Spill, they expect to ship more men in here this week. It seems as tho Millard County ought to promise enough men to do her own work and not be compeled to draw on Salt Lake and other northern towns for working men.

The people here have just placed an order for a town bell, which will cost delivered at Burtner $125.00

One of our popular young ladies was having a little wake with or by a garden and of course the time slipped by very rapidly, presently a little light streak was seen in the east just above the mountain top. Upon her return home an explanation was required, she said two of her lady friends insisted on her sleeping with them and of course she did'nt have the heart to refuse.

Mr. Horton S. Fisher is back from Los Angeles. Mr. Fisher says that Burtner is good enough for him.

Miss Nethalia Cooper is certainly a piano player and believe me, she is not slow when it comes to singing, in fact we will back her as the best singer in the county. Won't we Gib?

Millard County Progress
May 5, 1911

OAK CITY.

J. RAWLINSON, REPRESENTATIVE

To-day a number of our citizens are away to Lynn unloading a car of cement. House foundations, barn floors, and cellar walls will consume it.

On Friday last our district school closed. The year has been a very successful one. The attendance has been better and parents have shown greater interest in the school education than ever before perhaps.

In the afternoon a number of basket ball games were played while a very enjoyable dancing party, including refreshments, was given during the evening.

Most of the members of the eighth grade class are feeling hopeful as to the results of their final examination. It is not so much the way in which they answered the questions that gives them this encouragement, as it is the fact that while they were finishing the last subject, a mysterious inscription in many colors, suddenly appeared upon the blackboard, which, when properly interpreted, read,— "keep pegging away."

Miss Ethel Barton, our Primary teacher, who has been with our school the past three years returned to her home yesterday over the S. P. & L. A. and D. & R. G. R. R. It is said that there is hope of her leaving Panguich and coming to dwell with us forever. It is further asserted that John Lundahl accompanied her as far as Nephi. No one knows why he should go so "far and no farther."

Mrs. Annie L. Anderson has returned from the L. D. S. hospital, her condition is much improved.

Miss Silva Lovell is home from Salt Lake where she has spent the winter. Her health has been impaired of late, but she feels better since her return.

The other day while hitching a trace George E. Finlinson was painfully kicked upon the right arm. It was first thot to be broken, but proved only to be seriously torn. This will prevent him from taking part in the athletics at Hinckley. He was making a good mark at the shot event.

Deseret.

Mrs. E J. Whicker and family of Burtner spent the week with relatives.

After an illness covering the greater part of its brief life, the infant child of Mr. and Mrs. Orson Cahoon died early Tuesday morning, much sympathy is felt for the sorrowing family.

Mr. Jas. Stubbard of Neb. arrived early in the week and will assist in the settlement of the estate of his mother, the late Margaret M. Blythe.

It will be pleasant news for the many music lovers of this section to know that Mrs. O. A. Broaddus has been induced to take up active work among us. Mrs. Broaddus is an accomplished pianist and singer of musical charm.

Messrs. Hawkins and Sheppard of Payson who so successfully raised and marketed several tons of honey here last year are in town again. The gentlemen have taken the residence of O. F. Webb for the summer.

Oasis

SAMUEL RUTHERFORD REPRESENTATIVE.

The Sunday school was reorganized with Samuel Rutherford Supt. and O. O. Peare as first and Val Styler as second assistants.

We are still having some frost

everybody is wishing summer would come for good.

We can see teams leaving here early the last few days to Hinckley for the sports.

Tuesday was a grand success in the A. M. the orations were fine. Fred Pack was awarded

first and Maurice Lambert second The basket ball in the afternoon was won by the Meadow team. Wednesday the oral stories were fine and all present enjoyed them. The first prize was awarded Miss Laura Johnson of Oasis and second Miss Eunice Iverson of Deseret.

BURTNER.

A. O. SORENSON, REPRESENTATIVE

The dance given by the Commercial Club was the event of the season, every lady present expressed themselves as having the time of their lives. It is the clubs intention to have another dance in the near future.

A great many of our people are taking in the track meet at Hinkley this week.

Mrs. Ellen Wise of Fillmore is here visiting with her sisters and brother the Misses and Mr. Day. Mrs. Wise is not quite sure that she would like the pioneer life we Burtner people are living.

Last Monday Sheriff Black of Deseret brought a man down from Lynndal and placed him in our new jail, this is the first prisoner we have had confined in the Burtner jail.

Last week the Burtner Commercial Club shipped in 50,600 pounds of seed oats and distributed them among the farmers here, this will be the means of several hundred acres of land being put into grain this season, which otherwise would have laid dormant. Boost the Commercial Club and in return the Club will boost for you.

The train wreck which happened two miles north of our town cast a gloom over all the people of Burtner, the sad part was the life that was lost, and the lady corpse that was in the baggage car, had it not been for this we would not have cared so much, but this is a lesson to our Irrigation Co's, tho rather a sad one, who are now busy repairing and strengthening all weak points on their canal system and the writer doesn't look for any more serious accidents to happen.

You Burtnerites if you want a good paper that gets all the

news of Millard County, subscribe for the Progress-Review.

Two car loads of lumber, two car loads of oats and one car load of cement was unloaded at Burtner during the past six days this will give you an idea of the amount of business done at this point.

The grain in this vicinity is looking fine, the rye is heading out and indications are that we will have some large crops raised here this season.

The wages paid on our new spill way is $8.00 per day for four horse teams, $5.00 per day for two horse teams and $2.50 and board per day for single hands. These are the best wages paid in our state, if you want work come to Burtner, there is plenty of work here.

OAK CITY.

J. RAWLINSON, REPRESENTATIVE.

The new saw mill of Mr. Lee Anderson made its trial run last week. It gave entire satisfaction.

This is something our town has been in need of for many years, a good saw mill. There is much timber decaying each year that needs to be utilized. Besides a saw mill, the large wheel will furnish power for lighting. We much appreciate this move and wish Mr. Anderson success for his industry and enterprize.

An other consignment of 50,000 brook trout has been distributed in our canyon stream. This means several trout dinners. Thanks to Mr. Miah Day. Since

Mr. Day's appointment as district fish and game commissioner he has looked after our interests in a first class manner.

Mr. Willard Christensen, Lydia Roper and Charles G. Roper have returned from school. They report having spent a very pleasant winter in Hinckley.

Le Roy Walker is down from Logan to accompany our track team to Hinckley. You will perhaps hear more of him later. I have not seen him as yet and hence cannot give any correct account of his physical condition. Last year at Holden he played basket ball, high jumped and took part in the weight events.

This year he wrestles, playes ball, high jumps and handles the weights. He is over six feet and last year had a very respectable moustache, notwithstanding he is only nineteen.

John Lundahl has returned from Nephi, and will leave for Hinckley in good time for the long races. He is not worried about a chance to ride. Horses and buggies never trouble him. A run from here to Hinckley would be an enjoyable recreation for him.

Mr. Edward Ottley of Murry is with us again. He in connection with his sons, has to his credit a number of excellent pieces of work here. He is a carpenter, who having learned his trade in England, takes pride in good workmanship.

BURTNER.

Albert P. Wallace, Chronicle Representative.

Everybody is busy watering their crops. Some very promising crops are growing here now.

Burtner has one of the most efficient telephone systems that we know of. It can accommodate sixteen people on one line at once.

Engineer J. W. Thurston is very busy running lines and levels on the south tract of land belonging to the Delta Land & Water Co. They expect to have it opened up for settlement soon.

Miss Tillie McDonald, traveling saleswoman and demonstrator for the Hunts Perfect Baking Powder Co., has been in our town the last week canvassing the town and showing the merits of their product to the people. R. J. Law is the local salesman.

Jas. A. Melville was in town this week on business connected with the D. L. & W. Co.

Mr. and Mrs. H. J. Henry of Oasis were seen on our streets last Sunday.

Mr. T. Clark Callister and Noble Peterson of Fillmore were in Burtner on telephone business last Saturday.

Mrs. John Eardley returned to her home in St. George last week from an extended visit with her children of this place, John Erdley and Mrs. E. H. Bunker.

Our telephone line is connected with the depot here now. Patrons can now call and find out if their freight has come without the bother of making a long trip over there. R. J. Law is the only one of the merchants who has this convenience.

Quite a number of our people went to Hinckley to the track meet. They expressed themselves as having had a very good time.

THE NEWS FROM BURTNER

Albert P. Wallace, Chronicle Representative.

Last Sunday night Jas. A. Melville, chief selling agent for the Delta Land & Water Company, arrived here with two cars containing about sixty people from Los Angeles, Pasadena and San Diago, Cal., and up to the time of our writing they are here investigating the lands in and around Burtner. The company was gotten up by Mr. Dow Pitzel, of Los Angeles. Mr. Pitzel has been in our county before and has been very much pleased with all of his investigations. Everything was fixed up in great style for their arrival. General Manager Geo. A. Snow of the Delta Company came down from Salt Lake City. He brought with him a chef from Salt Lake, who immediately began to prepare a barbecue for their arrival.

Monday they visited the south tract, also went over through Hinckley. One man said: "I have seen more alfalfa today than I ever saw before," and as a whole they seeme to be pretty well satisfied with the place.

Mr. F. E. Manges, city ticket and passenger agent of Los Angeles, has the excursion in charge.

Mr. and Mrs. S. T. Allen, also W. I. Moody and wife were Burtner visitors last week.

Quite a number of the people are very much dissatisfied about the way the new company does about the pay checks. The 10th of each month was set apart as pay day. Well, the people get their money any time after that the company sees fit. It was the 17th this time, and there was quite a kick and part of it being held back for unknown reasons. The people need their pay and when pay day comes they would like to have it, and not wait so long and then only get part of it.

The Burtner Lumber Company is building themselves a new office building and get it completed. This will be a great improvement on the tents they are now using.

Frank L. Copening of Provo was in town the past week.

The water is being pumped out of the hole where the wreck occurred on May 5th.

William H. Gardner of Salem, Utah, came back to Burtner last Saturday. He expects to stay indefinitely.

Abner Johnson and George Matheson are the new ditch riders. Johnson has the day and Matheson the night shift.

Mr. V. M. Samuels made a trip to Salt Lake City Sunday night, returning Tuesday morning.

Harry Dresser came down from Salt Lake last week. He was at the Chronicle farm, learning something about irrigation.

Stewart Eccles & Son call special attention to their ladies furnishings this week. Next week they will have a discount sale of hardware and harness sundries.

BURTNER.

A. C. SORENSON, REPRESENTATIVE

On May 23rd one of the largest land deals ever made in the state of Utah was pulled off at Burtner, between a german colony from Los Angeles, California and The Delta Land and water Co. of this place. The deal covers some 10,000 acres of land and water. The land lies about four miles east of the town of Burtner. The price paid for the land and water was $50.50 per acre or a total of $505,000. Some 400 families are interested in deal. A few more deals like this and Burtner or Delta as it will be called, will forge to the front as one of the most thrifty and prosperous towns in the state.

After July1 it will be WATCH DELTA GROW.

Our new spill way that is being built by the Delta Land and Water Co. and the Melville Irrigation Co. is nearing completion this is one of the finest pieces of cement work of its kind ever built and is certainly a credit to these Co's.

S. R. Humphries, our enterprising lumber dealer is building him a nice office on the west side of the railroad track, just opposite the Depot.

Considerable town property at fancy prices was bought by Germans here during the past two weeks. If you care to buy you a lot you had better get a move on you, as the price of property is going up.

The talk of the town here is the stampede which took place at twelve A. M. Tuesday. The cause was that several hundred acres of land had been thrown open for homestead enteries. The land thrown open for entry lies along the Sevier River, between the Hinckley spill and the old Burtner spill and is some of the best in the state. It is a nice loamy soil and cover with a heavy growth of sage brush and greasewood.

Heber Mitchell of Fillmore was seen on our streets Sunday Mr. Mitchell is thinking of locating in this neighborhood. Come to Burtner Heb and bring all your friends, we have room for all of you.

The Burtner Commercial Club held a meeting Sunday evening for the purpose of interesting the people in a town organization another meeting was called for Sunday June 4th at 5 p. m.

Mr. R. E. Robison of Hinckley our County Commissioner, met with the Commercial Club here Sunday.

Francis M. Lyman and his son Richard and James A. Melville of Salt Lake are in town trying to locate some of the land thrown open for entry along the Sevier River.

OAK CITY.

S. J. Rawlinson, Representative

The Stake Primary Convention held here Sunday, May 28th was in every respect a success. So said the visiting members of the General Board. Many interesting parts were given from the various primaries of our stake Also in this connection was held the Stake Priesthood meeting on Saturday. Most wards were represented.

Among the social happenings of the week was the "shower given Mr. and Mrs. John Lundahl who were recently married at Panguitch, the home of the bride. A flood of presents of unique descriptions were handed the happy couple. Games were played and all report it as "a perfect success."

Upon that same evening a mysterious light appeared in the sky near the center of town. It was first pronounced another comet, but later was discovered to be a lantern hung upon the liberty pole to a height of about seventy five feet. Question after question, mingled with wonder, crossed the minds of weary homeward travelers, but none could guess.

It later developed that a certain wide-awake young gentleman of this place had taken his lantern to light his path to the "shower." It might also be added that this man was at one time a reporter of note, for the New York World, The San Francisco Examiner and the Millard Co. Chronicle.

Undoubtly he had hoped to gather a few items that no other person, without a lantern, would be likely to observe. Let his motive be what it may, the fact remains that after the "party" he was given the legal privilege of seeing a young lady home.

"Lanterns and girls do not go together." So saying he left the old for the new and journied towards the home of his bride's parents. It might be given as a further explanation that the distance was long with a three per cent grade most of the way. Some boys who stood ready to help when the lantern was left alone, decided that it would be nothing more than an act of charity to place the light at an elevation where the owner might view it from his destination; and thus during the perplexities of mind, which have caused many "speakers" to become bewildered and forlorn, might locate at least one familiar corner, and return home with praise and thanksgiving.

When he reached the liberty pole, he was greatly startled with seeing his lantern so far above him. Yet there it was and he must bring it down. He started to climb; the first twenty five feet were soon reached yet the lantern seemed no nearer. A stretch of ten feet more were added, he thought he had climbed fifty and the light above seemed no nearer. He made another effort but in vain. He began imaging the distance below when he turned dizzy and came carefully down. He now offers a handsome reward to the young man who will get his lantern.

Oasis

Samuel Rutherford Representative.

The weather has changed very much and it appears that summer has come at last.

Decoration day which has passed was a beautiful day and was observed by nearly all of the town there was 53 graves and nearly all were decorated but it appears that some have almost forgotten the ones who have passed away.

Wm. Ward who has been sick for some time now is no better and we extend our deepest sympathy for those who are closely connected and are bearing the trials of the long illness but we sincerely hope he will soon be able to be out again.

Mrs. S. M. Hawley will leave Tuesday for Salt Lake to be treated for her trouble we do hope she will come home in good health.

Earl Huff can be seen repairing the house on the Huff ranch and moving there for the summer.

It has been said that there would be a car load of honey bees unloaded in Oasis to stay and we have talked to some for 2 years at least to secure ground on which to place them. Why don't some of our own people take hold of this business? We know it will pay.

Millard County Chronicle
June 15, 1911

Albert P. Wallace, Chronicle Representative.

Mr. James A. Melville made a business trip to Salt Lake City last week.

Mr. F. M. Wilson of Abraham, passed through Burtner last Sunday evening on his way to Salt Lake City.

Some building was going on in Burtner last week. An addition was built on Will Jenkins' house. An automobile garage was built for the D. L. & W. Co. and a porch on Ray Bishop's house.

The new concrete spillway has been completed and it certainly is a dandy. They are making the fills and are preparing to turn the water over it. It was completed last Thursday.

The trouble between Ray Bishop and John Chidester has quieted down. Chidester moved off the land last Friday.

John E. Steel made a business trip to Salt Lake City this week.

Mr. Frank Taylor and Irene Lewis went to Fillmore Tuesday to procure a marriage license. They were married Wednesday evening at the home of the bride's parents. Mr. Taylor is from Wayne county. He came here about a year ago and is making this his home. Miss Lewis is one of Burtner's most highly esteemed young ladies.

We wish them all the joy and happiness in their new life.

Another carload of cement was unloaded Monday by the D. L. & W. Co.

Mr. Eugene Hilton of Hinckley is here painting Ray Bishop's house.

Word has just been received that the temporary spillway at the big cut built about the 20th of April, has washed out. They had the fills very nearly made to turn the water over the new spillway, but the water got the start of them and washed out the old one. It will delay the work for about three or four days. If the old spillway had held twenty-four hours longer they would have had men and teams tearing it out.

Millard County Progress
June 16, 1911

BURTNER.
A. O. SORENSON, REPRESENTATIVE

Elder Workman who has been laboring in the missionary field in Kansas arrived in Burtner the 9th. Monday evening a party was given in his honor, a beautiful program was rendered. Brother Workman made a short talk touching in brief on his experiences while in the missionary field which was very much appreciated and a treat to all present. After the program the chairs were removed and all participated in a dance which was not brought to a close until in the wee small hours of the morning.

Saturday evening a matched basket ball game was played between the Jr's. and Sr's. of our town. The game was well played but the juniors were a little to nimble for the seniors and they marched off with a victory to the tune of 29 to 14 points. Since the game was played the juniors heads have swelled considerable and you often hear them express themselves as, they could beat any Jr. team in Millard County.

Elder Workman who has just returned from a mission occupied the time at the chapel last Sunday, his topic was the fall of Adam and Eve.

Mr. George Billings Supt. of the Hinckley co-op and Miss Aba Workman of Burtner were married in the Salt Lake Temple Wednesday June 7th. Their many friends join in wishing them success and a pleasant journey down the stream of life and that the paths where ever they may roam may be strewn with roses and sunshine.

Our new cement spillway is completed and the people here feel that in the future their water supply is sure.

Oasis

SAMUEL RUTHERFORD REPRESENTATIVE.

The weather is warm now and we can begin to hear the click of the mower in the hay but as yet there are not many cutting but will soon be cutting everywhere.

Mr. A. W. Thompson was seen here this week, he came down to visit his children and other relatives but has returned to his labor in Salt Lake.

Mrs. Samuel Rutherford and Mrs. Gerald Bennett both of Oasis have been to Salt Lake as delegates for the Primary and M. I. A. Convention and are much enthused over the labor and the many very well attended meetings and splendid instructions they received while away.

The Y. L. M I. A. had a dance last night the proceeds to be used in helping befray the expenses of their delegates.

William Ward is still bed-fast no change that can be noticed.

Mrs. Peter Anderson has returned from Salt Lake City where she went to receive medical treatment and is much improved at this writing.

Mr. T. H. Church the aged stage driver who drives from here to Abraham is well again and out at his job as driver. He is now eighty seven years of age and is as spry and nimble as many who are only half that age and reads the news without glasses, how is that for his age?

OAK CITY.

S. J. RAWLINSON, REPRESENTATIVE

The twelfth annual commencement of the Millard County public schools was held here on the 9th inst.

One hundred three of the one hundred nine eighth grade graduates were present to receive their certificates. This is the largest class in the history of our county. It indicates the growth of our school.

The program as printed was carried out in every instance. Each part was indeed creditable and profitable.

The address to the graduates by Prof. R. L. McGhie was full of inspiration and could not fail to appeal to the young as well as the old.

Two thots well subdivided and carefully and eloquently delivered consisted his theme. They were (1) "You can become what you will in life" (2) Never fail to appreciate the efforts of your parents."

The professor commenced by saying that he did not feel like a professor but rather like a plain, little, Utah boy. He briefly referred to his own experience in attempting to gain an education and gave Prof. Wm. Stewart much praise for early impressions that he made upon his (Prof. R. L. McGhie's) life. He cited other characters and plainly demonstrated that money is not necessary to acquire education.

Parents are making great efforts to send their children to school, we must do kind deeds to show our true love for parents.

More than one hundred twenty five students, principals trustees and friends sat at banquet in the afternoon. Beef sandwich, lettuce salad, with bananas and oranges and strawberries were served.

Interesting toasts were given by Supt. A. J. Ashman, former Supt. Jos. Finlinson, Prof. Mc Ghie and others.

In the evening the commencement ball was given in the gymnasium. All present seemed to enjoy it.

Among the Millard principals present were: Alma Beckstrand of Meadow, Wm Gardner of Deseret, S. J. Rawlinson of Oak City, John Watts of Kanosh and Avery Bishop of Burtner.

We appreciate the educational advantages derived from such a gathering and invite more.

Of course we have the funny side in all such gatherings. It is said that two young ladies sat up all night because they were asked to sleep on the floor and I am told that the bed was not hard. Yet we would not be understood as being disgusted with our guests, where we have one of the type referred to above, we have a great number who are appreciative of what is done for them. A few remarks were made at the banquet by a certain one or two that were far from decent. And such will not be welcome at our table again. It was not because of our town, the same thing takes place at every such gathering.

This is certain to discourage hospitality and implant a certain degree of suspicion when it comes to entertaining company.

We do not meet on any occasion to enjoy luxury or admire new dresses. If such is our motive, thin indeed, is the crust of our education and culture. This one phase of education, our school must look to carefully. We are prone, with our free books, free materials, well graded classes, to not be sufficiently appreciative of what comes to us, and this condition never fails to bring one into extravagance and destroyes his economy.

We should know that education is nothing more than behavior. If we may observe your actions, we can easily judge of your education. Education is not grammer, arithmetic, history, geography nor any subject. But rather our interpretation of life through these subjects as a means to accomplish our own aim. It does little good if any for a child to memorize Washington's Rules of conduct if he has nothing of "conduct' in him. Nothing comes from repeating moral codes. Practice must play its part or art, taste, and refinement are empty terms.

Marriage License Issued.

Marriage License: Issued on Wednesday to Frank W. Taylor and Miss Irene Lewis, both of Burtner, Ut.

Was issued on Tuesday to John O. Smith of Fillmore and Miss Jetta Bennett of Holden.

Was issued to Arthur Jenson of Elsinore and Miss Violet Monroe of Scipio, Ut. The last named couple were married at the court house by Clerk N. A. Anderson.

NEWS NOTES OF SCIPIO

D. Grover Probert, Chronicle Representative

The election held here on the 27th resulted in the following: For sale of liquor, 14, against sale, 150. There were a number who did not vote at all. We are glad the majority of the people of Scipio are in favor of prohibition.

There have been two new grain-headers purchased here the last week. One by L. A. Robins and one by F. L. Wasden. Mr. Beckstrand from Meadow made the sale.

Seffel Fisher came up from Burtner Thursday on account of the illness of his mother.

Thomas Memmott Sr. has gone to Nephi to be present at the marriage of his grandson Alton.

Studebaker agent, Mr. Small was in town Wednesday.

Albert Johnson has returned home from Nephi.

Miss Vera Monroe has returned to Scipio after a week's visit in Sevier County.

J. D. Smith occupied most of the time in meeting last Sunday.

George Day is spending his spare time helping put up a new store building for himself in Delta. The basement with its cement walls is completed and the foundation walls are laid. The store will be 24x35 feet in size and made of cement blocks furnished by Mr. Koch of the Delta cement block works. Mr. Day expects to have the building complete and ready for occupancy in about a month. This is pretty good proof of Mr. Day's faith in Delta.

PIONEER DAY AT DELTA.

The people of Delta are showing their enterprise this year by providing for a two days celebration of Pioneer Day, Monday and Tuesday, July 24th and 25th. Committees are at work and great preparations are being made to provide such attractions as will draw the people from all parts of the county. Old Millard County people from elsewhere are invited to come back and meet their old friends on this occasion. Others interested in seeing the country around Delta are invited to come down and rigs will be provided to take them around. The following is the general program provided:

Hoisting of flag at sunrise by Marshal of the Day, John E. Sticele.

The people will gather at the amusement hall at 10 o'clock sharp where the following program will be rendered.

Singing by choir, "Utah Queen of the West."

Prayer by Chaplain Edgar W. Jeffery.

Duet by Miss Helen Callister and Miss Nathalia Cooper.

Speech of welcome by Miss Agnes Eardley, "Queen of the West."

Oration by Wm. Gardner.

Solo by Octava Murphy.

Recitation by Miss Lydia Workman.

The Growler, by Fred Barben

Song by the Underhill Girls.

Instrumental solo by Mrs. Bessie Law.

Pioneer speech by H. J. McCullough.

Male Quartette under the direction of S. W. Eccles.

Stump speech by N. S. Bishop.

Female Quartette under the direction of Mrs. La Myra Bishop.

Instrumental solo by Miss Cree Underhill.

Delta ten years hence by A. S. Workman.

Toasts by Volunteers.

Song by choir.

Benediction by Chaplain E. W. Jeffery.

Children's dance will begin at 2 o'clock.

At 4 o'clock there will be sports and races for the children where prizes will be rewarded.

A prize will be given the best looking baby under the age of one year. Western states represented by:

Utah, Queen of the West, by Miss Agnes Eardley.

Colorado, by Edna Bowman.

Wyoming, Venice Barben.

Montana, Orvilla Lewis.

Oregon, Olive Cook.

Washington, Phosia Humphries.

California, Ealsa Munns.

Nevada, Blanche Maxfield.

Arizona, Armelia Jacobs.

New Mexico, Eliza Hook.

Committee on decoration: Miss Helen Callister, Mr. M. H. Workman, Miss Ella Patten, Miss Mame Patten, Mr. Claude Billings, Mr. Norman Gardner.

General committee: Andrew C. Sorensen, Fred Barben, H. A. Knight, M. H. Workman, Mrs. Geo. Mathewson, Mrs. Tom Hook, Miss Helen Callister.

The program of races are as follows, and will take place at 4 o'clock: $10 purse for the fastest running horse in the county; $10 purse for the fastest pacing horse in the country; $10 for the second-class running race; $5 purse for the fastest trotting horse; $10 purse for the fastest saddle horse; $5 first prize, $2.50 second prize for 100 yard foot race.

There will also be a bucking broncho contest with a $10 prize for the best rider.

Everybody is invited to come to Delta and have a good time.

The Celebration At Delta.

The 24th of July celebration held at Delta was a decided success in every way and the visitors from other towns were treated right royally by the citizens of Delta. There were some very good races pulled off the principal ones being a quarter mile running race which was won by Walker's horse from Oak City.

Saddle horse won by S. W. Eccle's horse.

Saddle horse race won by Fay Theobald's horse.

A pacing race best 2 out of 3 heats won by O. L. Bunker's horse.

A trotting race which was won by Sam Stansworth's horse best 2 out of 3.

O. L. Bunker,s horse paced a ½ mile exhibition, no time given.

Walker's horse ran in a half mile exhibition in 55 seconds on a very slow track which is a good indication of what he could do on a fast track.

The 24th a ball game was played between the married and single men of Delta which was won by the married men by one run.

Oasis vs Delta, Oasis won by a small margin.

On the 25th a game was played Hinckley vs Abraham which was won by Hinckley.

Hinckley defeated Deseret the same day by a large majority.

It was estimated that there were fully 1500 people at the track on Tuesday and 500 people attended the dance given in the evening.

The whole town of Oasis closed on Tuesday in order that every one who wished could go to Delta and help celebrate.

F. L. Hickman while riding his horse in one of the races met with an accident. His horse saw the team and buggy belonging to Mr. Hickman and he flew the track and made for the team, throwing the rider against one of the buggy wheels and breaking every spoke out of it.

Dr. Dryden of Modena dressed the wounds and Mr. Hickman was able to proceed home.

The restaurant which is conducted by Mr. and Mrs. Cooper did a large business, Mrs. Cooper is an excellent cook and sets a good table.

Althogether everyone was well satisfied with the celebration and the general committee composed of H. A. Knight chairman Ed. Marshall and Cass Lewis are to be complimented on the way in which everything was handled. We are informed that nobody was asked for donations but the stores donated $5 each and a little from the Land Co. and that there was a small surplus left after all expenses were paid, this shows good management on the part of the committee.

Hurrah for Delta!

OAK CITY.

S. J. Rawlinson, Representative

Pioneer Day was well celebrated here yesterday. The weather was ideal. The meeting at 10 o'clock a. m. had many interesting features. The ball game, in the afternoon between Limbers and Stiffs was an interesting part of the day's program. Mr. Thomas of Lyndyll and John Watts of Kanosh formed the battery for the older fellows. The game was closely contested the first five innings. The limbers having a better quality of endurance finally were successful.

Among visitors present was our state's first Governor Hon. Heber M. Wells, also his brother Joseph and wife, Mr. and Mrs. Jas. Thomas of Lyndyll, Mr. and Mrs. Walter Johnson of Leamington and Mr. and Mrs. White of Beaver City.

Miss Millie Lyman, who is at present engaged at the L. D. S. Hospital from which institution she graduated last spring, is spending a two weeks vacation with us.

A number of our citizens were away Monday spending Pioneer Day with other towns. Undoubtly Geo. Finlinson will detail to us exactly what they did in Holden, while W. R. Walker and his bosom friend Mr. Timothy will bring to us speedily the good news from Delta.

On Sunday last our Sabbath school was visited by Stake board members Bros, Rigby and Whicker of Delta. They also gave some interesting words at Sacrement meeting.

On Wednesday evening last a welcome party was tendered Bert Roper. It was highly enjoyed by all present.

Next week will be most of our younger population, sprinkled with a few of the sager folk, resting under the canyon trees eating up the summers earnings.

Deseret.

D. S. Cahoon made a trip to the capitol last week.

Clark Allred and Mark Kelly were visitors at Holden and Meadow the first of the week.

Myron Black spent Pioneer Day in Scipio.

After a very pleasant visit of ten days with her aunt Mrs. Jno. Knider, Miss Peterson has returned to her home in Granger.

Mrs. Virgial Kelly is home from Salt Lake after a visit of several weeks with her daughter Mrs. A. D. Ryan.

Mrs. Marcus Jones wife of Prof. Jones of the Geological Survey of the Salt Lake division is the guest of her daugther Mrs. O. A. Broaddus.

Dr. and Mrs. Broaddus entertained on Thursday evening for their friend Miss Scranton who returned to her home in Salt Lake Friday morning.

Mr. and Mrs. Chas. Maw were down from Provo for the 24th.

Mrs Tim Harrington of Coleville arrived on the East bound train Monday morning, following a summons to the bed side of her father, D. O. Reid, who is dangerously ill at the home of his daughter, Mrs. I. N. Moody.

Mrs. Grace Hopkins, returned from summer school Sunday accompanied by Miss Ada Taylor of Salem. Miss Taylor taught in our school two years ago and has been engaged for the coming school year. For the present she is renewing old acquaintences and visiting her many friends.

The home of Bishop and Mrs. Damron was the scene of a pleasant party the afternoon of the 20, when their daughters Norma and Lucile entertained the MacDowell and Mendelssohn clubs. Mrs. O. A. Broaddus who organized the clubs furnished delightful music, among which a number of Bird songs by the noted English composer. Mrs. Liza Leham.

Probably the most successful celebration ever held in Deseret was that of Pioneer Day. Every one requested to furnish floats, responded most loyally making the parade a special feature.

The representation of the advent of the pioneers of 47 by Albert Hales, B. P. Crafts and their families was typical of conditions under which the early settlers traveled. The handcart company of of, 1856 under the direction of Marvin Black and Marvin Western, most vividly brought to mind the terrible suffering and hardships which that devout company endured. A veteran of the company Mrs. Hanna Allred in a speech readily verified all the picture portrayed. Misses Carrie Jensen and Lillian Peterson displayed the meager possibilities of furnishing flour for the early set-

tlers of Deseret by a not altho gether up-to-date fish wagon drawn by a more primative animal.

Mr. Wm Justensen brought out the present day possibilities of a deseret farm by a desert farm by a flat beautifully decorated with fragrant flowers and vegetables the equal of any thing in Millard County all products of his farm.

Following the parade a well rendered program was given in the meeting house. The afternoon and evening given over to the usual line of sports.

MARRIAGE LICENSE

was issued last week to Lecile D. Pace and Geneva Cook, both of Delta. They were married in the court house by Clerk N. A. Anderson.

Millard County Progress
August 11, 1911

OAK CITY.

S. J. RAWLINSON, REPRESENTATIVE

Mr. P. Callister of Delta was a caller here last week. While at the home of his sister, Mrs. Mary M. Lyman, he was desirious of talking with certain people of our place. He attempted to reach them by phone but received no answer. He was certainly a caller. Central finally responded with "they're in the canyon."

According to the census taken by Mr. Joseph Finlinson between 175 and 200 old and young people spent three of the funniest days of the summer at White Horse Resort.

Men who had long since said good-by to baseball foot racing etc. under the influence of heavy appetites for crystal spring water and delicious and savory foods, were glad to indulge in the most agile sports.

John E. Lovell, once a baseball man, proved beyond any doubting notion, that on a 50 yd. down hill track can yet make respectable racing. Bp. Jno. L. Anderson, who belongs to the fleshy class, was "day lighted" in 50 yds by his eldest son Otto.

Many other interesting things took place of a nonsensical nature which would intrest only those present.

"Many things taking place at the same time."

All are now home removing the coat of rust nature would be glad to see all wear.

Twenty teams after two days of hard work finished today our 1-2 mile race track. All horses are invited.

Mrs. Wm. Huff of Oasis is spending a week with us.

Ward conference was held here on Sunday last. Pres. A. A. Hinckley, Thompson and Finlinson gave interesting words at the sacrement meeting. Clerk Willis E. Robison was also present.

Oasis

SAMUEL RUTHERFORD REPRESENTATIVE.

Last Friday while ploughing Mr. S. M. Hawley of this place was attacked by some honey bees which are in the adjoining field of Samuel Rutherford.

The bees first attacked the team and they at once turned in fright and became so entangled in the traces that they both fell to the ground. Mr. Hawley at once tried to release the animals but was unable to do so as the bees at once turned their attention to him and he was compelled to flee for his own life, he at once ran to the home of Mr. Rutherford and told him in a few words what had happened and asked him to help release the animals then they both went with haste to the scene and found that one of the animals had freed itself enough to get up. After a hard fight for some time with smoke, the bees were forced from the animals but not until one of them had been stung so severe that he died some 6 hours later. The other animal we think will recover but is badly swollen yet from the stings.

The team consisted of a fine pair of bay mars as near mated as could be found and the one that died was only four years old. Mr. Hawley was always very proud of his fine team and the loss will be felt by him. Although the owners of the bees has proffered to pay for the animal, he will not soon get over the fright of the bees and the experience.

The men in charge of the bees said it was sure a miracle that the animals were rescued at all.

and both Mr. Hawley and Rutherford express themselves as never wishing to have the same experience and say that it is indescribe the way the small bees fought both them and the animals and if they had not been closely covered with mosquito bar no doubt would have been driven away.

At the present time prospects are very favorable for another fair crop of alfalfa seed and we hope this will continue till harvest time will be in September.

Alfred Stansworth left for Dixie and will be gone about a month.

Mrs. Ambrose Stansworth will leave for Salt Lake on the 14th where she expects to get medical treatment both for herself and child.

DELTA.

A. C. SORENSON, REPRESENTATIVE

Bunker, Sorenson and Patters started their threshing machine and threshed about two thousand bushels of rye. It is the farmers intention to plant this rye during the latter part of August.

As a rule the crops of Delta are looking fine. The farmers are busy cutting and stacking their grain, it is estimated that their will be between 60,000 and 80,000 bushels of grain raised here this season.

Wm Bunker's rye averaged 35 bushels to the acre, the lowest rye average to the acre here is 28 bushels, Not so bad is it.

During the past thirty days over twenty binders and one he der has been sold and unloaded at Delta.

It is not an uncommon thing to find oats in the fields here with heads from 18 inches to 21 inches long. Beat this if you can.

Mr. Roe Doddy who has been employed by The Delta Land Co. as an auto driver, has resigned his position. Mr. Doddy left for Salt Lake Sunday morning where he intends to make his home for the summer.

Two representatives of a Jewish Colony in the east have been in Delta the past few days looking over the land here. They are figuring on buying 8,000 acres of land from the Delta Land Co. At the rate land has been selling here of late, it will only take some sixty days longer for The Delta Land Co to unload of all the land they have for sale.

If you want a farm at Delta you had better hurry or you will be too late.

A number of the people here are intending to attend the County Fair at Fillmore this fall.

$1.50 pays for the Progress Review one year. Hand in your subscription to A. C. Sorenson and he will see that you get your paper.

Robison House Notes.

O. P. Hansen U. S. cream seperator salesman arrived Aug. 3rd left next day.

W. F. Greshner well driller, working for Mr. Westphal arrived Aug. 3rd. Mrs. Greshner arrived Monday, they expect to be here for some time.

W. D. Owen son and daughter were here last week for a short stay.

Mr. and Mrs. E. W. Ellis arrived here last Saturday left same day.

O. E. Summerhayes a stock buyer came on the 7th left next day.

The Cunning Company are with us during their engagement here.

Oasis

SAMUEL RUTHERFORD REPRESENTATIVE

Mr. Humphries of Salt Lake City is here at present.

We understand that a company is underway of getting new steam threshing machine in Oasis for this seasons work and we think this a very good move as we need a good thresher her

as we have a good outlook for another good crop of alfalfa seed as well as some grain.

Mr. Smyth is here unloading the big Drain Digger and is getting it out to work it will commence work as fast as possible. Although he got hurt yesterday while unloading the boiler which weighed about six tons he is able to be around to day and is on duty. We hope to see this machine at work soon on the first big drain which will commence at the south of Oasis and drive through the west central part of this place.

News was received here of the sudden death of Mrs. Dana Cropper Handerson of Hinckley who leaves a husband and five children to mourn her great loss.

She was a mother to all of her sisters and they will all miss her very much.

DELTA

A. O. SORENSON, REPRESENTATIVE

The writer interviewed Mr. James A. Melville, who gave him the following information:-

Mr. Melville said, "Delta will have a modern up-to date depot which will be built at once." It will be a frame building and will cost $5000. The material has all been ordered and he expects the actual work will commenced on the depot before this is published. As soon as the depot is built we will have a night operator.

There is some talk of a hotel being built, what about it Mr. Melville? Mr. Melville said the Delta Land and Water Co. has already had plans drawn and will begin at once on an up-to-date hotel, which will have ample capacity to accomodate the traveling public. The name of our hotel will be The Delta Hotel.

The above is good news as the traveling public have repeatedly suggested that a Hotel and livery barn be constructed to accommodate the many people who are visiting this place. The Delta Land and Water Co. now has two first class automobiles which are kept busy every day showing the home seekers over the company's lands.

Our Commercial Club is taking steps to have our town incorporated and a petition is being circulated for the purpose. The Club is also negotiating with the railroad officers to have the two American Express trains No. 3 and 4 stop at Delta. These are both day trains, No. 3 west bound passes through Delta at 6:45 p. m. and No. 4 east bound 10:6 a. m. If the Club is successful in having these day trains stop at Delta it will mean better accommodations to the traveling public.

N., Bishop has as fine a garden as can be found any place in the county for the amount of ground it covers. He has several loads of melons, sweet corn, potatoes, beets, onions, cabbage etc

Dr. A. Murphy is building him a fine furniture store on Clark St. The building will be frame and will have a 20 ft. frontage and 32 feet deep.

Honorable T. O. Callister made a flying trip to Salt Lake City.

S. R. Humphries was awarded the contract to build our new school house.

Mr. and Mrs. Hyrum Miller of Black Horse Nevada, are visiting with their daughter, Mrs. Chas Clawson. Mr. Miller said things are looking bright at Black Horse.

While riding a horse a few evenings ago. Leslie D. Pace met with a painfull accident. His horse stumbled and fell and threw him to the ground breaking his collar bone. Dr. Breddus of

Deseret was called, who set the fractured bone, but it seems the bone again worked out of place and Dr. Murphy was called in and reset the bone.

Thunder and lightning, hail and rain or an earthquake would be preferable to the noises we

heard here last Monday night. It was the young people of our town paying their respects to Mr. and Mrs. Douglas Lisonbee. Dug said he would give a dance and well, yes I think he will.

THE DOINGS AT DELTA

A. P. Wallace, Representative

Attorney J. Alex Melville of Salt Lake City was in Delta Sunday.

Mr. John Christianson of Spanish Fork came down to Delta last Thursday morning bringing with him Bishop Hanson and wife to look over the country here. Mr. Christianson is also representing the Provo Nurseries.

Some of the people are not sending their children to school yet. Mr. Rigby gave out notice in the meetings Sunday that all children of a school age must be in school at once, as, if they don't come on their own free will they will be compelled to.

John Steel is erecting himself a new house just south of the depot.

Stewart Eccles, one of our local merchants, made a trip to Salt Lake City the past week.

Bishop Ashby of Leamington was one of the speakers in church Sunday afternoon.

The new real estate office of McClain, Copening & Gull is nearing completion. It is just north of N. L. Bishop place, is 18x20 bungalo style with wide eaves and porches. It is a very neat little building and is a credit to our town.

The Reverands McClay and Herrick, Presbyterian ministers, held service in the hall here Sunday evening.

The water is flooded along some of our streets again. We suppose preparatory to being shut out of the canals for the season.

OCCURRENCES AT OAK CITY

W. R. Walker, Representative

LeRoy Walker and Lydia Roper left Sunday to attend school at Hinckley. Among the other Oak City students attending the M. S. A. are Miss Lucy Anderson, Loise Anderson, Don Anderson, Maggie and Zella Nielson and Willis J. Lyman. These are not all who will attend, the Bishop said the number would reach fifteen if he himself had to go.

Saturday night the Mexican Orchestra played for a dance in our Gym.

The musicale was without a doubt the best ever heard in this part of the country. They gave us a few pieces Sunday morning and departed for Lynndyl.

Our district school starts next Monday with Wm. Davis as principal and Miss Alice Deen of Beaver and Miss Jane Rawlinson as assistants.

Four molasses mills are busy day and night making molasses. A good crop is expected considering the dry weather we have been having.

"If" we get some rain between now and next year there will be a big crop of dry grain next year, but without some rain it will no doubt continue to be dry.

Clif Talbot has been working in Leamington the past week, also Clarence Nielson has gone to work there.

Thomas Talbot and wife attended the reception at Hinckley.

Mrs. Christen Christenson and Mrs. John Christenson of Aurora, Sevier County were visiting relatives and friends in Oak City last week.

Millard County Progress
September 29, 1911

OAK CITY.

S. J. Rawlinson, Representative

Molasses making, grain planting, and lumbering are claiming the attention of our citizens this week.

Four mills are busy manufacturing the sugar cane crop, which is exceeding all previous seasons. Arthur and Thomas Talbot have built a mill of their own, and hence will have to pay no toll.

The dry season, although bringing decreased harvests, has increased the faith of our dry farmers.

When grain will mature as it has done this summer under such hot skies, and parching winds blowing its roots from the ground, it is a safe conclusion that with an average amount of moisture we are sure of our bread. The dry seasons are doing much to teach us how to conserve moisture. O. H. Jacobson has already sown fifty acres, some of which is now peeping up. Peter Anderson's farm has 80 acres ready part of which is now drilled. John Nielson is putting in a patch of thirty five acres, and others are planting smaller lots.

Bishop Anderson is directing his energies toward the forest. He has purchased 10 m. feet of stumpage from the government, and will be in condition to furnish our town with the greater part of its lumber from now on. Quite a number are contemplating building barns this fall.

Fruit picking is almost over, yet the later varieties are still to be disposed of. Many have visited us for their fruit supply, still the rush has not been so great as some previous years.

Our merchant Mr. Jacobson, has returned from Fillmore where he spent a few days at the County Fair. He states that while Fillmore made lots of preparations, it was not patronized as it should be, throughout the county. This move although good, is yet new, and we are hardly able to realize its value.

In a sociable way, coming as a result of melodious music, nothing in the history of our new hall, has surpassed the party given last Saturday evening by a Spanish and Mexican orchestra. These we are informed are a part of the great orchestra that came to Salt Lake City about one mo. ago. They are musicians of note and it is well worth ones time and money to hear them. Our violinist, Mr. Ray Finlinson, who has an instinct for music when it enters the feet, as well as the heart and ear, happened to first hear this music in Leamington, he induced their leader to bring them here by offering free transportation, board and lodging. He (Ray) came early to the dance and was doing nothing between tunes, but instructing others to set their watches back and not to tell the bishop.

Sunday morning this same violinist was coaxing them to play and offered his team and services to haul them to Lynndel. Last mon night they played in that place and our musician left town at dark in company with three other music lovers to dance at Lynndel. I have not seen him since but trust he has returned.

He cannot help putting some of this renewed music into our own orchestra.

Last week the following young folk left us for the winter season to attend the M. S. Accademy at Hinckley: Lucy, Lois and Don Anderson, Lyda Roper, Willis J. Lyman and Le Roy Walker.

Others will leave us in the immediate future.

We have noticed in the last issues of both our county papers remarks concerning railroad points and also mail routes. We too have a suggestion, although perhaps a little out of season. It has been mentioned before—but not in a public way. Our county mail system could be much improved. The arguments set forth from Holden in the Chronicle last week are sufficiet. We can get answers to letters from our boarding states sooner than from our county towns. Although our town is small we should like to see one daily mail route from Kanosh to Lynndyl through all the towns on the eastern side of the county excepting Scipio. And a daily mail could be carried from there to Holden. With this route we could write and receive answers to letters, in many instances, the same day and no later than the next day from any town in the county. The road next to the mountains, with a little work, as all roads require, would be free from sand in summer and mud in the winter. The distance say from Fillmore to Lynndyl would be but some seven or eight miles farther than it would be to Clear Lane. The road site is a bigger consideration than the distance.

Again there are eight passenger trains that stop at Lynn as compared with any other point in the county. Six through and two locals. The passenger via Nephi, Provo etc. goes no farther south than Lynn, while the "limited" stops only at Lynn.

If the day of outomobiles is past then a system something after the old stage style could be used. Two large conveyances with horses enough, would render us a much better system than we have.

From a freight standpoint we believe many advantages are in its favor for some of our towns.

Millard County Chronicle
October 19, 1911

SOCIAL EVENTS IN DELTA.

Even though the people of West Delta have no amusement hall they do not lack for social entertainments. Besides the pleasant party at Jacob De Brees', already noted, Al Watts had a party at which every one greatly enjoyed themselves. The last one was held on Saturday evening at the home of J. J. Clark. About twenty of the neighbors were present and they were entertained with music and dancing, and during the evening refreshments were served. Mr. Clark is a great performer on the fiddle and he gave the old fashioned tunes in such lively style that it set everybody's feet to beating time if they didn't dance.

THE DELTA DEPOT ROBBED.

Last Sunday night the depot at Delta was broken into and $350 in gold coin was taken from the express box. F. F. Mansfield, a carpenter, who had been working for Marshall & Knight, is the one who is charged with the robbery. The man was standing by the side of the express car Sunday morning and saw the package handed to the agent. So Sunday evening during the absence of the agent he broke into the car and with the help of wire pliers pried open the flimsy express box that contained the money. The pliers were identified by H. A. Knight as belonging to Mansfield. He also stole a horse and buggy from Fred Barben to make his get-away in. This he tied up down by Oasis. The horse and buggy were located early Monday morning.

At the time of this writing nothing has been learned of his whereabouts. Sheriff Black is working on the case.

A DAY TRAIN.

The Development League of Utah made up of delegates from the Commercial Clubs of the State, met at Nephi last week to discuss matters of interest to the State. The clubs from the northern part of the State were pretty well represented, but the only delegate from any club south of Nephi was Wm. N. Gardner of Delta, who gave a good boost for his town and county. Douglas White, the industrial agent of the Salt Lake Route, was also present and made a good talk on the resources and opportunities of Millard County. Better than all, he gave assurance that Delta would soon have a day train, and also a through train from Provo via Lynn. This will be a very great convenience for Delta, as the present train service is about as poor as could be devised.

THE DOINGS AT DELTA

A. P. Wallace, Representative

Two carloads of imigrant movables were unloaded here last week. They came from California.

Mr. E. H. Dutweihler, of Steamboat Springs, Colo., arrived here Thursday evening with an imigrant car. His family came in on the train Saturday.

All trains have been quite late the last few days, and the hobos have been plentiful, both of which was a result of the strike, we suppose.

Mr. Wesley Lockyard of Los Angeles has moved to Delta to make it his home. He came last Thursday. Mr. Lockyard is a jeweler and watchmaker by trade. He will have his shop in connection with the Arcade Furniture Co. Mr. Lockyard should do well at his business, as there is not a first-class jeweler on this side of the county.

GOOD WORDS FOR MILLARD.

Postmaster Clove and a number of other people from Provo were in Delta looking over the Carey Acts land with a view of purchasing. In an interview with a newspaper he said that the Millard county district is forging ahead at a most rapid rate, and that the 80,000 acres of ground to be purchased will all be taken up in the course of next month. Carloads of people are coming into the state from Los Angeles and points in southern California, Oklahoma, Kansas, Nebraska, Iowa and other middle western states, and are buying these tracts of land all the way from forty to 160

In every case they are well satisfied with their purchases, and Delta, the principal town in the tract, will undoubtedly be a town of from 1,200 to

All the priesthood is requested to be present at the Priesthood meeting Sunday afternoon, as there is some very important business to be transacted, and your presence there is wanted.

The water has been shut out of the canals and as soon as they dry out the work of enlarging them will be commenced.

L. W. Gaisford, of Fillmore, formerly the East Side editor, was in town Monday selling peaches. He talks as thought he thought our town would amount to something yet—which is a kind word we don't get from everybody over there.

Word is being pushed on the new hotel as fast as possible. The lumber has not yet arrived, so that is delaying them some. The building is to be a two-story frame structure, with 15 rooms, besides two bath rooms, linen closet, hallways and basement. There will be a lobby, dining room, kitchen, living room, two bedrooms and _____ wash room on the lower floor. Nine bed rooms, linen closet, ladies wash room and bath on the second floor.

1,500 inhabitants by next spring. The land is mostly located south of Lynndyl, and takes up the Pahvant valley, the largest valley being brought under cultivation in this state. It contains three hundred square miles of agricultural ground.

In an interview with some of the farmers in that section Mr. Clove stated that they said they were raising better crops the first year than they had raised after years of cultivation in the states from which they came.

While the Utah people generally are not purchasing this valuable land at the government rates of $5 per acre

The building when complete will be a very nice structure. It will have hot and cold water for both bath rooms, kitchen and basement.

George Day made a trip to Salt Lake City last week on business.

Last Monday the Delta Company loaded one of their automobiles on a flat car and sent to to Salt Lake City to be overhauled and repaired.

Monday evening Leslie Lewis had the misfortune to accidentally shoot himself with a 38 Colts automatic pistol. The bullet passed through the knee joint. Dr. Murphy dressed the wound, and at the present time the patient is getting along very well.

Last week Dr. Underhill and wife made a trip through the settlements of the East Side doing dentist work. They report doing a good business.

I wish to thank my friends and the people of Delta for the liberal patronage they have accorded me in the past, and I assure them that in the future any business that they give me will be greatly appreciated, and I will do all in my power to merit any favors shown me. Very truly yours,

A. C. SORENSON & CO.

each after 1913 until $50 is paid, many Utah county farmers are buying forty and sixty-acre tracts. These farmers are trying to get the Salt Lake Route to put in a train service between Salt Lake and Milford via Provo in order to facilitate travel back and forth. When Mayor W. H. Ray was returning from delivering an address to the residents of Delta early in the week, he returned to Lynndyl with other Provo people, and none of them could secure accommodations, so were forced to spend the night in a box car station, as there are only twelve beds available for transients at the hotel at Lynndyl.

THE WEEK AT OASIS

Mrs. Mina Jackson, Representative

The alfalfa seed is rolling out this season similar to the gold that rolls out of the mine.

Mr. Nelson Bishop of Delta was a visitor here this week.

Milton Moody of Salt Lake is here visiting and recuperating in the fresh, cool air, and attending to business.

The little 9-year-old son of S. M. Hawley is reported as not doing well. The doctor fears his leg will have to be reset after two weeks.

Mrs. C. O. W. Pierson is reported to be improving after the operation she underwent on the 7th inst., and it is hoped this will end her sickness, and she will soon be able to return home.

Mr. L. W. Gaisford of Fillmore was seen on our streets this week.

Another feature that will be a marked improvement and that is when the mail route is changed from Fillmore via Oasis on the 23rd of this month. Our postmaster, J. P. Johnson, received the word this week to this effect.

Mrs. Herman McCosh has returned home from the hospital and is very much improved.

J. C. Hawley's new brick house is well under headway with William Critchley and Ira Clothia of Fillmore as masons.

Mrs. Alf Johnson has returned home from Lynndyl for the purpose of sending her children to school.

A number of our people went to Salt Lake City to enjoy the conference and also the fair.

A great show visited our town last week. Many were disappointed, though. They carried $1,000 out of town.

IN AND AROUND DELTA

The Week's News from the Coming Metropolis

Things have been very busy around here of late. Everybody is working hard to get all the work done that they an while we are having such good weather.

Last Monday quite a bunch of men and teams gathered at the hall to help with the work of excavating for the boiler house preparatory to putting in the new steam heating plant. The boiler house will be just back of the hall and will have main heating pipes running through the concrete floor of the rooms of the basement, and up to the radiators on the main floor.

Mr. John W. Thurston of Morgan was in town the first part of the week. He came down with more land buyers. Jack is a hustler and we are glad to see him working for our county. This is his second trip and he has sold over a section of land.

Dr. Dryden of Modena was up here last week and disposed of his Clark street property to S. W. Eccles. The same week Mr. Eccles sold it to our new blacksmith.

Last Saturday night the Delta Junior basketball team played a match game with the Millard Stake Academy First Year team. The game was a good one from start to finish, and ended with a victory of 32 to 31 in favor of the home team. The line-up was as follows:

First Years.—L. Abraham, r. f.; Clete Larsen, l. f.; R. Stott, c; W. Blake, r. g.; A. Workman, l. g.

Delta.—W. Gardner, r. f.; A. Humphries, l. f.; C. Billings, c.; H. Koch, r g.; D. Callister, l. g.

John Greener, referee.

Meltiah Workman, umpire.

Bushnell, score keeper.

The commendable plays that were made were as follows:

Stott, 11 field and 5 foul throws, making 27 points; Larsen, 2 field throws, which made their complete score. Gardner and Billings both made 6 field and 2 foul throws each. Humphries made 1 field and 2 foul throws, which made the 32 points for Delta.

The boys of both teams played a good game and especially the work of Koch to hold down his man, not a single score, as their r. f. man was the one they mostly feared.

Dr. Murphy has got only his first installment of furniture for the Arcade Furnishing House, but will soon have a complete up-to-date stock. A furniture store is a much needed acquisition for this section.

Attorey Melville was down from Salt Lake City last Sunday.

Prof. R. R. Lyman was down from the City this week on business pertaining to the county road from here to Fillmore.

We have another new railroad agent again. Mr. McEwan being called into Salt Lake City, and Mr. W. H. Hawes taking his place.

Last week David R. Stevens of Holden was in town and while here he disposed of his lots just east of N. S. Bishop's place, the one with the well on was purchased by Arthur Gull of Fillmore, and the one with the big red barn, to Edwin F. Bishop of Hinckley. The sale prices were $450 and $500 respectively.

Mrs. J. Winterrose and sons are among the new comers to Delta. They are from Heber, where Mrs. Winterrose has been in the millinery business for the past eight years. Her sons have taken up a farm at Delta and Mrs. Winterrose has opened a millinery shop in J. H. Riding's building. She can't make much of a show where she is, but will soon be in a fine cement block building of her own just west of her present location. She also does dressmaking.

If you want to buy any Delta property you had better buy it now, as the price of land is going up every day. The lands of the Delta Company that have heretofore been $40, $45 and $50 have all been raised $5 per acre, and it is expected that another raise will take place by the first of the year.

A new alfalfa huller has just been shipped here for use in threshing the alfalfa seed across the river. It is for the Payson people, who are threshing in Abraham this season.

Bunker & Sorensen have had their machine in town the last week threshing out the small jobs here while waiting on the oats on the west side, as all of the farmers had not got all their crops harvested.

Mr. O. B. Lackyard made a trip to Salt Lake City last week to order the paints for the new hotel.

W. H. Denison, the local plasterer, will start the plastering on the new hotel soon. He expects to do it up in very short order.

If Delta keeps growing like it is at the present time it will not be long till it will be the largest town in the county. People are coming here from everywhere. It is very seldom that a day passes that Delta does not add one or more people to her population. People are coming from other towns in covered wagons, bringing their belongings with them. They all seem to know a good thing when they see it, as they are all coming here.

Potatoes are selling for $1.00 per bushel now and are hard to get at that price. We hope that by another year we will raise plenty for our own wants and will not have to pay such extortionate prices for them.

Commenting on the new calendars which R. J. Law has got for his customers this season we wish to say that they are a long ways ahead of anything that we have ever seen around this locality.

Work is being pushed on the enlarging of the canal as fast as possible. The engineers are working early and late doing the surveying and team work will start some time about the latter part of this week.

The railroad strike has delayed Arthur Humphries' shipment of lumber, but by the time this reaches our readers the Delta Lumber Co. will probably have received four carloads of lumber, shingles and plaster. Others will soon follow until the yard is completely stocked.

Roy S. Dresser has gone into the horse business with Al Searls. They have bought up twenty-three brands of horses running the range and expect to gather in several hundred head this winter. Their first camp is at Clear Lake, and they expect to move over on the river in a few days.

J. M. Ashby, County Superintendent of Schools, was in Delta last week, and expects to visit most of the school of the county during the next two weeks.

The school at Clear Lake started up October 16 with Mary Peterson of Fillmore as teacher, and with 60 pupils.

W. J. Locke is a canny Scotchman who has been in Canada, the northwest, Mexico and South America, and finds Delta good enough for him. He has taken up 80 acres in West Delta, just north of the Abraham canal and is putting up a house to live in. He has made a good start this fall with 20 acres of fine looking rye.

The Bunker boys seem to know all about farming in Millard county. We don't think any of them have made a failure. Take C. T. Bunker, for instance, over on sections 3 and 4, north of the Abraham canal. A year ago this summer this land was in grease wood and this fall he has harvested 2,357 bushels of wheat and has got a nice stand of alfalfa started. He also raised the finest lot of potatoes you can see anywhere.

A bunch of about fifteen land buyers came into Delta last Saturday and Sunday to look over the prospects here. They were mostly Utah people. They think this country is all right and the majority will invest.

Two of our honorable county commissioners, Mr. Geo. Nixon of Holden and Edw. Bushnell of Meadow, were in Delta Sunday. Mr. Nixon and Bushnell ordered some improvements made in connection with our jail here. They also instructed Constable Soren I. Taylor to see that anyone guilty of breaking the law and sentenced to serve a term of imprisonment be locked up.

The writer had quite an extended talk with the county commissioners, and they assured him that they would only be too glad to help the people of Delta in any way that lay within their power. The writer asked them what became of our petition that we sent some time ago asking to grant us a town incorporation, and they answered: "We granted your petition, and if you haven't heard from it, then the fault lies with the county clerk." They further stated that the clerk had been sick, and they thought that was the reason we hadn't heard from him, but that they would see that it was attended to at once.

You ought to get a draw on the big candy raffle at A. C. Sorenson's store. It is by far the best raffle that has ever come in to the town, and every draw gets a prize. You also have a chance at the big 10-pound basket.

It is now estimated that Delta has the second largest population of any town in Millard County, and if the people continue to flock to Delta at the rate they are now coming, it will be less than six months from now when Delta will be able to boast of the largest population in this county.

IN AND AROUND DELTA

The Week's News from the Coming Metropolis

To prove to the public that land at Delta is selling rapidly, will give the amount sold by Jas. A. Melville in eight days. Mr. Melville told the writer that he sold 1040 acres alone in eight days. Besides the land sold by Mr. Melville, there has been a great amount sold by Mr. Poccart, Mr. Mahoney, Steele, Mr. Jack Thurston, Copening and McClain and others.

Mr. Jas. A. Melville who has been closely connected with the Delta Co. since it first come into existence, has handed in his resignation with that company, and after the 20th of this month he will devote all of his time to his personal affairs. Mr. Melville will spend the greater portion of his time here at Delta, as a great deal of his interests are here.

Abner and Bryant Johnson have joined the Commercial Club. They are both hustlers and good boosters, and will be a great help to the Club.

The Melville and Delta Irrigation Companies were in session all day Monday and Tuesday. The writer is unable to give any of the particulars at this time, except that they have decided to let contracts for building their main canals at once, and they expect to have them completed in ample time for the spring irrigation.

Monday the 13th, A. C. Sorenson sold five gresnoes, one to Avery Bishop, one to Ren Sampson, one to Anthony Steffenson, one to Ben Johnson and one to a California man. Mr. Sorenson claims he can sell scrapers cheaper than any dealer in Delta.

Mr. Taylor, Z. C. M. I. traveling hardware man, was in town a few days ago. Mr. Taylor reports a nice business in Delta.

The other morning Bunker's cow had left home. Bunker thought the cow had been stolen. People were out trying to locate either her or the thief. Among the gallant hunters was Joe Forest. Joe soon found the lost critter, but at the present he is compelled to eat his meals off the mantle piece. Joe explains matters as follows: "It was this way, Bunker's cow was stolen and I borrowed Avery's horse and went to hunt the cow. I was not used to riding horseback. I rode fast as I knew something had to be done quickly. I wore a union suit that was buttoned all the way around and I had to sit on one of them buttons. You see, the button done it all, and when I go riding again I won't wear a union suit, I can tell you that."

While all the threshing has not yet been done in West Delta, the results are proving very satisfactory to the farmers over there. A. A. Ackerman whose field of ripening oats the editor admired a few weeks ago yielded him 53 bushels to the acre, and it weighed 46 pounds to the bushel. If anyone can beat that on new land come to the front with your report.

Ed Johnson seems to be the champion wheat raiser, his yield was 46 bushels to the acre. Next.

IN AND AROUND DELTA

The Week's News from the Coming Metropolis

Mr. A. B. Ward from Tremonton, Utah, has purchased the S. W. corner lot in the D. R. Steven's block, on 1st North St. Mr. Ward will put up a livery barn on this property, and at this writing Knight & Marshall are figuring with Mr. Ward to put up his building. It will be a modern and up-to-date livery barn, and will be equipped with first-class rigs. In fact, Mr. Ward is now north buying his rigs and teams, and as soon as the barn is completed he will be ready to handle your livery and drayage business.

Mr. N. S. Bishop had a carload of coal come in this week, and it only took him three hours to dispose of it.

Mr. Geo. Billings, while lifting a sack of grain met with a very serious accident. Mr. Billings wrenched himself. Dr. Murphy and Dr. Harsh were called to attend to him; the two doctors were with Mr. Billings for several hours, and at this writing he is resting easier.

Mr. J. T. Brower is again seen on our streets. Mr. Brower has spent the summer in Canada.

Mr. Lesley Lewis, who some time ago had the misfortune to shoot himself through the leg is again able to be around town and shake hands with his many friends.

Mr. and Mrs. Frank Taylor, who have spent the summer in Sevier County has returned to Delta, where they expect to make their home.

Mr. Oda Day of Oasis was in Delta this week.

A. C. Sorenson, Jas. M. Rigby, Miss Milley Workman and Mrs. Riding have been selected as a committee to conduct the _____ and Oral stories _____ ____ expect to have ___ in this ___.

The County Commissioners have granted us a town incorporation and appointed the following town board: A. C. Sorenson, President; John E. Steele, E. S. Marshall, F. S. Lyman and Bert Johnson, directors.

MURDER SUSPECTS ARE UNDER ARREST

William S. Sandercock Is Slain By Burglars In Store at Garfield of Which He Was Manager

FIGHTS BRAVELY WITH SLAYERS

Body Marked By Blows and Bullet Wounds—Two Men Arrested at Lynndyl Being Brought to Salt Lake by Sheriff Sharp

BEATEN on the head with a chisel-pointed track hammer while he slept, and twice shot through the body, William S. Sandercock, forty-seven years old, was brutally murdered by burglars early yesterday morning in the store of the Sampson Meat & Grocery company at Garfield, of which he had been for two years the manager. He leaves a widow and three children at Austell, Cornwall, England.

Late yesterday afternoon word was sent to Sheriff Joseph C. Sharp that two men who were acting suspiciously were seen at Lynndyl, Utah, having arrived there some time during the day. The sheriff at once left for Lynndyl, arriving there at 9:30 last night. After a short search he came upon the men, who were under surveillance, and placed them under arrest upon suspicion of being the men who had committed the murder. They admitted, under a severe cross-examination, that they had been in Garfield the day before. Sheriff Sharp will bring the suspects to Salt Lake today.

...n mute evidence of the terrible
...uggle Sandercock had waged against
... assailants his dead body was
...und in the counter aisle of the gro-
...ry department of the store at 6:15
...clock yesterday morning by Theodore
...ndland, meat cutter of the butcher
...op. The dead man's hand was
...retched out toward a revolver which
...y on the floor almost within its
...rasp, and one foot was braced against
... counter partition in a position which
...med to suggest the desperation of
...he struggle the man had made to
...g himself within reach of the
...pon.
...he ugly wound on the head, and
...................from the bullet
............horrified the man
...made the discovery and, stepping
...ck, he twice called the name of his
...nager. No response came and
...ndland leaped out of the store and,
...nning down the streets of the set-
...lement, notified Deputy Sheriff
...Charles E. Wood of his startling dis-
...overy. Then he summoned Dr. D. L.
...arnard and together the three ran
...back to the store.
... After carefully studying the position
...of the body, Dr. Barnard examined the
...rounds. He found a deep indenta-
...on in the top of the skull, made with
...e track hammer which lay several
...rds away. A bullet had entered the

...e left arm, passing through the mus-
...es of the chest.
...The body was still warm and Dr.
...arnard declared the murder had been
...mmitted less than two hours prior
... its discovery.

Sheriff Summoned.

...Sheriff Joseph C. Sharp was sum-
...oned and the store and body of
...ndercock were not disturbed until
...e arrival of the officer. Deputy Sher-
...ff Wood searched Garfield for sus-
...cts and clews.
...Immediately upon the arrival of
...eriff Sharp a systematic examina-
...n was made of the premises. Through
...otprints it was almost clearly estab-
...hed that two burglars had attempt-
... to rob the store. In gaining en-
...nce one of them crawled upon a pile
... boxes at the entrance to the butch-
... shop and carefully picking a window
...t of a transom, peered through to
... if the door had been barred,
...ding that it had not, the men suc-
...ded in opening the door with a
...leton key
...eparating the butcher shop and gro-
...ry department is a broad archway
...ree-fourths down the store. Equipped
...th the track hammer, which prob-
...ly had been taken from the railroad
...ck shed, the burglars are believed
... have been feeling their way to the
...fe in the grocery department, when
...ey stumbled upon the cot occupied
... Sandercock.
...That the careful steps of the in-
...uders had not interrupted the sound
...eep of Sandercock is indicated by the
...nner in which it appears that he

MURDER SUSPECTS UNDER ARREST

William S. Sandercock Is Slain by Burglars in Store at Garfield.

(Continued From Page One.)

was attacked. It is presumed by Sheriff Sharp that the burglar leading the
way to the safe stepped upon the
cot unsuspectingly, and drove his hammer at Sandercock when the latter
raised his head in alarm.

Sandercock was a man of unusual
strength and vitality and that the
blow of the hammer did not kill him
outright is not surprising to his friends.
To avoid having to keep a watchman
in the store Sandercock had slept on
a cot in the counter aisle of the grocery department immediately under the
cash register. His position, as he slept,
was such that he could raise his right
hand to a revolver lying in a ledge under the register.

It is believed that when Sandercock
reached for the revolver after being
struck he fumbled the weapon, knocking it forward in the counter aisle,
and, in the effort to recover it, crawled
over the head of the cot to the floor
of the aisle. It was then, it is thought,
that the burglars opened fire on him,
stopping him with a bullet through his
head as he was about to grasp his
weapon.

Sheriff Sharp found six bullets in the
woodwork of the store; two that had
passed through Sandercock, and four
others, which missed their mark, but
had cut close to the body of the manager. All the bullets are of the deadly soft-nosed type and of .38-calibre.
These bullets may play a prominent
part in the search for the murderers.

Footprints Covered.

Heavy footprints indicate that the
burglars escaped through the door they
entered, but efforts to follow the
tracks proved futile, because the
streets already had been trodden by
hundreds of employes of the smelters
who passed the store on their way to
work an hour before the body of Sandercock was discovered.

...ercock was discovered.
That the motive of the crime was
robbery is indicated beyond a doubt
in the robbery of the cash register after Sandercock had been struck down.
It was known to contain 60 cents when
the manager retired.

The remainder of the money which
had been taken in at the store during
the evening was secreted upon the person of Sandercock. When his clothing
was examined, yesterday, it developed
that it had not been touched. The
amount was between $60 and $70. Because of the semi-monthly paydays at
the smelters business usually is heavy
for several days after the 15th of the
month and, cognizant of this fact, the
burglars probably had expected to find
large sums in the safe. However, Sandercock placed a large quantity of
money in a bank across the street from
the store at 5 o'clock Tuesday afternoon.

Sandercock was last seen in the
store at 11.30 o'clock Tuesday night,
when he concluded a long talk with
Arthur Baron, manager of the general
merchandise store of B. Baron & Co.,
two doors east of the Sampson grocery. During this conversation Baron
says Sandercock seemed gloomy and
confided with him an account of the
attentions he had been given by Miss
Mary O'Brien of Burlington, Ia., who
made her home at the Kensington
apartments during a recent visit to
Salt Lake.

"Sandercock was so gloomy as I
talked with him Tuesday night," said
Mr. Baron yesterday, "that when I first
learned he had been found dead in his
store I feared suicide. Finally he told
me that it was a letter from Miss
O'Brien and that in it she had invited
him to go to her home at Burlington
and enjoy Thanksgiving with members of her family.

"Then, stretching out his arms and
yawning, he told me that he had tired
of spending his days in Garfield and
soon hoped to go to some other part
of the country and continue his life
in a city of some consequence. When
I left him and went home 'Bill' tried
to smile his usual good-natured smile
as we shook hands, but it seemed that
he had to force the smile and when
I retired I was a bit worried about
him."

When Sheriff Sharp had concluded
his investigation about Garfield and
had satisfied himself that the murder-

ers were far away, the body was
brought to Salt Lake and placed in the
mortuary of Eber W. Hall, where it
will be prepared for funeral services
and burial.

W. Plummer, 119 South Main street,
who was a schoolday companion of
Sandercock, said last night that Sandercock was born in St. Blazey, Cornwall, England, forty-seven years ago.
Before coming to America he married,
and a widow and three children, now
residing at St. Austell, Cornwall, England, survive him. He also is survived
by one sister, Miss Helen Sandercock of
London, England.

During the spring of 1883 Sandercock came to America. Coming west,
he settled in Butte, Mont., the same
year and for a number of years worked
as a miner in the Alice mine. He came
to Utah from Butte and worked in the
mines at Park City, Fish Springs and
other mining centers and had engaged
extensively in prospecting. His latest
mining venture was at Austin, Nev.,
where, it is said, certain disagreements
prevented him from accruing a fortune.

Discouraged with mining, Sandercock returned to Salt Lake two years
ago and was made manager of the
Sampson Meat and Grocery company at
Garfield, of which Louis Sampson, of
the Oxford apartments here, is proprietor. By his congenial nature Sandercock won extensive popularity in
Garfield. When those who had gained
his friendship learned yesterday that
he had been murdered it was threatened that if his assailants are ever
captured attempts will be made to
lynch them.

"Sandercock was a rare type of a
man," said Mr. Sampson," his employer. "He had a way of making friend-
ships which it was hard to break; that
made him a model manager for a grocery. He could be sympathetic, jovial
and sad whenever the occasion required
as could no other man I had ever
known. He was courageous, but always diplomatic. Being thoroughly acquainted with the man, I can imagine
how desperately he fought against the
murderers, who had all the odds on
their side."

SHERIFF FINDS AN IMPORTANT CLEW

Bloody Handkerchief Discovered Near Scene of Sandercock Murder.

WOMAN TELLS A STORY

Overheard Two Men Talking at Garfield Station—Suspect Caught at Stockton.

Search for the murderers of William A. Sandercock, the store manager who was killed Tuesday night or early Wednesday morning at Garfield, centered yesterday about the whereabouts of a Willard Thomas, whose handkerchief, marked with his name, stained with blood and perforated with bullet holes was found on the railroad tracks at Garfield. Near where the handkerchief had been blown by passing trains a gunnysack, in which were nine half-sticks of giant powder, was found concealed by the high grass. That the bloody handkerchief may have belonged to one of the men who murdered the store manager, whom they found asleep in the store they had broken into, is the belief of Sheriff J. C. Sharp. That these two men also abandoned the giant powder is equally certain. Where they are and where they came from is an enigma for the solution of which there is now an aggregate reward of $1,500 offered.

William Findley, who was seen with Peter Mackey and William Lithgow, the two men arrested at Lynndyl and brought back to the county jail here, where they have been held while their suspicious actions the night of the murder are being investigated, was arrested at Stockton, Tooele county, yesterday afternoon. Deputy Sheriff Axel Steele went to Stockton last night to interview him. If he gives the same explanations of his actions the night of the murder as that given by Mackey and Lithgow he will be released. If not, he probably will be brought to Salt Lake and held until his movements can be investigated.

Findley was the man who was seen loitering about the Garfield depot before and after midnight Tuesday, and was with the other arrested men when they boarded the freight train going west after the murder is supposed to have been done. He was thrown off the train at Erda, a small town a few miles west of Garfield because the train brakeman declared, he was drunk. Mackey and Lithgow were allowed to ride on in to Lynndyl.

Reward Is Offered.

As soon as the newer developments in connection with the finding of the handkerchief and the giant powder at Garfield had almost dispelled the suspicion enveloping Mackey and Lithgow, Governor William Spry announced that the state would pay a reward of $500 for the arrest and conviction of the murderers of Sandercock. To this sum the county commissioners yesterday afternoon added another $500. T. W. Whiteley, president of the Garfield Improvement company, already had offered a reward of $500.

Mackey and Lithgow would have been released last night but for the arrest of Findley at Stockton. They probably will be released this morning unless some new light is thrown on the case by Findley.

Peter Mackey, sr., father of one of the boys, called upon the sheriff yesterday and asked that his son be released. The father is in business at Trenton, and there the son will have a home and a position as soon as the sheriff is through with him.

George Williams, an uncle of William Lithgow, the other young man, is a liveryman at Garfield, and he promised the sheriff that if his nephew were released he would see that employment was given him. Lithgow will be given into his uncle's keeping as soon as Findley's story is investigated. It is not thought probable that Findley will have anything to tell which could again cause Mackey and Lithgow to be suspected.

Woman Hears Conversation.

The most important development in the hunt for the murderers is the testimony of Mrs. William Dudley, wife of the station agent at Garfield. Mr. and Mrs. Dudley sleep in an addition to the freight depot close by the tracks, where the freight trains stop at Garfield.

Yesterday Mrs. Dudley related to the sheriff that Wednesday morning about 3 o'clock she was awakened by the sound of voices just outside her window. She did not look out, but she heard two men in conversation. One of them was weeping.

"The other man," said Mrs. Dudley, "I heard say, 'Come on, let's go back and get the rest of it.' The other man who was weeping answered: 'I won't do it. I've had enough of this. I'm going to get away from here.' The other man again tried to persuade his companion to 'come get the rest of it,' whatever they were talking about, and the one who cried refused again and said over and over again that 'he had had enough.'

"I am sure I could recognize the voices of the two men if I should hear them again, as I listened very closely, wondering if they were talking about anything in the freight house. I did not get up because I was afraid I would miss something they said. A few minutes after I first heard them the freight train, No. 81, came in and I did not hear them again."

The handkerchief found near this spot was discovered by a deputy sheriff who was searching for the revolver he thought the murderers might have thrown away near there. The handkerchief was caked with blood which was evidently not very old. The cloth was not powder-stained, but holes in it suggested at once that it had been used as a muffler for their revolver by the men who shot Sandercock.

Funeral services for Sandercock will be held at 1:30 o'clock Sunday afternoon from the mortuary chapel of Undertaken Eber W. Hall, 164 South West Temple street. Rev. P. A. Simpkin will officiate. Interment will take place in Mt. Olivet cemetery.

MORE LAND BUYERS.

Land seekers continue to arrive in Delta by nearly every train, and after looking over the ground they nearly all become buyers.

Copening & McClain report the following sales: J. F. Hamilton and Geo. W. Kerr of Kansas, have bought 120 acres southeast of Delta. Michael Caldwell of California is the buyer of 40 acres of improved land southwest of twon. An improved 40 acres has also been bought by W. W. Bowmer of Nevada. The land is just north of Delta. Harry Cole and Alfred Keely of Salt Lake have bought Carey Act lands on the west side. Geo. E. Schwartz is also a recent buyer in the same tract. They have also sold four town lots. They report 55 land seekers, mostly from various parts of Utah as having looked over the lands around Delta the past week. Fourteen outfits also arrived by team from Tooele. They had already taken up land in Sections 2, 3, and 4.

N. S. Bishop has also been showing land seekers over this section and reports a number of important deals nearly consummated. He is receiving an increasing number of enquiries from all over the country.

IN AND AROUND DELTA

The Week's News from the Coming Metropolis

The carpenters have nearly finished up their work on the lower floor of the Hotel Delta. The new furniture of the hotel is arriving and is being put in place as fast as room can be made for it. Mr. Cooper expects to give a turkey dinner next Sunday as a house warming.

George Day has been laid up with the grip and rheumatism for some time, and was too ill to be out of bed for a week. He crawled out Tuesday, however, to tell the editor that he was just getting in a big stock of dry goods and Christmas goods, and that his new line of rubbers and women's shoes couldn't be beat for price and quality anywhere.

Will H. Dennison has about finished plastering the basement of the amusement hall and is making a fine job of it. There is one large assembly hall and four smaller rooms in the basement, and their completion will add greatly to the usefulness of the building. The extension basement for the steam heating plant is finished and this much needed improvement is expected every day.

John Jimpson and D. A. Bunker of Salt Lake City, among the first land buyers in West Delta, were in town last week. They own 240 acres in section 4 which were all cleared three years ago. They were among the unfortunates who lost out the first two years, but they have never lost faith in the country. Their faith has been justified this year when from the part of their land that was cropped in grain they threshed 1955 bushels of wheat, 850 bushels of oats and 100 bushels of rye. Another harvest will put them to the good and their experience is that of dozens of other farmers on the west side.

S. W. Eccles has completed his new bake oven and is now turning out all sorts of bakery products.

We also note that he has just got in a fresh stock of groceries and is prepared for cold and muddy weather with a big stock of overshoes and rubbers.

The Delta Dramatic Club is practicing a new play which they expect to present to the public within the next two weeks. Watch the Chronicle for fuller particulars.

A. C. Sorenson & Co. expect to get into their new and more commodious quarters this week where they will be able to make a better display of their goods and wait on their customers with greater convenience. In the meantime ask about those celebrated Rouss Bros shoes just received direct from their factory in New York. Also those thick, warm, Utah made blankets; just the thing for these cold nights.

A. C. Browen, father of John T. Browen, who used to be a resident of Delta, was in town last week. Mr. Browen is an old timer of Utah, and built one of the first adobe houses in Salt Lake.

T. C. Gronning, our new blacksmith, has been kept so busy since located himself on the lot he purchased from Dr. Dryden, that he has not had time to finish his shop. He evidently fills a long felt want and though his wife says he hardly stops long enough to eat his meals, he's a week behind on his work. Mr. Gronning is not only an all 'round blacksmith, but is an experienced machinist as well, and can fix up boilers, engines and any kind of machinery. Although he just came from Oregon he is an old Millard County boy, having been raised in Scipio and his parents still live there.

As will be seen from a notice elsewhere Miss Octavia Murphy intends to start a dancing class in a short time. It is a class for young beginners, and Miss Murphy starts in by physical exercises, which develop graceful movement and strength of the limbs, which are the first requirements for graceful dancing. Miss Murphy is well qualified for the work, as she took lessons in this department in the Sacred Heart Academy for two years.

Job Riding, who has been over in Sevier County for the past month, came over for a couple of days last week with some land buyers.

Contracts for the enlargement of the main canal are being signed up and probably by the time this issue reaches our readers 200 teams and 150 men will be at work. There are 30 contractors so far and preference is given men owning land on the Delta tract, and the size of the contract is in proportion to their hodlings—a very fair arrangement. The prices paid is from 10 to 75 cents per yard, and those of the cnotractors we have talked with consider the price a very fair one. Unless the weather continues very cold or some unexpected difficulties arise good wages will be made, according to Engineer Martin the contracts run till March 1. This will provide much needed work for many men, put money in circulation and enable many men to make payment on their land who otherwise would be unable to do so.

The Arcade Furnishing House has got in some more new goods this week. Among them is a number of the celebrated White washers, one of the best washers on the market.

R. J. Law has just got in his first installment of holiday goods and is showing a fine assortment of toys, dolls, albums, toilet articles, etc., to please both young and old. He has already sold considerable, his customers evidently following the oft-repeated advice to do their Christmas shopping early.

Although things are not get settled at the Hotel Delta, Landlord Cooper is doing a rushing business and taking good care of everybody that comes. The tables are filled at every meal and in the evening the office presents a very busy appearance.

There has been such a demand for merchandise the past few weeks owing to the big influx of people that the merchants have run short on some goods. For a while there was a shortage of potatoes, sugar, butter and eggs, also coal. Eggs and all sorts of farmers produce will find a ready sale at the highest prices in Delta.

Wm. Hoff, who has done business all over the west, came from California a few weeks ago to look things over. They looked good to him and he bought 160 acres southeast of Delta. This week he began hauling lumber for his buildings and will begin at once to improve his land with the intention of putting it all in crops next spring.

Jno Dennam and J. J. Willets, from Salt Lake have also bought lands in the same section and will have improved farms next summer.

A. B. Ward is rushing his new livery stable up at a rapid rate and will soon be ready for business. He will go north in a day or two to bring down his horses and rigs.

E. J. Ednay and N. H. Folsom are the latest new-comers to Delta. They drove all the way from Green River, Utah, with their families and outfits. They were eleven days on the trip. Their farms are southeast of town.

County Clerk Nephi Anderson of Fillmore was over this week to see about the threshing on his farm east of Delta. He also went over the lands

of Delta. He also went over the lands in West Delta with a view of locating several families from Fillmore.

W. E. Bowman bought from McCloin & Co. this week 40 acres, a mile north of Delta, and a city lot near the depot. Mr. Bowman is in the merchandising and lumber business in Moapa, and expects to close out there and go into business in Delta in the spring.

Arthur Humphries is doing a rushing business in his lumber yard, and teams are driving out every day with loads of lumber.

The mail car goes north from Delta on the midnight train. This is a great improvement. Another improvement will be making Delta a money order office, which may be done the first of the year.

Have you noticed Geo. Day's windows? He has some attractive lettering on both sides and behind the windows are some Christmas goods that are also attractive. There is also a nurse girl in the window that bows an invitation for everyone to enter. She is quite a novelty.

Stewart Eccles & Son want to get out of the dry goods business and devote themselves exclusively to confectionery and bakery goods. They are therefore making a special sale and offering everything in this line at cost for cash. The sale begins next Saturday and continues through the month. Besides low prices every cash purchase on one dollars worth of goods gets a chance for a $10.00 set of silverware.

Jacob De Bree has just threshed his crop and got 3155 bushels of grain from 100 acres. This is pretty good for a first crop.

People on the west side don't spend all their time working, but enjoy themselves in social intercourse as well. Mr. and Mrs. "Denver" Smith entertained the Watts and Albro families at their Thanksgiving dinner, and Mrs.

Herman Munster had Mr. and Mrs. Ackerman to help eat their big Thanksgiving turkey. Jerome Tracy had J. J. Clark's family over for a similar occasion. There was also another very enjoyable party at J. J. Clark's a short time ago, about 40 people were present and music and dancing made the time pass very quickly and pleasantly.

The Water Users Association held their annual election last Saturday night and about 35 members were present. The officers are A. Watts, president; Frank Foot, Secretary-treasurer; Jas. Connelly, Jerome Tracy, M. A. Abbott and J. Thompson, executive committee. There are about 60 members at present and more are coming in all the time. The association want to get in every water user in this section so they can act as one man when action is necessary. They want a big attendance at their next meeting the first Saturday in January, as matters of importance are to be taken up.

Millard County Progress
December 8, 1911

OAK CITY
S. L. Rawlinson, Representative

The freezing nights, the sunny days, and the absence of snow, have furnished an excellent opportunity for wood hauling the past two weeks. Most of our citizens are taking advantage.

We have heard little in the past few years, concerning "bees" corn husking bees are gone, apple and peach bees have settled long since, rag bees are winter killed, but the old woodbee swarmed one week ago last Friday and settled in the near by cedars.

As a result thirty loads of wood with a few promises for more came tumbling into the school and church grounds.

One week later, the women swarmed. They flew in all directions. The men said nothing. For what man dares set his hand against the inevitable will of a women, if his stomach be empty and her actions promise food? I am told that some thirty chickens, with promises of more, "lost their heads" and hopped and flew into boiling pots and kettels, under the soporific charm of women. Flour was turned into sandwitches, pies and cakes and the hungry wood bees were feasted. Dancing was also indulged in.

Thanksgiving was fittingly celebrated here.

On Wednesday evening the schools rendered a creditable program, full of thanksgiving thoughts.

On Thursday evening a basket ball game begun the program, followed by dancing.

The game was our first this season, and showed well. It was full of exciting circumstances. The Juniors and Seniors have always been close players here and were none the less last Thursday. It was eithers game until near the last when the featherweights lost their endurance and left their score 30 to 29.

All of our students came home for Thanksgiving vacation.

William Prows who left our town 15 years ago, to take up his abode in Mexico, is here paying old timers a visit. He now resides in Garfield County.

IN AND AROUND DELTA

The Week's News from the Coming Metropolis

The Hub Mercantile and Produce Co. has had a big sign painted on the roof of its warehouse which attracts attention for a long distance. Manager Steele reports business picking up. He sold one of their celebrated Millburn wagons last week and with the large number of settlers coming in he expects a big call for farm machinery in the spring. Hay is so scarce and high here that he has ordered two carloads from Idaho.

S. W. Eccles has also decorated his store with a big sign—bakery being especially conspicuous. He is making arrangements to have his celebrated Pavant bread handled by the stores in the adjoining towns.

W. R. Walker, the Chronicle's valued representative at Oak City, was a caller at the office last Saturday.

The Delta town board held their first meeting last Saturday night. The board consists of A. C. Sorenson, president; John Steele, E. Marshall, B. F. Johnson and F. S. Lyman. They appointed M. Stapley as clerk, Anthony Stephenson, treasurer, Dr. A. Murphy, town physician and C. A. Clawson, marshal. All the officers will serve without pay for the first year at least. Their next meeting will be held on Thursday evening, when the question of revenue, town ordinances, etc., will be taken up.

Another Pioneer Laid To Rest.

It was no great surprise to the relatives and friends of Henry Judson McCullough when word came to Fillmore that he had finished his mortal work and died at Delta on the 17th, as he had been failing in health for some time, His remains were conveyed to Fillmore on Monday and funeral services were held in the Chapel on Tuesday. The speakers were Joseph V Robison and Joseph D Smith. Appropriate singing and music was furnished by the ward choir and conducted by Miss Katherine Woodhouse. We very much regret being unable to join with the rest of our community in paying a parting tribute of respect to that dear friend. And for many years co-laborer of ours in church work, owing to being confined to our room with sickness.

Henry J. McCullough was born in Jackson, Michigan, April 13, 1842. His parents having become members of the "Mormon Church" they with their children were among the exiles who had been driven from their homes by mobs and while on their way westward, the father was one of the 500 responding to a call by government representatives for a batalion to march to the seat of war in Mexico. Henry was then only 4 years old and the next year his mother died when the children had to be distributed among friends to be cared for in a way. The family came to Utah in 1852 and soon after made their home in Fillmore where Henry married Helen Mar Callister, who bore him 19 children, seven of whom with their mother survive him.

Our pleasant acqaintence with this good man dates back to 1889, when he returned from a mission to England and to the best of our knowlege he has been in the harness ever since. He never slid back. Always faithful and true. We have worked together in Sunday School, in Bishopric and High Council, and our associations have always been most agreeable. He was one of the most kindly and even tempered men we ever met His temper and disposition was like a beautiful spring morning and his character as spotless as the fallen snow.

The deceased had his home a few years in Loa, where he was postmaster and superintendant of Sunday School, after which he came back to Fillmore and shortly after moved to Burtner (Delta) where he held the position of postmaster when death came and relieved him.

TOWNSITE OF DELTA

The Plan of an Up-to-Date Town and How it is Laid Out.

A stranger who drops off at Delta and looks over the town can't see that it is laid out with any regularity. He sees houses scattered irregularly over an area of about a mile square and wonders why it has not been built up compactly from some common center. Most agricultural settlements have grown up on the four corners of two well traveled highways. But it was quite different with Delta.

In the spring of 1906 about fifteen of the owners of land in the 10,000 acre Melville tract met at Oasis to discuss the location and plan for a new town which they proposed to name Burtner in honor of the passenger agent of the Salt Lake Route, who had done much for this section of Millard county. The plan was substantially as given below, the site covering an area of one mile and a quarter. Through the center of the plot running east and west was Clark street, named in honor of Senator Clark, principal owner of the Salt Lake Route. North and south through the center was located Main street. Both of these streets were eight rods wide. The plot was divided into 110 blocks 20 rods square, containing about five acres each, with a two-rod alley running through it. One block was reserved in the center of each of the four quarters of the town for public purposes. One block was reserved in the center of the town as public square.

Another block at the corner of Main and Clark streets was reserved for school purposes and two blocks and two halves at the head of Main street were reserved for a public park. The streets were numbered east and west from Main street and north and south from Clark street as they are in Salt Lake City, and were six rods wide. As Clark street was intended for the business street of the new town, the alleys ran through the blocks parallel with this street so as to give access to the rear of every business house. The residence lots of the town,

about an acre and a quarter each, were distributed by lot, every owner of a forty acre farm being entitled to one lot. Of course this scattered the ownership of the lots all over the townsite, and when the owners got ready to build, the houses were of course considerably scattered. Many of the original owners have never built, or have sold out. One result of this method of distribution is that it has kept the value of lots at a pretty uniform price, as one could have neighbors in any part of the townsite.

The business lots on Clark street were sold to the highest bidders and it has developed according to the original plans, into the business street of the town. The business houses on this street are as follows: R. J. Law, corner of Main and Clark; E. W. Eccles, near the amusement hall; Job Riding, telephone exchange; Mrs. Wintorrose has the cement blocks for a building adjoining. Next west is the Arcade Furnishing House, then the Delta meat market. Across the street the Chronicle office, next to which the Hub Mercantile Co. expects to put up their new store building, and further east is A. C. Sorenson & Co.'s mercantile establishment and Knight & Marshall's new building, at present used as a carpenter shop. It is expected that the postoffice will be ultimately located on Clark street, its present location being on Second West and Third North. As the amusement hall is located on Clark street and the town and ultimately the county buildings will be located on the public square reserved for this purpose. This will naturally attract the business houses to this part of the town for several years to come or the lots are put up to a figure out of proportion to their real value. The quickest way to kill Clark street as a business center is to sell the lots for speculative purposes, or hold them out of use in expectation of a big profit through the improvements made

by other people. We think it will pay owners of these lots to sell some of their lots at cost to any one who will put up a good building, and we think this is the policy of all those who own lots on Clark street. Any man who wants a lot for business purposes and agrees to put up a good building can get a lot for from $75 to $300, according to the size and location. We think this is remarkably cheap, and is a great encouragement to those who want to go into business in Delta. There is very little speculation in land, the desire being rather to see the town grow along legitimate business lines.

As we stated the residence lots are about an acre and a quarter in size. This enables the home owner to have a garden and an orchard, have a stable and a cow, a team and some chickens and other things necessary to an agricultural community, as it will be during the early years of its development. The alley in the rear of each lot makes a convenient arrangement for all out-buildings to be in the rear of the lot so that the main streets will be kept clear of everything but residences. As the town grows these lots will undoubtedly be subdivided into smaller residence plots, the original owners reaping the benefit of the enhanced price arising from the growth of population.

The ownership of the lots being divided among so many people and having been obtained at so low a price, the prices are still remarkably cheap. Delta is not a one-man town or a corporation town laid out for speculative purposes. It is a town laid out by the owners of adjacent farms whose only desire is to see it develop into an attractive city of home owners. When we see that residence lots of an acre and a quarter can be had for from $60 to $300, according to location, we can see that unusual opportunities are offered to home seekers. Where can you find a new town where residence lots can be bought for as low a price per acre as farm lands are sold? It is also to be remembered that the irrigation system provides water for every lot.

We have heard it remarked that the streets six and eight rods wide will be too expensive to keep up; that they will be nothing but streaks of mud and dust between weed lined sidewalks. But we think this is a short sighted view. Delta is laid out with the expectation that it will before many years be the principal city south of

Salt Lake. No other town in the state has such an area of splendid farming land immediately surrounding it, and its founders laid it out with a knowledge of this fact. Is it not the wide streets that constitute the principal charm of Salt Lake City? Does any one doubt that in time Delta will have street cars running on its principal streets? That they will be lined with trees, covered with gravel from the nearby bluffs, sprinkled with water from a city water system drawing its supply from that pure and inexhaustable subterranean lake that underlies this whole valley? Being a town of home owners, made up of progressive people from every part of the country will they not be interested in beautifying their homes, and also see that we have a progressive city government, that the streets, alleys, ditches and public parks are kept in an attractive condition?

The town looks raw and unkept now. You can't locate its streets or parks or vacant lots today. For two years and over the people had a hard struggle for existence. It is only since the last harvest that they have begun to get on their feet. But now things are coming their way. By next spring several hundred new families will have settled in and around Delta. The town has just been incorporated. We have a live town board and the work of public improvement will go forward as rapidly as the revenues will permit. A fine new depot—the largest on the line south of Salt Lake—is nearly completed. A new modern hotel has just been built. From 30 to 85 land buyers come into Delta every week. About 4,000 acres of land were sold around Delta during December. Take another look at the plat of the townsite and see if Delta hasn't the making of a beautiful modern city. If you are looking for an opening either as a farmer or a business man, write the Delta Commercial Club or any of the Chronicle advertisers for information.

The laughing plant is not a flower that laughs, but one that creates laughter, if the printed accounts of travelers can be believed, says an English paper. It grows in Arabia and is called the laughing plant because the seeds produce effects like those caused by laughing gas. The flowers are of a bright yellow, and the seed pods are soft and woolly, while the seeds resemble small black beans. Only two or three grow in a pod. The natives dry and pulverize them, and the powder taken in small doses makes the soberest person behave like a circus clown or a madman, for he will dance, sing, and laugh most boisterously and cut the most fantastic capers and be in an uproariously ridiculous condition for about an hour. When the excitement ceases the exhausted exhibitor of these antics falls asleep, and when he awakens he has not the slightest remembrance of his frisky doings.

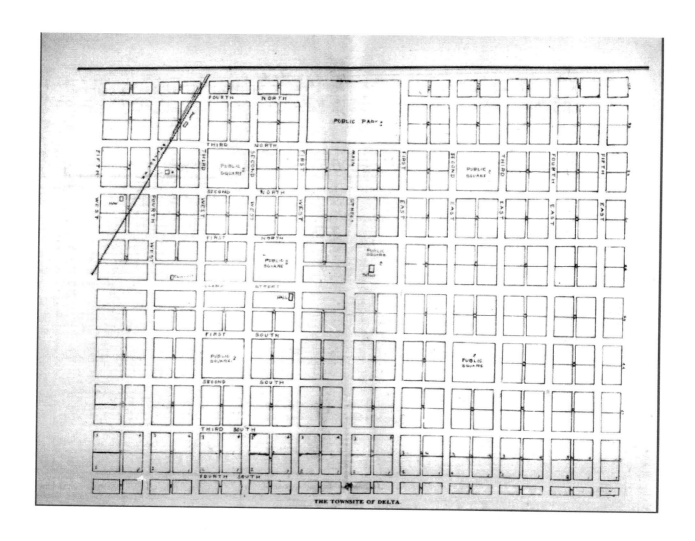

THE TOWNSITE OF DELTA.

IN AND AROUND DELTA

The Week's News from the Coming Metropolis

The oldest inhabitant of Delta does not remember to have experienced such a continuous spell of cold weather as we have had during the past six weeks. The thermometer has hung around zero most of the time. But there has been no wind, the days, for the most part have been bright and sunny and the night sky studded with scintillating stars. One does not suffer from the cold as in a humid climate, where the fierce winds pierce one like needles. There has also been a heavy snow fall all over the county which has served as a blanket to protect fall grain and young alfalfa, will supply the needed moisture to the thousands of acres of dry farms and assure plenty of water for every mountain stream to irrigate its tract of land.

The gates of the big Sevier bridge reservoir, which stores the water for all the Pavant valley irrigation systems, were closed the middle of October and the water has been accumulating at the rate of about 1,000 acre feet per day. When the water had risen to about ten feet of the top of the big dam the gates were raised and the water is now going down the river. As this is the dry season one can imagine the volume of water that flows in the spring, when the winter snows are melting. With more storage reservoirs enough water could be saved to water two or three times the amount of land now under canals. Recent surveys of the reservoir show that its capacity is 104,000 acre feet instead of 90,000, as the former survey gave. Millard can have the largest flow of water for irrigation purposes of any county and it has the largest area of fertile lands that can be watered by it of any county in the state.

One of the most notable social events of the holiday season was the musical party given on Thursday evening of last week by Mr. and Mrs. N. S. Bishop, the pioneer family of Delta. Miss Feral McClain, the accomplished daughter of Mr. McClain, senior member of the leading real estate firm of Delta, McClain & Copening, officiated at the piano in a very charming manner, playing and singing some of the most popular opera pieces. James A. Melville, of Salt Lake City, father of the Melville project, acquitted himself in a very creditable manner. Mr. N. S. Bishop sang a mowrie song in a very entertaining manner. Mrs. Nephi Stewart, of Salt Lake, gave a musical Norwegian song and Miss McClain sang several beautiful German songs. Mr. F. L. Copening, of Utah, give an amusing incident of real life, entitled, "What's Good for Grandfather and Father is Good Enough For Me." Mr. Rod McDonald, of Cincinnati, told us what Delta would be ten years hence. Mr. Bassett, of American Fork, rendered a recitation in a very effective manner. Solos and quartettes were given by other members of the party. At the conclusion of the program the hostess, Miss Anna Bishop, served a buffet luncheon to the guests. Every one declared it a rare and delightful evening's entertainment. The party was mainly for the visiting guests at the Hotel Delta and those present were James A. Melville, Mr. and Mrs. Nephi Albia, Iowa; Jack and Leo Thurston, Morgan, Utah; Dr. Baymiller, Thos. Poutaker, William Smith and daughter, Chicago; Mrs. Glosserman, Philadelphia.

Among the holiday visitors to Delta the past week were Will Willoughby, of Bingham, who has been visiting his brother, Henry; Mr. and Mrs. D. O. Wilcox, of Idaho, who have been visiting Mrs. Helen McCullough; Miss Ella Bassett and children, and Mr. and Mrs. Ingersoll, who have been visiting at the home of his sister, Mrs. E. S. Marshall.

John Alory has returned home from Garland, where he has been working in the sugar factory.

The Hub Mercantile Co. has just received the agency for the Reeves & Company traction engines, separators and plows. This firm has a big manufactory at Columbus, Ohio, and their machinery is among the most reliable made.

The ice harvest is on in full force at Delta and a large amount is being put up by different people. The Salt Lake Route is getting out several carloads for use on the road.

The Hub Mercantile Co. received two cars of hay this week, and N. S. Bishop, a car of Kemerer coal and four cars of Castle Gate coal are on the road. It takes a long time for freight to get to Delta these days.

Notwithstanding the holiday season about twenty-five land seekers have been in Delta the past week and the company's automobiles have been out every day, showing land to the visitors. About 1,000 acres has been sold the past week.

A. B. Ward has his new livery stable in operation and is prepared to furnish rigs for hire, to feed horses and sell hay and grain. The livery stable joins the growing ranks of Chronicle advertisers.

The farmers' demonstration train is billed to be in Delta on January 17. This train did excellent service last spring and will doubtless draw still larger crowds.

On another page will be found a cut of the town site of Delta and a descriptive write up. We think it will prove interesting to those who think Delta is a straggling looking town.

On Christmas Day Willie Bassett, local agent of the Saturday Evening Post received word from the publishers that he was second in the race for a premium of a Shetland pony, harness and cart. Number one was only seven copies ahead of him. The contest closes on January 27, and Willie hopes to be number one by that time. He is a rustler and it is hoped his many friends will help to make him a winner. Willie will also handle the Chronicle and we have no doubt he will make a success of that also.

Bert Johnson was the winner of the big rocking chair given away by the Arcade Furniture House, and Mrs. Delia Knight won the musical album given by A. C. Sorenson & Co. No. 35 was the lucky number.

During the past week the town board has been struggling with the new town ordinances. They have been fixing the occupation taxes which are to be levied on every business and graded according to the volume of business.

An enjoyable program was rendered at the Amusement hall on Christmas Day, which was greatly enjoyed by the audience of about 300 persons. The program was as follows: Address of welcome, by Bishop Maxfield; recitation, Mrs. Elija Hook; reading, Mrs. Cassie Riding; male quartet, Wilford McClellan and company; recitation, Miss Edith Bunker; a Christmas talk by John Steele. In the evening a dance was given for the children and one in the evening to the older ones. Both occasions were greatly enjoyed by the large crowds that attended.

Although the people of West Delta are somewhat isolated, they do not lack for social amusement. They hold a party at some of their homes every Friday evening and have for several months past. Two weeks ago one was held at Lyman Moulton's, and last week one was given at Frank Foot's new house. Everyone has a good time at these dancing parties.

Mrs. Ashby, of Woods Cross, has been visiting her son, Charles Ashby, and getting acquainted with her new grandchild.

Dr. W. W. Stockham, of Pioche, writes that he will be in Delta in a short time. He has ordered a stock of drugs and will open a drug store and practice his profession.

Nephi Stewart returned to Salt Lake Sunday night, after completing the job of plumbing for the Hotel Delta.

Miss Ferol McClain left for her home in Salt Lake Sunday night, after spending several days with her father, Charles McClain.

Dr. Dryden and wife, of Pioche, who formerly lived in Delta, paid the town a visit last week.

Bymiller Bros., of Delta, went to Salt Lake Sunday night to make some filings on government land on the West Side.

John Alory has returned home from Garland, where he has been working in the sugar factory.

The Hub Mercantile Co. has just received the agency for the Reeves & Company traction engines, separators and plows. This firm has a big manufactory at Columbus, Ohio, and their machinery is among the most reliable made.

The ice harvest is on in full force at Delta and a large amount is being put up by different people. The Salt Lake Route is getting out several carloads for use on the road.

John Avery Bishop took a business trip to Hinckley last Wednesday.

The Delta public school opened on Tuesday with a fair attendance.

R. H. Humphreys, L. L. Whiting and W. H. Ide, of Winchester, Cal., on New Years day were looking over the country, with a view to purchasing farms

R. J. Fischer, an old acquaintance of the editor's, was down from Salt Lake a couple of days looking for a business location.

The heating plant for the amusement hall has at last arrived and is being installed. It will certainly be appreciated as the hall is is hard to heat with one stove. Another badly needed improvement is a rack to hang hats, overcoats and wraps on. At present they have to be piled in the windows or on chairs.

Correspondents should send their matter in on Monday as the way trains are now running correspondence is not likely to get through in time if sent any later.

No. 227 won the candy basket at A. C. Sorenson & Co.'s. If the holder of the lucky number will call at the store he can get the prize.

The Young Ladies Mutual gave a leap year party on the evening of New Years day. There was a big crowd out and every one pronounced it a grand success. The young ladies were very impartial and the married men got as much dancing as the young fellows

OCCURRENCES AT OAK CITY

W. R. Walker, Representative

The Oak City Basket Ball team made a trip to Delta last Wednesday and brought back victory for their town.

The people of Delta gave their team poor support. There were hardly enough out to act as officials. No team can bring honors to their city without the support of their townspeople.

Oak City also defeated Delta in Oak City.

Saturday night a dance was held after the game and a big time was enjoyed by all present. The Oak City team wishes to thank the people of Delta for the royal time they were shown.

Last Friday night the people gave Mr. C. P. Christensen a welcome dance. A big time was had by everybody. He even showed his appreciation by showing one of our nice young ladies the time of her life.

"The Great Winterson Mine" was played to a great success. Mr. Eddie Jacobson as Simeon Stout, was an object for a good laugh. S. J. Rawlinson and Miss Silva Lovell, as Robert Melrose and Miss Grace Winterson, gave the young people, as well as the married ones, a good idea how to make love in the right way. Leo Lyman, as Eb. Winterson had them laughing all the time. The other actors all took their parts fine and everybody present said they got their money's worth.

Mr. Earnest Ottley came to spend the holidays with his many friends. Sunday he was showing the young ladies a nice sleigh ride, while the other boys looked on.

A nice program was rendered in Mutual Sunday night. It was an educational feast.

The girls are going to show the boys the "one" time of their lives, while the boys are anxiously waiting for such a time.

The men folks have declared war on the Jack Rabbit, and many are expected to lose their lives Wednesday.

The Old Folks were shown a big time last Thursday.

Millard County Chronicle
January 11, 1912

THE WEEK AT OASIS

Mrs. Mina Jackson, Representative

Cold! Well, I guess it is, the coldest weather in many years. The weather bureau estimates the temperature down to 18 below zero. That is going some.

A number of people are putting up ice for summer use. It looks as thought it would be plentiful next summer.

Miss Bell and Velora Styler are home from Caliente, where they spent the holidays.

Christmas passed off very quietly, the main feature being visiting among families. But on Christmas evening a very appropriate program was rendered by the Sunday school, which was enjoyed by all. After the program all participated in a dance till in the small hours of the night.

Miss Grace Davis was a visitor here this week from Fillmore.

On Wednesday afternoon the young people of this place went to Delta with the basket ball team, which played a game with Delta's junior team, the score being 20 to 25, in favor of Delta. The Oasis team was not in practice, hence their losing out.

On Thursday evening the young men's M. I. A. gave a social and it was the one feature of the holidays. All responded to the calls made of them and many sporty games followed, after which a delicious luncheon, together with hot chocolate, was served.

Miss Laura Johnson, of Oasis, has just returned home from Fillmore, where she has been spending her holidays.

On New Year's eve was given a grand leap year ball.

Born—To Mr. and Mrs. William Ward, a baby boy, on December 27. All concerned doing nicely. A Christmas present from Dr. Damron.

Mr. Sims and Jacob C. Hawley made a flying trip to Salt Lake on Sunday night.

Mr. Barton, our school teacher, has just opened up a first-class barber shop in Della Church's ice cream parlor building. He opens on Friday after school and all day on Saturday. He does good work.

Our place was visited with quite a blizzard from the north on Sunday last. Also very cold weather.

Mr. John Thornley, of Kaysville, was a visitor this week; also Mr. Baker, of the Baker Lumber company. The above company has just received three carloads of lumber and two of coal in the past ten days.

Miss Alta Huff has just returned home from a two weeks' visit in Salt Lake.

Miss Velora Styler, of Oasis, and Arthur James, of Black Rock, were joined in the bonds of wedlock on Wednesday, January 3rd, in the First Congregational church at Salt Lake City. We join in wishing them a happy union down the stream of life.

Mr. and Mrs. H. L. Jackson entertained a company at their home on January 4th. There will be an old peoples' party given next Friday, January 12, 1912.

Mr. F. H. Church is still in a poor condition of health. On January 20, the old gentleman will be 88 years of age.

Bishop John Beckstrand, of Meadow, was seen on our streets.

The district school resumed its work after a two-weeks' vacation.

A baby boy was born at the Jap foreman's last week, the first Japanese born in the county. Dr. Damron was in attendance.

The report of the ward was read in meeting yesterday, giving it a very good recommendation and in good condition.

Miss Erma Turner, of Holden, was here last week, visiting with friends.

Mrs. Barton's mother, from Park City, is here, visiting for a week.

IN AND AROUND DELTA

The Week's News from the Coming Metropolis

At the meeting of the Commercial club last Saturday evening several new members were received and quite a number of communications were received. One important matter the Commercial club has succeeded in accomplishing is getting the county commissioners to designate about 20 miles of county road tributary to Delta. One is through the West Delta tract and the other is a continuation of Clark street east and south across the canal. This will give a good outlet to our city and Holden. The secretary of the Salt Lake Commercial club wrote that the meeting of the Utah Development League and the Utah Press association would be held at Salt Lake on January 23, and wanted the club to be represented. The next meeting of the club will be held on Saturday next, at which the annual election of officers will be held. It is to be hoped that every member of the club will be present and that when the club begins its next year's work it will have the hearty co-operation interested in a bigger and better Delta.

The cold weather of the past few weeks has made a big demand for coal, and N. S. Bishop has disposed of four car loads in the past two weeks. It takes only about two days for a car load to be cleaned out, and if you delay getting your supply when a car comes in you are likely to go without. Mr. Bishop has several more cars on the way and a good many, including the editor, are anxiously awaiting it.

Although the new depot is not quite completed inside, Agent Hawes has moved in and he feels as proud as if ~~someone had given him a mansion~~. The old box cars have been removed and the coal shed in front has been taken up to the north end of the yard so the new depot looms up in fine style.

About forty land-buyers have been in Delta the past week. They come from different parts of Utah, from California and from the Eastern states. Everyone is satisfied with the country and every one buys land now or will buy in the near future. The Chronicle is getting a good many subscribers from the visitors. N. S. Bishop reports the sale of 40 acres of unimproved land two miles south of Delta for $50 per acre and three or four prospective buyers on the string.

The Delta Home Dramatic club will make its first appearance before the Delta public next Saturday afternoon and evening in the famous play, "The Old New Hampshire Home." They have sent for scenery, properties and costumes, and expect to present it in good shape. The money realized will be applied toward buying scenery for the hall, and other plays for the same purpose will be given during the winter. Come out and see a good play presented by your own young people. The following is the cast of characters: Farmer Winthrop, Fred S. Lyman; Edward Van Dusen, A. P. Wallace; Oliver Stanhope, Douglas Lisonbee; Zeb Watkins, Donald Callister; Mickey Mullins, William Vandervanter; Moser Jacinsky, A. E. Stephenson; Rawlings, Price Lewis; Mabel Winthrop, Helen Callister; Tilly, Eliza Hook; Mrs. Winthrop, Cassie Riding; Muffins, Lemira Bishop.

William Walker was over from Oak City this week. He has bought William Ottley's land over in West Delta and proposes to farm it the coming summer.

LOST—A gold watch fob. Will the finder kindly return to The Chronicle office.

The Chronicle has added a telephone to its equipment and when you want the editor ring two short and two long calls. This makes twenty-seven subscribers on the Delta exchange. The Chronicle is getting out a directory of every exchange in the county and when it is completed every subscriber in the county will get a copy. The business of the company is growing, so that it looks as if a central office soon will have to be put in on the west side.

M. M. Steele, a member of the State Land Board, was in Delta this week, visiting his son, John Steele.

George Snow, James A. Melville, Lloyd Seigler, Joseph A. Cannon, B. H. Baker, of the Baker Lumber Co., and Milton Moody were among the prominent people in Delta this week.

Milton Moody expects to open up a real estate office in Delta in a short time.

There has been an agreeable change in the weather this week, and the long spell of cold weather seems to have been broken.

IN AND AROUND DELTA

The Week's News from the Coming Metropolis

A. C. Sorenson, Hiram Knight and E. S. Marshal returned this week from Salt Lake where they have been for several days buying a big stock of goods for the new firm of the Delta Mercantile and Implement Co. They intend to occupy the store now occupied by A. C. Sorenson and also the adjoining frame building recently built by Knight and Marshal. They are going to have an up-to-date stock and you want to look out for their big announcement in a few weeks.

The cold weather has somewhat interfered with putting in the new heating plant at the amusement hall but men are now at work on it and it will be in place in a short time.

A gasoline engine has arrived for the Hotel Delta. It will be used to pump water up into the big tank over the well from whence it will be carried to the kitchen, wash room and bath room.

The cold weather seems to be over in Millard county and the snow is rapidly disappearing. One thing about sunny weather as we are now having this country is that a few days of ing quickly dries up the mud and we soon have good roads. Also that while we have had a long spell of cold weather it hasn't been as cold as in Colorado, Wisconsin, Idaho and many other states nor has it done any damage here. We hear of it killing the peach crop in Colorado, the orange crop in California and fruit trees elsewhere. Come to a country where you never lose a crop from frosts, blizzards, cyclones, droughts or floods.

The temporary frame structure to be occupied by the Chronicle printing office will be completed in a few days. It isn't any imposing building but we prefer to start small and grow with the growth of business. In a short time we will have in a stock of all the leading magazines, newspapers and fancy stationery.

Since the break in the cold weather most of the contractors have resumed work on the big canal and few work will now go forward without interruption.

Amusement hall was crowded last Saturday evening by an appreciative audience who came out to witness the ▓▓▓▓▓▓▓▓▓▓▓▓▓▓▓▓▓▓▓▓▓ New Hampshire Home." The play is an interesting one with a combination of comedy, sentiment and tragedy that was well portrayed by the performers. The comedy parts were well presented by Wm. Vandevanter, as "Mike Mullins," and Eliza Hook as "Tilly," the old maid. Bert Wallace's makeup as "Edward Van Dusen" was excellent and he took the part of the villain in a very realistic manner. Lemira Bishop's characterization of "Muffins" was excellent and her distinct enunciation was especially to be commended. Cassie Riding's, in the character of "Mrs. Winthrop," showed a thorough understanding of the part. The club desires to express their appreciation of the work of James Steele in coaching them in their parts. Mr. Steele is an old actor and thoroughly understands the business and was able to render them much assistance. The club will repeat the performance Saturday night and should draw out another good audience.

Cass Lewis has finished double-planking the bridge West Delta and it is now in first class condition. The Delta company is also repairing the bridges on their tract and putting in a number of new ones.

McClain & Copening have been busy the past week showing visitors over the country and report everyone enthusiastic over the showing made. Everyone who has the money becomes a buyer and those who haven't propose to get in as soon as possible.

About thirty out of town visitors registered in Delta this week. Among them were eleven from California, all of whom are or will be buyers.

Dr. W. W. Stockham, late of Pioche, is now a resident of Delta. He has part of his stock of drugs here and will begin the erection of his store building in a few days. Those who require his professional services will find him at the Hotel Delta. His card appears in another column.

Attorney James A. Melville has been in Delta this week on legal business. Mr. Melville has an office in Salt Lake but does a great deal of legal work in Delta and as soon as he can get an office will spend most of his time here.

Dr. Murphy has been interesting himself in getting a free traveling library for Delta and the first box of 870 volumes has arrived and is at Dr. Murphy's. Tuesday evening a temporary organization of a library club was formed. For the present the membership fee is fixed at 25 cents. The only expense is the freight charges on the books to and from Salt Lake. When the membership fees do not cover this expense a small assessment of ten or fifteen cents will be levied. Any member can borrow a book for two weeks. If held longer than that a fine of ten cents will be imposed. If enough interest is aroused monthly meetings will be held for the reading of papers and discussion of literary or other subjects. The books just received consist of standard fiction, history, biography,

science, etc., to suit all tastes and every one who cares for good reading ought to join the club.

LOST—A wallet containing a number of personal papers and a $5 bill. Finder will please return to the Chronicle office.

The editor goes to Salt Lake next Monday to attend the meeting of the Utah Press association, of which he is treasurer. He will be absent a week or ten days.

Jacob De Bree, of West Delta, has just completed a new house. J. H.

Frederick's new house is nearly finished. He has just returned from his old home in Illinois, where he spent the holidays.

A large amount of water is going over the spill. The river is getting so high that the water is up to the top of the fill at the west end of the West Delta bridge and Cass Lewis is raising the fill.

Farmer Wanted—To cultivate 80 acres of land in West Delta; cropped last year; cabin, stable, cellar; liberal terms to an experienced farmer. Address Chronicle, Delta.

AN ELECTRIC LIGHT PLANT.

P. J. Bammes, an electrical engineer, formerly with the electrical department of the Boston Con., mill was in town last week, looking up the proposition of putting in an electric plant for the Melville Co. The company owns a large amount of surplus Desert water and a power site to utilize it. This water would be carried down the joint canal to the flume where it would be turned back into the river through a stand-pipe. A fall of about 32 feet would be utilized and the water the company has would develop about 300 horse-power according to Engineer Bammes.

The proposed plan, however, is to start with a unit of 175 horse-power. The estimate cost of the plant would be about $50,000. It would have a turbine generator and about 30 miles of line covering Delta, Oasis, Deseret and Hinckley. The current would be transmitted at 4,000 volts and sets of transformers would reduce it at the delivery end to 110 or 220 volts.

To raise the funds for erecting the plant bonds would be issued and enough money would have to be realized from the first to pay the expense of operating—about $300 per month, and interest on the bonds. At a rate of 50 cents per light at least 1,000 lights would have to be subscribed for to start the enterprise. To these would be added public lights by the different towns and the use of the current for power purposes. Such a plant could furnish cheap power for a flouring mill and elevator at Delta and could be used at the cement block works, a seed cleaning plant and other industries.

While, of course, the plan is only being considered at present, it looks like a good thing and the first step will be to estimate the number of lights that can probably be rented. The company would not expect to make money at first, but if Delta and the tributary towns grow in population to the size the resources of this section indicate ultimately a good paying prospect. The beauty of the project is that it will be owned by our own home people and not by an outside corporation, with no object but to charge the highest rate, the people will submit to, and which will yield the greatest dividends. Success to the enterprise.

NEWS OF OUR NEIGHBORS

Gathered by the Editor in His Weekly Rounds

There are several cases of scarlet fever at Deseret but they are of a mild type and as they are kept closely looked after there is little danger of its spreading.

Mrs. Wm. V. Black has passed through a very painful experience, the outcome of which was in doubt for a time. She appeared to have a felon on her hand which daily grew more painful and was accompanied by fever. Dr. Broaddus decided to open the hand to liberate the puss that was evidently accumulating. Owing to the condition of her heart and lungs an anaesthetic could not be administered. It was only much deep cutting that the puss was liberated from the sheath of the sinews where it had gathered. Though still weak from the pain and shock of the operation, the patient is recovering, but it was a narrow escape from blood poisoning. Mr. Black expressed his deep appreciation of Dr. Broaddus' efficient service and constant attention.

Mrs. Maggie Ryan and her bright baby is spending the winter with her parents, Mr. and Mrs. Virgil Kelly. Mr. Ryan expects to abandon the railway service in the spring and come down to Deseret and go into farming.

We have seen very few good barns in Millard. Probably our dry summers and generally mild winters make expensive barns not as necessary as in the East. John Dewsnip has the best barn we have seen so far. It is 30x50 feet in size, built of matched siding, a cement floor covers the whole interior. There are ten stalls on one side and on the other side six open stalls and two box stalls. Behind the stalls is a sunken drain to carry out of the barn the drainage from the stalls. In the large loft overhead is room for forty tons of hay. Mr. Dewsnip believes the barn is a paying investment in reducing the amount of feed his stock requires and increasing the amount of milk his cows give.

There is a large accumulation of alfalfa seed at Deseret and very little demand. Dan Black gave it as his opinion that while last year the buyers came, the demand came for it, this year they are letting the farmers hold it, with a probability that it will be some time before they are able to dispose of it. This is pretty hard on the farmers as they have been depending upon their alfalfa seed money to pay their bills. Probably not half of the seed in the county has been sold. We think this points to the necessity of organizing a farmers' association to look after the selling end of seed raising. There is not an unlimited demand for alfalfa seed, nor a large number of buyers. Farmers have to take a chance in finding a market for their seed. An association could look up the market, keep informed as to the demand and the prices and act as a unit when it comes to selling. Growers of oranges, apples, peaches, grapes and other farm products have their organizations which look after the marketing of their products and find them of great value. We believe it would be of equal value to the seed raisers of Millard county and Utah.

Mr. and Mrs. Eccles and children took the train north a week ago Monday night. Mrs. Eccles and the three children will stop with Mr. Eccles' father in Ogden until a new home is prepared for them in Delta. Miss Munns also went and will remain with them. Mr. Eccles will return in a few days to get the tangled ends of his business together.

The annual shareholders' meeting of the Melville Irrigation Co. was held on Monday evening, January 8, and between thirty and forty stockholders were present. The principal business was to hear the annual financial report read. It showed a very satisfactory condition. Whereas the report last year showed a debt of $65,000, this year's report showed the debt reduced to $25,000, a new spillway built, the main canal enlarged and water contracts to the amount of $60,000 in the treasury. The subject of disposing of the 2,000 water shares in the treasury came up for consideration and after considerable discussion, it was decided to leave with the directors, to whom and what price they should be sold.

L. A. Patten and wife have returned to Delta after living at Logan for some time. They decided after a fair trial of the bigger town that Delta was good enough for them.

Bob Jenkins returned from Salt Lake last week.

Mrs. William Jenkins and child, who have been spending several days in the city, returned with him.

The week-old infant of Mrs. Ben Sampson died on Monday, January 8, and was buried Tuesday.

Bert Clawson, the automobile expert, from Salt Lake, was down last week overhauling the machines of the Delta company.

Now that we have a new depot the next necessity is a night agent. Agent Harnes is expected to put in fifteen hours a day, but he has so much to do that it takes him twenty hours and more to get through his work. All the trains that stop at Delta get here in the night and as it now is one can't get a ticket, have it validated or get baggage checked except in the day.

time. Passenger and freight business is steadily increasing and it is already too much for one man to handle. Mr. Manderfield has shown a willingness to meet the needs of this rapidly growing community and we have no doubt he will accede to the universally signed request of our citizens for a night man.

President Blake, of the Hinckley town board, tells the editor that the board intends to strictly enforce all quarantine and sanitary laws so that there shall be no epidemic of contagious diseases.

Last Saturday Hinckley presented a very animated appearance, there being so many visitors in town. The Wright House was so full that the guests had to eat in relays. The way young Orville Thompson assisted in the kitchen would lead one to believe that he had taken a course in domestic science.

Pratt Bros.' clearing sale has been a great success, as was to be expected from the low price asked for the goods. The sale lasts only a few days longer.

The Indian War Veterans will make their annual visit to the schools next week. On Wednesday they will be at the M. S. Academy. On succeeding days they will visit the district schools at Hinckley and Deseret, Oasis and Delta. Their itinerary will be decided upon Wednesday.

The people of Deseret had quite a scare Monday morning. Soon after Mr. Allred had started the fire in the school house he saw smoke issuing from the roof in all directions. He quickly gave the alarm and a crowd soon gathered. A hole was broken through the roof and the flames quickly extinguished with no other damage than the broken roof and some scorch-

ed hands. The fire started around the stove pipe, where it passed through the ceiling.

Damron & Hawley have just received a carload of Idaho oats which are so highly valued by the farmers here.

The stockholders of the State Bank of Oasis held their annual meeting on Monday. The old board of directors was reelected except Jens Peterson of Scipio, Geo. W. Cropper being elected in his place.

Word comes from Fillmore that the notorious Frank Hanson has been locked up in jail for safe keeping, as he has shown every indication of being crazy. He is to be examined by physicians and if the case demands it he will be sent to the asylum at Provo.

The annual meeting of the stockholders of the West Side Telephone Co, will be held at Deseret January 26.

Millard County Progress
January 18, 1912

A Colony From Sevier County.

A colony from Sevier County is preparing to locate at Delta as soon as the weather shall permit an exodus. They are selling their farms in Sevier at $150 to $200 per acre and are buying at Delta at $50 to $80 per acre. Sevier County is a good productive county but it has been demonstrated that Delta farms will yield larger returns with less work than the higher priced Sevier County lands Some of the best crops raised last year at Delta were by Sevier County farmers. They are getting ahead many of Millard County's people in taking opportunity by the fore-top at Delta. The selling agents of the Delta Land and Water Company report that Sevier and Sanpete Valley people have bought 5,000 acres of Delta lands this fall and winter.

Since the greater part of our taxes are consumed by our schools it may be of intrest to know who the school officers are Here is a list of our school boards.

Fillmore, Jas. A. Kelly, J. F. Holbrook, W. N. McBride.

Meadow, F. H. Stewart, Edwin Stott, Jas. C Beckstrand.

Hatton, Wm. Robison, E. Bird, J. C. Whitaker. Kanosh, A. A. Kimball, Anthony Paxton Albert Nadauld. Holden, Sidney P. Teeples, Edward F. Stevens, Lorenzo Stevens. Scipio, Ernest Brown, A. P. Peterson, Wm. Bradfield. Oak City, Wm. Lovell, Franklin Anderson Geo. Finlinson. Leamington, August Nielson, Louis Nielson, Jno. Greathouse. Hinckley, Delta, Hosea Stout, J. M. Rigby, Willis Robison. Oasis, Thos. S. Reid, C. W. Pierson, Lars Hansen.

The teachers in the county are:

Fillmore—J. F. Day, Carl Day Hazel Day, Stella Day, Ada Brunson, Isie Carling, Alonzo Huntsman, W. L. Jones, Thera Speakman, Katherin Woodhouse

Holden—L E. Acord, Nellie Hunter, Reid Mathews, Erma Turner.

Scipio—Oscar P. Bjorregaard, Milo Dyches, Marcelia Johnson, Jennie Robins.

Meadow—A. N. Beckstrand, Ezra Gull, Edith Lee.

Oasis—C. H. Barton, Florence Ellison.

Hinckley—Fred W. Pack, Miss Parker, Mary Cropper, Lillian Bishop.

Delta—Avery Bishop, Al线 Sperry, Millie Workman, Mable

Sperry,

Kanosh—Ray Barton, Winford Paxton, Florence Stevens, Lizzie Thompson.

Leamington—Chester Cheel, Mary Stevens.

Deseret—Mr. Petty, William Cheel.

Oak City—Wm E. Davis. Alice Dean, Jane Rawlinson.

Hatton—Hazel Giles.

Clear Lake—Mary Peterson

The names of the Faculty of the Stake Academy are not available.

IN AND AROUND DELTA

The Week's News from the Coming Metropolis

About fifty visitors registered at Delta the past week. They came mainly from California and Nebraska and nearly all of them bought land.

Last week Delta and all the other west-side towns suffered from a famine of coal oil. This week everybody is out of sugar.

No mail at all left Delta last Thursday, the sacks being left at the depot. That's why nobody outside of Delta got the Chronicle until Saturday. We have a letter postmarked Provo, January 7, that didn't get to Delta till January 10, and another letter was mailed the editor from Salt Lake Sunday afternoon and hadn't got to Delta when the editor left there Monday night. Tell us your experience and we will continue to expose our rotten mail service.

Bert Wallace is putting up the office building for Milton Moody, just north of N. S. Bishop's house. It will be 18x24, rustic style, with a main office 14x18 and two smaller rooms.

The Commercial club met at the school house last Saturday evening for the election of officers. Sixteen members were present. Secretary John Steele gave the financial report for the past year, and an account of the activities of the club, which showed that it had accomplished much good during the year. In the election of officers, E. S. Marshall was the unanimous choice for president, John Steele for secretary, and R. F. Law for treasurer. Cass Lewis received 10 votes and Dr. Harsh 6 votes for vice-president; H. E. Maxfield, S. W. Eccles and W. S. Bunker were elected directors and Hiram Knight a delegate to the meeting of the Development League and Press Association at Salt Lake. Now that every member has had a chance to vote for the new officers and they have been elected by acclamation, we hope they will be supported by every member. While the Chronicle has criticised some of the acts of the board, it recognizes the good intentions of the officers and will support their every effort to build up Delta. It hopes to give free publicity to all its doings and make public all inquiries about Delta. Let's drop our differences and all pull together.

George Day is advertising a big closing-out sale of winter goods, beginning next Monday. See his bills for the remarkable bargains he is offering. Now is the time to get winter goods at cost and below.

The editor greatly enjoyed the meeting of the Press Association and Development league at Salt Lake on Tuesday. He had several opportunities to put in some good words for Millard county. He will give a report of some of the most important matters discussed, next week.

For sale—One covered two-seated heavy spring wagon, good as new, cheap. Also set of double harness, all in good order. Inquire at Chronicle office.

A. C. Sorenson has finished stock-taking and the new store building to be added to the establishment of the Delta Mercantile & Implement Co. is rapidly approaching completion. They will have accommodations for a big stock of goods.

The installing of the new heating plant at the Amusement hall is nearly completed.

Serious Accident.

Last Wednesday Dr. Broaddus was called to Fillmore in consultation on an insanity case, but urgent calls to Abraham and to Delta on the same day made it impossible for him to go. The family of Mr. Dan Black was very thankful the next day that he had not gone, but was no farther than Hinckley at the time of one of the most horrible accidents that has occurred in Deseret.

Little 7-year-old Netta Black, while climbing into a buggy, slipped and fell so that her right leg went through the wheel just as the team started up. Before they could be stopped she had been whirled about several times by the revolving wheel and her little leg was so horribly mangled that her clothing had to be cut away in order to extricate her. Dr. Broaddus hurried from Hinckley as fast as his own team and Sam Stansworth's horse in relays could run, and found the leg broken below the knee and also above the knee and through the joint, the entire knee joint being laid open and the knee capsule torn open. The broken bone of the thigh was laid bare for 5 or 6 inches by the mangled flesh and the large main artery was completely severed, so that the child was very weak from the terrible loss of blood. As only an inch of skin and a bit of flesh held the upper and lower leg together, the wound was full of axle-grease and dirt, amputation became necessary at once. The operation was performed successfully by Dr. Broaddus and the child was taken to St. Mark's hospital for careful nursing. By Monday she was reported steadily improving. The miracle is that she was not killed outright. The Blacks have the sympathy of the entire community.

NEWS OF OUR NEIGHBORS

Gathered by the Editor in His Weekly Rounds

After being quarantined for about six weeks, Joseph Neilson's family has been liberated. On Monday the house looked as if a tornado had passed through it, but they were simply tearing things up and giving the house a thorough fumigation.

About 30 stockholders of the Deseret Irrigation Co., met at Hinckley Monday afternoon to discuss matters preliminary to the annual meeting which was to be held next Saturday, but may be postponed a week. Strong dissatisfaction was expressed with the actions of the president and directors in giving Henry Huff a rake-off of 15 and 25 cents on all flour sold at the mill. The belief was also expressed that the best interests of the company would be served by electing a president who lived here and did not have a divided interest. A committee was appointed to bring the matters complained of to the attention of the stockholders at their annual meeting.

Pratt Bros. are showing the biggest line and greatest variety of graniteware we have seen in Millard county. At the prices they are selling they must have picked up a snap.

The editor had a chance to listen to a debate at the Academy last Monday that was of special interest to him. The subject was, "Resolved, That under present conditions a temporary school building at Delta is preferable to a modern, up-to-date one." The affirmative was supported by Willis Lyman and William R. Stopley, and the negative by Clark Allred and Eugene Hilton. The boys had evidently studied the subject and some ingenious arguments were used. It was a very even debate and the judges, Profs. Maughn, Stott and Gardner decided in favor of the affirmative by a vote of two to one.

The basket-ball game was won last Saturday by the Academy team over the Beaver team. It was a fast game and the visitors were not in it at all. The Academy team has a good show for being one of the teams in the state meet.

The Hinckley Co-op has just received a big line of crockery which merits the attention of housekeepers who want something good but not expensive.

The college play of "Mr. Bob," presented by the M. S. A. Dramatic club last Friday, was a great success. The hall was crowded and over $60 was realized for the Academy. The comedy parts were well taken by Clark Allred, as "Robert Brown," Eugene Hilton, as "Jenkins," and Eda Cropper as "Patty." It is expected that other plays will be presented in the near future.

The 14-year-old son of Ora Lake, at Abraham, has been seriously ill with penumonia for the last two weeks. Dr. Broaddus was called out there twice, and now reports the boy to be rapidly convalescent.

The Hinckley meat market and grocery is the latest addition to our advertisers. We'll have 'em all in yet.

The warm weather has brought the bowlers out and the bowling alley is the busiest place in town.

Mrs. Joseph Damron and Mrs. Maggie Kelly Ryan's baby have been quite ill the past week, but are much better as this goes to press. Mr. Ryan has come down here to make his home.

The busiest postmaster we have seen is Postmaster Johnson at Oasis. He starts out at 6 o'clock a. m., with the mail from the north which he has to distribute for the mail driver for Deseret, Hinckley and Abraham and also the mail route to Fillmore, all of which leave before 9 o'clock. Then the mail from the eastern settlements gets in about 5 or 6 o'clock p. m. and the Fillmore stage not till 9, and sometimes a good deal later. This mail has to be made up to go north about midnight, so it keeps Mr. Johnson busy day and night. Still we have mighty poor mail service to and from Millard county, but we can't discover that any of it is the fault of our county postmasters.

IN AND AROUND DELTA

The Week's News from the Coming Metropolis

The neat bungalow office of the Utah Real Estate and Live Stock Co., otherwise Moody & Cropper, is nearly completed and will be ready for occupancy by Saturday. It will be an attractive addition to Delta's business houses.

Dr. Stockham is also preparing to put up a good sized building to be used as a drug store. He will build on the corner of Second North and Fourth West, near McClain & Copening's office.

The excavation has been made and material is on hand for a six-room, story and a half residence for Ed Bishop, opposite Avery Bishop's residence.

Arthur Humphries has gone to Idaho on business and during his absence Andrew Grunstod is looking after the business of the Delta Lumber Co.

N. S. Bishop is preparing to make quite a number of improvements on his farm west of Delta. He is having a four-room frame house put up, a stable 16-32 with stalls and a cement floor, a hay barn, his granary improved and a well dug. Mr. Bishop evidently intends to broaden out as an up-to-date farmer.

A. L. Bailey, local agent of the Baker Lumber Co., has received his first consignment of lumber. The yard is located just west of the warehouse of the Hub Mercantile Co. Bert Wallace bought the first bill of lumber from the new company.

B. E. Cooper of the Hotel Delta made a business trip to the city this week.

The new office of the Chronicle doesn't show very much style on the outside, but the interior is rather tony with are wall paper, shelves and fixtures. We have got all the latest magazines and papers, and a very attractive line of valentines. Our fancy stationery will be along in a few days.

Yes, last week's Chronicle was a pretty bum number. For one thing the editor was in Salt Lake all the week picking out his stock of stationery, valentines and new printing material for his printing office, and second on account of our bum mail service. About half of the correspondence failed to get to the office until after the paper was printed. The Chronicle is of such uniform excellence that a poor number raises a strenuous kick.

From ten to fifteen land seekers have been coming into Delta every day for the past week, and the Hotel Delta has had more guests than it could accommodate. The visitors came from California, Illinois, Colorado, Kentucky and various parts of Utah. Although a good many thousand acres have been sold the past two months, the visitors find there are plenty of desirable tracts still left. Every one is delighted with the country and the opportunities it affords. One Southern California man told the editor he found the climate here more desirable than in the Golden State. It would certainly be hard to beat the weather we have had in Millard county the past week or two.

No, Molly, the editor has not wiped Delta off the map, but it is evident from the kicks he has received that he will be wiped off the earth if he doesn't keep Delta on the map every week and all the time.

Wm. Manderfield has kept his word and a night man is now on duty at Delta, F. O. Bollinger taking the "grave yard shift" Monday night. The officials of the Salt Lake Route evidently recognize the importance of Delta and this new acquisition is greatly appreciated by the people.

The Felton farm of 120 acres on the west side, which has been operated by Jacob DeBree, has been sold to John A. Bolton, of Los Angeles. Mr. Bolton also bought the adjoining forty owned by Ed Johnson.

If our esteemed contemporary, the Progress-Review, would cut out about 75 inches of its cheap quack and foreign advertising matter which is only used as fillers to save setting up live news, end its partnership with a Salt Lake liquor house, which is an encouragement to the Fillmore boys to buy cheap whiskey, and then try to make the paper a real newspaper, it could accomplish more real good for its community than all its futile knocking of the Chronicle. This paper fills a long felt want in the county and is taking business away from the Progress-Review every week. Hence these heart-rending wails from the county seat. Take a tumble, Brother Anderson, and try and get out a real newspaper, if you know how.

Next week the Chronicle will publish an illustrated article on the great Rainbow Natural Bridge of southeastern Utah. It is written by Joseph E. Pogue of the U. S. National Museum, and will be found a very readable article. Utah has a great many natural wonders and the great bridge in the southeastern part of the state, hewn out by the wind and sand and water of centuries, are not the least remarkable.

LOST—On Tuesday, a red envelope containing invoice and shipping bill of hardware from Salt Lake Hardware Co. Finder please return to A. P. Wallace.

A. E. Gull this week sold 160 acres of land in Section 20 and 240 acres in Section 21, southeast of Delta. The buyers are six well to do Spanish Fork farmers who will bring down stock and implements to work the land. They may bring down a traction engine.

The Hotel Delta has just installed a fine cash register. Landlord Cooper is evidently getting in more money than he can carry in his pocket.

Work has been commenced on a well for the new depot. A twelve-inch pipe will be sunk.

FOR SALE—Twenty shares of Melville water stock. Enquire at the Chronicle office.

We learn from Engineer Morton that the Delta Co. will put in the new steel flume this season, and that work for it will be commenced at once. This will be good news to the west side farmers and will banish any fear that there will not be plenty of water for them the coming season.

Delay in getting the glass front for the new store of the Delta Mercantile and Implement Co. is holding back the completion of the fine new building.

Millard County Fruit.

Mr. Simeon Walker, who lives in Oak City, Utah, about 12 miles east of Delta, brought to town last week, which is undoubtedly the largest pear that was ever raised in Utah, or in fact, in the intermountain states. The pear measured 15 inches in circumference and weighed two pounds and one ounce. While this pear is larger than usual, it only demonstrates beyond a doubt that Millard county can and does produce the choicest of fruits, and that within the vicinity of Delta. So that you people who think Millard County is no good puts us in mind of a saying related hundred of years ago by our Master, "A prophet is not without honor, except in his own country." We also say, "that land is not without virtue except it be in Utah." Mr. Walker has a number of bushels of pears and some very choice apples for sale and is making shipments to California markets.

OASIS.

The little daughter of D. J. Blacks is getting along nicely. She will soon be able to leave the hospital and go to a rooming house.

Al. Nuxman of this place has purchased the northeast corner lot from Samuel Ruther, opposite Washington Rogers, and has commenced a new frame house on same.

Mrs. Agness Reid has been quite ill the past week, but is now able to be around the house again.

A very good audience was at meeting Sunday at Oasis hall for the purpose of listening to Elder J. S. Bennett of Deseret, also Ed Whicker of Delta. Both spoke very good. We cordially invite them to come again. Also conjoint Mutual was well attended in the evening and a very interesting programme rendered.

OAK CITY.

Judging from the amount of cedar posts that are coming into Oak City each day there will be great improvements along the line of fencing or the market will be supplied at Delta.

Mr. H. G. Ottley has gone to Salt Lake City on business.

The actors are counting on giving an exhibition on the skates Saturday afternoon.

Stage Manager S. J. Rawlinson has left for Salt Lake City to arrange for scenery and costumes for the actors. On the 14th of February they will play "The Noble Outcast" on the new stage. On the 16th they will play "The Great Winterson Mine" in Leamington and "The Noble Outcast" on the 17th.

Geo. Howard of Nephi and Ben Kenney of Holden were in town last week on some cattle business.

Bert Roper and Soren Anderson went to Fillmore and purchased a couple of fine milch cows.

After over a year of suffering with a cancer death came as a great relief to Bro. Alvin Roper on Jan. 29th. It may be truly said that he was a man with sunshine in his heart and carried the same feeling to any person whom he should happen to meet. He was loved and respected by both young and old. Through all his long suffering, which was great, he was cheerful and endured it with unsurpassable pattience to the end. He was a kind and loving father to his children as well as a faithful husband. He leaves a wife and nine children as well as a host of friends to mourn his departure.

IN AND AROUND DELTA

The Week's News from the Coming Metropolis

The get-acquainted party last Wednesday evening at Amusement Hall was a great success. 250 adults were present besides a large number of young people. Every one was given a tag with his name and a number so that no introductions were necessary to get acquainted. Avery Bishop was master of ceremonies and he kept something doing all the time—music, dancing, recitations, games, puzzles, etc.—all of which was very entertaining. A good many new-comers were present, but they were made to feel that they were not strangers. Quite a number were present from the adjoining towns.

Mr. Boyle of the Manufacturers' Association, has been giving illustrated lectures the past week in Delta and our neighboring towns. The illustrations were not first class but the talks were all right. They were on Utah and her resources, and his text was "Support the State that Supports You," and keep your money at home He said that there were 175 industrial institutions in the state making goods the people of Utah needed, and that some of them got a larger trade outside the state than from Utah. He urged them to patronize their local merchants instead of sending their money to mail order houses, and believed the local houses could duplicate most of the goods and prices of these concerns. The lectures were largely attended.

SEED WHEAT FOR SALE—Club and red chaff, clean and of good quality, $1 per bushel. E. C. Underhill, Delta.

Henry Vollhart was feeling pretty good when he came into town last Friday. The reason was that a fine baby boy—the first—made its appearance at his home at 11 o'clock the previous day. Here's hoping the baby will be as aimable as its mother and as handsome as its father. Mrs. Jerome Tracy was in attendance, assisted by Mrs. "Denver" Smith, and both mother and baby are getting along fine.

It is about settled that John Avery Bishop will be our next pastmaster as was expected by most people. We think the selection will be very generally satisfactory. Avery is fully capable, no one can say a word against his character and we have every reason to believe he will be an obliging and competent postmaster. The office will be located on the corner opposite his residence, which brings it within the limits where the mail has to be delivered by the railway company, one of the requirements of the department. The location is near to the center of town, to suit most people, even if it isn't on Clark street.

R. J. Law returned from Salt Lake last week after selecting a big stock of spring goods, consisting of dry goods, boots and shoes, underwear, ladies goods, etc. They will be along for your inspection in a few days.

Attorney Melville and wife are among the Elks excursionists who tour California this month. Mr. Melville goes on a combined pleasure and business trip and expects to return about February 20.

IN AND AROUND DELTA

The Week's News from the Coming Metropolis

We understand the sale of delinquent stock by the Melville Co. has been postponed one week.

From ten to fifteen people arrive daily in search of business openings or farm property and nearly everybody is able to find what he wants. The majority of outside people are from California and Nebraska.

J. W. Schwartz and family and his son W. E. Schwartz and family, from Iowa, are to make Delta their home. They brought along a car of household goods and a span of fine draft horses. They have invested in a farm on the west side and some city lots, which they will use for business purposes. When they left Iowa the temperature was below zero, with heavy snow and strong winds, and they find the climate of Millard county a very pleasant change.

McClain & Copening report a ready market for city lots and several sales made the past week. California parties have bought with a view of putting up a couple of business houses, and several Colorado people have purchased lots upon one of which a bank building will be erected.

The foundation for D. Stockham's two-story frame building is laid and it will be pushed to a speedy completion. It will be 44x60 feet, part of the ground floor for a restaurant and the other side a drug store, with a rooming house up stairs.

Call upon Roy S. Dresser at the Chronicle office for any kind of teaming.

The piano recital which was given by several of Mrs. Broaddus' pupils at Hinckley and Deseret will be repeated at Delta on March 1 or 2. The program is an interesting one and the performers show much skill and understanding of the instrument.

The first birth to be recorded in the South Delta tract occurred last week, when Mrs. Bud Galloway presented her husband with a fine baby boy. Mrs. Moore, of California, was there to welcome her lusty grandson. Hereafter we will keep close tab on the south and west side and see which will carry off the record for babies and brides.

The editor came over from Fillmore last Sunday afternoon with Mr. Clark Callister, in his automobile. The trip was made in two hours and thirty-five minutes. While the road is pretty fair, it would be greatly improved if run over with a drag and the hummocks taken off and the ruts filled.

The number of patrons of the telephone has increased so rapidly on the west side that Mr. Callister intends to install a switchboard at Delta, and alter the system into a four-party line plan. This will greatly increase the usefulness of the phone and widely extend its use.

Marshall & Knight have about finished up their new store building for the Delta Mercantile and Implement Co., and the shelves are being rapidly filled up with new goods which are arriving every week. Judging by the first shipments, they are going to be strong on shoes.

Another improvement on Clark street is Mrs. Winterrose's cement block building, the walls of which are nearly completed. Will Van Devanter has begun his new cement block buildings next to his present residence. Mrs. Van has just got in some new spring millinery and wants the new building to display it in.

We understand the Consolidated Wagon & Machine Co. has got a lot on the west end of Clark street and expect to put up a good sized warehouse on it. There are plenty of other desirable business sites on Clark street which prospective buyers should investigate. Those who have lots for sale on Clark street should put up some signs and advertise, for the lots won't sell themselves.

N. S. Bishop reports the sale of his 80 acres west of town to a Mr. Nell, from Eastern Canada. Forty acres of it is cleared. The price paid was $6,000. He also sold 40 acres of unimproved land south of town for $2,000. He sold two of his lots in the block east of Avery Bishop's for $800, and Avery Bishop sold the west half of his lot for $200.

Eighty dollars per acre is what Dr. Harsh received for his 80 acres of improved land west of town. He doesn't intend to leave, but is looking around for another 40 acres for a home.

Milton Moody has sold to Prof. L. F. Moench forty acres close to his present holdings east of the Deseret reservoirs.

We hope next week to give definite information about the new bank and the big store building that has been under consideration for some time.

The well at the depot is down about 175 feet and will be completed in a few days.

The Chronicle News Stand has all the leading magazines and newspapers and a small line of fancy stationery. This is the only news stand in the county. We believe we can get the people to read the popular magazines.

Farmer with teams and farm machinery to handle 80 acres of improved land. Chronicle.

Dr. Mitchell, of Ogden, vice-president and director of the Utah Aerial Navigation Co., has been selling stock in their company at Hinckley this week. They have a pretty good invention and we will tell something about it next week.

IN AND AROUND DELTA

The Week's News from the Coming Metropolis

There averaged one emigrant car each day last week for Delta.

Dr. W. W. Stockham returned last Sunday morning from Pioche, Nev., where he has been on business connected with his holdings in that place. He reports Pioche on the boom.

The Baker Lumber Co. received another car of lumber Tuesday. They expect soon to be able to furnish you anything in lumber that you may want.

Work is being rushed as fast as possible on the concrete headgates for the south tract of the Delta L. & W. Co.

Messrs. Moody and Williamson of the Utah Real Estate and Live Stock Co., are in Salt Lake City this week on business connected with their firm.

Mr. Lyon, our new barber, is now comfortably located in his new shop on First North and Third West. We are all glad to have him with us, as he fills a long felt want in our busy little town.

The work on Dr. Stockham's new drug store is progressing very nicely. It is being built of hollow fire clay building blocks. This is their first trial in this part of the country. They appear to be all right and make a good wall. People are watching them very close, for if they give satisfaction, a good many of them will be used here, as they are cheap, economical and fireproof.

A. P. Wallace received two carloads of building blocks for Dr. Stockham's store this week.

Most all of the contractor are through with their work up on the canal. Some few of them are still trying to get some of the fruits ▓▓▓▓ moved.

What was the matt▓▓ service last week? L▓ Delta ▓▓ the 19th ▓▓▓▓▓ nation in Salt Lake on the afternoon delivery of the 23rd.

Friday evening, March 1, Delta will be treated to a musical recital by several of Mrs. C. A. Broaddus' pupils. The program is quite varied and will be found very interesting to all music lovers. The first part will consist of piano solos and duets and vocal solos, the music being explained by Mrs. Broaddus. The second part will contain five numbers of dance music played as piano duets. To this music the audience will have the privilege of dancing. The pupils taking part in the recital are Cora and Geneva Robinson, Myrtle Langston, Afton Hinckley, Norma Moody, Norma Damron and Vera Day. The editor has heard these young ladies play and they certainly do well for beginners. Come out and hear them, and also Mrs. Broaddus' explanation of some celebrated music for there is something more in music than melody.

Among the recent new comers to Delta who have brought along their household goods, farm implements and some stock are Geo. E. Beech and C. M. Lewis of Salt Lake, who have 80 acres each southeast of Delta. G. A. Livington of the same place has sent down some horses and implements for work on his 80, but will continue to pound away in Zion until his farm is started. Many and Thomas, miners from Cripple Creek, have an 80 near Delta and will discontinue trying to make a living out of Mother Earth with dynamite and a pick, and turn to the use of the plow and harvester. In mining your capital is growing constantly less. In agriculture your capital is constantly increasing in value. The boys are wise to make the change. D. Rosenbaum, a merchant of Brigham City has been improving his eighty.

On Friday, February 16, Dr. Broaddus, of Deseret, was called to the home of R. L. Simkins, in Delta, and found two of his children suffering with diphtheria. The prompt administration of anti-toxin resulted in a speedy recovery of the little girl; but the little boy had been sick for two weeks and was already in the clutches of the deadly paralysis of tongue, heart and the organs of breathing, which is one of the most dreaded consequences of the poison which diphtheria throws into the blood unless it is checked by anti-toxin, given within the first few days of the disease. In spite of all efforts to save him, the little fellow died that same evening. During the past week Dr. Broaddus has been called several times to Delta by parents who did not wish to take any chances with their children's sore throats, but so far no other positive cases of diphtheria have developed.

The Delta public will have another treat Saturday evening when the Oak City Dramatic Club will give the four-act drama, "A Noble Outcast." It has been given several times at other places and was well received and should draw a crowded house at Delta where amateur theatricals are well patronized.

Six or seven thousand dollars has recently been distributed by the Melville Irrigation and the Delta Land & Water companies, which was much appreciated.

The sale of delinquent stock by the Melville Company has been continued till March 20.

NEWS OF OUR NEIGHBORS

Gathered by the Editor in His Weekly Rounds

Wednesday evening, February 21, Mr. Hanks, a former school friend of Mr. William Gardner, gave a delightful lecture in the Academy Auditorium. His subject, "From the Cradle to the Grave," was rightly illustrated by quotations from Shakespeare's plays. Mr. Hanks' visit must have been an inspiring example to the students of what perseverance can accomplish, even under crushing handicap. For, since a terrible accident which deprived Mr. Hanks of both eyes and both hands, he has not only learned to dress and feed himself, but has taken the courses of study in literature and elocution, fitting him for lecture work. Everyone was deeply impressed by his cheerful manner and unconquerable spirit.

Sunday afternoon, February 25, Dr. Broaddus presented Mr. and Mrs. Rich Cropper with a little 8½-pound girl. All are doing well.

On Washington's birthday the Hinckley district school gave a delightful program to a packed house. Each room was represented by several numbers, songs, recitations and drills. Of the very long program, two of the best numbers were Master Bunker's recitation of "Seein' Things at Night," and the four-act dramatization of Betsy Ross' days by Miss Justeson's pupils. The teachers, Mr. Pack, Miss Cropper, Miss Cluff, Miss Parker and Mrs. Bishop, had evidently spent a great deal of time and effort in preparation of the children, and deserve especial credit for such good results in such cramped quarters as the small stage offers.

The Hinckley Mutual gave quite an elaborate character ball in the Academy Auditorium Friday evening, February 23. Many of the young people had sent to Salt Lake for costumes and the gymnasium was gay with color.

The tie game between Millard Stake and the Cedar basket-ball teams will be played off in Delta on Wednesday, February 28. The Academy students will be excused from school in the afternoon to attend, for it will be an exciting game and a good deal is at stake. The winning team will go to Salt Lake to play in the league games.

Mrs. Broaddus has postponed her last lecture recital, the one on Faust, until Wednesday, March 6, at 8 o'clock, on account of the basket-ball tie game and dance in Delta Wednesday afternoon and evening.

C. L. Christiansen, of Provo, is canvassing the west side district, taking orders for trees and shrubbery. Last year Deseret, Oasis and Hinckley put out several thousand shade trees and will probably plant as many more this spring. Care should be taken in the selection, as some kinds do not thrive in this land, while others, noticeably the Carolina and silver poplars do exceptionally well.

Last Wednesday our district school devoted the afternoon to a friendly contest with the Hinckley school. A feature of the day was an old-fashioned spelling match, which should have been between the eighth grades only, but owing to lack of numbers Deseret was forced to recruit from the 6th and 7th grades. The match resulted in victory for Hinckley, but the outdoor sports all went to Deseret.

One of the largest real estate deals consummated in this section recently was the sale of the Pack farm to outside parties by N. L. Peterson. Mr. Peterson bought this property less than five years ago for $6,000, and after harvesting, each year, a small fortune in alfalfa seed, hay, grain and garden stuff, sold out for $16,000. It is understood that Mr. Peterson and family are to occupy the residence of Mr. C. F. Webb for a time. That they will find permanent footing here is confidently hoped by their many friends.

Damron & Hawley are in receipt of a car of fine seed oats and an elegant line of new spring dress goods and trimmings.

Mrs. H. S. Cahoon Jr. is said to be rapidly recovering from an operation which was performed at the Groves L. D. S. hospital in Salt Lake City.

It seems to be a very hard matter to stamp out the scarlet fever which got such a hold in the west side settlements this winter. Two new cases were reported last week. One at the home of George Croft and another at George Hale's.

A heavy snow storm visited the west side last Friday night and Saturday and a cold wave now covers the valley.

One of the most pleasant times was had last Friday, Feb. 22, at the character ball given at Oasis by the Young Ladies' M. I. A. The characters were very well represented, especially the butterfly, by Miss Clara Thompson, shamrock by Alta Huff, the fairies by Miss Hulda and Lillie Hansen, also the clowns, especially Mr. Charles Thompson. There were also others who did justice to the parts represented, especially Mr. George and Martha Washington. The prizes were awarded to Miss Clara Thompson and Mr. Charles Thompson.

The judges were Heber W. Beckstrand, Wm. Huff, T. G. Reid, Marcus Skeems, J. C. Hawley, Mrs. Gene Hawley and Mamie Pierson.

Mr. John Jackson of Provo is at Oasis in the interest of the Singer Sewing Machine Co. He reports business as being fairly good.

Mr. and Mrs. Henry Huff returned home Monday morning, after a month's stay in Southern California. They report having had an excellent trip and the time of their lives.

Mr. Alonzo Christenson returned home on Feb. 22, after being at the Deseret Gymnasium in Salt Lake, where he has been taking training for athletics.

Mrs. McCosh is reported very sick at this writing with quinsy. Miss Matilda Hales is nursing her.

Mr. J. W. Reid of Mammoth is at Oasis visiting his mother and friends.

OCCURRENCES AT OAK CITY

W. R. Walker, Representative

The correspondent has been away from town, which accounts for no news for some time from Oak City, but the town is still on the map.

Since the last correspondence the population of Oak City has increased to the extent of three. John Lundahl is father of a nice-looking girl; Dad Lundahl is the happiest man in all the land, and has now quit sitting up with his wife and has gone to walking with his daughter. He says she was afraid her lungs were going to be poor, so she is developing them early.

Born to William Jacobson and wife, a girl. C. W. Rawlinson and wife, a boy. All doing fine.

There has been a great deal of travel through Oak City. Drummers and other traveling men, representing different lines.

The district school gave an entertainment last Thursday evening, which pleased the large audience which was present. The acting of the pupils was good and great credit is due the teachers for the splendid work.

The Dramatic club played "The Great Winterson Mine" last week, and "The Noble Outcast" twice to a crowded house. Friday, in all the beautiful snow, they went to Leamington and played "The Great Winterson Mine," and "The Noble Outcast" on Saturday night. The Leamington people certainly treated us fine and showed us one of the times of our lives.

Sunday night a debate was held in Mutual. Subject, "Resolved, That the West will be developed more completely by dry farming than by irrigation."

W. R. Walker and Edgar Nielson had the affirmative and S. J. Rawlinson and Joseph S. Anderson had the negative. The judges were Mr. J. F. Bean, of Richfield and William Davis and Leo Lyman, of Oak City. The negative won the argument and English, while the affirmative won the delivery, leaving the negative champions. They will meet Holden in Oak City Friday night.

If arrangements can be made, the Dramatic Club will play, "The Noble Outcast" in Delta Saturday evening.

Miss Maggie Rawlinson has been to Salt Lake and purchased a nice stock of millinery and will open up the stock next Friday, March 1.

Most of the Oak City students at the M. S. A. were home for a few days. A number of others came along to see the Orchard City.

Millard County Progress
March 1, 1912

Jury List for the March Term of District Court.

On this 17th day of Feburary, 1912, after due notice, the County Treasurer and the Fillmore City Justice of the Peace (acting in the absence of the County Attorney) met at the County Clerks office in Fillmore City, Millard County, state of Utah to witness the drawing of trial jurors for the March term of the 5th Judicial District Court in and for the county of Millard. And after the jury box was shaken by the Clerk so as to thoroly mix the slips of paper upon which the names of the jurors were written the Clerk in the presence of said County Treasurer and Justice of the Peace publicly drew out of the jury box the following named jurors, towit:-

Antone Sorenson	Fillmore
Thomas F. Wasden dead	Scipio
Walter James	Black Rock
Nelson S. Bishop	Delta
F. T. Slaughter	Hinckley
Geo. Theobald	Hinckley
Gen. A. George	Kanosh
Charles Burke	Hinckley
John H. Hilton	Hinckley
Samuel Memmott	Scipio
Joseph Christensen	Kanosh
Hyrum S. Cahoon	Deseret
Anthony Stephenson	Holden
Edgar W. Jeffery	Delta
Juel Moody	Hinckley
William R. Thompson	Scipio
Geo. Finlinson Jr.	Oak City
Abel M. Roper	Oak City
Anthony Paxton Jr.	Kanosh
Joseph V. Black	Deseret
William R. Johnson	Holden
Samuel Probert	Scipio
Herbert Taylor	Abraham
Joseph S. Anderson	Oak City
H. E. Maxfield	Delta

State of Utah } SS
County of Millard }

We the undersigned do hereby certify that the foregoing list is a true and correct list of the names drawn this 17th day of February, 1912, to serve as trial jurors at the March term of court of the Fifth Judicial District, State of Utah, County of Millard

Nephi A. Anderson
County and District Clerk
Christian Anderson, Deputy
John Cooper, Treasurer
Joseph S. Giles, J. P.

Robison House Notes.

The following have registered here.

Mr. and Mrs. Carl Brown, Scipio; S. G. Godd, Nephi; E. Houtz, Salt Lake City; E. McMichen, Salt Lake; C. B. Blumanthal, Provo; B. C. Watkins, Salt Lake; Jean Wattt, Ora Paxton, James Abraham, Flora Bird Hyrum Prows, Ervy Prows, Walter Paxton, Kanosh; Mr. and Mrs. G. W. Baker, Deseret; Talbot and Theobald, Hinckley; Cushman Bros., Hinckley; Oscar Johnson. Salt Lake; M. Grover, Frisco; V. O. Stratton, Hinckley; L. H. Taylor, Abraham; D. J. Black, Deseret; N. I. Bliss, Hinckley; David Powell, Murry; Mr Demmick; A. Owen, New York.

EVENTS AT OAK CITY

W. R. Walker, Representative

Born to Bishop J. L. Anderson, a girl. Mother and baby are getting along fine. Mrs. Anderson's mother, Mrs. Broadhead, of Idaho, is down on a visit and is looking after the new-comer.

Mrs. C. W. Rawlinson has been quite sick the past week. Dr. Broaddus, of Deseret, was up and she is reported getting better. Miss Vera Stout, of Leamington, is acting as nurse.

Mr. and Mrs. C. Johnson, of Leamington, were over visiting with their daughter, Mrs. Thomas C. Talbot.

DESERET.

It has been requested that services at the L. D. S. meeting house next Sunday afternoon will be conducted under the auspices of the local Relief Society. The 70th anniversary of the general organization being the occasion for such observance. A program reminiscent of the progress of the society will be given.

The Relief Society gives a party in Petty's hall Friday night.

A case of scarlet fever is reported at the home of V. Wm. Kelly.

One of the most damaging fires occurring in Deseret in a long time was that which destroyed the warehouse and seed cleaning mills of Jno. Dewsnup the night of Feb. 25. The fire started some time after 11 o'clock and in an hour's time had consumed the building and a large amount of alfalfa seed which was being prepared for shipment. Aside from the loss amounting to several thousand dollars sustained by Mr. Dewsnup, a number of others lost heavily. Taylor brothers of Abraham are out $2,500. Mrs. C. Warnick's entire crop was in the fire along with many smaller amounts. Altogether the loss is estimated at about $20,000.

A message was received by Virgil Kelly Saturday, announcing the death of his brother, Joseph Kelly, of San Bernardino, Cal. In compliance with a request made by his brother at the last meeting Mr. Kelly went to San Bernardino by first train that he might be in attendance at the funeral service which was to be held Monday.

Baby boys have recently arrived at the homes of Jacob Croft, George Croft, Wilford Warnick and Benjamin Bennett.

IN AND AROUND DELTA

The Week's News from the Coming Metropolis

So many land buyers are coming to Delta these days that it's hard for the editor to keep track of them all the time. The Hotel Delta is full all the time and a good many have to find sleeping quarters elsewhere. Wednesdays, Saturdays and Sundays are the big days. California visitors usually coming Sunday, when the limited stops for their benefit. Sixteen California people stopped last Sunday. We learn that there is a good reason for so many California people buying land in Millard county. Every once in a while a frost comes along and ruins their orange or lemon crops, and then a drought finishes up their grain. On land costing from $300 to $1,000 per acre this is a pretty serious blow. California has many taxes, as does every other country, we don't often hear of them. Millard county may have some disadvantages, but crop failures is not one of them.

An Iowa man showed us a picture of his native town taken the week he left, which indicates one of the disadvantages of that splendid state. The snow was three or four feet deep on the street, and on one corner a drift as high as a man's head. This was probably exceptional. Millard never has this disadvantage. The snow this week is about as much as we ever get, and it is gone in two days. Of course it leaves the roads in bad shape, but this only lasts a few days. It is really surprising how quickly this sticky mud dries up.

Engineer Martin informs us that the piles for the new steel flume are on hand and as soon as the engine sinking the depot well is at liberty the work of driving them for the support of the piers will be commenced. The material for the abutments is arriving and the big steel flume is on the way, of which we will round, nine feet and a ▓▓f across and with a capacity of 250 second feet. It will probably be in place by the first of May, and is a guarantee that the farmers on the west side will have plenty of water this season.

J. W. Robb, representing a big bunch of farmers of Auburn, who own a large tract of land on the west side, is back from Nebraska. He wants all those who have borrowed plows, harrows and other tools from over there to bring them back. He don't mind lending them, but he don't expect to give them away.

Delta is doing more passenger and freight business now than any town south of Salt Lake. Last month beside our unusual amount of local freight, there were nineteen cars of settlers effects. There has averaged one car of settlers' effects this month, besides cars of lumber, coal, machinery, etc. This will give some idea of the way Delta is booming.

The Baker Lumber Co. has got in three more cars of lumber, including the material for the new lumber shed. This will be 44x120 feet, and when built all their lumber will be under cover. Manager Bailey says that while there are no storms in this country to damage lumber the continuous sunny weather is likely to check and warp it. The company has also got in a car of shingles and a quantity of nails and other builders' hardware. The large amount of building going on in and around Delta keeps Manager Baker busy from morning till night.

The new store of the Delta Mercantile and Implement Co. on Clark street is completed and all hands are busy unpacking goods and putting them away, and from the way the place is filling up they ought to add another twenty feet to the old store. The old building will contain their grocery and hardware department, and the dry goods, boots, hats, clothes, etc., will be in the new building. They are connected by a passage way in front. A car load of farm machinery will be in shortly and another car will be along in about a month. They will handle the celebrated Emerson plow and the Milwaukee machines, embracing every kind of machine and tool the farmer needs, including wagons and buggies. Hyrum Knight of the firm says they propose to carry one of the biggest stocks in the state.

Don't forget the entertainment of the Relief Society on Friday afternoon and evening. An interesting program will be furnished in the afternoon, which will be free, and fifty cents will be charged to the St. Patrick's dance in the evening. Don't forget that green is the color, and all silks, satins and dress suits are barred.

Simeon Walker, the Oak City orchardist and stock raiser, was in town last week with a fine team of Shire mares which he sold to Arthur Cordiner, a new settler, for $350. Mr. Walker has a few more of these horses for sale.

The new well at the depot has been completed at a depth of 253 feet. A three-inch pipe has been sunk and the water rises to within 30 feet of the surface.

A fine baby boy made its appearance at the home of Albert P. Wallace on the 23. Mother and baby are getting along fine and the father has acquired an added touch of dignity.

The heavy snow fall this week will be a fine thing for every farmer who has fall grain in, and also a great benefit to the man who has done his spring plowing, of whom there are a great many. On the dry land along the east bench it was about a foot deep. This with the heavy fall of last month assures big crops on the dry farms of the county.

The article in last week's and this week's Chronicle on the duty and measurement of water, construction of weirs, etc., by Engineer Bark in charge of irrigation investigations are most valuable papers, and we advise every user of water to cut them out for future reference.

We have received a number of guesses on who stole the money in the continued story, "The Lash of Circumstance," but the guessers are away off, so some one still has a chance to win the $5 prize for the correct guess.

John Steele reports increasing sales of farm implements and machinery, of which the Hub Mercantile and Produce Co. has a big stock. With the large acreage under cultivation this year there will be a growing demand for farm machinery.

Dr. Stockham is having a well put down back of his new store by the new well driving firm of J. E. Pratt and A. M. Rosenbaum. They have brought in a new well driving outfit with a nine and a half horse power gasoline engine, and are prepared to put down wells in any part of the district.

Quite an important discovery was made last week in sinking a well near the new townsite of Alfalfa in Section 29, 15 South, Range 7 West. An artesian vein was struck at a depth of 200 feet, the water rising two feet above the surface of the ground. If the artesian vein extends very far it will be a great thing for that section. The water is of the same unsurpassed quality found elsewhere in the valley.

Whicker Bros., who are now in partnership, have struck two flowing wells on the south tract that flow seven gallons per minute, rising two feet above the surface. They have also just completed four wells on the west side.

Settlers on the west side are growing more ambitious now that they have a county road laid out through the tract. They are going to try and get a rural mail route established. Sixty families are already located there and the number will probably be doubled in a few months. They also want to be set aside as a school district, either this year or next, so they can have a school. More than the requisite number of children of school age are in the proposed district. Most of them are now in the Abraham district.

J. W. Smith has purchased the big Rawley tractoin engine that has been standing all winter near the Delta Company's office. He will use it to plaw the 1200 acre tract of the Valley Orchard Company west of the Deseret reservoir. He suggests that some bridge across the river, preferably the one across the spillway, be made strong enough for traction engines, as there will probably be a number used in this section this year.

Rev. Josiah McClain, superintendent of Home Missions for the Presbyterian church in Utah, held services at the school house last Sunday evening. He announces a service for next Sunday, March 17. Sunday School at 2:30 and preaching at 7:30. Strangers are invited. The preparations for the building of a small chapel is now under way. New people interested in church work are invited to come out and make themselves known. "Come thou with us, and we will do thee good."

Whenever there is a lot of freight comes in there is sure to be a big consignment for R. J. Law. Some of his new spring arrivals are among them and the ladies will be sure to be pleased with the new dress goods he is showing. Other seasonable goods noted in his new ad elsewhere.

OAK CITY.

Mr. Ed. Lovell and wife of Idaho and Mr. and Mrs. Wm. Dutson of Leamington, were in town last week visiting relatives and friends.

Mr. Simeon Walker made a business trip to Nephi last Saturday.

John E. Lovell and wife have gone to Salt Lake to take the little boy, Clark, to the hospital.

Oak City is enjoying some nice wet weather. With every rain the dry farmers' smile grows a little longer. If the present weather keeps up there will be farmers with a double smile on their faces, the one reaching around twice.

Miss Sylva Lovell entertained a number of the young folks to a very enjoyable "nickle party" Sunday evening.

Saturday the Meadow junior basket ball team came up to play the local junior team. The Meadow team beat the Oak City team one point at the last track meet for the county championship. The home team was handicapped. The home team was handicapped on account of the lack of practice, but they put up a good game and made the Meadow boys work for the game. The line-up was as follows:

was one of the best ever played on the local floor. The Meadow boys were too much for the home team. They simply outplayed them. Their team work was better as was their basket pitching.

Meadow.		Oak City.
Leo. Stotts	R. E.	Talbot
B. Stotts	L. F.	Lealand Roper
R. Stotts	C.	Less Roper
Swallow	R. G.	Walker
Bushnell	L. G.	Allridge

Referee, W. R. Walker.

Final score, 40 to 24 in favor of Meadow.

IN AND AROUND DELTA

The Week's News from the Coming Metropolis

Cars with settlers' effects are coming into Delta nearly every day. Three came in on Sunday. One contained two outfits from Morgan county. Many settlers are living in tents until they can have more substantial buildings erected.

A. B. Ward's livery is doing a thriving business. Beside a great demand for rigs by land seekers, commercial travelers and others are patrons of the stables.

The sound of the saw and hammer are heard from morning till night in Delta, and building operations are active. Beside the new buildings on Clark street mentioned elsewhere, the following buildings are in course of construction on have been built in the last thirty days: House, barn and stable for N. S. Bishop just west of town; a neat residence for Ed Bishop; postoffice for John Avery Bishop; barber shop built for J. W. Schwartz; Dr. Stockham's drug store; Moody & Cropper's office building; house for W. C. Smith; house for V. V. Colvert;

residence just started for A. B. Ward; office building for Dr. Searight, a new arrival from Indiana. John Steele is also finishing up his attractive bungalow. The Delta Land & Water Co. is also putting up a new warehouse.

Win Walker was over from Oak City this week to get some stock.

Avery Bishop has received his commission as postmaster, and expects to take hold of the office April 1. The new building will be ready then and will be quite an improvement on the old quarters. Ninety-six lock boxes will be provided and other convenient features. It is also expected that it will soon be made a money order office. We learn from the [?] by for [?] of the railway mail [?] that a south-bound mail service will soon be provided. The sending of all the mail north has resulted in great delay and the change has long been needed.

A. C. Sorenson tells us that the Delta Mercantile & Implement Co. has secured the agency for the New York Tailors, one of the largest made-to-order suit builders in the country. See their fine line of spring samples.

Hay is in great demand in Delta owing to the large amount of stock being brought in by settlers. John Steele got in a car on Sunday from Leamington and it was all gone the same day.

The Baker Lumber company got in three more cars of lumber this week, rustic and dimension stuff being the principal items. They can now fill any kind of an order.

McClain & Copening now have a piano in their office and musical entertainments are of frequent occurrence in the evening.

Secretary Rigby attended a meeting of the district school board at Hinckley last week, the other members being R. E. Robinson and Hosea Stout. The question of making Delta a separate district came up. Hinckley is ready to make the separation, giving Delta the present buildings and assuming all the bonds, which is very fair, considering that Delta has got a good deal more out of the district than she has put in. The expenses of the school here will be between $3,000 and $4,000 next term, and it is believed that with her proportion of the railroad property for assessment purposes Delta will be able to support her own schools. The railroad pays about half the taxes. More accommodations are needed here for our growing school population, and it is not thought wise to put up any more temporary buildings and the town is not yet able to erect a large and permanent school building. It is therefore proposed to rent, if possible, a room in the basement hall for another department. This seems to be the most feasible way to provide the necessary accommodations at the least expense.

Among the big sales of real estate recently reported is that of 680 acres on the west side to W. T. Mason, representing himself and a number of others from the same state. They expect to go right to work and put it under cultivation this season.

L. W. Gaisford was over from Fillmore this week. He reports that about twenty-five Fillmore boys are working around Delta this spring.

When you are ready for garden and flower seeds Dr. Stockham will have a supply at his new drug store.

You ought to be getting ready to make a fight on the gophers, squirrels and other farmers' pests. The new drug store can supply you with bluestone, formaldehide, strychnine and other poisons.

If you are interested in fruit lands, orchards, dry land, irrigated land or a nice home on the east side, call at the Chronicle office for particulars.

Dr. W. W. Stockham made a trip to Salt Lake City this week on business connected with getting his new drug store stocked up.

F. D. B. Gay, publisher of the Travelers Guide and One Hundred Best Towns in Utah, was in town last week gathering up commercial cards for his paper.

Empty barrels for sale at A. P. Wallace.

L. R. Humphries received a carload of Jumbo Hardwall Plaster last week.

The new drug store of Dr. Stockham is nearing completion. The roof is on and the carpenters are getting the front enclosed. They expect to have the drug store ready for occupancy by the last of the week.

Delbert Searle made a trip to Provo this week on business. We can't get much out of him but from the way he is acting we think he is making a noise like a new butcher shop for our town.

If you are thinking of doing any papering this spring, you should see A. P. Wallace, as he has the most complete line of wall paper in southern Utah.

EVENTS AT OAK CITY

W. R. Walker, Representative

Born, to Mr. and Mrs. Thomas B. Talbot, a girl. Dr. Theobald of Hinckley was in attendance.

It has been raining or snowing very nearly every day the past week. Over three inches of rain is reported.

The first herd of sheep passed through Oak City Sunday, moving on their way to the summer range.

Hay is athing that is hard to get in Oak City. Many are hauling from Leamington and the western country.

The stormy, cold weather is holding back the peaches, which will no doubt save from the frost. This is all it takes to make a prosperous year for the farmers.

Most of the young people went to Leamington last Friday and returned Sunday. The usual good time was reported. They are learning to skate better now and less accidents are reported.

The saw mill is again running and any one wishing lumber can get it without the muddy drive to the west for it.

Millard County Progress
March 29, 1912

HINCKLEY

This is the birthday of the Hinckley ward and the birthday of Hinckley as well. for they are twins. A fact that may not generally be known and have this day attained their majority.

Twenty one years ago or to be more explicit March 22nd 1891 they were born in Deseret, christened under the direction of Apostle F. M. Lyman and their names enrolled among the list of wards of the Millard Stake of Zion Just which is the eldest we have been unable to find out for their history does not enlighten us. If we might judge by the population, the honor would go to Hinckley, but Oasis might present her claim in bank stock and lucerne seed so we will not quarrel about age as there is no birth-right to loose. Just what our little sister has been doing to day we do not know but Hinckley has been celebrating the event with songs and recitations toasts and reminicences which by contrast with the nice spread served by the Relief Society made us feel as hungry as we used to in the days of our infancy.

For we fell under the care of the sisters, for this was the day they had it set apart for their annual and our birthday was just an appendage tacked on as it were, for it was not thought of at the time their meeting was first announced but with a generosity characteristic of them they said like Annie Lee to Willie Grey "you may only carry half."

At the organization of the ward it numbered about eighty souls. The church record now shows a population of 729. Of the original 80, 20 answered to roll call to day. James P. Terry is our oldest man and Kindness Martudale the oldest woman, she favored us with a song which brought merited applause. Our old friend Jacob Langston with the costume fitingly arranged sang "My old wife and I" and "old wife" dressed in a sort of a monkish garb bore a striking resemblance to a Mr. Slaughter of Kanosh.

Wm. Gardner and wife, Mrs. Stout, Jones, James Blake and many others contributed to success of the entertainment which concluded with a dance in the evening at which "alaman left and "swing your partner" were conspicious features. We all feel well and no serious cases of sickness amon . A little of scarletina is still left as evidence by the yellow flags tacked to the gate posts, one of which decorats the entrance of president Hinckley's premises.

Robison House Notes.

Cushman Bros., Sewing Machine agents, Hinckley, Ernest Hurbert, Range rider, Scipio. Geo. Alma George Kanosh. Emery John Olear Lake, Hosea Stout, Hinckley, Mr. Stevens, Holden, Pearson Oasis, Lou Kimble, Kanosh, Axel Anderson Sterling, P. R. Wilson Nephi, Giles M. Donald, Heber City, O. D Basset Salt Lake. Wm. G O. Morrison Monroe, Dick Daley Manti. Mr. Crook, Ogden.

IN AND AROUND DELTA

The Week's News from the Coming Metropolis

It is a pretty busy place around the depot these days. It looks like a camping ground with the large number of settlers' tents and stock. Some idea of the way settlers are coming in can be judged by the fact that seventeen cars with stock and effects for the settlers around Delta have come in during the past week, and more are on the way. They come from all parts of the country.

D. A. Bunker and John Jimpson of the Hub Mercantile Co., were down from Salt Lake and spent several days looking around the country. They are surprised at the improvements that have been made since their last visit. They are contemplating the erection of a big store building on Clark street, but the matter has not been settled sufficiently to give anything definite this week.

The town board held their regular monthly meeting last Saturday night. Besides the routine business they passed an ordinance placing a tax of $1 on male dogs and $3 on females. They also decided to enforce the Sunday ordinance, so all general business houses are to remain closed hereafter on Sunday.

Agent Bolt also says that the Sunday closing applies to the depot as well. He will not handle any freight or express on that day, as he wants a little time to himself.

Dr. Stockham's new drug store is now open and ready for business. He has his first lot of goods in and can supply you with drugs, medicines, poisons for gophers, etc., garden and flower seeds and other goods in his line.

The new shed for the Baker Lumber Co. is nearly completed. It is 130 x44 feet in size, being the largest shed they have, and will keep all their lumber in out of the weather.

Postmaster Bishop took possession of the office on Monday, and is getting the run of things. Although the boxes for his new office were ordered the 11th of last month, they have not yet arrived, so the old quarters will have to serve for a while.

McClean & Copening report many sales of farm lands and city lots during the past week, and they have been busy showing lands during the day and making out deeds and contracts at night. Many enquiries are also coming from all parts of the country. People are beginning to realize the wonderful advantages of this country in nearness to markets, richness and depth of soil, our pure domestic water supply, abundance of water for irrigation and agreeabl and healthful climate. But the land is going off so rapidly that the opportunity will not long remain open.

Pratt & Rosenbaum's well-driving outfit is kept busy all the time. They have a nine horsepower gasoline engine, capable of driving a two and a half inch pipe, and are also provided with a 3,000 candle power acetelyn light so as to work nights as well as days. Their ad apeaprs in another place.

S. C. Farmer has put himself up a house opposite N. S. B. Bishops to retire to when he wants to enjoy town life when tired of the farm.

A fifteen horsepower oil engine was unloaded on Monday for T. W. Mason and has been demonstrating on the streets this week. It is not a very fast traveler, but can pull a big load. It will be used to clear and cultivate the 640 acres of land Mr. Mason owns on the west side.

Manager Smith of the Valley Orchard Co., also has his big steam Rumley engine at work. It can haul 24 plows and plow 30 acres per day. One hundred feet of iron flume is being laid from the turbine pump to connect with the ditch that is to water their 1200 acres of land.

You can't help but note the big new ad of the Delta Mercantile and Implement Co. this week. The new company has a big stock of goods and a great variety and they invite your trade.

C. W. Watts of Kanosh, president of the Utah Real Estate and Live Stock Co. spent several days in Delta this week. He says Kanosh is in a prosperous condition, that they have had an abundance of rain and snow this year and they look for big crops this season. About 1400 acres of dry farming land will be put in this year—twice what was in last year.

The Utah Real Estate and Live Stock Company has got in a car of seed potatoes and those who want some should call for them. They are also getting in some seed wheat and oats and a car of horses and mules for sale to the settlers. Their ad is also among our new ones this week.

Mr. and Mrs. Watts announce the engagement of their daughter Jean to Mr. Winford Paxton, the marriage to take place in May.

Among the new comers to Delta is Wm. Heatherly, of Dillon, Colo. Mr. Heatherly has a farm southeast of town and will have his family out before long. He says a good many people at Dillon are becoming interested in Delta.

The Hotel Delta is getting ready for the summer weather by getting in a fine new refrigerator.

A. P. Wallace was in the city last week to lay in a supply of builders hardware, paints, oils, etc. He has bought the building recently used by the Delta Lumber Co. and moved it on the lot north of the office of the Utah Real Estate and Live Stock So. and will carry a full line of goods.

R. L. Humphreys and family left this week for the north. Mr. Humphreys will establish himself in the lumber business in Idaho and will return this week to ship his goods. His friends met at the ball last Friday night and gave him a farewell party. Mr. Humphreys is one of the early settlers in Delta and his many friends wish him much success in his new field.

Mr. Hanks, the man who lost both eyes and hands in an explosion of primers eight years ago, lectured in the hall last Wednesday. His lecture was made up of humorous stories, noble sentiment eloquently expressed and beautiful word pictures. He has

got the largest part of his education since he lost his sight and is a wonderful example of what can be accomplished under great disadvantages. No one could be more cheerful.

Our article last week on school district consolidation meets with general approval. J. Frank Day of Fillmore who knows more about school conditions and needs than any other man in the county, says it is the only way to give every district a chance and unify the system. He made a strong talk in favor of it at Hinckley last Saturday.

A force of men is at work putting in the piles and making the approaches for the steel flume across the river. While the flume may not be ready as soon as the water is turned in it will be in place as soon as it is needed. The canals are being cleaned out and the water will probably be turned in about the 15th.

The editor has been busy this week getting out a lot of job printing. Come in with your orders. We are ready to handle them.

NEW DEPOT AT DELTA.

NEWS OF OUR NEIGHBORS

Gathered by the Editor in His Weekly Rounds

The debate at Hinckley last Saturday night was the event of the week, and a large crowd was in attendance. The Hinckley team took the affirmative of the question, "Resolved, That the Principals of the Initiative and Referendum should be Incorporated into the Legislative System of Utah," and the Fillmore team took the negative. Both teams handled the question in a very able manner and showed that they had studied the question deeply. The judges gave their decision in favor of the nega-

tive. While the editor would have given his decision for the affirmative, perhaps his strong convictions on that side would have influenced him. The judges thought the affirmative did not explain the subject fully enough or give sufficient authorities for their statements. It was generally admitted that Eugene Hilton made the strongest speech of any of the debaters.

As will be seen by a notice elsewhere teh stock of the Utah Aerial Navigation and Power Co. is to be advanced to 12½ cents after the 8th of April. Nearly 50,000 shares of stock have been sold in Millard county, a large share of it being in Hinckley, the home of the inventor. Mr. Flanigan has gone to Salt Lake to see about

the manufacture of the wind mills and they will soon be on the market. As they can be made of one-third the weight of the single wheel mills and consequently lower in price, there should be a big demand for the mills. The editor is not usually in favor of stock in inventions, but this looks like a good thing. It is something there will be a demand for, the [illegible] are reliable.

There is a new baby boy at the home of Mr. and Mrs. Frank Western, in Deseret, and a new little girl at Pres. Hinckley's. Dr. Broaddus says all are doing well.

Probably no athletic contest or entertainment this year has equalled in interest or value to the school as this debate. If a school could not turn out clear thinkers, what would it be good for?

Dr. Broaddus is getting quite nicely settled in his new drug store, next to Rich Cropper's barber shop in Hinckley.

During the past week the state road commissioner was in Deseret and together with the county commissioners, decided that the roads being graded

should be widened. The ploughing and scraping have been renewed to make the elevated portion of the roads broader. Between the grading and the stormy weather travel has been a real hardship.

The Hinckley Cash Drug Store has put in some of the finest candies in the region. Boys, come in and see the beautiful gift boxes that will melt her heart of stone. They are going fast. The drug store intends to carry a select stock—that includes the famous "Doctor Bars."

EVENTS AT OAK CITY

W. R. Walker, Representative

Mrs. Nellie G. Lyman left last Wednesday for her home in San Juan county. She has been visiting with relatives and friends for a number of weeks.

Lem Roper's nice dwelling house is now up to the square. It certainly will improve the east part of the city when completed.

Miss Maggie Rawlinson has been doing a big business in the hat line. No doubt, the boys will see a hat parade some of these fine Sundays.

Mrs. Ann Lyman has been quite ill of late. Dr. Stevens of Fillmore, was called to her bedside.

Mrs. Thomas E. Talbot also has been quite sick. Dr. Broaddus, of Deseret, was called on the case.

A number of Delta farmers have been to Oak City the past week buying horses. They found their wants sup-

plied at Simeon Walker's and are now giving them a trial at turning grease-wood under the sod.

Mr. John O. Dutson is home from school. He has been attending the M. I. A. at Hinckley and acting as chaprone to a number of Academy girls.

Mr. Clarence Nielson is ready to move into his nice cottage west of the city.

Eddie Jacobson is nearing completion his location along the main ditch leading to town.

Most of the Finlinson boys went to Fillmore to attend the funeral of their aunt.

Warm weather has come and the apple blossoms will soon be out. The horticultural inspectors should see that the law is enforced and the trees are sprayed properly, thus doing away

with wormy apples. It is poor inducement for an industrious farmer to spray his trees and take good care of them and then have to compete with some lazy farmer who finds it too much work to take care of his trees. He not only injures his neighbor, but he beats the person that buys his apples, besides he is a law-breaking citizen. If the inspector finds any such persons let him see that they obey the law. It is a fact that last year wormy apples were sold in the western country, many coming from the home of the inspector. Does this look like the law was being enforced? How many are there who would not pay more for good apples than those the worm has taken his dinner from, the leavings being left for the buyer. Let us hear from a consumer!

NEWS OF OUR NEIGHBORS

Gathered by the Editor in His Weekly Rounds

Professor Millard J. Andelin and Mrs. Andelin will give a concert in the Deseret meeting house next Friday evening (April 19). They will also sing in the Millard Stake Academy Saturday evening.

Professor Andelin has an excellent bass voice and when he sings the listeners can understand every word. He has recently returned from Europe, where he has been for five years, having his voice trained. He won distinction by singing on some of the large stages in Berlin and London.

Mrs. Andelin (formerly Miss Arvilla Clark) has also been studying while abroad.

We feel that the people of this vicinity are favored in having the privilege of hearing these artists. It is by good patronage that we can get them to come again.

Oasis continues to be the show ground for the land sellers of the Delta tract. Nearly every day prospective land buyers are taken through the lands around Oasis to show the capabilities of this section for raising alfalfa hay and seed. Some of the visitors get the idea that all they have to do is to plant the seed this spring and get a good crop of hay and seed this fall. They don't realize that our splendid fields of alfalfa have been cropped for years, and that it sometimes takes years to get a first-class stand of alfalfa, but they will find this out by experience, but it is hardly fair to give buyers the impression that they can start right in and make a crop from their hay and seed to meet their payments and expenses and a good profit besides.

Oasis is waking up and is organizing a commercial club to further the interests of this section. Among other improvements contemplated is a road straight east of the depot to connect with the road running south from Delta. Oasis is nearer to many of the new settlers than is Delta, and our southern neighbor proposes to furnish a short and direct route to their trade center over a good grade. Henry Huff has donated a long strip of land through his farm and it is expected that other farmers along the route will do likewise. Have good roads into your towns and good bridges and trade will follow.

The road from Oasis through Deseret and nearly to Hinckley has been widened, graded and put into better condition than any road on the west side. New culverts and bridges have been put in and the road rounded so that the water will run off. We have the best natural roads in Millard County of any section in Utah. There are no hills to dig down or gullies to fill. All it needs is for the roadway to be rounded up so the water will run off and they will keep in good condition all the year round. The expense is small, and the benefit in time saved, lessened wear of vehicles and horses, and the ability to haul heavier loads is incalculable.

Hosea Stout is getting in numerous shipments of trees for the west side settlements. Carolina poplars are the favorites for shade trees, but many are getting in other ornamental trees, and bushes for hedges, lawns, etc. Deseret is getting in a large share of them.

Deseret is the only place we have yet heard of that had a real celebration on Arbor Day, last Monday. Principal Petty took his pupils and two grades of the Hinckley school over to the old fort, cleared out the brush from part of it, raised the stars and stripes over it and had an interesting program. Sons of the old Indian war veterans were present and participated in the exercises. An effort is going to be made to have this historic monument of pioneer days restored and preserved for future generations. The people ought to see that this is done, for it is well worth preserving as a monument.

John Dewsnup tells us that he expects to rebuild his seed warehouse and cleaning plant. The new structure will be fire proof, so there will be no danger of a repetition of the former accident. Nothing was saved from the former fire, even the boiler being warped and rendered useless.

The ladies of Deseret are evidently like their sisters elsewhere—they love fine millinery, and judging by the assortment we saw at Mrs. D. J. Black's they will not have to go out of town for it. We couldn't see but what her stock was just as attractive as what we saw in Salt Lake, and when the ladies are decked out in her creations they will cut as big a swell as their sisters in the capital.

The Kelly Ryan Realty company, the new land merchants at Deseret, are doing a good business and report numerous sales and many enquiries for land. No better land can be found anywhere in Millard County than at Deseret, and when land sellers want to show what a splendid soil we have for vegetables they bring buyers down here. The 10,000 acre tract that is being opened up south of Deseret has been nearly all taken up. Dr. Mitchell of Ogden recently took up several hundred acres and will put a large portion of it under cultivation. The company expects to prove up on their water early next month.

Damron & Hawley have some men's, women's and children's suits that they are selling very cheap. They also have some special bargains in men's, women's and children's shoes that should prove attractive to the economical buyer.

FOR SALE—A fine Jersey-Durham cow in calf. A heavy milker and very gentle. Just the thing for a family cow. Enquire of Virgil Kelly.

Ora Lake of Abraham is seeding another 100 acres of his farm to alfalfa, and it is coming on fine. This will make 220 acres Mr. Lake has in alfalfa—the largest alfalfa farm in the valley.

H. L. Bishop of Hinckley has sold his old home of 160 acres west of Hinckley to a California man. Mr. Bishop has lived on this farm for over twenty-five years. But he has plenty of other land so will not have to leave to found another home.

EVENTS AT OAK CITY

W. R. Walker, Representative

Born to Mr. and Mrs. Leo Finlinson, a girl. Mrs. Theobold acted as nurse, and mother and child are getting along nicely.

Since the last correspondence, Mrs. Mary M. Lyman had traded homes with Joseph P. Callister, of Delta. We are sorry to lose Mrs. Lyman and her two boys, as they are a big help to the town. We like all we have got and hate to lose them and welcome all we can get. Mr. Callister and wife are formerly of Oak City and are no doubt glad to get back once more.

Walter Johnson and Alma Harder, of Leamington, have been doing the carpenter work on Lem Roper's house. Alma is learning to like the town, at least some of the people who live in it.

John Loundahl has moved to Leamington, where he is going to work this summer.

The Sunday services were taken up by the religion class. A very instructive program was given.

Mr. Daniel Stevens and R. W. King, of Fillmore, were here Sunday in the interest of the high school at Fillmore.

A farewell party was given Wednesday evening at the home of George K. Finlinson in honor of Miss Alice Dean, who has been teaching school here the past winter. A very enjoyable time was had.

The school children surprised Mr. William Davis Thursday night and gave him a nice party in his honor. They presented him with a nice rocking chair, so he might take things easy during the summer.

The district school closed Friday, after a most successful year.

A farewell dance was given Mr. Stanley Lovell Friday night. Mr. Lovell left Sunday morning for a mission in England. One hundred and twenty-three dollars was raised to start him on his journey.

Mr. Alfred Jacobson spent a week home. He is attending school at Provo.

A gentleman who is best known to the swearing and oath taking people of our community had the misfortune of losing his cows. An early start to the hills was made for them. They were soon located, but to the surprise of the "notary," one of his cows had been branded with an eleven (11) on the right ribs.

Arthur Talbot, who lives at the base of the lane leading to the hills, and who thought the people were losing their smiles for him, has raised a three cornered beard (on his chin), was aroused, but the smile that he brought to the fact of the "notary's" was of short endurance. Some one had branded his cow and an appeal for assistance was soon made and a call upon the next neighbor was in order. The correspondents of both county papers were called to assist and give a good account of the affair.

Every man branding with a brand resembling that of an 11, was called upon to show his iron. Fires were looked for all up and down the lane. The constable, who has not as yet had the privilege of making an arrest, was overflowing with pride on the prospects. The chief justice of Oak City was hurrying his calendar in order to make room for the case, but to the disappointed helpers, they found the cow had only "licked" herself a couple of times on the ribs. The guilty one was located and the case dismissed.

John C. Lovell, at present the "Hay King" of Oak City, thought he had discovered a thief the other week. His hay had been molested and leaves had been strung for a block and a half, where it was placed in a neighbor's sheep pen. He was doing some fine detective work on the case when it was discovered that mischievious boys had done it the night before. They certainly had the Hay King excited for a while.

William Chestnut, the "Bell Shark" of Oak City, is complaining over the town clock. He thinks it should be fixed so as to keep the correct time.

Millard County Progress
April 19, 1912

OAK CITY.

S. J. Rawlinson, Representative

Stormy weather continues, and while the vegetative growth is some what retarded, yet a prosperous outlook is before our community.

The fruit crop promises better than it has done for some years and if nothing unfortold happens, every variety will be produced this season.

We are informed that Mrs. Mary M. Lyman and sons have traded homes with Joseph P. Callister of Delta. We are glad to welcome Mr. Callister, in as much as we know him from his boyhood spent here, but our people will miss Mrs. Lyman very much, since she has been a very valuable citizen in all respects, here most of her life.

Last Sunday evening Mr. Daniel Stevens and Co. Atty. R. W. King of Fillmore, were speakers at the Priesthood meeting in interest of establishing a county high school at Fillmore. They set forth very logical reasons why the people of the county should support a high school at Fillmore. Not because it is the county seat but that it is a center of the eastern part of the county and also has the majority of the high school students as well as a building already constructed. They also pointed to the fact that a school established at Fillmore would not injure the Academy at Hinckley.

EVENTS AT OAK CITY

W. R. Walker, Representative

Names of contestants to enter in the M. S. A. track meet, to be held in Fillmore, May 14th, 1912:

Fillmore.

Junior Basket ball team

Waldon Lyman, Captain.

Amell Warner, Leutie Wade, Roy Saver, Willie Starley and Edgar Warner.

Track Men—Albert Robison, Carl Day, Nielson Cooper, John Smith, Elmer Carling, A. Huntsman, Archie Robison, Morse Lambert, Newel Warner, J. Speaksman, Milan Brunson, Grover Giles, Van McBride, Willard Day.

Oak City.

Senior Baseball Team.

LeRoy Walker, J. Lausdahl, S. Roper, C. Roper, W. E. Davis, L. Christensen, W. R. Walker, W. Christensen.

Track Team—Ray Finlinson, John Dutson, C. Dutson, S. J. Rawlinson, A. Christensen, Leland Roper, C. Talbot, Bert Roper, E. Anderson, Jos. Finlinson, Edgar Nielson, Lee Walker, Jos. Christensen, Geo. E. Finlinson.

Hinckley.

Basket Ball Teams—Senior and Junior D. Gourley, M. O. Maughan, M. Bishop, John Wright, A. Reeve, John Greener, Marvin Moody, L. Whitehead, C. Bishop, William Blake, William Pratt, H. Maxfield, H. Slaughter.

Track Men—L. Davis, E. Stout, C. Slaughter, C. Theobald, Fay Theobald, Don Bishop, E. Talbot, John Reeve, James Blake, Jr.; Wm. Camp, A.

Workman, Thomas Greener, B. Moody, E. Maughan, M. Draper, Geo. Talbot Jr., Leon Finlayson.

Leamington.

Senior Baseball Team.

Fred Greathouse, W. Stout, A. Dutson, S. Nielson, W. Nielson, Axel Johnson.

Track Men—Fred Nielson, A. Hardre.

Oasis.

Junior Baseball Team.

A. Christensen, A. Christensen, A. Standworth, M. Jackson, O. Cornwall, P. Peterson Jr., G. Huff, A. Jensen.

Track Team—V. Stayler, A. Jensen, H. Roundy, Wm. Ide.

Holden.

Junior Baseball Team.

Fred Johnson, W. Stevens, H. Stevens, E. Huffins, Grant Johnson, P. Stringham.

Deseret.

Track Men—George Cahoon, Arthur Cahoon, George Kelly, A. Petty, Edgar Petty.

Delta.

Junior Baseball Team.

P. Hawkins, N. Gardner, C. Billings, T. Bower, R. Hone, H. Koch and W. Callister.

Meadow.

Junior Baseball Team.

Leo Stott, A. Stott, R. Stott, Thomas Swallow, George Bushnell, D. Bushnell.

Track Men—Joseph Edwards, P. Bennett, F. Dame, Ely Bennett.

Hinckley.

Delayed in Transit.

Another one of Millard County's pioneers answers to the roll call and passes over the divide.

James V. Knight comonly and familiarly known in the early days of Fillmore as Jimmie Knight died in the Hospital in Salt Lake City on the 11th inst after undergoing what was supposed to be a successful surgical operation, but his enfeebled condition was unable to endure the strain and death came to his relief.

He was born in the state of New York in 1833 and came to Utah when about 17 years of age was a cousin of the McBride families and as a young man the writer remembers him and his mother living with old uncle Samy McBride in Fillmore.

He was of a jovil disposition and honest to a fault, his word was his bond and always redeemed. In the days of immigration across the plains, he made two trips to aid the worthy poor to come to Utah. He lived single for a long time but finaly married and with his wife moved to Kingston with the King family. And after the Order broke up which they went there to establish, he moved to Circle Valley where he lived for several years but finally came back to his home county again and settled in Hinckley where his remains were taken after his death. His funeral services were conducted by Bp. Wm. F. Pratt but virtualy turned over to the Indian war veterans who came from different places to pay their respects to a departed comrade. The speakers were Thomas Cropper, Samuel Bennett, Virgil Kelly, Joseph Nielson, T. O Callister, Lee Cropper and Bp. Pratt all of whom spoke words of comfort to his wife and family.

Although aged and infirm, he will be missed for his bent form scarred by the ravages of time was a familiar sight on the streets of Hinckley for he failed to realize that he was like Holmes'es last leaf on the tree, And felt that he still carried the responsibilities of a home and family. Sunday he always took his seat in the same place near the pulpit and was ever ready and willing to testify to the truth of the great Latter-day work and the divine mission of the prophet Joseph Smith whom he well remembered as a child in Nauvoo.

Retiring and unassuming in his nature, he sought for no conspicious place among his fellows and yet when the angel of resuresction shall call the roll the names of such men as James V.

Knight will be found listed among those who met the issues of life squarely and done their whole duty as they understood it.

Millard County Chronicle
May 9, 1912

NEWS OF OUR NEIGHBORS

Gathered by the Editor in His Weekly Rounds

There have been a number of visitors in Deseret recently, among them Mrs. Crandall of American Fork, visiting her brother, A. D. Ryan. Mrs. Staats of Salt Lake visiting her aunt, Mrs. Effie Moody.

A good many new settlers have moved into town and out on the flat between Deseret and Clear Lake. The desert is relieved by several cabins and tents.

The enterprising citizens of Deseret are expressing themselves in many useful ways. One day recently they got together and put in a lot of hitching posts in front of the Relief hall and in the lane between the meeting house and the river. An ideal hitching place has thus been secured where the teams and rigs are off the street. Another improvement bee was held in the park Saturday where the women served refreshments to the men who worked. Committees have also been canvassing the town in the interests of a new amusement hall. A good deal of money and work has already been subscribed. Bishop Damron has called several meetings of the townspeople to consider ways of beautifying and improving the town.

Mr. Braddus was seen returning from Clear Lake Friday morning in one of the coldest and worst blizzards we have had for a long time. Sand, mud, the Black Rock hill, a high wind and rain and snow put the little motor car to a severe test but it came through all right. Clear Lake has been bought up by several Kansas people who have moved out and settled. The illness which called the doctor was in the family of Mr. ___ the new owners. Why doesn't Clear Lake have a telephone? It is the only utterly isolated town in the county.

The funeral of Sister Baker was held last week in the Deseret meeting house. Mrs. Baker was taken to Salt Lake for operation as the only possible hope of recovery from her long ill health, but the condition of

her heart proved too serious for operation to be undertaken at all—so serious indeed that she died before she could be brought home again. The many friends of Mr. Baker extend their sincere sympathy to the bereaved family.

All the smallpox seems to have died out of Deseret. Fortunately it did not spread outside the family where it first developed.

A good many Desereters are at work down on the Black Rock bottoms, fencing, plowing and making ditches—and incidentally changing the road.

Deseret congratulates Miss Vernell Moody, its only graduate this year from the Academy Hinckley.

On Thursday evening, April 25, Dr. and Mrs. C. A. Broaddus entertained the Academy musical culture students at a unique and delightful music party. Between 35 and 40 students were present, the boys gallantly escorting two or three girls apiece. Mrs. Broaddus was assisted by Miss Fern Huff and Miss Ida Parker, two of the district school teachers who have shown an enthusiastic interest in the music work in Hinckley this winter.

Miss Lapriel Robinson won the prize in the first game which required a great deal of knowledge of musical history, and in the second general game of guessing composers by their pictures, seven or eight shared the prize—a box of McDonald's Red Dutch chocolates. Many other musical games were played in groups and dainty refreshments were served in the dining room, while music on the piano player and Victrola filled in all the spaces.

The first week of May was full of interesting affairs at the academy. One of the most dignified and carefully prepared entertainments was the delightful recital of spring music given Monday evening, April 29 by some of the piano pupils and musical culture students of Mrs. Broadus at the academy. The stage was made attractive and homelike and decorated with potted plants. The program as prefaced by brief comments on some of the numbers. The piano numbers were given by Ellen Kelly, Rosetta ___, Golden Huff, Norma Damron, ___ Moody; the vocal

solos, duets, trio and double quartets being furnished by Geneva Robinson, Norma Moody, Lapriel Robinson, Norma Damron, Myrtle Langston, Arthur Humphries, George Bushnell, Layton Harris, Rodney Stott and Mrs. Broaddus, with Mrs. Laura Robinson and baby assisting in the closing tableau. Mrs. Broaddus and some of the others on the program met all the expense of the evening including programs, giving the music with the compliments of the season to a crowded house.

Eddie Anderson's son, Marvin, was kicked Sunday morning by a horse, receiving a severe wound beside the ear. It was necessary for Dr. Broaddus to take three stitches to close the wound, but the boy is now getting along all right.

Have you seen the toilet articles the Hinckley cash drug store? Why not try some of their toilet water, face powder, cold cream, toilet soap and prophylactic tooth brushes? Two new shipments of fine candies are just in. Look at the "Pink Lady" window. Nothing could make a lovlier gift than a box of "Regents" or "de Luxe" chocolates.

Milton Moody is erecting a fine modern bungalow just west of the academy lane. Surely the bungalow is the most appropriate style for this broad, flat country.

EVENTS AT OAK CITY

W. R. Walker, Representative

Joseph Finlinson is feeling first class and carries a broad smile. When asked what made him so pleased he exclaimed, "Why, haven't you heard? I have another fine looking boy."

The weather has been making the people wear out their winter clothes before getting themselves some new summer ones.

The other night the young girls of our place deserted the boys of Oak City and took their abode at "Fool" City. They reported a fine time.

The students of the M. S. A. have returned home from school. They are looking fine and no doubt have enjoyed themselves the past winter.

Although the cold weather is still prevalent the water supply is good and a big crop is expected both in the fruit line and the field crops.

If the county commissioners and the county road inspector happened to make a trip from Oak City to Delta the road in the near future would take on an improved appearance. It is greatly needed.

IN AND AROUND DELTA

The Week's News from the Coming Metropolis

Additional lock boxes have been put in at the post office and there are now 170 altogether. The new ones are combination locks which do not need keys. Rent a box so you can get your mail at any time.

Delta will have a wholesale establishment as soon as S. W. Eccles' new establishment is open. He intends to make ice cream by the wholesale, so as to supply the neighboring towns. He will also want a large amount of cream from the farmers, so those who want to sell their cream should be prepared to keep Mr. Eccles supplied. Making his supply from pure and fresh cream, and having an excellent recipe Mr. Eccles will make a superior article and ought to have the trade. Patronize home industry is a good motto and ought to be applied in this case.

A cheap shoddy outfit was in town last week getting rid of some junk brought down from Commercial street, Salt Lake. While the prices are low the goods are dear at any price. People can't get something for nothing, when they pay cheap prices for anything they may be sure they are getting cheap goods. They may think they are getting the genuine article but they will soon find out that it is shoddy. Buy from your home merchants who help keep up the town and have a reputation to keep up. They will make good anything that does not prove to be as represented, but these traveling outfits that are here today and gone tomorrow don't stay long enough for the cheap character of their goods to be discovered. Patronize your home merchants and you will get the worth of your money.

We hear only good words for Engineer Roberts who is the water master on the west side. He is on the job from dawn till dark and the farmers have no trouble in getting all the water they want. They don't have to chase after him either. He calls on them to find out when they want water.

R. A. Nelson, who recently bought the Bishop homestead near Hinckley, has sold it and bought H. S. Stapleys place a mile east of Hinckley. Forty of it is in alfalfa. Millard county has a great attraction for California people. No wonder when they can get land here for $50 and $60 that is better than that for which they pay $250 and more in California.

A. C. Sorenson of the Delta Mercantile and Implement Co. reports that they have sold two carloads of farm machinery since they added that line to their business. The expect two more carloads this week and will, doubtless soon dispose of them as there is a big demand for farm machinery by the many new farmers in this section. See their new ad and note the special prices they are making on some staple groceries.

Mr. Harrison of the National Copper Bank of Salt Lake City spent a day looking over the town and surrounding country. He expressed his opinion that a great future was in store for this section. He said his bank had no expectation of starting a branch down here. He only came down to look the country over. We have heard considerable talk about a bank for Delta but it doesn't materialize very fast.

The store of the Hub mercantile and Produce Co. has been fixed up and more improvements are contemplated The interior has been wainscotted, more shelving and counters put in and a sanctum provided for Manager Steel. A square front will be added, the building will be newly roofed and painted and a fence built around the store and warehouse. The Hub now handles the goods of the Consolidated Wagon & Machine Co. The oldest and largest establishment of the kind in Utah. The Hub does a big business in farm implements and machinery and handles more hay and grain than any other firm. Manager Steel reports a splendid business, and they deserve it.

Things are shaping up for a big time here on the 4th and 5th. It is expected that some good purses will be offered so that it will be an inducement to attract some fast horses. A good band will be present, there will be a big dance in the evening and all sorts of attractions will be offered to entertain the visitors. If you want to have the time of your life come to Delta July 4th and 5th.

Chas. Pocock, representing the Pioneer Nursery, has put out 105 Carolina populars in the yard of the Delta Hotel. A good many trees have been set by others and in a few years Delta will present quite a different appearance. We also note that nearly every one on the west side is setting out some trees, both shade and fruit.

Manager J. H. Smith of the Valley Orchard Co., expects to put about 300 acres under cultivation this year. It will be principally oats and wheat, but he is going to put out some potatoes and a variety of garden stuff as an experiment.

Note the new ad of the Golden Rule Store this week. Day is making some prices on calicos and ginghams that ought to prove attractive to the ladies.

The Delta Mercantile and Implement Co. is selling the best flour made. It is from the Nephi dry farm wheat.

Theobald Bros. and Joseph Grue of Hinckley expect to build a real estate office in Delta and also go into the contracting and building business.

The paint, hardware and glass business of Bishop & Wallace seems to fill a long felt want and Bert Wallace seems to be busy all the time.

Although not as many land buyers are coming in now as during the winter a few drop off every week. If they can't find anything on the Carey act lands they usually get an improved or unimproved farm around Hinckley, Deseret or Oasis. They can hardly fail to get good land wherever they go in Millard county.

Hay continues to soar upwards and the latest quotation is $22. The next lot of oats will probably be $2.85 or more and barley will likely get up to $3 before every one is supplied. It is to be hoped the farmers will get somewhere near that price when they want to sell this fall.

Every one is looking forward to big crops this harvest. The abundance of moisture this spring, the absence of dry hot winds and the excellent condition of the soil, and the abundance of water for irrigation purposes ensures a rapid growth of everything as soon as steady warm weather comes.

Deputy Sheriff Huntsman informs us that the item of two weeks ago which stated that a free county boarder and another man were hurt playing ball was a mistake, in that it was not a free county boarder. The young man had served his time and was working for the deputy, and had been free for three months. He says that since he has been deputy he has not allowed his prisoners to mingle in public amusements or linger upon the streets. The only time they are not in close confinement is when they are working under his charge.

The Delta Implement and Mercantile Co. is offering 15 pounds of sugar for $1, and as you will note by their ad are making some other special prices this week.

W. D. Mason of the animal husbandry branch of the Agricultural department, has been making an examination of the sheep herds of the county to see if there was any scab or other disease among them. He reports all the herds in a healthy condition.

A picked up baseball team went down to Deseret last Saturday and had a game with their team and were badly defeated by a score of 21 to 5. They didn't mind that, however, as they were treated as if they were the Phillies. They were treated to ice cream on the grounds, were given a good supper by the good people of the town and then enjoyed a good dance in the evening. They are loud in their praises of the way they were treated. There will be a return game here next Saturday and they want to show the visitors as good a time as they had. The boys want to get up a good team at Delta. There are some good players here. Win and Roy Walker, two good players, will be here for the summer and there are some good players among the new comers from the east. With a team here, one at Deseret and another at Hinckley, there ought to be some good games pulled off this summer and a big series for the 4th and 5th of July, when we have our big race meeting.

J. A. Fenton of the Omaha Bee has been in the county the past week gathering data for some special articles about Utah. He is much impressed with the resources and prospects of Millard county.

Attorney Melville was in town last week. He has more and more calls to Delta and expects to locate here permanently about the first of June. He will have an office in the Stock-ham building, where N. S. Bishop will also have his real estate office. Delta needs a first class attorney and Alex Melville will certainly fill the bill. His excellent reputation as a lawyer and wide acquaintance in the county should assure him plenty of business.

Have you seen Bert Wallace's line of wall papers? He carries quite a stock, besides about 900 samples from which one can also make selections. We were surprised at the low prices he is asking. We know from experience that one can't do any better in Salt Lake City.

The boys are going to give a big dance on Saturday evening after the ball game. They say they are going to get the best music they can regardless of cost. And while we think of it why can't a good orchestra be organized in Delta? We understand there are quite a number of players on various instruments here, and all they need to do is to get together. They will have plenty of employment, not only in Delta, but in neighboring towns. Get together, boys.

Mrs. Mary Lyman and her boys have moved down from Oak City and are going into the poultry business on an extensive scale. They have four incubators with a capacity of about 500 eggs and raised at Oak City about 1500 chickens, many of which they sell at $10 per 100 when a day old. They are bringing several hundred down here where they have the advantage of being on the railroad and will go into the egg business. They raise White Leghorns exclusively, as they believe they are the heaviest egg producers. Conditions for the poultry business are ideal at Delta.

NEWS OF OUR NEIGHBORS

Gathered by the Editor in His Weekly Rounds

The presence of spring is much more manifest in Hinckley than in Delta. There are trees and lawns and gardens to put on their verdant garments, while the air is full of the odor of bud and blossom. Nearly everyone is putting out trees and the new streets will in a few years be shady avenues. There are a number of nice lawns, but the nicest one is Wm. Walkers' on Main street. There may be others just as nice but the editor didn't happen to see them. The blossom laden fruit trees in Joseph Blake's front yard are also noticeable.

The ditches in and around Hinckley are in excellent condition and we saw no mud puddles in the street as one sees in Delta. The flume across the streets are also sound and substantial. A good many concrete head gates have been put in.

Some notice should have been given the public that the bridge across the canal southwest of the Valley Orchard Co.'s land had been taken out and the road was impassable. The road to Hinckley now runs south along the canal beside the brickyard to the main county road running straight west to Hinckley. There is also a bad crossing on this road that needs fixing. That is one thing we are all deficient in—good bridges and crossings. No expensive work is required anywhere; just a few dollars worth of lumber and the prompt expenditure of a few day's labor would fix them all up. If the first break in a crossing was promptly repaired it would save expense and often prevent a breakdown.

Among the other seasonable goods of which we were shown samples are of ladies' shirt waists, skirts and dress goods. The firm carries such a big stock of goods that you are sure to always find just the quality and price of goods you want. They are doing a bigger business than ever and Mr. Pratt says they do less credit business than formerly, showing that there is more money in the county.

John Argue is a newcomer from California who is preparing to make his home in Hinckley. He has built a house for Joseph Neilson on his ranch west of town and the family moved out there this week. He has also built a house for Mr. Foulk, another California man who with his bride will try farming at Hinckley.

Golden, the lively young son of H. V. Wright, fell off the fence a few days ago and broke one of the bones of his leg below the knee. He wont be able to run around for a couple of weeks, but that will be the most serious result of the accident.

We found George Billings of the Hinckley Co-op, opening up several cases of ivory and cameo channeled ware, a new thing in cooking utensils. It is a big improvement over ordinary granite ware and is no more expensive. They have also been doing a big business in United States separators, having sold ten within the last week or so. They have just got in another lot. This seems to be the favorite machine for the farmers in this section.

We found D. A. Flanigan, the wind mill man at the blacksmith shop busy trying out a new pump he has just invented. It is a very simple contrivance having no piston, pump rod or suction valve. Nothing but a check valve operated by the weight and inertia of the water. He tells us that the Aeriel Power and Navigation Co. is having some wind mills made at Ogden and will have them on the market in a short time. A large number of people around Hinckley have put in orders for mills.

Hinckley isn't quite as lively appearing since the academy students and faculty have gone but everybody seems to be happy.

Next Friday, May 24th, a mother's program will be given to the married ladies of Hinckley, to which they are all invited. It will be held in the afternoon and the program will be musical and literary in character, and lunch will be served. In the evening a dance will be given with good music in attendance. The committee having the affair in charge consists of Mary Cropper, Sylvia Stout, Emmeline Stapley, Edith Reeve and Mabel Wright. Come out and have a good time.

N. E. Lewis, the expert harness maker, is always busy when the editor calls and never has any complaints of hard times. When he isn't busy making or mending horse millinery he is repairing footwear. He says he has a good market for his celebrated harness, single and double cinch saddles, horse blankets, collar pads, bridles, etc.

Roy Joice, who recently came here from California, thinks the climate here superior to that of the Golden State, and likes the country well. We don't find any of the newcomers making any complaint of Hinckley.

As the country around Hinckley becomes better known the demand for farms has increased and prices have gone up. A few years ago people wouldn't look at land west of Hinckley, although it was offered for $10 per acre. Now it sells readily for $50.

James Stapley and family are leaving Hinckley to make their home in Kannarra. We regret losing such citizens and wish them success in their new home.

Dr. Broaddus' new drug store will soon be equipped to do a hot weather business. He intends to put in a soda water fountain and carry ice cream, and will doubtless do a good business. By the way, this is one of the drug stores in the county where a man can't get a dose of whiskey by simply saying that he has a cramp in the stomach. The doctor can do all the business he wants to without running liquor on the side.

Miss Vera Carter of Provo, has been visiting friends in Hinckley. Mrs. Ben Black is visiting her sister, Mrs. Madge Robinson.

Miss Edna Cropper has gone to American Fork to visit friends.

The road from Hinckley to Deseret and on to Oasis is the only good piece of road making we have seen on the west side. The roadway is rounded up so it will shed water so there will never be any danger of mud holes. A road drag once in a while will keep it in good condition all the year round. The expense is not heavy and once fixed it will stay that way. We wish a few roads around Delta could be fixed that way.

William Black's orchard is a 'bower of sweetness and beauty. His apple, pear and crab trees and currant bushes are loaded as full of blossoms as they will hold, and if no frost comes he should have a large crop of fruit. Frost is the only drawback for fruit raising in this valley. A killing frost is likely to come the last two weeks of May, which means ruin to fruit. The years that frost does not come a good crop is assured.

The farmers of Millard county believe in good horses and many good stallions for breeding purposes have been imported. The finest stallion we have seen for general purposes is Virgil Kelly's French coach he has just brought in from California. It was imported from France at a cost of $2600 by Mr. Kelly's brother, recently deceased in California. It weighs about 1300, is a bay with a coat like satin, and is good for riding, driving or heavy work. He is gentle as a kitten and carries himself like the king of beasts.

Although Mrs. Dan Black has a small store, she does a surprisingly large business. She finds her quarters cramped and will enlarge the store this summer, also putting large plate glass window. While she specializes on millinery and dress goods she also handles a line of general merchandise. Judging by the large amount of millinery business she does she evidently suits the ladies' tastes to perfection.

W. H. Western is the only blacksmith in Deseret, Nick Faust having left. We always find him busy whenever we come to Deseret. He thoroughly understands his trade and knows how to do good work.

We found nearly everybody worked up over the scarcity of water. No one could tell the reason for it. There is plenty of water in the big reservoir and there is more snow in the mountains than for thirty years yet there is not enough coming down the river to fill the canals. It looks like very bad management somewhere.

Mr. and Mrs. Ryan are now occupying part of William Black's house.

Miss Norma Moody celebrated her sixteenth birthday last Friday by entertaining a number of her young friends. Music and games were indulged in and refreshments were served.

Mr. McRae and family, who spent the winter in Deseret for their health, have gone to Colorado.

Mrs. Margaret and her aids drove over to Holden to attend the primary conference last Sunday.

Miss Ariel Wood, the popular clerk at Damron & Hawleys has gone to Holden and when she returns it will be as Mrs. Penny. The many friends of the young people wish them long life and much happiness.

A. D. Ryan of the Kelly-Ryan Realty Co., reports a good business in farm lands. They are making sales every week and the buyers are mostly Salt Lake and Ogden people. They have an office in the Kearns building, Salt Lake, and one of them is there all the time. People only need to see their lands and prices to become buyers.

Nels Peterson, who recently sold his farm near Deseret, has bought the Huff hotel at Oasis.

Mrs. Damron and daughter Lucile have gone to Salt Lake and Plain City for a few weeks' visit. Bishop Damron also took a business trip to Salt Lake.

Irwin McDowell of Provo had quite an experience last week. He left Deseret in the morning to go to Osceola and Ely on his seven horse power motor cycle. He got lost on the desert, about 75 miles out, and had to lay out all night in a canyon with neither food or water. He had enough gasoline to get back to Deseret next day completely exhausted. After resting up a day and getting more explicit directions he started out again confident that he would get

through all right. A man has considerable nerve to tackle so long a journey through the desert.

The people of Deseret are a pretty public spirited lot. They get out every Sunday and fix up the streets, clean the ditches, repair the roads and crossings and put the town in presentable shape. The result is that the town makes a favorable impression on visitors. The town isn't incorporated and has no revenue. They have fixed up their amusement park in good shape and in a few years will have a nicely shaded park. Public spirit and united effort will accomplish wonders for a town.

IN AND AROUND DELTA

The Week's News from the Coming Metropolis

The best cash register outside of Salt Lake that we have seen is the new one just installed at the Hub Mercantile Co. It is a $200 machine and besides registering the cash, reg it ers ccount sales, who the salesman w s, gives the customer a coupon ti ket and can be made to do a number of other stunts. It perform. nearly all the functions of a bookkeeper and with a phonograph attachment would pretty near take the place of a salesman. The Hub evidently believes in being up to date in their equipment for doing business.

Although land buyers are not very numerous now days and land sales will be slow for the next three months a few prospective buyers are coming in every week. Last Saturday C. Adderly, Dr. J. W. Bracken and J. Keely came down from Bingham and spent the day looking around. There was a livelier movement in real estate that day than we have ever seen in Delta, but it was occasioned by a big wind from the south. It was the most disagreeable dust storm we have seen. The gentlemen are coming down again when the country can be seen to better advantage and expect to invest.

R. A. Nelson of California, who has considerable holdings in this vicinity, returned to Delta last week. Beasly Bros. and J. Verbaum returned with him and expect to invest here if they can find something that suits them.

The session of the town board last Saturday was taken up in considering the proposed franchise to the People's Telephone Co. and to Clark Callister's Telephone Co. One of the provisions of the franchises is that the companies are to run their lines through the alleys, and Mr. Callister is already at work changing his lines. He intends to have a switch board installed at A. B. Ward's and to convert the line into a four party system. This change is greatly needed and will result in a great improvement in the service and an increase in the number of customers.

Miss Emma Tozer is now officiating behind R. J. Law's counters and can show you as fine a line of ladies' white dress goods, scrims, ginghams, crepes, etc., as you will find anywhere. Mr. Law is also carrying a line of ladies' skirts that should prove attractive to his customers.

The walls of S. W. Eccles' new store are now up to the second story and it is going to be a handsome structure. It is made of the smooth white tile and is different from any other building in town. Mr. Eccles is going to have his establishment equipped with the latest machinery for making ice cream and candy and bakery goods, and will be in a position to do a wholesale business with neighboring towns.

There seems to be no good reason why the Melville Company should allow their ditches to overflow the streets as they are doing all the time. The street by Avery Bishops has been a mud hole ever since the water was turned in, and west of George Days the street is flooded for nearly a block. A few hours with a team and plow would throw up banks on either side of these ditches so that the water would not break over. The company has surely got enough money to put in at least one day's work. That's all it needs.

Have you seen those Ball Brand rubber boots for irrigating at R. J. Law's. You can't find anything better for the money.

It looks as if Delta was to have a good orchestra at last. It will consist of a violin, thrombone, clarinet and piano, and they have been practicing this week. They are all good players and when they have had a little practice working together they will be able to furnish first class music.

J. Kelly of Mills is excavating the cellar for his new building on Clark street across from the stores of the Delta Mercantile and Implement Co. It will be two stories high, 30x50 feet in size and of tile or cement blocks.

J. C. Dort, an employe of the Agricultural Department, is engaged in taking measurements o f the Sevier river and some of the canals to determine the flow of the river and the amount of water to be delivered to the various companies. He has just installed a measuring device in the river above the flume. A wire cable is stretched across the river on which runs a sort of car from which the operator makes his measurements. The depth of the river is measured every foot from one bank to the other. From this the area of the water is determined. By means of a revolving wheel placed at various depths and at frequent intervals across the river the average velocity of the stream is determined. When these two factors are known the volume of water passing in a given time is easily calculated. Measurements of water are being taken at a number of stations above the reservoir.

The Delta Company is very slow in getting in the necessary bridges on the west side. There are no bridges across the main canal from the road running west of the bridge on the river to a point five miles north. Those who have tried to cross the canal between these points have come to grief, as the editor can testify. Farmers north and east of the gravel hill find themselves entirely cut off by almost impassible canals and broken wagons and mired teams follow every attempt to get out. The engineering force is overworked now in building head gates and keeping the canals in order, and the force ought to be increased so that a few bridges could be built. The show road up through the center of the tract is in good order, but travelers would find themselves in a predicament if they were to get off that road. Get busy and fix up some bridges.

Nephi flour is the best made, and the Delta Mercantile and Implement Co. have sold three loads to Fillmore. They are hardly able to keep enough sugar on hand to supply the demand, which has been created by their price of $6.55 per hundred. Their fine new ginghams at three yards for a quarter has also proved a leader.

Raymond J. Rutt of the Home Missionary Board of the Presbyterian church is now stationed at Delta permanently and will conduct services in the school house every Sunday. Sunday School will be held at ten o'clock. Preaching services at 11 a. m. and 8 p. m. Everyone interested in these services is cordially invited to attend. They will be ethical rather than denominational in character, so that people of all and every creed will feel at home.

The Golden Rule store feels proud of their line of Sunflower shoes, which, for price and quality, cannot be surpassed. They are still selling men's bib overalls for 85c and waist overalls for 75c, and find plenty of people who know a good thing when they see it.

There will be a big dance at Amusement Hall on Friday, June 7, at which a Salt Lake orchestra will furnish music, and free refreshments will be provided. Prepare for a good time.

The Chronicle News Stand has received a lot of new books this week. Many of them have only just been published and all are lively and stirring stories. Come in and see them.

OCCURRENCES AT OAK CITY

W. R. Walker, Representative

Reporter Walker has been absent for the past three weeks. This accounts for no report from Oak City for some time.

We are having ideal weather at the present time. The crops are growing fine and the prospects for everything, especially for fruit, has never been better.

Last Thursday we had a fine shower which was much appreciated, although it interfered with our plans for Decoration day.

The water has been much higher this spring than ever before, and the farmers certainly have no cause for complaint.

Mae, the 14-months-old baby of Wm. and Caddie Lovell, was drowned in an irrigation ditch. It is not exactly known how she fell into the ditch, but it is supposed she was carried for some distance by the swift stream. When she was found she was so far gone nothing could be done. Her head was badly bruised and it is supposed she was knocked senseless when she fell in.

May 9th the Lovell family celebrated the one hundredth anniversary of Grandfather Lovell.

Last Friday evening a farewell party was given Ray Finlinson, who departed for a mission to the northwestern states the following Sunday.

During the party a program was rendered and refreshments were served. A purse of about one hundred and forty dollars was raised to help him on his way.

Mr. Finlinson will be greatly missed by our young people, as he was a general favorite.

Saturday a crowd of young people accompanied Mr. Finlinson to Leamington, where a dance was given in his honor. After the dance the crowd adjourned to the Nielson hotel, where all partook of a delicious chicken supper. This was enjoyed by all and we, of Oak City, express our thanks to the Leamington young people for the good time we had.

By the time supper was over it was time to bid Mr. Finlinson good bye.

If any more information of this affair is desired just ask Mr. John Watts. He is able to give every detail.

Mrs. Huldah Rawlinson, who has been ill for a few weeks, is reported some better.

Primary conference at Holden was well attended, there being eighteen officers in the association and fifteen present.

Mr. Veo Nielson is a visitor to our town. I supose he is here investigating the peach crop, as he spends most of his time at Anderson's.

The following are the graduates: Cliff Talbot, Clifton Airidge, Ruby Jacobson, Mandy Roper, and Gene Lovell.

OLD DOBE FORT AT DESERET.

Saturday was quite a sociable, busy day at Deseret. In the forenoon twenty-five or thirty men with eighteen teams scraped and leveled in the park and worked on the race track and grand stand. At noon a committee of ladies served lunch to the workers at Mrs. Petty's home and sports followed in the afternoon. The ball game between Delta and Deseret resulted in a score of 12 to 11 in favor of Delta.

Wm. Jenson has on his lot in Deseret one of the most beautiful patches of alfalfa in the community. It is very tall and nearly ready to blossom.

Early Tuesday morning Dr. Broaddus made a moonlight dash to Delta in his motor car, reaching there from Deseret in 20 minutes. He left a 7-pound girl at the home of Mr. and Mrs. Fred Wood, who are recently from Oklahoma.

Mrs. Virgil Kelly of Deseret and also her year-old baby, were quite ill during the past week.

Miss Adar Taylor, for several years a popular and successful teacher in Deseret, has returned as Mrs. Glen Cropper to make her home here.

Bob Whicker of Delta is driving a well on Dr. Broaddus' lot in Hinckley.

Hinckley seemed quite lively with students again Tuesday, and the air was full of their laughter and singing. In the afternoon were held the graduation exercises of the county eighth grade students. Many former academy students and parents also took occasion to visit in Hinckley. The Hinckley students served a delightful banquet to all the graduates in the academy rooms. A few of the nearly 70 graduates were unable to be present, but all who were here enjoyed a pleasant day. Mr. Pack was very busy for several days helping the visitors to find accommodations. In the afternoon Deseret and Hinckley played a game of baseball in which Deseret made one score. No one seems to know the Hinckley score somewhere from 17 to 27. The most interesting antics were those of Alma Langston and Arthur Reeves as pitcher and catcher. In the evening a big dance was held in the gymnasium. During the ball game Lucien Whitehead was struck back of the ear by a swift ball and hurt quite badly, though probably not dangerously.

Millard County Progress
August 17, 1912

Millard Stake Divided.

The action taken at the late stake conference held at Deseret deviding Millard Stake into two, is being commented upon as a progressive move, and meets with general satisfaction. Millard County, all of which has for 33 years constituted the ecclesiastical organization known as the Millard Stake of Zion, is geographically divided by a desert many miles in extent, making it somewhat inconvenient for the stake officers in their supervision over the church affairs in both sections.

The first ecclesiastical organization was effected shortly after the arrival of Anson Call with a colony of 30 Mormon families on Chalk Creek in the fall of 1851 There was no stake organization for a number of years, but Fillmore was organized as an ecclesiastical ward with N. W. Bartholomew as Bishop, and John A. Rap as presiding Elder At a later reorganization Bartholomew and Ray were released. Lewis Brunson was ordained a bishop and called to preside over the Fillmore ward. Bishop Brunson was later succeeded by Thomas Callister, who held the position, not only as Bishop of Fillmore ward, but as presiding Bishop of the diferent branches which were gradually being organized at Scipio. Holden, Meadow, Kanosh, Deseret and Oak Creek.

The stake organization was effected in March 1869, when Thomas Callister was chosen as the first president of the Millard Stake of Zion without counselors. A stake high council was organized at the same time of which we have not a complete list, but will give the names of as many as we can remember. Thomas R. King, Joseph V. Robison, Francis M. Lyman, James C. Owens, Allen Russell, Lyman Levitt, Charles Hall, B. H. Robinson, L. H. McCullough, William King.

On July 22, 1877, the Millard Stake was reorganized, president Callister and all other stake officers were released, and Ira N. Hinckley was chosen president with Edward Partridge as 1st and Joseph V. Robeson as second Counselor. A new High Council was organized as follows:- James C. Owens, Allen Russell, Nephi Pratt, Jessie B. Martin, Alexander Fortie, Christian Hanson, Richard Johnson, Reuben McBride, William H. Stott, William Wade, F. A. Weeb and James Abraham.

President of the High Priest quorum, Lewis Brunson with John Powell and William North as counselors.

Recorder and Historian, Lafayette Holbrook.

Fillmore was devided into two wards with Joseph D. Smith for Bishop of 1st ward, with Albert Robison and Alfred Gull as counselors.

Bishop of 2nd Ward, Alexander Melville, with Christian Anderson. and H. J. Mc Cullough as counselors.

Scipio was organized with Daniel Thomson as Bishop with Thomas Yates and Peter C. Nielsen as counselors

Holden Ward was organized with David R. Stevens as Bishop and Benjamin Bennett and A. P. Harmon as counselors.

Kanosh Ward was organized with Culbert King as Bishop and Lyman Levit and O. R. Hawes as counselors.

Oak Creek ward was organized with Platte D. Lyman as Bishop and John Lovell and George Finlinson as counselors.

Deseret Ward was organized with Joseph S. Black as Bishop and Hyrum Dewsnup and M. M. Bishop as counselors.

Deseret Ward was organized with Joseph S. Black as Bishop and Hyrum Dewsnup and M. M. Bishop as counselors.

Meadow Ward was organized with H. B. Bennett as Bishop and James Fisher and James Duncan as counselors.

There were changes made in the Stake Presidency High Council and Bishoprics at different times, but Ira N. Hinckley was retained in office until November 24, 1902, when he and his counselors Daniel Thompson and David R. Stevens were released, and were succeeded by Alonzo A. Hinckley as President with Thomas Callister and George A. Setman as counselors. Owing to removal and death, changes of counselors had taken place, so that the Stake Presidency at the time for division stood, Alonzo A. Hinckley President with Orvil L. Thompson as first, and Joseph T. Finlinson as Counselors. They were a cultured and scholarly trio, and had the affairs of the Stake well in hand.

At the reorganization Alonzo A Hinckley was retained as President of the Deseret Stake with Joseph F. Finlinson as 1st Counselors Orvil L. Thompson was promoted to President of the new Millard Stake with Bishop John A. Beckstrand of Meadow as 1st, and Bishop Peter L. Brunson of Fillmore as 2nd Counselor.

The promotion of Bishop Beck- strand and Brunson into the new Stake Presidency disorganized the bishoprics of Meadow and Fillmore wards, which are given Jesse J. Bennett as Bishop of the Meadow Ward with Howard B- Bushnell as 1st, and W. M. Stewart 2nd Counselor. Almon D. Robison as Bishop of Fillmore Ward, with Rufus Day as 1st and Richard T. Ashby as 2nd Counselor.

Salt Lake Telegram
August 19, 1912

EL PASO MORMON REFUGEES BEING SENT TO VARIOUS POINTS IN THE UNITED STATES

EL PASO, Tex., Aug. 19.—Because of the reduced rate of 1 cent per mile on railroads leaving El Paso, the Mormon refugees will be able to find temporary homes in Arizona, New Mexico, Colorado and Utah, without their transportation costing the government more than $10,000 of the $100,000 appropriated for their relief. A total of 230 has already been sent away and more will follow as rapidly as their temporary locations can be determined upon. The situation here so far as the Mormons are concerned remains the same. There is no immediate prospect of peace in Mexico and life would be worth little in the Mormon colonies now with the federals and rebels both harassing the country surrounding the Mormon settlements.

Those Coming to Utah.

The names of those of the refugees who have gone to points in Utah are:

Salt Lake—F. F. Hassell, Lila Hassell, N. M. Hassell, May Cluff, Jesse, Rosa, Cecil and Mildred Cluff.

Fairview—Travers Tucker, Will Mett, Wilhelm, Amass, Clifton, Lucille and Agnes Tucker.

Logan—Rasmus Larson, Sophia, Joseph and Alvin Larson.

Provo—Erastus Romney, Rhoda, Starwell, Willie, Iris, Grant and Harold Romney, Mary B. Eyring, Mary Eyring and G. O. Lebanon.

St. George—Samuel Jarvis, Frances and Clementina Jones.

Lehi—Benjamin, Mary and Esther Jarvis.

Nephi—Jarvis, Pearl, Hirum, Edwin and George Jarvis, Mary E. Millie, Grace, Joseph and S. W. Jarvis Jr.; Olive Melissa and John Walter Jarvis, Louise Haag, Ammon Lake and Mary Lake.

Payson—Neils Frederickson, wife and daughter, Philip Young, Mary and Beryl Young.

Richfield—H. M. Payne, Helena and A. D. Payne, Hollister James and Roxie Jacobson.

Friday's List.

The following refugees left El Paso Friday afternoon and night:

Aurora—Chloe, Austin, Hannah, Ruth, John and Earl Spencer, E. F. Nancy, E. Olive, Myrtle, Angelina, Ralph, Jabez and Effie Durfee, Reuben Wilson and Luella Wilson.

Delta—Roy Patten, Sarah Patten and Leroy Patten.

Fairview—Annie Jacobson, Arcadia Jacobson and Eldon Jacobson.

Kaysville—Phoebe Frank, Charles and Spencer Gallbraith.

Lynndyl (Oak City)—John, Mary E., Martha, Ellen, Adelia, Henry, George, Catherine and Laura Carlin and Martha Whetton.

Lund—George O., Jennie and Owen Naegle.

Fillmore—Clara A., Isaac, Ida L. and Anna Turley.

Monroe—Fred W., Jesse and Loren Jones, Ray Hurste and Agnes Hurste.

Mount Pleasant—Alice A., Bessie, Norman, Irene and Lucy Taylor.

Nephi—George A., Emma, Lydya Emma, George A., Themma and Newel Johnson.

Oasis—George W., Phoebe, Cleone, Hettie and George Rowley.

Price—Frank R., Mary and Charles Jones.

Provo—George L. Cluff, Clara Cluff, William C. McClellan, Alameda McClellan, Anne E. Leader, Mildred, Melvin, Mary, Ethel and Lester Taylor.

Richfield—William Foutz, Mary Foutz, Reuben, Maggie, Addie, Wilford, Vilate and Thomas Gurr, Nellie, Vera and Farley Rowley, Wallace Gurr, Bathspeda Gurr, Francis Bunker and Evelyn Bunker.

Salina—C. B. Desky, Benjamin and Anthon Cooley, J. A., Mary, Evelyn, Joseph and Hortenz Spencer.

Salt Lake—Ernest, Orissa and Ozella Rowley, Lurline Tenney, Annie Tenney, Arza Kartchner, Ada Kartchner, Mary S. Turley and daughter, Robert L. Scott, David, Emma and Owen Thyggrios, Mary B. Wall and Ella Wall.

Tooele—Annie, Rachel, Delta, Emma and Arnold Adams, Mary Boyce and three children.

OAK CITY.

S. J. RAWLINSON, REPRESENTATIVE

On Thursday and Friday last, the Christensen family held its Re-union in our town. The family of Christen Christensen now numbers 125. Of this number 101 were present to renew and reinforce the bond of family ties Members were present from Heber, Levan, Leamington, Aurora and Hinckley. Programs of speech, music, ball playing and dancing furnished ample amusement for all.

In the baseball game between the family and town, the former won with a score of 12 to 5 in its favor.

The family has a creditable orchestra of six pieces that furnished music part of the time at the dances.

Christen Christensen was born in Denmark in 1808. As a member of the Mormon faith he came to Utah in 1862. His first home was at Spanish Fork. Later he was called to Monroe, Sevier Co. to aid in its settlements.

He lived in Marysvalle. Richfield and Gunnison, but was unable to live in those places due to Indian troubles. He then removed to Scipio Millard Co., and thence to Oak City where he died on Aug. 4th 1880.

He was the father of seven children and to day but two survive him Anthony and Annie C Anderson of this place.

No one expressed any dissatisfied word, but all went away saying that the time was well spent.

The grain crop is now in the bins waiting the call of the miller.

The yield was exceptionally good this season.

The Elberta peaches are now ripening and if cool weather continues will be rushed upon in fear of frost getting the later ones.

Mr. H G. Ottley of Delta has been improving a little on the primises of Mr. Simeon Walter A new grainary in connection with an implements house is the result.

Dr. Christie has been kept very busy the past week also making improvements and disapprovements on various mouths of our citizens.

Tonight, Mon. the Republicans and Democrats will meet in separate primaries for the purpose of exhibiting their products at the co. convention held in conection with the co. fair on Sat. next.

Jos. Finlinson attended the Republican judicial convention held in Salt Lake the past week, while John E Tovell represented the Democrats. Both have returned in happy spirits.

Jury List for 1913

John A. Beckstrand and Jos. Finlinson Make Selection

Is Your Name Here?

ABRAHAM

Wm. S. Taylor, Ora Lake, N. L Westover, Charles Theobald.

BURBANK

George C. Richardson

CLEAR LAKE

Barclay John

DELTA

George S. Bunker, Bryant B. Johnson, A. C. Sorenson, John E. steele, E. F. Bishop, Robert Whicker, R. L. Simkins, Frank W Wood, Emery Peterson, Henry G. Ottley, Ervin Jeffery, A. Ackerman, G. D. shipley. N. A. Abbot and Albert Watts.

DESERET

Jacob Croft, Peter T. Black, Orson Cahoon, Oscar Warnick, Orson Erickson, John Rogers, Angus Allred, Joshua Bennett, Jr. and Joseph W. Damron, Jr.

FILLMORE

E M. Harsen, Heber Jackson, Ova Peterson, Almon Robison, James L Smith, Marion Owens, F. A. Robison, W. N. McBride. Frank Cooper, Louis B. Smith, Nephi A. Anderson. Thomas Hutton, John H. Davis, J, F Holbrook. F. O. Melville, James Swallow, Frank Warner, Robert Seguine, G. W. Black, Hans Petersoh, James Mitchell. Edward Trimble, Wm. A. Huntsman. Frank Partridge, Joseph Carling John W. Starley, Wm. H, Rasmussen, Geo. Rowley and Carl Day.

GARRISON

Thomas Dearden and Brigham Young.

HINCKLEY

Peter G. Peterson, Jacob H. Langston, Geo. A. Robison. H F Wright, R. E. Robinson, L. R. Cropper, Jr., Simon Webb, John Terry, H. F. Stout, Joseph M. Christensen, Thomas Pratt, Nathen B Badger, Thomas Greener Jr., Geo. H. Walker, J. P Mencham, C. A. Stratton, Hugh Hilton, Jedidiah Cox and Samuel Dutson.

LEAMINGTON

Brigham Clark, M C Dutson, Alma Harder, Alfred E Johnson and Fred Neilson.

LYNN

O T Meade

MEADOW

Peter W Pearson, John O Labrum, Neil M stewart, Jr., J Delbert Bushnell, Charles R Gull, Nephi D Beckstrand, Henry Stewart, Joseph H Fisher, Elmer J Duncan and Lawrence Barkdull.

OAK CITY

O H Jacobson, Anthony Christensen, Franklin Anderson, Arthur Talbot, John C Lovell John L Neilson and Simeon Walker.

OASIS

Henry Jackson, Samuel Rutherford, N L Peterson, Peter Peterson, John Styler and James Thompson.

SCIPIO

George Monroe, Adolph Hanseen, Earnest Brown, Carl Wasden, Samuel Memmott, Jr., Marion Robins, Lars Jensen, Joseph

Edward Bennet, Frank Badger, Simeon Stephenson, Edward Stevens, John Wood, John O. Poulsen, Lorenzo M. Stevens, Edgar Turner, Sidney P. Tuples and Leslie Thompson.

KANOSH

Hyrum P. Robison, Orson Whittaker, C W Watts, Jr. Daniel J Rogers, Alonza Geo., Henry Paxton, Harvey Cummings, H T

Stone Edson Robison, Frederic D Olson, Frederic Quanberg, Wm. H Bradfield, Anthone Peterson and J R Ivie.

SMITHVILLE

Issac Robison.

Rappleye, Harvey Watts, W B Fennimore, Albenida Abraham, Alonzo Roberts, Geo. D Hunter, Lewis Barney, Thomas Charlsworth and Henry Whatcott.

Last Friday Dr. Stevens was called to Hinckley in consultation with Dr. C. A. Braddus upon the little daughter of Mr. Chideston of that place. It was deemed necessary to operate immediately and they found general periotinits due to a ruptured appendix. At this writing the little patient is doing nicely and bright hopes are held for a speedy recovery.

Millard County Chronicle
January 23, 1913

OASIS.

The cold south wind has been blowing several days.

The past ten days Oasis people have been engaged in putting up ice.

The Pahvant Valley Creamery Co. has put up some 75 tons of ice. David Day 45 tons, Wm. Huff, 40 tons, Peterson Hotel, 40 tons, Samuel Rutherford, 25 tons. It looks as though Oasis would be supplied with ice the greater part of the summer.

Miss Cora Day of Fillmore is here visiting with her brother and family, Mr. Oda Day.

Miss Nora Styler went to Lynndyl on Sunday night, where she has been employed by Mr. Mead.

H. L. Jackson just returned from Salt Lake City, where he has been for a few days visit.

Many are complaining of colds and a grippe of late. A good storm would perhaps improve the atmosphere. It is reported that Herman McCosh has purchased the N. S. Peterson hotel and will soon take possession of the same. He expects to do a first class business.

The new auto company just formed has rented the old saloon building of Washington Rogers and is doing some remodeling, putting a large door in the front and expecting to use it for a garage for their auto. They expect to put in two more cars in the near future, also a large freight carrying car. This will be an ideal line via Holden to Fillmore and return to Oasis daily.

We also have an up to date blacksmith shop where all kinds of repairing is done.

LEAMINGTON.

Merlin Elder, the little 2 year old son of Mr. and Mrs. Parley Elder, was burned while putting chips into the stove. His mother had just left the house but although help was at once received he was seriously burned. His hands, face and legs were injured the most. Dr. Bennett of Nephi was in town, consequently the boy received prompt attention. He is improving nicely.

Forest, the six year old son of Mr. Charles Herrick, has been very sick for the past six weeks from an attack of spinal meningitis. He has had eleven convulsions since Jan. 10th. The last one he had was last Friday morning. We think from reports that he is on the improve.

Friday, February 1st. The Hinckley District School basket ball team, after defeating Oak City, paid us a visit and gave us the most exciting game of the year. Our players felt discouraged in the beginning but they took the defensive and a warm game followed. Through a mistake on our part, the game was called a draw.

Progress-Review.

Dear Editor:

We wish to congratulate you on the improvement of your paper. We believe that a County paper should be a means of betterment—educationally and financially—for the county. Since you have eliminated the non-important advertisements, we hope you keep your paper free from "cheap gossip", and the like. A student has said, "I think the Progress-Review is an interesting paper, it has made a great improvement the last month by leaving out many advertisements and putting news in the place."

We wish you every success in keeping your columns filled with the best possible news.

Leamington District School.

Hinckley.

Last Friday night Drs. Broaddus and Stevens performed an operation for appendicitus on Miss Lula Huber. As there wasn't a hospital available, the Relief Society Hall was prepared which served the purpose well. The case was very serious as the appendix had ruptured but she is improving rapidly.

Hinckley was given a rare treat in the form of an opera given by the Academy Choir under the direction of Prof. Stott. Prof. Stott may well feel proud of the way it was presented as every part was taken well. The chorus was beautiful. It is to be presented at Deseret Thursday night and Delta Friday night.

Early Saturday morning was a busy one for the Academy students. One could see buggies. autos and band wagon rolling toward the sand hills of Fillmore. Why such disturbances? The game, they cry!

They say that things over there at Fillmore went off swell, but—but—well the score and that will be made right on the 15th. Come over Fillmore and see the fun out.

The District School boys played Oak City Friday night, the score stood 24-14 in favor of Hinckley. They also went to Leamington Saturday night and played basket ball. The score 27-25 in their favor, showed they had to play some.

Sunday night the Conjoint session of the Y. L. and Y. M. I. A. Prof D. A. Stevens gave an excellent lecture on, "The Great Reformer, Martin Luther." Those that were not there missed a treat.

Hinckley.

We had a very exciting game here in the Millard Academy gym last Friday after-noon. The presence of a very enthusiastic cheering crowd from Fillmore made it all the more so. We wondered if they liked the score? Some seemed to be in such a hurry to get home to tell about something. Let us all see the fun out and be in Delta Saturday. It promises to be the best game of the season.

The opera "Sylva", was repeated here Saturday evening for the benefit of Lula Huber, who underwent an operation. This makes the fourth time it has been played, twice here and twice in the neighboring towns, and all seemed to enjoy it immensely.

A very sad death occured here last Saturday night. Mrs. Sim-on Webb died of pneumonia. She leaves a husband and seven children, three of whom are married. A very sad part of it was that her oldest daughter Mrs. Retta Jennings was unable to be here for her funeral as she is at present in New York with her husband, where he is attending college.

The funeral was held Tuesday 18th and was largely attended. The whole community mourns her loss.

IN AND AROUND DELTA

The Week's News from the Coming Metropolis

W. H. Warfield and N. H. Stevens were two visitors from California this week. Owing to the snowy weather they did not get around as much as they would like to have done, but they saw enough to convince them that the country was all right and they bought some land on the north tract.

Three cars of settlers' effects arrived the past week. Two of them came from California, and one from Bartlesville, Oklahoma. The latter contained goods for J. E. Childers and Nell White who have land northeast of Abraham.

Ed Bishop is rejoicing over the arrival of a fine nine and a half pound baby boy that arrived at his home on Tuesday.

J. E. Works of the Baker Lumber Co., went into Salt Lake Tuesday on a very important errand. He and Miss Hazel Huff of Oasis were married the following day. Both of the young people have many friends in this section who wish them a long and happy wedded life.

Attorney William Higgins of the firm of Higgins & Higgins was a visitor in Delta last Sunday. Mr. Higgins is located in Fillmore and with a member of the firm located in Salt Lake is able to handle the business of his customers at both places. They have had a wide experience in legal work and anything placed in their hands will be well looked after.

Mrs. Bert Johnson of West Delta died last Thursday. She had been ill for some time and her death was the result of a complication of diseases. She leaves a husband and two small children to mourn her untimely death. The funeral took place on Saturday and was attended by a large number of sympathizing friends.

S. W. Eccles, a former Delta resident, was a visitor in Delta this week and notes many improvements since he left here last summer. Mr. Eccles has been living in Austin, Oregon, the past winter and recently moved back to Ogden with his family.

Muddy weather is here and you want to be prepared for it by getting rubbers, overshoes and rubber boots and other wet weather goods. The Golden Rule Store is advertising them this week.

When we were in the Delta Bakery this week we noticed them unpacking another lot of fine candies. Mr. January says he finds plenty of sale for the very best candies. He has also got in some more oranges, lemons, dates and bananas.

The Delta Friendly Women have postponed their regular meeting from this Thursday to March 13. A Washington birthday party was planned but owing to the threatened sickness in town it was thought advisable not to meet this week.

Guy George returned to California Wednesday morning after having spent a couple of weeks in Delta. Mr. George is a great booster for this country.

The heavy snow this week is acceptable to the farmers and with the warmer weather that has followed the frost will soon be out of the ground so that plowing can soon be commenced.

Bishop & Wallace Co. have a small ditch scraper that is just the thing to clean out old ditches and make new ones. It can do more work and do it better than a dozen men could in the same time. They also call attention to some of the reasons why they advertise.

Avery Bishop and Roy Dresser returned Monday from Leamington, where they have been engaged the past ten days driving piles for the syphon that is to carry the water across the river at Lynndyl for the Sevier River Land and Irrigation Co.

OASIS.

The weather was again broken by a fine snow storm that has lasted about forty eight hours and as yet there is no prospect of any change. This is welcomed by all on account of our long dry winter although it prevents work for a short time, the farmers are all looking pleasant.

The members of the Commercial Club met last evening and chose the various officers necessary for the operation of such club, and the members of Oasis, Deseret and Hinckley will meet to night for full organization of the three districts the name of the club will be the Bannnl Commercial Club. We hope this will be for the betterment of our community in the way of streets, bridges and etc.

Miss Laura Johnson is here visiting relatives and doesn't look any the worse for having undergone an operation for appendicitus.

We understand that we will soon have a new merchant here as we learn that Oda J. Day is preparing to put in a full line of groceries as well as some dry goods and we will then have three stores and we welcome competition as it is the life of trade.

We understand that the creamery is doing a very good business at present.

We are all blessed with excellent good health at present.

Hinckley.

The play entitled "Down on the Farm" was presented in the Academy last Friday to a large audience. It was for the benefit of the ward choir.

Stake Conference was held here Saturday and Sunday. The visiting brethern were Apostle Heber J. Grant and Joseph W. McMurrin who gave us some timely instructions. The meetings on Sunday were well attended there being 600 present.

A sad death occured here Monday evening, taking away one of our beloved sisters, Miss Pearl Blake. About a year ago she was taken sick with Brights Disease and Dropsy. Every thing possible was done in her behalf but her father, James S. Blake finally took her to the Temple in Salt Lake where after she had been baptised for her health she practily recovered.

Pearl was a student of the Millard Academy where she enjoyed her studies until two weeks ago when she took a severe cold. This brought on Odema of the lungs with Brights Disease and Dropsy from which she died.

Pearl was born Dec. 18, 1894 at Hinckley where she has lived her entire life. She has been organist of the Primary, Sunday School and Mutual where she has served faithful until her release.

The entire community sympathizes with the Blake family in this their great sorrow.

The funeral will be held Wednesday at 2 o'clock.

The ward has bought twenty acres from H. F. Wright to be made into a sporting ground. There will be a race track, park, ball grounds etc. The men are at work now so it is expected to be finished for spring and summer work. It is estimated that it will cost $2500 when completed with grand stand. With a large dancing hall, now the town could well feel proud of its places of amusements.

The dance of the season was given last Friday in horor of the basket ball boys. The banquet was served at 7 o'clock. During the "M" dance as it was called, the sweaters were given to the team escored by the First Year girls. The hall was decorated beautiful. Some say the best the gym ever looked. Quite a compliment for the "Freshies."

There was quite a number of the members attended the Y. M. and Y. L. M. I. A. Conference at Delta. An enjoyable time was had by all.

Monday, the Anual Day was celebrated by the Relief Society a program and refreshments in the afternoon and a dance at night. All seemed to have a nice time.

The streets of Hinckley are taking on a different appearance, fences moved back so as to broaden them considerable, then cleared. It sure looks better and that is what gives the town a boost.

OAK CITY.

A man never realizes he's happy until he is married, and then it's too late." Said a certain witty man. W. R. Walker our chronicle correspondent, now realizes he is a happy man having just returned from St. George. where he was married to Miss Josephine Bunker of that place on the 6th inst. They will make their home at Delta, where Mr. Walker last year, purchased a good farm. We extend our sincerest congratulations and wish for their good fortune.

Mr. Leslie Raper has recently returned from a visit into Idaho He is convinced that it is a better place than where he now is and will dispose of his belongings here and take his wife father and mother into the northern climes. We dislike the idea of parting with our citizens and trust that this emigration spirit will soon cease to be. Mr. Eli Rawlinson, who has spent the past eight months in the employ of the Consolidated Wagon and Machine Co. in Salt Lake City, is again at home. and will work at home the coming summer.

Millard County Progress
April 11, 1913

Hinckley.

The Y. L. M. I. A. gave a social Friday night which was a success and everybody who went had an enjoyable time. The "Ladies Gloves" took a raise in price and yet some young men seemed to feel sad because they could not get one.

Saturday night the 4th years entertained the faculty. An enjoyable time was had by all who attended. The lunch being especially attractive.

Instead of the regular Conjoint Sunday night, the contest in Oral Stories and Reciting was given. The contestants for the oral story were Juanita Stout and Cleona Bunker. The decision was given in favor of Miss Bunker. The reciting was given by Lyle Cropper, Ruby Kelter, Fannie Cropper and Lillie Terry of Hinckley and Miss Lake from Abraham. Lyle Cropper got the decision in this. They were all good both oral stories and reciting and the girls are to be commended for their efforts.

Berrie Robison wore such a smile Saturday that some people thought that the "Paw-choos" stock must have taken a raise but Berrie declares it isn't that but that he is now "papa". The mother and baby girl are getting along nicely.

The improvement of streets still continues, moving fences, cleaning ditches, and making side walks etc. "Thanks to thee thou worthy men for the example thou dost set."

Salt Lake Tribune
April 13, 1913

MEAD—In a local hospital, this city, April 12, 1913, of pneumonia, Orlando T. Mead, a merchant at Lynndyl, Utah; born December 27, 1873, in Spanish Fork, Utah; son of Mr. and Mrs. Orlando F. Mead. The body was shipped by Joseph William Taylor this morning to Price, Utah, where the funeral services will be held.

Millard County Progress
May 2, 1913

DELTA.

Mrs. James A. Melville came to Delta with Mr. Melville on Wednesday, stopping at the Delta Hotel. We hope no such wind storms as visited us last week occur while she is here to give a bad impression to what is otherwise a most delightful climate.

Mrs. Frank Beckwith and youngest daughter spent ten days in Delta, returning to Salt Lake City on Monday. It is expected that she will return about July bringing the three children with her.

Business at the Delta Hotel has increased so fast that ten more rooms are to be added to this popular hostelry. Mrs. Cooper deserves great credit for the excellent management of this house, which is winning the traveling public to make Delta their headquarters. With the addition of more rooms the hotel will be able to accomodate all.

Our worthy and efficient Town Marshal, Brother Cass Lewis, is in the field as public Prosecutor of the Kangaroo Court, and H. A. Bramwell heads all tickets in the field—politics harmonized—as Judge. These worthies will attend to all matters within the jurisdiction of the Kangaroo court the fame of whose doings is spreading. Unearthing crime seems to be a specialty in which some men have a craving, and certainly these two artists have not reached a satiety.

OAK CITY.

After two citizen's meetings that went well into the midnight hours, and after a good deal of pro and con discussion it was decided to supply our town with a water system. The irrigation Co. will have the work in charge and will place the system with the understanding that the people own it after it is paid for. A distance of about four miles will bring what is known as "The First Springs" into our town. Other springs will be piped in connection with the First Springs for irrigation purposes. A good force of men and teams are now at work and it is hoped that before snow falls in its usual season that we will all be drinking our best health.

Bishop Lee Anderson, who recently has been compelled to make a number of trips to Salt Lake City, due to his wife's illness at the L. D. S. Hospital, somehow and somewhere came in "contact" with small pox? Last Friday he visited Dr. Broddus of Hinckley who made examinations and found it to be the above named disease. Unfortunally a great number have been exposed and it may result seriously. However, a most careful course will be followed, about 100 being vaccinated last Sunday, and with other due precautions it may avoid other cases.

Mr. Franklin Anderson of our city has become somewhat "blooded", of late; having purchased from Salt Lake Co. a first class yearling percheron stallion and also the old champion butter cow, from Cannon Bros. Jersey herd, known as Forest Dale Buttercup.

OASIS.

The weather still remains cool and everything very backward in growing while the alfalfa looks fine this spring it does not grow very much.

Mrs. Mark Skeem is in Salt Lake City and has under gone an operation for apendicitus and is reported as doing fine. Mrs. C. B. W. Pearson is also in the city.

Mr. Valentine Styler left for a mission to the southern states on the 7th we all wish him success in his labors.

There is still some building going on here. Alfred Nuzman has just completed an addition to his house. Also Carl Pearson has added an extra room and James Christensen is remodeling his home at the pres-ent and it is reported that Neils Anderson is going to build a new house at the close of our school this season.

Our very able teacher turned out seven graduates from the 8th grade out of 9 that took the examination. We feel proud of this and can see that our teacher must have worked very hard having only two teachers for eight grades.

Messrs. Goddard and Kimball have purchased a new automobile and we expect better service from them in the future.

Hinckley.

Arthur seems very lonely since the graduates have returned from Fillmore. For Mary chose to stay at the county seat awhile, to get renewed strength since school was out. She has had a successful year at Oasis.

The Young Ladies Mutual Association have outlined an interesting coarse for the summers work consisting of Domestic Science and Art, Culture and Art Needle Work. And we hope the Deseret Stake won't give up their trip to Oak City Canyon as we are anxious to join them in full blast for a grand time. It's the only thing.

Last Thursday night the Jenkins' Band played for a dance in the Academy. All reported having a good dance.

Mrs. Emma E. Robinson's baby has been very ill, but is reported to be improving slowly, at this writing.

Peace day was observed Sunday. Fred Pack gave an excellent talk at the afternoon services. Also the Stake Superintendency of the Sunday School were honorably released. And John Reeves sustained as the Supt. with Willis E. Robinson as first and J. H. Langston as second Counselors. Arthur Reeves as secretary.

Salt Lake Tribune
May 28, 1913

Keeps Cupid Busy.

Special to The Tribune.

PROVO, May 27.—Marriage permits have been issued to Ray D. Nichols of American Fork and Fern Scott of Lake View, Don C. Smith of Lynndyl and Mary I. Stevenson of Springville Sliad Koyle and Hannah Johnson of Spanish Fork.

Millard County Progress
May 30, 1913

Hinckley.

Sunday night in the Academy was given an excellent program for the two missionaries who are going to leave the first of June for the North Western States. Mission Bros. Eddie Anderson and Joseph Christenson. There will be a grand ball in the Academy gym. Thursday night for their benefit. A good turn out is expected. Friday night in Oak City they will be given a send off. Every body wishes them success in their labors and a safe journey.

Pres. A. A. Hinckley is in Lynn doing a big business in the land question. Lynn is bound to do well and go up. (Especially if the wind can blow it up)

Earnest Stout is sure wearing a broad smile and the correspondent has guessed the reason. For at the June Conference he will take upon himself the vows of Matrimony. He will return to Hinckley with his wife.

DESERET.

Lagrippe is again in our midst Bp. Damron, John Cahoon and the children of Dell Bennett are among the sick.

A bond Election was held in Deseret and Oasis Sat the 17th. The results were 16 to 40 in favor of Bonding.

Mrs Mary Petty of St. John is visiting relatives and friends.

Miss Bessie Eaton who has been with us since last Sept. teaching school, leaves Friday morning.

Mrs. Effie Moody reached home Wednesday last from Salt Lake where she was called to attend the funeral of her brother Laurence Reed, who died very suddenly of heart failure in Elko Nev. He leaves a young wife and babe, besides an aged mother, brothers and sisters to mourn his loss

The Primary Association is preparing an excellent program to be given in the near future.

Mr. Virgil Kelly left yesterday morning for the east side of the county on business.

The concert that will be given by the M. I. A. Sunday evening promises to be a success.

Wm. Justensen and family left several days ago for Southern California to make their home.

Miss Norma Moody leaves for Salt Lake in a few days on a visit.

NEWS OF A WEEK IN AND AROUND DELTA

Record of the Important Events of Past Seven Days in the Newest Town.

The family of Chas. McClain arrived from Salt Lake last week and are now settled in their handsome new cement block house east of the depot.

A. B. Walling, who has a farm on the north side, left with his family for the old home in Iowa. Mrs. Walling found the contrast too great between a new Millard county farm and her home town. Walling has leased his farm.

The Delta Bakery is doing a big trade in its pure home made ice cream. If you want the Bakery to make your ice cream on shares bring in your cream and have it made into ice cream on the bakery's engine driven ice cream freezer.

A fine baby girl was born to Mrs. Wm. Bunker last week. Everybody getting along nicely.

John Winterose was taken into Salt Lake last week to be operated on for apendicitis.

Word has been received from Salem that Leo Gardner was seriously hurt last week by a hay pole falling on him. His skull was fractured and little hope was entertained for his recovery.

J. Barras on the north tract jumped from a hay stack one day last week and landed on a large hay fork. One of the tines penetrated his thigh, inflicting a serious wound.

The seven-year-old son of J. R. Law got his finger tangled up in the chain of a bicycle and the end of the member was so badly lacerated that Dr. Broadus had to be called in to save it.

Mrs. Will Basset presented her husband with a fine baby girl last week.

Bob Whicker finished a well for Ed Marshall this week and then took his outfit to the new tract that is to be opened up west of Lynndyl, where he will sink two wells to see if the same strata of lithia water underlies that tract and what the character of the underlying soil is.

Mrs. Louis Moench, who has been teaching school in the northern part of the state, has joined her husband on his model farm near the reservoir.

S. W. Eccles has completed his new store on the west side and expects to open up next week with a big stock of new goods.

The five-year-old son of S. W. Eccles had a narrow escape from death last week. He climbed up on the front wheel of a load of lumber just as the team started off. He fell under the wheel which ran over his body from the right hip to the left shoulder. His father stopped the team when he heard his son cry and the wagon backed over his body again. While the little fellow was badly bruised no bones were broken, nor were any serious internal injuries inflicted. The only way to account for the narrow escape was that the weight was chiefly on the hind wheels.

Miller's furniture store is the place to get genuine bargains in furniture. Call and you will always find some bargain you want.

Mr. Clayton from Ogden is down irrigating his land on the west side near Herman Munster's. He has built himself a Millard County bungalow which he will live in while making final proof on his land.

The West Delta Telephone Company is preparing to consolidate with the company that will give it the best service, and to this end an effort is being made to consolidate all the telephone companies. We have the People's Telephone Company, the West Side Telephone Company, the West Delta Telephone Company and the Millard County Telephone Company. Much better service could be rendered if all these small companies were consolidated into one strong company. Mr. Callister of the Millard County Company says that whether consolidation is effected or not his company will put up a building at once with a first class switch board and two operators so they can give continuous service.

About 20 men are now employed on the Sevier Bridge Dam. They are getting the material ready to make the ten-foot raise. In a week or two the water will be lowered so that the turbine wheel and pump can be installed in the overflow tunnel preparatory to sluicing the earth on to the dam.

The West Side will soon have a postoffice. Win Walker has been appointed postmaster and he will put up a building and be ready for business as soon as his commission has been received.

In the contest for Goddess of Liberty for the Fourth of July Emma Tozer is still ahead. The contest closes at 12 o'clock Friday at the dance. It is rumored that two dark horses are to enter the contest and their supporters will make it interesting for all other candidates. Come prepared to make a stiff fight for your favorite.

The annual election of school trustees for the various districts of the county will occur on July 14.

Petitions in favor of the consolidation of the school districts of the county are being circulated in every district. Only registered voters sign them and from the way public sentiment has turned in favor of consolidation there is little doubt that the required majority can be obtained so that the commissioners can grant consolidation at their next meeting.

The band is faithfully practicing and it looks as if we were to have some inspiring music for the Fourth of July.

So many of the boys are away just now that it has been impossible so far to organize a baseball team in Delta. Perhaps one can be organized later.

EVENTS AT OAK CITY

The small shower of Monday was sure appreciated after such hot weather.

The Rev. M. McClain of Salt Lake City is here holding tent meetings. He is accompanied by Mr. Meaker of Mt. Pleasant and Miss Weaver of Ohio, who furnish very beautiful music for the meetings.

Our canyon is proving a very attractive place these days. Quite a number of people from Delta and Lynndyl were up enjoying the sights and fresh air.

A large number of our people attended conference at Deseret Sunday.

The following is the program for the Fourth of July:

Firing of cannons and bugle calls at daybreak by Capt. Walker and Adj. Dutson.

Hoisting of the Stars and Stripes at sunrise by Lieuts. Roper and Aldridge.

The band will play Rally Round the Flag as the flag is raised.

Ringing of the bell at 9:30, William Chestnut.

Meeting at 10:00.

Master of Ceremonies, Lorenzo Lovell.

Male quartette, national medley, Geo. E. Finlinson and company.

Prayer by Leo Lyman.

America, by band, under the direction of Prof. Eddie Q. Dutson.

Oration, Zella Nielson.

Flag drill, directed by Lydia Roper and Belva Lovell.

Patriotic speech, Brigham Lovell.

Solo, the Star-Spangled Banner, by Frank C. Stanley.

Speech, Uncle Sam, represented by Soren J. Rowlinson.

Columbia, represented by Gene Lovell.

Vocal solo, Columbia, the Gem of the Ocean, by Harry Macdonough.

Toasts, Eli Rawlinson, Lydia Finlinson and volunteers.

Music by orchestra.

Benediction, Bert Roper.

The committees have all been appointed and are working on their programs.

There will be horse races, foot races, baseball games and dances, so come one and all and have the time of your life.

Salt Lake Telegram
July 5, 1913

IN MILLARD COUNTY MADE AVAILABLE FOR PROFITABLE FARMING BY IRRIGATION

OUTLET TUNNEL AND GATES

LYNNDYL SIPHON PIPE

INTAKE OF LYNNDYL SIPHON, 60 INCH DIAMETER

WEST PORTAL INTAKE TUNNEL

Water Is Turned Into Ditch of Sevier River Land and Water Company at Lynndyl

SOME SOIL DOWN THERE

C. Overson of Leamington is one of the oldest residents of the Pahvant country in Millard county. Mr. Overson acquired land at the head of the valley in 1875 and moved to that location five years later, where he has since resided. He is one of the county's most enthusiastic "boosters," and has given active aid and financial assistance to every project for the reclamation by irrigation of the valley lands.

Mr. Overson was asked recently by a newcomer for advice relative to a contemplated purchase of land in that section. "I am thinking of buying forty acres and planting it in alfalfa," said the newcomer; "what do you think of it?" Mr. Overson said: "Do so by all means; but I would advise you to buy an additional forty acres on which to stack the product of the first forty." The veteran did not even smile when giving this astounding insight of the productivity of the soil.

Water is in the ditch at Lyndyl!

This news flashed over Millard county early Thursday, the telephones carrying the glad tidings and neighbors joyfully hastening to congratulate each other on the culmination of their hopes of many years. The news meant that after long and vexatious delays, water is at last available for 50,000 acres of the best land in Millard county, which is only another way of saying the best in the state. It means much for the growing town of Lyndyl, which is now expected to realize its hope of becoming "the largest and best town in the state, south of Salt Lake City."

The Sevier River Land and Water company began work on the great irrigation ditch a year ago. Lafayette Holbrook, president and general manager of the company, received word of the complete success of the project exactly a year from the date of beginning the work. The project is said to be the largest under private ownership in Utah and as it is more concentrated than any government project in the state, is expected to lead all in results accomplished.

The company has a large force of engineers at work engaged in extending laterals and water will be available for crops in a very short time. While the canal was completed more than a week ago, the water was turned in slowly in order to prevent damage to the new channel. The few soft places in the thirty-mile canal have been strengthened and the flow of water is being steadily increased. Landowners in the valley and on the benches around Lyndyl have plowed their land and are in readiness to irrigate and plant their crops in August and September.

Brigham Young's Prophecy.

When the immense area of Millard county is irrigated and brought under cultivation, one of the plans of the earlier pioneers will be consummated. The capital of Utah was first established at Fillmore in this valley, the immense area of rich soil and its central location commending itself to the men who were carving a new state out of the desert. Brigham Young declared that some day the valley would be the nation's granary and the arrival of water on the project this week marks the beginning of the realization of his prophecy.

The immensity of Millard county is beyond the ordinary conception. Standing on the high bench lands at the mouth of Sevier River canyon, one may see, as far as the eye may reach, beautiful benches and valleys stretching into the distance until the purple mountains eighty miles away check their progress. You realize then that Brigham Young's statement that the nation could be fed from the products of this valley is not a figure of speech. The main line of the Salt Lake Route runs through the heart of the great valley and transportation facilities await the products of the soil.

Water from the Sevier river will be used to irrigate the 50,000 acres of the Sevier River Land and Water company's project. To get this water on the land, the company has put in the best and most costly canal in the state. Beginning at a point six miles from the mouth of the canyon, a great side hill canal has been constructed. An immense diverting dam has been built at this point, the water from the river entering the canal through a portal cut in the living rock. This dam is built of reinforced concrete with a rock fill behind the body of the dam, immense boulders lending it added solidity. The spillway is a perfect example of the concrete maker's art. The structure cost $5000 and was three months in course of construction.

Seven Tunnels in Six Miles.

The canal hugs the southern walls of Sevier River canyon. Where the mountains intrude a shoulder in the path of the channel, the builders have boldly tunneled through, seven of such tunnels being found in the six miles of canal before it debouches from the canyon. The longest of these tunnels is 1260 feet and three of them are blasted through solid rock. Of the latter, two are more than 200 feet long and penetrate some of the hardest rock

that ever blunted a drill and withstood the shock of dynamite.

The canal itself, throughout its thirty miles of length is twelve feet in width at the bottom and thirty feet wide at the top. It is designed to carry five feet of water or about 400 second feet. An idea of the solidity of the structure may be gained from the fact that its retaining wall is so large that a 16-foot driveway has been constructed along the top. Four bridges have been constructed over the canal and they are of the strongest and most symmetrical structure, reinforced concrete again being used.

Leaving Sevier River canyon, the canal runs directly west for five miles to a point within one and one-quarter miles of Lyndyl, where it turns south. At this point, the most interesting and important part of the project is found. The canal is on the south bank of the river while the town of Lyndyl and thousands of acres of the best land in the valley are on the north side. It being necessary to convey a large portion of water across the river, an immense siphon has been constructed and it is through this great tube that the water is flowing into Lyndyl.

Siphon Described.

For the benefit of those who have never seen a siphon in operation, the following brief description is offered. A branch of the canal is brought to the edge of the bluff overlooking the river bottom and 140 feet above the river bed. A reinforced concrete intake on the very edge of the bluff terminates in a 80-inch wooden pipe with steel bands, built at a sharp angle down the hillside to the river's banks. A trestle carries the pipe, now diminished to forty inches in diameter, across the river and it proceeds upward at an equally abrupt angle to the high land on the north side of the stream. Here, for a distance of more than 200 feet, the conduit is built of reinforced concrete to stand the strain of the volume of water still excited by its dizzy glide and hurried climb. Emerging from the splendid masonry which marks the outlet, the sparkling water spreads peacefully through the laterals under the delighted eyes of the residents of Lyndyl.

This syphon cost the company in excess of $35,000.

But the syphon has an even greater mission in life than the irrigation of the 6000 acres around Lyndyl. The power generated by the hurried rush of the mountain stream is to be harnessed at this point and made to furnish light and power for all the towns of the valley. The company will begin in the near future the erection of a power plant which will in itself mean much for Millard county.

One of the first uses to which this plant will be put will be to furnish the motive power for a pumping plant to be located east of Lynndyl. One of the most beautiful stretches of bench land is to be found in the entire country lies along the base of the Pahvant mountain range, but unfortunately the water derived from the small mountain streams is insufficient to irrigate all of this section. The settlers have done wonders with the small supply of water and numerous thriving towns, settlements and ranches are to be found on this bench. Nearer the base of the mountain range and overlooking the great valley are the towns of Leamington at the canyon's mouth, Oak City, which enjoys the distinction of being the wealthiest town in the country, there being an average of $1500 in bank for every one of the 500 or more citizens, Scipio, Holden, Fillmore, Meadow, Petersburg, Kanosh and others.

Fool's Creek Flat.

That part of the bench land east of Lynndyl is known as "Fool's creek flat." The old residents tell an interesting tale of how this odd name was fastened on the locality. Two brothers, first to visit this country, idly speculated on the origin of the little stream, one venturing the guess that it originated in a range to the east and the other expressing the belief that it came from the western canyon. Argument waxed warm and they decided to investigate. It developed that neither was right, and they clasped hands, their anger forgotten, and formally christened the stream "Fool's creek."

The great area of this bench land without water is being dry farmed and an astonishing degree of success is rewarding the efforts of the farmers. With

water which will be available with the installation of the pumping plant, the entire bench will be brought under irrigation. Farmers throughout the state who have been exhibiting their products at the state fair and have been regular prize winners are notified that when the products of this section are placed on exhibition, others must be content with minor awards only.

A maximum of 1200 horsepower can be derived from the stream, which is ample for all purposes in Millard county for years to come.

While the earlier settlers located along the base of the mountain range, the later comers, with their irrigation projects, are building up towns in the valley. Lynndyl is the most striking example of the enterprise of the town builder, this pretty little town springing up on the prairie at the junction of the Salt Lake Route's lines to Salt Lake City both through Utah valley and through the Tintic district. Lynndyl is the division point for the road and the roundhouse of the company is located at this point. More than 125 men employed by the railroad company reside at this place and the monthly payroll is in excess of $15,000. It is planned to double the capacity of the shops in the near future, and it is a well known fact that nothing aids in the growth of a town more than "the tin bucket brigade." With cheap power available, following the construction of the power plant, other additions to the industrial life of the town are expected in the way of manufacturing enterprises.

Unite Under Carey Act.

Lynndyl has all the advantages of location, climate and tributary country to become one of the real cities of the state and not a resident of the valley, but what is firmly convinced of the future greatness of the town.

Other thriving towns in the northern portion of the county are Delta, Oasis, Deseret and Hinckley. All are thriving and prosperous, the only concern among the farmers being the appearance in the lowlands of some alkali caused by over-irrigation. The farmers are taking heroic measures to stamp out this evil and open drains have been dug, while tile drainage has been ordered by residents of Hinckley and nearby farms. J. P. Welch, agricultural college representative and farm demonstrator for Millard county, is doing efficient work in teaching the farmers of the lowlands methods for the prevention and cure of water logged lands. Meanwhile the residents of the high lands under the Sevier River Land and Water company's project, while extending sympathy to their neighbors, are rejoicing over their entire freedom from the menace of alkali.

The four great irrigation companies of Millard county have united in a plan under the Carey Act which will be put into operation, probably next year. The Delta, Deseret, Melville and Sevier concerns own about 158,000 acres of bench land north and east of Lynndyl. Of this tract, 20,500 acres on the north bench have been segregated and the combined companies will construct a canal, coming from the Sevier river along the north rim of the canyon to water this tract. This land is without possible question some of the best to be found in any country, needing only water to make it wonderfully

productive. It is pointed out that the soil is lasting; that while in other sections rotation of crops is necessary, one may plant the same crop year after year in this valley without ill effects. The high rank of this section as an alfalfa country is shown by the fact that at Leamington seed alfalfa nets the farmers as high as $255 an acre.

Some of the most attractive ranches and orchards of the state are to be found in Millard county. Sam McIntyre has a ranch near Leamington, on which some of the best cattle in the state are raised. August Nielson, C. Overson, the Sorensons, Ashbies, Finlaysons and others have model places. Mrs. Nielson runs Leamington's hotel, and residents of the valley drive far in order to enjoy her fare.

With the irrigation project a reality, the people of the Millard valley have the reward for a wonderful degree of patience. Many disappointments have been experienced. The project first formed in 1891 fell through by the death of Aaron Hirsch, who intended to send a large Jewish colony to this valley. Next, when success seemed in the grasp of the promoters, the bonds being already printed, war with Spain was declared in 1898 and the money was not forthcoming. Other disappointments followed and it was not until last year that L. Holbrook, F. D. Kimball and W. S. McCormick became actively interested when the plan became a reality. There is many a happy heart in Millard county today, some of the old residents making it the hope of their lives that some day irrigation would be a reality in this section.

Millard County Progress
August 1, 1913

DELTA.

Attorney Melville has gone to Fillmore on professional business.

The Delta Land & Water Co. have moved their office from Salt Lake to Delta, bringing with them all their furniture, books, records etc.

Mr. H. B. Proutt secty-treas. of the Delta Land and Water Company has come to take charge of their office and will remain with us permanently.

The people of Delta celebrated the 24th at Hinckley and reported a very enjoyable time.

Manager Geo. A. Snow of the Delta Land and Water Co. is in town and hereafter will make this his business quarters. He also has his family with him. They are stopping at the Delta Hotel.

Dentist F. S. Robinson of Fillmore is in Delta for a few days. He is located at the Delta Hotel.

Foster Funk returned from his trip to Snake Valley Tuesday morning.

Delta is deserted these days. Everyone is bound for Oak Creek Canyon. Everyone is going early so as to be on hand for the Mutual encampment and good times in the canyon.

Hinckley.

Pres. A. A. Hinckley has gone back to Lynn to take charge of the land work there.

There was a dance given Friday evening in the Academy Gymn but owing to the small crowd it was not much of a success.

There has been quite a bit of sickness in town amongst, those being Earl Bishop, Bro. Meacham and a few others but all reported as being able to be around again.

Mr. J. H. Langston bought 160 acres at Lynn and is building a cement home there.

John Greener and Eva Chamberlain made a flying trip to Fillmore last week, friends say, to get married. It turned out to be a practical joke on those friends for the couple returned still single.

There will be a big dance tonight in the Academy Gymn. A good orchestra has been engaged and a good time is assured all who attend.

Carlisle Reese fell from the grandstand and broke his arm last week, Dr. Broddus set the arm and says that the break is healing nicely.

The I. L. G. Club is now being conducted under the management of Mrs. Broaddus, wife of our physician. She is planging a number of good times for the Club and in the near future will conduct the club on an outing to the Oak City Canyon.

The people who have returned from Oak City Canyon say that over 600 people attended the recent outing and claim that Oak City has the best resort they have visited in Utah. All report having had the time of their lives.

OASIS.

Our Brass Band is progressing very nicely and we feel sure that they will furnish plenty of music in the near future. We understand that they placed a bid to play for the County Fair this fall at Deseret. And we hope they may be successful in getting this as it will be at home and we believe they will be able to give satisfaction.

There are prospects here now for a fair crop of alfalfa seed if something does not come to destroy it later.

Miss Millie Christensen and Miss Inga Jensen returned home last week from Provo where they have been for the last few weeks. The latter having gone under an opporation for her appendix.

Mr. Alf Johnson was seen on our streets Monday but he left for Lyndyle again before the next day.

There was a large number of our young people went with the mutual to Oak City canyon resort for an outing. They have all returned now and report having had a fine and enjoyable trip there and all express themselves as having been taken care of in a first class manner and they wish to go again the coming year.

Mrs. Alice Davis has gone to her home in Fillmore after having spent a week here in the canyon with friends and relatives.

DELTA.

Job Riding and family who have been camping for the past three weeks at the Sevier Dam returned Wednesday night.

O. R. Lambert who has been visiting his brother, Norman Lambert for a few days returned to his home at Toncia, Ill. Sunday night.

James A' Melville made a business trip to Salt Lake City and to Panguich last week.

Mr. and Mrs. Cox and Miss Lizzie Kelly of the Kelley Hotel are enjoying an outing in the Oak Creek Canyon. They intend to spend at least ten days there.

A large party of land seekers arrived from California last Friday. They all purchased land and are infatuated with the country.

Mrs. T. L. Richards of the City Drug store went to Salt Lake City on business last Friday. She expects to be gone a week. Mrs. Archer is running the drug store in her absence.

Take a drive out on the north tract if you want to see some beautiful crops, and see what Delta lands will do if they are cultivated.

O. D. Lackyard of Los Angles, Calif. who has been visiting his brother W. L. Lackyard for the past two months, went to Salt Lake City Sunday night.

Judge L. A. Hollenbeck made a business trip to Salt Lake City last Thursday returning Saturday morning.

Were you one of the many campers at the Canyon? Good! Now you can think of the nice cool trees up there and the cool afternoons you spent there and feel how nice it is to be here again where it is nice and hot.

OAK CITY.

Nothing, save the whistle of the chore man, the rounds of the water master, the neigh of the horse for his mate, the ball of the calf for its late supper, the early crow of chanticleer, and a few other natural occurances have constituted alone, the happenings in the village above named, the past week. Much like a hive, a hive of angry bees the humanity of the city, with camping outfits, on Monday and Tuesday last, made its debut into the new resort near the mouth of our main canyon. All that happenened I shall not report. Since I know not. And perhaps readers would not be interested in details. But so large was the crowd, that it is safe to conclude that there were many things taking place at the same time. Every town in the county had representatives save

Kanosh. And while not many were present from the eastern part of the county the west side was present in good numbers. Leamington furnished in the neighborhood of 75, Delta's delegation was above the 100 mark and Oasis and Deseret came forth fourth. In all as nearly as the count could be obtained, some 600 were at the resort on Wednesday, Thursday and Friday.

Some excellent base ball games between various towns were played. The championship, however was conceded to a picked team, calling themselves "has beens" and "yet to comes", "Scrubs" etc. etc. drawn up and coached by Wm. J. Finlinson of Leamington. They handled themselves well and played a very clean game considering the dirty and unsubdued grounds upon which they played. Wrestling, boxing, old folk hide and seek and other day amusements kept one busy between the long meals.

President Geo. E. Finlinson of the Deseret Stake mutual was in the best of spirits and fully demonstrated it in word, song and action.

On Wednesday evening the Walters Co. performed and from reports pleased the audience.

On Thursday night a program consisting of various parts furnished from different towns was indeed commendable.

On Friday evening a ball was held in the Oak City gym. and a large attendance closed the Stake Mutual Canyon outing.

Pres. A. A. Hinckley, of the Stake presidency and also Joseph Finlinson were present and complimented the mutuals on their efforts and the success of the occasion. Pres. Hinckley stated that he was happily surprised at the good conduct of the vast majority of the young while there and believe that it had and would prove to be a good social factor.

Millard County Progress
August 29, 1913

Evidence of Fraud.

Dr. Alexander, member of the State Board of Optometry, discovered evidence of fraud in Deseret and Hinckley during his trip in Millard County last week. Two smooth fakirs had sold several pairs of glasses of a very inferior grade for 25 per pair, telling people that they were pebble lenses and that no change in glasses would ever be needed. In testing the eye they used a trick as old as time itself using a double prism making the patient see double with one eye and only one object with the other. Thus in some cases frightening the patient so badly that they were willing to pay almost any price for supposed relief.

This goes to show that people should be careful in dealing with anybody they do not know either in this or any other. The names of the alleged fakirs are Messrs Word and Worley, although they do not scruple to use aliases in some place. Warrents have been sworn out for their arrest and it is only a matter of time when they will be brought to justice.

DELTA.

Will Killpack returned from Manti Saturday bringing with him Mr. Funk's family. Miss Loge of Salt Lake who has been visiting Mrs. Guss Faust for the past week returned Friday.

A fine baby boy arrived at the home of Ray Bishop Wednesday Aug. 20. Mother and babe are doing fine.

W. I. Moody Jr. of Salt Lake City was in Delta on business the fore part of this week.

Dr. C. H. Richards made a business trip to Salt Lake City the fore part of this week.

Mrs. Sadie Dailey passed away Thursday Aug. 21, at the home of J. H. Riding of leakage of the heart. Her home was in Panguitch. Herself and husband had been visiting relatives Mr. John Daily and family. She leaves two small children, a husband, mother, father and several brothers and sisters to mourn her untimely death. J. H. Riding and John Daily accompanied the remains, which was taken overland, to Panguitch.

Earnest Johnson returned from Leamington where he has been working on canal work for the past two months.

Millard County Progress
September 5, 1913

DESERET.

Mrs. D. J. Black, accompanied by her daughter Mrs. Marion Western left for Salt Lake a few days ago. Mrs. Western had to undergo an operation. It is reported she is improving.

Carl Day of Fillmore was a visitor recently also Frank Hinckley of Provo.

Mrs. Effie Moody spent last week in Salt Lake taking in the carnival and visiting relatives and friends.

A base ball game was pulled off Saturday afternoon between west Delta and Deseret. The score being 1 to 9 in favor of our home team. Ice cream, cake and sandwiches were served by the committee.

Leigh Moody and wife, Sarah Cahoon and Eva Moody are visiting in Salt Lake this week.

Geo. Cahoon has gone to Montana for the winter.

Miss Eeil Western is serving the people at the post office, Eliza Black having to go with her father to Milford.

Dora Black has returned home after an absence of several months in Idaho.

Mrs. Arthur Henry Miller of Idaho is the guest of her sister Ruby Black.

DELTA.

Mrs. J. A. Melville left Wednesday for Salt Lake City where she will spend a month visiting her daughters. Jas. A. Melville made a business trip to Salt Lake City Friday.

A fine baby boy arrived at the home John A. Bishop Wednesday noon. Mother and child doing fine. Now THAT explains that broad smile on John A's face.

Guss Faust is now working in Bishop, Wallace & Co. Hardware Store taking the place of his father, James A. Faust who is taking a months vacation in the Escalante Valley.

Professor Richard Lyman of Salt Lake City arrived Monday morning.

John A. Bryant of Los Angeles arrived with a party of land men Sunday night.

Mrs. James Faust left for Salt Lake City the latter part of the week where she will spend a month visiting with relatives and friends.

Mr. H. B. Prout and son left for Salt Lake City Saturday night spending Sunday, Monday and Tuesday visiting his family and attending to Company business.

Mr. and Mrs. Guss Faust moved into the front part of the Nels Bishop residence last week.

Mrs. J. H. Hall of the Iron Mountain Ranch was taken very ill Sunday evening and it was found necessary to remove her to the Holy Cross Hospital at Salt Lake City. Dr. Richards accompanying the patient. We were pleased to receive news today that the patient is much better.

N. B. Dresser, Editor of the Millard County Chronicle has been in Salt Lake City for the past week, on business.

Mr. and Mrs. Guy Hire of Dalton, Colo., are spending a week their uncle L. Hire of the South Tract.

Miss Arvilla Lewis returned Monday from the Yuba Dam where she has been visiting her father, sister and brother for the past two weeks.

We learn that Mr. Chas. Clawson has been appointed City Marshall taking the place vacated by Cass Lewis, who resigned.

Abraham and vicinity and west Delta have experienced very heavy rains for the past week.

We are sorry to learn that Miss Oree Underhill is slightly under the weather.

Mr. Stewart had his thumb crushed in the binder last week. Dr. Richards found it necessary to take three stitches in it.

Salt Lake Telegram
September 12, 1913

UTAH POSTMASTERS.

WASHINGTON, Sept. 12.—The following postoffice appointments for Utah were made yesterday by the postmaster general: Anna M. Decker, Bluff, vice U. A. Nielson, resigned; Sarah A. Waggstaff, Charleston, vice H. J. Waggstaff, deceased; Oscar W. Paswaters, Lynndyl, vice O. T. Mead, deceased.

Millard County Progress

DELTA.

H. B. Prout returned from Salt Lake Thursday noon, his daughter returning with him for a short visit.

Dr. O. H. Richards returned wednesday noon from Salt Lake City where he has been on medical business.

Loyd Seigler made a business trip to Milford Monday morning.

James A. Melville returned from Shelley Idaho where he has been visiting his son Harvey.

Miss Rose Terry of Hinckley is visiting her sister, Mrs. Guss Faust.

We are pleased to learn that Mrs. J. H. Hall who has been at the Holy Cross Hospital at Salt Lake City for the past two weeks is rapidly recovering and will soon return home.

The concert given by the Beck sisters of the South Tract will be given in the Marsoni Hall next Friday night. We anticipate a very enjoyable time and it will be worth attending. Everybody invited. It is given for the benefit of the South Tract Literary Club.

Miss Pearl Tozier departed Tuesday night for Mount Pleasant where she expects to attend

school this winter.

Dr. O. H. Richards, Conductor Deacon and Brakeman Hall went to Fillmore Friday morning as witness for the State in the Loechner case. They returned Friday night.

Mr. Archer Brown is organizing a Socialist party here. A meeting was held Saturday night. They have seven members.

The State Drug Inspector Evans passed through Delta and surrounding towns this week.

Judge Greenwood of Nephi made a business trip to Delta Tuesday night going on South Wednesday morning.

Oasis.

Mr. Lars Hanson who for over 30 years has been a resident of this place died at the L. D. S. Hospital at Salt Lake Sept. 6th, following an operation for bladder trouble performed 6 days before. Mr. Hanson was born in Denmark May 21st 1844, came to Utah 40 years ago and shortly after came and settled here where he has resided continually ever since. He became a member of the church of Jesus Christ of Latterday Saints about the year 1880. And for many years he was first counselor in the Bishopric of the ward and he was a high priest at the time

of his death. He leaves a wife and 7 children. 5 daughters and two sons and 4 grandchildren and 5 children having proceeded him to the great beyond. He died as he had lived a faithfull latter day saint. His funeral will be held to morrow at 2 P. M.

Mr. and Mrs. A. J. Henry have returned home again after an absence of three months in Idaho.

Mrs. John Iverson is very ill at this writing.

Mrs. Harriet Church who has been seriously ill is reported to be some what on the improve.

The Oasis Brass band under the leadersip of Mr. Beck are making rapid progress and we think Oasis will soon be able to

boast of the best band in the county. Great credit is due the young men who have given so much of their time and means to make this band a success and it is to be hoped that the people of this place will be able to appreciate the worth of a good band and give them their hearty support in the future.

The prospects of a good crop of alfalfa seed is very good providing the frost stays off another ten or twelve days.

The Oasis threshing machine is busy at its fall work, having threshed most of the grain here and is now threshing grain at Delta.

Mr. Neals Anderson's aged father, whose home is in Provo is paying his son a visit. He is 93 years old and is still hale and hearty.

Charged With Assault and Battery.

Sheriff Dorrity returned from a trip to Lynndyl last Tuesday evening bringing with him as a prisoner, H. H. Bunce who was convicted in the Justice Court of Wm. Noble on a charge of assault and battery. It was proven to the satisfaction of the court that Mr. Bunce was guilty of striking and hurting severely the person of 15 year old Layton Johnson of that place. Justice Noble sentenced Bunce to pay a fine of $25 in default of which he was committed to the care of the Sheriff until such fine has been served out at the rate of $1.00 per day. He is at present sojourning in the County jail at Fillmore.

Hinckley.

The District School started Monday morning with a genuine corps of teachers. They are as follows: Mr. Tibits as principal, Clark Allred, Florence Stevens, Mattie Stevens, Junneta Stout and Erma Turner. It is believed by the trustees that they will have a successful year.

Last Friday in the school house was an exhibit given by the Primary. Each class had a booth beautifully decorated and the work they had done was commendable. They sold every thing except a few articles. The association realized about $55. which was remarkable considering that the the Primary has been discouraged several times lately. A dance was given in the evening but there was such a small crowd, of boys especially, that they went behind.

Deseret is doing herself proud in the way they are fixing up for the Fair and deserve a large turn out.

Did any one ever hear a violin talk? If not you should of been to the dance Friday night and heard Al Stout's violin. It would sing out and then if one would listen closely, they could hear it say, "Little baby boy, little baby boy at our house."

Born at the home of J. H. Langston a baby girl, but those who claim this bouncing girl are Alma and Jennie Langston. They are very proud of the same.

Oasis.

The funeral of Larse Hanson one of the largest ever held here was held at the Relief Hall Sept. 9th. The Hall was filled to overflow, as many were present from neighboring towns. Singing was furnished by the Deseret choir and the speakers were Bishop Skeen of Oasis and Bishop Damron, of Deseret, Milton Moody and Bishop John Styler all spoke of the useful life lived by Bro. Hanson and of his faithful labors in the church. The casket was banked with flowers. A large cortage followed the remains to the Oasis Cemetary, where the interment was made.

The M. I. A. Convention of the Deseret Stake was held here last Sunday, there were present a large number of officers and workers of the Mutuals of the different wards in the Stake and Bro. Partridge and Miss Demond of the General Board were here to give instructions.

Miss Nina Hawley, the 16 year old daughter of Mr. and Mrs. S. M. Hawley, was taken to Salt Lake City last night to undergo an operation for appendicitis.

Born to Mr. and Mrs. Virgil Kelly, a baby girl.

DELTA.

Miss Farrel McClain entertained a few of her lady friends Thursday, in honor of Miss Clara Prout of Salt Lake City.

Miss Clara Prout who has been visiting her father for the past two weeks returned to her home in Salt Lake City Saturday morning.

The concert given by the Beck sisters was a perfect success. The young ladies are certainly talented singers. They were accompanied on the piano by Mrs. Garnett January who also recited.

James A. Kelly and son of Fillmore were Delta visitors Saturday.

The dance last Friday night was well attended. A large crowd of young folks from Hinckley and Oasis came up.

Mrs. Clyde Maxfield who has been visiting relatives in Fillmore returned Tuesday night.

Miah Day of Fillmore was in Delta on business Saturday.

Mr. and Mrs. Loyd Seigler went to Milford Wednesday.

Mrs. S. N. Christenson of Salt Lake City and her daughter Mrs. J. R. Laminon of Zanesville, Ohio, who have been visiting sister and daughter Mrs. Cronholm of west Delta for the past week returned to Salt Lake Tuesday night. Mrs. J. R. Laminon will remain a week with her mother then return to her home in Ohio.

Mr. W. T. Threfall who recently moved here from San Diego, Cal., has been very ill and at this writing lies at the point of death.

The Delta Hotel reports a fine business. It seems that all the commercial men and travelers know where they can receive the best service.

Marriage Licenses Issued.

The following marriage licenses were issued by the county clerk during the week just passed.

Mr. Olive Bassett to Miss Margie Warner, the ceremony being performed at the home of the bride by the Co. Clerk.

Mr. Norman R. Lambert to Miss Ethel May Ward both of Delta, the ceremony being performed by the Co. Clerk at the court house.

Mr. Hugh Hurst of Logan and Miss Melissa Stephenson of Holden, these young people will undoubtedly be married in the Temple at Logan, Utah.

Millard County Progress
October 3, 1913

DESERET.

While David H. Palmer was trying to water his bull several days ago. The animal became unmanageable, attacked Mr. Palmer breaking a number of his ribs, and giving him a good shaking up. The same day it cornered John H. Western bruising him up considerably, as a consequence he has been confined to his bed since.

A number of our young people attended the shower given in Oasis Sunday evening in honor of Miss Hilda Styler whose marriage takes place in the near future.

Mr. and Mrs. Wm. Mc Leod of Santaquin and Mrs. Fred Warnick of Provo are guests of their parents Mr. and Mrs. W. V. Black.

Mr. and Mrs. Carl Day have located in the Peterson residence for the winter.

Our District school commenced Monday morning with R. L. Woodard as Principal and Mrs. Hazel Day and Hellen Stanford as assistants.

There are now about 15 or 20 men employed on the new Central School building, we expect it completed and ready for use by the 1st of the year.

Mrs. Lillian Peterson of Moapa came to attend the fair and visit relatives and friends, also her sister Phoebe Reid of Leamington was among the many visitors.

Mrs. C. A. Reed of Salt Lake is visiting her daughter Mrs. G. M. Moody this week.

M. H. Webb of Baker, Nev. was in town last week, also his daughter Alice Roberts accompanied him here and took the train for Salt Lake.

The Misses Maud and Madge Larson of St. George are with us for an indefinite time.

Mr. and Mrs. Maroni Palmer announce the marriage of their daughter Ruby to Frank Scott. The marriage to take place in the Salt Lake Temple the 3rd.

The Millard County Fair was a success in every way. The little daughter of Ed. Bishop won the $10 prize for being the prettiest baby at the fair.

The Misses Laura and Ada Hinckley of Provo were visiting relatives and friends last week.

Mrs. Ellen Howell of Salt Lake will deliver a lecture tomorrow on health, to the ladies.

DELTA.

Mrs. Archer Brown who has been a resident of Delta for the past six months stored her household goods and went to Lyndyl Thursday morning to accept a position there.

James A. Melville made a business trip to Salt Lake City Wednesday returning Saturday. He also tells us he has a new grandson. Now we know why he wore such a broad smile upon his return.

School was closed Friday so that all school children might attend the fair. That was a fine thing and we hope all the children embraced the opportunity as it is a great help to the children to see all the different products raised through out the country, it is a good object lesson to them. Of course we hope that none of the youngsters observed the condition that a number of the young men were in and follow their example as one of the most disgusting sights is to see a fine young man intoxicated.

H. B. Prout Sec. and Treas. of the Delta Land & Water Co. made a business trip to Salt Lake the fore part of the week.

Mrs. A. P. Wallace and little ones returned Thursday from Garfield County where they have been visiting friends and relatives for the past three weeks.

Mr. and Mrs. M. J. Greenwood and little ones of Salt Lake City are spending a week with Mrs. Greenwood's father James A. Melville at the Delta Hotel.

James Faust returned Friday from his trip to Garfield County where he has been for the past three weeks. He has taken his position in the Bishop and Wallace Hardware store again.

Mr. and Mrs. Robert Jenkins went to Salt City Sunday where they will attend conference and also go through the Temple.

Mrs. J. W. Winterrose has opened her millinery store on Clark Street and has a fine display of fall and winter hats in the latest style. See her before buying elsewhere. The right hat for the right price.

Some of these days two of our most honorable young folks are going to take the train for Salt Lake and be united in the holy bonds of matrimony. Watch the next paper.

Mr. and Mrs. Hollenbeck are visiting their daughter Mrs. Frank Johnson near Abraham.

Mr. Job Riding left Wednesday morning for the Yuba Dam where he will secure work.

James A. Kelly has purchased and erected a fine new street lamp in front of his hotel. It is certainly fine and a great help to any one walking along the streets at night as the streets are so full of holes and no bridges across the ditches. If we don't have something done to the streets before long we will need a street lamp at every corner to insure our safety after dark.

Mr. Walker agent for the Mutual Life Insurance Company has been in town for the past week.

Mrs. Albro of Topeka, Kansas, who has a farm out on the North Tract spent Sunday with Mrs. John Dailey, leaving Tuesday morning for California to spend the winter with her daughter.

Alma Greenwood of American fork was a guest at the Delta Hotel also attended the county fair at Deseret.

A fine rain settled the weather and the dust Tuesday night and was appreciated by everyone.

Foster Funk of the stage line made a business trip to Salt Lake Monday.

Mr. and Mrs. Edson of Boston are here to purchase a farm at this writing.

Mr. Lee assistant Traffic Manager and Mr. Donahue Train Master of the Salt Lake Route were here Wednesday.

DIED.—On Thursday morning at Oasis Mrs. Elizabeth Rutherford only living sister to the wife of our County Treasurer. Funeral arrangements have not as yet been completed.

Millard County Progress
October 24, 1913

Alonzo Billings of Hinckley Hurt.

While at work on Tuesday morning of this week Mr. Alonzo Billings of Hinckley, Supt. of the work at Yuba Dam, fell a distance of 20 feet from a scaffold on which he was working onto a pile of rock and was pretty badly bruised all over besides suffering a fracture of two bones of the forearm and badly bruising his right foot. Messrs Robinson and Anderson were on their way to Salt Lake in their auto and when they reached the dam were asked to take the victim to Fillmore for surgical treatment. This they did and Dr. Stevens dressed Mr. Billing's wounds and said he would get along nicely providing no complications set in.

OAK CITY.

Our entire community was grieved and caused to sympathize greatly over the death of Mrs. Rachel F. Nielson, which occured on Monday night Oct. 13th at her home in this town. Heart trouble was the cause of her death.

Deceased was thirty two years of age and was born and raised in this town. As a girl she was highly respected and useful in the duties that fall to community life.

Ten years ago last December she was married in the Manti Temple. to John L. Nielson. Four little girls survive her, the youngest being but three weeks when its mother died.

Funeral services were held in the town hall on Wednesday following. The attendance was large, which showed the esteem in which she was held. The choir furnished appropriate songs and the speakers, Elders, Christensen, Lyman, Roper and Anderson all spoke good thots and showed that many merits belonged to the life of the young mother. Friends and relatives were in attendance from Fillmore, Holden, Leamington and Hinckley.

Rachel was a third daughter of George and Susan Finlinson. Her father and older sister Maggie, have within the past three years preceded her.

In disposition, it may truthfully be said that deceased was an exceptional mother in the government of her young family. Those who were intimate with her declare that she never became angry enough, in all her life to lose her poise. And at the same time had exceptional control over her children. She will be greatly missed not only in her home, but in the community as well.

The sympathy of all extends to the sorrowing father and children.

DELTA.

Dr. O. H. Richards went to Fillmore Monday as witness in the murder trial which is being held there this week.

Mrs. James Melville who has been visiting relatives in Salt Lake for the past month returned Saturday.

Mrs. F. L. Copening's mother is reported quite ill at this writing.

Mrs. G. A. Faust who has been on the sick list for the past two weeks is some better at this writing. Her mother and sister of Hinckley came up Sunday and took her home for a weeks visit.

The Ben Hur Show Company was here Monday and Tuesday They left for Milford Thursday.

Mrs. J. W. Winterrose has leased her building to Mr. and Mrs. Garnet January. They will have a confectionary and Bakery there. They expect to move into the building the fore part of next week. Mrs. Winterrose will leave for her home in Heber City in a few days.

Bishop and Wallace Hardware Co. have sold out to the Eccles Co operative Merchantile Institution. We wish the company success.

W. L. Lackyard, has in a fine stock of Jewelry, everything in the line of Xmas goods to be had for reasonable prices.

Millard County Progress
October 31, 1913

DELTA.

Will Killpack made a business trip to Salt Lake the fore part of the week.

Mrs. Win Walker of West Delta is seriously ill at this writing.

Tuggles are selling out their household goods and poultry. They intend to spend the winter in California.

Dentist F. S. Robinson of Fillmore is at the Delta hotel this week and is prepared to do all kinds of dental work.

Mrs. Archer Gardner returned Sunday from Salt Lake and Provo where she has been visiting friends and relatives.

Mr. and Mrs. Wilkins and family of Hinckley spent Saturday and Sunday with their relatives Mr. and Mrs. James O. Wilkins.

Geo. A. Snow and wife of Salt Lake and their daughter Mrs. Gentsch of Spokane Wash. arrived in their automobile Friday night returning Sunday.

Mrs. John Jimpson of Salt Lake arrived Sunday morning.

Miss Ada Wilkins spent Sunday with relatives in Hinckley.

Mrs. J. W. Winterrose is adding a large addition to her building on Clark Street for the convenience of Mr. January.

James Melville made a business trip to Salt Lake Wednesday.

The Misses Vera and Lisle McKinney returned to the their home in Fairfield, Utah County, Tuesday morning.

Miss Inez Wilkins of Lyndyl spent Sunday with her cousins Misses Ada and Amy Wilkins.

Mr. F. G. Barrows of Los Angeles and Mr. J. W. Furness of San Francisco were in Delta on business.

Dr. O. H. Richards is having his drug store building remodled also putting a new metal ceiling and adding new fixtures.

F. W. Taylor who has been working on the Yuba Dam for the past two months came down for a few days visit with his family.

The Jolly Stitchers of West Delta and Abraham met with Mrs. Clark of Abraham last Tuesday.

Mrs. Tozier entertained the Delta Friendly Women last Thursday.

Hinckley.

Although we haven't been heard from for a while, we are not quite dead as yet.

The Millard Academy gave a fine program Thanksgiving morning to the general public.

The Murdock Basket Ball Team met the M. S. A. Team at 8:30. The score being in favor of the Murdock Team. The day closed with a ball in the evening. The Academy orchestra furnishing the music for the dancers.

The stork has visited homes of several families within the last few weeks, in Hinckley.

M. I. A. Stake Pres. Geo. Finlinson and Kirkham were here in interest of Mutual work, reorganizing the Y. M. M. I. A. with Dean Peterson Pres. Phyletus Jones 1st counselor, Arthur Reeves 2nd counselor.

Thrashing is now drawing to a close here, there has been four thrashers running the past two months. Some people are or feel so, very much richer before thrashing than after.

Oasis.

We were visited with a light fall of snow here on the 1st inst. Last week thrashing machines were seen traveling through here on their way home. Thrashing is nearly over, we have only one more job in Oasis and as soon as the weather will permit this will be done.

We understand that there is to be a hubu or seed machine in Oasis soon and that nearly all of the alfalfa chaff that has been thrashed with grain machines will be thrashed over with this machine.

There was a fine dinner served at the ward house last Thursday, Thanksgiving day, everyone seemed to enjoy themselves. Much praise is due to the sisters of the Relief Society as they were directing the whole affair. A fine program was rendered after dinner.

There has been too or three cars of alfalfa seed shipped from this point and local buyers are still looking for more but the price is not satisfactory and most everyone is holding for a raise in prices.

Miss Reta Stevens of Holden has been a visitor here for a few days, but has returned home.

The stork visited the home of Mr. and Mrs. Samuel Rutherford and left a fine baby girl at 6 o'clock A. M. on Thanksgiving morning. This little stranger was welcomed by all of the family because it was the first of its sex in fifteen years at their home. Mother and child doing fine.

Grand and Petit Jurors for the Year 1914.

In the District Court of the Fifth Judicial District of the State of Utah, in and for the County of Millard.

List of names from which the Grand and Petit Jurors shall be drawn to serve in the District Court, in and for Millard County. State of Utah, during the

Concluded on following Page

Grand and Petit Jurors for the Year 1914.

(Concluded)

next succeeding calendar year, to-wit:- the year 1914.

Abraham. Donald Hogan, Allen Young, LeRoy Young, Herman Talbot.

Clear Lake. Byrum J. Bond.

Burbank. Brick P. Hockman.

Deseret. John R. Bennett, Hyrum S. Cahoon, Jos. F. Western, Wm. R. Black, Virgil Kelly, O. W. Pack, Chas. F. Webb, Noah Rogers, James Mace.

Delta, Edgar W. Jeffery, Ezra Burker, Arthur Gull, A. J. Knight, Abner Johnson, Chas. A. Ashby, T. C. McCollough, Ed. J. Whicker, J. F. Sampson, Cass Lewis, Wm. H. Riding, Hyrum O. Gardner, Del Searle B. J. Johnson, W.F. Taylor

Fillmore. Verne Bartholomew, Elmer Day, Earnest Carling, David A. Melville, Charles Ashman Albert E. Deardon, M. B.

Seguine, James Anderson, A. F. Robison, Daniel A. Kelly, Peter L. Brunson, Ed. Davis Sr. Martin Anderson, James C. Peterson, Alfred Swallow, Hazen F. Stevens, Daniel Melville, John J. Starley, Peter Shields. Jessie B. Giles, Wm. Cooper, James Day, Alonzo Beauregard, Chr. Anderson, Joseph S. Smith, E. M. Hanson, Wm. Jackson, John Rowley, Wm. Frampton.

Garrison. Walter T. Rowley Jr. James Robison.

Hinckley, Johnathan B. Pratt, John Hilton, W. F. Pratt, Robert E. Slaughter, Joel Moody, Miles Greener, Chas. Burke, Heber L. Bishop, John W. Hutchinson, John C. Webb, John M. Wright, Joseph W. Blake, Alfred Bliss, Allen F. Stout, J. Jarvis, B. Robison, O. R. Cox, Geo. O. Whitehead, John Reeve.

Holden, Benj. Kenney, Geo. H. Stevens, Orson R. Johnson, Richard S. Nixon, Geo. W. Badger, John Alma Stevens, Anthony R. Stepheson, John Crosland, Byrum B. Johnson, James A. Stephenson.

Kanosh, D. S. Dorrity Sr. Jesse A. LaFevre, Wm, Staples, Parley Kimble, Frank Christenson, Parley Rappleye, James C. Paxton, O. W. Hopkins, Geo. W. Rogers, Wesley George,

James Abraham, Anthony Whatcott, J. Percy Gardner, Andrew Christianson, Jacob Hopkins, B. J. Roberts.

Leamington. August Nielson, Nathaniel Ashby, John Strange, John Nielson, Jens Jensen.

Lynndyl, Wm. Scannel.

Meadow, John A. Beckstrand, Joseph L. Stott, Chas. Swallow, Joseph Dame, James Stewart, Allison A. Stott, Asel Fisher, Lewis Brunson, Harry A. Johnson, John B. Bushnell.

Oak City, Augustus Carlson, Jos.L. Anderson, James Rawlinson, Joseph H. Lovell. Jos. Finlinson, Thos. E. Talbot, Eddy Q. Dutson.

Oasis. Jacob C. Hawley, Wm. Buff, M. H. McJosh, Thomas Reed, David Rutherford, Wm, Ide.

Scipio. Thos. F. Robins, Neils Lavritzen, Louis Johnson, Wm. R. Thompson, F. L. Wasden, James Sorenson, Wm. Bradfield Jr., Moroni Monroe, James E. Johnson, Hans Ecklund, Marvin M. Hatch, James Allen, Carl Wasden, Carl Brown

Smithville, Wm. Meecham.

DELTA.

Miss B. M. Parker returned from Salt Lake and Ogden Monday morning.

Mrs. O. H. Richards, went to Salt Lake Monday morning to meet her husband who is on his way from Chicago.

Miss Sylvia Turner returned from Salem where she spent the holidays.

The Ward Hall is receiving a new coat of paint which will certainly add to its beauty. Also the wood work inside is being finished up.

Atty. L. A. Hollenbeck made a business trip to Lynndyl Tuesday morning.

Miss Marie Kelly is visiting friends at Lynndyl.

Mr. and Mrs. Carl Elmer have taken a suite of rooms at the Dunsmore hotel.

Mr. Eugene Gardner returned from Salem where he spent the holidays with his relatives.

Everybody wants to remember railroad day at Delta Jan. 15th and be sure to come.

A new reading room has opened up at the school house. Everybody is invited.

Miss Sue Jenkins who has been visiting her brothers here for the past three months returned to Salt Lake last Friday night.

OAK CITY.

The Christmas vacation came to us this year with his usual congenial cheer. With the home coming of a number of our townsmen engaged in various pursuits, is sure to come again that Christmas benediction that we all feel as no other time can bring us.

The delegation from Hinckley attending school and many of them away from home for the first time and also having had no two day Thanksgiving vacation, were radiating even through their winter garbs the warmth of the kindlier heart and the truer hand.

The Christmas eve program under the direction of the young men was interesting and of course when Santa came Mrs. Santa was with him and the couple showed but very slight effects of the wear of 1913. If anything the wife looked to enjoy even better health than last year. They were very liberal with our boys and girls this time which of course proves the goodness of the children.

Dancing was the principal feature of amusement. On Wednesday evening Dec. 31, a leap year dance was given. The women and girls did full justice to the occasion, it wasn't long until every man's brow was wet with honest sweat, but not earning bread, and again woman gets the blame.

On Friday evening Jan. 2 the Delta basket ball shooters fought out a game with our boys and spent the remainder of the evening dancing. The victory was carried away by the Mountaineers who had a few advantages over the valley chaps.

Saturday evening closed the season with a production of "The Circus Folk" by our home Dramatic Club.

Considering the tax of many late hours of holiday times on the players, it was very creditably done.

Among visitors with us were Mr. and Mrs. John Lundahl of Lynndyl, Miss Hazel Barton of Panguich, Mr. and Mrs. H. G. Ottley of Delta, Miss Myrtle Frisbby of Eureka, Mrs. Leland Janes of Bluff, Mr. Rulon Nielson of Axtel.

Miss Curtis of Richfield and a student at the B. Y. U. of Provo spent the last week of her vacution with her aunt Mrs. Lee Anderson. It is said that during her stay here that George Anderson was continually calling on the bishop.

Eldon Anderson was reported on the sick list during the first week of holidays but spent the second week in Beaver City where his health seemed to improve.

A shadow of gloom however, came to our townspeople in the death of Melvin Lovell son of Mrs. Brigham Lovell, on Sunday The burial took place on Monday following at 12:30 P. M.

Melvin was eight years of age he has suffered for nearly two years with heart and dropsy troubles and gradually failed until death ended his suffering. The people of the entire community extend their sympathies to the bereaved parents and family.

Oasis.

The weather has turned out very mixed after our recent cold snap and the ground that a short time ago was covered with snow is all mud and water and the present indications are that there will not be much chance for those wishing to put up ice.

Miss Laura Johnson and Mrs. Enoch Gillen are here spending Xmas holidays.

Miss Dora Henry has returned to Salt Lake after spending the holidays with her parents here.

A baby girl arrived at the home of Mr. and Mrs. Wm. Ide all concerned doing nicely. This is their first.

Alfred Stansworth and Miss Ethel Merrill took a trip to the County Seat and returned as man and wife. This was rather a surprise to us but we all join in wishing them a happy journey through life and it looks like another of our young men will soon surprise his friend in very much the same way.

Miss Norma Rutherford has returned home after spending Xmas week at Fillmore.

Ten of our young people who attend the Millard Stake Academy at Hinckley have returned to school after their two weeks vacation.

LEAMINGTON.

Our Representative has been "dumb" the past few weeks owing to a slight carelessness of "not having had time". But anyway not much has been missed, as the happenings of Leamington have been few the last few weeks. Although the holidays were passed very enjoyably. A number of the students were home visiting parents and friends. Including Mable J. Overson, her daughters Leta, Sina, and Manilla from the Hinckley Academy. Myrtle and Fred Greathouse from the L. D. S. University and Bessie Greathouse from Plain City where she has been teaching school.

Mr. and Mrs. Earl Davis of Bingham, were also visiting here for a few days.

The various dances and moving picture shows of holidays were attended by all and all reported having had a good time.

Dec. 31, 1913 a large "rabbit hunt" was indulged in by the able men and boys of the town.

The result was a "hot chase" and the loosing side giving a dance.

A number of men and boys are employed under Wells Nielson in repairing and making stronger the recent break in the canal.

Tuesday and Wednesday were buisy days for the men of Oak City.

They have been hauling pipe from here for their new water system. They expect to have it piped into town by summer. If possible every town in Millard Co. should have this way of obtaining pure water.

DESERET.

Monday the fifth Principal R. L. Woodward presented Dora Palmer with a prize being won

by having the best time of Xmas day.

All the Students seemed to have had a pretty good time during holidays as it took them a day or two to get to studying again.

It seems that there has been quite a little chicken roasting here during the past week. The remains of such will be found in the park if it has not yet been removed.

Thursday the Deseret and Oasis schools played a game of

latter.

The last few days Mr. Virgil Kelly has been on the improve and it is hoped he will soon recover.

Thursday evening the parents of Deseret met in a parents meeting. Principal R. L. Woodard wishing to talk to the parents on a few things pretaininh to school.

On account of the parents needing their childrens help in the spring and school running so late it was decided that school would be held on Saturdays as there are just 15 Saturdays school will be let out 3 weeks earlier, All grades except the sixth, seventh and eighth will

only be held one one-half a day also.

It has been decided also that the new school between Deseret and Oasis be called the A. O. Nelson School and the Deseret-Oasis District.

While in Salt Lake during the holidays Principal R. L. Woodard obtained about $150 for various prizes for the boys and girls clubs and is intending to obtain more.

The last few days Bp. Damron's baby has been ill but is improving.

Tuesday evening Jan. 13th, Black Dick or The Brand of Cain will be presented here by The Gem Dramatic Co. of Fillmore.

DESERET.

Holidays passed off quietly here.

Mr. and Mrs. Carl Day returned Saturday from Fillmore they report having had an enjoyable time during their vacation.

Mr. R. L. Woodard returned last week, she having gone to Roosevelt to visit with her mother for a short time.

Mrs. Helen Stanford returned Monday after an absence of two weeks in Salt Lake City and Ephraim. Did you notice the smile on Angus face?

Miss Eunice Iverson was a visitor last week, the guest of Vernell Moody.

Mrs. Maggie Huff an old time resident of Deseret spent the holidays here.

Mr. Geo. Kelly of Springville has been visiting his brother, Virgil Kelly.

The party given by the Bishopric last Friday evening was a big success both socially and financially. All had an enjoyable time.

Miss Vernell Moody left for

Redmond Saturday to resume her work.

J. M. Moody and family spent Xmas week in Salt Lake with relatives.

The Central school building is progressing rapidly. It is now ready for the plasters. Supt. McCornick expects to have it completed by the middle of February.

The M. I. A. expects to present a "Cantata in the near future.

John W. Reid of Leamington is in town.

Mr. Virgil Kelly is some better at this writing.

Millard County Progress
February 13, 1914

DESERET.

(Arrived too late for last week)

Mr. George Littlewood from Meadow was here on business last week.

R. R. Lyman, G. L. Morgan,

H. E. Maxfield were here Saturday on business concerning roads.

Hyrum Cahoohn has just returned from Los Vagas, Nev.

Mrs. Emily Black just returned from Fillmore where she has been for t e past month.

In a conjoint meeting held Sunday night, Mr. Thomas Sponberg from the Academy of Hinckley lectured to us.

On the 20th of this month the school will give a program in which will be given many interesting points.

NEWS FROM OAK CITY.

(Jos. H. Christenson, Rep.)

Mr. Smythe of Fillmore, the candy man, was here last week.

John H. Lundahl and family of Lynndyl, were here last week visiting relatives and greeting friends.

W. R. Walker of Sutherland was here the past week visiting his parents and greeting old acquaintances.

Monday and Tuesday were busy days for people here, as most of us were putting up our ice supply for summer use.

Geo. E. and Joseph Finlinson went to Fillmore last week to pay their respects at the funeral of their uncle, Jos. Trimble.

A number of our young folks went to Hinckley to witness the big basket ball contests pulled off there last Friday and Saturday nights.

Albert Christenson made a flying trip to Delta one day the last week and instead of bringing his girl back as he intended, brought a disc plow.

We have two taps in use on the new water system, A. M. Roper and Jos. Finlinson are the lucky ones. The remaining taps will be made so soon as the fixtures reach here.

A number of our young girls have organized a sewing society and will meet each Tuesday evening at a selected home for the purpose of learning to do fine stitching, patching and the like. This is a move in the right direction and the knowledge acquired in this manner will prove quite helpful to them in the not distant future. Their last meeting was with Miss Ella Carlson.

Abraham Lincoln's birthday was celebrated last Thursday in a fitting manner by splendid program rendered by the school children, a number of the parents having called in to enjoy it. The feature of the program was a warmly debated question by 8th grade pupils as to which was the greater man and which did the more for our country—George Washington or Abraham Lincoln? The negatives got the decision.

—Old fashioned hoar-hound stick candy at 20 cents per pound. At the Delta Bakery.

NEWS FROM OAK CITY.

(Jos. H. Christenson, Rep.)

Kirt Roper made a trip to Leamington recently

Mrs W. R. Walker is here from Sutherland visiting relatives and friends

Several went from here to attend Priesthood ceremonies at Hinckley, Saturday.

LeRoy Webb of Hinckley, was here Sunday, the guest of W. Aldridge and looking over his homestead.

LeRoy Walker made a trip to Abraham recently to look after some cattle, which he is having fed over there.

Mrs. Maggie Duncan left Monday for Eureka for a short visit with her husband, who has employment there.

C W. Rawlinson, a resident of this vicinity for the past 40 years declares the roads to be in worst shape he ever saw them.

Thos B. Talbott and son are on the sick list, the changeable weather of late has been causing considerable sickness here.

We are very much in need of a better road to Lynndyl. J. Lee Anderson has taken the matter up with T. C. Callister, agent for Sevier Land & Water Co., in that town, and together they will select and open up a road.

Our phone system has been in bad condition for some time on account of tree limbs coming in contact with the wires. E L Lyman, C Roper and Jos. Finlinson have been chosen as a committee to get the lines in shape.

This part of Millard county is experiencing a steady, healthy growth—water is being put on some fine land between here and Lynndyl, which signifies there'll be some excellent farming within a short time on these virgin lands, where the soil is adapted to fruits and most all farm products.

Thousands of rabbits have been poisoned around here and we believe that our vexations with the pests are over for a time at least. 1 ounce of strychnine to ½ bushel of alfalfa leaves did the business. John E. Lovell informs us that on a recent trip he saw three dead rabbits to every live one.

Prof. Jos P Welch, farm demonstrator, spent a couple days here the past week, offering suggestions and advising with our worthy farmers. He gave us a number of good instructions in the trimming and care of fruit trees, and said in his opinion that Oak City could produce as fine a quality as could be grown in the state by proper care.

A movement is on foot to organize the farmers here into an association, as in unity there is strength and much more can be accomplished. A committee of five— Lorenzo Lovell, J. E. Lovell, Peter Neilson, J. C. Lovell and J. Lee Anderson, have been selected to push the matter. They are all exceptionally good farmers and will no doubt meet with success in perfecting a farmers' organization.

Lynndyl Headlights.

Mr. Simeon Walker is building two small houses to rent.

T. C. Callister left for a short business trip to Salt Lake Monday.

Mr. Carl O. Scannell went to Delta Friday We think he danced.

The Land Company expect to have water on the occupied farms this spring. The canals are all in excellent condition.

Roscoe Willis has his plans for a new building which he intends erecting for a dwelling and a first class barber shop.

Mr. Ernest Scannell, of Salt Lake, was an over Sunday visitor at Lynndyl. He says he likes the place and may locate here.

Messrs. Harder and Johnson, of Leamington have been in town the past few days helping in the erection of the new jail here.

Louis Neilson, of Leamington, has been working on his basement. He will erect a two story building to be occupied by a clothing store and furnished rooms.

The drug store, to be erected for Dr. Murray will be started this week. It is to be a one-story building and will be occupied by Dr. Murray's office as well as drug store. We are sure pleased to have a booster here like Dr. Murray. It helps.

For the last few days we have been having some fine spring weather. It has caused a building boom in town. The material for the new picture show and dance hall is on the ground and will soon be in place. The building is being put up by Frank L. Copening. Mr. Copening is also figuring on the erection of two or three small houses.

NEWSY NOTES ABOUT FOLKS

Floyd Hickman returned Friday from a business trip to Salt Lake

G. W. Cropper of Deseret, was a Delta visitor the end of last week.

Daniel Stevens and Wm. B Higgins of Fillmore were Saturday visitors in Delta.

John Workman returned Sunday from a business trip to our growing sister town, Lynndyl.

Mrs Jeff Clark's mother returned to her Kansas City home Friday, having spent the winter here.

William Jenkins returned Monday from a business trip to Salt Lake City, having went up last Thursday.

M. M. Steele made a hasty business trip to Salt Lake City Sunday, going up on the 12 30 and returning on the 1 30.

Mrs. R. R. Carey returned to her home at Hinckley, Sunday, after an enjoyable visit with friends at Lynndyl.

Sheriff Dorrity took the train here for San Pete Friday to bring back a man wanted at Lynndyl, for assault and battery.

Miss E. L. Lake, arrived the end of last week from Salt Lake, to visit her parents, Mr. and Mrs. Ora L. Lake of Abraham.

Mrs. Jas. Kelley has went up to the Kelley ranch at Mills to spend several weeks, to see that the ranch-hands were well fed

Geo. A. Snow came in Wednesday from California, where he had been for a couple of weeks on business pertaining to land matters.

Joseph Neilson, a desirable, industrious farmer of Hinckley, was shaking hands with friends and looking after personal interests in Delta, Saturday.

The town has been full of land seekers the past week from all corners of the globe. She's 20,000 and you can't stop'er, is not any of your pipe dreams.

Misses Ellen and Anna Larson of Chicago, arrived here Monday to make some needed improvements on their respective farms in the north tract and also make final proof.

T. Clark Callister, manager of the Millard County Telephone Exchange, was looking after interests of the company here Saturday, going on to his home at Fillmore, Sunday.

A. P. Wallace, the insurance man, deputy game-warden and all around good fellow, was in the East Millard soliciting business in the way of insurance, the first of the week.

Dr. Verne Bartholomew of Fillmore was in Delta, the end of last week, greeting friends and attending to personal business. Dr. Bartholomew owns a valuable farm adjoining Delta townsite on the north.

Irvin and Edgar Jeffery are new members of the Delta Commercial Club. Such enterprising, public spirited men as these two are valuable additions. We need more just such men, as members.

C. A. Clawson shipped an eight weeks-old thoroughbred Duroc Jersey male pig to a party in Sevier, Saturday receiving $25 for it. He has one left of this litter and being anxious to dispose of it has cut the price to $10

The basket ball team of Delta School went to Oak City Friday evening and defeated a like team there by a score of 40 to 37. Legrande Law sustained a minor injury to one of his lower limbs during the game.

Mrs. Mary E Taylor, left on Thursday last, for an extended visit with children residing at Provo, Salt Lake City and other points. Her many friends are glad to note that she has so improved in health as to permit her to enjoy a visit.

H. A. Lund, of Los Angeles, Calif., has accepted a position with the Delta Land & Water Co., as book keeper. Mr. Lund is the owner of a farm in the north tract, and has come to West Millard County to remain permanently.

Paul T. Bammes of New House Utah, was here Saturday, attending to personal business matters Mr. Bammes owns a good farm near Hinckley and spent several days there looking after some improvements that he was having made thereon. He will in all probabilities move to his farm and become a citizen of West Millard next year

O. L. Robinson and other gentlemen of Fillmore were here Saturday negotiating with the directors of the different water companies for 50,000-acre-feet of water, which was to have been sold that day, but owing to a disagreement among the directors, the water was not sold, and it appears that the water will be divided if a compromise is not reached.

DESERET.

Mr. W. Batty from Dixie, Earl Viele of Fillmore, and Mr. Mitchell of Ogden are visitors at Deseret.

Friday afternoon a spelling match was held at Hinckley between the eighth grades of Hinckley and Deseret, which was won by the latter. Both oral and written tests were given, the purpose being to give the students practice.

Mr. James Bennett and wife have been called away on account of the latters brother being ill.

Mr. Christensen, a sheep man of Salt Lake is here visiting.

Messrs. Hatton and Robison of Fillmore have a large herd of cattle which they are feeding near here, as has Austin Ashby of Holden also.

Mr. Bagely of Springfield is here taking pictures. Tuesday the school had their pictures taken but the machine is still in good condition.

It seems the sheep men and the people don't agree on the weather as the sheep men want

more rain and the people want it about as it is for we have been having splendid weather the past few days.

Two of the basket ball players have had to be taken out of the team. The girls have organized a basket ball team and expect to begin playing soon.

The third accidental shooting to happen in the Craft family occurred this week when one of the boys had his right hand injured so badly as to make amputation at the wrist necessary. The wound is healing rapidly, however at this writing.

Deseret Doings.

Mrs. Carl Day spent Saturday and Sunday in Fillmore.

Prof. Maw, of the B. Y. U Provo, was in town on business recently.

Amos Maxfield of Pleasant Green, made a visit to his old home last week.

Mr. and Mrs. Copening, of Delta, were guests of Bishop and Mrs. Damron Sunday.

Dr. C. A. Broaddus attended the arrival of a bouncing boy at the home of J. H. Western a few days since.

Dr. Talmage and J. Golden Kimball were entertained at the home of M. J. Hales during their attendance at conference.

Mrs. R. L. Woodward who accompanied her daughter, Mrs Jensey, back to Provo, on the 16th returned Sunday morning

Mrs. Victoria Christanson, a nurse from the L. D. S. Hospital is visiting her parents, Mr. and Mrs. Wm. V. Black. Mrs. Christainson expects to take a trip east this summer. She will specialize in some particular line connected with nursing.

Mr. and Mrs Pay. and Mr. Hunter of Lynndyl, were in attendance at the Stake conference Sunday. Their visit, aside from its importance to the newly organized ward, Lynnydl, was to Mr. Pay, the occasin of unexpectedly meeting an old friend and missionary companion Angus Allred. The gentlemen had not met since their return from Florida.

Jho. Batty of Toquerville, who spent the summer here last year in the interest of the Ogden Bee and Honey Co., has concluded this a good country in which to live, as evidenced by his return with his family and household goods. Mr. Batty who has already proved himself capable and industrious, is, with his family, heartily welcomed by our citizens.

Chas. Baker, recently of Chicago, but now a resident on the lower Deseret project, assisted by Mr. Lovelers of Hinckley, is at work on a three piece set of scenery for the stage in the new school building. Mr. Baker, whose several years experience as designer and decorator, as well as being an artist of no small degree of talent, should assure the school board a valuable piece of work as well as one that will add to the beauty of the interior of the building.

Deseret Stake Conference was held here on the 21st. and 22nd., while not well attended Saturday due doubtlessly to the press of spring work, was largely attended Sunday, and at both evening sessions, which were devoted to Sunday School work. The Sunday School officers are to be congratulated for presenting a program of so many excellent numbers. The appearance of Miss Wooley in kindergarten work and Dr. Broaddus in his able talk on the Care of the Eye, the timely talk of Golden Kimball, and the excellent musical numbers all go to prove that the S. S. is intended to meet the needs of every day life as well as developing the spirital and talented, Dr. Talmage of the quorum of apostels and J. Golden Kimball added deep interest to the regular sessions of the conference, with their excellent address and timely advice. Ward organizations were effected for Lynndyl, and Sutherland which, by the by is to the north and the Abaham ward was reorganized.

The pupils of the eighth grade and their enterprising principal, R. L. Woodward were instrmental in bringing Prof. Creer, supt., of Utah county schools, here for a lecture one night last week. Prof. Creer proved himself an interesting and able speaker, and thoroughly well posted on educational conditions and achievements, not only in our state, but throughout the United States. Could his talk have been given before the people of the county much of the feeling against consolidation would have been elimated. His points along this thought were well drawn and conclusive. The speaker was pleasantly surprised to find the movement for better schools so manifest in our community and most heartily congratulated the taxpayers of Deseret, and Oasis, on their motive and energy in building the magnificent school building, which, is now nearly completed Prof. Creer express the hope of many thinking people of both towns when he suggested the school should be the neucelus for, not only better work and study, but that it should become a social center where old as well as young might partake of the spirit education.

Oak City News Budget.

(Jos. H. Christenson, Rep.)

This vicinity was blessed with a nice rain Monday.

W. Rawlinson left last week to work his farm near Delta.

Miss Lorena Polson of Holden is here working at Jos. L. Andersons'.

Everybody is busy here cleaning their correll and fertilizing the soil.

Dr. C. A. Broaddus of Hinckley was here a couple of days the past week administering to the ailing ones.

Joseph Dutson and his two sisters has left for Idaho, after an extended visit with relatives and friends here.

C. Larson of Lavan and two sons are here at present and are treating P. Neilson's house to a coat of paint.

Parley Roper has finished the winter course at the M.S.A., and has returned here to look after his father's store.

A number of our people are afflicted with sore-throats, as a result of the sudden changes of weather recently.

Miss Edna Anderson spent Saturday and Sunday with homefolks. Miss Edna is a student at the Hinckley Academy.

Most of our young folks went to Lynndyl to the big opening dance, and all report a dandy fine time, especially agoin' an' comin'.

Strangers are seen in our city every day of late—some of them are working on the canal, while others are breaking up new farms hereabout.

LeRoy and Lester Webb of Hinckley were up here making improvements on LeRoy's homestead last week. He expects to move his family up in the near future.

W. R. Walker of Sutherland was here the past week and purchased several dozen chickens—he must be going to engage in the poultry business as he picked out some fine bred fowls.

The legend stork put in his appearance here again one day the past week—the 27th, and left a dandy, chubby-fisted baby boy with Mr. and Mrs. C. Neilson; all concerned are doing nicely.

Peter Anderson one of our best farmers, continues to poison the quimps and is having good luck; he recommends using poisoned oats this time of the year as the birds do not bother oats like they would wheat. If we had more farmers like Peter, these destructive pests and the rabbits would be extinct in a few years.

Oak City News Budget.

(Jos. H. Christenson, Rep.)

C. Dutson is reported as being sick.

P. Elder is here visiting T. B. Talbott.

Miss Eva Anderson is reported as being quite sick.

Eddie O. Dutson was a visitor to Lesmington, Saturday.

G. Howard of Nephi was here buying beef cattle last week.

LeRoy Webb has moved onto his homestead, coming up from Hinckley.

John Carling is busy as can be planting a crop on his homestead down near the river.

Miss Rea Neilson of Leamington was visiting admiring friends here the past week.

Miss Golda Anderson of Hinckley was visiting friends here for a few days last week.

Lee Walker a student of the M.S. A. this winter has returned home for the summer.

Clifton Aldredge has returned from a month's stay over at Fool Creek, and is now busy farming.

S. J. Rawlinson, who is teaching at Leamington, visited here with parents Saturday and Sunday.

Oak City boys are getting in trim for the track meet by practicing daily out on the public square.

A number went from here to attend conference at Salt Lake City, among which were Mr. and Mrs. Lee Anderson.

A big dance was enjoyed here Friday night. The young folks of Lynndyl were present to help swell the attendance.

J. Peterson has been bothered with rheumatics in one arm and one leg but he has too much grit to quit work and keeps agoin'.

Sheep are being drove through here in great flocks nearly every day—going from the desert to the summer range on the mountain sides.

A farewell party was given Miss A. Trumbo, who expects to return to her Salt Lake City home in the near future, having spent a year here with relatives.

Mrs. Jos. L. Anderson, who has been very poorly of late, has gone to Salt Lake to consult a specialist in regard to her ailments and receive treatment.

Charley Talbott and wife of Hinckley were here the past week visiting his brother, Thomas Talbott and wife; together they enjoyed a trip up the mountains.

E. Jacobson, who has been attending school at Logan the past winter, has returned home for the summer. Says he's feeling as happy as a little boy with a new red wagon.

We had another rain storm on Saturday night accompanied with considerable thunder and lightning. Lightning struck Joshua Finlinson's shed, killing two fine thorough-bred pigs therein.

The Laurel Club met at the hospitable home of S. Walker and a fine time was had. The boys had prepared a gorgeous feast for the occasion which consisted of roast chicken, pies, cakes with all the trimmings, the boys cooked it all and did splendidly.

Our water system is in operation but the anticipated celebration hasn't been pulled off yet. We feel that the completion of our water system was one of the most progressive accomplishments ever made in our little village, and we should celebrate.

Oak City's reporter made a trip down along the river recently and found that most all the land had been homesteaded and is being put under cultivation. It is surprising to note how rapidly the country is being developed, and in the course of a few years this entire scope of country will be densely populated—without the least doubt.

Lynndyl Headlights.

T. Clark Callister went to Salt Lake Sunday.

J. H. Baker was in town on business last week.

Frank Copening was in town on business Tuesday of this week.

Dr. W. P. Murray was in Salt Lake on business last week.

Mr. and Mrs. Callister have been Salt Lake visitors for the past few days.

Mrs. Clarence Newman has returned from a visit with her mother at Pleasant Grove.

Quite a number of Lynndyl's younger set made a trip to Oak City to the dance last Friday.

T. C. Callister, Miss Nola Callister, Grant Lyman, James Chesby and cheif engineer C. S. Jarvis motored to Fillmore Sunday.

F. Nielson of Leamington, has just let a contract to the Baker Lumber Company for the material for three cottages to be built at once.

An unknown Mexican was so badly hurt, while trying to board a freight train just north of town, that he lived, but two hours.

Ernest Scannell has given up his position with the Salt Lake Route and is intending to go in business with his father, W. D. Scannell of this city.

A. Harder informs us that he has the contrast for building a two story brick building for Mr. Louis Neilson. Mr. Neilson already has his cellar dug.

W. D. Scannell and Mrs. O. T. Mead spent Saturday and Sunday in Salt Lake City. Carl Scannell took charge of the business during their absence.

A large force of men have begun work on the Sevier Land & Water Co's ditch north of town. The Company has turned the water in town and are expecting to plant some new trees soon.

C. S. Jarvis, chief engineer for the Land Company, has been spending most of his time for the past two weeks superintending the work of turning water into the new canals and building bridges and headgates.

Frank L. Copening has material on the ground for three cottages he intends putting up soon. The dance hall and picture show is about complete. He tells us that he will open the pictureshow about the first of next week.

Millard County Progress
April 17, 1914

DESERET.

A little baby boy came to visit Mrs. May Petty the other day while she was staying with her mother, Mrs. Maggie Bennett.

Mr. Virgil Kelly Senior has had to return home from work again on account of sickness.

Mrs. Susie Bennett has a new baby girl which is very much welcomed.

Mr. Price was kicked by a horse the other day and has now quite a deformed face and body but seems to be on the improve.

The last few days have been quite rainy with a little sprinkling of wind in between.

Mrs. Western has also been presented with another baby boy.

While in Salt Lake at conference Principal R. L. Woodard obtained gravel and cinders for the roads on road day also some beet seeds for the beet contest.

Friday the eighth grade will go to Hinckley to the eighth grade day to be held at the Academy, everything free. The basket ball boys will accompany them to play a picked team of the county that is the best in the county.

The thirteen pictures gotten last year in the Art Exhibit by the school have been taken to Salt Lake to be framed ready for the new school house.

Mr. Williams and family after selling his place in Oasis is living in Deseret until he can decide where to make his future home.

Mr. Lard from Drum is here visiting.

The sunday school second intermediate class has joined the Liberty Bell Club whose motto is "Protect Our Feathered Friends".

Wednesday evening a troupe of players are going to put on a comic play.

Several of our citizens attended conference at Salt Lake.

Mrs. Isabell Bennett who has been in Idaho visiting her daughter has now returned.

Mr. George Cropper has been in Salt Lake on business.

NEWSY NOTES ABOUT FOLKS

Frank L. Copening was in Lyndyl Monday.

Edgar Jeffery is reported as being quite ill.

Thos. C. Callister of Lynndyl was a Delta visitor, Tuesday.

Robert Robinson, a desirable citizen of Oasis, was a Saturday visitor in Delta.

A Mr. Wilkinson, who recently came from California, found the altitude too high, and has returned there.

S. T. Sinclair, a successful poultryman, of near Hinckley, was a Delta visitor Monday, favoring The Chronicle man with a call while here.

Ben R. Eldridge, expert dairyman of the state agricultural college and Farm Demonstrator Jos. P. Welch of Hinckley, left here Monday for points in east Millard to enlighten farmers along these special lines.

Attorney J. Alex Melville has been employed by the four irrigation companies interested, to examine the abstracts of title to the lands that will be submerged by the enlargement of the Sevier Bridge Reservior.

The Band Boys are going to entertain you royally at the Maisoni Saturday evening. Delicious refreshments will be served, music will be plentiful and if you dance you can do so. A special invitation extended to all and a delightful evening's entertainment is assured.

Jas. A. Melville, the man who has always had the utmost confidence in West Millard, and witnessed a supposedly desolate waste transformed into a valley of profitable farms, went to Salt Lake Saturday, to visit his wife and attend to business requiring his attention.

A. Billings has as fine an 80 acre field of wheat, immediately south of town, as we ever saw. He has a splendid stand, healthy looking in color and entirely free from weeds. There's nothin' to it, soil like this, tended by a a good farmer like Mr. Billings, can't be discounted anywhere.

Mr. and Mrs. Neils P. Jensen of Oasis, were Delta visitors on Saturday. They have been residents of Utah for 31 years, having came from Denmark; they are among our best and most valuable citizens, are public spirited and are pleased to see West Millard waking-up and forging to the front.

Jacob C. Hawley, one of the county's most influential and respected citizens, residing at the substantial and growing village of Oasis, was transacting personal business and greeting his many warm friends in Delta, last Friday. Mr. Hawley has ever been identified with the progressive element in the upbuilding of West Millard County.

Atty. G. E. Banks of Los Angeles, arrived here Saturday to see the town and surrounding country with the intention of buying a 40 acre farm close-in and also establish a law office in this city, and conduct the two together. He met up with that recent arrival who has gained a distinction of being as hard a knocker as old Jack Johnson, the pugilist; but Mr. Banks took in his unfavorable, false remarks with salts, has sized up the country himself, sees a most wonderful future for it—and is now out looking for a suitable forty and expresses an intention of locating here soon.

NEWSY NOTES ABOUT FOLKS

Thos. C. Callister of Lynndyl was here, Monday.

Co. Atty. R. W. King of Fillmore, was a Delta visitor, Thursday of last week.

F. S. Robinson, the Fillmore dentist, was registered at the Hotel Delta, Sunday.

A. T. Moon was here from Salt Lake, Sunday, looking after his land interests hereabout.

Avery, Ed and Don Bishop received a splendid Duroc male pig from Payson, the first of the week.

Mr. and Mrs. P. M. Anderson of Oasis, were Delta visitors on Wednesday. They are among our most desirable citizens.

Milton Moody returned Tuesday from the Yuba dam, reporting that all was well up there and that the work was progressing nicely.

M. M. Steele went to Salt Lake City, Tuesday, to be present at district court, being interested in a law suit on the docket to come to trial early that day.

Mrs. Hall and daughter, Mrs. Wyatt arrived from Tremonton, Wednesday, for a visit with the sons and brothers, Jim and Millard Hall, south of town.

Sir Richard D'Caulhns returned to his castle here Friday, having been at Milford for 10 days doing carpenter work. Dick declares Milford not in it with Delta town.

Albert Leuthaeuser returned Saturday from a three weeks visit at his old home in Nebraska. His daughter, Miss Martha, who had been there attending school, accompanied him home.

N. R. Lambert is down from Salt Lake this week, remaining at the bedside of his wife, Mrs. Ethel Ward-Lambert, who has been seriously ill, but we are pleased to state that under the care of Dr. Broaddus is regaining gradually.

The Walters Stock Co. will be at the Marsoni for several nights next week—watch bills for exact date. This is a strong company and you will get your money's worth—in the way of genuine amusement.

A. O. Thomas of Karney, Neb., arrived Wednesday, to oversee the planting of his 160 acre farm near Omaha, to grain. Mr. Thomas is president of the normal school at Karney. This is his third trip here and he was agreeably surprised at the growth and improvement of the country—made since his last visit, one year ago.

A. Anderson of near Oasis, was a Delta visitor, Tuesday. Mr. Anderson is an early pioneer of this section, having been here the past 28 years, he owns one of the very best farms in the county, has 85 acres of alfalfa, 40 acres of which was sown 25 years ago; he raises alfalfa seed extensively and profitably, has his farm well improved and asserts that there's a fortune awaiting the man in this soil, for all who will work for it. Mr. Anderson is not only one of our best farmers but a highly desirable citizen as well. There's room a plenty here for such men as Mr. Anderson, and they are headed this way, our misfits will be forced to move on and make place for those who do things.

Prof. Moench of Ogden was here the end of last week looking after his 120 acre farm 2½ miles from Delta, stopping at the Kelley Hotel, while here. His farm is as level as a sheet of paper, 80 acres is plowed and ready for the drill. He is well pleased with the work done by Clyde Underhill and Carl Elmer, who have charge of the work thereon. The other 40 acres will be plowed later and sown to fall wheat. Prof. Moench believes in improvement, has a fine cozy cottage erected and has engaged Whicker Bros. to get a flowing well, which he claims will add at least $1000 in value to his farm. He speaks highly of the country and believes Delta has a great future before her. He remarked that places a few years ago appeared desolate and valueless are today, to his great surprise, covered with a healthy growth of alfalfa and grain. In short, land that was offered for $30 to $10 an acre two years ago have now jumped up to $75 and $100 an acre. He noted our increase in population and said at the gait we were going, it wasn't a hard matter to foretell what this vicinity will be in 10 years. Just exactly what her name indicates The Delta of Utah.—Contributed

---

Oak City News Budget.

(Jos. H. Christenson, Rep.)

A number went from here to Priesthood meeting at Hinckley, Saturday.

Mrs. Martha and Miss Ida Roper spent a few days with friends in Hinckley, the past week.

We have been favored with another abundant rainfall the past week, which makes us all happy.

Edgar Nelson went to Lynndyl Sunday to assist Geo. E. Finlinson in organizing a Y. M. M. L Association over there.

The Oak City Primary Association gave an entertainment Friday evening, rendering an interesting program which was enjoyed by all. Different games were played afterward.

Jesse Peterson and Elmer Duncan made a trip to Eureka, the past week, after his furniture; he has rented Wm. Alldredge house for the summer and Mr. Alldredge has moved onto his homestead east of town.

A fierce pugilistic bout occured in the north part of town one day the past week, which from all reports was a lively affair, full details are unobtainable, but it was not for championship honors. We hope they will make public their next engagement in advance.

NEWSY NOTES ABOUT FOLKS

C. A. Tush of Milford, is a visitor here, today.

H. B. Prout was a business visitor to Milford, Sunday.

Ray Bishop had his ankle dislocated Tuesday, while working.

An old-fashioned dance at the ward hall tomorrow—Friday eve.

N. A. Anderson of Fillmore, was a Delta visitor, Wednesday.

S. W. Eccles made a business trip to Salt Lake City, last Friday.

Sheriff Dorrity and G. A. Robinson of Fillmore, were Delta visitors Tuesday.

Jas. W. Walton was fortunate in securing a flowing well on his north tract farm.

Jas. A. Melville and M. M. Steele were business visitors to Clear Lake, last Friday.

Jas. A. Melville went to Salt Lake City Sunday, for a few days visit with relatives.

F. L. Copening and Wm. N. Garden were Lynndyl business visitors, Saturday.

Bert Chambers went to Salt Lake City, last week to look up a suitable position.

Postoffice Inspectors, Messrs. Hamilton and Hood of Provo, were Delta visitors, Friday.

Geo. A. Snow arrived on this morning's train to look after business interests on the project.

Miss Daisy McClary came from Salt Lake Wednesday for a short visit with Miss Bertha Parker.

A. H. Land, L. A. Sorenson, and C. E. Ferre of Gunnison, were Delta visitors Wednesday.

State Engineer W. D. Beers of Salt Lake, arrived here this morning to attend to official matters requiring his attention.

Mrs. C. W. Moffitt is expected to return tomorrow—Friday from a visit with her parents at Beaver for the past month.

A. C. Brown of Beaver City, was here the end of last week, making arrangments to have his eighty on the south tract sown to alfalfa.

Assistant General Passenger Agent Joe Manderfield and Prof. Louis A. Merrill of Salt Lake, were prominent and distinguished Delta visitors, last Friday.

Albert Leuthaeuser consigned a car of Millard County swine to the Ogden market, Friday. He accompanied the shipment, returning Monday.

Mrs. Garretts returned to San Diego, Cal., Monday to remain with her mother, until her husband selects a suitable farm and erects a house thereon.

Jacob Schwartz is down from Salt Lake this week, looking after improvements on his farm, he has engaged Dobson Bros. to put down a well thereon, also.

Milton Moody made a business trip to Salt Lake, Tuesday. Mr. Moody is a gentleman in every sense that term applies and his friends can be numbered by his acquaintances.

The Chronicle force very much appreciated a nice, fragrant bouquet of pansies and lilacs, sent in by Mrs. O. Gustaveson of Holden last Saturday. Many thanks, kind lady.

T. Hersleff, a youngman of the Woodrow vicinity, went SaltLake Saturday, to undergo an operation for appendicitus. Hersleff is the crack catcher of the Woodrow ball team.

Mrs. Dora Cooper and daughter, Mrs. Wesley Lackyard were Salt Lake City visitors from Friday till Sunday. The latter consulting a specialist in regard to ailments peculiar to her sex.

N. E. Lewis, the harness and saddle maker of Hinckley, was a Delta visitor, Saturday. He reports his business good and that he anticipates opening another shop here, before a great while.

Our good friend, Mayor Sorenson put one over on us Saturday, simply by attending to business while we was not. N. E. Lewis of Hinckley knocked at our office door intending to give us a nice fat trout; yes opportunity knocked at our door for a swell feed, we were not present to grasp it, so Mr Lewis found the Honorable Mayor attending to business and gave him the trout instead.

DESERET.

Tuesday we had a nice little shower which will be a great benefit to the grain farmers.

Last evening Maletta Woodard got kicked by a horse on the eye although it is not injured.

A few days ago Conk's dike was washed out causing quite a flood down there.

The report of the Yuba dam on the verge of collapse has caused great excitement here. The people are getting ready to move as soon as it goes.

Last Thursday a social was held at Jerald Bennett's home every one seemed to enjoy themselves very much.

The people are beginning to plant their beets now although the school boys who are going to contest have not yet begun planting theirs.

Mr. Ben R. Eldredge visited the school Wednesday and while there spoke very interesting on the dairy cow showing how much benefit it was to raise dairy cows in preference to beef cows.

The students are busy preparing for the last day of school and the commencement exercises to be held this week.

Results Very Gratifying.

Following is a list of the Eighth Grade Graduates in all the different District Schools of Millard County for the term just ended. This is the largest number of graduates in this county in years and the results are very gratifying to County Superintendant Asaman.

Names of Graduates.

HINCKLEY Carrie Wright Ila Anderson LeRoy Cahoon Maud Badger Ruby Kellar Ruby Stout Stella Wright Victor Terry Carrie Langston Etta Meecham Wayne Lisonbee Sadie Lisonbee Lillian Loveland Mina Wright Minnie Wilkins Aften Greener Myron Theobald.

FILLMORE Noble Day Ellen Beckwith Fred Burt Adrian Frampton Plat Trimble Nicholas Day Fern Ashby Jane McBride Myrtle Brunson Eva Swallow Wells Starley Clark Greenway Ray Warner Freeman Brunson Joel Black Alton Owens

KANOSH Gilda Paxton Bertha Christensen Rulon Dorrity Lloyd Rogers Clemoth Whatcott Wilford Watts Velma Dorrity Myron Abraham Thelma Hatton Levi Hopkins Meredith Erickson Edith Erickson Veatrice Rappleye.

DELTA LeGrand Law Melva Turner Viola Turner Florence Cook Eliza Hook Gerald Billings Vernon Tozer Alfonzo Gronning Helen Aller Helen Maxfield Dewey Sanford.

HOLDEN Miriam Stephenson Luella Teeples Chloe McKee Jesse Stephenson Gertrude Wood Ruby Jones Elza Hunter Floyd Hofheins Nettie Johnson Edwin Stephenson.

DESERET Inez Western Ora Hales Mansel Warnick Lucile Damron Hulda Hales Isabel Bennett Raymond Cahoon Martha Schoenberger Henry Bennett.

SCIPIO Emil Peterson Max Robins Myrtle Peterson Virga Olson Alta Robins Beatrice Quarnberg Merle Peterson Eloise Ivy Maggie Hatch.

LEAMINGTON Myrtle Strange Eleanor Ashby Earl Greathouse Leda Finlinson Winnie Strange Maria Nelson Clyde Overson Leonard Dutson Shelby Nielson.

OAK CITY Clara Walker Eva Lovell Ellis Anderson Elsie Talbot Jesse Sheriff Pearl Christensen Ellie Roper.

MEADOW Leah Duncan Howard Stott Ordell Gull Arland Beckstrand Wendl Iverson Howard Bennett.

ROOK Richard Thompson Harold Connelly Oscar Houman Marie Barben.

OASIS Lorenzo Christensen George Rogers Frances Beach Alice Howell

MALONE Lillie Johnson Daisy Raymond Eunice Stott.

ABRAHAM Guy Watts Effie Clark.

SUTHERLAND Maud Heise.

BLACK ROOK Verna r Hock.

Oasis.

Farmers are rejoicing here this spring as we have had enough moisture this season to supply the crops with plenty water and now we have had nearly 24 hours of steady rainfall so we don't expect to use any water for some time, yet this will allow us to hold our supply of water until such times as we may need it.

Mr. James Ide who has been in the sheep business for over 20 years has sustained such heavy losses this spring that he has been forced to retire from the sheep business. While crossing the desert a disease caught his flock and took them so fast that he returned here and has returned the sheep he had of other parties that he had leased for fear he would lose them all.

We regret very much his heavy losses but hope he may be able to start out again in the near future.

Mr. Edmond Williams who sold his farm here some time ago has now purchased the farm that belonged to Washington Rogers and expects to make his home here with us again we learned the price paid for the place was thirty five hundred dollars.

A fine baby girl arrived at the home of Mr. and Mrs. Nephi Peterson. Mother and child doing nicely.

A very pretty wedding occured at the home of J. O. Hawley in honor of their daughter Janneta who was married Thursday to Mr. Earl Blackburn of Hinckley, the ceremony being performed by Bp. Marcus Skeen, there were present about 75 invited guests. Their many friends join in wishing them a happy journey through life.

Black Rock

Mr. F. S. Van Veghtan of Hastings, Neb. and Mr. John Anderson and Mr. Law of St. Paul Mich. spent a few days at the Deer Lodge Ranch with Mr. Hogson.

Mr. Wm. Crane of Riverton shipped two train loads of sheep from this point to Soda Springs, Idaho.

We have some more new neighbors now. The section boss at Pummic recently went to Seattle where he met his bride, married her there and they are now settled here at Black Rock.

Dr. and Mrs. Broadhurst accompanied by Mrs. J. O. Jordon came from Mt. Pleasant in their machine, on account of the heavy roads, it took a day and a half to make the trip.

Mr. T. W. Jones of Salt Lake City shipped a train load of sheep from here to the northern part of the state.

Mr. Wm. Lee of the Salt Lake Route has been a frequent visitor here during this busy season of sheep shearing, sheep dipping wool loading and sheep shipping.

Mr. and Mrs. H. A. Stahl have moved back to their farm. They spent the winter here in order that John might attend school.

The heavy and continued rains have been a great benefit to the country and farmers are smiling.

Mr. F. J. Johnson recenty arrived from California. It took 5 weeks to make the trip with six mules. He encountered the bad roads in places. He was warned not to try Caliente canyon as it was impassable but he managed to get through.

Mr. Robert E. Cotx arrived from Los Angeles, he expects to remain for some time on his farm.

Mr. M. M. Moody of Deseret brought some men down to look at his mine.

Dr. and Mrs. Broadhurst visited Beaver and Milford Sunday.

Mr. and Mrs. J. O. Jordan have been visiting Walter James and family. They returned to their home in Mt. Pleasant with Dr. and Mrs. Broadhurst in their car.

Owing to the necessity of dipping his sheep the second time, R. L. Wasden of Mt. Pleasant was the last sheepman to leave Black Rock for the Spring.

Millard County Progress
May 15, 1914

DESERET.

Wednesday morning the books were handed in and in the evening a school program was held. A great many were out from Deseret and Oasis with a few from Hinckley. This was the first entertainment held in the new A. O. Nelson school house.

Thursday evening the eighth grades of the two towns gave a program in the new building which was enjoyed by all who attended.

Friday morning all the eighth grades of the county met at the church and marched to the new school house where a very interesting program was rendered.

In the afternoon there was contesting in sports for the winning of a trophy. The trophy being won by Deseret.

In the evening a wrestling match took place which was followed by a dance where the electric lights of the new building were used for the first time. The gymnasium was filled to overflowing by the many visitors.

Sunday a light shower visited us which seemed to fall in streaks, as in some places it was heavier than in others.

Sunday Mr. Virgil Kelly went to Salt Lake to be operated on.

Monday and Tuesday evening a theater was given in the new school house.

Wednesday evening a moving picture show will be given in Petty's hall.

Mrs. Simmons is a visitor at Deseret, intending to stay for several weeks.

Mr. Hugh Hales from Gandy is another of our visitors this week.

Sunday the principal of the Academy at Hinckley with two other teachers of the same school spoke here showing how much it paid to send the boys and girls to school.

NEWSY NOTES ABOUT FOLKS

Joe Davis went to Milford on Monday.

Harry Aller was a visitor to Milford, Saturday.

J. E. Yates of Provo was a visitor here, Monday.

P. J. Adams of Milford, was a Delta visitor, Saturday.

Milton Moody made a business trip to Salt Lake, Tuesday.

Mr. Willoughby of Newhouse, was visiting homefolks here, the past week.

Wm. D. Livington of Nephi, is here again this week, 'ooking after land interests.

Robert Stewart of Logan and Prof. L. A. Merrill of Salt Lake, were distinguished visitors in our city, Sunday and Monday.

County Treasurer John Cooper took the auto stage here Monday for his home at Fillmore, having been at Salt Lake on business.

H. S. Joseph and Geo. B. Hancock of Salt Lake, were taking a peep at the Pahvant, the first of the week and declared it a dandy.

Messrs. Rivers and Gibson, of Salt Lake were here several days the forepart of the week, looking over the valley and pronounced it a comer.

Mrs. Jas. A. Melville came in from Salt Lake Tuesday to visit for several weeks and listen to Uncle Jim predict the future of this vicinity.

Fred Rock sold a fine Duroc Jersey brood sow to the Delta Land & Water Co. Monday, for $1.25. This Co. will put the sow on their demonstration farm at Milford.

John Heppler and wife, who had been here since Sunday visiting the wife's parents, Mr. and Mrs. Isaac Jacobs and other relatives, departed Wednesday for their Canada home.

Ira D. Wines of Salt Lake is here this week looking after his farming interests, owning 1000 acres hereabout, including one of the largest and most productive alfalfa farms in the state.

John Alvery went to Lynndyl Monday to work at his trade for three weeks, that of making and repairing shoes. During his absence, the wife and babe will visit relatives at Leamington.

George Webster of Sutherland, went to Salt Lake Tuesday morning, having received a telegram informing him that his wife was in a critical condition, after undergoing an operation for throat afflictions.

T. L. Johns has sold his barber shop to a Mr. Dyer, who arrived last Friday from Corina, Cal. Mr. Dyer is a first-class barber and we welcome him to our city. Mr. Johns will move onto his farm near Woodrow, this fall.

Atty. Geo. E. Banks has rented the building opposite the post office and will open up a law and real estate office therein. Atty. Banks has practiced law for 25 years in the states of Wisconsin, Nebraska and California, he is a lawyer of wide experience and of marked ability, and we join with all others in extending to him a he rty welcome. He expects to move his family to Delta within a s ort time.

Juvenile Judge, Thos. H. Burton of Nephi, was here Tuesday and held court, four young boys were brought before him charged with burglary, having recently entered Law's store, helping themselves to about $3 worth of eatables. The boys admitted their guilt, having gained entrance by a skeleton key. Three of the boys were sentenced to the industrial school, this being their second offense but were paroled, four however paid a $10 fine. We have been asked not to make public the boys names.

Deseret Doings.

The Kawleigh man was a visitor this week.

J. E. Petty is a business visitor in Salt Lake City this week.

M. C. Webb and family will move to Holden for the summer.

Mrs. James Mace from Gunnison is here visiting her son for a few days.

Frank Black who has been working in Ely, Nev. returned home last week.

Mr. and Mrs. Geo. Kelly are down from Lynndyl visiting relatives and friends.

Arthur Cahoon returned home from Malta, Mont., where he has been the past two months.

Miss Blanche Dewsnup leaves next week for a two months visit with her parents in Eden, Ida.

The stork visited the home of Mr. and Mrs. Roy Justensen, May 13th and left a fine baby girl.

The farmers are busy irrigating their crops, and will begin cutting their alfalfa by the first of June.

No Sunday services were held here Sunday on account of the funeral of Sister Emma Robinson at Hinckley.

The Y. L. M. I. A. of Oasis gave a dance in the new A. C. Nelson Monday evening which was enjoyed by all.

I. M. Petty of St. John's Utah has purchased 30 acres of alfalfa of V. W. Kelley; we hope he will come into our midst to live.

A crowd of twenty-four friends and relatives very pleasantly surprised Mrs. Ann E. Bishop Wed. night at her home in Delta the occasion being her 57th birthday. The refreshments served were ice cream, cake and punch.

NEWSY NOTES ABOUT FOLKS

T. T. Thompson of Provo, was in the city last Friday.

Miss McClary and Mr. McPher- went to Millford Sunday.

County Attorney King of Fillmore, was in Delta Friday night.

F. S. Robinson, the dentist of Fillmore, was a visitor in this city, the end of last week.

Carl Scannell of Lynndyl was here Sunday, basking in the captivating smiles of one of our nice, goodlooking Delta girls.

A. D. Lisonbee of Kelso, Wash., arrived here the end of last week to visit his brother, Douglas for a few days.

The Moffitt Brothers were down from Lynndyl again over Sunday. They expect to conclude their work there this week.

F. L. Copening's horse was struck by a through train Friday night and now Frank must depend on his Ford altogether for a conveyance.

Miss Millie Workman, who taught school at Bingham the past year, came home one day last week for a short visit before entering summer school at Salt Lake.

Mr. and Mrs. Jas. A. Melville were over at Fillmore, from Friday till Sunday, visiting relatives and former neighbors. They were residents of Fillmore for a number of years.

Atty. Geo. E. Banks has opened his office, opposite the postoffice and is ready for business. Besides practicing law, he will peddle West Millard County dirt, expecting to bring several wealthy landbuyers up from the coast towns in the early fall.

Mr. Frank Beckwith, banker, journalist, lawyer and an all around clever good fellow, went to Salt Lake Friday morning and remained till Monday morning visiting with his family. Ed Pearson looked after the affairs of the bank during his absence.

J. H. Baker, president and general manager of the Baker Lumber Co., with yards at Lynndyl, Oasis, Milford and Delta on the Salt Lake Route, was a Delta visitor, the end of last week. Mr. Baker like most fat folks has a cheerful, optimistic disposition and always greets his friend with a hearty handshake and an optimistic smile. He has great faith in the city of Delta, believes it will make a city of several thousand inhabitants, and that before a great while.

John Dewsnup, proprietor of the Cash store at Deseret and also the Cash Store at Oasis, was transacting personal business and greeting friends in this city last Thursday afternoon. While here he leased his hall at Deseret to Princess Amusement Co. for a year. Mr. Dewsnup has been a resident of Millard County since in the early seventies residing at Fillmore for a number of years before taking up his residence at Deseret. He has an extensive acquaintance throughout the county and is quite influential politically. He is too big and broad a man to harbor ill will against any section of the Delta Country, delights in seeing the entire westside grow.

N. S. Holloday, traveling salesman for a wholesale grocery house of Salt Lake, was here the past week, making improvements and sowing alfalfa on his forty acre farm out on the north tract, Sec. 13, which he purchased a couple of week ago. Mr. Holloday says that his business has taken him over all of Utah, the southern portion of Idaho, most of Nevada and a part of Wyoming and that the Delta Country looks more promising and inviting to him than any of the other projects seen in his travels. He purchased this farm solely as an investment, believing it will increase in value to at least $150 per acre within the next three years and pay him good dividends in the meantime from the crops raised thereon. Traveling salesmen are a pretty wise bunch of men and they seldom pass a good thing and a sure thing by; they know a good thing every time they see it.

Oak City News Budget.

(Jos. H. Christenson, Rep.)

Don Anderson is reported very sick at this writing.

Miss Lynn of Fillmore is here this week visiting relatives.

Dr. Booth, the Nephi dentist was here doing work, the past week.

Walter Carlsod went to Lynndyl last Thursday, to get his new wagon.

Peter Nielson was a business visitor to Fillmore, one day the past week.

Elmer Duncan went to Lynndyl Thursday to get an organ for John E. Lovell.

Miss Eleanor Ashby of Leamington, was here Monday, attending primary exercises.

Our newly organized band is coming along fine, and expect to liven things up hereabout July 4.

Miss Clara Walker has returned from a three weeks' visit with her brother, W. A., at Sutherland.

A number of young girls met and organized a social club, naming it the I. S. Club. Zella Nielson was chosen president, Ella Carlson, vice-president and Gene Lovell secretary.

Hinckley Happenings.

Paul T. Bammes is down with typhoid pneumonia.

Willie Stapley of Kanarra, was here visiting his parents here the past week.

Lawrence Draper, a small boy fell from a cultivator recently, getting his foot badly cut.

Jesse and George Dobson of Delta are planting potatoes on their farm in this garden spot, this week.

Punch Judia is rigging up an outfit to make a trip to California overland. His wife and children have went through by rail.

Homeseekers should visit the garden spot and become convinced that this is a country of unequaled opportunities—you can't beat it.

The young ladies of Hinckley will entertain with a dance at the Academy June 10th. Refreshments will be served. The public in general is invited.

We do not have a desire to dictate to the real estate agents but it's only fair to let buyers see the whole of the delta country; so bring 'em down to the garden spot.

A little boy has put the query: "When Delta, Hinckley, Oasis and Deseret all grow and become transformed into one large city, then what you going to call it?— Mr. Editor, can you give it an appropriate name?" (That's easy. call it Paradise.—Editor.)

We have organized a brass band in the garden spot, with our popular druggist, Charles N. Anderson as president and Ward Moody as secretary and treasurer, the latter being the only young man here with more money than he needs. We will soon be asking other bands of the delta country to come over and hear some real swell band music.

The M. I. A. musical concert held last Thursday evening was all that could be desired; every number was excellent, and there was a fair sized audience present to enjoy it. We have as good musical talent in the garden spot as can be found anywhere. To say that Mrs. Broaddus is an efficient music teacher would be putting it lightly, she and her pupils are masters of the art.

I hitched up and took a ride to Deseret last Friday morning, and on down to the Conk settlement, here I partook of a good dinner with one of the Conk families and made to feel welcome by Mr. Conk. He showed me samples of gold-oar taken from Sawtooth mountain and they looked good to me; I inspected the gardens in the vicinity and was quite surprised to find such nice gardens, in such low, soggy lands. We found crops looking good over that way and everyone apparently happy and contented. Bob Whicker, one of the well-drilling magnates, was putting down a well for Mrs. Black at Deseret at 22½ cts. per foot. Poor Bob, he has fallen from grace and the trust has evidently busted. I also called upon Peter Peterson south of Oasis, he is not a member of the trust and gets all the drilling he can do at 25cts. per foot.

Deseret Doings.

L. R. Cropper has been very ill, but has recovered sufficiently to be able to ride from his farm into town.

Nels L. Peterson made a business trip to Fillmore Tuesday incidentally taking a few passengers. Mr. Peterson drives a Lexington.

In connection with other improvements which John Dewsnup has under way at his ice plant, R. L. Whicker has the contract for drilling a well. Mr. Whicker was recently successful in getting an artesian well on the town property of Mrs. Caroline Black.

E. L. Cropper, for several years principal of the Midvale schools, Salt Lake County, is in town visiting his parents, Mr. and Mrs. Lehigh Cropper. Mr. Cropper is said to be gathering data of the early history of Millard Co., in quest of which, he will probably visit neighboring towns before returning home.

E. J. Eliason of this place and Miss Lois Robinson of Fillmore, were married in the Salt Lake Temple Wed., June 3rd. Mrs. Eliason, the daughter of Mr. and Mrs. L. Robison was one of Fillmore's extremely popular girls, while Eph. has a record for substantial and worthy citizenship. Their many friends, while extending heartiest congratulations are delighted to welcome the bride in our midst.

Virgil Kelly, who has been under treatment at the Holy Cross Hospital, at Salt Lake City, for some time, returned last week, attended by his daughter, Mrs. J. W. Damron, who accompanied him to the City. Mr. Kelly is now lying ill at the home of Bishop Damron. Though his illness is of a curious nature hopes are entertained that he will shortly be able to return, to Salt Lake for further treatment.

The Millard Co., Fair Association with a number of subordinate committees are busily engaged on arrangements for a big celebration for Independence Day. It is pleasing to note the willingness with which the Chronicle proposes the co-operation of the people of Delta. They may rest assured that everything required to make a jolly good day of sport will be supplied.

Mr. John Dewsnup, one of our enterprising merchants gives voice to a long felt want by proposing the erection of an ice plant. Mr. Dewsnup will erect the building near his Social Hall and Club room across from Damron and Hawley's. In fact, excavations have already begun and work will be hurried, in anticipation of the near summer season. The custom of supplying ice from the river by storage has proven inadequate in view of the rapidly increasing population of this large valley, hence it is safe to predict immediate success for this new undertaking.

Hinckley Happenings.

Leland Neilson is a victim of rheumatics and is bed-fast.

Pres. A. A. Hinckley returned Monday from a business trip to the capitol city

Our band has been appropriately named—"The Garden Spot Cornet Band."

A. A. Hinckley's two daughters accompanied him to SaltLake City, for a visit with friends.

There are numerous little green worms damaging vegetation in an alarming manner hereabout.

Our farmers are busy as bees in getting up hay; while the crop is not so heavy, it is of exceptionally fine quality.

Our band is practicing regularly and they will be playing fine by July 4th. Hoo-ray for the garden spot band.

Misses Lottie Nielson, Lapriel Robinson, Genevive and Eleanor Wright are away visiting relative in the northern part of the state.

H. F. Stout has sold his blacksmith shop to W.S Jackson, who hails from California, his family will arrive soon, we bid them a welcome.

Mrs. Geo. Kelly of Lynndyl, is here visiting her parents, Mr and Mrs. R. E Robinson, while Geo. her husband, is at the bedside of his father, Virgil Kelly in Deseret

Mrs. Hardy has opened a tonsorial parlor on the northside of her house; a free hair-cut to the needy and seedy ones. Get it cut before our July 4th celebration.

Your Hinckley reporter is getting onto the nack of procuring a full feed, same as a banker and editor. I enjoyed a most sumptuous dinner with Mr. and Mrs. Neily on Tuesday, which I most heartily relished. I want it known that lemon pie suits me too.

Miss Myrtle Blackburn sustained severe burns on her face and hands recenty by the accidental ignition of a quantity of gasoline in which she was cleaning a nice dress. She is recovering nicely and all are rejoicing that it was not near so serious as it might have been.

The popular and hustling manager of the Hinckley Co-Operative store, George Billings, is in Salt Lake transacting business this week, among other things purchasing new goods for the many satisfied customers of this store, where you are treated fair and get dependable merchandise always.

(Received too late last week)

A. A. Hinckley made business trip to Fillmore, the first of the week.

A hail storm did some damage to gardens here Sunday afternoon.

George L. Stewart and wife are visiting his folks at Meadow this week.

Mrs. Mable Larsen of Leamington, is here visiting her father, H. L. Stout.

Miss Ruby Law of California is here visiting her aunt, Mrs. Jennie Bishop

George E. Talbott enjoyed his mess of green peas from his nice garden, June 4th.

Mr. Biehler got fine a flowing well for Mrs. Erickson, having a flow of a gallon per minute.

Miss Clara Holbrook of Fillmore is visiting her grandparents Mr. and Mrs. Heber Mitchell.

Murrel Blake is planting a lawn and trimming his hedge, beautifying his home immensely.

Mrs. S. T. Robinson, who had been visiting her daughter and friends, has returned to her home at Fillmore.

F. L. Hickman of American Fork, was here visiting Mr. and Mrs. J. W. Hutchison and looking after property interests.

Druggist Anderson and George Billings light their places of business with electric lights, by generating the juice with a gas engine.

Miss Lillian Terry of this city and Gene Stevens of Holden, have gone to Salt Lake to be married and will make their home there.

A man by the name of Smith from Ogden, has purchased the farm known as the Pack place from N. Peterson, lying Southwest of the garden spot.

Oh, how it rains; our clever watermaster, Jas S. Blake is kept busy riding the canals to prevent the heavy precipitations from breaking over the canal banks.

It is gratifying to see the orchards of the garden spot, the trees of all varities are loaded to their fulest capacity with choice healty looking fruit. Joseph W. Blake has the best orchard that we have seen.

The garden spot boasts of a real genius, in the five year old son of Mr. and Mrs. G. A. Robinson. Alden has constructed an auto, steamboat, sailboat, flying machine and a telephone; and besides he is more familiar with ancient history than most grown folks are

Abraham Articles.

Mr. Petty of Deseret, was an Abraham visitor Saturday.

Miller Bros. have sold out their farm and crops to California men.

Miss Florence Fullmer visited in Delta Sunday at Turner home.

Miss Laura Wilcken left Sat-for Salt Lake City, where she will visit indefinitely.

Miss Dorothy Hansen, who has been staying at Leamington the last few weeks came in last Sun. to spend a week with home folks

Mrs. R. T Patterson was quite ill Sunday evening, suffering with bronchial trouble. Dr. Broaddus was summoned and she has since been improving.

Mr. and Mrs. Underhill and Mrs. Underhill's parents from Mo. who came on a visit to their daughter were entertained Sunday by Mr. and Mrs. C. M. Hickman at the home ranch.

Sutherland and Abraham ball teams crossed bats Saturday on the latter's diamond. Walker, Abbott, Smith and Robison were Sutherland's battery and did excellent work, while Fullmer and Reed for the home team were in their usual good form and kept the visitors guessing. The score was 9 to 15 in favor of Abraham. The Abraham ball team goes to Hinckley Saturday and a good is expected, game to be called at 3.30, we want all the players present on due time. We invite the public to attend these games.

Wedded in the Temple.

Miss Fern Steele, eldest daughter of Mr. and Mrs. M. M. Steele, Jr., of this city and Mr. Edgar A. Henry of Panguitch, were united in marriage at Salt Lake City in the Temple, on Wednesday, June 17th. The bride is one of our most popular and highly esteemed young ladies, well equipped in every way to take up the duties and responsibilities of governing a home of her own. The groom is a prosperous young farmer of near Panguitch and we understand is deserving of the good fortune that has fell to his lot. The Chronicle joins with relatives and friends in wishing for them all the joys to be derived from a wedded life.

Millard County Chronicles
July 2, 1914

NEWSY NOTES ABOUT FOLKS

A. C. Jones of Salida, Colo., arrived here Saturday to look after land interests.

Another fine dance was enjoyed at the Marsoni Saturday evening the attendance is increasing each week.

Mrs. and Mrs. Fred Stephenson of Pioche, Nevada, were here the first of the week, looking after property interests.

The wife and daughter of L. F. Schultze, a settler on the Bench, arrived here Tuesday to join him in his new home.

Albert Leuthaeuser, Frank Koch, John Neutsch were visitors to Fillmore Tuesday. T. C. Gronning drove them over.

The Moffitts are moving to Lynndyl this week. We regret to have these people move away, but wish them well in their new location.

E. J. Whicker reports that he has sold a Ford to Sims Hawley at Oasis. Mr. Hawley is the new mail carrier from Oasis to Fillmore.

Mrs. N. A. Anderson of Fillmore passed through here Saturday, presumably enroute to the capitol city, where she visits quite frequently.

H. F. Aller and Frank Beckwith and their wives spent a very delightful day Sunday at the home of Mr. and Mrs. J. W. Underhill, south of this city.

The Princess Amusement Co. have started a war on flies; they are offering a ticket to the show to all that will bring them five hundred dead flies. Get busy kids.

J. H. Alison returned Tuesday from Milford, where he has been for several weeks doing some carpenter work for the Delta Land & Water Co. Mr. Alison is a rapid and thorough workman and his services are always in demand.

The honorable way to stop a newspaper is to pay up your back subscription when ordering the paper discontinued. Yet, there are some who have the nerve to quit the paper and say nothing about what they owe the publisher.

Our City fathers are sweating blood these nights, they have two electric light companies knocking at our door for admission, asking for a franchise to light our town. We hope this matter will be settled for the future welfare of our town.

Fillmore has perfected all arrangements for a grand big time there on July 23-24-25th, called the "Home-Coming." They are expecting some fifteen hundred former residents to return there on these days and indulge in the festivities of one monstrous event.

C. E. Tobey of Shandon, Cal., arrived here Monday to look over our valley with a veiw of purchasing land and becoming a resident. He is of the opinion that The Imperial has nothing on the Pahvant; judging from the complimentary remarks made regarding our country in general, it is a good bet that he will become a resident.

A real enjoyable time was had at the Presbyterian church social last Friday evening; the art study was unique and the other games and contests were interestingly amusing. The men folks gave the ladies a few lessons of instruction along the art of threading needles and sewing button holes. The refreshments served consisted of punch and cake.

The bridge across the Sevier on the Delta Branch has been completed and work in constructing the track from the bridge on to Omaha will commence at once. No information has leaked out as to where this branch is to go further than to Omaha. The track is of heavy steel rails, something unusual for a spur or branch line of minor importance, so we can rest assured that at some future time, the R. R. Co. fully intends to extend the line to some place, but the officials only know where.

Sutherland Searchlights

Win Walker is in Oak City getting out shed timber this week.

Bishop and Mrs. Geo. Shipley attended conference at Leamington.

Lawrence Abbott sustained a broken shoulder last week while mounting a bronco horse, it has been quite painful.

Mrs. A. K. Moulton left for her home in Heber last week, to find cooler and more comfortable climate for the summer.

D. A. Bunker has made a trip to his home in Salt Lake City to bring his wife and baby to the country for their health.

The beet crop is certainly looking fine, when we consider that as yet all crops are being grown on unfertilized land, it certainly looks fine.

A Postoffice Inspector was out around our country last week to consider the advisability of rural routes, we have not heard yet the results of his visit.

Mrs. M. A. Abbott, Mrs. Ward Robinson and Geo. Abbott have gone to Richfield for a visit, hoping the change will be benifical to Mrs. Abbott's health.

Guy Lewis, a banker from Richfield, was here on a visit recently and to look after property interests. Mr. Lewis was especially interested in the beet culture.

Abraham Articles.

Most of our people will celebrate at Hinckley.

Haying is almost over here, the crop was excellent.

Mrs. Bills of Salt Lake, is here visiting her son, Roy and family.

Miss Myra Turner of Delta was calling on friends here, Monday.

Prof. Tibbetts of Provo, was an over-Sunday visitor at the O. M. Fullmer home.

Ed Clark and family moved to their homestead in West Abraham last Saturday.

Mr. Van Eura of Marquette, Michigan, is visiting O. L. Lake, manager of the VanEura ranch.

Mrs. William Nott and children came from Salt Lake last week to join the husband on his Abraham farm.

Nathan Lake returned from Salt Lake City, last week, where he has been visiting and taking music lessons.

Bishop Hogan and wife and Florence and John Fullmer were among those who attended L. D. S. Conference at Leamington on Saturday and Sunday.

Ora Lake met with a painful accident last week, while riding a wild bronco, he was thrown to the ground with much force and suffered a fracture of the forearm.

Hinckley Happenings.

Fred Moody of Los Angeles, is here visiting his cousin, Ward Moody.

Mrs. Mary Spinlove of Dixie, is here visiting her daughter, Mrs S. E. Wright.

Richard Parker and J. E. Wright have the nicest gardens we have seen down this way.

Miss Edna Cropper has returned from Provo, where she was a student at the B. Y. U., during the past school year.

From the hustle and stir in the garden spot, one would know that July 4th was near at hand and that we are going to celebrate.

Several went from here to conference at Leamington, the end of last week, among which were Bishop J. B. and Frank Pratt and their families.

The little three year old daughter of Mr. and Mrs. J. P. Mecham fell and cut an ugly gash in her forehead, it was necessary for the doctor to take three stitches to close the cut.

L. R. Cropper, our miller, has purchased a car of Turkey Red wheat seed for sale. Folks that are wanting to sow wheat will do well to see Mr. Cropper—if he tells you it's good -enuf sed.

Hon. A. J. Ashman, who won highest honors in the state oratorical contest and carried off first place in number of contests will be the orator of the day here July 4th. Don't fail to hear him.

George Theobald has purchased a gas engine to pump water for his stock. Mr. Theobald is one of the garden spot's most prosperous and well-to-do farmers, he has a nice bunch of horses.

Bob Slaughter, Jr. and Miss Fannie Losey of West Delta, were happily married Monday night; Elder Bob Slaughter, Sr., performing the ceremony. They will make their home in the garden spot.

The ball game played Saturday evening by the local nine and Sutherland, resulted in a victory for the home team. Lookout boys, they might turn the table on you July 4th and get away with the purse.

Peter Nielson of Leamington and others are here training the horses for the races July 4th. We are going to witness some fast racing alrighty, and take this tip from us—Peter is going to get away with some of the purses.

According to reports the garden spot has a first-class blacksmith in J. A. Jackson, recently of California. He has purchased a home and also a lot on which he will erect a new shop. We are glad to have him locate permanently in our growing country.

John Ray and Miss Jaunita Stout were united in marriage in the Salt Lake temple last Tuesday. The groom has been attending college at Provo, the past year, while the bride has taught school in the Hinckley graded school for the past two years. We have not learned the future intentions of these highly respected young people, but hope they will make their home in the garden spot.

Mrs. Harriett Spendlove, one of our oldest residents passed to the great beyond Saturday a. m. at the home of her daughter Mrs Stanworth. She had been failing in health for some time but was feeling as good as usual, she was at the table eating when she became choked on a piece of meat and the shock was so great that attempts to revive her proved futile. The remains were put to rest in the Hinckley cemetary Sunday afternoon. Peace be to her ashes.

Oak City News Budget.

(Jos. H. Christenson, Rep.)

Franklin Anderson is reported seriously ill.

The Laurel club enjoyed a nice time at the home of Geo. E. Finlinson, a weed ago Sunday night.

Miss Amy Nelson of Leamington, is here visiting relatives and friends.

A dandy ten pound baby boy arrived at the home of Mr. and Mrs. William Jacobson, April 22. All concerned are doing fine.

The L. S. club girls met Tuesday night with Miss Arbie Talbot; the evening was consumed sewing, afterwards a fine lunch was enjoyed.

Miss Gladys Lundahl who went to Provo to visit her sister, Mrs. A. Johnson sometime ago, is at present detained there on account of small-pox in the family.

Jessie Pederson, who has been under the care of a Dr. at Provo for sometime, has returned home again and we hope that he will continue to regain his health.

A large delegation of our people attended conference Friday and Saturday at Leamington. E. O. Duston and his choir were there to help out in song services and a good meeting was had.

Following is the program for our July 4th celebration: Hoisting of stars and stripes at sunrise by Clifford Talbot and Cliff Alldredge, while the band plays—"We will rally around the flag." Saluting the flag by Lee Walker and John Alldredge, the powder monkeys. Tolling of bell at 9:30 by Wm. Chestnut. Chas. Roper Sr., marshal of day. Meeting at the hall at 10 o'clock: Singing by choir; Prayer by Chaplin Collier Lovell; Music by band; Oration by Geo. H. Anderson; Junior Girls Chorus, Lydia Roper, Director; Comic recitation by Oklan Dutson; Piano duet by Arbie Talbot; Paper on the past, present and future of Oak City by S. J. Rawlinson; Music by orchestra; Toasts by Brigham Lovell, Leroy Walker, Evan Jacobson and El-

mer Duncan; Tinker and Tailor by C. W. Rawlinson; Comic reading by Leo Lyman; How they celebrate July 4th in England by Stanley Lovell; Volunteer songs, toasts, recitations, etc.; Singing America by choir and congregation; Refreshments will be served at hall and at sporting ground throughout the day; A grand ball afford entertainment in the evening. The following committees were appointed: Decoration, Parley Roper, Eva Anderson, Ella Carlson, Amy Finlinson, Wanda Roper, Elmer Anderson, Martin Sheriff and Alvin Lovell. Sport and Amusement: LeRoy Walker, Geo. E. Finlinson, Louis Somers, Eliza Olsen, Frankie Roper and Jane Rawlinson. Finance: Albert Christenson, Alfred Jacobson, L. Roper and Don Anderson.

There will be fun for all and the public in general is invited to celebrate at Oak City.

Millard County Chronicle

July 9, 1914

Abraham Articles.

Mrs. Taylor is reported quite poorly at this writing.

Ed Taylor returned Monday from Salt Lake, where he has had employment for sometime.

Miss Afton Duncan of Pleasant Grove, is here visiting her sister, Mrs. Donald Hogan and family.

Miss Marguerittee Biehler, who has been attending school at Salt Lake for the past two months, came Monday for a visit with the homefolks.

Miss Effie, the accomplished and lovable daughter of Mr. and Mrs. Ora Lake of this place, and

Mr. Charles Filby of Salt Lake, were married at the latter place, one day last week.

The Abraham ball team met defeat at the hands of the Hinckley team for the purse the 4th and while we can't account for the unusual bum playing of our boys we have yet to hear of a team that don't play bad ball once in awhile; anyway we are betting our last thirty cents on Abraham. [Come to Delta July 24th, we believe you boys can glom that $30 purse, even though you did lose our last thirty cents for us at Hinckley. -Editor.]

Deseret Doings.

County Supt. of Schools, A. J. Ashman was a recent visitor.

The Petty orchestra was employed in Lynndyl on the Fourth.

Gibson Cowan of Nephi, was renewing old acquaintances here recently.

Miss Ora Hales is the guest of her aunt, Mrs. John Peterson in Fillmore this week.

Miss Blanche Dewsnup returned early in the week from a visit to her parents in Millner, Ida.

Horace Hales and family of Redmond are visiting Mr. Hales mother, Mrs M. J. Hales this week.

Miss Robinson while on the return trip from Salt Lake to Fillmore paid a visit to her sister, Mrs. E. J. Eliason.

Mr. Geo. Kelly, Mrs. Mariam Crandall, Commander Westwood, Geo. Harrison and Albert Harmer, who were in attendance at the funeral of Virgil Kelly returned on the early morning train Monday to their homes in Springville. Mrs. W. R. McTavish another party went to Yellowstone, Montana.

Mr. Virgil Kelly died at the home of his daughter, Mrs. Jos. W. Damron, shortly after five o'clock Thursday afternoon, July 2nd. The illness which proved fatal is believed to date from an injury he received when thrown from a horse while in Montana last September. Impressive funeral services were held in the Deseret Ward Chaple, Sunday afternoon. The building was filled to its capacity and many were unable to gain admittance. A profusion of floral offerings paid mute tribute to the high regard in which the departed was held.

Mr. Kelly had felt for weeks that death alone would end his suffering, which had extended over a period of nine months and calmly talked to his family and friends of his passing on. It was his desire that the Indian War Vetrans should conduct the funeral. The service, in every detail as he had arranged it, was conducted by Commander Lehigh R. Cropper of the Deseret Post. Geo. Harrison, State Chorister, assisted by Genevive Robinson, Bishop, the war veterans and Ward choir, sang with tenderness several numbers. Mrs. C. A. Broaddus and her double quartette feelingly rendered "Gently Lead us."

Resolutions of respect from Fillmore and Millard Co. organizations of I. W. V. were read by Frank Slaughter. The speakers Pres. A. A. Hinckley, State Commander Westwood of Springville A. J. Robinson of Fillmore, L. R. Cropper and Jos. W. Damron Sr., all paid tribute to the many excellent qualities and character of the decedent. The service closed with prayers by Wm. V. Black and James Terry of Hinckley. Mrs Broaddus at the organ played the march for the departing friends and the band from Hinckley solemly rendered the air America. Interment took place in the city cemetery. Mr. Kelly was born in Cottonwood, Oct. 10, 1851, two weeks after his parents arrived in Utah. He was left motherless at the tender age of three, but was more fortunate than many in that he was reared and loved by one of exceptionally strong and sympathic character, and to whom he ever attributed the best in life. Mr. Kelly

was well known throughout the west, having traveled the entire western states and pioneered through Nevada and northern Arizona. To the latter state he was called in 1877, in connection with his wife's father, A. F. Barron, to labor among the indians. He met with marked success in this mission. As a member of his church and citizen Mr. Kelly held various offices of trust. He served as sheriff of Millard Co., two terms and at the present filled the office of chairman of Old folks Committee of the Deseret Stake. He was also 1st Vice Commander of the I. W. V. of the State of Utah. In this capacity he spent his best efforts, to see the aged Veterans of the Black Hawk war receive their rightful dues was his most ardent desire.

Mr. Kelly is survived by his widow and the following children —Mrs. J. W. Damron, Virgil Wm. Kelly, Mrs. A. D. Ryan, Geo. L. Kelly, of Lynndyll and Marcus O. Kelly. Two children, an infant and Mrs. Roe Kelly Erickson having preceded him.

CARD OF THANKS.

To the host of friends who with their presence and many expressions of sympathy and kindly assistance so nobly aided during the many weeks of suffering of their late and lamented father, the family of Mrs. Virgil Kelly wish to extend their thanks and deepest obligation.

News Notes From Oasis.

Most all of our people celebrated at Hinckley and reported a glorious good time.

Miss Ella Jeremy of Salt Lake City has been here the past week visiting Mrs. C. O. W. Pierson.

We had a nice here last Wednesday which laid the dust and freshened up everthing, humanity included.

A dance is scheduled to take place at the Nelson school house, Friday evening, July 10th; the best of music under instruction of Prof. Sauer will be had.

The Oasis ball team went to the South Tract Sunday and defeated the Mountain Giants by a score of 22 to 14. This makes 2 games won for Oasis out of three played.

The Hinckley band visited in our city last Thursday and favored us with a few choice selections as a source of advertising the ball games to be played there on the following day.

Two new autos have been sold here the past week, S. M. Hawley and David Day are the proud owners. The Ford cars are taking up the place of the horse and buggy little by little hereabout, and we expect to see many new cars in this neighborhood before a great while.

The Deseret roller mill has received a car of fine dry-land turkey red wheat seed; in order to keep up our standard of wheat, it will be sold at $1 a bushel at the mill without one cent of profit to the mill, this is done to encourage the farmers to raise more and better wheat.

The directors of the Deseret Irrigation Co. held a business meeting here July 6th. They went from here to Delta in the afternoon to meet the Melville Co. and together discussed the proposition of placing their surplus water out on the bench. An agreement was reached and a committee selected to investigate the feasibility and approximate the cost of such an undertaking.

Wm. A. Stehenson, a student of agricultural college of Utah, will spend the summer months in Delta, where he will practice veterinary work; his headquarters will be at residence of N. S. Bishop.

Sutherland Searchlights

Mesdames Abbott and Robinson returned Tuesday from a visit at their former home in Sevier Co.

Jas. A. Kelley is now carrying the mail 6 times a week between Delta and Woodrow, according to schedule.

Beet thinning is now on in full blast—children are finding employment along with their elders in this industry.

Mr. and Mrs. Elliot, sister and brother-in-law of Wallace Clark, are here for several days visiting relatives and friends. They are guests at the Clark home.

People from here who attended the 4th celebration at Woodrow report a very enjoyable time. The affair was under the managment of the Water User's Association.

Most of our people spent the 4th in Hinckley and all report a fine time, in spite of the fact that certain causes, perhaps unavoidable, we failed to do our part in the parade.

Gus Neumyer has leased his farm to Mr. Armbruster of California for a year, and will spend a year in Kansas on his wife's farm, hoping to have her health restored by the change.

A number of people of Omaha were visitors at the ward meeting here Sunday, among whom were—Mr. and Mrs. Dibbs, Mr. and Mrs. Jacob, Mr. and Mrs. Sill and Messrs. Jaderholm and Barnett.

Mr. Hayes of California, who recently purchased the Bolton property, is erecting a nice house and barn and has employed men to plow under the summer growth of weeds. Looks like he intends to do things as they should be done.

Sutherland and Woodrow ball teams played a game on the latter's diamond on the morning of the 4th; the score 9 to 5 in favor of Sutherland For some reason the $5 prize, that was to have been awarded the winning team, has not been paid.

M. M. Steele left last evening for an extended business trip to Panguitch.

Wm. Hoff, an industrious and desirable farmer on the south tract spent the Fourth in Salt Lake City. Mr. Hoff gave up a a position at $200 a month in Arizonia to take up his residence on his farm here and he has never regretted it; he has through his industry and thrift made good on his farm although he knew but little about the farming game, he has his farm in excellent shape, his crops are good and he is prospering. Mr. Hoff says the delta country is alright and that he is here to stay.

Hinckley Happenings.

Ward Moody departed Sunday, for a two years mission in New Zealand.

Peter Peterson of Oasis, is driving a well for Sam Stanworth, this week

Our ball team met defeat at Abraham Saturday by the close score of 11 to 9

Mrs. J. P. Meecham is at Lynndyl, visiting her daughter, Louie, this week

J. W. Workman and wife of the St. George country, are visiting relatives here, this week.

Lafie, the nine year old son of Mr and Mrs. Jos. Nielson was thrown from a horse last Friday and sustained broken leg just above the knee

Mrs. T R. Greener was taken to the L. D. S. hospital at Salt Lake, Tues-

day morning to undergo an operation for the removal of a tumor on her side.

Atty. Geo. A. Cole of Salt Lake City, was here the forepart of the week, looking after farming interests, during his stay was the guest of Mr. and Mrs. Jos Neilson.

The first load of apples for this year was on our streets Monday, coming in from Meadow, they were the Early Harvest variety and nice for the kind, they sold at $1 per bushel.

I was out viewing the orchards in the garden spot the other day and found all loaded with choice fruit, young trees too are bearing well, especially pear trees.

L. R. Cropper has the best orchard to my notion, his ripe plums of the Wild Goose variety were dandy. Certainly, this is the Garden Spot. E Watker and Lyle Cropper both have lovely flower gardens, I think by odds the nicest in town.

I took a drive down to what they call the boggy lands the other day and to my surprise I saw some of the best grain in the county, it is being demonstrated that these lands are the very best in the valley—haystacks and fine fields of waving grain everywhere you look and the Rogers boys raise as good lucern seed as was ever grown I'm convinced that the entirity of the greater delta country is all good and am willing to boost any part of it.

Deseret Doings.

Mrs. Scott of Murray, and her two daughters are visiting with Mrs. H. S. Cahoon.

Mr. and Mrs. Jerold Bennett are welcoming a second little daughter, who arrived this week

Pres. Carrie Jenson entertained the members of the M. I. A. at her residence Tuesday afternoon.

Nels L. Peterson was a business visitor to the city Tuesday. He anticipates a trip to Los Angeles soon.

Mrs. Emily Black and Alpin Allred, completely surprised their friends by announcing their marriage which took place during a recent visit to Salt Lake.

The old social hall bought and removed from its old stand by P. T. Black to a lot north of his residence, has been converted into a new and attractive office building of two rooms, housing the Post Office and barbershop.

These long hot days bring fondly to mind "the old swimming hole." We are also reminded of the swimming pool in the A. C. Nelson School and we wouldn't mind a good clear splash there any afternoon. Turn the water on!

A damaging fire swept the barn yards of W. R. Black last Friday, completely destroying sheds, corrals and a valuable stack of hay. For a time the fire threatened the residence. A good stream of water in a near irrigation ditch together with the timely assistance of all the available men in town saved further loss.

NEWSY NOTES ABOUT FOLKS

Elder J. H. Hall returned Friday from two years spent in Indiana on a mission.

A big, bouncing baby boy arrived at the home of Mr. and Mrs. Emery Peterson, Saturday, July the 11th.

County Atty. King and Sheriff Dorrity came from Fillmore yesterday to attend to some official duties at different points on this side of the county.

Miss Marie Kelley went up to the Kelley ranch at Mills, Tues., to get a fast gaited saddle pony in order to compete for the prize money here, July 24th.

Many from here are attending the M. I. A. Outing at the Oak Creek Canyon; several having gone yesterday, several to-day and more are planning to go to-morrow.

Mrs. Maggie Kelley of Salt Lake City, arrived Tuesday for an extended visit with her sister, Mrs. N. S. Bishop and other kinfolks here, at Hinckley and Fillmore.

J. H. Baker, president of the Baker Lbr. Co., was here from Salt Lake, Tuesday, conferring with the local manager, J. E. Works on matters concerning the local business.

Dr. E. C. Underhill of Denver, Colo., arrived Tuesday for a visit with his parents, Mr. and Mrs. J. W. Underhill and his little daughters, who make their home with their grandparents.

Mrs. F. L. Copening is suffering with a severe attack of quinzey, which is severly painful. Dr. Richards is in attendance and she is improving as radily as could be expected.

The Presbytery of Southern Utah will begin its summer tent work this week at Holden. Rev. C. H. Hamilton of Delta will assist in starting the work but will be in Delta and Abraham for service Sunday.

Dr. F. S. Robinson, the Fillmore dentist passed through here Tuesday, enroute home from a visit in the east. He placed a professional card in the Chronicle, and solicits the patronage of the public of the westside.

Att. Geo. A. Cole of Salt Lake City, arrived Sunday to look after farming interests near the garden spot, owning 240 acres near Hinckley. He was graciously entertained by one of Delta's charming young ladies at the home of C. G. Hoyt, during the greater part of his stay.

Wesley Lackyard and wife returned the first part of the week from a two weeks visit with his parents in California, enjoying the gentle sea breeze, bathing in the surf of the roaring old Pacific and gazing at the historic sights to be seen at the different beach resorts.

Fred Turner, Inspector of Pure Food and dairy products, was in Delta yesterday, looking after sanitary conditions. He is not altogether suited with the butter question. Later on, something further will be heard from him along these lines through these columns.

Harold N. Banks of LosAngeles, junior member of the Summerland Farms Co. is expected to arrive in Delta, early next week, and will actively engage in the business of the company, that of dealing in lands generally; we bespeak for the company an active fall campaign with many sales to its credit.

Chas. A. McClain, who has been in California for the past four months talking West Millard and Milford lands to prospective purchasers, representing the Western Security Co., arrived home Sunday for a two weeks visit with his family. Seems good to have Charlie around again, kiddin' and makin' things lively.

A. Fred Weye, President of the Abraham Irrigation Co., who resides at Salt Lake, in company with J. J. Cammons, manager of the National Savings Bank Co. of that city, were here Saturday looking over the country and attending a meeting of the Abraham Irrigation Co. at Abraham. They are financially interested both in water stock and lands in the Delta Country and say they are positive that West Millard has a most illuminating future, more so than any other section in the state.

On his farm at the north edge of town, Mr. Lewis F. Koch has a variety of products which speak well for this valley; he has Spanish Pea Nuts, Dew Berries, Raspberries, Currants, Cherries (which ripened), Silver Leaf Poplars, a Linden Tree, and a small orchard, on which were growing some peaches, but the boys would not let them come to maturity, so anxious were they to rob the trees. Mr. Koch is a firm believer that in time the bench will be the orchard spot of the Greater Delta Country.

Millard County Chronicle
July 23, 1914

Thomas J. Jones Passes Away.

Thomas J. Jones, age seventy-six years, passed from this life at his home in West Delta last Saturday afternoon, after suffering with pneumonia for two weeks and after ailing in health for the past three years. The deceased was an early pioneer to Utah, having come in the early fifties and for a number of years freighted with ox trains between the Missouri river and Salt Lake City, enduring many hardships and exposing himself to all kinds of weather which would have caused the death of one less rugged and hardy, years ago, undoubtedly. Mr. Jones and his family took up their residence here two years ago, coming from Overton, Nev., where he had resided for several years, serving as President of the Stake at three different times and also served in the capacity of Bishop for several years.

Besides his wife, he left behind to mourn his going six children, namely: Jefferson, Calvin, and Joseph all of this county, Mrs. Effie Earl of Delta, Mrs. Lillian Hill of Fayette and Miss Louisa, a younger daughter.

It was the deceased's desire to be burried at Overton, and the remains were shipped to that point for interment on Tuesday morning.

NEWSY NOTES ABOUT FOLKS

H. E. Maxfield and Jas. A. Melville returned Friday from a business trip to Salt Lake.

Miss Florence Shimmings of Salt Lake City was here visiting her sister, Mrs. C. T. Bunker, from Thursday till Tuesday.

Atty. Jas. Alex Melville is in Los Angeles, Cal., this week attending to professional business, but will only be absent for a few days.

Miss Florence Thayne of Dixie is here for an extended visit with her friend, Miss Amy Wilkins, the competent and industrious assistant typo on the Chronicle staff.

M. M. Steele Jr., returned on Tuesday morning's train from a two week's trip to different points in Utah. He says crops are good at every place visited, but that the crops here are not to be beaten anywhere.

John Bryant was up from California with two prospective land buyers the end of last week, and the Utah Real Estate Co. showed them over the valley; although they expressed themselves as liking this country, they returned home without buying.

Thomas C. Callister and daughter, Nola, of Lynndyl, passed through here Wednesday enroute to Fillmore, where they will join Mrs. Callister who has been visiting there for sometime past. They will remain in Fillmore until after the home-coming.

Bartley John of Swan Lake, was a Delta visitor, Saturday. He informed us that he was going to endeavor to get a good seed crop off his 240 acre field of alfalfa this fall and that to date conditions were very favorable for a large and excellent seed crop. Mr. John has resided in Millard for the past 17 years, coming from Illinois. He conducted a newspaper at Clear Lake at one time.

The Dunsmore Hotel is being remodeled and converted into an apartment house to contain five apartments, each apartment has two rooms and is to be adequately furnished for light-housekeeping. Mrs. J. E. Andrews will continue in charge which is assurance that things will be kept neat and tidy throughout making the Dunsmore a home-like and comfortable place for tenants.

H. F. Stout has completed taking the school census in this district and reports a total of 570 children of school age, of this number 338 live west of the river, an increase of 46 pupils over last year. In this part of district east of river there are 232 pupils of school age as compared to 167 last year or an increase of 65, a net increase of 111 children of school age in this district within the past year. Of the 570 pupils enumerated there are 300 boys and 270 girls in this district.

Those who were in attendance at the M. I. A. Outing held at the Oak Creek canyon last week, from this vicinity, returned Sunday evening and declare that they enjoyed the time of their lives; that all were loath to leave such a delightful spot—where there were no "skeeters" nor flies to annoy and where the exhilirating atmosphere, gurgling, sparkling mountain streams and charming scenery together with the entrancing occupation of angling for trout, makes the canyon an enticing place for anyone wanting recreation and fun. There were over 300 attended the Outing; the Oak City band furnished music for the occasion and the various programs as rendered kept things lively.

D. M. Anderson resigned as leader of the band last Monday evening in order that he might return to his former home at Morgan. During the last year of his stay in Delta he organized and developed the Delta Band and the success he attained in this respect was demonstrated at Hinckley July 24th and at other public gatherings. "Morg" as he is familiarly called, possesses the rare ability or faculty of creating the required enthusiasm to hold the members of a band together where there is no cash consideration. The town and the members of the band feel grateful to Mr. Anderson for services cheerfully contributed by him and hope for his return to Delta.

Hinckley Happenings.

Earnest Nelson of Leamington was here one day the past week visiting John Talbott.

Mrs. Jas. Tellis and two sons of Pinto, Utah, are here visiting Mr. and Mrs. Don Bishop.

Joe Ivey and wife of Delta was here Sunday visiting his brother, Jerome Ivey and family.

Mrs. Ellen Mangle and daughter of Salt Lake are here visiting her sister, Mrs. N. R. Stewart.

F. L. Hickman of American Fork, is here on business and is the guest of John Hutchison during his stay.

Mr. and Mrs. John Hunter of Holden was here last Sunday, visiting at the hospitable home of J. M. Wright's.

Peter Peterson is driving a well for Geo. Webb. He got a fine flow for Sammy Stanworth, one of the best in town.

Mrs. Annie Higs and two sons, Stewart and Loa of Salt Lake, are visiting with her parents, Mr. and Mrs. Richard Parker, in this city.

There were 58 Hinckley-ites attended the M. I. A. Outing at Oak Creek canyon last week, all reporting a jolly good time, upon their return home.

At the school election held the 13th, H. F. Stout was re-elected trustee without opposition which is evidence that he is the right man for this important position.

Mr. Jones, the bugman, sent out by the A. C. to collect up the various kinds of bugs is still in town, stopping at the Wright hotel to the delight of the drummers and traveling public.

Mrs. Mary Spinlove, who is visiting friends here, had a fainting spell in front of Pratt Bros. store one day recently, she was carried into John E. Wright's where she was revived and at last accounts she is doing well.

Abraham Articles.

W. J. Cary and Dalton Reed were business visitors at Holden last week.

Mrs. Leroy Bills who has been quite sick for the past few days is improving.

Norman Bliss returned home Monday from Dixie, where he had been to attend the funeral of his sister.

Mr. and Mrs. Luther Franklin of Michigan came in last Friday to visit at the home of his cousin Mrs. W. J. Cary.

Abraham people are going to Delta on the 24th, and the base ball team are in good spirit and hope to play a winning game.

Mrs. Taylor who has been sick so long, is at this writing in a serious condition and is expected to pass away any time.

Mrs. Franklin of Forsythe, Montana, came Sunday to make an extended visit with her son and daughter, Mr. Payne Franklin and Mrs. Wes Cary.

Mr. Wilson Biehler and sister, Miss Elizabeth who have employment in Salt Lake City, also Mr. Yearsley, a friend are expected this week, on a visit to their parents, Mr. and Mrs. Ed Biehler.

The friends of Miss Margurite Biehler and Mr. Ed Taylor were much surprised last week to learn of their wedding, which took place at Farmington, Utah, July 3rd. Miss Margurite is the third daughter of Mr. and Mrs. E. J. Biehler of this place and is a beautiful and accomplished young lady. Ed is a splendid young man and we predict for them a happy future. The writer joins with thier many friends in congratulations.

Sutherland Searchlights

Keith Lewis and Lyman Williams, who have been here, returned to their home in Richfield.

We enjoyed a nice, quiet rain Monday evening. The weatherman knows when it is time to hay.

The Flint Thrashing Machine is all set and ready to begin thrashing on the Ackerman farm as soon as the weather will permit.

Mrs. H. G. Ottley and Miss Mary Perry who attended the outing at the Oak City Canyon report having had a splendid time.

C. T. Bunker and the crowd of young people that took to the canyon, are home again ready for work, feeling much better for having had such a delightful trip.

Geo. Webster and family have moved to Delta where he is working in the E. C. M. I., since the recent burn out. The effects saved from the fire were moved last week.

Judge Chidester and family are over from Richfield in their car looking after farming interests north of here. They were the guests of M. A. Abbott Monday. Mr. Chidester is at present a member of the State Land Board.

Deseret Doings.

Why yes, everybody goes to Delta, Pioneer Day.

Among recent visitors were Wm. and Chester Cheel of Kanosh.

Guy Robinson, representative of the Marshall-Pike Co. of Salt Lake, was in town Tuesday.

The genial Mr. Sommers of Oak City appeared with the first load of real peaches Tuesday.

Miss Norma Damron is the guest of Miss Ethel Day, during the home-coming at Fillmore.

V. W. Kelly left over the westbound train Saturday for San Bernardino and other Southern California points.

Miss Martha Schoenberger has been severely afflicted with rheumatism since the 4th, but is now said to be improving.

Mrs. Caroline Reed and daughter, Mrs. Laurel Stats are down from Salt Lake, visiting Mrs. Reed's daughter, Mrs. J. M. Moody.

Max C. Webb has added material improvment to his town property by the erection of a nice barn and screening the porch of his residence.

The re-seating of the social hall and installation of electric fans should add much to the comfort of the patrons of the Princess Amusement Co.

Nels L. Peterson and Mrs. Isabelle Bennett departed for Los Angeles, Cal., Sunday, over the Salt Route; Mrs. Bennett will visit with relatives, while Mr. Peterson profitably combines business with pleasure.

J. C. Hawley of Oasis, senior member of the firm of Damron & Hawley, who made a speculative visit to Los Angeles recently, returned to that city again early in the week with the intentions of interesting himself with his brother Henry, in construction and contract work.

Millard County Chronicles
August 6, 1914

Abraham Articles.

Mr. Norman Bliss recently sold 20 tons of hay at $14 per ton.

The Needle Craft Club meets at the home of Mrs. Ed Biehler this week.

Farm Demonstrator Welch visited a few of the Abraham farmers last week.

Mr. Needham, one of our prosperous farmers has treated himself to a new Ford auto.

Mr. Elmer of South Tract, is helping C. M. Hickman put up his second cutting of hay.

Mr. Priestman of Los Angeles, has been looking over Abraham lands this week with a view of locating.

Hinckley Happenings.

Mrs. Refiee of Indiana is here visiting her aunt, Mrs Mary Lee.

Charles Anderson was a business visitor to Salt Lake City, the past week.

Miss Wilhe and James Blake returned Monday from a visit to Lynndyl.

Geo. L. Stewart made a combined business and pleasure trip to Meadow, last Friday.

Atty. Geo. A. Cole was a visitor from Salt Lake, Monday, the guest of Joseph Neilson.

Miss Lapriel Robinson returned Monday from a visit with relatives and friends in and near Provo.

The Stork visited the Garden Spot again and left a nice, sweet little lady with Mr. and Mrs John Talbott.

G. W. Wright made a flying trip to Salt Lake City on business one day the past week; he didn't go in an airship, however.

J. P. Peterson, the Scipio merchant has traded for a house and lot in the garden spot; probably he intends to move over here and open up a store?

Joseph W. Blake was in town Monday, the first time in a long while, having been busily engaged all summer on his farm down on the west ditch.

Lafie Neilson, who unforaunatly fell from a horse and had his right leg broken several weeks ago, is improving rapidly and will soon be out and around.

Mr. Jones, the bugman has returned home; he says that among other truths that the bible does not contain is—that a man should not live away from his wife

Insurance men or adjusters arrived here Tuesday to make an adjustment of the fire loss with the owners of the Hinckley Co-Op. I haven't been able to learn whether the business will be resumed here or not.

Farm Demonstrater Welch informs us that the rust has laid waste a greater part of the late spring wheat and that the wise farmer will stick closer to fall wheat hereafter; it is the only safe way and should be planted before Sept. 15th.

M. Perhab and Alf. Johnson, both of Oakland, Cal., have purchased 40 acres each in the garden spot of this great delta country; they will move their families up soon and we are confident that they will bless the day that they moved to this healthful, beautiful, growing country.

Mrs. Earnest Nelson of Leamington, who has been here for sometime visiting her parents, Mr. and Mrs. Chas. Talbott, gave birth to a fine, bouncing baby boy one night the past week and the happy father came down to rejoice with the doting mother and elated grandparents over its arrival.

In last week's items a local read that J. W. Hawkins passed through here with 150 five gallon cans of honey, when it should have read 750 five gallon cans, or 3,750 gallons of honey. Possibly the Chronicle typo doesn't realize that this is a great country for honey, there is several car loads shipped out every year.

Several homeseekers from California and other points, have been here looking over the country with a view of purchasing and locating, during the past few days. We hope they will find a suitable farm and become numbered among our most satisfied residents. This is a wonderful valley and remarkable opportunities which abound in and around the garden spot for all who may come. We need more good industrious, well versed farmers in this valley.

A movement is under headway to build a good road from here to Omaho via Delta. I understand that the county commissioners have expressed their intentions of allowing funds to buy material and put in the bridges & culverts necessary; this coupled with the labor volunteered by the farmers along the new road to do the grading, is assurance that a good road will soon connect these important places. There is nothing that will tend to upbuild a country more than good roads and will enhance the value of abutting property to a great extent. Let us build more and better roads in Millard County.

News Notes From Oasis.

A dance is announced for Friday night, Aug. 7th, at the A. C. Nelson school house.

The public is invited to attend the grand concert to be given at the Nelson school house, Sunday evening, Aug. 9th, at 8.30 p. m.

The Lightning base ball team of Oasis defeated the Mountain Giants of the South Tract by a 10 to 8 score.

The outlook for a good alfalfa seed crop was never brighter than at present.

The old Stork delivered an assistant postmaster to the home of Mr. and Mrs. M. H. McCosh, one night the past week.

Carl Pearson drove over to Abraham Sunday, and spent the day visiting friends and viewing the crops; he reports conditions there as entirely satisfactory.

Oak City News Budget.

(Jos. H. Christenson, Rep.)

Mrs. C. C Green from Salt Lake is here visiting relatives and friends.

Mrs. Delia Jacobson is reported ill at this writing. We hope for her a speedy recovery.

Mrs. Ellen N. Lyman and her sister, Margret Neilson, made a trip to Hinckley last week.

There was a large number of people from our neighboring towns visiting here Sunday.

Henry Roper has returned home after a visit in Mayfield with his cousin, Ezra Lyman.

Mrs. Caroline Hartley and daughters, Irene and Lily, returned home last week after an enjoyable time spent in Salt Lake.

A big wedding dance was given last Friday night by LeRoy Walker and bride. Everybody speaks of having had an enjoyable time. A wedding dance is something new in Oak City.

Fawntella, the little daughter of A. J. Talbott, met with a very painful accident Saturday. While playing around a wagon she fell and broke her arm. Dr. Leavenworth from Hinckley was called to set it.

A crowd of our young people went out to swim last Saturday night, but while there, Parley Roper had a hard time getting back to shore. He worked until he was exhausted, then had to trust to the breeze which helped him to shore. The young folks better have some good swimmers along next time.

Sheriff Dorrity of Fillmore was in this city, Saturday attending to some official duties. Sheriff Dorrity has made good as a law enforcement officer in Millard County and in all probabilities he will be a candidate for re-election; should his party nominate him, he will be a hard man to beat at the polls, regardless of whom the opposition may nominate.

Attorney Cole was here the first of the week looking after his farming interests hereabout. Mr. Cole was a candidate for county attorney here two years ago and many of his friends of his own political faith are urging him to make the race again this fall; he is a brilliant young lawyer, a clever fellow and with his pleasing personalities would give the opposition some worry, to say the least.

C. T. Leachman and David Porter arrived here last Thursday from Pomona, Cal., with a car of their belongings to establish themselves as farmers on their eighty, three miles north of Omaha. They are now busy erecting two houses thereon, and are expecting their families to arrive most any day now. Mr. Leachman is a civil engineer and surveyor and expects to do work of this nature at times.

Sutherland Searchlights

Grandma Bunker is in Delta visiting since the 24th.

Lamond Bunker and Wayne Lisonbee made a short visit to Oak City last Friday.

W. R. Walker and Co. intend putting in a General Merchandise Store in the near future.

J. W. Hall has taken up his abode among us, on his farm. He lately returned from a mission.

Much of the spring grain is lacking in its yield owing to the rust, wheat having suffered the most.

There were a number of fruit wagons on the north tract last week, from Holden, Fillmore and Oak City.

Henry Freese is having a house erected. He has been living in his spacious grainery, but will need it now for his grain.

A number of farmers are hauling grain away, mostly to the mill, as yet there seems to be few active buyers in the field.

Mr. Hayes and family have moved on their farm, having lived at the Kelly Hotel in Delta while their house was being built.

The Jolly Stitchers met with Mrs. Jackson last Friday and enjoyed a very pleasant afternoon. They will meet again in three weeks at Mrs. Campbell.

W. E. Davis is again at his farm after a recent visit to Meadow. His father came Sunday from Nephi to look over conditions in the valley. We have not learned his opinion, but think it could not be otherwise than good.

A gathering of a very pleasant nature took place at the home of Mr. and Mrs. Geo. Webster in Delta Sunday evening. When the people of Sutherland paid respects to Mr. Webster who recently managed the Sutherland E. C. M. I. branch store.

Oak City Offerings.

(Jos. H. Christenson, Rep.)

Leo Carlson returned home Wednesday from Delta.

Dr. Leavenworth from Hinckley was with us again last week.

Belvia Lovell has returned home after her visit in Salt Lake.

Lydia Roper has gone to Sutherland, where she will work for some time.

Eva Anderson returned home last Tuesday after her visit in Leamington.

Marion Terry returned to Ogden last week, after a short visit with his mother.

Willis Lyman was seen here Sunday. He came to take his mother back to Delta.

Mrs. Lee Christenson from Delta, was here last week visiting the Christenson family.

Mr. and Mrs. Johnnie Christenson are here visiting with A. C. Christenson this week.

A number of our young folks went to Leamington last Friday night to attend the big dance.

A big birthday dinner was held by the Lymans last week in favor of Sister Mary Lyman of Delta.

Miss Dean and Miss White both from Beaver, were here last week visiting with their many friends.

Mrs. Lydia Theobald and children from Hinckley, were here last week visiting with her mother, Mrs. T. B. Talbot.

S. J. Rawlinson and his two sisters, Maggie and Eliza, left here last week for a visit in Gunnison with their uncle.

The Stork remembered us again leaving with Mr and Mrs. Walter Rawlinson a nice 9½ pound baby boy. Mother and baby are doing fine.

Mr. and Mrs. Joseph Lyman and four of their children from Mayfield were here the past week visiting their many friends and relatives.

Sunday evening a very interesting party was given by the I. S. and Laurel Clubs in favor of Gene Lovell, who is going to leave this week for Salt Lake to resume her school work.

Hinckley Happenings.

E. Talbot returned Sunday from a business trip to Snake Valley.

Chas. Anderson, the druggist will sell 7 bars of Bob White soap Saturday for 25cts.

Mrs. C. R. Johnson and children of Provo, are here visiting her daughter, Mrs. Earnest Theobald.

Jack Greener of Lynndyl was a Garden Spot visitor Sunday, coming down to get more bait for Robbins.

We are wondering where the weed man is, would like to see him come to the garden spot and see where he would start to enforce the weed law.

John Christenson and wife of Aurora, was the guest of Neils Christenson for several days the end of last week, going on to Oak City Monday to visit other relatives.

William Stapley of Kanarrah has sold out at that place and moved to the garden spot, where he will make his future home. His father accompanied him here for an extended stay also. Gladly welcome, to such clever men as Will.

Come down Mr. Editor and we will go gold hunting; our community is worked up to a fever heat over the discovery of gold in the Saw Tooth mountains; one man picked up a rock that tested better than 25 per cent gold and found nuggets as large as No. 1. buckshot. There is a rush for those hills.

Jas. Bennett and Wm. Bishop recently returned from a pleasure trip to the Grand Canyon of Arizona, taking with them a number of school teachers on a sight-seeing trip. Mr. Emmett is familiar with the country between here and the canyon, having been an Indian fighter and guide in the early days.

Mrs. J. W. Schwartz happened to quite a serious accident last Friday evening sustaining other painful bruises besides getting her left arm broken just above the wrist. Mrs. Schwartz and her daughter, Mrs. McCurdy were in Hinckley trading and just as they were getting ready to start for home a fruit wagon backed into their spring wagon upsetting it with the above results. Mrs. McCurdy also sustained slight bruises.

Dr. C. A. Broaddus is expected home Sept. 15 in time for the County Fair at Deseret. He has been very busy all summer at most interesting and valuable work in the hospitals of Cleveland, Ohio,— City Hospital, Charity Hospital, The Babies' Dispensary, Rainbow Hospital for Crippled and convalescent children, while the latter part of the summer he has spent chiefly in abdominal surgery in Lakeside Hospital. He writes that he has enjoyed greatly his postgraduate work and will be glad to get back to his friends and patients in Millard County. Dr. Leavenworth, his substitute for the summer, will leave for Cleveland as soon as possible after Dr. Broaddus' arrival.

NEWSY NOTES ABOUT FOLKS

Mrs. H. J. Meyers made a shopping expedition to Salt Lake, Wednesday.

Mrs. Jack Thurston returned Wednesday from a visit with her husband's parents at Morgan.

William Emmett with his neice, Miss McGown returned Monday from a trip through Texas, Okla. and Colorado.

A band dance and the music furnished by the band is announced for Saturday night at the Marsoni.

D. A. Bunker left Wednesday for Salt Lake and Bingham, where personal business demanded his attention.

Mr. Ricker came in from California Wednesday to look after the erection of a grainery on his farm in the north tract.

Richard Smith took advantage of the excursion rates to the home-coming at Spanish Fork and left for there Tuesday to greet former neighbors and friends.

Frank Beckwith and wife, Mrs. J. E. Andrews, Mrs. N. B. Robinson and Jack Thurston were entertained in a very agreeable manner by Mrs. A. B. Ward at luncheon Sunday.

Mr. and Mrs. Ogden and Miss Emma Christenson of Richfield, arrived here last Friday and visited with the former's daughter, Mrs. George Dobson until Tuesday, having made the trip overland.

Mrs. D. E. Hogan and children of Abraham, took the train here Wednesday morning for Salt Lake, where they will visit her parents for several weeks.

Mrs. N. B. Robinson, formerly a resident of Delta but now a resident of Salt Lake is spending the week here with friends, the guest of Mrs. A. B. Ward and Mrs. Garnett January.

Mrs. J. E. Andrews has secured the agency for the Troy Laundry of Salt Lake City and solicits your patronage in this line, assuring perfect satisfaction and prompt return of all bundles sent.

David Rosenbaum of Brigham City arrived last Friday to look after his farming interests out on the south tract, which is tended by Fred Haumann, a popular young batchelor of that progressive community.

Joseph Manderfield and L. A. Merrill were here Sunday and took a trip out over the north tract viewing the growing crops, especially the sugar beets and sizing up the many stacks of fall grain. These gentlemen are firm believers in the delta country, predicting it to become the greatest agricultural region of the great west when it is developed and properly farmed. Come to the delta country.

CAPTURES TWO HORSE THIEVES

Sheriff Dorrity returned here Monday with two horse thieves whom he captured at Spanish Fork, Saturday. Last Thursday Mr. A. D. Dimmrick of Lynndyl reported to the sheriff that he had four horses stolen from his place near Lynndyl on Wednesday and the sheriff hit their trail in all haste, tracking them to Eurerka, where they had disposed of one animal and from there to Spanish Fork, where he over-took the theives and after arresting the culprits recovered possession of all the horses. The two arrested were identified as Barney Trainer who had been loitering around Lynndyl for several weeks and the other a boy of eighteen years named George Minsor who lived with his parents in that city. It is thought that Trainer is a hardened criminal, judging from his actions as he made a desperate attempt to get away after being detected, however he was not armed and proved "easy pickin'" for our fearless sheriff who yanked him from a straw stack where he had hidden himself. The two fellows were taken to the county jail at Fillmore, chaperoned by Bishop Maxfield, where they will await the action of the district court at its next setting. Sheriff Dorrity has that enviable distinction of being the best officer Millard ever had in the capacity of sheriff; he is a wide-awake, fearless gentleman, capable of handling the affairs and duties of the office to the satisfaction of all. The lawless has poor luck getting away from him.

Deseret Doings.

Born to Mr. and Mrs. Frank Scott on the 18th a baby girl all concerned doing well.

We are pleased to have with us again Miss Delora Reid, who is to be our new Post-mistress this winter.

Wm. Justesen formerly of this place but now of Gridley, Cal. is visiting with his children and other relatives here.

Mrs. Hammond and Nina Scott of Salt Lake, were the guests of their aunt, Mrs. H. S. Cahoon during the past week.

Archie D. Ryan left for Salt Lake yesterday morning to undergo an operation. His freinds hope for a speedy recovery.

Every one seems busy getting up their third crop of hay also alfalfa seed. The last few days have been ideal for such work.

Miss Norma Moody leaves for Provo the latter part of the week to resume her studies in music and other branches of learning.

Mrs. Hannah Allred left Friday night for a visit with relatives and friends at Spring City. Her grand-daughter, Thelma Black accompanied her.

The many friends of Mrs. Virgil Kelley Jr. will be pleased to learn of her return home after having spent several weeks in the Holy Cross Hospital, where she was operated on for appendicitis.

The combined schools of Deseret and Oasis will open Mon. next at the new school house, with an up to date school building such as the A. C. the children should make rapid progress this coming year. Although we are several weeks behind most of schools in the State in commencing.

The Deseret Stake Quarterly Conference Convened at the A. C. Nelson building Sat. and Sun. the 26th. and 27th. Among the visitors were Apostle Ivans and Chas. Hart and Miss Agnes Campbell of the Y. L. M. I. A. General Board who spoke splendidly. All present enjoyed a spiritual feast.

The parties given Friday and Saturday were a decided success, especially the one Sat. evening, under the auspices of the Mutuals. Refreshments were served all visitors. The booths were attractively decorated and delicious punch was served by the Junior members of the Young Ladies from both wards.

Oak City Offerings.

(Jos. H. Christenson, Rep.)

Booth, the Nephi dentist, has returned home.

Mrs. Simeon Walker is reported as quite ill at this writing.

Walter Rawlinson is at his farm near Delta, planting fall grain.

Jos. S. Anderson made a business trip to Lynndyl, Thursday.

John Talbot of Hinckley, was here Friday after a load of fruit.

Threshing is being delayed this week, awaiting repairs for the engine.

Jos. H. Christenson made a trip to Lynndyl Monday to get a new wagon.

Miss Wanda Alldredge has returned home from Hinckley, to start school.

Earnest Nelson was here Sunday visiting his sister, Mrs. August Carlson.

August Nielson of Leamington was a visitor here Monday, coming down in his auto.

Soren Anderson and wife visited with her parents at Oasis, a few days the past week.

The Laurel Club had another enjoyable time Friday night when they serenaded the town.

We were favored with a nice rain Sunday night, which delighted our dry and farmers.

Some of the younger girls had a splendid time Friday evening at the home of Mandy Roper.

A number of the young folks enjoyed themselves dancing at band practice Saturday night.

Co. Com. Anderson was at the county seat the first of the week, attending commissioner's court.

Golda Anderson of Hinckley, was here Friday, visiting her grandmother, Mrs. Peter Anderson.

A number of our towns-people went to Deseret to attend quarterly conference, Saturday and Sunday.

A number of our children left for Hinckley Sunday, to enroll as students, the following day, at the Academy.

S. J. Rawlinson left for Leamington Sunday, to enter upon his duties as principal in the schools there for this term.

Miss Lydia Roper has gone to Salt Lake City, to take training to become a nurse, expecting to be away till next June.

Six cases of two quart cans arrived here last week, which are to be filled with choice fruit by the young ladies and sent to the L. D. S. hospital for use.

The democrats and republicans got together here on Wednesday night, nominating a fusion ticket for precinct offices — LeRoy Walker, a democrat, was nominated as justice of the peace and Leo Finlinson, republican, as constable.

Sutherland Searchlights

Herman Holdridge is having his house plastered and partitioned.

Mr. Hunter of Holden is visiting his uncle, Bert Johnson for a few days.

A fine baby girl arrived at the home of Mr. and Mrs. Lawrence Abbott Sept. 26th. Mother and babe doing fine.

The shower which came Monday and Tuesday settled the dust and brightened things up considerably.

The ward party of Sept. 25th, was a success. After a good program from 10 to 11 o'clock a. m. the crowd did justice to a fine feast spread on long tables. The afternoon passed with sports and games and visiting. A good crowd was in attendance at the dance in the evening.

NEWSY NOTES ABOUT FOLKS

Mrs. R. R. Betz is enjoying a visit from her father of California, he having arrived here Wednesday.

Mrs. Jas. A. Melville returned to Salt Lake City, Tuesday, to visit with her children till after the fair.

Frank L. Copening, who had spent the past three weeks at Nephi, purchasing grain, returned home Sunday.

Deputy United States Marshal Thompson of Salt Lake City was in Delta on official business the end of last week.

Uncle Jim Melville informs us that the gravel will soon arrive to put on Broadway which was recently graded. Let the good things continue to come.

Dr. F. S. Robison left yesterday for Hinckley to await on customers desiring tooth carpentry for several days. Dr. Robison enjoyed a lucrative practice here during the past ten days.

Mrs. H. F. Aller and daughter, Miss Helen, returned Wednesday from a month's stay at Salt Lake City, greatly to the delight of Mr. Aller. Miss Helen expects to enter the Millard Academy as a student of music next week.

W. D. Livingston and son, E. E. of Salt Lake City, in company with J. W. Edwards of Gunnison, arrived here Tuesday evening by auto, the former to look after land holdings and the latter to look over the valley with a view of investing in Millard County soil. Mr. Edwards expressed himself as being well pleased with our country and will probably purchase a farm.

Say You, if you do not register, you are apt to miss something that you will be sorry for ever afterwards. Possibly a county division, a county seat location or something else of great importance will come to an election during the next year, but if you have not registered you will not get to express your desire at such an election. Four more registration days are left in which to register, viz: Oct. 6, 7, 13, and 27.

Dr. W. B. Hamilton of Milford, was here Tuesday, looking over the town with a view of locating to practice his profession. He was favorably impressed, so we are informed, and leased Foster Funk's dwelling, expecting to move up in the very near future. Dr. Hamilton was at one time located at Deseret, having sold his practice to Dr. Broaddus three years ago. We are told that he is a skilled physician and a live, energetic citizen, therefore he will receive a most hearty welcome in this growing locality.

R. J. Law took the train this Thursday morning for Salt Lake City.

Jas. A. Melville left for Salt Lake City, this Thursday morning to remain until after the fair.

Mr. and Mrs. J. W. Crock of Abraham took the train here Thursday morning for Salt Lake City, to attend Conference, visit relatives and take in the fair.

Bishop H. E. Maxfield was chosen by Gov. Spry to represent the State at the National Irrigation Congress to convene at Calvery, Canada, on the 5th inst., and also by the Chairman of the Board of County Commissioners as a delegate to represent Millard County, but owing to pressing business matters here at home Bishop Maxfield will not be able to go.

Millard County Chronicles
October 8, 1914

Oak City Offerings.

(Jos. H. Christenson, Rep.)

Mrs. Simeon Walker is still reported very ill.

Jack Alldrege made a trip to Hinckley last week.

A dance was given last Friday night in honor of our Orchestra.

A number of our people have gone to Salt Lake to attend conference.

Mr. and Mrs. Bert Roper have moved in from their home at Fool City.

Roe Willey has been at Delta the past week working on Walter Rawlinson's farm.

Henry Carlson took Elmer Duncan to Lynndyl where he will take the train for Tintic.

Albert Christenson made a trip to Hinckley last week to take his sister, Pearl to the Academy.

Eva Stepheson of Holden is here visiting for a few days with her sister, Mrs. Mary Anderson.

A number of our men folks have been trying their luck at deer hunting. Reports are not very favorable.

All our batchelor boys are returning to their home-steads, but one and he has taken up school teaching instead.

The stork visited the home of Mr. and Mrs. Leo Lyman, on the 28th, leaving with them an 11½ pound baby boy. Mother and babe doing fine.

Deseret Doings.

School commenced with a very large attendance Monday morning.

It is reported by our local sportsmen that hunting was never better.

The Bonwell Dramatic Co. played Friday and Saturday evenings, to a small audience due to bad weather and a great many away to Salt Lake.

The wedding of Fay Theobald of Hinckley and Ethel Webb of Deseret was solemnized in Fillmore on Wednesday. They have hearty congratulations from many friends.

Mr. Chas. Gunn left for Salt Lake City last Wednesday and died there on Thursday. He had been a sufferer for the past year of stomach trouble, and came here for his health, where he seemed to improve for a time. A widow and several children are bereft of husband and father, who have the sincere sympathy of the entire community.

The marriage of Mr. Spencer Bennet and Miss Ecil Western took place at the home of the bride, last Thursday afternoon. The home was prettily decorated a bounteous dinner was served in the Relief Hall to about seventy-five guests. The many friends of Mr. and Mrs. Bennett wish them a long and prosperous life over the matrimonial sea.

NEWSY NOTES ABOUT FOLKS

Editor Smith was here Wednesday, on his way home from the state fair.

Mrs. C. H. Richards was visiting in Salt Lake City, the past week, going up Saturday.

E. H. Hibbard sold his farm to a Mr. Buzzard of Oklahoma, the first of the week, for $85 an acre.

L. Anderson of Riverside, Cal., arrived here Monday to look after his farming interests out on the north tract.

Bishop H. E. Maxfield left for Salt Lake Saturday morning to attend Conference and take in the sights at the Fair.

Atty. J. W. Kelso was a legal business visitor to Salt Lake the fore part of the week. Judge Kelso is meeting with a hearty welcome here and is commanding a fair practice.

Mr. Smith arrived Sunday with two prospective landbuyers from California, who seem well pleased with the valley and are looking at several farms listed for sale by our real estate men.

The dance given by the Ladies Relief Society Friday evening was largely attended and a fine time was had; the luncheon consisted of sandwiches, pie, cake and cocoa, and was heartily relished by all.

Mrs. R. H. Becknell left for Salt Lake City Saturday to remain with relatives and friends till after the fair. Mrs. Becknell was chosen as queen to represent Millard County in the parade on Monday evening.

County Clerk Ashby was here Thursday, attending a meeting of the republican central committee. He continued his trip to Tooele that night, also expecting to attend the state fair at Salt Lake before returning home.

The hunters report that ducks are scarce in this locality at present, but few have had any big hauls to report since the season opened, Oct. 1st, when everybody and their brothers went for a duck hunt. There has not been sufficient cold weather to bring the water fowls this way.

The Chronicle force is not making much of a pretense toward getting out as newsy a paper as usual this week as we are getting out the sheet on Wednesday afternoon, so we will be permitted to attend the state fair for a few days; all items received too late for publication this week will appear in next week's issue.

In response to a call by County Chairman Abbott, the republican county central committee met in Delta last Thursday and organized a campaign committee for the purpose of waging a vigorous and successful campaign in Millard county. It is the intention of the campaign committee to secure Senator Smoot and other prominent republicans to tour the county and tell the "deer peepul" why they should vote a straight republican ticket. The stalwart republicans are not napping and are continually making medicine. You demmys had better whip up or you will be left at the post on a November morn.

Millard County Chronicle
October 29, 1914

Oak City Offerings.

(Jos. H. Christenson, Rep)

Maggie Rawlinson was a Leamington visitor Thursday.

Mrs. Simeon Walker is somewhat improved at this writing.

Alfred Jacobson was home from Provo School, last week.

Ruby Jacobson made a business trip to Nephi, last week.

L. Sommers was a business visitor at Lynndyl, last week.

The Finlinson Bros. are busy molding dobies this nice weather.

Mr. and Mrs. Elmer Duncan have moved to Tintic, for the winter.

Mrs. L. Olson, who has been very sick, is reported on the improve.

Joseph L. Anderson was attending court affairs in Fillmore, last week.

The welcome home party given Elder Ray Finlinson Friday night was well attended.

Mrs. Ellen N. Lyman left Saturday on a trip to San Wan on business. Willis Lyman of Delta accompanied her.

Joseph Finlinson and Lorenzo Lovell made a trip to Scipio last week after cattle, getting a good bunch of Oak City stock.

Hinckley Happenings.

Jacob Felix has moved his family to Lynndyl.

Del. Cox is building a 4-room cottage on his town lot.

The thrasher is busy all about here with alfalfa seed.

Eugene Hilton has returned from a two years mission in the eastern states.

Rev. and Mrs. C. H. Hamilton of Delta were guests of Dr. and Mrs. Broaddus, Tuesday for dinner.

Zira Terry had his left arm broken Thursday, when his team ranaway throwing him out of the wagon.

Helen Aller and Mrs. Ethel E. Lambert of Delta, are among Mrs Broaddus' music pupils this term.

Dr. Broaddus is continuing his examination of the school children, being now occupied with the pupils of the 6th grade.

The stork has been quite busy this week, leaving babies for Mr. and Mrs. C. Mitchell, Mr. and Mrs Milton Moody, Mr. and Mrs. H. Stout Jr., and Mr. and Mrs. Lorin Taylor.

The many friends of Mrs. John Reeve of Hinckley, will be pleased to learn that she underwent an operation successfully in Salt Lake City, last week, and is now recovering as rapidly as could be hoped for.

Young Aroet Meacham, who sustained a serious eye injury by being kicked by a colt two weeks ago, has made a rapid recovery. The gashes about the eye which had to be closed with stitches did not even leave a scar, and altho' the iris of the eye ball was ruptured, the vision has been regained and the pupil restored to its normal size under persistent daily treatments at Dr. Broaddus' office.

The beautiful neighborly kindness of a country community was shown again when 20 or 30 young people left the dance Friday evening in response to Bishop Pratt's call for volunteer help and in the middle of the night emptied and thoroughly cleaned the Relief Hall, transforming it into a temporary hospital for the operation on young Merrill Blake Saturday morning. Although he had been sick since Tuesday, his condition had not been considered serious, but when the doctor was first called Friday, he found a serious condition of peritonitis with the appendix already ruptured. The parents and friends would not consent to taking him to Salt Lake fearing that in such a critical condition he could not withstand the trip but insisted on having Dr. Broaddus operate here with what local nurse help he could get. On account of the poisoning from the appendix's having been bursted so long, the operation was very serious and there was paralysis of the bowels for 36 hours, but at the present his condition is more hopeful though still critical. He rallied well from the operation and Dr. Broaddus was fortunate in securing on Sunday the services of a trained nurse, Mrs. Christenson, who was visiting her parents in Deseret.

Sutherland Searchlights

Lyman Moulton is putting a new roof on his barn.

W. R. Walker & Co's store building is nearing completion.

The pleasant weather still continues although the nights are cold.

Mr. and Mrs. Jed Cox of Hinckley were visitors at Sutherland Tuesday.

Lindsay Steele and family have moved into the home recently-vacated by the Dalys.

Perry Abbott returned to his home at Richfield Tuesday after a visit of several weeks with his parents and family.

Mr. and Mrs. W. R. Walker spent several days of the past week in Oak City attending the funeral of Mr. Walker's mother.

A birthday party was given Mrs. Abbott last Friday by a number of neighbors and friends. All report having had a jolly, good time.

Mr. Hayes has added a new fence along with other improvements on his farm which makes it appear as one of the neatest around here.

Mrs. M. A. Abbott and son, Howard, are planning to leave this week on a visit to her aged father and other relatives in Washington County.

John Daly and family left for their future home in Panguitch this week. They were given a farewell party at the Sutherland school house on the night of election. A nice program and dancing furnished the entertainment. All regret the Dalys leaving as they were among the first and most desirable settlers, however, best wishes for success go with them from all their former associates.

It seems that some of our people find it hard to drive in the road from Ottley's corner on the north and continually running into and breaking telephone poles. The last driver to have such luck steered into a pole set on the fence line of Mr. Riding's farm, entirely out of his way, and you can never find out who it was. It might appear just a bit courteous if they'd report and offer to help repair damages.

The above is the picture of Carl Hays, who has not been heard from since May 24, 1914. Any one seeing him will please notify Morton Miller, C of R of the Improved Order of Red Men, Bloomington, Ind., R. R. No. 4.

NEWSY NOTES ABOUT FOLKS

Mrs. Sarah Johnson of Holden is spending the week here, visiting relatives and friends.

Miss Myrtle Stansworth of Hinckley has accepted a position at the Hotel Delta.

Bartley John of Clear Lake was here again Monday, to take home a span of fine horses which he had purchased from F. H. Neil.

Uncle Jim Melville returned Monday from a business trip to Salt Lake. Uncle Jim talks Delta, no matter where he goes and he impresses 'em that "Delta is the place."

Mrs. H. F. Aller departed last Thursday for a three months visit with relatives in Illinois and Ohio, expecting to return home along about the first of the year.

Andrew Sorenson and Ed Marshall have returned from the eastside of the county, where they have been thrashing for several weeks. They expect to take their machine to Abraham this week where they have several jobs contracted, thrashing lucern seed.

The Delta-Fillmore Auto Stage has been discontinued, Billie Kilpack having turned the business over to S. M. Hawley, the mail carrier out of Oasis. Mr. Hawley makes Delta daily to get eastside passengers and returning delivers westside passengers either at Delta or Oasis, as they desire.

J. A. Daly and family left the first of the week for Panguitch, where they will abide hereafter, having traded his farm here for a residence there. The Daly family were well liked here and had prospered, but inasmuch as they desired a change, we hope that they will realize to their fullest expectations in their new home.

Bartley John of Clear Lake was here Saturday attending to business matters of a personal nature and greeting friends. In as much as Bartley is of the republican faith he was well pleased with the result in the senatorial race in Utah, but on the other hand was a little disappointed to see a few of his own political faith slaughtered in the race for county officers.

The Continental Oil Co. have purchased a building site north of the depot near the track and are going to establish a distributing plant here for Millard County, expecting to put on an oil wagon and deliver their products to the surrounding towns in this county. The Continental Co. is one of the biggest oil concerns doing business in the west and selecting Delta as one of its principal distributing points will be a benefit to our town and the surrounding country.

J. W. Damron, Sr., of Deseret was a Delta visitor Monday, favoring this office with an agreeable call while here. Mr. Damron has been a resident of Deseret for the past 39 years, having lived at Kanosh prior to taking up his residence there, for years. He served as an Indian War Veteran and suffered many hardships in those early days, yet he is apparently hale and hearty for a gentleman who has reached his seventy-fourth milestone. There is nothing suits us better than to set down and chat with one of those elderly men, who have by their grit, intelligence, frugality and sterling qualities of character, helped to convert this once wild and wooly west into a most peaceable, desirable place of abode.

Deseret Doings.

Mrs. Maggie Ryan was called to Hinckley Saturday to help Dr. Broaddus with an operation.

We are pleased to state that W. R. Black is slowly recovering from an attack of typhoid fever

The Savage brothers of Salt Lake were down to the funeral of their grandfather, J. H. Kinder, also Chas. and Robert Kinder.

One would imagine by the number of autos buzzing around town today conveying land seekers to various placer, that the desert would soon blossom as a rose. One man from Missouri was so favorably impressed with the country that he purchased over 200 acres of land and soon expects to take up his abode here

Mr Woodward has announced a parents' meeting of the two wards, Deseret and Oasis to be held Friday at 7.30 at the Nelson school house. A short meeting is to be held in which plans will be presented for improving the health of the school children and babies of Deseret and Oasis, and following it a social and dance for all the married people will be given. All the married people of the two wards are cordially invited to be present.

John H. Kinder, a highly respected citizen and War Veteran of this place, died very suddenly Sunday morning, Nov. 1st. He leaves a wife, 2 sons and 4 daughters to mourn his demise. The funeral services took place Wednesday in the ward chapel, Bishop Damron officiating. H. S. Cahoon, L R. Cropper and N. L. Peterson were the speakers. Mrs. Dr. Broaddus rendered "My Jesus as Thou Wilt" and the War Veterans, of which he was a member, sang "When the Angel Calls the Roll." Benediction was pronounced by W. V. Black after which the remains were conveyed to its last resting place.

The 81st birthday of Mrs. A. L George was celebrated at the home of her oldest daughter Mrs. Amelia A. Cahoon, Monday, Nov. 9th. Mrs. George is one of the pioneers of Utah having come across the plains with the Wm. Taylor and D. P. Kirtus company in 1854. She was also one of the Dixie pioneers having gone to St. George in 1861, and was a member of the first choir in the old tabernacle in Salt Lake City The members of her family in attendance were. Mrs. Amelia A. Cahoon, Mrs. Esther L. Scott, Mrs. Charlotte M. Birch and Heber Larson. Mr. Larson has been absent from home for 28 years. This is the first time he has seen his mother in that time. There were about 23 other members of the party besides many of the great grand children.

Oak City Offerings.

(Jos. H. Christenson, Rep.)

Ed Jacobson has moved to his home-stead east of town.

L. Christenson and wife were here visiting, last week.

Mrs. Burk and son of Hinckley were here last week visiting.

Henry Carling is home from his home-stead helping his father for a few days.

Henry Lyman and wife who have been here this summer have returned to their home in Mayfield.

Mr. and Mrs. O. H. Jacobson and daughter, Ruby, have gone to Aurora to visit their daughter, Mary Christenson.

Sister, Ann E. Walker who has

been ill for some time, passed away quietly last Wednesday, Nov. 4th, at five o'clock p. m. The funeral services were held Saturday at 1 o'clock. The speakers were: A. M. Ruper, Jeff Finlinson, Joseph Finlinson, Wm. Lovell and Lee Anderson, all gave some interesting talks on the life of Sister Walker. After which the remains were taken to the cemetery for burial. Never has there been a grave in Oak City so completely covered with flowers as was this one. Among those attending the funeral were: Mr. and Mrs. Harry Ottley of Delta, Mr. and Mrs. Jed Watts of Kanosh, Mr. and Mrs. Wm

Walker of of Hinckley, Mr. and Mrs W. R. Walker of Sutherland and a large number from Murray and Idaho

J. W. Evans of Ontario, Cal., arrived Wednesday to visit his son William on South Tract.

—$1600 cash down and $1500 on time payments will buy 60 acres with water, situated ¼ mile of Delta, all cleared and 40 acres in winter wheat; this is a rare bargain.—N. S. Bishop, Delta.

Excursion rates account Nat'l and Utah Wool Growers Assn'. Convention.

To Salt Lake City via Salt Lake Route Nov. 9th to 13th inclusive. Return limit Nov. 16th. Ask for tickets via Salt Lake Route.

NEWSY NOTES ABOUT FOLKS

Marcus Skeems, Bishop at Oasis, was a Salt Lake visitor this week.

J. E. Quinn and J. E. Shettle of Lynndyl were in Delta on a business mission Saturday.

J. W. Kelso made a business trip to Lynndyl Tuesday, in the interests of a client at that place.

J. S. Black and Mr. Peterson, the popular Real estate dealer of Deseret, were in Salt Lake last week.

James Melville, the jolly Daddy of Delta, returned from a business trip to Salt Lake and other points, Wednesday.

Mr. and Mrs. Ray Bishop left Thursday morning for Salt Lake City, where Mrs. Bishop will undergo an operation.

Attorney J. Alex Melville has just returned from a trip to Junction, Piute County, where he has been foreclosing a mortgage for one of his clients.

Mrs. Mary Lyman left Sunday morning for Salt Lake City to be at the bedside of her daughter, who had been taken to the hospital for surgical treatment.

The Salt Lake Route has dispensed with the services of a night operator and R. R. Betz, who has been serving in that capacity has been transferred to Oasis, for the present; however he will continue to reside in Delta, expecting that the office here will again be opened within a few months.

Mrs. N. T. Maxfield, Joseph and Alonzo Sampson arrived Monday from their homes in Rabbit Valley to attend the funeral services of their father, who died last Saturday. Also Mrs. Myrtle Meneray of Milford, daughter of the deceased, arrived Sunday morning to attend the the funeral.

While Bert King the County Attorney did not get it in the neck as far as votes were concerned, he got it in the neck from

a carbuncle. The vote was so close between Bert and Mr. Higgins that Bert says he is in a measure glad that he had the carbuncle, it kept him from worrying about the final count.

Verne Bartholemew of Fillmore was in Delta Saturday and Sunday in his official capacity as Quarantine Inspector, to pass upon the live stock of Harris, Nutsch and Koch, who are leaving for the east, of which mention is made elsewhere in these columns. Mr. Bartholemew reports a delicious turkey dinner prepared by Mrs. John W. Starley on Sunday, to which full justice was done.

Clarence L. Webster returned home Wednesday from the hospital in Salt Lake, where he has been receiving treatment for his foot which was injured some time ago. The Dr. who was in charge of the case informs Mr. Webster that it will be sometime before the injured member will be well again. An operation was performed on the injured member but Mr. Webester was not appraised of the exact nature of the same.

Sutherland Searchlights

Grandma Shipley is again better after a severe illness.

Miss Leda Finilson of Leamington is a Sutherland visitor this week.

Mrs. Dall Huntaman who has been rather ill is recovering nicely under the care of Dr. Tracy.

M. A. Abbott and M. M. Steele Jr. returned last week from a short business trip to Salt Lake City.

Simeon Walker of Oak City was attending to business matters this week in Sutherland and Oasis.

Miss Lula Johnson of Holden,

who has been staying with her sister, Mrs. Huntsman has returned to her home.

B. F. Johnson has been buying hogs for Mr. Hunter of Holden. The car left Oasis Monday morning for Goldfield, Nevada.

There are several new comers in the vicinity. Mr. Titus of California is building a new frame building on his forty east of Burt Johnson and intends moving his family very soon.

There seems to be a hearty response to the question of beet raising for next year by the answers being sent in to the Delta Land and Water Company on the cards they sent out for the information.

W. R. Walker and Company

are moving into their new building this week which is a much more attractive place than the quarters recently occupied. The building is of brick 32x20 ft. with a cement basement. The front of glass and the interior painted a flat green adds much to the appearance.

The wide grade from the Ottley corner to the end of Moulton's farm is going to make appearances better for Sutherland. The telephone poles are being moved and the grading will be completed with a steam roller at once Now when we get our rail road work completed and a siding in we will feel like we are on the map.

Oak City Offerings.

(Jos. H. Christenson, Rep.)

S. J. Rawlinson spent Saturday and Sunday in Oak City.

The E. Q. band will play for a dance in Leamington, Friday, Dec. 4th.

Mr. L. Webb of Hinckley, is here helping his brother, L. R. Webb, on his farm.

Mr. and Mrs. Jeff Finlinson of Leamington, spent Thanksgiving in Oak City.

Miss V. Lovell is enjoying a visit from her friend, Miss V. Talbot of Hinckley.

Mr. A. Hansen of Sucker Town, is spending a few days with Miss E. Carlson.

The Stork has again made his appearance in Oak City leaving a baby boy at the J. C. Anderson home.

J. Lee Anderson is building a house over his saw mill, in order to do his winter work under shelter.

The M. S. A. students were home for Thanksgiving, returning, Sunday, to their school work at Hinckley.

Edna Anderson and Ella Carlson are spending a week at Mills, to see how they like their future home.

Mrs. Ellen N. Lyman, while taking the top off a fruit bottle broke the top off and badly cut her fingers.

Jessie Peterson, who has been unable to work the past year on account of his leg, has received a large assortment of books for sale. Write, phone or call on him at any time.

Parley Elder reports finding a valuable mine running in high priced ore about five miles east of Oak City. We hope his reports are true as it will help this part of the county very much in many different ways.

Thanksgiving was thoroughly enjoyed by everybody in Oak City. The band was out and played a few selections. There was a dance at night free to all, the Orchestra, String band and Brass band furnishing the music. After the dance Mrs. Florence V. Neilson entertained her relatives and friends at a thanksgiving supper, all satisfying their appetites with all kinds of danties. Susan Finlinson also entertained at a party of the same kind after the dance.

Deseret Doings.

Miss Delora Reid left Sunday evening for home in Payson.

Seymore L. Brunson of Meadow was a visitor during the week.

The Jenkins Orchestra played to a crowded house on the 26 and 28.

Arthur Ryan in company with Mr. Stubbans made a flying trip to Fillmore Friday.

A number of our town sports are leaving for Crafton this afternoon for another hunt.

Raymond Ray and Sam Greenwood came up from the Salt Marsh Friday in their auto after a number of hunters from Salt Lake.

Miss Norma Moody, who is attending the B. Y. U. came down to spend Thanksgiving with parents and friends, returning Sunday night.

Mr. and Mrs. Maloy, who have been visiting with relatives for a couple of weeks, returned to their home in El Paso, Texas, the latter part of the week.

Preparations are being made by Teachers and School Board for the dedication of the A. C. Nelson School building next Friday. It is expected that Gov. Spry will be in attendance also a number of our leading Educators of the State. Services will commence at 2 o'clock p. m., a banquet will be served to the visitors in the evening, followed by a grand ball.

NEWSY NOTES ABOUT FOLKS

D. J. Black of Deseret, was a visitor to Fillmore, Tuesday.

Judge J. W. Kelso and his brother, L. V., were business visitors to Lynndyl, Monday.

Roy Dresser, brother of former editor, N. B., arrived here Saturday for an indefinite stay.

Jas. Williamson and wife of Fillmore were in Delta Monday, the husband peddling honey about town.

Mrs. A. Staley of Ogden, who had been visiting her daughter, Mrs. Jas. Williamson at Fillmore, returned home Monday night.

Mr. and Mrs. R. R. Betz leave the first of next week for Ohio and Maryland to spend the Yuletide with relatives and friends.

Mrs. Jas. A. Kelley and son, James, who have spent the summer and fall on the Kelley ranch, at Mills, returned here Saturday for the winter months.

The Cloninger Theatrical Co. failed to put in their appearance here Dec. 7th, as advertised, but will be here Saturday night and stage "Peg O' My Heart" at the Marsoni, sure.

Mrs. Zina Gray and daughter, Miss Jennie, returned Monday from Richfield, where they had accompanied the remains of their husband and father for interment, last Tuesday.

Prof. Calvin Fletcher of Provo, was here on Saturday, visiting Eugene Gardner and F. L. Copening and family, having been at Deseret on Friday attending the dedication of the A. C. Nelson.

The Ladies Relief Society will give a dance at the Ward Hall in Delta, Friday evening, Dec. 11th, the Delta band having been engaged to furnish the music for the occasion. Everybody invited.

J. H. Robison and son Isaac, of Gandy, were marketing alfalfa seed and purchasing ranch supplies at Deseret, the forepart of the week. They were well pleased with the price they received for their seed by the local buyer.

Mrs. Ray Bishop successfully underwent an operation for ailments peculiar to her sex in a Salt Lake hospital last Saturday, and the latest reports regarding her condition is that she is improving as rapidly as could be hoped for.

C. M. Graham's father of California, arrived here Monday to spend several months with him. They have purchased a well rig for drilling purposes both for flowing wells and oil wells and will operate in the vicinity of Holden, where they have a large ranch.

J. H. Baker, superintendent and general manager of a string of Baker and Co. lumber yards, located along the Salt Lake Route, was here the first of the week, conferring with the local manager, J. E. Works on business concerning the yard at this point.

Carl Elmer, who was operated upon for appendicitis at a hospital in Salt Lake, a week ago Tuesday, surprised his relatives and anxious friends Monday by returning home, having recovered from the effects of the operation in the remarkably short time of five days.

Albert Leuthaeuser shipped a car of hogs to the Los Angeles market Saturday and expects to ship another car the end of this week. Fred Tingleaf of Woodrow went with the shipment, taking advantage of a free trip down to visit his family at Riverside, for a month or six weeks.

The A. C. Nelson School was dedicated with appropriate ceremonies and a splendid program followed by a banquet last Friday evening. This school house is the handsomest, costliest and most substantial structure in this part of the state and the people of Oasis and Deseret are justly proud of it.

R. W. Butt arrived from California, Tuesday, with an emigrant car containing his belongings to establish himself as a resident of this valley, having purchased the Tuggle farm 2 miles west of this town last summer. This is certainly a dandy farm, is well improved and Mr. Butt will undoubtedly make good from the start.

A communication imparts the information that a 10½ pound boy was born to Mr. and Mrs. Gus Neymeyer at Hill City, Kansas, December 1st. The Neymeyers were former residents of the north tract and Gus wants his old neighbors to know that he can do something besides raising wheat averaging 45 bu. an acre.

A letter received from Miss Cora Heise, daughter of Mr. and Mrs. Frank Heise of Woodrow, states that she is teaching school at Center, Colorado, this year, and directs that we send The Chronicle to her address for three months, in order that she may keep in touch with the interesting happenings hereabout.

Henry Huff informs us that an abundance of of lucern and sweet clover seed has been markered at Oasis during the past several weeks and the buyers have paid a good long price for it, competition having been keen. Stores at Oasis and Deseret are very busy waiting on customers and things are very much alive down that way from a business standpoint.

R. R. Betz deciding that walking to his work at Oasis, each evening and returning home in the morning was entirely too strenuous for his shanks horses, rented a house at Oasis and moved down there Monday. We are all truly sorry to have Mr. and Mrs. Betz move away from Delta; they are a congenial, neighborly pair, liked and respected by all acquaintances.

Sometimes it rains on the just and unjust, but last Sunday it snowed on the "just" when three inches fell out on the north tract, covering a scope of country one-half mile south of Sutherland to beyond Omaha, which will be of untold benefit to the many fields of fall wheat in that neighborhood. It tried hard to snow all during the day in this vicinity Sunday but failed, however a light snow fell here Tuesday morning with a promise of some more.

E. J. Tuck, one of the industrious farmers and desirable entry-men on the south tract, was marketing hogs in Delta last Saturday. Mr. Tuck came here from Oklahoma four years ago, and while he has met with numerous discouragements since setting here, he now has his farm on a paying basis with several acres of good lucern, four milch cows and a good start in hogs of the Duroc strain. He has 40 acres to fall wheat and will put from 5 to 10 acres to sugar beets next spring.

The D. J. Black store at Deseret is showing as nifty a line of holiday goods this year as may be seen south of Salt Lake City. The stock consists of nearly every gift imaginable, from the inexpensive to the costliest. All the goods are bright and new, no old shelf-worn articles of whatsoever nature will be found there. The store is crammed with seasonable goods and Christmas shoppers will find it a distinct advantage as well as a pleasure to select gifts there; just go in and look around for yourself, everything is attractively displayed.

Our genial good friend, Dennis Black of Deseret was a business visitor in Delta, Saturday. Dennis was a member of a hunting party recently that went for a hunt down on Craft's Lake and successfully bagged over 200 ducks and he has not been heard "quacking" much about this remarkably large haul either. Dennis is sure that he got the limit each day; the limit set by most of the duck hunters hereabout has been from 1 to 3 ducks, of course, they could have gotten more, but they run out of shells, couldn't find the fowl after shooting it or well maybe the ducks are scarce.

Orson Sprague of Nevada, is here visiting the Sampson family.

Oak City Offerings.

(Jos. H. Christenson, Rep.)

Lots of snow falling in the mountains.

L. R. Webb has gone to Hinckley to visit his family.

Walter Carlson has just received a new grist mill.

Thos. C. Lyman is hauling fence post to Delta for Mr. Bender.

Miss Ruby Jacobs has been very sick but is now improving.

J. Lyman and son of Mayfield are here visiting relatives and friends.

Mrs. J. Lee Anderson is on the sick list and we hope for her speedy recovery.

Nearly everybody is busy putting in corral taps for their stock this winter.

The Oak City school has had two students added to its number, they being Indian boys.

The Finlinson brothers are erecting a brick house on their ranch at Fool-creek-flat.

Mr. and Mrs. O. H. Jacobson and Mr. A. Christenson left Friday for Aurora, to be at the bedside of their grand-daughter, a young girl 14 years old, who is very low with brights desease.

The A. Carlson home was saved from fire, Wednesday. The stovepipe near the roof had become rusty and worn and the blaze had caught the roof which was noticed in time to save the building.

A number of men are preparing to start work on the new canal west of Oak City, while others are busy clearing their land which will be watered by the canal. It is excellent land, has never been cultivated on account of the water supply by our mountain stream being so limited.

Sutherland Searchlights

Saturday night and Sunday brought us about two inches of snow, all which thawed, however, on Monday.

The new road from Delta to Omaha is still soft and unpacked and does not delight the auto men who drive over it.

A. Ackerman & Co., who recently made up a hunting party to Clear Lake, returned last Saturday and reports having had a fine trip with very good results.

Mrs. M. A. Abbott and son, Howard, returned from their visit to Dixie, last week, having had a very pleasant visit greeting old friends and neighbors all along the route.

There is a good program planned for Xmas eve to be held at the Sutherland school house. Everybody is expected to come and help make a good time. Bring the little toys and see Santa Claus.

THE HINCKLEY HAPPENINGS

People are anxious about their tax money.

Mrs. Frank Pratt is recovering from a sick spell.

Eugene Hilton is out of school, suffering with erysipelas.

Cleaning of alfalfa seed seems to be in vogue just now.

Percy Nelson returned Tuesday from a visit to Salt Lake.

Prof. Brooks of the Millard Academy is arranging to put on an operetta soon.

Dr. Broaddus has made two professional trips to Leamington, during the past week.

A very enjoyable dance took place Friday evening. The Jenkins Orchestra furnished the music.

Mrs. Georgia Cropper Johnson and her two children are guests of her parents, Mr. and Mrs. T. W. Cropper.

The Stork called at the home of Mr. and Mrs. Arthur Reeve and left an eight pound baby boy, Nov. 23rd.

Hosea F. Stout, who has long and faithfully acted as Ward Chorister, has been honorably released and John Brooks chosen to act in his stead.

Elders Hall and Spendlove from Hurricane, returning from missions to the Southern States, stopped off for a few days visit with relatives in Hinckley.

Friday, Nov. 26th, the Millard Academy Faculty with their wives, gathered at the Academy, where they enjoyed an afternoon of recreation. Games and luncheon being the main features.

Mr. and Mrs. George T. Holdaway of Aurora, made a trip to Hinckley in their auto, where they spent Thanksgiving with their daughter, Mrs. J. J. Spendlove. They reported the roads as being in a very bad condition.

A committee of six was chosen last Sunday from the Parents class of the Sabbath School to arrange for the distribution of presents among the worthies by Santa Claus at Christmas time and for a fitting celebration by the public.

Dr. C. A. Broaddus has taken three patients from here to Salt Lake, during the last week, where they have undergone operations for appendicitis. Those who are suffering from the disease are: Amy Cox, Fern and Robert Reeve.

Farm Demonstrator, J. P. Welch, has recently purchased the 40 acre farm belonging to Samuel Dutson, which is situated one-half mile south of town. Mr. Welch intends to erect a residence on his property sometime this winter.

The many friends of Mrs. John Reeve will be pleased to hear that she has sufficiently recovered from her recent operation in the L. D. S. hospital in Salt Lake, to be removed to her home, where she is rapidly regaining her strength.

Sunday evening the townspeople were highly entertained with a lecture on "The Life of Joseph Smith and the Rise of the Church" by Mr. Christensen. The lecture was illustrated by a number of oil paintings of scenes connected with Church History.

One of the most successful events of the week was a social given by Mrs. Mary E. Lee and her daughter, Mrs. Rose Jarvis. A number of old friends and the Academy faculty were the guests. The evening was one of laughter and fun; many unique games were introduced. Among the refreshments served were grapes, almonds, figs and pomegranates from Dixie.

The first Parents and Teachers meeting was held Sunday evening with a large attendance. Problems pertaining to the welfare of the school were discussed and the eighth grade rendered a pleasing program. Principal Tippetts in his report of the work being accomplished, stated that he believed the school to be thirty percent more efficient this year than last.

The Millard Academy joined with the towns people of Hinckley and made a success of the Thanksgiving celebration. A pleasing program was rendered in the Academy at 10 a. m. Among the most interesting parts given were: "The History of Thanksgiving" by Mrs. C. A. Broaddus in which many new facts and ideas were brought out; the heart to heart talk on "What we have to be Thankful for" by President Hinckley and the beautiful solos sang by Elmer Stout. At 2 p. m. the Millard Academy and town contested in a game of foot ball, which proved to be a very close game the score being 2 to 8 in favor of the Academy. In the evening the old and young joined in one of the most successful balls of the season.

During the past week 5 young people have required operation for appendicitis. On Sunday,

Jennie Johnson of Deseret, who had been sick for several days with an attack of rheumatism and appendicitis, was sufficiently recovered to follow the doctor's advice and go to Salt Lake. Within two days Dr. Broaddus was obliged to go himself to operate on Robert Reeve and Carl Elmer, and again Saturday night, operating Sunday morning on Fern Reeve and Amy Cox. On all of these cases Dr. Broaddus was called in early in the attack and by proper medical treatment and the application of ice bags was

able to control and reduce the inflamation, thus preventing the appendix from bursting and making the operation a comparatively safe and easy one; the most serious one, that performed on Amy Cox, taking only about 20 minutes; Carl Elmer has already returned home safe and sound In practically all of these terrible cases of peritonitis from a ruptured appendix, the whole trouble has been caused by the fact that the people have applied heat, which only increases the inflamation and causes the appendix to

burst. Many people have recently asked the doctor what precautions against appendicitis can be taken. First of all he says, never allow yourself to become constipated, regulate your body's house cleaning by proper foods, exercise, regular habits and by drinking plenty of water. Never regard lightly any severe pain or tenderness in the abdomen, but find out from a reliable physician the causes of the disturbance. If you get caught with appendicitis never apply anything hot but use cold applications over the tender area.

Abraham Articles.

Mrs. Leroy bulls is quite sick. Her many friends hope for a speedy recovery.

There will be a Ward celebration at Abraham on Saturday, Dec. 19th Come out and enjoy the day with us.

Mr. and Mrs. Marcus Dasche are rejoicing over the arrival of a fine son, born Dec. 2nd. All doing nicely at this writing.

There is to be a picture show, Wednesday evening at the Abraham school house illustrating the arrival of the Pioneers in the Salt Lake Valley.

All the threshing is done in Abraham district. The acreage cut for alfalfa seed was small, but the yield was good. C. M. Hickman, O. M. Fullmer, John Crooks, Payne Franklin, Parker and Pasche having near 100 bushel each. R. T. Patterson, Leroy Young and Donald Hogan having near 200 bushels each. The seed is of excellent quality.

Millard County Chronicle
December 17, 1914

Oak City Offerings.

(Jos. H. Christenson, Rep.)

Mr. and Mrs. John Lundahl of Lynndyl have moved here for the winter.

Ruby and Evan Jacobson and Sylvia Christenson made a trip to Aurora, the past week to attend the funeral of their neice.

A practice dance was had last Wednesday evening in order to get some of the new dances going again.

The Mutual gave a dance Friday night which was enjoyed by all present.

Elder C. C. A. Christensen gave a Historical picture show here Saturday evening, explaining Mormonism. Everyone present enjoyed it to a full extent.

Mr. J. Lyman and son, Alvin, have purchased the A. M. Roper & Son's store.

Alvin Lyman returned to his home in Mayfield to spend a few days with his family. Mrs. Martha Roper, Kirt Roper and J. P. Callister accompanied him.

Simeon Walker returned the first of the week from a visit at Lewisville, Idaho, with his mother who is 97 years old, and other relatives at other points.

Ella Carlson and Edna Anderson returned from their visit to Mills and report a very enjoyable time.

The program for Xmas Eve is as follows: quartette, Mandy Roper and Co.; prayer, Joseph P. Callister; music, E. Q. Band; speech, Leroy Walker; stump speech, E. Q. Dutson; music, String Band; recitation, Oakland Dutson; piano duet, Angie Finlinson and Mable Roper; violin solo, Ray Finlinson; comic reading, J. L. Nielson; song, Eldon Anderson; Xmas sentiments, Nellie Roper, Elma Nielson, Doris Alldredge, Esdras Finlinson, Clabbe Lovell, and Guy Sheriff; master of ceremonies, Lorenzo Lovell. The day program, Dec. 25th, is as follows:—Christmas Chimes at 8.30, Wm. Chestnut; Band serenade at 9 a. m.; basket ball game at 11 a. m., under the direction of Geo. Finlinson and LeRoy Walker. A dance in the evening at 8 sharp. A childrens dance will be given Monday, Dec. 28th, at 1 p. m.

Abraham Articles.

If present plans develope we can soon boast of a fine new hall.

Mr. and Mrs. Clyde Underhill of Woodrow, were guests of Mr. and Mrs. C. M. Hickman, Sunday.

Our school will close Dec. 18th for a two weeks vacation. The teachers will spend Xmas with home folks at Provo and Santaquin.

The Primary teachers and children will give an entertainment, Dec. 23rd. They have prepared a good program, come out and show your appreciation.

"A Fight Against Fate" was staged here Saturday night by home talent and was enjoyed by a good sized audience. Those taking part deserve much praise. Our hustling real estate dealer,

Floyd Hickman, recently sold 120 acres of land near Abraham to a California party and we understand the buyer will move here in the near future.

We understand that O. L. Lake has purchased E. H. Biehler's resident property in north Abraham. This will go well in connection with Ora's Abraham farm. Mr. Biehler anticipates moving on his desert farm west of here.

Deseret Doings.

A number of sheepmen are in town enroute for the desert.

Mrs. R. L. Woodward is reported very sick at this writing

Mr. Cone and Albert Bishop are in from Trout Creek hunting up seed buyers.

Mr. Freedman of Salt Lake was a visitor Saturday, also Mr. Lunt of Cedar City.

Jim and Ike Robison of Gandy found a first class market here for their seed crop.

Miss Jennie Johnson, who recently underwent an operation in Salt Lake, has returned home and is said to be doing nicely.

Mr. and Mrs. Alfred Bishop and little son, Lawrence, arrived from Calio, Friday, on their way to Los Angeles to spend the winter. They will visit the Fair before returning in the spring.

Billy Meechum and son, Emery, of Snake Valley, is in town disposing of their crop of alfalfa seed and transacting other business. Mr. Meechum received 12½ cents per pound for his crop of seed.

Dan Simonson has been shaking hands with friends and relatives, here, for several days. He left for his home at Baker, Nev., Monday morning. Mr. and Mrs. Simonson expect to soon leave for Oregon to spend the winter.

John Dewsnup has recently had the amusement hall plastered and installed electric lights, making it one of the best opera houses in the county. He is expecting to get his ice-plant in operation by early spring, having already purchased an equipment with a sufficient capacity to supply the trade of the entire county.

NEWSY NOTES ABOUT FOLKS

W. N. Gardner the movie man made a business trip to Lynndyl Friday and Sat.

Edward Pearson is handling the bank until Mr. Beckwith returns from a visit to Salt Lake.

Mrs. H. F. Aller returned, Thursday morning, from Ohio where she has been visiting for several weeks.

Miss Carrie Leigh, one of our school teachers, left Wednesday for her home in Cedar City to spend the holidays.

Mr. and Mrs Hibbard of near Omaha took the train here, Wednesday morning, for Chatham, Mass., where they will make an indefinit stay.

Mrs. George Tozer and children, Pearl, Vernon and Mrs. Emma Barras of Salt Lake City, returned Saturday to spend the Xmas vacation.

Mrs. Mary Lyman returned from Salt Lake, Sunday, where she had been in attendance with her daughter, who had been taking treatment in the Hospital.

W. B. Higgins the leading practicioner and barrister of Fillmore was in Delta Sat. enroute to Iron County where he has several matters pending in Court.

Reports received from Mr. Graham, who was severely injured by having the bones in his hand broken in the well machine, are to the effect that he is progressing favorably.

Dr. G. W. Richards D.S.S. of Salt Lake City formerly of Colorado has arrived in the city and will take care of your teeth for you. Give him a trial when in need of Dental work.

Reduced Rates for Holidays via Salt Lake Route. Excursion tickets on sale at all stations. Salt Lake Route Dec. 18 to 25th inc—Dec. 31st and Jan. 1st - Good returning until Jan. 4, 1915.

Christmas and New Year excursions via Salt Lake Route. Excursion tickets on sale at all Utah stations on Salt Lake Route Dec. 18 to 25th inc—Dec. 31 and Jan. 1st—Return limit Jan. 4th, 1915.

Mrs. Jeff Clark left Delta Sat. morning for a holiday visit with her people in Garnett, Kans. Mrs. Clark has been absent from the old folks for 9 years and this occasion will be a reunion as well as a visit.

—FOR SALE—Three good work horses cheap, one mare in foal. Fifty acres of land for rent, with or without stock, 20 acres in alfalfa, 15 acres in fall wheat, a good 8 room house, barn and chicken house.—E. E. LaDuke, Abraham, Utah.

Mr. Beckwith reports having had a very enjoyable dinner of wild duck, last Sunday, at the home of Mr and Mrs. Ward Cotterll of the South Tract. The afternoon was spent wholly in conversation and passed all too quickly. Mr. Beckwith feels deeply indebted for this social pleasure.

Geo B Campbell of Woodrow left for Grand Junction, Colo. to attend the sixtieth anniversary of his parents This is remarkable as we but seldom hear of a sixtieth anniversary; the fiftieth is hardly common, and the sixtieth rare indeed. And it so happens that George is the baby of the family.

—Dr. Christie, Dentist, will be in Scipio, Jan. 4th, prepared to do dental work. Holden, Jan. 11th; Fillmore, Jan. 18th; Meadow, Jan. 25th; Kanosh, Feb. 1st; Delta, Feb. 8th. He requests those needing his service, to come to his office immediately upon his arrival in your town, as his time is limited.

The family of Mr. Britt arrived from Cal. Thursday. Mr. Britt has taken up his residence on his fine ranch west of town which he purchased from Mr. Tuggle. Mr. Britt has visited many of the irrigated projects of the western states but is satisfied that the Delta project is the one for him.

Sutherland Searchlights

Too late for last issue.

Mrs. Harry Ottley entertained at a quilting party Tuesday.

Sadie Lisonbee is just recovering from quite a sick spell.

The condition of Grandma Foote continues about the same.

The Relief Society Stake officers visited the ward Society, Friday.

J. W. Hall is home after spending sometime in Hinckley doing carpenter work.

J. W. Critchlow has returned to his home in Ogden, after proving up on his farm.

The Club met with Mrs. Perry last Friday and enjoyed a very pleasant afternoon.

Mr. and Mrs. Wm. Walker of Hinckley were visiting at Wm Walker's, Monday.

School closes Friday for a two weeks vacation Our teachers will spend the Holidays with their parents in Provo and Sevier County.

Leo Ivman of Oak City visited the L. D. S. Sunday School, last Sunday. Jas Blake of Hinckley was an afternoon visitor in the interest of the Religion Class.

Abraham Articles.

The Needle Craft Club meets next week at the home of Mrs. Biehler

C. M. Hickman and wife took Christmas dinner at the home of Mrs. Cavanaugh.

Mrs. Martha Stout of Leamington is here visiting her mother, Mrs. Hansen.

The ward celebration at Abraham was well attended and a good time reported.

R. T. Patterson presented his family with a fine concert piano as a Christmas present.

Several from here attended the play given by the Abraham dramatic Club at Delta Tuesday night.

Mrs. Elizabeth Yearsley of Salt Lake arrived Monday and will spend the holidays with her parents, Mr. and Mrs. E. H. Biehler.

Ed Taylor and Wilson Biehler have a first class well drill and can put down a hole from two to six inches in diameter and guarantee to please.

Millard County Chronicle
January 7, 1915

THE HINCKLEY HAPPENINGS

Bob Slaughter has a new baby girl.

Arvilla Theobald's broken arm is doing nicely.

T. R. Greener has added another auto to the town collection.

Mrs. C. H. Anderson is entertaining two of her brothers this week.

Alfred Bliss's new baby girl is the fourth granddaughter in a large family of boys.

Principal A. I. Tibbets spent the vacation with relatives and friends in Utah County.

Mr. and Mrs. Clarence Bishop are visiting the lady's grandparents at Circleville, Utah.

Work at Millard Academy was resumed Monday with a full attendance of teachers and students.

Dr. and Mrs. C. A. Broaddus and Miss Rena Reeve were Salt Lake visitors for a few days last week.

One of the especially successful dances was the basket supper dance given by the relief society, Friday night.

George Anderson of Oak City and Sadie Curtis of Richfield, were guests of Mrs. Rose Anderson last Thursday.

Mrs. Cora Kelly, Mrs. Louie Loveland, and Mr. and Mrs. Leonard Meecham of Lynndyl, were holiday visitors to Hinckley.

Wilford Welch returned Sunday to resume his work in the district school, after spending two weeks with relatives in Cache County.

The four upper departments District School resumed work Monday. Three lower grades will not reopen until the whooping cough epidemic which is raging here subsides.

Lucille, the eight year daughter of Mr. and Mrs. [...]ard Parker died Saturda[...]ing of pneumonia. Fu[...]vices where held Mon[...] Relief Hall and was [...] many sympathizing[...] friends of the fam[...]

An especiall[...] was given in [...] Sunday ev[...] and Eln[...] duett[...] told [...] bu[...] F [...]

Miss Gladys Bishop, who has not been very well for a year or so, was taken to Salt Lake for X-ray examination last week. Dr. Broaddus was unwilling to advise operation unless absolutely necessary. Careful examination in consultation with Dr. Ralph Richards did not seem to justify immediate operation although medical treatment will be continued. Surgeons are so often

accused of operating hastily, that we are glad to be re-assured that there are plenty of surgeons who care far more for the patients than for an operating fee.

Two months ago Mrs. John Reeve was taken to Salt Lake by Dr. Broaddus for X-ray examination for a complicated and serious condition, where rapidly growing cancerous growths in the intestines, pelvis and stomach made it evident that the case was

hopeless. An operation for temporary relief was performed and the relatives tried hard to keep from Mrs. Reeve the knowledge of her real condition. It has been one of the most pitiful cases of unavoidable tragedy and brave heroism and the sympathy of the entire community goes out to Mr. Reeve and his family in their bereavement. The funeral was held Wednesday, Jan. 6th.

Oak City Offerings.

(Jos. H. Christenson. Rep.)

Manda Roper was visiting in Holden last week.

Lydia Roper returned to her work in Salt Lake, Saturday.

Stanley Lovell and sister made a trip to Hinckley the past week.

Mr. and Mrs. Eli Rawlinson were home to spend the holidays.

Miss Bushnel of Meadow was here visiting Lee Walker last week.

Don Anderson and Evan Jacobson made a trip to Fillmore last week.

Our school teachers have returned to resume their school work.

The Mutual gave a dance last Wednesday which was enjoyed by all.

The old fashioned calico dance given Thursday night was indeed a success.

Hazel Stephenson of Holden spent part of the holidays here

with Leland Roper.

Ruby and Edith Neilson of Leamington was here visiting during the holidays.

C. Johnson of Leamington was here last week visiting his daughter, Mrs. T. E. Talbot.

Gean Lovell spent the holidays with her parents. She is attending school in Salt Lake.

Sutherland Searchlights

Leda Finlinson returned home last Sunday.

Cleone Bunker is on the sick list this week.

Jed Watts of Oak City was in Sutherland last week.

M. M. Steele Jr. spent a few days in Salt Lake last week.

Our high school students have returned to Hinckley to resume their school work.

Several teams have gone to Whiskey Creek to get out posts for fencing purposes.

We had a nice snow fall Monday which looks good to the farmers who have fall grain in.

George S. Bunker has gone to Cedar City to attend the funeral of his brother, Edward Bunker, Sr.

John Ierslif had the misfortune to get his leg run over with a loaded wagon while out in the hills for posts.

Geo. Campbell returned home from a visit to his aged parents, in the best of health, having enjoyed the trip very much.

Mr. Titus and Frank Belestone are employed to put in the new Co. telephone line from Delta to their new hotel on the north tract.

Miss Brickey is back again after a very pleasant vacation

spent in Provo, ready to resume her work in the school room again.

Pery Abbott and James Barney returned to Sevier County, Sunday, the latter to take up his school work again and the former to spend a short time with his people.

Mrs. Denver Smith entertained Mr. and Mrs. Boardman at supper New Years Eve. A very pleasant evening was spent until the old year departed and the New came in.

Deseret Doings.

Minnie and Bessie Iverson of Provo, were Deseret visitors last week.

The Stork left a sweet little baby girl at the home of Mr. and Mrs. Alpin Allred.

Mr. and Mrs. A. D. Ryan entertained a number of their friends, Saturday evening, in honor of Mr. and Mrs. Mark Kelly.

Mary Stoddard and Nora Damron of Idaho, spent the holidays

here with relatives and friends, returning to their home New Years Eve.

The married folks dance New Years evening was a decided success. A jolly good crowd and good music made it one of the best dances during holidays.

Last Thursday evening, the Deseret Dramatic Co. presented to the public "Rocky Ford," to the public which was greatly enjoyed by a large audience.

Mr. and Mrs. R. L. Woodward

left for the north last Wednesday evening, for pleasure and business combined. Mrs. Woodward will stay for an indefinite length of time.

An out of town event of interest was the marriage of Mark Kelley and Maud Larsen, which took place at Bloomington, Dec. 31st, at the home of the bride's parents. Both are popular young people and their many friends wish them a happy voyage over the matrimonial sea.

Oasis.

Mr. David Day is confined to his bed and very ill as a result of a bad fall on the ice and snow his knee is badly bruised and his leg very badly swollen.

Mr. Thomas Church celebrated his ninty first birthday on the 20th of January. And his family and friends gathered at his home to do honor to the occasion. He is the father of 11 children all living and all but 3 of them were present at the party. In addition to his 11 children he has 36 living grand children and 6 great grand children. He is hale and hearty in spite of his many years and can read a news paper with out glasses. We all join with his family in wishing him many happy returns of the day.

The Oasis Dramatic Company will present the four act drama intitled the "Merry Cobbler" at Hinckley Thursday evening.

Born to Mr. and Mrs. Earl Blackburn an eight pound baby boy Sunday morning.

The stork also brought a little baby boy to the home of James Ode. But Jim says this little stranger is claimed by his daughter and her husband, Mr. and Mrs. Thornton.

Mrs. Mary Clegg is here visiting her parents who she has not seen for 18 years.

Paul the 12 year old son of of Mr. and Mrs. S. M. Hawley who had such a narrow escape from being burned to death some three weeks ago is so far recovered from his burns as to be out again.

Mr. O. J Day is enlarging and remodling his store.

OAK CITY.

Winter weather now prevails in Oak City, we have received the long looked for storm, which not only causes a broad smile to appear on the faces of the dry farmers, but it is a time of rejoicing for those who are so fond of taking water, even in wet weather.

Evidently the recent storm, falling as it has upon the frozen ground, partly covered with snow, will make good sleigh riding and we trust no one will let the opportunity slip by with out taking a spin through the balmy atmosphere.

Cold weather has prevailed for some time in this quarter, 2 degrees below zero being the coldest night we had.

From observation and close observance of tones and sounds ringing from various parts of the village, one would naturally conclude that the musical age had dawned upon the people of Oak City, for it appears that there are a collection of two or three instruments in every home.

Saturday night the brass band met at the home of Pres. Soren J. Rawlinson and enjoyed a practice coupled with a famous oyster supper. We are proud of our band and the rapid progress they are making, and wish them continued success in their work.

In November last a string band was organized with Ray Finlinson as president and instructor and Sam Roper as Secretary and treasurer. This delegation consists of fifteen members at present some play the violin, mandolin guitar and piano. The progress made by them since commencing is wonderful and we commend them for the zeal and energy with which they are working, and wish them to continue that more people may get to hear their music.

The Mutual Social Committee is putting on a play entitled, "The Hand of The Law." A real good entertainment is assured the people when this is staged.

Joseph Finlinson has resumed work on his new barn, according to the plans of a local architect. This edifice is nearing completion and even now is of great value to the proprietor who I suppose should rightfully be termed architect, designer, builder and all.

Martha Lynnox has spent the the past few days in Leamington.

Simeon Walker left town on the 25th for a trip to Kanosh.

Leo Finlinson spent the past week in Leamington feeding stock.

Oak City Offerings.

(Jos. H. Christenson, Rep.)

A. Hanson of Mills was a visitor at the Carling home, Sunday.

J. Lee Anderson was a business visitor to Hinckley, one day last week.

Gee. H. and Eldon Anderson made a business trip to Delta, on Monday of last week.

Six inches of snow fell here, the end of last week; snow in the mountains is reported 2 to 4 feet in depth.

John H. Lundahl, who has employment at Lynndyl, spent several days with his family here, the past week.

The Sewing Club girls were charmingly entertained by Miss Wanda Dutson. Delicious refreshments were served.

The Oak City basket ball team defeated the Millard High School team in a lively, snappy contest here Saturday night by a score of 35 to 21.

The eighteen months old baby boy of Mr. and Mrs. Lem Roper died in Salt Lake last Friday, the victim of pneumonia, having been taken there for treatment. The body was brought back here on Saturday, the funeral services and interment taking place the following day. This is the second child Mr. and Mrs. Roper have lost, and they have the heartfelt sympathy of this vicinity.

A purse of $75 was raised here Sunday, Jan. 20th, to aid the suffering humanity in Belgium. We as a nation should feel proud to live in this land of peace and plenty, enjoying ourselves at our different vocations without fear of a Kaiser or a King's desire to destroy our lives, our homes, our all. It's terrible to think of the horribleness of the existing conditions brought on by the great war—women and children left without husband and father, no home, no nothing—left to face starvation, entirely dependent upon Americans liberality. Let us be glad that we were able to help the needy in this method.

Abraham Articles.

Roy Bills is erecting a dwelling on his farm near Abraham.

The Needle Craft meets with Mrs. Marcus Fuscht, next week.

Albert Reid is building a bungalow on his farm in West Abraham.

O. M. Fullmer is improving from an attack of ear and throat trouble.

Mrs. Oscar Fullmer of Idaho, was a recent visitor at the home of O. M. Fullmer.

The Abraham Orchestra, made up of seven pieces, are producing some excellent music.

Chas. Vorwaller and wife returned Tuesday, from a ten days visit with relatives in Salt Lake.

Ed Soules of Salt Lake and two real estate dealers of California, were visitors at the home of O. L. Lake last week.

Mrs. Flossie Porter returned Wed. of last week to her home in Idaho after a few weeks visit with her sister, Mrs. Allen Young and other relatives.

A local stockholders meeting of the Abraham Irrigation Company was held last week to converse on matters pertaining to needs of the company.

Mrs. John Alva of Delta, who has been staying with her mother, Mrs. Hansen for the past two months, gave birth to a fine boy Wednesday of last week.

On Thursday of last week, a baby girl came to brighten the home of W. J. Carey and wife. All are doing well at this writing and Wes is stepping high.

Sutherland Searchlights

Mr. and Mrs E. L. Abbott are visiting in Holden.

Born to Mr. and Mrs. Ward Robinson a fine baby girl. Mother and babe doing fine.

Fritz Freese was given a surprise party Monday night. A pleasant time was spent.

Colds and Lagrippe are very prevalent. Whooping cough appears to be spreading amongst the children.

Misses Florence and Ira Holdridge entertained their Sunday school class Friday evening at an oyster supper.

Real estate still moving in Sutherland, regardless of no land agents in the vicinity doing active business.

Mrs. Mary Finlinson of Leamington, was visiting her brother, W. R. Walker and family Saturday and Sunday.

Wallace Clark has qualified as constable. He is at present trying to locate the guilty party who has been flooding the roads.

Saturday night a crowd of the male population of the district met at the school house and spent the evening in wrestling and boxing.

Chas. Simpkins has gone home to Circleville, for the summer. Dan Simpkins and family are home again after a visit with friends in Circleville.

Born, a son to Mr. and Mrs. Harvey Pocock at Tooele, Utah. Mr. and Mrs. Pocock who left Sutherland, late last fall for Tooele, have a number of friends who are pleased to hear of the new arrival.

A supposed tragedy has been explained. Recently people passing the home of Geo. Smith heard such a series of groans and cries that very uncertain rumors have been going the rounds as to its cause. The matter has been hushed up out of respect to Mr. Smith as he is one of our desirable citizens. However when we learn that it was merely Add Austin having a tooth pulled we rest easy again.

Found Among My Relics.

(Genevieve McClain.)

Softly I lay each one aside. An old slate sunbonnet, the one I wore to church, a piece of faded ribbon sent to me on my birthday, a string of watermelon seeds my only pair of beads when I was a child, a few of old torn and faded letters and a little booklet written on stiff paper and written in a childish hand. Back flooded the memories of many years when as a child I wrote by the dim light of a tiny candle these many experiences happening each day. Slowly I turn each stained and ragged page.

Oct. 24, 1868. Monday 7:25 p.m.

Today I went to school and we girls have all decided to keep a "Diery." It is to be our best secret.

Oct. 25, 1868. Tuesday 6:00 p.m.

I saw a red man sneaking through the forest when I went to the spring. He did not harm me but ran swiftly away. Father fears the Indians are getting ready for an attack. I have a new homespun dress I have worked two months on.

Oct. 26, 1868. Wednesday 5:30 p.m.

My aunt and uncle are here for the night with their three girls as the Indians are expected. A small band have been sneaking around near the village. Father shot a big, brown bear while he was chopping wood in the forest. Mother has called me to go spread the bed so I will say good-bye to you for to-night dear little book.

Oct. 27, 1868. Thursday 7:00 p.m.

Indians sneaked up on us last night but we soon chased them away. They stole a sack of grain but nothing else. Our old dog, Ned, died while guarding the sheep to-day and we burried him under the old elm tree and put flowers on his grave. The wolves can't find him and eat him now.

Oct. 28, 1868. Friday 7:30 p.m.—

I have to write in my own little room to keep it a secret and to-night it is very cold up here alone. All the men in the community have been busy today building our first meeting house.

A new preacher and his family are expected soon.

Oct. 29, 1868. Saturday 6:00 p.m.

The boys all went hunting this morning so I had to help father in the fields. I tied and piled up the grain. We are all going to a husking party tonight and expect to have a nice time. The new preacher has come. Good-night little book.

Oct. 30, 1868. Sunday 5:00 p.m.

We went to church this morning but I could not keep still so I have been kept in my room all day. The boys came home from their hunting trip but they did not seem to have found anything. Mother made them hang their clothes on the line and go to bed.

I laid the little book aside and sat dreaming of a little girl in homespun and thick stockings and rough shoes. Her little brow wrinkled up as she bends over her little book.

MARRIAGE LICENSES.

Myron Alexander of Salt Lake and Molly Knoop of Springfield, Mo.; Edward L. Muller of Lynndyl and Martineau E. Conley of Philadelphia; E. L. Simmons and Neta Seabury, both of Payson; Harold J. Hay and Sophia Palfreyman, both of Salt Lake; Clarence Evans and Sylvia Halvorsen, both of Salt Lake.

Millard County Progress
February 5, 1915

OAK CITY.

It seems that many changes can occur in the course of a weeks time. While at this writing we are pleased to report that every body is enjoying good health, yet we are sorry to report the loss of Alvin Fay Roper a child of Lem and Libbie Roper.

The child had contracted a cold which turned into pneumonia and that affecting his intestines. Upon securing the aid of a doctor, his condition was found to be very serious. He was taken to Salt Lake City for an operation but being so weak was not able to under go the operation and while in the City he quietly departed his life. The parents brought the body home Saturday.

Sunday January 31st the services were held over the remains. The speakers at the meeting were Elders Joseph A. Lyman, Ray Finlinson and Geo. H. Anderson, all giving some comforting as well a interesting remarks. The people of Oak City, one and all, join in extending their most heartfelt sympathy to brother and sister Roper in their time of trouble.

For the past 60 or 70 days real cold weather has prevailed in and around this region. It has been the longest cold spell we have had in a number of years, though judging from present conditions it appears that a warmer period is beginning to dawn and that the coldest weather has passed over.

The latter part of last week Leo and Ellen Lyman, Joseph and Geo. E. Finlinson made trips to Hinckley and attended the Monthly Priesthood meeting. A number of others fully intended to go but upon arising early Saturday morning discovered that a very severe storm was at hand which prevented their going.

Saturday night we were favored with a visit from the Fillmore High School basket ball team. It was rumored and also remarked by the high school boys that if they had lost a game in Hinckley at the M. S. A. by a score of 25 to 24, they would gain an easy victory over the Oak City boys. But to their sorrow they met defeat by a much greater degree than at

Hinckley the score being 35 to 21 in favor of Oak City. The line ups were for the high school Lyman, Rodgers R. F., Stott L. F., Beckstrand O, Pearson R. G. Holbrook L. G.; for Oak City, Leland Roper, O. Aldridge, K. Roper, Lee Walker, and Jack Aldridge.

Both teams played good and are to be commended on the manner in which they handled the ball.

Simeon Walker returned recently from Kanosh where he has been for a short time on business.

Joseph Finlinson who has been to Leamington feeding cattle returned to Oak City on Monday.

Millard County Chronicle
February 11, 1915

Deseret Doings.

Mrs. Maggie Maw of Provo, is visiting her parents, Mr. and Mrs. Nels Peterson.

Considerable mud slinging has taken place the past week, literally, not figuratively.

Only one week now to prepare for the mask ball. Masks and costumes can be had at Damron & Hawley's

Mrs. May Petty is here visiting relatives and friends. She will return to her home at Stockton to-morrow.

Conk Bros. have brought ore for shipment from the Sawtooth Mts., which promises to yield a large percent of gold.

A social was held at the home of John R. Bennett on Saturday evening in honor of his daughter, Mrs. May Petty.

The Spanish Fork High School bask't ball team came down Frida and defeated the local team to the tune of 54 to 24.

Jos. Moody has gone to his mine at Antelope Mt. to bring home the men who have been working his property there.

There is an epidemic of colds and grippe in town at present. Mrs. Woodward, Lee Moody and wife, Myron Black and Annie Webb's family are among the afflicted.

NEWSY NOTES ABOUT FOLKS

James A. Melville was a visitor to Fillmore, Tuesday.

H. B. Prout was attending court at Fillmore, the first of the week, being interested in a case which came to trial.

Charles H. Rossman of Orange, Cal., bargained for a 40 acre tract near Sutherland, Monday, through the Western Security Co.

Mr. and Mrs. Cass Lewis were in attendance at an old settlers gathering at Oasis, Tuesday, they having resided there at one time.

Messrs. R. J. Law, J. A. Bishop and Irwin Jeffery were in Fillmore, the past week, serving as jurors at this term of district court.

R. A. Nelson of near Hinckley was a Delta visitor Wednesday. He says farmers are finding it a hard matter to find a hay market down that way.

H. A. Knight, the only licensed embalmer and funeral director in Millard County, was transacting business in Salt Lake, the end of last week.

Abraham Lincoln's birthday will be celebrated at the Ward Hall, Friday evening with an appropriate program, to be followed by a dance. Everyone is invited.

Ellis Jacob, who was operated upon for appendicitis in a Salt Lake Hospital, several days ago, is recovering as rapidly as could be expected. The appendix bursted just previous to his arrival at the hospital.

Joseph Neilson of Hinckley, was in town Saturday, on his way home from Salt Lake, where he had been attending to matters fo a personal nature, favoring this office with a short but appreciative call while here.

A fine baby girl, weighing nine pounds arrived to bless and brighten the home of Mr. and Mrs. Geo. E. Billings, Monday morning, February 8th. Dr. Broaddus of Hinckley was the accoucheur, and reports mother and babe as doing nicely.

Herman Nutsch of Morrowville, Kansas, arrived here Wednesday to make some improvements and final proof on his Carey Act farm out on the north tract. He is a brother of the other Nutsch boys, residing here.

John Reeve and Joseph Welch of Hinckley, were here Monday meeting with Jas. A. Melville and Bishop H. E. Maxfield and perfecting plans to make the Farmers Round Up and Housekeepers Conference, a stunning success in every particular.

A number of the friends of Miss Bertha Sampson assembled at the Sampson home on the evening of the sixth, and celebrated her twenty-first birthday. A joyful good time and lots of good things to eat, made the occasion one long to be remembered by the happy guests and they long for a return of the event.

O. Wood and sons, Herald and Edward, arrived here last week to take up their residence on the 80 acres purchased last fall out on the south tract. They came from Santa Barbara, Cal. and are former Kansans. A nephew, Artie Johnson of the same place arrived also to take charge of an adjoining 80 acre farm which his father had purchased last fall.

Josesh Overson, a prosperous and honorable resident of Leamington, passed through here on Tuesday, having been to the Deseret mill, exchanging wheat for flour. He tells us that the year 1914 was a prosperous one for Leamington with abundant fruit and grain crops. Mr. Overson is the owner of a fine quarter section which will be judiciously watered under the new canal.

D. W. Scannell, an enterprising merchant of Lynndyl in company with O. W. Paswaters, the clever postmaster, were in Delta Tuesday, attending to business affairs. They report business a little quiet but are optimistic in their belief that Lynndyl and Delta will expand to such proportions that it will be found convenient to relocate the county seat on the railroad, before long

A. M. McPherson, Field Supt for the Delta Co., made a trip to Salt Lake City, last Friday, to confer with the Idaho-Utah Sugar Co. in rdgard to the contracting of sugar beets in Millard County this year. We understand that he was successful in making the necessary arrangements for a representative of the sugar company to spend several days in Delta, thereby enabling the farmers who desire to contract their beets, a chance to do so.

—HOGS—I will pay highest market price for hogs that ar ready for market, weighing from 165 to 225 pounds. Phone or see me before selling what you have Alb. Leuthaeuser, Delta, Utah.

Sutherland Searchlights

Little Leslie Holdredge is ill with pneumonia.

Miss Agnes Hersliff was a week end visitor at the D. Smith home.

Miss Clara Walker will visit in Oak City, and Leamington the end of this week.

Miss Clara Clark of Woodrow, is employed at the home of Mrs. Ralph Simpkins.

M. M. Steele, Jr. has rented 40 acres to Japs for the cultivation of sugar beets.

M. M. Steele, Jr., and A. L. Simons have phones intsalled in their homes this week.

Mr. and Mrs. A. L. Simons left Monday for Payson, to attend the funeral of Mr. Simon's sister-in-law.

Art Nelson of Salt Lake City, is again seen on the streets of Sutherland. Too bad Art! Five years is a long time to wait, But Mr. Perry says it must be so.

The Atheletic Club is planning to make a base ball diamond on the public square. The ground lately vacated by the E. C. M. I. and taken over by the school trustees will give ample room.

Ross Simpkins of Sutherland, is stepping high—And no wonder when we found out the rea-son why—Mr. Stork had happened nigh—And left a girl to be rocked bye, bye—With big blue eyes and dark brown hair—A plump "nine pounder" fair and square.

Stepping into the store at Sutherland a day or so ago the tho't struck me very forcably as I gazed upon the peeled nose of W. R. Walker that the Roper hands of Baby Walker had already begun to show "Daddy" who is "Boss at our house." But upon inquiry I found to my great surprise that (Win) our real athelete had found his match at the Sutherland wrestling and boxing Club which held their regular meeting the night before.

THE HINCKLEY HAPPENINGS

Farm Demonstrator Welch is home again, after attending the U. A. C. "Round Up."

Earl and Marion Bishop were business visitors to the county seat during the week.

John Jackaway and family have returned to their home in Nevada, after spending the past four months in Hinckley.

Mrs George Paxton has returned to her home in Kanosh, after spending two weeks as the guest of her father, H. F. Stout, Sr.

Roy Webb and family have returned to their home in Oak City, after having spent the greater part of the winter in Hinckley.

Milton Moody left for Salt Lake City on Tuesday. Mr. Moody has had very poor health lately and is going north for medical aid.

Percy Nelson, Wallace Wilkins and Harrison Slaughter left Monday for Callio, Utah, where they have employment for the spring and summer months.

The many friends of Preston Meecham will be pleased to hear that he has so far recovered from a serious attack of pneumonia, to be able to be about the house again.

On Friday, Feb. 12, at 2 p. m. the new presidency of the Relief Society will give a party in honor of the retiring presidency. All members are respectfully invited to be present.

Mrs. Elizabeth Walker left recently for California, where she will remain for sometime visiting with her sister, who lives in Los Angeles. She will also attend the Panama Pacific Exposition.

Our population is steadily in-creasing, Mr. and Mrs. Dean Peterson are the proud parents of a baby girl which arrived Sunday, and Mr. and Mrs James Blake, Jr., are rejoicing over the arrival of a fine baby boy.

Through the courtesy of Wm. Gardner, a three reel photo-play drama entitled "The Star of Bethlehem" was given instead of the regular conjoint M. I. A. programme, last Sunday Evening. The house was filled to capacity and the evening's entertainment was enjoyed by all present.

There was a very large attendance at the Parent's and Teacher's meeting held last Thursday evening. Principal L. A. Stevens gave an interesting talk on "What the High School Expects from the District School." The "Trip Around the World" by Miss Cropper's Fifth Grade was very interesting and was warmly applauded.

Oak City Offerings.

(Jos. H. Christenson, Rep.)

The Seventies conference was held in Oak City, Sunday.

Leroy Webb has returned to his farm east of Oak City.

The baby boy of Eddie Jacobson is reported critically ill.

The Oak City Dramatic Co. put their play on in Oak City last Saturday.

Cliff and Arbie Talbot, students of the Academy, are home visiting with their parents.

Jense. C. Anderson is recovering nicely from a serious illness of two weeks duration.

Jos. A. Lyman has bought the P. N. Neilson store and will consolidate the two stocks, making one good general store for Oak City, hereafter.

The Holden Dramatic Co. put on a play here, on the night of Feb. 3rd, which pleased all present, they performed their parts exceedingly well for ameteurs.

The farmers in this vicinity are rejoicing over the big snowfall of last week, which is an assurance of a sufficient water supply necessary for bounteous crops.

The M. I. A. Dramatic Co. of this place, staged "The Hand of the Law," at Leamington, last Thursday evening, and they were greeted with a large and appreciative audience.

Oak City basket ball team made a trip to Fillmore last Friday and played a game of ball with the High School and were defeated 20 to 36. After the game a grand ball was given.

Several are devoting their time to the poisoning of rabbits these days, and Joseph Anderson says he has killed hundreds in this manner. If there was a bounty placed on these pests, say a sufficient amount to cover on the cost of the poison, more concerted effort would be put forth, and the rabbits would soon be gotten rid of.

Oak City Offerings.

(Jos. H. Christenson, Rep.)

Two horse buyers were in town last week buying work horses.

The biggest snowfall of the season fell here last Friday night.

The Oak City Dramatic Co., at the request of several, re-staged their play Saturday night and a fair sized audience was out to enjoy it.

The Oak City Dramatic Co. put on their play at Holden and report a satisfactory turn out, the proceeds paying them well for their trip.

Clara Walker, who has been at Sutherland for some time, clerking in the Walker & Co. store, is here visiting relatives and admiring friends.

The Stork visited our city February 11th, leaving a fine little girl at the home of Mr. and Mrs. Geo. E. Finlinson. All concerned are reported as doing nicely.

The Sewing Club girls met last Thursday with Ella Carlson, who proved to be a queenly hostess; dainty refreshments were served and all enjoyed the meeting.

A number of the younger folks enjoyed a candy pull at the home of Edna Anderson, Friday night. Games of all kinds afforded entertainment. Edna is a most clever hostess.

Mrs. C. Hartley and Henry Carlson, both of Salt Lake, were visiting relatives and friends last week, they stayed at the home of Franklin Anderson, the greater part of the time.

A number of Delta teams are now at work on the new canal west of town and it looks now as though the canal will be completed as far as Holden in time to irrigate the tributary lands by early spring.

THE HINCKLEY HAPPENINGS

Mr. and Mrs. Thomas A. Ellison have gone to Salt Lake City. While there Mrs. Ellison will undergo an operation.

The family of Frank Webb has been increased by the arrival of a fine baby boy. Mother and child getting along nicely.

Mrs. M. J. Alldredge, one of our oldest and most highly respected citizens, has been very ill for the past week.

Layton Harris of Springville, has spent the past week in Hinckley, the guest of his sister, Mrs. D. A. Morris, Jr.

Mrs. A. A. Hinckley and infant daughter left Friday for Salt Lake City, where they will spend sometime visiting with relatives.

Jacob Felix and family are again located at their residence, after spending the winter in Lynndyl, where Mr. Felix has had employment in the railway yard.

Wilford Welch, one of our district school teachers has been on the sick list. Miss Pearl Mortenson took charge of his school on Thursday and Friday of last week.

The Relief Society party, last Friday in honor of the retiring presidency was a complete success. It was very well attended and a very entertaining program was rendered. Each retiring officer was presented with a token of respect in the form of some useful article. Dainty refreshments were served and all report having enjoyed the afternoon thoroughly.

One of our respected townsmen, Mr. Judd Wilkins, died very suddenly on Sunday last. He had been in poor health for sometime past, but his condition was not regarded as serious. Some years ago he was employed at the Delamar mines and some people are of the opinion that the poison taken into his system while there, was in a large measure responsible for his death. He has been a citizen of this town for the past six years and has always been known as an honest, industrious man. His first wife was Mary Jackaway who died many years ago, leaving a son, Frank, who survives his father. Some years ago he married Mrs. Mary Ann Bagshaw who survives him, together with their three children, Heber, Delia and Mary. Funeral Services were held in the Relief Society Hall on Tuesday and were well attended. The following speakers spoke consolingly to the bereaved: Charles Webb, Richard Parker and Bishop John B. Pratt. A large cortege followed the remains to the Hinckley cemetery, where they were interred.

NEWSY NOTES ABOUT FOLKS

B. E. Cooper was a business visitor to the capital city, the end of last week.

Marion Kilpack was in Oasis, Sunday, paying his regards to one of the most lovely young ladies of that town.

Alb. Leuthauser returned last Thursday, from a trip to Los Angeles, where he had been marketing a load of porkers.

Mrs. H. J. Myers of Abraham, took the train here Tuesday evening, for Salt Lake City, to visit friends and do some necessary shopping.

Mrs. Laura Furrer, of Woodrow, left Saturday for Salt Lake, where she expects to remain for a couple of weeks, to receive treatment from a specialist, for ailments peculiar to her sex.

Uncle Jim Melville spent Saturday and Sunday with relatives in the Lake, returning Monday, in order that he might put his shoulder to the wheel in making arrangments for the Round Up, next week.

Mr. and Mrs. J. O. Wilkins were called to Hinckley, Sunday morning, Mr. Wilkin's brother, Jud, having passed away early Sunday morning. Interment is to take place today. Our heart goes out in sympathy to the bereaved relatives in this intance.

In response to a telegram conveying the information that her mother was seriously ill, last Saturday night, Mrs. Geo. Meinhardt of Sutherland, took the train Sunday morning for Franklin, Iowa, to render such care and assistance as a dutiful daughter could to aid a stricken mother.

Abraham Gibson, a newspaper man of Nephi, was a Delta visitor Sunday. Mr. Gibson said that he had heard so many flattering reports of the greater delta country; that he had concluded to see it with his own eyes. It goes without saying that he was highly impressed with Delta's past, present and future.

The U. S. Weather Bureau issued for January gives the snowfall in West Millard County during January, as 14 inches, while at Fillmore, a trifle less than 7 inches was reported. Oak City averaged slightly over 15 inches and Scipio a fraction over 16 inches. The precipitation during the same month is given as 1 to 2 inches, varying considerable in the different localities of the county.

Mr. Lant, representing the Utah-Idaho Sugar Co. of Salt Lake City, is spending the week here, contracting with the farmers for the planting and marketing of sugar beets. Several of the settlers have already called upon Mr. Lant at the Delta Co. office and made arrangements to grow beets this year. We will endeavor to ascertain for next week's issue, the total acreage contracted.

Following a precipitations of approximately 2 inches on Wednesday and Thursday, a 3 inch snowfall fell here, Thursday night of last week. It looks as though February was trying to out do the month of January both in rainfall and snowfall. Our cement sidewalks are appreciated more than ever before just at present, but the crossings are not kept as clean as they should be.

Little Miss Ruth Cottrell celebrated her fifth birthday Saturday, March 13th, from 2 to o'clock. The little guests enjoyed the occasion in playing childish games and were treated to refreshments consisting of egg and peanut-butter sandwiches, bananas and whipped-cream, cake and cocoa, also one individual box of fancy candy. Little Ruth received several nice presents from her little guests.

Peter Hauman left Saturday for Idaho, where he will make his home for a time at least. Peter did not put forth the necessary efforts to make a successful farmer, he devoted the most of his time, so we are informed by nearby neighbors, in finding fault with the country and everything in general; otherwise he was a very good citizen, even if he did leave the country without paying what he owed the printer for the Chronicle.

Thirty-five ladies of the Relief Society of the Delta Ward, with about half as many babies in their arms, together with basket after basket of good, wholesome 'chuckaway,' loaded themselves into a hayrack Monday morning and rode out to the home of Mr. J. M. Rigby, two miles south of town; despite the fearful muddy roads, and gave Mrs. Rigby a unexpected, yet happy surprise. After stowing away a huge dinner, a nice program and social converse afforded entertainment for the remainder of the afternoon.

Millard County Chronicle
February 25, 1915

Oak City Offerings.

(Jos. H. Christenson, Rep.)

Mrs. Lamiah Rawlinson is visiting her daughter at Joseph.

Edna Anderson is visiting her friend, Miss Shuttle of Lynndyl.

Lem Roper is on the sick list, having been confined to his room with rheumatism.

J. Lee Anderson and Joshua Finlinson are attending the two Panama Exposition in California.

The Stork visited the Sparksman home, leaving a nice baby girl. All concerned doing nicely.

Cliff and Arby Talbot returned last week, to resume their work at the M. S. A., after a week's visit with home folks.

Jas. Overson of Leamington, has taken a contract on the new canal. The main force is now working two miles west of Oak City.

Joseph Neilson and Charley Williams of Leamington, passed through here on his way to do some contract work on the new canal.

The Misses Margret and Zella Neilson, Students of the M.S.A., spent a few days visiting home folks. They were accompanied by Clemont Dutson.

Miss Edna Anderson entertained the Young Ladies' Sewing Club at a Chicken Supper, Tuesday evening, which was heartily relished by all present.

THOMAS HOOK DIED THURSD'Y

Thomas Hook of this city, died Thursday, February 18th, at 7 o'clock, after suffering one year with Brights desease and other complications, which had confined him to his bed for eight montht. The Death Angle came giving him relief from his sufferings in the presence of his wife and children and a number of his intimate friends, beckoning him to a brighter shore, where the ravages of desease and earthly troubles are not known. He had lived such a life that he was ready to meet the Master of all things willingly and uncomplainingly; he had realized that there was no chance for his recovery sometime ago, yet he had remained cheerful to the last, in the thought that all would be well over there.

Thomas Hook was born at Tooele, Jan. 22nd, 1868, where he grew to manhood: in the year 1896 he was united in marriage to Miss Eliza Smith of that city, and to this union three daughters were born. In the year 1904 with his family he moved to Canada, returning in 1906 and locating at Holden. He was one of the first to locate on the Melville project in the year 1908, after assisting in the work of constructing the Uba dam the two years before.

The deceased was a gentleman in every sense that term would imply; he was industrious, persevering; honest with himself and his fellowmen; he was prompt in meeting his obligations at all times; had a kind word of cheer for everyone; provided well for his family and was held in the highest esteem by all acquaintances.

Mr. Hook had professed Christianity when a mere boy and had lived as a faithful, consistent Christian to the last, and was a member of the Church of the Delta Ward. He leaves behind to mourn his departure his wife, three daughters and five sisters, besides many friends and neighbors.

Funeral services occured at the Ward hall, Saturday at 2 o'clock p.m., the speakers were Abraham S. Workman, Jr., Levi H. McCullough, Mell Workman and Edgar Jeffery, all of whom spoke in the highest terms of the deceased and offered comforting words to the bereaved wife and children. The remains were burried in the Delta cemetery following the services.

THE HINCKLEY HAPPENINGS

Milton Moody left Tuesday for Heber City, where he will look after some business.

Clark Bishop, who was operated on for appendicitis in a Salt Lake Hospital last week, is reported as recovering rapidly.

Mrs. Della Bagshaw and two children arrived here Sunday from Salt Lake City, to join Mr. Bagshaw. The family intend making their home in Hinckley.

Preston Meecham, who was recovering from a severe attack of pneumonia is again confined to his bed. His daughter, May of Grantsville, arrived Sunday, to help nurse her father back to health.

Last Saturday, The Parent's Class gave a social in the gymnasium to all the married folks in the town. The afternoon was spent in listening to a program, eating refreshments and dancing.

A large audience assembled in the Academy auditorium Monday, to hear Dr. Widtsoe, but on account of the roads being in such a bad condition he was unable to reach here, so after listening to excellent piano duets by Prof. Brook and Miss Mercy Blackburn, those assembled adjourned to the gymnasuim, where a dancing matinee was enjoyed until 12:30 p. m. At three p. m. a large crowd again assembled to see the M. I. A. scout team win in a basket ball game from the Academy team, by a margin of ten points.

NEWSY NOTES ABOUT FOLKS

J. Avery Bishop was a Salt Lake City, visitor, the forepart of the week.

H. B. Prout, A. M. McPherson and Fred Cottrell were visitors to Salt Lake City, Tuesday.

Miss Amy Wilkins has returned from a two weeks visit with admiring friends at Cedar City.

Mrs. Myrtle Meneary of Milford, is here this week, visiting relatives and attending the Round Up.

Fred Keim, has returned here for the summer, having spent the winter months with relatives in Colorado.

Mrs. Jas. A. Melville is down from Salt Lake, this week, participating in the festivities of Round Up week.

Miss Lottie Burger of Lynndyl is the guest of Miss Marie Kelley this week, enjoying the festivities of the Round Up.

Mrs. Wm. F. Osterling left Wednesday, for a three weeks visit with relatives and former neighbors in Los Angeles.

Born to Mr. and Mrs. Noah Rogers of Deseret, on Feb. 15, a twelve pound baby girl. Dr. W. B. Hamilton of Milford in attendance.

Chris Beck is down from his claim near Mills, this week, taking in the Round Up and visiting friends. Chris has a good dryland farm up there.

Dr. Mason of Chicago, who had been in California for sometime, arrived here Monday, for a brief visit with his sister-in-law, Mrs. W. T. Mason and nephew, Robert, out at Abraham.

A letter received from S. C. McCormick of Los Angeles, informs us that he expects to move to his forty acre farm near Woodrow, the first of March. His arrival will be gladly welcomed by the good people of that locality.

Jack Childers has been employed at the Hub, the past week, arranging the stock and marking new goods. Jack has had considerable experience as a merchant and has succeeded in getting the stock nicely and conveniently arranged at the Hub.

R. R. Betz of Oasis, spent Monday in Delta, attending to business matters and extending the glad hand to his many friends. Betz is a congenial fellow, always happy and smiling, and is liked universally by his acquaintances.

The information has been tipped off to the publisher, that R. H. Becknell and family, who are now at Minersville, will again take up their residence at Delta, along the first of March sometime. They are fine people, and their many friends will warmly welcome their return.

Banker Frank Beckwith was with his family in Salt Lake from Saturday till Tuesday, celebrating Washington's birthday. Frank has never been accused of being more honest than Washington, but if he isn't on the square with his fellowmen, the printer hasn't heard to the contrary.

Miss Mae Huntsman entertained the O.Z.O. Club at the Delta Bakery, Monday night. A very pleasant evening was spent in reading, sewing and social converse. Later in the evening, a delicious lunch was served, and the remainder of the evening was spent in singing and a jolly good time was had.

A card received from H. E. Hunt at Anaheim, Cal., conveys the information that he has disposed of his farm immediately north of Delta to Mr. H. L. Haverland of that place; he will move up and take up his residence soon thereon. Mr. Hunt adds that Mr. Haverland is a good substantial farmer and will be a credit to the vicinity.

David Rosenbaum of Brigham, arrived here Wednesday, to remain on his good farm on the South Tract for a number of weeks and make final proof. He has forty acres to fall wheat and it is looking fine. Mr. Rosenbaum is going to rent his farm to a man from Brigham, the coming year, who will move down in the very near future.

Geo. W. Nixon and H. B. Johnson, two of Holden's good and influential citizens, are here this week, attending the Round Up and greeting friends. They are both of the opinion that Uncle Sam should order all American merchant vessels and other ships home, place an embargo on all exports, and thereby diminish the food supply of the warring nations to such an extent as to make them clamor for peace. If all the neutral countries would take action in this manner, there is no question but what the belligerents would soon adjust their difficulties by the hunger route.

Millard County Chronicle
March 4, 1915

Oak City Offerings.

(Jos. H. Christenson, Rep.)

Miss Edna Anderson has returned from her visit in Lynndyl.

A number of our young people attended the Round Up at Delta, last week.

Every one enjoyed the dance given here on Washington's birthday.

John E. and Lorenzo Lovell made a business trip to Fillmore, last week.

Jos. Lyman left for his home in Mayfield, last week, to the bedside of his sick wife.

J. Lee Anderson and Joshua Finlinson have returned from their trip to California.

Messrs. Smith and Warren of Fillmore, are here doing some work for Mrs. A. Lyman.

Sunday night Joshua Finlinson gave a very entertaining lecture on his trip, which was enjoyed by all.

The Sewing Club Girls met last Thursday with Louis Anderson. Dainty refreshments were served after sewing time was over.

The many friends of Sister Robinson are glad to see her cheerful face with us once more. She is the guest of Mrs. Anne Lyman.

Sutherland Searchlights

Ward Robinson and family were visiting at Hinckley, this week.

Mrs. Della Lisonbee is preparing to move on to her ranch soon as spring arrives.

Alva Tanner recently returned from a visit with homefolks at Grantsville, Utah.

Bert Johnson is buying enough marketable hogs to make a shipment of two cars for Thursday.

Born to Mr. and Mrs. Jesse Hultz on February 25th, a fine baby girl. All concerned doing nicely.

Joseph Ayers is again brightening up Sutherland with his sunny smile, after a stay in the mountains.

Mr. Crosland and family have moved from the Bert Johnson farm on to Ackerman's place, where he has employment for the season.

A number of people from this vicinity attended the Round Up at Delta, all reporting it as being very beneficial; a much better attendance would have been present had the weather permitted.

Owing to whooping cough and colds being so prevalent, the entertainment planned for Washington's birthday was postponed indefinitely. Social life is very dull, but it will brighten-up with more favorable weather.

THE HINCKLEY HAPPENINGS

Mrs. Mary E. Stout is reported as being very sick.

J. F. Brumund has traded his Studebaker automobile to Will Taylor of Abraham.

Mr. Amy Elkington of Tooele, is the guest of her parents, Mr. and Mrs. Carson Draper.

Milton Moody spent Saturday and Sunday here with his family. He returned to Heber City, Monday.

Last Saturday afternoon the Primary Association entertained all the little folks of the town at a dancing matinee.

Mrs. Allen Stout left recently for ElPaso, Texas, for an extended visit with her parents, who are Mexican refugees, residing at that place.

Mrs. Ella Meecham has returned to her home in Lynndyl, after spending a few days at the home of her parents, Mr. and Mrs. Jacob Langston.

Next Saturday evening the local home dramatic club will present the play entitled, "The Little Savage." The proceeds for the benifit of the Ward organizations.

On Monday and Tuesday nearly all of our most public spirited citizens turned out in full force to repair the sidewalks. This makes the town look much better and makes it easier to walk from one part of the town to another.

NEWSY NOTES ABOUT FOLKS

Jeff Clark of Woodrow, made a business trip to Salt Lake, last Thursday evening, returning Saturday night.

Jack Sly and Charles Sampson, both residents of the South Tract, are crowing over the arrival of new born sons at their homes. All concerned reported as getting along well.

S. W. Eccles, one of our live and energetic merchants was transacting business matters in Salt Lake and Ogden, the past week, leaving for those points last Thursday night and returning today.

Miss Carrie Leigh entertained the O. Z. O. Club at her apartments at the Dunsmore, Monday evening. A jolly good time was had after the business meeting by playing cards and eating delicious home-made candies served by the hostess.

Joseph Nielson, one of the desirable and progressive farmers of Hinckley, was a visitor here, Monday. He attended the Round Up last week and said he gained much knowledge that would be both useful and profitable to him in his farming duties.

L. E. Perrine of Los Angeles, is here looking after his farming interests out on the bench, and will probably remain throughout the spring and summer, till his bumper wheat crop is harvested at any rate. He will make some improvements on his ranch also.

L. F. Kimball, a young man of Los Angeles, Cal., has arrived here to take charge of his father's 40 acre ranch, near Sugarville, for the summer, intending to make some extensive and permanent improvements thereon, as soon as the weather and road conditions will permit.

J. W. Evans, Jr., out on the south tract, is keeping up with the procession in the way of increasing the population of Millard. A dandy, big fisted, nine pound boy arrived at his home Thursday night, Feb. 25th. Mother and child are reported as doing nicely. Dr. Broaddus was in attendance.

J. J. King of Pasadena, Cal., was here the end of last week, looking at ranch property for which he was considering trading California property. He was non-communicative upon being approached as to his decision about the trade, but thought this was a coming country, so far as he could judge by observation.

F. E. Sanders of Oasis, was a visitor in our city, Monday. He has resigned as manager of the Baker Lbr. Co. at Oasis and expects to engage in the business on his own hook, as he expressed himself, in the very near future; intending to deal directly with the mills in furnishing lumber and building material to the trade.

J. H. Allison, the master carpenter of West Millard, has completed the plans and specifications for the large new building to be erected at Woodrow. By employing Mr. Allison to do the work thereon, the owners of the new building, are aware of the fact that the construction will be satisfactory, workmanship first-class and the charges nominal.

W. G. Crum arrived the end of last week with a car of his belongings to become a permanent resident on his eighty acre ranch out on the bench east of this city. He comes from California and we are informed that he was recently married to an Ogden girl. We bid them a most hearty welcome, and believe and hope they will realize to their fullest expectations in this favored locality.

THE HINCKLEY HAPPENINGS

Jesse Stott of Meadow was a business visitor to our town last week.

Milton Moody returned home Sunday from a business trip to Salt Lake City.

The people of this place have been highly entertained the past week by four good dramas.

Arthur Reeve has been appointed Post master at this place and has already entered upon his duties in that capacity.

Roland Curtis is home again after spending the winter in Provo where he took advantage of the B. Y. U. midwinter term.

The family of Edwin Workman has been increased by the arrival of a baby. Mother and child are reported as progressing rapidly.

That the population of our town is steadily increasing was shown last Sunday when four infants were blessed in Sacrament meeting.

Jacob H. Langton and daughter, Tressa are spending a few days in Lynndyl this week as the guests of Mr. and Mrs. Leonard Meechum.

The Hinckley Dramatic Company played to a very large audience Saturday evening. The play was a military drama, "The Little Savage."

Quite a number of Hinckley people attended the wedding reception given in honor of Mr. and Mrs. Hyrum Maxfield in Deseret last Thursday evening.

Miss Reva Hunt is again at the home of her Grandfather, Willis E. Robison, after spending several months in Richfield with her uncle, Berry Robison.

Mrs. Neils Christenson is now in Salt Lake City where she was recently operated on for appendicitis. All the townspeople are interested in her and hope for her immediate recovery.

The many friends of Mrs. Thomas A. Ellison and of Clark Bishop will be pleased to learn that both have so far recovered from recent operations in Salt Lake City hospitals, as to be able to return to their homes where they are rapidly regaining their strength.

Mr. and Mrs. Claude Tripp and their children, Vera and Harold, arrived Monday from Calio, Utah for an extended visit with Mrs. Tripp's parents, Mr. and Mrs. Fred Wilkins. Mr. Tripp left Tuesday for Salt Lake City he will spend a few days attending to business affairs.

Monday evening the Walters Company presented "The Country Girl." It was well played and well liked by all. The parts of the Country Girl and her aged father were exceptionally rendered by Miss Bunzell and Mr. Cosgrave. On Tuesday evening the same troupe played the temperance drama "Ten Nights in a Bar Room" with good success.

Everyone here is enjoying the delightful spring weather, all are glad that the mud is fast disappearing, and the farmers are taking advantage of the pleasant days to begin their farm work for another season. Many of the citizens are doing spring cleaning about their premises which makes the homes more comfortable and gives the town a more tidy appearance.

Abraham Articles.

Mrs. Ed Soules visited with Mrs. Cavanaugh, Sunday.

Wallace Black has a large class taking lessons on the violin.

Joseph Fullmer is much improved from a recent illness.

The Needle Craft Club met with Mrs. R. T. Patterson, this week.

The industrious farmers of Abraham are beginning to till the soil.

E. H. Biehler and wife were the guests of W. J. Cary and family, Sunday.

Mrs. Ed Soules of Salt Lake is here visiting her brother, Ora Lake and family.

Mr. and Mrs. Pete Christenson of Deseret were Abraham visitors the first of the week.

The members of the orchestra were entertained at the home of O. L. Lake, Sunday evening.

The Abraham Dramatic Club put on a good play Monday evening. The specialties were fine and enjoyed by all.

Mr. and Mrs. Sherrick gave a taffy pulling Friday night which was much enjoyed by the young people of Abraham.

Mr. and Mrs. H. E. Sherrick entertained Mr. and Mrs. Jeff Clark and Mr. and Mrs. Clyde Underhill of Woodrow at Sunday dinner.

NEWSY NOTES ABOUT FOLKS

Mrs. Luther Buchanan presented her husband with a bouncing baby girl, last Sunday.

Mrs. Aller, wife of Agent Aller of the local station, left Sunday morning for a visit at Salt Lake City.

Jas. A. Melville was down from Salt Lake this week looking after business affairs and shaking hands with his many friends.

Mrs. Emery Peterson entertained at her home, last week, in honor of her husband's birthday. A short program, games and a dainty luncheon was enjoyed by all present.

Homer G. Busenbark, former editor of the Chronicle, and family, left Monday morning for Raton, New Mexico where they expect to reside in the future. He contemplates the purchase of a paper at the place mentioned.

Wm. Pratt and M. J. Moody were over from Hinckley Monday soliciting ads for the Millard Stake Academy 1915 Year Book. The year book is always a beautiful piece of work and a good advertisement for the school and surrounding country.

Robert Allison, brother of Jim Allison, one of Delta's enthusiastic citizens, came in the first of the week from his home in Chicago for a visit with his brother and to get a little western ozone which he realizes will be good for his constitution after his long city residence. Incidently he is looking for a better place than the city in which to live and will no doubt locate here in time.

Mr. F. W. Stout, the enterprising manager of the Studebaker Co., we notice has been busy this week caring for a full car of wagons and buggies the company has just delivered to the local establishment. This looks like the Studebaker people had unbounded faith in the prosperity of "The Delta" country and this is the largest single consignment of wagons and buggies ever shipped to this part of the country by the company.

The H. G. L. Girls held their first meeting, Tuesday night, at the home of Miss Mae Hoyt. The name was decided upon and a number of other business matters attended to. The girls also got a good start in their embroidery work and "finished up" a pan of popcorn which was prepared by the hostess. They are a jolly good "bunch" and will make a success of their Club.

Spring time is coming on. Clean up the house and get your wall paper at the Delta Furniture Store. 43-2t.

A fire occured in the big Huntsman department store at Fillmore early Wednesday morning of last week. Indications point to its having started from coals falling from the stove. The fire was quickly extinguished after being discovered but damages to the extent of $75,000 is said to have resulted, caused mostly by water. It is not known here whether or not the loss is covered by insurance but it is presumed it is.

HOGS—I will pay highest market price for hogs that are ready for market, weighing from 165 to 225 pounds. Phone or see me before selling what you have. Alb. Leuthaeuser, Delta, Utah.

Mr. and Mrs. F. L. Copening and Mr. John E. Steele left today for Los Angeles and 'Frisco where they will take in the fairs. Frank took an arm load of "Delta Country" literature along with him and proposes to let more of the out side world learn of the good things to be found in this "neck-o'-the-woods."

The Foster Funk residence in the southern part of town has been sold to R. H. Becknell, watermaster for the Delta Land & Water Co. Mr. Becknell has been here long enough to thoroughly size up conditions and has reached the conclusion that this place will do to tie to and reiterates his faith by the purchase and determination to reside here permanently.

Suits cleaned and pressed 75c. and up; 1 suit a week for month at contract price of $2.00. Suits called for and delivered in city. All work guaranteed satisfactory or money refunded.—A. L. Broderick, on Clark St. 41-4t

Hinckley.

Everyone here is enjoying the delightful spring weather. All are glad that the mud is fast disappearing, and the farmers are taking advantage of the pleasant days to begin their farm work for another season. Many of the citizens are doing spring cleaning about their premises which makes the homes more comfortable and gives the town a better appearance.

Mr. Milton Moody returned home Sunday from a business trip to Salt Lake City.

The many friends of Mrs. Thomas A. Ellison and of Olark Bishop will be pleased to learn that both have so far recovered from recent operations in Salt Lake City hospitals to be able to return to their homes where they are rapidly regaining their strength.

Mr. and Mrs. Olaude Tripp and their children, Vera and Harold arrived here Monday from Onlio, Utah for an extended visit with Mrs. Tripp's parents, Mr. and Mrs. Fred W. Wilkins. Mr. Tripp left Tuesday for Salt Lake City where he will spend a few days attending to business affairs.

Mrs. Neils Christenson is now in Salt Lake City where she was recently operated on for appendicitis. All the towns people are interested in her and hope for her immediate recovery.

The family of Edwin Workman has been increased by the arrival of a baby. Mother and child are reported as progressing rapidly.

That the population of our town is steadily increasing was shown last Sunday when four infants were blessed in Sacrament meeting.

Mr. Arthur Reeve has been appointed Postmaster at this place and has already entered upon his duties in that capacity.

Quite a number of Hinckley people attended the wedding reception given in honor of Mr. and Mrs. Hyrum Maxfield in Deseret last Thursday evening.

Mr. Jacob H. Langston and daughter Tressa are spending a few days in Lynndyl this week as the guests of Mr. and Mrs. Lenard Mucham.

Mr. Roland Ourtis is home again after spending the winter in Provo where he took advantage of the B. Y. U. midwinter term.

Miss Reva Hunt is again at the home of her grandfather. Willis E. Robison, after spending several months in Richfield, with her uncle, Berry Robison.

Mr. Jesse Stott of Meadow was a business visitor to our town last week.

The people of this place have been highly entertained the past week by four good dramas.

The Junior Class of the Millard Academy presented the lively college comedy called "Aaron Boggs, Freshman" and pleased everyone with their splendid rendition of the play. Their work was very good for amateurs.

The Hinckley Dramatic Company played to a very large audience Saturday evening. The play was a military drama, "The Little Savage."

Monday evening the Walters Company presented, "The Country Girl." It was well played and well liked by all. The parts of the Country Girl and her aged father were exceptionally well rendered by Miss Bunzell and Mr. Cosgrave.

On Tuesday evening the same troupe played the temperance drama, "Ten Nights in a Bar Room," with good success.

DELTA.

Mrs. Ingersoll and children from American Fork are visiting her parents Mr. and Mrs. N. S. Bishop.

There has been a new 25 piece band organized here the past week.

The Christian Scien. Church was organized here a ek ago last Sunday and will hold services in The Mission Chapel at 2:30 every Sunday afternoon.

L. Anderson of Riverside, California, arrived here Friday morning for the purpose of attending to his farm which is located on the North Tract.

W. G. Norris of Los Angeles is looking over the Delta Project for the purpose of purchasing a farm.

Alex Melville, Atty., made a business trip to Delta the latter part of last week.

W. I. Moody, Jr. and wife arrived from Los Angeles, Cal., Thursday morning where they had been attending to business matters of the Company. Mr. Moody has charge of the new hotel recently completed on the North Tract.

J. H. Baker of the Baker Lumber Company was here the latter part of the past week.

Mrs. J. W. Winterrose of Heber City is here attending to business concerning her town property and visiting friends.

James A. Melville returned from a business trip to Salt Lake City Sunday morning.

Nephi A. Anderson of Salt Lake City arrived the latter part of the past week with two land seekers Edgar G. Johnston and Gen. S. Burt both of Ogden and succeeded in selling both parties.

F. L. Copening and wife left here last week to visit the fairs at San Diego and San Francisco, California. John E. Steele accompanied them.

Sam Dorrity, Sheriff, was here on business last week.

Mrs. William Osterling returned from Los Angeles, Cal. Saturday morning where she has been visiting relatives and friends.

Messrs. Roy Cowan salesman for the Simms Utah Grocery Co. and Pob Elto salesman for the McPonald Candy Co., made a business call on the merchants Saturday.

Oasis.

We are having most beautiful spring weather at present and the roads are dry again after being wet and muddy for so long.

Whooping cough and mumps are still raging and new cases of both these diseases are developing every day, there are at present about 45 cases of whooping cough and 20 cases of mumps.

Walter, the 8 year old son of Mr. and Mrs. David Rutherford, who has been very ill with leakage of the heart and whooping cough is very much improved at this writing.

Geo. Jensen is confined to his bed with an attack of rheumatism but we hope he will soon be out again.

The Millard Lumber Co. is building a sample room to display their vehicles and machinery. This indicates prosperity with the company and we wish them success.

The Deseret Irrigation Company are changing one of their main canals leading to Deseret the old one not being large enough to carry the needed supply of water now used in that section of the the country owing to the many new farms being cultivated south and southwest of Deseret.

A little 6 year old boy of Mr. and Mrs. Charley Thompson is seriously ill and but little hope is entertained for his recovery He is suffering from pneumonia and whooping cough.

The angel of death visited the home of Mr. and Mrs. Earl Blackburn and took from them their little six weeks old baby boy. The cause of the death of this little one was whooping cough which turned to pneumonia. The funeral services was held at the Ward meeting house Sunday afternoon at one o'clock. Beautiful and appropriate music was rendered by the Ward Choir. And consoling remarks was made by Bishop John Styler, Joseph Damron Sr., and R. L. Woodward. Burrial was in the Oasis cemetary.

LEAMINGTON.

(Concluded from last week.)

Fool creek flat, Oak City Whiskey creek, Holden and on Fillmore, Meadow, and Kanosh whirled over good road on land already raising crops to his liking. No wonder country booming has not been successful in this County when it is a well known fact that the first impression is always most lasting, and it never will be, till methods are changed for inviting the stranger to our land. You gave us a broad hint in a recent issue of your paper that the R. R. officials were considering going to the east side, not through the mud but from Leamington, and in the mean time if the mail service was from the same place, developing a long line of country producing traffic and tonage would and will be the means of inducing the building of a road to the east side. Let's all get together on this proposition of putting the mail service on a substantial road before another muddy season finds similar or worse condition existing than those just past.

THE HINCKLEY HAPPENINGS

Milton Moody is in the State Capital again looking after business interests.

Walter Bagshaw has gone out west where he has been employed to shear sheep.

Mr. J. J. Spendlove has moved from the residence of L. R. Cropper, Jr., to the home of James P. Terry.

Born to Mr. and Mrs. Samuel T. Webb on March 29th a fine baby girl. Dr. C. A. Broaddus attending.

Mrs. Chas. Burke left Monday evening for Provo where she will spend a week as the guest of her mother, Mrs. Mary E. Peterson.

Mrs. Thomas Talbot, Sr. and Mrs. Thomas Talbot, Jr. of Oak City, spent a few days last week as the guests of Mr. and Mrs. George Talbot.

Bishop and Mrs. A. Y. Stephenson and Mr. and Mrs. Chas. Wood came down from Holden by automobile last Saturday and returned Sunday.

Principal and Mrs. L. A. Stevens are rejoicing over the arrival of a baby boy at their home on March 30th. Both mother and infant are progressing nicely.

Miss Sylvia Christensen of Oak City has returned to her home after spending the past three weeks in Hinckley, caring for the family of her brother Neils, during the recent illness of his wife.

Mr. and Mrs. J. H. Langston and daughter, Sarah, have returned from Lynndyl. They have decided not to move to their farm at that place for the summer but to stay in Hinckley.

Mr. and Mrs. Robt. E. Robinson pleasantly entertained a number of their friends at their home Monday evening. The evening was spent in parlor games and toothsome viands were served.

It is announced that the M. I. A. meet of the Deseret Stake will be held in Hinckley on April 30th and May 1st. Besides the regular events there will be a contest in Dramatics and athletic events between the scout patrols.

Quarterly conference of the Deseret Stake was held here last Saturday and Sunday. The conference was very largely attended, there being six hundred and thirty eight present at the Sunday afternoon session. All the people had a spiritual treat in listening to the timely and inspiring sermons delivered by Apostles Grant and McMurrin and Elders, Wm. A. Morton and Oscar Kirkham.

The Scouts of the Hinckley Ward took their first hike last Friday. The spillway grove was the place selected for the camp and forty eight, boys, carrying their bedding and provisions, under the direction of Scout Master, A. I. Tippits, left Hinckley on Friday afternoon. Mr. Oscar Kirkham, who has all the Scout work in charge, visited the scouts in camp and complimented them very highly on their work. The whole affair went off without a hitch and all who made the trip declare they had the time of their lives.

Sutherland Searchlights

Our roads are fine now. Come out and try them.

Geo. Billings was a buisness visitor here Tuesday.

The Jolly Stitchers will meet with Mrs. Boardman this week.

Tom Moulton, of Heber City, is spending the spring with his brother, Lyman Moulton.

Mr. Mason of Abraham has been in our town several days of the past week attending to business.

Mr. Simeon Walkor of Oak City and Mrs. Von of Salt Lake City, were Sutherland visitors last Monday.

The epidemic of whooping cough that has been in our midst is about a thing of the past now. The health of the people seems to be fine.

A number of people from here attended the conference at Hinckley last Saturday and Sunday and report having had a splendid time.

M. M. Steele, Jr., is spending considerable time as a real estate booster lately. Goes whizzing by in his auto quite often with prospective land buyers.

The repairing of the canals seems to have been completed around Sutherland and the force of men under Geo. Smith have been moved farther north.

Ben Bunker, of Delta, who has spent the winter in Dixie and who just returned from a trip to the fair at San Francisco was looking after buisness and visiting with his sister Mrs. W. R. Walker, of Sutherland, Monday.

Mr. E. L. Abbott recently purchased forty acres of land of a Mr. Sorenson of Sevier Co. Mr. Abbott is delighted with acquiring such a good piece of land in what he considers the most desirable portion of the north tract.

We learn that the Holdredge and Hayes farms are about to change hands. We hardly understand why these very desirable citizens are anxious to leave us, but if they do we certainly hope they will leave as good neighbors and men in the community as they have been.

The Abraham school boys came over last Friday and played a game of basket ball with Sutherland school boys, which resulted in a victory for our boys, after which a game between the school girls and a team of outside girls was played, but the outside team didn't even have a look in with the big husky school girls we have. Report are of how severe Mr. Barney is in insisting on his pupils putting forth good efforts at their studies, but he certainly has not weakened them physically at all.

Deseret Doings.

Lucile Damron has the mumps.

The youngsters are still whooping it up.

Edgar Petty will leave for Lynndyl on April 1st.

Dr. Conkling is doing a rushing buisness in the dental line.

A good many of our people attended Conference at Hinckley.

Elmer Petty and wife have moved to their ranch on the bogs.

George Kelly and wife of Lynndyl were visitors in town this week.

Bruder, the great magician performs at the A. C. Nelson school Monday night.

Oscar Kirkham of Salt Lake gave a splendid lecture on Boy Scout work on Saturday evening.

Peter Christensen has gone to Salt Lake to secure medical aid. He has been ailing for some time.

Mrs. Woodward has recovered from her serious illness and leaves to visit relatives in Northern towns on Wednesday.

Mr. Edwards of the Inter-Mountain Insurance Co., is in town doing buisness in connection with their local agent, T. B. Allerd.

Oak City Offerings.

(Jos. H. Christenson, Rep.)

T. C. Lyman has retuned from his trip to Delta.

Mrs. F. Anderson is on the sick list at this writing.

B. L. Robins from Scipio, the range rider, was seen again in our midst.

A. Hansen from Mills was visiting with Miss E. Carlson last Sunday.

A large attendance of our people spent Conference at Hinckley Saturday the 27th.

Alvin Lyman and his brother Alton from Mayfield are here visiting friends and relatives.

Mr. Evans of Nephi, repersenting the Consolidoted W. and M. Co. was in town again last week.

Mr. J. Aldridge has been spending some time at Lemington, working for Mr. J. Finlinson.

Farm work is on in full blast in our vicinity. It looks as if spring had come to stay this time.

Miss Frankie Roper has returned home from Nephi where she was getting some dental work done.

Last Tuesday some of our young ladies spent the afternoon with Mrs. Ethel Lundahl, to do some sewing for her.

The sewing club girls met last Friday afternoon with Belva Lovell. A very delicious luncheon was served after sewing.

Mr. J. E. Lovell received a wrench in his back while working on his farm and has been unable to be out for a few days.

Mr. Lem Roper is still in a bad condition. He was taken to Delta last week to see the Dr. We wish for him a speedy recovery.

J. D. Smith from Fillmore was here the past week visiting friends and old acquaintances, also attending to his drummer buisness.

LeRoy Walker is going into the hog buisness right. He has now purchased some thorobred stuff and expects to make a success along that line.

The Oak City B. B. team went to Leamington Friday night the 26th and found their mates at last, Leamington winning the game 29 to 20. Now boys cheer up and see it through. You'll get 'em yet.

Friday night the Oak City boy scouts gave an entertainment showing some of their work, after which a big dance followed. All present had a good time. A number of the scouts received their pins.

Leslie Booth, while riding a horse the other day met with an accident. The horse became frightened and ran away, turning a corner too fast to keep his balance. The horse fell at full speed and the rider struck on his shoulder. He is still unable to be around.

Delta Young Couple Marry

Miss Amy Wilkins and Mr. Ernest Pierce left this morning for Salt Lake City where they will be married in the Mormon Temple tomorrow. After their marriage the young couple will go to Carbon county for a short visit with the groom's mother, after which they will take up their residence on the E. W. Jeffery ranch a mile and a half south of Delta, where the groom has been employed for the past three years.

The bride is one of Delta's estimable young ladies who has resided in Delta for some years past and who has been an efficient employee of the Chronicle office for the past year.

The groom is an industrous and pains-taking young man of sterling worth, and a trusted employee of Mr. Jeffery.

Our best wishes for a long and happy wedded life go with them.

Born:—To Mr. and Mrs. F. W. Cottrell Wennesday morning a brand new girl.

Woodrow Writings.

Henry Volhart is occupying his new home in Woodrow.

The "Willing Wives of Woodrow" will meet at Dr. Tracy's as usual. A full attendance is requested.

John Barnett was given a surprise party last week, and a general good time was enjoyed by all present.

The regular monthly meeting of the Water Users' Association will be held in Woodrow Saturday, April 3rd, at 8:00 p.m.

Mrs. Laura Furrer who has returned from a hospital in Salt Lake, greatly improved in health is receiving greetings from her friends.

S. H. Thompson and Jerome Tracy, representing the Water Users' Association, took a trip to Ogden and Salt Lake City last week.

The hummer Dramatic Association will make their debut in for Delta, Friday, p.m. We hope as cordial a reception in the sister town as they were at home.

A. N. Wright and wife who have been spending the summer in California, have returned home with their new baby and are heartily greeted by all their friends.

Special Easter services will be held by the Woodrow Sunday School next Sunday. The Parents of the children are especially requested to attend. Services at 10:30 a. m.

Mrs. Rural Wright met with a painful accident last week by running the tine of a pitchfork in her foot. Symptoms of blood poisoning developed but were quickly under control.

The genial tax assessor, Mr. Rapelye of Kanosh, has been visiting Woodrow the past week. We are glad to see him every spring even if we are compelled to pay for his visit in the fall.

Roy Jones has gone away for several days and we have excellent authority for the statement that he will return home with a better half. Mr. Jones is a prosperous industrious young man with hosts of friends and the young couple are attended by hearty good wishes for the success of their journey through life together.

Millard County Progress
April 2, 1915

HINCKLEY.

Mrs. Charley Burke left Monday evening for Provo where she will spend a week as the guest of Mary E. Peterson.

Principal and Mrs. L. A. Stevens are rejoicing over the arrival of a baby boy at their home on March 30th. Both mother and infant are progressing nicely.

Born to Samuel T. Webb and wife on March 29th a fine baby girl; Dr. O. A. Broaddus in attendance.

Mrs. Thomas Talbot Sr. and Mrs. Thomas Talbot Jr. of Oak City spent a few days last week as the guests of George E. Talbot and wife.

Bishop and Mrs. A. Y. Stephenson and Charles Wood and wife came down from Holden by automobile last Saturday and returned Sunday.

Mrs. Neils Christensen has so fully recovered from her recent operation that she is able to be at her home again.

Mrs. Sylvia Christensen of Oak City has returned to her home after spending the past three weeks in Hinckley caring for the family of her brother, Neils, during the recent illness of his wife.

Milton Moody is in the State Capital again looking after business interests.

Walter Bagshaw has gone out west where he has been employed to shear sheep.

J. J. Spendlove has moved from the residence of L. R. Cropper Jr. to the home of James Terry.

J. F. Brumund is expecting his brother and wife from California this week. They are come into the country with a view of locating here.

J. H. Langston and wife and their daughter Sarah have returned from Lynndyl. They have decided not to move to their farm at that place for the summer, but to remain in Hinckley.

The scouts of the Hinckley ward took their first hike last Friday. The spillway grove was the place selected for the camp and fortyeight boys carrying their bedding and provisions under direction of Scout Master A. I. Tippetts left Hinckley on Friday afternoon. Oscar Kirkham who has all the Scout work throughout the church in charge visited the scouts in camp and complimented them very highly on their work. The whole affair went off without a hitch and all who made the trip declare they had the time of their lives.

Quarterly Conference of the Deseret Stake was held here last Saturday and Sunday. The conference was very largely attended, there being six hundred and thirty eight present at the Sunday afternoon session. All the people had a spiritual treat in listening to the timely and inspiring remarks delivered by Apostles Grant and M. S. Murrin and by Elders Wm. A. Morton and Oscar Kirkham.

It is announced that the M. I. A. meet of the Deseret Stake will be held in Hinckley on April 30th and May 1st. Besides the regular events there will be a contest in dramatics and athletic events between the scout patrols.

Robert E. Robinson and wife pleasantly entertained a number of their friends at their home monday evening. The evening was spent in parlor game and toothsome viands were served.

DELTA.

(Continued from last week.)

Mr. F. D. Kimball, a banker of Salt Lake City and James A. Melville came from Salt Lake City with the purpose of transacting business in connection with the East Millard Irrigation Project.

Donald Hogan of Abraham shipped a carload of alfalfa hay to Bingham the fore part of the week.

Among the arrivals on Saturday were the following business men from Salt Lake City, J. J. Cannon, O. Tyng, W. D. Livingston and L. Anderson who held a business meeting at the Delta Hotel until very late hours Saturday night.

Blaine Wines, the son of a Utah Banker, came down from Salt Lake and has taken charge of his fathers ranch near Abraham.

H. F. Haviland of Anaheim, Cal. arrived here with a carload of household effects and farm implements and has located on a farm one mile north of Delta which he purchased a short time ago.

Bishop Maxfield has had trouble with his vocal organs and he can only speak in a whisper. Nothing serious, however, and expects to be in a normal condition soon.

A. Hanson's family in Oasis are ill with the mumps. Their 16 year old son is very ill. Dr. H. A. Abbott of Delta was called to attend the case.

D. A. Bunker of Salt Lake and a number of his associates reached Delta Sunday for the purpose of developing their large ranch on the west side of the river, and to purchase 200 acres more land that joins their ranch.

The Railroad officials report that Delta shipped 75 per cent of all the hogs shipped out of the State of Utah during the year 1914. Speaks good for Delta.

Chas. Winebriner of the west side of Delta is very busy improving the ground surrounding the Utah Realestate and Livestock Company Building.

Miss Ferrel McClain was taken suddenly ill Sunday evening and Dr. Abbott was called. She is on the improve at this writing.

D. F. Kimball of Los Angeles arrived the latter part of last week to take charge of his ranch on the North Tract.

If you want to know how the roads are from Delta to Hinckley, Deseret and Oasis ask B. E. Cooper he makes the drive daily with commercial men from the Delta Hotel.

This weeks news.

George A. Snow of Salt Lake City, President of the Delta Land and Water Co. was here on Company business the past week.

Mr. Lackyard of California is now clerking in the Delta Furniture Store. Mr. Miller is attending to his farm.

Joseph Wall moved his family into the January residence the forepart of the week.

O. H. Erickson salesman for the Sweet Candy Co. and Heber R. Woolley salesman for the Stavell Paterson Co. made a business call upon the merchants of Delta, Woodrow and Southerland the latter part of last week.

A. N. Rosenbaum accompanied two land seekers to Delta last week. It is understood that both parties bought and were very much taken up with the country. They will look a long time before they ever find as fine a land and conditions as they will find on the Delta Projects.

Mrs. O. H. Richards who has been ill for the past week is now on the improve at this writing.

James A. Melville left for Salt Lake Sunday morning to spend a few days with his wife and family.

F. H. Niel of Ontario, Canada is here for the purpose of attending to his farms. Mr. Niel has some fine farms on the Delta Project.

O. R. Platner of Gooding, Idaho, was here the fore part of the week buying hogs for the Los Angeles market.

D. M. Jackson of San Diego, California, arrived the fore part of the week to spend the summer here. Mr. Jackson has a fine farm on the north tract and will attend to the putting of the summer crop in shape.

Mrs. W. T. Vaughan of Salt Lake City, was here the fore part of the week for the purpose of purchasing a farm and also to look up the hotel business.

Mr. Simeon Walker of Oak City was a visitor in Delta the fore part of the week.

Jean Bakeman of Los Angeles made a step over at Delta while on her way to Salt Lake the fore part of the week.

Miss Ferrel McClain who has had a bad attack of nerve troubles is on the improve at this writing.

Mark Johnson and Dave Hunter of Provo were here on business the first of the week.

OAK CITY.

A goodly number of our towns people were in attendance at the Stake Quarterly Conference held in Hinckley March 27 and 28th and all reported having had a very successful as well as an enjoyable time. Brother Mc-Mussin, Wm. O. Morton, Apostle Heber J. Grant and Oscar Kirkham were present from Salt Lake City and all gave some very timely remarks.

Last Friday night some of our basket ball players went to Leamington and played an interesting game with them. The score was 29 to 20 in favor of Leamington.

Frankie Roper spent a few days in Nephi during the past week having some dental work done.

On Saturday Jim Peters was in town buying cattle. He purchased in the neighborhood of a hundred head from different parts and paid a real good figure for them. The following day he went to Leamington and there bought a good bunch also.

Soren J. Rawlinson who is Principal of the Leamington school spent Saturday and Sunday with his relatives in Oak City.

Lafe Olson spent the past week plastering the house recently erected by Finlinson Bros. on Fool Creek Flat.

Lem Roper who is now in Delta under the doctor's care is reported considerably improved.

The recent storm that swept this portion of the country will be a grand thing for the farmers as it will be a wonderful help to the fall grain as well as giving the spring grain a good start Conditions throughout the country depend largely upon the farmers because they are the producers and when crops are good everybody and everything in general is benefited.

OASIS.

Charley, the little seven year old son of Mr. and Mrs. Chas. Thompson, who has been very ill with whooping cough which afterwards turned to pneumonia passed away Thursday morning. Funeral services were held Friday afternoon. We all extend our heart felt sympathy to the bereaved parents.

Even Hansen is reported very ill with the mumps.

More flags are going up for the mumps and whooping cough.

While riding over the South Tract Sunday we saw many nice wheat fields but above them all was Edgar Jefferies wheat field Mr. Jefferies has one of the best wheat fields in the country.

Mr. H. E. Beck had the misfortune of losing a large work horse last week.

Threen Scipes left for Salt Lake last week.

We made a good trade when we traded weather and got this last bunch.

Mr. Stapley and his drag has made us a good road from the Oasis corner into Delta.

We see that Walter Saunders is again with us on South Tract and making arrangements to make his share of the South Tract blossom as a rose.

We understand that Colonel Wm. Hoff has gone to Colorado to induce a lady to come home with him to act as house wife and be a full partner in the farming stunt

Fred Kime is working for E. A. Hire and we think some hustling real estate man should get a hold of him and sell him a piece of land so as to locate him properly.

Mr. Tomlinson's farm is rented and now Walter can go right ahead making Los Angeles candy and everything will go merrily on during his absences.

Mr. Carl Elmer and wife are again with us on South Tract. Carl is hustling the dirt for all he is worth. He has 80 acres of fall wheat in and is preparing to put in 70 acres more in spring wheat.

Hinckley Happenings

Funeral services over the remains of Foster Slaughter were held in the Millard Academy and were largely attended. The ward choir furnished appropriate numbers, "Shall we meet beyond the river" and "Oh! my Father." The Ladies' Double Quartette under the direction of Mrs. C. A. Broaddus rendered very pleasingly. "One Sweetly Solemn Thought." Mrs. Broaddus sang, "Lead Kindly Lights" and James Blake and Amy Cox sang, "Unanswered Yet." The following speakers spoke words of praise in behalf of the young man whose life was so suddenly ended. James Faust, Jacob H. Langston, H. P. Stout, Sr. Geo. Terry and James Blake. All of these men had for a long time been intimately acquainted with the young man and bore testimony to the goodness of his life. Many sorrowing relatives followed the remains to the Hinckley cemetery where all that is mortal of Foster Slaughter was consigned to it's last resting place.

A large corps of Sunday School workers attended Sunday School Uniou meeting in Delta last Sunday afternoon.

A. I. Tippetts, principal of the Hinckley schools, spent the week end in Payson visiting with his mother.

Mr. and Mrs. Carl Brummund, of California, arrived last week to make their home here.

Miss Myrl Robinson has again returned home after spending some time in Salt Lake City.

Mrs. A. B. Hardy arrived Wednesday from California for an extended visit with her son Raymond Hardy, one of our fellow townsmen.

Roy Webb, of Oak City, spent a couple of days here last week.

Leonard Meecham of Lynndyl was in Hinckley one day last week.

Milton Moody has returned from California where he has spent two weeks combinding business and pleasure.

Mrs. Artiemissie Black returned Sunday from Moapa, where she was called to her mother's bedside. She reports that her mother is now very much improved.

Harvey Loveland has purchased the Alma Langston residence in the northeast part of town and intends to make it his home.

Mary E. Lee was a Delta visitor last Monday.

Samuel Knight who has had poor health for some time past has had to quit school and go to work on a farm in hopes of regaining his strength.

Warren Cox of Salt Lake City was the guest of his sister, Mrs. Mary E. Lee, for a few days last week.

Alfred Bishop, of Salt Lake City was a business visitor to our town this week. He was a guest at the home of his uncle, J. C. Webb while here.

Oak City Offerings.

(Jos. H. Christenson, Rep.)

Miss Frankie Roper has gone to Sutherland to help W. R. Walker with his mercantile buisness.

Bill Dutson and children from Idaho are here visiting their

many friends and relatives.

LeRoy Webb made a buisness trip to Hinckley last week.

Dr. Broadus was called to the sick daughter of Mr. and Mrs. John Lundahl last week. The child is not on the improve much at this writing.

Jos. L. Anderson made a trip to Holden last week to get his wife and baby. We all welcome sister Anderson home again.

A number of our towns people attended conference at Salt Lake last week.

Alton Lyman, from Mayfield, is here to help his father in the mercantile buisness.

Miss Alice Bennett, of Holden, is here working for Mrs. Jos. L. Anderson.

Dean Peterson, County Supt. of schools, was here visiting onr schools last week. He reports them in fine condition.

The S. S. club met last Friday with Miss Silvia Christensen. A dainty luncheon was served after sewing.

Mr. and Mrs. Charley Roberts of Leamington were here visiting with friends and relatives the past week.

Farr Nelson, of Leamington, spent Sunday in Oak City.

Oak City correspondent made a trip to Hinckley last week, and passing through Delta saw some very nice fields of grain and hay, also some very nice crops at Hinckley. The crops around Oak City are looking fine this year; also the fruit crop is in a very favorable condition.

Mrs. L. Roper left Sunday night for Salt Lake City, to visit her husband, who is there in the hospital.

S. Walker made a business trip to Delta last week.

Former Delta Resident Dies

The sad news as indicated in the heading of this article, was received last week by Delta people.

Rev. Rutt was the first Presbyterian minister assigned to Delta and helped to construct the Chapel here. He was a bright young man with a very pleasing personality and the news of his wife's death willbe a shock to his many friends here.

At the time of her death he was attending the seminary in Omaha and he will graduate this spring. He has been assigned work at Corning, Iowa, and was planning to take it up at the time of her death, which was caused by pluresy-pneumonia.

Her death deprives a husband and two small children of her care and protection. He left Delta about two years and six months ago.

Her many friends here extend to the bereaved ones their heartfelt sympathy.

Death of a New Resident

Death visited the home of one of our new and highly respected settlers last Tuesday evening and took away one of its members, L. Arnold who recently came here from San Diego, Cal., with his son, C. M. and wife, who cently purchased a place near Abraham, but who are for the present living just west of town. Mr. Arnold was about fifty four years of age and was very low with Bright's disease when he arrived, coming here for his health. His affliction, however, had obtained too great a hold on him and climate and water were of no avail. At this time arrangements for interment have not been perfected, but a daughter is expected today from California after which they will be arranged, burial taking place in the Delta cemetery. We are all sorry to learn of Mr. Arnold's death and the sympathy of the community goes out to the sorrowing ones left to moirn their loss.

At the Copening Home

Mrs. Belle T. Copening entertined last Friday evening in honor of Mrs. Frank Beckwith. Those present were Mr. and Mrs. Law, Mr. and Mrs. John E. Steele, Mr. and Mrs. M. M. Steele Sr., and Mr. and Mrs. H. F. Aller. The hostess provided a very fine chicken supper and after doing it full justice the guests withdrew to the parlor where speeches were made by the guests in turn, interspersed with humorous stories. A very pleasant and agreeable evening was spent by all and the kind hostess was thanked for her hospitality.

Abraham Articles.

W. J. Cary anp family spent Sunday at the new resort on Drow Mountain.

The Needle Craft Club meets next Wednesday at the home of Mrs. Swartz in South Abraham.

We understand that Abraham will soon begin grading. on the Spur line.

H. B. Lake and wife came in from Los Angeles, Cal., last week to spend the summer. They will reside on the farm of Ora Lake adjoining Aberham.

Mrs. Mattson of Payson is here visiting her daughter Mrs. Ernest Houser. Mrs. housers sister is also here.

The baby of Mr. and Mrs. Marcus Fox was quite sick the first of the week.

NEWSY NOTES ABOUT FOLKS

F. C. Lanham from Parsons, Kansas was here the first of the week.

Sheriff Dorrity and Albert King were here from Fillmore on Monday.

The public schools of Delta will have a half holiday tomorrow, as it is Arbor day.

FOR SALE:—A 12 h.-p. Fairbank-Morris gasoline engine, good as new. Art. C. Tunison, Holden, Ut.

For Sale or Trade:—Thorobred 2-yr.-old Jersey heifer. Will trade for fresh cow or sell.
Geo. Minehardt, Abraham.

Dr. and Mrs. Richards were at Salt Lake last week and the fore part of this, recreating and purchasing some new goods for their drug buisness.

The Salt Lake Nursery Co. has a few fruit trees on hand. Any one wishing trees , call at once. C. F. Winebrenner, Utah Real Estate Office.

Mr. and Mrs. Peary of Provo City were here this week. Mr. Peary has charge of the work of of putting in the cement headgates for the Sevier Land and Water Company.

D. O. Thurston went up to Morgan, Utah. the last of the week, and returned Wednesday with a team of horses and a cow for the farm out on the South Tract.

E. C. Perrin of California, came in Saturday with a car of emigrant goods, and moved them out to his placs near Woodrow, where he will put in a crop and arrange to make his futnre home.

Contractors: If railroad location on Delta Land & Water Co. North Tract is changed will want to get in touch with local contractors at once for construction of grade, about 60,000 yards. See a15-22   Delta Land & Water Co.

The building across the railroad track west of the Hub building, formerly used for restaurant purposes, but now vacant has been raised upready to move. It will be taken over on Clark street east of the Mission where it will be used by Miss Jacobs of Woodrow as a millinery store. Cass Lewis has the moving in charge.

Geo. A. Snow, vice-president of the Delta Land & Water Co, visited at the headquarters of the Company. the first of the week, and left Weenesday for Milford, where he will look after Company affairs.

Mr. and Mrs. Ernest Pierce returned home Tuesday morning from Salt Lake City where they were married. and other Utah points which they visited after the wedding. which took place in the temple the second of April.

Mrs. Frank Beckwith after a very pleasant visit with her husdand, of the Delta State Bank and her many Delta friends returned to Salt Lake last Sunday where their two daughters are attending school,.

Win Walker, the aristocratic Sutherland merchant, in his meanderings around our city yesterday, lost a ten dollar William, which some how slipped off from his pile of greenbacks. No, we didn't find it, and we don't know that it was found.

Attorney J. Alex Melville last week purchased a fine new five passenger Buick Touring car of the latest model. Mr. Melville reports that he finds the car a great time and labor saver in his many trips over the country; besides affording a great deal of pleasure.

Mr. and Mrs. Luther Buchannon had the misfortune to lose their little five-week-old girl of whooping cough Wednesday morning. At time of going to press the funeral arrangements were not complete. Mr. Buchannon, who has been working in Ogden, arrived home Wednesday morning. The sympathy of all is with the parents.

Mr. Eugene Gardner proved a most genial host, and his "take off" of a certain instructor was witty, to the point, and characteristic. Those present were Willis Lyman and Sylvia Turner, Gus Faust and mother, Dr. G.W. Richards and Miss Ferol McClain, Mr. and Mrs. Frank Beckwith, Miss Jennie Grey, Eugene Gardner and Myra Turner, and the hostess, Mrs. Walter M. Gardner. A very pleasant time was spent, and Mr. Mrs. Beckwith return thanks to the host, hostess and the class.

Walter I, Moody, whose new house was recently completed near the Woodrow school house, is now comfortably located in it with his new bride, This is one of the fine new residences of the project an we expect soon to have a likeness of it in the paper. While it is thot by some to have been erected for hotel purposes, such is not the case, It is the residence of Mr. Moody and a most beautiful home,

The Delta State Bank expects, from present indications, to declare a small dividend this coming July. We are glad to record this as it betokens prosperity for this new part of the country, and in a great measure foreshows yet greater possibilities when our community builds into its own.

Millard County Progress
April 16, 1915

Hinckley.

Funeral Services over the remains of Foster Slaughter were held in the Millard Academy and were well attended. The Ward Choir furnished two appropriate numbers "Shall We Meet Beyond the River" and "Oh, My Father." The ladies double quartett. under the direction of Mrs. O. A. Broaddus, rendered very pleasingly "One Sweetly Solemn Thought." Mrs. O. A. Broaddus sang "Lead Kindly Light" and James S. Blake and Amy Cox rendered the duet, "Unanswered Yet." The following speakers spoke words of praise in behalf of the young man whose life was so suddenly ended: James Faust, Jacob H. Langston, H. F. Stout Sr., George Torry and J. S. Blake. All of these men had for a long time been intimately aquainted with the young man and bore testimony to the goodness of his life.

Many sorrowing relatives and friends followed the remains to the Hinckley cemetary where all that is mortal of Foster Slaughter was consigned to its last resting place.

A large corps of Sunday School workers attended Sunday School Union meeting in Delta last Sunday afternoon.

A. I. Tippetts, principal of the Hinckley schools, spent the week end in Payson visiting with his mother.

Carl Brumund and wife of California arrived last week to make their home here.

Miss Myrl Robison has again returned home after spending some time in Salt Lake City.

Mrs. A. B. Hardy arrived Wednesday from California for an extended visit with her son, Raymond Hardy, one of our fellow townsmen.

Roy Webb of Oak City spent a couple of days here last week.

Lenard Mucham of Lynndyl was in Hinckley one day last week.

Milton Moody has returned from California where he spent two weeks combining business and pleasure.

Mrs. Artiemissie Black returned Sunday from Moapa, where she was called to her mother's bedside. She reports that her mother is now much improved.

Harvey Loveland has purchased the Alma Langston residence in the north east part of town and intends to make his home there.

Mrs. Mary E. Lee was a Delta visitor last Monday.

Samuel Knight who has had poor health for some time past has had to quit school and go to work on a farm in hopes of regaining his strength.

Warren Cox of Salt Lake City was the guest of his sister, Mary E. Lee, for a few days last week.

Alfred Bishop of Salt Lake City was a business visitor to our town this week. He was a guest at the home of his Uncle J. O. Webb while here.

Thomas Pratt our genial merchant is in Salt Lake City this week looking after business for his firm.

Miss Dora Richards is again at her post in Pratt's store after spending ten days in Salt Lake City and Provo.

County Superintendent Dean Peterson, left Monday for the east side of the county where he will visit schools.

Farm Demonstrator J. P. Welch is in Eastern Millard this week doing work with the farmers along the line of selecting and preparing seed potatoes.

OAK CITY.

A number of our town people were in attendance at the general conference of the Church held in Salt Lake City April 4. 5, and 6th, and upon their return all reported it as being the most profitable as well as interesting conference they ever attended. Some who were there called to see Bro. Lem Roper who is at the L. D. S. Hospital. They stated that his condition is gradually improving, which we are all delighted to hear, and we sincerly trust that as soon as he leaves the Hospital he will have a speedy recovery.

The items that were touched upon at the Conference relative the war situation in Europe, seems to impress one abating somewhat, especially in England Denmark and the countries to the north. Providing such is the case it will be a grand opportunity to spread the truth in those various countries as it has been revealed to the Later Day Prophet (Joseph Smith,) and we under stand that experienced missionaries are in great demand to carry on the foreign missionary work.

Mrs. Lem Roper and Miss Maggie Jacobson left for Salt Lake City last Sunday.

Charley Iaver the Juvenile Judge was in town Sunday and Monday starting a sort of a reformative era for the sole benefit of some of the juvenile offenders. This experience will unquestionably be a safe guard and a good example for other boys.

Joseph Finlinson made a business trip to Fillmore Saturday, returning home the day following.

The County Assessor arrived in town to day and has commenced taking inventory of all live stock and included in his catalog will also be a complete list of fixtures necessary for farm work.

Brother William Dutson and wife who have been here on a visit for some time left today for Leamington where they will board the train that will take them to their home in Lorenzo, Idaho.

The farmers have all been extremely busy of late planting their spring grain.

DELTA.

A brother of Mr. Chrelholm arrived here from the east for a short visit with relatives.

Geo. Moffitt made a trip to Salt Lake City last week for the purpose of having some dental work done.

Dr. McDonald, Optician, was here the past week making his headquarters at the Delta Hotel.

Mrs. Gray and daughter Jennie moved into the Cooper Building on Clark Street last week.

Lettie Burger who has been visiting her friend Marie Kelley returned to her home at Lynn Junction.

Mrs. Frank Beckwith of Salt Lake City spent Easter week with her husband who is cashier of the Delta State Bank.

A. W. Allen of Salt Lake City is here visiting Mrs Bjerklund.

J. T. Lunt and wife of Salt Lake City were Delta visitors the past week.

WOODROW.

Last Friday night a chivare was given on Roy Jones and his new bride. After treats at the house all marched down to the school house where the time was spent in dancing and a few songs sung by the bride. Every one had a grand time.

Fred Ohronholm is visiting with his brother Thure Chronholm in hopes of gaining better health as he has been poorly for some time.

A large crowd enjoyed the dance at Woodrow Saturday evening with music by Ruel Hibbards victorola.

Mrs. Ruel Wright entertained Mr. Jones and wife at dinner Monday night. After dinner a large crowd came in and surprised them. The evening was spent in parlor games and fun.

Last Friday evening the young peoples Sunday school class held their club meeting at Russel Perry's. After a business meeting games and lunch were enjoyed. Adjourning to meet at Mr. Thompson's next meeting.

A masquerade ball will be held the 14th by the Thimble Club at the Sugar City school house. A good time is being planned.

The Tat and Chatter Club met with Miss Olga Thompson on Saturday afternoon. After an hour of fancy work, lunch and a few games were enjoyed. All dispersed to meet with Miss Verla Oppenhimer on the 28th.

The Woodrow school term ended Friday and on account of whooping cough being so bad in the school, they were obliged to change their plan of an evening entertainment. So a dinner was planned and an afternoon entertainment for the pupils and their parents. All enjoyed this very much.

Miss Etahel Iverson and her mother returned Wednesday from a long visit to Ephriam. Their many friends gladly welcome them home.

Miss Hilda Wicklund has gone to help Mrs. Lake with her work.

Mrs. Esther Pritchett made a visit to Mrs. Will Carry, Monday.

Mrs. Laura Furrer made a trip to Delta and spent a couple of days there.

Millard County Chronicle
April 22, 1915

Sutherland Searchlights

Ray Finilson and Miss Angie Finilson were visiting in Sutherland Sunday.

Roy Basset of Ogden has taken up his residence on the Chritchlow forty west of Foot's.

Burt F. Johnson recently returned to this valley with a wife, which greatly surprised the good folks. However we are glad to have him and his family reunited and wish Mr. and Mrs. Johnson a pleasant journey through life. He will give a wedding dance in the school house Tuesday night.

The school ground presents a very pleasing appearance with the new fence around it and the park of trees set out Saturday April 10th by the men of the district, which workers were fed by the Ladies Relief Society, to which feed all did ample justice.

Fall grain certainly looks fine and there is a good acreage of land being got ready for beets.

Trees and gardens are being planted and conditions in general look fine.

Mrs. Shipley and Mrs. Walker will entertain the jolly stitchers April 30th. The last meeting was held with Mrs. Hickman of Abraham and a very enjoyable time was spent.

Miss Frank Roper is employed as a clerk in Walker & Co. store. Miss Mildred Locke is ill with pneumonia.

Oak City Offerings.

(Jos. H. Christenson, Rep.)

Monday April 12, the town united together to put in L. Roper's crops for him as he is in the hospital and is unable to do his own work.

B. L. Robins has been busy up in the canyon the past week making preparations to plant some trees which he expects right away.

The Juvenile court officers of Millard County were in town last week attending to some small difficulties among the boys. The main event was chickens. We presume the boys got hungry at midnight and prefered a lunch.

A. Hansen of Mills and Ella Carlson of Oak City were married Thursday. We wish them a happy battle through life together.

J. Lee Anderson and others are busy loading a car of wheat.

The "All the time visitor" Mr. Stork, again made his call at the home of Mr. and Mrs. Walter Carlson leaving a nice baby girl. Mother and baby doing nicely.

John E. Lovell took another load of trout up in the canyon to keep the creek well stocked.

Mr. Erwin Jacobson who has been up north attending school the past winter, has returned home for the summer.

Saturday a few men and teams started on a new road up Dry creek canyon, which will be an improvement and make the road shorter than the old one has been.

The Hinckley Dramatic Club put on the play "Escaped from the Law." All present reported a good time and their time well spent.

John and Willard Lundahl came over from Lynndyl to spend Sunday with their folks.

Mr. C. W. Rawlinson and family have moved up on their farm east of town where they expect to make their future home.

Mrs. Rachel Roper is reported very sick at this writing. Dr. Broadus was called to her bedside Saturday.

Mrs. Lem Roper who went to Salt Lake to see her husband a week ago had her only son undergo an operation for tonsilitus. The boy is reported doing fine. Mr. Roper has not yet undergone his operation as he is still too weak to stand it. We wish them the best of good luck as Mrs. Roper has certainly got a hard trial before her at present. It has not been long since they lost one of their baby boys.

We have been having some nice spring rains the past week.

FOR SALE:—A 12 h.-p. Fairbank-Morris gasoline engine, good as new. Art. C. Tunison, Holden, Ut.

For Sale or Trade:—Thorobred 2-yr.-old Jersey heifer. Will trade for fresh cow or sell.
Geo. Minehardt, Abraham.

—List your property for quick sale. Summerland Farms Company, Opposite Post Office, Delta, Utah.

—FOR SALE—Five forties with water right joining Delta on the north, or will rent to grow sugar beets. Verne Bartholomew, Fillmore, Utah. M25-tf.

FOR SALE:—A good three quarter blood Jersey cow. Mrs. Eliza Hook. A8-29

Millard County Chronicle
May 13, 1915

Deseret Doings

Last evening an excellent program was rendered in honor of Mother's day, Apostles Grant and Rulon S. Wells, Mrs. Alice Merrill Horne, Marguerite Summerhays and Edith Hunter were visitors and assisted in the program.

Virgil Kelly is very low at this writing with pneumonia.

The little son of Mr. and Mrs. P. T. Black, who has been dangerously ill, is improving.

Orvil Bennett, cut his foot severely yesterday on a bottle and lost a great deal of blood before the flow could be checked.

Albert Petty had the misfortune to fall from his wheel while trying to avoid running into an automobile, breaking his thumb.

D. J. Black and family left for Scipio this morning in his new car.

Norma Damron is at home nursing the mumps.

Geo. Kelly, came down from Lynndyl this afternoon to visit his brother.

Archie Ryan, accompanied by a number of land seekers, left

his morning to look over new fields.

Mrs. Gunn left for Salt Lake City the 1st. of the week on business and pleasure. She was accompanied by her son Walter who will remain there for the summer.

Mrs. Lois Erving, who has been in Milford for the past two weeks under Dr. Hamiltons care, is said to be improving.

Otto Stewart, has gone to the Lake for the summer.

Blanche Deswnup, is reported the sick list.

Oak City Offerings.

(Jos. H. Christenson, Rep.)

Rosabel Anderson, daughter of Janse Anderson and wife passed away Tuesday evening. Funeral services were held Friday after which the remains were taken to the cemetery for burial.

A. Christensen, from Lavan, is spending a visit with Anthery Christenson, of Oak City.

S. J. Rawlinson went to Leamington last Saturday to give his students an examination on their past winters work.

Mrs. Annie L. Anderson is reported quite ill at this writing.

John Alldredge, who has been at Leamington for some time, is visiting with parents and friends here again.

Brigham Lovell and daughter, Vera, made a trip to Lynndyl Saturday.

Mr. Larson and son, Ornald, are here again improving some of the houses in town. At present they are at work on the S. C. Anderson residences.

After an investigation of the fruit it is learned that the frost did not get it all. It was kind enough to leave a sample.

L. Olsen is preparing to have a nice, big garden this year. He was going to have an early melon patch but some little worms got in and destroyed the seeds so a new planting is necessary.

Leo Finlinson is preparing to build a nice, new, up-to-date bungalow this summer. The foundation now being layed.

Marian Terry took Leslie Booth, our district school principal, to Lynndyl Sunday. He is returning to his home at Nephi. It has not been learned, yet, who of the Eighth grade pupils will graduate yet, but Mr. Booth reports that there will be about seven graduates. If so it will be one hundred per cent of the class.

The tree planting up in the Oak Creek Canyon is completed, 16,000 trees were set out under the direction of B. L. Robbins and F. H. Koomey, the rest of the tree planting party were as follows: B. Lovell, Joseph H. Christensen, H. Roper, K. Roper, of Oak City and C. Walch and and C. Robins, of Scipio. It is reported that these white pines will bear seed in about 20 years and it will improve the canyon and some of us will easily see that time come. More trees will be planted each year.

L. R. Webb, of Joe Town, has gone to Delta to work on the new rail-road.

The resort in the canyon is now surveyed, and it is expected in the future each party will have a certain place to camp each year, by so doing each party can beautify their place and by all doing this it will improve the resort and make a pretty place to spend some of the hot summer days. This place is for all who spend summer vacations there: Leamington. Oak City, Delta, Oasis, Deseret, Abraham, Hinckley and all other places not mentioned, are given this resort by the goverment.

Last summer some of the young boys did some chopping with axes on some of the nice trees that give comfortable shade. It would be a good thing for the older ones to watch and avoid this, as the trees after being barked soon die and this will not beautify our resort. Let's all try to improve our summer resort and have a beautiful place to come to, and enjoy each others partnership in a pretty place, and have a good time thgether.

Hinckley Happenings.

Our genial merchant, Mr. Thomas Pratt is home again after spending a month in Salt Lake City.

Mr. Joseph Christenson has returned home after spending two years in the Northern States Mission. Mrs. Christenson went to Seattle to meet him and the two made the return trip by way of California.

Mr. and Mrs. Earnest Stout are the proud parents of a baby girl. The new arrival was born at the home of Mrs. Stout's parents in Murray, Utah.

Mr. and Mrs. Bruce Stephenson visited with Principal and Mrs. L. A. Stephenson for a few days last week on their return from St. George where they recently married. Both are well known here; the bride, formerly Miss Hattie Mackelprang, taught school here one year, and Mr. Stephenson was a student at the Millard Academy. The townspeople all wish them a pleasant voyage on the sea of matrimony.

Willford Welch, who has been employed as a school teacher here the past year, returned to his home in Paradise, Utah last week.

Two of the children of President Alonzo A. Hinckley, Arza and Nellie are reported as being very ill. Dr. Broaddus is in attendance.

Mr. and Mrs. Freely, of Salt Lake City are the guests of Mrs. John Brook for the rest of this week.

Mr. and Mrs. L. R. Cropper Jr.

are rejoicing over the arrival of a fine baby boy. Dr. Broaddus was in attendance and mother and infant are progressing nicely.

Prof. C. R. Johnson of Provo was here last week to officiate as judge at the M. I. A. District contest.

R. E. Robinson has returned from a business trip into Sanpete and Juab Counties.

The District M. I. A. Contest held here last Friday was rather a one-sided affair. The contestants of Millard and Moapa Stakes failing to appear. The Deseret Stake Contestants won by default and will now represent this District at the church M. I. A. Contests to be held in Salt Lake in June.

Mother's Day was fittingly observed here last Sunday. Special services were conducted in the afternoon at which a special Mother's day lecture was given by Mrs. Mary Cropper-Reeve. Special musical numbers were furnished by Professor Freely and by the Primary Children.

A welcome home party was given last Sunday evening in honor of Mrs. Jos. Christenson. The welcome address was given by Bishop J. B. Pratt. The missionary responded. Mr. Freely gave a violin solo and the evening's entertainment was concluded by an illustrated lecture, "The Granduer of the Rockies" by Miss Eda Cropper, which was very instructive as well as highly entertaining.

On Wednesday evening a musical recital was given in the Academy auditorum by Prof. J. Brook and Prof. and Mrs. Freely. After the recital a dance was given in the gym. which was enjoyed by all.

Mrs. Hannah L. Cropper and daughter Eda leave next Friday for Aurora, where they will be the guests of Mr. and Mrs. Willard R. Johnson.

Mrs. M. M. Horne and her son Aaron, and Mrs. Margaret Richards are planning to spend next week in Richfield.

Miss Sulia Curtis leaves this week for Aurora after having spent the past two years in Hinckley with her sister, Mrs. Joseph Christenson.

Mrs. Alfred Bliss has returned to her home in Hinckley after undergoing an operation for appendicitis in a Salt Lake City Hospital.

Mr. and Mrs. Joseph Blake entertained at a suprise party in honor of the birthday of Erma Turner. The evening was pleasantly spent in games, musical selections, etc. The hostess served dainty refreshments consisting of sandwiches, crackers, cake, ice cream and punch. The guests were Prof. John Brook and wife, Prof. Freely and wife, H. F. Stout and wife, R. E. Robinson and wife, G. A. Robinson, and the Misses Bertha Stevens, Erma Turner, Eda Cropper, and Nettie Hunter.

Deseret Doings

N. L. Peterson came home from Los Angeles to visit with his family for a few days before going to New Castle where he is working in the real estate business.

James Bennett and wife have gone to New Castle for the summer.

H. S. Cahoon and Warre Moody made a flying trip to Saw Tooth Mountains, returning the last of the week.

Messers. Passey & Thomas of Provo, are located at Petty's hall with a large stock of goods, which will be sold at reasonable prices.

Chas. Kimball, representative of a Chicago house was doing business with our merchants this week.

Mr. Scowcroft of Ogden, was a visitor Saturday in the interest of his firm.

William Ashman and wife entertained at a dinner last week in honor of their wedding anniversay.

The Primary Officers are preparing an excellent program to be given the 1st of June. Everyone welcome.

Hugh Hales after an absence of several months in the Southern part of the State has returned home.

Harry Pierson and Hannah Johnson were visitors on Sunday.

Messers. Edgar Petty and Geo. Kelly were down from Lynndyl Sunday.

Virgil Kelly who is suffering from pneumonia, is reported as being much better now.

Isaac Robinson and wife accompanied by their two children from Gandy, arrived in town on Wednesday. They motored to Salt Lake on Thursday where they will remain until the last of the week, when they will return bringing with them a new car.

A number of our neighbors from Snake Valley are at the Moody House, among them Jim Robison, Dan Simonson and son, Geo. Bishop, Billy and Claud Meecham.

Tne Mountain Giants suffered a second defeat Sunday afternoon by the Deseret Braves taking the game. The score being 15 to 5.

Miss Minnie Iverson of Salem, was a visitor at eht Damron home on Wednesday. Miss Iverson has been engaged to teacn here this year.

Charles A. Conkling, the Deseret Dentist has been very busy the past two months but never too busy to attend to your wants in that line.   m13-12

Born:—To Mr. and Mrs. Eli Rawlinson, May 9th, a boy,

—FOR SALE:— A span of mares. m13-20   Mrs. Eliza Hook.

Ratchel Bennett is here from Holden visiting her sister, Mrs. Andrew Sorenson.

Attorney Melville left Delta today for the county seat where he will attend to legal matters.

Reuben Turner left Friday for Wayne county where he will attend to some business matters.

The past three days have been rainy and all out-door work has been retarded but the rain has surely done a great deal of good to all crops, as there has been enough fall to soak up the ground.

FOR SALE—5 head good Jersey Milch cows. 1 Thoroughbred Bull, few calves, No. 17 De-Laval Separtaor with power attachment and cream can. m13.tf H. J. Myer, Abraham.

LOST,—A 10 gallon milk can, red top, with "property of the Continental Oil Co." stamped on plate. Reward for return to James Wilkins, Delta.   m20-2t

Mrs. E. H. Detwiler and Mrs. J. W. Underhill visited Mrs. Frank Beckwith in Salt Lake from last Thursday until Sunday morning. The ladies went the city for the purpose of having their eyes fitted by an optician, and combined business with a very pleasant visit.

Mrs. A. B. Ward has gone to Aberdeen, Idaho, for a visit with her daughter, Mrs. L. C. Blades, who is the proud possessor of a new daughter. Grandpa Ward says it doesn't matter if it rains or shines, "he ban grandpa, all the same, two time." Then he honks, honks and you should see the mud fly.

—HOGS I will pay highest market price for hogs that are ready for market, weighing from 165 to 225 pounds. Phone or see me before selling what you have. Leuthaeuser and Lyman. See Willis Lyman, Delta, Utah.   tf

J. P. Neilson of Riverside, Cal., came in Thursday with a car of household goods and farm equipment, to take up his residence on the piece of land he recently purchased from James M. Hibbard of that place. Mr. Hibbard has not entirely disconnected himself with the project, but is figuring on a trade which will put him in possession of another fine piece of Delta land.

Miss Elsie Jacob and Mrs. Geo. Day have opened up a Millinery shop on Clark street first door east of the Presbyterian church. Hats made to order, repaired, cleaned and trimmed; also feathers cleaned and curled. Call and see us. A new line of ladies, misses' and children's just arrived.   a22-tf

Abraham Articles

All grain crops in this vicinity are in excellent condition, and alfalfa hay cutting will begin soon.

The small child of William Nott and wife had the misfortune to fall from a buggy last week, breaking an arm. The doctor was called and reduced the fracture and reported it doing nicely.

Mrs. Wesley Cary entertained the Needlecraft club Wednesday. Dainty refreshment swere served and all report a jolly time.

Ed Taylor and wife are the proud parents of a baby boy, born Friday, May 14. All reported doing well.

The Abraham baseball club won in a hotly contested game with the Sutherland team last Saturday, the score being 7 to 6.

Mrs. Maud Westover has been on the sick list the past week.

Marcus Fox and wife were guests at the Patterson home Sunday.

Born:—May 10th, to Mr. and Mrs. Levi McColough, a boy.

Mrs. S. W. Eccles, of Ogden is here visiting her son, S. W., Jr. of the Eccles Co-op Co.

Price Lewis left last Sunday for St. Anthony, Idaho, where he will visit with his brother.

Mr. and Mrs. H. A. Knight have gone to Hanksville, Utah, for a visit with Mrs. Knight's relatives and friends.

Millie Workman, who has been teaching school in Boxelder county has returned to her home for the summer.

Minnie Iverson, who has been visiting her sister, Mrs. Wm. N. Gardner, has returned to her home at Salem, Utah.

—FOR SALE:-A new $15 22-cal. Repeating Rifle $11. Enquire at the Chronicle office.   m13tf

H. B. Lake and wife recently moved into their new bungalow on West Main St., Abraham.

Joe Palmer and wife visited Sunday with C. A. Varwaller and wife.

Albert Reed is suffering with a bad case of tonsilitis.

John Fullmer, Ruffy Westover, and Low Taylor have contracted 3000 yds. R. R. work. They are all first class paddy's and will soon complete the job.

Joe Palmer, Chas. Varwaller and Reed Bros.. have bought a new Case threshing outfit to be delivered about June 20th. This is the latest improved machine and fully equipped for threshing either grain or alfalfa seed. They are all experienced machine men.

Sutherland Searchlights

Mrs. Holdridge entertained the Heise family last Sunday.

Wm. Bunker and wife were Sutherland visitore Monday.

Mildred Locks is on the improve after a short run of the typhoid fever.

Miss Ida Ropper is visiting with her sister Miss Frankie Ropper at the Walker home.

Leslie Abbott has gone to Ogden and Salt Lake to visit relatives and see the cities.

The Eighth grade students took the final exam. at Woodrow but as yet have not heard who the graduates are.

In our notes of last week we told of the recent activites of the Midland land boosters which never found its way into print.

Mr. Edwards, of the Midland project has gone home for a few day's stay, leaving one son here to look after his interests on the ranch.

Susie Sanford is home again after spending the winter in Hinckley with her brothers, Ralph and Dewy, who have been attending the Academy.

Ross Simpkins and family have gone to Summit, Iron Co., to visit with Mrs. Simpkin's people from which place they will go to Circleville to visit with his parents before returning home.

Mesdames G. D. Shipley and W. R. Walker entertained the jolly Stitchers last Friday in a very pleasant manner. The next meeting will be held with Mrs. Isles in two weeks.

Abraham and Sutherland played a very interesting game of base ball on the latter's grounds Saturday, the score was six to seven in favor of Abraham. One of the best games we have seen Sutherland play as they have not as yet chosen a regular team and for a try out game, it went off fine.

(Left over from last week)

M. M. Steele, Jr., is doing a rushing business in real estate on the Midland Project, having sold 880 acres in one day, locating many local people among whom are Abbotts, Bunkers, Bert Ottley, John Herslifl and others. The terms of payment each fall of one half the crop, makes it a very desirable investment.

Rail Road work is progressing nicely across the Steele farm, the grading being done by Hinckley teams mostly.

Burt Johnson is buying and shipping another car of hogs for Mr. Hunter, of Holden.

The Delta Depot, where you first land on coming to the "Greater" Delta Country

Woodrow Items

Mrs. David Porter returned last week from California where she had been called by the recent illness and death of her mother. Much sympathy is expressed for Mrs. Porter in her recent bereavement.

The mother and sister of the Messrs, Barnett came to their attractive ranch last Monday for an extended visit.

Mrs. Christenson, of Salt Lake City, is visiting her daughter, Mrs. Esther Cronholm.

The eighth grade pupils of Sutherland, Sunflower and Woodrow districts met last Friday at the Woodrow school for their final examination as graduates of the grammar school of Millard Co. The examination was conducted by the Woodrow Principal, and we understand that all of the pupils made a very creditable showing.

Many new families are settling in our midst. The families of Messrs Parker, Kyes, Hogan, Tyler and Hilliard are recent arrivals from California. Mr. Johns of Delta, has moved his family to his Woodrow ranch and John Nutsch of Kansas has arrived to look after his business interests here. We bespeak for the newcomers a hearty welcome.

Monday May 11th, the Trustee's of the District Schools of Millard Co., were relieved of their responsibilities, control having passed into the hands of a board of five County Trustee's in compliance with the school law passed by the recent state legislature. Messrs S. H. Thompson,

J. J. Clark and Mrs. Jerome Tracy are to be congratulated upon the efficient and harmonious result of their activities. We hope that our excellent principal of last year, Mrs. Clyde Underhill, may be returned by the new Board and that future results will justify the sweeping change in school control made by the new law.

(Too late for last week's issue)

Preaching services at Woodrow next Sunday at 3, p. m.

S. C. McCormick was called to Los Angeles last week as a witness on an important law case.

Mr. Jasper of Missouri is visiting his daughter, Mrs. Geo. Campbell.

Mr. Wind was called home last week by a telegram announcing the sudden death of his father in Nebraska.

Mothers' day was observed at the Woodrow Union Sunday School last Sunday with appropriate exercises which were enjoyed by a large audience.

The Strickley Bros. have taken up a homestead on the desert claim, two miles east of Woodrow and have built them a new home preparatory to dry farming in that section.

The Misses Inez and Doyne Underhill were happily surprised Tuesday afternoon by a large crowd of their girl friends who took possession of their home temporarily and had a joyous time.

Mrs. Jeff Clark has been quite sick during the past week.

Oak City Offerings.

(Jos. H. Christenson, Rep.)

We believe spring has come this time to stay after having a big snow storm to wind up winter.

All the farmers are busy getting in their crops at present.

A number of teams and men are busy working on the new road west of Oak City to Delta. It is believed this will be a much better route than where the road has been and also closer.

On Friday, May 14th, the Oak City Brass Band gave a benefit dance for Mr. Lem Roper, who is still in Salt Lake City in a critical condition. Ice cream was served, and while no price was set on tickets, all donated freely and the proceeds amounted to about $50. We feel to thank Leamington for such a big turn out to our party on this occasion for it helped us out very much,

and we hope they will not call that their last visit with us. Come again and have a good time. All present had a good jolly time.

Oak City Band boys played the scouts a game of base ball Saturday, the score being 18 to 17 in favor of the Band team. This was a starter for this season. We are going to play the game from now on providing anyone can get out to play.

John Alldridge has returned to Oak City for the summer but he makes a trip to Leamington each Sunday just the same. The reason for this can easily be guessed, as Leamington has some nice young ladies over there.

Our young boys are sorry to see the bounty go off on the ground squirrels as they have a great deal of fun catching these fellows, and it is also a good thing for the farmers. It would

be a good thing if this bounty could keep up all the season as we do not have time to thin them out enough. The rabbits are now working on the crops pretty hard and that means a big reduction by harvest time. We have all got to fight this pest to a finish, so keep after them boys.

All of the school students that have been attending the M. S. A. Academy at Hinckley the past winter have returned home for the summer. We are always pleased to have our town folks with us and they are also glad to return to Oak City.

Miss Carlo Lyman, of Mayfield, is here helping her father in the mercantile business. Mrs. Maggie Rawlinson, who has been in the store for some time has quit and gone to gardening.

South Tract Review

Miss Hannah Johnson took the train for some point in Wyoming, last Sunday evening. We are very sorry to loose her from among us for the summer.

Road flooding seems to be the order of the day. A good many have been complained of and many have complained on themselves and have been fined. In most cases road flooding comes

from carelessness, and "I dont care if I do" feeling.

The South Tract Sunday School had an unusually large attendance last Sabbath.

Mrs. Horace Crawford is out of the neighborhood for a few days.

Harry Parsons driver will soon be rested up now and it won't be long till it will look as good as ever.

The social held at the home of Mr. and Mrs. H. E. Beck, by the

neighborhood, on Saturday night was, to the writer, a very injoyable affair. After a few games a short program was given, consisting of solos by Hugh Mulvaney and Edna Beck, a well rendered reading and comeback by Hannah Johnson, and some sweet instrumental music by Horace Crawford and wife. A light luncheon was then served and taking it all around it made a very pleasant evening. The next one will be held at the home of Mr. and Mrs. Chas. Hardin

and we'll have a good time I am sure.

A base ball league has been organized, consisting of the following teams: Abraham, Sutherland, Hinckley, Deseret, Oak City and the South Tract. Our first game will be with Suther-

land on our own diamond, on May 29th. at 4, p. m. The league rules say we must charge an admission so we will ask of each one who attends a small donation. Each team will play ten games and say, there will be some fun ere it is all over.

BLACK ROCK.

Pleasant G. Taylor, who has finished his Freshman year at the Weber Academy at Ogden, has come home to spend the summer with his parents Mr. and Mrs. O. S. Taylor.

Messrs. Goddard and Scowcroft traveling in the interests of the Scowcroft Co. of Ogden were here on business this week.

Richard Travis of Montrose, Col., stock buyer and contractor was here looking over the sheep industry. He was the guest of Walter James and wife.

One of the Japs employed by Shims, the section boss at Pumice, left quite suddenly a few days ago, and with him, watches guns, razors, and other portable stuff disappeared. Allen Hedges of Milford, special officer for the Salt Lake Route, came to Black Rock in search of the thief. It is to be hoped he will be successful in catching him.

Frank Singleton, Tom Burns, Walter James, and A. R. Travers spent some time lately exploring several mines in Beaver Lake mining District. They are are all firm in the conviction that with the aid of a little capital well paying mines could be developed there. The whole region seems to be highly mineralized.

Leo Seely of Mt. Pleasant came to Black Rock a few days ago in the interest of his father's business.

Daily rains for more than a week have been our portion and still it rains and the farmers smile.

Sunday night Walter James and wife entertained at dinner in honor of J. H. Manderfield of the Salt Lake Route and T. J. Meachan of the Salt Lake Evening Telegram. Covers were laid for seven. Those present were J. H. Manderfield, T. J. Meachan, Don Helwig, Mel McEathron, Geo. Dhyso, and Mr. and Mrs. James. The Misses Helen James and Gladys Taylor were waitresses. The decorations were in native wild flowers, bench mallow and daisies which were effective and pretty.

OAK CITY.

The much needed storm which came the past week is the cause of great rejoicing among the farmers in this locality, because it not only assists materially in the growth of all crops but it helps the range feed and assists in various ways that will tend to make prosperous times in this section of the country.

1.07 inches was the amount of rainfall during this storm, this alone is sufficient to assure us reasonably good crops but we feel that more will follow which will surely be welcome.

A number of teams have been working the past four or five days on the new road to Delta. This is a short cut through the sand and it is reported by those who were at the work that a good road will be made and that it will be especially good for winter and rainy seasons. Lorenzo Lovell, the road supervisor, for Oak City has the work in charge.

Our townsmen loaded a car of rye at Leamington and on their return trips hauled to Oak City a car load of cement for building purposes.

Pres. Geo. E. Finlinson and Edgar Nielson were in Sutherland Sunday May 23rd for the purpose of organizing a Mutual for the young men.

Mrs. Libbie Roper has returned from Salt Lake City where she has been with her husband Lem, who is at present receiving treatment at the L. D. S. Hospital. Bro. Roper is still at the Hospital and is reported as slowly but gradually improving which we are all glad to hear.

Miss Eda Roper spent the past week visiting in Sutherland. She and Frankie, her sister, who has been working there returned home May 23rd.

J. Lee Anderson, Franklin Anderson and Ray Finlinson were summoned to act as jurors in the Fifth Judicial Court for County of Millard. They left here for Fillmore Monday morning May 24th.

Our Eighth Grade graduates went to Holden to attend commencement exercises scheduled for May 24. They were also accompanied by a number of our young people who have interests at heart in Holden.

Lee Walker Jr. made a trip to Nephi recently, but as to the nature or extent of his visits none can find out.

WOODROW.

The mass meeting last Saturday was well attended.

Mrs. Ohelson and baby arrived from Riverside, California. Sunday to join her husband who has provided a home for them here.

Mrs. Will Carey has the pleasure of having her daughter and family from Missouri with her They intend to spend the summer here in hopes of improving her daughter's health.

Mrs. Furrer moved to Delta Monday where she will make her home.

Mr. Thompson left for Fillmore Tuesday to meet with the school comissioners on business.

The Southerland baseball team played with Abraham on the formers' grounds and were beaten by a score of 2 to 6. Southerland will play the Southtract Saturday on the former's grounds.

Delta's baseball team played Lynn Sunday and many of our citizens witnessed it and enjoyed the trip.

Mr. Wicklund made a business trip to Fillmore Tuesday.

Mr. Johns of Delta has moved out on his farm at Woodrow.

Mr. Hillard and family of California arrived here a few weeks ago and are now settled on a farm east of Sugarville school house.

Mr. Barker and wife of California have moved to Woodrow on their farm. Mr. Barker is a Chicago White-sox and is now engaged to pitch for Southerland's baseball team.

Miss Ethel Iverson has been employed by Mrs. Cooper of the Delta Hotel. We are very sorry not to have Ethel in our midst even though she is not very far away.

Mr. Hamilton preached at Woodrow Sunday.

The Nutch brothers gave a party to many of their little friends Sunday. All report a fine time.

The Jolly Stitchers will meet at Mrs. Isles Friday. A nice time is assured.

The Thimble club had to postpone their meeting on account of the heavy rain.

Mrs. Ohronholm was the guest of Mrs. Thompson Monday.

Ruel Hibbard wears a broad smile this week as he has received word of a nine pound girl in California. He expects his wife and baby here in a couple of weeks.

Miss Margarette Thompson was a visitor at the home of Mrs. Wright this week.

The Woodrow Sunday school is preparing a program for children's day.

LYMAN --- REEVE

Miss Mary Lyman and Mr. John Reeve both of Hinckley, were married in the Salt Lake Temple at noon on May 18th. The ceremony was performed by the bride's uncle, Pres. F. M. Lyman At 1 P.M. a very pretty wedding breakfast was given in their honor by Mrs. Joseph Wells, cousin of the bride. The bride and groom spent a very pleasant ten day honeymoon visiting friends and relatives in Salt Lake City, Provo and Richfield.

An exciting runaway occured here last Saturday when the horse belonging to Jacob Davies got frightened at an auto and ran away. Luckily no one was in the buggy and the horse ran for several blocks before being stopped by Mr. George Rowley. The best part of it is that not even the buggy was injured.

HINCKLEY.

The Misses LaPreal Robinson and Nina Pratt returned home Friday from Provo where they have been attending the Brigham Young University.

Jack Greener returned home Tuesday from Logan where he has been a student at the A. C. during the past year.

Miss Eda Cropper has returned to her home after an absence of three weeks. She has visited her sister Mrs. W. R. Johnson of Aurora and her aunt, Mrs. Jas. Woodard of Fillmore during her absence.

Miss Elsie Richards and Miss Oleone Bunker left last week for Provo where they will attend the B. Y. U. Summer School.

Mrs. Samuel Dutson has been confined to her bed the past month, but is now reported as improving.

Lafayette C. Lee and Miss Pearl Mortenson, two of our most respected young people were married in the Salt Lake Temple recently.

Miss Myrtle Langston and Joseph M. Wright, and Miss Sarah Langston and Clarence Mortenson were married in the Salt Lake Temple last week. All of these young people are well and favorably known here, the brides being daughters of Mr. and Mrs. Jacob Langson. The best wishes of the community accompany these couples in their voyage over the sea of matrimony.

Aaron Horne has gone to Millville, Cache Co., to spend the summer working on his brother's farm.

Mrs. Margaret Richards and Mrs. Elizabeth Walker left Wednesday for Salt Lake City where they will spend some time working in the Temple.

Mrs. Jackson, wife of our enterprising blacksmith, is confined to her bed as a result of having both legs run over by a buggy. In driving from Oasis to Hinckley she dropped one of the lines and in attempting to jump from the buggy to get the line, she slipped and fell beneath the wheels of the vehicle.

A couple of ministers, sometimes known as "wagon missionaries" are here for the purpose of holding meetings. They in-

Hinckley.

(Concluded from page 1.)

Thomas W. Cropper, John and Noah Bogers sold a couple of carloads of fine fat steers to John E. Hunter of Holden.

The Pavant Valley Scouts organized June 1st with the following officers:

Lealand Neilson, Scout Master; George Terry, Assistant Scout Master; Ianthus Wright, Cleamont Dutson, Fenton, Reeve, Verle Maxfield and Victor Terry, Troupe Committee.

These enterprising young men and other scouts spent a day cleaning up the cemetary and repairing the roads in that vicinity.

Miss Birdie Bushnell of Meadow is here to spend a few days as the guest of William Blake.

Black Rock

Miss Alice Ray had the misfortune to be thrown from a wagon while riding from Antelope Springs toward home, the heavy wheel passing over her ankle caused a very painful if not serious injury.

A. E. Gibson of Storrs, Utah, accompanied by two others, were business visitors here early in the week.

Wm. D. Livingston, R. R. Agent of this place, made a business trip to Fillmore. Owing to the continued heavy rains the roads were in a bad condition, making the trip a hard one.

Karl Kettelson made another trip to Black Rock this week and out to Antelope.

Messrs. Ryan and Batty who are interested in mining in Antelope Mts. feel greatly encouraged with their findings and are confident that a little money and labor would be well rewarded in that district.

Walter James went to Caliente, Nev. last Saturday his business there will detain him a number of days.

Mrs. W. D. Livingston, the R. R. night operator has gone to her ranch near Anaheim, California. From there she expects to go to San Diego and also to San Francisco to visit the Exposit-

ions. Mrs. Frank Beane of Terahouti, Ind., will be Mrs. Livingston's substitute during her absence.

The Misses Zona and Verna Pollock have gone to Salt Lake City for a visit. They will also visit in Provo before they return.

O. S. Taylor just returned from a trip to Cedar City, New Harmony and other southern points in time to go on to Salt Lake where he will attend Summer school.

D. S. Dorrity, Jr., our genial sheriff, accompanied by J. H. Beckstrand and son were looking over the roads in this part of County last week. It would certainly be appreciated by the people if something was done of this nature out here.

WOODROW.

Miss Weaver Clark and Mr. Frank Needham were happily united in wed-lock Wednesday at Fillmore. They were accompanied by the bride's sister Clara Clark and the grooms brother, Fay Needham. A dance was given by them at Woodrow Monday evening which was attended by a large crowd of friends. The orchestra was hired to furnish the music. All wish Mr. and Mrs. Needham a happy journey through life together.

Mrs. F. Roch gave a nice dinner in honor of the Pritchett family, the guests being Mr. Pritchett, wife and sons, LaRue and Donloy, Mr. W. Oppenheimer, S. H. Thompson and wife.

Miss Marie Barben arrived home from Heber, where she has been on a long visit, last Monday.

Dr. Tracy has been very busy lately attending sick calls.

W. Titus is visiting his parents at Sutherland. He has a good position in California.

Mr. and Mrs. Oppenhiemer were the guests of Mr. and Mrs. Bussards Sunday.

The Public Library which was started by the Thimble Club is now open at the home of Mrs. Ohronholm for the present time, and she is in charge of it. There is a good stock of the latest books.

We are glad to see the sun shine again, as every body is putting up hay.

Mr. Pederson of the Oasis Lumber Co. was in our neighborhood Monday looking over business.

Grain around here is looking very fine and promising.

OAK CITY.

The Farmers of Oak City have commenced cutting their first crop of alfalfa while it is not as good as it generally is we wefeel assured that there will be a good second cutting for the reason that the land has been properly taken care of. The cause of the shortage in the first crop was the frost which came in the fore part of May and the pesck lucern weavel, although the weavel is not as bad here as it is in neighboring localities.

In talking with a man from the northern part of the State, the writer has learned that in Salt Lake and Utah Counties where the weavel first started they have none at all. This condition is propably due to properly cultivating the land. So if they have succeeded in bringing about a move of this kind, I trust the people of this section might work with the same motive and determination to keep the weavel from going

(Concluded on page 8.)

OAK CITY.

(Concluded from page 6.) South.

Eddie Q. Dutson, the Ward Choirister, is laboring earnestly with all the choir members and is preparing some new anthems, hymns etc. to be sung at the Quarterly Conference of the Deseret Stake which will be held in Oak City, June 26th and 27th.

Maggie Rawlinson, Wanda Dutson and Soren J. Rawlinson spent the past week in Sevier, visiting with relatives and friends.

Carlie, Lola and Alvin Lyman returned home Sunday after a week's travel or a visit to Mayfield.

Lydia Roper has returned home after spending 8 months in Salt Lake City. She has been taking a special course that was given there. Mandy has also been in Salt Lake City the past two weeks.

HINCKLEY.

Dr. and Mrs. O. A. Broaddus, Hugh Hilton and Miss Rena Reeve motored to Salt Lake City last week to attend the M. I. A. Contests. They returned Sunday and report having had a very pleasant trip.

Thomas W. Cropper, wife and their daughter Lyle, are spending a fortnight in the north visiting with Robert Ashby and wife of American Fork and with Mark Reynolds of Springville. Miss Lyle represented this div-

(Concluded on page 8.)

Hinckley.

(Concluded from page 1,)

ision in the M. I. A. Junior Retold story contest and scored the highest number of points but was disqualified because of exceeding the time limit by a few seconds.

The Scout Boys Chorus won second place in the contests in Salt Lake City. The chorus was composed of Victor Torry, Leroy Cahoon, Francis Stout, Virgil Hilton, Richard Terry, Golden Webb, Manton Moody, Clement Hilton, Marion Slaughter and Ashael Wright.

Other Hinckley people who attended the contests in Salt Lake City were Mrs. Wm. F. Pratt, and daughter Rosie, Mrs. Eda Bishop, Mrs. Nora Bishop, Miss Amy Cox, Mrs. Charles Cahoon, Mrs. Clara Stewart, Roy Hilton, the Misses Bly Moody, Stella and Letha Wright, Grace and Eureko Robinson, Ruby Stout, Fauntella Cahoon, Rose and Loren Terry and Carrie Langston.

Irvin Tippetts, principal of the Hinckley public school spent a few days here last week. He has just returned from a two month's motorcycle tour of Cal-

ifornia. He visited the Panama Pacific Exposition and the San Diego Exposition. He reports having had a splendid trip and feels well paid for the time spent.

O. T. Bishop & wife are rejoicing over the arrival of an infant at their home. Both mother and child are getting along splendidly.

Mrs. Carson Draper is entertaining as her guest Mrs. Dalton of Southern Utah.

Base ball seems to be the order of the day here. Several games have been played and the teams are practicing hard. We all hope to see some exciting games in the near future.

We are having delightful weather now. Most of the farmers are busily engaged in putting up the alfalfa crop. Heavy frosts have made the crop lighter than usual but all are hoping for a better second crop.

Alton Anderson of Salt Lake City is here to spend the summer with his brother O. H. Anderson, proprietor of the drug store.

Fay Theobald is erecting him a neat little dwelling house on his property in the northern part of town. We are glad to have this additional evidence of the fact that Hinckley is growing.

WOODROW.

Wednesday evening, Mrs. Oppenheimer entertained several of her friends at dinner.

Wednesday afternoon, Miss Margarette Thompson gave her Sunday School Class a party and the children sure had a good time.

Mr. Hillyard is erecting a fine new house, has three carpenters from Santa Ana, Cal., building it.

Last Saturday Mrs. Pritchett entertained a number of her friends at dinner.

Children's Day was observed by the Union Sunday School, Sunday and the program was very pleasing.

Miss Dorothy McCollum was a guest of Margarette Thompson at Sunday dinner.

Sunday night Miss Margarette Thompson entertained a number of young folk in honor of LaRue and Douly Pritchett. After supper that evening was spent in jolly games and music.

Rev. Hamilton preached at Woodrow Sunday and had a good audience.

Mrs. S. H. Thompson entertained a number of friends at dinner Tuesday in honor of Mr. Pritchett and wife.

The boys have cleared and made a new ball diamond, and had a good game Sunday, played by a pick up team.

Sutherland has mutual every Sunday evening.

Mrs. Agnes Sherrick was a guest of Miss Helen Smith the week end.

Mr. Hamilton and wife of Delta spent last week visiting in and around Woodrow.

Black Rock

Al. Wilkes and Jack Travers came in from Mt. Home on business.

Burton G. Clay came over from Burbank to deliver some mules at Black Rock.

Mr. A. G. James and wife were visiting here for a couple of days, Mrs. James is now in Milford visiting with her sisters.

J. H. Wittuer was doing business here this week, his line being nursery stock, he went to Delta from here.

The Misses Beniti and Thekla James have returned home from Salt Lake where they have been in school. They motored home Leslie Clay was the chauffeur. They were accompanied by Miss Alice Grun, daughter of Dr. James Grun of Parawan.

James Burtner of Riverside California was a visitor here this week.

Deseret Doings

Lois, the little 15-month old daughter of Mr. and Mrs. John H. Western, died last week. The burial took place on Saturday. The family have the sympathy of the entire community.

Independence Day was fittingly celebrated yesterday. A splendidly arranged program was rendered in the fore noon at the A. C. Neilson building. In the afternoon various sports were given at the City Park, and a game of base ball between Hinckley and Deseret was played. Both sides played well, Deseret winning by a small majority, the score being 4 to 7. A big hop in the gymnasium concluded the program for the day.

Mrs. Mary Garity of Salt Lake City is a guest of Mrs. Josephene Petty for the week.

Archie D. Ryan left for Salt Lake last evening.

J. H. Witner has been in town the past week doing a good business for the Salt Sake Nursery Co. No doubt, that Deseret will look more beautiful when all the trees and shrubery grow.

Mr. Clive "the mining Expert" has been sojourning here the past week. He is one of the promoters of the Joy District and just sent a nice car of high grade ore to the smelter.

Angus Alred and John Cahoon leave the 10th. for the coast. They will visit both fairs before returning.

Among the visitors Monday were Mrs. Rich Cropper, and Mr. and Mrs. Amos Maxfield, old residents of this place. Come again.

The Deseret Braves are making arrangements to leave for Milford on Friday of this week to play the Milford team. Success boys.

Mr. and Mrs. Edgar Petty were down from Lynndyl to spend Independence Day with relatives, also Messrs. George Kelly and Bryan Petty.

A birth-day party was given at the home of Mrs. J. M. Moody on Sunday, July 4th, in honor of Mrs. C. A Reed. The rooms were decorated in the national colors, the color scheme being carried out in the menu and place cards. Musical numbers were rendered and social chats were indulged in for a couple of hours. Each guest was given a piece of birthday cake on their departure, tied with red, white, and blue ribbon. The following were present:—

Messrs. and Mesdames, L. R. Cropper, Jos. W. Damaron, A. J Henry, H. S Cahoon, Amanda Kelly, Hannah Allred, Geo. and Arthur Cahoon, and Miss Neva Cropper.

Millard County Chronicle
July 15, 1915

Fined $100.

Last Monday and Tuesday were busy days in Judge Faust's court. Dr. Murray, whose trial on the charge of selling liquor in violation to the local option law was brought here from Fillmore on a change of venue occupied all day Monday and Tuesday and the jury was out Tuesday evening until about ten o'clock before bringing a verdict against the defendant. Attorney Higgens of Fillmore acted as council for the defense and County Attorney King and Associate Council Alex. Melville prosecuted the case for the state.

The penalty in cases of this kind, runs from $50 to $299 with a jail sentence up to six months. He was assessed $100 by the judge, but the doctor served notice on the court that an appeal would be taken to the district court which will be held in October.

The plea of the defense was that in the case in question the man who had obtained the liquor procured it on the plea that he had cramps and was asking for it as a medicine.

Those who composed the jury were Chas. Ashby, John Starley, Avery Bishop, and Abner Johnson. Those attending the trial from Lynndyl were Harry Hedgee, Julius Samuelson, O. W. Passwater, Ed. Creelman. Mr. Marsh, Mr. Jones and Dr. and Mrs. Murray.

This was a hard fought battle and the attorneys for both defense and prosecution worked hard for conviction and acquital, the attorney for the state making every effort possible to fulfill his oath of office.

Lynndyl Lines

The Lynndyl base ball clu[b] could not manage to go to Leva[n] last Sunday to play the retur[n] game, and upon inquiries Mana[ger] Haley states that quite a fe[w] of his star players were compel[l]ed to work on this date, whic[h] prevented them from filling th[e] engagement.

A case of poisoning occure[d] here the other day, and woul[d] certainly have ended very se[r]iously had it not been for th[e] timely efforts of Dr. Murray. [It] appears that one of two youn[g] men passing through the tow[n] was feeling sick and complaine[d] of the fact to his companio[n] This companion claimed to hav[e] some pills which were reporte[d] to be good and just what th[e] sick man needed. He took fo[ur] of the pills, which immediatel[y] caused terrible pains, and hea[r]ing there was a Dr. in town, h[e] went to him. Dr. found th[e] pills, or tablets to be bichlorid[e] and he worked on the man f[or] six or seven hours before relie[ved] ing him. It appears that the young man is the son of a D. & R. G. engineer by name of Baldwin, living in Salt Lake City, and Special Officer Hedges got into communication with the man's father regarding his son's condition. Young Baldwin was in such condition the following morning that he was able to go to Salt Lake City. No trace of the man who gave Baldwin the pills has been found since.

Messrs Earl Jones, Richard Jones and W. E. White took in the sights and pleasures of Salt Lake City last week.

Dr. Murray has gone to Delta on business.

Woodrow Items

In November 1909, the grease-wood plain 14 miles from "Burt-ner", (it being necessary t[o] cross the Sevier at the spillway[)] was ornamented by a crude 1[4] by 20 foot dwelling christene[d] "Tracy's Dream" (of a home[)] Six months later 80 teams use[d] in construction work camped a[t] the Tracy well. One year passe[d] and a wife, whose nearest neigh[b]or was two and one-half mile[s] away, shared the "dream". To[-]day the dream has materialize[d] in the settlement of Woodro[w] whose inhabitants are so pro[-]gressive, and whose soil is s[o] fertile, whose water is so pur[e] and whose activities are so we[ll] known that she requires n[o] boosting.

The many friends of Frit[z] Nutsch will be glad to learn tha[t] he is now convalescent from a[n] attact of the serious malad[y] known as "Rocky Mountain Spot-ted Fever". Fritz has been th[e] first one to suffer from its rav-ages in the Pahvant valley an[d] we congratulate him on his re-covery.

Harvest is on. Many of ou[r] progressive farmers have invest-ed in headers and are thus har-vesting their abundant crops others are binding. All are hap[-]py. There are but two seriou[s] problems confronting this com[-]mon wealth, and the sooner som[e] concerted effort is directed t[o]ward combaling these evils th[e] better it will be for all concerne[d] We refer to the weed nuisanc[e] and the lack of a drainage sys-tem. Proper drainage is abs[o]lutely essential to health, an[d] weed free fields are esential t[o] good crops.

The Jolly Stitchers met enforc[ed] with Mrs. Robert Jenkins an[d] enjoyed a good time. The nex[t] meeting will be at the home [of] Mrs. Clyde Underhill, Frida[y] July 23rd.

Walter Barben is mourning th[e] loss of an open face watch [at] Sugarville July 4th. He woul[d] gladly give suitable reward upo[n] its recovery.

Oak City Offerings

(Jos. H. Christenson, Rep.)

The Oak City base ball team played a lively game of ball with Leamington, Friday the 9th. On the ninth inning the game was 17 to 17, and on the tenth Leam-ington run in two points and Oak City fanned, on the eleventh Oak City run in three points and Leamington fanned out, the score being 19 to 20 in favor of Oak City. A large crowd came over to root for Leamington. All joined in a big dance at night and everybody had a time of the season.

Miss Viola Pratt, of Salt Lake City, is spending a visit with her aunt, Mrs. Eliza Anderson.

Mr. Joseph Finlinson made a business trip to Fillmore last week.

Mr. William I. Alldredge, left for Salt Lake last week to under-go an operation for his eyes, that is if after consulting an eye specialist it appears favorab'e.

Mrs. Mamie Wells and some of her friends from Salt Lake City, have come to spend a pleasure trip in the canyon for some time.

Mr. Peters, a cattle buyer, was in town again last week gather-ing up beef stuff.

Mr. Alvin Lyman has erected a nice new house on 1st north and 2nd west.

Mr. Joseph Finlinson is also building an addition on his resi-dence.

Mr. Joshua Finlinson is ad-ding a couple of rooms to his building.

Mr. Jesse Peterson has started a fruit and ice cream stand on main street. Everybody seems to enjoy gathering there and having a good fill up.

A big time is expected up in the canyon on the 24th of July. A program is being prepared for the celebration.

J. Lee Anderson is preparing to build a nice big house in the near future, on main street between 2nd and 3rd north.

The next 10 days will see most of the grain cut as it is ripening very fast this hot weather, and a good crop is reported all around here this year.

Mr. Walter Carlson left for the McIntyre ranch at Leamington last week.

Sugarville Siftings

David Porter is the first victim of the Pahvant plague this season.

The Misses Hillyard entertained a few young folks at their home last Saturday evening.

Chas Iverson left Tuesday for Salt Lake City where he will join the Utah State Gaurds for a months camping at Fort Douglas.

The farmers are busy getting their headers in readiness for heading the winter wheat. Many have already begun, and the crops bid fair to be the best yet ever harvested.

The Ladie's Relief Society meet each Tuesday afternoon, instead of each afternoon as stated in last week's items.

There is probably but few farmers who have any wheat left from last year, except Mr. Hib

bard, who we understand is marketing a car load and realizing 91c. per bushel.

Mr. Harry Pedricks returned a few days ago from California where he has been since last November. He is much improved in health and ready for harvest work.

The celebration at Sugarville July 5th was a grand success. The day was ideal, and people from Woodrow, Sotherland and Sunflower were on hand to join in the pleasures of the day. Over 200 people partook of the picnic supper which would certainly have been inviting to a king. The sports were enjoyed by everybody, and those winning prizes were as follows:—

Girls' race, between 12 and 1 yrs., Blanche Remington.

Men's 50 yd. race, Walter Wright.

Boys' race, between 12 anb 1 yrs., Carl Nutsch.

Girls' race, under 12 yrs. Emma Clark.

Boys' race, under 12 yrs., Jo Nutsch.

Three legged race, Walter Barben.

Night shirt race, Payne Franklin.

Backing buggy race, Payn Franklin.

Boys pony race, Frank Hiese.

Prize waltz, R. M. Wright an Mrs. Fred Barben.

Ball game between Woodrow and Sugarville boys was a victory for Woodrow.

Pony Express Rider

E. H. Maxfield, father of our fellowtownsman, Bishop Maxfield, together with Geo. Chappel of Lyman, paid the Bishop and our town a visit last week. Mr. Maxfield is an old timer in the west, and in early days was one of the Pony Express riders, his station being out at Deer creek, Wyo. He is also a veteran of the Black Hawk and Walker Indian wars of Utah and a man of very bright mind and interesting coversation, although he has reached the age of eighty-three.

He has a store of very interesting and exciting reminiscences of early western days, some we hope later to be able to reproduce for our readers. Mr. Chappel while here took an option on an 80 and says that he has eight sons whom he hopes some day to have located in the Delta county. After an extensive trip over the valley both expressed themselves as highly taken up with the country and went home greatly pleased with what they had seen. Mr. Maxfield has been a resident of Wayne County for the past 35 years.

LOCAL NEWS

E. D. Knight went to Lyman Monday to attend to business matters.

BORN:—To Mr. and Mrs. Ray Bishop, last Tuesday p. m., a boy. All well.

First class work done at Empire Photo Studio, and Millinery Emporium, Delta, Give us a call.
j15-tf

Mr. and Mrs. R. J. Law went to Draper last Saturday night for a visit with Mrs. Law's sister.

A. M. McPherson, field superintendent of the Delta Co., went to Salt Lake Monday night to meet with some of the officials of the company.

Miss Lillian Larsen of Washington, Utah, arrived in Delta last Monday for an extended visit with her Uncle, L. Turner and family.

Passenger tarriffic on the San-Pedro is quite heavy at present. Several extras are being pulled over the line almost every day on account of the expositions in California.

Gilbert F. Miller, of Boone, Iowa, will join the ranks of the irrigationists of the Delta North Tract, having this week purchased an eighty-acre tract of land near Woodrow.

First Vice-president, Geo. A. Snow and consulting Engineer C. A. Tush, of the Delta Land & Water Co., came in Wednesday from Salt Lake for a visit on the Delta project.

Miss Bertha M. Parker, who has been connected with the office force of the Delta Land & Water Co., for some time, left for Salt Lake the first of the week where she will reside.

J. H. Turner, chairman of the Salt Lake county Bull Moose trail committee, and State Senator Mont. Ferry, of Salt Lake county, are visitors to Delta this week. These gentlmen are on an inspection trip and have interests in this viciniy.

When you have anyone visiting you or anything transpires which you are interested in, call in and tell us about it, or at least call us up on the phone. We are always glad to publish all the news. However, our field is so large that we can't cover it all ourselves and must have your assistance to some extent.

Bring the folks down to the Hub for Sunday dinner. It is worth while and is only 35c

A proposition to supply our county seat with electric lights and fuel is well under way and seems likely to meet with success.

Herbert Abbot son of Dr. Abbot, left Saturday for California where he will reside in the future. He was accompanied part way on his trip by his father.

Allen Kirkman, son-in-law of Mrs. M. E. Nebeker, came down from Santaquin the first of the week to visit with his wife who is visiting her mother at the Dunsmore.

The readjustment of salaries for postmasters has resulted in an increase for postmaster Faust of the Delta office of $200 per year. The salary of rural delivery carriers has also been raised to $1,200 per year.

Manager Works of the Baker Lumber Co. made a business trip to the yard at Lynndyl the first of the week Mr Works has charge of all the yards in this part of the county and is doing valuable work for the company.

N. Lambert has taken Ed. Pierson's place as manager of the Baker Lumber Co. yard at Delta, Ed. has retired to the farm where he will hereafter do the "agricultural" stunt. We expect soon to hear of him in the Luther Burbanks class.

We notice by the (Idaho) Rupert Pioneer-Record that L. R. Humphries, and son who formerly resided here, had left Rupert where they now reside, for Idaho Falls where they have the contract for the erection of a six roomed residence.

J. W. Thurston was at Lynndyl the first of the week where he met the government official in charge of water measurements for this part of Utah. Mr Thurston has been in charge of government measurements in this locality and the first of the week met the governmen man at Leamington to turn in his observations.

It is reported that some grass hoppers are showing up in some parts of the valley. It is also said that the alfalfa weevi has been imported to this coun try. It would be well for al to give this pest and its eradication a close study. Watch the fields closely and the minute i is discovered make a determined fight for its destruction.

Bill Goddard while in Delta Wednesday had the misfortune to have a horse he was riding slip on the pavement and fall on his left foot, dislocating the ankle.

E. J. Milne, Sec'y Juvenile Court Commission, of Salt Lake in company with Judge O. F. McChane, Judge of the juvenile court of Southern Utah, of Beaver, were Delta visitors Tuesday and Wednesday. The Judge is making a tour of this district in order to see how things are going and to get in touch with the people and conditions. We are pleased to acknowledge a call from these gentlemen and find them highly intelligent and pleasing men to meet.

BLACK ROCK.

Mrs. L. A. Fints of Richfield arrived on No. 19 to go out on the homestead where her family is already located for the season.

Among the teachers in our neighborhood who expect to teach next year are Mr. and Mrs. Murry, Mr. O. S. Taylor, and Miss Runyon. The three former have just returned from attending the Summer school at the "U." Miss Runyn took the teacher's examination at Fillmore last week.

Henderson of San Francisco carrying a fine line of Buckingham, Hecht shoes was doing business here last Wednesday.

Walter James is in Salt Lake City this week on business. He will visit Park City before his return.

Miss Ada Bentley one of the Salt Lake City teachers is spending her vacation with Mrs. Walter James. Miss Bentley spent a summer in Black Rock some years ago, since that time she has been two years in Honolulu.

O. O. Barry of Los Angeles, Auditor for the S.P.L.A. and S. L. R.R. spent the day at Black Rock on Monday.

F.B. McCrosky of Los Angeles is here with F. J. Johnson. Mr. Johnson has been making extensive improvement on Mr. McCroskys dry farm.

Frank Kiefoxer of Notus, Idaho, arrived here a few days ago. He expects to remain for some time at the Deer Lodge Farm, where he is employed by L. E. Hodgson.

OAK CITY.

The people of Oak City have been extremely busy the past two weeks harvesting the grain crop which is unusually good this season, owing to the favorableness of the climatic conditions that have prevailed. While the first cutting of hay was somewhat light on account of the frost, weavel, etc., the crop which is now ready for cutting is better in every way.

During the previous week a number, in fact a great majority of our towns people spent a few days of real enjoyment at the Oak Creek Meadow Resort. On Friday Pioneer Day was fittingly observed and celebrated in that place, and in a manner that offered a great amount of pleasure to all who were present. The parade which consisted of numerous demonstrations of overland transportation, such as hand-carts, ox-carts, go-carts without the go, etc., and a fair example of the once famous rim-fire hupmobile used by the Indians, which is two poles wired to the horse and the baggage stored on the rear end of the machine. The latter exhibit was represented by two Indians and Three Squaws from the tribe they call the Narajo.

Following the parade was a meeting in which an interesting program was rendered.

The afternoon was spent in playing ball. horse-back riding, racing and so on. Music was furnished by the Oak City Brass Band and we wish to thank them for the splendid musical selections that they rendered.

Most of the people returned home Saturday; had a ball game in the afternoon and a dance in the evening, where all expressed themselves as having a good time.

Mrs. Mammie Wells and family with some friends from Salt Lake City are spending a week or so in the canyon.

Lem Roper who for some time has been on the sick list is also in the Canyon and is getting along real well.

Wm. Aldridge who went to Salt Lake recently to have his eyes treated is reported as being greatly improved.

Visitors at our canyon outing were Misses Nancy Badger, Hazel Stephenson and Ellis Bennet from Holden; Samuel Night, Clemont Dutson, and Heber Bishop from Hinckley; Miss Mattie Parks and younger sister from Nephi.

Kirt Ropper spent the 24th in Nephi.

Lynndyl Lines

Talk about "Good Old Summer Time," we haven't heard of anyone with nerve enough to warble that song for some time, around here.

Base ball in Lynndyl has not yet lost its savor; Our boys report having enjoyed a fine time with the Milford team on the latter's diamond last Sunday. The final count was determined somewhat in the Milford team's favor, but Milford says they are in no way proud of it. Our team has played two games this season with Milford and reports they never have met a more congenial bunch, nor have been shown more hospitality than at Milford.

Some real life is shown amoung our citizens in that they have started a movement to incorperate the town. The object being that we could better impove the local conditions and cause our town to clean up and stay clean.

Some of the finest wheat crops have been grown here this season that Utah has enjoyed anywhere. A. A. Hinckley, Lawrence Hinckley and John Greathouse are especially there with the goods and we are proud to point new home seekers to these farms and prove what we have and it is a feeling of much satisfaction to know, ourselves, that within the very near future, without the least bit of doubt, Lynndyl will be surrounded with fine fields of grain, and the result is no guess any longer.

Geo. R. Mayer, an eastern farmer, with the kind of push that we need in this country, has purchased the Fay Holbrook farm just south of the village and is already making his new farm show the effect of knowelege and work.

The post office at this point is now second to none in the state in its class, as a brand new steel cabinet has just been installed. This is another feature of progress in the vicinity.

H. E. Wilkes has been transfered, temporarily, to the Milford yards to look after the inspection of cars at that point pending the absence of tho regular foreman there.

Mrs. Parley Peay of Provo is visiting with her husband here this week and they are contemplating making their future home at this point. Parley is a rustler and says that the field is good here.

The way Dr. Murray has demonstrated the fact that shrubbery will thrive and beautify in one season has put a quietus on the fellow who we, so short a time ago, had to listen to saying, that "there aint any use of a fellow fooling his time away in this here place trying to raise any thing fer I've had too much uf this kind of country and I know". Oh, when will the kicking, knocking balker quit or die? Either would help the country. And just the same we are glad that the optomist is never really effected by the howler when he can see the real truth thru the clear future that the pessimist cannot possibly see because he has so twisted and knotted his optic nerve that nothing but darkness can penertrate it.

J. F. Belliston, the local tonsoriel professor, is on the batching list this week as his wife and family are visiting in Nephi.

E R. Johnson recently returned from quite an extensive trip through the northern part of this State and Idaho. He reports conditions great in Idaho and says that there is no doubt but that it will soon be one of the leading states in the west. Ernald has now gone back to his duties with the Pedro and is stationed at the present at Tintic.

G. P. Ealy and family will soon leave for California where they will take in the fair and many other interesting features of the coast.

The Excelsor Mer. Co. is having some conspicious lettering done on their store and this firm, together with the D. W. Scannell's, Gen. Merchandise store, makes Lynndyl one of the leading towns of this part of Utah to shop. We notice many teams driving into Lynndyl every week to bring the people from the surrounding country to do their trading and the reason is that we have the goods here and our merchants are up to date and prices seem to be one of the principal features.

The Neilson two story brick hotel is now complete and will soon be swinging its doors to accommodate the public. This is one thing that Lynndyl has long felt the need of.

Geo. W. Sudburry, manager of the Excelsor mercantile Co. store, has moved his family from Nephi to their new home here and will make this their permanent home.

Allen Keller, of Hinckley, who has been employed on the McIntyre ranch near Leamington for sometime, appeared at Dr. Murry's office the other morning with a game arm. On examination the doctor found a broken bone and immediately set the fractured parts. Allen went on his way rejoicing that it was not his neck.

Hinckley Happenings.

"Yes, indeed," says some of our prominent citizens of Hinckley, "we would be delighted to read in the Chronicle some news from our town, for the people in the nearby settlements have no idea of the many interesting things that happen here. If we could tell them of an event once in awhile, perhaps they would think we were alive anyway."

One of the future's most promising events that has happened is the organization of the Home Economics Association. Miss White, who is representing the Extention Division of the A. C. in this county, is, we think, a very competent and efficient person to organize this work. The work of the Extention Division is progressing and indeed interesting for a large portion of the housewives and housekeepers. Under the competent leadership of Mrs. C. A. Broaddus, we have cause to believe that this work will grow and flourish in this community, and that a mutual benefit will be derived therefrom. The various committees are now fully organized and are ready for efficient, active work. Join with them, all the home-makers of Hinckley and make this organization a success. You can only do this by your hearty support and with the one thot that "In unity there is strength."

Miss Gertrude Ingells, who has just returned from the Oberlin Conservatory of Music, in Ohio, is here spending part of her vacation with Mrs. C. A. Broaddus. Miss Ingells teaches in the L. D. S. University the coming winter.

The Stork has visited the homes of Mrs. Reed Cary, and Mrs. Bammes, leaving at each place a baby boy.

Mr. Eldredge of the A. C., is in our community again visiting the farmers and giving valuable information. His special line of work is with the dairymen. A week ago Sunday in the parents class of the Sunday School, he talked upon the subject of beautifying the homes and their surroundings. Let us, as citizens, show our appreciation to such men by acting upon their suggestions. This is what will bring about our civic improvements.

We certainly have some fun loving, as well as willing workers in the Hinckley Young Men's and Ladie's M. I. A., judging from the way they participated

(Continued on page 8.)

Hinckley Happenings

]Continued from page 1.)
in a canyon trip the last week. Each swarm of the Bee Hive girls and all the scouts had chapheron's. Over fifty people, both young and old, were there and enjoyed the cool, balmy breezes, mountain hikes, fishing, gathering berries, and at night playing games, singing and dancing around huge bonfires.

Hinckley has made an acquisition in the form of a new butcher shop, which the proprietor, Wm. Drysdale, believes to be as clean and hygenic as anything in the county. Read his ad in this week's Chronicle.

Dr. Anna Louise Strong, prominent lecturer and worker for the National Bureau of Labor and Child Welfare, spent a few hours of last Thursday in our little town. She visited at the home of Dr. and Mrs. Broaddus.

Our skilled blacksmith, Mr. Jackson is in Salt Lake, at the present writing.

Emil, son of Nate Badger, sustained a rather severe injury last week when he fell from a wagon, breaking his right leg.

Our town is certainly getting prosperous. There are three new automobiles flashing along our roads; a Ford belonging to Will Bishop, and an Overland and a Regal belonging respectively to R. A. Cary and Fay Theobald.

Lyman Curtis, of Provo, came down recentla to help his father on the farm.

Sugarville Siftings

Albert Watts had the misfortune to lose one of his best cows last week, from bloating on alfalfa.

Mrs. Iverson and son Alvin ate Sunday dinner with Mr. and Mrs. Cronholm.

A party of young people picniced at Hot Springs last Sunday.

Saturday evening is regular meeting of the Commercial Club. A special business is to come before the club and all members are requested to be present.

Oak City Offerings

(Jos. H. Christenson, Rep.)

Born to Mr. and Mrs. J. Watts, a baby girl. All doing nicely.

Tuesday night a farewell party was given Mr. and Mrs. F. S. Lyman. A large program and refreshments were served, also a dance. Every body had a dandy good time. We all regret to see them leave as it is hard to part with our best friends. But we wish them the best of good luck and hope some day they will be back with us again as they are ever welcome. They expect to make their future home in San Juan County. Miss Zola Lyman, who has spent the past year or more with us, will accompany them home to see her parents and friends.

The little daughter of J. L. Neilson met with an accident while swinging in a swing, losing her holt and falling on a sharp edge of a tub which she had pulled over to get into the swing with. She struck the side of her head just below the temple. If it had been a little higher it might have been very serious.

The farmers are still busy at the second crop of hay. Some are done and some expect to raise some alfalfa seed. It looks favorable at present.

Rusticators are seen every day going and coming from the canyon. This hot weather makes it nice to be in the canyon enjoying the shade.

Saturday Oak City made a trip to South Tract and played a game of base ball. The game was rather one sided as Oak City was to much for South Tract team, the score being 15 to 5 in favor of Oak City.

Sheriff Dorrity and Co. Attorney King were doing business here and at Lynndyl the first of the week.

E. E. Smith, solicitor for exhibits for the stait fair, was here again the first of the week looking after exhibits.

Mr. and Mrs. S. H. Smith are the proud possessors of a baby girl, born on the ninth.

Mrs. Myrtle Manary of Milford spent several days last week visiting home folks here.

R. L. Turner, who went to Salt Lake Monday to take his infant daughter for medical treatment returned home Thursday. Mrs. Dr. Tracy who accompanied them there remained with the little one.

Miss Emily Price of Beaver is here visiting Mrs. Walter Moffit.

M. M. Steel visited Salt Lake City the last of last week.

FOR SALE: 80 head of good, thrifty pigs and shoats. Hi Holdredge, Sutherland.   a12-19

Dr. F. I. Kimball of Los Angeles, who has been here for a couple of weeks visiting his son Don., who is developing a place on the North Tractin which he and his father are interested in, returned home the first of the week. Mr. Kimball sees many improvements since his former visit here, and before his departure, after having viewed the crops and seeing the great possibilities in store for this country he looks for a mighty step forward in all lines within the next two years.

N. D. Thompson, one of Green River's prominent sheep men, was here the last of last week, for the purpose of looking after his large farm southeast of Delta and puting it in cultivation. Mr. Thompson purchased the land several years ago and was formerly a resident of Scipio. He said he always had great faith in Delta and the Delta country but was pleasently surprised at the progress the town and surrounding country has made since his last visit.

Mr. and Mrs. H. E. Soule entertained Mr. and Mrs. Beckwith and family last Saturday evening and at Sunday dinner. After supper Saturday an enjoyable evening was spent inspecting Mr. Soule's farm and visiting his neighbors on a "get acquainted trip." It is a pleasure to pay the Soule Farm a visit and to see the methods of farming, and a treat indeed to enjoy their hospitality, for which Mr and Mrs. Beckwith are deeply indebted.

—FOR SALE:-Carbon Copying Paper at the Chronicle office.
m13tf

Settler's Attention.

All Carey Act settlers should take in hand their proofs and attend to them now. If a final proof is due, the publication requires five weeks, and as most are due by April 1st, each final necessary should be begun at once. The yearly proofs should be attended to promptly.

WOODROW.

To late for last week.

A large crowd enjoyed the Birthday party of Mrs. Ruel Wright Monday evening. And all wish her many more happy birthdays.

The Friend-ship Thimble Club met with Mrs. Swartz on Wednesday. An election was held and a lovely four course luncheon was served by the hostess in honor of their first anniversary. The decorations being sunflowers. The members having had a lovely time adjourned to meet with Mrs. Watts next Wednesday.

Sunday evening a crowd of young folks took luncheon and canoes and went down to the ake and Spillway Grove and enjoyed a moon light boat ride.

Miss Corra Heise received three of her friends from Nebraska who will make a short visit here while on their way to the San Francisco Fair.

Mr. Charlie Iverson being a militia-man from the north, was called to join the militia on a trip to the Frisco Fair.

We are glad to have Mr. Hewlett up and around with us again after such a nervous breakdown.

A camp-fire supper was given at the Holdridge Ranch on Wednesday evening by Mrs. Holdridge and Mrs. Smith. A large crowd enjoyed it and also the evening's entertainment very much.

Mrs. Hibbard entertained a crowd of young folks at a dance and luncheon in her new home. At a late hour all dispersed with the thought of having had a dandy time and hoping the new house will remain warm during the winter.

Robert Jenkins spent several days in Salt Lake attending to some business matters and having his tonsils removed.

Mrs. Eaf Losey left to spend a short time visiting her mother Mrs. Skelton in Tooele.

Mr. Kyes is moving on the the Harper Ranch which he has just purchased by a trade with some Riverside, Cal., property.

Mr. Jeff Clark is moving on one of Mr. Kyes places, formerly known as the Pocock place.

News for this week.

Mrs. Oppenheimer entertained Messrs. Tingleleaf, Seams, and Baxter and the Misses Della and Vida Hillyard and Margarette Thompson at a most delicious supper Sunday evening.

The Jolly Stitchers met with Mrs. Campbell Wednesday, with a very large attendance. A delightful afternoon was spent, with a very delicious luncheon.

A surprise party was given on the McCullum sisters Tuesday evening. The evening was spent in jolly games and refreshments At a late hour all dispersed after having enjoyed themselves immensely.

Saturday morning a large crowd of young folks left for an outing in Oak City Canyon accompanied by Mrs. Lambert and Mrs. Herslelf as chaperons.

Last Saturday evening the Thimble club gave an ice cream social in the Sunflower school house. The lucky ice-cream tickets were drawn by Frank Schradder and Mrs. Tracy. Frank getting a fancy sofa pillow and Mrs. Tracy a lovely box of candy The entertainment was delightful and many lively games were played.

We are very sorry to hear that Mr. Ohelson is ill with the Pahvant Plague.

The harvest days are here, but not very disappointing. Many are heading and stacking while some are thrashing in the field. The report is very good, being from 40 to 50 bushels per acre.

The Tat and Chat Club met with Miss Olga Thompson Wednesday afternoon. There was a good attendance and after refreshments all adjourned to meet with Miss Verda Oppenheimer.

A crowd of young folks took dinner and left on Sunday morning to visit the hot Springs.

Horse-back riding seems to be a great sport for Sunday afternoon amongst the young folks.

Crowds both young and old gather at the flume by the sand hills from various places every Sunday and have great sport bathing.

Miss Athena Beckwith was a week end visitor of Miss Corra Heise. The rest of the Beckwith family joining them over Sunday.

LIST OF TEACHERS EMPLOYED IN COUNTY FOR 1915-16.

The following is a list of teachers employed for the Millard County School District for the school year 1915-16 as furnished to us by County Superintendent:

MILLARD CO. HIGH SCHOOL

FILLMORE

H. O. Lewis, Principal, F. E. Stott, J. F. Anderson, W. L. Jones, Etta Nelson, and E. K. Basset.

MEADOW

W. E. Davis Prin., Leo Stott, Flora Fisher, Rulon Stott.

KANOSH

W. A. Paxton, Prin., Herman O. Bement, Isabell Whatcott, Edith Bennett, and Elsie Gardner.

HATTON

Maurice Lambert.

HOLDEN

M. T. Dyches, Prin., Leonard Wood, Fay Wood, and Hattie Bennett.

SCIPIO

DeVere Childs, Prin., J. Major Rees, Alice E. Childs, Clara Thompson.

SUGARVILLE

M. M. Runyan.

LEAMINGTON

Mr. Winn, Prin., Bessie Greathouse, Stella Strange.

CENTRAL

S. F. Stephenson, Prin., Hannah Johnson, Vernell Moody, Marcia Beck, Hazel Giles, Merle Andrus, and Minne Iverson.

DELTA

Eugene Gardner, Prin., Eugene Hilton, Eli Rawlinson, Edna Beck, Millie Workman, Elizabeth Childester, Annie R. Salmon.

SUNFLOWER

Cora Heise.

CLEAR LAKE

Jane Rawlinson.

FILLMORE

E. F. Pack, Prin., H. E. Day Stanley Robins, Lillian Beauregard, Ella Robison, Nellie Holbrook, Geneva Ashby, Helen Brunson and Laura Callister.

LYNNDYL

Helen Beck, Prin. and LaNola Callister.

BURBANK

M. H. Madsen.

MALONE

W. W. Murray.

OAK CITY

Leslie Booth, Prin., Ada Smith, and Margaret Nielson.

HINCKLEY

A. I. Tippetts, Prin., George Beal, Eda Cropper, LaPriel Robinson, Carrie Leigh, Mattie Stephenson, Lora Shepherd, and Irene Michelprang.

SUTHERLAND

James Barney, Prin., and Helen Bunker.

ABRAHAM

W. H. Jones, Prin., and Daisy DuBois.

ROOK

Etta B. Underhill

BLACK ROOK

O. W. Taylor.

Oak City Offerings

(Crowded out last week)

Mr. C. W. Rawlison is busy erecting a new house in the east end of town.

Miss Maggie Jacobson, who has spent the past summer in Idaho, has again returned home.

A good grain crop is reported by our farmers out on the new project between Oak City and Lynndyl.

W. I. Alldredge has returned from Salt Lake where he has been to have his eye operated on. He is now able to see where he is going again.

Tuesday night a big crowd attended a dance at Leamington, the music being furnished by the Oak City string band, all had a dandy good time.

Miss Jane Rawlinson who has been in Salt Lake City the past summer has returned home. We are always glad to see our young folks back with us.

Thursday night a party was given by the Bee Hive Girls, at the home of Miss Arbie Talbert. Lunch was served by the girls. All present had a good time.

One of the most interesting base ball games of the season was played here between Oak City and Abraham, the score being 4 to 6 in favor of the visiting team.

Our new post master, Leroy Walker, is right on his job getting things straightened up. He expects to soon move the Post Office down on his place between Main St. and 1st East and 2nd North.

Sugarville Siftings

Mrs Jim Shepard is visiting her parents at Springville.

Iver Iverson from Ephriam is visiting his mother and brothers at the Eagle ranch.

Mrs. Fred Barben will entertain the Friendship Thimble Club next Wednesday afternoon.

John Fentress moved his family to Delta the first of the week where they will enjoy city life a few weeks before returnig to their old home in Kansas.

A few young people gave Alvin Iverson a pleasant surprise last Saturday evening to remind him that it was his birthday, a balloon ascension being part of the evenings enjoyment.

At the Sugarville school house Saturday evening, commencing at 8:30, sharp, The Thimble Club will give a miscellaneous recital followed by a dance, for the benefit of the new library. Admission 10c. for all over 12 years. Ice cream and cake 10c. Every body come.

Mr. G. E. Frevert, the expert dairyman, has just finished visiting and getting the manufacturers to co-operate with him in improving the quality of Utah cheese. He says that he finds the manufacturers anxious to learn the best and latest methods of cheese making, and that the quality of the cheese is really good. With the proper facilities for cooling the milk, the cheese will be much improved.

Hinckley Happenings

Our druggist, C. H. Anderson, is in Salt Lake on business.

Miss Hodges from Beaver, is here clerking in Mr. Woodbury's store.

A bounteous crop of wheat has been harvested by Milton and Joel Moody—an average yield of 38 bu. to the acre.

Eugene and Wilford Hilton have returned home after having worked all summer for an Aluminum Co. They seem to think there is no place like home.

Miss Eda Cropper and A. I. Tippets have just returned from their summer vacation. They seem to be exceedingly happy. We wonder if it's because school is so soon to start?

Last Saturday an exciting game of base ball was played at Deseret between Hinckley and the home team, Hinckley winning by a score of 6 to 9. This makes the second game Hinckley has won from them. Get busy Deseret because you will have to play a little harder next time.

A unique, informal ladies dancing party was given at the home of Mrs. C. A. Broaddus, Miss Rena Reeve acting as hostess, last Wednesday evening lasting from 8 o'clock, p. m., to 11. There were no special lights provided as the full moon did his best to make the dancers trip lightly and gay over the floor of the tennis court. Delicious refreshments were served and all the guests left feeling that they had had a most delightful time

Those being present were Afton Hinckley, Bly Moody, Laverna Wright, Laverna Nelson, Mrs. Geneva Bishop, Mrs. Myrtle Wright, Lapriel Robinson, Rena Reeve, Mrs. C. A. Broaddus, Clara Stewart, Lottie Bishop, Mabel and Wealthy Parker, Claris Erickson, and Esther and Fern Reeve.

The people of this community were very much astonished when they heard of the return of Allen Keller from Fillmore, bringing with him his bride, Miss Lillie Loveland, and no doubt they were in turn surprised the first night after their arrival with the various noises that were heard around the house. We wish this young couple a prosperous and happy life.

A lecture was given last Sunday night at Deseret by Demonstrator Welch to the Home Economics Ass'n. We are quite sure that the result of this lecture will be a general clean-up of the town of Deseret preparatory to the county fair. We also think that his lecture given in Hinckley has resulted in a vast amount of good already. Many people have begun to clean their own back yards and free their lots frhm the weeds and filth. A very sanitary movement. Keep it up citizens and let's have our town clean.

Farm Demonstrator, Welch and Prof. G. E. Frevert, of the Western Dairy Division, have been visiting the cheese factories of Millard Co. this week. Millard county has six cheese factories

all of which are producing good cheese. The Farm Demonstrator secured the assistance of Mr. Frevert because he is an expert in cheese making and can be of much assistance to the cheese makers of our Co. Mr. Frevert will begin a special line of cooperative educational work with these men which we believe will result, eventually, in Millard Co. producing cheese of equal quality to that from the eastern states.

The B. G. H. girls took another lay off from the regular meeting to have a corn and potato roast. It was a jolly bunch that sat around the fire, each with a long stick, with a cob of corn attached to it. With another stick they turned potatoes occasionally. Here let us add, if anyone wants marhmallows they can get them at the Cash Drug, but don't fail to soak them over night. Pudge thinks eats cooked out of doors better not happen too often, because "It takes on too much fat."

After such a sporty time the week before the B. G. H.'s thot they couldent settle down to a plain business meeting so a sleeping party was arranged. Toward evening girls from all parts of town were seen with a quilt, pillow and can of pork and beans. The table was spread for the following Mabel and Wealthy Parker, Mary and Fannie Cropper, Gladys Bishop, Nina Pratt, Nellie Bishop, Claris Erickson, Elsie Richards, Verna Nelson, Lapriel Robinson, Bly Moody and Laverna Wright. One girl had a birthday. She brot the cake with a thousand candles, which served as centerpiece. Peaches go well with birthday cake so Wealthy and Bly think everybody seemed to enjoy them equally as much, even if they didnt get so many.

A family bed was then made. About three o'clock there was a slight lull of voices, and some visirors thinking them asleep, showered them with water, after which the time was spent in sleeping.

Mrs. Bell T. Copening, her mother, Mrs. Mary E. Taylor, and the daughters, Mary and Ellen, little Miss Nina, and son Frank, will shortly leave Delta for Provo in order that the children may attend school there. Mr. Copening has property there,

so that the family will occupy their own home. Mr. Copening will remain in Delta and look after his business interests. Mrs. Copening entetained Mr. and Mrs. Beckwith at a chicken dinner, one of several to be given by her before leaving. The Misses Ellen and Mary will take up their school work at once

with the fall term, giving especial attention to instrumental and vocal training; these charming and talented young ladies need only skillful directions to their abilities to reach a high place in music. All the many friends of the Copenings are sorry to loose them from here, but the best wishes of all go with them.

Millard County Progress
September 10, 1915

The 5th Annual Millard County Fair.

COMMITTEES

GENERAL:- P T. Black, Pres., O.A Damron, Vice-Pres., Geo. W. Cahoon Sec. and Treas., J.H. Western, Joshua K. Bennett, Geo. W. Baker, P.P. Warnick, Daniel Stevens, G. W. Black, C. Day, R. T. Ashby, R.W. King, O. Anderson, Verne Bartholomew, Wm. N. McBride, Peter Shields, S. E. Brunson H. C. Lewis, Ed. Trimble, Don Wixom Committeemen.

AGRICULTURAL:- John R. Bennett Chairman, Deseret, Richard Parker, Hinckley, Frank Christensen, Kanosh, D. O. Wixom, Fillmore, Frank Badger Holden, Edwin Ivey, Scipio, J.L. Stott and E. B. Bushnell, Meadow, J. Hulse Southerland, Roy Bills, Abraham, A.M. McPherson, Delta, Wm. Hoff, South Tract, Sam Rutherford and J. C. Hawley, Oasis, Albert Watts, Woodrow and Sugarville, Peter Nelson, Oak City, R B. Ashby, Leamington.

LIVESTOCK:- C.O. Warnick, Chairman, Deseret, D. F. Peterson, Hinckley, O. F. Christenson, Kanosh, Vern Bartholomew, Fillmore, Richard Nixon Holden, Samuel Memmott, Scipio, J. A. Beckstrand and E. Lindsey, Meadow John Jimpson, Sutherland, Roy Bills, Abraham, Nelse Bishop, Delta, Chester Hire, Soth Tract, V. Styler, Oasis, Sugarville and Woodrow, Geo. Finlinson, Oak City, A. E. Johnson, Leamington.

DOMESTIC ART:- Grace O. Warnick Chairman Deseret, Wealthy and Mits Bunker, Hinckley, Belle Whacott, Kanosh, R. W. King, Fillmore, Mrs. Emily McKee, Holden, Mrs. O. L. Thompson, Scipio, Philip Barkdull and Flora Fisher, Meadow, Mrs. Mary A. Bourdman, Sutherland, Roy Bills, Abraham, Mrs. Avery Bishop, Delta, Mrs. Crawford, South Tract, Mamie Pierson Oasis, Mrs Tracy, Woodrow and Sugarville, Stella Nielson, Oak City.

SPORTS:- W. R. & D. J. Black, S.L. Brunson, Peter Nellson, and Geo. E. Beech, Chairmen, Joel Floody, Hinckley, Hyrum Prows, Kanosh, G. W. Black, Fillmore, S. P. Teeples, Holden Don Probert, Scipio, H. U. Beckstrand and Leo Stott, Meadow, Clifton Bunker, Sutherland, Roy Bills, Abraham, A. Johnson, Delta, Geo. E. Beech, South Tract, A. Standsworth, Oasis, Geo. L. Kelly, Lynndyle, Fred Nielson, Leamington, George Finlinson, Oak City.

Special attention will be paid to Agricultural, Livestock and Domestic Art exhibits,

Space will be reserved for every town in the county, and each town is earnestly requested to have an exhibit at the Fair.

September 23, 24, 25.

Oak City Offerings

Oak City was first settled in 1864, about three miles above where the town is now located, at the mouth of the Canyon.

The families of Alvin Prows, J. W. Radford, C. Green and J. Croft, were amoung the first to locate in this valley, coming from Deseret. The dam that supplied the irrigation water for Deseret went out, and the settlers were without water, so they became scattered, some coming to Oak Creek, as it was then called, because of the oak trees that lined the banks of the stream.

At first the settlers did not farm, but had cows which supplied them with butter and cheese. They used to take their dairy products to San pete County, and trade for clothing, and such other things as they needed. Their houses were dugouts.

After about two years, others came in to the settlement, and the town site was laid out. Some built adobe houses, and others built log cabins, and then they commenced to farm on a small scale. The first crops were corn and molasses cane. Later, as the community grew, other crops were planted, and now nearly everything in the line of farm and garden products is grown here.

Mr. J. Partridge built the first sawmill, which was run by water power, and this was later replaced by Lyman Bros.' steam sawmill.

In the early days, it seems there was no music to be obtained for the dances and parties, so the people used to beat tin pans and boilers, and they enjoyed themselver as much or more than if they had had the finest orchestra.

Oak City, as it is called now, is essentially a farming community, and the people are prosperous, and progressive. Fruit, vegetables, and garden stuff, form the bulk of the produce, but a great deal of butter is made, and eggs are also a source of income.

*

Oak City is twelve miles from Delta, and about the same distance from Lynndyl.

Most of the farmers have been busy the past week putting in their fall grain.

Mr. Jos. A. Lyman has returned to Mayfield, where he expects to stay a while. His leg has been bothering him so he has not been able to attend to his work in the store for some time.

Mr. Willard Christenson, went to Delta last week to help his brothers Mr. Edward and Lorenzo Christenson with their thrashing.

Contractors on the new school house are busy building forms for the foundation.

Mr. Bert L. Robins, and wife, of Scipio were in town last week. They were up in the canyon looking over the plot of white pines that was planted last spring. Owing to the long dry summer, Mr. Robin's has made a count of the trees and reports 75% of them living and doing fine. The government expects to put in another crop next spring also.

Music for the dance Friday night was furnished by the Oak City Brass Band. Punch and cake were sold and a dandy good time was had by all.

A number of our young folks attended a circus at Leamington last week. Mr. S. J. Rawlinson reports seeing it, and got home safe again. His entire expenses were $1.00. He did not say he wanted to go again.

Mr. Walter Rawlinson and family have moved to Delta for the winter.

Elder John Dutson, who has spent the past 27 months in the northwestern State Mission, has returned home. He reports the best time of his life while in the mission field. We are all glad to see him back and hear his reports as he gives them.

Oak City went to Leamington last Saturday and played them a game of Base Ball. The game was won 3 to 16 in favor of Oak City. A grand ball was had in the evening in Mr. John Anderson's hall. All had a fine time. We invite Leamington to come over and play ball with us on safe grounds.

Mr. Clinton Dutson, made a business trip to Lynndyl last week.

A. M. Roper, and his son Henry have been busy on their farm out on Talvor's flat plowing the past week.

Mr. Leroy Walker, our new post master, has nearly got his new Post Office completed.

Our District Schools start September 29th

Abraham Articles

The farmers in Abraham all wear a broad smile when they look over their harvest fields. The threshers are in our midst again and every farmer reports having a good crop of grain. Very little lucerne seed raised here this year, but an abundance of grain and hay.

Wm. Fullmer, who recently underwent an operation for appendicitis at the L. D. S. hospital at Salt Lake, after several weeks of suffering, is back with us again and getting along very nicely.

The most enjoyable programs of the season were those given by the Primary Sunday afternoon and Sunday evening by representatives from the Hinckley Academy.

We hear wedding bells at Fullmers.

Mr. and Mrs. Egdar Taylor's Baby is still on the sick list.

Several men and teams left here this morning to do more railroad work.

Mr. and Mrs. Marcus Fox are going back on the desert for a couple of months.

Mr. and Mrs. Ruffie Westover are preparing to move in their new home this week.

Leroy Bills will have his new house finished by the last of the week.

We welcome our School teachers back again to start their work Monday Sept. the 20th.

A New Store For Delta Open, the 25th.

Ben Douglas, formerly of Bingham and Silver City, whose ad. appeared in last week's issue and this week's also, returned to Delta Monday to prepare for the opening of his store which will occur on the 25th of this month.

Mr. Douglas will put in a complete and up-to-date line of Gents', Ladies' and Children's Furnishings and Clothing. He has leased the Jenkins' building for six months where he will open his store. Mr. Douglas has been in the Mercantile business in Utah for the past eight years and recently returned from a purchasing trip to New York.

He has great faith in the "Greater" Delta Country and expects to make Delta his future home. He is a live advertiser and it will pay you to keep your eye on his ads. in the Chronicle.

Wedding Bells.

Cards are out announcing the marriage of Miss Bertha May, daughter of Mr. and Mrs. Wm. Perry, west of Delta, to Arthur O. Nilsson.

The Weding day has been set for September 25th.

Miss Perry is one of the many pretty and refined little ladies to be found in the "Greater" Delta Country and came from California about two years ago with her parents. Mr. Nilsson came from Salt Lake and has spent the past two years here making his home and being employed by Mr. Perry. He is a manly, industrious and enterprising young man who will make good and we are glad to see this young couple begin laying the foundation of their future home.

Sugarville Siftings

Mr. and Mrs. Clarence Chelson are the proud parents of fine baby boy.

A few neighbors and friend of Mr. and Mrs. Presnall, gav them a pleasant surprise o Wednesday evening.

The Friendship Thimble Clu will meet with Mrs. J. B. Seam next Wednesday afternoon.

Mr. and Mrs. E. Jaderhol are entertaining their thre

LOCAL NEWS

R. J. Law, was a Salt Lake business visitor the last of last week.

S. W. Eccles was attending to business matters in Ogden this week and last.

Don't fail to read our classified ad. column this week. It represents some good bargains.

Quite a number of our young people are attending the Millard Academy this year.

H. B. Prout returned the first of the week from attending the fair at San Francisco.

Dancing at the Delta Opera House. Tomorrow night especially, good dance with fine music.

Mrs. L. C. Blades and baby leave today for their home in Aberdeen, Ida., after visit with the ladies parents, Mr. and Mrs. A. B. Ward.

C. F. Winebrenner went to Salt Lake the first of the week to visit Mrs. Winebrenner who is convalesing an operation.

Ormon Wilkins, of Washington, Utah, son of Jas. O. Wilkins, arrived Wednesday evening with a load of "Dixie" grapes.

Mrs. Jack Childers and Mrs. Arnold, leave today for California, where they will take in the fair and spend the winter.

Bishop Maxfield, F. W. Cottrell and Edgar Jeffery went up to the Uba Dam Wednesday to take measurement of the water.

Dr. C. O. Gates of San Jacinto, Cali., has filed on a 160 acres North West of Sugarville, and will have the entire tract into fall grain.

M. M. Steel, Sr., is erecting a four-room cement block cottage which he will occupy when completed, just north of F. W. Cottrell's residence.

Keep your Hogs in a healthy and thrifty condition by using Allright" Dip and Re.nedy for sale by Leuthaeuser* & Lyman. See Willis Lyman, Delta, Utah.

The Ladies' Economic club sent down a fine arts exhibit to the fair this week as did also the Girls' club send some sewing and the Boys club some vegetables.

J. W. Walton, of Lakeside, Cali., who is quite heavily interested in land here came up the first of the week to look after the crops raised on his farms.

The Chronicle is sporting a new office desk, the handy work of J. H. Allison, who, when it comes to general carpentry and cabinet work is there like a brick house.

Go to the Delta Furniture store for Bed Springs, Mattresses and Cotts.   s23-30

Rev. Wm Alter and wife of near Pittsberg, Pa., stopped off in Delta the first of the week for a short visit with Rev. Hamilton and wife while on their way to visit the California Exposition.

Dr. Von Harten, Optometrist of the above company will be at:-

Commercial Hotel, Oasis, Sunday from 3 to 6, Sept. 26.

Moody Hotel, Deseret, Monday from 10 to 12, Sept. 27.

Wright Hotel, Hinckley, Monday from 3 to 6, Sept. 27.

Delta Hotel, Delta, Tuesday Sept. 28.

Will call on our customers at Lynndyl, Wednesday forenoon Sept. 29.

Neilson Hotel, Leamington, Wednesday from 3 to 6, Sept. 29.

Those having any trouble whatever with their eyes should not fail to call.

If you want a Kitchen Table, fall leaf, or an Extention Table, call at the Delta Furniture, Clark St.   s23-30

Mrs. Elizabeth Finch, who with her three sons, purchased a considerable acreage of land west of Sugarville, has arrived from her former home in Santa Ana, to take up her residence on her place. We understand the family contemplates some improvements in the near future.

Hinckley.

Almost every inhabitant of Hinckley is busy these days, harvesting crops and planting fall grain. The yield of all crops this year has been unusually good in this vicinity. Perhaps the largest wheat crop in the history of the town has has been gathered this year and many of the farmers have good yields of alfalfa seed. There would have been much more alfalfa seed had it not been for the fact that an early frost did a considerable damage.

There is a good attendance of pupils at the Millard Academy this term and many more will register as soon as the rush of fall work is over. With one exception the faculty this year is entirely new, but all of them are well qualified for their positions and a most successful school year is anticipated. Several new courses have been added to the curriculum among them Elocution and Physical Education for women.

Practically two hundred and fifty pupils are registered in the District school this term. The assembly hall has been partitioned making two more class rooms thereby making it possible to have a teacher for each grade. The faculty this year is as follows Principal, A. Irvin Tippetts, George Beal, Iren Mackelprang, Eda Cropper, Laura Shepherd, Carrie Leigh, LaPriel Robinson and Mattie Stephenson.

Mr. and Mrs. Wm Frank Pratt and Grandma Wright motored to Salt Lake City to attend Conference and the State Fair.

Other Conference visitors were John Reeves and wife and Robert E. Robinson and wife.

A farewell party was given last Wednesday evening in honor of Elder Harold Hinckley who left on a mission to New Zealand on Oct 6. The affair was in the nature of a dancing party. A good programe was rendered and refreshments were sold. A considerable sum of money was raised to give to the departing missionary.

Quite a number of our young people are attending college this year. College at the A. C. U. Eugene Hilton, Claris Erickson, Laverna Wright and Marvin Moody have gone to the B. Y. U and Mabel Parker is attending the U. of U.

A fine baby boy arrived at the home of Mr. and Mr. Isaac Elkington last Sunday evening mother and infant doing well.

Mr. Wilford Pratt has returned from Salt Lake City where he recently underwent an operation for a growth of bone on his nose The operation was successful and he is improving rapidly.

The Y. M. M. I. A. has been reorganized with Jacob Felix as President and Eddie Anderson and Don A. Bishop as counsellors.

Quite a number of Hinckley's male population spent the first few days of October at the Lakes, hunting ducks and geese.

The boy scouts of the town are improving its appearance by cleaning the weeds and debris from the lot formerly occupied by the Co-op Store.

BURBANK

On the 23rd. of Sept. the stork called at the home of J. F. Robinson of Garrison and left a fine boy.

Dr. Cook with his wife and daughter accompanied by Mrs. J. F. Christopherson and daughter motored to Ely and returned in the last few days.

J. E. Christopherson with Bert Christopherson, Doyle Huntsman and Samuel Ketcham motored to Atlantic, Nev. yesterday and returned to-day.

Oak City Offerings

Most of the conference people have returned home from Salt Lake and all report being well paid for their trip.

J. Alldredge went to Hinckley last week to get some turkey red wheat for seed.

L. Booth made a flying trip to Lynndyl last week on business.

L. R. Webb has returned from Hinckley where he has been for a few days.

Alfred Jacobson and Miss Ruby Jacobson, who are attending school at Provo, spent a few days with Mr. and Mrs. O. P. Jacobson who accompanied them back to Provo by team.

Miss Edna Anderson has returned home from her visit in Leamington. Her cousin, Miss Beatrice Neilson, accompanied her back and is visiting relatives and friends while here.

F. Neilson of Leamington, was here visiting relatives and friends and attending to business matters.

LeRoy Walker, our new postmaster, has moved the post office from Main st. down on his place on 1st W. st. between Main and 1st E. street.

A number from here attended conference at Hinckley Sunday.

Work on the new school house is being delayed on account of inability to get lumber which is needed before work can go on.

Bishop J. Lee Anderson now has the brick work on his new house done.

Mr. and Mrs. Milton Lovell, of Eureka, are visiting with their parents, Mr. and Mrs. Brigham Lovell, also relatives and friends.

A welcome party was given Elder John Q Dutson Friday 8th. A large crowd was out and everybody had a good time dancing.

Delta's First Car Autos

Mr. W. S. Pace Agent for the Ford Automobile, on Tuesday last, received his first consignment of Ford Automobiles, consisting of one car-load. This is the largest consignment of automobiles ever unloaded in Delta, there being seven in a car. The most of the cars are already sold, among the purchasers being Co. Supt. D. F. Peterson, of Hinckley, Jas. Woodward, of Fillmore, Wm McBride of Fillmore, and James Kelly of Delta. Mr. Pace expects to have another car of Fords in about a month.

Hinckley Happenings.

The Academy opened with life from the first. The vice president of the student body elected last spring did not return to school. It was therefor necessary to hold a new election. Wealthy Parker was the sucessful canidate. She and the president, Roy Hilton, took their oath of office last Wednesday morning and are now busily engaged in selecting the other officers of the student body.

The Girls Club was reorganized with Bly Moody as president, Blanche Sawyer, vice president, Rena Reeve, Secretary and Treasurer, Lyle Cropper, Myrtle Blackburn and Lois Blake Program committee.

Last Friday evening the faculty entertained in a splendid manner, the students, their friends and parents. Light refreshments were served to all present.

A special feature of the evening was the grand march, led by the faculty, in which an N and A were formed.

The home Economics association of Hinckley had a good attendance at their meeting last Friday. The needs of school chilrden were presented in talks and discussed, special attention being given to their clothing, sleeping accommodations, study hours, home meals and lunches. The speakers were Mrs. Susie Theobald and Mrs. Geneva Bishop. It was an exceedingly interesting meeting with a number of new comers present. The next regular meeting will be held on the 4th Fridsy of the month, Oct. 22, at 2:30, p. m., instead of 4, p. m., as heretofore. The papers to be given are on "How to spend Christmas at Home," "Christmas Candy Making," and "Suggestions for Christmas Gifts." Every one should bring one valuable suggestion for the open discussion.

My! what a busy time it is for the farmers. Many of them even think they don't have time to speak to you on the street. We are exceedingly glad to know of them being so busy, perhaps it means better crops, and especially the beet crop next year. Some industrious farmers have nearly all their grain in and watered, and some of it is nearly three inches high. But what speaks so well about the farming industry in this locality is that the farmers each year are trying to get just a little more land in cultivation, and broadening their interests and trying to see why the farm cannot pay large dividends. This tends to make farming more scientific. And until scientific methods can be used and practiced on the farm, it will not pay for the time and energy of the farmer.

Next Friday night, Oct. 15th, the Y. M. M. I. A. will give a weigh dance. The ladies are to bring luncheons to serve to the young men after they have paid ½ cent per lb. for the young lady whose name he draws. All come and enjoy the fun.

Mrs. Carrie H Clay of Iowa Falls, Iowa, who spent eight months in Hinckley three years ago, is here again to spend the winter with her niece, Mrs. C. A. Broaddus.

As the Academy was unable to secure a music teacher after the late resignation of last year's teacher, arrangements have been made with Mrs. Broaddus to take the pupils in piano and voice, the students to receive Academy credit for their work. Fourteen Music pupils are already well started on their semester's work.

Dr. Broaddus suffered a very severe shock one day last week, which may result in his remaining in this country a year or two longer, when a man paid him $10 two months in advance on a confinement case. The country is surely improving.

There is a new baby at the home of Mrs. Wright of Garfield (a daughter of Mrs. Fan Terry.)

Woodrow Items

Mr. and Mrs. Geo. Miller contemplate spending the winter in California.

Roy Stephens will rent Mr. Miller's land for the coming year.

The Jolly Stitchers meet Friday at the home of Mrs. Harry Ottley.

The Young People's League had a good attendance last Sunday, p. m., and a very pleasing meeting under the leadership of Mr. Osborne. Next Sunday evening Miss Mabel Richter will lead. All young people are cordially invited.

Mr. and Mrs. Remington are rejoicing in the arrival of a 9 lb. girl.

The farmers of West Delta shipped two car loads of fine porkers to the Los Angeles market last Tuesday.

Geo. S. Hoffecker, who has been spending the summer with Mrs. Tracy and Mrs. Fredricks, left Tuesday to seek a warmer climate for the winter season.

Mr. Hoffecker's health improved greatly while here and he may return next year as a permanent settler.

Mr. and Mrs. Geo. Miller gave the first turkey dinner of the season last week.

Mrs. Ella Connelly returned home Monday after an extended visit in Tintic.

All kinds of job work done at the Chronicle office in first class style.

Hall - Yates

On Thursday, October the seventh was solemnized the "tie that binds" when Bishop Shipley joined the hands of John W. Hall and Miss Cathrine Yates in marriage at his home at Sutherland in the presence of thirty-eight of their friends.

Mr. Hall is one of the sturdy and pushing settlers of Sutherland who came here from Michigan several years ago to carve for himself a home in this great stretch of reclaimed desert which he is making good at, and in doing so has won unto himself one of Utah's fair daughters.

Miss Yates comes from Logan here and has visited on the project for some time. She is one of Logan's charming young ladies with a bright pleasing personality.

The evening after the wedding ceremony was spent in songs, recitations and lunch with a tin can bengrade serenade.

We offer congratulations and extend to the newly weds best wishes and hopes for a long and happy married life.

Sugarville Siftings

Miss Vera Weatherby was an over Sunday guest of Miss Leona Seams.

Mrs. E. H. Hibbard will entertain the Friendship Thimble Club next Wednesday afternoon.

Mrs. Tillie Olds and Grandma Olds spent Sunday with Mrs. J. B. Seams.

A party of young people visited the hot springs last Sunday.

Word has been received from Miss Runyon that she is slowly recovering.

Mr. Gautherovx of San Diego arrived Sunday to look after his interests here. He is very favorabley impressed with this country and says for the future prospects are that it will necessitate two railroads in the near future to handle the outgoing products.

Saturday evening, Oct. 19, there will be a Tacky dance at the school house and every lady is to bring a box with supper for two which will be auctioned to the highest bidder. Coffee will

beserved. Now do your best to lookyour worst. A prize will be given for the tackiest costume, also aprize waltz. Every body come. Proceeds to buy books for the Library.

Born:—To Mr. and Mrs. S. W. Eccles, Oct. 9, a baby girl.

Born:—October the 8th, to Mr. and Mrs. Gus Billings, a girl.

Mr. and Mrs. A. L. Broderick are the proud parents of a baby girl born Monday the 11th,

FOR SALE:—Two Oak City Lots with water, terms reasonable L. R. Walker.   o7tf

Postmaster Paswater and Dr. Murray were down from Lynndyl last Friday.

Elmeda Johnson and Mr. and Mrs. J. E. Hunter, of Holden, were registered at the Delta Hotel the last of last week.

Mr. and Mrs. Harry Aller returned Wednesday from Baker City Oregon where they made an extended visit with Mrs. Aller's mother.

John F. Christopher of Tabor came in the last of last week and will make proof on a piece of land he purchased from a Mr. Wall of the same place.

As a result of adopting a cash basis and cutting down retail prices the Delta Merc. is now doing a big volume of business to the advantage of both buyer and seller.   o14lt

Mr. and Mrs. Branson Brinton motored down from Salt Lake Wednesday and passed thru Delta on their way to the Crescent farm where they will visit Mrs. Brinton's parents, Mr. and Mrs. A. L. Simmons.

Dr. Murray, accompanied by a number of witnesses and a Salt Lake attorney got off of the south bound train Tuesday afternoon and were autoed to Fillmore where the Dr. will defend himself in the liquor cases brot against him by the county some time ago.

Messers. Cottrell, Maxfield, Melville and Davis formed a party which paid a visit to the Sevier Bridge Dam last Sunday. The trip was made in Mr. Cottrell's car. The gentlemen report that affairs at the dam are progressing nicely, and if the kodak worked all right we expect to have some illustrations of the dam and some descriptive matter for next week's paper.

Millard County Progress
October 22, 1915

Hinckley.

Mrs. Catherine A. Allred, an aged resident of this place, died last Tuesday morning after a lingering. She was a woman of sterling qualities and was possessed of much scholarly ability having held several positions of trust in the community in which resided. She was the widow of the late T. B. Allred, Sr., and is survived by two children, Mr. P. Mrs. Emmelie A. Stapley of Hinckley. One daughter, Mrs. Martha Allred Greener, has preceded her to for the funeral have not yet been made but interrment will likely be held in the Hinckley cemetery.

Mrs. Workman of Idaho and Mrs. Martindaleof Tooele have spent the past ten days here visiting with their sister and brother, Mrs. Wm. A. Reeve and Mr. John E. Wright whom they had not seen for twelve years. While herr they were entertained byMrs. Arthur Reeve at dinner and on Sunday evening, Mrs. Wm. A. Reeve entertained in their honor at

an informal party. The two guests of honor had formerly resided in Dixie and mosgt of the guests were their former neighbors, among them Richard Parker and wife, John Hilton and wife, John M. Wright and wife, Edward Workman and wife, John E. Wright and wife and Arthur were served and an enjoyable time was had by all who were present.

On Otober 15th a "Weigh Dance" was given under the auspices of the Y.M.M.I.A. Fre luncheon was served by the young ladies and the dance was well patronized.

Next Friday evening a farewell party will be given in the Academy Auditorium in honor of Mrs. Lafayate C. Lee who leave on Saturday for a mission to Japan. Both of these young people graduated from the Millard Academy with the clas of 1915.

rompleted two modern cottages for James E. Blake. These houses are built with the idea of renting to Millard Academy students or teachers Mr. Blako has set a good example which should be followed by other enterprising citizens.

Teacher's nistitute for the Millard County School District will be held in Hinckley on October 29 and 30.

The teachers ofy the Hinckle school are making arrangements for the the Hallowe'en ball to be given in the Academy gymnasium. There will be special features for the entertainment of the patrons and dancing will be indulged in.

Parley Stapley and family of Kanarrahave arrived in Hinckley and intending to make their home here

Bishop and Mrs. A.Y. Stepheson of Holdenmotored over here last Sunday to spend a short time with their son Malben who is a student at the Millard Academy.

Last Friday a game of basebal was played between the eighth grade of the district school and the Fresh men of the Academy resulting in a victory for the former by a score of 6 to 1

On Friday of last week Miss Croppers fifth grade entertained the mothers, regular school work was demonstrated and topics pertaining to home and school relations were discussed.

DELTA.

Mr. and Mrs. Harry Aller have returned from Baker City, Oregon where they spent a very pleasant visit with Mrs. Aller's reatives. They also stopped over a few days in Salt Lake iCty to visit with Mr. Aller's mother and sister.

We understand that a number of the male citizens of Delta have been making hunting trips for ducks and geese but they say that the game is very scarce.

Dr. J.F. West, a Chicago doctor is now located at the City Drug Store and prepared to answer all medical calls.

Dr. C.H. Richards returned from Salt Lake City in his new Haines car which he purchased while in Salt Lake. Mrs. Richards accompanied him.

J.M. Davis, field superintendant for the Utah-Idaho Sugar Co. is in town looking after the interest of the company. According to Mr. Davis,s report that although there were tw hundred acres of beets planted here last fall on account of the late frosts here will be only some 6** or 7** acres harvested.

Frank Beckwith, cashier of the Delta State Bank, made a business trip to Salt Lake City returning the fore part of the week.

Mrs. W.L. Lackyard and Mrs. R. L. Bates spent Sunday in Lynndyle isiting friends there.

Mr. A.M. McPherson made a trip to the Sevier Damin the interest of the Delta Land & Water Co. He was accompanied by Mr. W.L. Lackyard.

Miss Williams who has been visiting Mr. and Mrs. M.M. Stapley, returned to her home in Lund thefore part of the week.

A number of the traveling men out of Salt Lake wholesale houses made business calls upon the Delta merchants the fore part of the week.

BURBANK

Dr. Conk, who has been undecided as t his future residence, has decided t locate at Garrison.

Miss Mattie Heckethrne is duly installed as Postmistress at Garrison

Mr. Shepard and Mr. Simonson made a tip to Milford the latter also visiting Black Rock.

Dr. W.D. Mason, the Nevada State veterinarian, has been going over the eastern part of White line County. He with his wife has spent a few days with us.

Henry Deardon who has been carrying the mail fom Garrison to Ely for the past 18 months, has moved to Newhouse fo the Inter.

OAK CITY.

The great amount of building which is being done in Oak City at present and along with the harvesting of the late crops is keeping the people extremely busy. The new school building which is being erected is progressing very rapidly due to the experienced workmen carpenters and brick layers who are employed by Mr. Williams the contractor. The building when completed will inded be a credit to Oak City and its people. It is located on the east side of the public square, a very beautiful location.

Leo Finlinson,s new home is now complete and he is expecting to move into it as soon as it is convenyenient.

Joshua Finlinson is also building a four room addition on to his home the brick work was done by John Collins of Leamington and the carpenter work was done by Contractor Harder of Leamington.

Messers Willis and Kendal of Nephi have contracted the plumbing of all the buildings, the work is already done on George E. Finlinson,s and they have proven their efficiency as skilled workmen.

Dr. Booth of Nephi has spent the past few days in our city doing dentist work.

Our townspeople who were in attendance at the General Conference of hto Mormon Church held in Salt Lake City October 3rd to 5th report it as being the most successful time and the largest gathering in all the history of the church.

Ray Finlinson and Frankie Roper who were married in the Salt Lake Temple October 1st spent two weeks at the World,s Panama Exposition in California. They were accompanied on their trip by Mr. and Mrs. Peter Neilson of Leamington They returned October 17th and report a very enjoyabe time during their travels.

Mr. Parleye Elder and Maggi Rawlinson left this morning for Manti where they will be joined in wedlock and we wish them a happy and prosperous life together.

Black Rock

John Bushnell of Meadow and Frank Paxton of Kanosh spent a number of days here lately cutting out and selling fat lambs and later lipping their herds.

Wm. Clifford of Soda Springs, Idaho, spent some time in our midst receiving a consignment of sheep. He also went on to Milford, Miners these points. He was accompanied by Walter James and Lester Allman, the latter drove the car on the trip.

W.H. Yull returned to Park City after spending some time here. He likes the northern part of the state better than these parts

Mr. and Mrs. A.T. James have gone to Milford to visit Mrs. James sisters who reside there.

Mr. J.D. Simonson of Warm Creek Snake Valley was a recent Black Rock visitor.

Mr. and Mrs. L.G. Clay spent several days in Milford on business.

Mr. and Mrs. J.W. Pollock just received the news of their son Raymond's wedding at Los Vegas where he is employed. The young people intend making their home at that place.

Roy Gale who has been here working for E.R. Niles was summoned brother of his recently suffered an accident.

J.W. Pollock was a business visitor to Milford the last of the week.

WOODROW.

NORTH TRACT NEWS
TO LATE FOR LAST WEEK

Mr. Anderson arrived with with California Wednesday and was the first new settler who has moved in over the new railroad. He is located west of the townsite of Ucalla better known as Sugarville.

Mr. Buelar shipped a carload of wheat to Redlands, California over the new railroad.

The Literary Society met Saturday evening and a very large audience was entertained by the fine program which was rendered. Everybody enjoyed the debate which was given by two married men and two single men. The married men discussing why men should marry and the single men why men should not marry. Many funny points were given which caused much laughter. The negative won. After the program all enjoyed a short dance.

Mrs. Crnholm spent Thursday wit Mrs. S.H. Thompson of Woodrow.

Many new settlers are moving in and many nice houses are being built so that it looks like an old project. Not a desert like it was 5 years ago.

Sunday a crowd of young folks took dinner and visited the hot springs, twelve miles north of Sugarville or Ucalla.

The Sunday evening song serivce was much enjoyed by all and we find Mr. Osborn a good leader and a good chorister. Miss Mable Richter will lead the next Sunday evening service.

Much of the Midland tract has been cleared and prepared for fall crop.

Mr. George Erickson has erected a new house on his farm and is now looking for a housekeeper.

Many of the people have been ill with severe coldswhich seems to be an epidemic caused by the dust.

Miss Ruby Lambert was a guest of Miss Verda Oppenbelmer the week end.

Mr. Charles Connelly left for a visit to Tintic this week.

Mr. Holliday is down from Salt Lake building a new grainery on his placenear Woodrow.

The well drillers keep quite busy drilling wells for the new settlers. They have just completed a well for Will Cary near Ucalla.

THIS WEEKS NEWS

Mrs. J. J. Clark ad little daughter left for Califor. to visit an ill grand-daughter Mon. y.

Mrs. Connelly arrived from Tintic where she has been spending the summer.

The orchestra met and practiced at the Hillyard home on Tuesday evening. Several of the young folks came in and all enjoyed the music while a few sang songs. All helped themselves to a number of varieties of home made candies which are delicious.

Miss Cora Heise has purchased a art so that she can now drive from her home to the school where she teaches.

The Jolly Stitchers met at the home of Mrs. Harry Ottley Friday and gave a strk shower on one of their members. Ice cream and cake were served and all had a lovely time.

Miss Richer of Ucalla left for California Friday where she will spend the winter. She has been here to see her crop harvested which went 41 bushels to the acre. Mr. James Shields farming it the previous year

The people within two and a half miles of Ucalla or Sugarville received welcome letters giving them a lot at Sugarville for each frty acres they owned.

A parcel social was given at Sutherland Friday evening by the Y.L. and Y.MM.I.A. with a dance afterwards. All seemed to enjoy themselves.

The surveyors have changed their boarding place to that of the Oppenbelmer home.

A box social or tackie party was given by the Thimble Club on Saturday evening. And it was indet a merry time for all. The boxes went like hot cakes and at very good prices.

The prizes for the tackiest dressed were awarded to Mrs. Albert Watts and after supper all enjoyed the big dance.

Saturday afternoon a surprise party was given on Mrs. Miller by the neighbor ladies. A very pleasand afternoon was spent and at a late hour delicious refreshments were served.

Tuesday morning Mr. and Mrs. George Miller left for California. We were sorry to see them go, they were such good nethusiastic people, but hope they will return here some day.

Mr. Stephens and family are moving on the Miller ranch as they have leased it for a year.

Mr. Samuel Playford and wife are moving on Struan Robinson' ranch which Stephens just vacated.

Mr. Tracy and several neighbors together shipped a car of hogs Monday. Mr. Bert Johnson is taking them down to California.

The items printed under the head of "Newsy News From the Grwing town of Woodrow" a week ago were not fromWoodrow alone, but from Ucalla or better say from the North Tract. Woodrow is not a town, it was merely the name of the post office which is gone now since the mail route or the rural delivery started. Although the little neighborhood will go by that name and will work for the town of Ucalla.

The meeting or song service Sunday was well attended by a full hous and a motion made to form themselves into a Christian Endeavor Soety. A decision was made to have a Hallov e'en party on October 30th g and a committee appointed to arrange for it. Miss Cora Heise will be leader next Sunday evening

The Home Economics Club met with Mrs. Abbott Thursday afternen. Their topic for discussion being on lunches, school lunches and all kinds of lunches. This is a very good sciety and we hpe every twn in this vicinity will son have one.

The friends f Mr Iver Iverson were happily surprised when Iver went to the depot and met his bride Friday mrning. May thy live long and be happy with much prosperity.

Mr. and Mrs. Hillyard are visitin California, but are expected back son.

The thrashers are still busy thrashing arund here as there is a very large crop and the people arund Pucalla ar very glad anther thrashing machine has arrived so htey can have their grain thrashed.

OAK CITY.

At the regular monthly Priesthood meeting, which was held in Hinckley the last Saturday in October, many items of interest and worth were discussed in a satisfactory manner before the Stake Officers, and timely remarks given by Pres. Hinckley were of such a nature that it is believed they will encourage and undoubtedly bring abou . closer observance of many thin s taught and advocated by the Mormon Church. A good representation was in attendance from Oak City and all express themselves as being well repaid for going.

Saturday night being Hallowe'en, waag fittingly observed by a number of characters who indeed had aghostley appearance. Pumkin devils permeated the atmosphere and aroused within the hearts of many a discontented, superstitious feeling, especially when coming in contact with the one who played so well the part of the originator of the ghostly family.

The services held Sunday were well attended. In the evening Mutual an announcement was made relative to the farewell party which will be given Friday evening, November

6th for Leo Walker, who leaves on the 9th as a missionary to the Northwestern States.

Our towns people are busy harvesting their late crops of corn and potatoes, which are comparatively good.

Our school teachers, Mr. Booth, Miss Smith and Miss Margarette Nielson were at Hinckley last Friday and Saturday to attend the Teacher's Institute.

Black Rock.

C. W. Hodgson of Park City is visiting with his brother, L. E. Hodgson His faithful little Ford came through in good shape.

Miss Mamie Sawyer went to Hinckley the latter part of the week to attend Teacher's Institute held at that place.

R. W. Price, auditor for the American Express Co., spent a day here last week.

Frank Paxton of Kanosh and Ray Hamilton of Beaver arrived here with some fine rams from Pendleton, Oregon. Mr. Paxton drove his to his herds and Mr. Hamilton reloaded

the remainder on board cars and shipped further south.

Verne Sanderson of Fairview took the train here a few evenings ago to visit his home.

Alex Pace of Nephi has returned home after having spent some time with his brother who is mining in the Cricket Mountain just north of here.

On November 1st Mr. and Mrs. W. D. Livingston took their departure for Anaheim, California, where they own a beautiful home. After so many years of faithful service in the

employ of the Salt Lake Route they will be greatly missed.

Hert Christopherson and Tim Mulhall of Burbank came to Black Rock with a bunch of horses.

A. J. Sieber, wife and small son are settled here. Mr. Sieber is the new R.R. Agent. They came from San Bernardino.

W. J. Briggs of Beaver was a business visitor here one day last week.

Walter James, Jack Travis and George Dixxo spent a couple of days on business at the Black Rock mine.

Lloyd Schwab of San Bernardino, Cal., is visiting with his sister Mrs. A. J. Sieber.

DELTA.

Born to Mr. and Mrs. Hyrum Tanner, October 19th a fine bba ygirl.

Dr. J. F. West, wife and family, who have been visiting the Doctor's sister, Mrs. C. H. Richards, returned to his home in Chicago, Illinois, on Wednesday morning.

Three of the Delta hunters, Messers R. C. Bates, Harry Aller, W. L. Lackyard and Mr. Stewart, the water master were each successful in the bagging of a large goose last Sunday.

The little daughter of Fred Cottrell has been quite ill the past week.

Miss Lillian Williams of Oasis was a Delta visitor the forepart of the week.

Sam Dorrity, our County Sheriff was in Delta on business the forepart of the week.

W. L. Lackyard, the jeweler has in a fine stock of Christmas goods.

S. W. Eccles made a business trip to Salt Lake City and Ogden last week to make new purchases for the store and to attend to business interests in Ogden.

Gene Johnson, who is doing the cement work on the new school house in Oak City, made a business trip to Delta the forepart of the week

A fine boy arrived at the home of Mr. and Mrs. Ed. Whicker on the 6th of the month. Yes, that is why Ed. walks around here and doesn't know any of his old friends.

Aller & Co., had a car of fine potatoes shipped in here Monday and Tuesday a carload of fine apples Jonathans, Parmaines, Wineaps and Gános. Mr. Aller tells us that he expects two more cars of potatoes in the next ten days.

Mr. Ted Moore has purchased of our local agent here, W. H. Pace, a new Ford 'runabout. Ted says no more quiet evenings down on the farm for him and Mrs. Moore.

Messers Jim Villers, Clarence Gouder, Chess Jacobs and Ray Tozier returned the latter part of last week from up in the hills by and around Whiskey Creek, each having captured a deer in the hunt.

BURBANK

Machinery for the new mill on the tungsten property, north of Warm Creek, will be installed in the near future as it is already on the ground. Very promising prospects of tungsten carrying gold have been found

in the vicinity of Osceola by the Titford brothers and Richard Millick. Don Taylor has struck a vein of shelite at the head of Snake Creek

Joseph Deardon, Mail Contractor between Newhouse and Ely has purchased a new truck in Salt Lake City for use on the line.

Abraham Articles

The people of Abraham seem to be enjoying health and prosperity.

This vicinity has a car load of Turkeys ready for market.

Mr. E. H. Nichols, of Spanish Fork, was in Abraham on business last week.

The Vanevera Bros., have in 140 acres fall wheat.

Mrs. Albert Reed was visiting her mother Mrs. Wilkens last week.

Mr. William Nott will leave soon for Salt Lake to join his family where they will reside. O. L. Lake will take charge of Mr. Nott's fine farm here.

Mrs. Martha Stoutt and two children, of Lynndyl, are here visiting her mother Mrs. Mary Hansen.

Needham Bros., delivered a car of hogs in Delta last week.

The big Toe dance at Abraham Saturday night was a grand success.

Mrs. Robert Fullmer was called to Payson last week by the illness of her mother.

County School Supt., D. F. Peterson, in company with Mr. Hoganson, was visiting our school Friday.

Mrs. Geo., Whitehead will move to Hinckley soon so the children can attend school at that place.

Mr. and Mrs. Swartz were visiting Sunday at the McCurdy home near Hinckley.

Mrs. Ed Soules, of Salt Lake, came in Saturday and will spend the winter with her father H. B. Lake.

Mrs. Needham and sons, Fay and Guy, left Tuesday for Salt Lake where they will reside for the winter.

A sister and family of Mr. W. J. Cary, is expected this week from Montana on a visit.

Dan Black, of Deseret, was looking after Abraham interests Monday.

Mrs. Laura Petty and husband, are visiting Mrs. Petty's mother this week.

Grandma Hogan is here to make an extended visit at the home of her son Donald and family.

Mrs. Dubois of Santaquin is here visiting her daughter Miss Daisy who is primary teacher in our school.

Mr. and Mrs. John Crook are busy packing turkeys for the Salt Lake market.

Popular Couple Married

Last Monday evening at the home of the brides mother occurred the marriage of Miss Jennie Gray to Mr. Will Cook. The cermony was solemnized in the presence of the relatives and immediate friends of the young couple at the home prepared for them by the groom on Clark street.

Miss Gray is one of Delta's most popular and most comely young ladies. She has been employed for a long time as head clerk at the Eccles Cooperative Inst., where she was highly prized by her employer and where she made a host of friends by her obliging ways and sunny disposition. These will greatly miss her at the store but will be pleased to learn of new relations Mrs. Cook is the daughter of Mrs. Zina Gray, who with her husband and Jennie came here from Beaver and settled on a farm near Sutherland three years ago, Mr. Gray having departed this life one year ago.

Mr. Cook is a son of J. H. Cook, who lives just north of Delta. He is an industrious and prosperous farmer and owns a farm just northwest of Delta.

To this happy young couple we take pleasure in extending the congratulations and best wishes of the Chronicle and its readers and wish them a long and happy wedded life.

LOCAL NEWS

Jim Villers has been wrestling with pnemonia but improving

Born:—Monday, the 15th, a baby girl, to Mr. and Mrs. Ernest Pierce.

Mrs. Wm. Prince, of Buehl, Ida., is here visiting her aunt, Mrs. James Wilkins Jr.

E. D. Knight has just had a fine flowing well put down on his farm two miles south of Delta.

Mrs. J. H. Hall and son, of the South Tract have gone to Salt Lake where they will spend the winter.

Mr. and Mrs. James Turner of Delta are the proud parents of a new baby girl, born last Saturday.

Leonard Broadrick is down with a near attack of pnemonia, and about every other person is tussling with a cold of more or less severity.

H. A. Williams, wife and son of Imperial, Cali., arrived here the first of the week to look for a farm in the "Greater" Delta Country.

Buy the good house wife the best washer on the market and

save her many back aches and much drudgery:—Delta Furniture Store.

FOR SALE:—Feed grinding and Chopping, for toll or cash, at Snowcrest ranch. Capacity, 40 bushels per hour, ground and elevated to wagon. Ted Moore.
n18d30

Miss Cullison, who has been bookkeeping at the Eccles Co-operative Merc. Inst., for the past several months, is taking a vacation and has gone to San Francisco to visit the exposition.

R. J. Law reports his store building at Sugarville progressing nicely and the plasterers now putting on the plaster. He expects soon to open for business but at present cannot state the exact date.

The Improvement Ass'n gave Miss Jennie Gray a bundle shower last Saturday at the home of her mother. A goodly turnout was had and Miss Gray was presented with many useful articles.

Mrs. Theodore Britt came in from Cali. last Monday and was followed Wednesday by her husband with a car of goods. They have purchased land near Sugarville and will take up residence on it as soon as Mr. Britt can erect a dwelling.

C. A. Smead, who is located near Woodrow left last Sunday morning for Francitas Texas, where he will spend the winter. Mr. Smead was called to Texas last spring by the illness and death of his father and is now returning to help settle the family estate.

J. A. Faust Jr., of Pioche, Nev., is here visiting his parents during his mother's illness, who is quite sick with la grippe and for a time was threatened with pneumonia. Mr. Faust says that he sees a big change in the country since his last visit to Delta and thinks the country has made great progress. He may decide to remain here.

Mr. and Mrs. Willard Corry, of Cedar City, visited here the last of last week with Arthur Bunker and family, Mrs. Carey and Mr. bunker being brother and sister. Mr. Cary was here in the interest of the Consolidated Wagon & Machine Co. of which he is collector. They are traveling by auto and continued their journey on to Nephi.

P. L. Brunson of Fillmore, the monument man, was a Delta visitor this week. Mr. Brunson says the future looks bright for the Fillmore district on account of the great success they are meeting with in bringing in artesion wells. Four have already been brot in, furnishing big flows and there are three big

rigs on the ground drilling. Mr. Brunson was here looking over the ground with an idea of getting a lot and next spring putting in a marble yard.

Don Kimball, who has a farm near Abraham, left last Saturday for Los Angeles where he will spend the winter with his parents. He will return in the early spring to tackle the farming proposition again. Don has

always lived in the city until coming to the "Greater" Delta country but likes the change and is one of the active young men who are helping to carve out a great destiny for this valley, as well as himself.

County Agent Welch, after reading the article in a recent issue of the Chronicle relative to the possible importation of dairy

cattle, states that he will be glad at any time to lend his assistance and experience to either individuals or committees who wish to pass on the qualities of cattle for dairy purposes. He is also at the command of all farmers who wish to avail themselves of any knowledge he may have relative to farming or the live stock industry.

Delta Man Marries in California

The following, clipped from the San Francisco Chronicle, announces the marriage of one of the early settlers of the South Tract.

Mr Hoff left here a couple of weeks ago after having leased his ranch, which he has redeemed from a desert to fine productive farm, to spend the winter in California.

His many friends here will be greatly pleased to learn of his marriage and wish him great happiness.

"W. M. Hoff, a retired rancher of Delta, Utah, and Mrs. Wilda Kelter, a wealthy widow of Meeker, Colo., were married by the Reverend J. M. Caldwell in a parlor suite at the Manx hotel yesterday. W. M. Hoff Jr., a student at St. Mary's College, was best man.

The bride was attended by Mrs. Madge Hamilton and Mrs. Belle Russell of Long Beach.

The bride and groom, both of whom are 56 years of age, intend making a honeymoon tour of California that is to last through the winter, and will then go to their summer home on White river, near Meeker Colo."

Millard County Chronicle
December 9, 1915

ak City Offerings

(Too late for last week.)

Leo Lyman accompanied ife to Salt Lake City where she entered the L. D. S. hospital on account of illness. We all wish her a success.

August Neilson, of Leamington, was in town one day last week on business.

Born:—To Mr. and Mrs. T. B. Talbot, a big baby girl. Mother and baby doing nicely.

Miss Vivian Talbot, of Hinckley, is visiting with her cousin, Miss Vera Lovell.

Tuesday night a bundle shower was given Mr. and Mrs. Ray Finlinson at the home of Leo Finlinson. A big supper was served and Geo. E. Finlinson sang some very interesting songs. Ray thanked all present for their gifts. All had a good time. Eighty persons were present at the party.

Wednesday night Mr. and Mrs. Ray Finlinson gave their wedding dance. They had the Nephi Orchestra to play and they certainly furnished some very fine music.

Peter Nelson and wife, of Leamington attended the big dance of Mr. and Mrs. Finlinson.

On Thanksgiving a big ball game was played between the District School boys and the Stiffs, the score being 9 to 11 in favor of the boys. At night a dance was enjoyed.

Friday night the Oak City Orchestra went over to Lynndyl and played for a dance. A number of our young folks accompanied them.

Mr. and Mrs. Jess Peterson visited with friends and relatives at Hinckley last week.

Saturday night a bundle shower was given Mr. and Mrs. Parley Elder at the home of Mr. and Mrs. L. Olson.

Mr. and Mrs. Jeff Finlinson, of Leamington, were here last week visiting relatives and friends.

Killed in Runaway

Joe Moody, of Oasis, had the misfortune to lose a horse out of his team last Tuesday when after driving up to one of the stores in Oasis, he dropped the lines and went into the store, the horses taking fright ran away and after going a short distance they ran into a tree injuring one of them to the extent that they were compelled to put it out of misery.

Abraham Articles

Under the direction of Prof. W. H. Jones and Miss Daisy DuBois, Nov. 24, the school gave a program and dance for the children and parents. Each part was rendered well.

Thursday evening a program was given by the Ward at the Abraham hall. Aftere the program a dance, at which the best dancer was awarded a prize. Mr. Elmer Fullmer and Daisy DuBois were the lucky ones. Music was furnished by Mrs. Roy Bills and Co. All was a decided success.

Mr. and Mrs. M. L. Tuchs entertained the needlecraft and families at a Thanksgiving dinner, Nov. 25. Every body enjoyed themselves.

We are glad to see the Needham Brothers again among us, after an extended visit at the metropolis of the state.

Last Saturday a fine big baby girl arrived at the home of Mr. and Mrs. Reid. Mother and baby are doing well.

The Ward Reunion celebration (that should have been held Dec. 19th.) has been postponed until Jan. 1st.

Last Sunday afternoon at the L. D. S. Church, people were pleasantly surprised to have among them as visitors, Messrs Morris and Blake, of Hinckley.

Mrs. Soules of Salt Lake, has come to Abraham to visit with Mr. Lake for the winter.

Mr. and Mrs. Roy Bills were in Delta Tuesday on business.

Mrs. Robert Fullmer has returned home from Payson, where she has been visiting her mother.

Mrs. Madsen, of Payson, arrived in Abraham last week for an extended visit with her daughters, Mesdames Houser and Fullmer.

FOR SALE:—A brand new Xray Incubator, or for trade for chickens. For further particulars see or write C. M. Cochran, North Tract, Delta R. D. No. 1, Box 86   d9-23

Millard County Chronicle
December 23, 1915

Abraham Articles

The Stork has been very busy out here. Three new babies have been born within the last two weeks. Last week a fine boy arrived at the home of Bishop Donald Hogan and this week he dropped another at the home of Herbert Taylor.

Mrs. Allen Young has been very ill the last ten days; but we are glad to hear she is convalescing.

The primary grades were dismissed for Monday as their teacher, Miss Daisy DuBois, was sick.

Sugarville Siftings

Alvin Iverson is spending the holidays at Ephriam.

Mrs. Thure Cronholm is visiting her mother at Salt Lake.

Mrs. R. N. Wright left last Wednesday for Los Angeles Cal., having received word of the serious illness of her mother.

Mr. and Mrs. Anderson entertained at dinner on Christmas, Mr. and Mrs. Clarence Chelson and Fred Tingleaf.

Lou Carpenter, who has been working for John Law, left last week for his home at Orunge Call., to spend the winter.

There will be a leapyear dance at the school house Saturday evening, Jan. 2nd. Refreshments will be served by the gentlemen and the ladies will pay for the dance, 25 cents.

Another Pioneer Called

Mr. and Mrs. J. H. Schwartz of the North Tract, were called on to spend a very sorrowful Christmas this year, having been summoned to Spanish Fork last week to attend the last sad rites of Mrs. Schwartz's mother, Mrs. Matilda Robertson, who died there last Thursday morning.

Mrs. Robertson was one of the early pioneers of Utah and crossed the plains with the hand-cart brigade when but a small girl of 9 years and at the time of her death she was seventy-nine years old. Mr. and Mrs. Schwartz have the sympathy of all in their sorrow.

WOODROW ITEMS

The Jolly Stitchers will hold an all day meeting at the home of Mrs. Robt. Britt, January 19th.

* * * *

The Literary Society will be held January 20th. A fine program is assured. Come and see.

* * * *

A married folks' dance was given at Woodrow last Friday evening, which was well attended and much enjoyed despite the cold weather.

* * * *

Rodney Shields, the 12 year old son of Mr. and Mrs. James Shields, unfortunately broke his right forearm while trying to crank the automobile last Sunday morning. At present he is apparently faring well, however.

* * * *

Woodrow has stood the cold snap with fortitude but we will confess it is beginning to get on our nerve. Tuesday a. m. the thermometer scared us when we saw it standing at 23 below zero, with the sun away up in the sky.

* * * *

January 10th a party of Woodrow gentlemen surprised Geo. Webster with a stag oyster supper and a general good time. George says he hopes they will come again but will return home in time for him to open the store.

* * * *

Some of our enterprising citizens wrote out a subscription pledge Monday and made a house to house canvas for subscriptions to be used in building an amusement hall. They obtained a building site and $800.00 in cash, upon which a mass meeting of the citizens was called for Wednesday evening and plans formulated for the immediate erection of a hall. Hurrah for Woodrow!

Millard County Progress
December 24, 1915

JURY LIST FOR THE YEAR 1916.

In the District Court of the Fifth Judicial District, County of Millard, State of Utah.

List of names from which the Grand and petit jurors shall be drawn to serve in the District Court, in and for Millard County, State of Utah, during the next succeeding calendar year, towit 1916.

ABRAHAM.

O. M. Fulmp, Donald Hogan and C. M. Hickman.

CLEAR LAKE.

Emoy John

BLACK ROCK.

Hoace A. Stohl, Athur G. James

BURBANK.

J. F. Christopherson

DELTA.

George Day, J. D. Works, Levi W. McCullough, A. B. Ward, William N. Gardner, Raymond S. Bishop, John E. Steele, Robert Whicker, Don E. Bishop, Nelson S. Bishop, William Bunker, J. W. Underhill, George S. Boyack, Willis Lyman, Fred Cottrell, Orson Erickson.

DESERET.

George F. Croft, N. L. Peterson, E. J. Elliason, Joseph V. Black, H. S. Cahoon, Jr., J. M. Moody, Angus Allred, John Henry Western, John A. Bennett.

FILLMORE.

Orrin C. Black, James W. Frampton, F. C. Melville, Lars Rasmussen, George W. Black, Frank H. Partridge, Willard Rogers, Don C. Wixom, Joseph Beeston, Cuthbert Trimble, Henry Hanson, John A. Peterson, N. J. Bearegard, Daniel Stevens, J. Frank Day, Alonzo Huntsman, Parker Robison, Edward Trimble, Newel Warner, George C. Velle, John H. Davis, Hyrum S. Mitchell William H. Rassmussen, Porter Hatton, J. F. Holbrook, John Carling, Wm. Speaksman Harrison Anderson, Lorenzo Hanson, Jacob B. Davis, J. W. Payne, Charles Christopherson.

GARRISON.

Leo B. Rowley.

HINCKLEY

Heber J. Mitchel, Frank Wright, E. H. Theobald, Thomas H. Pratt, Daniel Morris Jr., Ed. Humphries, John T. Jacobs, James Blake, Jacob Felix, Edwin P. Anderson, A. A. Hinckley, Willie E. Robison, Samuel C. Dutson, Nephi Stewart, Lester C. Neely, Nathaniel Badger, Norman L. Bliss, C. E. Humphries, Hugh Hilton.

KANOSH

James Charlesworth, E. T. Rappleye, William Cummings Jr., C. F. Christensen, Alonza George, Henry Paxton, Antony Paxton Jr., George Chesley, Lewis Barney, Frank Slaughter, Weldo George, Will Paxton, Frank J. Christensen, John A. Watts, Joseph Whicker, William Penny, John Rogers.

HOLDEN.

Charles Wood, Jr., Edgar Turner, Austin Ashby, Franklin Badger, Wm. T. Bennett, Joseph Hunter, Richard S. Nixon, William F. Stevens, J. Ray Stingham, G. M. Mills.

LEAMINGTON.

Fred Nielson, Rodney B. Ashby, Brigham Clark, William J. Finlinson, John W. Anderson.

LYNNDYLE.

Thomas C. Callister, J. Alma Langston, Leonard Meecham.

MEADOW.

James Labrum, David W. Duncan, Edward Stott, Jr., Hyrum Gull, Joseph H. Fisher, Edward B. Dushnell, Joseph Beckstrand, Elmer Duncan, Emil K. Pearson, Paul Stott.

OAK CITY.

Joseph P. Callister, Edward L. Lyman, Lorenzo Lovell, John E. Lovell, Ray Finlinson, Arthur Talbott, Eddie Jacobson.

OASIS.

Marcus Skeem, S. M. Hawley, John Styler, David Day, Henry Jackson, Henry Huff.

SCIPIO.

William R. Thompson, F. S. Wasden, Adolph Hanseen, Carl Brown, Carl Robins, William Memmott, Wm. Bradfield, Jr., Hans Esklund, Curtis Johnson, Erwin M. Brown, Marvin M. Hatch, Bruce R. Mathews, Niels Lawritzen, Antone P. Peterson, Wells Robins.

SMITHVILLE.

Daniel J. Simonson.

SOUTHERLAND.

G. I. Smith, M. A. Abbott, W. R. Walke, Marr D. Simons, Volney H. King.

WOODROW.

Jerome Tracy, Fred Barben, Jesse Sill, John Wind.

Black Rock

Miss Della Nay has returned to her home at Monroe, after spending several months in this vicinity.

Walter James was called to Salt Lake on business. On his return he was accompanied by his daughters the Misses Denitl and Thekla, who have been attending school at Westminster College.

The Black Rock school closed for the holidays last Friday. Miss Sawyer, the teacher, has gone to her home in Hinckley to spend the vacation.

Mrs. A. J. Sieber and small son Glenn have gone to San Bernardino to visit Mrs. Sieber's mother and incidentally to do a little Christmas shopping.

J. H. Templeton of Seattle was a Black Rock visitor last week. He was sent out by the Stewart-Calvert Co., of Seattle. Walter James accompanied Mr. Templeton to the mineral deposit which he wished to examine. There is no lack of quantity and if the samples secured prove to be as good as desired, there is a chance that some extensive work may be done.

One day last week E. R. Niles, accompanied by Charles Malmberg went to his city of the saints. On their return they brought another with them. Mrs. Niles did not object to the new comer but welcomed the "Tin Lizzie" and has grown so fond of "Lizzie" she will keep her in the family.

Jack B. Travers is spending a few days in Salt Lake.

After spending three years on his dry farm and receiving title to his land, Lester Afluisi has gone to his home in New York City to spend X-mas with his parents and sisters.

A. J. Sieber was a Milford visitor one day this week. Judging by the number of parcels he was carrying upon his return, we infer that he expects to play the part of Santa Claus to a small boy.

We regret that Herbert Kruse the 11 year old son of Nicholas Kruse, has been suffering severely of rheumatism. However he is feeling a little better now and it is hoped that he will soon be well.

OFFICIAL DIRECTORY

Millard County Chronicle
January 20, 1916

Geo. Wise Cropper

George Wise Cropper was born May 4, 1347, at Spring Creek, Harris County, Texas, and died in Salt Lake City, Jan., 11, 1916, in the L. D. S. hospital, leaving two sons and five daughters. His wife, two daughters and one son preceeded him to the great beyond. He also leaves two brothers, Thomas W. Cropper of Hinckley, Utah, and Leigh R. Cropper of Deseret, Utah, one sister, Mrs. Kate Webb of Los Angeles, California, and a host of relatives and friends.

The funeral was held in the Deseret Chapel, under the direction of the Bishopric, conducted by first councilor, P. T. Black, and assisted by the Indian War Veterans. On January 15, 1916, he was laid to rest in the Oasis cemetery, by his wife and children.

His people emigrated to Utah in the year 1856, his father having died in Texas in the year 1851. He settled in Fillmore, Millard County, Utah. Later his folks moved to Deseret, in the year 1861, and his step-father, Jacob Croft, and brothers superintended the building of the first dam in the Sevier river.

After a number of years the dam went out and the place was abondoned. Then again in the winter of 1875-76, Gilbert Webb and Mr. Cropper and brothers, with some others rebuilt it. After some time Mr. Webb, who had put up money for building the dam became bankrupt.

Then the Deseret Irrigation was formed. They bought Webb's rights; a committee on the work under the George W. Cropper consisting of, William Byrum snup. Mr. Cropper working for the up building of Millard Co. until the day of his death.

Mr. Cropper always had great faith in the future of this broad county. He served as Sheriff of Millard for many years and assisted in the arrests of some of the most desperate characters or desperados that ever visited this part of Utah. He knew no fears. He also took part, and was active in the early settling of Utah, especially during Indian times. He was always among the ones defending the people.

With the passing of Mr. Cropper closes a life which was always active in the interest of the people of this community and the state of Utah; a life that was full of thrilling pioneer incidents and hard ships, always looking to the betterment of mankind and the world at large, the passing of which will bring sorrow to his hosts of acquaintances and relatives and with a reflection of his past life of usefulness which will stand as a password for the better things to come.

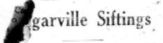

garville Siftings

. J. Clark and family, of Woodrow, spent Sunday with Mr. and Mrs. Albert Watts.

Alvin Iverson returned Monday from his visit to Ephriam.

Mr. and Mrs. E. Pierce and son, of Sunflower, left Sunday morning for Indiana.

Mr. and Mrs. Iver Iverson attended the basket ball game at Delta Saturday evening.

The Friendship Thimble Club will be entertained at the home of Mrs. Olds next Wednesday.

Literary next Saturday evening. After the exercises the Ladies will dispose of their quilts and pillow and serve coffee with a box supper, every lady to bring a box, with supper, to be auctioned off. The proceeds go for the literary fund. Be sure and get there by 7:30.

Oak City Offerings

The new school house is completed and will be ready for use soon as it is accepted. It will be highly appreciated, as the old school house is now too small.

A number of our men folk are working on the canal below town. It is expected that a few more will commence work next week.

Laval Elder, daughter of Pa ey Elder, died last Sunday nigh The doctor pronounced it dip theria that caused her dea But there isn't any new cases present.

Anthony Christensen has be ill with the neuraliga in his he He is now improving.

Bert Robins and wife w here on business last week.

George Anderson has retur from Salt Lake where he m a business trip.

Sutherland Searchlights

Messers Jeff Clark and Burt Johnson are buying hogs now for the market. The prices they offer this week is $5.35. Coming up!

Simeon Walker is here looking after business matters.

The main topic of the day now is the sugar factory, Pro and Con. Some for and some without faith.

Mr. Davis, the representative of the Utah Idaho Sugar Co., is now in the field looking after Co's interest.—Tending to ect.

Mr. Patton of the Intermountain Fal Credit Ass'n is again in th vicinity looking after busine

W. D. Liviston is down from Salt Lake C to look after affairs on the land tract. There are several families who have recent located thereon, among them Walters family from near Pa

Howard Att, Ward Robinson and Lon is, have gone to the woods trap for coyotes, and cut posts wood, should they run out job trapping.

Bishop G. Ripley is expected home this wk from Ogden where he has en to receive medical treat He is improved a littl health with promises of a e speedy recovery with ri are.

We are pleas see the bills of the recital given Wednesday night elta by Miss Helene Davis ur town as it proves that son ood can come out of Sutherl er all.

ONE OF MILLARD COUNTY'S BRAVEST SONS CALLED HOME.

George Wise Cropper was born May 4, 1847, at Spring Creek, Harris County, Texas and died in Salt Lake City, Utah, January 11, 1916, in the L. D. S. Hospital, leaving two sons and five daughters; his wife, one son and two daughters having preceeded him to the Great Beyond. He also leaves two brothers, Thomas W. Cropper of Hinckley, Utah, and Leigh R. Cropper of Deseret, Utah, one sister, Mrs. Kate Webb of Los Angeles, Cal., and a host of relatives and friends to mourn his demise.

The funeral was held in the Deseret L. D. S. Chapel on January 15th under the direction of the Bishopric and was conducted by First Councelor P. T. Black, assisted by the Indian War Vetrans Association of which he was a member. He was laid to rest in the Oasis Cemetary beside the graves of his wife and children.

Mr. Cropper came to Utah with his

mother in the year 1856, his father having died in Texas in the year 1851, and settled in Fillmore, Millard County, Utah, where he lived with his folks until the year 1861, when they moved to Deseret, where he and his brothers and step-father Jacob Croft superintended the building of the first dam in the Sevier river. After a number of years the dam went out and the place was abandoned. Then again in the winter of 1875 and 1876, Gilbert Webb and Mr. Cropper and brothers and some others rebuilt it. It was this venture which caused he bankruptcy of Gilbert Webb, who had furnished the funds for the undertaking. The Deseret Irrigation Co., was then formed and they bought the Dam of Mr. Webb and all his rights, under the direction of a committee composed of the following: George W. Cropper, William V. Black and Hyrum Dewsnup.

George Wise Cropper has always been an ardent worker in the interest of the west side of Millard and had great faith in its future. For many years he served as sheriff of the county and arrested or assisted in arresting some of the most desperate characters that have ever visited this part of the country. It was mainly thro' his labors that the notorious "Ben Tasker" gang was finally exterminated. He knew not the meaning of the word fear. He also took an active part in the Indian Wars of that time and in the first settling of Utah.

Burbank.

We will all miss our friend and neighbor, Mrs. Ketcham, Who left the valley on the 7th for California. She was accompanied by her son Samuel Ketcham and her brother James Jardine.

Mr. E. M. Smith, accompanied by his daughters, Annie and Virgie, left the valley on the 7th for California, where they will spend the winter.

A turkey dinner, with all the trimmings was given at the Simonson residence on the 8th, as it was the birthday of Mrs. Simonson. Covers were laid for seven. Those present were Mr. and Mrs. Simonson, Mrs. Schumacher, Mrs. Heckethorn, Mr. and Mrs. Clay and Burton Clay.

Rumor says that the Bonita mine at Bonita closed down on the 8th. The mill is still working on concentrates, and will continue until March 1st.

A heavy south wind accompanied by rain and snow visited the valley on the 8th and 9th.

Millard County Chronicle
February 3, 1916

Oak City Offerings

The stork visited the home of Mr. and Mrs. Clarence Nielson last Tuesday and left with them a fine girl. All concerned are getting along nicely.

Lorenzo Christensen and wife of Delta, spent a few days here last week visiting with relatives.

Eva Stephenson is here visiting with her sister Mary E. Anderson.

Lige Talbot and wife of Hinckley were here visiting with relatives.

Mr. Lewis of Delta, spent Sunday here.

Joseph A. Lyman and part of his family arrived here from their home in Mayfield the other day. They expect to stay here the remainder of the winter.

Lydia and Leland Roper left last week for Idaho where they will visit for a while with relatives.

The sewing club girls were entertained at the home of Sylvia Lovell Saturday night.

Jennie Harwood who has been here all winter has just left for her home at Mountain Home.

A dance was given last Friday night.

Sleigh riding is the main pastime at present

Woodrow Items

John Quincy Adams and family have settled in Woodrow, having traveled overland from Gridley, Calif., their former home. Mr. Adams was obliged to go 200 miles out of his purposed line of travel because of the snow which blocked the mountain passes. The family have been two months making the trip and are glad to anchor in a safe and sane harbor like Woodrow.

Mrs. Elizabeth Humphries, of Tooele, is visiting her granddaughter, Mrs. Robt. Jenkins. Mrs. Humphries is 82 years of age and was persuaded to make the trip in the inclement weather in order to be present when her daughter, Mrs. J. Q. Adams arrived in Woodrow. The mother and daughter had not met for 28 years and the joyous reunion may better be imagined than described.

Mrs. E. T. Lambert, with her daughter Ruby and son Merritt, leave Friday for their old home in Nebraska for an indefinite length of time. Their many friends greatly regret their departure but hope they may meet with success and happiness in their new home. Mr. Lambert remained in Woodrow for the present.

A very pleasant cottage meeting was held with Grandma Matthews last Wednesday evening. As "Grandma" is unable to attend meeting during the inclement season, she greatly appreciated having the meeting brought to her.

The Jolly Stitchers had a very pleasant meeting at the home of Dr. Louise Richter. Their next meeting will be Feb'y. 4th at the home of Dr. Tracy.

A Valentine Social will be given Friday, Feb'y. the 11th, in Woodrow, under the auspices of the Christian Endeavor Society. All are invited.

We bespeak for Miss Davis, a full attendance at her recital Saturday evening. Miss Davis is an entertainer of rare ability and none can afford to miss such a treat.

A correspondent from Sugarville heads her letter "The sweetest town in Utah". We agree that Sugarville is the "sweetest" and claim that Woodrow is the "spiciest".

Delta Company's Farm Sold

Roy Van Warmer, who has been chauffeur at the Delta Land & Water farm at Woodrow, has moved to Milford where he will continue in the employ of the Western Securities Co. H. H. Emrick, of Washington, has purchased the Company farm at Woodrow. Mr. Emrick has been traveling around for the past three months looking for a good location. When he struck the Delta Country it took him only three days to make up his mind to cast his lot with us.

The entertainment to have been given by Miss Helene Davis at Woodrow Saturday evening has been postponed until Monday evening Feb. 7th.

We need a good correspondent at Hinckley, Oasis and Deseret. And would appreciate it if some one would communicate with us about them.

Mr. Legg of Landes Machine Co. of Salt Lake, is here and informs us that the company has just closed the sale of another 25-horse power gas tractor for farm work with Stuck Bros. of the North Tract, who come here from California last fall.

Abraham Articles

Last Friday night the I. W. F. W. I. presented "A man from Denver" to the largest and most enthusiastic crowd that has been gathered in Abraham for many years. The parts were rendered excellently and were cast as follows: Roy Bills was "The Man from Denver", Paine Franklin, Manuel Clare, Junior partner in Wynn & Co., Daisy DuBois, Jimmy Black, the office boy, and was a rip roarer. Ed. Taylor, Archibald Wynn, Millionare Banker, Charles Vorwaller Bill Williams, a Nevada miner, Low Taylor, Major Millington,

Ruff Westover, Jim Goddard, Station Agent. Alf Biehler, Hop Sing. Mrs. Roy Bills, Grace Wynn, daughter of Archibald Wynn. Cora Vorwaller, Hetty Primrose. Maud Westover, Peaches. After the drama a dance was given, at which every one seemed to enjoy themselves immensely.

Wallace Black is attending school at Hinckley.

Mr. and Mrs. Duncan, parents of Mrs. Donald Hogan, of Farmington, arrived in Abraham last Tuesday for a ten days sojourn.

Mr. and Mrs. Ed. Taylor have gone to Hinckley to visit Mr. Taylor's sister, Mrs. Humphrey,

The I. W. F. W. I. gave one of the most successful balls, January 21, that has been given this season. A large crowd attended.

Bob Whicker and Mr. Cook have been at Mr. Bills for the past week driving a well. They will have it completed in the near future. The well will no doubt be appreciated.

Many people from Woodrow were over to Abraham to attend the show given by the I. W. F. W. I. They expressed the opinion that Millard Co. did not need traveling troups to put on a thrilling drama.

Mr. and Mrs. Lorin Taylor are now residing at the Crook ranch.

Sugarville Siftings

Don't forget the Literary Saturday evening.

Mr. Delano has rented his ranch and expects soon to return to California.

Mr. and Mrs. E. H. Hibbard entertained Mr. and Mrs. Oppenheimer and Mr. and Mrs. Seams at dinner last Sunday.

The Friendship Thimble club will meet at the home of Mrs. J. B. Seams next Wednesday.

Mr. and Mrs. E. H. Hibbard and Mr. and Mrs. Heulett visited at David Porter's last Friday.

Jim Boyle and family are moving into their new bungalow just west of the lumber yard.

Leuthaeuser and Lyman shipped two car loads of hogs from Sugarville Monday.

J. B. Seams left Monday for Los Angeles, Cali.

We are glad there are some fortunate enough to hold their wheat, and are now receiving a much better price. E. Olds sold his last week for $1.05.

24 below zero is pretty cold for one week old chicks. But Mrs. Albert Watts has 12 chicks from a setting of 13 eggs, and says mother and babies are doing fine.

Hinckley Happenings.

The next regular meeting of the Hinckley Home Economics Ass'n will be held on the fourth Friday of the month, Feb'y 25th, at 2:30, p. m. The program will be of especial interest and every woman will want to be there. We could not all go to the Logan Round-up, but we can get the best of it at this meeting as Mrs. C. H. Hamilton, of Delta, will give us a full report of it all. We shall probably also have a discussion of the spring cleaning campaign led by Mrs. Tom Pratt, chairman of our civics committee.

Saturday, Feb. 9th every man in town is wanted out on the Hinckley streets to help with some work on the public roads and grounds. Men with teams for hauling dirt and men with shovels can all be used. For supper the women will provide something good to eat. The mayor and members of the town council will meet the workers near the academy just after breakfast and tell them what is to be done.

Pres. Hinckley has just received the fourteenth addition to his family. This time a 10 pound girl.

Mrs. Geo. Talbot is improving from a rather protracted illness.

Abraham Articles

The most successful children's party that has ever been in Abraham was given Saturday by Mrs. Roy Bills and Daisy DuBois. Games were played and refreshments served, then a dance was given, at which prizes were awarded for the six best dancers among children. The first prize was awarded to Miss Henrietta Biehler and Lean Vorwaller, and the four remaining prizes were awarded to the Misses Elizabeth Orr and Amy Lake and Messrs. Armon Hampton and James Bohn. It was a decided success and everyone seemed to enjoy themselves immensely. We trust that this up-building work will be continued as it is greatly appreciated by the parents as well as the children of this place.

Miss Daisy DuBois was very ill last week but we are glad to hear she is improving.

The heroic rabbit hunters of Abraham (who were defeated) gave a successful dance and oyster supper at the town hall last Friday evening. A program was also rendered very nicely and everything from the dancing of "Siamese Twins," from Michigan, to a stump speech by "One Paine," of our city, was good.

Abraham farmers are somewhat regretting the fine weather, as it means work, work.

The many friends of Mrs. Roy Bills are glad to hear she is better after a short illness.

Woodrow Items

Much sympathy is expressed for the family of Fred Barben in the loss of their two months old daughter. The little one, after a brave struggle for life passed away last Thursday, a. m. Funeral services were held at the Barben home Saturday morning and were attended by a large number of Mr. Barben's neighbors and friends. Messrs. Jaderholm and Sill gave some very impressive talks on immortality. The remains of little Henrietta were laid to rest in in the Delta cemetery.

The Jolly Stitchers will be entertained Feb'y 18th, by Mesdames Sampley and Simmons at the home of Mrs. Simmons.

An entertaining Literary Society was held at Woodrow, Saturday, p. m. A permanent organization was effected with Mr. Lampert as president. The next meeting of the Society will be held Saturday Feb'y 26th, at 8, p. m. A debate on the question of "Preparedness" is scheduled. All are invited to attend.

The Woodrow Sunday School is increasing in interest and attendance. Sunday the 20th will be Temperance Day. There will be special songs and recitations, followed by an illustrated 30 minute talk by Mrs. Kyes, and a solo by Miss Kyes. The parents of the children are requested to attend. Mrs. Kyes is a speaker of rare ability, having been State Lecturer in California for the W. C. E. U. We are fortunate in having such talent in our midst and hope a large audience will profit by it.

Deseret Doings

After an absence of 2½ years spent in the Eastern states doing missionary work, Dudley Crafts arrived home yesterday.

The officers of the Y. M. and Y. L. M. I. A., have taken a step in the right direction in procuring a new piano for the Ward and should have the support of the community.

Under the auspices of the 8th grade pupils, a Character Ball was given Monday evening at the A. C. Nelson. Prizes were awarded for the best represent-ed characters. Good music and first class refreshments were served. All report a jolly good time.

Bishop Hugh Harvey of Heber City, was a visitor here last week.

James Wilson, the pioneer miner of the Tintic District, was registered at the Moody house this week.

J. R. Stockings and Brother residents of Draper came in from sheep camps on the desert and report conditions greatly improved among the flocks since the thaw.

Grandpa Damron was compelled to leave for Salt Lake to consult an eye specialist. Trust he will soon be able to return.

LeRoy Conk is reported suffering from an attack of pneumonia.

Bishop J. W. Damron left last evening for Salt Lake where he is serving as a juryman.

N. L. Peterson and Eph Eliason left for the Co. Seat on business.

Miss Minnie Iverson spent Saturday and Sunday in Delta with her sister Mrs. Wm. Gardner.

Oak City Offerings

It looks as though spring has come to stay as we have had regular spring weather over a week. We all hope it will not get the fruit trees too far along or there will be danger of another fruit crop failure this year.

A number of Leamington people are busy working on the canal below town.

A short play and dance was given here Friday night by some colored gentlemen. They certainly showed the people a lively time.

The married men and boys, called "The Stiffs and Limbers," challenged one another for a rabbit hunt a week ago Tuesday. The stiffs won by a few ears. Something over 2300 rabbits were killed. That ought to help the crops a little this summer. A dance and supper was given given by the boys. All report having an enjoyable time.

Men were busy hauling ice a few days last week. We were afraid there was not going to be any to store away for summer use, but the last cold spell settled the question for us.

Alvin and Alton Lyman have gone to Idaho on a business and sight seeing trip.

Niels Christenson and family are here visiting with relatives.

Hilda Anderson has gone to Oasis to visit with her folks a few days.

A number of students are home again visiting with their folks and enjoying the spring weather.

Agnes Lyman who has been ill for some time is on the improve.

Millard County Chronicle
March 9, 1916

Hinckley Happenings.

A new farmers' organization has been effected, with Peter E. Anderson, Pres., Richard Parker, vice Pres., G. A. Robinson, Sec.-Treas. This will bring produce direct to the farmers and do away with the middle man.

A car of potatoes has been ordered already.

On Feb. 26th the towns people were entertained by the scouts in which patrol work, signling and aid to the injured, were demonstrated, and the boys did some skilled work which showed the good training done by Scout master A. I. Tippets. After the scout display the ladies of the Home Economics, served a delicious lunch after which old time dancing was indulged in.

Principal and Mrs. Tippets have returned from Lake View where they have been to attend the death and burial of his mother. All extend their sympathy to them.

Sugarville Siftings

Gec. Vinzent, who came from Long Beach, Cali., last week to look this country over, is working for J. B. Seams.

Mrs. Albert Watts received the sad news last week of the serious illness of her father, at Riverside, Cali.

C. A. Iverson returned Sunday from a two weeks visit at Ephriam, where he attended a meeting of the state guards, he was accompanied home by his mother who has been spending the winter at that place.

J. B. Seams went to Sait Lake the first of the week to attend a meeting of the State Board Land Commissioners.

Mr. Ashby and Dale who came here a few weeks ago and start-ed building on their place, but were called back to Cali., by the sudden death of Mr. Ashby's father, will return soon with a car of emigrant goods.

See Billings for a Jack-Jr., to do your odd jobs.   d30-tf

Copper and galvanized Wash boilers, tubs, Pails and Foot Tubs at the Delta Furniture Store.

Sutherland Searchlights

Lay Abbott is down with appendicitis, but at this writing is recovering nicely.

A good number of our male population were attending the Water Users meeting at Woodrow last Saturday. There is another meeting at the same place next week to discuss items of advantage to the farmers.

Don't forget the meeting of the Ladies Home Economics Club to be held at Mrs. Abbott's this week.

Miss Helen Bunker spent Saturday in Delta, taking the teachers' examination.

Laurence Abbott is erecting an addition to his house.

Miss Agnes Hersliff is visiting Miss Helen Smith this week.

The Jolly Stitchers met with Mrs. W. R. Walker last Friday. Their next meeting will be at the home of Mrs. Brown.

Mr. and Mrs. Art Nillson have returned after spending the winter in Salt Lake City. Mr. Nillson will take up farming again if he finds a proposition suitable to him.

The new home of M. M. Steele, Jr., is nearing completion. It is a frame building of five rooms, plastered inside and altogether a neat little residence.

Mr. and Mrs. Ed Henry of Panguitch, Utah, have come here with a view to making their home if they find a farm to suit them. Mr. Henry already owns 40 acres on the Midland Tract and is looking over the Tucker farm with a view to buying that property.

Mr. Tucker still continues to be very frail.

Oak City Offerings

We are having real March weather at present.

School is closed at present on account of diphtheria, as there are a few cases in town.

Alvin Lyman and family, have moved to Idaho where they expect to make their home.

Jed Watts has sold out and moved to Leamington.

Walter Carlson has sold his home east of town and bought a city lot in town.

E. T. Rappleye, assessor, spent last week assessing the town, for all its worth.

Elder Callier Z. Dutson of Wyoming, who is on his return home from his mission in the Eastern states, is here visiting with relatives.

Miss Ada Smith and Leslie Booth, the school teachers, have gone home while school is closed.

Geo. H. Anderson is now in Salt Lake City.

Pearl Christensen has come home from Hinckley where she has been attending school.

The Oak City M. I. A. Dramatic Co. played "A Bachelor's Elopement" here Thursday night.

Miss Edna Anderson spent a few days in Leamington last week.

Joseph H. Christenson and John and Cliff Alldredge have been in Delta working.

John S. Tucker Dies

John S. Tucker of Sutherland, age 75, an old and respected citizen of that place passed away last Wednesday evening at 7:30 after a natural decline of some period, caused by old age. The funeral services will be held at Sutherland and burial will take place in the Delta cemetery. His widow and son Delbert, residing here, and a daughter in Colorado survive him. Just before Mr. Tucker's death, he disposed of his farm at Sutherland to Edward Henrie of Panguitch.

Abraham Articles

The many friends of Oscar Bohn, were sadly surprised to hear of his sudden death, March 3rd. Mr. Bohn left home Friday morning, Feb. 25, apparently well. He was going to a neighboring town for a load of grain. When he got as far as Whiskey Creek, he took suddenly ill, help was summoned and he was brot to Hinckley. The doctor could do nothing for him so he, accompanied by his brother-in-law, Mr. Greener, was rushed to the L. D. S. Hospital in Salt Lake. He was operated on for appendicitis and lived but a few days. His body was sent back to Abraham where the funeral was held Friday, March 4th. A large crowd was present. President Hinckley and Willis Robinson of Hinckley, were the principal speakers. The body was buried in the Hinckley cemetery.

He leaves a wife and seven children to mourn his death. In behalf of them the town got up a collection of $112 and gave to Mrs. Bohn. They have the sympathy of the entire community.

Miss Daisy DuBois was called suddenly home last Friday evening, due to the illness of her mother. She returned home the fore part of the week and we are glad to hear that her mother is improving.

Don't forget the grand ball that will be given in the Abraham hall, Friday, March 17th. Refreshments will be served and a prize given to the best waltzer. Remember it is St. Patrick's Day. Come dressed in your green. The dance will be given under the direction of the ball team and all the neighboring leagues are cordially invited.

W. H. Jones was called Friday evening to Nephi on a business trip.

The many friends of Mrs. Needham are glad to hear she is up and around after suffering with an attack of blood poisoning.

Miss Rose Terry of Hinckley, has been visiting W. H. Jones the past few days.

Millard County Chronicle
March 16, 1916

Obituary

John S. Tucker was born Sept. 16, 1841, at Greenwich, Washington County, New York. He died at Delta, Utah, March 8, 1916, at 7:30, p. m., at the age of 74 years, 5 mo. and 22 days. On March 9, 1878, Mr. Tucker was married to Jennie S. Loomis of Jefferson, Ohio, moving direct to Edison, Ohio, where he went into the General Mercantile business where he stayed for 20 years. While in the mercantile business he lost his health and, selling out moved to southern Montana, where he engaged in light farming, fruit growing and poultry raising. Later, himself, wife and son moved to Texas, from there to Arkansaw, thence to his last home in Sutherland, Utah.

On August 27, 1862, he enlisted in the Fedral Navy. Serving 3 months. He was honorably discharged Nov. 26, 1862.

Woodrow Items

Woodrow is receiving its share of the new settlers and the carpenter and wall drivers are being kept busy. Messrs Hargis and Patten are camping on the old Robinson ranch until their house one mile east is completed. The Mulvy's have settled on the Koch ranch recently purchased by them. A new family is preparing to build at the Myres ranch, and a new home is being constructed on the land originally bought by Mr. Thralfall. We are glad to welcome these new comers. We hope they will join in our activities and thus add to the "good times" we all so much enjoy.

Saturday, March 11th was a great day for Woodrow. A large number of our citizens attended the trial which opened at 10, a. m., and continued until 3, p. m., with one hour for intermission for luncheon. The water Users' Association held a rousing meeting from 2 to 5, p. m., in which much enthusiasm was shown and important business was transacted. At 8, p. m., the usual bi-weekly Literary Society meeting was held and a packed house was entertained for two and one-half hours with a program which was so good that even the children were so well entertained they did not become restless. The music was so well rendered that every selection was encored. An able violinist was called back three times. We are surely proud of the intelligent and cooperative spirit shown in our little community, and if it continues to prevail we need fear nothing for our future well being and happiness.

The case of Jeff Clark, vs. Andrew Eiszele, in which the discision was taken under advisement by the Judge, has been given to the Plaintiff.

Mrs. Alice Clark, who has been spending the winter months in California, returned home last week and expresses herself as glad to get back to the Pahvant valley once more.

Mr. and Mrs. Jeff Clark, accompanied by their father J. J. Clark, spent last week in Salt Lake City.

The Hinckley district school band was an attraction on the street of Delta Wednesday evening and attracted a good deal of notice and comment. They certainly did play well and deserves all the bouquets handed them. One little fellow with a big horn we noticed was so small he had to look around for a bump or clod to stand on so he could get action on the horn. The occasion was a theatrical play from Hinckley.

Miss Edna Beck entertained the O. Z. O. club at their regular monthly social Wednesday evening. Games were played and supper was served to ten members of the club. The table decorations and menu were both suggestive of St Patrick's Day.

Word was received yesterday of the death of Mrs. Shipley, mother of Bishop G. D. Shipley of Sutherland, who died at his home Wednesday morning. Mrs. Shipley was eighty-one years old at the time of her death and had made her home with the Bishop since he settled in the Delta country three years ago. Her body will be cared for by an Ogden undertaker, and will be taken there for interment.

Sutherland Searchlights

Mrs. F. N. Davis and Daughter Helene, returned Sunday from Cali. where they have been to bury her husband. Miss Davis is out on her pony as usual and says she is glad to get back to the farm.

Mr. and Mrs. Edwards, old friends of the Davises, are here from the east making them a visit.

W. R. Walker exchanged his race horse with Mr. Myers of Abraham, for his Studebaker car. Mr. Walker will make a truck of the machine.

Burt Johnson and family motored over to Holden Saturday to attend the funeral of Mr. Johnson's little niece.

A. Ackerman went over the Sevier Land & Co. water system this week to look the matter over before he accepted a position with the company.

Hunter Austin's family, who have been living in Delta since their arrival, have moved onto their farm.

Bert Ottley and Howard Abbott and family have gone to the Sevier Bridge Dam to work.

The Sutherland Ward has sent for a new piano for church and amusement purposes. The instrument will arrive this week.

Millard County Progress
March 24, 1916

Black Rock

Mr. and Mrs. T. H. Vincent and nephew Allen Vincent of McAllister, Montana were Black Rock visitors last week. They had been spending the winter in southern California and stopped over here for a visit with Mr. and Mrs. Walter James. Mrs. Vincent and Mrs. James were girlhood friends and had not seen each other since they were married, so it was a very happy meeting.

A most enjoyable affair was the masquerade ball given in the Malone school house on St. Patrick's Day. Some very pretty costumes were seen and a good many mirth provoking characters were represented. No prizes were given as all the money collected which amounted to about $30 was donated for the benefit of Gerald Williams, the young man who accidentally shot himself in the leg and is now in the L. D. S. Hospital in Salt Lake. The thigh bone was badly shattered but the injury is so high up amputation was impossible. His sufferings were severe and it was uncertain, for some days, whether his life could be saved. However the last advices from the hospital are that he is progressing nicely. The young man being without money or friends the good people of this vicinity are doing all in their power to aid him financially.

Wm. King of Lund who has been visiting with his nephew Nicholas Kruse, returned home this morning.

Mr. and Mrs. J. W. Pollock entertained very pleasantly at a dinner the last of the week. The invited guests were Mesdames Kruse and James and Miss Marnie Sawyer.

Commercial travelers have been frequent visitors of late among them we notice J. H. Henderson of San Francisco, John Smith of Fillmore who is with the Startup Candy Co. of Provo, P. L. Greenhalgh with Hewlett Bros. and Lewis Smith of the Z. C. M. I. of Salt Lake City.

Millard County Chronicle
March 30, 1916

Sutherland Searchlights

The new piano has arrived for the Sutherland Ward. And the instrument is a credit to any community. Piano evening is planned right away, when a nice musical will be given free to all. The date is not certain yet on account of people taking part on the program having previous engagments for this week.

Born, to Mr. and Mrs. Marr D. Simons, Sunday, March 26, a girl. All concerned doing nicely.

The infant of Mrs. Lon Davises is quite sick with bronchitis.

Mr. and Mrs. Ed Henrie have gone to Panguitch on a short trip to look after their business matters there.

A. Ackerman has begun his work as water master on the Sevier Land & Water Co. project at Lynndyl.

Mr. Davis, the beet man, made a trip home and spent Sunday with his family. He is looking for a house in this vicinity to rent so he may move his family here with him.

Hinckley Happenings.

(Delayed last week.)

Dr. Broaddus has visited homes where children are ill and made a thorough inspection of the town, and says there are only three cases of scarlet feaver and these are light and under quarantine. The school house with all the books have been fumigated so all public gatherings are continued with the Dr's consent.

The Stork made a flying trip to Hinckley the last of the week, leaving baby girls at the homes of Messrs and Mesdames Fay Theobald, Leon Abbot, John Reeve and Harvey Loveland.

On the 17 of March the Junior Prom was given which was the biggest event of the year. The colors being white and green, in keeping with St. Patrick's Day. Over three thousand green and white carnations were used in decoration. The Academy never has been so clean and beautifuly decorated in the history of the school. 65 plates were laid at the banquet which was served with skill by the second year girls. A large crowd attended the ball. The whole affair was a thorough success.

Owing to illness in Miss Cropper's family, Mrs. Maxfield is tending the Millinery store for the Misses Cropper and Pratt. They have a large assortment of hats and report doing a lively business.

The Third Years presented the play "Billies Bungalow" to a crowded house. The players did well. They also played in the neighboring towns.

Miss Fannie Cropper came home from the B. Y. U. for a week's visit.

Sugarville Siftings

Ernest Baxter moved his belongings to the Presnall place the first of the week.

The Thimble Club will meet next Wednesday afternoon with Mrs. C. T. Brown.

Word has been received from Grandma Olds that she reached her destination safely and had a pleasant trip.

Mr. Dale's emigrant car arrived Sunday. His brother and wife are also on the road from Cali., making the trip in their automobile.

"It's a Long Long Way to Tipperay," also a long long way to Delta, as a letter mailed here on Tuesday did not reach there until Thursday.

Every week brings one or more emigrant cars to the North Tract. Surely the country is settling up fast, as people are coming in by train, camp-wagons and automobiles.

Saturday evening will be the last Literary meeting at Sugarville. The Friendship Thimble Club will furnish the entertainment, and after the program a tamale supper will be served for the benefit of the Library hall fund. The shadow sale will cause much amusement. Everybody come.

Word has just been received here of the sudden death of Walter Wright, who was found dead in his bed at Kaine, Kansas. As gas was escaping in the room, death is supposed to have been accidental through carelessness in not tightening the gas jet properly. While here he lived with his sister, Mrs. Ralph Buehler, and went with them to Kansas early in the winter, to join their parents. Word also came that an older brother had one foot crushed by a truck, which will make him a cripple for life. The boys were well known here and the family has the sympathy of all here.

(Delayed last week.)

Born, to Mr. and Mrs. J. Boyle, Sunday, March 12th, a 9½ lb. girl.

Mr. Buhler of Pomona, Cali., has rented the Lamson place for the coming year.

J. B. Seams made a business trip to Salt Lake the first of the week.

Messrs Brady and Myers of Corona, Cali., have rented the Buehler place for the season.

Miss Ethel Iverson is home for a few weeks vacation.

Mrs. Marlow and daughter came Sunday to join her husband who is in charge of the lumber business here.

Little Pauline Seams, who was very sick last week, is up and around again.

The Friendship Thimble Club will furnish the literary program for Saturday evening, April 1st, after which they will serve a hot-tamalle supper. Each lady's shadow will be sold to the highest bidder. Every body come.

The Telephone line has been extended as far as R. J. Law's Store, and many of the people are anxious to have it in their homes.

Grandma Olds, left Monday morning for her home in Indiana.

Deseret Doings

The funeral services of Thomas Conk, who died suddenly last Tuesday evening, were held Thursday afternoon in the Ward Chapel. Mr. Conk had been in ill health for several years. He is survived by a wife and four children.

Mrs. M. C. Webb has been suffering with la grippe the past week.

Mrs. Amanda Conk and her brother-in-law, Wm. Conk, were taken to the Hospital last night, both to undergo operations for appendicitis.

Geo. A. Hone is in town on business.

Messrs Geo. and Mark Kelly are home again, after spending a couple of months at Joy.

Deseret now boasts of an up-to-date Soda Fountain and Confectionery Store, which is installed at Jos. A. Passey's place. Bring your wives and sweethearts for a dish of cream.

Mrs. Wm. Damron of Pocatello, Ida., formerly a resident of this place, is here visiting with relatives.

Robt. Munn, manager of the mining property at Cricket mountain, came up Wednesday of last week and reports everything in camp favorable.

Wm. Batty returned from the Antelope mining district last week. He took a couple of mining experts down to look at his property.

Bp. J. W. Damron is home to stay, having been excused from the Federal jury, where he served the past two months.

Millard County Progress
April 7, 1916

HINCKLEY MAN COMMITS SUICIDE.

Mr. David L. Blackburn, formerly of Loa, Wayne County, Utah, but a resident of Hinckley for the past two years, ended his life last Friday by slashing his throat with a razor.

Some years ago, while chopping wood, Mr. Blackburn had the misfortune to get a sliver into one of his eyes, since then his eye sight has failed to such an extent that he completely lost the sight of one eye and was gradually becoming blind in the other eye. The pain from his eyes affected his nervous system to such an extent that he suffered the most intense pain. Last winter he spent three months in a Salt Lake Hospital hoping to get relief but without results. He was therefore much discouraged. He had also been sick for a few days prior to the time the act was committed. At the time of his death he was at his farm three miles west of Hinckley, his son Earl had gone to town for a load of hay but was within a half a mile of the house when the tragedy occured. Mrs. C. C. Draper and Mrs. F. W. Wilkins were driving past in a buggy when they were horrified to see Mr. Blackburn walking from the house with a razor in his hand and with blood streaming from his throat. He motioned for them to stop but they were afraid to do so. They drove as fast as possible for a short distance and met Earl coming with the hay. The three went back as fast as possible, but by the time they arrived, Mr. Blackburn had fallen to the ground, and had lost so much blood that he was to weak to speak. He expired in a few moments.

The body was removed to the Delta Undertaking parlors and from there was taken by the family in an automobile to Loa, where the funeral was held and interment took place this week.

Mr. Blackburn was an honorable man and a good worker who had many friends in this community. He is survived by a widow and the following children, Mrs. Benjamin Black, Mrs. Berry Robison, Earl, Ray, Myrtle, Pearl, Iona and Leland Blackburn.

Hinckley.

The scarlet fever scare is subsiding, only two of the families quarantined have had the disease. The other suspected cases all turned out to be a bad form of the La Grippe.

Mr. and Mrs. Norman Bliss have a new baby boy. All concerned are doing nicely.

A fine little girl arrived at the home of Demonstrator and Mrs. Welch last week, mother and infant are getting along fine.

Verle Maxfield, a student of the Millard Academy, had the misfortune to fracture his right arm just above the wrist, while pole vaulting on the Academy campus one day last week. Dr. Broadus set the broken limb, and Verle is again able to attend school.

Ernest Jackson and family have moved to the place formerly occupied by Richard Gammes.

C. A. Stratton has sold his home on Main Street to Mrs. D. L. Blackburn and has purchased the Wm. Curtis place two blocks west of his former location. Mr. Stratton and family moved to their new home last week.

Mrs. John R. Terry is in Salt Lake City for an extended visit with her daughter Mrs. Lester Smith.

Mr. and Mrs. Isaac Elkington and children have returned to Hinckley for the summer after having spent the winter in Tooele where Mr. Elkington has been employed in the mines.

Mr. T. George Theobald made a trip to Fillmore on his motorcycle this week. His trip is of a business nature.

Mrs. Joseph W. Blake and Mrs. Wm. F. Pratt have gone to Salt Lake to spend a couple of weeks.

Mrs. Nerone Damron of Inkom, Idaho, is the guest of her relative Mrs. Juel Moody.

Hinckley.

Concluded From Last Issue.

Our Progressive merchant, Thomas Pratt has purchased the Dodge automobile formerly owned by John Reeve.

Miss LaPriel Robinson went to Salt Lake to hear the Boston Grand Opera Company Mrs. Mary C. Reeve is teaching school in her absence.

O. B. Farrel and wife have returned from the east where they spent three months visiting with relatives and friends.

A. F. and Ernest Stout have gone to the Swayzee Mountains on a prospecting trip. They expect t obe gone about ten days.

Toupe No. 1 of the Hinckley Boy Scouts are making things move. Weekly meetings are being held and several hikes have been taken. A suitable headquarters for meeting purposes is soon to be provided by Scoutmaster Tippetts au dthe troupe. Demonstrator Welch has purchased a new Ford runabout. This will assist him in making his runs about the county.

Claude Tripp and wife of Callio, Nevada have spent the past ten days as guests of Mrs. Tripp's parents. Mr. and Mrs. Fred Wilkins. They report everything prosperous in the western part of the country.

Mr. Green and son are visiting at the home of Mr. and Mrs. Robt. E. Robinson.

The Home Economics Club held a very pleasant social one evening last week for the members and their husbands. It was greatly enjoyed by all present.

R. E. Robinson is busily engaged in making assessments for he tax list of Millard County. Mr. Robinson is basing all the assessments on the full cash valuation of the property which will be a fair basis for all tax payers.

Through the efforts of the Home Economics Association our twn is beginning t present an appearance of cleanliness. Many of the most enterprising citizens are making great improvements about their places, About April 20, all citizens of the town are to form in procession and visit every house and yard in the community. A prize will be awarded the one adjudged to be the cleanest, and those whose premises are judged to be unsanitary will be invited to clean them up immediately.

This Week's News.

Dr. and Mrs. C. A. Broadus, Misses Rena Reeve, Wealthy Parker and LaPriel Robinson went to Salt Lake City to hear the Boston Grand Opera Company present several famous operas and to see Madame Pavlowa dance. They are all very enthusiastic in their praises of what they saw and heard.

A number of the Millard Academy teachers and students attended General Conference in Salt Lake last week. Among them are Prof. McClellan, Prof. Huffaker and the misses Dean Marsden, Vivian Peterson and Reva Hawley.

Prominent among our town people who were Salt Lake visitors this week are President A. A. Hinckley, Bp. John P. Pratt, Frank Pratt and wife, H. P. Wright, J. C. Emmett, Mrs. John Jacobs. Mrs. Rich Cropper, Mrs. Celestial Knight, Mrs. Margaretta Richards. Mrs. Lucinda Greiner, Mrs. George Walker and son Beslie.

Marvin Moody and the Misses Clara Erickson and Laverna Wright spent a few days with their parents during their spring vacation week. They are students at the B. Y. U. at Provo.

Mrs. Shaw of California has returned to her home after spending sometime visiting her sons, Wm. B. and Stanley Shaw

Mrs. Ethel Green of Salt Lake City is here to visit with her mother, Mrs. Fannie Terry.

Dr. C. A. Broadus has just purchased a fine new Buick car to take

Consitded on Page b.

the place of his faithful old Ford.

Mrs. Alfred Bliss is reported to be very ill at present writing. Her many friends hope for her immediate recovery.

Mr. and Mrs. C. E. Humphries have returned from Salt Lake, where they took their 18 months old infant for medical treatment. The child swallowed a nut shell, which lodged in the wind pipe making breathing difficult.

Mrs. Henrietta Hunter and baby of Holden are guests this week at the home of Mrs. M. C. Richards.

The M. I. A. party last Wednesday evening was a very enjoyable affair.

A. D. Dimmick is here to visit with his boys for a few days.

George Whitehead was taken to Salt Lake to undergo an operation for appendicitus. His friends are anxious for his speedy recovery.

Principal Eugene Gardner of Delta visited the Hinckley district school last Friday.

The debates between the Millard Academy and the Millard High School teams took place last Friday night. The question, Resolved, that the Monroe Doctrine should be Abandoned" was ably discussed by Messers Walch and Stevens of the Affirmative and Messrs. Sprout and Theobald of the Negative. The judges rendered their decision in favor of the Affirmative. At Deseret, Mr. Crafts and Mr. Moody upheld the Affirmative and Mr. Starley and Mr. Holbrook took the negative. In this debate the Affirmative was victorious. The judges were Prof. J. C. Swenson of the B. Y. U.; Principal A. H. Tippetts of the Hinckley district school and Principal Eugene Gardner of the Delta district school.

Prior to the debate the Millard Academy Domestic Science girls served a banquet to the debators.

OLD RESIDENT PASSES

Another of our old pioneers has gone to her last resting place. Mrs. Zuriah Shall, maiden name, Hatum, was born in Staffordshire, England, 75 years ago and while there embraced the Mormon faith, being blessed by President Brigham Young while he was on a mission to that country. In 1862 she migrated to America and joined one of the numerous handcart companies bound for Utah arriving in Fillmore, she has lived here ever since until the recent death of her husband when she moved to Deseret. In 1862 she married George A. Shall of which union 8 children resulted 4 of whom are now living. They are Mrs. Sarah Cahoon of Deseret, Mrs. Maria Nelson of Friday Harbor, Wash., James A. Shall of Rexburg, Idaho and John Shall of Fillmore. The funeral was held in the L. D. S. Chapel in Fillmore on Saturday last Mrs. Shall having died at Deseret on the preceding Thursday. The body was followed to the Fillmore Cemetary by a host of relatives and friends.

Hinckley Happenings.

All of our townspeople who went to Salt Lake for conference have returned home except Mrs. Celestial Knight, who remained at the bedside of her brother who will be operated on at a hospital.

The Stork visited the home of Mr. and Mrs. Joseph Wright, April 13th leaving a fine baby girl.

The students and faculty of the M. A. are rejoicing over the victories they won at the tract meet at Fillmore. All report a good time.

Wm. Walker was called to Oak City this morning to the bedside of his father, Simeon Walker, who is reported very ill.

There is considerable excitement over the mining prospect out in the west mountains. Among those interested are A. Stout, W. F. Pratt and C. C. Draper.

The Home Economics Association is actively engaged in the clean town campaign. Our slogan is "make Hinckley the cleanest town on the map." Early in the spring when the first flies appeared, the civics committee began to pay for all flies destroyed and in this way hope to help

control the fly nuisance for the summer. The social given recently by the club for the members and their husbands awakened considerable enthusiasm and civic pride. Mr. Welch gave a fine talk on clean milk and much discussion followed. The men folk present resolved to make a greater effort to provide better and more sanitary housing facilities for their stock. On May 1st there will be a May Day excursion. At 10, a. m., the citizens will assemble at the school ground and from there will proceed to visit the premises of all the people of the town and cash prizes will be awarded to

LOCAL NEWS

Mr. and Mrs. Edwards and son, of the Grand Junction, Colo., country are here for the summer visiting Mrs. Flora Davis and family of the Sutnerland district. Mrs. Edwards stopped off here with the Davis family last fall when they came up from California. They may decide to locate permanently.

L. A. Wilcox, who purchased land near Sugarville, came in the first of the week with a car of emigrant goods from California and has taken up his residence on his land.

Delta is after a sugar factory. North Sanpete was too, but we don't hear much of it at present. What's the matter folks? Keep it going. —Manti Messenger.

Born:—To Mr. and Mrs. Geo. Sampson, of the South Tract, Sunday night, a boy.

James Christensen was up Wednesday attending the big Demonstration train meeting. Mr. Christensen reports considerable damage done the fruit around Oasis by the late frosts.

M. A. Hutchings has errected a building on 1st West just west of George Day's store and will occupy it with a blacksmith shop. Mr. Hutchings is a good workman and we predict for him success.

D. H. Jordan, a contractor and builder from Florida and a friend of Ray Jones has located in Delta and will follow his trade. Mr. Jordan is a fine cabinet maker as well as a builder. He left the last of last week for Logan, where he visited his family a few days and will bring them to Delta to live.

Lightening struck the Delta Co's private phone line near Woodrow during Tuesday's storm and shattered a number of poles and burned ont several phones on the line. The damage is being repaired today and the line has recently been extended to near Sugarville.

LEAMINGTON

Ernest Nelson is the happy father of a bouncing baby girl. Mother and child are doing fine and with good care Ernest is expected to recover.

James McArdell and Miss Margaret Iverson were married at Nephi on the 29th. Miss Iverson is from Littlefield, Arizona and James hails from Leamington. We extend our good wishes to the happy pair.

Mr. Walter Johnson died at the L. D. S. Hospital and his body was sent to his home town for burial. His baby also preceeded him to the great beyond. The bereaved wife and 8 children which survive him has our heart felt sympathy.

Irrigating has commenced on the McIntyre Ranch and the grain and alfalfa are looking fine.

A number of men and teams have just completed 9 miles of canals under the direction of our genial foreman, Peter Nelson.

Miss Irene Penney has just returned from a visit to Kanosh, where she went to see her parents.

Mrs. Ida Collins has returned from Delta where she has been visiting with her daughter Mrs. Velma Davis.

After attending the M. A. all winter, Miss Leda Finlinson returned to her home this week from Hinckley.

Dr. Conklin is doing a rushing business in the dentistry line at Leamington.

Charles Nelson and wife have gone to California to visit with friends and relatives. They expect to be gone for a month or more.

The bundle shower and dance given by James McArdle and wife last week was a pronounced success. Many useful presents were given them.

Black Rock

Messrs. Allnisi and Waddoups made a business trip in from the west side a few days ago. They are doing some contract plowing and seeding over there and report that they are progressing nicely.

Chas. Bird of Hatton and Herman Whitaker of Kanosh spent several days in this vicinity last week.

Mrs. Nicholas Krause has returned from Milford where she spent a week under the physician's care. She feels somewhat improved in health, but Dr. Swanson recommends a change of climate and altitude in her case.

Mrs. Wm. Knox and baby daughter have returned to their home in Salt Lake City after spending ten days very pleasantly visiting at the home of Walter James. She was accompanied by the Misses Benita and Thekla James who have returned to their studies after spending their spring vacation at home.

Miss Mamie Sawyer spent a few days visiting in Milford. She returned in time to open school as usual on Monday.

The bond election received very few votes either for or against in this precinct. Some of the people paid taxes in 1915 but were not here the last time registration took place. Others were registered, but through no fault of theirs had never been honored by a visit from the assessor. In both cases the persons interested feel themselves agrieved as they were deprived of their vote.

Mr. and Mrs. Walter James made a trip to Richfield in their car. They were accompanied by their daughter Benita and Earl Tillson, the latter two took turns driving. They report roads on this side rough and the canon badly cut up and rocky, but the roads in Sevier Valley are all that could be desired and fill the Millard County autoist with envy.

Jack Murdock of Beaver was riding after cattle in this section a few days ago and incidentally calling on a schoolmate with whom he attended Westminster College.

Woodrow Items

Mrs. J. E. Berger has settled on the Reuben Erickson ranch and is farming with a vim.

Miss Leah Meinhardt met with a very painful accident last Friday night when she was thrown from her pony sustaining a dislocation of the elbow. The accident occured near Herman Munster's, where the young lady was carried and medical aid summoned. At present she is recovering as well as could be hoped.

The Jolly stitchers met Friday with Mrs. S. H. Thompson where they were royally entertained. Their next meeting will be at the home of Mrs. Chas Hickman.

A happy party of young folks with their parents and teacher, Mrs. Underhill, returned from Deseret last Friday where they had been called to attend commencement exercises. The graduating class, viz. Misses Annie Black and Venice Barben and Hugo Thompson, did not know whether they had passed their examinations until their arrival in Deseret, therefor their enthusiasm was the greater when they discovered that all had passed with high standing and no condition.

Miss Clara Clark went to Cali. Tuesday morning to spend the summer.

The Hummer Dramatic Co. presents their interesting play "Civil Service" at Woodrow Saturday, May 6th. Sugarville Tuesday, May 9th. Abraham Thursday, May 11th, and Sutherland Saturday, May 13th. Proceeds are for the purpose of purchasing a new piano. Admission 25 and 15 cents.

LOCAL NEWS

Mr. and Mrs. Orman Wilkins arrived in Delta Tuesday from Washington county. They will make their home here.

John Baker, who has been baking at the Delta Bakery for the last three months, went to Salt Lake Wednesday night.

A. C. Sorenson has started the erection of a nice four-room cement block bungalow on his lots three blocks south and one east of the Ward hall.

Ted Moore has moved to town from the Snow Crest ranch and has become affiliated with W. H. Pace as salesman for the Ford car. Teddy expects to remain in Delta permanently and may branch out into other lines later.

Millard County Progress
May 5, 1916

NAMES OF THE EIGHTH GRADE GRADUATES.

The eigth grade graduating exercises which were held in Deseret last Thursday and Friday was among the most enthusiastic gatherings of this nature ever held in this county. Prof. Lewis, Principal of our high school made the principal address of the day and his remarks were listened to with rapt attention by both the graduates and the patrons of our schools who were in attendance. The number of graduates this year sets a new record for this county as there were more than twice as many graduated this year than in any former year.

The high standard of the work of the pupils themselves is very encouraging and our advice to the pupils is that they continue on in high school with the same energy and vim which marked their progress through the grades. Following is a list of the names f the graduates in the different towns in the county of Millard.

FILLMORE, E. F. Pack, Prin.,
Lucy Robison, Loren Warner, Wm. Mitchell, Roy Huntsman, Alta Stevens, Phyllis Paxton, Lumena Dontre, Nora Warner, Theodore Rogers, Vera Huntsman, Cecil Warner Edmond Swallow, Ervin Warner, Pauline Rasmussen, Emily Crape, Arrilla Davies, Olive Chritchley, Adrian Davies, Ward Phillpps, George Huntsman.

Owen Warner, Ben Speakman, Ada Rasmussen, Addie Smith, Olive Burte Blouise King, James Eagan.

MEADOW, W. E. Davies, Prin.
Noreen Swallow, Grace Stewart, Lorell Bushnell, Lemar Bennett, Grant Beckstrand, Herbert Stott, Geneva Bennett, Elda Safford, Annott Iverson Cyriel Bennott, Albert Stewart, Leon Gull, Yorda Stott, Vilate Lindsey, Velma Bushnell, Karl Stott, Leroy Gull.

KANOSH, W. A. Paxton, Prin.
George Christensen, Bryant Hatton, Hollis Hunter, Novella Paxton, Atheila George, Eugene George, Golden Black, Manila Abrahams, Grace Rogers, Grace George, Noble Kimpaloma Whitaker.
hall, Dovello Whatcott, Ila Black.
HATTON, Maurice Lambert, Prin.
Clarke Stowe
HOLDEN, M. T. Dyches, Prin.
Lilian Paul, Louise McKee, Maymie Johnson, Otto Hunter, Stanley Poulson, Royal Bennett, Lucretia Hothines, Reta Stevens, Jessie Christenson, Harold Wood, Lorus Mills, Aaral Bennett, Leda Stevens, Dean Mills, Kenneth Olsen, Ruth Harmon. George Croesland.

SCIPIO, Devere Childs, Prin.
Burton Thompson, Mildred Robins, Riley Thompson, Joyce Hanscott, Bert Webb, Virl Ivie, Viola Yates, Merle Allen, Mildred Eskland, Lola Wasden, Zella Walch, Fay Johnson, Emily Peterson.

HINCKLEY, A. I. Tippets, Prin.
Aveline Pratt, Elwin Theobald, Edna Theobald, Grace Robinson, Oren Bliss, Willard Hardy, Harold Theobald, Layton Maxfield, Maude Whight Nellie Hanson, Boud Sawyer, Elmer Bishop, Florence Reeve, Golden Webb Richard Terry, Blanche Workman, Ila Dutson, Leatha Wright, Mary Brummond, Norman Terry, Clarke Bishop, Ether Reeve, Florence Mc Glellen, Harvie Jackson, Utah Terry, Floyd Loveland, Joan Slaughter Myrtle Reeve, Mary Draper, Olive Hansworth.

A. C. NELSON SCHOOL, S. F.
Stephcuson, Prin.
Lancie Peterson, Mary Larson Wm. Doach, Sommars Thompson John Webb, Alvin Hales, Josie Chris tensen, Lincoln Cropper, Alta Cahoon Irma Cropper, Novel Christenson Ray Moody, Abriah Kelly, Vera Day. Rulon Jackson, Nels Black
CLEAR LAKE, Jane Rawlinson Bernard Collins,
MALONE, W. W. Murray, Prin.
Isabell Oliver, John Oliver, Mollie Hacker.
BURBANK, Pearl Freemyer, Lloyd Christopherson
OAK CITY, Leslie Both, Prin.
Angle Finlinson, Alta Talbot, Alvin Lovell, Thelma Lovell, Geneva Wiley, Clisby Lovell, Mabel Roper, Otto Anderson, Murin Roper.

ABRAHAM, W. H. Jones, Prin.
Louisa Young, Louisa Perhap.

LEAMINGTON, R. E. Wian, Prin
Amy Nelson, Pearl Johnson,
Blanche Clark, Lety't Ashby, Mina
Johnson, Evelin Dutson, Alta Great-
house, Louise Overson, Mamie Over-
son.

DELTA, Eugene Gardner, Prin.
Alma Anderson, Arthur Warner,
Glenna Riding, Caroline Tanner, The-
odore Gardiner, Arena Law, Nota
Stewart, Wm. Kelly, Blanch Maxfield
Malba Steele.

SUTHERLAND, James Barney

George Campbell, Laurence Titus,
Rosaline Minchardt, Wayne Shipley,
Florence Holdridge, Cecil Sherer, Os-
car Herrick, Ive Holdridge.

HOCK, Etta B. Underhill, Prin.
Annie Clark, Venice Barber, Hugo
Thompson.

SUGARVILLE, Iver Iverson.
Wm. McKenna, Blanche Remington, Leona Seams.

SUNFLOWER, Cora Helse Prin,
Vera Weatherly, Cora Bronner,
Frederick Nutch, Carl Nutch.

NIGHT CAR INSPECTOR KILLED AT LYNN.

Thomas E. Williams, night car inspector for the Salt Lake Route at
Lynndyle in Millard County was
caught and crushed to death between
a switch-engine and a coach on Monday night of this week. Mr. Williams who was but 27 years old is survived by a widow and two small children all of whom reside at Lynndyle
his mother, a sister and two brothers
who reside n Sepo. Details in the
case are lacking and it is not known
just how the accident happened.

The members of the bereaved family have our heartfelt sympathy.

Millard County Chronicle
May 18, 1916

The Passing of Grandma Bunker

The passing of Grandma Bunker last Tuesday closes the long
career of another one of the early
pioneers of the west and Utah.

Sarah Ann Browning-Lang
Bunker was born on October 10th
1830 in Sumner county, Tenn.
She was united in marriage to
Edward Bunker in 1852. To her
was born nine children, two by
her first husband and seven by
Mr. Bunker. She migrated with
her family to Utah in the year of
1863, settling at Toquerville.
Later the family moved to Santa
Clara and subsequently to Annabell, Sevier county. From there
she moved to Delta where she
has spent the past five years.
Grandma Bunker was left a
widow in 1901, her husband having died in Mexico at that time.

Funeral services were held at
the Delta Ward Hall Thursday
afternoon at 2:00, and interment
took place in the Delta cemetery.

Five of her nine children were
present at the services. They
were William, Clifton and Mrs.
Della Lisonbee of Delta, James
of Gunlock and D. A. Bunker of
Salt Lake City.

Chief Police, Browning, of Ogden, a nephew, was also present
at the funeral services.

Mrs. Bunker was converted
and came to Utah as one of the
early Mormon settlers. She was
very devout and proved her sin-
cerity by a long life of faithfulness and constant endeavor for
the betterment of all with whom
she came in contact, and her
many friends feel that her's has
been a long noble life, full of
many good deeds and well rounded out.

Woodrow Items

The Hummer Dramatic Associ
ation presented their play, "Civ
il Service" to large and appreci
ative audiences at Woodrow, Sug
arville and Abraham last week
Judging from the statement
made by all the audiences who
have so far witnessed this, this is
the best local talent play which
has been presented in this com
munity. Upon the recovery o
Miss Helen Davis, who is now
convalescent, the play will be
presented in Delta and Deseret
We solicit your patronage, as the
proceeds are to be used to purchase a much-needed piano for
Woodrow.

Rev. and Mrs. Robert Elmore
of Chili are spending the summer with Mrs. Elmore's mother,
Mrs. Mary Isles, at the Foote
ranch. Mr. Elmore will address the Sunday School at
Woodrow next Sunday morning,
May 21st. Sunday evening the
German Lutheran Minister from
Salt Lake will preach at 8, p. m.
Sunday May 28th, Rev. Robt. El
more will deliver an address at
8, p. m. We hope for a large attendance at all of these meetings.

The Jolly Stitchers met at the
home of Mrs. C. M. Hickman, in
Abraham last Friday and were
royally entertained. They will
be entertained by Mrs. George
Campbell Friday, June 2nd.

The ladies of the Woodrow
Sunday School met at the home
of Dr. Tracy last Wednesday to
sew on the "Kiddies Kit",
which the Sunday school is furnishing for an eight year old or-
phaned Belgian girl.

In spite of the unseasonably
cold weather of the past week,
crops are looking well and everybody is cheerful in Woodrow.

Sugarville Siftings

Mrs. Thure Cronholm is entertaining her mother, Mr. Christenson, of Salt Lake City.

Don't forget the musical entertainment Saturday evening, given by the Thomas' and Carey's, for the Library fund. Admission 25c and 10c. Dance after. Everybody come.

John Mutsch is here from Kansas, looking after his ranch.

Mr. and Mrs. Brice entertained their friend, Mullins of Pomona, Cali., the first of the week. Mr. Mullins was looking over the project with the view of locating here and was much pleased with the country.

E. J. Hart, who was reported sick with pneumonia, was taken suddenly worse and had to be taken to Salt Lake to undergo an operation for an abscess. We all hope for his speedy recovery.

Ethel Iverson went to Delta Sunday to take a position at the Delta Bakery.

Abraham Articles

Mrs. Job Riding has been very ill the past week.

Miss Ida Orr, the hello girl at Delta, spent Sunday with home folks.

The Farm Bureau Organization had quite a successful meeting Friday night. Everybody come and help the good work along.

Mrs. Zola Soules is on the sick list.

Mrs. Hattie Forsythe of Salt Lake, is visiting at the home of her parents, Mr. and Mrs. O. M. Fullmer.

The Jolly Stitchers met with Mrs. C. M. Hickman, last week.

William Fullmer, who was sick last week with pneumonia, is much improved at this writing.

The Hummer Dramatic Co. of Woodrow, presented the play "Civil Service" to a large audience Thursday night. The play was a grand success with not a trace of the ameteur in sight. Come again, Woodrow.

Quite a number from Abraham attended preaching services at Sunflower on Sunday.

O. L. Lake, our local real estate dealer reports a number of sales recently.

Payne Franklin says he can trip the light fantastic much easier than he used to.

E. H. Biehler and family are moving this week to their farm west of Abrahrm. A Mr. Hall will occupy the residence made vacant by them.

Mrs. Laura Petty is here visiting her mother, Mrs. Wilcken.

Seventeen cars of hay have recently been shipped from the Abraham switch on the spur line, ranging in price from $14 to $18 per ton.

The Needle Craft Club met last week with Mrs Ora Lake. All report a very interesting meeting.

The Abraham and Sugarville Base Ball teams are contending for supremacy. Both teams are playing good ball. Come out and encourage the boys in their sport.

LOCAL NEWS

Born:—To Mr. and Mrs. T. C. Grunning, Tuesday morning, a boy.

Mrs. J. W. Thurston entertained the O. Z. O. Club Wednesday evening.

Stephen A. Bunker, step-son of Grandma Bunker's came up from St. George the first of the week to attend her funeral.

Miss Paxton, an experienced dressmaker from Fawler, Colo, who has been visiting her sister Mrs. Chas. Rodmon of Lynndy for some time, has come to Delt and will do dressmaking here She can be found at A. B Ward's residence.

Mr. and Mrs. Fred L. Baker of South Tract, entertained a dinner Sunday, May 7. The guests were Mr. and Mrs. Murray Jefferies and Family and Mrs. Martha Hunter of Grantsville.

Ted Moore returned last week from a trip to Denver and bro with him from Salt Lake one o the new Studebaker touring cars We understand that Ted is t handle the Studebaker car i this locality.

Hinckley Happenings.

ENTERTAINMENT, MAY 31

Hinckley is going to have a little excitement to break the monotony of a dull summer and incidentally to help on the improvements in our town. Next Wednesday evening at 8 o'clock, there will be a jolly good entertainment at the Academy Auditorium; tickets 10c and 15c so that everybody can afford to come and have a good time. Come early because a number of people want to catch that night train for Provo to attend Commencement there. Everybody in neighboring towns are invited to join us. There will be piano music, vocal solos and vocal duets by trained singers, a chorus trio, a beautiful ballet dance by a group of pink fairies, a Greek statuary posing drill by some Amazons (the ancient warrior women), some clog dancing, a monologue "The wooing of Hiawiatha," by Miss Helene Davis, with musical accompaniment, and a side-splitting farce—Shakespeare's burlesque of "Pyramus and Thisbe" from "A Midsummer Night's Dream" with the following cast:

Prologue - - - Jas. Welch
Wall - - Tom Greener
Moonshine - Ed Humphries
Lion - - Ted Davis
Pyramus - Dr. Broaddus
Thisbe - John Hutchinson

For further excitement the Home Demonstrator for this district will award the prize for the recent H. E. A. contest on clean premises.

Frank Wright is having a new well driven near his house.

Mr. and Mrs. Ed Anderson have a new baby boy, and Mr. and Mrs. Peter Peterson also have a new baby.

This Friday the H. E. A. will be the guests of Mrs. E. A. Smith for their social meeting and cooking demonstration, beginning at 3 p. m.

Automobiles are thick in Hinckley. Already this spring Mr. Welch has a new Ford, Dr. Broaddus a new Buick, Frank Pratt a Saxon, Milton Moody a Studebaker, Glen Cropper a Studebaker Four.

The Boy Scouts have been busy the past two weeks visiting every home in Hinckley with their score cards to score yards, corrals, wells and out buildings. Prizes are to be awarded for the places scoring higest. Come to the entertainment Wednesday night and see who gets it.

Miss Hettie White, the Home Demonstrator, spent over a week in and around Hinckley helping members of the Economics Ass'n with many of their home problems and now is on the east side of the county. She plans to be in Hinckley May 31, to make further arrangements with Dr. Broaddus and the H. E. A. for a Better Baby Convention the last part of June.

The Stork Stirring

The stork flew off its roost last Saturday Morning and visited the homes of Ray Jones, the Studebaker man, and A. C. Sorenson of the Delta Merc. No sooner had Jones found out that the stork had been there than he jumped onto A. B. Ward's old red rooster and pulled half the feathers out of his tail and stuck them in his hat and tried to make everybody in town believe that he was the only stork around their home. Ed Marshall says he caught Andrew out behind the store with his head down in a barrel helloing "papa", and listening to the echo come back to see how it would sound to hear himself called papa. Mrs. Jones and Mrs. Sorenson are both doing nicely and meekly allowing their lords to carry away all the honors.

Sugarville Siftings

Sugarville is planning a big celebration for the Fourth of July.

J. S. Law returned to his home at Banning, Cal., last week.

Mr and Mrs. Bale entertained their cousins Mr. and Mrs. J. C. Roland of Chandilar, Arizona last Saturday and Sunday.

W. G. McKittrick left Monday evening for his home in San Diego, Calif.

James Shields and wife spent last week at Tooele.

The Union Sunday School will observe Childrens' day Sunday afternoon at 2:30. Every body welcome.

The Friendship Thimble Club will meet with Mrs. Cochren

Sutherland Searchlights

We have been waiting for a warm day that we might say, lets cut our heavy, first crop of hay, thin out the beets, and run the hoe, so our bounteous crop might rush and grow, but mother nature answers "no", and in reply a cold north wind just whizzes by.

W. R. Walker and Mr. and Mrs. M. A. Abbott, spent two days last week visiting in Fillmore during Well Days celebration and went over to take a look at the U. B. Dam.

Jode Steward entertained a crowd of relatives and friends Monday, a number among them were here to look over the country and its projebts.

Hy Sherrer made a trip by auto to Salt Lake last week, taking Mr. Keeler who needed imediate medical attention.

Misses Era and Fern Holdrige entertained the little girls' tatting club last Friday.

The Jolly Stitchers will meet with Mrs. Wm. Perry Friday of this week.

Howard Abbott has moved his family from the dam, and himself and Wayne Lisonbee have gone to Uinta Basin to look for employment and the prospects for a home.

The water controversy of the Midland Tract seems to be in a more settled condition. People are still planting late crops such as oats etc. Shacks and cottages are springing up all over the tract. We have not learned the names of all the new comers but we hope to get acquainted with all in time and wish them success and prosperity in their farming.

Mrs. Mable Kenny just arrived from San Francisco, for an extended visit with her mother and family, Mrs. May Smith. Mr. Smith will follow latter.

Two Mr. Christensens and families were visiting Sunday with their brother-in-law and family, E. L. Abbott.

The first crop of hay, tho very light, is being cut. Crops are growing very slowly on account of the continued cold weather.

A Ackerman, Arthur Ackerman and Lou Davis, made a short trip to Salt Lake last week. Miss Annie Ackerman went over with her father to stay for some time and visit with relatives.

Mr. and Mrs. Lou Davis have moved into Burt Johnson house.

The Bee Hive Girls are taking up their work for the summer. A number of them enjoyed riding horse back last week. A wagon trip is planned for this week.

E. H. Bunker, who has sold out will move to Delta in the near future and Mr. Schlappy will take posession of the property.

Woodrow Items

Mr. and Mrs. John Wind are joyfully welcoming a fine baby girl.

Robt. Elmore will preach at Woodrow next Sunday evening at 8, p. m.

Mrs. Gertrude Stewart and daughter, Sarah, from Philadelphia, Pa., arrived in Woodrow last Sunday morning for a prolonged visit with Mrs. Harmon Fredricks. Mrs. Stewart has been in poor health for several years, and was finally ordered West by her physician for change of climate. Already she shows marked improvement. We wish that this valley was better known to Eastern invalids. Mr. Geo. S. Hoffecker who spent last summer with Dr. Tracy, is so much better in health that he is able to remain home with his family this summer for the first time in 20 years.

The Jolly Stitchers meet Friday with Mrs. W. E. Perry.

Master Milton Lills, son of Bishop Lills, who suffered a dislocation of the elbow, is improving nicely, and will soon be able to climb once more, but he says he will never again be so careless as to fall off a building.

Mrs. Clyde Underhill and Miss Cora Heise, have left the Woodrow metropolis to rusticate for a month in the village of Provo. They will attend summer school there. Already they have written home of some of their school girl pranks and of their delight in being scholars once more instead of teachers.

A party of men arrived in Woodrow this week trying to engage teams to haul ore from Deseret mountain on the north and Drum mountain on the west, to Sugarville.

Hinckley Happenings.

May 30th, the primary celebrated May Day by the braiding of the May pole and crowning the queen.

Mrs. Kate Hutchinson and Mrs. Lula Cropper and daughters, were in Provo for commencement exercises.

Afton Hinckley, Claris Erickson, Fannie Cropper and Laverna Wright, have returned home from where they have been attending the B. Y. U.

T. G. Theabold was seriously hurt while riding his motorcycle, he run into a calf and was thrown off breaking his collar bone and shoulder blade, Dr. Broaddus did the setting of the bones.

Mrs. Hanna Cropper has just returned from Fillmore where she has been receiving treatment from Dr. Stevens for a blood poisoned finger.

Sunday afternoon a social was held at Charle Burke's home in honor of his daughter, Jocosa, who has lest with her affiance to be married in the St. George Temple.

H. M. Bishop from Idaho, is visiting with his sister, Lula Cropper.

Mrs. A. P. Stout has been very ill the last few days.

Mrs. Alfbert Scott was visiting friends in Hinckley Saturday.

A large part of the town made a flying trip to Fillmore for the celebration of Well Days, among whom was our miller who actually took time to leave the town.

Everything is doing fine, the gardens are growing fast.

(Too late for last week)

Miss Bly Moody and George Beal returned Thursday morning from a trip north.

Miss Lapriel Robinson left on Wednesday evening's train for the summer term in the B. Y. U.

A number of Hinckley citizens including Mrs. Cropper and Mrs. Hutchison have gone north for a spring visit.

Friday May 26, was Home Economics social day. Six autos carried loads of women to Mrs. Smith's home about two miles west of town. The genial hostess did much to promote sociability and scatter good ideas among the 35 women present. The demonstration was a sponge cake of excellent texture and simple make. Ice cream was served with the cake.

A very "nifty" little entertainment was given at Hinckley Wednesday evening by the Home Economics Association. The program included much from music of a high order to burlesque of a rich order, fairy dancing, Amazon drill, clog dancing, solos, duetts, and an exceeding realistic production of the burlesque of and Thisbee in Shakespeare's Mid-summer Night's Dream.

The scoring of the town by the boy scouts under the direction of the Home Economics Association, has been completed. Nothing except sanitation was taken into account. Corrals, including pigpens, stables and corrals proper, yards considering also the well and outhouses, screening, removable vaults, and hinged lids, were the chief points taken into consideration, hence passing up beauty for utility.

In the town scoring, 5 was the lowest number of points given, 86 was the highest; 53 was the average of the 96 homes scored. A second scoring of those qualifying (80 or above) resulted in awarding the first prize of $5 to J. A. Jackson on a score of 80, while the second prize of $3 was divided between Ed Workman, John Pratt and T. H. Pratt who each scored 77. It was felt much good was accomplished by calling the attention of the citizens to a proper value of sanitation.

Hinckley.

The recent "Well Days" celebration at Fillmore attracted many Hinckley citizens all of whom returned with words of praise for Fillmore and an enthusiastic report of the splendid time they enjoyed. Among the visitors were, Milton Moody wife and family, Juel Moody and family Rich Cropper and family, Dr. C. A. Broadus and wife, Mrs. Wm. F. Pratt and family, Miss Lyle Cropper, Miss Ilena Reeve, Stanley and Wm. Shaw and George Beal.

Five new automobiles have recently been purchased by Hinckley citizens, W. F. Pra' has a "Saxon Six". Milton Moody and Glen Cropper "Studebaker seven passenger cars". Chas. Burke an "Overland" and William Walker a "Ford."

Charles E. McClellan, Mrs. Alice T. Bishop, Miss Bly Moody. Jacob Felix and George Beal have been appointed as a committee to arrange for the proper observance of the Nation's Birthday in Hinckley.

Miss Dora Burgess of St. George, is the guest of her sisters Mrs. Raymont Hardy and Mr. Frank Jarvis for the summer.

Mrs. Samuel Dutson entertained at a bundle shower for Mr. and Mrs. Sam Knight last Saturday. Many useful and beautiful gifts were presented o the newlyweds.

Mrs. Lulu Cropper, her daughter, Miss Mary and Roy Hilton attended the B. Y. U. Commencement exercises at Provo. -

Miss LaPriel Robinson has gone o Provo to attend the B. Y. U. summer school.

The Misses Afton Hinckley, Fannie Cropper and Laverna Wright have returned home from Provo where they spen the past year attending school .

Miss Elsie Richards is home from Heber where she taught school the past school year.

Mr. and Mrs. Charles Burke entertained a few friends last Sunday in honor of he marriage of their daughter, Jacosa, to a young man from orthern Utah.

Miss Anna Verna Nelson is home again after teaching school in West Jordan during the past school year.

A dance was given last Saturday night in the Academy Gymnasium. Music was furnished by Beal's Orchestra.

One of our highly esteemed citizens, T. George Theobald, had the misfortune to collide with a calf while riding his motocycle last week. He was thrown heavily to the ground and his collar bone broken. Dr. Broadus attended Mr. Theobald and he is rapidly recovering.

Mr. Harry Mathews of Salt Lake is visiting with George T 'y's family for a short time.

Quite a number of Hinckley people took advantage of the recent excursion rate to Salt Lake and spent several days working in the Temple.

Mr. and Mrs. Thomas W. Cropper entertained Mr. and Mrs. Leigh Cropper of Deseret at their home last Thursday.

Elmer and Ernest Stout and Reed Carey have returned from an extensive automobile trip through northern Utah and southern Idaho.

Some of the farmers are cutting their first crop of alfalfa, but due to the late frosts there is scarcely half a crop some of it being to short to rake. From all appearances there will be a shortage of hay in this section. Hay is at present selling for $12 per ton in the field. From present indications the grain crop will also be far below the average.

Hinckley Happenings.

The social meeting of the Home Economics club held at the home of Mrs. E. Smith, was well attended and much enjoyed by the members. Mrs. Smith has one of the most modern and best furnished homes in the country. The demonstration was the making of a sponge cake which was served with ice cream.

Last Thursday, twenty nine members of the club were conveyed in automobiles to the home of Mrs. Janett Joyce, where they were most profitably and pleasantly entertained by Mrs. Joyce and Mrs. Nelson. Miss White demonstrated the different uses of milk and a dainty lunch was served.

Mr. Wm. Gardner's automobile seems to be rather balky. While speeding along the highway it rolled over into the ditch but Mr. Gardner managed to keep his head out of the water. Frank Slaughter was quite uncomfortably shaken up. One wheel and the top were broken. If Mr. Gardner could just do it over again we are sure it would make a very entertaining reel for the movies.

In the stork's visit only one baby was left, Mr. and Mrs. Geo. Wright, Jr., being the lucky guardians.

Don't forget the big farewell party Friday night for Mr. Robert Robinson, who will leave for a mission to the northern states.

The B. B. Orchestra is making quite a hit, furnishing the best music in the west.

Mrs. C. A. Broaddus, Mrs. W. Bishop, Mrs. C. Cahoon and others were visitors in Salt Lake City the past week.

Mrs. Abbie Paxton is visiting friends and relatives here this week.

Mr. Beal has evidently fallen in love with our little town as we still see him here and Bly is so much interested in cooking recipes we expect to see her mo-Bealing away most any day.

Hinckley will furnish the program the second day of the Indian War Veterans Entertainment in Deseret.

Jack Greener came home from the southern part of the state very ill with typhoid fever.

Deseret Doings

After several days spent in business and pleasure Geo. Cahoon returned from Provo Tuesday morning.

One doesn't have to hunt altitude to find a variation of climate in this country. We boast everything from the torrid to the frigid zone all in a week.

The first cutting hay crop is the shortest known in this district in thirty years.

It is understood that the officers of the West Side Telephone Co., have definitely decided to have a central building in Deseret serving the entire company. Much better service will undoubtedly result from this action.

Mrs. I. N. Hinckley, ot Provo, was a passenger on the Joy stage this week. Mrs. Hinckley joins her husband who is interested in mining property in that vicinity.

The many friends of B. P. Crofts regret the death of his father which occured at the old home at Cedar Fort, recently.

Arrangements are underway for a real celebration on Independence Day.

A large number of interested mothers are in attendance at the Better Babies' Conference at Hinckley.

A. D. Ryan and C. L. Stubbins made a flying trip to Salt Lake in their car last Wednesday and returned home Monday.

Mrs. L. G. Kelly has been ill the past week but is now recovering.

Miss Hettie White of the Home Economics Department of the A. C. College, Logan, lectured before the women of the Relief Society Tuesday afternoon. Miss White's talks are always interesting.

Mr. and Mrs. Lon A. Robinson, of Fillmore on their way from Salt Lake, stopped over for a few days visit with their daughter, Mrs. E. J. Eliason.

Mrs. M. E. Proctor of Panguitch is the guest of her sister, Mrs. Amanda Kelley.

Geo. Beal, who so successfully organized and directed a Junior Band at Hinckley last winter, succeeded in interesting so large a number of Deseret boys in the work, that orders were placed for about 30 instruments.

A slight injury on the foot developed into a rather serious infection for M. L. Peterson. He has been confined to his room for three weeks.

Sugarville Siftings

Celebration at Sugarville July 4th. Program of the day will be published next week.

The Friendship Thimble club will meet with Mrs. E. E. Olds next Wednesday.

Mr. and Mrs. John Barker entertained friends from Redlands, Calif., last week end.

George Vinzant spent Saturday and Sunday with his cousin in Delta.

Union Sunday School every Sunday at 2:30, p. m., at the school house.

Saturday evening is the time of the Thomas and Carey musical entertainment. Admission 25 and 10 cents. A dance afterward.

Miss Effie Clark spent Saturday and Sunday in Delta, as the guest of Miss Eliza Hook.

Many of our young people attended the O. Z. O. dance in Delta Friday night and report a most excellent time.

Millard County Chronicle
June 29, 1916

Suhterland Searchlights

Ross Simpkins and family spent part of last week in Piute county, having made the trip in their new machine.

Miss Roseline Meinhardt entertained her Sunday School class last Friday evening. Refreshments were served and all report having a most pleasant evening.

Mrs. Gilbert and little daughter of New York, are visiting at the home of J. W. Smith. Mr. Smith is her Uncle.

Mrs. George Boardman, mother, sister and little niece are visiting in Salt Lake this week.

The Bee Hive girls had a slumber party last Thusrday night.

They toasted wiennies and had fun until the wee small hours.

Woodrow sure knows how to have a good time and the young —some older ones to—of Sutherland joined them in their picnic at the home of C. W. Hickman at Abraham. There were about two hundred in all, also plenty of good things to eat and about forty gallons of ice cream.

Miss Hattie Ward of Delta, was a guest at the home of Miss Helene Davis on Wednesday.

Mr. and Mrs. Elmore leave Saturday for Butte, Montana, and in September will return to their home in Cali. They have been here only a short time but have made many friends who regret to see them go.

Mrs. Burger, north of here is expected tomorrow from Placentia. She was called there by the death of her husband.

A crowd of young folks went to the flume Wednesday afternoon.

Result of Better Baby Contest June 22-23

During the past week the Fourth of July committees have been busy with plans for the celebration, and the Home Economics Association has been extremly busy with the aid of our Home Demonstrator, Miss White, conducting a Better Baby contest for the whole county. The cold snap made it difficult for babies from a distance to enter but over 50 babies from 6 months to 3 years of age were examined. Dr. and Mrs. Broaddus gave practically their entire time for three days giving the physical and mental tests, and making measurments. Miss White constructed an excellent Baby Health Exhibit covering all the problems of baby care and feeding, using the instructive charts furnished by the Woman's Home Companion and much original material. Especially helpful were the tables containing model were the tables containing model meals for babies of different ages, and a table of "baby killers". The men attending the contest showed especial interest in the charts and exhibits.

There was a fairly good attendance Thursday night at the stereopticon lecture by Dr. Beatty of Salt Lake, on "The Health of the Community". He talked in detail on Hinckley's rating in last year's clean town contest, congratulated us on our water supply, urged us to keep the manure hauled out of the corrals every ten days during the fly season. He commended the improvements in sanitation, for which the H. E. A. has been working, emphasizing that the sanitary disposal of all waste and garbage, and clean milk were of first importance. He hoped we could then add to the beauty of the town by more lawns and better fences. The lighting of the school house could be easily improved by rearrangement of the seating of desks.

On account of the failure of three of our out-of-town speakers the rest of the program had to be given by Dr. Broaddus, Mrs. Broaddus, Mrs. Lovell and Miss White. Dr. Broaddus spoke Thursday on "Pre natal Care", emphasizing the importance of outdoor exercise, good health and elimination and a nappy frame of mind; on "Weaning the Baby",

urging gradual weaning, ration feeding and the importance milk throughout the second yes On Friday he discussed cont gion among children, urging outdoor playhouse which co be used for immediate isolati of any child showing any sym toms of illness. He insist that most diseases are preven able and explained the comm means of prevention and bett hygiene.

Miss White explained t necessity of sterilizing ever thing used in the care and fee ing of the baby.

Mrs. Lovell of Oak City, ga a fine talk on the "Sick Room and the importance of fresh ai sun-light, and absolute clean ness. She urged freer use soap and water and continuo disinfecting during sickness.

Mrs. Broaddus in discussir "Training the Baby" stated th the real problem was "Trainir the Mother;" that the ide should be the baby's ultima good, physical, mental and mor and never the convenience a comfort of the mother. A mot er without broad education, reg ular habits, self-control, hig ideal and common-sense, ca never have a well-trained baby A number of special problems care and discipline were discuss ed.

The results of the contest a reported by the scoring commi tee, Mrs. Neeley and Mrs. Ti petts, are as follows:

Highest scoring girl and bo in the contest

Martha Christianson, Delta, 9
Edward Lovell, Oak City, 95.

To these, beautiful bronz medals are awarded by th Woman's Home Companion.

Division I under one year o age, highest girl and boy.

Pearl Cox, Hinckley, 9
Verdell Bishop, Delta, 9

Division II, between 1 and years, highest girl and boy.

Rosa May Thurston, South Tract, 9
Ladd Cropper, Hinckley, 9

Division III, 2 to 3 years.

Blaine Cropper, Deseret, 9
Charlotte Blake, Hinckley, 90.

To all these babies diploma will be given by the Woman' Home Companion. Duplicat score cards and certificates, dip lomas etc. will be mailed to con testants by the Hinckley H. E A., as soon as the committee ca do so.

Black Hawk War Veterans at Deseret

The Indian War Veterans of Millard county gave one of their chrracteristic entertainments here last week affecting a reorganization of the Millard Post at the same time. Excellent programs were furnished Wednesday and Thursday by the Deseret and Hinckley sons and daughters of veterans. Veterans and their wives as guests of the resident members were conveyed over much of the newly developed country by auto Thursday afternoon. The entire day Friday was devoted to the election of officers and reminiscent talks by the aged comrades, many of whom are now past eighty years.

The Black Hawk war began late in '63 when over some personal trouble, two whites were killed by Indians near Gunnison Bend, Utah. Black Hawk, chief of the Indians, becoming alarmed declared open hostilities. The white settlers referred their trouble to the Governor of Utah, who in turn asked the government for assistance. The president of the United States then ordered the Governor to call out the State Malitia. At that time no such body of men existed in the state of Utah, hence the citizens were called to arms in their own defense.

This trouble with the Indians continued over a period of three years, all this time the citizens doing active service without renumeration from the state or nation. Men furnished their own arms and commissaries were supplied from the homes of the people. It was many years after, before any effort was made to gain recognition for the men who sacrificed so much to guard home and border development. Since the organization of its veterans at Springville, Utah, several years ago, much has been done by the ernest body of officers and the constant effort of Congressman, Howell to gain some acknowledgment for our Pioneer soldiers as has been gained for the same service in other states. It is hoped this recognition will not come too late.

Mr. and Mrs. Jos. Damron, Sr., leave for Inkom, Idaho, Saturday morning, where they will visit with relatives for some time.

Mrs. Isabelle Bennett expects to spend the summer with her daughter, Mrs. George Hunt, in Burley, Idaho.

After an absence of six weeks Mrs. J. C. Hawley, of Oasis, returned Monday from Iowa Hot Springs, Ida., where she has been under the care of Dr. Prouse. Mrs. Hawley has been extremely ill but has hope for a complete recovery.

John Dewsnip drove a new Maxwell touring car home, from Salt Lake last week.

Chas. Baker and the Conk boys are doing some fine developing on their mining claims in Saw Tooth range. They report the property looking fine.

C. L. Judd, of the Dep't. of Prehistorical Research of the National Museum, which is in Washington, D. C., who has been for several months making extensive investigations of the cliff and mound dwellings of Southern Utah, was in town Wednesday and he in company with Bishop Damron, went out to the Hot Springs north of Abraham to look over the ground which is reported to bear strong evidence of a very old civilization.

Hinckley.

The Base Ball Dance given last Saturday evening was a decided success in both financial and social ways.

Miss Theuckla Blackburn of Delta spent Saturday and Sunday as the guest of Miss Lyle Cropper.

Vernon Moody, son of Juel Moody, left this morning (Tuesday) for Manti to respond to the call for Utah Militia to mobolize. Mr. Moody joined a company while attending school at Ephriam last year.

The Independence Day committee have things well underway for a glorious "Fourth" at Hinckley. The town has been divided into two sections, the South and the North and all athletic events and all sports will be contests between these two factions. Mr. A. L. Tippetts and Dr. O. A. Broaddus have been appointed Commanders-in-chief and with these two enhusiastic gentlemen at the head something exciting is promised. The Goddess of Liberty will be elected by vote. Miss Blanche Sawyer being the candidate from the North, and Miss Verna Nelson the candidate of the South.

Mrs. Janette Joyce entertained the Home Economics Association at her home last Wednesday. The trip was made to the Joyce farm by thirty ladies in automobiles.

Miss Hetty White of the U. A. C. Extension Division demonstrated several ways of preparing "Cottage Cheese" and also a delicious "Tomato Timble." Mrs. Joyce assisted by Miss White and Mrs. R. A. Nelson served toothsome refreshments.

That the association is getting results was shown by the fact that nearly all the ladies were trying at home the recipes that are demonstrated at every club meeting.

Mrs. O. A. Broaddus spent a few days in Salt Lake City last week, combining business and pleasure. While there she attended the meeting of the State Board of Health. She will make a detailed report to the Hinckley Town Board in regard to steps taken by the Board to make the towns of the State clean and sanitary.

The "Better Baby Contest" to be held this week under the direction of Miss Hetty White and Dr. O. A. Broaddus promises to be highly educational to all mothers. It is a splendid opportunity to have the babies scored for physicial and mental efficiency.

A farewell party for Elder Robert E. Robinson Jr. who leaves soon to fulfill a mission in the Northern States, will be held in the Academy next Friday evening. A program will be given at 8 P. M. after which dancing will be enjoyed in the Gymnasium.

That automobile accidents may even happen in quiet little Hinckley was demonstrated last week when the Ford car belonging to Wm. N. Gardner and driven by Frank Slaughter, decided to leave the road and fell bottom side up into the canal just north of Charles Burke's residence. Mr. Gardner and Mr. Slaughter had a fine bath and escaped without injury. The Ford also had a bath and lost a wheel which was soon replaced with a new one from the Delta Garage after which the gentlemen proceeded on their way.

H. H. Pederson of Oasis had a similar experience in the same spot some three weeks ago. Mr. Pederson was uninjured and the car was not damaged in the least.

Wm. F. Pratt was a business visitor to Salt Lake City last week.

Miss Annie Lund of Salt Lake City is spending a few weeks in hi vicinity, the guest of Miss Fauntella Cahoon.

HINCKLEY.

The Nation's Birthday was appropriately celebrated at Hinckley. At 9 A. M. a street parade was formed in which all patriotic citizens were invited to participate. This was followed by the sports for the children and a demonstration of fire making, tent pitching and flag signaling by the Boy Scouts under the direction of Scout Master A. I. Tippetts.

At 10.30 citizens of Hinckley, Delta and Abraham filled to overflowing the Academy Auditorium, where they listened to a spicy, patriotic program.

The Thirteen Original States were represented by thirteen of Hinckley's most popular young ladies, who led the congregation in singing "America," and "Columbia, The Gem of the Ocean." A. A. Hinckley offered the opening prayer which was followed by Miss Lavorna Wright singing, "My Own United States." Miss Blanche Sawyer was Goddess of Liberty and Elmer Stout represented Uncle Sam.

Mr. A. I. Tippetts was orator of the day and gave a spirited, patriotic address which was enthusiastically received. A chorus composed of Lily Moody, Elsie Richards, Europa Robinson, Clara Walker, Wilford Pratt, Afton Greener, Cleamont Dutson, Alma Western, Ivan Hilton and Ira Stout rendered the "Flag Without a Stain," under the direction of Mrs. C. A. Broadus. A playlet "The Making of the First Flag" was presented by some of the smaller boys and girls and the exercises were closed by Mrs. Marion Bishop singing "The Star Spangled Banner." Taking it all in all it was the most splendid program that has been given in Hinckley.

The afternoon program of sports were intensely interesting. A game of baseball bewteen the North and the South in which the South was victorious, was he first number. All sorts of horse races, and a motorcycle race between Dr. Broadus and William Shaw interested the onlookers. A game of baseball between Hinckley and Abraham teams resulted in a victory for the home team. The days festivities closed with a grand ball in the Millard Academy Gymnasium.

The band under the leadership of Mr. George Beal gave a serenade in the morning and entertained the crowd with splendid music throughout the day.

Miss Dora Richards and gentleman friend came down from th uncinityle Ranch to spend the "Fourth."

The dance given on July 3rd was a splendid success. Music was furnished by the B. B. orchestra and the Hinckley band. Dancing was continuous.

Mr. Rollo Calloway of Provo who has spent the past two years in New York City as a student, is the guest of his friend Mr. A. I Tippetts for a few days. Mr. Calloway is enroute to his father's mines in Arizona.

Miss Thenolda Blackburn of Delta spent several days this week as the guest of her friend Miss Lyle Cropper

Elder Robert E. Robison, Jr., left last week for a mission to the Central States. He was accompanied as far as Salt Lake City by Mrs. Robison and their son, Ross.

Mr. Wallace Holman of Provo spent the fourth with Miss Verna Nelson at Hinckley.

Mr. Jack Greener is home again after spending the winter at the A C. U., and the time since then as a salesman for the "Wearever" Aluminum Co., in Carbon county. He was obliged to return home on account of poor health but his friends are gratified to know that he has completely recovered.

Mr. Percy Nelson is home after having spent some time working in a Salt Lake City Assay office.

Messers Fred Wilkins, Ernest Jackson and George Webb have gone to Antelope to work in the mines.

Mr. Charles Talbott, Sr., is reported as being on the sick list.

LEAMINGTON

While engaged in a friendly wrestling match with Bruce Moore, Mr Jerome Ivie was thrown heavily to the ground sustaining a fractured collar bone and shoulder blade. Dr. Murry of Lynndyle was called who set the injured members.

Mr. and Mrs. Rodney H. Ashby have the sympathy of this entire community in the sad hour of their bereavement in losing their little baby girl, who departed this life on July 1st and whose burial took place on July 2nd in the Leamington Cemetery. Bishop and Mrs. Ashby take this means of expressing their heartfelt thanks to all those friends who so kindly assisted them during the illness and recent death of their little daugher.

Mrs. Amanda Stout, 56 years of age passed peacefully away on June 28, of acute Bright's Disease. She leaves the following son and daughters to mourn her demise. Lewis, Walter, Elvira, Lydia, and Mattie.

She was a woman with a lovable disposition and was greatly loved and respected in this community. Mr. Louis Stout wishes to thank one and all for the kind assistance rendered to the family during he recent illness and death of their loving mother.

Pioneer Day at Hinckley
Program

Solute ot daybreak.

Hoisting Stars and Stripes at sunrise.

Sernade by the band.

10, a. m.,—Program in Academy Auditorium, as follows:

Utah the Queen of the West
By congregation.

Invocation.

Quartett,
Utah, the Star of the West.

Orator of the Day,
Hon Nephi L. Morris,
(Utah's Prospective Gov.)

Cornet Solo,
Albert Christensen,
(Band Master)

Reading,
Eda Cropper-Tippits.

Utah, We Love Thee

Benediction

2, p. m.,—Childrens' sports at Relief lawn.

3:30, p. m.,—City Park.

Catching greased pig.

100 yd. race,   Boys 16 of age.
100   "   open to all.
75   "   30 to 40 years.
50   "   40 to 50 years.
40   "   50 to 60 years.
25   "   over 60 years.

Egg race,   single and married women.

Peanut race,   single and married women.

Relay race,   Single and marrid women.

Relay race,   single and married men.

Sack race,   Single and married men.

Jumping and running relay, 10 men, single and married.

Horse Races.

Orange race, 25, 50, 75, 100 yds.

¼ mile race,   Two year old.
¼   "   race,   work horses.
¼   "   harness race, free for all.
¼   "   go,   free for all.

Baseball game.   Limber nine and stiff nine.

8:30, p. m.,—Grand Ball in Gym. Best music in the Land.

Something doing all the time. Everybody invited.

———

Geo. Bishop and Jim Robison are in from the west, to attend court at Fillmore.

T. H. Pratt and family arrived home Sunday night from a week's visit with Mrs. Pratt's sister in Richfield.

A twelve-pound boy arrived on the 11th, at George Walker's place.

Dr. Broaddus motored up to the city with his family, but returned home on the train, having broken his car down on the trip. They brought back with them Mrs. Broaddus' friend, Miss Gertrude Ingalls, who will visit with them for some time.

Next H. E. A. will be held on the 28th of July at Mrs. J. A. Jackson's home, where she will demonstrate the making of vinegar dumplings and cheese sandwiches. All members who fail to come will be sure to miss a sociable time as Mrs. Jackson is a very pleasing hostess.

Our Junior band is doing good work under the leadership of Mr. Albert Christenson of Ephraim, Ut., who was called here to take Mr. Beal's place, as he had to go to the city for an operation on his lip. We are a very fortunate community indeed to have such an able leader, who can have the patience to train such a band successfully, and we need to give them all the support and appreciation we can. Let us profit by past experiences and not let this band die out for lack of money and support. Let us show both on the morning of the twenty fourth when they serenade us, by showing them the best we have is none too good for them. Our town has the talant, and is going to be the musical center of the "Greater" Delta country.

New families moving in town are Mr. Clarence Woodbury and a Mr. Naylor who is occupying one of Jim Blakes bungalows.

A very successful festival was held on the Relief lawn by the Primary children Monday afternoon. A table covered with sand and other things to represent the old pioneer trail was very cleverly done. The children in their funny costumes of pioneers danced, sang and did a number of other things to show what the pioneers did. The old folks or pioneers, were taken to and from the grounds in autos and treated to ice cream and punch. A very striking part was illustrated by the children of the call made by the Government for five hundred volunteers to go to Mexico, and Brigham Young's reply, "You shall have your men Captain Allen, if there are not enough young men the old can go and then if not enough we will take the women"

The Junior band, altho minus a leader, helped to make things lively. Great credit must be given the officers for their untiring and unselfish work.

Deseret Doings

The little son, Max, of Mr. and Mrs. Don Bishop of Hinckley, came near drowning while its parents were making a call at Mrs. Geo. Kelly's Sunday. Only out of sight for a moment the child was found head first in the barrell at the well.

A. D. Ryan and O. W. Kelly spent a good part of last week showing California home seekers over the country.

A. D. Ryan was called to Salt Lake Tuesday of last week, to attend his wife who is ill at the L. D. S. Hospital.

Mrs. Olla Webster and daughter, Ore, of Central, Arizona, and mother, Mrs. Hester Damron of Thatcher, Arizona, who have for the last two months been visiting relatives and friends in Nephi, Fillmore and Deseret, left Monday morning for Los Angeles, Cali., where they will remain sometime before returning home.

County Road Supervisor J. P. Bennett with Mrs. Bennett, and their son, Adelbert, wife and two children, left by auto Monday of last week, for Salt Lake. They will spend a week in Ogden canyon before returning.

The Sego swarm of Bee Hive girls were guests of the Misses Mamie and Molly Cropper, Thursday afternoon. The girls had an old fashioned quilting bee.

The Blue Bird Swarm of Bee Hive girls spent Wednesday afternoon at the Callmore Cropper home, guests of Edna and Izma Cropper. Folk dancing was a feature of the entertainment.

H. S. Cahoon was called to Salt Lake Wednesday to attend funeral services of two uncles, Charles Spencer and Richard Maxfield.

Mr. and Mrs. Frank Scott retuened from Murray Sunday, accompanied by Mr. Scott's mother, who came to arrange for the erection of a bungalow on her city property.

Miss Stella Jacobson of Pine Valley, Utah, who arrived here Saturday morning will visit for a time with her sister, Mrs. Pearl Bennett, and many friends. Miss Jacobson's amiable character, and ability as a teacher won for her many friends here a few years back.

J. V. Black and W. R. Bennett who are are doing some contract work at Swan Lake, were in town early in the week for supplies.

Clarence Nelson, son of the late A. C. Nelson, Superintendant of schools, representing the J. A. Folger Co., of San Francisco was in town Saturday.

Many families are preparing for a few days or weeks in the canyon. Among those to leave this week are Mr. and Mrs. Wil Warnick and Mr. and Mrs. Albert Bliss and families.

Mrs. Leigh Cropper, surrounded by her children and grandchildren celebrated her seventy first birthday on the 16th.

The Primary Association, on Monday last, at the A. C. Nelson gave a realistic demonstration of the travels and early day conditions incident to the life of the Pioneers in the west.

M. Wolfolk and brother of Virginia, who are doing some systematic development work in their mining property in the Cricket range, are in town for a short time. The gentlemen are enthused with prospects in that vicinity and predict a real live camp for Crickets at no distant day.

The entire Pioneer day celebration is under the direction of the Sunday School. The program as printed gives promise of a rousing good time. Preparations are under way to care for a big crowd and a hearty welcome is assured.

N. L. Peterson, our well known real estate dealer, and Mrs. Peterson, who are planning a trip to California, will probably leave the last of this week.

Mr. Jos. Dewsnip leaves soon for his cattle ranch near Milner, Idaho.

Mrs. Christina Warnick is visiting her son Fred, in Provo.

Quite a large party of residents foom Snake Valley passed here Saturday on their way to Fillmore where they are to attend court which is now in session. James H. Robinson of the party stopped over Saturday night in Deseret.

Sugarville Siftings

Mr. and Mrs. Roy Jones are enjoying a new buggy.

W. G. McKittrick returned from San Diego last Saturday to look after the harvest work on his ranch.

Despite the fact that some people are leaving the valley for various reasons, new ones are coming to take their place. Mr. Bruns and family came in a few weeks ago and have their house nearly completed.

LOCAL NEWS

P. M. Sanders has been appointed the position of P. M. at Oasis.

L. R. Walker has resigned the position of postmaster at Oak City and has been succeeded by Miss Sylvia Lovel.

July 24th being a legal holiday in this State, the Delta State Bank will be closed all day Monday next.　jy20-1t

Professor C. E. McClellan of the Millard Academy, and John Reeve, chairman of Millard County Drainage District No. 1, were Delta visitors last Saturday.

Mr. and Mrs. Ed. Bunker and family, who have been spending about a month here, the guests of Mr. and Mrs. John Eardley, left Monday for their home at Delta, Millard Co.—St. George News.

The last contingent of the Ut. troops passed thru Delta last Friday for the border, and word comes from Nogales that they have arrived there and are now comfortably located. All the Utah troops are together at Nogales.

This week will be found in the Chronicle the first installment of a new serial story, "Beyond the Frontier," a story of the early pioneers of the west. It is reported to be an excellent story and as it treats of our own country should be well worth reading.

Harold Koch, son of Lewis Koch, wife and baby, arrived here Saturday from Manassa, Colo., and will make their future home here.

Sanders & Thompson, painters and decorators, of Oasis, are engaged in refinishing the interior and exterior of the Delta Hotel. They are doing the interior in white and brown calcimine and are making a neat job of it. They are experienced men and have quite a job at the Delta.

L. E. McCann, of Ontario, Cal., arrived in this city Tuesday to look the country over with a view to obtaining farms for his three sons, and looking up a location for a commercial establishment of some sort. Mr. McCann is a thoro business man and he will find no more promising field in the Intermountain country for his operations than the "Greater Delta" country we are sure and no better chance for getting in on the top floor in an agricultural way.

Last Sunday, friends gathered at the home of Mr. and Mrs. George Meinhardt at Sutherland, to enjoy dinner and spend the day in sociability. Those present were the families of Mr. and Mrs. Frank Heise, and of Mr. and Mrs. Frank Beckwith with Miss Mary Johnson who is visiting with Miss Athena Beckwith, and the family of Henry Freese. After dinner of chicken and other good things, the autos took the party over to the flume for a swim. The day was very pleasantly spent, and all thank the hostess.

FOR EXCHANGE:—Five passenger Oakland car 30 H. P. to trade for good team horses, will be at Delta Hotel Saturday and Sunday. W. P. Walker.　j201t-p

About fifteen teams from the east side came into Delta loaded with hogs to be shipped to market. They were bot by Bert Johnson who will ship out four cars this week.

The case of Ted Moore, charged with assault on the person, Mrs. Parley Stapley of Hinckley, was tried in justice court at Fillmore last week and Moore was fined $150 and costs, having plead guilty to the charge. Moore paid his fine and he and his wife left last Sunday for Chicago.

Rev. and Mrs. Hamilton have returned from an extended trip to the east and services will be held at the Presbyterian chapel next Sunday evening. While in the east they attended the national Presbyterian at Atlantic City, and visited relatives in a number of the eastern states.

Hinckley Happenings.

Our gardens and crops are looking better since the warm weather began, after having such a long cold dry spring.

Mrs. Alta Morris was very ill Sunday but is improving slowly now.

We have a number of visitors in town now. Mrs. Nancy Stansworth of Grafton Utah, is here visiting her sons. Mrs. Walter Stout of Hurricane is visiting her aunt, Mrs. J. E. Wright. Will Wright, an old resident of Hinckley, is here also.

Mr. and Mrs. Leonard Mecham, Mrs. Sarah Mortensen and J. H. Langston and family from Lynndyl, were all celebrating the twenty fourth here.

New houses recently built are one each for the Christenson,

Wilson and Swayer families, north of town. Jim Blake is building another bungalow for renting perposes. One for Frank Wright, wife and mother.

The drainage system is going merrily on. The surveyors can be seen with their striped poles in all parts of the town during the day.

The Y. L. M. I. A. was recently organized with Mrs. Rose Jarvis as President, Delta Blake and Mattie Knight as counselors, Nina Pratt secretary and Ruby Stout organist.

A powerful and interesting sermon was delivered Sunday by a Dr. Caldwell of Brooklyn, Mass., who is a recent convert to the Mormon church. He is a friend of Jene Hilton, who brought him down from Salt Lake in his car. Wilford Hilton is also here and we are pleased to welcome them both back home after a long stay in the north.

The weather man is at last favoring us with a nice rain.

Our twenty fourth celebration was ushered in by the firing of guns and raising of the flag and serenading by the band. The citizens of the town, after being awakened to the necessity of supporting the band, treated them very royally. They gave them candy, nuts, ice ceam, soda water, beer, cake, apples and a great many expressions of of appreciation, also six dollars in cash.

The program was successfully carried out. The oration being very masterly and forceful as well as instructively given. The song, Utah We Love Thee, by Bly Moody, cornet solo, by Albert Christenson and original poem by Eda Tippetts, were very well rendered. The sports in the afternoon were only just begun when ended by the storm The dance at night closed a celebration that was charaterized by a greater patriotism and enthusiastic spirit than has hitherto been exhibited in former celebrations.

Deseret Doings

Otto Stuart is home after several months in Salt Lake.

Miss Cora Nelson, who with her parents, motored from their California home to their ranch on the South Tract in June, was a guest of Miss Lucile Damror Pioneer Day.

No one in Deseret has said anything about being in the field for the governor's chair, but a lot is being said about the votes the man will get who stands for prohibition.

Jas. H. Robinson, Isaac Robinson, Geo. and Alfred Bishop and Mr. and Mrs. Albert Bishop, le for their homes at Gandy and ty of the Western Pacific R. R extension thru Deep Creek, wil undoubtedly mean a continuation of the road thru Snake Val

Smithville, Tuesday. These residents of western Millard all spoke interestingly of conditions in Snake Valley. The Probabililey making their dream of access to the larger markets of the State come true.

Pioneer Day was fittingly observed, beginning with a parade of citizens and representative floats, followed by service at 10:30 in the meeting house, and an afternoon of sports, which was to some extent deferred, owing to the heavy rain which continued for several hours.

Miss Edna Cropper took census of school population this week.

D. J. Black left by auto for Milner, Idaho, last week. His daughter, Dora, who has been there since the first of June, will return with him.

Mr. and Mrs. Glen Cropper, motored to Salem for a few days visit covering Pioneer day.

Mrs. Geo. A. Hone and two children, arrived from the north Monday going directly on to Drum by stage where she is to join Mr. Hone, who has the management of the Martha mine in the Drum district.

U. S. district attorney, W. W. Ray, while on his way to Salt Lake from Fillmore made a hurried call on a few old acquaintances, expressing himself as being delighted to visit the old home again.

Messrs Stubbins, Ryan and Baily of the Alpha Farm Co. came in from Salt Lake, Monday.

Mr. and Mrs. H. McCosh, who have had the managment of the Clifton Hotel at Oasis for the last three years, left for their old home in Nebraska last week where they will take up their future residence. Mr. McCosh held the office of post master at Oasis. Since his resignation the office is being filled by F. E. Saunders.

Abraham Crop Report

An interesting letter on conditions of alfalfa and sugar beets by A. W. Reed.

Harvesting is in full blast in this vicinity. Crops are somewhat short on accout of cold spring but the assured high price of grain will make up for this. Prospects for an alfalfa seed crop was never better.

The farmers of Abraham have organized a Water Users' Association for the purpose of looking after the interests of the Abraham Irrigation Co. The sugar beets planted in this part as an experiment are certainly looking fine. They tell the story, that beet culture is no longer an experiment but a grand success. The writer planted one and one half acres on what is known as the worst alkalied land in the county and we are glad to report that the sugar beet is king of alkali. These beets are flourishing without water, having never been watered since planted. And we will say to those who have signed up with the Southern Utah Co., to prepare to make good this contract as there is no risk to run. When considering planting sugar beets we must look beyond personal interest as it will increase the valuation of real estate all over Millard county.

The taxes on such an industry will help build up our schools and roads, and make Delta a trading center. It will draw the attention of moneyed men, as one great industry calls for another, and last, but not least, all kinds of stock do well fed on sugar beets.

Sutherland Searchlights

Mrs. Reed is visiting her sister Mrs. Hy Sherer.

W. R. Walker and Miss Helen Bunker, were visiting friends in Salt Lake.

Mrs. May Burger of Woodrow spent several days in Sutherland visiting friends.

After this glorious rain the dust is nowhere to be seen and the air is real clean for once.

Nearly everyone from here spent the 24th at Delta and report having had a fine time.

James A. Edwards is having a rest, also a change from farm life by spending several days in Delta.

Several of the farmers have headed their grain and report crops as very light.

A very enjoyable program was held Sunday evening at the church.

The Bishopric of Sutherland Ward, very pleasantly entertained the officers and teachers of their ward at the home of Bishop G. D. Shipley. Some fifty people were present and all enjoyed the encouraging remarks by the Bishopric and ward officers, also the program and refreshments of ice cream and cake.

Millard County Chronicle
August 3, 1916

140 Attend Bunker Family Reunion

Excellent Program is Rendered and Guests Feast on Dixie Fruit

The Edward Bunker family, to the number of one hundred for , including a few invited guests assembled at the Ward Hall to commemorate the 94th anniversary of his birth. A full days program was rendered with intermissions for refreshments. The program was opened in the morning with a song service "Utah We Love Thee", by the congregation and was followed by historical sketches from various members of the family interspread with vocal and intrumental music, readings and recitations Intermission was had for a fine spread in the basement of the hall at 2, p. m., after which the program was continued until evening when it was again adjourned to meet in the evening for a big fruit festival and the completion of the program.

The entertainment furnished was most excellent and pleasing and all those who took part, did so with great credit to themselves. M. M. Steele, Sr., recited an intensely interesting history of father Bunker, following his travels and labors down from his boyhood days in the state of Maine to the time of his death in old Mexico in 1901. M. A. Bunker, who was a delegate to the Bunker reunion in Boston gave a pleasant account of his trip back to the "Hub" and of meeting that branch of the family, and of the historical old fort which was built on the farm of the original sire of the American Bunkers. The fort is now in ruins but Mr. Bunker stated that at the Boston meeting, steps had been taken which would probably lead to the purchase of the land on which it is located, and its re-construction, the idea being to rebuild it and turn it over to the state as a historic relic.

Mesdames Corey and Miner rendered some excellent vocal and instrumental music for the entertainment of the audience. Aunt Betsy Goodwin, a convert of Edward Bunker's during his mission days in Scotland, read a pleasing poetic sketch of his life, as did others. The performances of all who took part on the program are well worthy of mention only for lack of time and space.

The refreshments served by the ladies of the family, in the basement of the hall were excellent and all that the heart and (stomach) could desire.

The fruit festival served in the evening consisted of delicious fruits brot from the Dixie country by members of the family, who reside in that famous fruit region—cantelopes, white and purple grapes and peaches. These were devoured with great relish by all present and; while there was lots of the fruit left, it was only by reason of insufficient capacity to store it all away that it was not all devoured.

Those present from a distance were John M. Bunker, Overton, Nev., M. A. and Robert Bunker, and wives, St. Thomas, Nevada, S. A. Bunker, Glencove, Utah, Irene and Owenia Grover, Beaver, Utah, Beulah Crosby, Panguitch, Willard Corey and wife, Cedar City, Mrs. Paul Miner, Springville, Utah, Violate Rumley, Cornish, Utah, and Aunt Betsy Goodwin, Beaver, Utah.

The Bunker family as a whole is one of the largest in the U. S., the Utah branch numbering over 300 decendents.

Following is a brief history of the father of the Utah branch of Bunkers:

Father Bunker was born in Penobscot, Maine, August 1st 1822. He came to Illinois and joined the Mormon Church in 1843. Afterwards enlisting in the Mexican war of 1846. He marched to California and there served during the war in the defense of his country. After his duties as a soldier were performed, he returned to Council Bluffs, Iowa, by way of Salt Lake City, in 1847. Having remained there a short time, he again returned to Utah in 1849, making his home in Ogden. He was one of the early pioneers of this state and for some years a Bishop in the Mormon church.

After living in Ogden for some time, he moved to Dixie in the year of 1861, and settled in Toquerville first. He was later called to Santa Clara, where he served as a bishop, and where he remained for sixteen years. From there he went to Nevada where he established the town of Bunkerville, and which bears his name.

In 1901, he crossed the border into old Mexico, where he settled at Morrelas. After reaching his destination, he only lived three weeks, and there his remains were laid to rest at the ripe old age of 79 years.

Sutherland Searchlights

A large crowd enjoyed their swim Sunday in the flume and river.

Marvin Greathouse spent Sunday in Sugarville.

There has been several on the sick list the past week—Mrs. F. N. Davis, Mrs. C. M. Hickman, and Bryan Smith.

Tiny Barker has sold his machine to Mr. Hy Sherer.

It sure keeps a fellow guessing whether he'll be roast pork in the day or an icicle at night. There was a heavy rain here last Friday and, thanks be, it settled the dust.

Frank Foote spent Saturday and Sunday in Whiskey Creek with Mr. Day of Delta.

Roy Walker and sister, Clara, are visiting their brother W. R. Walker, our merchant with the always smiling face.

Lawrence Abbott gave a talk on prohibition Sunday evening at the church.

There was a family reunion of the Bunker's in Delta Tuesday. As the Bunker's are one of the oldest families here there is a large number of them. Mr. and Mrs. W. R. Walker, and the Misses Helen and Hazel Bunker attended.

The Jolly Stitchers met with Mrs. Irvine Greathouse and report a lovely visit. There is a rumor that they are going to have their husbands with them at R. W. Britt's home sometime in August.

Mrs. James Edwards, and Mrs. Davis enjoyed a birthday dinner at Mrs. Cavanaugh's at Abraham.

Make your arrangements for Fall Sewing while I still have open dates. Miss Paxton, Delta Hotel.   a3-10

NOTICE

To Whom It May Concern.

Notice is hereby given that at a meeting of The Republican Central Committee in and for Millard County, Utah, held at Delta, Utah, July 26, 1916, the following apportionment for the election of delegates to The Republican State Convention to be held at Ogden, Utah, Aug. 8th, 1916, and The Republican Congressional Convention for The First Congressional District to be held at Ogden, Utah, Aug. 9th, 1916, was made:

Precinct	State		Congressional
Delta	1	”	2
Sutherland, Abrahan and Woodrow	1	Primary to be held at Sutherland	1
Hinckley	1		1
Deseret and Snake Valley	1	Primary held at Deseret	1
Oasis and Clear Lake	1	Primary held at Oasis	1
Leamington and Lynndyl	1	” ” Leamington	1
Oak City	1		1
Scipio	1		2
Holden	1		1
Fillmore	2		3
Meadow and Blackrock	1	Primary held at Meadow	1
Kanosh	1		1

And that Saturday, August 5th, 1916, at 8, p. m., has been designated and set as the time for holding the primaries in the aforesaid precincts for the election of delegates as set forth above and the chairman of each precinct is hereby instructed to provide proper meeting places for holding said primaries, and notify the Republican voters of his precinct of the place where said primary will be held.

By order of The Republican Central Committee Millard County, Ut.

j27a3   M. A. Abbott, Chairman.   M. M. Steele, Jr., Secretary.

The Anderson Farm

I spent Sunday at the farm of Louis Anderson on the North Tract, just west of Sugarville.

I am right good and glad to have my vision corrected. I had been seeing things blue for a long time, and listening to howls, until I was nicely in tune to both. But Mr. Anderson is so keenly alive to the other side, and so full of it, that it is catching, and it serves as a fine corrective. So I'll pass it along.

Mr. Anderson has 120 acres of land, a very fine quality of black soil, which he works by discing (not plowing) into a deep mulch, and thereby keeps it from baking into cracks and crusting. He says that's the secret,—got it from a Government Year Book, tried it out in practice, and will hereafter farm that way entirely. He fits his land, even for grain, like a seed bed. Disced the land now growing wheat, that I went through, four times, seven inches deep, and for this year, the stand is good. The heads are much better than the average, and the stand above the common lot.

And not one single weed: He had rented the place before, and has only been here himself since last fall, coming to find the place run with weeds, ditches thick, the field badly weeded, and he set to with a vigor and determination to clean the place of them. He did. What I have ridden over this year does not compare with this farm for freeness from weeds. Some of the grain has been in, too, for the fifth crop, so that no one need rise in the back seat and bawl me out with "New land is always clean, Mister:—wait until it's been cropped a time or two."

I walked out into the alfalfa, 25 acres, two years old and as pretty a crop as ever lay outdoors. No weevil as yet, even a little above knee high, and a beauty-crop.

Now I want to dwell for a minute or two on the land itself: There is a streak of land running from the southwest to the northeast through that section of the project that is A1; it is dark colored, not gumbo, a little loose, not too much alkali, though a little, and classed by everybody as choice land. Schwartz, Anderson, Leutheauser, Seams—these good people are on that belt, and some others. Results are coming to them. Ask any of them. I talked with Schwartz this a. m., as I am writing this up, and he joins in what I say, I'll bet—Schwartz likes the country, is doing well, and looks to coming out nicely. So, the land quality known, we can pass to man and methods.

Anderson believes in fitting his land. He spends money and labor fitting and preparing the land for crop. He has farmed in Illinois and Nebraska, and did well both places. He has sold farms and also done well. He has gathered experience in his sixty seven years, and likewise coin of the realm, for Anderson is well to do and prosperous.

The farm is for the boys, an independence they couldn't get slinging ink or shoving a pencil for others, and an income for them in keeping. Like the Van Evera Brothers at Abraham, here is a farm large enough for full ambition, and an opportunity to make a stake. Under the father's tutelage I believe the farm will make good, and the boys see it, which means they'll plug.

Now Anderson believes in that deep mulch, got only from discing, and done lots of times. He claims it will prevent crusting and baking. It proves so with him. Why not others try it out? He believes in short water runs; easy irrigation, all covered, and saving on water. He hears with a deaf ear much of the rant that is being talked—and steadily plugs at his own ends, makes his land, gets crops, and boosts. Why it was fine to listen to all the good men he knew, who were good farmers, who had nice crops, whose trees were pretty, whose farms showed they savvied, and where prosperity

was in the habit of hanging around. He spoke of the excellent sugar beet crop Schiffer Bros. have; and I jotted down the names of Elmer Golden, J. B. and Earl F. Seams, Chelson, Tingleaf, Cary, Roy Jones and Sampley, all good beet crops. And Charlie Ashby's; and Abbott's trees; and Hillyard's house;—and in fact, he has an eye out to all good things, and laid them by handy—but the bad features, the discouraging things, he tucked away into dimly lighted pigeon holes of memory, as unhandy as possible, with the hope that forgetfulness would spin a web of oblivion over their resting places. Leastwise, that's the impression I got, and I'm thankful for it—it corrected too much of the other.

I noted the nice house and the furnishings. But I was sick and could only eat eleven helpings of chicken—nothing near my usual self. Too bad. And following the advice of my physician I stopped on the third platter of ice cream. Well, aint belts a nuisance anyway?

Anderson has a nice basement under the house, and no trouble with surface water. A dandy granary, built on a cute scheme, making it just right to get grain from.

And once more I repeat, small acreage and lots of money. If not, ruin, though it may take years to spell it. For this 120 acres it takes Anderson's money. May he do well, build it into a producer, and hand to the boys his skill of getting there.

I thank Mr. Anderson and family for such a pleasant visit, and cannot conclude without mentioning little Fern Cornelius, the eighteen months old grandchild. This remarkably pretty little girl won first prize in Riverside, Cal., at the age of fifteen months, in a better baby contest, and I am sure the judges saw well, too.

Frank Beckwith.

School Census

We are given the results of the school census recently gathered by J. Avery Bishop, member of the Millard County Board, which are as follows: Delta, boys, 136, girls, 138, total 274; Sugarville, boys 45, girls 31, total 76; Sutherland, boys 52, girls 49, total 101; Sunflower, boys 17, girls 10, total 27. Rock, boys 17, girls 20, total 37; Abraham, boys 39, girls 29, total 68. The grand total for the above territory is 583 pupils. A high school building could be used for this territory right now to advantage and it will be only a very few years before the demand will be so great that it will actually have to come.

HINCKLEY.

Concluded from last issue.

Messrs. Eugene and Wilford Hilton, who are salesmen for the Wear Ever Aluminium Co spent the "Twenty Fourth" with their parents. They brought with them, Dr. Frank Caldwell, until recently of New York City, but now of Salt Lake City, who was a very warm friend of Eugene Hilton during his labors in the Eastren States Mission.

Miss La Priel Robinson is home again after spending the summer in Provo, where she attended the B. Y. U. Summer School. She has a position as teacher in the Hinckley schools.

Mr. Lealand Neilson left for Salt Lake City last week. He will spend a week in having a jolly good time.

Miss Dora Richards came down from the McIntyre Ranch to see her mother and to celebrate Pioneer Day.

Mrs. John Loveless and children have gone to "Dixie" for a visit with relatives.

Mr. and Mrs. Leonard Meecham, Mrs. Clarence Mortensen and Charles Langston of Lynndyl are spending a few days with their parents, Mr. and Mrs J. H. Langston.

The Young Ladies Mutual Improvement Association has been reorganized with Rose Jarvis as President, Delta Blake and Mattie Knight as Counselors.

A conjoint session of the M. I. A. was held Sunday evening O. E. McClellan and A. I. Tippetts gave exceedingly interesting and valuable talks on interesting topics.

Mrs. Ann Pratt is having a new residence built near the home of her daughter Mrs. Frank Wright.

OASIS.

A great many people from Oasis are leaving their home town and going to the mountains, where they may obtain the clear cold water and cool mountain breezes.

A truck load of young people left here Sunday morning to visit the hot springs and other points of interest at Eastern Millard.

Mrs. Laura Johnson and mother from Lynndyl are visiting with friends and relatives this week.

The mother of Mr. A. Stansworth is spending a few weeks here with her son.

Mrs Lorraine Hawley just returned from Salt Lake City where she has been studying Elocution under the direction of Miss Babcock. She will go back in a few days. Mr. and Mrs. Marion Killpack were visitors of Mrs. Killpack's mother, Mrs. E. Williams, Sunday.

Allen Pederson has returned some after having been absent nearly one year. We believe he can not find any other place he likes better than his home town.

John A. Richardson spent a few days here last week visiting friends.

Oscar Cornwall of Salt Lake City is an Oasis visitor this week.

Appearantly, this is a good year for alfalfa seed, if Jack Frost will be so considerate as to make his call just a little later than he has been accustomed doing.

Mr. Will Killpack and Fauster Funk were in town Monday, they bought one of Mr. Hawley's Buick trucks.

Hinckley Happenings.

At last threshing season has begun and the amount of grain that has been threshed shows that the crops this year lacks a great deal of being a failure. Norman I. Bliss threshed 778 bushels of wheat from about 15 acres of ground, which averages a little better than 51 bushels to the acre. This is just a sample of what can be produced from this land with the right kind of care. There are also first-class prospects for a heavy crop of lucern seed. Many farmers are rejoicing, inwardly, mostly, and hoping that Jack Frost will please keep low for a few weeks longer.

How delightful it would be to passersby if they could look upon each individual's home in this community and see no weeds, just clean yards, gardens, sidewalks and streets. The effect that such a sight would cause can hardly be estimated. Civic pride is what is needed to make clean, attractive and healthful homes. And such homes make successful communities. So do get busy and let's have a clean town. Now is the time to begin, before the weeds seed and plant their crops for the coming year.

Mabel Parker is again seen in the ranks with her Hinckley

(Continued on last page)

Hinckler Happenings

(Continued from first page)

friends. She has just returned from her second year college work at the U. of U. We are delighted to have her here.

The 16 months old child of Mr. and Mrs. Sam Webb was found lodged in a headgate of the canal by Preston Mecham, the water master. Everything that could be done to restore life was tried, but was too late. The doctor thot the child must have been dead some time before it was discovered.

A birthday dinner was given in honor of Mr. and Mrs. Chas. S. Talbot, by their children 14 grandchildren and two great-grandchildren, at the home of their daughter, Mrs. Annie Walker. Their daughter, Mrs. Lizzie Nelson, of Leamington, was there.

Mr. and Mrs. A. I. Tippetts, Lyle Cropper and Wilford Pratt have just returned from a canyon trip. A serious mishap occured to them which caused a speedy return,—a wildcat walked into their camp and ate all their food.

Prospects for drainage in Hinckley look very favorable. Most of the surveying has been done, a Buckeye trenching machine has been ordered and actual construction work will begin in the near future.

Hinckley is still improving. There is a small bungalow home for Mrs. Ann Pratt being completed and a new granary and buggy shed for Jos. Christensen.

The last H. E. A. club was entertained at the home of Mrs. Jackson. The hostess' demonstration was well received and appreciated by those present. The next meeting will be held at Mrs. Richard Parker's, Aug. 11th.

Delna, the 2-year old daughter of Mr. and Mrs. Geo. Stewart, has been seriously ill the past week, suffering from an absess of the throat.

Elizabeth, daughter of Mr. and Mrs. Preston Mecham, fell from a house last Sunday and broke her arm.

Mr. and Mrs. Samuel Webb wish to thank most kindly the people of Hinckley who were so thotful and considerate of them in their deep sorrow, and desire to make them feel that all that was done was surely appreciated.

South Tract Review

W. H. Tomlinson, who has been employed by the Delta Land & Water Co., for some time, is now taking a short vacation to haul himself some hay and do up a number of home jobs.

The social at W. H. Evans' was well attended and the occasion was enjoyed by all present.

R. J. Whicker completed a fine well for F. B. Johnson last Saturday. It flows ten gallons per minute of the precious lithia, the best water on earth.

The threshing machine made its first set the South Tract, on Wednesday morning, at N. H. Folsom's. Quite a number of farmers are ready and will thresh while the machine is here.

We are simply overjoyed to get our mail delivered at our door. It has been promised so long that we had almost lost faith in Uncle Sam.

This fall is a fine time for the Delta Land & water Co. to put on a selling campaign as the land they are putting to sweet clover and wheat looks fine and much better than it will look in a year from now.

We understand one of Mr. Cramer's engineers, Rob't Patterson, is going to leave for other fields of labor sometime this week.

Chas. Perry, who has been in the neighborhood since last winter has gone back to Salt Lake and his mother.

Oak City Offerings

Jess Peterson still makes his weekly business trips to Lynndyl.

John Dutson has gone to Eureka to work.

Miss Margaret Nielson has returned home from Salt Lake, where she has been attending summer school.

Mr. and Mrs. Jos. Wells were here visiting friends and relatives for the 24th of July.

Born to Mr. and Mrs. Ray Finlinson, July 23rd, a boy. All concerned doing fine.

Parley Elder has gone to Lynndyl to work.

A shower was given last week at the home of Lee Anderson in honor of Mr. and Mrs. Geo. Anderson. All present had an enjoyable time.

A baby boy was born to Mr. and Mrs. Leo Finlinson, July 23rd.

A birthday party was given Miss Belva Lovell, last Tuesday evening, at the home of Miss Edna Anderson.

A fine rain storm visited this town last week which did much good.

Fred S. Lyman, of Grayson, Utah, is here visiting friends and relatives.

Miss Zola Lyman is again in our little town, and expects to stay here all winter.

Relief Society Conference was held here last Wednesday. There was a large attendance, with many out of town visitors.

Dr. Broaddus visited Oak City again last week.

Mrs. Lily Reed from Salt Lake is here visiting her sister, Mrs. Eliza Anderson.

Alton Lyman and wife have left us. We are sorry to part with them, but wish them the best of luck.

Fred Hartley from Salt Lake, was a visitor here last week.

Simeon Walker made a trip to Lynndyl Sunday.

Miss Pearl Christensen has returned home from Delta, where she has been visiting for some time.

Mrs. Jos. L. Anderson has been on the sick list of late, but we are glad to state that she is improving.

Sutherland Searchlights

Mrs. Jackson and George Boardman have been under the weather with the Pahvant Plague.

Everyone has been watching to see how these combines were going to work, but they aren't a success and people had to go backto the binders and headers.

Mr. and Mrs. Boardman gave a turkey dinner on Sunday, with Mr. and Mrs. Wolfe and Mr. and Mrs. Hickman as guests.

A number of young people are planning to attend the dance at Delta, given by the O. Z. O. club on Wednesday.

A number of boys went to the spillway Sunday afternoon and had a fine boat ride.

Mr. and Mrs. Boardman and Mr. and Mrs. Hickman enjoyed a chicken dinner at the home of Mrs. Cavanaugh of Abraham.

The Jolly Stitchers are going to entertain their husbands and friends, Friday evening, at the home of R. W. Britt. This is an annual affair and those who have attended before have informed the newcomers of the good times in the past and everyone is looking forward to the event.

Sugarville Siftings

Mrs. Ray Beardsley left last week for California and her husband will follow with a car in a few days.

Albert Watts and family, have gone to Cherry Creek on a camping trip this week.

Mr. and Mrs. Iver Iverson of Ephriam, but formerly of Sugarville, are rejoicing over the arrival of a little daughter.

Mrs. Cornelius and little daughter returned to her home in Riverside, Cal., last Thursday, after spending the last five weeks at the home of her parents, L. Anderson and wife.

The Thimble club will give an entertainment Saturday evening, August 12th, at the Sugarville school house. They will also dispose of the two beautiful quilts and rugs which they have just finished.

E. R. McCoy received word last week of the death of E. J. Hart, at his home in Pasadena, Cal. Mr. Hart was sick for some time in Delta last spring and was finally taken to Salt Lake where he underwent an operation for an abscess. It was hoped he would fully recover, but after returning to his home in Pasadena it broke out again and proved fatal.

E. Cady returned last week from Los Angeles, making the trip with his Ford. He was accompanied by his sister and sister-in-law and her daughter. After a few days out on the road they got in company with Clair Dale and wife, who were also making the trip in their machine. They all arrived home safely last Wednesday.

David Porter is the first to have his threshing done, but many are ready to fall in line, in order to have the wheat to feed.

At the last meeting of the Thimble club, which was held at the home of Mrs. Roy Jones, officers were elected for the coming year; Mrs. Louie Seams, president, Mrs. Rebecca Cady, vice-president, Mrs. Pearl Sampley, secretary, and Miss Myrtle Anderson, Treasurer. The ladies voted to entertain the boys that played base ball on the Fourth, to a supper, in the near future.

Hinckley Happenings.

Glen Cropper is suffering with a broken arm.

Mrs. Mary C. Reeve and Mrs. Belle Hardy both have babies. The town of Hinckley is certainly prospering.

Wm. Walker reports having a first class beet crop, some being more than 5 inches in diamenter. We only wish that such large crops were more numerous throout the state, so as it would help lower the price of sugar.

Chas. Talbot, who has had such a long seige of rheumatism, has been to the hot springs the past week for his health.

Many of our citizens are anticipating a most excellent time in the canyon this coming week. We think that a canyon trip is well worth taking, as it revives your spirits and drives away the monotony of farm life to the farmer or dull care to those in any other profession. So lets all get ready and be in the canyon for a week.

Mrs. Alice Isom, from Dixie has been visiting with her friends, and Mrs. Emma Wright has gone to Dixie to see friends and her aged parents.

We are delighted to see another new building being erected. It will be for rent to the Academy students and teachers. We think that James Blake is doing something to help build up the town by erecting such modern bungalow houses. If only more citizens could do this it would sure be appreciated.

The H. E. club was highly entertained at the home of Mrs. Betsy Parker, Friday, August 11th. Miss White gave samples of fruit from the Northern Fruit Canning Co., and from the Leeds Canning Co. to the members so they could judge from what source they had better send for fruit, so anyone desiring to order their winter's fruit, apply to the H. E. A. for further information. A literary sketch was given by Mrs. Florence Neely on the life and works of James Whitcomb Riley, who so recently died. She recited several of his poems and then had three played on the phonograph. These were spoken by Riley himself. Such demonstrations of a poets works makes people love the poet and appreciate his works. We are sorry that no more were there to hear such splendid things. An art exhibit was then arranged for the county fair and a committee was ap-

pointed to further investigate what can be done. Refreshments were then served.

The Sunflower Swarm of the Hinckley Bee Hive girls spent a very pleasant evening last Thursday. The girls took a moonlight drive out to the Wilson farm, where they were entertained by the Y. L. M. I. A. Stake President, Mrs. J. H. Riding. After the program games were played and a delicious luncheon was served by the Misses Mary and Zina Wright.

The No. II Bee Hive girls spent a very enjoyable afternoon at the home of Mable Hinckley, last Thursday at 3, p. m. A program was rendered and games enjoyed until 5, o'clock when popcorn balls were made. Light refreshments were served by Misses Mable Hinckley and Carrie Langston, after which the popcorn balls were sold.

Hinckley is planning to devote the rest of August to a general town-cleaning with especial attention to weeds and rubbish. This year we hope to catch the weeds before they go to seed. All the organizations in town are joining together in this movement. Allready individual cleaning has begun and Tuesday a large number of men turned

out at the call of the Bishop, to clean and weed the public school, Academy and meeting house grounds and try to stop the spread of the Russian thistle. Mayor Blake is organizing some volunteer work and some special work for the Marshal in notifying those who don't clean up voluntarily. The H. E. A. has money in its treasury from its summer entertainment and is financing the undertaking. A mass meeting and town social will be held this week, Wednesday evening, when messages from the State Board of Health and a report from the State Health Officers Convention will be heard and discussed, definite plans for the clean-up campaign will be made and prizes offered by the H. E. A. for the cleanest premises. There will be plenty of music and a good time generally, with sandwiches ice cream and waffles for refreshments. The contest is to close Sept. 1st, and it is planned to give a big dance for the married people for which a free ticket will be given to every one who has put in a full day of cleaning up the town, including his own premises.

Woodrow Items

(Too late for last week)

Rev. and Mrs. Hamilton are visiting in Woodrow this week. Mr. Hamilton preached to a large audience. Monday evening a display of pictures, representing a missionary tour of the world, was much enjoyed by all present.

The Jolly Stitchers entertained their husbands at the home of Mrs. Robt. Britt, Friday, Aug. 11th. The next regular meeting of the clnb will be held at the home of Dr. Tracy, Mrs. Lamson will be the hostess.

Mr. and Mrs. Jerome Tracy took to the hills Tuesday, remaining until Saturday p. m. They were accompanied by Mervin and David Webster, and report having had a good time. Thursday p. m. a cloud burst overtook them at Rockwell's ranch. Owing, however to the hospitality of the Cox family at the ranch, no serious difficulties were experienced and the sight was certainly awe inspiring. Chas. Connelley and son Harold were overtaken by the storm six miles out, and they came in on horseback and had to dig the wagon out the next day.

Mrs. Irvin Greathouse was out Sunday for the first time, after a ten days illness from appendicitis.

A letter has been received from Mrs. Campbell, giving their permanent address as Johnson City, Tenn. Mrs. Campbell states that they are pleasantly located at 1700 ft. elevation, have a good climate, fine drinking water, and all they lack for happiness is a chance to visit once in a while with their Woodrow friends.

Mrs. Herman Fredricks is on the sick list.

Mr. and Mrs. Stewart have rented their ranch for the ensuing year and leave for their old home this week. The Ontko ranch has been traded for California property, and Mr. and Mrs. Ontko will leave shortly for California.

Oak City Offerings

Mrs. Alice Jacobson who has been very ill is now on the improve.

Farewell Hartley from Leamington was a visitor here last week.

Miss Gladys Lundahl, who has been in Provo for some time, has returned home.

Miss Nielson from Grayson is here visiting friends and relatives.

The Bee Hive Girls presented the play "A Southern Cinderella" last Friday night to a large attendance. Everyone present enjoyed themselves.

S. G. Rawlinson made a business trip to Lynndyl last Saturday.

The lightning, which came with the big storm last Thursday, did some damage to our phones, cutting the wires in several places.

Threshing has commenced here. The Williams & Evan's machine is here from Leamington.

The Bee Hive Girls visited Leamington and Lynndyl last week with their play, which was a success.

Miss H. White gave very interesting talks while here last week, also gave some lessons on canning. We all hope she will visit us again.

The big time in the canyon this year will be on 22, 23, 24, and 25 of August. Many people will attend.

Mrs. Lily Reed has returded to her home in Salt Lake.

Franklin Anderson made trip to Oasis last week.

Mr. and Mrs. Fred Lyman have gone home. They were called home on account of sickness.

Miss Eva Anderson went to Delta last week.

Miss Margret Nielson has gone to San Jaun County to visit with her sister for a while.

A tractor engine was seen going thru here last week pulling two hay racks full of furniture.

The Finlinson Brothers, Leo, Joshua, and Joseph, were called to Grayson last week by the sickness of their sister, who is at the point of death.

Many of our towns 'people are suffering with colds at present which we hope will soon leave.

Deseret Doings

(Crowded out last week.)

Mrs. Christena Warnick is home from Provo, where she spent several weeks with her son, Fred, and family.

Mrs. Laura Peterson of Eureka, and sister, Mrs. Nora Peterson, of Benjamin, Utah, are visiting at the home of their father, W. R. Black.

Mr. and Mrs. V. W. Kelly, A. D. Ryan, and Mrs. Elizabeth Procter left for Salt Lake by auto early Tuesday morning. They expect to make the trip by way of Richfield, where Mrs. Procter is to visit relatives before returning to her home in Panguitch.

The D. D. girls were guests at a birthday dinner in honor of Miss Clarice Erickson, at the home of her aunt, Mrs. Jonn Hutchinson, of Hinckley, last Sunday. Those present were the Misses Afton Hinckley, Laverna Wright, Wealthy Parker, Edna Cropper, LaVern Croft, Norma Damron and Elsie Richards. The club entertained again this week at the spill, inviting a wide circle of friends.

Bishop and Mrs. Damron, Mr. Erickson, and the Misses Norma Damron and Verna Nelson were guests of the South Tract at a delightful social at the home of Mr. and Mrs. R. Evans, Saturday evening. The members of the party expressed themselves as having a very pleasant time and are all agreed to "hats off" to the South Tract hospitality.

Two auto loads of relatives of Mr. and Mrs. H. S. Cahoon arrived from Salt Sake last week staying over Monday. The party is touring the Southern part of the state and will extend their trip sometime yet before returning to Salt Lake.

Services at the church Sunday evening was very pleasing. Several musical numbers were especially well received.

Mrs. M. Wolfolk and son, Edward, of Virginia, who have been at the Moody hotel for a fortnight, were met by Mr. Wolfolk Friday, who took them by stage to his camp out in the Cricket Range.

Mrs. Howard Durham arrived Sunday afternoon from Salt Lake, for a visit with her parents, Mr. and Mrs. S. W. Western.

It is understood that the county Commissioners have recently taken favorable action toward making the road from here into Snake Valley, a part of the state highway. This is hearty good news to residents of this section as well as those of the western end of the county, as it will not only shorten the distance materially but will bring a vast amount of traffic and travel this way that now of necessity goes thru Juab and south thru Frisco.

Sugarville Siftings

Mr. and Mrs. Clair Dale moved into their new house last Thursday.

Union Sunday school every Sunday at 2:30, p. m., Rev. Hamilton has promised to preach for us every fourth Sunday, after Sunday school, commencing with Aug. 20th.

Several of our young people spent last Sunday at the Hot springs. A fine picnic dinner was the main feature of the day, they gathered many petrified specimans, took snap shots, and with many other amusements, the day passed all too quickly.

The Relief Society will give a benefit social and dance Saturday Eve., August 19, at Sugarville school house. Ice cream will be served. Dance 25 cents. Everybody come.

The Friendship Thimbele club will meet with Mrs. J. B. Seams next Wednesday afternoon. All members are requested to come early.

Adam and Martin Shiffers are entertaining their sister who arrived from Los Angeles last Saturday.

Sutherland Searchlights

We have two new arrivals at Sutherland. One is a fine boy that came to Mr. and Mrs. Lawrence Abbott the other is a girl at Mr. and Mrs. John Meinhardt. Those who have been on the sick list this week are Alta Simpkins and Master Ferrill Walker.

Mr. and Mrs. Boardman, Mrs. Weldon and Mr. and Mrs. Hickman enjoyed an auto ride Sunday afternoon and then had dinner with Mr. and Mrs. Hickman.

Frank Foote left last week for Butte, Montana, for an indefinite stay. His brother is expected to arrive this week from there to spend his vacation.

There was a severe storm visited here last night but did no serious damage.

The annual affair held by the Jolly Stitchers at the R. W. Britt home was enjoyed by all. Games were played, then came a guessing contest. Harry Ottley was awarded first prize which proved to be an immense stick of candy, while W. J. Edwards received the booby. Refreshments of ice cream and cake were served.

HINCKLEY.

The infant daughter of Mr. and Mrs. Samuel Webb, aged fifteen month was drowned in the city irrigation ditch last week. The child was playing near its home with its brothers and sisters and slipped away unnoticed. Its body was recovered by Preston Meecham, city water master when he began an investigation to see why the stream of water was failing. Upon raising the head gate the little body floated down the steam. Mr. Meecham took the child to Dr. Broaddus office and its parents were notified. Dr. Broaddus was not at home but friends and neighbors tried all known methods of resastication. Later the Doctor arrived and did all in his power but without success. The funeral was held the day following in the Relief Society Hall and was largely attended by sympathizing relatives and friends. Interment took place in the Hinckley cemetary.

Mss. Thomas Higgs of Salt Lake City came down to visit with her parents Mr. and Mrs. Richard Parker. She took back with her her sons Stewart and Lowell, who have been spending their vacation with their grand parents.

Miss Mabel Parker is home from Salt Lake City to spend a month before returning to resume her studies at the University of Utah.

Mr. and Mrs. A. I. Tippetts, Miss Lyle Cropper and Wilford Pratt spent last week in Oak City Canyon. They report having had a most enjoyable time while there.

Amos Maxfield and wife entertained two automobile loads of their friends and relatives from Salt Lake City this week. The party included Reeds and Spencers. They are much taken up with this part of the country and predict a splendid future for it.

Miss Wealthy Parker has gone to Salt Lake City to s end a month with her sisters Mrs. Annie Higgs and Mrs. Marie Keil.

Miss Nina Pratt has left for Provo for an extended visit with her Aunt, Mrs. O. R. Johnson.

Miss Zella Pratt is home after spending the past three months with her aunt Mrs. O. R. Johnson of Provo. She was accompanied home by her cousin Miss Clover Johnson who will be a visitor at the Pratt home for sometime.

The baseball dance given last Friday night was well attended and was a success from both a social and a commercial standpoint. Music was furnished by the Hinckley Orchestra.

When it comes to obtaining results we respectively your attention to Farm Demonstrator, J. P. Welch, who has just thrashed a splendid crop of Turkey Red wheat from his farm at west of town. When Mr. Welch bought the place in 1915 everybody considered it a water logged salaratus bed that would raise nothing but tumble weed. Mr. Welch has put considerable of his college theory, lots of his good sound judgment and quite a bit of his sturdy Irish elbow grease into use and from all appearnces will make his place one of the garden spots of Millard. We would like more men like Mr. Welch in our community.

We regret the resignation of County Superintendent of schools Dean F. Peterson. His work in this County has been of a high order and his efforts for improvement untiring. He is a man of honorable principles and if his services could have been retained we are sure the schools would have shown marked improvement. We hope the Board of Education will find a good man to fill the vacancy but feel that it will be a hard matter to find any one to take the place of Supt. Peterson.

Active work on the drainage system of Drainage District No. 1 has begun. The lines have all been surveyed by E. B. Theobald and some of the open drain is being made. This will surely result in much improvement to this part of the country.

HINCKLEY.

Delma, the three year old daughter of Mr. and Mrs. George Stewart has fully recovered from her recent illness caused by an abcess in her throat

Mr. and Mrs. Arthur Reeve are re

joicing over the arriva lof a new baby boy on August 11. Dr. W. B. Hamilton of Milford and Miss Matilda Hales of Deseret In attendance.

Raymond Hardy and wife are the proud parents of a nine pound boy, Mother and child progressing nicely.

Mrs. Alice Howells of Lynndyle, who is at the home of her aunt, Mrs. Charles Cahoon, gave birth to a baby aat Wednesday

R. R Carey and Elmer Stout have gone to Salt Lake City to attend to business connected wih heir mining propery.

A Democratic Primary wa aheld in th aHinckley school house, August 12 John Reeve acting as temporary chr.

A permanent organization was made with Thomas W. Cropper as chairman and N. B. Badger as Vice- chairnan. John Reeve was elected delegate and Wm. F. Pratt alternae to the Democratic State Convenion. Mr. Reeve lef on Wednesday. for Ogden.

Architect R. L. Ashby of American Fork was a guest at the home of Thomas W .Cropper last Thursday.

Mr. Sorenson, connected with the Deseret News was in Hinckley making collections for that paper · this week.

Mrs. Emma H. Wright has gone to Dixie for an extended visit with her parents

Members o fthe Millard Academy Faculty are beginning to arrive. Miss Iorda Geo of Provo, who will have charge of Elocution and Physical Edication is in town and Prof. Alva Woodward, who teaches music has arrived bringing with him Mrs. Woodward and the children. Prof Woodward has been very ill since his arrival suffering from hemorage caused by having a tooth extreated. Dr. Broadus Is in attendance and we hope for Prof. Woodward's speed yrecovery

Everything is in readines sfor the Millard Academy outing in Oak City Canyon and a goodly percentage of Hinckley people will be in attendance

Millard County Progress
September 1, 1916

HINCKLEY

Continued from last Issue.

The dance in the A. O. Nelson at Deseret last Friday evening was well attended by Hinckley young people who report an enjoyable time.

Mrs. Ann Pratt has moved into her now home in the rear of her daughter's, Mrs. Frank Wright's home.

That Hinckley is steadily improving and growing is shown by the fact that Jas. S. Blake has had a fine new four room bungalow built for rental.

Mr. and Mrs. J. Avery Bishop motored down fro mDelta to visit with relatives last Thursday evening.

L. R. Cropper, Jr., has opened a Meat Market in his shop near his residence and reports business as good..

Little Elizebeth Meacham ,daughter of Preston Mecham had the misfrtune to fall and break her arm about ten days ago,Dr. Broadus reduced the fracture and she is getting along nicely. However she was attempting to pour some boiling water from the teakettle and having the use of onl yone arm had the misfortune to scald her leg very badly. All poss ible comforts are being given the child and her friends are hoping for her speedy recovery.

Last Wednesday evening the Home Economics Association entertained al lthe "Grownups" at a social in the School House. Plans were discussed for improving the sanitary conditions of the town and delightfully toothsome refreshments were served. ·

Mrs. Richard Parker entertained the Home Economics Association at her home last Friday. A delightful sketch of the life of James Whitcomb Riley was read by Mrs. Florence Jones Neeley, together with several of Riley's poems. Refreshments were served and a most enjoyable afternoon was spent.

The Millard Academy Faculty met with the people of Hir ay Ward on Sunday evening. President A. A. Hinckley and President C .E. McClellan made talks an dMrs. Alva Woodward sang two solos. Prof. Woodward played two piano solos and Miss Gorda Gee and Miss Mae Mortenson each gave two readings. The meeting was of a high order and was well attended.

Mrs. Val Black of Abraham gave birth to a baby recently. She is staying at the home of Mrs. Phoebe Mecham.

Miss Mae Mortensen, Instructor in the Cassia Stake Academy is here for a visit with her sisters, Mrs. C. E. McClellan and Mrs. Alfred Stout.

Hinckley

Concluded From Page 1.

Threshing is now on in full swing several machines are running in this vicinity and much grain is being threshed, the yield being up to the average.

Miss Ruby Stout has gone to Mammoth to work until the opening of school.

Mr. Richard Torry has returned from Salt Lake City where he has been working at the L. D. S. hospital.

Attorney Daniel Harrington and wife sister and two children Russel and Mary motored dow nfrom Salt Lake City to spend the week end with Mr. Harrington's cousin, Mrs. T. W. Cropper.

Mrs. Mary J .Wright and little daughter Lavell have gone to Dixie for a visit with relatives. They made the trip by auto with relatives who had been here to visit hem. Tracy Stout also went with them for a visit un tlschool begins.

Black Rock

Mrs. A. J. Siber and small son Glenn have returned after a month's vacation in Indianapolis, Ind. Mrs. Siber's mother accompanied them on their return. She has now gone to her home in San Bernardino, Cal. All look greatly improved by the change and rest. C. C. Williamson who was night man during Mrs. Siber's absence is now stationed at Delta. Mr. Jones and family went to Salt Lake.

Mr. and Mrs. J. J. Milliken of Colorado Springs are visiting with their parents, Mr. and Mrs. H. A. Stahl. Their coming seems very opportune, as Hele nStahl is very ill and their

company an dhelp are doubly appreciated at thi stime.

Mr. W. H. Foreman an deon of Elgin, Nevada, spent a couple of days here enroute to Monroe where Mr. Foreman was called by th eillness of a sister who resides there.

Walter James has gone to the northern part of the state on business.

Joseph Coleman of Los Angeles, Calif., spent some time in this neighborhood looking after his land here.

Mrs. A. F. Callahan accompanies Mrs. Phoebe Singleton and her daughter to Dixie where they will visit for a few days and incidentally feast on the fine fruit of that section.

Millard County Progress
November 3, 1916

LYNNDYLE

In making our bow as a correspondent of the Progress, we ask the indulgence of its readers, in view of our first attempt at newspaper work. However, we will endeavor to supply teh news impartially and fully, as the circumstances will permit.

The Hallowe'en party given last special costumes were worn by Mr. and Mrs. O. A. Golden, the former impersonating a "tramp" and Mrs. Golden the character of Aunt 'Gemima' were the first prize winners. Two Harem girls represented by Misses Onn Kuballo and Edith Webb. Guy Campbell was awarded the booby prize as a negro wench. Mrs. Sudbury in the character of "death" was especially good. Miss Balfe, a recent arrival, was pretty in the character of the Gypsy Princess. The list of attractive and handsome costumes would make to long a list to mention in detail. The decorations were in keeping with Hallowe'en. The hall was trimmed with crepe paper and corn shucks, and with Jack-o'-lanterns gave a decided imposing effect. Lunch was served by Miss Agnes Hughes and Mrs. E. L. Peay.

Monday night was a very enjoyable and highly successful affair. The costumes were unique and tasty. About 27 men and women indulged in the entertainment, 50 couples in all. The

The L. D. S. Sunday school of Lynndyle was reorganized with the election of Parnell Hinchley, Supt.; Albert Hurst first councilor and Frank Belliston as second councilor.

Our society was enhanced by the arrival of Miss Balfe of Sprague, Wash., a niece of Dr. Murry, who will spend the winter.

D. W. Scannel and wife spent several days in Salt Lake last week.

O. W. Paswater, who recently suffered the loss of his home and business by fire, has reopened his confectionary establishment, much to the delight of those who are inclined to "take a chance."

Frank O. and Laura Johnson are the successors of D. W. Scannell in the grocery department of the former Scannell-Mead Co. The postoffice has been installed therein. Mr. Scannell wil continue the dry gods and gent's furnishing department in the same building.

The new hotel building erected by Mr. Neilson of Leamington is being repaired and remodeled with a view to occupancy. This wil be a much desired benefit to our little city.

Mrs. Hary Wilkie is home from a short trip to Nephi, where she visited with her parents.

Mrs. E. L. Peay returned from Provo, after attending the funeral of Joseph Cook, her cousin.

Mrs. E. A. Jacob and Miss Greathouse, our local teachers, attended the teachers institute at Fillmore last Saturday.

Politics have been somewhat strenuous the past few weeks. Both political parties giving numerous entertainments. The speakers presented by both sides were of a high character and we are pleased to say that none of the metings savored of personalities.

A Boys and Girls basket ball team

has ben organized and judgeing from the enthusiasm manifested considerable amusement is in store for the younger people.

Dr. Murphy, assistant surgeon of the Salt Lake Route lectured on Saturday night to an interested audience His subject was "First Aid to the Injured."

A primary organization is in contemplation which will be of a beneficial character for the little folks of the town. It is hoped that all parents will lend their support to this worthy cause.

The initial dance of the M. I. A. will be given next Saturday night, November 4th. This is preparatory to the opening of their winter's work.

W. A. Stafford, a violinist of some note, furnished the music for the Hallowe'een dance. He was assisted by Babo McNamara and Curl Scannel.

OAK CITY

To Late For Last Issue.

In November to make a final cleanup here of the stuff he did not take.

We have had 2 or 3 rallys here which has served to kindle the old political feelings and engendered in the minds of many a reasoning that is felt in all communities nearing election time.

The stork visited Mr. and Mrs. Jos ?. Callister during the week leaving at their home a fine baby boy all concerned doing well.

A number of M. A. students were home to visit with relatives and friends Saturday and Sunday.

Much work has been accomplished in this locality since our recent storms as it has moistened up the earth and made the plowing superior to what it has been for several years.

The grain that was planted in September is beginning to show and it is evident now that the dry farm grain will turn out better next year than what it has this season.

For a number of years the potato crop in this neighborhood has been a complete failure but we are happy to state that the much improved conditions are prevalent this year. The red willow, early Ohio will yield especially good. Where the land has cultivated and the potatoes properly taken care of we will get from 250 to 300 bushels per acre and the corn crop is also good. A number of our citizens have been hauling potatoes to Delta, Lynndyl and elsewhere realizing what we term a good figure 1½ to 2 cents a lb. The pig market has

been flush for several weeks but is somewhat on the decline at present. Willis J. Lyman of Delta was in town Saturday and purchased a carload, 40 or 50 being taken to Delta today.

Jim Peters has made a recent trip to our town and purchased 100 head of cattle paying the top price. Mr. Peters is among the best buyers that make this country. 150 head left here for Mills today and he will be back

Millard County Chronicle
August 24, 1916

South Tract Review

N. H. Folsom is having a well put down, and no doubt is near the end, as he has in over three hundred feet of pipe. He has now a 2-gallon flow but wants more. R. L. Whicker is doing the work.

James and Miller Hall have raised oats this year of the best quality that I have yet seen raised in Utah.

It surely does one's heart good to drive about and see the immense stacks of hay on a great many South Tract farms and smaller ones on a great many more. This hay comes from practically new meadows.

Mrs. W. J. Evans contemplates a visit on the Pacific coast with her parents-in-law in the near future. We wish for her a good visit and joyous time.

Lawrence Nelson, who has been doing Idaho and Oregon for the past few weeks, returned home last Saturday and he is very much pleased with conditions in Oregon.

Mrs. E. A. Brush who has been quite poorly for some time is up and around again, which we are glad to chronicle.

The Delta Land & Water Co. have now planted and watered over one thousand acres of sweet clover and Mr. Saunders says it is coming up fairly well.

Our neighbor Stapley is surely having his share of tough luck in regard to loosing horses and colts by some unknown disease.

Some of our young folks have made some very pleasant trips of late, such as visiting the Fillmore wells, the big dam, the ice caves near Fillmore and Oak Creek canyon, using Mr. Hawley's auto truck to make the trips.

Robert Patterson of the Delta Land and Water Co. engineers, has gone to Salt Lake to attend the wedding of his brother.

The Photo Studio will be closed after Oct. 1st, for three months. All wishing work done should come at once.   a17-31

Turner-Steele

Miss Myra Turner and Parley Steele boarded the train last Monday night for Salt Lake City, where they were married Wednesday in the Salt Lake Temple. The happy pair will return the last of the week and go to housekeeping in the Copening residence which Mr. Steele purchased in anticipation of the happy event. Congratulations and best wishes are extended by the Chronicle.

Sutherland Searchlights

While playing with the children last Saturday, R. W. Britt knocked his knee out of joint. It has gone back in place but is very badly swollen and painfull.

Mr. Joe V. Palmer was called to his home in Redondo, Cali., by the illness of his father. He has been here for the past eight months and left with many regrets. He said maybe he would come back next spring.

A number of ladies attended the meeting of the Jolly Stitchers at the home of Dr. Tracy with Mrs. Lamson as hostess. All report a very pleasant afternoon. The next meeting will be with Mrs. Hillyard at Sugarville.

Word has been received that Frank Strickley is worse again. He was reported as getting along fine. He is in the hospital in Salt Lake. Ralph Sanford who went there last week to be operated on for appendicitis is reported doing fine.

Little Miss Alta Simpkins is reported doing fine. She has a very bad case of tonsilitis.

The Misses Helen and Nina Bunker, Clarence Abbott and Bishop and Mrs. Shipley, left for Oak City yesterday to attend the Chatauqua. Mr. Hulse and family will go up later this week.

M. A. Abbott has returned from a trip to Montana. He reports crops there fairly good but it is a bad year. He says it's a nice place to live but he's glad to get back here among his friends also to see his new grandson.

W. R. Walker said Jeff Clark bought a couple of halters for his mules as they were getting too familiar with him. We take it they have been showing Mr. Clark that they are alive and kicking.

The thresher is busy in this part of the country and crops seem heavier than everyone thot. The heaviest yield so far is that of Adolph Ackerman which averaged forty two and one half bu to the acre. Nothing the matter with that, is there?

Ben Bunker has sold his place on the Midland to Howard Abbott for a consideration of $7 an acre. Mr. Abbott is going to move to the place as soon as arrangements can be made. Wallace Mitchell now occupies the place but is undecided as to where he is going.

Dentist at Hinckley

Dr. Stains of Delta will be at Hinckley Wednesdays of each week hereafter. a24-31

Oak City Offerings

Roe Willey from Circleville is here visiting with friends and relatives. We notice Miss Anderson smiling to see him back.

Mrs. Alice Jacobson is still on the sick list. We hope she will soon recover.

Miss Silva Lovell, who has been in Beaver visiting for some time, has returned home again.

Mr. Jones the agent, for the Con. Wagon & Machine Co., was here last week.

Our dance hall will soon be complete, painting is all that is needed now, and we will have a hall to be proud of.

Willis Lyman, from Delta, was seen in his car here last Sunday.

Wayne Lyman from Mayfield is here visiting friends and relatives.

Miss Thelma Lovell has gone to a Salt Lake hospital. Word was received that she is doing fine. Also the little son of Mr. and Mrs. H. Ludahl was taken at the same time to be operated on.

Mr. William Lovell and son Alvin returned home from Salt Lake last week where Alvin was taken to see the doctor. We hope our sick folks soon all be well.

Mrs. Geo. Anderson is visiting in Salt Lake.

The Economy Store from Deseret is here selling goods. We hope they will do well so they will visit us again.

Don Anderson and Ernest Ottley left last week for Salt Lake City to attend the training camp. We wish the boys lots of luck.

Ed. Renolds has returned from Salt Lake City.

John E. Lovell has returned home from Ogden, where he attended the Democratic Convention.

Eldon Anderson visited in Beaver last week.

John Dutson has returned home from Eureka.

Woodrow Items

Rev. C. H. Hamilton preached in Woodrow last Sunday, p. m. Next Sunday preaching by Rev. Schmoek of Salt Lake.

Mr. and Mrs. Tibben are rejoicing in the safe arrival of a fine baby boy.

Fred Barben, who was so unfortunate as to dislocate his knee as well as to suffer otherwise from severe bruises when a hay pole fell on him two weeks ago, is now traveling around again as smiling as ever.

J. J. Clark has 30 acres of fine beets that are well worth visiting by any one who feels discouraged.

Messrs Hyes & Co. also Thompson & Co., who are the proud owners of Combined Harvesters, are delighted with them. They state that the work done by them is eminently satisfactory. The waste is nil and the crops of wheat thus harvested have been good, far exceeding their expectations.

Mrs. Irvin Greathouse whose contined ill health has been a source of anxiety to her many friends, left last week for Los Angeles where she arrived safely, feeling no worse for the long journey.

The new Library at Woodrow is now in full operation. We have a new bookcase which will accommodate more books, and donations will be gratefully received. Those desiring to obtain books should call upon Mrs. Philip Lamson.

A telegram has just been received here by H. F. Aller from J. P. Sprunt announcing, that Judge Quinton had succeeded in financing the Delta sugar factory and that construction work would begin as soon as details could be arranged, which would be in a very short time. The factory is to be of 10,000 tons capacity and cost in the neighborhood of $1,000,000. More details are promised soon.

Mesdames Tracy and Fredricks have received the sad intelligence that their neice, 8 years old, has fallen a victim to Infantile Paralysis in New York. Passing away in less than 24 hours after being attacked by that dreadfull disease.

Sutherland Searchlights

Howard Abbott and family have moved into his place on the Midland and Mr. Mitchell has moved his family to Hinckley.

The Stork visited here last week and left a girl at the home of Mr. and Mrs. Hall.

Ross Simkins is going to take his family to Iron County for a visit with his people and attend the wedding of his brother whose home is in Nevada.

Mr. and Mrs. Boardman, Mrs. Wellman, Mr. and Mrs. Hickman and Helene Davis made a trip to Rockwell ranch, Sunday in Mr. Rockwell's machine. The road across the desert is much better than around here. Mr. Cox invited them to make themselves at home and the fine lunch under the trees was enjoyed by all.

Ralph Sanford returned Sunday night and is much better since his operation.

Miss Nina Bunker left Saturday for St. George for a week. Miss Leda Finlinson is taking her place in the store.

Mr. and Mrs. M. A. Abbott left Monday for Enterprise called there by the death of his brother.

The Ackerman family moved back on their place last Thursday.

The friends of Mrs. Bifigland and Wallace Mitchell will be surprised to learn of their trip to Fillmore where they were married. Their many friends are wishing them all kinds of happiness.

Winn Walker says Will Titus is going to paint signs on his granary to tell it from his house as people are making mistakes. That comes by having things fixed up—painted and kept clean around the granary as well as the house.

Oak City Offerings

Mrs. Harry Johnson of Lynndyl was here last week visiting with her parents and friends.

Miss Gene Lovell made a pleasure trip to Delta last week.

Kirt Roper has gone back to Mayfield.

People of Oak City are begining to enjoy the big melon feasts again.

Mr. and Mrs. A. Hanson made a trip to Delta last week to visit the Dentist.

The little son of Mr. and Mrs. H. Lundahl who was taken to Salt Lake Hospital has returned home feeling fine.

Parley Elder, who is working in Lynndyl, spent a few days home last week.

Mr. and Mrs. Wm. Aldredge made a trip to Deseret last week. They intend to move down there for the winter.

Jack Aldredge has gone to Delta to work.

Leo Carlson, who is working in Delta, visited home Sunday.

The threshing will soon be done for this year and we hope the Leamington machine will come again.

Woodrow Items

Until further notice Rev. C. H. Hamilton will preach at Woodrow at 8 p.m., on the second and fourth Sundays of each month.

The Jolly Stitchers were royally entertained by Mesdames Wright and Hilliard at the Hilliard home in Sugarville, last Friday. Next meeting will be Sept. 15th at the home of Mrs. Titus in Sutherland.

The Woodrow Sunday School will give a Fatsy Swap social Sept. 13th at 8 p.m. Ice Cream and cake for sale. Admission ½ cent per inch waist measure of each adult. All are invited. A good programme will be rendered and much fun is waiting for all.

Miss Paxton of Delta is visiting Mrs. Underhill and Mrs. Jeff Clark.

Affairs of Oasis

Mrs. Oda Day has been very ill for the past week but is some better at this writing.

Henry Huff has returned home from a business trip to Fillmore.

The prospects for alfalfa seed are immense this year. Every one is expecting a good crop if the frost will stay away.

A number of the young folks enjoyed the corn roast and Water melon feast at J. C. Hawley's residence sunday evening.

Our post office has been moved into part of the Huff store, on account of the room being wanted at the hotel.

A car of peaches has been unloaded the past two days.

James Christensen has been ill but is on the improve-

John Iverson was bitten by a small bug and has since been suffering with blood poison but is some better now.

The McCosh Hotel has changed hands and is being remodeled, papered and painted. It has the look now of an up-to-date place and will soon open and be able to accommodate every body.

Venus, the small daughter of Mr. and Mrs. Chas. Thompson has the past week been suffering with abscesses of the head but is reported some better the past few days.

South Tract Review

Taking the South Tract all over, there never has been so much wheat raised as there has been this year especially hay, and everything is a rousing good price.

The ladies of the H. E. A., in celebration of the first anniversary of their club, held a banquet at the school house. The only ones invited outside of the membership were the husbands of the ladies. Place cards directed each couple to their proper location. After all had reached their places, and before sitting down, they all sang America with rousing good cheer, with Mrs. Parks at the organ. After taking our seats we were immediately waited on to the first course which consisted of fresh fruit served on plates. Then the only imposition of the evening began, which continued throughout the serving of the four courses, and that was the calling on the men to reply to toasts by the president. The second course was roast pork, pressed chicken, potato salad, sliced tomatoes with dressing, pickles and olives, butter and rolls and ice tea. The third course consisted of ice cream and cake, and the last course warmed us up with coffee and wafers. The table was decorated with center pieces and beautiful boquets of sweet peas and pansies. After working all summer in mud and water, hot sunshine and dust, in the hay and harvest field, also the threshing, then to be treated to such a magnificient spread, which was in every way a complete and striking success, was almost more than flesh and blood could stand and a great shock to the capacity and nervous system of we poor hungry men.

Mrs. Chas. Hardin will accompany her parents, Mr. and Mrs. Nelson, to their home in Englewood, Cali., starting today. They will go overland by auto. They have had a good visit with the Hardins and their two sons, Lawrence and Lowell for two and a half months.

Mrs. W. H. Evans will leave on the 18th inst. to visit Will's parents in Cali., and will go from there to Galveston, Texas, for a protracted visit with her own parents.

No happier thought for centralizing public interests could be suggesttd than that suggested by the Chronicle editor in last weeks issue in regard to a park.

We opine that Messrs W. H. Evans and Chas. Hardin will be inmates of the mad house if their wives extend their visits over any great length of time.

Deseret Doings

There was a time—not so many years ago—when the farmers of this vicinity, looked on the alfalfa seed crop as a matter of luck, and a very lucky person was he who chanced to let his hay crop go long enough without cutting to determine the extent of his possibilities. Thru intensive cultivation and more scientific management, men have learned that alfalfa seed can be a dependable, annual crop, whereas, formerly a seed crop once in five or six years was about all the best farmers hoped to get. Today the crop is practically assured, barring an early frost.

Notwithstanding the delay of spring and general unfavorable weather conditions this year, it is conservativly estimated that Deseret and Oasis will have the largest seed harvest in the history of the valley. Among those whose prospects are more than fair, is Geo. Croft with a ninety acre piece. This is considered one of the best seed tracts and will run a high average of bu. per acre. S. W. Western, who boasted one of the bumper seed crops last year, expects a heavier yield this. If—It's all "as a man thinketh." If there will be no frost says Mr. Western, J. R. Bennett, J. H. Western, J. M. Moody, the Erickson Bros. and many others with less acreage, are all to benefit largly from the culture of alfalfa seed. While grain is a secondary crop, that raised this season is of good quality. Corn has grown especially well and we note some the largest corn fields ever planted in Deseret. Potatoes, as if ashamed of the blight of the last two years, are yielding better and bigger than ever before.

Infant sons have arrived at the homes of Mr. and Mrs. Geo. Sporr, and Mr. and Mrs. Jesse Western.

Miss Dora Black who has been with relatives in Idaho the last three months, returned home Monday.

Arthur Palmer returned from American Fork Sunday, bringing a bride.

Mr. and Mrs. A. D. Ryan who have occupied the Kelly residence for two years are going over to Hinckley for the winter.

Nelson Cooper and Frank Rasmasson of Fillmore disposed of a car of Alberta peaches this week.

Everybody is talking about the Millard County Fair, and sure, everybody is going to be there. Take your hogs and embroidery and go 'long; you might learn how to better 'em next year.

Latest model $27.50 pump gun, good as new $20.00 Enquire at the Chronicle office.

Oak City Offerings

Mr. and Mrs. Lem Roper visited in Sevier County last week.

Miss Maudy Stephenson from Holden is here visiting her sister, Mrs. Jos. L. Anderson.

Bro. Nielson who has been visiting here most of the summer, has returned to Leamington.

Mr. and Mrs. Miles from Richfield were here on business last week.

Mrs. H. White and children from Beaver were here visiting with her sister, Mrs. L. Summers.

Mrs. W. R. Walker from Sutherland was visiting here last week.

Marion Terry has returned home from Eureka.

Misses Pearl and Silva Christenson were visiting in Delta last week.

Gus Faust and Willis Lyman were here last Saturday and Sunday, visiting with the young folks and enjoying chicken roasts.

Mrs. R. Ashby from Leamington was in town last Saturday.

Mr. and Mrs. Leo Lyman were seen here in their car last Sunday.

The Walters Co. presented their plays Friday and Saturday nights, which were Sowing the Wind and Coranton. Many of our towns people enjoyed them and we hope they will meet with us again.

Mr. and Mrs. Nels Christenson from Hinckley were here the past week visiting relatives and friends.

Mr. Peters the cattle buyer is here again.

Many out of town people are coming here to get peaches, and Oak City has some very fine peaches this year.

The Alldredge family have moved to Deseret for the winter.

Miss Margret Nielson has returned home from San Juan County. She reports having had an enjoyable time on her visit.

Woodrow Items

Richard Thompson has gone to Mt. Pleasant to attend school for the winter.

Senator Sutherland and T. C. Hoyt honored Woodrow with a visit Tuesday holding a political meeting. Prominent Politicians from all over the state accompanied them. Senator Sutherland made a fine address, discussing the Rural Credits Bill, and the Emergency Currency Act. T. C. Hoyt pleased all with a forceful talk about the policies of the present administeration, dwelling upon the Mexican situation.

Mr. and Mrs. Meade Tillotson are very happy in the welcoming of a fine baby girl.

A rousing Democratic meeting will be held at Woodrow Sept. 28th. Judge King and W. H. Welling of Salt Lake will be the speakers.

The Tacky Swap Social Wed. evening proved a great success both socially and financially.

The Jolly Stitchers will meet Friday with Mrs. Robt. Britt instead of with Mrs. Titus as was formerly announced.

Mr. Philip Lamson has the sincere sympathy of the entire community in his sad bereavement. His father passed away Monday in his home at Plainfield, New Jersey in his 73rd year. His death followed the third stroke of paralysis. He was born in Windsor, Vt., and in the prime of life he came to Salt Lake where he remained for 17 years. After the first stroke of paralysis he went back east to pass his last days among his old friends and be laid to rest among his ancestors.

Hinckley Happenings.

The D. D. Girls gave a bundle shower to Miss Bly Moody and then accompanied her and Mr. Beal to the depot where they boarded the train for Salt Lake to be married in the temple. The club members brot many nice and servicable presents. They also carried out their color scheme, pink and white, both in the decoration and lunch.

After Bly's and Mr. Beal's honey-moon trip to Ephraim, the couple will return to Hinckley where Mr. Beal will teach in the District School.

The wedding dinner will be served at the bride's home, Sept. 15th. Over 100 guests have been invited and 75 will be seated at the table at once. Some of Mr. Beal's folks from Ephraim are expected to be present.

The townspeople are turning out en mase to clean up their premises from weeds. The Town Board and the H. E. A. are at the head of a grand pro-ceeding Friday night. There is going to be a dance given. All those who have spent at least one day cleaning up around their own homes or public property will be entitled to a free ticket. There will be lunches served from a mysterious menu and also laughable sideshows will be had for people to see. So all come out and have a jolly, mysterious time.

The last H. E. A. meeting was held at Mrs. Lulu Cropper's home. The election of officers was postponed until next session. Songs were rendered by Bly Moody and Fannie Terry, and a recitation by Fannie Cropper. The refreshments served were very delicious.

The Academy will start Sept. 18. Most of the Faculty members are here. It is expected that this year will be better and more efficient than ever before, and we only hope that our beliefs will be realized.

Mr. and Mrs. J. Alma Langston are in our circles again and he is quite sure he has come to stay.

Miss Lulu Cropper has gone to Salt Lake to study the milliner's trade. She expects to have a first-class up-to-date line of fall and winter hats.

Mrs. Clara Stewart has returned from the city and is slowly improving from her serious health condition.

Work on the drain will commence in a very short time. The trenching machine has arrived and a demonstrator is on his way here to demonstrate the working of the trenches and then definite work will begin.

We see Ingof Norman on our streets again. We can also see new paint begining to appear on the residences. Civic improvement has started to show results.

Jack Frost didn't stay away very long after all. But we believe that a good share of the lucern seed has been cut. The gardens look black and desolate, for which the citizens feel sorry as the tomatoes, melons and cantalopes had just begun to get ripe. There was a splendid crop of tomatoes, but now there will be mostly green ones.

A surprise party was given by the children of Mrs. Mary Ann Wright on her 77th birthday at the home of her eldest son, John M. Wright. A most enjoyable time was had in playing games and having music. Light refreshments were also served.

Dr. and Mrs. Broaddus have gone to Salt Lake in their car to attend the funeral of Mrs. Broaddus' mother, who died recently.

LOCAL NEWS

Herald Banks has gone to Los Angeles where he will spend the winter.

A good Chiffonier, second-hand, at the Delta Furniture Store.   s14-21

Hugh Mulvaney who has spent the summer in Ogden has returned to Delta.

Arvilla Lewis left last Monday morning for Salt Lake where she will attend school this winter.

Miss May Hoyt left this week for Mt. Pleasant where she will continue her school duties for another season.

Get your stove repair order in now. Don't wait until you need the stove, because it takes a long time to get them. Right now is the time. Delta Furniture store.   s14-21

The coon show that stopped off here last night showed to about the biggest crowd that has been together since we came to town. It was the same old story lots of colored folks and plenty of old stale jokes.

Some one has turned a poor, little old blind mule out to prey on the public or starve to death. Such acts are anything but commendable. Instead of turning this animal out it should be taken out and shot. The city officials should look after such affairs.

Messrs D. J. Black and Nels Peterson of Deseret were doing business in Delta today and dropped into the Chronicle office for a short visit, contracting for a nice space in the paper for the purpose of bringing to the attention of the public the excellent quality of dry goods and general merchandise handled by the D. J. Black store at Deseret. Look their ad over and watch it for further information relative to their store business.

W. S. Callister of Blackfoot, Idaho, is an arrival in the Delta country this week with a car of emigrant goods.

Jim Wilkins, the Continental oil man, paid a visit to Salt Lake the first of the week, returning Wednesday.

Mrs. James A. Melville is down from Salt Lake this week visiting her son Harvy and other relatives and friends.

Dr. Stains has moved into a part of the Furrer residence now owned by Mrs. Lizzie Chidester and her sister, Miss Millie Workman.

Richard Thompson, son of S. H. Thompson of the North Tract left last Monday for Mt. Pleasant where he will attend college the coming winter.

Hogs and grain are on the move this week in great style. Last Sunday there were eight cars of hogs shipped to the Omaha market and Tuesday another car was shipped to Kansas City. Quite a number of hogs which went out Sunday came from the east side of the county.

Dr. F. S. Harris of the Utah Agricultural College, was here last Thursday looking over the country in company with Farm Demonstrator Welch, and taking sample of soil for testing. He took back to the college forty samples of soil.

Indications are now that there will be a pretty large acreage of sugar beets planted in this valley next season. From the talk we have heard the farmers of the valley are coming to the belief that sugar beet raising offers better and surer remuneration than most any other crop and we have heard quite a number of them express a determination to put in more beets next year, and several who have not heretofore raised them, are planning on a good acreage for the coming season. The crop this year is very promising and there are some excellent fields in the valley.

Millard County Chronicle
September 28, 1916

Abraham Articles

Hello Folks:—

Now that I've started writing to you als, I jes can't stop. I'm agoin to try and tell you everything I know and some I don't.

First I'm going to tell you that Miss Helen Smith of Sutherland is visiting with Mr. and Mrs. Sherrick and has been since last Sunday.

Mr. Mel Adkin has returned to Hinckley and is then going on south (?) with Wallace Slaughter of Hinckley.

Oh! yes, Sunday Mrs. Chas. Hickman had a lovely dinner, Mrs. Wellman being the guest of honor. Mrs. Welman has been spending the summer with her daughter, Mrs. Boardman, of Sutherland, and expects to leave for her home in Hollywood, Cal. about the fifth of October.

When you go past the school house see if it don't remind you of Louisa M. Alcott's "Little Men" when they sang:
Summer days are over,
    Summer work is done
Harvests have been gathered,
    Gayly one by one.

Helen Davis and brother, Edward, spent several days with the Hickman's and had lots of fun riding on the loads of hay Mr. Hickman is putting up ready for the thresher.

Say, while I think of it, I guess you remember how it thundered and lightened also rained the other day--well Frank Nutsch lost two of his fine horses.

Before I forget I want to tell you that Mr. John Franklin of Colorado is here visiting relatives. He expects to stay all winter.

I've told you all I can think of this week so will write another letter next Friday.

Peggy from Abraham.

Sutherland Searchlights

Ross Simpkins and family returned last Monday from a visit in Summit, New Castle and Circleville. They report having several punctures and once the machine went down hill backwards, but fortunately no damage was done. Miss Langford of Summit, returned with them. She is a graduate of the B. A. C. High School and a very fine musician.

Mr. and Mrs. Sherrick of Abraham spent Sunday at S. W. Smith's.

Saturday night seventeen young folks met at the home of Mr. Huntsman and went in a body to the home of Laurence Titus and gave him the surprise of his life in honor of his eighteenth birthday. All had a most pleasant evening and after delicious refreshments were served the guests wished him lots of happy birthdays and cheery goodnights were heard.

School did not start last Wednesday as reported but waited until Monday. They are working on the new building and hope to have it finished in a few weeks.

The Jolly stitchers meet this Friday at the home of Mrs. Will Titus. All are looking forward to a very pleasant afternoon.

Helene Davis has been sick in bed for several days with the grippe, but is out again.

Frank Belston left Monday for Salt Lake. He said "I'm going to get my wife and bring her down here," but he has told us that so many times we'll have to be shown now.

There wasn't any Sunday school Sunday as so many were attending Conference in Deseret.

Talk about thunder, lightening and rain, well, Friday Old Mother Nature showed us that she hadn't forgotten anything about any of them. Mr. Keyes had a sholder blade broken in two places as a result of the lightening.

Miss Helen Bunker who was reported last week as quite sick is about again and has her sunny smile as of old and we're all glad to see it.

Master Teddy Kenny has been quite sick with bronchitis.

Mr. and Mrs. Walker and Miss Helen Bunker, made a trip to the mines out north and report a hot dusty trip.

A little party was given Sunday evening at the home of Ross Simpkins in honor of Miss Martha Langford. A most pleasant evening was enjoyed by all.

Miss Agnes Hersleff of Woodrow, was a visitor last week at the home of Miss Helen Smith.

Mrs. Perry and son, Russel, are expected home this week from San Diego, Cali., where she has been for several months. Russel left here a couple of weeks ago to make the return trip with her.

The Relief Society met Tuesday afternoon with Mrs. Hulse. The Subject for the afternoon was "Home Economics."

Affairs of Oasis

Mrs. E. F. Sanders left Monday evening for her home in Kansas City, to attend the funeral of her brother who was killed in an automobile accident.

Mrs. C. F. Dellenbeck, and Mr. and Mrs. J. Brown, returned to their home in Michigan, after a short visit here.

Miss Maud Styler has gone to Milford to visit with her sister.

Born, to Mr. and Mrs. James Stubbert, on the 21st of Sept., a boy.

The A. C. Nelson school has started and we believe we have a very competent corps of teachers this year.

Mrs. V. Styler has returned from Holden where she has been visiting with her parents.

Mrs. J. C. Hawley and daughter, Reva, returned the last of the week from Cali.

Conference was held in the A. C. Nelson School building Saturday, and Sunday.

Nels Skeems of Nephi spent a few days with relatives here.

Quite a number of young folks are planning to take the fair in at Fillmore.

Sugarville Siftings

Ralph Duncan returned last Sunday from Los Angeles where he has been visiting for some time.

The pupils of the fifth, sixth seventh and eighth grades are waiting anxiously for the school room to be made ready for use.

Beginning with Sunday, October 1st, the Union Sunday school will be held in the Castle store school room, at 10:30, a. m., each Sunday. Everybody come.

Last Wednesday afternoon the Friendship Thimble club was entertained by Mrs. Hillyard and Mrs. Cady at the home of the former. The afternoon was spent in comfort tearing and sewing carpet rags for the hostess. Besides the club members many visitors were present, and as well as being a jolly good time, it was a farewell party for several of the members, three of whom are to leave in a few days, so a surprise was planned at which about 35 gathered at the home of E. E. Olds last Saturday evening. Dainty refreshments were served on both occasions. The next meeting of the club will be with Mrs. Anson and Mrs. Nutsch at the home of Mrs. Nutsch, October, 4th.

Oak City Offerings

Many of our town people went to Deseret last Saturday to attend conference.

Mrs. Jed Watts from Leamington was here visiting with her father, Mr. Sim Walker, last week.

Dr. Christie the dentist, is here this week doing dental work.

Jos. H. Christenson spent last Sunday home with the folks.

Don Anderson and Ernest Ottley have returned home from the training camp at Salt Lake.

Mrs. Jos A. Lyman from Mayfield is here visiting and taking her daughter's place in the store while she is at home.

Miss Zella Nielson left last Sunday for Provo where she will attend school this winter.

Miss Silva Christenson and her brother Albert, made a trip to Hinckley last week.

A. Hanson visited home last Sunday.

Parley Elder made a trip to Delta last Monday with fence posts.

South Tract Review

Mrs. Hardin, with her parents, who went to Cali. overland via a Studebaker, arrived all O. K. and had a very pleasant trip.

The road from the lone tree corner into Oasis looks fine. The farmers, most of them along that road, have cleaned out the brush and weeds along their fences and it gives the whole roadway a mighty fine appearance. It paid to do it, just for the looks of it.

There is a steady come and go of laboring men to and from the works of the Delta Land & Water company. A few days work for the floating laborer is quite a plenty so they soon get up and go. But the fellows who stick and get the money are the farmers who live there.

F. B. Johnson, one of the contractors for the Delta Co's ditch work, told me that he had ridden a Martain ditching machine over seven hundred miles this summer.

Chas. Hardin is still a lone widower, doing his own cooking but W. H. Evans has hired a cook. Its a cinch he don't know how.

Folsom's have taken the contract for planting the Delta Co's fall grain and they are a busy bunch.

The Andersons and Dorsies will leave us next week and will make their home in Cali.

The South Tract school started on the 18th inst., with a full attendance, and Miss Marcia Beck at the helm.

The Management of the telephone Company, tells me that as soon as the system is reorganized in Delta, a line will be run out onto the South Tract. Then won't we talk some? Just think, we havn't said a word for most five years.

Alfalfa seed sown this fall is producing a fine stand. Better than usual and the plants are bigger and more thrifty than heretofore. Lots of acres are being planted.

Mr. Ericson and family from Lehi, are now domiciled on the Coffin and Lane ranch and we hope they will like it and remain.

Edward Folsom is attending school at the A. C. Nelson and Lewis Beck at the Millard Academy.

LOCAL NEWS

Wm. Lovell of Oak City, was a Delta visitor Wednesday.

Simeon Walker was over from Oak City Thursday of last week.

Come in and see those nice Bed Steads at the Delta Furniture Store.   s2805

Mrs. Irene Taylor entertained the O. Z. O. club Wednesday evening.

LeGrande Law left last Sunday for Provo where he will attend the B. Y. U.

L. C. Blades has the carpenters at work on his new house, just west of J. A. Bishop, and has it all inclosed.

Haven Paxman and Glenna Riding left for St. George last Saturday where they will attend the Dixie academy.

Engineer E. A. Porter and family, who have been living temporarily at Gunnison, have moved back to their home in the south part of town.

Miss Arvilla Lewis returned from Salt Lake this morning and instead of going to school there as intended at first, she will attend the Millard Academy.

There will be a Married People's Party at the Ward Hall next Wednesday evening, commencing at 8:00, p. m. Everybody over the age of fourteen years are invited.

Mr. and Mrs. Arthur Bunker and Mr. and Mrs. David Terry are visiting with relatives and friends in Washington and Iron counties. They drove down in Mr. Terry's car.

A fine shower visited this valley last Friday and was greatly appreciated. It laid the dust which was fierce, but we could have appreciated it more had these been about three times as much.

Uncle Jim Melville, A. M. McPherson and E. A. Porter, have been appointed as delegates to the International Irrigation Congress by Governor Spry. The meeting convenes at El Paso, Texas, Oct. 1st to 18th.

I. E. Deihl, editor of the Mammoth Record, was down attending the state senatorial convention and paid this office a very pleasant call. In conversation with Mr. Deihl we discovered that we were almost old friends, we having known two of his brothers in Idaho and worked in the same office with them.

The Walters Co. played Corianton to a good sized house last Saturday evening at the Opera house. The company has some new scenery which they have had made especially for the play and which fitted in nicely with the story. The play was well received and the company received considerable encoring.

The executive meeting of the Home Economics Ass'n will be held at five o'clock Monday, October 2nd, at the Chapel, instead of Friday on account of the fair. All officers are requested to attend. Next regular business meeting of the Ass'n will be held Friday, October 6th, at 3, p. m., in the Chapel. A good program will be prepared and all ladies interested in the work are especially invited to be present.

Ira Heffelman, who owns a 120 farm just north of Woodrow, arrived in Delta Monday morning with a car of emigrant goods and has moved them out to his

Miss Cecil Stuart, cousin of F. S. L. Patterson, who has been visiting him here at the Delta Hotel for some time past has gone to Salt Lake where she will make her home during the winter.

W. H. Pace, the Ford auto man, has received another car of autos. They are of the 1917 model and have oval shaped fenders and sloping engine hoods similar to the late model larger machines.

farm. Mr. Heffelman left his family at his old home in Modesto, Cali., where he has two daughters attending high school. The family will join him in the spring.

Some of the members of the Utah-Idaho Sugar Company were here last Thursday looking over the field and studying conditions relative to the establishment of a sugar factory in the Delta country. They did not make their observations and con-

Oak City Offerings

Mrs. Anna Lyman made a business trip to Delta last week.

Mrs. Soren Anderson is visiting in Oasis with her sister.

Mr. and Mrs. Jones were here the past week, Mr. Jones doing business for the Continental Wagon and Machine Co.

Many of our farmers attended the big water meeting at Fool Creek last Thursday.

Parley Roper made a trip to Hinckley last week with his brother, Henry, who is going to school there.

Misses Mable Roper and Arlene Trumbo are visiting their aunt, Mrs. W. W. Rawlinson, of Delta.

Ezra Lyman and his girl friend and Kirt Roper were seen here the past week.

Sim Walker made a business trip to Fillmore last week.

Miss Carlie Lyman has returned from her home in Mayfield.

Anna L. Anderson and daughter Ethelyn made a trip to Hinckley last Saturday.

Some of our farmers are now very busy, getting their molasses made.

Mrs. Ella Hanson and Miss Edna Anderson made a pleasure trip to Delta last week.

Mr. Harmon, the Supt. of the district schools visited here Sunday and gave a very interesting talk in church Sunday afternoon which was enjoyed by all.

A very exciting event occured last week at Brigg Lovell's when a coyote came in one evening and killed twenty-three chickens and three turkeys for them.

LOCAL NEWS

Register next Tuesday Wednesday or Thursday. Don't forget.

Miss Millie Workman visited Salt Lake City over Sunday.

R. J. Law and Geo. Moffitt are visitors to Salt Lake this week.

R. H. Becknell visited his family in Salt Lake over Sunday.

The O. Z. O. club was entertained Tuesday evening by Mrs. Nathalia Lackyard.

An item we overlooked last week is the birth of a baby boy to Mr. and Mrs. Wm. Cook.

Recent advance of 50 cents a ton on sugar beets will amount to $400,000.

Mr. Eugene Markham of Benjamin, Utah, is here visiting with Miss Edith Bunker.

Jim and Ormon Wilkins and wives went to Salt Lake last Friday to take in the Fair.

Mrs. C. E. Stewart and her father-in-law went to Zion last Saturday morning for a visit.

Mr. and Mrs. James A. Melville went to Salt Lake the first of the week.

Don't fail to see a real theatrical treat in "On Government Service," Delta Opera house, Monday evening.

Miss Rowena Hatch, of Springville, came Tuesday morning and will visit with her sisters, Mesdames Bjarnson and Murdock.

Mrs. John Steele and daughter, Clora, went to Salt Lake Saturday night to attend Conference and take in the State fair.

Apostle Heber J. Grant was visiting the Delta L. D. S. church last Sunday night and addressed the congregation.

Porter Martin, who has been here for the past six week visiting friends, has returned to his home in Ogden.

Mr. and Mrs. A. E. Stephensen are the proud posessors of a fine baby boy born Wednesday morning.

Mrs. C. H. Aller went to Salt Lake Monday for a visit with relatives and to see the wonders of the State Fair.

The Forest Taylor & Ada Daniels Co., will please you in "On Government Service" at the Delta Opera house next Monday evening.

The County Commissioners met in regular session last Tuesday and went thru their regular routine of work. There was nothing of particular interest to the public before the board.

Mrs. Angelo Hansen and Miss Edna Anderson of Oak City, who were visiting at the home of Leo Lyman the last of last week, were pleasant callers at the Chronicle office last Friday. Mrs. Hansen is our representative in Oak City and sends in some good reports from that locality.

Woodrow Items

(Left out last week)

Mr. and Mrs. Schwartz and Mr. and Mrs. McCurdy of Abraham, spent Sunday in Woodrow, guests of Mr. and Mrs. Philip Lamson.

Mr. Hanna and family of Riverside, Cali., after an auto trip to the Pahvant valley, are camping near Sutherland. They were welcome visitors to the Woodrow Sunday School last Sunday morning. Mr. Hanna delivered a fine address, to the delight of all present.

Mr. and Mrs. William Jones are happy in the safe arrival of a fine baby boy. The little one arrived as a birthday gift to his father.

Lightning played some very serious pranks in Woodrow during the storm last Friday afternoon. Mr. Henry Kyes was struck while walking from the train to the house.

The house of Mr. Jackson was struck, the lightning playing some interesting freaks around the stovepipe and a gun on the wall. There were four persons in the room but none were injured.

Fritz Nutsch is mourning the loss of his riding pony which was struck by lightning while in the field. Another horse was stunned but recovered.

Mr. C. H. Hamilton will preach at Woodrow next Sunday at 7:45, p. m.

Mrs. Wm. Oppenheimer has gone for a three week's visit to her parents in Cali.

Mrs. Geo. Webster and son, Jack, are spending the week in Salt Lake.

Hon. Simon Bamberger, democratic candidate for governor, will speak at Woodrow Thursday afternoon, Oct. 12, at 3:30.

The rain of Sunday morning interfered with the plans of several families who were planning to visit the State Fair by auto. Mr. and Mrs. Schwartz and Hugo Thompson and Lawrence Titus went by train instead and are having a glorious time we are assured.

Mr. and Mrs. R. C. King have a daughter. Mr. and Mrs. Robt. Jenkins and Mr. and Mrs. Wm. Jones each have fine boys.

The three-year old son of Mr. and Mrs. Radcliff is recovering from a very severe scalp wound received last Friday by falling on an iron bed stead.

The many friends of Mr and Mrs. Wm. Mulvy will be shocked to learn that their only child, Maxine, died suddenly of heart failure at their home in California last week.

Sugarville Siftings

Mr. and Mrs. Cline left Monday morning for Nevada.

Owing to the bad weather Sunday morning there was a small attendence at the Union Sunday school. But those who did attend highly appreciate the new school room and hope there will be a full attendance each Sunday at 10:30, a. m.

Frank Buhler, who has been here for the past month looking after his ranch, returned to his home in Redlands, Cali., last Sunday.

Saturday evening, Oct. 7. the Thimble club will have an experience social at the school house, the club members are to give their experience of earning $1.00 to give to the club. There will be a program and other amusements for the evening. Everybody come.

Mr. and Mrs. Andrew Eisle have a daughter visiting them from Cali.

Mr. and Mrs. E. E. Olds left the first of the week for their old home in Indiana where Mr. Olds has a good position awaiting him.

Hinckley Happenings.

A rousing Democratic rally was held here last week. Mr. Bamberger and his party entertained the audiance with speeches, songs and jokes. They certainly made a big "hit" so far as their jokes were concerned, as the people report having a most laughable time.

There is to be a Republican rally here Wednesday, Oct. 18th. We are anxious to hear their side of the story now that we have heard the Democrat's. Politics seems to be the main issue of the day, judging from the large crowds that assemble in front of the stores and blockade the sidewalks so that ladies are obliged to force their way past. Even when the rain was pouring in torrents, they still stood in the streets and loudly declared their views about politics. There will be peaceful days after election.

Thomas Pratt is having a cement cellar and a number of new rooms added to his old residence.

Chas Stratton and wife took a trip to Dixieland last week.

Mr. and Mrs. Frank Hinckley are here visiting friends.

Allen Stout and wife, also Mr. and Mrs. Chas. Webb, have just returned from Salt Lake. Mr Webb has been serving on the Grand Jury.

The students of the 7th grade gave a surprise peanut shower for Mr. Beal.

A new baby has arrived at the home of Mrs. Maude Westover. Also a new girl at Mrs. John Jacobs'.

Mrs. Naomi Theobald died Monday night. She has lived in Hinckley 29 yrs., and was one of the first to settle here. The people of Hinckley will certainly miss her as she was always such a good faithful friend to everybody. The young people that have been getting married for the last 3-4 years were taught by her in the Kindergarten class in Sunday School. Her casket was strewn with a most beautiful floral display. The speakers were Pres. Hinckley, Bishop Pratt, Frank Pratt and W. E. Robison. They all gave a like sentiment of Sister Theobald's integrity and worth. She was 52 years old, and has taught in the Sunday School 25 years and was a worker in the Relief Society 20 years.

At the last H. E. A. meeting held Oct. 13, the election of new officers took place. Mrs. Broaddus was unaminously re-elected with Mrs. Ryan as her vice-president. Mrs. Neely Sec'y-Treasurer and Mrs. Nelson her assistant. Mrs. Welsh chairman of program committee, Mrs. Jackson chairman of Entertainment, and Mrs. Jane Pratt chairman of the Civics work.

Miss Hettie White, the H. E. A. demonstrator, conducted the re-election and afterwards spoke of the splendidly efficient work that had been done by the H. E. A. in one year, said that we were right to the front and doing as much or more than the similiar organizations in other parts of the state that had been organized for a number of years. The next meeting will be held at Mrs. Broaddus' Oct. 27, at 3 o'clock, p. m. All the members are cordially invited to attend.

About a dozen guests consisting of the District school teachers and some of the Academy teachers and graduate students assembled at the home of Dr. Broaddus. It was a "get acquainted" party. Music and pop corn were served.

Abraham Articles

Hello Folks;

Say it's been a long time since I "writ" a letter to you all—about three weeks. I'm going to tell you all I know of your business and some I don't.

Everyone will be sorry to hear that John Fulmer underwent an operation for appendicitis, last week in Salt Lake. He is reported as doing nicely.

Mrs. Soules spent last week in Salt Lake.

Oh say! Last week Dr. Richards came out here in his auto and got stuck in the mud and finally had to leave his machine and "bum" a ride home.

Everyone extend their sympathy to Mr. Childs who buried his mother last week.

Everyone will be sorry to hear that Mrs. Patterson is very sick with stomach trouble.

Mrs. Davis, her daughter Helene and son Edward, spent Sunday and Monday at the home of Mr. and Mrs. Chas. Hickman.

The club which was to have met with Mrs. Patterson will meet with Mrs. Reed instead. All the members are looking forward to a pleasant afternoon.

Miss Ivy Holdridge, who has been working on the Wilson ranch, returned to her home in Sutherland yesterday and Miss Florence expects to return home next Monday.

Oh say, a young lady saw Mr. Frank Lake and seemed head over heels in love with him at first sight. She asked so many questions and asked them so fast I could'nt answer them all. To get her to shut up, a fellow told her he had a wife and eleven children but he was suing for a divorce and after he got it he would introduce her. She hasn't asked any more questions. I'm sorry Mr. Lake if we've spoiled a love affair for you.

I've written all I can find out so I think I'd better ring off before some one eats me up or I'm in trouble. I'll write next week—really I will.
As ever
Your happy-go-lucky,
Peggy.

Sutherland Searchlights

Miss Charlesworth of Redlands, stopped here for a two days visit at the Titus home. All who met her regretted that her stay was so short.

Mr. Hanna and family expect to leave today for their home in Riverside, Cali. They have been proving up on their place here. They came thru in their car and will return the same way.

Last Friday the Jolly Stitchers met with Mesdames Bassett and Kincaid at the home of the former. A most enjoyable time was had. At the close delicious refreshments were served. The next regular meeting will be in the nature of a hallowe'en party at the home of Mrs. Davis.

Mrs. Wellman left for her home in Hollywood, Calif., after a delightful visit of several months with her daughter, Mrs. Boardman.

A large crowd from here attended the Democrat rally in Delta and were very favorably impressed with the addresses.

Mrs. Maria Smith has taken the agency for the Thomas hosiery which is of a very good quality and we wish her success.

R. W. Britt, who had the misfortune to dislocate his knee early this summer is having trouble with it again and at times it is very painful.

Wm. R. Livingston, of Salt Lake is here for a few days on business.

Last Wednesday evening at the home of W. R. Walker, there was a big "Chicken Feed". A number were there from Delta.

Mr. Burgess, son-in-law and family have moved on the place across from the Bowles place. I am sorry I do not know their name but we understand they are going to live there permanantly.

It is indeed a pleasure to drive to Delta and not be hitting bumps and chucks in the road and when we get there to find the culverts and bridges fixed.

The young folks that attended the "kid dance" in Delta last Friday night report having had lots of fun dancing and eating all-day-suckers.

Little Ina Simpkins had the misfortune to run a pitchfork in her foot last week, causing her to be absent from school for several days.

Mrs. Davis has rented the Bowles place, and Fred Kenney and family have moved on to it. Mr. Kenny will tend that place and Novilla place for Mrs. Davis.

W. R. Walker is having an addition put on his house which will add to the appearance of the place.

LOCAL NEWS

Next Registration Day Oct. 31st.

Born, to Mr. and Mrs. J. H. Riding a baby boy, Monday Oct. 16th.

Mrs. R. H. Becknell came down from Salt Lake for a few days' visit with Mr. Becknell.

If you have anything to sell, or want to buy anything, put a reader in the Chronicle. It brings results.

Mrs. C. E. Stewart returned from Salt Lake Sunday, after visiting with relatives for the past two weeks.

Theodore Wambold, after harvesting the crops on his two places here, has returned to his home at Los Angeles.

C. J. Ludwig, who has been here looking after his farm during the summer, has returned to his home at Campbell, Cali., for the winter.

If you want your hair comdings made into a switch, transformation curls, etc., leave your order with Mrs. VanDevanter Millinery. o12n2

Mr. and Mrs. W. E. Allen of Los Angeles, who have been here making proof on their Carey-act farm just east of Sugarville, left for their home last Monday evening.

Ed Bunker and family have returned from Eden, Idaho, where they went a couple of months ago, and are living in their residence just west of Kilpack's barber shop.

J. W. Walton, who has been in Delta most of the time during the summer looking after his farm here, returned to his home at Riverside, Cali., last Friday where he will remain during the winter.

On account of the shortage of cars at present we are unable to get our car of potatoes here. But later Mr. Melville expects to go to Idaho and select a car of the best seed potatoes. Melville and Searle.

Leo Lyman is erecting a modern six-roomed residence of gray pressed brick, in bungalow style. The house will be of the most modern design and equipped with the latest conveniences and will have a large basement.

Carl and Leon Rogers, sons of R. M. Rogers, Delta's cement block manufacturer, came down from Salt Lake, where they have been doing contracting, the last of last week and will help Mr. Rogers, who has more work than he is able to handle.

R. C. Bates, our efficient local agent at the Salt Lake Route station, left the last of last week for his old home in Michigan where he will join his wife, who has been visiting in the east for some time and they will put in another month visiting after which they will return to Delta.

Oak City Offerings

Mr. Thomas B. Talbot went to the City last week to attend the funeral services of his sister.

All of our teachers attended teachers institute at Fillmore last Friday.

Mr. and Mrs. Leroy Walker and Joseph H. Christenson made a flying trip to Fillmore last week.

Miss Edna Anderson is visiting in Hinckley.

Miss Gladys Lundahl left for Provo last Friday for an extended visit with her sister.

Mr. Geo. Terry who has been working in Eureka all summer, has returned home.

Mrs. Chris Overson who died at her home in Leamington last Friday was brought here for burial. Short services were held here for her Sunday afternoon and afterwards she was taken to the cemetery.

Our farmers are now busy gathering their potato crops. There is a fine crop of good potatoes here this year.

Mrs. Anne Lyman is on the sick list but we hope she will soon recover. Mrs. S. T. Finlinson is also reported ill.

Many of the Leamington people were here last Sunday to see sister Overson laid away.

Mr. and Mrs. Thomas E. Talbot visited in Hinckley last week.

Some of our town people attended conference at Hinckley.

Sutherland Searchlights

Every one will be glad to hear that George Boardman is up and about again.

Thelma Simkins was on the sick list last week.

Mr. and Mrs. John Hersleff are on their place in Woodrow during the beet season.

Everyone will be glad to hear that Mrs. Marie Smith has added dress goods and underwear to her agency.

M. A. Abbott left last week for Los Angeles to be a witness for the Delta Land & Water Co. in the Finch case.

The Jolly Stitchers met last Friday with Mesdames Smith and Davis at the home of the latter. Next Friday they will give a party at the home of Mrs. Brown, Mrs. Lamson being the guest of honor.

Last Monday evening there was a republican rally at the school house. Lawrence Abbott, the chairman, introduced Mr. Taylor, candidate for Sheriff; Ed Bishop, candidate for county assessor and T. Clark Callister of Fillmore, who is running for representative. M. M. Steele Jr. also gave a talk.

Just before the light was lit Mr. Steele started to walk across the floor but finally decided to roll across instead as he stepped in the coal bucket and had a mix up with the coal. No siree, he hadn't had anything to drink—he wasn't seeing things—if he had been, he'd have seen the coal bucket.

Every one will be sorry to hear that, owing to Bishop Shipley's health, they had to leave for Ogden Wednesday morning.

W. A. Hays left for his home in Covina, Cali., after a week's stay here.

Mr. Freeze has bought the forty acres of him that used to belong to Tiny Barker.

There was a large crowd from Deltahere and attended the chicken dinner and dance last Saturday night. They cleared about twenty-five dollars which will be applied on the piano.

A number of young folks from here attended the dance in Hinckley Tuesday evening but the majority went to Delta and had the best time ever.

There is lots of sugar beets passing here every day and are being loaded on at the Steele station.

The best place to buy shoes is at Walker's. The best clerk to fit you is Mr. Walker. If you don't believe me ask Mr. Britt. You must buy both shoes for the left foot and one a size larger than the other. That makes the best fit.

Tuesday afternoon the teachers gave a party for the kiddies and they report a fine time.

Mr. and Mrs. A. D. Bunker, who have been here visiting relatives, left for their home in Salt Lake the first of the week.

Schedule of Preaching Service

Conducted by Rev. C. H. Hamilton.

1st Sunday of month, 3 p. m., Hinckley; 7:30 p. m., Delta.

2nd Sunday of month, 3 p. m., Sunflower; 7:30 p. m., Woodrow.

3rd Sunday of month, 3 p. m., South Delta; 7:30 p. m., Delta.

4th Sunday of month, 3 p. m., Sugarville; 7:30 p. m., Woodrow.

Abraham Articles

Howdee Folks:—

Say what do you think. I wrote you'ns all a letter last week and lost it on my way to Delta. I had lots of news last week but you know I've been so all-fired busy this week I hardly know whether I'm goin' or comin'.

Say what do you think. Frank Lake says he'd jest like to know who the feller is that writes to you all. I guess he is kinder peeved at what I told you about him but I didn't mean any harm honest I didn't.

You know that Mrs. Soules and Miss Fannie Reed are working on the Alpha ranch. If you didn't know it before, you know it now.

Everyone will be glad to hear that Mrs. Patterson is very much improved. Mrs. Cary is with her this afternoon.

Several from here went duck hunting Saturday but I havent heard whether they killed anything (I mean ducks or geese—not soldiers) or not.

Everyone will be sorry that Mrs. Cavanaugh and nephew, Joiner Cassidy, leave Sunday for Nebraska, where they will spend the winter.

Oh yes, I almost forgot to tell you that Mr. and Mrs. Hickman celebrated their thirtieth wedding anniversary last Sunday. We hope they will celebrate more of them too.

I've run out of paper so guess I'll have to close whether I want to or not.

Your happy-go-lucky,
Peggy.

Woodrow Items

Rev. Schmock of Salt Lake will preach in Woodrow next Sunday evening.

Jack Losee passed away last week after a a short illness in Mammoth, where he was at work in the mines.

A special meeting of the Jolly Stitchers will be held at the home of Mrs. Argo Brown, Friday, October the 3rd, to bid farewell to Mrs. Philip Lamson, who will depart for her new home in Newport, West Virginia, immediately after casting her ballot for the next president.

West Delta was well represented at the Teachers Institute, in Fillmore last week. Mesdames Underhill and Lewis with Misses Cora Heise and Mable Richter formed a jolly party and report it to be the best institute ever held in Millard county.

Mrs. Percy Kyes entertained a few friends Tuesday afternoon as a farewell handkecheif shower for Mrs. Lamson. All present spent a delightful afternoon and were happy to greet Harry Kyes who has recoved from his severe illness and broken shoulder, caused by lightning six weeks ago.

Walter Barben is enjoying life in his new buzz wagon. Walter is always glad to give his neighbors pleasure and when you see his car coming it is filled with a jolly party.

The new weighing station 1½ miles west of Woodrow is a busy point these days. Tons of beets are being emptied into the cars awaiting them and other tons have been piled along the track when no cars were in evidence and will have to be reloaded.

LOCAL NEWS

LaMond Bunker is visiting in Spanish Fork.

Hank Warner left last Monday to join his family in Orange, Cali.

Marion Kilpack visited his old home in Sterling, the first of the week.

Mr. Richards, the dentist, is here visiting. He is located in Richfield now.

Mrs. Cass Lewis entertained a number of friends at a social Wednesday afternoon.

Abner Johnson is contemplating the construction of three more rooms to his residence.

Born:—Thursday, Oct. 26th, a girl, to Mr. and Mrs. Dean Peterson. All concerned doing fine.

Mrs. Andrew Sprowl of Washington, came Tuesday night for an extended visit with her children here.

Mr. and Mrs. Norm. Lambert returned last Saturday from an extended visit to Mr. Lambert's home in Illinois.

We figure that we will be a day late next week on account of the delay occasioned in getting in a report of the election.

F. H. Aller, who is buying wheat for the Sperry Milling Co. of San Francisco, informs us that he is now paying $1.50 for first-class milling wheat.

Mesdames Hamilton of Delta and Neely of Hinckley, left last Monday for Ogden where they will attend the State Sunday School convention.

The Home Economics Association of Sutherland will meet with Mrs. Fredericks on Wednesday, Nov. 8th, at 2:30, p. m.
Mrs. S. E. Boardman, Pres.

L. C. Neely of Hinckley was in town the first of the week and we understand that he is contemplating opening a garage in Delta and was looking for a location.

Mr. and Mrs. R. C. Bates, who have been visiting in their homes in Michigan and Illinois for some time, are expected back tomorrow. Mr. Bates is our local railroad agent.

Miss Sylvia Turner of the Chronicle office, visited her brother, Lorin, who is clerking for the Sudberry Merc. Co., of Lynndyl. Lorin accompanied Miss Sylvia home.

Frank Beckwith took a spin on his motor cycle to Fillmore last Saturday and spent Sunday there. He says our neighboring city is taking on metropolitan airs quite fast these days.

Jack Thurston left last Monday for Los Angeles where he will be a witness in a case of the Delta Land & Water Co. and some California parties who purchased land under the North side canals.

Mrs. O. B. Lackyard, mother of W. L., our jeweler, who has been visiting in her old home in Indiana and who stopped off here to visit Mr. and Mrs. Lackyard, left for her home in Los Angeles last Sunday morning.

A man named Dumont, who was recently operator at the Delta station for a short time, fell from a D. & R. G. passenger train at Provo the other day and had his leg cut off. He was on his way to Denver and was riding the blind.

Uncle Jim Melville came down from Salt Lake last Sunday, having returned from Cuba the day before. He says he had a splendid trip and enjoyed the scenery of the sunny south but for a place to make his home and enjoy life, Utah and Millard county are good enough for him.

The West Side Millard County Farm Bureau expected to hold a meeting next Saturday for the purpose of discussing the Federal Farm Loan law, but owing to the inability of one of the prominent speakers, a Prof. of the U. A. C., to be here as planned, the meeting will be postponed until after election.

Dr. Paul of the U. of U. was a Delta visitor Sunday and Monday and lectured before the congregation of the L. D. S. church Sunday on bird life and the usefulness and uselessness thereof. Monday he spoke on the same subject before the schools. The professor in his talk was assisted by the use of a large collection of mounted specimens.

Mrs. Walter Moffitt and Mrs. A. M. McPherson, entertained Thursday afternoon in honor of Mrs. Philip Lamson who is going away to West Virginia. Delightful refreshments were served after a pleasant afternoon sewing. Those present were Mesdames Philip Lamson, Harry Aller, James Works, R. C. Bates, Marion Kilpack, A. B. Ward, Parley Steele, Charles Hamilton and Miss Stringer.

V. V. Calvert says that we misrepresented him in the article we published in last week's Chronicle relative to his giving the Greeks $178 for the trouble he caused them in bringing suit against them. This was the way it was given to us. But Mr. Calvert says that he brot action against them for the reason that they were not living up to their contract in the manner in which they were farming and taking care of stock intrusted to them in the contract. The Greeks failed to appear as sighted in Calvert's action but after that applie for a new trial and he gave them the $178 to get off the place and drop appeal for a new trial.

Millard County Chronicle
November 9, 1916

Delta Precinct and County Vote

With all the precincts in the county except Snake Valley, in the extreme west, Millard County shows a substantial Democratic majority for all state officers except Lincoln J. Kelly, for Sec'y of State, who polled a majority over his democratic opponent of 32 votes. 4-year term county commissioner, Thompson, Republican, leads by 19 votes, Clerk Ashby, leads by 1 vote and Recorder Ashby, leads by 193 votes and is practically sure of a majority even when all precincts have reported.

With Snake Valley, which has formerely had a considerable tendency toward democracy, to be heard from it is very probable that Thompson and Clerk Ashby will find themselves a few votes short of the majority. So there is a probability that by the time all votes are counted there will be but one republican office holder in the county, Mrs. Jennie Ashby, Recorder.

Following are the returns of the county outside of Snake Valley. These returns we expected to give the people by precincts but found we were short of figures and time to handle them:

	For President		
	Delta	County	Majority
Hughs, R.	115	1283	
Wilson, D.	225	1736	453
	For Governor		
Morris, R.	154	1515	
Bamberger, D.	184	1526	11
	For U. S. Senator		
Sutherland, R.	133	1325	
King, D.	204	1698	373
	For U. S. Representative		
Hoyt, R.	133	1343	
Welling, D.	215	1672	229

For State Senator			
Hinckley, R.	158	1375	
Stevens, D.	178	1708	333
For State Representative			
Callister, R.	147	1405	
Pratt, D.	188	1667	262
For District Judge			
Lund, R.	103	1281	
Greenwood, D.	235	1786	505
For 4-Year Commissioner			
Thompson, R.	131	1548	19
Brown, D.	204	1529	
For 2-Year Commissioner			
Skeems, R.	42	1501	
Maxfield, D.	296	1573	72
For County Clerk			
Ashby, R.	143	1540	1
Pack, D.	193	1539	
For County Treasurer			
Day, R.	134	1417	
Lambert, D.	204	1590	173
For County Recorder			
Mrs. Ashby, R.	137	1637	193
Mrs. Pitts, D.	198	1444	
For County Assessor			
Bishop, R.	234	1444	
Peterson, D.	103	1619	175
For County Attorney			
Peterson, R.	141	1395	
Giles, D.	195	1683	288

For County Sheriff			
Taylor, R.	186	1251	
Dorrity, D.	152	1829	578
For County Surveyer			
Geo. Theobald	141	1405	
Ernest Theobald	195	1644	239

New Editor Arrives

The editor and Mrs. Davis are rejoicing over the arrival of a fine 8½ pound boy, this morning. All doing fine. Andrew Sorenson was seen sneaking around our back door at an early hour this morning trying to get back on the editor, but we were careful that any stunts we pulled off, on account of our enthusiasm over the event, were done behind closed doors. But we really were sorry we didn't have a rain barrel handy to hollow in. Ray Jones is also reported to be pesticating around in this neighborhood but Mr. Ward's old red rooster hasn't grown any more tail feathers so we were out of luck there. Looks like the other "guys" around this town had pulled off about all the funny stunts there was. Just guess we'll cut our suspenders and see if we can't Zepplin.

Oak City Offerings

The little daughter of Mr. and Mrs. Thomas E. Talbot was severely burnt last week and had to be taken to the Dr. for care.

Martin Lewis and Miss Maggie Jacobson were married in the Manti Temple last week.

Mr. and Mrs. Lyman Overson from Leamington were here visiting last Saturday.

The first snow storm that we had this season came last Sunday.

Mr. Cliff Talbot made a trip to Hinckley last Sunday.

Mr. and Mrs. Henry Lyman from Mayfield were here visiting with relatives and friends.

Jos. H. Christenson and Mrs. El'a Hanson made a trip to Delta last Tuesday.

A big party was had at the home of Ida Roper on the 31st, which was injoyed by all.

Jos. A. Lyman has returned from a visit to his home in Mayfield.

Mr. Jones, the agent for the Con. Wagon & Machine Co. from Nephi, was here last week.

Abraham Articles

Howdee Folks:—

Well, how be ye today? Feeling pretty good after the election? There was a large crowd attended the dance at the school house last night and as usual had a good time till one thirty.

Mrs. Patterson is up and around and feeling fine to the delight of her many friends.

Mrs. Hickman has been having such a cold she sometimes can't speak above a whisper. I'm glad I can because I would be in a terrible perdicament if I couldn't talk.

Oh say folks, it is rumored that the small boys' baseball team of Sutherland is going to play the small boys of Abraham on the home grounds Friday afternoon.

Warwick Taylor of Salt Lake spent last Friday with the Pattersons. Of course he liked this country, why shouldn't he.

Everyone is talking nothing but "election" and don't know any news for me so I'm not going to write any more today.

As ever,
Your happy-go-lucky
Peggy.

Sutherland Searchlights

M. A. Abbott has returned from California, the land of sunshine, fruit and flowers. He was very much pleased with it and wants to take his better half down.

Last Saturday evening while Mr. and Mrs. Boardman were calling at the Holdredge home someone walked away with their machine. I say "walked" because thats what they did—pushed it by hand as far as Walker's store so no one would hear the sound of the machine. It is thot someone wished to go joy-riding. The would-be joy-riders got away but without their ride.

The Jolly Stitchers meet this afternoon with Mrs. Isles and Mrs. Keeler at the home of the former. Everyone is looking forward to a pleasant afternoon.

A large crowd of young folks from here attended the dances on Monday and Tuesday nights at Delta and all had a dandy fine time.

Mr. Walker made arrangements to get election returns here Tuesday night and the Jolly Stitchers sold wiennie sandwiches, coffee and pie until after three o'clock.

The Democrats carried Sutherland and M. A. Abbott was elected Justice of the Peace and Mr. Bassett Constable.

Ross Simpkins returned Sunday evening from Kansas City, where he took two car loads of hogs.

A number of ladies from here attended the meeting of the Home Economies at the home of Mrs. Tracy and report an interesting meeting.

Millard County Chronicle
November 16, 1916

Oak City Offerings

Wednesday night a big chicken supper was given by Misses Ida and Carlie Roper in behalf of the democratic party. All the young folks were invited. After suppor was over games were played and all report a good time.

Marion Terry has returned home from Hinckley where he has been working.

Farewell Hartley from Leamington, is here visiting his daughter, Mrs. Franklin Anderson.

A big time was given the old folks last Saturday and they all injoyed it to a full extent.

Edward Christensen from Delta, was here last week visiting relatives and friends.

The Oak City young folks presented the play, "The Dust of the Earth," last Saturday night which was enjoyed by all.

A large number of the students from the M. A. at Hinckley spent Saturday and Sunday home last week.

Sutherland Searchlights

Mr. Harry Ottley is making improvements on his house.

Sunday evening Miss Cleon Bunker entertained about twenty of her friends with a chicken "feed". They report a dandy fine time and say it was the best chicken they ever ate.

Everyone will be sorry to learn that Mr. and Mrs. Boardman are going to leave in about two weeks for California after selling their place to Mr. Livingston of Salt Lake City. They went to Salt Lake Tuesday evening and expect to be gone several days, combining business and pleasure.

The Jolly Stitchers met last Friday with Mrs. Keeler and Mrs. Isles at the home of the latter. A very pleasant afternoon was spent in laughing at riddles and stories. These ladies are making great plans for a bazaar to be given the early part of December at the Woodrow school house. There will be aprons, candy and all kinds of booths as well as a program and fishpond.

Mrs. Marie Smith is in Delta and helping take care of C. O. Davis' new boy.

I understand that Harold and Doyle Steele are going to Logan to school.

A large crowd from here attended the beet meeting in Delta Monday evening.

Some going in by autos. Oh, yes, one party burned out their lights and tied a lantern on in front. If you don't believe me ask Ross Simkins.

Mrs. Denver Smith has the right idea about entertaining the young people. She has an ice rink in front of their place to skate on.

Perry Abbott returned Tuesday evening from Richfield and says he has the finest baby girl in the country. He'll have to show us as we're from Missouri.

Oh yes, Mr. Holdridge thinks the mule is the finest animal in the U. S. since the election. He has several that bray exceedingly loud for Wilson which is contrary to his politics.

Affairs of Oasis

The A. C. Nelson school gave a Japanese Ball election night. The hall was decorated with Japanese lanterns, fans and parasols. Punch was served from the Japanese tea garden by six Japanese girls. An exceedingly large crowd attended and the teachers were delighted with the success of their first ball.

Miss Norma Rutherford and Henry Bennett were quietly married Nov. 1. All their many friends wish them success through life.

Mrs. Carl Pierson returned after a month's visit with her parents at Murray, Ut.

J. C. Hawley has recently bought a new ford car.

Henry Church has sold his home and will move to Eureka for the winter.

Friday the 3rd, a bundle shower was given Mr. and Mrs. Henry Bennett at the A. C. Nelson. a large number of relatives and friends were invited, and the Bride and Groom received many useful and beautiful presents. After ten o'clock every body was invited to attend the free dance. All reported having a good time.

Hinckley Happenings.

(Too late for last week)

At the last meeting of the H. E. A. a most delightful time was had. Our president, Mrs. Broaddus, was our hostess and endeavored to make all those present feel comfortable and at home. The method of keeping "tab" on its members and enrolling them was discussed from every standpoint, and the big thot that was uppermost in the minds of all was to have on the roll just as many names as possible and then to try and interest them enough to get them to be on the active membership roll. The hostess demonstrated the fireless cooker by serving to the ladies Boston baked beans and Boston brown bread which was very delicious. All women are cordially invited to attend these H. E. A. meetings and become economically benefited.

Killing at Lynndyl

A shooting occurred in Lynndyl about 2 o'clock Tuesday morning. A fellow named Davis and Mike Dancer and John Kelling had been celebrating and quarreled. Davis went home and to bed, and the other two come to his cabin, kicked in the door, beat him up and took a few shots at him with a 22. Davis got his shot gun, went out on the streets and found them, shooting Dancer in the head and shoulder, wounding him considerably. He then found Kelling and shot him twice, the first charge entering his heart and killing him instantly. Davis boarded No. 7, which was late. He was thrown off and took to the cedars but came in Wednesday and gave himself up.

LOCAL NEWS

Harry Aller got a goose on the reservoir Tuesday morning, with a rifle.

Irene Taylor's baby almost choked to death on an apple pealing one day the last of the week.

Mr. and Mrs. W. G. Norris of the North Tract left yesterday for Los Angeles where they will spend the winter.

Mrs. Emily Jensen, of Panguitch, Utah, came Saturday evening to visit with her parents, Mr. and Mrs. M. M. Steele, Sr.

Miss Nina Hoyt entertained the O. Z. O. club Wednesday evening at the home of Mrs. W. L. Lackyard. Dainty refrreshments were served.

J. P. Sprunt and Mr. Stearns went to Salt Lake Tuesday night to arrange with the Salt Lake Route for putting a siding into the factory grounds.

There is a stray St. Bernard dog running around causing an endless amount of trouble. A shot from the town marshall would relieve the situation to the satisfaction of tre populance. "Nuff sed."

Wm. Warner, who has been at the head of the Chicago office of the Salt Lake Route for some time past has been appointed to fill the office of A. G. P. & F. A. for the road at Salt Lake vs. J. H. Manderfield resigned.

Wentworth Lewis, who has been working for the Sevier Land & Water Co. at Lynndyl, came home Sunday evening very sick and has been confined to his bed since. He is thot to have been poisoned by eating canned goods.

Mr. Harris of Nephi, who did threshing on the North Tract this summer, came down from Nephi with a bunch of horses which he is pasturing here this winter. We understand that a number of others are bringing stock here from the North where they will be pastured.

Mrs. Ward and her son-in-law, Jack Thurston got a little reck-'less over the outcome of the election and made a wager that the one who lost would have to haul the other thru the streets on a hand cart. Mrs. Ward was on the wrong side of the fence and last Saturday she paid her debt by borrowing Mr. Miller's cart and giving Jack a ride up Clark street.

E. G. Skiliris of the firm of Skliris & Co., have just sent word to the sugar factory builders as we go to press that he will be here the first of the week and assure the growers that he will furnish all the necessary help in the fields to take care of the beet crops when the factory is built. He will furnish any nationality they desire and will meet with the growers at several places while here—Delte. Woodrow and any other place which will let him know.

Narrowly Escapes Death

Last Saturday afternoon Alton Steele, the ten-year-old son of Mr. and Mr. John Steele came near losing his life. He was playing in an elavator bin. When the wheat was started, being drawn from the bin the boy was unable to extracate himself from the flowing grain and was drawn under. His little brother, who was with him grabbed his hand and cried for help. Parley Steele, their uncle, who is attending the elevator, heard him and ran to his assistance, but was unable to pull him from the wheat, he having sank down; until nothing could be seen but the arm his brother had hold of. Other help was summoned and the boy was rescued more dead than alive, having been sufficated until he was black. Dr. Broaddus had been summoned and was on hand soon after the boy was rescued, and soon had him on his way to recovery.

Weather Report

The following report of temperature for last week is recorded by Sam'l W. Western, U. S. Observer, at Deseret.

Date	Temperature	
	Highest	Lowest
5	63	38
6	53	27
7	42	26
8	46	20
9	52	19
10	56	19
11	40	18

LYNNDYL

O. A. Golden was called to Provo last week on "professional" business. He succeeded in resurrecting a dead engine.

I. N. Hinckley was down from Salt Lake, Sunday. In company with his son Lawrence, he went to Oasis, on business.

The Sunday School will give a dance on Friday night. The proceds are to be devoted to the purchase of books.

Leland Kimball, who has been on the border for several months past is expected to return within the next few days to resume his duties as Chief Engineer of the Sevier Land & Water Co.

Ben Lovell, employed on the farm of President Hinckley, was so unfortunate as to break his leg last week. The accident was occasioned by reason of Mr. Lovell standing on the wrong end of a limb he was sawing.

Dr. Murry made his usual visits to Leamington, during the week. The voting population of the little "burg" promises to be materially enhanced in the course of time.

Charles Langston was a Fillmore visitor last week.

Foreman Papeke of the railroad shops is off on a vacation.

There is a dearth of news since election. The people seem to have subsided into a "safe and sane" existence once more, apparently satisfied with the result all around. The society offerings will be rather unimportant until some thing new is inaugurated.

SHEEPHERDER SHOT AND INSTANTLY KILLED AT LYNNDYL.

John Keating, a sheepherder, was shot at instantly killed at an early hour Tuesday morning, by Carl Davis, a local carpenter. It seems that Keating, who is known as a bootlegger, Mike Dancer, a rancher and Davis had been drinking around the town during the evening and all became quite intoxicated.

Some time during the night, as nearly as can be ascertained, Dancer and Keating went to the cabin of Davis, breaking in the door and a fight ensued, in which Davis was badly beaten up. While Keating was later standing in the doorway of the Sudberry store Davis approached and shot him through the heart. It was ascertained sometime after this occurance that Dancer had been shot also, but not dangerously, a few shot having lodged inhis neck.

Sheriff Dorrity is on the ground investigating, but at this time the facts are so meager that it is impossible to get the real conditions surrounding the affair. It evidently was merely a drunken row. Davis was seen south of town this morning, but the search of Sheriff Dorrity and and Deputy Hedges, has so far failed to locate him. Dancer refuses to talk. The antecedents of Keating are unknown at this writing.

LYNNDYL

D. W. Scannel and wife attended the annual excercises of the Odd Fellows at Milford on Sunday.

C. E. Freer and wife, Mr. Wilkes and Carl Scannel are to give a big Thanksgiving Ball, with the Tipperary Orchestra, of Deseret, as ther drawing card in the musical line.

T. C. Callister was called to Salt Lake, to attend the funeral of his brother-in-law, Francis M. Lyman.

The North Pole Basket Ball Team vs the Lynndyl Team, was an interesting but one-sided affair last week. The boys from the rural districts not only proved their superiority, but their goneralship.

Rev. T. M. Kenasoff, a native of Bulgaria, but American educated, has been among us for a few days in the interest of the American Bible Society and the Sunday School. He is a very interesting gentleman and deserves success.

Hinckley Happenings

John Jakeway and Edward Humphries have received new additions in their family—a new baby. All concerned very happy.

We are always glad to report anything that is being done about the building up and improvement of our town. Marion Bishop is having a screen porch and concrete cellar built on the back of his little home. Also Geo. A. Webb is to have 2 modern bungalow rooms built. Spencer Wright, who left us so suddenly to get married, determined to make his home elsewhere, has returned and will build a very neat bungalow cottage up-on his lot 3 blocks west of the Academy. We only wish that all of the young people who get married from Hinckley would do likewise, and build up our community with modern homes and wide awake citizens.

We are glad to welcome Mr. and Mrs. A. I. Tippetts back again.

Elmer Stout and company have just returned from Salt Lake in his car where they spent a most delightful time and transacted business.

Mrs. Broaddus has also returned.

Our last H. E. A. meeting was held at Mrs. Jennie Langston's. An instructive and enjoyable time was had. A book report was given by Mrs. Jackson, and a demontration on the care and bathing of the baby was given by Mrs. Maggie Ryan. Light refreshments were served.

A farewell party was given Wilford Hilton Friday night—a musical program and dance.

It seems to be an epidemic of sickness of la grippe and colds that is taking this town by storm. Beware of those dreadful disease germs and don't get sick.

The second week in December will be the study meeting of the H. E. A. A demonstration on the making and cutting of sandwiches, and the furnishing of a sick room, will be given.

Sutherland Searchlights

While riding a beet plaw last Friday, Mr. Perry was thrown beneath it and dragged quite a distance. He is out around the yard but unable to do anything as yet.

Charles Simkins of Circle Ville, Piute Co., has been visiting relatives here. While here he and Dan purchased a Ford and left for his home. Dan and his family returned the early part of the week.

Master Teddy Kenney tipped his high chair backwards and sat on a red hot stove which burned him terribly and causes him a great deal of suffering.

M. M. Steele, Jr., and W. R. Walker, are business visitors in Salt Lake.

Mr. and Mrs. Boardman went to Fillmore last Tuesday on business.

Ross Simkins was a business visitor last week to Downey, Idaho.

The Stork visited the home of W. R. Walker and left a fine baby girl. Miss Clare Walker of Oak City came down to see it and says its the finest girl in the valley.

John Wind has bought Geo. Boardman's Ford and with his family are joy-riding around the country.

The Parent-Teachers association gave a program Monday evening at the school house. Several of the little folks taking part. Dean Peterson gave a talk on the benefits derived by the cooperation of parents and teacher's.

The Jolly Stitchers met last Friday with Mrs. Sampley and Mrs. oppenheimer at the home of the latter. A good time was enjoyed by all. Everyone is making great plans for the bazaar and the club is going to hold a special meeting Friday with Mrs Heyes and Norris, at the home of the former.

Every one will be glad to hear that Bishop Shipley is gaining in strength and expects to be home in about two weeks.

The Boardman's entertained with the Hickman's and Davis' on thanksgiving.

In my last news items I said Mr. Holdridge's mules were braying for Wilson, but I made a mistake, they are crying because Hughes didn't get elected.

Abraham Articles

Hello Folks:
Here I am again and I don't know nothing.

Tuesday evening there was a program and dance given at the school house. All had a good time.

Someone says Paine Franklin had a stomach ache from eating so much goose. If that gave him a stomach ache, what will he have after he eats the Turkey on Thanksgiving, I'd like to know. Cheer up, Paine, the worst is yet to come.

Everyone will be sorry to learn that Mrs. Palmer has been sick with la grippe and rheumatism.

It took sixteen to help move the Meyer's house over on the Steele place.

Well, I'm going to quit now.

Oh! yes, Mr. Parker had seven hundred (700) bushels of seed. Just think of it. Let's hold him up when he goes to the bank.

Oh! yes, Mr. John Franklin returned to his home in Colorado last week after visiting here all summer with relatives.

Doggone, I'm gettin' tired, I'm going to quit right now.
Peggy.

Woodrow Items

Messrs Jack and Frank Strickley have returned to their home in Salt Lake for the winter.

Mr. and Mrs. John Hersleff are preparing to spend the winter in Sutherland.

Don't fail to vote for school trustee at the Woodrow school house, Wednesday, December 6th, from 2 till 5, p. m.

Mr. and Mrs. Quinn accompanied their visitors, Mr. and Mrs. Hill, to Salt Lake City last Friday, returning home Tuesday of this week.

The Jolly Stitchers were royally entertained by the Mesdames Sampley and Oppenheimer last Friday. This week they will be entertained at the home of Mrs. Percy Kyes.

Mr. and Mrs. Henry Kyes, with their daughter, Miss Vera, returned to Riverside, California, for the winter.

Mr. and Mrs. Theodore Britt are planning to settle in Woodrow for the winter.

All Sutherland was shocked last week when the Chronicle appeared without the announcement that Mr. and Mrs. Win Walker are the happy parents of a bouncing baby girl. Win actually shed tears of disapointment it is said.

Woodrow is to be the center of attraction next week as the Rev. Dr. Paden, of Salt Lake, and Rev. C. H. Hamilton and wife of Delta are to spend the week with us conducting a series of sermons. Dr. Paden will preach every evening at 7:30, p. m. The first of the series will be held Sunday at 11, a. m., and will take the place of the regular Sunday school. Rev. A. D. Schmoch of Salt Lake is expected to preach at 8, p. m. Sunday evening. All are cordially invited to attend these meetings. Dr. Paden was with us last winter and we rejoice at the opportunity of having him again.

The Jolly Stitchers will hold a bazaar at Woodrow Dec. 16th, afternoon and evening. Come prepared to have a good time, get a cafeteria luncheon and buy Christmas presents cheaper than you could make them.

A married folks' dance at Woodrow Thanksgiving night was well attended.

Deseret Doings

Mrs. Hannah Allred returned home last week from Gridley, Cali., where she has been visiting with her daughter, Mrs. Wm. Justesen.

Wm. Barney of Spring City, Utah, has been visiting with his mother, Mrs. Hannah Allred and other relatives for the past few days.

These days are lovely but nights and mornings are cool. It looks as tho Jack Frost has come to stay.

B. P. Craft's new home is nearing completion and will surely be a credit to Mr. Craft as well as a comfortable and commodious dwelling.

SOUTH TRACT SAYINGS.

Seed threshing is almost done. It has been rather a tough job as the hay seemed to contain more moisture than usual. There is lots of seed but so far not much of a price.

Mesdames Evans and Burt Whitmore have returned to their respective homes, and when we get Mrs. Harden back we will be complete again.

The tile hauling for the South Tract draining is all done and the tile will soon be all in the ground.

We hear that there is a case of smallpox at the Delta Land & Water camp.

A wonderful amount of wood is being hauled from the cedars at present. The shortage of coal has compelled many people, who prefer to burn coal, to supply themselves with wood.

I have been keeping a tabulated account for some time, of the drivers of autos that I have met on the public highways and it is distressing to give the small per cent of careful, respectful or even decent drivers. If your team wont hold your half the road but shys off, then the driver of the auto almost invariably takes the whole road, forcing your team down into the barrow pit and weeds. An average of one out of ten drivers of autos is the very best you can get who shows any consideration for the man, woman or child who is driving a horse vehicle. It seems that when most men purchase an auto it develops in them a proprietary right to the public highway which they never had before and makes it only possible to spell their names with three big capital letters—H O G.

It looks odd, and is unusual to see teams from the East Side towns hauling hay from off the flat. We understand that Mr. Rosenbaum has quite a lot of hay to sell.

PUTS IN ELECTRIC LIGHTING SYSTEM

Mr. Myers, agent for the Delco gasoline lighting system, has been in town the past week installing one of the plants at W. H. Pace's garage and demonstrating it to the public. This is a new system and one of the most compact and best plants for individual lighting and power we have seen. The plant is conected with a storage batterywhich, when charged, will carry 20 16-candle power lights for eight hours without the aid of the generator. The whole plant retails at $235. It is capable of carrying 50 16-candle power lights with the generator in operation.

BENNETT FAMILY REUNION

On November 30th, 1916, the 2nd Annual Reunion of the Samuel Bennett family, of Holden was held at the home of Heber L. Bishop, of Hinckley.

At 1:00 p. m., tables were spread for twenty-four guests, and a sumptuous Thanksgiving dinner was enjoyed by all.

During dinner father spoke on organization, he also said the gospel first came to his family in 1860, when Brigham Young brought the message to his grandfather in the little town of Harding, Flintshire county, North Wales. After having laid due respect to the turkey and cranberry sauce, we passed into the parlor, where under the direction of master of ceremonies, Heber L. Bishop, a very appropriate program was rendered.

An organization of the Bennett family was affected as follows:

Samuel Bennett, Pres., Samuel Bennett, Jr., 1st vice-pres., Lorenzo Christensen, 2nd vice-pres., Andrew and Martha Sorenson and Leah Christensen, Sec'y and Treasurer John and Hilda Bennett, Coresponding Sec'y., Heber and Mary Bishop Lawrence and Josephine Abbott, Genealogical Committee, Temple Committee Father and mother, Samuel Joseph, Lena, and Hettie Bennett, and Edward and Ida Christensen, Social Committee, Ratchel, Artemesia and Lena Bennett and Bennett Bishop.

On motion the Pres. Vice-pres. and Sec'y are to meet in the near future and formulate by-laws by which the associations are ot be governed.

It was decided that the next annual meeting should be held Sept. 10th, 1917, at the home of A. C. Sorenson at Delta, Utah.

After having spent a very enjoyable day, the whole family joined in singing the closing hymn, Sing we now at parting.

Leah B. Christensen, Sec'y.

WOODROW ITEMS

The Bazaar held by the Jolly Stitchers last Saturday afternoon and evening was a very enjoyable affair, and netted the ladies a handsome sum.

A Christmas cantata will be rendered by the Woodrow Sunday school, in Woodrow, Sunday, evening, December 24th, at 7:30 p. m. All are invited.

Mr. Weigner, of Iowa, is visiting his daughter, Mrs. John Meinhardt.

Mr. and Mrs. Herman Munster will spend the winter with relatives, in St. Louis, Mo.

Messrs J. B. Seams, Argo Brown, and Jerome Tracy took a trip to Salt Lake last week, with Adolph Ackerman, in the latter's car, returning Saturday evening in time for supper at the Bazaar. They found 90 miles of the route to be covered with snow. They attended the great Democrat Banquet Friday p. m., and report a good time.

Woodrow has been fortunate the past week in having present, Dr. Wm. Paden, of Salt Lake City, and Mr. and Mrs. Chas. Hamilton. Dr. Paden preached to a large and appreciative audience every night during the week except Saturday.

Letters received from Mrs. Philip Lamson state that they are charmed with New Port News and are reveling in their opportunity of viewing the Atlantic Squadron and viewing the great war vessels.

The friends of Mr. and Mrs. Geo. Miller, who are visiting in California, will be pleased to learn that they are the proud parents of a fine son.

Mr. and Mrs. Losee, with their family started for the Mammoth mines during the recent cold period and reports from the mines state that upon their arrival Mrs. Losee and her young baby were so nearly frozen that they are resuscitated with difficulty by the Mammoth physicians.

ABRAHAM ARTICLES

Well Howdee Folks:

Everybody's been so busy agettin ready for Christmas they ain't agoin' no place nor acomin' any place either. You know I writ to you last week but so many people hadn't paid their taxes it took all the paper so couldn't send it to you.

Mrs. Young has returned from the Alpha ranch, where she has been for some time. If I'da knowed she was was cooking I'll bet I'd gone down there and got something to eat wouldn't you?

Mrs. Polmer is jest a feelin' fine now. I wonder if she feels like Mrs. Patterson. She has been a tryin' to get me to come over and play leap-frog with her, but I haint agoin' to do it.

Oh say, Paine how long can a goose stand on one leg?

The ladies club met Wednesday afternoon with Mrs. Cary, and all report a good time.

Mrs. Baker narrowly escaped serious injuries when she fell in the cellar one night last week.

There was great excitement last Friday night when Mr. and Mrs. Riding lost their little girl. She forgot to wait for her mother to come to school for her. She was found about 7:30 that evening at the Steele ranch.

Well Paine have you found out how long a goose can stand on one leg? Try it and see.

Gosh, I'm agoin' to quit right now before I get my foot into it. Into what? Why trouble.

Oh yes, Mr. and Mrs. Vorwaller had a grand Thanksgiving in the form of an eleven pound girl.

Your happy-go-lucky,

Peggy.

P. S. Oh yes, I'm agoin' to California next week and the three weeks I'm away, Lila Lake is going to write to you. The paper will be sent to me and if you don't be good I won't write to you while I'm gone.

Peggy.

SUTHERLAND SEARCHLIGHTS

The Jolly Stitchers Bazaar, which was held last Saturday afternoon and evening at Woodrow proved to be a howling success.

The Messrs Dan and Ross Simpkins and Vess Neilson have returned from the cedars with wood.

Mrs. Marie Smith had a cold settle in her right shoulder and can hardly move it.

Everyone will be glad to know that Mrs. Walker is out and around again.

Most of the small children are sick with lagrippe and colds.

Mrs. Helms is expected home Sunday from Ogden, where she was called by the death of her father.

Mrs. John Hersleff is home with her parents for awhile.

M. M. Steele, Jr., has returned from a business trip to Salt Lake.

The school children are looking forward to their Christmas vacation which begins next week.

The Wolf's have sold their place to Dan Livingston, of Salt Lake and have bought the place across from Jackson's.

Howard Abbott's baby has been very ill but is reported now as better.

The stork visited the Reuben Turner home last Tuesday and left a fine baby girl.

Hy Sherer and A. D. Ackerman went duck hunting with Jeff Clarke, Clyde Underhill and George Webster, to Clear Lake on Wednesday.

SOME LOCAL SAYINGS

School will be discontinued tomorrow for the Christmas holidays.

Mr. and Mrs. Harvey Melville and family will leave Saturday for Shelly, Idaho, where they will spend the holidays with Mrs. Melville's parents.

Remember that there is a first class garage located at Deseret that can take care of your auto troubles when they occur in that vicinity. d14-1t

A postal from Uncle Jim Melville states that he is now in Coronado, Cali., attending to business matters but will be home the last of the week.

Procter Robison and Will Kilpack, who have been attending a reunion of the Willey-Knight Auto Co., returned home the first of the week.

The railroads say it is the mining companies' fault and that there are plenty of cars for coal, and the coal companies say it's the railroads' fault. But that don't help the fellow with the empty coal bin.

See Tom Christy's all white minstrels, Delta Opera House, Wednesday, December 20th.

W. H. Gardner of Salem, came down this morning and brot the casket for Mrs. Alonzo Billing's body.

The Dewsnup garage of Deseret, wishes to announce that they are now open to the public and ready to do all kinds of auto repair work. A competent mechanic in charge, and gasoline, oil and accessories for sale. d14-1t

It is reported that local parties have been riding some of the freight trains out of Delta and throwing coal off between the two towns, after which it was gathered up and sold and were later apprehended. They were arrested by the R. R. detectives from Lynndyl.

H. H. Emrick, who purchased the Company ranch near Woodrow came down from Waterville, Washington and made final proof on his Carey-Act claim. He returned to Washington last Saturday, after having disposed of his place to his father, who expects to go quite heavily into sugar beets next year.

The town was filled with lawyers last Monday, when court convened to try a water case between the various companies hereabout and the Swan Lake Co. which is contending for a prior right. Judge Greenwood later in the day took the case to Nephi on account of the lack of a commodious place to hold court this time of the year. However, court is expected to re-convene here in the spring and take the testimony of the witnesses for the defense.

D. H. Madsen, of Provo, candidate for State Treasurer, on the Republican ticket last fall was here the first of the week looking over the country with an idea of investing in some real estate, on account of the proposed sugar factory. There will be dozens more come as soon as the question is fully settled.

Attorney Hartman and T. B. Stearns, of the new sugar Co. are expected to arrive in Salt Lake the last of the week to make further arrangements for the beginning of work on the factory, and will come to Delta to attend the meeting of the stockholders of the Melville Irrigation Co. which is called for 2:00 p. m. Monday. All stockholders should be present.

Millard County Chronicle
December 21, 1916

Hinckley Happenings

The program for the next H. E. A. to be held at Mrs. Jane Pratt's Dec. 29th, is as follows:

1. Shetch of Dicken's "Xmas Carol," by Miss White.
2. Review of some Xmas. books, by Mary J. Wright.
3. Demonstration by hostess.

The Relief Society dance that was given to raise funds for a new meeting house, was almost a failure. Why was it? Can those who were not loyal to the cause tell us why?

Mrs. Joyce is in California where she has undergone a serious operation. She is reported as slowly improving.

Mrs. Broaddus, Rena Reeve and Bernard Broaddus have gone to El Paso, Texas, to visit Dr. Broaddus' folks. The Dr. is expecting to follow in their wake as soon as the people say he can leave.

John Terry has just returned from Salt Lake where he attended the funeral of his daughter, Melvina's, baby.

This community is still growing because of the fact that another member has been added to each of the following families: Mrs. Frank Jarvis—a girl, Mrs. Fanny Terry—a girl, and Mrs. Alfred Bliss—a boy.

At the recent conference held here, a most enjoyable and instructive time was had. Large audiences greeted the speakers and gave them their best attention.

A most entertaining program was given by the grammar grades Thursday, Dec. 14. The auditorium was crowded with parents and students. The pupils and teachers are to be congratulated.

The faculty of the District school is very enthusiastic about giving a night school for the parents. If they give it, which is most likely as the majority of the school board are in favor of it, it will depend entirely upon the parents whether or not it is a success. Give them aid by being in attendance, that is all they ask. Lets get in and boost for the night school. Those subjects which the citizens desire will be taught. Take hold of this opportunity.

A farewell program and dance was given for Charles Langston. An enjoyable time was had. He goes on a mission to the Tonga Islands. We wish him success and a safe journey.

Miss Mamie Sawyer entertained some guests at her bundle shower recently. She is to be married soon. May happiness be hers in her married life.

Sugarville Siftings

Mr. and Mrs. Elmer Golden left Tuesday night for Seneca, Mo., for an extended visit with Mr. Golden's parents.

The next meeting of the Sugarville Literary will be Saturday evening, December 30th.

The schools are planning a fine entertainment, also a Christmas tree for Friday evening, December 22nd.

Thos. Dibb and family left the first of the week for a place near Salt Lake where they have rented a ranch.

Roy Jones will spend the holidays at Morgan, Utah, his wife having gone there several weeks ago.

The Bazaar given by the Thimble Club was an enjoyable occasion. The Ladies feel well paid for their work as receipts were about $80.

Mr. Sampley had the misfortune to lose one of his horses last week with bronichial pneumonia.

Mrs. Clara Dale and Mrs. James Shields are on the sick list.

The many friends of Ralph Millican will be pleased to learn of his marriage on Saturday Dec. 16th to a lady in Ohio where he went a few months ago. All extend congratulations and best wishes.

Oasis Affairs

The A. C. Nelson school gave a Christmas entertainment Friday night, the 15th. The children did exceedingly well and a large crowd was in attendance.

The little son of Mr. and Mrs. D. B. Rutherford passed away early Sunday morning after suffering the past two years with heart tronble. Their many friends sympathize with them in their sad bereavement.

The measles are again in our town, but we hope we will soon have all the flags down.

Born:— to Mr. and Mrs. Al Nuzman, a boy. Unfortunately it lived only a few hours after birth.

Mrs. J. V. Styler is visiting with her mother in Holden and will remain there until after the holidays.

Ed Sanders has finished his painting at Fillmore and is home with us again.

Mr. and Mrs. John Styler have returned from a visit to Black Rock, Utah, with their daughter, Mrs. A. G. James.

Jim Robison and his son, Ike, from Gandy were seen on our streets the past week.

Miss Lorian Hawley is at Deseret clerking at the Damron & Hawley store.

Lynndyl News

John Lundahl and family have moved into town for the winter months.

Ernest Nelson and James McCardell were seen here last week.

Miss Verl Ivie from Scipio is here working for her aunt, Mrs. A. Hanson.

Eddie Jacobson from Oak City was here on business last Saturday.

Cliff Talbot and Kirt Roper from Oak City, have been here the past week.

Jess Nelson and wife made a trip to Leamington to visit relatives.

Sim and Leroy Walker make their weekly trips here to sell beef and pork.

Tom Christys Minstrels visited us last Saturday evening. All present enjoyed themselves.

Christmas is near and every one busy so that accounts for not much news from Lynndyl.

Sutherland Searchlights

Miss Helen and Cleon Bunker left Tuesday evening for Salt Lake to attend teachers institute.

Little Mary Simkins has been quite sick the past week.

The Stork visited the home of Mr. and Mrs. Fred Kenny and left a fine boy.

Mrs. Davis and daughter gave a dinner Sunday, the guests being the Hickmans of Abraham and the Boardman's and Wolfes.

Master Richard Perry has been sick for several days.

Harold Steele is home for the holidays from Logan where he is a student.

The Home Economics met last Thursday with Mrs. Davis. Miss White gave Christmas cake receipts and served two kinds of cake which proved she knew what she was talking about.

Mr. and Mrs. Wolf left Thursday for Provo to spend the holidays.

A number of the young people from here attended the dance in Delta Friday evening and report a fine time.

The Cornwalls have moved into their new home which they erected on the Keystone Ranch.

Those who attended the bazaar at Sugarville report a dandy fine time.

Bert Ottley returned Friday night from Aurora where he has been visiting.

Bishop Shipley returned last Friday from Ogden where he went for his health and is improved a little.

South Tract Items

The regular meeting of the Economic Ass'n was held with Mrs. W. H. Evans last week.

Chas. Hardin is buying up a bunch of pigs which he believes will be good property in the near future. Why not?

The South Delta Loan Ass'n will hold a special meeting at an early date, to transact business which will be of interest to all members. All will receive notice, so make it your business to come out.

Two of the tile machines have finished their work and pulled into camp and the other will get through about the 21st.

Mr. Many, also the Hall Bro's, have lost all the horses they had by what the veterinary calls forage poisoning.

Miss Helen Beck is at home from Gandy where she is teaching, to take in the teachers institute at Salt Lake and spend the following week with home folks.

Jo. Fidel has completed his long job with the D. L. and W. Co. and will go at once to his old home in Colorado on a visit. Now Jo may be going home to visit his mother or maybe his sister, and yet there is a chance that he is going to see somebody els's sister. I am sure Jo thinks a great deal of his folks but he has never before deemed it necessary to make two visits inside of six months on account of his great love for his people. Watch his smoke.

The Fred Baker family is quite under the weather, particularly Mr. Baker.

Pearson Bro's have added to the north side of their granary, a nice, large, roomy shed in which to store their farm machinery. That is what we would all like to have.

Mr. Stapley and L. E. Johnson are putting additions to their dwellings.

We are very sorry to have to chronicle the death of one of our neighbors, Mrs. Alonzo Billings. Our sympathy surely goes out to Mr. Billings and family in their sorrow and bereavement.

It will be demonstrated beyond peradventure this year whether the South Tract will raise sugar beets or not. There will be a large acreage planted and if properly cared for and a good stand is secured there is no doubt of the result.

Woodrow Items

School closed December 15th. The closing entertainment however will be held Saturday December 23rd, at 7:30, p. m. After the entertainment a Christmas tree will be unveiled for the Sunday school. Santa Clause will be there for sure and all the kiddies will go home happy.

Don't forget the Christmas cantata next Sunday evening at 7:30. All invited.

Mrs. Chas. Connelley came from Pioche last Friday for her daughter, Lucille who will attend school in that prosperous city.

The Jolly Stitchers are planning a fine Christmas party for their husbands and children, at the home of Mrs. Flora Davis, December 27th, 8 p. m.

Mrs. George Webster very pleasingly entertained a large party of Woodrow ladies last Wednesday afternoon in honor of Mrs. Whitenack, of Delaware.

The family of J. Q. Adams are moving from the Connelly ranch to the property owned by Guy Lewis of Richfield.

Arthur Anderson has returned to his home in California for the winter. We understand he expects to bring his mother and brother to Utah next spring.

Mr. Heffelman has completed a substantial dwelling on the forty acres east of Jerome Tracy and proposes to bring his family from California to occupy it in the early spring.

Much sympathy is felt for Mr. and Mrs. Lossee in the loss of their infant son at Mammoth, Utah.

Death of Mrs. Alonzo Billings

Mrs. Alonzo Billings, south of Delta, passed away Tuesday night, at twelve o'clock, after a short illness. Mrs. Billings' death was caused by a severe cold contracted a few days ago and she only lived about three days after taking down. However, she had been a sufferer for a good many years and fell an easy prey to her recent affliction. The funeral services will occur at the Ward Hall Friday at 11:00, a. m. We will try and have her obituary in the Chronicle of next week. Mr. Billings and the children have the sympathy of the community in their sad loss.

Pahvant Farm Loan Association

The above has been designated as the name of the Federal Farm Loan Association which has just been perfected with headquarters in Delta. W. N. Gardner who has been instrumental in bringing about the formation of the association has accomplished a good work in this as well as in the efforts he has made in helping to bring about the erection of a sugar factory for which he, with others worked unceasingly and did all he possibly could to help Mr. Sprunt and those interested later in getting contracts and getting mutual understandings in matters pertaining to the erection of the factory.

The association met at the Ward Hall last Monday and completed their organization by the election of the following officers:

President, J. A. Faust.

Vice-president, Jos. Neilson of Hinckley.

Sec'y-Treas., W. N. Gardner.

The directors for the association are as follows:

J. A. Faust, Pres.,
Jos. Neilson, V-pres.,
Ray S. Bishop,
Lorenzo Sampson,
F. G. Wells,
Geo. F. Boyack.

Within the association as formed at the time there has been applications made for $96,000.

At the time of the meeting there were forty-three members enrolled as charter members and there are still others who are desirous of joining and who will be cared for as soon as they make application. New members who wish to take advantage of the Federal farm loan law will be admitted to this organization at any time they see fit to come in.

As every rural credits association which is formed must have certain boundary lines, the Pahvant Farm Loan Ass'n has designated the whole of Millard county as its limit. This, however, does not limit the formation of other organizations within this same territory and any one else who has one in the process of formation need not

DELTA

Mr. and Mr. C. H. Aller are visiting in Salt Lake this week.

R. H. Becknell will leave Friday to spend Christmas with his family in Salt Lake.

J. P. Sprunt and T. B. Stearns and son, Burt returned Tuesday evening to Salt Lake.

Rile Johnson is building a modern cement bungalow on his place in the eastern part of town.

Ed Erickson of Brigham City, has been here the past week, the guest of Miss Millie Workman.

Miss Helene Davis of Sutherland left Wednesday evening for Los Angeles where she will spend the holidays.

Mary A. Wilkins left Saturday for Salt Lake to spend Christmas holidays with her daughter, Mrs. R. C. Graham.

J. Avery Bishop went up to Salt Lake Tuesday evening to take in the nstitute as a member of the school trustees.

Mrs. Gertrude Thomas, mother of Mrs. C. O. Davis came down from Ogden last Sunday for a visit with her daughter and family.

Pearl and Vernon Tozer are home from Mt. Pleasant, where they are attending school, to spend the Christmas holidays with home folks.

A. B. Ward left yesterday for Los Angeles where he will visit for two or three weeks with his mother who is ill. She is now in her eighty-fifth year.

Mrs. Geo. Dobson and children have gone to Richfield where they will spend the holidays with relatives. Geo. will join them the last of the week.

Ed. Bishop has the material on the ground and is preparing to erect himself a nice four-roomed brick bungalow just south of Geo. Dobsons residence.

Mr. and Mrs. Orson Sprages left the last of last week for Bunkerville, Nevada, to attend the funeral of Mr. Sprages' brother who was killed in a mine there.

Tuesday night's train to Salt Lake was loaded down with Millard county school teachers going to the institute and others going to Salt Lake and other places to spend the holidays.

Elmo and Leonard Sprowl left Wednesday morning for Washington, Utah, to spend the Christmas vacation. They have been attending school at the Millard Academy.

STRAYED:—Last Sunday, a 7-months-old blue roan bull calf, no marks visable. Any one knowing its whereabouts, please notify Henry Freese, Sutherland, and receive reward.   d21-28

The school entertainment given by the pupils Tuesday night entitled "Old School Days" was pronounced excellent by those who witnessed it and was also a financial success to the extent of over $15.

Albert Hales and son were in town Wednesday from their home in Deseret, arranging with the Chronicle for the publication of a legal notice. Mr. Hales subscribed for the Chronicle and will hereafter keep posted on the doings in the valley.

W. G. Emmett has gone to Santa Ana, Cali., to spend the holidays and will be forwarded a bunch of Chronicles of this week's issue and spread the good news that we are to have a big new sugar factory for the 1917 campaign.

The Primary Association is arranging to give a children's dance at the Delta Opera House, at 3 o'clock, p. m., Christmas day. Good music will be furnished and a fee of five cents will be charged to defray the expense of the orchestra.

LYNNDYL

Sheriff Dorrity has been over here several times during the past week on official business.

Engineer Daggett with Ray Tozier and Price Lewis of the Sevier Land and Water Co., are here for the present.

There has been an epidemic of La Grippe in our midst for some time past. A number of our people have had quite an eloquent touch of the plague.

F. W. Belliston and wife, G. O. Golden and wife, Mrs. Harry Wilkin and others of our local residents contemplate spending the Holidays at

Nephi.

The Christy minstrels, all white, gave a fairly pleasing entertainment on Saturday. They were greeted by a goodly sized audience.

The Primary entertains on Friday evening and it is expected there will be an attendance of visiting officers who will introduce some new and novel dances to the little folks.

We inadvertantly omitted to mention the arrival of a baby boy at the

home of Justice of the Peace elect Passwaters, last week. A baby girl has also arrived at the home of Mr. Lure Turner.

are underway, consequently there is but slight news, as all seem to be awaiting the important event. It is likely that there will be considerable to note in the social whirl in our next.

OFFICIAL JURY LIST OF MILLARD COUNTY FOR 1917.

In the District Court of the Fifth Judicial District of the State of Utah in and for the County of Millard.

Lists of names from which the Grand and Petit Jurors shall be drawn to serve in the District Court, in and for the County of Millard, State of Utah, during the next succeeding calendar year, to-wit the year, 1917.

ABRAHAM

Leroy Young, A. W. Reid, O. M. Fullmer.

BLACK ROCK

John Travers, George Dhyse

BURBANK

E. W. Clay

CLEAR LAKE

H. C. Snyder

DELTA

Allen Searles, Nels H. Christensen, M. M. Stapley, Hans S. Olson, J. E. Works, Benjamin Bunker, William H. Riding, Robert J. Law, Andrew Sorenson, William Jenkins, Bert L. Johnson, Raymond S. Bishop, Robert L. Whicker, Edwin Whicker, E. W. Jeffory, E. E. Gardner, John B. Steele B. E. Cooper, William H. Pace, Geo. E. Billings.

DESERET

Hyrum S. Cahoon, David H. Palmer Clifton C. Dickerson, Jacob Croft, Charles O. Warnick, Marion Black, Owen J. Conk, George W. Baker, John W. Western.

FILLMORE

Marvin W. Peterson, M. H. Seguine, Lars Rasmussen, Daniel A. Kelly, William Jackson, James Mitchell, Wm. N. McBride, Peter L. Branson, Jr., Peter A. Shields, Henry Hanson, Henry Hatton, Ruben A. Melville, Willie D. Tomkinson, Geo. Rowley, T. Clark Callister, James Swallow, Joseph S. Smith, Abe Carling, Joseph W. Swallow, Jesse H. Giles, Charles A. Brunson, Fred Cummings, Frank M. Warner, James A. Kelly, P. H. Robison, Hazen F. Stevens, Alonzo Beauregard, Jacob B. Davies, William Critchely, John A. Peterson.

GARRISON

Leo D. Rowley

HINCKLEY

John E. Wright, John D. Pratt, Charles E. Humphries, Charles Christensen, E. M. Workman, Peer Peterson, William H. Walker, T. George Theobald, Thomas R. Greener, Daniel A. Morris, Jr., Jacob H. Langston, Jedediah Cox, John W. Hutchinson, Ray Slaughter, Joseph E. Spendlove, Nephi R. Stewart, Charles A. Stratton, Don A. Bishop, S. T. Webb.

SCIPIO

Leonard F. Robins, William F. McArthur, Lars B. Peterson, William S. Walsh, Daniel Johnson, Lewis P. Brown, George Monroe, Bruce Mathews, Lars Jenson, Earl Wasden, William I. Hatch, William F. Memmott, Carl Robins, Lewis Johnson, Henry Miller, Carl M. Anderson.

HOLDEN

William Stevens, Jr., John C. Poulson, Andrew P. Christensen, Benjamin Kinney, Alma Stevens, George W. Nixon, Jr., Edward Wood, Sidney P. Teeples, James B. Stephenson, Frank Badger.

KANOSH

James A. LaFevre, Henry Paxton, Harvey F. Watts, Hyrum Iverson, Wesley George, J. Alonzo Roberts, Percy Gardner, William Penney, Henry Holmes, Bert Robison, Milton H. Whitaker, B. F. Kimball, Daniel Rogers, J. Andy Avery, Abinadi Abraham, Grant Staples, Wm. A. Cummings.

LEAMINGTON

James C. Overson, Fred Nielson, Alfred E. Johnson, H. P. E. Anderson Brigham Clark, Rodney B. Ashby.

MEADOW

Byron Porter, Rulon Stott, Joseph Edwards, William A. Labrum, Thomas Swallow, Henry Robison, Peter W Pearson, Ernest Bushnell, J. Alonzo Duncan, William Reay.

LYNNDYL

William D. Scannell, Thos. C. Callister, O. W. Passwater.

OASIS

Nephi M. Peterson, Antone Anderson, Jr., Peter Anderson, O. J. Day, Lars Hanson, Jr.

OAK CITY

Joseph S. Anderson, Abe M. Roper, Edgar Nielson, George Finlinson, George H. Anderson, Eddie Q. Dutson, Jedediah Watts.

SMITHVILLE

Daniel J. Simondson

SOUTHERLAND

W. R. Walker, G. I. Smith, M. A. Abbott, Merr D. Simons, Volney H. King.

Hinckley Happenings

Beginning January 10th, at 3 p. m., at Hinckley, Miss Hettie White the Home demonstrator for Millard Co., offers a course of twelve lessons at the rate of one lesson per week to the mothers.

The outline of the course, (subject to change by the class members) is here given. A slight fee of $1.00 will be charged to defray expenses. An attempt will be made to provide a nursery for children during the class so as to free the mothers during that hour.

The course will be as follows: Lessons 1-6, Principles of nutrition and serving.

7. Principle of Home building or remodeling.

8. Home decoration.

9. Home management.

10. Home nursing.

11. Invalid diet.

12. Entertaining in the home.

Abraham Articles

The entertainment given by Miss Helene Davis was a success there being a large crowd out. Every body seemed to enjoy themselves.

Mr. and Mrs. Fuchs and Mr. and Mrs. Childs left Tuesday evening for Salt Lake where Mr. and Mrs. Childs will stay during Xmas holidays. Mr. and Mrs. Fuchs go on to Oklahoma. We wish them a Merry Christmas and a pleasant trip.

Mr. and Mrs. Palmer and daughter Lucy left Thursday for Ogden where they will spend Christmas.

Lorin Taylor has another fine baby to buy presents for this Christmas.

There was a dance last Friday night given by Fanny Reid and Wallace Black. Candy and nuts were sold.

Mrs. C. W. Filby, daughter of O. L. Lake whom he has been looking for for some time, arrived a week ago last Sunday with her two children just in time to join a merry party.

Messrs Wilckens and Lake took their picture machine to Woodrow, Thursday night but on account of their films the people missed a reel and a half.

Mrs. Orpha Leffingwell, O. L. Lake's sister-in-law, arrived Friday.

I heard Paine Franklin had lost his team and buggy. It must of gone over to Reids.

The Van Evera Bros. have a new Stewart phonograph.

It took four teams to move a house from Baxters over to C. E. Lewis'. Who says Lewis' are going to move out of Abraham?

Well Merry Christmas and Happy New Year.

Peggy's assistant.

Mr. and Mrs. Marcus Fox and little son, Carrol, left last week for a month's visit in Oklahoma.

Mrs. Valentine Black gave a party to a number of young folks Saturday night.

A baby has arrived at the Pace home. All reported doing well.

Remember the Abraham Water User's Association meets again on New Year's day. Want all to be present as there are important matters to attend to.

A number of good yields of alfalfa seed are reported as follows:

Parker and Fox,	700 bu.
W. J. Cary,	300 bu.
R. T. Patterson,	290 bu.
O. M. Fullmer.	190 bu,
C. M. Hickman,	180 bu.

And a number of others not reported, a conservative estimate places the Amt. produced in this locality at 2500 bu., present price ranging from 12¢ to 15¢ per lb.

Rustic Rambles

We appreciate the fact tha we have in the Chronicle a med ium through which we can ex press ourselves on all matter pertaining to the condition of ou community.

La grippe is very common among the people.

Allen Young left Monday for Salt Lake with a prospective case of appendicitis. We wish him a successful trip.

Christmas celebration at Sun flower was one of the most social affairs your honorable servant

ever had the pleasure of attend ing. As a matter of fact there was not much sun that day as the snow had covered all the flowers and the heavy clouds from the south driven by one of the coldest winds of the season, obscured the sun. Nevertheless the meeting was conducted by Chas. Schappel in such a way

that we all felt the sunshine of "Peace on earth good will to men." The program was fine, a large number of the Sunday school students taking part, and last, but not least, the table that was spread was ample proof of the harmony, peace and prosperity these people enjoy.

Since reading the last issue of the Chronicle that the beet fac tory was a sure thing, the

suspence which a great many of us have been laboring under has passed away and we have taken on a double portion of am bition which we will need to meet the requirements that this great enterprise will demand. Here we take the liberty to voice the sentiments of our people in thanking the Chronicle, H. F. Aller, the Delta Commercial

Club, and a host of others, too numerous to mention, for the in terest they took in the wellfare of all the people. For this we hope they will reap a personal reward.

In reading this don't think for a moment that we mean to tress pass on the rights of our Dear Peggy, for such is beyond every ability.

Rustic.

Millard County Chronicle
March 29, 1917

DESERET DOINGS

A meeting will be held Tuesday evening for the purpose of consider ing town incorporation. If the movement goes through men will be selected for the various offices.

* * * *

Mr. and Mrs. Jacob Croft are the proud parents of a fine baby boy, born Sunday last.

* * * *

The Annual Day program of the Relief Society, March 23rd was well patronized and was a success in every way. Much credit is due those in charge.

* * * *

George Kelly came home Sunday from Lynndyl for a visit with his family, returning Tuesday.

* * * *

Clive Black, one of our town boys has enlisted as a volunteer in the U. S. army. We admire his bravery and patroitic spirit to serve his state and country, but would rather see the war cease and our boys remain at home.

* * * *

J. V. Black, who has spent the last few months at Joy has returned home.

* * * *

The O. N. E. club members were entertained by the Misses Vernel and Norma Moody at their home Thurs day evening. Progressive five-hun dred was played after which dainty refreshments were served.

* * * *

Mr. Neal of Portland, Oregon, was a visitor during the week looking ov er the drainage district, with a view of buying bonds.

* * * *

Saturday evening the students of the Millard Academy presented the Opera "H. M. S. Pinafore", in the A. C. Nelson school to a large and ap preciative audience, after which dancing was indulged in for a short time.

* * * *

Frank Hinckley, a resident of San dy spent a few days here looking over his interests.

* * * *

Mrs. Hazel Stephensen has return ed home from Fillmore.

(Delayed from last week)

The club dance given last Sat urday night, celebrating St. Patrick's day was well attended and a pleasant evening was enjoyed by those par ticipating. The proceeds will go toward the erection of a tennis court for the O. N. E. girls.

* * * *

A number of people from Deseret attended conference at Delta last Sun day.

* * * *

Mrs. J. A. Passey, accompanied by Miss Evva Cahoon visited relatives and friends in Provo for a week, re turning Monday.

* * * *

The West Side Telephone Co. held

HINCKLEY HAPPENINGS.

A. N. E. Lewis has returned from Salt Lake City, where he went to arrange for the pensions for the Indian War Veterans.

* * * *

Those who attended the Minstrel show last week seemed to enjoy it and report that it was better than the average show of that kind.

* * * *

The big snow storm that came upon us so suddenly last Wednesday was responsible for the small attendance at the R. S. social. But those who did attend enjoyed the short but interesting program that

was given and the old fashioned dances, also the delicious refreshments.

* * * *

A rare treat was given the people in the form of a band concert given by the Academy. Solos and duets were given as well as pieces by the whole band. Altogether it was pleasing and entertaining.

* * * *

Superintendent Cummings of the church schools was here Monday and delivered a fine lecture to the students at devotional.

* * * *

It will be Girls Day at the Academy March 30th. Look out for there will be something doing on that day.

* * * *

The Academy faculty are all very grateful that April Fool's day comes on Sunday.

* * * *

Dr. Broaddus was to have given

a talk on bottle fed babies to the R. S. Tuesday but was called away suddenly and Mrs. Broaddus delivered it in his place.

* * * *

A very interesting social meeting was held at the home of Mrs. Broaddus last Friday. Some interesting practical talks given at the Round-up were sketched by Miss White. The few songs sang by Mrs. Broaddus and the selections on the Victrola were splendid. Also the brown meat stew that had been cooked in the fireless cooker was nutricious and delicious and was enjoyed by all. A game was played that tested the taste of the players and was won by Mrs Joseph Blake. It was educational as well as funny. The club members all decided to meet Friday at the park grounds and start a grove. Next social meeting to be held at Sarah Slaughter's.

RECEPTION FOR RETURNED MISSIONARY

The following is a program which will be given in honor of Elder Claude Billings who has just returned from a mission on the Samoan Islands. It will take place Friday evening at the Delta Opera House,

commencing at 8:30 p. m.
Chorus by all returned missionaries.
Prayer.
Speech of welcome by Bishop H. E. Maxfield.
Duet by Mrs. Davis and Company.
Anachronistic by Mrs. Law.
Short speeches, jokes or songs in

diversified languages.
Speech by Elder Billings.
Chorus by returned missionaries.

The program will be followed by a dance of old time dances, like we danced when Elder Billings left for the mission field. Refreshments will be served under the auspices of the Relief Society.

WOODROW ITEMS

George Webster returned last Saturday evening from Salt Lake City, where his stay had been prolonged by an infected hand.

* * * *

Mrs. Argo Brown is seen again on our boulevard in her auto. She reports a fine winter in California but is glad to get back to the Pahvants.

* * * *

A fine session of the Sunday School was held in the new hall last Sunday, fifty-six being present.

* * * *

The original building committee have been elected as a board of trustees to care for the new hall. The board is composed of Messrs. Thompson, Sherer, Freese, Ackerman and

Oppenheimer.

* * * *

Woodrowites are excited over a play by local talent which is to be staged here in the near future. Watch for posters.

* * * *

The most encouraging sign of progress we have noted is the pleasure with which our citizens who have been spending the winter in California return to the Pahvant Valley. Mesdames Watts, Kyes, Norris, Brown, and Cavanaugh all express themselves as being delighted to return home.

* * * *

A large delegation from Woodrow is hoping to be able to attend the Quarterly conference in Delta at the Mission Chapel next Saturday, March

31st.

* * * *

Wayne Shipley who has been suffering for weeks from a severe attack of rheumatic fever, followed by endocarditis is improving, much to the delight of his many friends.

* * * *

Mr. and Mrs. Percy Carter have added a husky male citizen to the ranks of Utah. We do not need a better baby contest in Woodrow, as they are all the best and can not be improved upon.

SOUTH TRACT SAYINGS

The farmers are making a start toward preparing their land for the beet crop, which we hope will be a signal success.

* * * *

The South Tract Sunday School is going along nicely with good attendance and lots of interest. Mrs. Fred Baker is superintendent, and no doubt she is the right one for the place.

* * * *

E. A. Brush will put out quite an extensive truck garden this spring. His experiences of a year ago convinces him that he can raise any sort of garden truck that he desires. If we watch him closely I think that we will discover that he is making a success o it ere the season closes.

* * *

LOST:—Between M. M. Stapley's and H. E. Beck's, a spear of good bright alfalfa hay, first cutting. Finder will please leave it at Chronicle and receive reward.

* * * *

Coffin and Lane are the right sort for the Delta Country. Misfortune of various kinds, loss of stock, etc., don't daunt them in the least; they move steadily on us if nothing had happened. They have just finished the second dwelling on their ranch, with the usual outbuildings, and they are adding more horses to take the place of those that died last winter, and I understand they will stock up with registered hogs. Mr Coffin has located his son on one eighty and we are sure glad to welcome them into our community and hope they will come among us and help us to enjoy life socially.

* * * *

When Fred Kelm took possession of the Schofield place which he bought this spring the neighbors decided to help him warm his house for a starter. So about fifty or sixty with lots of good stuff to eat and drink and without asking Fred or even telling him they were coming went in, the very first evening and took possession. To say we had a jolly time only partly explains it.

Mr. Crawford, who was Director General kept things moving in a dignified manner until late in the evening when he bade us good night. Fred said if we just kept coming he didn't care whether he raised any crop or not this year.

* * * *

Things are beginning to move again at the Delta Land & Water camp.

* * * *

Our friend, Mr. Rogers, from Delta has bought land among us and is grubbing brush, burning weeds and has a man putting down a well.

ABRAHAM ARTICLES

Howdee Folks:

Here we be again. We can sure sing "Spring's a coomin" or has come now.

Mr. Hansen went to Leamington the first of the week for a visit. His mother, who has been visiting there returned home with him.

A number of our young people—also some old ones—attended the dance at Woodrow Friday night. Say folkses I'm going to whisper in your ear—listening? Well Mr. Hickman is learning to dance.

You folks don't want to forget that there's going to be a masquerade dance at Sugarville Friday night.

Mrs. Cavanaugh and Joiner Cassidy returned Friday from Omaha, where they spent the winter.

Happy-go-lucky,

Peggy

SUTHERLAND SEARCHLIGHTS

Mr. Perry made a trip to Salt Lake last week and came home with a new Metz car, which the family is enjoying.

* * * *

A. Ackerman came home last week but has returned to Salt Lake City, for treatments.

* * * *

Ross Simpkins' family spent Sunday in Hinckley.

* * * *

A large crowd attended the dance at Woodrow Friday and had a good time as usual.

A sister and brother of the Ottleys are visiting them this week.

* * * *

The Jolly Stitchers meet Friday with Mrs. Wolfe and every one is loooking forward to a most pleasant day.

* * * *

Enid Ottley was sick the first of the week but is better now.

* * * *

Mr. Austin is able to resume his work on the sugar factory after his accident.

* * * *

The Porter's have moved to their new home on the forty they purchased from Mr. Calvert.

* * * *

The C. C. C. Girls met Tuesday evening with Miss Susie Sanford as hostess. A good time was had by all. A delicious luncheon was served about 10:30.

* * * *

Mr. Walker and family spent Sunday in Oak City.

* * * *

The Cantata "A day in the Woods" will be given Saturday evening, Mar 31st, at the school house.

* * * *

The Home Economic Association held a very interesting meeting—also a very pleasant afternoon with Mrs. Titus.

Personal Items

Ezra Bunker, who spent the winter in Nevada, came home last week.

—)(—

It is reported that the farm loan rate of interest will be 5 per cent.

—)(—

Miss Effie Clark of Salt Lake is here visiting her brothers, Oren and Andy.

—)(—

N. A. Hays, a former North Tract resident, is here from California, looking after his business affairs.

—)(—

Miss Louise Fuller entertained the O. Z. O. club Tuesday evening at the Delta Bakery. Several new members were initiated into the club.

—)(—

Harry Coon, of Milford is now employed at the local office of the Delta Land & Water Co. as water recorder and for general office work.

—)(—

Herman Gaster, who is located on the North Tract, and who spent the winter in California, returned Monday and will look after his farm this summer.

—)(—

W. H. Lee, industrial agent for the Salt Lake Route was here Friday looking after the wants of the road's patrons. Mr. Lee is one of the road's busiest and most accomodating officials and we are always glad to welcome him as Delta's guest.

—)(—

It is reported that patents for carey-act land in this locality will be issued as soon as the clerical force at the Land Board's office can get the work on them done. This is thot to mean that patents will reach the land owners some time during the coming month.

busy with some carpenter work, failing to appear, a change of venue was taken to Hinckley where the justice rendered a verdict in favor of the defendant.

—)(—

R. A. Nelson was up from Hinckley yesterday and gave us a short call. Mr. Nelson has just closed a deal with James Emmett for a forty acre tract of land just north and west of the Deseret Mill. He will put twenty or twenty-five acres of it into sugar beets this year. Mr. Nelson grows alfalfa seed on his home ranch and raised a record crop last year. He is a booster for the new sugar company and believes every one in the valley should stand squarely for them and raise all the beets they can. He came from a country in California where they went thru an experience just like we are going thru and he knows what a factory with the proper encouragement will do for us.

—)(—

Those who were in the vicinity of the railroad last Friday morning got a glimpse of an immense coast defense gun which passed thru Delta on its way to San Pedro, California. It was a 14-inch gun of the model of 1910. The barrel was over 50 feet in length and its weight was 136,825 pounds, or about 68 tons.

—)(—

Mrs. James E. Works and Mrs. J. W. Thurston entertained the O. Z. O. club and their escorts at a dancing party in the Bonneville Lumber Co's new office and hardware building. The music was furnished by Mr. and Mrs. Work's new Victrola and was enjoyed very much by all. Refreshments of ice cream and cake were served. The party broke up at a late hour voting many thanks to the ladies for a pleasant evening.

Last Monday Frank Slaughter and June Overson were arranged before the justice at Delta on the charge of housebreaking. They entered a plea of not guilty and their trial was set for next Monday. George W. Bradford was the complaintant and charged btem with entering his house at Leamington on the 17th day of March and carrying off household goods and halters and robes. Duputy Sheriff, Cass Lewis made the arrests and reports finding some of the goods at Hinckley and some of them in the rooms of the men at the Hub Rooming house. The men had gone to work at the sugar factory at the time of the arrest. The amount of goods taken was about $75. J. S. Giles appeared as attorney for the county and Harold Youell was retained by the deendents as their atterney.

OASIS AFFAIRS

John Church is in town visiting with his mother and friends.

* * * *

Mr. and Mrs. Edmond Willams have returned from the city where they both underwent operious.

* * * *

Several automobile loads of people from the East side came to Oasis last evening to take the train for Salt Lake City.

Salt Lake City to attend conference.

* * * *

Several people from Oasis are going to Conference.

* * * *

A jolly crowd was entertained at the City tonight to purchase an auto. until train time Many jokes were sprung and a good time was had.

* * * *

Ambrose Hunter is going to the City tonight to purchase an auo.

Hinckley Happenings

Friday, the 30th, was the day set aside for the members of H. E. A. to to plant trees on the park grounds. Although we were enjoying one of our March breezes, seven loyal members assembled , kept their pledge.

Yes, they did more; they planted three nice trees each .If we allow such small things as a wind storm to discourage us, our park will always remain an alkali fit.

A.D.Ryan and L. C. Stubbins made a trip to Salt Lake last week. while there, Mr. Ryan purchased a Ford turing car. He reports the road between here and Salt Lake in excellent condition.

The stork played rather an unusual trick on Mr. and Mrs.S.T.Webb April Fool day ,by leaving a fine baby girl at their house. Mother and baby doing nicely.

* * * *

Girls' day at the Academy proved an unusual success.

* * * *

The new store erected by Mr. Passey is a credit t Main Street. They have one of the finest lighting systems in Millard County.

* * * *

Last week A. D. Ryan sold the one hundred and twenty acre farm belonging to R. E. Baker, of Abraham to Salt Lake parties.

* * * *

We regret to hear that Mr. Joyce has sold his farm west of town, and expects to leave for California the first of the week.

* * * *

Mr. and Mrs. J. E. Wright leave Thursday for Circleville, Piute Co. Their daughter, Larema, who has been teaching schoolthere, will accompany them home.

* * * *

It is reported that R. E. Robinson has sold his farm to Salt Lake parties...We are glad to state, however, that Mr. Robinson does not ntiend to leave here.

* * * *

Mr. and Mrs. Joseph M. Wright expect to move to Oasis in the near future, where Mr. Wright has taken a position with the Millard Lumber Co.

* * * *

The next meeting of the H. E. A will be held Friday, April 6th...The program is one every woman should hear. .It includes Diet for Invalids members.

SUTHERLAND SEARCHLIGHTS

The Messrs Fulmer of Springville arrived the first of the week and are working on their Midland place.

Miss Nina Bunker and W. R. Walker are visitors in Salt Lake this week.

* * * *

The many friends of Miss Erickson are glad she has returned to this country. Mr. Erickson said, "there is six here now, and more coming soon." So we will speak of their district as Ericksonville. We hope they'll like it here as well as Miss Erickson does.

* * * *

The Eugene Gray's entertained the Helm and Walker families last Sunday evening. .A greater part of the evening was spent in listening to Gray's "Cornish".

* * * *

Mr. Humphreys of Idaho, and Mr. Williams of Denyer are here canvasing for the Chicago Art Co.

* * * *

Mrs. Ackerman left Tuesday morning for Salt Lake City.

Mr. and Mrs. Bassett are very happy over the arrival on Friday, of a bouncing boy weighing 10½pounds. Mr. Bassett said it was reading the Chronicle yesterday. It's some boy.

* * * *

Mrs. Walker has ben troubled with neuralgia.

* * * *

There was a large crowd in attendance at the school program last Saturday evening. The program consisted of a song by Miss Helen Bunker's room,a flag drill by the girls of Miss Cleon's, and the contata.

The men of this district are going to work on the roads tomorrow.

The Farm Bureau meets tomorrow evening.

Everyone will regret to learn that Helm's expect to leave Saturday for Acequia in Minidoka County where Mr. Helm will continue with another month of school. Mrs. Helm and children will visit a short while in Salt Lake City with relatives.

Last Thursday when Ernest Ottley returned to Oak City he took his dog with him. Saturday night he returned. Even the dog knows a good country? No slams meant against Oak City, either.

There will be a social gathering for the teachers, Thursday evening.

Despite Mr. North wind, a number of the Jolly Stitchers spent the day with Mrs. Wolf,and had such a lovely time. There were two guessing contests and Mrs. Lewis won two first prizes, and Mrs. Harris one booby prize and Mrs. Davis the other. The next meeting will be with Mrs. Hickman.

Those who attended the masquerade at Sugarville report having had a fine time.

The Sherer family are visitors in Salt Lake this week, going there in their machine.

Mr. Lawrence Abbott hashad a well drilled on his place which is not only an improvement, but a great convenience to the family.

Mr. Harry Ottley made a business trip to Oak City last Saturda y.

Mr. Walker is fencing his place on the Midland.

SUGARVILLE SIFTINGS

Mr. Baker, who bought the Adamson place, took posession last week and expected his family to arrive last Monday.

Saturday night will be the last Literary. Don't miss seing the mock trial play, "The Case Against Casey."

Mr. and Mrs. Hanson of Delta, called on Mrs. Elsie Iverson and family last Sunday.

Oscar Anderson returned from the Deseret mine last Friday, and will remain home for the summer.

Miss Millie Jones of Morgan is visiting at the home of her brother Roy Jones.

J. B. Seams was in Salt Lake on business the first of the week.

If the mail carrier had not left the letter containing the items in the box the day they were supposed to have gone out, last week, they would have been published.

Mrs. Dale, who has been seriously ill of pneumonia the past week, is a little better at this writing. Her daughter and little grandson arrived Monday, from California.

The Adamsons have moved into the Handcock house, as they were disapointed in the proposition they had in view at Tooela. We understand they expect to stay here.

ABRAHAM ARTICLES

Hello Folks:-

Well sir, do you know I met Paine the other day and he said he heard the worst commotion outside other night, and what do you s'posu, saw the matter? Welslr, one of his mules had found a green stem of alfalfa in the hay, and the rest fo the stock were trying to take it away from him.

* * * *

Mr. Hogan shipped a car of hay the the first of the week.

The Vorwaller's expect to move into their new house the first of the week. Mr. Robbins of Delta, did the plastering.

* * * *

The Van Evera's are entertaining Mr. Roberts and Mr. O'Brien of Salt Lake, and are also showing them the beauties of Pahvant Valley in the new Ford.

* * * *

Miss Lila Lake has blood poison in her arm caused by being cut with a tin can.

* * * *

Mr. Gerard was taken to Salt Lake to the hospital lastweek.

Illinman Lake's have moved into the house on Bills' place.

* * * *

The Baker's left Friday for their old home in Imperial Valley, Cal.

* * * *

People from Hinckley are baling hay at Hickman's.

* * * *

Mr. and Mrs. Keeler and son, Wilson, of Sutherland spent Sunday with the Harrises.

* * * *

Mr. Riding left Wednesday for Salt Lake on business.
Salt Lake n business.
Your Happy-go-lucky Peggy.

WOODROW ITEMS

Mrs. Webster is spending the conference week in Slt Lake City.

Messrs. J. B. Seams, Jerome Tracy and C. B. Cornwall are in Salt Lake City on business for the settlers on the North Tract.

The Sunday School will render a special program of Easter music and recitations at Wodrow Sunday morning at 10:30 A. M. An invitation is issued to the parents and friends of the children to be present. Rev C. H. Hamilton will prech at 7:45 P. M.

Mr. Baker, who purchased the Adamson Ranch at Sugarville recently was joined by his wife and family from Curtis, Nebraska, last Sunday, and is now more than usually jovial.

The Woodrow school is progressing finely. The pupils are apparently desirous of showing that they appreciate the parents' scrifice in keeping the school open.

Mrs. Ephriam Blackburn was taken to be operated for appendicitis in one of the Salt Lake hospitals the first of the week.

Local News Notes

George Billings has built himself a new home two blocks south of the Ward Hall.

—)(—

Earl Stewart is here from California to look after his farm on the North Tract.

—)(—

Born last Friday, to Mr. and Mrs. Wm. Bassett of the North Tract, a fine baby boy.

—)(—

We can use a young lady or good young man who wishes to learn a trade at the Chronicle Office.

—)(—

A large crowd from Delta and vicinity is in Salt Lake this week visiting and attending Conference.

—)(—

Mrs. Frank Beckwith came down from Salt Lake the last of last week to spend a few days with Frank.

—)(—

Jack has a new residence under way just north of the new residence erected last spring by Norm Lambert.

—)(—

Mr. and Mrs. John Alvey have gone to Salt Lake to attend a meeting of the National Fraternity of Deaf People.

—)(—

R. R. Betz, who has been operator at the Salt Lake station since last fall, has been transferred to Lynndyl and F. M. Glassner has taken his place.

The Ladies' Auxiliary of the Farm Bureau gave a social at the Ward Hall last Wednesday night. A very pleasant time is reported by all present.

—)(—

Messrs Geo. A. Snow and W. I. Moody of the Delta Land & Water Co. were here the last of last week looking over matters pertaining to the company's business.

—)(—

H. Graham has been detailed as extra man at the local station. There is too much business being done eby the railroad Co. at this point for the regular force to handle, why the increase.

—)(—

Robt. Campbell who is interested in land on the North Tract, came in the first of the week from his home at Campbell, Calf., and will look after his holdings here during the summer.

—)(—

Mr. F. H. Neil of Lucan, Ontario, Canada, who has been here the past week making arrangements for spring work on his farm near town, has gone to Salt Lake City to tend the big stock show.

—)(—

A man walked into the bank the other day and rented a safety deposit box at $6.00 per, to put two wisps of hay in it. The income tax collector is going to arrest Beckwith to make him divulge the name of that rich guy.

—)(—

James Kinne of Pomenia, Calf., who traded for is known as the "Kicker" Johnson farm on the North Tract, came in the fore part of the week with a car of goods and

has taken up his residence on his farm.

—)(—

J. H. Jenkins, local manager of the Delta Beet Sugar Corporation, returned Tuesday evening from a business trip to Denver and Pueblo. He was accompanied on his return by Mrs. Jenkins.

—)(—

L. A. Broderick is having an excavation made for a two story brick just east of the bank on Clark street. He contemplates a structure 60 feet deep and will use it for a short order and confectionery and have rooms on the second floor.

—)(—

The Farm Bureau is having a lot of seed potatoes shipped into the farmers of the valley. We wish to caution those obtain these potatoes that they have been treated with corosive sublimate, a deadly poison. Don't use any of these potatoes for the table. It will be the means of saving funeral expenses.

—)(—

Miss Sylvia Turner, who is the main stay of the Chronice office and who is the only real linotype operator in the shop, is laid up with a throat affection and this home comfort is in a deplorable condition this week. So if you don't find as much news in it this week as usual blame the doctor.

It is reported that Dan Stevens of Fillmore has rented one of the vacant rooms in the McCornick building and will put in a line of general merchandise about the first of June. The other room is reported to have been let to a drug firm who will soon install an up-to-date store.

—)(—

The H. M. F. Pinafore opera which was presented in Delta last Saturday evening by the students of the Millard Academy is reported to have been exceptionally good and to have been a performance for those who participated in it to be proud of.

—)(—

Wednesday morning F. G. Wells of the Island Farm received two fine specimens of registered Berkshire brood sows by express from California. These are bred to one

of the most highly prized hogs in the U. S., and Mr. Wells expects to make this breed and the Poland China a specialty on his fine farm.

—)(—

Wednesday Evening, March 25th. the 'Boys' of Delta, entertained the O. Z. O. Club with a dancing party at the new Woodrow Hall. The evevening was spent in dancing all the late dances. The guests were served by the hosts with coffee, cake and ice cream.

At a late hour the party broke up all having had a very enjoyable time. Melody "6" furnished the music.

—)(—

Mr. and Mrs. O. L. Crawford of Deseret were in Delta Wednesday, and in conversation with Mr. Crawford, we learn that the big 25,000 acre drainage tract in that territory has a fine chance for going thru. We are glad to be assured of this fact as it means the salvation of that territory, and with a little push and energy it will also mean a sugar

factory for Deseret before many years roll by.

—)(—

The firm of Carpenters, contractors, who built the original McCornick block here in Delta, have a contract for building two more rooms to it on the south. Each of the rooms will have a frontage of 40 feet, and one of them will be occupied by the Con. Wagon & Machine Cooper Garage, & Auto Livery whose Co. while the other will be added to business has outgrown its present and it has been compelled to enlarge its floor space. An eighty foot frontage in a business of this kind is seldom found.

—)(—

Henry Freese and family had a mighty lucky accident last Thursday when they went to pull around a load of balled hay north of Hinckley with their car. They pulled out of the road just before they came to a ditch crossing and there was not room enough to get back to the road before they reached the ditch. The car struck the edge of the bridge and toppled over into the ditch in which there was water. The three occupants extricated themselves none the worse for the experience.

—)(—

Mr. and Mrs. W. G. Norris returned yesterday from a winter's visit in California. They report a nice time and also notice a big change in Delta. ... ...

—)(—

Mrs. Robard, wife of the mechanical man at the Cooper Garage, who has been spending the winter in California, returned home the first of the week.

Millard County Chronicle
April 12, 1917

HINCKLEY HAPPENINGS

Miss White gave an Easter dinner at the Mother's class this week at the home of Dora Webb.

* * * *

I suppose Will Bishop's trip to Salt Lake was just one of his periodical pleasure sprees.

* * * *

Nathan Badger and wife took their baby, Ruth to Salt Lake last week to have her eyes operated on.

* * * *

Leland Neilson made a trip to Ogden the last of last week to take an examination for forest ranger.

* * * *

An epidemic of measles has broken out amongst us again. All public gatherings have been closed so as to prevent further exposure.

* * * *

The April sunshine and showers we have had are bringing up the lawn grass and making every thing look green and beautiful.

* * * *

C. E. McClellan went to Salt Lake last week for the purpose of attending conference and securing teachers for the coming year.

* * * *

We certainly will have a shady and beautiful town if all the trees that have been delivered here the past week and the other shipments that have been ordered are planted.

* * * *

Mrs. Broaddus gave an Easter party to the Ryan's Neely's, and Nelson's the past week, which was very successful and enjoyed by those invited.

* * * *

Floyd G. Eyre and LaPriel Robinson went to Salt Lake together to embark on the sea of matrimony, so people said, but they must have been frightened of submarines and hidden mines as they returned without doing so.

* * * *

Even if we can't have electric lights to light up the street, others can be substituted that do almost as well, as was demonstrated Tuesday night when some dozen gasoline lanterns were strung along the streets for a half mile north and south of the school house. The lights were paid for by enterprising citizens, by subscriptions and were installed by L. S. Naylor.

* * * *

The following people attended conference at Salt Lake last week: Pres. A. A. Hinckley, Pres. Frank Pratt, Bishop John Pratt, John Jarvis, Mary Lee and mother, Mrs. Cox, Robert Slaughter and son Earl, and Eddie Anderson and wife, Richard Cropper and wife, Milton Moody and wife, Alfred Bliss and wife, Mr. and Mrs. Howells, James P. Terry and Fannie Terry.

ABRAHAM ARTICLES

Abraham, Utah.

Hello Folks:—
Well how are you after the rain? Feeling good of course.

* * * *

The Ora Lake's have moved to Abraham.

* * * *

Mr. Riding has returned from Salt Lake where he went on business.

* * * *

Miss Emily Carpe, of Fillmore is working at the Wilson ranch.

* * * *

A number from here attended the Relief Society at Sutherland Tuesday.

* * * *

Mr. Forgeuson was taken to Salt Lake to be operated on for appendicitis.

Mr. and Mrs. Bills were in Abraham this week, visiting and looking after business.

* * * *

The Jolly Stitchers met Friday afternoon, with Mrs. C. M. Hickman as hostess, and a program of readings and music was planned—also a good time.

* * * *

Mr. Roberts has been hauling lumber from Delta this week but I haven't learned what he is going to do with it.

* * * *

Well I am in a hurry so as I don't know any more, might as well quit.
Your happy-go-lucky,
Peggy.

SUTHERLAND SEARCHLIGHTS

Mr. Bunker is visiting with the Walker's.

* * * *

Mr. Rogers of Delta is working on the Wallace house.

* * * *

The Potters are having a well drilled on their place.

* * * *

Mrs. Lloyd left Tuesday for Panguitch to be gone for several months.

* * * *

The Geo. Meinhardt's entertained a number of their friends with an Easter dinner. A lovely time was had by all present.

* * * *

Everyone regretted to see the Helm's leave but wish them success and as many friends or more, if that is possible, in their new home.

* * * *

Mrs. Martin and daughter, Belle who have been very sick are just fine now. Mr. Martin says she must be, as she ate only four eggs for breakfast.

* * * *

Friday evening the P. T. A. gave a farewell party to the teachers. There was a short program and games after which lemonade and cake were served.

* * * *

Say, did you know it rained Monday night? So does Mr. Freese. He was returning from Salt Lake and right in front of Calvert's they had a blowout, but even at that I'll bet he's glad to get back again.

Nina Bunker and Winn Walker returned Tuesday from Salt Lake and report a grand time. Nina says there's lots of good looking fellows in Salt Lake, but they'll have to go some to beat our young fellows in looks.

* * * *

The Ackerman's returned Saturday from Salt Lake, bringing Anna with them, to the delight of her many friends. Anna has been in Nebraska attending school and Mr. Ackerman in Salt Lake receiving medical treatment.

* * * *

* * * *

If you want to imagine yourself on the good roads around Fillmore and that part of the country or on a boulevard out of Salt Lake just get in your Lizzie and spin around on the roads our men graded and fixed up. Now who says Sutherland is asleep?

* * * *

On Wednesday there will be a class in expression and vocal from 9:30 to 10:30 for which there will be a charge of 25c. each, with Miss Helene Davis as teacher., and from 10:30 the mothers are taking turns to hold school so that the children will not lose their interest.

* * * *

Mrs. Ottley and Mrs. Davis entertained for Mr. and Mrs. Helm at dinner Saturday evening. Helen Bunker took them and a number of children to Delta to see them off.

* * * *

The Country Cousins, formally known as the C. C. C's, met with Helen and Nina Bunker on Tuesday evening. A delightful time was had by all.

REAL ESTATE TRANSFERS

Anes L. Udy has purchased the John Swartz 80, also the Garard 40 acre tract adjoining it, thru C. F. Winebrenner as agent.

Mr. Potter and Mr. Watson have taken options on the Miller farm, located in the Abraham district.

Mrs. Alice Jones has sold her residence in the south part of town to Wm. Blackwell. Mr. Blackwell recently sold his farm on the North Tract to Jeff Jones.

DESERET DOINGS

DELTA

You ask us what town is the best.
DELTA
To us she's fairest in the West
DELTA
It's growth you can see on every hand,
She has so much of nice, good land
And buildings on it that are grand
DELTA
The county seat it soon will be
DELTA
And Fillmore then no more we'll see, just

DELTA

For Delta is the fairest place,
That was ever given the human race,
And it has such a lovely grace;
DELTA
The sugar beets will soon be green at
DELTA
The sugar factory soon be seen at
DELTA
Oh, wont the farmers wear a smile
On their broad faces all the while,
Oh, wont the sugar begin to "bile" at
DELTA

Personal Items

Get your potatoes at the Drug Store. $4.50 per 100.

—)(—

Eugene Gardner went to Salt Lake Saturday night.

—)(—

Don't forget that the Chronicle has maps of Utah on sale for 25 c.

—)(—

J. E. Steele was a visitor in Salt Lake the first of the week.

—)(—

C. H. Blake left Sunday for his home in Provo.

—)(—

The contractors have resumed work on the new public school building.

—)(—

J. H. Peterson has returned from Salt Lake where he went to attend conference.

—)(—

Mrs. Emily Jensen returned Monday night from Salt Lake where she attended conference.

—)(—

The stork visited both Joe and Maurice Briggs this week and left a baby at each place.

—)(—

Mrs. Harold Koch left Saturday evening for Salt Lake City, where she will remain for several months.

—)(—

T. B. Stearns of the Delta Beet Sugar Company is here looking after affairs connected with the company.

—)(—

If you need a Crib, Sanitary Couch, Cot, Bedstead or Mattresses, call at the Delta Furniture Store. a12-19

—)(—

Mr. and Mrs. C. E. Stewart and family have moved to their homestead north of town and will spend the summer there.

—)(—

Mr. and Mrs. Ben Douglas have taken up their residence in the McClain house, recently vacated by A. M. McPherson.

—)(—

A. B. Walker, brother of W. P. Walker, is here from Saratoga, Wyo. looking after his land holdings on the North Tract.

—)(—

W. I. Moody and A. M. McPherson of the Delta Land & Water Co. are in town attending to business matters pertaining to the company.

—)(—

T. C. Gronning and family left Sunday for Milford, where Mr. Gronning has a position with the Delta Land & Water Co. repairing machinery.

—)(—

The Delta Furniture Store has Pails, Tubs, Wash-boards, Bread-mixers, Coal oil and Gasoline Stoves and Ovens. Call and see them. a12-19

—)(—

The material for the addition to the McCornick block which will have a frontage of 80 feet on Broadway, is arriving and construction work will begin at once.

—)(—

Prof. J. Q. McQuarrie, who has been teaching in the B. Y. U. at Provo is here looking over the country with a view of investing and visiting.

—)(—

C. A. Clawson has traded his house and lot in town to L. D. Pace for a part of his farm west of town. Mr. Clawson moved to his farm the fore part of the week.

—)(—

Mr. and Mrs. A. L. Simons are in Salt Lake visiting. Mr. Simons has just delivered a car of hogs to the new Cudahy Packing Co. and received 13 cents per pound for them.

—)(—

Harry Coons, who has been working at the Delta Land $ Water office for the past month, went to Milford for a visit with his parents and while there enlisted in the army.

—)(—

D. D. Rogers left Saturday evening for his home in Kanosh where he will visit for a week with home folks before returning to Delta, where he will remain during the summer.

—)(—

Last Wednesday night the parents entertained the Delta school teachers at a social in the Ward hall. A short program was rendered, and games played, after which cake and ice cream were served.

—)(—

J. W. Walton and son, J. W., Jr., drove in Tuesday in their car, from Riverside, California. Mr. Walton will spend the summer here, looking after his farms on the North Tract and east of town.

—)(—

Wm. N. Gardner, Secretary of one of the local Farm Loan Associations, is in receipt of the following letter, from Burrell G. White, President of the Federal Land Bank at Berkeley, California.

—)(—

Misses Viola Turner and Verna Schlappy entertained the O. Z. O. girls Tuesday night at the home of the former. About ten members were present and the evening was spent in sewing and music, after which refreshments were served.

—)(—

Chris Beck was the victim of a very painful accident Wednesday while helping Mr. Robbins to plaster a small closet. A large piece of wet plaster fell into his eye. Dr. Broaddus was called and it is hoped that the injury will not prove serious.

ABRAHAM ARTICLES

Abraham.

Well, hello, folks!

How are you these fine days? Feelin' Hunkey Dory?

* * * *

Mrs. Hickman has been suffering with rheumatism.

* * * *

We understand that Mr. Gerard has sold his place.

* * * *

Charlie Vorwaller has sold a carload of hay and loaded the car the first of the week.

* * * *

Whitehead's have moved to Hinckley to the regret of their many friends.

* * * *

Now, when you're irrigating, don't get your feet wet; be sure and do a good job irrigating.

* * * *

There has been quite a bit of going and coming at the Livingston ranch the past week. Mr. Duffen of Provo is working there. Mr. Livingston was there Sunday.

* * * *

Mrs. Alven Jensen of Delta spent several days with her sister, Mrs. Riding, before leaving for her home in Panguitch. Mr. Riding was a business visitor in Panguitch last week. They are building a kitchen and dining room for the help.

Don't you think that's a whole lot for one place?

Yours, Happy-go-Lucky Peggy.

SOUTH TRACT SAYINGS

Considerable activity is being shown at the D. L. & W. Co. camp and the work is progressing nicely.

* * * *

Joe Fidel is talking of enlisting as a soldier of the U. S. army. One of his brothers has already gone.

* * * *

Talk about making peace with Germany. I would rather make peace with the men who have hay to sell. It's more to the point.

* * * *

The South Tract Federal Farm Loan Association has received all blanks necessary to going forward with making loans, which will be done at once.

* * * *

Considerable brush is disappearing this spring and the ground is being prepared for beets. Beet acreage is still increasing on the South Tract.

* * * *

If you want to keep tab on Delta you must go there every day as the changes are so frequent and continuous. After an absence of twenty-four hours you have to make application for information and start all over again.

* * * *

The children of the Brush family have been quite under the weather with some sort of sore mouth. The inside of the mouth being infected with blisters. We are glad to note, however, that at this writing they are better.

* * * *

Enoch Folsom, who went away about a year ago, has spent the time carrying the U. S. mail over a twenty-five mile route with a sledge and four dogs. His route was in Idaho near the Yellowstone Park and his traveling was mostly done on skis. He says he came home to get thawed out.

* * * *

Our next Farm Bureau meeting will be on Saturday at 2 p. m., May 5th. Let each member make it his business to be there as this organization is of vital importance to us all. If you are not a member get ashamed of it as quickly as you can and get your name on the roll so as to be able to get your share of the advantages it brings to your door.

* * * *

Donald F. Beck, son of H. E. Beck, who was here five years ago, returned some two weeks ago and expresses himself as very much surprised at the development of Millard County. He has spent the intervening time in the north-western States and says that nowhere has he found such opportunity for investment or work as in Utah and especially in Millard County.

* * * *

On the 18th of this month, in the company of Mr. and Mrs. H. E. Beck, Don and Edna, Frank B. Johnson and Marcia E. Beck were married at Fillmore, by R. T. Ashby, County Clerk. On the same evening a reception was given the bride and groom at the home of the bride and was attended by their many friends. On Saturday evening a shower was given them at the home of Mr. and Mrs. Chas. Hardin by the community in general, where they received many useful and beautiful presents. During the festivities at the shower, some of their friends went to the home of the bride and groom and fixed the house and furnishings so that it took them most of the balance of the night to get in and get to bed. Frank said he thought they had more fun re-arranging their house than the boys did disarranging it.

SUGARVILLE SIFTINGS

The Friendship Thimble club will meet next Wednesday afternoon with Mrs. Cronholm and Mrs. Iverson at the home of the former.

* * * *

There will be a big dance at the F. T. C. Library hall Saturday evening. Music by the "Melody 6". Refreshments will be served. Everyone come and have a good time.

* * * *

Rev. Hamilton and wife were out on the North Tract this week making their farewell calls as they leave in about three weeks for their summer work in the southern part of the State.

* * * *

The local Farm Bureau will meet the first and third Wednesday evening of each month at the F. T. C. Library hall, so don't forget next Wednesday evening. Interesting topics are always discussed and each meeting is very beneficial to all farmers. Officers of the association are as follows: Ed. Cady, president; J. B. Seams, vice-president, and J. F. Boyle, secretary.

WOODROW WRITINGS.

Mr. Herring is here from Salt Lake and is vigorously improving his Woodrow ranch.

* * * *

Mr. De Lapp has suffered from a relapse of the rheumatic fever, but at present writing is again improving.

* * * *

Mr. and Mrs. Jeff Clark took a trip to Joy Mountain last Monday in their new Overland, returning about 4 p. m. Some class to our car!

* * * *

Rev. C. H. Hamilton was out in his new Ford car Sunday, preaching at Woodrow and Sugarville to appreciative audiences.

* * * *

Mr. Perry is busy in our midst, demonstrating the virtues of his new Metz. Wait till we harvest the beets next fall and you will see more cars in Woodrow than there are individuals.

* * * *

John Wind received the sad news this week that his 13-year-old nephew had died suddenly in Nebraska of an attack of apoplexy occurring during a severe illness from the measles.

* * * *

The Jolly Stitchers will have a meeting in the Woodrow hall Friday afternoon commemorative of their lives twenty years ago. They will dress according to the fashions of that date. A short program will be given and the old songs rendered.

* * * *

The young ladies of Woodrow are going to entertain at a dance in the New Hall, Saturday evening, May 5. Music will be furnished by the Tipperary Band of Deseret. Refreshments will be served, and a general good time is anticipated.

* * * *

Little Ruby Turner, who was operated upon almost two years ago for talipes, demonstrated her ability to walk alone last Tuesday, since which time she has only been off her feet long enough to sleep, so proud is she of her new ability to go it alone.

SUTHERLAND SEARCHLIGHTS.

The Schlappy's of Delta have moved on their place on the Midland.

* * * *

Little Grace Kinney, who has been quite sick, is out again.

* * * *

Mrs. Walker returned Monday from Dixie where she has been visiting.

* * * *

Bert Wallace had the misfortune to drop a harrow, running one of the spikes thru his foot.

* * * *

Mr. and Mrs. Dan Simkins are very proud and happy over the arrival of a nine pound boy.

* * * *

Jennie Bridges was quite sick last week but is out again enjoying this beautiful weather.

* * * *

Mrs. Martin is on the sick list again to the regret of her many friends.

* * * *

The measles have been visiting our district. The Bunkers have been in quarantine.

* * * *

The stork visited the Jimpson and Bunker ranch Tuesday and left a ten pound boy to Mr. and Mrs. Wallace Mitchell.

* * * *

There will be a program given at the school house Tuesday evening, May 1st, by the school children. Be sure and come.

* * * *

Lyman Molten has purchased the forty acres on the Midland owned by Perry Abbott and a forty of Lawrence Abbott.

* * * *

The patriotic meeting held Tuesday evening was well attended and enjoyed by all. Mr. Tibbets of Fillmore, Mr. Welch and Miss White of Hinckley, Mr. Foote and Mr. Cornwall were the speakers of the evening and gave very interesting talks. Mr. Tibbets will organize a boys' and girls' club and they are requested to meet at the baseball grounds Saturday afternoon at three o'clock. Winn Walker says there's a baseball game to be pulled off, too. Be sure and come.

COMMISSIONERS FOR MILLARD COUNTY

Hiett E. Maxfield, Chairman, Delt.
John Beckstrand, Meadow.
Carl Brown, Scipio.

DELTA TOWN OFFICERS.

Pres. of the Board, F. W. Cottrell.
Members:—W. E. Bunker, James Wilkins, George Dobson, Avery Bishop.
Clerk, Geo. E. Banks.
Treasurer, A. L. Broderick.

DELTA COMMERCIAL CLUB.

A. C. Sorenson, President.
O. A. Anderson, Vice-President.
Rev. C. H. Hamilton, Secretary.

DELTA FARM BUREAU

D. F. Peterson, President.
E. L. Lyman, Vice-President.
A. P. Wallace, Secretary-Treasurer

Personal Items

Mrs. M. M. Wilkins is adding two rooms to her residence on Main St.

—) (—

H. A. Hansen, contractor, has the job of building five residences for R. L. Whicker.

—) (—

Mrs. Marion Kilpack visited relatives and friends in Cedar City last week and the first of this.

—) (—

Mrs. Ben Douglas returned home the last of last week from Lehi, where she has been visiting with relatives.

—) (—

Miss Ella Patten visited friends in Delta last Tuesday, returning to her home in Eureka Wednesday morning.

—) (—

A good Royal Western Blacksmith's Blower, one foot in diameter, cheap at the Delta Furniture Store.   a19-26

—) (—

N. S. Bishop and family drove over to Fillmore the latter part of last week where they visited until last Tuesday.

—) (—

As a result of contributions which were recently taken up, the star spangled banner now floats over the new school house.

C. W. Madsen of the sugar factory force is having a two-roomed residence erected east of Bert Johnson's home.

—) (—

R. K. Stewart returned home yesterday from Southern Utah, where he has been working for the past several months for the Government.

—) (—

The four room residence of Walter Moffitts is nearing completion and will be ready for occupancy in the very near future.

—) (—

Alma Rosenberg, father of Mrs. H. A. Hansen, who has been wintering his sheep near Clear Lake, visited Delta the first of the week.

—) (—

The big sheds which have recently been built by McCrnick's for the use of machinery by the Consolidated W. & M. Co. blew down during last night's wind storm.

—) (—

A. L. Broderick has started the erection of his two-story brick building just east of the bank on Clark Street. Eugene Gardner has the contract for the brick work.

—) (—

Mrs. T. C. Gronning and children came up from Milford in their car and was accompanied from this point to Salina and Scipio by her sister's Miss Louise Fuller and Mrs. Wm. Stanley, of Baker, Oregon, where they will make a short visit with relatives.

Robert Wicker is about the most enterprising resident we have in Delta these days. He has already rected two residences for rent and has let the contract for five more.

—) (—

S. A. Bunker, Ben Bunker, Mrs. Josephine Walker and Miss Helen Bunker arrived here from Delta last Friday and will spend some time here, visiting.—News, St. George.

—) (—

Mesdames Norm Lambert and J. W. Thurston entertained the O. Z. O. club at the home of the former last night. A good crowd was present and a delightful evening was spent.

—) (—

The Delta Beet Sugar Corporation is arranging to move its office in the corner room of the McCornick building which will be temporary quarters until their office building at the factory is completed.

—) (—

Mrs. Leslie Lewis, of St. Anthony, Idaho, came last Friday evening for an extended visit with Mr. Lewis' parents, Mr. and Mrs. Cass Lewis. Leslie will join her here in about three weeks.

—) (—

Attorney Edw. D. Dunn was down the first of the week looking after his farm in the Abraham district. While here he received a Case gas-tractor and will put in about fifty acres of alfalfa this spring. He was accompanied by A. Hochguertel of Franklin, Mont., who will operate the engine.

Millard County Chronicle
May 3, 1917

DESERET DOINGS

Spencer Bennett, who was taken very ill Sunday last with appendicitis, was taken to Salt Lake Tuesday to be operated on, accompanied by his father. We hope for a speedy recovery.

* * * *

Mr. and Mrs. Frank Hinckley, former residents of Deseret, have returned and are occupying the residence of Mrs. Virgil Kelly on Main Street.

* * * *

A. R. Crownover is in Salt Lake on a business trip.

* * * *

The members of the O. N. E. club entertained at a "High Jinks" party Saturday evening. A jolly ride in a "Ford Special" was enjoyed, after which dainty refreshments were served, and dancing indulged in for a short time at the Passey Confectionery, Hinckley. The invited guests were: Messrs. Arthur Cahoon, Ernest Black, Clarence Moody, Axel Jensen, John Cahoon, Carl Theobald, William Shaw, George Cahoon, A. R. Crownover and Mark Dunn.

* * * *

M. C. Webb, who is suffering from dropsy, is confined to his room at this writing.

* * * *

Mrs. J. M. Moody returned Thursday from a ten days' visit to Salt Lake.

The M. I. A. meet will be held in Deseret Friday, May 4th. The committee in charge assures everyone a good time.

* * * *

Hyrum Cahoon, Jr., has returned to Joy.

* * * *

Last Friday evening a farewell party was given for Bryan Petty, one of our most popular young men, who with Alvin Peterson enlisted to serve their country. The hall was decorated in the national colors. A large crowd was in attendance, and many friends accompanied the boys to the train to wish them good luck and safe return.

* * * *

Mrs. Josephine Petty left Tuesday evening to bid her son good-bye before leaving for San Francisco.

Delta News Notes.

Call at the Delta Furniture Store for Gasoline and Oil Stoves. (m3-10)

—)(—

Born, on April 28th, to Mr. and Mrs. Sam Smith of Delta, a 11-pound girl.

—)(—

Attorney Higgins of Fillmore was in town last Saturday looking after legal business.

—)(—

Mrs. C. O. Davis and son Billie leave tomorrow for a visit with relatives in Ogden.

—)(—

Dave Conger and Willard Lee of Moapa Valley are here looking for farming locations.

—)(—

Born, to Mr. and Mrs. Chas. Sampson of the South Tract, on April the 24th, a fine girl baby.

—)(—

Mrs. H. F. Aller and daughter are here this week from Salt Lake, visiting Mr. Aller and others.

—)(—

Alma Greenwood came in Monday from his home at American Fork and is looking after his land interests.

—)(—

Supt. C. D. Fulmer, of the Sugar factory, accompanied by Mrs. Fulmer made a business trip to Provo and Payson.

—)(—

Superintendent Fulmer did the hoisting, after which a verse of "My Country, 'Tis of Thee" was sung by those present.

—)(—

Bishop Maxfield was called to the city this morning on matter pertaining to the Sevier Land & Water Co.'s irrigation work.

County Commissioner Maxfield went to Fillmore Monday to attend the regular monthly meeting of the Board of Commissioners.

—)(—

J. H. Jenkins, manager of the Delta Beet Sugar Corporation, and Mrs. Jenkins are in Salt Lake this week. Mrs. Jenkins will return to her home in Pueblo temporarily.

—)(—

D. J. Diton, bookkeeper for the Delta Beet Sugar Corporation, is expected here the last of the week from Pueblo and will make Delta his future home.

—)(—

The boys and girls who passed the Eighth grade this spring were Hattie Ward, Verda Turner, Verdell Rigby, Owen Bunker and Alfred Lisonbee.

—)(—

D. D. Rogers, who has been employed in the Delta schools, leaves today for his home in Kanosh, where he will put in the summer working on the farm.

—)(—

Miss Ella Callister and children, of Blackfoot, Idaho, has been visiting relatives here for the past week. Mr. Callister is looking for a location in Millard county.

—)(—

Word comes from Panguitch, Utah, of the death of John Daly, a former well respected resident of this place. He died very suddenly, April 21st, of heart failure.

—)(—

The latest recruits to the army are Went. Lewis and a lad named Helmet Olson.

"A Lass of the Lumberlands." A big new serial play starting in Delta next Monday evening. Be there and see the first episode. A punch in every reel.

—)(—

Rev. Hamilton expects a student minister here the last of the week to fill his pulpit while he and Mrs. Hamilton are on their missionary trip in the southern part of the State this spring.

—)(—

The big production of "Civilization" at the Princess Theatre drew a large audience, Saturday night, and those we heard express themselves said it was a marvelous production.

—)(—

We have experienced some fine showers the past week which will materially aid in the bringing on of crops and hay. Over on the East Side they had some very heavy rains the last of the week.

—)(—

Misses Sylvia Turner and Louisa Jones left this morning for Salt Lake. Miss Turner will visit in the city and in Payson for a few days and return home. Miss Jones expects to make a more extended stay in the city.

—)(—

Mrs. Bill Sprunt, who is an employee at the Sugar factory, is here looking for a house to rent. Their goods together with those of Russel Sprunt, manager of the Delta Lumber & Hardware Co., are on the road to Delta.

—)(—

H. G. Busenbark, former editor of the Chronicle, is here visiting old friends and looking up a paper location. Mr. Busenbark notes a marked improvement in the country since he left here over two years ago and is very enthusiastic over its future.

—)(—

People who shoot around with twenty-two rifles should be careful as to the direction their bullets take. The first of the week while Irene Lewis was in the backyard of the hotel some one fired a gun and the shot struck the ground not more than two feet from her.

—)(—

The last of last week we received a box of about the finest asparagus we have ever tasted, from Moapa Garden Co., of Logan, Nevada, which is preparing to do a mail order business in fruits and vegetables in this part of the country. See the ad. in the Chronicle relating thereto.

Misses Sylvia, Viola and Melva Turner entertained at a May Day party at their home Tuesday evening. The rooms were decorated in blue and white. Games and music were enjoyed, after which luncheon was served. About thirty guests were present and a fine time was had.

—)(—

Last Saturday was flag-raising day at the Delta Sugar fetory. A handsome silk flag, a present from the F. J. Burch Tent & Awning Co. of Pueblo, Colo., was used for the occasion, and was raised in the presence of about one hundred twenty-five of the employees and a few citizens from town. The raising was an impromptu affair, or more people from town would have attended.

HINCKLEY HAPPENINGS

Geo. E. Hume, of the First National Bank of Oxnard, Cal., accompanied by his wife, has been visiting at the home of R. A. Nelson and family of Hinckley. Mr. and Mrs. Hume are taking a trip through the Eastern States and Canada and will return by the C. P. Railroad to their home in Oxnard.

* * * *

Geo. L. Tucker, who recently moved to Hinckley from California, and who was lathing a house for Bill Blake a mile and a half west of town, had a very exciting time last Wednesday with a "Bob" cat. The wildcat came into the house and made a jump for him. He had some lathes in his hand and knocked it from the scaffold to the floor. The cat was pretty badly used up for the time being and made off and crawled under the water trough. Mr. Tucker closed him in there and thot he would wait for assistance to finish him. After being there for some time the animal got out and attacked a horse in the lot, jumping and catching it by the throat. It failed to get a good hold on the horse and fell to the ground, making off thru the field where Mr. Blake was plowing. It stopped at an irrigation ditch for a drink and was dispatched by him with a shovel.

SUGARVILLE SIFTINGS

Ruff and John Clark are putting in grain on the Lamson place.

* * * *

Mrs. Christianson of Salt Lake is visiting her daughter, Mrs. T. Chronholm.

* * * *

Mr. and Mrs. Roy Jones are the proud parents of a fine baby boy born May 3rd.

* * * *

Fred Ashby, of California, is visiting his sister Mrs. Dale; also looking after his land interests here.

* * * *

The Friendship Thimble Club will meet next Wednesday afternoon with Mrs. Anson and Mrs. Bruner at the home of the former.

* * * *

Don't forget there will be a big dance at Sugarville Saturday evening, May 26th. Further notice next week.

* * * *

Herman Gater is here from San Jose, California, looking after his ranch. He says the fruit in that section is hurt by frost much worse than reported.

Death of Spencer Bennett.

Spencer Bennett, son of Mr. and Mrs. John R. Bennett of Deseret, who has been working on the sugar factory, died in a hospital in Salt Lake City last Thursday and was buried in Deseret Saturday.

He became sick the latter part of week before last and was taken to his home where he seemed to improve for a short time. He later became much worse and was taken to Salt Lake where an operation for appendicitis was performed Wednesday morning and he died Thursday.

Spencer Bennett was married and leaves a wife and child to mourn their loss. The sympathy of the community is extended to them and to the bereaved parents.

WOODROW ITEMS

George Webster has been on the sick list during the past week, but is now convalescent.

* * * *

Some of our enterprising neighbors are planting out trees, we notice. We wish more were doing so.

* * * *

Preaching by C. H. Hamilton at Woodrow Sunday at 11:45 a. m. immediately following the Sunday school. All are cordially invited.

* * * *

A dance will be held in the new hall Saturday evening, May 12th, for the benefit of the Woodrow band. The boys hope for a fine turnout to support our home talent.

* * * *

The Calico ball of last Friday evening was a marked success, and attracted many visitors from Delta, Hinckley, Deseret and Abraham. The hall is none too large to accommodate the people.

* * * *

We are still hoping for real spring weather sometime in the near future. We are highly favored, however, over other places in America. We read of a heavy snow storm in Texas or elsewhere and are thankful we are in the Pahvant valley.

* * * *

The Pritchett family, who sold their ranch in Woodrow two years ago to Argo Brown, are touring through Utah on their way to Powell, Wyoming, in an auto car. They are making an extended visit to Mr. and Mrs. Rock and are receiving a glad welcome from their many friends. They state that the marked improvements during their absence are a great surprise and pleasure to them, and they are very glad to get back to the Pahvant, if only for a short visit.

TRUE BLUE.

Recruits from Millard county have been more numerous of late and the martial and patriotic spirit has begun to swell within the bosoms of many of our citizens. Yesterday June Williams and Lawrence Christensen, of Oasis, and Stanley Shaw of Hinckley, joined the colors and went to Salt Lake to be sworn into the service. They were given a big send-off by the people of their towns.

The latest recruits from Delta are Went Lewis, son of Mr. and Mrs. Cass Lewis; Johnny Miller, son of A. Miller, of the Delta Furniture store, and Ward Love, son of S. E. Love of the harness shop. The boys have gone to Salt Lake and taken the examination for the navy and all passed. They returned the fore part of the week and are awaiting orders to report. All training stations being full now, they may be called to their duties at any time within a month. When the time comes for them to go we should give them a big farewell.

Delta News Items.

A nice Commode and Kitchen Safe at the Delta Furniture Store. (m3-10

—)(—

W. H. Livingston was down from Salt Lake the first of the week looking after his business affairs.

—)(—

Mrs. Zina Grey left Sunday for Beaver, where she will make an extended visit with relatives.

—)(—

The infant daughter of Mr. and Mrs. Jim Turner died Tuesday. The body was taken to Fillmore for burial.

—)(—

Miss Glenna Riding has returned home from St. George, where she has been attending the Dixie Academy the past winter.

—)(—

Bishop Maxfield was again called to Salt Lake the first of the week on business matters pertaining to the Sevier Land & Water Co.

—)(—

Jas. Jenkins and I. E. Gardner, brothers-in-law of Wm. N. Gardner, are here from Provo visiting and looking over the country with a view of investing.

—)(—

Wm. H. Gardner came down from Salem the first of the week to help with the construction of A. L. Broderick's brick building, which is going up on Clark Street.

—)(—

Miss Melba Steele, who has been attending the academy at St. George for the past nine months, returned home the first of the week and is assisting at the Hub Merc.

—)(—

The Alpha farm boys have been having a lot of grief lately as a result of their caterpillar tractor sliding into an irrigation ditch. They broke it pretty badly in getting it out and have just received their repairs for it.

—)(—

Frank Copening, accompanied by Mrs. Copening, were Delta visitors the fore part of the week. Mr. and Mrs. Copening and family expect to go to Cuba in June where Frank will be busy for the coming year with his oil interests.

Mrs. C. B. Penniston and two children arrived from Omaha the last of last week and will make their future home in Delta. They will live in the house west of the Delta hotel formerly occupied by W. J. Robbins. Mr. Penniston is employed as bookkeeper at the Delta Land & Water Co. office.

—)(—

We need a lot a live correspondents for the Chronicle in this valley to help boost things. If your community is not represented in the paper take it up with us. We've got the ball rolling. Get in and help us make 'er grow. It's for the good of all.

—)(—

We have just received the details of the big oil well recently brot in near Havana, Cuba, by Frank Copening thru having visited in Delta this week and thru a Havana daily paper. We will probably give our readers the details next week, they having been crowded out this week.

—)(—

F. D. Kimball, Salt Lake banker and also a heavy stockholder in the Sevier Land & Water Co., was in town the last of the week and accompanied by Bishop Maxfield made a trip to Fillmore to meet a number of citizens who are interested in getting water thru this company.

—)(—

The Messrs. Clyde Bunker and Ralph Sanford, have gone to Cedar City to attend the Commencement exercises of the Branch Agricultural College, from which institution Ralph is graduating this spring and of which Clyde is a member of the Alumni association.

—)(—

The editor thinks he has one of the classiest autos in the country now in one of the beautiful Overland "Country Clubs," which Agent R. H. Robison brot down from Salt Lake Monday. Agent Robison and the Overland people on the other hand think (and right at that) that they have struck an excellent proposition in the advertising columns of the Chronicle which space they have contracted for. They will soon be telling its readers of the many virtues of the "Country Club" and other Overland makes. Watch for their ads.

Millard County Chronicle
May 17, 1917

ABRAHAM ARTICLES

Mrs. Bohn's boy Dan had the misfortune of getting his leg broken. While out riding, Mr. Hogan's team ran away and ran into the horse which Dan was on, knocking it down. Dan will be in bed for some eight weeks.

* * * *

The Abraham ball boys played ball in Sugarville, Sunday, and came home beten. 13 to 11; but the next time they play they win.

Will Fullmer and Nathan Lake were Delta visitors Sunday. They enjoyed their ride in, but not their walk back.

* * * *

There ws quite a crowd of young folks that went to Hinckley Friday to attend a dance, but as there wasn't any they came back disappointed.

* * * *

Miss Etta Meecham of Hinckley

has been in Abraham visiting the Young's since Friday.

* * * *

Mrs. Sherick had the misfortune of losing her $20 turkey gobbler.

* * * *

Harry Hall's brother has been visiting Abraham the past few days and expects to buy some land here.

* * * *

Mr. Leroy Young expects to leave for Salt Lake in a few days.

DESERET DOINGS

Mr. and Mrs. John H. Western and family motored to Fillmore Tuesday on business.

* * * *

Mrs. M. C. Webb, who has been ill for some time, is not well at this writing.

* * * *

Miss Mable Anderson, of Fillmore is spending the week in Deseret, the guest of Miss Norma Moody.

* * * *

The O. N. E. girls were entertained at the home of Miss Blanche Dewsnup last week.

* * * *

Mrs. Josephine Petty, Mrs. Dora Western, and the Misses Edna and Isma Cropper have gone to Mammoth to attend the wedding reception of Mr. Leroy Hanson and Miss Rowena Larson.

* * * *

Mother's Day was very fittingly celebrated here last Sunday.

* * * *

We are looking forward to the Whittaker musical, which will be given soon. It promises to be a real treat.

* * * *

'r. Geo. A. Hone is in town for a few days. His family expect to join him soon, and locate at Joy for the summer.

* * * *

Elmer Petty is building a five-roomed house on East Main Street. He expects to have it ready for occupancy by the first of the month.

* * * *

Mr Cline and Mr. Green passed through Friday last, enroute to Joy to continue work on their mine.

* * * *

A number of our townspeople visited the Demonstration train at Delta last Thursday.

* * * *

Miss Ada Hinckley arrived last Sunday to spend the summer with her parents, Mr and Mrs. Frank Hinckley.

DELTA NEWS NOTES.

W. W. Warnock of Hinckley is erecting a brick house in Hinckley.

—)(—

Chas. Blake, of Provo, is visiting in Delta for a few days.

—)(—

County Commissioner Maxfield is in Fillmore this week attending to county business.

—)(—

Come out and enjoy the best serial yet, "The Lass of the Lumberland." Just starting. m17-1t

—)(—

Jas. Works, manager of the Bonneville Lumber Co., is in Fillmore this week on jury duty.

—)(—

The infant son of Mr. and Mrs. Elmer Bjarnson died Tuesday morning.

—)(—

John Baker, of Salt Lake, is visiting with his sister, Mrs. R. C. Bates.

—)(—

G. L. Huff, son of Henry Huff of Oasis, has been engaged to work in the Bonneville Lumber yards of Delta.

—)(—

C. C. Lauck, of Bingham, and Mrs. G. E. Jones, of Salt Lake City, are here attending to business matters concerning real estate.

—)(—

The murder trial of Davis, the fellow who killed Kelling at Lynndyl last November, is now being tried at the county seat.

—)(—

W. H. Pace received a car of Fords Tuesday. He reports that the shipment was over a month late in getting around.

—)(—

An item we overlooked last week was the birth of a baby boy to Mr. and Mrs. A. L. Anderson, of the South Tract.

Lorin Turner was in Delta Wednesday on his way to Fillmore where he will be a witness in the Kelling murder case.

—)(—

Miss Stringer, of the Delta Land & Water office force, was here from Milford the last of last week and the first of this.

—)(—

Messrs. Stearns and Schwarz of the Stearns-Roger Co. arrived here today on a tour of inspection of the sugar factories the firm is constructing.

—)(—

"The Lass of the Lumberland" contains more thrilling and beautiful scenes than any other serial ever shown in Delta. m17-1t

—)(—

A. Billings and son George are in Salt Lake City where Mr. Billings is taking treatment for condition of the jaw which came about thru some badly ulcerated teeth.

—)(—

Mrs. Wm. Stanley, who has been visiting Mrs. Harry Aller and Miss Louise Fuller, her sisters, left Wednesday for her home in La Grande, Oregon.

—)(—

Ralph Saanford returned the first of the week from Cedar City where Ralph graduated from the Branch Agricultural college. He also visited St. George while away.

—)(—

Dr. and Mrs. Hamilton of Milford were here Wednesday looking for a residence in which to move. The Doctor is contemplating locating here for the practice of medicine.

—)(—

Don't miss seeing the Serial, "The Lass of the Lumberland" at the Princess Theatre, Delta, each Monday night. The peer of all serials. Just starting. m17-1t

—)(—

The Delta bank building is being equipped with hot and cold water system. The move is of great convenience to the bank and the Bank hotel and will be fully appreciated by all.

E. H. Clarke, who recently sold his farm near Abraham to D. H. Livingston, and family left last Thursday for Oakland, Calif., near where they expect to make their future home.

—)(—

As an illustration of the magnitude of the work which is being done at the sugar factory and the immensity of the thing itself, last Tuesday there were fourteen cars of construction material switched onto the factory sidings. Some enterprise, eh?

—)(—

Work began the last of last week on the new picture play-house, and from the way they are rushing things it will but a short time until we will have a picture house of the most modern type. Its completion will also add two nice, modern store-rooms to the business section of Delta.

—)(—

Hirum Chitterden, of Canada, has purchased eighty acres of H. E. Duffin's farm two and one-half miles south of Delta. Mr. Chitterden and family have already taken possession of their farm. He has left for Hurricane where he expects to find a climate more congenial to his wife's health.

—)(—

A. D. Ryan reports the following land sales which he has closed recently: 20 acres R. T. Patterson, 20 acres Mrs. Marshall Shapp, Omaha, and 40 acres Mrs. Tillie Cattern, Lincoln, Neb., to D. H. Livingston. Mr. Ryan says he has having many calls for farm loans for improvement purposes which he is able to handle on land with clear titles.

—)(—

We would like to see a little work done on the roads and bridges around Delta. They are in an abominable shape. Some of the bridges across some of the canals are practically impassable. One we call to mind in particular is about a mile east on Clark Street. The roads in this vicinity are worse than in any other part of the valley and if any is responsible for their condition they should be fixed at once.

SUGARVILLE SIFTINGS

Big dance at Sugarville May 26th.

* * * *

W. G. McKittrick is here from San Diego, Calif., to look after his ranch.

* * * *

Mr. McLane and family motored to the mountins last Sunday. They visited the Deseret Mines, then took the trail up in the narrow canyons. Leona Seams accompanied them and all reported a fine time.

* * * *

The Abraham boys came to Sugarville Sunday with a ball team picked from Abraham, Deseret and Sutherland and were trimmed to the tune of 14 to 7 by the home team. The Sugarville team will play Sutherland on Saturday, May 26th, at Sutherland. Don't forget the date. Everyone come!

SUTHERLAND SEARCHLIGHTS

The Lloyds are erecting a five-roomed house upon their place.

* * * *

Miss Florence Holdredge is working at Britt's.

* * * *

Miss Leota Clark spent several days at Novilla Place.

* * * *

Mr. Sanford has the posts in the ground and is going to fence his place.

Mr. Adams was taken seriously ill while working in the field last Saturday.

* * * *

Little June Bassett is having a serious time with erysipelas in her left foot and leg.

* * * *

Harry Ottley's entertained the Davis family and Miss Leota Clark of Woodrow on Sunday.

* * * *

Mr. and Mrs. Rogers and daughter and Mr. Wright of Delta were guests Sunday at the Davis ranch.

Word has been received from Mrs. Lloyd that her health is much improved since she has been at Provo.

* * * *

The Bee Hive girls went on a hike Wednesday afternoon. They started from Sanfords and hiked to the river, then back to Mrs. Walker's, where they were entertained with a delicious lunch. The next meeting will be held at the school house on Wednesday evening.

Millard County Chronicle
May 31, 1917

OAK CITY HAPPENINGS

Oak City is still on the map. The reason you have not heard from us for so long is because so many of the young folks have been away. Now that they have returned home things have brightened up and the town seems different.

After one week of heavy rain storms, the sun has again made its appearance and practically all of the gardens are up and are looking fine. If frost does not interfere we will have a heavy fruit crop.

Leland Neilson, of Hinckley was the guest of Miss Wanda Dutson last Sunday.

Ervin Jacobson and wife have returned from Idaho, where they have been spending a few of the winter months with Mrs. Jacobson's parents.

The "Helo" swarm of bee-hive girls are preparing a celebration for Registration Day. The following is the program for the day:

The dawning of the day will be ushered in by volleys and thunders from the Germans. Hoisting of the flag by swarm, during which bugle calls and salutes will be rendered. Serenading of the town by the band.

Millard County Chronicle
June 7, 1917

ABRAHAM ARTICLES

Oscar Bohn is now working at the Livingston Ranch.

Ora Lake's big black mare has been very sick the past few days.

Con Faragson, who has been working on the Livingston ranch, departed for his home two or three days ago.

Bill Fullmer and Nate Lake leave for Milford the first of June, where they intend to spend the summer.

Roy, the youngest son of Mr. and Mrs. Young has been quite sick the past few days.

There was quite a bit of excitement Tuesday afternoon when the team belonging to Val Black ran away. They ran from C. A. Vorwaller's and past Young's but were finally stopped by Ora Lake.

Mrs. Norman Nation of Salt Lake City, has been visiting her friends of Abraham, the H.B. and Ora Lakes, since Sunday, but returned to Deseret Tuesday evening, where her husband is in business with the Deseret Garage.

Mr. and Mrs. Walter Stout of Leamington had the sad misfortune of losing their oldest son, Douglas, with pneumonia. He had chicken pox also. Mrs. Stout was a former resident of Abraham and they have the deepest sympathy of this community.

Big Land Deal Pending.

John Merrill of Onterio, Calif., was here this week with J. Q. Ayers looking over the country. Mr. Merrill is one of the big farmers of California and was here as a representative of interests which are looking for a 1000-acre farm on which to raise sugar beets and do general farming. He said he found the country looking 100 per cent better than he had expected to find it and took options on 1000 acres in the Abraham district, near the McCornick-Livingston ranch. Others interested are expected soon to look over the proposition and close the deal.

Born, to Mr. and Mrs. Henry Bennett, Tuesday 5th, a baby girl.

—)(—

Eugene Gardner spent last Sunday in Oak City.

—)(—

Tom Chapman is building a residence in the extreme southern part of the city.

—)(—

FOUND:—Mud chain for large car. Call at Chas. Ashby's, north of Delta. j7-1t

—)(—

LaGrand Law returned from Provo Sunday, where he has been attending school at the B. Y. U.

—)(—

FOR SALE:—$75 Stewart steel Range, cheap, used three weeks. Bank Hotel. j7tf

—)(—

Born, to Mr. and Mrs. R. W. Britt, of Sutherland district, Wednesday, a baby boy.

—)(—

Three aliens were arrested in Delta for not registering. They were Mexicans.

—)(—

Mrs. Wm. N. Gardner left last week for Salem, Utah, where she will make an extended visit with hers and Mr. Gardner's parents.

—)(—

GREEN PEAS:—Best wrinkled sort at 6½cts per pound in second zone. B. Jarvis, Jr., St. George. Ut. j7-1tp.

—)(—

Mr. and Mrs. James Smith, of Kaysville was here the first of the week looking after some land they have on the North Tract.

—)(—

Mr. and Mrs. Edgar Jeffery left Wednesday for Salt Lake t attend conference. They drove thru in their car.

—)(—

Misses Orena Law and Louise Fuller left this morning for Salt Lake, where they will visit for some time with relatives and friends.

—)(—

Those who were not out to the concert, rendered by the Whitaker family missed a fine treat. The entertainment was most enjoyable and pleasing to all who were there.

G. Campbell, of Evans, Idaho, arrived here the last of last week with an emigrant car and had it sent out to Sugarville where he will make his home.

—)(—

W. H. Pace, of the Pace Auto Agency has moved his family here from Price and they are occupying the J. H. Riding house just east of the Bakery, on Clark St.

—)(—

J. Q. Ayers, who has been here several times in the last two years as a real estate agent, came up the last of the past week with a party looking for land.

—)(—

R. M. Rogers drove up to Salt Lake in his car last week and on his return was accompanied by his daughter, Miss Evadeen, who will visit with him for some time.

—)(—

Word comes from Bunkerville, Nevada that Mr. and Mrs. Orson Sprague are the proud parents of a 9 pound baby boy. Mr. and Mrs. Sprague resided here before going to Nevada.

—)(—

The Social Betterment Club gave a dance in the Delta Opera House last Friday night. Ice cream was sold during the evening. There was a good crowd present and everyone seemed to have a good time.

—)(—

FOR SALE:—Canned Yellow Peaches per doz. qts., $2.25, Canned Beef Steaks, 1 pound cans per doz, $2.35, and 2 pound cans, per dozen $4.20, by mail prepaid in 2nd zone. Southern Utah Packing Co., Leeds, Utah. j7tt

—)(—

On account of there being a case of diptheria in Sutherland the C. C. club girls were compelled to postpone their dance, which was scheduled for last Saturday night. They do not know definately when they can give it.

—)(—

A. D. Ryan of Hinckley who made application some time ago to join the U. S. engineer corps, received word the other day that his services were not needed at this time, this arm of the army being already supplied.

—)(—

Among those leaving for Salt Lake today for conference were Mr.

and Mrs. J. Avery Bishop and children, Mrs. E. D. Knight and daughter, Clara, and Mrs. Abner Johnson and daughter Chloe.

—)(—

Frank Copening has let the contract for three modern four-roomed bungalows which will be erected on his lots just north of his present residence. Moffitt Bros. have the contract for the construction and are already busy with the excavation.

—)(—

D. A. Bunker came down from Bingham Sunday and was accompanied by Geo. Chandler of the same place and Jack Rockledge, his son-in-law of Salt Lake. Mr. Chandler is a financier of Utah and was here looking over the town and country in regard to some investments.

—)(—

The Delta State Bank reports the sale of the first Liberty Bonds subscribed for in Delta. This speaks well for the spirit prompting the purchase, and it is sincerely to be hoped that others will follow this good example and likewise take some of these Government securities.

—)(—

O. W. Israelsen, irrigation expert with the Agricultural College experiment station, is here and on the East Side this week studying Millard County's irrigation systems in connection with Co. Agent Welch. Mr. Israelsen is here to give any assistance he may be able to render to all who have irrigation problems to solve.

—)(—

Carl McQuown and family of Los Angeles came in last week and will remain here during the summer. Mrs. McQuown is a sister of C. Webster south of town. Mr. McQuown has disposed of his interests in California and will look around here for a farm. They are living on the Webster farm.

—)(—

M. J. Greenwood and family came down from Salt Lake the first of the week for a visit with Uncle Jim Melville and family and other relatives. Mrs. Greenwood being a daughter of Mr. and Mrs. Melville. Mr. Greenwood and Mr. Melville went to Salt Lake yesterday on a business mission and will return the last of the week.

C. M. Hansen of the Nelson-Ricks Creamery Company was here the last of last week and made arrangements with S. E. Love to take charge of a creamery station which the company will open in a short time in Delta. Mr. Hansen says the station will be open as soon as material can be had with which to supply the station.

—)(—

Wm. Evans, of McGill, Nev., has purchased the Calvert place of Mr. Mulford of Richmond, Kansas, who but recently bought it of Mr. Calvert. Mr. Evans was here just before Mr. Mulford bought the place and it looked good to him. He came back last week with the idea of buying and found it already sold but persuaded Mr. Mulford to sell it to him at an advanced price.

—)(—

Mr. and Mrs. W. G. Bickley left Tuesday morning for their home at Beaver after spending ten days with their daughter, Mrs. R. J. Law.

Mr. Bickley directed the oratorio, which was given at the Ward Hall last Sunday night. The proceeds from it amounted to $66.65. This will go toward buying a new church organ.

—)(—

The case of Chas. E. Norton, vs. the Delta Land & Water, and a number of settlers on the North Tract will be argued in the Supreme court on June 11th. Attorney Melville, who represents a number of the settlers states that the former court failed to reach a decision in this and about thirty other cases before the change in the personel of the court, and that all these cases will be re-argued and not re-tried as we mentioned in our last issue.

—)(—

The Salt Lake Tribune reports that a number of subscribers for stock in the Intermountain Rural Credit Association have started suit to recover the money they paid on their subscriptions, attorney Melville states that he has started suit against the same company to recover promisory notes which of other clients he will file petition for an order permitting his clients to join in the suit in Salt Lake City.

—)(—

OATS:—Idaho Oats on hand all the time for feed or seed. A. B. Ward & Co. a12tf

---

Death of Fredrick Freese.

The whole community was shocked by the sudden death of one of its popular young men when Frederick Freese, the eldest son of Mr. and Mrs. Henry Freese of Sutherland passed away Friday, p. m., after an illness of 36 hours, with diptheria.

Mr. Freese was 18 years of age. A young man of exemplary character and industrious habits, who will be sorely missed socially.

Much sympathy is expressed to his bereaved parents, as was evidenced by the large number of families represented when his remains were laid at rest in Delta, Saturday afternoon in spite of the private funeral necessitated by the contagious nature of the disease.

The Reverend Geo. Caldwell was at the grave and in a few well-chosen words consigned all that was mortal of Fritz to the earth, but gave to the sorrowing relatives and friends the assurance that Fritz still lives and that the life so abruptly ended on the earthly plane continues to exist under perfect conditions in the spiritual realm.

There is a day of sunny rest,
For every dark and troubled night
And grief may bide an evening guest,
But joy shall come with early light.
And thou who o'er thy son's low bier
Sheddeth the bitter tears like rain,
Know thou, a brighter happier sphere
Will give him to thou arms again.

OFFICIAL FIGURES OF REGISTRATION IN MILLARD.

Following are the official figures of the number of registrations of youths in Millard County between the ages of 21 and 30 both inclusive.

Fillmore, 102; Meadow 41; Kanosh 49; Deseret 38; Oak City 31; Leamington 23; Holden 43; Scipio 58; Oasis 29; Hinckley 78; Burbank 11; Smithville 8; Abraham 8; Clear Lake 4; Black Rock 18; Garrison 9; Delta 116; Lynndyl 52; Sutherland 29; Woodrow 47, making a total of 808 in the entire county. No disturbance of any nature marred the day in the County.

OAK CITY HAPPENINGS.

The celebration of June 5th was a great success. The "Helo" swarm of the Bee Hive girls were highly complemented upon their work. With the exception of one girl, everyone was loyal to the celebration.

* * * *

Great excitement was aroused was aroused Wednesday morning, when a man was found in a near by field asleep. He was thot to be a German spy at first but upon further investigation he was proved to be only the "quiter" who caused one girl's disloyalty of the "Turn about is Fair Play" dance.

* * * *

The Whittaker family gave a concert Thursday night. Following it was a dance. Everyone reports a good time.

* * * *

Dr. and Mrs. Broaddus were in town Saturday.

* * * *

Lynndyl played our boys a game of baseball Saturday. They won by one point. It was a very interesting game and we hope they will come again. The dance which followed was enjoyed by all, especially by Marthy, Lizzie and Dolly.

HINCKLEY HAPPENINGS

Miss Claris Erickson and Leon Finlayson were married last week at Salt Lake.

* * * *

Miss Dean Marsden, former teacher in the Millard Academy, and David Richards went to Salt Lake last week and were married.

* * * *

The H. E. A. is again holding their regular meetings after the busy season and will meet on the Relief Society lawn at 3, p. m., Friday. They will visit the nearby gardens and gather points from the owners, after which they will return and discuss garden problems.

* * * *

A baby girl was born to Mr. and Mrs. Spencer Wright last week. Mother and little one doing fine.

* * * *

Mr. and Mrs. Carter have a new baby at their home.

* * * *

Mrs. Richard Parker has gone to Idaho, where she will visit some time with her parents and those of Mr. Parker.

* * * *

Mrs. Isabelle Hinton is here visiting her parents, Mr. and Mrs. John Hilton.

* * * *

Many Hinckley people went to Salt Lake to attend the June conference.

SUGARVILLE SIFTINGS

Mr. and Mrs. Ira Creek are entertaining two of Mr. Creek's sisters from Montpelier, Ohio.

* * * *

The Sunflower Sunday school contest was won by the "Blue" and they will entertain the "Red" with an ice cream party Friday evening at the home of Mr. and Mrs. Kinney.

* * * *

Don't forget the Vaudeville entertainment Saturday evening, June 16th, at the F. T. C. Library hall. Admission 25 and 15 cents. Refreshments free.

* * * *

Mr. and Mrs. Baker returned Wednesday to spend the summer at their ranch, north of Sugarville. They have been spending the winter in Pomona, Calif.

Despite the showers Sunday afternoon a very interesting game was played between the Deseret and Sugarville ball teams, the score being 8 to 5 in favor of Sugarville.

DELTA FORGING AHEAD

In last week's issue I spoke of the building conditions at Delta, and of the showing of prosperity reflected in the erection of business buildings and dwelling houses.

It is now the condition of business that attract others to us, that will be the subject of this article.

Delta is coming to its own. It is beginning to get recognition, and is conceded a place on the map. Notice is being taken of it. Business firms in the centers are canvassing it for trade or expectant trade; banks are looking to it; money lending firms are already in the field with agents beating the brush for borrowers to scoot out. Take it all in all the conditions are remarkably opposite to what formerly held.

Now the particular phase of the beckoning that Delta gives is found in the attractions it has for our neighbors.

Dr. Broaddus moves in from Hinckley, and makes a wise step.

Dan A. Kelly buys out Delbert Searle, and launches the incentive for Fillmore to mingle with us.

Next comes Noble G. PetPerson who owns the moving picture play house at Fillmore sees the possibilities ahead of him at Delta, and gets in the swim.

Next comes one of Fillmore's staunchest business men, Dan Stevens, into the field, whose clear insight into business, actual and potential sees this as the proper field. Dan Stevens is the moving spirit in the Stevens Mercantile Company of Fillmore, a man of high ideals, clear cut, schrewd and of unquestioned integrity; just such a man as Delta most needs, welcomes and will be proud of.

Big business knows that success is based on repeaters. Service must be rendered, satisfaction given, and the pleased customer willing to repeat. Once stung, twice shy is so true, so pat, that business to be big and to remain big, must give such good value that the customer is pleased with the transaction, the goods and the price and comes back. The best advertisement is the good-will of the trade.

Toward that end Dan Stevens has built up the large and successful business the firm has at Fillmore. Occupying one of the largest stores of that town, he commands a patronage in measure to his investment, and from the measure of success he has achieved has the wherewithal to establish himself here. A credit is the business man's best asset. We

bankers read, and read on the run. Dan Stevens merits the credit standing he has won.

The store he will establish will be on a strictly cash basis, no credit. His prices will invite the trade, his service will keep it.

He will open a big store, with stock large enough to meet the demand, finding at times a call for what mands of the populace to be served, is not carried, will promptly get it in.

That conditions in Delta are such as to attract merchants of varied lines, speaks well for the substantiality of the town. Those conditions are seen as actual, and felt to possess even greater possibilities for the future. One thing that spreads the good gospel better than any other medium is printer's ink. Dan Stevens uses it (and space) in the Progress of Fillmore, and gets results. He will use it here; and advertising will get the trade from it. Watch the columns of the Chronicle for his announcements.

We take pleasure in welcoming Mr. Stevens to us, and find it more than a pleasure to introduce him and his establishment to our readers. May he achieve the success he merits and may he find in Delta all the rewards he expects.

Frank Beckwith.

Bundle Shower Given.

Miss Olive Cook entertained at a bundle shower Tuesday evening, at her home north of town in honor of her sister Florence, who was married the 6th of this month in the Salt Lake Temple to John Workman. The house and lawn was beautifully decorated and lighted with lanterns. The guests assembled on the lawn, where games were played, music, recitations and songs enjoyed, also a few old time dances. Delicious refreshments were served after which the guests departed for the parlor, where the bundles were opened. The bride and groom received many beautiful and useful presents, one of which is worthy of special mention, it being a beautiful tatted piano scarf.

Mr. and Mrs. Workman will make Delta their home. They have the sincere wishes of the community for a long and happy married life.

SUGARVILLE SIFTINGS

Big dance at Sugarville Saturday evening, June 30th.

* * * *

Albert Watts was in Salt Lake last week on business.

* * * *

The entertainment given by the F. T. C. was a grand success and listened to by a large audience.

* * * *

J. B. Seams spent Saturday and Sunday with Ed Pearson and Fred Tingleaf on the South Tract.

* * * *

The Friendship Thimble club will be entertained next Wednesday afternoon by Mrs. Johnson and Mrs. Cochran at the house of the former.

* * * *

Rev. Caldwell will preach at the F. T. C. hall at 3. p. m. Sunday the 24th. His sermons are good and we hope everyone will turn out to hear them.

* * * *

E. D. Cady received the sad news on Tuesday of the death of his brother-in-law, Mr. Noble of California. Mrs. Noble, who spent several months at the Cady ranch last summer has been called to part with both, husband and daughter since returning to California. Our sympathy goes out to her.

* * * *

Last Monday, while raking hay, Byron Jacobs narrowly escaped a serious accident. The line of the harness broke and Mr. Jacobs stepped between the horses to fix it when they became frightened and started to run breaking the rake and slightly cutting one of the horses. Fortunately Byron escaped injury.

WOODROW ITEMS

Miss Ivie Holdredge is spending the week with Mrs. Webster.

* * * *

The Jolly Stitchers will be entertained by Mrs. Barben next Friday.

* * * *

Ludwig Vollhart is building a new residence on the Vollhart ranch.

* * * *

Mr. and Mrs. Wilbur Pervine, nee Helene Davis, spent Sunday in Woodrow.

* * * *

Preaching at Woodrow Sunday, June 24th at 8, p. m., by the Rev. Geo. Caldwell. All are cordially invited to attend.

* * * *

If you want to hear a fish story about the fish that took two men to haul it out of the water ask Mr. Webster.

* * * *

Mr. and Mrs. Jeff Clark and Miss Anna Clark took a trip to Fillmore last Thursday to attend the wedding of Miss Davis and Mr. Pervine.

* * * *

Mr. and Mrs. Geo. Webster, Mr. and Mrs. McLane and Mr. and Mrs. Theodore Britt spent a pleasant day at the spillway Sunday on a fishing trip.

* * * *

Miss Venice Barben, who has been visiting her former home at Midway, Utah, returned in time to assist the young ladies in entertaining the Friendship Thimble club at Sugarville last Wednesday.

* * * *

The Pritchett family have been obliged to defer their contemplated trip to Wyoming until next month, because of the heavy snow still remaining in a pass through which they wish to travel in their touring car.

* * * *

July 4th will be celebrated in Woodrow by a patroitic meeting in the community hall. Program at 1. Picnic supper at 5, p.m. Athletic games in the afternoon and an entertainment at night. The public is requested to participate in any way possible to make the day a success.

* * * *

So far everything looks promising for a good crop on all lines. The first cutting of alfalfa is now harvested and is far in excess of the same cutting last year. The beets are looking fine and the grain, both fall and spring crops are much more promising than at the same time last year.

SUTHERLAND SEARCHLIGHTS

Mr. Banks has moved his house on his place he bought out at Sugarville.

* * * *

Mr. and Mrs. Simeon Walker of Oak City spent Sunday in Sutherland.

* * * *

Mr. and Mrs. Simpkins and their sons, Charles, Ed and Clarence of Circleville visited Dan and Ross Simpkins for a few days.

* * * *

Messrs Titus, Robison, Moulton and Ackerman were in Provo this week. They went in Mr. Ackerman's car.

* * * *

Mr. and Mrs. Walker returned Thursday after visiting a week in Salt Lake.

* * * *

Dan Simpkins and family started for Circleville Saturday in their "fliver" but near Mud Lake they had a blowout and had to come back, but Sunday they went to Fillmore, taking Mrs. Willy, Mrs. Simpkins' mother.

* * * *

The Jolly Stitchers meet Friday with Mrs. Barker and Mrs. Osborn at the home of the former.

* * * *

Mrs. H. G. Ottley entertained the Mesdames Wolf, Kesler, Titus, Davis, Pervine and Miss Anna Clark of Woodrow last Friday.

* * * *

The Kyes family, Ross Simpkins', Jeff Clarks, Wolfs, Mr. and Mrs. Smith, Mr. and Mrs. Holdrerge and Mr. Banks spent Saturday at Novilla place.

* * * *

Don't forget the C. C. dance at Woodrow Saturday evening.

* * * *

Miss Ann Clark spent several days at Novilla Place last week.

* * * *

The Mothers of Sutherland held a meeting Wednesday afternoon to start Red Cross work.

* * * *

Mrs. Bert Ottley and baby Phyllis arrived last week and Bert has a smile that wont come off.

* * * *

The Britt family have been having the measles.

* * * *

Mr. Stephenson and two children have moved to their ranch.

* * * *

The C. C. club met with Susie Sanford Tuesday in honor of her birthday.

SOUTH TRACT SAYINGS

The ladies of the H. E. A. and their families were entertained by the men of the Farm Bureau on Saturday night, June 15th, at the school house. The treat fell to the ladies as the winners of a spelling match a few weeks previous. The guests were entertained during the evening with instramental music by Mr. and Mrs. Horace Crawford. The refreshments consisted of coffee and sandwiches followed by delicious ice cream and wafers. After a few patroitic songs, sung with spirit and enthusiasm the guests departed to their homes.

* * * *

A baby boy was born to Mr. and Mrs. Henry Botts June the 11th.

* * * *

Mr. and Mrs. Bert Whitmore were dinner guests of Mr. and Mrs. Chas. Hardin last Sunday.

* * * *

Miss Francis Beach, daughter of Mr. and Mrs. George Beach, left last week for New York City, where time with her aunt.

* * * *

Miss Minnie Russel of Salt Lake City is here to spend the summer with her sister, Mrs. Botts.

* * * *

H. E. Bock has been doing Farm Loan Organization work in Milford for the past two weeks and has not yet returned.

* * * *

Miss Ivy Mortison and younger sister are here spending the summer with their sister, Mrs. Bert Whitmore.

* * * *

Word has lately been received that Theron Sipes has joined the aviation corps.

* * * *

The Ladies Home Economics club was entertained last week at the home of Mrs. Charles Hardin. Mrs. Chester Hire will entertain in two weeks.

* * * *

The afternoon church services, held at the school house last Sunday conducted by Rev. Caldwell were well attended.

* * * *

The beet fields over the Tract are looking good. Cultivating and thinning are in progress now and will go on rapidly.

* * * *

Mr. and Mrs. Bert Whitmore will entertain at a neighborhood social on June 30th.

OAK CITY HAPPENINGS.

Mrs. Caroline Hartley from Salt Lake City is here visiting with her daughter, Mrs. Franklin Anderson.

* * * *

A fine baby girl arrived at the home of Joseph E. Finlinson last Saturday.

* * * *

Mrs. Guyman and son are here from Provo visiting with her daughter, Mrs. Jesse Higgins.

* * * *

A large number of our town residents attended the June Conference in Salt Lake City.

* * * *

The Misses Angie Finlinson and Ida Loper are spending this week in Delta.

A number of our boys and girls are preparing to go to Delta, where they will work in the beet fields.

* * * *

At dawn Friday morning the younger swarm of bee hive girls left town with their fishing lines and followed the creek up to the canyon.

* * * *

Mr. A. M. Woodbury has returned home after going to St. George for his family, where they have been visiting. Mrs. Woodbury's sister returned with them.

* * * *

The weather has also proved ideal for haying. The clicking noises of mowing machines can be heard any time. A good crop of goose berries and strawberries are coming on now and the English currants will be ready next week. The house wives are getting a large supply of fruit jars now in order to be ready for the big fruit crop as it comes on.

* * * *

June the 15th was surely an ideal day for fishing. The weather was exceptionally good. Buggies, wagons and automobiles kept a continual string to the canyon. One man that was there counted as many as thirty-five automobiles that were there at one time. Many fishers stayed up there two and three days. The high water which is some what muddy yet, made it a little disagreeable for fishing.

ABRAHAM ARTICLES

Oscar Bohn is now working at home.

* * * *

Mr. Frank Needham went to Ohio to attend the funeral of his father.

* * * *

James Bohn is able to be out again but surely shows that he has been sick.

* * * *

The Pattersons and Carys started on their tour on the 10th. We wish them success and happiness on their trip.

* * * *

Halley Young was reported to be very ill Sunday, having a very high fever. Some time ago she was bitten by a deer fly which is now giving her much pain.

* * * *

Every one was shocked and sorry to hear of the sad death of Mrs. Martha Stout. She was a brave and honest woman and will be missed by all.

* * * *

Mr. and Mrs. Christensen met with the sad misfortune of their oldest son drowning. Mrs. Christensen is the sister of Martha Stout and was formerly Dorthy Hanson.

Weather Report

The following report of temperature for last week is recorded by Saml. Western, U. S. Observer, at Deseret, Utah:

	Temperature	
Date	Highest	Lowest
10	75	50
11	73	51
12	76	39
13	74	31
14	89	39
15	89	44
16	92	49

Millard County Chronicle
June 28, 1917

A Man Drops Dead In Yard -

C. A. Miller, brother of John Miller, passed suddenly away last Sunday at 6, p. m., of heart failure, at the home of his brother. Mr. Miller had not been feeling very good for some time until Saturday, the day previous to his death, when he felt much better and was preparing to go into the hay fields Monday morning, at the time of his death. He went out in the yard and was standing by the house when he fell dead.

Mr. Miller was 62 years old. He came here from Emery County last December and has been living with his brother and family since that time. Burial was in the Delta cemetery. Funeral services being held there, conducted by Bishop Maxfield.

Dr. Broaddus Locates in Delta

Dr. Broaddus has established his residence in his office at his new home in the south part of Delta and will hereafter make that his headquarters. Mrs. Broaddus will remain in Hinckley for a short time until their new residence is completed, when the family will take up their permanent residence in their beautiful new bungalow in Delta.

SUTHERLAND SEARCHLIGHTS

Mr. and Mrs. Wolfe have two nephews from Provo with them.

* * * *

Frank Purdy of Delta is working at Novilla place.

* * * *

Mrs. Robard and son, Charles of Delta spent several days here with friends last week.

* * * *

Jennings Banks of Spanish Fork, is here with his brother and helping tend his father's place.

* * * *

The Messrs Foote, Huntsman and Smith tok a trip to Fillmore Sunday with Mr. Ackerman's car.

* * * *

All those who attended the dance at Woodrow, Saturday night, given by the C. C. club, report a lovely time.

* * * *

It was reported by the doctor that the Britt family had the measles but later the doctor decided it wasn't.

OASIS AFFAIRS

Golden Huff returned from the city a few days ago bringing with him a swell Roadster car.

* * * *

Herman Pederson left for Salt Lake on the 25th, where he will be set apart for a mission to the Eastern States. His father and mother accompanied him to Salt Lake.

* * * *

Mr. Leonard Holman was killed in an automobile accident at Baker on the 13th and was brought to Oasis by J. S. Singleton, of American Fork. He was buried last Sunday and a very large crowd attended the funeral. Mr. Holman leaves a wife and one boy aged five. Mrs. Holman wishes to thank all those rendering assistance and for the many floral offerings.

OAK CITY HAPPENINGS.

Collier Dutson is here from Wyo. visiting with friends and relatives.

* * * *

Miss Belva Lovell, who has been away several months visiting in Salt Lake and Idaho, is back home again.

* * * *

Mrs. Jens Anderson has gone to Salina with her brother to visit with friends and relatives.

* * * *

Martin Sheriff got kicked on the foot by a horse, hurting his ankle and breaking one of his toes.

* * * *

Miss Silva Lovell has gone to Salt Lake City to visit with her sister, Mrs. Jos. S. Wells.

* * * *

Mrs. A. M. Woodbury's mother, Mrs. Atkins is here visiting with her.

Mrs. Guyman and son, who have been visiting Mrs. Jesse Higgins, have returned to her home in Provo.

* * * *

Mrs. Hettie Johnson and family are here visiting her mother, Mrs. Martha Roper.

* * * *

Our baseball game with Lynndyl last Saturday fell short a few points in score for our favor, the score being 14-9 in favor of Lynndyl.

* * * *

Our town was well represented at Quarterly conference held at Leamington last Saturday and Sunday.

* * * *

We are expecting a big celebration here on the 4th of July. An exceptionally good program is being prepared for that day.

* * * *

Susan, the little daughter of John L. Nielson, was thrown from a horse while riding from one farm to another. She was found unconscious and remained so most of that night. One of her arms was quite badly hurt.

HINCKLEY HAPPENINGS

A. D. Ryan has been away for a week or more on business in and near Salt Lake.

* * * *

Joseph Neilson and family have gone in their car to Circleville to attend a family re-union.

* * * *

Dr. Broaddus and family accepted the invitation of Miss Ida and Mrs. Martha Roper to spend the Fourth in Oak City.

* * * *

It is reported that another young couple recently married are Miss Lavern Croft and Mr. Carl Theobald. The matrimonial fever seems to be quite an epidemic this spring.

* * * *

Former Misses Amy and Lynn Wright and their young husbands of Salt Lake are guests at Geo. Talbots and are visiting their many relatives in town.

* * * *

Messrs Tippetts, C. E. McClellan and Richard Parker are very busy with the boys' beet thinning clubs. Girls clubs have also been organized and they are at work.

* * * *

Monday evening, at the school house a farewell party was given for Vernon Moody, who left Wednesday night for the war. We fear many more will follow soon, but hope they may soon all be with us again.

* * * *

The Union Sunday School had a delightful lawn social last Wednesday evening on the Broaddus lawn, with Mesdames Broaddus and Ryan as hostesses. Jolly games, music, ice-cream and cake filled the evening with fun. An unusually large number of young folks were present.

* * * *

Mr. Passey is about to build on to his store building another room to be used by Dr. Broaddus as his Hinckley office. The doctor will keep office hours here as many days a week as the need requires and will leave perscriptions, etc., with Mr. Passey, where patients can conveniently obtain them.

* * * *

Mr. and Mrs. Leon Finlayson have been the recipients of a number of social attentions, among them a large reception at the home of Mr. and Mrs. John Hutchinson. On Wednesday, June 27th a 500 party and luncheon in their honor was given by the Misses Mable and Wealthy Parker, to which sixteen guests were invited.

* * * *

The town of Hinckley has an ordinance against allowing any animals loose on the streets and yet the town Marshall had 31 animals in the estray pound last week and was out for more. Aren't we loyal, patriotic enough citizens to see that every animal is securely corralled where it cannot get loose? The women have responded to the call of raising garden stuff, but isn't it outrageous to have it destroyed and eaten up in the night by loose cows after all the hard work of raising it? Several gardens last week were hopelessly damaged by the cows, one garden loosing one-fourth of a large patch of pop-corn and another having 130 hills of sweet corn up high eaten off to the ground, to say nothing of the plants tramped to death. It isn't fair to let animals out in the night to feed free on the streets and your neighbor's garden. Everyone can excuse an accident, but this regular night-prowling of loose animals is not accidental and should be stopped by everyone.

Section of Delta's First Manufacturing Enterprise, Now Under Construction

The above photograph shows a section of the new 1200-ton sugar factory, now under construction on the outskirts of Delta. This factory lies in the center of 125,000 acres of rich irrigated sugar beet land and will handle during the coming campaign 10,000 acres of beets of high sugar content and a stand which promises to be phenominal. More settlers are needed here to secure their own farms and grow beets.

Millard County Progress
July 13, 1917

HINCKLEY MAN CHARGED WITH ASSAULT.

As we were going to press with our last issue word came to us that there had been a shooting affair over in Hinckley on Thursday afternoon. Our informant was misinformed as to the name of the party that did the shooting but the balance of the article was correct. We have since learned that the affair took place over the trespass of a horse belonging to J. H. Hilton who on seeing his horse in the grain field belonging to H. E. Sherrick went over to get him, but was refused permission to do so by Mr. Sherrick. Mr. Hilton said that he was going to get the horse and Mr. Sherrick said that he would keep the animal until the bill for damages he had against the horse was paid. Mr. Hilton grasping a short iron bar said that if Sherrck didn't stand out of the way he would level the bumps on his (Sherrick's) head. With that Mr. Sherrick went to the house and returned with a revolver of small cal., iler and as Mr. Hilton essayed to pass him, he shot him once in the right arm just under the shoulder blade, the wound while not dangerous as yet may develop into something serious as the doctor could not remove it without endangering Mr. Hilton's life.

County Atorney Giles went over to Delta and formaly arraigned Mr. Sherrick on a charge of "Assault with a deadly weapon with intent to do bodily harm, Mr. Sherrick having given himself up to Sheriff Dorrity soon after the shooting and the Sheriff having taken him to the jail at Delta. Mr. Sherrck was released on a $300 bond which was furnishe and the preliminary hearing wil be heard at Delta on Saurday next. Attorney, J. A. Melville is representing Mr. Sherrick in the case.

Millard County Chronicle
July 19, 1917

Wedding Bells.

Last Wednesday in the Manti temple, the wedding of Miss Gene Lovell and Mr. Eugene Gardner was solemnized.

Miss Lovell is the daughter of Mr. and Mrs. John E. Lovell of Oak City and is loved and respected by all who know her. Mr. Gardner is the son of Mr. and Mrs. Wm. H. Gardner of Salem, but he has lived in Delta for the past several years, having taught school here for five years. He has a farm here and is now employed in the Delta State Bank. The happy couple will make this their home. The Chronicle joins in wishing them a long and happy married life.

Dick Smith and Irene Lewis went to Salt Lake last week and while there embarked on the "Sea of Matrimony." They spent some time in the city visiting, returning home the first of last week and will make their home here. The wishes of the community go out to them for a happy married life.

OAK CITY ITEMS.

Mrs. Agustus Carlson made a flying trip to Lynndyl to see her daughters.

* * * *

After a short visit at her home, Angie Finlinson returned to her work at Delta.

* * * *

Alma Christensen of Oasis, came up for the dance Saturday night and spent Sunday in town.

* * * *

Jeff Finlinson and family motored over from Leamington Saturday, returning the following day.

* * * *

Mrs. Will Lovell spent a few days last week at the home of her sister in Lynndyl.

* * * *

Mrs. Hettie Johnson is visiting at the home of her mother, Mrs. Martha Roper, for a efw days.

* * * *

Mr. Hague of the Con. Wagon & Machine Co. was in town setting up a new binder for the Jacobsen Bros.

* * * *

Mrs. William Alldredge and her daughter, Wanda made an extended visit in Hinckley, with relatives and friends.

* * * *

Mrs. Joseph S. Wells came to attend the wedding of her sister, Gene Lovell. She will remain visiting relatives and friends for a few weeks.

* * * *

Mrs. Clarence Nielson, accompanied by Mandy Roper and Martin Sheriff left for an extended visit in Idaho last Monday night.

* * * *

Quite a number of our towns people spent Sunday afternoon in the canyon, enjoying the mountain scenery.

* * * *

Joseph S. Anderson while working on his farm was overcome with the heat and was confined to his bed for a few days.

* * * *

Leo Finlinson and family with Mrs. Mary Lyman made a flying trip to Delta Saturday morning, returning the same day.

* * * *

J. Lee Anderson went to Delta Monday morning on a business trip.

Bishop Anderson and family will leave for Idaho Thursday of this week.

Cleamont and Ila Dutson of Hinckley attended the dance Saturday night. They spent Sunday with relatives and friends, returning home Monday.

* * * *

Strangers were seen on our streets during the past week. Gus Faust and Willis Lyman extended their visit over Saturday night and spent Sunday in the canyon catching trout. (?)

* * * *

Eugene Gardner and Gene Lovell were married Wednesday of last week in the Manti temple. Saturday a reception was given them at the home of the bride's father. Only the immediate family was present. Saturday night a dance was given by the "newly weds". An enjoyable time was had. Quite a number

WOODROW ITEMS

Miss Margaret Thompson is visiting in Salt Lake City for a few days.

* * * *

Rev. George Caldwell will preach in Woodrow next Sunday evening. All are invited.

* * * *

Mr. and Mrs. Elmer Golden are receiving congratulations upon the arrival of their 9½ pound son.

* * * *

Mrs. Helen Hersleff is improving after a serious illness, dating from the Fourth of July.

* * * *

Miss Etta Fletcher of California is spending the summer with Mrs. Berger at the Berger Villa in Woodrow.

* * * *

Roscoe P. Jackson, of Oklahoma, is here looking over his ranch and is being gladly welcomed by his old friends in Woodrow and Sutherland.

* * * *

Mrs. Robison of Hinckley who has been assisting at the boys' camp was called home Sunday by the illness of his sister.

* * * *

Johnnie Kozina was made happy Sunday by the arrival of his mother from California who will keep house for him during the summer. Mrs. Kozina was accompanied by several of Johnie's small brothers and sisters to help entertain them.

SOUTH TRACT SAYINGS

George Beach has been on the sick list the past week.

* * * *

Mrs. Russel and daughter, Minnie who have been visiting H. A. Botts have returned to Salt Lake City.

* * * *

Mr. and Mrs. Carl Elmer in company with Mr. and Mrs. Underhill left on Wednesday of this week for an extended auto trip into the northern part of the state.

* * * *

Mrs. F. B. Johnson entertained the Home Economic's club at the home of Mrs. Carl Elmer last Thursday afternoon. Refreshments consisted of ice lemonade and wafers.

* * * *

Miss Hannah Johnson entertained a few of her friends at a "500" party at her home last Wednesday evening. Strawberries and cake were served at the tables.

* * * *

Mr. and Mrs. J. E. Whitmore entertained on Saturday evening, July the 14th with the community social, at their home. The guests were delightfully entertained. Refreshments consisted of ice tea and cake.

* * * *

Mr. and Mrs. B. W. Whitmore entertained a number of friends at dinner Sunday, in honor of the birthday of Mrs. F. B. Johnson and Mrs. Whitmore. The invited guests were Mr. and Mrs. J. E. Whitmore, Mr. and Mrs. F. B. Johnson, Miss Ivy Mortinson and Messrs Harry and Edward Pearson.

Personal Items

Miss Myra Underhill is here visiting with relatives and friends.

—)(—

Born, Saturday, July 14th, to Mr. and Mrs. Chas. Ashby, a boy.

—)(—

A dance is reported at Sugarville for next Saturday night.

—)(—

Mrs. T. C. Gronning and children have been visiting with relatives and friends for the past week.

—)(—

Mr. and Mrs. A. O. Gardner visited in Provo with Mrs. Gardner's parents, this week.

—)(—

A Gardner re-union was held at the grove last Sunday, being present.

—)(—

Prof. Richard R. Lyman, of Salt Lake City is in Delta, looking after his business interests.

—)(—

Ed Reynolds left Tuesday for Salt Lake City, where he will attend to business affairs.

—)(—

Three cars of hogs were shipped from Delta Tuesday by the Livingston ranch and Wills Lyman.

—)(—

Dan Kelley, of the Delta Meat Market was attending to business in Salt Lake the last of last week.

—)(—

L. F. Koch has sold half of his lot on 3rd west to M. J. Greenwood, of Salt Lake for $1000.00.

—)(—

Born, to Mr. and Mrs. David Nichols of Oasis, Friday July the 13th, a girl.

—)(—

The small son of Mr. and Mrs. Jesse Hulse was very badly hurt last week when a motorcycle fell on him.

—)(—

Mr. and Mrs. Artie Wade have returned to Delta after spending the Fourth in Beaver with Mrs. Wade's parents.

—)(—

The neat three-roomed bungalow, belonging to S. E. Powell is completed and the family are moving into it this week.

—)(—

R. R. Betz was here Tuesday from Lynndyl visiting Mrs. Betz and shaking hands with old friends.

—)(—

City Drug Store is closing out their stock of cured meats and other groceries. Call and get special prices. Salt Side 27½ cts.   jy192t

—)(—

Misses Vera and Genevieve Swenson, who have made an extended visit here, returned to their home at Sterling Tuesday night.

—)(—

Attorney J. Alex Melville was here Saturday as attorney for H. E. Sherrick in the shooting trial held here Saturday.

—)(—

The City Drug Store is closing out their stock of Baldwin Pianos. Call and get special prices, on monthly terms.   jy192t

—)(—

Mr. and Mrs. L. D. Pace and children and Mr. and Mrs. J. D. Pace and son, Woodie, went to Salina the last of last week for a short visit with relatives.

—)(—

Mr. Ed Reynolds has received word that his cousin has been killed on the Western front in France, after two and one-half years of active service in the army.

—)(—

Mr. and Mrs. Lute Wade have returned to Fillmore, where, we understand Mr. Wade is going to manage the James A. Kelly meat market. Mr. Wade was employed at the Dan Kelley meat market here.

—)(—

Joseph Ogden of Richfield drove to Delta in his car Sunday and was accompanied home the following day by his daughter, Mrs. Geo. Dobson, and children. Mrs. Dobson will make an extended visit there.

—)(—

The case of H. E. Sherrick, who was arrested on the charge of shooting John Hilton north of Hinckley was tried in Justice court last Saturday and the charge changed to ordinary assault which Sherrick pleaded guilty and was assessed $125.00. The case grow out of Sherrick's horse getting into Hilton's field and ill feeling arose in which Hilton attacked Sherrick with an iron and Sherrick shot him with a 22 pistol.

—)(—

Sec'y State Road Commission, and State Road Engineer Browning and State Road Commissioner Irving were in the valley the latter part of last week looking over road conditions.

—)(—

Jennie Sampson, of Lyman, who has been visiting relatives in Delta for some time was taken suddenly ill last Wednesday with appendicitis, and was taken to Salt Lake that night, by her uncle, Jack Sly, where she will be operated on.

—)(—

Mrs. Marie Porter and daughter, Amy, who have been here visiting their daughter and sister, Mrs. Nellie Workman, left Tuesday for her home. She will return in the near future and make her home with Mr. and Mrs. Workman.

—)(—

While being helped on a horse last Wednesday, by her mother, Erma Sampson, the little daughter of Mr. and Mrs. Ren Sampson fell to the ground and broke her arm in two places below the elbow. The Dr. was summoned immediately and the arm set and she is getting along nicely.

—)(—

Editor Smith of the Progress Review, District Attorney Murdock of Beaver City and County Attorney Grover Giles were here representing the state in the Sherrick-Hilton shooting scrape and Mr. Smith was admiring the tall buildings and rapid growth of our city.

—)(—

Mrs. W. H. Gardner, Mr. and Mrs. Leo Gardner, Mr. and Mrs. Dell Gardner, of Salem and Mr. and Mrs. J. Stout, wife and children, of Leland, Utah, Mr. and Mrs. W. Stout of Canada, Mrs. Albert Peterson and Mrs. Hattie Stout of Idaho came down to attend the wedding reception of Mr. Eugene Gardner last Saturday.

DELTA NEWS NOTES.

Mrs. Lizzie Chidester has returned home from Summer school.

—)(—

Ed. Erickson is visiting in Delta, the guest of Miss Millie Workman.

—)(—

Don Hoyt returned from Salt Lake the last of last week.

—)(—

Coal Oil and Gasoline stoves at the Delta Furniture Store.   jy26a2

—)(—

Miss Helen Bunker is here from St. George visiting relatives.

—)(—

Dewey Sanford spent a few days last week in Springville with relatives.

—)(—

Cash will buy Bed Springs and Mattresses cheap at the Delta Furniture Store.   jy26a2

—)(—

Miss Margaret Cramer, daughter of Engineer Cramer, in charge of the Delta Co's work on the South Tract, has been engaged in the Delta office of the company.

—)(—

Pearl Tozer, who has been assisting Rev. and Mrs. Hamilton with missionary work in Southern Utah, returned home last Thursday night. Mr. and Mrs. Hamilton will follow later in their car.

—)(—

J. W. Walton has gone to Riverside, California, to attend to business matters and visit his family. He expects to return in a short time to look after his crops and may move his family to Salt Lake to be nearer to them during his farming operations here.

—)(—

Mr. and Mrs. Theodore Christensen who started for Fish Lake to spend the 24th, were compelled to abandon the trip owing to weather conditions. They spent a few days with Mr. Christensen's parents in Wales and returned home Saturday night.

—)(—

Last Friday night a bundle shower was given in honor of Mr. and Mrs. Eugene Gardner, at their home on Clark St. They received many nice presents. Music and games were enjoyed during the evening and refreshments, consisting of ice cream and cake were served.

—)(—

The first person to bring in a pair of shoes to be sent to the destitute in France was L. E. Johnson, of the South Tract, he having brot them in last Saturday. Shoes must be in Salt Lake by August 10th, and we want enough to make a showing when we ship them. It's only a small chore to gather up your old shoes, if you have any and bring them into the Chronicle office. Do it now.

—)(—

The farmers on the North Tract between Delta and Sutherland are busy grading and leveling the road from the river west to where the highway crosses the Sugarville branch of the Salt Lake Route. They are also doing some work on the road which branches off and leads to Sutherland and some work around Sutherland. This is a very commendable act and if the people of Delta showed as much enterprise we might be able to induce more people to come here to trade.

SOUTH TRACT SAYINGS

(Too late for last week.)

H. E. Beck returned from Milford Saturday morning of last week.

* * * *

Miss Folsom and Mrs. Drake of Ohio are here visiting the Folsom family.

* * * *

Mrs. Leo Thurston, who has been visiting in Morgan with Mr. Thurston's folks has returned.

* * * *

Miss Ivy Martinson was the guest of Mrs. Charles Hardin a few days last week.

* * * *

Mrs. C. A. Hire returned from Slt Lake last week where she has been the past several weeks with Mr. Hire who is in the city on business.

* * * *

Roy Mortison is here visiting his sisters, Ivy Martison and Mrs. B. W. Whitmore, for a few days before going away to join the army service.

* * * *

J. P. Fidel returned from Salt Lake City last week where he went to be examined for enlistment ien the engineer corps. Sixty men out of the four hundred examined will make up the total requirement.

* * * *

Carl Elmer was taken sick Thursday of last week, the day on which he had planned to start on an auto trip to the northern part of the state. Mr. Elmer is much improved now and he and Mrs. Elmer will postpone their trip until he is fully recovered.

* * * *

Miss Ivy Martinson entertained a few friends at the home of B. W. Whitmore on Sunday July 22. A delicious luncheon of ice cream and cake, followed by ice tea was served to twelve guests, by the hostess. The guests indulged in tennis at the courts in the evening.

SUGARVILLE SIFTINGS

Big dance at F. T. C. hall Saturday evening, August 4th.

* * * *

The Friendship Thimble club will meet with Mrs. Sampley next Wednesday afternoon.

* * * *

Rev. Swenson preached a very interesting sermon last Sunday and has promised to preach next Sunday at 3, p. m. Everyone invited. Come and hear him, it will be worth your time.   Union Sunday school at 2, on Sundays when there is preaching.

* * * *

The following letter was received by J. B. Seams from a mother of one of the boys of Camp No. 2, which was in charge of W. G. McKitterick. This camp broke up about a week ago and those boys who stayed to the end were the ones who were proud of their earnings.

Salt Lake City, July 23th, 1917.

Dear Sir:

I feel it my duty to write and thank you for your kindness in every way to my son Alvin Pocock. Mrs. Duke also wishes to thank you as her boy was with mine. They talk about their good boss and the good things they had to eat and how they enjoyed their trip.   My boy brot back a nice piece of money and made good use of it. He bot himself some good clothes and put the rest in the bank.   I hope he earned it justly and did his true part to the farmers.

I was proud of my boy being called a soldier of the soil, and want this letter to be an acknowledgment of good treatment to him.

Yours very truly,

Mrs. Pocock.

CORRECTIONS IN THE MILITARY DRAFT LIST.

Following are the corrections of the official list of drafted men for Millard County. The list contained in our last issue is now the official one with the exception of the corrections herein contained.

Add Platt Trimble to Fillmore list Arvid F. Anderson to Delta, Everett Robins to Sciplo, Horace Monroe to Scipio and take off Milo T. Dyches. Take off Lucien Robison Whitehead of Hinckley, and put on Manuel Martinez of Lynndyl; add the names of J. W. Lewis and Owen Y. George to the Kanosh list, and take out David Nichols of Oasis; add Charles W. Lewis of Leamington and take out Cload Nielson of the same place; add K. Yasukawa on Deseret and take out James F. Robison of Garrison; add Wilford Johnson to Holden and take off Dalton M. Reid of Abraham; add to the Malone list the name of Paul Cline and you have the complete official list for Millard County.

HINCKLEY HAPPENINGS

Wm. Pratt, one of our young men, recently returned from a mission is with us again and we are glad to see him.

* * * *

Car owners are keeping Mr. Jackson so busy repairing their machines that he can scarcely find time for blacksmith work. It is interesting to see how people seek out a good workman wherever he may be.

* * * *

Mr. and Mrs. J. A. Jackson, and Mr. and Mrs. Ernest Jackson and their families spent the week-end camping in the Oak Creek canyon, and report having had a splendid time.

The little two-year old baby of Mr. and Mrs. Leavitt fell off the bed Friday, breaking both bones of the arm. Dr. Broaddus quickly set it, however, under a brief anaesthetic, and it is getting along nicely.

* * * *

Mr. Gardner's new picture show building is fast nearing completion It has a fine inclined floor, a gallery and a good big stage with orchestra pit. Dr. Broaddus' office just east of Passey's store will soon be completed also.

* * * *

Within the past two weeks Dr. Broaddus has performed a number of tonsil operations with great success in every instance. The people of this district are very fortunate in having so capable a physician available.

* * * *

Tuesday afternoon, Aug. 14th, the Relief Society entertained with games, program and refreshments in honor of the older women of Hinckley. Those especially honored were Grandmas Wright, Pratt, Reeve, Slaughter and Martindale.

* * * *

On the evening of the first Wednesday in August, Mrs. Nelson and Mrs. Neely entertained the Union Sunday School in their monthly social. Quite a large crowd was present and games and delicious icecream and cake made a very delightful evening.

* * * *

Bishop John Pratt and Mayor Jos. Blake have been on the road sides and the Academy lot moving weeds. Let the work speed up! The weeds are getting ahead of us. In the neighborhood of the Academy the Russian thistle is getting alarmingly thick. Everybody get busy before the town inspector comes.

* * * *

On August 8th an informal reception was held in the gym of the Academy, when two hundred of the inhabitants of Hinckley assembled to express their regret that Dr. and Mrs. Broaddus were going to move to Delta. A Program consisting of songs, speeches and dancing was enjoyed. Those present voted it the most enjoyable time of the summer.

* * * *

The Farm Bureau, under their live, hustling president, Eddie Anderson has done a fine work in completing the railroad grade for the Hinckley spur. In spite of the busy season there is scarcely a man in Hinckley who has not contributed money, or labor to the work and Eddie Anderson and Amos Maxfield have been almost constantly on the job.

* * * *

The energetic women of Hinckley are certainly doing their part in the way of raising gardens. Among those coming under the observation of the writer are Mesdames Will Bunker, Hannah Reeves, John Wright, and Mrs. John Hilton. Not only these young women but one at least past the limit of three score years and ten, a great grand mother, in fact, Grandma Wright, who has done all the work, weeding and hoeing with her own hands has one of the finest.

* * * *

In place of the regular H. E. A. meeting Aug. 10, Miss White conducted 4 sessions of vegetables and meat canning in the Academy kitchen, August 10th and 11th. A large number of Hinckley women attended bringing their own vegetables and bottles and doing their own work, under Miss White's direction. Most of the canning was done by the cold-pack boiler method altho the pressure cooker was also used. Miss White has done an enormous amount of good in educating us to better methods of preservation of vegetables and meat as well as fruits. The next social meeting of the H. E. A. on the 4th Friday in August is to be at the home of Mrs. Richard Cropper. None of the women can afford to miss these cozy sociable afternoons.

More Soldiers Called For.

Clerk Ashby, Sheriff Dorrity, Dr. Stevens, of Fillmore, and Dr. Broaddus, constituting the Examining Board, held forth at the Delta school house Tuesday, Wednesday and Thursday and examined the following persons for an additional draft.

Guy C. Campbell, Lynndyl, Geo. A. Sampson, Delta, Jos. R. Briggs, Delta, John D. Strickley, Delta, Chas. Hardin, Delta, Myron L. Western, Deseret, Joss Draper, Lynndyl, Lawrence Nelson, Delta, Myron Pratt, Hinckley, Leon Abbott, Delta, Milton Lovell, Oak City, A. L. Cahoon, Deseret, Parley Roper, Oak City, Hyrum Chittenden, Jr. Delta, James Stubbert, Oasis, Theodore Bougas, Delta, Reyes Garcia, Delta, Alfred Damron, Deseret, Alma Western, Hinckley, GGeorge Sipes, Delta, A. E. Reed, Abraham, Oscar W. Anderson, Delta, Frank Sanford, Delta, Edwin R. Westover, Abraham, J. D. Thompson, Delta, Carl Elmer, Delta, Fred Harada, Delta, John Kozina, Delta, Willard S. Lee, Delta, John Dutson, Oak City, Willard Christensen, Oak City, Jesse C. Works, Delta, A. W. Mitchell, Delta, Don Taylor Bishop, Hinckley, GG. L. Massall, Delta, Chas. Eddie, Delta, Leland Roper, Oak City, R. F. Mason, Abraham, Lebrado Guadian, Lynndyl, Enoch L. Folsom, Delta, Fred R. Greathouse, Leamington, Peter F. Anderson, Leamington, Walter Gardner, Delta, A. A. Folsom, Delta, Ernest Baxter, Delta, W. H. Walloston, Hinckley, Jesus Rodriquez, Clear Lake, Roy Betz, Lynndyl, C. Talbot, Oak City, A. M. Black, Deseret, Glen Stewart, Delta, K. Nanawa, Lynndyl, I. O. McMillen, Delta, Rupert Morrell, Lynndyl, Martin Marque, Pummice, Hugh Kelly, Delta, Oxel Johnson, Leamington, Clifton Simmons, Delta, Peter J. Hersleff, Delta, J. Textorious, Leamington, L. A. Pritchett, Delta, D. G. Pritchett, Delta, A. Jensen Oasis, James H. Abbott, Delta, Harold Morris, Hinckley, Andy R. Owens, Oasis, E. G. Kimball, Delta, J. V. Styler, Oasis, Cleveland Mitchell, Hinckley, M. W. Clark, Delta, B. F. Riding, Delta, W. Robison, Delta, Clement K. Porter, Abraham, Archie Maxfield, Delta, T. J. Greener, Hinckley, J. E. West, Lynndyl, James E. Works, Delta, W. B. Shaw, Hinckley, B. H. Jacobs, Delta, Oscar F. Loveland, Hinckley, Ben Galogos, Delta, J. S. Neilson, Hinckley, F. H. Palmer, Delta, G. W. Dobson, Delta, Leslie H. Morrell, Delta, A. Koenig, Dan A. Kelly, Delta, S. W. Lovell, Oak City, M. J. Dunn, Deseret, E. W. Berger, Lynndyl, Chris Teller, Delta, J. Panogos, Delta, Hugh P. Grahm, Delta, C. M.Draper, Lynndyl, T. J. Dale, Delta, Arvine M. Stillson, Delta, A. M. Becker, Deseret, A. I. Tippetts, Hinckley, Norris M. Lockwood, Delta, T. M. Broderick, Delta, H. N. Allen, Lynndyl, Otto H. Luch, Delta, G. A. Gillispie, Malone, Bert Roper, Oak City, A. C. Eliott, Lynndyl, H. Slaughter, Hinckley, Adonrian Hagan, Delta, I. Ellis Jacob, Delta, H. Williamson, Delta, A. C. Christenson, Oak City, Lindsay Steele, Delta, R. C. Bunker, Delta, Luther Buchanan, Delta, R. Jenkins, Delta, Percy Carter, Delta, R. P. Larson, Lynndyl, H. C. Hawley, Oasis, Melliar Workman, Delta, F. H. Tanner, Delta, I. P. Hinckley, Lynndyl, H. J. Ottley, Delta, Jean Sperry, Delta, Elmer Stout, Oasis, V. C. Kantz, Delta, Ray Nakamara, Delta,

LOCAL NEWS

Mrs. Harry Aller spent the week-end in Salt Lake City.

—) (—

Fresh vegetables every Saturday at D. Stevens & Co. Store.   a2-tf

—) (—

Ralph Prout is down from Salt Lake and is employed at the Sugar Factory.

—) (—

Miss Thenelda Blackburn left Saturday night for Payson, where she will make an extended visit with relatives and friends.

—) (—

Dudley Wells left last Saturday for Salt Lake where he was called to take the selective draft examination.

—) (—

Mrs. Rufus Stoddard left last week for Duchesne county where she will visit for some time with her mother and other relatives.

—) (—

A pleasant afternoon was spent at the home of Mrs. Arthur Bunker, Friday, the 11th. Lemonade and fresh Dixie grapes were enjoyed by all.

—) (—

Mrs. P. M. Purdy, formerly Miss Marie Kelly and little son, Philip are here from Salt Lake visiting with Mrs. Purdy's parents, Mr. and Mrs. James Kelly.

—) (—

Miss Vida Earl of Bunkerville, Nevada, stopped off in Delta, on her way home from Summer School in Salt Lake to visit with relatives for some time.

—) (—

Arthur Bunker returned to Delta from Nevada the last of last week, to get his family who will go there with him to remain for some time to help take care of the grape crop. They left for that place Monday.

—) (—

Will Gardner and family accompanied his father and family, who have been here visiting the boys for some time to their home in Salem. Mrs. Gardner and the children remained there fo ra visit with her parents and Will came home Monday.

—) (—

The Delta Land & Water Company is busy now forwarding their settlers deeds to them to their land. These have finally been or or being issued by the land board after a delay of months and are being recorded at the county seat and sent to the land owners, thru the company.

—) (—

Russell Sprunt of the Delta Hardware and Lumber Co., was in Salt Lake the last of last week, attending to the company's business. The company now has an extra fine line of lumber and building material on hand and are adding to their up-to-date line of shelf hardware and cutlery.

SECOND DRAWING IN MILLARD COUNTY DRAFT

The following named persons are hereby notified that, pursuant to the Act of Congress approved May 18, 1917, they are called for military service of the United States by this local Board.

All those residing on the West side of Millard County, will report at Delta for Examination on the 15th and 16th days of August, 1917. All those residing on the East side of Millard County will report at Fillmore Utah, for Examination on the 17th and 18th days of August, 1917.

SCIPIO.

350—Milo T. Dyches; 685—Ralph M. Monroe; 71—Roy Elkins; 17—Edwin Johnson; 122—James Lawson 202—Leffel Fisher; 650—Eugene Memmott; 32—Bert F. Johnson; 287—Perry Memmott.

HOLDEN.

212—Ralph E. Jones; 438—Leon E. Dobson; 725—Bruce S. Stephenson 663—Austin G. Ashby; 832—Delbert Hoffhines; 759—Leonard A. Wood. 240—Joseph Bennett; 272—Sydney O. Hunter; 214—Carl S. Johnson; 629—Carl Nixon; 449—Elm D. Hoffhines; 88—Wilford S. Badger; 150—Thaddeus O. Johnson.

FILLMORE.

336—Wilford J. Anderson; 822—Arnold N. Rasmussen; 441—Arron Wayne Robison; 331—Clinton Day; 86—Willard R. Huntsman; 235—Brigham L. Melville; 410—Marvin W Peterson; 299—Richard S. Webber; 58—Thomas W. Trimble; 4—Rudwin W. Jackson; 328—Carl H. Day; 624—Archie Robison; 378—Will Kilpack; 776—Joseph D. Pyper; 311—Oreon L. Huntsman; 829—Arnell Warner; 326—Philander B. Day; 393—W. Clark Colegrove; 766—John Smith; 157—Orvil R. Warner; 647—M. Henry Hanson; 29—Wm. E. Greenway; 35—Wm. F. Williams; 827—Jay Speakman.

MEADOW.

102—Edwin A. Lindsey; 257—Joseph H. Edwards; 186—E. D. Bushnell; 416—Howard N. Barkdull 100—Lewis H. Duncan; 712—Neil M. Stowart, Jr.; 237—Edmond Bodle 36—Parley A. Adams; 236—Albert B. Bennett.

HATTON.

187—Charles E. Bird; 742—Dennis Smith.

KANOSH.

305—Chas. A. Malouf; 23—Weldo George; 750—Clarence A. Whatcott 430—Chas. A. Robert; 593—George T. Prows; 526—Andy Levi; 316—Ira J. Hopkins; 41—James R. Whatcott.

LYNNDYL.

278—Guy C. Campbell; 323—Jess Draper; 211—Labrado Gundlan; 13 Fred R. Greathouse; 115—Peter F. Anderson; 544—Roy R. Betz; 635—K. Naniwa; 802—Rupert Morrell; 76—John E. West; 540—Edwin L. Berger; 342—Darnel R. Johnson; 460—Carson M. Draper; 114—Harry N. Allen; 209—Almon G. Ellett; 224—Rasmus P. A. Larsen; 640—Ira P. Hinckley.

LEAMINGTON.

344—Oxel L. Johnson; 52—Takanori Yoshimura; 164—Josiah Textorius.

OAK CITY.

662—P. L. Roper; 715—M. B. Lovell; 436—John Dutson; 396—W. R. Christensen; 560—Loland Roper; 747—Clifford Talbott; 613—Stanley W. Lovell; 603—Bert Roper; 362—A. C. Christensen.

DELTA.

524—Geo. A. Sampson; 532—Joseph R. Briggs; 49—John K. Strickley; 557—Chas. R. Hardin; 357—L. Nelson; 565—Wm. L. Abbott; 501—Hyrum Chittenden, Jr.; 555—Theodore Bougas; 506—Reyes Garcia; 713—George G. Sypes; 113—Oscar W. Anderson; 156—Frank J. Sanford; 780—James D. Thompson; 267 Carl Elmer; 567—Fred Harada; 421—John Kozina; 169—Wm. S. Lee; 155—Jesse C. Works; 284—Albert W. Mitchell; 807—George L. MaMass. ell; 265—Charles D. Eddle; 229—Enoch L. Folson; 306—W. Gardner,

Jr.; 228—A. A. Folson; 91—G. C Stewart; 633—I. O. McMillen; 619—Hugh Kelly; 824—G. C Simmons; 412—P. J. Herslof; 208—L. A. Pritchett; 407—D. G. Pritchett; 566—James H. Abbott; 421—D. J. F. Bill; 499—Mitchell W. Clark; 590—Don F. Riding; 444—W. A. Robison; 735—P. Valenzula; 634—Archie H. Maxfield; 158—James E. Works; 1—H. H. Jacobs; 836—Chn Gallagoz; 418—F. H. Palmer; 456—G. W. Dobson; 806—L. H. Morrell; 416—Alfred Koenig; 609—Daniel A. Kelly;

Concluded on Page 8.

Concluded from Page 1.
134—Cris Teller; 711—James Panagos; 205—H. P. Graham; 427—T. J. Dale; 656—A. M. Stillson; 100—A. W. Lockwood; 533—T. A. Broaderick; 151—O H. Lucy; 33—A. B. Hagan; 63—I E. Jacobs; 816—Linsey Stoele, Jr.; 371—R. C. Bunker; 29—L. Buchanan; 64—Robert Jenkins; 382—Percy Carter; 702—M. H. Workman; 48—F. A. Tanner; 127—H. J. Ottley; 668—Jean Sperry 173—V. C. Kautz; 686—Ray Nakamura; 768—Herbert Williamson.

OASIS.

714—J. J. Stubbert; 262—Andrew Jensen; 124—Andy R. Owens; 744—J. V. Styler; 818—J. K. Hawley; 743 —Elmer Stout.

DESERET.

781—M. L. Western; 539—A. L. Cahoon; 434—A. R. Damron; 138—A. M. Black; 241—A. M. Baker; 374 —M. J. Dunn.

HINCKLEY

492—Marion A. Crafts; 681—Alma Western; 133—D. T. Bishop; 96 —W. H. Wollaston; 581—H. R. Morris; 582—Cleveland Mitchell; 447—J. T. Greenor; 778—Wm. B. Shaw; 105—O. F. Loveland; 352—J. S Neilson; 40—A I. Tippetts; 777—Harrison Slaughter.

ABRAHAM.

450—A. E. Reed; 808—E. R. Westover; 303—R. F. Masca, 136—E. L. Baxter; 636—C. K Porter.

CLEAR LAKE.

570—Jesus Rodriquez.

BLACK ROCK.

672—E. Torrez.

MALONE.

61—Gilbert A. Gillespie.

GARRISON.

8—W. S. Heckethorne; 349—Wm. Davies; 272—G. A. Richardson.

GANDY

Alonzo A. Miller.

BURBANK.

617—Arthur L. Murray; 618—Paul S. McQuarrie.

PLUMBICE.

691—Martin Marquez.

Millard County Progress
August 24, 1917

Following is a list of the men who have been accepted for military service under the draft regulations of 1917. This list is subject to a further slight revision and to the addition of a few names not as yet passed upon by the local board.

FILLMORE

739—Park E. Smith; 623—Almon Dee Robison; 6—Arnell W. Jackson; 406—J. Albert Robison; 336—Wilford Anderson; 622—A. Newton Rasmusson; 331—Clinton C. Day; 86—Willard R. Huntsman; 624—Archie Robison; 776—Joseph D. Pyper; 311—O. Lawrence Huntsman; 452—Harnell R. Roldson; 54—Platt Trimble; 90—Stanley C. Maycock.

HOLDEN

379—Erastus L. Christensen; 550—James W. Crosland; 64—Parley C. Turner; 175—Wilford Johnson; 72—Bruce S. Stephenson; 150—Thadeus Johnson; 572—Sydney O. Hunter; 629—Carl Nixon; 449—Elm D. Hoffhines.

SCIPIO

606—Henry Miller; 675—Marion G. Thompson; 677—Edward C. Peterson; 585—Ralph M. Monroe; 202—Leffel Fisher.

MEADOW.

258—John E. Edwards; 185—Edward Dee Bushnell.

KANOSH.

760—Clarence A. Whatcott.

LYNNDYL

278—Guy C. Campbell; 116—Peter F. Anderson; 549—Edwin L. Berger; 342—Earnel Johnson; 640—Ira Parnell Hinckley.

LEAMINGTON.

19—Fred R. Greathouse.

OAK CITY.

437—Clinton C. Dutson; 320—Eldon Anderson; 436—John Dutson; 396—Willard R. Christensen; 613—Stanley W. Lovell; 362—Albert C Christensen; 717—Martin H. Sheriff

DELTA.

786—Arthur A. Hochgnerial; 770—George A. McNutt; 183—Emory Bridges; 792—Raymond S. Tozier; 549—Myron C. Olive; 637—Cyril H Chur; 571—George M. Hampton; 112—Arvid F. Anderson; 505—Clarence Prestwick; 46—John R. Strickley; 357—Lawrence oNelson; 421—John Kozina; 266—Charles D. Eddie; 229—Enoch L. Folsom; 136—E. Le

roy Baxter; 96—Wm. H. Wollasten; 633—I. O. McMillen; 619—Hugh Kelly; 824—Clifton C. Simmons; 499—Mitchell W Clark; 590—Benj. F. Riding; 636—Clement K. Porter; 734—Chris Teller; 33—Adonlian D Hagan.

OASIS.

33—Amos J. Peterson; 262—Andrew Jenson.

DESERET.

51—Francis H. Black; 530—Arthur L. Cahoon; 241—Allen M. Baker.

HINCKLEY.

784—John W. Wright; 194—Chas. Burke; 46—Carl G. Theobald; 116 Roy Parker Hilton; 392—J. A. Crawshaw; 581—Harold R. Morris; 352—Joseph S. Nielson; 460—Carson M. Draper; 777—Harrison Slaughter.

MALONE.

548—Paul Cline.

ABRAHAM.

809—George O. Wilcken.

BURBANK.

617—Arthur Lee Maurry.

Millard County Chronicle
September 13, 1917

The School Year---Over 300 Enrolled

The kids are much in evidence now as the district school commenced last Monday and they have begun to concentrate on the streets. Co. Supt. Hammond was here visiting the school and states that the new building is an excellent addition to the school facilities of Delta, being well constructed and a blessing to the teachers and pupils. There are already a little over three hundred pupils enrolled and more coming in all the time. Eight teachers are employed and another will have to be added and possibly two more. In this event all available rooms in the building will be taken up and we will soon have to figure on another building to accommodate the increasing attendance. Supt. Hammond's idea of the next move is that it should be a Junior High School. The school census of the Delta District, taken during the summer, showed 372 children of school age. Hinckley district is only one behind us. In the county there are 2834 children of school age.

The teachers of the West Side are as follows:

Clear Lake:—Charlotte Gallyer.

A. C. Nelson School:—A. I. Tippetts, Malda Stewart, Ella Curtis, Laverna Wright, Elsie Richards, Hazel Nelson.

Hinckley:—Stanley Goats, Otis Walsh, Eleanor Johnson, Afton Hinckley, Mrs. Arita Black, Lois Blake and Vivian Smith.

Delta:—Clark Allred, Rulon Starley, Murial Erickson, Hannah Johnson, Maude Smith, Cleo Pierce, Edna Beck and Mrs. Elizabeth Chidester.

Sutherland:—Prof. Pratt, Fannie Cropper, Lila Peterson.

Woodrow:—Mrs. Etta B. Underhill.

Sugarville:—Alfreda Gunnerson.

Sunflower:—Cora Heise.

Abraham:—Oran Oppenshaw and Mrs. Mertie Lewis.

South Tract:—Miss Mary Runyon.

Oak City:—Jesse Higgins, Mrs. Alice Anderson and Zella Neilson.

Leamington:—R. E. Winn, Lessie Greathouse and Ethel Olsen.

Lynndyl:—Mrs. Jacob.

SUGARVILE SIFTINGS.

There will be a drainage meeting at Woodrow Saturday evening, Sept. 15th. Everyone invited to come.

We were quite surprised to learn that our storekeeper had taken unto himself a wife. We extend congratulations.

Albert Watts and family spent Sunday at the home of J. S. Barker.

Mrs. E. R. McCoy and son, Ernest spent Thursday in Delta, to visit with a friend who stopped off for the day, while on his way from California to her home in the East.

The Friendship Thimble club will be entertained next Wednesday by Mrs. Barker and Mrs. Hoyt at the hall. At the last meeting it was decided that the ladies would entertain their husbands and families at their hall Saturday evening, Sept. 22nd. A committee was appointed to arrange a program and all members are requested to be present next Wednesday to make the final arrangements.

WOODROW ITEMS

Mr. and Mrs. Endle, nee Miss Minnie Clark with their children are visiting Mr. and Mrs. J. J. Clark.

* * * *

Miss Clara Clark, who has been spending the summer in California, returned home last week.

* * * *

Master Edward Heise was accidentally cut on his knee by a hoe last week and is unable to attend school this week.

* * * *

The babies of John Wind, Chas. Barker, Meade Tillotson, and Frank Nutsch have been on the sick list for the past week.

* * * *

Mrs. N. B. Dresser, who has been spending the summer with Mr. Dresser on his ranch, recently returned to her home in Salt Lake City.

* * * *

Rev. and Mrs. Hamilton were gladly welcomed last Sunday at their first service in Woodrow since leaving for the summer work in Gospel tent.

Sunday, Sept. 30th has been selected for Rally day for the Wodrow Sunday school.

* * * *

Rev. Mr. Leinhardt preached a fine sermon in Woodrow Sunday afternoon. Mr. Leinhardt is a Lutheran Minister, who is here attending to business interests.

* * * *

Quite a party of North Tract young people will make things lively for the Mt. Pleasant Academy this winter. Among those attending are Ethel Heffleman, Beatrice Bracewell, Leona Seams, Cora Brunner, Maude Heise, Richard Thompson and Verda Oppenheimer.

* * * *

School opened Monday with Mrs. Underhill in charge. About 40 pupils are in attendance. Wodrow requested a second teacher for the primary department but the Board of Trustees have decided to deny their request. We should not complain, however, as after three years of requesting we still have our cattail and mosquito pond to decorate the landscape. Woodrow knows how to be grafted for the many favors received from the County, including the broken bridges and road repairs that fail of accomplishment.

* * * *

A very enjoyable farewell party was given to our boys who have been called to the service last Tuesday, p. m. A fine program was rendered which consisted of instrumental music, by the Schiffer brothers and by Mrs. Pervine and Mrs. Kyes, vocal duets by Mrs. Pervine and Mr. Banks. Recitation by Miss Mable Foote, interspersed with songs by the male quartette. In the absence of Delta talent which was to have made the farewell address, Mr. Cady of Sugarville was called upon and made a very impressing farewell speech.

Woodrow was hard-hit by the draft. From those registering within a radius of one mile, were taken the following: Mitchell Clark, Geo. McNutt, Adrian and Clinton Hagan, Donald and LuRu Pritchett, John Kozina and John Strickley. We are proud of our boys, but sorry of Woodrow's loss. However, when they return as Colonels, Captains, and generals, which they surely will, for the stuff of which these officers are made is in them, we will dry our tears and rejoice at the honor thus reflected upon Woodrow.

MORE WEDDING BELLS.

Mr. Norman Gardner and Miss Verna Schlappy went to Salt Lake City last Sunday night where they were married in the Salt Lake Temple yesterday.

Miss Schlappy is the charming daughter of Mr. and Mrs. H. J. Schlappy, of the North Tract, and is well known in Delta, having filled a position of clerk in the Golden Rule store for the past year.

Mr. Gardner is also very well known in this community, having lived here since the first settlers came. He is now employed by R. J. Law and is managing his store at Sugarville.

The happy young couple will visit relatives and friends in Salt Lake City and Payson for several days, after which they will return to Delta where they intend to make their home.

They were accompanied to Salt Lake by Mr. Gardner's mother.

Congratulations and best wishes go out to them in their new venture.

In the Salt Lake temple, Wednesday, September the 12th, occured the marriage of Miss Silva Christensen, of Oak City and Mr. Alma Christensen, of Oasis.

Mr. and Mrs. Christenson are people of unquestionable character and have hosts of friends in the communities where they reside.

They were accompanied to Salt Lake by Mr. Christensen's sister, Mrs. C. H. Jones, of Delta.

After a sojourn of a few days in Salt Lake they will return to their home at Oasis.

SOUTH TRACT SAYINGS

Threshing is about done south and east of Delta.

* * * *

The H. E. Beck family recently enjoyed a splendid visit of ten days with a neice and her daughter from the old home in Illinois.

* * * *

E. A. Brush and family are delighted over a visit with Mr. Brushes father, mother and sister. We hope they will stay with us for a good long time.

* * * *

Miss Mary E. Runyon, who comes to us as a well-qualified teacher is now at work at the East Central school on the South Tract. We wish for both the teacher and the pupils a most successful school year. Let us do all we can to encourage and help the school along.

Joseph Fidel has purchased from J. W. Evans the alfalfa seed and beet crop on the Evans farm. He is now cutting the seed.

* * * *

Mr. Whitmore, Sr. has commenced operations on the new piece of land purchased from the Delta Land & Water Co. last spring. It joins Fred Keim's land on the east.

* * * *

Delta News Notes.

Joe Briggs and family have moved to Salt Lake City.

—)(—

Miss Thenelda Blackburn is employed at the Dan Stevens Store.

—)(—

Mrs. Gene Gardner is visiting with her parents in Oak City.

—)(—

T. C. Gronning of Milford was a Delta visitor this week.

—)(—

H. McKnight, of Keever, Idaho, is here looking over the country with the idea of buying land.

—)(—

Mr. and Mrs. S. E. Jacobs returned Tuesday night from Salt Lake, having visited there for the past several days.

—)(—

Richard Smith returned the first of the week from Salt Lake, where he has been attending to business.

—)(—

Milton Moody returned from a business trip to Salt Lake, the first of the week.

—)(—

Miss Pearl Tozer has resigned her position in Steven's store and has gone to Salt Lake to school.

—)(—

Spencer Crookston returned to his home in Logan the first of the week.

—)(—

Last Monday we were visited by a fine rain, which lasted most of the day.

—)(—

Ralph Sanford left Tuesday morning for St. George where he will attend the Dixie Fruit Festival.

—)(—

L. F. Koch returned from a five-week's stay in Salt Lake City last Saturday.

—)(—

W. J. Carey, and family returned the first of the week from an extended trip to their old home in the east. They report a fine trip.

—)(—

Mrs. M. E. Koch and daughter, Mrs. Lola Beck, are visiting relatives in Delta. Mrs. Beck may spend the winter here.

—)(—

George Searle of Montana, brother-in-law of Mrs. J. H. Peterson, visited in Delta one day the first of the week, leaving Tuesday morning.

—)(—

The Jass orchestra of Fillmore, played for dances here Monday and Tuesday nights, good crowds being present on both occasions.

—)(—

Don't fail to read the ad of D. J. Black, Millinery, Dress goods, General merchandise and Groceries. There are things in it which will interest you greatly.   s13o4

—)(—

Mrs. C. H. Aller and Miss Louise Fuller returned the first of the week from Oregon, where they went to attend the funeral of their brother, who was killed in a railroad wreck.

—)(—

Our ad talks straight to you. Come in and we'll do business straight with you.   At your service. J. D. Black, Gen'l merchandise, Deseret.   s13o4.

—)(—

R. T. Patterson and family returned Saturday from a trip of about three months thru Missouri, Iowa, Kansas and Oklahoma, where they went at the same time W. J. Carey and family. Mr. Patterson and family made the trip in their Dodge and report a fine time and the best of luck all the way along.

—)(—

Read J. D. Black's Gen'l store ad in Deseret. There are some excellent bargains in it for you.   s13o4

—)(—

Richard R. Lyman, who is erecting a number of residences west of the Delta Land & Water office building. is having pavement built to connect them with the city pavement.

—)(—

H. F. Aller is again seen on the streets of our city.   He is at his old stand buying grain and produce. Mr. Aller was called to Ohio on account of the illness of his father.   He reported him much improved when he returned to Delta.   The new sugar company, at Rigby, Idaho, Mr. Aller says is progressing nicely and will be in shape to handle beets next year.

—)(—

The Princess Theatre announces that the Photo play, "Pots and Pans Peggie", which was advertised for Wednesday night but the reels of which failed to appear in time, has been postponed until Friday evening to give preference to the free play at the new play house. Remember the date, Friday night at the Princess, and come out and see the splendid acting of Gladys Hulette, whose clever performance you will remember having recently seen in the play, "The Shine Girl". Gladys is one of the cleverest girls on the stage and will please you immensely.

Dr. F. I. Kimball of Los Angeles,

Millard County Chronicle
September 20, 1917

Rally Round the Flag, Boys!

With all Utah putting forth every possible effort to let the boys who were called on the selective draft know before their departure that the heart of the state is with them in the sacrifices they are making for the sake of humanity, Millard County was not lagging. Wednesday, the day of the departure of the first quota for their training station at American Lake, Washington, was given up by patriotic citizens of the county in preparation of a big event in their honor.

By six o'clock in the evening all the boys were assembled at Delta, and the home Economics Association with the assistance of their friends, under the leadership of Miss White, had prepared an excellent banquet in the Opera House for the boys, free of charge and for all others who wished to partake at a most considerate fee. The ladies worked hard and long to prepare the sumptuous repast and are to be congratulated on the success, and most earnestly thanked for the labor in its preparation.

Sheriff Dorrity and the County Commissioners, as well as their friends and assistants and the Fillmore orchestra showed their patriotic spirit in their efforts to make the occasion a success.

After the banquet was served, patriotic speeches were made by a number of prominent people of the county and solos were sung by Messrs Huntsman and Bannon. Next dancing was indulged in until train time, when the boys, accompanied by one of the largest crowds ever congregated at the depot, were escorted to the station where last farewells were exchanged and the future soldiers of Right, Justice and Liberty were on their way to uphold these principals against the most ruthless, inconsiderate, and inhuman foe civilaztion and the theory of right between man and man has ever known.

The hearts of the people of the whole nation except I. W. Ws, and thank God we have but few of them here go with them and fear not, but that they will do their duty to their country.

Following are the names of the boys who left last night:

John E. Edwards, Fillmore, John W. Wright, Hinckley, Amos J. Peterson, Leamington, Henry Miller, Scipio, Marion Glen Thompson, Scipio, Edward Carl Peterson, Scipio, Raymond S. Tozer, Delta, Platt Trimble, Fillmore, Arnell W. Jackson, Fillmore, Roy Parker Hilton, Hinckley, Jesse Allen Crowshaw, Hinckley, Stanley C. Maycock, Fillmore, J. Wilford Anderson, Fillmore, Arnold H. Rasmussen, Fillmore, Ralph Monroe, Scipio, Lawrence Nelson, Delta, Willard R. Huntsman, Fillmore, Edward D. Bushnell, Meadow, Chas. D. Eddie, Enoch L. Felsom, Delta, Clarence Whatcott, Kanosh, Fred R. Greathouse, Leamington, Peter F. Anderson, Oak City, Wm. H. Wollaston, Glen C. Stewart, Delta, I. O. McMillen, Delta, Joseph D. Pyper, Fillmore, Harold Morris, Hinckley, Orson Huntsman, Fillmore, Benjamin F. Riding, Delta, Joseph S. Neilson, Leamington, Harris Lockwood, Lynndyl.

Master Edde Heise has been suffering from a severe attack of dysentry and Master Bernard Munster from a facial abscess due to an ulcerated tooth.

* * * *

Miss Beatrice Bracewell has recovered from the Pahvant Plauge and joined the Woodrow contingent at the Mt. Pleasant Academy Monday morning.

* * * *

The Jolly Stitchers will be entertained at the Woodrow hall Friday the 28th by Mesdames Ludwig and Heinlein. We hope all members will be present.

* * * *

We are sorry for those who have sold their teams for autos and find themselves marooned on a desert island because their neighbors have flooded the roads in all dierctions. It seems strang, that after living 2000 years under the "Golden Rule", a whole community would care so little for their neighbor's welfare.

* * * *

A very exciting runaway rendered the nerves of our Woodrowites somewhat unsteady last Sunday morning when those who had gathered for Sunday school saw the team of Mrs. Mary Isles tearing down the road, evidently uncontrolled. Mrs. Isles was accompanied by her two neices and nephew for whom the situation looked serious. Fortunately a group of men happened to be talking by the roadside and the panic of the horses subsided when they found themselves faced by about a dozen stalwart citizens. The trouble was caused by a broken shaft, which was striking the horses heels.

Millard County Chronicle
October 4, 1917

SOUTH TRACT SAYINGS

H. E. Beck is expecting a visit from Mrs. Beck's brother from Oakland, Calif., in the very near future.

* * * *

We are sorry to note that Henry Ericson and family, who are farming the Coffin and Lane ranch will vacate the ranch sometime next month.

* * * *

Ed Pierson finished his labors at the Delta State Bank last week, and is now the book keeper at the Delta Land & Water camp on the South Tract.

* * * *

The South Tract is becoming very much divided up. It seems that the neighbors are going together in small clans, to wage war on the beet fields. About three families to a clan and the way they will deliver beets to the Delta sugar factory, won't be slow.

* * * *

Mr. and Mrs. Fred Baker and family are moving into Delta for the winter to get next to the Delta school. We will miss them while they are gone, both socially and in our little school.

* * * *

C. A. Hire and wife have returned from their sojourn in Salt Lake City, and are with us again heart and hand. Ray says batching is alright but too much of it isn't nice.

* * * *

A farewell party will be given at Mr. and Mrs. Whitmore's for Ivy Mortensen, who goes to her home in Salt Lake City in the near future. She has enjoyed an all-summer visit at Bert's, Mrs. Whitmore being her sister.

* * * *

The only safe way to get about Delta no wis with hip boots. The writer has seen two autos stuck in the mud on two of the main streets in the heart of the town and had to be pulled out. All this without any rain too.

On last Saturday the Delta Sugar Company added another star to their already luminous crown out on the South Tract about 9 a. m., and gathering up about twenty-six farmers, who greatly enjoyed the day, both as an outing and an opportunity to gather informtion in regard to growing beets, as well as to see what was possible in the way of tonage. The field men chaperoned by Frank Roberts, are a bunch of highly honorable and dignified pleasant men, who understand beet culture and are a bunch of good chauffeurs. Incidentally about noon they pulled up at the Woodrow store, where we were royally served with luncheon. Flatly refusing to allow us to have any part in settling for same. I don't think Mr. Roberts got enough of the luncheon, for when we got to Hinckley, he secured a stock of sorgum, and ate on that the balance of the way home. I am sure, judging

Personal Items

Born:—To Mr. and Mrs. M. M. Stapley, on the 17th, a fine baby girl.

—)(—

Silas Earl, of Fayette, Utah, is here visiting his brother, Orange and family.

—)(—

Read J. D. Black's Gen'l store ad in Deseret. There are some excellent bargains in it for you.   s13o4

—)(—

Miss Wanda Boyack has returned from Spanish Fork, after an extended visit with relatives.

—)(—

LOST:—A Ladies' gold wrist watch. Name "Sylvia" engraved on back. Finder please return to Chronicle office and receive reward.

—)(—

Mrs. E. J. Biehler of Abraham, has her sister, Mrs. R. A. Kennedy, of New York, her daughter, Mrs. R. E. Dansfield, and son of Chicago and daughter, Mrs. G. Yearsley and daughter of Salt Lake City making her a visit. Mrs. Biehler will return as far as Salt Lake City with them.

—)(—

Mrs. E. M. Gibson, and daughter, Miss Jessie, of Chillicothe, Mo., arrived in Delta the last of last week to visit for a few days with Mrs. Gibson's brother, E. H. Detwiler.

—)(—

Oscar Bohn, of Abraham, who has been working in Delta during the summer was brot in and taken to Salt Lake on Tuesday night's train to have an operation performed for appendicitis.

—)(—

O. L. Lake, Abraham's real estate man and farmer was in town the first of the week and says the Abraham district is looking fine and that there is some very nice stands of beets being grown there this year.

—)(—

Jeff Clark has just received word that on and after October 1st, the price of the Twentieth Century tractor attachment goes to $200. By ordering now you will be saving $15 on the tractor.   s20tt

—)(—

Jeff Clark has closed a deal in real estate whereby he sold the forty acres belonging to the American Trust Company, just east of M. M. Steele's Jr. to Wm. H. Riding and Scott Armstrong of the sugar company, jointly.

Mrs. W. H. Riding left Monday for Brigham City, where she will visit with her mother for a week.

—)(—

Mr. and Mrs. Jesse Knight and son Kenneth, are visiting for a few days with relatives here.

—)(—

We are indebted to Wm. N. Gardner for two fine watermelons sent him from his father's farm at Salem.

—)(—

The Studebaker establishment has moved to their new home on Clark street.

—)(—

The Delta Merc. has installed a new gasoline pump infront of their store.

—)(—

I have just received a fine line of Matresses, good ones and cheap ones. My motto is "The Best is None too Good for My Customers". You can find them at the Delta Furniture Store.   s20-27

—)(—

The Misses Jetta Bunker, Orena Law, Sadie Lisonbee, Vida Anderson, and Melba and Flora Steele, left the last of last week for Provo, where they will attend school at the B. Y. U. the coming winter.

—)(—

Don't fail to read the ad of D. J. Black, Millinery. Dress goods, General merchandise and Groceries. There are things in it which will interest you greatly.   s13o4

ACCIDENT AT HINCKLEY.

A very sad accident accompanied the opening season for the hunting of ducks and geese, when Sam Webb, of Hinckley, met with an accident which will mark him for life and may yet cause his death.

Last Monday, about 2, o'clock while a party of three, consisting of Will Bishop, Will Shaw and Sam Webb were returning from a hunt down near Craft's lake. Mr. Webb's gun exploded, the charge striking him in the right cheek. Mr. Webb was sitting in the back seat of the car alone and the butt of the gun, which was a single shot gun, was leaning against the door, when the door came open and allowed the gun to slip out. It was loaded and was supposed to have been discharged by the hammer striking as the gun descended. A part of the charge struck Mr. Webb in the cheek, making a very painful and dangerous wound. To just what extent it could not be determined at the time of our interview with those in possession of the facts.

When Mr. Webb received the shot, he fell from the car. He was picked up and he was rushed into Hinckley, and Dr. Broadhus was summoned as soon as possible.

NEWLY WEDS.

Dainty announcements are out, announcing the marriage of Mr. Gus Faust and Miss Amy Finlinson, Wednesday, October 3rd, in the Salt Lake temple.

Mr. Faust is the son of Mr. and Mrs. Jas. A. Faust and is known to all to be an honest and industrious fellow. He has lived here for several years and has the good will of all who know him.

Miss Finlinson is the eldest daughter of Mr. and Mrs. Geo. E. Finlinson of Oak City, and is very popular with the young people of that place, and respected by the community at large.

The best wishes of the community go out to them for a long and successful married life.

They will make their home in Delta, where Gus is having a house erected north of town, near his work.

ABRAHAM ARTICLES.

There was quite a number of young folks went to Salt Lake last week. Those who have returned report a pleasant time there.

—)(—

Miss Lila Lake and her sister, Mrs. Filby and children returned from Salt Lake last week.

* * * *

Some people from here attended conference in Oak City last Sunday.

* * * *

Louisa Young went to Oak City for fruit last week.

* * * *

Mrs. Bohn returned from Joseph last week where she has been canning fruit. She brought back with her a nice lot of fresh fruit.

* * * *

Mrs. Young and family are going to Salt Lake Saturday where she is going to do temple work.

* * * *

Henry Vorwaller is located at Mare Island, California where he is training. Says he feels fine.

WOODROW ITEMS

Mrs. W. J. Strickley, of Salt Lake is visiting at the Strickley ranch.

* * * *

Mr. J. DeLapp of Nauvoo, Illinois, who has been spending the winter on the coast, stopped off in Delta for a week's visit with his son, John De-Lapp, of Woodrow, on his return to Nauvoo.

Mr. Herring and his visitors and Mr. and Mrs. Herman Fredericks were guests at dinner with the Webster and Tracy families Thursday evening. The basis of the bill-of-fare was 11 wild ducks, the product of Monday's sport, enjoyed by Messrs. Tracy and Webster.

* * * *

We are very sorry to announce that Mr. Webster has again changed his mind, and will leave for Carbon Co.,

this week. The mercantile firm in Helper made a new offer, which was too tempting for Mr. Webster to turn down.

* * * *

The Jolly Stitchers are buisily engaged rehearsing a play, known as the "Old Maid's Convention", which will be staged Saturday evening, October 13th. Don't fail to come, and wear loose clothing so that you may laugh with comfort, as the play is a side-splitting farce.

HINCKLEY HAPPENINGS

Last Tuesday evening a primary was held for the purpose of selecting the names of the forthcoming town officials. As the business of the meeting was not completed the names of the different officers are not ready for announcement.

* * * *

Tuesday evening also witnessed the opening of Hinckley's new play house. A large crowd was present and the management may be sure that that efforts to give the town a modern show house will be fully appreciated.

* * * *

The district school teachers have shown their enterprise by securing for their school, a good victrola. The

teachers and students alike are loud in their praise of the service it is rendering to the institution.

* * * *

Last Friday many of the townspeople, as well as the students, enjoyed listening to stirring appeals from Pres. Geo. H. Brimhall and Supt. H. H. Cummings, who were urging loyalty to the cause of the Liberty Loan. The Lectures were given in the Academy, under the auspices of the Student Body.

* * * *

The new railroad recently built into Hinckley has already taken on a business like air. The beet dump just east of town is the scene of activity from early morn until late at night. A huge pile of beets is being accumulated at the dump ready for transportation to the factory at Delta in the near future.

Our hustling blacksmith, J. A. Jackson, is being worked overtime, trying to supply the demand for wagon boxes, in which to haul the beets and the farmers, in turn, are being rushed by the season and the scarcity of laborers, in their efforts to harvest the beets before severe cold weather sets in.

* * * *

James S. Blake, C. E. McClellan and Milton Moody have been named as a committee to solicit subscriptions to the Liberty Loan fund. They have made a house to house visit, over most of the precinct. In many instances they meet with a ready response to their appeals, but too many citizens seem not to realize the seriousness of the call made upon them. On Wednesday evening there was a mass meeting and a Liberty Loan dance in the Millard Academy. At this time a substantial increase was added to the loan.

Man Found Dead.

Last Saturday morning the people of Delta were shocked at the report of some boys having discovered the body of a man in a straw stack, near the cemetery and just east of the sugar factory. On examination, the report was confirmed, and an investigation by the authorities revealed

the fact that the man had been sick and was seen about the factory some days before. He had gone out to the straw stack and crawled into it in his depleted condition and probably chilled to death. When found, the body had been badly trampled upon by cattle, which had fed at the straw stack, and it is thot that it had lain here from two to four days after life had departed. The coroner's jury entered a ver-

dict that he came to death by natural causes. With the exception of a small kit of eating utensils there was nothing found on his body. No papers or marks of any kind to identify him.

He was a man of near sixty with a beard covering his face, and was very thin from ravages of disease.

His body was turned over to undertaker Knight for disposal and now occupies an unnamed grave in the cemetery.

SUGARVILLE SAYINGS.

J. S. Law and R. O. Marton left Monday for Banning, California.

* * * *

The Friendship Thimble Club will be entertained next Wednesday afternoon by Mesdames Shields and Huelett at the home of the former.

* * * *

Word has been received from Er-

nest Baxter that he did not pass the examination at Camp Lewis, so he will be home in a about two weeks.

* * * *

You must not forget the big Halloween entertainment at the F. T. C. hall, Saturday evening, October 27th. which will commence at 8:30, p. m. Be sure to shake hands with the lady at the door. The witch will brush

your shoes and the lady in white will escort you thru the varius apartments. Get your fortune told and find what is in store for you. Many stunts and contests will be carried out during the evening. Refreshments, consisting of pumpkin pie and coffee, all thru the evening, also a refreshing drink with cookies served on a broom stick. There will be a dance after. Admission is free. Everybody come.

Personal Items

E. S. Marshall is addending to business in Salt Lake.

—)(—

H. F. Aller is a Salt Lake visitor this week.

—)(—

Miss Eva Gardner is employed at the Delta Lumber and Hardware store as stenographer.

—)(—

A choice line of Monarch Ranges to choose from at the Delta Furniture Store.   o18-25

—)(—

Mr. and Mrs. W. E. Bunker have moved to their farm one mile east of town.

—)(—

Mrs. Emma Barrass is here from Illinois, for a visit with her parents, Mr. and Mrs. George Tozer.

—)(—

S. W. Eccles returned this morning from an extended business mission in Ogden.

—)(—

Mrs. A. L. Broderick went to Salt Lake this week to visit Mr. Broderick, who is in the hospital there.

—)(—

Lorin Turner, who has been working at Manti for the past four months, returned to Delta Tuesday morning.

—)(—

Mr. and Mrs. Abner Johnson have moved on to their farm, recently purchased from E. H. Detwiler south and west of Delta.

—)(—

Theodore Wambold left the first of the week for Salt Lake for a short visit before returning to his home in Los Angeles.

Next Wednesday, October 30th is the last day you can register if you wish to vote at the coming city election. Books open at the Delta Merc. Store.

—)(—

In our last issue we stated that the next Commercial club meeting would be held on October 31st. This was an error. The next regular meeting will be held on the first Wednesday in November. (the 7th.)

—)(—

A party was given last night in the Ward hall in honor of Ervin Jeffery, who recently returned from a mission. A program, consisting of music and speeches, games, dancing and refreshments furnished the evening's, entertainment.

—)(—

The Community Social of the South Tract will be held at the residence of George Beach on Halloween night. All members of the Literary Society are requested to be present. The H. E. A. of the South Tract will sell comforts and a few home products, the proceeds to be used for the Red Cross.

All are welcome.

—)(—

The prospective Town Board, consisting of J. W. Thurston, President, Dr. Broaddus, J. E. Works, A. B. Ward, and O. A. Anderson, forms a list of excellent progressive men who will see to it that the affairs of the city are properly looked after and that all possible improvements in walks, roads and other matters are attended to. They will see to it that the integrity and dignity of the town is unheld and allow no immoral or improper practices to degrade our city.

The case of Walker Bros. vs. Wm. N. Gardner and Mrs. Eliza Jackson, condemning ditch right-of-way thru the Gardner and Jackson farms for a canal, supplying a part of the water to the Hashimoto farm, the court granted a right-of-way to Walker Bros. and assessed them $205 damages for Gardner and $93 for Mrs. Jackson. This is the ditch over which a controversy arose between Mr. Gardner and Hashimoto's men some time ago in which Mr. Gardner was reported to have dynamited the ditch.

—)(—

Mrs. F. G. Wells of the Island Farm, returned from Salt Lake Tuesday, where she went to take Mr. Wells to the hospital. Mr. Wells was kicked by a colt last spring and underwent a very delicate operation at the time. He has never recovered from the wound and has been in a very bad condition ever since. Recently he lost the use of his entire right side and it is thot at the hospital that it may be a blood clot on his brain, which they have hopes may clear up.

—)(—

A. P. Wallace received a letter from his sister near Garland the last of last week, notifying him that his father had been killed the Saturday before at a flag station just this side of Tremonton. He was trying to flag the train, and it being dark and with no light to use he stood too close to the train and was struck by the engine.

A telegram was sent Mr. Wallace at the time of the accident, asking him to come to the funeral last Saturday, but the telegram had not yet arrived and the letter from his sister was the first intimation that he had received of his father's death.

Millard County Chronicle
November 1, 1917

WOODROW ITEMS

Dr. Wm. M. Paden of Salt Lake City accompanied Mr. Hamilton on his rounds Sunday and preached very acceptably to the people of Woodrow.

* * * *

Burton Alward is prospering toward complete recovery from his severe attack of typhoid fever.

* * * *

The Woodmen of the World are gaining new recruits from our Woodrow young men.

* * * *

The Jolly Stitchers will meet with Mrs. Heinlein Friday November 9th. The meeting will be in the way of a farewell party for Mrs. Marie Smith and Mrs. Robert Britt, who will leave soon for their new home in Oregon. Refreshments will be served.

NEW BABIES.

Mr. and Mrs. Jos. A. Frampton, Delta, a boy, October 25th.

Mr. and Mrs. H. E. Markham, Delta, a girl, October 28th, a girl.

Mr. and Mrs. C. A. Stratton, Hinckley, a boy, October 28th.

Mr. and Mrs. Alma Western, Hinckley, a boy, October 28th.

Mrs. and Mrs. Carl Wasden, Delta, a boy, October 29th.

Personal Items

Miss Gertrude Swenson, of Sterling, Utah, is visiting with her aunt, Mrs. Jesse Works.

—)(—

Miss Tora Jaderholm visited with Miss Effie Clark the first of the week.

—)(—

Miss Clora Farnsworth has accepted a position at the Delta Drug store as clerk.

—)(—

Three train loads of soldiers passed thru Delta Tuesday and Wednesday, enroute to the training camp in Southern California.

—)(—

Cyril Cluff and A. I. McMullin returned home from American Lake, Washington the first of the week, having failed to pass the examination there.

—)(—

What was supposed to be an airship, was seen Wednesday evening over Sawtooth mountain, west of Hinckley. These phenomena are getting to be almost common.

Frank Helse, of the North Tract, went to Salt Lake on business last Monday.

—)(—

Simeon Walker, of Oak City, was in town Tuesday yith a load of fine apples.

—)(—

Theodore Wambold, who has been looking after his harvest, left last evening for his home in Los Angeles.

—)(—

The Chronicle office turned out a fine job of two-page bills for the Golden Rule store the last of last week, advertising its big fall opening.

—)(—

Next Tuesday is election day, for the city, and we understand another ticket has been placed in the field, which promises to make a most interesting day.

—)(—

A party headed by John A. Widstoe, president of the University of Utah, visited the valley Friday, investigating matters in connection with Rural Credits. Their findings were not made known.

Miss Lulu Johnson, who has been our faithful correspondent at Holden for a number of years, passed thru our city last Saturday as Mrs. Roy Morgan, on her way to the Uinta Valley, accompanied by her husband, where they expect to make their future home.

—)(—

Engineer Diehl, who has been installing an electric plant at the Delta Club, has finished his work and left for Salt Lake Tuesday evening. A fifty light system, generated from a gasoline engine is now in operation at the club and makes a most favorable impression, and adds greatly to the convenience of the house.

—)(—

During the past week, Dr. and Mrs. Broaddus enjoyed a visit from the doctor's parents and his sister, Mrs. T. C. Sexton and her two children, all of Las Cruces, New Mexico. They found this country much like their own, near the big Elephant Butte Dam, and in about the same stage of development. The New Mexico climate is milder, but their sugar factory is not yet built, the beets being still in the experimental stage.

Millard County Chronicle
November 8, 1917

WOODROW ITEMS

Rev. C. H. Hamilton will preach in Woodrow at 11:30 a. m. Sunday, Nov. 11th.

* * * *

The meeting of the Jolly Stitchers on Friday, Nov. 9th, has been changed to the home of Mrs. Perry in Sutherland instead of at Mrs. Heinlein as was formerly announced.

* * * *

The Ackermans, Titus', and the

Denver Smiths left Tuesday a. m. in their auto cars to tour California during the winter months.

* * * *

Mr. Geo. Webster is back in the old stand, smiling and happy, and so are all of the patrons of the Woodrow store.

* * * *

The beet harvest continues unabated with many acres yet unharvested. We are fortunate in having no fall storms as yet. But oh! those roads!!!

* * *

Messrs. John S. Strickley of Woodrow and Emery Bridges of Suther-

land left Friday night to join our local contingent of soldier boys at American Lake.

* * *

Mr. and Mrs. James Johnson of the South Tract are the fond parents of a nine-pound boy.

* * * *

Willis Leroy, the 3 weeks old infant of Mr. and Mrs. Jesse Hulse, passed away suddenly Thursday evening of last week and was buried Saturday afternoon in Delta. Mr. Hulse's sister from Salt Lake attended the funeral. Very impressive services were held. The speakers being Mr. Jackson and Lawrence Abbott. Mr. Cornwall sang a beautiful solo.

Millard County Chronicle
November 22, 1917

DESERET, THE FIRST TOWN

Deseret, the oldest town in the valley, was first settled in 1865. It was later abandoned on account of the settlers being unable to build a permanent dam to turn water onto their land. In 1876, Gilbert Webb took up the proposition of constructing a dam and the territory around Deseret was again populated. Conditions became somewhat brighter after this but still adverse conditions prevailed many times on account of not being able to control the waters of the river.

The old fort, a short distance south of the present town was constructed of mud bricks in nine days and the walls of the fort can still be seen standing in part. The men building the fort, chose up sides and each took certain portions of it, the side which beat were given a free dance by the losers. No attacks by Indians were ever made on the fort.

The first men coming out into the desert to begin settlement were John Ray, Jacob Croft and Alexander F. Barron. They came by team from Fillmore and were hauled over by Uncle Lee Cropper, then a boy of 15

years.

Deseret is blessed with an up-to-date garage, a barber shop, Damron and Hawley's general store, D. J. Black's general store, John Dewsnup's general store, Joseph Passey's furnishing and notion store and refreshment parlor and a first-class picture play house.

A fine central school lies half way between Oasis and Deseret. This school is one of the most complete schools in the county with a swimming pool, lecture room, water system and electric lights.

HINCKLEY, THE ACADEMY CITY

In the beginning of the development of this valley, the land around Hinckley was a part of the Deseret Ward of the Mormon church, whose people first settled in the valley. Later the community was made a ward of itself and the ward and town received their names from Ira N. Hinckley, the first bishop of the ward. It was in the year of 1906 that a canal was built from the Deseret Irrigation Co's canal and water made available for this community, which slowly grew, until it is now quite an imposing village, with many fine houses and yards surrounded by stately trees and beautiful flowers, shrubbery and fruit trees tastily decorating the yards and adjoining gardens.

Hinckley is a very pretty place to visit in the summer.

The business establishments consist of the Pratt Mercantile Co's big general store, where one's wants may be satisfied in almost any line. Joseph Passey's grocery, furnishing and notion store, a harness shop and a blacksmith shop.

The Millard Academy is also located here and enjoys a large enrollment of students from all over the valley.

Besides the Academy, the town of Hinckley has a comfortable grade school, employing a number of teachers.

A spur of the Salt Lake Route was built into Hinckley this fall and a beet dump erected adjoining the town for the beet growers' convenience.

Those around Hinckley are highly pleased with their experience at beet culture this year, altho they realize they have something yet to learn in their propagation and look forward to a much larger yield next year.

WOODROW ITEMS

Preaching services by Rev. C. H. Hamilton Sunday, a. m. at 11:30.

* * * *

Clinton Hagan is visiting here, while on a furlough from Ft. Douglas.

* * * *

Mrs. George Webster is spending the week in Salt Lake City.

* * * *

Mrs. Kozina and children have returned to their home in California.

* * * *

Mr. and Mrs. George Clemons (nee Miss Margaret Thompson) have moved to California.

* * * *

Ed Herrring is building a residence on his land, and preparing to become one of our permanent citizens.

* * * *

Mr. and Mrs. Lambert, formerly of Woodrow, but now residents of Lincoln, Nebr., stopped off in Woodrow last week to visit with old friends while enroute to California, where they will spend the winter months for Mrs. Lambert's health.

Many Other Towns

A number of towns in close proximity to Delta and allied with the growth of Millard County, which we should like to take up separately, but are unable to on account of space, are, first, Sutherland, located on the Delta Land & Water Co's North Tract five miles north of Delta, at which there is a general store Woodrow three miles farther on at which there is a general store and a large public hall, Sugarville three miles northwest of Woodrow, where there is another general store and public hall and Abraham 5 and one-half miles west of Sutherland at which place there is a postoffice, a nice two-roomed school house and a number of dwellings. These communities are all fairly well settled with people from various parts of the United States

Fillmore, thirty-seven miles southeast of Delta is a town of 1200 inhabitants, at the foot of the mountains, and is experiencing quite a growth on account of the large number of artesian wells recently brot in in the locality, an increased supply of water for irrigation from the Sevier Land & Water Co. ditch, oil drilling. Etc.

Holden and Scipio, both of which lie some distance southeast of us, and are very prosperous and substantially built communities.

Oak City, which nestles at the foot of the mountains, twelve miles east of us is a beautiful little village of 350 people, where everybody raises an abundance of early fruit and vegetables, hay grain and stock. The town has a fine system of waterworks and many beautiful homes

Leamington is snuggled away at the mouth of the canyon, where the Sevier River enters the Pahvant valley. It is twenty-two miles northeast of Delta, and the locality is noted for alfalfa seed raising, fruit, hay and livestock. The town numbers about three hundred and fifty and is now installing a $25,000 water system.

Lynndyl, a railroad division of the Salt Lake Route, lies 17 miles north of Delta and is like the rest of the towns of the valley, in the making. Water was recently supplied to the land around Lynndyl by the Sevier Land & Water Co.

Oasis Large Shipping Point

Oasis lies five miles southwest of Delta, on the Salt Lake Route, and is the shipping point for a large surrounding territory as well as for a considerable part of the east side of the county. The mail leaves there every day for Fillmore and adjacent points. Here is located two hotels, two general stores, a warehouse, the Bonneville Lumber Co. has a branch yard there and there is a neat, up-to-date bank there doing a thriving business.

The Pahvant Valley Creamery is also located in Oasis.

The community around Oasis was originally a part of the Deseret Ward but was later made a Ward to itself. After the coming of the railroad, affairs centered around the station and now a village of twenty-five or thirty families constitute the town.

Commodious Home of N. S. Bishop, Delta.

ABRAHAM ARTICLES.

Recent rains have put winter wheat in first class condition.

* * * *

Several thousand head of sheep are feeding in the fields at Abraham.

* * * *

Grain threshing is slowly progressing. We hope to get through by Christmas.

* * * *

Mrs. O. M. Fullmer returned from a 4-month's visit in Idaho and northern Utah last Saturday.

* * * *

O. M. Fullmer had a short visit from a brother from Idaho, whom he had not seen for 25 years.

* * * *

Sugar beets are about all harvested in this locality. Some fields are showing a very satisfactory tonnage.

* * * *

The Abraham school is progressing nicely under the leadership of Prof. Oppenshaw and Mrs. Lewis.

* * * *

Mr. and Mrs. Charles Jensen were called to Delta Saturday by the serious illness of Mr. Dimmick, a brother-in-law.

* * * *

It is rumored that E. R. Westover has traded his farm for the R. J.

Law stock of merchandise at Sugarville.

* * * *

Chris Larsen who is feeding 400 head of cattle in this vicinity shipped 60 head to the Salt Lake market last week.

* * * *

Van Evera Brothers have leased their farm to the Beet Sugar Co., and will leave for Michigan as soon as their crops are disposed of.

* * * *

The big dinner to be given by the Abraham Water Users' Association on the 17th of this month was postponed until Saturday, December 1st.

* * * *

Schraeppel and Lewis have leased their fine farm for a term of five years to the Delta Beet Sugar Corporation. They leave for Southern California the fore part of December.

SOUTH TRACT SAYINGS

Miss Mary Runyan was sick Monday and unable to teach school.

* * * *

Theron Sipes is visiting his mother, Mrs. Geo. Beach and family.

* * * *

Miss Francis Beach is home after spending the summer at the old Beach home in Auburn, N. Y.

* * * *

Roy is now head weigh-master for the Beet Sugar Co., at Delta.

* * * *

The Hall brothers have been working at the sugar factory and living in town this winter. We miss their friendly faces here.

* * * *

Most of the farmers are finishing up harvesting their beets this week. The rain storms put them behind some in the work.

* * * *

We see quite a number of land buyers out this way lately and we understand some have bought land.

* * * *

H. E. Beck is weighing beets at the Oasis dumps.

Ed Pierson is now bookkeeper in the Delta Land & Water Co's South Tract office.

* * * *

Charles Hardin and family are going to spend the winter in California.

Delta's Big 1,200 ton Sugar Factory; Electrical Thruout.   Built in 1917.

Millard County Chronicle
December 6, 1917

SOUTH TRACT.

The snow on the mountains has been warning us for some time to look out for winter in the valley and now, this Monday morning, it is all about us, mud and snow combined.

* * * *

Mr. and Mrs. Chas. Hardin will leave us on the 6th for California, where they will spend the winter. We seriously object to their going, as we need them to help us spend the long winter months socially.

* * * *

Harry Pearson has gone to Salt Lake. The community question now being asked is, what for? He didn't say anything about having any business to attend to there, he hasn't any relatives there, but someone says, perhaps he has a friend there, and, come to think of it, I believe he has. However, we will have to wait for time to put us wise.

Miss Nira, one of the Beck sisters, who went from here to Hayward, Cal., four years ago, has returned to help eat Thanksgiving turkey and have a general good visit under the parental roof.

* * * *

We understand that Nelson, Kelm and Hire will move the large pile of beets onto cars at the Billings' dump for the sugar factory, and Fred and Guss Hauman will load the pile at Oasis.

* * * *

There were lots of fine beets delivered from the South Tract this year. The tonnage, per acre, however, was very light. The best beets raised on the South Tract this year that came under the observation of the writer, was raised by Carl Elmer on the Van Winkle place. Let's get a better stand and better beets next year. The sugar content of the South Tract beets is away up and should demand a good price.

* * * *

The Home Economics ass'n is arranging for a bazaar in the near future.

* * * *

G. F. Porter and sons will go to the mountains soon for the winter, to cut and deliver posts.

* * * *

The rest of our boys that registered have been called.

* * * *

Work at the D. L. & W. Co. camp is coming to a close and men are getting scarce about there, only about twenty on the payroll now beside the regulars.

* * * *

H. E. Beck says that his friend Emmerson is about the easiest greenhead to decoy that he has seen this fall, calling him in from a mile away, through the marshes and over the hills and even had to go up over the bank and say, "good morning, Si," to keep him from shooting his decoys.

* * * *

It doesn't seem natural to go into the Chronicle office and not see Miss Turner there, on the job as usual. I will go along and help, Mr. Editor, if you want to kidnap her and bring her back.

N. H. Folsom received a photo of his son Enoch who is quartered at American Lake. He is dressed in his soldier uniform and looks the specimen of a fine American soldier.

* * * *

The D. L. & W. Co. are selling considerable of land to newcomers which means that we are going to have lots of new neighbors. We will sure be glad to welcome them as a part of our community.

LOCAL NEWS ITEMS

G. W. Webster, of Woodrow, has opened up a picture show in the Woodrow hall. He has equipped the building with electric lights and uses the same for his projecting machine. He is showing pictures every Tuesday and Friday evening. While Mr. Webster is new at the business and it may take him a little time to find himself, he has the requisite of a hustler and will make the proposition a go and give the people of that community a good show if they will stay by him.

—)(—

D. H. Livingston is here this week from Salt Lake looking after his many interests.

—)(—

John Beckstrand has disposed of his 40 acre tract of land at the edge of the reservoir and the termination of Clark street, to J. W. Schwartz who will make it his home.

—)(—

J. W. Walton, who has been spending the past two weeks with his family in Salt Lake, returned the first of the week to look after his farms.

—)(—

M. F. Goble, of Park City, Montana, who has been looking the country over for the past few weeks, has decided to cast his lot with us and has opened up a first-class shoe and harness repair shop. He is located in the old Broderick restaurant bldg. and guarantees you an A1 job in his line.

—)(—

Mr. Weeter of Salt Lake, who is interested in the Delta Lumber & Hardware Co., is here looking after business matters.

—)(—

The Dale Engineering Co. has just completed the installation of a steam heating system in the Ward hotel and it now represents one of the most modern hotels in this part of the country, having steam heat in every room. The firm has also just closed a contract for overhauling the steam heating plant at the A. C. Nelson schoolhouse.

—)(—

Rufus Clark, who enlisted in the army recently, went to Salt Lake City Sunday evening to join his regiment.

Mrs. W. N. Gardner from Salem, Utah county, who is spending the fall with Mr. Gardner who is working in that locality, was here the first of the week attending to business matters.

—)(—

H. B. Prout, vice-president of the Delta Land & Water Co., is attending to business matters in Salt Lake City.

—)(—

Judge L. A. Hollenbeck, who formerly lived in the valley, is here from Duchesne. Mr. Hollenbeck is still considerably interested in this locality.

—)(—

The city officials have teams busy filling in on the sides of the sidewalk crossings. This move fills a long-felt want and will save a number of atmospheric punctures by sulphuric phrases. Now, if someone would give a few sharp prods to those responsible for the abominable road conditions in this neck-o'-the-woods—and 'abominable' expresses it lightly in some instances—maybe there would be at least some degree of comfort in driving over them if not any pleasure. Who is responsible, anyhow? Is anybody, or isn't there any money to do anything with? And if not, why not? Let's find out. Let's start something—a good roads movement —whether we are able to finish gracefully or not.

ABRAHAM ARTICLES.

Donald Hogan returned from Tintic, Friday.

* * * *

Mrs. Cavanaugh and nephew, Joiner Cassady, were Thanksgiving guests at the Ottley home near Delta.

* * * *

H. D. Lake, his son Frank and Paine Franklin took dinner Thanksgiving with Mrs. Zola Soules.

* * * *

The attendance at the water users' association dinner, Saturday, was not as good as it should have been. We wonder why.

If you want to secure the services of good gentlemen dressmakers, ring 6 shorts on the Abraham line.

* * * *

Sherman Tolbert and wife left on Wednesday for Salt Lake City and other points in Utah.

* * *

Chris Larsen shipped 100 head of fat cattle to the Omaha market, this week.

* * *

O. L. Lake is remodeling his residence in Abraham.

* * *

Robt. Fullmer and wife visited on Sunday at the O. M. Fullmer home.

WOODROW ITEMS

Woodrow has a real up to date 1st class picture show under the ownership, and management of Geo. Webster. Tuesday and Friday of each week are show nights.

* * *

Dr. Wm. N. Paden of Salt Lake City preached very acceptably to the Woodrowites last Sunday at 11:30 a. m.

* * *

Rev. W. N Paden, Rev. and Mrs. Hamilton, Dr. and Mrs. Tracy were handsomely entertained by the De Lapps last Wednesday.

* * *

The Jolly Stitchers will meet with Mrs. Tracy, Friday, December 21st, to finish the organization of the Red Cross Auxiliary and plan for an evening entertainment during the holidays.

* * *

Mesdames Osborn and Underhill are drilling the childrn for one of Woodrow's famous Christmas entertainments.

* * *

Mr. and Mrs. Howard Abbott are the fond possessors of a bouncing baby boy.

* * *

Sutherland has been almost depopulated for ten days as the families of M. A. Abbott, Lawrence Abbott, Ward Robinson and Lyman Moulton in their respective automobiles took a trip to Dixie where there was a great Abbott reunion on the occasion of the unveiling of a statue erected to the memory of M. A. Abbott's father at Bunkerville, Nevada. The respective families made the trip and returned without accident, and they report a most delightful occasion at the gathering of Abbott clans from near and far.

* * *

Mr. J. W. Hall is recovering from a serious illness.

* * *

The Munsters entertained the whole east side to a social dinner last Sunday.

Millard County Chronicle
December 20, 1917

Personal Items

Henry Freese of the North Tract is visiting in southern California.

—)(—

Mrs. C. O. Davis and son have returned from a visit to Ogden.

—)(—

Mrs. Dora Cooper has gone to Salt Lake for a visit and rest until Christmas.

—)(—

The Lincoln Theatre is having a swell new advertising curtain painted for the stage.

—)(—

A carload of Nephi "Gem" flour just in. Prices far below the average. D. Stevens & Co., Delta. (d20tf

—)(—

Our new serial, "King of the Khyber Rifles," begins this week. It is said to be an excellent story based on German intrigue in India.

—)(—

A big Red Cross drive is being made. 500 members for the West Side is planned, and of this number 100 joined last Monday. The membership fee is $1.

—)(—

Barber Hoganlober of Deseret had the misfortune this a. m. to shoot the second and third toes from his left foot and otherwise disfigure that member, while carrying a loaded shot gun on a horse.

—)(—

Bishop Maxfield, who has been in the hospital in Salt Lake for the past two weeks on account of an injury to his knee, returned last Saturday and is now using a crutch and cane as supplementary propellers.

—)(—

In this issue appears a letter written by Charles MacKnight Sain. It is worth reading, and while some may say it is visionary—and is, perhaps—yet just such things are being contemplated in a greater or less measure and we may live to see this very thing put thru by the government—at least in a modified way.

—)(—

While Geo. Cropper's little children were playing around the barn at their home at Deseret one of the little ones ran against a pitch-fork which was being used by the other to throw manure from the barn. The fork ran into the neck for some distance but was deflected from piercing the windpipe.

—)(—

Mr. Watson, an employee of the sugar factory, working at the Oasis beet dump, smashed his foot the first of the week while trying to stop a car on the siding with a pinch bar. The car running up onto the bar with sufficient force to jerk it from his hand and slam the end of it down onto his foot, resulting in badly injuring it. Mr. Watson is a brother-in-law of Mrs. O. L. Crawford and they recently came here on a visit.

ABRAHAM ARTICLES

C. E. Lewis and wife left last week for Fort Collins, Colo.

* * *

Raynier Van Evera made a business trip to Salt Lake this week.

* * *

The Schroeppel & Lewis auction sale was well attended and fair prices realized. Jeff Clark did the auctioneering and behaved very well.

* * *

D. H. Livingston is making some extensive improvements on his fine Abraham ranch by installing water works and various necessities.

John Fullmer is freighting oats to the sheep camps in Drum Mountains.

* * *

It is rumored that W. J. Carey has leased his fine alfalfa farm to the Sugar Co. and will leave soon for Arkansas.

* * *

Frank Lake made a hurried trip to Milford last week.

* * *

The school children will give Xmas program at the school house, Friday evening, Dec. 21. All welcome.

* * *

The sheep and cattle which are feeding on alfalfa hay in this vicinity are taking on flesh very rapidly.

* * *

Mr. and Mrs. Schroeppel left Wednesday for Los Angeles, accompanied by Mr. and Mrs. Osborne of Sugarville. They go overland via Arrowhead route.

* * *

Dee Van Evera, who recently enlisted in the army, has joined the Aviation Corps.

* * *

Geo. Q. Wilcken, one of our army boys, has crossed the continent to New York, and is now on his way to the Sunny South.

WOODROW WRITINGS.

Rev. and Mrs. C. H. Hamilton are to become Woodrow residents for the winter months, residing in the Sampley home during their stay in California. Mr. Hamilton will preach Sunday a. m. at 11:30.

* * *

The Christmas entertainment by the children of the public school and the Sunday school will be held at 8 p. m., Christmas eve. Santa Claus will be there, and a big Xmas tree. All invited.

* * *

Little Hazel Heise was accidentally shot by an air rifle during play on last Sunday. The B. B. shot penetrated her upper lip and everyone is congratulating her that it was her lip instead of her eye that was injured.

* * *

Mr. and Mrs. Osborn, and Mr. and Mrs. Greathouse accompanying the Schroeppels, left early Wednesday morning for an auto trip to California. The Schroeppels will remain, but the Osborns and Greathouses will return after the holidays.

The Misses Agnes and Marie Horsleff are entertaining their sister from Kansas. Miss Horsleff will remain in Utah for several weeks and then visit the coast before her return to Kansas.

* * *

Several of our most husky appearing lads have been turned down upon physical examination by Uncle Sam's representatives.

* * *

There is to be a grand ball in Woodrow on New Year's eve., the proceeds to go to toward finishing the hall. Admission price $1.00 per couple. Refreshments served.

* * *

Lawrence Abbott went last week to San Francisco to engage in a six months' mission in California.

* * *

Mrs. Iva Haffleman leaves on the 23rd to spend the winter with her daughter in California.

* * *

S. H. Thompson expects to join Mrs. Thompson in Kansas City for Xmas dinner.

Millard County Progress
December 28, 1917

Marriage licence was this week issued to Miss Carry Langston and Mr. Harold Theobald both of Hinckley. The ceremony was performed by the County Clerk.

Miss Larsen and Mr. Oliver Olson of Delta received their marriage licence on Monday and were married later at the home of the bride.

First Accident at Factory to Cause Death

Acil Wright of Hinckley is Caught in Beet Washer Dies in Few Hours

A deplorable accident happened at the sugar factory at three o'clock on Saturday afternoon which resulted in the death of Acil Wright, 15-year-old son of Mr. and Mrs. John Ed Wright of Hinckley.

Acil, who was a large boy for his age and who had been attending school at Hinckley, came up to the factory and applied for work during the holidays with the idea of adding to his pocket money. Being a large boy he was put to work in the sugar room at first. Later a helper being needed at the beet washer he was transferred there to assist in cleaning out grease wood which would float down and become entangled in the washer. For this work hooks on long handles are ordinarily used but it became necessary to get into the washer at times to remove pieces which get fast. The washer is a long trough conveyor with big iron paddles attached to a shaft running thru the middle of it. It is used to wash the beets as they are on their way to the knives. The paddles turn around in .e trough by means of an electric motor which operates the belt and which is stopped and started by a lever. It had been the custom of the two that when one had to get into the washer the other would stand and hold the lever to make doubly sure the belt would not play back on the light pulley.

At the time of the accident a signal had been given that there was plenty of beets on hand and the washer was shut down and Mr. Gates and the boy began removing the grease wood from the washer with their washer, Mr. Gates being under the impression that everything had been done and that the machine was ready to start again; when he reached the other end the signal whistle for more beets blew, and without looking around to see where Acil was he threw on the belt.

In the meantime apparently the boy saw some more greasewood in the corner of the washer and went into it to remove it.

The second the power is turned on the big steel paddles begin to move around within the trough and there is no chance to avoid them. Altho the boy gave a warning cry and the paddles revolved only a part of the way round one caught him on the hip and tore the flesh open to the bone while another caught him in the groin and opened the flesh into the lower abdomen. He was immediately taken out and cared for at the factory and a doctor telephoned for at once. Dr. Hamilton responded and dressed the wounds. He found evidence of internal injuries but expressed the hope that the wounds might not be fatal. However, at five o'clock Sunday morning the boy breathed his last.

His parents were telephoned to at once and were with him to the last. Everything possible was done to save his life.

There seems to be no real blame attached to any one and it is only another of those sad, fatal affairs which attaches to human efforts and the onward move of the commercial world.

The funeral was held at Hinckley, Tuesday afternoon, and the boys at the factory expressed their feelings hooks and had worked their way thru the length of the washer, concluding their work as Mr. Gates thot.

At that moment someone came along and engaged Mr. Gates in conversation and he and the party walked back to the other end of the and sympathy for the sorrowing family with a most beautiful floral tribute.

We all feel the pangs and heartaches of bereaved parents and bow our heads in sorrow and sympathy with them.

Indian Girls Kidnaped at Delta

The following is relative to two Indian girls who were here working in the beet fields. Sheriff Darrity left yesterday to bring them and the Mexican back.

That two—even a. Julia Launey, 17, and her —o inc— a John, 14 years old, had been — —ed at Delta, Ut., and brought to Salt Lake City by an armed Mexican was revealed to the police yesterday. The incident became known to the officers when the girls attempted to borrow $10 at the Continental National Bank with which to pay their fare back to Delta On their description Frank Tobar, 18, a Mexican, was arrested in a down town lodging house and is held in the city jail.

According to the police, the girls say they were enticed to appear at the depot at Delta by the Mexican, who was known to them only as Frank. As the train approached the station the girls said that the Mexican drew a revolver and told them if they did not consent to accompany him to Salt Lake he would kill them instantly. Afraid to do otherwise, the girls boarded the train.

Upon their arrival in Salt Lake the girls said, according to the police, that the man gave them money with which to rent a room and got one for himself directly across the hall where he could guard them. Yesterday he left them in their room saying that he was going after his brother, who would take charge of the younger sister, and that together they would go to Mexico. When he had gone the girls escaped from the room by jumping out of the window.

The federal authorities are investigating the case.

SOUTH TRACT ITEMS

Horace Crawford is spending these fine winter days working on his dry farm which lies straight east of the D. L. & W. Co. camp. We understand he contemplates putting in some crop up there. We hope it will be a success.

* * *

Our teacher, Miss Mary Runyan, after taking the usual holiday vacation, is back and at again.

* * *

Harry Pearson, during the holiday week, went to Salt Lake and at the home of Mrs. Mortenson was presented with a most beautiful and useful Christmas gift. The gift was a young lady of Harry's own choosing, and a sister of Mrs. Burt Whitmore. To look at Harry you would be sure that he thinks he received the finest present possible.

* * *

At the regular meeting of our Farm Bureau, Jan. 5th, at 2 p.m. and 7:30 p.m., we were visited by officers of our County Farm Bureau, Dean Peterson and M. Cornwall, also County Agent Welch, besides two representatives of our Agricultural College at Logan. We were asked to raise more meat in the shape of beef and pork of which the county is short, and were taught how to feed and care for the animals intended for meat. Mr. Cornwall told us, among several other things, of the uses and abuse of our county money and the extreme necessity for our loyalty to our sugar company. President Peterson told us of the past year's business of the County Farm Bureau, which we thot was splendid for the first year. Mr. Welch made a few very useful and practical remarks and distributed bulletins on farm management and sheep husbandry. We certainly enjoyed their visit and profited thereby. Please don't miss us the next time 'round.

* * *

We are glad to know that there will be quite an exodus into the drained portion of the South Tract next spring. This will be of much value to our community as we are not thickly enough populated. The D. L. & W. Co. is selling quite a bit of land and we hope it will be settled on.

* * *

The community in general have taken to the Red Cross movement. Not all have joined as yet, but more will follow. All are loyal to the movement.

* * *

How any farmer can raise a crop of beets for any other than the Delta Sugar Co. and call himself a loyal citizen to the Delta country is more than figures or words will prove.

* * *

The South Tract Farm Bureau held their annual election of officers on the evening of the 5th inst. H. E. Bock, president; Geo. R. Beach, vice-president, and Harry Pearson, secretary-treasurer. Our membership is almost one hundred per cent of our population.

* * *

The Economics Association, will hold their next meeting on the 10th at the home of N. H. Folsom.

* * *

Joseph Fidel says his cattle are taking to the hay and pulp in good shape and are doing fine.

* * *

We very much fear that we are going to lose Ed Pearson from our midst. There is something radically wrong about this kind of an arrangement and we sincerely hope his plans may be changed so he can stay with us or at least soon return.

DIED

Mrs. Julia Rhoane Elder, daughter of Mr. and Mrs. A. S. Workman, Sr., at the home of her parents, January 7th, at 10:30 a. m.

Mrs. Elder was thirty-seven years of age and leaves a husband and six children, the eldest being eighteen years of age and the youngest seven years of age, to mourn their loss. Death came as a relief after continued suffering from tuberculosis.

The funeral services were held from the Ward hall on the ninth at 2:00 o'clock p. m. Interment was made in the Delta cemetery.

The relatives have the sympathy of all in their trial and sorrow.

Miron Theobald Succumbs

Miron L. Theobald of Hinckley, 19-year-old son of Geo. Theobald, was brot to Delta, Tuesday, by Dr. Hamilton suffering from an obstruction of the bowels. The trouble was aggravated presumably from riding after horses which had strayed. As he was very low it was necessary that an operation be performed and he was taken from here Tuesday afternoon in an auto with Dr. Hamilton in charge in the hope that Provo could be reached and relief administered. He died, however, before the auto reached Nephi. The body was taken on to that town where it was prepared for burial and returned to Hinckley on the Wednesday morning train. Mr. Theobald has been very unfortunate in his household regarding the grim reaper. About a year ago his wife was called and altogether six of his family have been laid to rest. The sincere sympathy of all those who know him is his.

ABRAHAM ARTICLES

Leroy Bills and wife left for their home at Grantsville, Friday.

* * *

Frank Beckwith and family took dinner with Payne Franklin and wife Saturday.

* * *

Chris Larsen, who has had several hundred head of cattle in this vicinity for the past three months, will drive them overland to his home at Ephraim, this week.

* * *

Prof. Openshaw returned Monday from a holiday vacation with friends in Salt Lake City.

* * *

Miss Florence Fullmer of Salt Lake City came in Monday for a visit with her parents, Mr. and Mrs. O. M. Fullmer.

* * *

W. J. Cary, who is in a Salt Lake City hospital, is reported much improved at this writing.

Grand and Petit Jurors

The following is the official list from which the Grand and Petit jurors will be called during the current year:

ABRAHAM

A. W. Reid, William S. Taylor, J. H. Riding, John R. Riding.

BLACK ROCK

Thomas Johnson, H. E. Adams, Malone, Utah; Arthur G. James, of Black Rock.

CLEAR LAKE

Charles Ireland.

DELTA

Allen Searles, Nels H. Christenson, Hans Olsen, Benjamin Bunker, William H. Riding, Andrew C. Sorenson, Bert L. Johnson, Edgar W. Jeffery, Eugene Gardner, Burt E. Cooper, William H. Pace, Archie Gardner, John E. Steele, Clark S. Wood, Charles A. Clawson, Marion Kilpack, Edward Bishop, Lorin I. Taylor, Empson S. Marshall, A. B. Ward, Nelson S. Bishop.

DESERET

Hyrum S. Cahoon, David H. Palmer, John W. Western, Daniel J. Black, Jerold S. Bennett, T. B. Allred, Joseph B. Dowsnip, Warren W. Moody, O. L. Crawford, William R. Black.

HINCKLEY

John E. Wright, Jonathan B. Pratt, E. M. Workman, Peter G. Peterson, William H. Walker, T. George Theobald, Thomas R. Greener, Jedediah Cox, John W. Hutchinson, Charles E. Stratton, Don A. Bishop, Simon T. Webb, Charles Burke, William R. Shaw, John T. Jarvis, Marion Bishop, Hugh Hilton, William T. Stanley, R. E. Nelson.

HOLDEN

William Stevens, Jr., Benjamin Kinney, George W. Nixon, Jr., Edward Wood, James B. Stephenson, Frank Badger, Moroni Stevens, Carl Johnson, William T. Bennett, Jos. R. Stringham, Edward Jones, Arthur Tunison.

LEAMINGTON

Brigham Clark, John D. Evans, August Nielson, Benjamin Lovell, Nathaniel Ashby, Albert Textorius.

LYNNDYL

E. A. Jacobs, John Greathouse, Louis B. Noble, Leo Meecham, Alfred Johnson, J. Austin Hunter, H. C. Larson.

OASIS

Anton Anderson, O. J. Day, John V. Styler, Ray Owens, William Norton, Samuel Rutherford, Henry Huff, Charles Thompson.

OAK CITY

Joseph S. Anderson, Abel Roper, George Finlinson, John L. Nielson, Lorenzo Lovell, Leroy Walker, Jesse Peterson.

SCIPIO

Leonard F. Robins, Lars P. Peterson, William F. McArthur, Daniel Johnson, Lewis P. Brown, Bruce Mathews, Lars Jenson, William I. Hatch, Carl M. Anderson, F. Lewis Wasden, Erwin M. Brown, W. S. Walch, James A. Ivie, Frederick Quarnberg, Antone P. Peterson, Adolph Hanseen.

SUTHERLAND

W. R. Walker, G. I. Smith, George R. Johnson, Walter Roberts, Ward Robison, Dan Simpkins.

WOODROW

John Winn, Alberta Watte, George Webster.

Personal Items

Mrs. J. A. Faust is reported as being sick this morning.

—) (—

Isaac P. Robison of Gandy was a Delta visitor the first of the week.

—) (—

R. C. Strong of Indian Valley was registered at the Delta Club the first of the week.

—) (—

T. B. Stearns arrived last evening from Denver to attend to matters pertaining to the sugar factory.

—) (—

Ila Swensen of Sterling, sister of Mrs. J. C. Works, has accepted a position in the City Drug store.

—) (—

Jimmie Canally, son of Mrs. I. V. Many, has gone to Salt Lake where he will take a business course this winter.

—) (—

Mrs. I. V. Many of the South Tract left Saturday evening for a ten day visit with relatives and friends in Salt Lake City.

—) (—

A Mr. Hendrickson was here the first of the week from Sevier county looking the country over for a farming location.

—) (—

Mrs. Bates is assisting at Mrs. Cooper's lunch counter for a few days on account of Mrs. Lackyard being sick with the grip.

—) (—

R. S. Wood and W. S. Woodbury of Ogden were here the first of the week and closed a deal with the Melville Land Co. for a 140 acre farm near Hinckley.

—) (—

A. D. Ryan, who is now with the U. S. Geological Survey engaged in classifying government lands, was in town Thursday of last week. The work is in Utah at the present time.

—) (—

H. F. Aller has returned to the old stamping grounds after spending his holidays with the family in Salt Lake City. H. F. is some sport and says he had a big time in the city.

—) (—

O. W. Paswaters of Lynndyl has been appointed Explosive Licensing Agent, a government position created for the purpose of keeping tab on all explosives used, authority for their purchase and use can be obtained thru him.

—) (—

Attorney Joseph Sampson of the Sugar Co. returned Sunday evening from a business trip to Denver. Joe called on the recruiting officers while in Denver and tried to get into the army but the M. D. found a slight defect in his physical makeup and turned him down. He still has hopes, however, of getting to the front in some capacity.

—) (—

Wm. Williams of Fillmore died the fore part of last week. He was born at Deseret in 1862 and had been a resident of this locality all his life. He was married to Miss Annie Rutherford of Oasis in 1885 and leaves seven children and a wife to mourn their loss. Two small children at home, Frank of Delta, Reynold at home, Elmer, Moab; Arnold and Mrs. Eva Brooks, Salt Lake.

—) (—

Report comes from Fillmore that one of the electrical engineers who are installing the light system for the town was killed the first of the week by coming in contact with a live wire.

HINCKLEY BOY MEETS DEATH AT SUGAR FACTORY AT DELTA.

What was probably one of the saddest accidents and deaths which the people of Millard County have heard of in some time was that which occured at the Delta Sugar Factory on Saturday last, when Mr. Asael Wright son of Mr. and Mrs. John E. Wright of Hinckley, got caught in the machinery of the Beet Bath and had his lower limbs and abdomen so badly crushed that he later died of his injuries.

It seems that the foreman of that part of the factory and Mr. Wright were engaged in cleaning out the Bath of sticks which had been blown in by the wind, and had completed their task and were climbing out of the Bath preparatory to starting the machinery.

The foreman was in the lead and supposed that Mr. Wright was following him out of the bath, as indeed was the case, and the foreman threw in the clutch which started the machinery in motion. As he did so, Mr. Wright noticed another stick in the bath and turned around to go after the stick as the machinery started. He was caught in the giant maws of the beet slicer with the result as above stated.

The machinery was at once stopped and the young man extricated from it, Dr. C. A. Broadus at the same time being hurriedly called. It was at first thought that the young man's life could be saved and everything possible was done for him toward that end, but the internal injuries received caused his death within three hours after the accident happened.

Mr. Asael Wright was but 17 years old at the time of the accident and was a high school student at the Millard Academy at Hinckley and had been working at the factory during holidays in order to get money to assist him through his studies. It has cast a pall of gloom over the tudents of the Academy, with whom he was a prime favorite. The funeral was held on Monday from the L. D. S. Chapel at Hinckley and interment took place in the Hinckley cemetary the remains being followed to their last resting place by scores of friends and aquaintances.

Our sincere sympathy is extended ceased and we greatly deplore the sudden taking off of one whose whole life had shown that he was destined to become a leader among his people. May his spirit rest in peace.

FORD TURNS OVER INJURES DELTA WOMAN.

While on his way to the meeting of the Millard County Board of Education held in Fillmore this week, Mr. Avery Bishop of Delta, and a member of said Board, had the misfortune to have his Ford car turn over with him at or near the Haw Bush. Mr. Bishop's mother was in the machine as were also two other occupants, but as far as can be learned the only one to suffer severe injury from the accident, was Mrs. Bishop. The lady sustained a broken collar bone and two broken ribs, while the others, including Mr. Bishop got off with slight bruises.

It was at or near the Haw Bush where the accident occurred. Mr. Bishop, who was driving, got the car into a deep rut and essayed to get the wheels out of it, and in making the turn was successful, but got the machine too far over on the opposite side of the road, and in getting it back up on the grade, the car skidded and turned completely over, breaking the top an smashing the wind shield.

The mail car driven by Golden Hawley, brought Mrs. Bishop and the others into Fillmore where Dr. Stevers gave the lady immediate attention and assured Mr. Bishop, that unless complications set in, Mr. Bishop would soon recover from her indisposition.

At last reports the lady was resting easily and the doctor gave out assurance that she would soon recover.

Millard County Chronicle
January 24, 1918

Sugarville Sayings.

Mrs. Willis Byers of Delta is spending a few days with her people, J. H. Dale and family.

* * *

A new baby girl at E. R. Westover's.

* * *

Mr. and Mrs. Albert Watts and J. S. Barker and family spent Sunday at J. B. Stevens.

* * *

Ernest McCoy and mother ate Sunday dinner with Harry Anson and wife.

The Athletic club will give a boxing and wrestling contest at the F. T. C. Hall next Thursday evening. McLane of Springville and Terry of Hinckley will be the main feature of the evening.

* * *

At the last meeting of the Sugarville Farm Bureau, held Jan. 16th, the following officers were elected for the coming year: E. Cady, president; J. B. Seams, vice president; James Boyle, secretary and treasurer. Committees were also appointed for the various branches of work. Every farmer should be a member of the Farm Bureau. Remember the meetings are the first and third Wednesday evenings of each month at F. T. C. Hall at 8:30.

Abraham Articles.

Miss Erma Tolbert has been clerking in the E. R. Westover store at Sugarville.

* * *

Harvey Graham came down from Idaho this week on a visit to his sister, Mrs. Charles Vorwaller.

* * *

Miss Lila Lake returned home on Tuesday from Salt Lake City where she has had employment.

* * *

Raynier Van Evera made a business trip to Salt Lake City this week.

* * *

Clinton Tolbert, the 15-year old son of Mr. and Mrs. Sherman Tolbert, was taken to Salt Lake City on Wednesday to undergo an operation for appendicitis.

Mr. Porter and son-in-law, Jesse Cain, of the South Tract, moved this week to the R. J. Law ranch, recently vacated by E. R. Westover.

* * *

Mrs. Maggie Hogan died at the family home Sunday, Jan. 20, after a brief illness, with pneumonia. She was the wife of Bishop Donald Hogan and the mother of eight little children, the eldest being 12 years and the youngest a babe of 5 months. Besides husband and children she leaves parents, brothers, and sisters to mourn her departure. The funeral was held Wednesday at the school house which was filled to overflowing with a sad and sympathetic gathering of people. The remains were then shipped to Mr. Hogan's old home at Woods Cross for burial, and accompanied by him. Those attending from a distance were Austin Duncan of Farmington, a brother of the deceased, and Mr. Hogan's mother and brothers Charles and Lester and wife of West Jordan, Clarence Duncan and wife of Eureka, who are looking after the welfare of Mr. Hogan's children during his absence. Four of the little ones are down with colds.

Mr. Hogan is heartbroken at the loss of his helpmate and being one of our best respected and most upright citizens has the deepest sympathy of the community at large.

OAK CITY NEWS ITEMS

Lorenzo T. Lovell has returned from the hospital in Salt Lake City. He is improving nicely.

* * *

E. L. Lyman, Jr., and family motored up from Delta and spent Sunday with friends and relatives.

* * *

Mrs. George E. Finlinsson is visiting her daughter, Mrs. George A. Faust, of Delta.

* * *

Mr. and Mrs. Roe Wiley gave a wedding dance Friday night. A very enjoyable time was had.

* * *

An epidemic of la grippe is in our community. Nearly everybody has had a touch of it, and several babies are very sick.

* * *

Parley Roper has returned from Camp Lewis where he went to join the army. But Uncle Sam decided he did not want him. He left for Hinckley to resume his studies in the Millard Academy.

* * *

Miss Mable Roper is working for her uncle, Ely Rawlinsson, at Delta.

* * *

Ernest Ottley and John Eldridge gave a party for the young people at Joseph S. Anderson's. All present had an enjoyable time.

* * *

S. J. Rawlinson was home from Leamington to spend Saturday and Sunday with his mother.

* * *

Misses Sylvia Roper and Zella Nelson went to Delta to attend the Sunday School Union meeting Sunday.

* * *

Mr. and Mrs. Alma Christenson of Oasis were here and spent Sunday with friends and relatives.

* * *

Parley Elder is home for a few days. He has been working in Leamington canyon.

DELTA NEWS NOTES.

Dr. Stephensen has gone to Logan to attend the State Veterinarian Association meet.

—) (—

Manager J. H. Jenkins of the Delta Beet Sugar Corporation, is transacting business in Salt Lake City this week.

—) (—

Miss Clara Farnsworth who is clerking at the Delta Drug Co. store, left last week for Lyman, where she will visit relatives until the firsat of February.

—) (—

Attorney Joe Sampson of the sugar company has resigned his position and gone to Chicago where he has accepted a position with a big advertising firm which handles street car advertising, etc. Joe expects to have the management of their Denver office at a big salary.

—) (—

The Delta State Bank recently received a cabinet of safety deposit boxes. These have been installed in their new bank vault. The boxes are large, roomy ones and their yearly rental runs from $2.00 up. They have individual keys for patrons and guarantee one perfect safety from loss by fire, burglary or misplacement of your papers of value.

—) (—

J. W. Schwartz informs us that he recently received a letter from his daughter, Mrs. Lamson and in it Mrs. Lamson stated that she was unable to purchase more than two pounds of sugar. She said a thousand pounds of coal at a time is all that they can get and then an order has to be obtained in order to get it. Mrs. Lamson lives at Newport News, Va.

—) (—

We met Joe Fidel in town yesterday and he informed us that Tuesday evening he started a fire in the house on his farm and picked up the milk bucket and went out to "pail" the cow. When he returned to the house it was all ablaze, having caught from the flue, Joe thinks. He rushed in and secured his best clothes and his papers but his house and all his other belongings went up in smoke. The loss is about six or seven hundred dollars.

—) (—

The people of Sutherland are incorporating with the idea of buying Hi Holdrege's eighty acre farm and dividing it into lots which will be sold to the framers of the locality for residence purposes. The idea is to bring the community together for social purposes and give them the benefit of city conveniences such as light, water, phone connections, etc.

—) (—

Dr. Stephensen has the distinction of having administered the first Pasteur treatment for rabies yet to be given in the State. It takes six days to treat an animal for rabies and the serum is sent each day. The animal treated belonged to John Hunter of Holden and was bitten on the nose nineteen days ago. Bitten in the head by a rabid animal the disease usually shows on another in ten or fifteen days and the case will be watched with much interest.

—) (—

Abner Johnson was in Salt Lake last week with a bunch of fat cattle.

—) (—

Ye editor went to the city last week with the idea of attending the Utah Press Association meeting. The meeting, however, had been postponed until conference time in April. The idea of having the boys all meet in Salt Lake at this time is a good one and should be productive of a large attendance.

—) (—

J. H. Hemmerly, who has taken over the electrical business conducted by Bill Shaw, who is now busily engaged in screwing up his courage to cut his suspenders and join the aviation corps, is installing electric lights in the Delta Opera house. The plant which was used in the Ward hall is being used. Later there will be a line run to the Delta Mercantile store and their establishment lighted by the same plant. Mr. Hemmerly is an experienced electrician and worked for the sugar company installing their plant.

—) (—

Mr. and Mrs. Will Warnick of the West Side, entertained the following persons at a 12 o'clock luncheon last Sunday: Messrs. and Mesdames Geo. Beach, Horace Crawford, Glen Cropper and Miss Frances Beach and Geo. Sipes. A most enjoyable time was reported by the guests.

OAK CITY

The summer weather has turned to winter and we are having some rather cold nights. The men of the town have filled the ice pond with water in the hopes of getting some ice for next summer.

Mrs. George O. Finlinson has gone to Delta to visit with her daughter Mrs. George A. Faust.

Mr. Parley Roper who was notified to appear at American Lake returned home last Wednesday.

Work has again been begun on the town telephone line and we hope to have it completed soon.

The young folks of the town were entertained at an oyster supper at the home of Miss Eva Anderson on Saturday night. They report having had a very enjoyable time.

Mr. and Mrs. Robert Wylie gave their wedding dance on Friday night last and a very enjoyable time was had.

Mrs. Harriet J. Lovell was called to Salt Lake City on account of the illness of her grandson.

Miss Mable Roper has gone to Delta to stay a short time with her aunt Mrs. Eli Rawlinson.

Mr. Bert Roper, who had the misfortune to break his leg on Thanksgiving Day, has returned home from Delta where he has been under the care of Dr. Broadus, and is improving nicely.

The health of the people in general is very good at this time except for a few colds.

Mr. Lorenzo Lovell who was operated on at the L. D. S. Hospital in Salt Lake City some two weeks ago has returned to his home and is reported to be feeling as well as could be expected.

Mr. and Mrs. Alma Christensen from Oasis were here Sunday visiting friends and relatives as were also Mr. and Mrs. Leo Lyman of Delta

Mr. Willis J. Lyman of Delta made a business trip to our town last Thursday and remained over for the dance Friday night.

The Misses Eva Lovell and Mandy Roper have returned home after spending the week at Hinckley.

OASIS

Mr. George Stansworth has returned from Salt Lake City where he has been working for the last six weeks.

Mr. and Mrs. A. J. Henry have returned from Salt Lake City where they have been visiting with their daughter.

Mrs. Nina Huff returned from Fillmore Sunday, afternoon for a short visit with friends and relatives.

A dance was given Tuesday evening in the A. C. Nelson Hall by the Sego Lily Club. Everyone reported having had a jolly good time.

The Income Tax Collector spent Saturday in Oasis collecting taxes from the prosperous men of this and neighboring towns.

Mrs. E. F. Sanders has returned from the East where she has been visiting with her mother.

OAK CITY NEWS ITEMS

A number of our boys have been to Fillmore to be examined for military service.

* * *

Ernest Ottley is in Meadow visiting her sister.

* * *

Evan Jacobson has returned home from Provo where he has been attending school. He expected to be drafted soon.

* * *

A number of our people have been to Hinckley to mill the last week.

Miss Belva Lovell of Oak City and Jefferson Jones of Delta were married in the Salt Lake temple last Wednesday. We wish them a long and happy married life.

Willis J. Lyman is making his regular trip to Oak City. The other Delta boys have won out here. Keep coming, Willis.

* * *

A number of Oak City people attended priesthood meeting at Hinckley, Saturday.

Sugarville Sayings.

Dance at Sugarville Saturday evening, Feb. 2. Be sure and come.

* * *

Mr. and Mrs. Simmons are staying a few days with Ira Creek and family, before leaving for Arizona.

* * *

Mrs. Dewit Hewlett entertained Mrs. Barben and daughter and Mrs. J. B. Seams at dinner last Monday.

* * *

The Friendship Thimble Club will meet with Mrs. W. L. Cary and daughters next Wednesday afternoon at their home.

* * *

Mr. and Mrs. E. H. Hibbard are rejoicing over the arrival of a little daughter.

* * *

Mr. and Mrs. G. C. Sampley returned home last Saturday from Indiana where they have been visiting their people for the past six weeks. Mrs. Sampley's mother and a brother of Mr. Sampley accompanied them home.

- - -

Mrs. Roy Jones returned Friday from Morgan where she has been visiting her people since Christmas.

* * *

J. B. Seams is in Delta and Fillmore this week looking after the drainage work.

SOUTH TRACT ITEMS

Farmers, don't forget our next Farm Bureau meeting, Saturday, the 2nd of February, at 2 o'clock p. m. Come out and help put our membership up to one hundred per cent. This will give us the benefit derived from such an organization and will insure our receiving the Farm Bureau News each month which is of interest to all of us.

* * *

Harry Pearson is still nursing his broken foot which he says is doing well, but it is noticed he does not bear any weight on it yet.

* * *

Leceil Nelson says he is going to do one of three things and that pretty soon. He says he is either going to war or going to Idaho or going to get married. He seems to prefer the latter.

* * *

Jack Sly has returned from a trip to Dr. Richards' dental office where he lost all of his original teeth. Jack is not dangerous now, for he can't even bite bread.

* * *

J. E. Whitmore has his house almost ready for occupancy and will move into it some time this week. They will have a comfortable and roomy house with a nice big porch on the east 10x26 feet, screened in. They will pipe the water from their flowing well into the kitchen and bathroom. They will be near neighbors of Pearson brothers and Fred Keim.

* * *

The Hire folks received a letter from their old home in Indiana stating that their father was very ill. Roy took the train on the following day to go to the assistance of the old folks. We hope he finds his father's health much improved.

* * *

Miller Hall showed his usual good judgement one day last week by taking as his bride, one of the nice girls of Oasis, Miss Clara Thompson. We wish to join the community in wishing them a lifelong happiness.

* * *

Joseph Fidel who was so unfortunate as to lose his house by fire one evening last week has purchased the house at the D. L. & W. Co. camp belonging to Mr. Cramer. This will make for a good home.

* * *

We are sorry to say that we are going to lose the Cramer family from our neighborhood, but where we have the loss some other community will have a gain wherever they may decide to locate.

* * *

Will Beach and Geo. Sipos are spending the winter in southern California with Walt Saunders. They expect to obe back about the first of March.

* * *

A young gentleman who has not yet received a front name arrived at the home of Mr. and Mrs. A. E. Brush on the 29th inst. He has picked out a good home and will undoubtedly stay there. He is a lucky chap.

Abraham Articles.

Miss Florence Fullmer is clerking in the E. R. Westover store at Sugarville.

* * *

Bishop Hogan returned home Sunday.

* * *

Frank Needham loaded a car of wheat last week.

* * *

The two-weeks-old babe of Mr. and Mrs. Pace died Sunday, Jan. 27th.

* * *

Frank Lake, Joseph Fullmer and Nathan Lake have gone to Butte, Montana, presumably in search of gold.

* * *

Mrs. E. J. Biehler, who has been quite sick is reported much better.

* * *

Raynier Van Evera is visiting Salt Lake City again this week.

* * *

W. J. Cary's many friends will be glad to know he was able to come home from the hospital, Sunday.

* * *

The little Misses Ruth Hogan and Maxine Patterson were under the doctor's care this week; in fact, nearly every child in the neighborhood has been tussling with disease of some sort, the most prevalent being German measles.

* * *

Mr. and Mrs. Clarence Hogan have returned to their home at Eureka.

* * *

Clinton Colbert is recovering nicely from his recent operation for appendicitis.

BIRTHS

To Mr. and Mrs. Rowland Stewart, on Jan. 27, a girl.

To Mr. and Mrs. Ed. Brush of the South Tract, on Jan. 30, a 13 pound boy.

Personal Items

Mrs. Lizzie Garrison, sister of Mrs. J. A. Faust, Jr., is here visiting from Pioche, Nev.

—)(—

Aliens who are required to register should apply at the postoffice where they get their mail.

—)(—

Gus. Faust, who has been with the Studebaker branch here, has been promoted and given charge of this branch.

—)(—

A fine library table, two writing desks, two kitchen cabinets and center table at the Delta Furniture Store.   j31f7

—)(—

Jesse Hulse has rented his place just across the river to a Mr. Henry of Milford for five years and has moved to Murray.

—)(—

Frank Larkin, who has been in charge of the Delta branch of the Studebaker Co., has been given charge of the branch at Idaho Falls.

—)(—

There will be a W. O. W. business meeting held in the Chronicle office at 8 o'clock Friday evening. Members are urgently requested to be on hand.

—)(—

Dr. Green and companions of Cedar City are developing a big coal mine in that locality with the idea of inducing a railroad to build to the mine and put the coal on the market.

—)(—

Mr. and Mrs. L. C. Blades went to Salt Lake last week, Mrs. Blades entering a hospital for medical treatment, while Mr. Blades returned on Sunday. Mrs. Blades expects to return soon, an operation not being necessary.

Mrs. Horace Crawford of the South Tract has received a beautiful one hundred and fifty dollar violin, a present from her brother, J. S. Null of Montana, and for volume and sweetness of tone it is said to be unexcelled. She is very proud of her gift.

—)(—

A German named Hecker, who has been working on the railroad bridge between Delta and Lynndyl, was reported by his fellow workmen to have been continually making derogatory statements about the President and the U. S. government. He was taken in hand by Deputy Lewis the last of the week and will be turned over to the U. S. officers.

—)(—

Ward Love, who was one of the first Delta boys to answer the call for volunteers, is getting to the front in the navy. He is now stationed at the Norfolk navy yards and has been appointed a junior instructor. In commenting on his duties, in a letter to his parents, he says he is instructing a company of 3rd class firemen in which there is 108 men, none of which weigh less than 175 pounds, stripped.

—)(—

The Howard Foster Theatrical Co. played "Arizona" Friday night and "Queena" last Saturday evening at the Lincoln Theatre. Mr. Foster always carries a clean, gentlemanly and ladylike troupe with him who are endowed with dramatic ability. The company was well up to standard on this occasion and their playing, costumes and special scenery fitted in harmoniously and pleasingly with our new opera house. Come again, folks; we always like to go to a good play produced by real actors and actresses.

—)(—

The United States has withdrawn all government land around Hurricane and has the reclamation service engineers on the ground making surveys of the proposed 2,500 acre irrigation project in that vicinity with the idea of taking it over and putting it thru if possible.

—)(—

J. J. Bessinger has been put in charge of the Bonneville Lumber yards, while J. E. Works and wife are spending a month in Salt Lake City. Mr. Bessinger was with Manager Works in the yard here for some time last spring but was later transferred to the management of their yard at Oasis.

—)(—

Samuel Stark, treasurer of the People's Sugar Co., which erected a factory at Moroni this year, was in town Sunday on his way to California. Mr. Stark informs us that while they had a fair run the factory did not turn out near as much sugar as figured on and that every other factory in the intermountain States fell down on production.

—)(—

Hon Steele had a steer at his ranch which became sick the first of the week and in his efforts to administer to it Mr. Steele received a number of scratches on his hand which he put in the steer's mouth. Later the animal showed unmistakable signs of rabies and died in convulsions. The head was sent to Dr. Beatty for analysis.

—)(—

Deputy Sheriff Lewis has been entertaining a couple of young men since the last of last week who were supposed to be slackers. Lannie Vaughn of Attica, Ind., was found to be under age and was turned loose. Clinton C. Thompson of Dupree, So. Dak., was found to be a registrant who had not returned his questionaire. He will be turned over to the Federal officers.

Millard County Progress
February 1, 1918

OAK CITY

Mr. Erven Jacobson is down from Provo visiting friends and relatives.

Mrs. Martha Roper who has been down to Hinckley visiting her daughter, Mrs. Wm. Lovell, returned home Saturday.

A number of our towns people attended the monthly Priesthood meeting Saturday at Hinckley.

Mrs. Mary M. Lyman was here on Sunday visiting with her children.

Miss Belva Lovell and Jefferson Jones were married last Wednesday in the Salt Lake Temple.

Word has been received here that Mr. Kirt Roper, our volunteer soldier had the misfortune to break his ankle and is now in the hospital at the Presidio, California.

OASIS

A concer and dance twas given in the A. C. Nelson School House Saturday night by the Millard Academy studenst. Everyone reported having enjoyed themselves hmmensely.

Mrs. Lars Hansen, Sr., was called to Salt Lake Sunday evening on account of the illness of her daughter Mrs. Frank Dillenbeck.

It is reported that Miss Clara Thompson and Mr. James Hall are married. The young couple are living in Salt Lake at present.

Millard County Chronicle
February 14, 1918

DELTA NEWS NOTES.

Mrs. Dora Cooper visited Salt Lake last week.

—) (—

Will Kilpack was here from Fillmore last Sunday.

—) (—

See our line of Waterman Ideal Fountain pens. W. L. Lackyard, Jeweler. j31f14

—) (—

The time in which you have to report your income has been extended ot April first.

—) (—

Born, this morning, to Mr. and Mrs. Frank Johnson of the South Tract, a fine son.

—) (—

Fred Haumann has returned from a visit with his parents who live east of Alliance, Neb.

—) (—

The Millard County School Board met in Delta yesterday and transacted routine business.

—) (—

G. T. Olson of Emery was here this week looking over the country with an idea of investing.

—) (—

Sam and Ed Van Schmitz of Syracuse, Neb., are here looking the valley over with a view of locating.

—) (—

Mrs. Hautz has gone to Eureka for a month's visit with her husband who is working in the mines there.

—) (—

J. W. Walton came down from Salt Lake Wednesday where he has been staying with the family for the past month.

—) (—

Mrs. M. M. Stapley and daughter Lelu returned the first of the week from a visit with relatives at Kanarraville.

—) (—

J. E. Whitmore, who has purchased a farm a quarter of a mile east of Pearson Bros., is moving to his new persessions.

There is still time for aliens who have not yet registered to do so. You can learn the particulars by applying at the postoffice.

—) (—

Turah Folsom, daughter of N. H. Folsom of the South Tract, was taken to Salt Lake Wednesday morning to be operated on for appendicitis.

—) (—

R. J. Gardner of Pine Valley, father of J. X. Gardner, civil engineer, well known in this locality, was a Delta visitor the first of the week.

—) (—

Steel for the Delta-Lynndyl road has arrived and the bridge builders are at work putting it up. The bridge will be ready for travel in about two weeks.

—) (—

We have at last secured a correspondent for Hinckley who we believe will stick to the job and furnish a lot of interesting news from that town each week.

—) (—

Paint now, and paint right. Dennis & Ormandy, Delta, Painters, Paperhangers and Calciminers, will do your work and guarantee it. Phone No. 3-y. Po. O. Box 71. (f14-28p)

—) (—

Chas. McClain, who has spent the past month in Delta and Salt Lake City, has returned to his home at Pomona, Cali. Ho has disposed of most of his holdings here to F. L. Copening.

—) (—

Chas. Burke of Hinckley has closed a deal thru Jeff Clark of the Melville Land Co. for the sale of his fine farm just south of that town to Messrs. Wood and Woodbury of Ogden who will soon take possession of it.

—) (—

There is a bunch of horses running loose around Delta pestering the life out of all who have hay. The horses should be put in the pound. It is hard enough for one to keep their own stock fed without feeding a dozen strays.

Bill Shaw, one of the valley's popular young men who has a farm just south of the reservoir and who has been engaged in electrical work in Delta for the past year, has gone to San Diego where he will visit his parents before going to to the front.

—) (—

H. H. Holdredge, who recently sold his farm in Sutherland to the Church for settlement and who expects to leave soon for a visit with relatives at Peona, Colo., will have a public sale at his farm on Saturday, Feb. 23rd. He has a good list of farm machinery, stock, etc., to dispose of. Watch for bills and ad in the Chronicle.

—) (—

Members of the State Labor Board —Rich, Neboker and Davey—were here Monday taking testimony in the case of Asil Wright who was killed at the sugar factory, with the idea of adjusting the compensation to be allowed the parents for their loss.

—) (—

The Delta ladies of the West Millard County Chapter of Red Cross sent away this week their first box of wristlets, socks and sweaters, and expect to send out another box in a few days. The ladies will meet at Mrs. Beckwith's again Friday, and all Red Cross ladies are welcome. There is always something to do.

—) (—

The Henry Freese public sale, which took place last Monday, is reported by the crowd to have been the best advertised and arranged, biggest crowd and most successful sale ever held in the Pahvant valley. Henry has rented out his place and is going to Santa Rosa, where he has bot a small farm and will take life easy for a while. He is a good farmer and citizen and we dislike to see him go.

Judge Bartow of Gordon, Neb., was here the first of the week in the interest of a colony of Nebraska farmers looking over the valley with the idea of having the colony locate here. He went from Delta to Lynndyl but at the time had not made any conclusions as to what his report to those interested would be. He was well pleased with the country, however.

OAK CITY NEWS ITEMS

Born, to Mr. and Mrs. William Jacobson, a nine pound baby boy.

* * *

The Oak City M. I. A. Dramatic company presented a military drama, "By the Enemy's Hand," to an appreciative audience.

* * *

Miss Sylvia Lovell, our postmistress, has gone to California for a vacation.

* * *

Miss Lydia Roper has gone to Beaver for an extended visit.

* * *

Mr. and Mrs. George A. Faust of Delta were here and spent Sunday with friends and relatives.

* * *

Alonzo Billings and J. H. Peterson of Delta were home, missionaries here Sunday.

* * *

Miss Mabel Roper has returned home from Delta.

* * *

Mrs. Walter Rawlinson of Delta was here visiting with relatives and friends.

* * *

A number of our students from the M. A. were home to spend Saturday and Sunday.

Sugarville Sayings.

Farmers, don't forget the Farm Bureau meeting next Wednesday eve.

* * *

Mrs. E. D. Cady and sister returned last week from Ohio, and they say they are glad to be back as it is like summer here compared to the winter there.

* * *

Mrs. C. M. Cochran will entertain the Thimble club next Wednesday afternoon at her home and she requests the ladies to come early.

* * *

Feb. 22nd the L. D. S. Sunday school will give a concert and children's dance in the afternoon, and dance in the evening at the F. T. C. Library hall. Everybody come.

* * *

March 14th the Friendship Thimble club will celebrate the anniversary of their hall. Remember the date and watch for further announcement of what will be doing.

Former Resident of Centerfield Passes Away

Mrs. Christina Ostlund Hanson passed away on the morning of Feb. 10th, 1918, from a paralytic stroke in her left side. She was 76 years old on Dec. 10, 1917, and had resided with her daughter, Mrs. Clara E. Jeffery, since the death of her husband seven years ago. She was born near Stockholm, Sweden, Dec. 10, 1842, and heard the Gospel message in her native land. She came to Utah in the early 70's, remaining for a time in Salt Lake City. She was married to P. C. Hanson in Feb. 1878 in the Endowment House in Salt Lake City. One daughter came to bless this union. She made her home in Sanpete County, living first in Gunnison and later moving to Centerfield.

She was a noble woman. "None knew her but to love her." On the evening of Feb. 7th she was knitting stockings for the soldiers, busy and useful to the last.

Funeral services were held on Feb. 12th at 10 a. m. in the L. D. S. chapel. Interment took place in the Delta cemetery.

Millard County Chronicle
February 21, 1918

DELTA NEWS NOTES.

Onions one cent per pound. D. Stevens & Co.   f21-1t

—)(—

Mrs. Noble Peterson is visiting her parents at Fillmore.

—)(—

Born, to Mr. and Mrs. J. M. Davis, February 13th, a boy.

—)(—

Miss Belle Oates left yesterday for a ten-days' visit at Salina.

—)(—

Born, to Mr. and Mrs. Ingolf Norman of Delta, a girl, Thursday of last week.

—)(—

Parley Steele has gone to Lynn, where he is employed with the Delta-Lynn road survey crew.

—)(—

R. F. Runzel, who instituted the Pahvant Lodge W. O. W., was in town the first of the week visiting the boys.

—)(—

Frank Beckwith departed this morning for Oakley, Idaho, where he will assume the duties of cashier of the bank at that place.

—)(—

Mr. and Mrs. W. H. Pace returned Monday from a visit at Los Angeles. W. H. says it is a fine place to visit and he enjoyed the trip fine but when one gets his visit out, Utah looks good for a place of refuge.

—)(—

W. L. Lackyard returned Wednesday from a visit with his parents in Los Angeles. "Wes" is pretty well satisfied, tho, with just a visit and prefers Utah in which to do business.

—)(—

The Delta Merc. report a great deal of interest in their new cash purchase reward of dishes. They say the idea is proving a big drawing card for the store and results in well satisfied cash customers.

—)(—

Mr. and Mrs. Al. Fonda of Onoco, Neb., who have been visiting their daughter in Salt Lake City and spending the winter on the coast, stopped off in Delta Wednesday for a visit with old friends, Mr. and Mrs. B. E. Cooper and daughter, Mrs. Lackyard.

—)(—

Wm. Perry of the North Tract has sold his place to Oliver L. Wilcox of Enterprise for $120 an acre and is preparing to go to California to make his home there. The family will leave in about two weeks. Mr. Perry is now in the sunny south looking for a location.

—)(—

A. B. Ward is remodeling his livery barn and will fix up the front for use by Goble & Turner as a Secondhand store and Shoe and Harness repair shop. The new firm will also handle new harness. In connection with their store business they will run a feed yard in the rear. Mr. Goble now runs the repair shop in the Broderick building. Mr. Turner is a brother of Lorenzo Turner.

—)(—

WOODROW JOLLY STITCHERS CHANGE TO RED CROSS

At the last meeting of the Jolly Stitchers it was voted to suspend that club for an indefinite period in favor of the Red Cross Auxiliary and to devote all time and energy to Red Cross work. The Auxiliary will meet with Mrs. Win Walker, March 1st. An all day meeting will be held and all members are requested to be present.

OAK CITY NEWS ITEMS

The measles are spreading rapidly in our locality. This could likely have been checked had the quarantine law been observed.

* * *

The Oak City M. I. A. Dramatic company returned home on Sunday from Holden and Scipio, where they had presented the play entitled "By the Enemy's Hand."

* * *

A bundle shower was given for Mr. and Mrs. Jefferson Jones on Saturday evening at the home of Jessie Higgins. Many valuable presents were received.

* * *

The ice crop has been harvested here. It was very light.

* * *

Dr. J. E. Stains, dentist, of Delta, was here last week doing dental work.

* * *

Dr. Wm. A. Stephenson, veterinarian of Delta, was here twice last week.

* * *

Bishop H. E. Maxfield, of Delta, has a gang of men working for the S. R. L. & W. Co. on their reservoir north of Oak City.

HINCKLEY HAPPENINGS

Mrs. Claud Tripp is here on a visit with her mother, Mrs. F. W. Wilkins.

* * *

On the 12th inst. "The Eyes of the World" was played to a large and appreciative audience. Mr. Passey deserves credit for the high-class plays he is presenting to the public. It is something Hinckley has needed for some time. He informs us he has a return engagement on the 28th.

* * *

Another game of basketball in name only was played in the M. A. Gym. between Delta and the M. A. The Academy was victorious by 21 points. We think we have some team at the M. A. this year and that the Delta High School League will find them "hard to catch."

* * *

The draining machine has been doing business again and seems to be traveling right along regardless of frozen ground. Things generally move when T. G. gets behind them.

* * *

Afton Greenes went to Salt Lake to enlist(?) but has returned. Don't know what happened. Tell us about it, Tad.

* * *

Geo. Tripp of Callao is in town. We suppose, on business.

* * *

The many friends of Mrs. J. A. Jackson will be grieved to learn of her death at Salt Lake City on the 16th. She was a loving wife and mother and was loved by all who knew her. Mr. Jackson and family have the sympathy of the entire community. This makes the second loss of its kind for him, he having lost a former wife some years ago. Mrs. Jackson leaves a family of eight children—six by the former wife and two of her own. Her presence will be sadly missed by the people of Hinckley and her wide circle of friends.

* * *

The wrestling match between Terry and McLane was staged at the Lyric Theatre on the 14th. After a struggle of about three hours the referee called it a draw as neither man was able to get a fall. We hear they are to try it again in the near future.

* * *

Mr. R. A. Nelson has sold his farm in the east part of town to Parley Warnick and has moved to the Island farm, which place he has leased for five years. Sorry to lose you, Bob.

WOODROW WRITINGS

Woodrow has been out of the Chronicle for several weeks, but rest assured she is not off the map. She was a little stunned two weeks ago, when she broke her bank voting on Ida Underhill as the prettiest girl in Utah and Sugarville went her one better and the cake was carried off by Miss Blanche Remington of Sugarville. Woodrow was restored to consciousness, however, when she learned that $107.00 had been realized for the Hall. These Sugarville boys are surely NOT pikers.

* * *

The stork has been on the job for the past week with the following record: Bishop Walter Roberts and wife, a daughter; John Hersloff and wife (nee Helen Smith), a daughter; Lindsey Steele and wife, a son.

* * *

The Needle Craft club of Abraham won the heart of every member of the Red Cross Auxiliary No. 1 by presenting to them the handsome gift of a $50 Liberty Bond. Hurrah for Abraham!

* * *

Frank Foote dropped in on us suddenly last Thursday for a few days' visit and delighted his many friends. Frank is on his way to South Africa under a two-years' contract to take charge of a diamond mine. We all wish him good luck and hope some day to see a big diamond on the finger of a lucky girl.

* * *

Mr. and Mrs. Frank Beckwith have been the honored guests at numerous farewell banquets on the North Tract during the last week. We refrain from writing them up, hoping that Frank in spite of his overfeeding, which would break the heart of Hoover, should it reach his ear, will still be able to wield his pen and write them up in his own inimitable style.

* * *

We hear by letter that Sid Trailey, having spent one year in the hospital undr treatment for rheumatism, is so far recovered that he hopes to be able to visit his ranch here in a few weeks.

* * *

Geo. Webster is suffering from a severely sprained ankle, but is still able to run the picture show.

HINCKLEY HAPPENINGS

Will someone kindly tell us what kind of weather we are having?

* * *

Stake priesthood meeting was held in the M. A., Saturday. People from all over the Stake were in attendance.

* * *

Jim Emmett and Edw. Davis have gone to Dixie on a prospecting trip. They went via Ford.

* * *

Mrs. Sweat and son, of Uinta, are here visiting with Mrs. Sweat's brother, J. H. Langston.

* * *

Alfred Bliss, who has been living in H. F. Stout's place this winter, has moved to his farm east of town.

* * *

Thursday night the M. I. A. gave a party in the District School House. About 100 persons were out and everybody seemed to have a jolly good time.

* * *

Last week the paper quoted us as saying that the Delta High School League would find the M. A. boys hard to catch. This should have read the State High School instead of Delta.

* * *

Yes, we have found out what business Geo. Tripp had in Hinckley. After he had disappeared the people awoke to the fact that one of our popular young ladies, Miss Inez Wilkins, had also disappeared. Now we don't propose to put up with any more of such doin's; we don't care if young men marry our girls, but to take them away to some other country when we have plenty of room here for all comers, did you ever hear of such nerve?

* * *

R. E. Robinson went riding with A. A. Hinckley in his Ford and the car hit a hole and R. E. hit the bow over his head which resulted in a badly bruised nose and a black eye for R. E. Haven't heard of the car being damaged any by the accident.

* * *

Friday night Mr. and Mrs. Ray Slaughter entertained a few of their friends and relatives in honor of Mr. Slaughter's sister, Rose, it being her birthday. Games and dancing were indulged in until a late hour, after which a dainty lunch was served by the hostess.

* * *

Monday, the 18th, the funeral of Mrs. J. A. Jackson was held in the Academy. Counselor Stewart was in charge. The speakers were: Willis E. Robison, Rev. C. H. Hamilton and A. A. Hinckley. They all spoke of the high character of Mrs. Jackson. The choir rendered the following: "I Need Thee Every Hour," "Rock of Ages" and "Nearer, My God, to Thee." Mrs. Jennie Bishop sang, "Oh, my Father," and Mrs. Jennie Langston sang "Face to Face." The pall-bearers were Wm. Webb, Edw. Anderson, Alonzo Leavitt, A. F. Bliss, C. A. Stratton and Hosea Stout, Jr. Interment took place in Hinckley cemetery.

Sugarville Sayings.

Mrs. Johnson, who has been spending the past year with her son, Gus. Johnson, returned to California this week.

* * *

Mrs. Dewitt Howlett is out again after tusseling for some tome with the grippe. Those on the grippe list this week are Mrs. C. M. Cochran and Mrs. J. B. Seams.

* * *

Pauline Seams had a narrow escape one evening last week. While playing she ran into a barbed wire fence, cutting a two-inch gash on her neck which just missed the jugular vein. It was necessary to have five stitches taken.

* * *

The Friendship Thimble club will meet with Mrs. Cronholm and Mrs. Iverson at the home of the former next Wednesday afternoon.

* * *

On March 14th the Friendship Thimble club will have a bow dance, each lady to wear a small bow and place a mate to it in an envelope, to be drawn out by the gentlemen to secure their partners for supper. Com and have some fun. Regular price for dance; nice supper 25 cents. Everybody invited.

* * *

Farm Bureau meeting next Wednesday evening.

ABRAHAM ARTICLES.

Prof. Openshaw returned from Salt Lake, Sunday, where he went to have his eyes treated.

* * *

Raynier Van Evera left Monday for Fillmore to be examined for the army.

* * *

Bishop Donald Hogan is suffering from blood poisoning in one of his hands.

* * *

Van Evera Bros.' auction sale was largely attended and articles sold readily, T. Payne Franklin as auctioneer did excellent work. The ladies of Red Cross realized a goodly sum from the luncheon served and also from the sale of a roll top desk which was donated by Van Evera Bros.

* * *

W. J. Carey and family have moved to Delta and will occupy one of N. S. Bishop's tenant houses on the west side. Success to the ins and outs.

* * *

D. H. Livingston is putting a hog tight fence around his fine Abraham ranch.

* * *

Mrs. Ed Clark was unable to teach school Wednesday on account of some throat trouble.

* * *

Marcus Fox and Chris Hansen made a business trip to Delta, Wednesday.

* * *

T. Payne Franklin is tuning his voice for the big auction sale of Needham Bros., Saturday.

* * *

Quite a number of our farmers are plowing for the spring crops.

* * *

Herbert Taylor is on the sick list this week.

DELTA NEWS NOTES.

Jeff Clark and P. H. Robison visited Fillmore Monday.

—) (—

Mr. and Mrs. Wm. Starley are visiting in Fillmore this week.

—) (—

Prof. Howells of the Millard Academy was a Delta visitor, Monday.

—) (—

Onions one cent per pound. D Stevens & Co.   f21-1t

—) (—

It looks like the ice harvest is all over. A short crop of very thin ice was gathered.

—) (—

Court is in session this week and a number from the West Side are in attendance.

—) (—

Pratt Mercantile Co. of Hinckley are advertising attractive spring bargains in the Chronicle this week.

—) (—

R. M. Rogers has sold his residence property south of the Presbyterian mission to Ray Dresser.

—) (—

E. A. Stott of the Millard Academy has been appointed County Agent for San Juan county.

—) (—

Noble Peterson has purchased the Lincoln Theatre Confectionery stand from Geo. Billings.

—) (—

Earl Robard and P. H. Robison went to Salt Lake the first of the week to take in the Auto show.

—) (—

The Delta Canal Co. is getting ready to begin work cleaning out and overhauling their canal system.

—) (—

Mesdames Freer and Lewis of Lynn met with the Red Cross officers Tuesday to lay plans for work of the Lynn Auxiliary.

—) (—

The store of Joseph Passey of Hinckley has been turned over to the Credit Men's Ass'n for the adjustment of claims.

—) (—

Miss Ila Slaughter came down from Salt Lake, Sunday, and went to Fillmore on Monday to attend court. She is attending business college in the city.

—) (—

Fred Tingleaf, who has been spending the winter in Riverside, Calif., has returned and will act as water master on the South Tract the coming season.

—) (—

Owing to a misunderstanding in dates, Needham Bros. & Baxter have postponed their farm sale until March 5th. Read their list in this week's Chronicle.   f28-1t

—) (—

Jas. S. Blake of Hinckley has been appointed Government License Explosive Agent for this territory. Any one wishing to purchase explosives should take the matter up with him in order to obtain permission.

—) (—

Mr. Whitehead, representing the Aultman-Taylor tractors, was in town the fore part of the week looking after the tractor possibilities. The Delta Merc. Co. are agents for the Aultman-Taylor tractor in this locality.

—) (—

While no date has yet been set for calling of the second draft, it is announced that class A men will very likely be called in April. The delay in the call has been on account of lack of quarters and equipment.

—) (—

H. B. Prout., vice president of the Delta Land & Water Co., came up from Milford the first of the week to attend to company matters. He was joined here by Attorneys Ryan and Frank Holman of Salt Lake and together they made a trip to Fillmore.

—) (—

Dr. F. J. Alexander, of the Alexander Optical Co., Salt Lake City, will be at Delta Hotel Saturday and Sunday, March 2 and 3; at Day Hotel, Oasis, Monday, March 4th, all day Those having any trouble with their eyes should not fail to call. (f28-1tp)

—) (—

Mrs. Walter Moffitt entertained on Friday the 22nd, from 2 until 4, in honor of little Helma Mitchell's birthday. Tables were decorated with dainty little red hatchets and hearts. After playing and enjoying the afternoon with games of different kinds, dainty refreshments were served.

—) (—

The Delta Ladies' Red Cross Auxiliary held its last meeting at Mrs. Frank Beckwith's. Mrs. R. C. Bates and Mrs. Ben Douglas entertained. Plans were completed for the big dance Friday, March 1st. The meeting this week will be held Thursday, Feb. 28th, on account of the dance Friday.

—) (—

Attorney O. P. Soule of the firm of Soule & Spalding of Salt Lake City, is in the Valley attending to business connected with Drainage Districts No. 2 and No. 3. Mr. Soule is highly pleased with the successful placing of No. 2's bonds and is very hopeful of placing No. 3's bonds with the same house.

—) (—

This year there will be a $2 poll tax collected thruout Millard county. The county road commissioner will look after the tax outside of incorporated towns, and the town boards will collect and expend all such monies within the town. The poll tax is due before the 3rd week in April and will be used to build roads. No poll tax has been collected the past two years.

OAK CITY.

The program given by the school children on Washington's birthday was largely attended by the people.

The cooperative handling of cattle on Forest Reserves was discussed by R. J. Becraft here last Thursday to all the stockmen of Oak City.

Miss Sylvia Lovell reurned home f.·· California last Tuesday and re-p· .d having had a very good time.

.uss Angie Finlinson made a special business trip to Delta last week.

Dr. C. A. Broadus was called here to attend the son of Mr. and Mrs. John C. Lovell who is seriously ill of Erysipelas.

Bishop J. Leo Anderson has gone to attend a school convention in New York and expects to be gone two or three weeks.

Mr Abner Johnson was here on Friday night buying cattle.

Mr. and Mrs. Frank Dillonbeck have returned from Salt Lake where they have been living for the past few months.

OASIS

A big dance was enjoyed in the A. C. Nelson Hall last Friday evening in honor of Washington's birthday.

Mr. Hilton Kelly has left for a visit with relatives in Salt Lake City

Mr. Marvin Jackson left for Provo on Monday night where he will be examined for military service.

Mr. C. M. Hanson has been in town the last few days reinstating Mr. Frank Dillenbeck in the cream station.

Mr. J. A. Phillips has been buying hay for the past ten days in this vicinity and shipping it to other points from here.

OAK CITY.

We are having spring weather the past week and the farmers are getting ready to plant their spring grain.

Born to Mr and Mrs Franklin Anderson a baby girl on Wednesday last the 27th.

Word has been received from Mr. Stanley W. Lovell and Clinton Dutson that they have reached England safely.

A bouncing baby girl arrived at the home of Mr. and Mrs. Arthur Talbott on March 4th.

The M. I. A. Dramatic Company of Scipio presented the play "A Noble Outcast," here last Friday night to a large and appreciative audience.

The sewing club meets with Miss Louis Anderson on Tuesday night.

Miss Mabel Roper is reported on the sick list this week.

Electric Light for Millard Towns

Oasis, Deseret, Hinckley and Abraham are to have electric lights. This fact was made known the first of the week when the Deseret Irrigation Co. closed a contract for the installation of a hundred-horse power lighting plant with eleven miles of transmission line. They have also contracted for the installation of a complete refrigerator plant of ten tons capacity, including cold storage compartments. In addition to this, contracts have been made for future delivery for a two hundred and twenty-five horse power lighting plant to run in connection with the present system. The present power for generating lectricity will be furnished from distillate.

The Deseret Irrigation Co. is to be congratulated for its thrift and enterprise in launching this modern and much needed enterprise on such a large scale and at a great expense and it is expected and hoped that all who are within reach of the transmission lines will give the company their support and assistance by their patronage. We are also advised that all house wiring for lights and power must be done in accordance with the Underwriters' rules before connection to the premises will be made by the company, as required by the laws of Utah.

The plant is expected to be in operation within ninety days.

DELTA NEWS NOTES.

, Dora Cooper left Monday for
..ake for medical treatment.

—)(—

se fine new Monarch Ranges
ust arrived at the Delta Furni-
tore.   (m7-14)

—)(—

t week begins a new serial, the
n Trail." It is said to be an
nt story.

—)(—

have the most complete line of
ms ever displayed in Delta.
vens & Co.   m14-1t

—)(—

. Lackyard has a nice line of
Society   embroidery   articles
.as for sale.   m14-21

—)(—

Chronicle is in the market for
ch of soft, clean cotton rags
a on its presses.

—)(—

Bright of Lewiston, Utah, has
sed the R. W. Hibbard 80 in
oodrow district.

—)(—

. Whip," now playing at the
ake Theatre, is booked at the
. Theatre, Delta, for April 6th.

—)(—

you going to build or fence?
r prices on wire, nails, and sta-
D. Stevens & Co.   m14-1t

—)(—

ne fumed oak buffet, kitchen
. and splendid $14.50 oak chif-
at the Delta Furniture Store.
                          (m7-14)
mpson came down from Bing-
uesday, to see how things on
nker-Jimpson ranch were go-

—)(—

. Prout of the Delta Land &
Co. was here Monday from
. looking after company busi-

—)(—

t fall to see "Womanhood."

20th and 21st. The newest
.c picture. See contest condi-
h ad.

—)(—

will not have another oppor-
in a long time like that of-
t Black's store, Deseret. which
Saturday night.   (m14-1t

—)(—

als in groceries: Pansy rais-
.ks. for 25c; Dutch cookies, 2
.r 25c; McLaughlin's coffee,
.; D. Stevens & Co. (m14-1t

—)(—

. Riding left Saturday for
.tch with his car to bring Mrs.
and the little ones, who have
.ere visiting for some time.

—)(—

Turner, manager of the Des-
.ines Co., was here Tuesday
.ednesday, going out to the
.o see how things were run-

—)(—

Dr. Richards has left Delta
.rned over the store to W. G.
t to be closed out. Mr. Em-
.as disposed of most of the
.l in the building.

big sale at Black's Store, Des-
offering you advantages you
.nd anywhere else in the val-
' you haven't taken advantage
.etter do so before it closes.
                          m14-1t

—)(—

Cowen, who lives north of
.y, returned recently from
Colo., where he went last fall
.is wife. He informs us that
.owen died of goitre early in
.

—)(—

.ret Auxiliary of the Red Cross
.ning a big supper, dance and
.sale at the A. C. Nelson bldg.
.day evening, March 20. Every
.ould be out to it, have a good
.nd help along a good cause.

—)(—

.y Warnick, who recently pur-

chased the Nelson farm between
Delta and Hinckley, has let a contract to the Dale Engineering Company for the piping of water into his
residence.

—)(—

Arthur Bunker and family, who
have spent the past year on their
grape vineyard near Moapa, returned
to Delta the last of last week and
have taken up their residence in their
home south of the Delta Lumber &
Hardware Co. yards.

—)(—

J. S. Wood and W. S. Woodbury of
Ogden arrived in Delta   Saturday
with their farming equipment and
household goods and moved to their
farm north of Hinckley recently
purchased thru Jeff Clark of the
Melville Land Co. from Chas. Burke.

—)(—

Mr. and Mrs. Forest E. Hart of
of Bakersfield, Cali., arrived in Delta
last Thursday to take up their residence on their farm in the Woodrow
district. Mr. Hart was here last fall
and   purchased the place of Jeff
Clark.

—)(—

Mr. and Mrs. J. E. Works returned
Friday from Salt Lake where they
have been for the past few weeks.
They brot back with them a fine girl.
Jim says he figured on a boy, but the
call of our country for soldiers has
increased the demand over the supply.

—)(—

O. P. Hull of Corona, Cali., was
here last week and closed a deal thru
the Melville Land & Water Co. with
Lulu B. Howlett whereby he takes
over her 80-acre farm north of Sugarville in exchange for Chino and
Balboa, California, property. The
change will be made in the near future.

—)(—

The Beaver County News says that
"Mr. Cotes, project manager, and
Mr. Crookston, farm manager for the
Delta Land & Water Co., have taken
their positions with the company."

Mr. Crookston, who is Mrs. Dean F.
Peterson's father, was up looking
over affairs of the company at Delta
the first of the week. A. M. Mc-
Pherson, former project manager, is
now with the Jesse Knight interests
on a project in the Uintah county.

—)(—

Word reaches us thru the Delta
Land & Water Co. that the case of
Attorney Norton against that company and certain settlers under the
old Oasis Irrigation Co., in which
Norton was suing for a large service
fee, has come up in the district court
and been thrown out. This ends another of our settlers' tribulations
which has long been a thorn in their
side.

J. H. Zimmerman and John Wilson of Carbondale, Colo., and J. J.
Oldham of Denver are here buying
stock cattle for the Colorado range.
They purchased 160 of cattle from
the Livingston Land & Live Stock
Co., which were loaded out Tuesday
night and. are looking over the Oak
City and Scipio stuff.

—)(—

Cyril Cluff and Veda Wilkins hied
themselves off to Salt Lake and
were married in the temple, Wednesday of last week. After a visit in the
city they will return to Delta for a
short stay and from here go to Wash-

ington, D. C., where Cyril has a
stenographic position with the government. We wish the happy young
couple long life, prosperity and lots
of bliss.

—)(—

An item we overlooked last week
was the fall A. B. Ward received last
Thursday morning. He had run a
splinter in his thumb the day before
and the pain it gave him sent him to
Dr. Hamilton's office to have it removed. While the operation was being performed the doctor turned
from the chair. As he did so Mr.
Ward fainted and fell forward, striking his forehead on the window sill
and cutting a gash just above the
right eye which required three stitches to close. The fall also resulted in
a bad bruise on his right cheek bone.

ABRAHAM ARTICLES.

Mrs. Christianson of Idaho is here visiting her sister, Mrs. C. A. Verwaller.

* * *

Mr. Larson of Delta moved last week to the Van Evera ranch.

* * *

John Walters of Greeley, Colo., has taken charge of the W. J. Carey ranch.

* * *

The youngsters of this vicinity enjoyed a candy pulling at the Alex. Reid home Saturday evening.

* * *

Miss Florence Fullmer of Sugarville visited over Sunday with home folks.

* * *

You land owners, come out Saturday and vote your sentiments on bonding the district for one and a quarter million dollars for drainage purposes.

* * *

Tiny Baker is again in this region with his caterpillar plowing outfit and is doing creditable work.

* * *

George Q. Wilcken, one of our soldier boys, is now in France.

* * *

Misses McCheyne and White were out last week explaining to the ladies the urgent need of conserving food and clothing. Some of the ladies have been trying out Miss White's recipes on war bread and report favorable results.

HINCKLEY HAPPENINGS

About the most important event of recent happenings is the real estate deal between R. E. Robinson and C. R. Woodbury, the former having sold his home at South Main Street to the latter. Mr. Robinson will move onto his ranch east of town which he recently bot from Clarence Pack. Mr. Woodbury is one of our local merchants.

* * *

The draining machine is idle again owing to the scarcity of tile, but more tile is expected soon and work will be resumed.

* * *

The Relief Society is preparing to put on play entitled "Lighthouse Nan." They have an excellent cast and will guarantee your money's worth. Bryant Moody and Fannie Cooper are taking the leading characters, and anyone who has seen those two young people on the stage will know that the play is bound to be a success.

* * *

Nephi Marquardson and wife of Richfield, Utah, are here staying with Mrs. Marquardson's father and mother, Mr. and Mrs. W. J. Carter; Mr. Marquardson has been in this locality before and the country looked so good that he has decided to locate here permanently. He is now looking around for a place to rent for this year and will buy later on.

* * *

Pratt Wright, who has been attending the A. C. College at Logan, has returned home.

* * *

Quite a number of our town people have been attending court at Fillmore the last two weeks.

* * *

The infant daughter of Mrs. Hazel Whitehead has been seriously ill with pneumonia, but is reported better at this writing.

* * *

Chas. Burke and Mrs. Richard Parker have been to Idaho to attend the funeral of their father, who died recently.

* * *

Farmers are busy plowing and preparing to put in their spring crops. From present indications the farmers are preparing to carry on their end of the war by putting in every available acre. May their efforts not be in vain.

DESERET DOINGS

Old Mister Wind is becoming such a frequent visitor in Deseret, that the good housewives can't even keep their clothes on the clothes-line, and even some of our promising young "horseshoe players" have had to stop practicing.

Mrs. Howard Richardson of Pocatello, Idaho, is visiting her grandmother, Mrs. J. W. Damron, Sr. She is accompanied by her little daughter, June.

* * *

There are several cases of pneumonia here at present. We are glad to know that some of the patients are improving, and hope for speedy recovery of all.

* * *

Miss Rose Conk and Mr. Elmer Dewsnup were married last week. We wish them much joy and happiness.

* * *

Mrs. Norma Wright entertained the Elite Club last Tuesday night. The story of Verdi's opera "Rigoletto" was told, and all records obtainable were played on the Victrola.

* * *

A very interesting meeting was held Saturday by Misses White and McCheyne. They spoke on the conservation of food, clothing, time and energy, and gave some splendid ideas on the subject.

* * *

"The Broken Oar," played here on Thursday night by the Millard Academy, was a great success. We hope they will come again.

* * *

An auction sale will be held this week for the purpose of helping the Red Cross. Everybody must be loyal and bring a purse full of money.

Sugarville Sayings.

Fred Tingleaf was a welcome visitor with his many friends a few days last week.

* * *

The Friendship Thimble Club will be entertained next Wednesday afternoon by Mrs. Sampley and Mrs. Jones at the home of the former.

* * *

The Sugarville Auxiliary of the Red Cross was presented with a pony by Needham & Baxter at their sale. It sold for $38.

* * *

Ernest Baxter enlisted in the coast artillery and left for San Francisco the first of the week.

WOODROW WRITINGS.

The Loyal League and Red Cross Auxiliary will meet at the home of Mrs. Hy Sherer tomorrow at 1 p. m.

* * *

A meeting of the Jolly Stitchers is called for Friday, March 22, at 2 p. m., at the home of Mrs. Harry Ottley. Business of great importance is to come before the meeting.

* * *

Mr. and Mrs. Geo. Clemens have returned to Utah after a month's stay in California. They have been visiting during the past week with Mrs. Clemens' parents, Mr. and Mrs. S. H. Thompson, where their many friends have gladly welcomed them.

* * *

The little two months' old infant of Wm. Remington, whose life was despaired of, is convalescing and bids fair to make a permanent recovery.

* * *

Woodrow has lost two of its esteemed citizens, Mr. and Mrs. Meade Tillotson, who moved onto the Holdredge ranch at Sutherland last week. The Tillotson home, however, is occupied by Renal Hibbard and family, whom we are glad to have that much nearer us.

* * *

Mr. and Mrs. Ward Robison are proud of a new daughter.

Abraham Articles

Little Miss Bonnie Bishop, who is staying at the Riding ranch, was under the doctor's care this week.

* * *

Rynier Van Evera was down from Salt Lake this week, on business.

* * *

Mrs. Robert Fullmer, who has been visiting in Payson the past few weeks, arrived home Sunday.

* * *

Mrs. Christenson, who has been visiting at C. A. Vorwaller's, returned to her home in Idaho, Tuesday.

* * *

Mr. and Mrs. C. M. Hickman were guests at the Underhill home near Delta, Sunday.

* * *

Donald Hogan returned from Salt Lake City, Tuesday, where he had been taking treatment for blood poisoning in his hand.

* * *

Mrs. Hattie Forsythe and Joe Fullmer arrived from Salt Lake City Friday, on a visit to their parents, Mr. and Mrs. O. M. Fullmer. Mrs. Forsythe returned home Tuesday.

HINCKLEY HAPPENINGS

Born to Mr. and Mrs. Marquardson, March 10th, a boy. Mother and child doing fine. (Father may recover.)

WOODROW WRITINGS.

Sunday school at 10:30 a. m. Preaching by Rev. O. H. Hamilton next Sunday at 11:30 a. m. All invited.

* * *

Dance at the hall next Saturday night; proceeds for the hall fund.

* * *

Called meeting of the Jolly Stitchers at Mrs. Ottley's, Friday afternoon at 2 o'clock.

* * *

Mrs. Percy Kyes gave a delightful afternoon reception last Saturday at which Mrs. Argo Brown was guest of honor. Mrs. Brown was presented by the ladies with an Ideal Fountain pen, which she promises to wield faithfully in keeping us informed as to affairs in Colorado Springs, where Mr. Brown is going in search of relief from the asthma.

* * *

A large party of friends from Sutherland, Sugarville and Abraham as well as the Woodrowites, swooped down on Mr. and Mrs. Argo Brown last Monday night in a surprise farewell party at their home. In spite of the sadness in our hearts at the parting with these good friends and neighbors, a rollicking good time was enjoyed by all, and heartiest wishes were extended to Mr. and Mrs. Brown that they may be as truly loved and appreciated in their new home as they have been in Woodrow.

Mr. and Mrs. Kinne left last week for a visit to Pomona, Cal., expecting to return after the March winds have blown themselves to death.

* * *

James Webster has been visiting with his brother George at the Woodrow store this week.

* * *

The Junior Red Cross is drilling for an entertainment to be given on the 30th of March in the Woodrow hall, for the purpose of buying thrift stamps to help out Uncle Sam, as well as the school. The entertainment is to be of a unique character and unusually good, and we hope the youngsters will be encouraged by a full house on that evening.

NEWS OF OASIS

The Liberty Social Club was organized on the 5th of February. The members meet at each home where the luncheon is served in a pleasing manner.

* * *

Mrs. Clara Hall is expected home from Salt Lake.

* * *

Mrs. Carl Pierson left for Sandy to be gone for a short time.

* * *

We are very glad we have prospects of a new butcher shop, under the firm name of Dillonbeck & Hansen. We surely need competition in this line. Success!

* * *

There have been 75 cars of hay shipped from our neighborhood to Texas.

* * *

Bishop Skeems has moved into his new home which certainly adds to the looks of our town.

* * *

Mr. and Mrs. Henry Huff returned home from California.

* * *

Mr. and Mrs. Clark Huff were seen in our midst.

* * *

Some dirty sneak in our community is again at his old trade poisoning animals. Ambrose Hunter lost a valuable dog. There has been $50 reward offered for the conviction of the party putting out poison. (Dogs should not be allowed to eat any poisoned quimps.)

Sommers Thompson is working at the Commercial hotel.

* * *

Henry Jackson is all smiles and is paying 30c a dozen for eggs.

* * *

James Christenson is sporting a new car.

* * *

We have quite an epidemic of measles and chicken pox. Otherwise our little hamlet is blessed with good health.

* * *

We are certainly having beautiful weather.

DELTA NEWS NOTES.

Jeff. Pace is visiting his mother in Loa.

—)(—

La Grande Law. visited in St. George last week.

—)(—

Norm Lambert is in Salt Lake this week.

—)(—

Cass Lewis has been appointed city marshal by the town board.

—)(—

A line of knee pant suits for boys; the new styles. D. Stevens & Co. m21-1t

—)(—

Born, to Mr. and Mrs. Verg. Justesen, Monday the 18th, a fine girl baby.

—)(—

Born, on March the 18th, to Mr. and Mrs. A. S. Workman, Jr., a baby girl.

—)(—

A petition is being circulated for the admission of plat B into the corporate limits.

—)(—

A new American high-speed, easy-running washer at the Delta Furniture store. m21-28

—)(—

A. B. Ward is preparing to remodel the upper story of his barn for a lodge room.

—)(—

Don't forget Douglass Fairbanks and W. S. Hart at the Lincoln Theatre next week.

—)(—

Mrs. Lackyard has a nice line of Royal Society embroidery articles and floss for sale. m14-21

—)(—

E. D. Hashimoto was in the valley the first of the week looking after his big farm south of town.

—)(—

Arthur Dennis has had a very sick baby the past week, but it is reported better now.

—)(—

Jeff Clark held a successful auction sale at Ward's barn last Saturday and a goodly number of articles changed hands.

—)(—

The engineers for Drainage District No. 2 are now busy putting down the test holes preparatory to beginning construction work.

—)(—

County Attorney Grover Giles was in town the fore part of the week representing the county in a liquor care from Deseret.

—)(—

Walter Huntsman of Farmington is now employed at the local Studebaker branch as salesman and collector.

—)(—

Miss Louisa Jones, who spent last summer with a Salt Lake family and accompanied them to Los Angeles last fall, returned Tuesday from the latter place.

—)(—

O. B. Ferrell will start construction work this week on a neat 4-room residence for J. W. Schwartz on his farm at the end of Clark Street near the reservoir.

—)(—

Beginning Friday afternoon (Mar. 29th) we will hold a two-for-one sale on stationery and tablets. You buy one, and we give you one free. D. Stevens & Co. m22-1t

—)(—

A number of ladies met Wednesday at the Presbyterian mission and made wash rags for a soldiers' hospital at Newport News in response to an appeal from Mrs. Lamson.

—)(—

Scott Grunden, of the 20th Infantry, located at Fort Douglas, was here the first of the week visiting Mrs. Grunden (nee Miss Christensen of Holden).

—)(—

The Imperial Lead Mine will install at once a 500 or 600 foot tramway from their mine to their loading station which they will equip with convenient bins and loading devices.

—)(—

The rush will soon begin. Have your painting, paperhanging and calcimining done now by Dennis & Ormandy, Painters; phone 3-Y; P. O. box 71, Delta.

—)(—

Mrs. E. H. Lewis, of Denver, Red Cross inspector for the Mountain Division, was here looking over the Red Cross progress in the valley. She reports the work moving along splendidly and was well pleased with the showing made.

—)(—

B. B. Ramey, Geo. Holmberg, and Geo. Johnson have just been up to the Imperial Lead Mine. These gentlemen made the trip for the purpose of looking over the mining possibilities of the district.

—)(—

Mrs. Frank Beckwith wishes all Red Cross workers who are now working on sewed or knit goods for the association, to finish them up, if possible, and have them in by the 28th of this month so that they can be forwarded that day to the divisional headquarters.

—)(—

The bond election in Drainage District No. 3 carried last Saturday by a vote of 158 for to 9 against, and Attorney Soule and J. B. Seams went to the county seat Monday to have the ballots canvassed and prepare for further proceedings regarding the bonding of the district.

—)(—

Agent J. C. Selvert of the Delta station has taken a month's leave and with Mrs. Selvert will visit Denver and southern Texas in the hope of bettering the lady's health. Harry Aller will act as agent during Mr. Selvert's absence and H. F. will perform the duties of cashier.

—)(—

Marion Grundy, one of the partners in the Delta Flour mill, was in town the first of the week looking after his interests. He was unable to say when the mill would be ready for operation as the machinery is still tied up in the East with small prospects of getting it thu any way soon.

The 5-year old girl of N. B. Badger while running across some plowed ground fell and broke a leg. Dr. Broaddus set the broken limb and the little girl is doing fine.

Friends of J. A. Jackson will be pleased to learn that the doctors of the hospital think that his boy Johnnie is slowly recovering, altho his condition is still very critical.

Mrs. Tracy Stout is here after an extended visit with her husband at San Francisco. She left the boys feeling fine, she says, and awaiting the word to sail for "over there."

OAK CITY

Most of our townspeople attended Conofrence at Delta last Sunday but it was found to be impossible to hold meeting in the afternoon.

Miss Lydia Roper has returned home from Beaver where she has been for the past six weeks.

The Primary is going to have an Easter party next Saturday all are invited to attend.

Miss Elva Lovell is spending the week at Hinckley.

Mr. Charlie Roper and Miss Arbie Talbott attended the dance in Delta Monday night, also Mr. John Dutson and Eva Anderson.

The Talbott family celebrated brother Talbott's birthday Monday afternoon.

HINCKLEY HAPPENINGS

Ruby Duncan, formerly Miss Ruby Kellar, is visiting with her mother, Mrs. Christina Kellar.

* * *

Mr. and Mrs. Jas. Ross and family of Delta were visiting with Mr. and Mrs. W. J. Carter, Sunday.

* * *

The ward reunion on the 30th of March was a grand success in every way. About 300 people were there and enjoyed the program, dinner, dance, etc. Considerable credit is due the various committees for their work.

* * *

Sunday, the 24th of March, Hinckley looked like a deserted village, the occasion being conference at Delta.

Everybody and their dog seemed to be in Delta and it was hard to find anybody to get up a war conversation with.

* * *

H. F. Stout, while driving a tractor to Levan for John Jacobs, had the misfortune of tipping over and being pinned beneath the machine. He escaped, however, with a few scratches and bruises but is laid up for the present.

* * *

Friday's string of autos was seen going thru town with horn tooting, flags flying, and banners waving. A stop was made at Pratt's store and we were able to decipher the banners which announced a big dance at Delta. They had a brass band with them and their music was appreciated by our town. Come again, boys; you are over welcome.

* * *

Yesnesday night, March 27, "Down in Dixie" was presented by the Hinckley Dramatic club to a crowded house. Everybody took their parts like professionals, and the closing scene ended with singing the last two lines of the chorus to "The Star Spangled Banner," the audience rising and joining in the song. The play was staged at the A. C. Nelson hall at Deseret Monday night, the 1st of April. There is some thot of taking it to Delta, but no permanent arrangements have been made.

SOUTH TRACT ITEMS

Spring is now on the South Tract and urging us farmers to get into our fields to start the early work.

* * *

Everybody about us is showing signs of uneasiness about getting into their fields and a good many are already there.

* * *

The South Tract Farm Bureau is getting in a quantity of seed grain which has been shipped from Salt Lake. This seed will be here very soon and everyone should be ready for it when it comes. Keep in touch with your purchasing committee, Messrs. Beach, Brush and Hire so as to know just when the grain arrives.

* * *

Misses Edna and Helen Beck entertained three of the lady school teachers from Delta last Saturday and Sunday. Sir Hinkum, Tennis and horseback riding was the order of the day and a big noise at night. A mighty nice bunch. Come again, please.

* * *

The South Tract ladies of the South Tract are meeting each Thursday afternoon at the home of Mrs. H. E. Beck to cut and sew garments for the above order. All ladies, especially members of the Red Cross, are requested to attend and help in the good work.

Mr. and Mrs. Chas. Hardin and son Kenneth have returned from their winter's sojourn in California, to their farm here. We are glad to have them back and hereby extend to them a hearty welcome from the entire neighborhood.

* * *

Miss Nealy, our school teacher, has organized a Junior Red Cross in her school, and they are doing good work. Look out, boys, we hear murmurings of a coming box supper to aid the kiddies in their noble work. Be ready, and if it should materialize let us all be there and encourage them.

* * *

April 6th, at 8 o'clock p. m. will be our next regular farm bureau meeting; let us have a full attendance.

Sugarville Sayings.

(Too late for last week's issue)

Your correspondent was sick with the measles last week, so some of these items may be a week old.

Mrs. Cropper is here from Pomona, Calif., caring for her new granddaughter at the home of Mr. and Mrs. Ronner.

James Shields is in Tooele on business this week.

Mr. and Mrs. Struene Robertson are moving to the Judge Lambert place. Mr. Robertson is able to be around with the aid of crutches.

We understand the oldest son of Mr. Emmett has typhoid fever.

Willie Schiffer returned last week from Los Angeles, Calif., where he has been spending the winter with his parents. He was accompanied back by his sister Maria, who will look after the household for her brother this summer.

Last Saturday evening a number of friends and neighbors of Dewitt Hewlett and wife gave them a pleasant surprise. The evening was spent with games and music and as Mr. and Mrs. Hewlett have traded their place for property in California and expect soon to leave here, there were many remarks of regret at losing such good people and hopes that they would see their mistake of moving and return here soon.

On March 14th Earl F. Seams and Miss Myrtle Anderson wended their way to Fillmore, as they thot, unsight and unseen. But on their return Friday their many friends were ready with hearty congratulations and had planned a neat surprise on them for the following Tuesday evening at the Hall, which trap they stepped easily into by inviting themselves to accompany the party, who had the scheme in charge, to the picture show and, then, instead, were taken to the hall where the crowd awaited them. The evening was spent in dancing. Refreshments were served and all report a fine time.

DELTA NEWS NOTES.

Born, at Mr. and Mrs. Chas. Jensen last Saturday, a boy.

—)(—

Mrs. Clark Allred has assumed Edna Beck's duties as teacher in the Delta schools.

—)(—

Chas. Schroeppel and family were here the last of last week on their way to Mt. Carroll, Ill.

—)(—

Mr. and Mrs. Jim Smith are rejoicing over the arrival of a son who arrived at their home last Saturday.

—)(—

Messrs. J. B. Seams and M. A. Abbott went to Salt Lake Monday to attend a meeting of the board of directors of Drainage Dist. No. 3.

—)(—

The band boys escorted Sergeant Stump and the boys who enlisted last week around the horn in autos with flags flying and the band playing.

—)(—

Miss Edna Beck has resigned her position as teacher in the Delta school and accepted a position with the Delta Land & Water Co. in their local office.

—)(—

Miss Veda Anderson, who is attending the B. Y. U. at Provo, spent the past week with her parents, Mr.

and Mrs. O. A. Anderson. She returned to school Sunday evening.

—)(—

Cyril Cluff received a telegram last Saturday calling him to Washington, D. C., for service in the Quartermaster's Dept. as a clerk. He left that evening accompanied by Mrs. Cluff.

—)(—

D. S. Dorrity, Jr., formerly sheriff of Millard county, reported at the office of the United States marshal Tuesday morning for duty as a deputy marshal. Mr. Dorrity takes the place of David Thomas, who was promoted as chief deputy to fill the vacancy caused by the resignation of Lucian H. Smyth.—Telegram.

—)(—

The committee appointed to secure signers of the land owners under the Melville Irrigation tract (proposed Drainage District No. 4) went to Fillmore Tuesday) to lay the petition before the County Commissioners and ask for organization of the proposed district. The committee consists of A. Billings, O. A. Anderson and D. F. Peterson.

—)(—

Miss Emma Leona Christensen, who, with her sister, Mrs. Scott Grunden, lived in the Dick Collins house last winter and whose parents live at Holden, was married in Ogden March

the 29th to Reuben E. Weaver of Fort Worth, Texas. Mr. Weaver was in the employ of the Sevier Land & Water Co. for a number of years at Lynndyl. They will make their home in Salt Lake City. Mrs. Weaver is a sister of Mrs. Arthur Dennis.

—)(—

Come to the Delta Furniture Store for Pails, Tubs, Wash Boilers and Washing machines   a4-11

—)(—

Jos. D. Mercer, our affable druggist, has purchased Norm Lambert's residence, and dame rumor has it that Jos. is making some elaborate plans for the near future. He looks sheepish when approached on the subject and doesn't seem inclined to give up the whole story. That's all right, Jos., we were young and foolish once ourself.

—)(—

Mrs. R. J. Law, who has composed the following songs: "When the Meadow Lark is Singing in the Spring Time," "Fifty Times the Roses Bloomed," and "America, My Own Dear Land." has recently received the last named from the publishers and it is making quite a hit. She has already received a large number of orders from dealers out of town and the song is selling freely locally.

Millard County Progress
April 12, 1918

OASIS

Mrs. H. L. Jackson returned from Idaho where she attended the funeral of her sister-in-law Mrs. Ella Henry.

Mr. David Day has gone to Fillmore on business.

Mr. Freeman Brunson and Mr. O'Dell Gull have been visitors in Oasis the last few days.

Mr. Frank Dillonbeck has started

a new butcehr shop in Oasis. We wish him success.

The following program followed by an auction sale was held in the Oasis Ward Hall Tuesday evening for the benefit of the Red Cross.

1, Star Spangled Banner, by the audience; 2. Reading by Wallace Reid; 3. Song by Whilma Ward and Thelma Bennett; 4. Story, Elvin Anderson. Song, Kate Day; 6. Reading

Glida Gillen; 7. Instrumental Vera Day; 8. Vocal Duett, Deloy and Thelmas Reid; 9. Violin Solo, Stanford Cluff; 10. Instrumental Inez Thompson; Song Marcia Reid; Talk by Mr Jeff Clark, the auctioneer; Vocal Duet Emma Ward and Hilda Dillonbeck.

We are pleased to say that the Red Cross netted about $175 on the auction sale, that much more going to help the boys "Over There."

OAK CITY

The Relief Society and Young Ladies Mutual have joined together and organized a unit of the Red Cross with Mrs. Lorenzo Lovell as president and Silvia Lovell as vice president.

Mr. and Mrs. John Laundell were here Monday night visiting friend.

and relatives as Mr. Laundell leaves for Los Angeles where he has been engaged to serve Uncle Sam in the shipyards. He is an expert boiler maker.

Mr. and Mrs. George A. Faust are here visiting friends and relatives Mr. Faust is engaged in the Studebaker business and is working up a trade here.

On the 1t and 2nd a snow fell to a depth of 6 inches. Some of the fruit trees were in bloom but the frost which followed made them duck their heads in shame.

Bishop J. Leo Anderson and wife also Pres. Joseph Finlinson, Mrs Elmer Anderson and Ruby Jackobson were conference visitors in Salt Lake last week.

Mr. and Mrs. Jens C. Anderson went to Leamington Sunday afternoon and returned home on Monday

Millard County Chronicle
April 18, 1918

HINCKLEY HAPPENINGS

David Richards has gone to Parowan to see his wife who is at that place visiting her parents.

* * *

Quite a representation of Hinckley people went to conference in Delta last week and report a fine time.

* * *

It is reported that the M. A. will close this week and the district school will close the week following.

* * *

Mrs. F. W. Wilkins has gone to Callao to visit her husband and two daughters who are at that place.

* * *

S. T. Knight and wife have been visiting with Mrs. Knight's parents at Holden the past week.

* * *

No word from Hinckley last week. Well, I guess it's up to me to apologize. Cause? Just laziness, I guess, so forget and forgive and we will try not to let it happen again.

* * *

Geo. Whitehead and Chas. Burke are shipping their furniture, cattle, horses, machinery etc., to Idaho and will follow with their families in a few days.

* * *

Did you see "The Whip" at the Lyric on the 8th? If you didn't, you certainly missed a treat. Everybody that saw it says it was the best ever.

* * *

Word was received from Francis Stout at San Francisco, by his folks, that he had got poisoned eating canned goods and had been removed to a private ward in the hospital, but that he was recovering slowly.

* * *

Eddie Anderson is moving his family to Leamington where he has bot 80 acres of land under the new high line canal. He is keeping his 80 here and no doubt will come back at some future date.

* * *

Mrs. N. I. Bliss entertained, April 1st, in honor of her husband, it being his birthday anniversary. Games, music, singing, speaking, etc., were indulged in until the wee small hours when the guests left, wishing Mr. Bliss many happy returns of the day.

* * *

The Hinckley Dramatic troupe went to Delta and played "Down in Dixie" for the Red Cross. We understand that about $25 was realized from the trip. The troupe report good treatment from Delta and an appreciative audience.

* * *

The recruiting officer was seen in our town the past week and some of our young boys were soon dodging around and shaking their heads as tho very undecided, but we understand that he made quite an impression on a few and we will be able to give a more definite report next week.

* * *

The mail gets into Oasis at 6 o'clock a. m., and usually reaches Hinckley about 10 a. m. The people generally get their mail about 11:30 o'clock, just 6½ hours after arriving in Oasis, four miles away. We don't know where the fault lies but do know that the service could be greatly improved with a little effort.

Mrs. Malinda Aldredge died on the 6th inst. at the age of 83 years. Her husband died twelve years ago and since that time she has been living with her daughter, Mrs. Sadie Talbot. Mr. and Mrs. Aldredge were among the early settlers in Hinckley. having lived here about 35 years. She is survived by the following children: Mrs. Sadie Talbot, Mrs. Emily Wright and Wm. J. Aldredge of Oak City.

Abraham Articles

Sugar beet planting is progressing nicely.

* * *

Dick Reid, who has been working at the mines in Butte, Montana, is expected home this week.

* * *

Herbert Taylor and family motored to Murray last week to attend the funeral of Mrs. Taylor's brother.

* * *

"Tiny" Barker and his big caterpillar tractor are doing the plowing act on the Hickman ranch.

* * *

Wayne Patterson whose poem "Victory" was published in last week's Chronicle, says he don't mind the name Peterson so much, but has serious objections to the editor calling him a girl.

* * *

Mr. and Mrs. Fred Vorwaller left for Salt Lake Wednesday, where Mrs. Vorwaller underwent an operation for appendicitis Saturday morning. Their little daughter who was being cared for at the home of Mr. C. A. Vorwaller, took sick Friday, and on Saturday was in convulsions for seven hours, but at this writing is able to be up and at play.

DESERET DOINGS

Our District School celebrated Arbor Day very loyally. Every student seemed to be anxious to respond to the call of Uncle Sam, and plant trees and war-gardens.

* * *

John Petty, a brother to Albert Petty, is here visiting friends and relatives. He has not been here since he left thirty-two years ago, and reports that he sees much improvement in our town.

* * *

Mrs. La Cleod Nielson, formerly Ellenor Ashby, was guest of Miss Lucile Damron last Saturday.

* * *

The rally held for the purpose of promoting the Liberty Loan, was a great success. Pres. A. A. Hinckley gave a very good, patriotic talk, and Mr. Mitchell of the Academy rendered several very pleasing musical selections, both vocal and clarinet.

* * *

Mrs. Thomas Howells of Hinckley spent a very pleasant day with Mrs. J. A. Christenson, Monday.

* * *

Come to the big dance in the A. C. Nelson Wednesday night.

WOODROW WRITINGS.

Mrs. Ella Bassett has been appointed chairman of the Woman's Liberty Loan Fund for the North Tract. It is hoped that all women's organizations, and all women who can do so as individuals, will take out Liberty loan bonds in their individual names.

* * *

The Red Cross met with Mrs. Irvic Greathouse last Friday afternoon and incidentally turned in much finished work which had been made at home since the last meeting.

* * *

Miss Thelma Tinsley dislocated her wrist last Friday by falling as she slipped from the running board of an automobile before it had reached a full stop.

* * *

A little daughter was born at the home of Mr. and Mrs. R. Yamaki Monday morning.

* * *

DELTA NEWS NOTES.

—)(—

Mr. and Mrs. Noble Peterson returned from Salt Lake, Tuesday.

—)(—

The Chronicle is in the market for some clean soft cotton rags. Five cents per pound given. a18-25

—)(—

A fine line of Center tables, fumed oak. Also Extension tables, 6 and 8 feet lengths, at the Delta Furniture Store. a18-26

—)(—

Mayor Thurston went to Hinckley Tuesday evening to assist in the organization of a Home guard in that locality.

—)(—

The Delta Bakery has discontinued business on account of too much work and confinement for Mr. and Mrs. Aller.

—)(—

T. R. Sprunt of the Delta Lumber & Hardware Co., is building a residence just south of Bishop Maxfield's home.

—)(—

The raising of the Liberty pole and the Liberty Loan celebration Saturday was handicapped to a considerable extent by a shower of rain.

—)(—

Atty. Edw. D. Dunn was down from Salt Lake the first of the week preparing to start farming operations on his Abraham farm.

—)(—

Cleve Sedoris, who has come land on the North Tract, is here attending to business affairs and making proof on his homestead.

—)(—

The machinery for the mill has arrived and the proprietors, Messrs. Grundy and Willes, are here putting it in place. They expect to have the mill in operation about June the first.

Call at the Delta Furniture Store and get a fine Reed Rocker, or a Golden Oak or Mahogany finished one. They make pleasing wedding presents. a18-26

—)(—

Beginning Saturday, April 20th, the Delta State Bank will observe the usual custom of closing at 12 o'clock on Saturdays and continue so during the summer months. (ap11-18)

—)(—

A letter from Cyril Cluff to the Chronicle informs us that he is in the Supply and Equipment division of the Q. M. Department in Washington and orders the Chronicle sent to his address, that he may keep informed of Delta doings.

—)(—

J. H. Turner, who is interested in the Deseret Mountain and the Imperial Lead of Death canyon, was in town last Friday on his return from an inspection trip to these properties.

—)(—

H. A. Knight, who has a farm just south of Delta, is elated over a well which he recently had put down. The water raised to four feet above the surface and flows a nice stream of several gallons per minute.

—)(—

On a wager last week Noble Peterson carried four 100-lb. sacks of cement from the Delta Lumber & Hdw. yards to T. R. Sprunt's new residence being constructed south of Bishop Maxfield's residence. Some Sampson!

—)(—

Some of our town boys were up before Police Justice Steele yesterday for gambling and were fined $2 each. We understand they will appeal the case. The question at law is just what there is in a "stuff" game.

The Delta Town Board has taken over the irrigation within the city limits. They are also doing some good work on the roads, leveling them up, dragging them and putting in culverts. Seth Jacobs has the work in charge and will see that it is done right.

—)(—

The Hinckley Academy will play the opera "The Sorcerer" at the Lincoln Theatre Saturday night. Special music will be a feature of the program. This production come highly recommended and the Academy deserves your patronage.

—)(—

The Cooper Café and Refreshment Parlor have their fountain and cream business in operation. All kinds of drinks and cooling dishes served. Clean and nifty and open after the theatre for your convenience. (a18-11

—)(—

E. L. Chaplin, cheese export for the government, was here Tuesday and accompanied by Farm Demonstrator Welch went over to the East Side for a visit to the cheese factories there. He is endeavoring to unify the product of the various factories with the idea of a more profitable market.

—)(—

An item which slipped by us last week was the arrival at the M. J. Kilpack home of a new boy. Also the death of Alfred Lisenbee who was suddenly called away by an attack of pneumonia. Alfred was an industrious boy of sixteen and will be greatly missed by his widowed mother and brothers and sister.

—)(—

Miss Louise Fuller left last night for Denver where she will be married to Mr. Glenn Da Shiell. Mr. Dal Shiell was employed at the local factory and went from here to Colorado. He is now employed at the Longmont factory. Best wishes of the community go with Miss Fuller. Mrs. Harry Aller accompanied her sister, Miss Fuller, as far as Salt Lake.

Millard County Chronicle
April 25, 1918

HINCKLEY HAPPENINGS

The main topic for the week seems to be bonds, bonds and—more bonds. Hinckley "went over the top" in fine style by subscribing something like $7,000, while our allotment was only $5,000. Not so bad for 'poor' people.

* * *

Two more of Hinckley's young men have enlisted with Uncle Samuel the past week; Afton Greener and Clarence Bliss being the ones who have donned the khaki uniform.

* * *

The Millard Academy closed one of the most successful years it has ever known, last Friday. We don't know how many of the present faculty will be with us again next year but hope to see them at their old stand next term.

* * *

F. L. Hickman of Salt Lake City, one of our former citizens, was seen on our streets for a few days. He and another man, whose name we were unable to learn, have bought the stock of goods at the Passey store.

* * *

A farewell party for Geo. Whitehead and family was given in the Relief Society hall on the 15th; they left for Idaho the following day to be gone for a year or so; but have not sold out here, so we expect to see them back by another year. Chas. Burke and family also left for Idaho the past week.

* * *

J. A. Passey has been in Salt Lake City the past week on business.

DESERET DOINGS

Deseret boasts four graduates from the Millard Academy this year. The names of the students are: Inez Western, Lucile Damron, Ora Hales and James Western.

* * *

Mrs. Axel Jensen has returned from the hospital this week, and is on the improve.

* * *

The Elite Club was delightfully entertained by Miss Elsie Richards and Miss Stewart, this week. Many of the members are leaving town this week, and a reorganization will take place next meeting.

* * *

Born, to Mr. and Mrs. P. T. Black, a baby girl. All concerned doing nicely.

* * *

A farewell party was given for Geo. Bennett, who is leaving to join the army, Wednesday night.

* * *

Abraham Articles

A number of the young folks enjoyed a party at the home of Paine Franklin, Wednesday evening of last week.

A farewell party was given Thursday evening for Oren Oppenshaw and Wilson Biehler, who leave Friday— Oren for his home at Santaquin, and Wilson for the army training camp.

DELTA NEWS NOTES

The Delta School closes this week for the summer.

—) (—

Dr. C. A. Broaddus is in Salt Lake to meet his new son.

—) (—

Postmaster Faust is in Salt Lake this week taking medical treatment.

—) (—

B. E. Cooper went to Salt Lake Tuesday for a day's business operations.

—) (—

Born, to Dr. and Mrs. C. A. Broaddus, in Salt Lake, April 20th, a seven pound boy.

—) (—

Regular $1.25 brooms for 88c at the Delta Lumber & Hardware Co. store.   (ap25m2)

—) (—

A farewell dance will be given to the boys who are to leave for the training camp.

—) (—

Miss Viola Turner has returned from Salina, where she attended school during the winter.

—) (—

Jeff Clark of the Melville Land & Water Co. is doing some missionary work over in Sevier valley this week.

—) (—

Earl Robard went to Salt Lake last week and took the examination for a tank driver in the army.

—) (—

Gus. Neymeyer and wife of the North Tract are rejoicing over the arrival of a boy which arrived Sunday.

—) (—

Manager Jenkins, Chief Clerk R. P. Jones and Cashier Townsend of the sugar factory are in Fillmore today.

—) (—

The stores of the valley have agreed to close their business places at 7 p. m. week days and 9 p. m. Saturday.

—) (—

L. C. Stubbins is down this week looking after his big ranch, the Alpha farms. He has been crippled up the past month with rheumatism.

—) (—

Jesse Hulse is down from Murray this week looking after the building of a fence along the right-of-way thru his farm on the North Tract.

—) (—

Call at the Delta Furniture Store and get a fine Reed Rocker, or a Golden Oak or Mahogany finished one. They make pleasing wedding presents.   a18-26

—) (—

Leonard Blade was taken to Salt Lake last Saturday and operated on at the L. D. S. hospital Sunday for appendicitis. He was accompanied by Mrs. Blades, and report from him the first of the week indicates that he is getting along nicely.

—) (—

J. W. Thurston has been appointed local representative of the Utah Div. Food Administration. He will begin a campaign at once to see to it that the 50-50 flour measure is lived up to and advises all stores to supply themselves with substitutes.

Sugarville Sayings.

Mr. and Mrs. Dewitt Hulett have sold their belongings, and left the middle of the week for Los Angeles, Calif.

* * *

Mrs. Albert Watts will entertain the Thimble Club next Wednesday afternoon.

* * *

There will be a May dance Saturday evening, April 27th, at the F. T. C. Hall. The ladies are to buy the dance tickets and the gentlemen to bring lunch, of not more than three things, in a May basket for his lady. All come and have a good time. The ladies can show you a good time, boys.

Millard County Progress
April 26, 1918

NEW SOLDIERS TO LEAVE SATURDAY.

All registrants desiring deferred induction into the Army on account of Agricultural pursuits, must submit their claims in affidavit form with the Local Board at Fillmore, Utah, before they receive their official call. No registrant will be given deferred induction after he receives his notice. Application blanks for furlough for agricultural purposes of men in the Army, may be obtained at the Local Board's office. After the blanks have been filled out, they should be returned to the Local Board for approval.

Millard County's quota in the next call of the draft will leave for Camp Lewis, Washington Sunday morning April 28th. Following are the thirteen men selected by the Board to fill this allotment:

Joseph Fielding Riding, Delta.
George Baris, Delta.
Ralph Clyde Bunker, Delta.
Ivin Seamour Dimmick, Delta.

John Alldredge, Oak City.
Wilson Biehler, Abraham.
George Albert Bennett, Deseret.
Peter Johnson, Oasis.
H. P. Arnold Larson, Lynndyl.
Mark L. Bennett, Holden.
Donel William Peterson, Scipio.
Gilbert Penney, Kanosh.
William B. Pratt, Hinckley.

The Local Board also received a call to entrain three men for Fort McDowell, California on May 10th J. Ralph Wood, and Clayton A. Wood of Holden, and Maurel J. Warner of Fillmore were selected by the Board to represent Millard County's quota.

OAK CITY.

The Red Cross had a rummage sale Friday night, the 19th.

Last Tuesday night, the 19th, the Liberty Loan Committee held a meeting and had a programe. After the meeting the people all gathered on the square around a bon fire and burned the Kaiser in effigy.

Mr. and Mrs. Nielson moved out on their farm at Fool Creek, this week.

Messrs. Chalse Trimble and Harry Roper went to Fillmore Monday.

Mrs. Joseph S Wells who has been in California for some time returned here Sunday and expects to remain here this summer.

Mrs. Annie L. Anderson, her son Don, and daughter Ethelyn made a trip to Manti last week. They stopped in Mayfield to visit relatives on the way.

All the students have again come home fro mschool and we are glad to see them back.

Mr. Winslow Walker spent Sunday afternoon here visiting friends and relatives.

Miss Wanda Aldridge is home after spending the winter in Sutherland.

Mr. John Q. Dutson, Miss Eva Anderson and Miss Wanda Dutson went to Delta Monday.

Mr. Clifton Aldridge has returned home after working in Hinckley.

the amount used in the territory and if our investigations prove that we are right, we will immediately nstall a refinery with at least 100 barrels a day capacity.

"We plan to furnish gasoline, kerosene and distillate for the territory between Fillmore and St. George, and think we can furnish it at a less price tha nit can be shipped in from outside points. So far we have met with much kerosine. We learn that n the neighborhood of 20,000 gallons of gasoline per month is hauled into the St. George and Cedar City

Millard County Chronicle
May 9, 1918

HINCKLEY HAPPENINGS

H. E. Sherrick, Delta, has plenty of Sweet Clover seed left for sale cheap.

* * *

Water has been turned into the town ditch, and people are busy putting in garden seed and trees and otherwise keeping busy. Indications are that this will be a favorable summer for gardens. The fruit in this locality has most all been frozen.

* * *

Mr. Dean, proprietor of the Hinckley Confectionery, has gone south on business and also to visit the Dixie oil fields and sulphur springs at Laverkin.

* * *

Mrs. Letitia Wilkins, who has been visiting her husband and children at Callao, has returned.

* * *

Wm. Walker, who has been under the care of a physician in Salt Lake City, has returned and says he is feeling much better. He has an affliction of the spine, one of the vertebræ being misplaced.

* * *

Chas. A. Stratton has purchased a car and is busy trying to learn the "durn" thing to run straight and smooth. But up to the present time he has been unable to get results. He says he never saw such a stubborn critter.

* * *

Word has been received from David Richards that his wife is critically ill, having lost her baby at birth. She is with her parents at Parowan and everything possible is being done for her.

* * *

We would like to know if West Millard is going to see any baseball playing this summer. What is the matter of the towns getting together and forming a baseball league and playing regular ball? Of course, most of our young men have gone to war, but we old stiffs could fly around and tell what we have done and try to see what we can do, yet, and let people laugh at us anyway. In these serious times a little fun is a mighty big relief and we need it now as bad or worse than ever. What say you, boys?

WOODROW WRITINGS.

Mrs. Robbins and daughter of Delta, Mrs Fredricks and Dr. Tracy of Woodrow were entertained by Mrs. Fred Rick, Monday.

* * *

Mrs. Fredricks disposed of her household effects Wednesday at public auction sale and will leave for California to join her husband, Friday.

* * *

Red Cross and Jolly Stitchers held a joint meeting Friday afternoon at Mrs. S. H. Thompson's.

* * *

The Webster family went to Salt Lake in their car Sunday and will be gone for ten days.

* * *

Mr. Griffith has purchased the 40 acres recently bought by Guy Watts and has moved his family into the farm house.

* * *

Guy Watts is actively training with Uncle Sam's obys at Camp Kearney, California.

Sugarville Sayings.

Farm Bureau meetings are held the first and third Wednesday evening of each month.

* * *

J. B. Seams, H. E. Anson and Harry Pedsick were down to Fillmore on business the first of the week.

* * *

Sugarville Red Cross meeting this week, Friday afternoon.

* * *

Roy Jones was called to Morgan, Utah, last week, by the death of his mother.

* * *

The Friendship Thimble club will meet next Wednesday afternoon with Mrs. J. B. Seams and Mrs. J. L. Barker at the home of the former.

* * *

Miss Ethel Iversen spent Saturday and Sunday with her mother and brother at Sugarville, also called on friends and neighbors. She was accompanied by her friend Mr. Wagner.

* * *

Mr. and Mrs. Erick Jaderholm are enjoying a visit from their three daughters from Salt Lake City this week.

DELTA NEWS NOTES

Corporal H. G. Potter of the veterinary corps, stationed at Fort Riley, Kansas, came in Wednesday evening for a short visit with his mother, Mrs. W. J. oCnger, who is living on N. S. Bishop's place west. Mr. and Mrs. Conger recently purchased a farm west of town and came here from Rigby, Idaho. Mrs. Conger has three sons in the service, they having enlisted in Idaho. One of the other boys is in the navy and the other in the signal service. They are both thot to be in France now. The corporal s enthusiastic over his experience in the army and talks interiatedly of army life as seen at Ft. Riley. He says that they have a reservation at this post twelve miles square and the work-outs they receive are exactly the same as on the firing line except for the bullets.

—)(—

Sergeant Wm. D. Manca of the marine corps is in town this week, coming down from the marine recruiting station in Salt Lake for the purpose of instructing the home guards in the manual of arms and company drill. Meetings were held

Monday, Tuesday and Wednesday evenings and will bo hold this evening and Friday evening, after which the sergeant will return to his post and leave further instruction to the guard officers.

—) (—

Sergeant Stumpf, who has became a person known to most of our people here, having been here a number of times on recruiting service, was down the first of the week to accompany the Abraham boys who recently enlisted to the recruiting station. While here he took the applications of Max Pace, Willie Pace, Marcus Morrel (of Loa), and Jack Webb of Deseret back with him. These boys will leave about Friday to be examined.

—) (—

Attorney Edw. D. Dunn was down the last of last week looking after his Abraham farm. He was accompanied by E. H. Hill of the Bronson-Hill Investment Co. who was looking over the country in a business way.

—) (—

Earl Robard left last Sunday evening for Salt Lake for duty with Uncle Sam's sammies. He was joined Tuesday by Mrs. Robard and they will journey together to Portland, where Mrs. Robard will visit with Earl's parents and he will report at Vancouver barracks for duty.

Dan Livingston was down, the first of the week and shipped eight cars of fat cattle from the feed yards at the sugar factory to the Denver market. Ten cars were shipped the week before. There remain several cars to be shipped later.

—) (—

The W. O. W. met in regular session last Tuesday evening and decided that hereafter their meetings would be held each first and third Tuesday of the month. Their next meeting will be held Tuesday evening, May 21, at which they plan a social entertainment in connection with the regular meeting.

—) (—

At the Home Guard meeting Monday evening Dr. Broaddus was elected medical adviser with the rank of major. Ed Marshall was appointed to the captaincy, made vacant by the Doctor's appointment. The captains have been ordered to have their men meet and drill in squads every two weeks.

—) (—

The big attraction at the Lincoln Theatre next week is the melodrama "Come Through," which will be presented Wednesday and Thursday. See ad. on back page of this issue of the Chronicle.

—) (—

Messrs. Prout and Penniston of the Delta Land & Water office force of Milford spent Saturday and Sunday in town looking after company business.

Miss Datty Robbins and grandparents, Mr. and Mrs. Peter Hughes, who spent the winter in California, returned overland this week to Delta.

—) (—

Miss Sylvia Larson of Deseret expects to leave the last of the week for Salt Lake to enter the Red Cross service as a nurse.

—) (—

Dennis & Ormandy are busy these days calcimining. They are experts at the business and have time to attend to your wants.   (m9-1t)

—) (—

Ye Editor lost his glasses last week and will reward any one returning them to him. They were xylonite frames with cable bows.

—) (—

A fine line of Glassware, Crockery, Granite and Tin Ware at the Delta Furniture Store.   m9-1t

—) (—

Mrs. R. C. Graham left Saturday evening to join her husband who is a government saddle maker in California.

—) (—

Attorney J. A. Melville, Jr., was here attending to legal matters this week and left Wednesday evening for Salt Lake.

—) (—

Miss Pearl Tozer has returned from her winter studies at Mt. Pleasant.

Millard County Progress
May 17, 1918

MILLARD'S QUOTA TO LEAVE MAY 27TH.

The Local Board of Millard County entrained Maurel J. Warner of Fillmore, Utah, and Harold Anton Petersson of Scipio, Utah, Wednesday the 15th for the University of Colorado, at Boulder, Colorado, where they will receive training as expert Mechanics.

Chester L. Bowers of Nashville, Tenn., formerly of Lynndyl, Utah, was ordered to report to Fort Benjamin Harrison, Indianapolis, Indianna May 17th, as a locomotive engineer, by the Local Board of Millard Co.

Millard County's quota of the next increment of the draft, to entrain for Camp Lewis, American Lake, Wash., on the morning of the 27th at Oasis at 7.25 A. M., will be 33 men. Following are the men selected by the Board to fill this quota:

307. Marcus James Dunn, Provo.
406 Alma Evan Jacobson. Oak City.
535 Robert W. Nesbitt, Provo.
536 Noah Eugene Stowe, Hatton.
557 Ernest Hunter, Kanosh.
599 Edward Erastus Johnson, Deseret.
611 John Archie McMullen, Ogden.
614 Tage Andreas Hersleff, Delta.
623 Earl Lionell Webb, Lynndyl.
631 Philip H. Barkdull, Meadow.
635 Axel Jensen, Oasis.
638 Clyde A. Sampson, Delta.
643 James A. Faust, Delta.
648 John Golden Hanssen, Scipio.
650 Francis Harmon Eaklund, Scipio.
659 Jesse Stott, Meadow.
663 Bryant Moody, Hinckley.

670 Benjamin Elmer Bennett, Holden.
677 John D. Cole, Los Angeles.
680 Walter W. Barbou, Delta.
708 George August Faust, Delta.
709 Wm. A. P. Heise, Delta.
734 George Macaire, San Francisco.
735 Leigh Richmond Allred, Deseret.
737 Arnold R. Workman, Hinckley.
744 Willis J. Lyman, Delta.
751 Rolland M. Black, Abraham.
771 Clarence Moody, Deseret.
775 Clive Black, Deseret.
777 Ausmond Willden, Scipio.
780 Jesse M. Nichols, Fillmore.
794 W. Helgo Johnson, Spanish Fork.
804 Parley Ivie, Scipio.
811 Albert M. Peterson, Scipio.
817 Milo Peter Johnson, Lehi.
835 James A. Downs, Oklahoma City.

OAK CITY

A number of people have gone to Manti to work in the Temple this week.

Mrs. Fred S. Lyman's baby is seriously ill at this writing but we hope it will soon be improving.

The stork visited the home of Mr. and Mrs. Jesse R. Higgins last week and left a fine baby boy. Mother and child are getting along fine.

Mr. Willard Christensen is home on a six week's furlough.

The bundle shower given Mr. and Mrs. Willis J. Lyman was a success and they received many beautiful and useful presents.

Mrs. Eugene Gardener of Delta is here visiting friends and relatives.

Brother Leo Lyman of Delta and Brother Christensen of Oasis were the speakers in our Sacrement meeting on Sunday last.

Lester Johnson of Lynndyl is here spending the week with relatives and friends.

The fine rain storm improved the crops which were suffering for the want of water.

Millard County Chronicle
May 23, 1918

DESERET DOINGS

A farewell testimonial for the boys leaving for the training camps was held at A. C. Nelson hall Wednesday evening. The guests of honor were: Ed. Johnson, Leigh Allred Clarence Moody, Cline Black, of Deseret; Axel and George Jensen, brothers, Jack Nelson, of Oasis, and Joe Fidel of the South Tract, all of whom were presented with a comfort kit by the Mutual Improvement Association of their respective wards.

County Attorney Grover Giles of Fillmore was in town on legal business Tuesday.

Another recruit arrived at the home of Mr. and Mrs. Averno Black last week.

A little daughter made its appearance at the home of Mr. and Mrs. Henry Dewsnup recently.

Mrs. Jam Boyack of Delta, chairman of the "Bee Hive" girls of the Deseret Stake, visited the Deseret ward association Monday, outlining the new features of the work for this summer, prominently among which is "thrift service" and "child welfare" work.

The committee handling the Red Cross drive for funds submitted to the central committee at Delta the sum of $357.73 Monday afternoon Much more has been pledged.

Mrs. Hester Scott is down from Murray for a short visit with relatives. It is understood Mrs. Scott will sell her home here and settle permanently in Murray, her former home.

Miss Mary A. Hales left Tuesday for Salt Lake City, where she will visit for some time. Her little niece, Mable Crafts, accompanied her.

Arthur Cahoon, who has been at Camp Lewis since last October, is due to arrive home on a short leave of absence.

Services at the chapel, Sunday afternoon, were devoted to the Red Cross. Aside from the spiritual and musical uplift the time spent proved a financial success inasmuch as the allotment to Deseret of $165 was far exceeded in the contribution made after the services. President A. A. Hinckley was the speaker of the afternoon and made a stirring appeal for the Red Cross and for the many peoples who need its succor.

The Deseret Red Cross Auxiliary delivered to the West Millard Chapter, this week, 202 refugee garments, five pajamas and 30 pairs of socks.

HINCKLEY HAPPENINGS

Born, to Mr. and Mrs. Floyd G. Eyre, a girl. All concerned doing fine.

The following boys have secured farm furloughs and are home for a short time: Carl Theobald, Harold Morris, and Vess Nelson. The boys are certainly looking fine and are loud in their praises of treatment accorded them from Uncle Samuel.

Mrs. Fannie Hilton has gone to Camp Lewis to visit her husband who is with the boys in training at that place.

The following boys will leave on the 24th for training camps from Hinckley: Arnold Workman, Bryant Moody, Mark Dunn and Peter Keise; more will follow soon.

J. A. Jackson, our congenial blacksmith, is putting in a cement floor in his shop and is otherwise preparing to run an up-to-date garage. Those having bad work done by him seem to have got satisfaction, as they invariably come back when they are in need of more repairs.

The management of the local theatre, known as the Lyric, is offering a prize of one dollar and a free ticket for one month for a name for the show house. They report business good and are highly pleased with their investment so far.

It is reported that three of our influential citizens are selling out and preparing to move to other places in the near future. They are A. A. Hinckley, who will locate at Lynndyl; W. F. Pratt, who is going to Springville, and Jacob Felix, who is going either to Leamington or Springville. These are all good men and we are sorry, indeed, to see them go; but we hope their moves will be for the best.

The dance given by the Liberty orchestra on the 17th was certainly a grand success and everyone is boosting for the young musicians and wishing them the best of success.

J. M. Rigby has been quite ill for a week or so, but is on the improve at this writing. There seems to be quite an epidemic of La Grippe or something similar going around, and those having it say it is no joke.

Deputy Sheriff Chas. Theobald made a flying trip to Gold Hill last week and brot back a couple of young men who are wanted by local merchants and business men for jumping some bills. We refrain from mentioning any names but hope the matter will be straightened out without any serious trouble.

State Road Agent F. F. Slaughter is seen in town and we hope he notices the big water hole, frogpond or lake at the south end of Main St. It is certainly a nice breeding place for disease.

Abraham Articles

Samuel Miller has gone to Columbus, Ohio, to attend a Synod of Presbyterian church as a representative of southern Utah.

* * *

Mrs. M. J. Hansen returned from Salt Lake City last week where she had gone to meet her son Hans, who was on his way home from a two years' mission in Illinois.

* * *

Frank and Nathan Lake arrived last week from Butte, Mont., where they have had employment for the last two months.

O. M. Fullmer purchased a Dodge Bros. auto from Oscar Warnick of Deseret.

* * *

A farewell party will be given Thursday evening of this week in honor of Hansen and Rulon Black who leave for the army.

* * *

The National weighing and measuring test for children under school age will be held the afternoon of Wednesday, May 29th, at the home of R. T. Peterson. Everyone living in Abraham district please bring all children under this age.

R. J. Law of Delta was out the first of the week, inspecting his fine Abraham farm.

* * *

Mrs. J. H. Palmer of Abraham gave a delightful party in honor of her daughter Lucy's 8th birthday on Thursday, May 16. Those present were: Lillie Vorwaller, Maud Hampton, Leon Bohn, Irma Hampton, Nola Bohn, Myral Young, Ernestine Hall, Phebe Taylor, Madoline Spare. The little girls sang patriotic songs and enjoyed themselves in games and dancing. Ice cream and cake were served to all. Miss Ida Orr and Mrs. Phoebe Hills assisted in entertaining the children.

WOODROW WRITINGS.

A large representation from Woodrow attended the Red Cross dance at Leamington last Saturday evening in their respective auto cars. They partook of a campfire supper after the dance and returned home in the early morning, reporting a fine time.

* * *

There will be a Red Cross dance at Woodrow Saturday, May 25th. All invited.

* * *

A number of our young men have been called to the service of their country, leaving here on the 24th. Among them are Tage Hersleff, William Heise, Walter Barben and Dick Clark. We are proud of our boys, but oh, how we miss them!

* * *

Word was received from Tampe, Arizona, that Jacob De Bree, well known to the original settlers of the North Tract, had died suddenly at the dinner table last Sunday at his home near Tampe. Mr. and Mrs. De Bree have many friends in Woodrow who are saddened at the news and who wish to extend sympathy to Mrs. De Bree in her hour of sorrow.

* * *

The Jolly Stitchers will meet with Mrs. C. C. Sampley, Friday, May 24, at 2 p. m.

* * *

Preaching at Woodrow next Sunday at 11:30 a. m. Sunday school at 10:30. New theme: all invited.

* * *

Henry Vollbard, who has been working in Los Angeles, is now in the hospital suffering from an injured hand. He writes that he will be at home for the summer as soon as he recovers.

* * *

Leon Abbott, who was operated upon in Salt Lake City two weeks ago for appendicitis, is expected home this week.

BOOZE TRAFFICKERS COME TO GRIEF

Sheriff Cass Lewis Assisted by Home Guard Confiscate an Immense Amount.

FINES TOTAL OVER $500.00

Tire Trouble Makes Capture an Easy Matter---Destination Thot to be Salt Lake.

Sheriff Cass Lewis and the Home Guard are responsible for one of the biggest wet hauls in the State, capturing two auto loads of almost 1000 pints of joy water last Thursday evening.

A week ago last Saturday night two men, giving their names as Martin and Williams, routed T. H. Pratt of the Pratt Merc. Co. of Hinckley out of bed to secure gasoline for their cars, each having a big Studebaker car. The next day Sheriff Lewis was in the store and heard Mr. Pratt remark that he had been called out of bed the night before to supply some stragglers with gasoline and remembered one of the car numbers. The sheriff asked him to keep his eyes open for them, figuring that they were on a mission for booze over in Nevada and that they would be back Friday.

Mr. Pratt was called on Thursday afternoon of last week to supply the same two cars with gasoline again and they were piled high with something covered with quilts. He noted the number on one and it was the same as on one of the cars he had supplied with gasoline the Saturday night before.

He tried to reach the sheriff by phone but he was in Fillmore or on his way back to Delta, figuring that Friday would be about the time the cars would return.

Mr. Pratt then thot of Mr. Shields of Sugarville, captain of one squad of the Home Guards, and, the autos having headed that way, telephoned to him to be on the lookout. Mr. Shields phoned to Fred Barben to keep his weather eyes open and just about that time two autos passing Mr. Barben's place stopped near there to repair a puncture. He telephoned Mr. Shields and went out to investigate. The pair was caught with the goods on them and when Mr. Shields arrived were arrested and brot to town. They were turned over to the sheriff who had arrived by that time.

Their trials were held the last of the week and the two of them were fined $510, which fine was paid the first of the week and the men took their cars and hiked, minus their booze, and sadder "Bud-weisser." There was 934 pints of beer and whiskey which at present prices would have brot them nearly $4,000 retail had they succeeded in getting by with it.

It is supposed they got it at Ely, Nev., and were taking it to Salt Lake City.

HINCKLEY HAPPENINGS

The Red Cross drive in Hinckley was a grand success. This town went over the top Sunday night and the money was all in at that time. Next!

* * *

Word has been received from Hurricane, Utah, that Thomas Reeve had died following a operation for appendicitis. Tom was well known here and has a mother and two sisters, a brother and several other relatives here. Our sympathy goes out to the bereaved.

* * *

Last Thursday nearly every mother in town could be seen with their babies going in the direction of Mrs. Lula Cooper's, the occasion being a weighing and measuring of the said offsprings by Miss White.

* * *

John Church of Eureka was down for a few days last week and brot with him Mrs. Miner Peterson and Mrs. Jas. Morgan.

* * *

John Jarvis and family have returned from Logan where John has been attending school the past winter.

* * *

Simon Webb was called to Heber to attend the funeral of the infant son of Mr. and Mrs. Giles McDonald. Mrs. McDonald was formerly Miss Mandie Webb. Parents of the babe have the sympathy of the community.

* * *

One of the Hinckley Home Guard saw a couple of autos going thru town from out west and suspected something, so phoned to Chas. Theobald, our local captain, who immediately telephoned to Sutherland and had them stopped and searched and found them loaded with booze. They were taken to Delta and Justice Billings gave them a fine of $250 each, so we understand. It don't pay to fool with Uncle Sam these days, boys. Better tie a tin can on such carryings-on.

* * *

S. T. Webb has gone to Snake valley to do some work for Geo. Bishop, and will be gone about two weeks.

* * *

Little Norma Phillps, daughter of our genial harness maker, won the prize for the name for our local theatre, which will be known as the Star Theatre hereafter.

* * *

Born, on the 25th, to Mr. and Mrs. J. A. Knight, a boy. Mother and babe doing finely.

* * *

Edwin Stevenson of Holden is here visiting his aunt, Mrs. S. T. Knight. We suppose this is the purpose of his visit but have heard that Geo. Wright has bot a bulldog and a shotgun.

* * *

Two more Hinckley boys have gone to help Uncle Sam in the army. They are Frank and Call Slaughter. Call spent a year with the troops on the Mexican border, but was sent home on account of sickness.

* * *

Our boys from Camp Lewis, who came home on farm furloughs, have been suddenly called back and will have to report to their companies on or before May 30. They believe this means a trip to France before long.

* * *

Mrs. Golda Jackson has been at Leamington for a week or so, visiting her mother, Mrs. Eddie Anderson.

* * *

Jacob Felix has sold his home in Hinckley to Alfred Bliss, who lives just east of town.

* * *

PERSONAL PARAGRAPHS

Mrs. Dr. Broddus' father who was passing thru Delta for Salt Lake in his car, stopped over for a day's visit Sunday.

—)(—

Mr. and Mrs. J. A. Knight of Hinckley are the parents of a nine-pound boy, which registered at their home Sunday morning.

—)(—

A few copies of the song "America, Our Own Dear Land," composed by Mrs. R. J. Law, remain on hand and can be procured at Law's store.

(m30-1t)

—)(—

H. F. Aller, who went up to Rigby last week to attend a meeting of the stockholders of the Beet Growers' Sugar Co., returned home the first of the week.

—)(—

Arthur Dennis and family motored over to Marysvale last week for a visit with relatives. They returned home Saturday accompanied by Mr. Dennis' brother, who came over in his car.

—)(—

P. M. Purdy has arrived from Bingham and announces that he will have everything at the Bank Hotel in apple pie order and ready to serve meals by the first of the coming week.

Mr. and Mrs. W. J. Shillington of Oxnard, Cali., old friends of Mr. and Mrs. R. A. Nelson of the Island farm, who are making a tour of the country, stopped for a few days the last of last week for a visit with their old friends.

—)(—

We are pleased to chronicle the marriage, last Thursday at Fillmore, of Mr. O. L. Lake of Abraham and Mrs. Laura Rose of Ogden. We extend the bride a hearty welcome to this new commonwealth and wish them both long life and happiness.

—)(—

Miss Hettie White, head of the women's work in the county, was in town Saturday and took the weight and measurements of the little ones under five years old for statistical purposes in the child saving move being carried on thruout the United States.

—)(—

Lorenzo Christensen, brother of Mrs. Calvin Jones, who enlisted in the army about a year ago from Oasis, arrived in Delta the last of the week for a visit with his sister. He is now a member of the cavalry force and expects to make the trip to France before long.

—)(—

Mrs. R. J. Law has composed a song entitled "Somewhere in France" which is in the hands of the publishers and is expected soon to be ready for distribution. She has met with good success with her former compositions and, judging from the title, the one now about to appear should meet with great favor.

Dr. H. L. Evans, chiropractor, formerly of American Fork, has located in Delta and is making his headquarters at the Ward Hotel temporarily. He expects to be here about a month, and if his business justifies it will procure office rooms and locate here permanently and move his family here. Read his ad. in this week's paper.

—)(—

The Jolly Stitchers have handed their copy in to the Chronicle office for a new cook book which will contain about one hundred pages and have all the latest recipes for food saving brot about by the war. The book will be of great value to housewives and will be covered with oil-cloth of washable material to prevent soiling. The ladies expect to divert the proceeds of the book into war channels. Better see them and speak for a book at once. It will be off the press the latter part of the coming month.

PERSONAL PARAGRAPHS

Coal Oil and Gas Stoves. Monarch Ranges—the best on the market—can be had at the Delta Furniture Store. j13-20

—)(—

J. M. Van Winckle of Oklahoma, who has a fine farm on the South side, is here looking after his interests.

—)(—

Mrs. Gertrude Thomas, and Gertrude Irish, mother and neice of Mrs. C. O. Davis, are here from Ogden visiting in the Davis home.

—)(—

Dave Richards of Hinckley has accepted a position with the Delta Milling Company and will move his family to Delta.

—)(—

The body of Mr. Arnold, who died about two years ago on the Niel farm just west of Delta, was exhumed the last of last week and shipped to his old home in Kansas.

Cashier Pierson of the Oasis State State Bank and wife are rejoicing over the arrival of a ten pound boy who reported at their home last Saturday for duty.

—)(—

Watch for the first installment of Lieutennant O'Brien's own story of his remarkable adventure. It will appear June 27th.

—)(—

Mrs. C. A. Hire left Tuesday morning for Etna Green, Ind., where she will visit relatives during the summer.

—)(—

The Friday Auxiliary concert given at the Ward Hall Wednesday evening is reported to have been an excellent musical entertainment in which all the participants did fine. A large crowd would have been acceptable.

—)(—

John Knight of Clear Lake has rented the Willoughby farm east of town and Mr. and Mrs. Willoughby are having a sale of their effects today and will soon leave for Southern California where they will look around for a pleasant place to rest.

—)(—

John Jimpson is moving into the Eccles home this week. Mr. Jimpson is heavily interested in this valley, having an interest in one of the largest farms in the North tract. He is a booster for Delta and the valley and we welcome Mr. and Mrs. Jimpson to our community.

—)(—

The Jolly Dozen attended a lawn party Sunday at the home of Miss Arvilla Lewis where they had an enjoyable time. The guests were Miss Bell Gates, Thenelda Blackburn May Peterson, Reva Pane, Alta Stevens of Fillmore and Messrs Golden Hawley, Lad Damron, Clint Black, and Paul Hawley.

—)(—

J. W. Thurston's sister, Mrs. Allie Riter and children, stopped off at Delta the last of last week for a short visit with him while on her way from her home in Ogden to Southern California where she will spend the summer.

—)(—

J. C. Jones, manager of the Western Newspaper Union branch at Salt Lake paid the Chronicle office home a pleasant visit between trains Tuesday evening. Mr. Jones is a very pleasant man and always solicitous of the country printer's welfare.

SUTHERLAND SEARCHLIGHTS.

The Jolly Stitchers and L. L. Red Cross Auxiliary spent a very enjoyable afternoon with Mrs. Titus. Next

Jolly Stitchers meeting to be at the Woodrow Hall with Mesdames Keyes and Norris as hostesses, Friday the 21st.

* * *

Mrs. J. T. Britt has resigned as chairman of the L. L. Red Cross

Auxiliary. Mrs. R. G. Ottley was elected to fill the vacancy. Anyone wishing to do Red Cross work may get it at the home of Mrs. Ottley.

* * *

The Jolly Stitchers have decided to let Sugarville have the Fourth of July celebration.

* * *

W. S. S. solicitors have been busy and allotments were received cheerfully, with promises to go over the top by a strong margin.

* * *

Haying is on in full swing and a great many are busy in the beet fields thinning beets.

* * *

Harry Ottley had the misfortune to loose a horse last week. It attempted to jump a fence and alighted on top of a post piercing its intestines, necessitating shooting it.

* * *

It has been reported that the cut worms have been doing considerable damage in the beets this season.

* * *

Bishop Roberts, Wm. Walker and Mr. Livingston and wives took a trip to Gunnison by auto.

DELTA NEWS NOTES.

Miss Margerie Littledyke of Fillmore is working at the Bank Hotel.

—) (—

Mrs. Rhoda Melville of Fillmore visited with friends in Delta yesterday.

—) (—

Mrs. Harry Aller and party, who made a trip to Ely, have returned. They were accompanied by relatives.

—) (—

J. Baker, brother of Mrs. R. C. Bates, came down from Salt Lake the first of the week and he together with Mr. and Mrs. Bates and Miss Gwen Johns have gone to the canyon for an outing.

—) (—

A big rain is reported to have fallen on the bench and east of town yesterday. It was a real down pour those who got mixed up in it report, but it only reached the edge of town.

—) (—

Mr and Mrs. A. L. Broderick and family and Delbert Searles left yesterday by auto for Fish Lake where they will spend several days enjoying the great outdoors, after which they will visit with relatives in Wayne county. During their absence the Broderick business is being managed by Miss May J. Peterson, a sister of Mrs. Broderick.

—) (—

Seth Jacobs brot us in a sample of cherries yesterday which were raised on his home place in Delta. Seth says he has quite a nice crop on his young trees and that it is only a matter of knowing how to handle the trees and getting them to the bearing point when we will have all the home grown cherries we can consume.

—) (—

Mrs. Frank Copening visited Delta friends Monday and attended to business matters. Mrs. Copening and the girls are now living in Salt Lake. Frank is still in Cuba but expects to return to Utah next month. Mrs. Copening will live in the city where the girls will finish their education. She says the time spent in Cuba was very pleasant and she enjoyed it greatly.

Millard County Chronicle
June 27, 1918

SUTHERLAND SEARCHLIGHTS.

Mr. and Mrs. W. R. Walker entertained the family Saturday evening in honor Lee Walker who expects to leave Thursday to enter the service of his country.

* * *

Mr. and Mrs. Tilletson from California are spending a few days with their son, Meadé. They are on their way into Colorado by auto.

* * *

W. R. Walker spent last week in Salt Lake on business.

* * *

A number of our citizens are taking a vacation at Fish Lake. Among them are Mr. and Mrs. M. A. Abbott and Mr. and Mrs. H. Sherer.

* * *

Mrs. Rachel Roper of Oak City is ill at the Walker home.

* * *

The "Jolly Stitchers" and the L. L. Red Cross Auxiliary will meet with Mrs. Webster at the Woodrow Hall, July 5.

* * *

Mrs. Jefferson Jones has returned from Salt Lake City, where she has been attending her sister, Miss Nell Lovell, who underwent an operation for appendicitis and the removal of her tonsils.

* * *

Ernest Ottley was in Sutherland Wednesday bidding friends and relatives good-bye. He is on his way to Vancouver, Washington, where he will work for Uncle Sam.

ABRAHAM ARTICLES

The prospects for grain and sugar beet crops were never better.

* * *

Miss Lila Lake left for Salt Lake last week, for an extended visit.

* * *

John Walters returned home Monday from Salt Lake.

* * *

Mr. and Mrs. Sherrick and Miss Nellie McBride are spending a week in Provo canning cherries, etc.

* * *

Mr. and Mrs. C. M. Hickman received word from their son Floyd of Camp Lewis, Washington, that he had been rejected for overseas service on account of his feet.

* * *

Alex Reid and daughter, Fern, left Tuesday for Salt Lake City where Mr. Reid went to consult an eye specialist.

* * *

Joseph Palmer and family are moving this week to their new bungalow on South Main.

* * *

The local Red Cross meets Friday, July 5th, at the School House.

* * *

John Lucas is visiting in Salt Lake this week.

WOODROW WRITINGS

Born to Mr. and Mrs. Ruel Hibbard, a daughter. To Mr. and Mrs. Jacob Ritter, a daughter.

* * *

The Misses Laura and Thelma Tinsley are visiting in Provo and incidentally picking fine fruit to ship by parcels post to all who want it.

* * *

Mrs. La Rue Pritchett, nee Cora Heise, writes from Camp Lewis that the Millard county boys are all well and doing fine work at the camp.

* * *

Hereafter the Woodrow store closes promptly at 6 P.M., according to government regulations.

* * *

Oscar Wiklund met with a serious accident last week when a pitch fork penetrated his fore arm to a depth of several inches.

* * *

The Clyde Underbills and the Chas. Barker's are camping at Fish Lake this week.

* * *

Mr. and Mrs. E. H. Lambert received the sad intelligence by telegram that their little grandson had passed away in California.

* * *

The weevil they are evil with persistance of the "Devil." They have eaten up the first crop of hay. If the second crop is like it, down the road afoot we'll hike it, in such numbers that no one can lose his way.

ABRAHAM ARTICLES

Mrs. Minerva Hampton and children left Sunday for a visit to relatives in Lowell, Wyoming.

* * *

Sherman Talbert is moving this week to the W. J. Cary farm.

* * *

Harry Hall and family left Monday for a ten days' visit at Joseph, Utah.

* * *

Samuel Miller arrived home Friday from a two months' visit in Ohio, Missouri, Kansas and other states.

* * *

Mr. and Mrs. Udy left Monday on a visit to points in northern Utah.

* * *

Alex Reid and daughter, Fern, left for Salt Lake Monday, where Mr. Reid went to receive medical treatment for his eyes.

* * *

Mr. and Mrs. Waymant of Ogden, spent the Fourth here with their daughter, Mrs. Ora Lake.

* * *

The Red Cross ladies are making a house to house canvass this week soliciting funds to be able to meet the demands of Uncle Sam.

* * *

Mrs. Porter of the South Tract is here visiting her daughter, Mrs. Jesse Cain.

* * *

Mr. "Bert" has gone to Milford, where he has employment as a plasterer.

* * *

Mr. and Mrs. McCullom of Washington, are here visiting Mrs. McCullom's parents, Mr. and Mrs. White.

* * *

Mr. and Mrs. Hutchins have taken charge of the W. D. Livingston ranch.

* * *

O. L. Lake purchased the Emery LaDuke farm this week.

* * *

The Postoffice was moved this week to the home of Mrs. Hallie Young.

3 at the school house. Mr. Forrest gave a very interesting talk on soil fertility.

* * *

Mrs. Jefferson Jones is visiting relatives in Oak City.

* * *

Mrs. Geo. Dunker is in Provo canning fruit.

* * *

The "Jolly Stitchers" and L. L. Red Cross Auxiliary met with Mrs. Geo. Webster and Dr. Tracy at the Woodrow Hall, Friday last. A very enjoyable afternoon was spent. Next meeting to be in two weeks with Mrs. De Lapp and Mrs. Wind as hostess.

* * *

The Abbotts, Robisons and Shorers have returned from Fish Lake. They report the fishing fine and having had a most enjoyable vacation.

* * *

Mrs. Roper was able to return to her home in Oak City last week.

* * *

Sutherland was well represented in Delta and Hinckley on the 4th of July, all reporting a good time.

* * *

The Sutherland Relief Society will meet Tuesday, July 9. Meetings will be postponed one month. The members to devote the meeting time to Red Cross work or visiting the sick or other beneficial work.

* * *

Mrs. Jefferson Jones is on the sick list.

tion in Delta postponing their trip on that account.

* * *

John Jones, the youngest son of Mr. and Mrs. Edward Jones, was shot through the lower part of the body last Saturday with a 22-caliber rifle by Riley McKee. The boys were out hunting rabbits and the McKee boys' gun being accidentally discharged, the bullet passed entirely through John's body. It it has not penetrated any of the vital organs, John may soon be around again.

* * *

The state presidency spent Sunday at Holden Ward visiting with the people in their several meetings.

YOUNG DEFENDERS
JOIN THE COLORS

Sergeant Clark of the U. S. A., who recently returned to Salt Lake from a recruiting trip to Delta and vicinity, paid this district the following compliment in Wednesday morning's Tribune:

"I never saw so patriotic a town as Delta," said Sergeant Clark, "Every man, young and old, wanted to take a crack at the kaiser, and had I another man with me to take some of the labor of examining the men off my shoulders, Uncle Sam's army would have been larger today by at least forty huskies. They came in wagons and autos, Delta contributing the most of the men, but little Deseret, with only a handful of eligibles, turned in four. What impressed me more than anything, though I was visibly touched by the display of love of country and patriotism, was the going away of the boys when the whole town turned out.

"Saturday evening at about seven o'clock the boys and myself were banqueted, and with dancing and speeches everybody had a good time. A collection was also taken up for the boys and each one received a goodly sum."

The following boys from this valley accompanied Mr. Clark who was here for the Fourth celebration and on recruiting duty to Salt Lake and enlisted in the army: Allen F. Crafts and Nels C. Black, Deseret; Geo. C. Bunker, Hinckley; Lammond Bunker, Delta; Lincoln Cropper, Deseret, Delbert E. and Geo. E. Patter, Delta; Bert A. Sharp and Donald C. Hoyt, Delta; Ervin R. Stoddard, Sutherland; Romulus Shields, Sugarville; Doyle and Harold Steele and George M. Abbott, Sutherland.

These are boys of less than draft age. While America was slow to get into this war, now, with every young man of the country surging on the bitto get at the atrocious Hun and nearly every family represented in the army here or in France, there will be no quit until he is thoroughly licked.

The boys were all passed and sent to Ft. Logan, Colo.

OAK CITY NEWS.

Collier Lovell has purchased a new Ford.

Leland Neilson has been here since the Fourth, visiting with Miss Wanda Dutson.

Mr. and Mrs. Charles Roper left for Idaho Sunday morning where they will visit relatives and friends. They were accompanied by their daughter, Nellie and son Murlin.

Everybody is busy poisoning grasshoppers, which have been a great pest in destroying their crops.

Mr. and Mrs. Henry Roper came home to spend the Fourth with their parents. They are taking care of Joseph Finlinson's farm this summer in Leamington.

Edwin Smith and Miss Eva White were here last week visiting friends. Misses Melba and Kate White came with them to visit relatives and friends.

The Fourth of July was a great success. Many people from neighboring towns passed through going to the canyon.

TRAGIC DEATH
OF DELTA GIRL

GLADYS POWELL PERISHES WHILE BATHING.

A cloud was cast over this community last Saturday evening as the news spread that little Gladys Powell had met death by drowning near the spillway of the Deseret Irrigation Co. reservoir a couple of miles southwest of Delta.

After supper, Mrs. Powell and daughters, Florence and Gladys and Mr. and Mrs. Wm. Askee went down to the reservoir to bath as do a number of persons each evening. They went to the point that projects out into the big pond just after crossing the bridge. At this point Mr. Powell had taken his family a number of times before for a bath.

He had cautioned those with him that at a certain place in the water there was a step-off and not to get out too far. The water in the reservoir at the present time, however, is quite low, and Gladys, who was first to get into the water was deceived by the stage of the water with regard to the step-off.

She could swim a little and when she found she was beyond the shallow water she started to swim back. Thinking she had reached a point where she could touch bottom she let down and went under. This coupled with the exertion probably excited her and she lost control of herself. Mr. Askee ran to her assistance and had secured her and started for shallow water.

He was having some difficulty in getting back to where he could wade and Mrs. Powell seeing things apparently going against him became frantic in her efforts to aid got beyond her depth.

Mr. Askee in his attempts to save the mother lost hold of Gladys. Mrs. Askee and Florence formed a chain from the shallow water with Mr. Askee and Mrs. Powell was saved. By this time Gladys had disappeared and a call was sent to a number of men bathing at the bridge. It was something like twenty minutes, however, when J. W. Thurston brought her body to the surface after a dive.

The body was taken to the home of A. S. Workman, nearby, where friends and doctors worked with it for a number of hours in an effort to restore life, and while some encouragement was apparent, the efforts were all in vain.

Gladys Blanche Powell was the daughter of Mr. and Mrs. S. E. Powell of this city. She was born at Oberlin, Kansas, December 12, 1905 and was twelve years old at the time of her death, July 6th, 1918.

She came to Delta three years ago with her parents and was known to all those of school age and most of our townspeople.

She was an amiable little lady and a dutiful sister and daughter, who took her part in life beautifully and pleasingly. Her death was a great loss and shock to all who knew her as well as to the members of her family.

The hearts of all go out in sympathy to Mr. and Mrs. Powell and

we all mourn alike for the beauti young life which has just been so tragically separated from its natural course.

Funeral services were held at the Ward Hall at two-thirty Tuesday afternoon, conducted by Rev. Hamilton, assisted by J. H. Melville. The hall was crowded with sorrowing friends. The floral offerings by the children were particularly impressive and were added to by those of the older ones.

Interment was made in the Delta cemetery.

MILLARD'S ROLL OF HONOR.

Following is the list of boys of Millard County, who, having reached the age of twenty-one registered for service, June 5th. First nuber is the order in which they will be drawn. The last number is that of registration:

1. William Arnold Rasmussen, Fillmore, Utah, 10.

2. Cyrus Grant Stevens, Holden, Utah, 29.

3. Callie Memmott, Scipio, Utah, 17.

4. George Quail Terry, Sutherland, Utah, 57.

5. Wells Brunson, Fillmore, Utah, 4.

6. George Washington Stanworth, Oasis, Utah, 70.

7. Cloon B. Stott, Meadow, Utah, 28.

8. James Hyrum Hopworth, Leamington, Utah, 65.

9. George Isaac Carling, Lynndyl, Utah, 45.

10. Glenn Albert Patten, Gandy, Utah, 72.

11. Walter Ward Bishop, Delta, Utah, 61.

12. Ernest E. Blackburn, Delta, Utah, 51.

13. Edward Everett McNutt, Delta, Utah, 63.

14. Evan Burgess Theobald, Hinckley, Utah, 41.

15. Wallace A. Wood, Holden, Ut., 32.

16. Richard John Smith, Delta, Utah, 66.

17. Roscoe Blaine Thompson, Scipio, Utah, 16.

18. Henry Arnold Schlappy, Delta, Utah, 56.

19. Morris Hunter, Kanosh, Utah, 33.

20. John Henry Jenson, Delta, Utah, 56.

21. Raymond Earl Kaminska, Malone, Utah, 48.

22. Nolen Frederick Robison, Fillmore, Utah, 13.

23. Richard Eugene Ashby, Fillmore, Utah, 3.

24. Alfred Frank Biehler, Abraham, Utah, 64.

25. Orvil Lewis Starley, Fillmore, Utah, 11.

26. Myron Abraham, Kanosh, Utah, 69.

27. Arron Almon Penney, Kanosh, Utah, 35.

28. Edgar Rollo Moody, Deseret, Utah, 62.

29. Rex B. Peterson, Scipio, Utah, 18.

30. Charles Wallace Cahoon, Hinckley, Utah, 54.

31. Clifton I. Alldredge, Oak City, Utah, 29.

32. Frank Garr Stephenson, Holden, Utah, 30.

33. Frank Alan Strickley, Delta, Utah, 43.

34. Leonard Stott, Meadow, Utah, 25.

35. Edwin Imer Christiansen, Oasis, Utah, 58.

36. Rulon Fay Starley, Fillmore, Utah, 12.

37. Clinton Penney, Kanosh, Utah, 34.

38. Willis Eugene Black, Fillmore, Utah, 2.

39. Justle George Peterson, Delta, Utah, 46.

40. Carl Everett Christopherson, Fillmore, Utah, 8.

41. Oliver Sophus Olson, Delta, Utah, 67.

42. Ira Dee Talbot Leamington, Utah, 40.

43. Ivan Hilton, Hinckley, Utah, 44.

44. Carl Cahoon Bishop, Fillmore, Utah, 27.

45. Jesse Lyman Duncan, Meadow, Utah, 27.

46. Thomas Clark Greenway, Fillmore, Utah, 1.

47. Philip Hinton Kelly, Oasis, Utah, 52.

48. Nolan William Huntsmen, Fillmore, Utah, 6.

49. Angus Stewart, Meadow, Utah, 24.

50. Marion Clinton Martindale, Fillmore, Utah, 14.

51. Joseph Clem Duncan, Meadow, Utah, 71.

52. William Glen Allen, Scipio, Utah, 19.

53. Henry Lemont Miller, Lynndyl, Utah, 59.

54. Lars Hansen, Oasis, Utah, 37.

55. Thomas Alfred Whatcott, Kanosh, Utah 36.

56. Robert Andrew Wiley, Lynndyl, Utah, 68.

57. Lelland Rider Wright, Hinckley, Utah, 44.

58. Waldo George Robins, Scipio, Utah, 15.

59. Sterling John Bennett, Meadow, Utah, 15.

60. Clyde Leroy Wood, Holden, Utah, 31.

61. James Lougy Smith, Delta, Utah, 53.

62. Waldo Clyde King, Malone, Utah, 43.

63. Joseph Clifton Beckstrand, Meadow, Utah, 23.

64. Orvil E. Beckstrand, Meadow, Utah, 22.

65. Irvin George Monroe, Scipio, Utah, 21.

66. Pedro Elizondo, Delta, Utah, 50.

67. Elton Ashmer Miller, Delta, Utah, 47.

68. George C. Terry, Oak City, Utah, 60.

69. Jacob Perry Huntsman, Fillmore, Utah, 9.

70. Otis Probert Walch, Scipio, Utah, 20.

71. Lawrence James Frampton, Fillmore, Utah, 5.

72. Farail Kesler, Cove Fort, Ut., 42.

SUGARVILLE SIFTINGS

(Too Late for Last Issue.)

E. Jaderholm and Mr. Ashby are slowly recovering from a severe attack of the plague.

* * *

Mrs. Elizabeth Lee and little daughter, of Salt Lake, are visiting her parents, Mr. and Mrs. E. Jaderholm.

* * *

J. F. McLane and family and W. W. Baker and family left for Fish Lake Monday morning for a ten days' outing.

* * *

The little daughter of Wm. Remington was badly burned one day last week by pulling a tea kettle of hot water over on herself.

* * *

Mr. and Mrs. Ed. Cady and Miss Libble Milton left this week for California to be present at a reunion of Mr. Cady's family as five of the relatives are to leave for the army in August.

* * *

Another little girl has come to live at the Thure Cronholm home.

SUTHERLAND SEARCHLIGHTS.

Miss Nina Bunker and Wanda Allredge entertained at a party Tuesday night at the Walker's residence, Sutherland, in honor of Arnold Schlappy and Pratt Wright, who leave shortly to join Uncle Sam's army. The room was decorated in the national colors. Games were played and a delightful lunch was served. The invited guests were: Arnold Schlappy, Pratt Wright, Rulow Hinckley, Edw. Workman, Ianthus Wright, Dewey Sanford, Orwin Memmott, Anna Wilcox, Susie Sanford, Nell Peterson, Priscilla Leavitt and Wanda Boyack.

SUGARVILLE SIFTINGS

The Friendship Thimble Club will meet with Mrs. Cary and daughter Edna next Wednesday.

* * *

The Red Cross Auxiliary has changed the day of meeting from Friday to Wednesday of same week.

* * *

Fred Tingleaf of the South Tract is visiting friends at Sugarville this week.

* * *

Mr. and Mrs. E. D. Cady have returned from a three weeks' visit in California.

* * *

Thurston Dale and wife and Fred Ashby and family are enjoying a few days outing at Oak Creek Canyon this week.

* * *

Quite a number around here have their land ready for fall wheat and are waiting for the threshers so as to obtain seed.

* * *

Friends of Ernest Baxter will be interested to hear that he has been sent to the Philippine Islands for training.

* * *

Engineer Caldwell and wife drove down from Salt Lake Tuesday, and stopped at J. B. Seams for dinner, en route to Delta.

ABRAHAM ARTICLES

Mr. and Mrs. O. M. Fullmer, their son Joe and daughter Florence, returned Monday from a three weeks' auto trip through Utah and Southern Idaho.

* * *

Mr. Wilkins of San Bernardino, Cal., is here visiting his daughter, Mrs. Hattie Young, their first meeting in thirty-five years.

* * *

O. L. Lake and family will move soon to their new home at Ogden, Utah.

* * *

A big dance is scheduled Friday night, August 16th at Abraham School House for the benefit of the Red Cross. Good music and refreshments. Everybody welcome.

* * *

Miss Veda Rose is under the doctor's care this week.

* * *

Wanted—A good threshing machine to thresh our wheat crop.

* * *

Fred Vorwaller is packing his household goods preparatory to moving north. Destination not known.

* * *

Miss Ida Orr of Delta, was visiting at the Palmer home Sunday.

* * *

George Wayment is now a resident of the beautiful city.

* * *

Quite a number of the Abraham boys are fighting their way into long pants.

* * *

Mrs. Worthington of Grantsville, is here visiting her daughter, Mrs. Leroy Bills.

WOODROW WRITINGS

The thresher has appeared in our midst. Both the Flint and Harris machines are working on full time.

* * *

We are lucky to be living in Utah. A letter from the eastern coast says that sugar is an unobtainable luxury, but whisky is being sold on every corner.

* * *

Gus Neymeyer escaped a serious accident by a narrow margin when he became caught in the gasoline engine at his home Sunday morning. With rare presence of mind he seized the belt, and, luckily succeeded in breaking it, thereby, escaping with nothing more serious than a badly bruised and lacerated arm with a dislocation at the elbow joint.

* * *

The Jolly Stitchers met at the at the Woodrow Hall on Friday, August 16th at 2:00 p.m. Election of officers. A full attendance is requested.

* * *

The two-year-old daughter of Jas. Boyle is recovering nicely from a broken forearm.

* * *

The electrical storm of Sunday afternoon put the Woodrow telephones out of business, and so they remain until the present writing.

* * *

Mr. Fred Stevens, who came recently for a short visit to his brother Roy, has decided to remain a month or two and help in the autumn harvest fields.

* * *

Mr. and Mrs. Kinne are established in the Frank Koch residence in Woodrow to the delight of their many friends.

PERSONAL PARAGRAPHS

Ethel Iverson is again at the Liberty Parlor assisting in dispensing of cooling drinks and confections.

—) (—

Mrs. Art Botton of Salt Lake City is spending several days visiting with her sister, Mrs. Alf. Bunker.

—) (—

A report from Rufus Clark who is in France, states he has nothing to do but bake bread and then more bread.

—) (—

Corporal Frank Slaughter of Camp Lewis is visiting his people in Hinckley for a short time.

—) (—

Mrs. W. L. Lackyard made a flying trip to Salt Lake City Saturday for a short visit with her husband who accompanied her back.

—) (—

Geo. Meinhardt and Joseph Kaiser of the North Tract, left Tuesday for a two weeks visit with relatives and friends in California.

—) (—

Donald Searle, son of Allan Searle, had his tonsils removed by Dr. C. A. Broaddus last Wednesday forenoon.

—) (—

Mr. and Mrs. Edwin Larsen of Abraham have moved to Gunnison, where they have purchased land and will reside permanently.

—) (—

Editor C. O. Davis returned home Wednesday evening. He reports that his mother is not greatly improved, but hopes to have better news soon.

—) (—

Miss Thenelda Blackburn, who has been wrestling with an attack of diphtheria for the past two weeks has returned to her work at D. Stevens & Co.'s store.

—) (—

Matthias Koch left Sunday night to join Uncle Sam's army. A crowd of friends and relatives were at the station to see him off and wish him good luck.

—) (—

Mrs. Della Kennedy and small son, arrived the last of last week from Burley, Idaho, to spend a few months with her sister, Mrs. Struen Robertson.

—) (—

Mrs. Rose Dugett of Emery, a friend from childhood of A. L. Broderick, paid his family a short visit last week. Mrs. Dugett proceeded to Hinckley to visit with her mother and other members of her family.

—) (—

Ben Douglas of the Golden Rule Store, accompanied by his wife, left the first part of the week for Salt Lake City and various points in the state. Mr. Douglas and wife expect to be absent for about ten days, and during his absence, his business will be looked after by the Misses Viola Turner and Blanche Maxfield.

—) (—

The Delta Relief Society met Tuesday, August 13, at the Ward Hall and in connection with the regular meeting held a short program was rendered to about 100 guests after which refreshments of ice cream and crackers were served. A very enjoyable time was reported by all.

—) (—

O. L. Lake of Abraham has rented his place to his brother-in-law, Neil Wayment, and will move with his family to farm at a point about 12 miles west of Odgen. Owing to a rumor that has been circulated, Mr. Lake wishes to state that his daughter, Lila, is employed as housekeeper for a family in Salt Lake.

—) (—

Increased activity in land sales and exchanges is reported by our local land agent Jeff Clark. Mr. Clark attributes this activity to the abundant crops in Millard County. News having been spread far and wide of the wonderful possibilities afforded the farmer at Delta, and not withstanding our national troubles, Millard County continues to grow.

The Red Cross will give a dance at Sugarville on Saturday evening, August the 24th.

—) (—

Mrs. F. E. Dale returned last week from a month's visit with her daughter in Denver. Mrs. Dale left her son George in Denver when she returned.

—) (—

Edgar Moody, who will be remembered as one of the local teachers here last year, having had charge of the 6th grade, left Tuesday night for Salt Lake to enter the service of Uncle Sam. A number of Mr. Moody's friends gave a farewell party for him at the Deseret Meeting House just prior to his departure. We extend our best wishes for safe and speedy return.

Millard County Chronicle
September 5, 1918

SCHOOL DAYS, SCHOOL DAYS, GOOD OLD GOLDEN RULE DAYS.

The Delta Schools opened last Monday with a house chucked full of students, there eing 315 pupils present at the opening. During the year a number of more will drift in. It is evident that there will have to be more room provided for the next school year and it is now time for the people of this district to begin advances for a new building to provide for the overflow for next year and to incorporate in their advances a demand for a high school. Knowing that there is a demand for such an institution here it is also time for the County School Board to begin planning for these without further effort on the part of the citizens of the district.

The seventh and eighth grades have already been arranged on the Junior High plan.

The following teachers have been elected for the year:

Clark Allred, Principal.

Miss Flavo McMullen, Sandy, 7th grade.

Mrs. Bertha M. Wells, Delta, 6th grade.

Mrs. Fannie Hilton, Hinckley, 5th grade.

Miss Muriel Erickson, Grantsville, 5th grade.

Miss Cleo Pierce, Springville, 4th grade.

Miss Maude Smith, Springville, 3rd grade.

Miss Grace Priesbrey, St. George, 2nd grade, "B."

Miss Evlyn Palmer, Cedar City, 2nd grade, "A."

Miss Lela Peterson, Springville, 1st grade.

Assistant to the first grade teacher has not yet been provided for.

WOODROW WRITINGS.

Wedding bells have been ringing in Woodrow figuratively speaking for the past week.

* * *

Leo Davis (Furrer) of the Aviation Corps, stationed in Florida, obtained a furlough of twenty days and returned to Woodrow to wed his fiancee, Miss Venice Barben, daughter of Mr. and Mrs. Fred Barben. After a happy honeymoon of ten days duration, Mr. Davis has returned to camp leaving his bride with her parents. Their wedding dance at community hall last Wednesday night was a social event, and congratulations and best wishes were showered upon the plucky bride and groom.

* * *

Mrs. La Rue Pritchett nee (Cora Heise) returned to her home in Woodrow last week to remain while her husband is "over there." She was given a surprise Miscellaneous Shower by her many friends last Friday afternoon. Handsome presents good wishes and hearty cheer were in evidence.

* * *

Wednesday P. M. Mrs DeLapp entertained all the ladies west of the main canal to a dish towel shower in honor of Mrs. La Rue Pritchett. A fine time was enjoyed by all present.

* * *

The Jolly Stitchers and Red Cross are to meet in the Woodrow hall Sept 16th, with Mrs. Greathouse and Mrs. Hickman as entertainers.

* * *

Harold Watts and Fred Kenney are the latest victims of the Pavhant Plague.

* * *

Ed McWatt, George Clements, Oscar Anderson and Chas. Barker left us for Uncle Sam's service.

Men Between 18 and 45 Must Register

All male persons within the United States who shall have attained their eighteenth birthday and shall not have attained their forty-sixth birthday on the Twelfth day of September 1918, must register. The only exceptions are those that have previously registered either on June 5th 1917, June 5th 1918, or August 24th 1918, and officers and enlisted men of the Regular Army, Navy and Marines. The time of registration will be between the hours of 7 a. m and 9 p. m. on Thursday the 12th day of September.

Any person temporarily absent from the jurisdiction of his local board will report to the office of the nearest local board, where he will receive a registeration card. This will be filled out and sworn to by a member of the Local Board. The registrant is instructed to mail the reg. istration card himself to his local board of origin, allowing sufficient time for the registration card to reach his local board by September 12th. This applies to only those who are so far distant from their local boards that it will be impossible for them to return for registration.

Registration officers have been appointed by the Governor of Utah, in each voting precinct within the County. Registrants will go before the nearest registrar and register. Following is the list of registrars for Millard County:

Fillmore: C. H. Day; Frank L. Stewart; Floyd Ashman.

Holden: Sidney Teeples, J. Alma Stevens.

Scipio: Carl Brown; C. A. Memmott.

Meadow: J. Azonzo Duncan.

Kanosh: John Watts.

Oak City: Joseph L. Anderson.

Leamington: John B. Evans.

Lynndyl: E. A. Jacobs.

Delta: F. W. Cottrell; A. P. Wallace; J. Avery Bishop.

Hinckley: R. E. Robinson; H. F. Wright.

Deseret: E. J. Eliason.

Oasis: C. O. W. Pearson.

Clear Lake: H. J. Bond.

Black Rock: Benitta James.

Malone: H. E. Adams.

Burbank: A. Frank Robison; L. C. Winder.

Garrison: James F. Robison.

Abraham: Donald Hogan.

Sutherland: W. R. Walker.

Woodrow: Albert Watts.

Delta Sugar Factory: R. C. Bates.

Any person who fails to register on the day of registration will be subject to one years imprisonment, or involuntary induction into the Army.

All registrars are requested to submit to the Local Board, immediately, an estimate of the approximate number of registrants with their respective districts.

Millard County Chronicle
October 3, 1918

SUGARVILLE SIFTINGS.

The Sugarville Red Cross met at the home of Mrs. Cady last wednesday afternoon. A new name was decided upon for the Auxiliary and it will hereafter be known as the Liberty League Auxiliary. The next meeting place will be with Mrs. J. B. Seams when more work is expected and every member should be present.

* * *

Kenneth Seams had the misfortune to be kicked in the cheek by a horse Sunday afternoon, but is getting along fine.

* * *

Misses Edna Cary and Blanche Remington and Messrs. Alvin Iverson and Clyde Cary are taking in the sights at the fair at Salt Lake this week.

INFLUENZA AND PNEUMONIA TAKE ALARMING TOLL.

Eight Citizens Dramatically Taken From Our Midst in the Past Nine Days.

Influenza in Delta as well as in other parts of the country has continued to take its toll of victims the past week at an alarming rate.

Since last week's issue six deaths have occured in Delta and vicinity. Most of those who have fallen victim to the disease have been big, hearty men, with the best part of life still ahead of them. They have been men who would least expect to be taken by disease of this kind.

Those who have just passed away from among us represented some of our best and most trustworthy citizens and we all mourn their loss as brothers' and deeply sympathize with those who have been deprived of their help and comfort in their homes and daily work. Our hearts as a community feel in particular the great sorrow and gloom that has been cast over the little ones and their mothers in being deprived of the guidance and care of the strong hands which have heretofore watched over them. Let us be more kind and helpful to these in the future that we may in turn impart to them at least some degree of the help and comfort they have been deprived of and that we still enjoy.

There being no gatherings nor intercourse one with another except just what is necessary we have not been able to go fully into details of each death:

GEORGE E. BILLINGS

who had been very sick at his home when the hospital was established was moved there the last of the week and died of influenza Saturday morning at three o'clock. Tuesday at twelve o'clock, after being reviewed by relatives, the body was laid away in the Delta cemetery with appropriate services and the loving care of friends. He leaves a wife, who is now very low with the same disease and four little girls. His father three brothers and two sisters also survive him. At the time of his death George was just turning thirty-one years of age. He was a man who always worked for what he thot to be the good of the community. He will be greatly missed by the community as well as by his more intimate friends and his family.

DICK SMITH

died in the hospital after having been moved there the last of last week, in a serious condition. His death occured Sunday at 5:30, p. m. The funeral occured today at 2. p. m. Left to mourn his loss is his young wife and three small children besides his father, seven sisters and one brother. His age at the time of his death was twenty-one years. He was the son of Dick Smith, Sr., who lives on the South Tract and a brother-in-law of Maurice and Joe Briggs, and was engaged in the threshing business at the time of his death.

MAURICE BRIGGS

died at his home south of Delta of influenza Tuesday at 10:30. He was twenty-seven years of age and he leaves a wife and three small children to mourn his loss. He was engaged in threshing with his brother-in-law, Dick Smith. His father and mother and brother, Joe and wife of Salt Lake came down when notified of his condition. A double funeral occurred today when he and his brother-in-law, Dick Smith, were buried at 2:00 p. m., by sorrowing friends and relatives with appropriate services.

CHARLES PHILBRICK.

Charles Philbrick, of Wymore, Neb., electrical engineer at the sugar factory contracted influenza at the factory and was moved to the hospital the last of last week while in a very serious condition. He died at two on the morning of Monday. He was thirty-three years of age. His brother-in-law arrived from the east a few hours before his passing away and his sister Miss Christie Philbrick arrived that night. Mr. Philbrick was a Mason and carried some insurance. His sister left on Wednesday night with the remains for Nebraska.

ERBIN STEWART

Erbin Stewart was an employee at the factory and was twenty years of age, and was moved to the hospital in a precarious condition and died Wednesday night at 5:00 p.m. He was alone in the vicinity, his mother living in St. George. She was communicated with and gave instructions that the boy be temporarily buried in the Delta cemetary.

JAMES A. SMITH.

James A. Smith of Delta, who had been in the hospital and returned to his home in the east part of town died Wednesday night at midnight of influenza and asthmatic complications. He was past middle age and leaves a wife and nine children. His funeral will take place as soon as the casket can be obtained.

LUTHER BUCHANAN.

Word reaches us just as we go to press that Luther Buchanan has passed away, leaving a wife and several children.

ELECTION RETURNS

Democrats and Republicans of County Divide Honors. State Goes Democratic. Nation Apparently Goes Republican

The recent election was void of much enthusiasm, apart from the immense amount of publicity given it by the party organizations. The masses were content to go to the poles and vote as they saw fit, those who went at all.

The Delta precinct went Democratic by from twenty-five to thirty majority in most cases. For supreme Judge the Socialists cast fifteen votes in the county for Parsons.

The State went Democratic for both U. S. Representatives.

The completion of the lower house seems to be Republican and the upper house is in doubt the dicision of its politics remaining in the hands of Michigan, Idaho and New Mexico.

The vote in Millard County shows the following votes for respective candidates:

U. S. Congressman, Dist. No. 1.
M. H. Welling, Dem., 1012
Wm. H. Wattis, Rep. 961

District Judge.
D. H. Morris, Rep. 866
L. A. Miner, Dem. 807

Supreme Judge. (3)
Samuel Thurman, Dem. 994
J. W. Cherry, Rep. 913
— Parsons, Socialist, 15

Valentine Giddeon, Dem. 979
A. E. Bower, Rep. 929
A. J. Weber, Dem., 974
J. E. Frick, Rep., 942

The results of the County ticket is as follows:
State Representative:
Jos. Finlinson, Leamington, Rep., 1017
H. E. Maxfield, Delta, Dem., 897

Commissioner, 4-yr. term.
R. E. Robinson, Hinckley, Rep. 930
Oscar Warnick, Oasis, Dem., 975

Commissioner, 2-yr. term.
H. Watts, Kanosh, Rep., 827
F. C. Christensen, Kanosh, Dem., 1070

County Clerk.
Carl Day, Fillmore, Rep., 971
Maurice Lambert, Fillmore, Dem., 949

County Assessor.
A. T. Rappley, Kanosh, Rep., 950
N. L. Peterson, Deseret, Dem., 915

County Treasurer.
Frank Partridge, Fillmore, Rep., 940
Harrison Anderson, Fillmore, Dem., 971

County Attorney.
M. M. Steele, Jr., Delta, Rep., 937
G. A. Giles, Fillmore, Dem., 979

Sheriff
Geo. W. Cropper, Deseret, Rep., 1075
Cass Lewis, Delta, Dem., 837

Surveyor.
C. Theobald, Hinckley, Dem., 975
T. Geo. Theobald, Hinckley, Rep., 951

Constable.
Seth Jacobs, no opposition.

Justice of the Peace.
N. S. Bishop.

Indications point to all three of the Constitutional Amendments having carried.

DEATHS OF THE PAST WEEK.

Mr. Norton was one of the employees at the sugar factory, who recently moved to Delta from Nevada and lived in the second house below R. J. Law's store. The family consisted of his wife and his wife and his son. and his wife. The remains were interred in the local cemetery with appropriate services.

Chester Patterson, a young man of eighteen, who came from Beaver to work in the factory, died last Monday. His mother was with him at the time of his death. He was unmarried and his body was taken to Beaver for burial. His father's name is Edward Patterson.

George L. Schow, who has been with the Delta Beet Sugar Corporation since it first started its first operations, as a fieldman, died Friday Night of pneumonia coupled with other ailments of long standing. Mr. Schow was thirty-nine years of age and was a brother of Mrs. Frank Roberts, whose husband is field superintendent for the sugar company. He leaves a wife but no children. The body was taken to Lehi, his boyhood home, for burial. Mrs. Schow will go to California where she will make her future home.

Those who have been so severely afflicted have the deepest sympathy of the community.

SUTHERLAND SEARCHLIGHTS.

The Shipleys are rejoicing over the arrival of a fine baby boy.

* * *

Mr. and Mrs. Frank Belston are sick with the "flu".

* * *

The late snow storm did not please our farmers.

* * *

* * *

News is hard to get as everyone stays at home as much as possible.

* * *

Allen Lloyd had the misfortune to break his leg last week. His horses backed a load of beets off the beet dump, at Steele. Allen jumped when he saw the load was going over or it would have killed him. The horses were badly shaken up and part of the railing was torn from the drive way to the dump.

Millard County Chronicle
November 21, 1918

WEATHER REPORT.

The following report of temperature for last week is recorded by Saml. Western, U. S. Observer, at Deseret, Utah:

Date	Temperature Highest	Lowest
27	.59	23
28	.53	42
29	.58	23
30	.65	23
31	.68	24
1	.73	27
2	.70	31

Hinckley Soldier Dies in France

Youngest Son of Mr. and Mrs. H. L. Bishop Falls Victim of Pneumonia.

Word was received last Saturday of the death of Elmer Bishop, the 18-year-old son of Mr. and Mrs. Heber L. Bishop of Hinckley, in France, as the result of pneumonia, which was preceded by a severe attack of Spanish influenza.

Elmer Bishop left his home in Hinckley on the 11th day of July last and enlisted in the 145th Utah Artillery the following day, having passed a 100 per cent physical examination. He was sent to Fort Logan, Colo., for training where by close application and strict attention to duties he received recognition. A vacancy occurring gave him the opportunity to get over-seas at once should he be able to pass the final exam. This examination he passed successfully and was bound for duty in France within one month after his enlistment. An achievement reflecting much credit on the young soldier.

Young Bishop was in France over two months before he fell a victim to the fatal pneumonia and word received by his relatives were full of enthusiasm and encouragement and mentioned how fortunate he felt at being able to get into the fray within such a short period of time.

Elmer Bishop was the youngest of nine children, having seven brothers all residents of Millard County, and a sister at present a resident of Rifle, Colorado, and engaged in business at that place. He was born in Hinckley and was a graduate of the Millard Academy at that point, and was among the most popular of the younger set, and held in high esteem by all with whom he came in contact, and his passing away is deeply felt by all who knew him, and his family have the sincerest sympathy of the entire community in the loss of their soldier boy and baby brother.

PERSONAL PARAGRAPHS

W. E. Evans, Bank Commissioner of Utah, was in Delta Wednesday.

—)(—

Homer Hansen has rented the Frank Nutsch farm for the next season.

—)(—

Born—To Mr. and Mrs. T. C. Gronning, Wednesday, November 13th, a girl.

—)(—

Mrs. C. H. Blake left last night for Camp Kearny where she will visit with her husband who is in the army.

—)(—

Leland Snorr of Salt Lake, cousin of Mrs. T. C. Gronning and Lottie Aller is spending a few days in Delta.

—)(—

Mr. and Mrs. G. W. Norris expect to leave for Los Angeles within the next two weeks to spend the winter there.

—)(—

A whopping big bargain in a $25 Economy Heating Stove for $22.50. I want to get rid of this one. Call at Delta Furniture Store. n21-28

—)(—

Rye For Sale—135 bushels Feed Rye, one-fourth wheat at $1.80 per bushel. W. G. Norris, 1 1-2 miles north of Woodrow. n21-28p

—)(—

Attorney J. A. Melville, Jr., will be in Delta on Friday and Saturday of this week attending to business for his clients.

—)(—

Mr. and Mrs. A. S. Rogers, cashier at the Delta State Bank, and family have gone to Oklahoma for a three-week's visit with Mr. Roger's parents.

—)(—

D. Rosenbaum has leased his place to Mr. Justesen of Salt Lake who hasland near him and will reside in Brigham City. Mr. Justesen has already taken possession of the place.

—)(—

Attorney J. A. Melville, Jr., Engineer R. A. Hart and Engineer Caldwell came down from Salt Lake this evening and will attend a meeting of the Board of Supervisors of Drainage District No. 4, Friday.

—)(—

Herbert Hoover has set aside the first week in December as Food Conservation Week as a means of supplying the needy of Europe who will suffer unless supplied food by the U. S. A.

—)(—

Lewis Koch has disposed of his homeplace in Delta to Tom Starley and his farm southwest of town to S. E. Love. He will travel some this winter in the hope of finding relief from rheumatism.

—)(—

Alfred Dolin for many months a resident of Delta, employed by W. L. Aired in his well drilling operations, left for McGill, Nevada, on Wednesday last, where he has accepted a position with a mining concern.

Vernon W. Tozer, Well Known Delta Resident, Is Victim of Influenza

Vernon W. Tozer, son of Mr. and Mrs. George W. Tozer, residents of very-highly esteemed here, died of influenza at the Ft. Douglass hospital in Salt Lake City, Wednesday evening. The young man had answered the call of his country last fall by entering the S. A. T. C. of the University of Utah. After that institution had been closed in consequence of the influenza epidemic, Vernon came back to Delta and was here up until a little more than a week ago when he was called back into the service. He had been back at the U. but a few days when word was received that he had been taken down by the disease and had been sent to the hospital at Ft. Douglass. Wednesday morning, Mrs. Hoyt, sister of the lad, received word from Mr. and Mrs. Tozer who had both left for Salt Lake some time earlier, that the case was not so bad as it was at first thought. The following-morning a telegram was received that the young man was dead.

Vernon was born in Bertrand, Nebr., in which state he lived until six years ago, when he came with his family to Delta. He received a high school education in the Wacatch academy, where he was graduated in the spring of 1918. He has spent his vacations here and has played an active part in many of the local activities. He has won many friends and his loss is mourned deeply.

Friday evening Mr. and Mrs. Tozer returned from Salt Lake. The memorial service is to be held at the Delta cemetery, which will be the only one, has not been definitely arranged for yet. It is hoped that the brother of the deceased, George, who is en route from a training camp in Kentucky, will arrive in time for the burial service. Beside this brother, the deceased is survived by his father and mother, Mr. and Mrs. Geo. W. Tozer, a brother, Ray, who is now in France, and two sisters, Mrs. Emma Barrass and Mrs. Pearl Hoyt.

DELTA BOY SLIGHTLY WOUNDED IN BATTLE.

Mr. and Mrs. A. H. Riding received word recently that their son, Joseph H. Riding had been slightly wounded on the firing line in Frnce. A Letter from him says that he had just chased four Huns out of a dugout with a grenade and gone out to the firing line, being there but an hour when he was struck in the hand and received a slight wound on the head from a shell. He left the firing line of his own accord without reporting and was therefor reported "missing in action" some time ago.

RECENT BIRTHS

To Mr. and Mrs. D. F. Peterson, Thursday, November 12th, a boy.

To Dr. and Mrs. W. A. Stephensen, December 3rd, a boy.

To Mr. and Mrs. Walter Bagshaw, November 13th, a boy.

To Mr. and Mrs. Herold Hoyt. November 22nd, a boy. This is a war baby. Mr. Hoyt onw being in France in the service of his country.

PERSONAL PARAGRAPHS

WANTED—Second-hand typewriter, address Box 182, Route A, Delta.
d3-1tp

—) (—

C. D. Fullmer, former superintendent of the Delta sugar factory, is now in Cuba in the same business.

—) (—

Go to the Delta Furniture Store for Lunch boxes, Turkey Roasters, Granitware and Lamp Chimnies.
d5-12

Misses Stella Kuphaldt and Thelma Ree are here from Salt Lake visiting in the home of Mr. and Mrs. C. R. Johns.

—) (—

Mrs. W. L. Lackyard is closing out her stock of jewelry, toilet articles, etc., at cost. They must all go before Christmas.
d5-19

Born, to Mr. and Mrs. Theo. Christensen. December 9th, a girl. To Mr. and Mrs. Billy Van de Vanter, December 12, a girl.

—) (—

T. D. Stearns was here this week looking over his interests in connection with the Delta sugar factory and his land investments.

—) (—

Children's Aluminum Dishes and a fine line of Hard Painted Japanese Chinaware at the Delta Furniture Store.
d5-13

DOINGS AT OASIS.

Lots of mud, but we are still on top and hope the "flu" will soon be a thing of the past. So we will soon be able to hold public gatherings and begin our schools.

* * *

Stylers J. C. Hawley and Stansworth have the Spanish influenza in light form. All are doing fine.

* * *

Our genial Postmaster, Mr. Sanders is building a new home on E. Main street.

* * *

Several new families have located in Oasis. We are glad to welcome them.

* * *

Our electric plant is running night and day and is giving splendid service, which adds greatly to our comfort.

* * *

We still hear the hum of the threshing machine.

* * *

William Huff, who represents Northup, King & Co., of Minneapolis, has shipped out 190,000 pounds of alfalfa and clover seed, and is still in the market for more seed.

* * *

Dr. Hamilton is busy innoculating most of Oasis as a preventative of influenza.

Tells of Conflict

Writes Interesting Account to Brother, W. R. Walker of Woodrow.

Rescues His Bunkie But is Himself Overcome by the Hun's Gas.

Lee R. Walker who for several months past has been seeing actual service in the trenches in France has sent some interesting letters to his brother, W. R. Walker, of Woodrow.

Upon arriving in France he was anxious to get into the fray in a hurry. He received an opportunity to volunteer with the 1st Regiment of New York, and seized it. He almost immediately got into the thick of it. For almost a solid two months he was in the trenches near Sedan when the heaviest fighting centered about that place. Mr. Walker volunteered to go over the top several times. On one occasion when he went over the top his bunkie and pal was struck by a fragment of a shell and severely wounded. Mr. Walker was given orders to take him to the rear. He had proceeded but a short distance with his burden when gas was sent over. Mr. Walker stopped to put a mask on his friend. By this time he had done this he himself had breathed some, and was himself removed from the field unconscious. He is fully recovered.

On another occasion when he went over the top an enormous shell struck not 20 feet way from him. He was completely covered by the earth thrown up and had to dig himself out. "Talk about quimps," writes Mr. Walker in description of the incident, "when I get back to Delta I can outdig any quimp in all Millard county."

Millard County Chronicle
January 2, 1919

SUTHERLAND SEARCHLIGHTS.

Mr. Walter Roberts sold his team of Percher mares ()one is a thoroughbred) to Mr. George Dunker for $600.

* * *

Mr. Simeon Walker was in Sutherland visiting last week.

* * *

Mr. and Mrs. R. E. Wolfe spent Christmas in Provo with relatives.

* * *

The Memmott family is spending Christmas week in Holden.

* * *

Sanford's have the roof on their new home.

* * *

Arnold Schlappy is home for the holidays.

* * *

Mrs. Abbey Steele Preswick's husband is home on a fourteen-day furlough, having been wounded in the shoulder, he has to return to the hospital for treatment.

BIRTHS.

Born—To Mr. and Mrs. Leo Lyman, December 24th, a son. To Mr. and Mrs. Robert Graham, December 27th, a daughter.

DESERET DOINGS

Mr. George Cropper, head cattle man for the Livingston Co., has fully recovered from a recent attack of influenza and is again able to attend to business.

* * *

Mr. and Mrs. W. W. Moody and family of four children are all up and around again after a scourge of "Flu". Donald, their son, who was so dangerously ill of the disease is well on the road to recovery.

* * *

Miss Ada Hinckly who has been in Salt Lake for the past several months is home for holiday vacation.

* * *

Bearing the names of the Deseret boys who entered the service of their country, the Service flag calendar issued by John Dewsnup Company, makes a fitting appropriate gift for the close of 1918.

In the recent Red Cross drive Deseret came out with a membership more than double that of last year.

* * *

Those of our boys to receive honorable discharge and return home from the army training camps are as follows: Lieut. Bryan Petty, son of Mr. and Mrs. Albion Petty, enlisted April, 1917, and spent a year in San Diego, Cal.; transferred to Camp Pike (Arkansas) Officers' Training school, from which place he received his commission and discharge, returning home November last. Corp. Dudley Crafts, son of B. P. Crafts, entered U. of U. training reserve in June, 1918; transferred to Fort Zachery Taylor, Ky.; discharged early in December, 1918. Dean Petty, brother of Lieut. Petty, and Ray Cahoon, son of Mr. and Mrs. Orson Cahoon, both entering S. A. T. C. of Provo;

transferred later to Texas for further training; returned together December 20th. Clarence and Rollo Moody, sons of Mr. and Mrs. W. W. Moody, from Camp Lewis, Wash., and Camp Wise, Va., are home, Clarence preceeding Rollo by a month.

* * *

The Misses Ora and Hulda Hales will resume their studies at the B. Y. U. at Provo the first of the year.

* * *

Mr. and Mrs. Will Warnick gave a reception to their many friends Saturday night, December 28th, at their beautiful new Riverside home, commerating their crystal wedding.

* * *

After many months of separation, Mrs. Josephine Petty was happy in the reunion of her family Christmas day, including her two soldier boys.

* * *

Bishop Joseph W. Damron, who met with the County School Board at Fillmore on December 28th, says the superintendent of schools feels justified in opening the schools January 6th, health boards permitting.

PERSONAL PARAGRAPHS

Norma Lambert left Christmas night for Shelby, Idaho, where he will have charge of a lumber yard. Mrs. Lambert will follow soon. Norm is a hustler and the firm which avails itself of his services will sure find him an asset to their business. Mr. and Mrs. Lambert have a host of friends here, who regret their departure.

—)(—

Attorney J. A. Melville, Jr., has moved his Salt Lake office from the Felt Building to the new Deseret Bank Building. He has engaged the corner suite of rooms facing Main and First South streets on the sixth

floor, Nos. 605-6, and states that his clients and friends are welcome to make his offices their headquarters while in Salt Lake City.

—)(—

While it looked dubious for a time about the latter end of the beet crop being saved on account of the cold weather and scarcity of help, practically the whole crop was recovered. The factory figures on completing the season's run in about two weeks.

—)(—

Misses Maudie Holm and Georgie Meinhardt and Wilson Keeler left the last of last week for Salt Lake City, where they will attend school. Mrs. Keeler went with them and will keep

house for the young folks.

—)(—

Edgar and Delbert Potter, who have been in the training at Camp Logan, Colorado, for the past six months, were honorably discharged from the service last week, and reached home Sunday evening.

—)(—

Sunday night Mrs. R. C. Bates gave a dinner party to a few of her friends. Among her guests were Mr. and Mrs. Jim Faust. Mr. Faust has but recently returned from service in the army.

—)(—

Mr. and Mrs. Glen Miller, of Lorane, Wyo., of whom the latter was formerly Gwendolyn Johns, are spending the holiday season with the bride's parents, Mr. and Mrs. T. L. Johns.

Lieut. Dr. Baker, brother of Mrs. R. C. Bates, expects to conclude his visit to her here Thursday, when he will go to Salt Lake and follow his profession in Holy Cross hospital.

—)(—

Dick Purdy, the little fellow who chronicles good luck to the players at the pool hall, has gone off to visit his granddady, James A. Kelley, at Mills, Utah, for a week or two.

—)(—

Joe Riding, wh was wounded in battle in France, and who has been in the Fort Douglas hospital, was home on a leave and ate Christmas dinner with his parents.

Dr. and Mrs. W. H. Woodring, of Bingham, Utah, have been the guests of Mr. and Mrs. John Jimpson during the holiday season.

—)(—

Mr and Mrs. Henry Brantley came down from Salt Lake last Sunday. Mr. Brantley has accepted a position with the Chronicle.

—)(—

Attorney Hill, of the Salt Lake Route, was in town Saturday checking up the company's interests in Paving District No. 2.

—)(—

Mrs. Theodore Schultz and daughter, Edith Louise, of Chicago, are visiting the former's sister Mrs. E. J. Blehler at Abrahams.

Miss Emma Clark arrived from Kaysville last Sunday for an indefinite sojourn with friends and relatives in Delta.

—)(—

Mrs. Oliver Olson and Mrs. Blaine Johnson have left for California to join their husbands who are at Camp Kearney.

—)(—

Funeral Services were conducted over the remains of the infant child of Mrs. John Taylor, on Monday December 30th.

—)(—

R. C. Orr went to Salt Lake Saturday morning, where he may go to work.

ELECTRIC LIGHT AND POWER COMING SOON

The Deseret and Melville Irrigation Companies Join Hands to Light the Valley—Power From Oasis Plant Now. Later From Deversion Dam—Here In 60 Days.

A deal which has been pending for some time which is very important to Delta in particular, and the West Side in general was closed on Thursday of last week when a joint meeting of the Deseret and Melville Irrigation Boards was held at Oasis, in which an agreement was made and signed up by the officers of the boards to consolidate the two companies for the purpose of furnishing electrical power and lights for the West Side.

A committee was appointed to order equipment and begin work at once.

A survey and map of Delta and an estimate made of the cost of the tow line and distributing system is $10,000. It is said that work on this can be completed by the last of February or fore part of March.

The Deseret Irrigation Company already has a completely equipped electrical plant installed at Oasis, which has been in successful operation since last fall, and which has sufficient capacity for all purposes for some time to come.

It is the intention of the two companies to later develop the Melville Company power site at the diversion dam, and connect these two systems so that during the major portion of the year power and light can be generated by water and the steam plant which is located at Oasis, will be used as a reserve when that time comes.

The need of such an establishment has been keenly felt for some years, and its installation will be a big factor here, inducing industrial development and adding to the conveniences of those already on the ground.

The evidence of growth and prosperity of the Pahvant Valley has been very noticeable the past two years, and the strenuous labor of the pioneers has now begun to stand out and will continue to show more each year.

Mr. and Mrs. Walter Huntsman spent Christmas visiting in Salt Lake City.

—){(—

Born—to Mrs. Oscar Graham, Dec. 29th, a girl.

—){(—

Miss Lizzie Kelley, of Bingham, Utah, is in town visiting relatives at the Bank Hotel.

—){(—

Mrs. T. R. Sprunt has gone to Salt Lake for the holiday season.

—){(—

Mr. and Mrs. Ben Douglas have gone to Nephi, Utah, where they will be with friends over New Year's.

—){(—

Born—To Mrs. H. J. Cook; a girl. Mr. Cook is at present in France.

Millard County Chronicle
January 9, 1919

BOYS' AND GIRLS' BEET-ACRE CONTEST—1918 PRIZE WINNERS.

Prize	Tons-Lbs.	Am't	Bonus	Amount Prize	Total
1 Edwin Heise, Woodrow	24-1025	$245.12	$4.50	$50.00	$299.62
2 George Meinhardt, S'erland	24- 800	244.00	4.40	20.00	268.40
3 Myrtle Wood, Hinckley	22- 319	221.59	2.16	15.00	238.75
4 Ova Christenson, Delta	21- 938	214.69	1.47	10.00	226.16
5 Deloy Elder, Delta	20-1072	205.36	.54	5.00	210.90
6 Glen I. John, Woodrow	19- 526	192.03	.....	2.50	195.13
7 Romola Bunker, Delta	19- 414	192.07	.....	2.50	194.57
8 Dennis Lloyd, Sutherland	18-1321	186.60	.....	2.50	189.10
9 Verl Baker, Sugarville	18- 882	184.41	.....	2.50	186.91
10 Veda Webb, Hinckley	17-1716	178.58	.....	1.00	179.58
11 Glen Rawlinson, Delta	17- 413	172.07	.....	1.00	173.07
12 Owen Bunker, Delta	17- 362	171.81	.....	1.00	172.81
13 Leon T. Wayment, Hinckley	16-1958	169.79	.....	1.00	170.79
14 Earl Bliss, Hinckley	16-1610	168.05	.....	1.00	169.05
15 Emily Billings, Delta	16-1510	167.55	.....	1.00	168.55
16 Roka Bunker, Delta	16- 967	164.84	.....	1.00	165.84
17 Bethyl Bracewell, Woodrow	16- 958	164.79	.....	1.00	165.79
18 Derald Clawson, Delta	16- 810	164.05	.....	1.00	165.05
19 Frank Lloyd, Sutherland	16- 719	163.60	.....	1.00	164.60
20 Kenneth Wayment, Hinckley	15-1897	159.49	.....	1.00	160.49
21 Evan Ashby, Leamington	15-1646	158.25	.....	1.00	159.23
22 Dolbert Ashby, Delta	15- 207	151.04	.....	1.00	152.04
23 Bros Roberts, Sutherland	15- 183	150.92	.....	1.00	151.92
24 Robert Stevens, Woodrow	14-1489	147.45	.....	1.00	148.45

PERSHING REWARDS
HINCKLEY SOLDIER

General Pershing has awarded the distinguished service cross to Corporal Carl C. Theobald of Hinckley, Utah, First batalion, intelligence section, 31st Infantry. Corporal Theobald is thus honored for extraordinary heroism in action near Gesne, France, October 10. While on liaison patrol with Private Ivan Y. Baily of Montana, Corporal Theobald and his companion attacked and captured a hostile machine-gun nest and its entire crew.

Carl is the son of T. George Theobald, and joined the colors a year ago the first of January. He is still on duty in France.

Mitchell Clark, brother of our townsman Jeff Clark, and son of J. J. Clark of the North Tract, arrived in Delta last Friday evening from overseas.

Mitchell is the second of our local boys to arrive at home from France, Thierry and Argonne Forest, and was severly wounded at Argonne Forrest, and was among the first soldiers sent home.

Mitch was in France over a year as the two gold bars on his sleeve indicate, and has had a number of thrilling experiences, being among the first of the American Expeditionery Forces to leave the United States; He took part in the battles of Chateau Thierry and argonne Forest, and was slightly wounded in the latter. The transport on which he made the trip to France was afterwards sunk by a submarine.

Mitch says that the United States is the best of all, and he is glad to be at home again.

SUGARVILLE SIFTINGS.

James W. Walton, Jr. whose interesting letter appeared in the Chronicle two weeks ago, is the son Mr. and Mrs. J. W. Walton of Sugarville. He worked on his father's ranch here before enlisting last April, and is now in Bordeaux, France.

James Shields made a trip to Tooele last week.

Mrs. Clarence Chelson received a telegram from her brother, Lawrence Norlen, that he had landed in New York from the steamer Orizaba on Jan. 23rd. He has been overseas with the Headquarters Detachment of 116th Engineers, 91st division (famous Wild West) which figured so brilliantly in the last weeks of the war. He was one of the contingent of boys which left Delta October 3rd, 1917, for Camp Lewis. Mrs. Chelson expects her brother here for a short visit soon.

The Liberty League Auxiliary will meet on Wednesday, Feburary 5th, at the home of Mrs. Hoyt.

The Liberty League met at the home of Mrs. Cady on January 11th and elected the following officers: Chairman, Mrs. E. D. Cady, reelected, Vice Chairman, Mrs. J. W. Warton Secretary, E. H. Hibbard, Treasurer, Mrs. C. J. Chelson, Inspector, Mrs. C. G. Hoyt.

Mr. and Mrs. L. C. Dale have come out from town and are residing on their ranch.

Mr. and Mrs. Chronholm have gone to their new home in New Plymouth, Idaho.

Mr. and Mrs. H. C. Anson entertained at dinner last Sunday The guests being Mr. and Mrs. Gust Johnson, Mr. and Mrs. Cochran, Newton Anderson and Danny Pedrick.

Mr. and Mrs. Gust Johnson have moved their buildings and are located south-east of Sugarville.

WOODROW WRITINGS

Two of our popular residents, viz. Mitchell Clark and Guy Watts have returned hale and hearty from "over there", and are being royally greeted by their friends. Others are on their way home. Up to date all who wnet from here are safe and sound, and the whole community is filled with gratitude.

At last we have two school rooms and two teachers for our thirty five pupils. We extend our thanks to the school board. "Better late than Never".

Mr and Mrs. Griffiths are rejoicing over the birth of a son. Mr. Griffiths daughter, and husband Mr. Earl Horton of Beaver, are visiting Mrs. Horton's parents Mr. Horton left his bride two years ago at the call of the church, and has spent that time in the mission field, and the happy couple are now off on their honey-moon.

Mr. and Mrs. Rawlins have rented the house left vacant by W. G. Norris. Mr. Rawlins is still wearing the uniform of Uncle Sam, having been discharged from the service about two weeks ago.

Our thrifty bachelor, John Barnett, took a trip to Bountiful after his crops were harvested and announces the fact that he has married the finest woman in the world, and will bring her home in the near future.

Mr. and Mrs. Caldwell who have been visiting the Powell's in Delta for several months, have cast their lot with the Woodrowites. They will move into the Given house immediately.

Joe Alward is sick with the "Flu" contracted while on a trip to Salt Lake City.

The Oppenheimer's and the Thorpe's are enjoying their new autos Our roads which have been a disgrace to Utah for three months, are undergoing repairs and we hope it will be possible in the near future to take a spin for a few miles without having a bill for repairs before the journey is over.

Mr. and Mrs. Frank Strickloy (nee Miss Agnes Hersleff) are the parents of a fine daughter.

The Woodrow Sunday School is now open at 10:30 each Sunday Preaching by the Rev. Hamilton on the second and fourth Sundays of each month.

George Hoffecker, who has spent a summer in Woodrow has just received word from Washington that his only child, John D. Hoffecker, died July 12th, from wounds received in action in France. Jack was one of the first to enlist when the war commenced.

T. R. Sprunt made a visit to Salt Lake City first of the week.

—) (—

Excellent Jersey cow for sale, cheap. Inquire at this office. j9-2t

—) (—

Clyde Sampson has returned to his home on the north tract from service in the army.

—) (—

Mrs. Norman Lambert and little daughter left last Friday for Shelly, Idaho to make their future home.

—) (—

Less Pace, the Rural Route mail carrier went to Salt Lake the first of the week. During his absscence el Hibbard is carring the mail.

—) (—

Dr. J J Buswell Ophthalmic Specialist of Salt Lake will be at the Ward Hotel Wednesday February 5th. No charge for testing eyes. References. Glasses are worn for health as well as well as vision. j30-1t

—) (—

R.H. Becknell, formerly engineer for the Delta Land and Water Co., is now chief engineer for a new railroad being promoted from Lund to. Cedar City and beyond. Mr. Becknell was one of most highly respected citizens while here and his many friends will be pleased to learn of his good luck.

Some one tried to destroy Mr. Forrest's car last Thursday night by setting fire to the gas tank. Failing to accomplish their end by this method they secured a heavy bar and battered the engine and body up until it is almost past repair. The car had been abdoned on the road on the north tract and left for the night. Sherriff Cropper was hot on the vandal's trail the last we heard of the case.

—) (—

Cyril Cluff has accepted a position with the Melville Land Co.

—) (—

Mrs. Russell Sprunt left for California Wednesday evening for an extended visit.

—) (—

A letter from Gus Faust, who is still in France, says that he expects to sail for home in a short time. He says that the mud is knee deep where he is.

—) (—

A letter from Archie Maxfield, who is in the Marines, and who was reported missing in action, and later reported as being on duty, states that he is now on the Rhine. This is the first word received from Aachie for some time, and his friends will be pleased to hear that he is all right.

SUTHERLAND SEARCHLIGHTS.

Mr. and Mrs. Lawerence Abbott are rejoicing over the arrival of a fine baby boy

* * *

Earnest Ottley is visiting relatives in Southerland having been released from the Spruce Division, in Uncle Sam's service.

* * *

Mrs. Lee Walker has gone to Salt Lake to meet Lee who is on his way home from Ft. Logan.

The Sanfords are moving into their new home.

Millard County Progress
January 31, 1919

BURBANK

A party was given at the elegant home on the I. H. L. ranch on the evening of the 23rd in honor of Thomas Johansen a young soldier who received his honorable discharge from Camp Kearney and has returned The evening was spent in pleasant games, dancing and music at midnight a fine super was served by the genial hostes, Mrs. Ipsen, assisted by Mrs. Johansen and Mrs. Showalter. Covers were laid for over 20 invited guests. Among them we noticed bside Mr. and Mrs. Neil Ipson, Mr. and Mrs. James Showalter, Mrs. Johansen, Thomas and Wesley Johanson, Mr. and Mrs. E. W. Clay, Mrs. L Schumacher, L. G. Clay, Mr. and Mrs. F. Loper, Mr. and Mrs. E. Christopherson, Mr. R. Pace, Don Taylor, Alfred Hocker, G. Hayes and P. Mc Quorie.

The death of Mr. Kinney, an elderly man occurred at Smithville on the 25th. of pneumonia. His remains will be laid at final rest at the Garrison Cemetary on the 27th.

Although our community was seriously visited this winter by the general epidemic, it seems to be fro from it now, and general good halth prevails.

HINC

This week records one of the saddest events which has taken place in Hinckley for sometime. The death of Keith, Pauline, and Katherine Stratton, son and two daughters of Mr. and Mrs. Charles Stitton. They all died within twenty-four hours. The parents are now bereft of their four oldest children. Mrs. Stratton was in a very critical condition for sometime but is much better this morning These are the first deaths Hinckley has suffered from the "Flu."

President Hinckley and his family are al out and around again.

A new case of "Flu" comes unawares once in a while in spite of all the precautionary measures which have been taken.

School, if not opened Monday February 3, will be closed for the year.

Many of the academy students have gone home for the year.

A welcome is heartily extended to our returned soldiers altho no public demostrations is possible.

Arnold Workman, returned from overseas with the "145th," reached home Friday January 25th. Mr. Heb Bishop arrived from Camp Lewis Monday January 27th. Boys, we extend to you our hearty congratulations for duty well done and an unbounded gratitude for services rendered to our Country and to your friends, and to the righteous cause of freedom of mankind.

Mrs. Thomas Hatton entertained at a dinner party Sunday evening in honor of Mr. Russell Hatton who arrived recently from overseas. Nearly 50 friends and relatives were present

---

James M. Stewart, a well known ranchman of Meadow, was in town yesterday on important business. Mr. Stewart is one of the oldest men residing in that section and is still hale and hearty.

C. F. Christensen of Kanosh, County Commissioner and director of the Pahvant Irrigation District, was a business visitor here yesterday.

Two of Kanosh's prominent young men, came into town in their car on Monday of this week, and proceeded to take two of Fillmore's young ladies for a joy ride, thereby breaking the City's quarantine laws. They were arrested by Marshal Jackson and the case was tried before City Justice John Cooper on Tuesday, who fined boys $4.00 each. The young ladies were quarantined in their homes for the usual 4 days.

Mr. Frank Strange of Hallock, Nevada, was a visitor this week at the home of his wife's mother, Mrs. Jessie Gasquin.

Millard County Chronicle
February 20, 1919

Chronicle Under New Management

With the change of management of the Millard County Chronicle, a word or two may not be amiss as to the future policy of the paper.

The Chronicle will be conducted as heretofore; in politics, as near the middle of the road as possible, open to both sides for full expression of their views; in news, alive, cheery, and printing all that happens; in boosting, the best medium the Greater Delta Country has yet had, at all times putting the best forward for the towns of Millard County.

The policy of the paper will be such that its snappiness will attract readers. It will build in subscription list, and hence, will be the best advertising medium that can be got in this region. Its advertisements will be prominent, individual, and speaking of the distinctiveness that will win this paper a foremost place for merchants and everybody to use.

The sugar factory will find these columns a willing exponent of its efforts to reach the farmers, and no time or labor will be spared to aid in the good work of making the Delta Beet region a success.

From time to time, good farmers will be chosen, and write-ups given as heretofore. Not that the editor of this paper is a farmer—far from it—(farming the farmer that farms the farm is as near as he ever got to it,) but he is at the service to put into print all the good things that can be spoken of this country. For four years he made it his pleasant work to give space in these columns for articles of interest, intended to attract others to our community. And there are more than four years ahead of him yet before the topic is exhausted.

For the present Mrs. Beckwith will have charge of the paper while Mr. Beckwith is so arranging the affairs of the bank he is in at Oakely, Idaho, as to be relieved. During that period indulgence is asked for the paper in all its auspects. But give it your hearty local support, and with that support given, the greater Delta Country will find the Chronicle fully up to expectations.

Read it. Advertise in it.

The new management wishes at this time to thank the former editor of the Chronicle, Mr. Chas. O. Davis, for the large space always cheerfully accorded him heretofore, and for the many courtisies extended, which have produced an intimate friendship, so that the succeeding editor is quite sincere in wishing Mr. Davis success in his new field, and the very best of good health.

FRANK BECKWITH.

DELTA NEWS NOTES.

Willis Lyman came home last week from duty in the army.

—)(—

County Attorney Grover Giles, of Fillmore, was in Delta the first of the week.

—)(—

Mr. and Mrs. Powell are the proud parents of a fine baby boy, born Saturday Feb. 15th.

—)(—

Mrs. Geo. Tozer and Mrs. Harold Hoyt returned from Salt Lake on Wednesday the 12th.

—)(—

Miss Marin Kelly of Delta, and William Stowell, were married in Salt Lake last week.

—)(—

C. D. Penniston, of the Delta Land and Water Co., at Milford was a visitor in Delta last Tuesday.

—)(—

Mr. Russel Sprunt received word California Sunday that his little daughter Betty was very ill with bronchial pneumonia.

—)(—

Mrs. Frank Beckwith, and daughter Athena, arrived in town Thursday the 13th. They have taken Mrs. Leslie Pace's house, and will make their home here.

Mrs. Phil Purdy, and Miss Lizzie Kelley went up to Mills last week to see their brother, James Kelley who had returned from the front. Jim has seen some real fighting, but he doesn't say much about it.

—)(—

The last payment on the Fourth Issue of Liberty Bonds was due Jan. 30th. If you are among those who have neglected to meet this payment, please attend to it now, at the Delta State Bank.

—)(—

The Board of Directors of Delta Canal Company, with the newly elected directors, Mr. James W. Walton and Hy Sherrer, participating, held a meeting at the company's office on Tuesday. An assessment of sixty cents was levied and the notice of such assessment elsewhere in this issue The Company's Income and Expense Statement for the past year will also be found in this issue.

The O. Z. O. Club was entertained at the Bluebird Cottage Wednesday evening. The club enjoyed itself immensely that evening quite unaware of the lanky prowler, who was snooping around their windows. Regular old Sherlock.

—)(—

The dance on the 14th was a success, according to the girls. There were as many boys as girls, and even a few left over.

The Delta Bakery was sold this week, to Mr. Hill of Gunnison. Mr. Hill intends to start the ovens working again.

—)(—

Dont' be surprised if Mr. Mercer of the Delta Drug Co. asks you for the ribbons off your candy boxes. He says he wants them for his little daughter, who is now two weeks old.

SUTHERLAND SEARCHLIGHTS

Ross Simkins and family of Circleville are visiting friends and relatives in Sutherland.

* * *

Mr. Lee Walker has taken up his residence in Sutherland again having returned from France.

* * *

Wm. Gull and sons of Meadow are putting up a building in Sutherland to house their threshing machine. The machine is a new one making its first run last fall, and giving perfect satisfaction. Mr. Gull expects to stay in the threshing game on this side of the County.

* * *

Sunday School and meeting were held in Sutherland Ward last Sunday for the first time since the epidemic. Everyone seems to be glad to get out again.

* * *

The Sutherland Farm Bureau held its regular meeting at the school house. Wednesday evening February 19th.

Mrs. Anthony Stephensen is very ill this week with influenza.

—)(—

Mrs Birdie Thurston was under the weather the first of the week but is better now.

—)(—

Let us get our heads together and think up a rip-roaring good time for returning soldier boys.

—)(—

Wealthy Beckwith arrived Wednesday night, she had been in Salt Lake visiting her aunt until Mrs. Beckwith found a house.

—)(—

Miss Hettie White here holding some interesting meetings, with the ladies of West Millard County, and will have a meeting at the School house Saturday at 2 P. M. and would like to have all the ladies there who are interested in the Farm Bureau Work.

—)(—

Salt grows on the greaswood in our county. So when the salt cellar is empty, all you have to do is run across the way, and shake some of the greaswood. That is, you can do that if that is the kind of of shrubbery you raise. Now just south of Deseret, where the open drain cuts thru a lake, the greaswood is coated with salt like a heavy frost. If scoois believing with you, just step into the Chronicle office. We will prove it.

Millard County Progress
February 21, 1919

HINCKLEY

Hinckley is again free from the "Flu"; high hopes are entertained that we will not be revisited by it.

Our field man, Mr. Prestlerch, is busy taking contracts for next year's beets. The farmers intend to produce an enormous increase the coming season.

All public affairs have been resumed. Business is being carried on. Church services have been resumed picture shows are again in style The district school is running with a new impetus.

The Millard Academy is making rapid progress in its work. A larger registration than was expected and a surpassing zeal and interest put pep and life into thes chool work. Last Thursday evening, February 13th, we enjoyed a practice basket-ball game with the Delta team in their hall. The results were a new determination to take the State Championship and a score of 12 to 29 in favor of the Academy. This visit will be returned Thursday evening, February 20, and another victory is almost

positive. Our team is fresh but the members are working with a will and determination which will accomplish desired results. With the exception of the "subs" the men are veteran players of previous years. Friday, February 21st, will be the opening day of social life of the school, the get acquainted dance will be given unless some unforeseen thing happens to prevent. To school was honored today, February 17th by a visit from Supt. of Church Schools Cummings.

DESERET.

(To Late For Last Issue.)

Again the A. C. Nelson has opened its doors. Monday school began with over one-fourth of its pupils, while Tuesday it swelled to over 50 per cent, with a steady increase throughout the week. It is hoped that there will be no future outbreaks, especially that the people will not bring the influenza into town, or the Board of Health permit outside people to come here with it.

Sacremental meeting was held on Sunday for the first time since January 5th. A goodly crowd was out; the speakers being Bp. J. W. Dameron and Principal Ezra Gull.

The Webb brothers of Brigham City and Nevada stopped here enroute to Fillmore where they buried their father. He died suddenly and without pain which, due to his advanced age was not unlooked for, and assuredly a desired way to leave this earth. Peace be with him!

The Deseret Dramatic Club is preparing to stage, "Because I Love You" a drama of exceptional worth and one sure to please.

The wind has blown here 4 days each succeeding day gaining strength It twill soon have to repeat itself, or ———stop!

(This Week's News.)

Sunday was duly celebrated as British Day, having been postponed until now, due to the rigid quarantine S. W. Western reviewed the events of the war showing the great work done by the English. Miss Norma Moody rendered a piano solo and Jas. H. Western sang "Mother McCree." Part of the services were given to the Academy in its campaign for more students. Lieut. Bryan Petty, Privt-Raymond Cahoon and Dean Petty spoke well on the service of the Academy is rendering, and appealed to the young to avail themselves of this splendid opportunity to gain knowledge. Lieut. Petty reviewed his life as a soldier and paid glowing tribute to th officers of the American Army.

Mr. Petty was one of the first Millard County volunteers and thru tireless efforts rose from private to a Lieutenant having just received his commission to overseas service when the armistice was signed.

Mr. Gull reports a steady increase in attendance at the A. C. Nelson. Monday there were 131 out of a possible 181, the maximum enrollment before the vacation. Each day new students enroll, so it is expected that all will be back by next week.

The A. C. Nelson will give a big dance on Friday evening. Excellent music has been secured and a good time is assured.

Mr. and Mrs. D. J. Black have gone to California. While there they will visit their two sons-in-law and daughter Mr. and Mrs. Webb and Elder Western.

Good at to repair men are in great demand. Several garages in Utah and Idaho are trying to induce Mr Johnson of the Deseret Garage to go there saying hat they have better positions for him. We need and a man here: so get in and boost and help Mr. Dewenly keep him to render the automobile owner of Des res and neighboring towns high class service.

MANY FRIENDS ATTEND FUNERAL

Funeral services were held here on Saturday last for Almon Robison in the L. D. S. Chapel with Bishop Rufus Day in charge. The speakers were Christian Anderson, James A. Kelly, Joshua Greenwood, James A. Melville, J. Alex Melville and William P. Payne al of whom spoke of the stalwart character and business integrity of the deceased. The last 4 speakers whose names are given above journied from afar to attend the last rites over the remains, the deceased having been numbered among their best friends during his lifetime.

Appropriate music was furnished by the Ward Choir and vocal solos were rendered by Mrs. Helen Derrick and Mrs. Katherine Rasmussen. Many beautiful floral tributes were in evidence and the service was very largely attended.

Mr. Robison, as narrated in our last issue, was the son of Joseph and Lucretia Hancock Robison, and was born at Crete, Ill., May 5, 1845. He crossed the plains with his parents in 1854 and came almost direct to Fillmore. In 1864 Mr. Robison recrossed the plains and returned with a large body of immigrants. Since that time, by persistent effort and good business management, he succeeded in building up a very large fortune and at the time of his death was accounted one of the richest men in southern Utah.

In commenting upon his life the speakers laid great emphasis upon his faithfulness to his friends, and many a man, who today is independently well off in this world's goods, has Mr. Robison to thank for the start he gave them in life. Many there are, no doubt, who will miss his wise council in business affairs and farming pursuits, for he was responsible for many changes being promulgated in this section in an agricultural way.

After more music by the choir, the funeral cortege wended its way to our

Concluded on Page 8.

DESERET DOINGS

Mrs. Verne Cahoon presented her husband with a fine girl baby Tuesday morning.

* * *

Wit the grandfather, P. T. Black, so long in the government service; the father, Mr. Larson, so recently home from a training camp in Texas—the new arrival at the postoffice will probably become a president of the United States. Of course, it is a boy, 8½ pounds, and all well.

* * *

Welcome to the Beckwiths, much as we regret the departure of C. O. Davis and family.

* * *

Ed Johnson, our last recruit to be released from the training camps, returned from Camp Kearny, Calif., a week ago. While Ed would have gone the limit for Uncle Sam and his country, he expresses himself quite willing to walk the advances of peace.

* * *

After eighteen months service with the I. M. C. auto section in camps from San Antonio, Tex., to New York, Corp. George Cahoon was honorably discharged and returned home Sunday, the 16th, having spent a few days enroute with relatives in Salt Lake City.

* * *

Knowell Cahoon, who underwent an operation for appendicitis some four weeks ago at the L. D. S. hospital in Salt Lake, is reported convalescing from his serious condition.

* * *

Mrs. Effie Moody was a recent visitor to Salt Lake.

* * *

Miss Grace Prisbury is back again at her post as teacher of 2nd grade at the A. C. Nelson School. Miss Prisbry went home at the time influenza was so prevalent.

* * *

The A. C. Nelson School is running again with almost a full attendance.

* * *

Washington's Birthday was appropriately celebrated at the school Friday, and a party of social games and dancing was given by the 8th grade pupils at night.

* * *

The sale at Damron's Merc., beginning last Tuesday, has been a howling success, and continues the week with lots of specials for Saturday. Plenty of goods yet.   f27

SOUTH TRACT ITEMS

Our old neighbor J. P. Fidel, who has received his honorable discharge from the service of the U. S., came home a few days ago. Joe is looking fine and feeling well after his very severe attack of the Flu. He will visit his people in Colorado, after which he will probably go to Wyoming in the employ of the government.

* * *

The Delta Land & Water Co. has made some decided improvements in the working of its drainage system this spring.

* * *

George E. Beach was appointed by the executive committee of the Central Farm Bureau as chairman of the "farm management" project. Leo Coffin will be his coworker, appointed from our local bureau. Other members appointed were: E. A. Brush with Abner Johnson chairman; O. L. Crawford, with J. B. Seams; B. W. Whitmore, with Geo. S. Forest; F. B. Johnson, with Harry T. Baker; Fred Hauman, with Ed Cady; Harry Pearson, with H. E. Beck; J. M. Ross, with A. M. Cornwall; Benjamin Finch, with Leo Lyman; Miss Frances Beach, with Mrs. H. G. Ottley; Mrs. B. W. Whitmore, with Mrs. Clark Allred; Mr. Fred Keim, with A. J. Thurston.

* * *

It is reported that the Gus Hauman family will move onto the Folsom place.

* * *

E. A. Brush is feeding out some fine looking beef cattle.

* * *

Our membership committee in the farm bureau reports a membership at the present time of forty-four, and more to follow.

* * *

Our socials held every two weeks at the Camp Mess House, are well attended and a pleasure to all.

* * *

Mr. and Mrs. O. L. Crawford, Mr. and Mrs. J. E. Whitmore, Mr. and Mrs. F. B. Johnson and Mr. William Lawson took luncheon with Mr. and Mrs. H. E. Beck last Sunday afternoon.

* * *

Don't let anything keep you from our Farm Bureau meeting on next Saturday at 2 o'clock p.m. at the school house—March 1st.

* * *

Mrs. Geo. E. Beach left on Wednesday of this week for California to make a visit with a sister.

* * *

Lewis I. Beck is teaching the South Tract school and has a very full attendance.

* * *

Mrs. Russell of Salt Lake City is making her daughter, Mrs. Henry Bott, a visit, which is a great pleasure to Marie.

* * *

Lowell Nelson has just returned from an all winter visit at Englewood, Calif., with his parents, brothers and sisters. He had the Utah Flu before he went, and when he got among the home folks he took a shot at the California brand, which he claims is much worse than our brand.

SUTHERLAND SEARCHLIGHTS.

Edward Ottley is in Sutherland looking after his interests and visiting relatives and friends.

* * *

James Barney and family are here visiting friends.

* * *

Lee Walker related his experiences while in France, at the Sutherland ward meeting last Sunday.

Charles Simkins is with us again; he contemplates making his home in Sutherland.

* * *

The Sutherland Farm Bureau will meet at the school house Tuesday evening, March 4. Everyone invited. Ladies are especially invited to decide and outline their year's work.

* * *

The Relief Society began their weekly meetings Tuesday, February 25th. The meetings are held at the home of Sister Walker.

* * *

The Jolly Stitchers held their first meeting with Mrs. Oppenheimer at Woodrow Wednesday afternoon, Feb. 26.

WOODROW WRITINGS.

All hail to Editor Beckwith! Woodrow is awaiting a visit and a write-up from ye editor in his own onemical style, as soon as the Flu has flown.

* * *

Woodrow has been paralyzed for a month from and extensive outbreak of the Flu. At present writing, however, all have recovered and there have been no new cases in two weeks. Hence the lid is lifted, and we hope to make up for lost time socially.

* * *

The Jolly Stitchers and Red Cross organizations met Wednesday afternoon at the home of Mrs. Oppenheimer to organize after a three months enforced vacation.

* * *

Mr. Oppenheimer has disposed of the southern half of his large ranch and is now building on the northern portion, preparing to move there in the near future.

* * *

The Misses Verda Oppenheimer, Olga Thompson and Ethel Heffleman together with Floyd Heinleen, who have traveled forth and back to school several times this winter, only to meet a new quarantine and travel home again, have finally given up and are to remain at home for the remainder of the school year.

* * *

There will be a dance in Woodrow Saturday night, at which our returned soldier boys will be cordially welcomed. The khaki-clad wanderers who have returned to date include: Mitchell Clark, Guy Watts, Earl Horton, Mark Rawlins, George Clemons, Pat Hagan, Louis Titus, Bryan Smith, Royal Erickson, Chas. Erickson, and Leo Davis

The Underhills and the Jeff Clarks met with Hy Shearer for dinner Sunday afternoon. We know by their jolly faces as seen in Woodrow Sunday evening that the dinner was a big success

* * *

Mr. and Mrs. Mark Rawlins are proudly showing a new son. While Mr. and Mrs. Allen are just as proud of their new daughter.

* * *

Church and Sunday School are re-established in Woodrow and Sugarville. All cordially invited.

* * *

The many friends of Mrs. Percy Kyes, Mr. Caldwell, Mrs. Arthur Rawlins, and Miss Margaret Griffith, all of whom have been dangerously ill with complications resulting from the Flu, will be delighted to know and are ready to greet their friends once more.

* * *

The Athletic association organized in Woodrow last Monday evening, and gives promise of valuable recreation for our lads in the future.

Millard County Progress
February 28, 1919

HINCKLEY.

Since last week's report went in we have had three more new cases of "Flu". Nothing serious has yet developed.

The basketball game with Delta was called off as two of Delta's players were down with the "Flu." Some of the old Academy stars still know how to hit the hoop and we had a rousing good game with them. The score was 33 to 18 in favor of the school team.

The first league game is to be played here with Milford on Friday, February 28th. Another game will be played with the old stars sometime next week. They are practicing every night and the hardest game of the season is anticipated.

No evil effects have yet followed our dance. It was an invitational affair. The hall was well filled, the school orchestra furnishing the music. Someone said we had forgotten how to dance, but we guess they will now change their tune.

Next Friday following the basketball game the faculty and the board will give their dance to the students and the parents.

The business of draining this country is being attended to and work will soon commence.

DESERET DOINGS

Mr. Barney Fawcett of Wallsburg, Utah, was this week registered at the Moody hotel.

* * *

We are pleased to record the advent of a son at the home of Mr. and Mrs. Nels L. Peterson.

* * *

With Ezra Gull, principal of our school, at the head, we have a real live reading club organized. A number of books have been sent for beside those in circulation.

* * *

The teachers of the A. C. Nelson School gave a dancing party last Thursday. This is the first dance given at the gymnasium in many months and marks renewed activity in a number of social ways.

* * *

Mr. Chas. Dewsnup has rented his house and in connection with Will Bunker of Hinckley will move to Sutherland soon, where they are to run one of the big sugar beet farms.

* * *

Bryan and Dean Petty, members of the M. A. Basketball team which played Milford High, Saturday the 8th, report a victory for their team. This brings the Millard Academy boys in battle against the B. A. C. champions of the southern half of the Southern division. They are to meet at Milford, neutral ground, next Monday night.

* * *

Miss Mary Larson, who has been serving as Red Cross nurse several months in Salt Lake City, returned last week.

* * *

Marvin Jackson met with a painful accident one day last week when, in making a broad jump, he wrenched his knee and tendons of the leg to such an extent that an operation was was in attendance and says Mr. Jackson will be laid up for some time.

* * *

A number of improvements are noted at the A. C. Nelson School, among which feature the reslating of the blackboards in all class rooms. The steam heating plant is undergoing repairs and it is hoped it will be in running order soon again.

* * *

Elmer Croft, five-year old son of George F. and Mary Croft, died Saturday morning as a result of a severe attack of influenza-pneumonia which nearly cost his life some eight weeks ago, at which time his mother died of the same disease. This is the third death to occur in Mr. Croft's immediate family since last April. Many friends and acquaintances grieve with the bereaved in their great loss. Funeral services were held Monday afternoon.

Prof. A. C. Christensen, of the Millard Academy, Hinckley, lectured before a large and appreciative audience, Sunday evening. By request his subject was the "League of Nations." His knowledge of history ancient and modern, his clear citation of world conditions of today—such as selfishness, anarchy and the revolutionary spirit—left his hearers in no doubt as to Prof. Christensen's ability to entertain. It is suggested that the M. I. A. follow up this lecture with a discussion of the constitution for the League of Nations as presented by President Wilson.

* * *

SERVICES POSTPONED

Owing to the illness of Mr. and Mrs. H. S. Cahoon, memorial services for their son Arthur and Geo. Western are delayed indefinitely.

SUGARVILLE SIFTINGS.

Mr. J. W. Walton left last week for Oklahoma, where he will attend to business matters.

* * *

The Liberty League Auxiliary of the Red Cross will meet next Wednesday afternoon with Mrs. Chelson. There will be yarn on hand for those who want to knit.

All who paid the Liberty Committee their dollar during the Christmas Drive, are members of that auxiliary for this year, and are invited to attend each meeting so they can receive their share of the work assigned to the auxiliary.

* * *

Mrs. Chelson is expecting her brother from Riverside, California, this week. He just recently returned from duty in France.

* * *

Watch for the date of the Community Sale and Bazaar to be held at Sugarville for the benefit of the Hall. The ladies have added a bazaar and will serve lunch at noon, also ice cream. Everybody come. Something for all. If you don't see anything you want, come anyway, as things are being entered every day, and there will more than is listed, so come and make it a day of pleasure as well as business.

* * *

April being the month for the annual report of the F. F. C. library, the club is anxious that all books out be returned to the hall or handed to Edna Cary, librarian, by April 1st.

* * *

Ivan E. Jacobs arrived safely from France Tuesday, and is now stationed at Camp Mills. Ivan enlisted in California and was sent from there to France.

DIED.

Funeral services were held Monday, the 10th, for George A. Rice, who died here, from a complication of diseases, last Thursday, the 6th. Mr. Rice was fifty-six years of age, and leaves a widow, Mrs. Lillie Rice, and five children—Agnes, George Jr., Emma, Eva, and Henry. His brother and sister, from Caliente, Mr. Hyrum Rice, and Mrs. James Ryan, came to Delta for the services. They were accompanied by Mr. E. A. Pilcher, an old friend of the family. Mr. Rice came to Delta from Uinta Basin. His home is in Spokane. We deeply regret the loss of this worthy man. The W. O. W., of which Mr. Rice was a member, took charge of the funeral services.

DELTA NEWS NOTES.

There will be an dance in Delta Friday night. Be there.

—)(—

Mr. and Mrs. Edwin S. Bishop have a new baby boy at their house.

—)(—

Miss Maude Smith spent the week-end at her home in Springville.

—)(—

Noble Peterson was a Salt Lake visitor this week. He didn't tell the editor why.

—)(—

Henry Baab is back on the job again in the Delta State Bank, after a severe attack of rheumatism.

—)(—

Mabel Davidson, from the sugar factory, went to Milford and brought back her grandmother, who is going to live here now.

—)(—

W. P. Walker, formerly with Studebaker here, is now located at Tremonton, where he has charge of the local Studebaker branch there.

—)(—

The Red Cross will print their new knitting instruction next week. Watch the paper, you women who knit.

—)(—

Mr. and Mrs. H. O. Mills are visiting at A. M. Anderson's home. Mr. and Mrs. Mills stopped on their way east from California.

—)(—

James Angell of New York spent the biggest part of last week in Delta with his old school friend S. D. Forward.

—)(—

R. A. Hart, Supervising Drainage Engineer, came to Delta last Friday to meet with Mr. Bullock and Mr. Neale.

—)(—

Mr. and Mrs. Martin of Oklahoma City have come to Delta to make their home. They are going to take the Van Winkle place.

—)(—

Oliver Olsen came home from San Diego last Monday, the 3rd. He was with the Field Artillery. By some mistake this item missed last week's paper.

—)(—

The O. Z. O. club is giving a big dance on the 17th. This is going to be the biggest dance of the year. Don't miss it. Whether you wear a Shamrock or not, be there.

—)(—

Mrs. Russel Sprunt arrived home from Los Angeles last Thursday. She was accompanied by her sister, Mrs. Conrad, of Salt Lake, who will visit in Delta for a few days.

—)(—

Mrs. Russel Sprunt entertained at her home Wednesday evening for her sister, Mrs. Conrad, who is here visiting in Delta. The evening was spent playing cards and dancing.

—)(—

Don't forget the Parents-Teachers' meeting at the School house, Friday evening, the 14th. We want a Junior High school. Be there and express your views.

—)(—

L. M. Fernly of Salt Lake has accepted a position in the Delta State Bank. He will take over the duties of Shelby Forward, who is leaving Delta for the coast in the near future.

—)(—

Mayor Thurston was in Salt Lake the fore part of the week. We can't say whether it was a business or a pleasure trip. There is an auto show in Salt Lake this week.

—)(—

Mrs. Fred Schwartz gave a party Wednesday evening in honor of Mr. Dudley R. Parker, who is down from Salt Lake. There were a large number of guests, and they spent the evening at "five hundred".

Mr. Ed Pearson, with "the boys over there," writes us from Cannes, France, that he is located now on the Mediterranean, and that he thinks often of the contrast of us here in the Rockies plowing through the recent snow, while he is in his shirt sleeves. Quite a difference, surely.

—)(—

A large party of Delta's young folks spent a very pleasant evening last Monday at the home of H. E. Beck, on the South Tract. The evening was spent playing cards and dancing, and was over only too soon. The guests of honor were Frank and Clarence Thurston, who have just returned from the service.

—)(—

Miss Crystal Crane from San Francisco, arrived in Delta this week, to visit with her aunt, Mrs. Dr. Charles Miss Crane is a trained nurse, a graduate of the University of California Hospital, and expects to remain here some time. She will help Doctor Charles with his work.

—)(—

Tuesday evening, March 18th, at 7:30 p. m., the Delta Relief Society will celebrate their annual day at the Ward hall. An interesting Victory program has been prepared for the occasion. A cordial invitation to come is extended to all. Members of the R. S. are requested to bring either sandwiches, cake, or pie.

—)(—

Mr. and Mrs. Harry Willoughby arrived in Delta Wednesday morning. Mr. Willoughby will remain in Delta, while Mrs. Willoughby is to leave Friday morning, for New York. She expects to sail from New York about the 20th for England, to visit with her relatives.

—)(—

J. W. Thurston was paid a visit last week end by his brothers Frank and Clarence Thurston, as they were on their way home from Mare Island where they have been in the service. Frank Thurston was an inspector on the rifle range there. Clarence was a member of the Marine band.

—)(—

Mr. W. P. Bullock, representing the Hanchett Bonding Co. of Chicago, was in Delta Friday. With him was Mr. John D. Neale of the Lumbermen's Trust Co., Portland. Mr. Bullock bought the bonds of Drainage District No. 4. Mr. Neale bought those for District No. 1.

—)(—

Mr. T. J. Britt has sold his belongings here in Delta, and Wednesday morning he and Mrs. Britt left Delta for Texas. Mr. Britt has long been a resident of Delta, and this valley, and we are sorry to lose him now. But we wish him the best of luck, wherever he goes.

The Red Cross are making another "old clothes" drive, and are asking all the women to look over the family wardrobe carefully, and decide just what you can give for the refugees. A complete list of the garments called for will be published next week. The committee on this work are Mrs. Cass Lewis, Mrs. C. H. Hamilton, and Mrs. Wells.

NEWS FROM OUR SISTER TOWNS.

Owing to the bad condition of the roads this news was not recieved in time for last issue.

HINCKLEY

Since last report the "Flu" has taken another member from among us, George Terry.

Academy basket ball team did themselves proud Friday last. In combat with Milford we came out victorious, score 61 to 16. We only have to "lay it over" Cedar this year and then we go to the State tournament. We can already see our banner swaving high as our team comes home crowned with glory.

School work is very strenuous. Every student is exerting himself to the limit. Such determination and pluck as have been shown this year should prove that we have the men and women of tomorrow nearly ready to begin their work.

Due to circumstances arising, the Faculty and Board of Education postponed their reception one week. It will be given Friday March 21st. All parents and past patrons of the school are cordially invited to attend

Stake Conference will be held in this ward March 22nd, and 23rd.

THIS WEEKS NEWS

The weather is delightful. Farmers are very busy with their spring work

Elder Ward Moody has recently returned from a four years and seven months mission in New Zealand. Elder Moody is a son of Mr. and Mrs. Milton Moody. His spirit speaks well for the work he did. Two of his friends, Elders Maw and Patrick came home with him for a short visit. Elder Patrick of Salt Lake City, was a teacher in the Maori Agricultural College. He is well acquainted with Elder F. Earl Stott and his family of whom he speaks very highly.

day was clean up day at the Academy, both the grounds and the building were thoroly cleaned. In the evening an overall and gingham apron dance was enjoyed by all.

Sunday afternoon services were held in Memoriam to those who have been taken from us during this epidemic of Influenza. Those remembered were: Kleth, Pauline, and Kathereine Stratton, Son and two Daughters of Mr. and Mrs. Charles Stratton; Mrs. Eliza Terry and her Son, Mr. Elmer Bishop, Son of Hober Bishop and Elder Charles Langston Son of Mr. and Mrs. Jacob Langston. who died abroad. Mr. Elmer died in the service. He was a member of the 145th Utah in high standing. He was buried in a grave in one of the most beautiful spots in France. Mr. Arnold Workman, a member of the same regiment, spoke in his memory.

Elder Langston died in the South Sea Islands in the service of his God. His resting place is one of the beautiful on earth. The warm climate, the luxuriant vegetation and the gentle breezes made it almost a garden of Eden, as Elder Thomas Pratt who spoke to the memory of this brother, put it. Elder Langston was doing a wonderful work.

Our heartfelt sympathy is extended to all of the bereaved. The Relief Society Annual, held Monday March 18th, 1919 was a grand succes The M. A. Boys met B. A. C. in Beaver Monday March 17th. It was a battle royal, the score standing 42 to 43.

SOUTH TRACT ITEMS

Very severe attacks of spring fever are now quite common, but as yet no serious results have been reported.

* * *

Mrs. Joseph Russel, who has been visiting her daughter, Mrs. Henry Bott, has returned to her home in Salt Lake City. She says she would like to stay down here and farm.

* * *

Our farmers are busy on their alfalfa fields with the spring tooth harrow and find that a great many young buds are showing up through the warming soil.

* * *

H. E. Beck attended a state farm bureau meeting, held on the 17th inst. at the Hotel Utah in Salt Lake City. The annual election of officers resulted in the election of D. D. McKay, president; Mr. Burton, vice president, and Mr. Taylor of Payson, sec.-treasurer. Two other members at large were added, to complete the executive board, which were H. E. Beck and a member from Sanpete county. It was a meeting full of interest to the agriculturist, and was very much alive on all farm topics.

* * *

Dr. H. Tomlinson, who has spent the past fall and winter in Idaho, is among us for a short visit, when he will again leave for his old home in Illinois with his father for the summer.

* * *

Some new neighbors are coming in on the South Tract; so far, a Mr. Martin on the Van Winkle place and a Mr. Potter on the Will Evans place. We hope more will settle here.

* * *

Mrs. Leo Coffin is enjoying a visit by a sister from Idaho.

* * *

A merry party, coming in three autos, invaded the home of Mr. and Mrs. H. E. Beck on the evening of the 19th inst., and to say that the Beck folk enjoyed their coming very much, is only mildly expressing it.

* * *

The Misses Mildred Forrest and Helen E. Beck spent the last weekend at the home of Miss Helen, coming down on horseback. On Sunday they were joined on their horseback ride by Miss Florence Beck and all had a fine time.

DELTA NEWS NOTES.

Have you seen the new Victory stamp?

—) (—

Mrs. Dr. Charles has her mother, Mrs. Jameson, here visiting with her.

—) (—

August Miller is in Salt Lake this week on a buying trip.

—) (—

Attorney Ivory, of Fillmore, was in Delta over Saturday.

—) (—

Sheet iron work of all kinds at the Delta Furniture Store.   m?!

—) (—

Mrs. A. B. Ward made a trip to Salt Lake this week, to spend a few days.

—) (—

March seems to be going out like a lamb, but maybe we'd better knock wood.

—) (—

H. F. Aller left Delta for Salt Lake Tuesday night for a visit with his family.

—) (—

The Delta School has spoken for the first Victory Loan Bond. Who gets the second?

—) (—

Don't miss the Millinery Opening at Black's Store, in Deseret. You'll rue it if you do.

—) (—

Mr. R. H. Orr was called to Grantsville suddenly, on account of the serious illness of his mother.

—) (—

Mrs. Jetta Cook, and her sister-in-law, Miss Ardella Cook, are visiting in Spanish Fork for a few days.

—) (—

Mrs. Nathalia Lackyard arrived in Delta last Thursday to spend a few days with her mother, Mrs. Cooper.

—) (—

Mrs. Harry T. Baker returned to Delta last week, after a long visit spent in Colorado with her relatives.

—) (—

Lewis Koch was in Delta a day or two this week. Mr. Koch has been in Salt Lake a month, for his health.

—) (—

Broom special 98 cents. Regular $1.50 quality. Delta Lumber & Hdw. Co.   m20-27

—) (—

Ward Love arrived home Monday night. He has been in the Navy two years. He is the son of Mr. and Mrs. S. E. Love.

—) (—

Mrs. W. L. Allred is returning to Delta soon. Mr. Allred is building the new cabaret, going up west of the Meat Market.

—) (—

Mr. Emmett of Hinckley, president of Drainage District No. 1, and Mr. Wright, secretary, were callers at the Chronicle office Saturday.

—) (—

The O. Z. O. Club were entertained at the home of Mrs. R. C. Bates, Wednesday evening. The girls enjoyed a very jolly evening.

—) (—

Judging from the sounds coming from the Hall at Band practise Wednesday evening, we're going to have a real band here pretty soon.

—) (—

Mrs. Pearson has opened her dress making shop next door to the Clark Street Market, and can give you good service.   m27p

—) (—

The members of the Union Church held their Quarterly Congregation Meeting Saturday afternoon at the Presbyterian Chapel. This meeting was for business and pleasure both.

—) (—

Coming! "The Camouflage of Shirley," comedy drama in three acts, new 1919 military play, will be presented by the H. B. Dramatic club in Hickley, April 2, 1919; in Delta, Lincoln theatre, April 4, 1919.

—) (—

Gerald Mc Clain came thru Delta Friday, with a troop train bound for the Coast. He had just time to get off and shake hands with a few of his friends who were at the depot.

—) (—

Shelby D. Forward, who has held the position of book-keeper in the Delta State Bank for the past year, is shaking the Delta dust from his heels this Saturday. He is leaving for California. So long, Shelby.

—) (—

Mr. J. H. Jenkins, from the Sugar Factory, left Monday, for California, where he will join Mrs. Jenkins, who has been there about two weeks. They expect to spend about a month in California.

—) (—

Mrs. R. R. Betz was in Delta a few hours Saturday, visiting with friends. Mrs. Betz has a splendid position in the railroad offices at Tintic, where she has been while her husband, Cpl. R. R. Betz was in France.

—) (—

Mr. Frank Conrad came down from Salt Lake last week to look over this country. Mr. Conrad seemed to be favorably impressed. He was stopping with Mr. and Mrs. T. R. Sprunt, Mrs. Sprunt being his sister-in-law.

—) (—

Mrs. Palmer, of Cedar City, and her niece, Miss Brown, stopped off in Delta on their way to Salt Lake, to visit with Mrs. W. H. Pace. Mrs. Palmer is Mrs. Pace's sister, and her daughter, Miss Evelyn Palmer, is teaching in the Delta School.

—) (—

Mrs. Ben Douglas returned to Delta Monday night, after a six weeks' visit in New York with her family. Mr. Douglas went to Salt Lake to meet Mrs. Douglas, and they spent Sunday visiting with relatives at Lehi.

WOODROW WRITINGS.

Messrs. Hugo and Richard Thompson, who have been spending the winter in California have returned to Woodrow for the summer prepared to raise sugar beets.

* * *

Mr. Mc Cormack of California is in Woodrow this week looking over his business interests here.

* * *

Once more everybody has recovered from the Flu.

* * *

The Miller family of Spanish Fork have taken possession of the Tinsley ranch, and the Tinsley family have moved on the Ralph King ranch in Woodrow.

* * *

Mr. and Mrs. Horton, who have been visiting the Griffith and Rollins families returned to their home in Beaver last Wednesday.

We hear that Clinton Hagan has gone into partnership with Austin and Purdy in cultivating beets on the Austin and Davis ranches in Sutherland.

* * *

SCHOOL ITEMS

The Woodrow school is having a series of debates on Friday afternoons. Parents are invited to attend.

Mr. J. Earl Horton gave the school an interesting talk upon his travels through the East last Friday afternoon.

The civic class had an entertaining and instructive afternoon a week ago when Sheriff Riter arrested one of the members for a misdemeanor and he was tried in school with Mr. Tracy acting as judge. The prosecuting attorney, Glenn Johnson, made out a good case, but the lad's eminent attorneys, Callie Clark and Orel Griffith, with their skillful defense so appealed to the jury that a verdict of

SUTHERLAND SEARCHLIGHTS.

Mrs. Evan Evans has returned to her home in Sutherland.

* * *

Mr. and Mrs. John E. Lovell, Mrs. Wells, and Hattie Lovell, have been staying with their daughter and sister, Mrs. Jeff Jones, while attending conference. Hattie expects to remain for a while.

* * *

Mr. Chris. Christiansen, who recently purchased the Britt place from Mr. Cliff Bunker, met with a painful accident Saturday afternoon while spreading manure. He drove through a ditch, was thrown to the ground, and the manure spreader went over him. No bones were broken, and it is thought there are no internal injuries, but he is badly bruised and shaken up.

* * *

DELTA NEWS NOTES.

Marion Kilpack went to Sterling last week, to see his father.

—)(—

H. F. Aller returned from Salt Lake last Friday.

—)(—

Miss Edna Beck was in town last week, for several days.

—)(—

Don't forget the Junior Prom at Hinckley, April the 4th.

—)(—

Mr. and Mrs. Cyril B. Cluff are the proud parents of a fine baby boy, born a week ago Wednesday.

—)(—

Stray sorrel horse about 12 yrs. old, two brands on left thigh. Delta pen.

—)(—

Miss Mildred Forrest spent the week-end with Miss Verna Nelson on the Island Farm.

—)(—

Miss Ethel Iverson is in Delta this week, managing Cooper's Cafe, while Mrs. Cooper is in Salt Lake.

—)(—

John Sage and Joe Mercer left for Eureka Thursday afternoon, by auto, and will be gone several days.

—)(—

I will have a new supply of furniture in; you can save money by buying for cash at the Delta Furniture store.   ap3

—)(—

A new line of extension tables, kitchen and drop leaf tables, will be in next week at the Delta Furniture Store.   ap3

—)(—

Mrs. Zina Gray left Delta, Sunday, to go to Beaver, to visit with her son. Mrs. Gray expects to remain away all summer.

—)(—

D. Landows left for Salt Lake City Wednesday on a business trip. Mr. Landows is going to start work right away on his building.

Ed Marshall returned to Delta last week after spending the winter in Salt Lake taking treatment for his health.

—)(—

Mrs. Louise Christian returned to Pioche Monday, after a short stay in Delta with her sister, Mrs. Lena Faust.

—)(—

Coming!! Friday night, April 4th. "The Camouflage of Shirley", at the Lincoln Theatre, for the benefit of the Stake Mutual.

—)(—

The O. Z. O. Club met Wednesday night with Mis Athena Beckwith. At this meeting the club mixed both business and pleasure.

—)(—

Mrs. Dora Cooper went to Salt Lake Monday night, to spend a few days with her daughter, Mrs. W. L. Lackyard.

—)(—

Frank E. Lanham arrived in town Monday, to go on his farm on the South Tract. Sergeant Lanham has been in the service two years, with the 145th Field Artillery.

—)(—

Miss Verna Nelson gave an April Fool's party, April 1st, to celebrate her birthday. The evening was spent playing practical jokes, the biggest joke being the trip home.

—)(—

A car load of new Fordson tractors are here now. Their agent, W. H. Pace, sold five tractors at the first demonstration, to Mr. Rodges, of Deseret.

—)(—

Ben Douglas and Jeff Clark left for Salt Lake Monday morning in Mr. Clark's car. Mr. Douglas is making a spring buying trip, and Mr. Clark had business to attend to.

—)(—

Mrs. Russell Sprunt was given a surprise party last Friday evening, by her many friends. The occasion was Mrs. Sprunt's birthday, and the guests enjoyed a very jolly evening.

—)(—

A. F. King left for California on Wednesday, to start work out at Hollywood, in the R. R. offices. Mr. King has been up at Lynndyl for some time, tho previous to that he was operator here at the depot.

—)(—

Don't forget the big nine-reel extra Saturday night at the Lincoln—"God's Man," in seven parts, is a remarkable story of New York's Broadway and elite underworld. A two-reel comedy will also be shown. 10 and 20 cents.

—)(—

If you want to buy a watch, buy from your local watchmaker, as I have proven to the people of Delta, as I have fixed the very best watches there are around here—Elgin, Waltham, Howard, Hamilton, Hampden, Ill. Watches sold at the very lowest prices. D. Landows, expert watchmaker and jeweler.   ap3

SUTHERLAND SEARCHLIGHTS.

Mr. and Mrs. W. R. Walker went to Salt Lake City on a business trip last week.

* * *

We hear that Mr. Schlappy has sold his farm in Sutherland. We wish him success wherever he decides to locate.

* * *

Mr. Taylor, who has just returned from France, took up the time in meeting Sunday, telling of his experiences, and explaining the gas mask. It was greatly appreciated by all.

* * *

The trial between Mr. Belston and Mrs. Davis was held last Saturday. The judge decided in Mrs. Davis' favor. Mrs. Davis intends looking after her farm this summer; her man is already cleaning the weeds off the place.

SUGARVILLE SIFTINGS.

The Friendship Thimble Club held a very interesting meeting at the home of Mrs. Cochran. Gardening was the subject up for discussion. The next meeting will be held at the home of Mrs. Hibbard, when Poultry Raising will be discussed. Topics similar to these are discussed at each meeting. Everyone invited.

* * *

J. H. Burtner of Riverside, Cal., an old time friend and brother of the editor, was in Milford Monday for the purpose of making final proof on his enlarged homestead at Reed. Mr. Burton has a choice one-half section which he is very proud of. He is an old time Salt Lake agent and is still connected with that line. At one time the town of Delta was known as Burtner and the post office was Burtner for a number of years in the good old days, but owing to a confusion of names, between Burton and Burtner, the name was changed to Delta. He is very enthusiastic over the future prospect of this valley and is one of the many friends of Milford has in Southern California.

DELTA NEWS NOTES.

Enoch Folsom arrived in New York last Tuesday from overseas.

—)(—

Get your Deed properly drawn by Frank Beckwith.

—)(—

A. L. Broderick went to Salt Lake on business a day or two this week.

—)(—

Mr. Otto Rydman and Ed Reynolds spent Easter Sunday in Zion.

—)(—

Miss Mildred Forrest and Miss Athena Beckwith were guests at the Beck rancho over Easter Sunday.

—)(—

Miss Gwen Slaughter spent the week-end at the Island Farm, with the Nelson family.

—)(—

Wm. Heise arrived in New York Thursday from France, on the ship "Mexican," with the 91st division.

—)(—

Mr. and Mrs. T. J. Hetland and their family are here visiting with Mrs. Hetland's parents, Mr. and Mrs. J. S. Forrest.

—)(—

Take your Contract, Sale Agreement or other Legal Work to Frank Beckwith.

—)(—

W. H. Pace and Roy Dresser have bought a seven-foot cement mixer. There is so much building activity going on that such a machine will find plenty of work.

—)(—

A fine writing desk, just the thing for farmers. It has six pigeon holes, two spaces for writing paper, and four spaces for long books. A letter file, two small drawers, and three large ones. There is nothing better for the money. Only $22.00 for cash. Delta Furniture Store.

Ground has been broken by Allred on the lot west of W. H. Pace's garage, for the erection of a nice brick business building. Also Mercer's construction work has commenced. Delta is humming.

—)(—

Up to the hour of going to press Delta's quota to the Victory Loan is is lagging. We urge the people not to fall down on this loan; the government has spent the money and it is up to us to subscribe for the bonds. Do your duty.

—)(—

A committee was appointed this week to make plans for a reception to our returned soldiers. We should all heartily join in making this the biggest event Delta has yet given, and show the boys a real welcome. Arrangements will be completed by the committee soon, when full details will be given.

—)(—

If you want to buy a watch, buy from your local watchmaker, as I have proven to the people of Delta as I have fixed the very best watches there are around here. Elgin, Waltham Howard, Hamilton, Hampden, Ill. Watches sold at the very lowest prices. D. Landows, expert watchmaker and jeweler. ap24

—)(—

At the preliminary meeting held at Hinckley Monday night last, the matter of the election for additional drainage bonds was thoroughly discussed. The sentiment of the meeting was strongly in favor. The arguments were ably put by Engineer Hart, and the meeting given over to a full discussion. A further meeting will be held Saturday night, and there is no doubt but that election for the new bond issue will be carried. As this matter is vital to the district, it should receive the ardent support of all voters.

New Monarch Ranges just came in. Good discount for cash at the Delta Furniture Store. ap24-m1

—)(—

Delta is very proud indeed to note among its honored sons the high distinction given to Glenn Stewart as champion machine gunner of the A. E. F. That's a nifty mark, Glenn, and you have our warmest handclasp in congratulation.

—)(—

R. E. Caldwell of Caldwell and Richards was in town last week. Messrs. Caldwell and Richards are engineers in charge of the drainage work in Districts Nos. 2, 3 and 4, besides being similarly employed in six other districts in the state, making in all ten drainage districts on which this firm is doing the construction work. At the present time they are actively employed in Salt Lake, Sevier and Millard counties.

—)(—

Albert Watts from Woodrow paid us a pleasant visit last week. Albert reports the morale of the North Tract the highest yet, and prospects for this year exceedingly good. The outlook for beets is excellent, and he thinks this will be the best year yet had. Albert asks that the County Commissioners print their monthly proceedings in the Chronicle for the benefit of this region.

—)(—

Ray Tozer, son of Mr. and Mrs. Geo. Tozer arrived in Delta from France Tuesday evening. Ray has been with the 348th F. A. and was in France about nine months. Ray says Delta looks mighty good to him.

—)(—

A little drop on some of my furniture and galvanized ware at the Delta Furniture Store. ap24-m1

—)(—

FRANK BECKWITH
Conveyancing and Legal Work.

DESERET DOINGS

Arbor Day and Clean-up day were merged into one by the teachers and pupils of the A. C. Nelson school. A commendable feature of the day was in the planting of a tree on the school grounds in honor of each soldier from Deseret and Oasis who served, or is now serving in the U. S. Army. The citizens of this school district will support any movement to fence and beautify and care for the A. C. Nelson school property.

* * *

Mrs. Caroline Black has been seriously ill for about ten days. In consequence of her condition the daughters living at a distance were called to her bedside. They are: Mrs. John W. Reid, of Payson, Mrs. Nels Peterson, Moapa. Nevada; Mrs. Diantha Hansen and Mrs. Peter Jensen of Mammoth.

* * *

Miss Eva Cahoon returned from a short visit to Salt Lake and other northern points last Saturday.

The marked success of those who did war gardening last year has proven beyond a doubt that our soil is well adapted to the growth of almost all kinds of vegetables. Many are taking this knowledge to heart and are arranging for more extensive and intensive gardening. With but ordinary care we predict that the local farmers could make it quite unnecessary for dealers to ship in any but the very early vegetables.

* * *

Corpl. Ray Black, son of Mr. and Mrs. Dennis Black, is home on a short furlough, arriving last Sunday. Ray was one of our earliest volunteers and served for a long time in training at Camp Dodge, Iowa. He was later transferred to New York where he and companion—Dewey Miksell—did guard duty for many months. Corpl. Black is to return to New York May 1st when he will sail for France, being one of the army who will relieve the boys who are overseas.

* * *

At the instigation of some of Oasis'

and Deseret's more enterprising citizens, Mr. Jenkins, of the Delta Sugar factory made a trip of investigation over our farming district south and west of town. It is the opinion of those who know, that this section of the country is better adapted to beet culture than any other part of the valley, and it is earnestly hoped that Mr. Jenkins and his field men will be able to contract with our landholders for a very considerable acreage this spring.

SUGARVILLE SIFTINGS.

The Liberty League Red Cross will meet with Mrs. Anson next Wednesday afternoon.

* * *

Arvid Anderson, son of Mr. and Mrs. L. Anderson, returned Tuesday from service in the U. S. army.

* * *

Rev. Hamilton will preach at Sugarville next Sunday afternoon, after Sunday School. Everybody is welcome.

Fred Tingleaf is a welcome visitor in our community this week. He has been spending the winter with his people in Riverside, California, and while there had a pretty bad case of "flu."

* * *

The people of Sugarville were very much surprised and needless to say pleased, with a twenty dollar contribution toward their Community Building, presented by Mr. Crowl, for the Delta Beet Sugar Corporation. Many thanks.

Mr. and Mrs. Cochran entertained at dinner Easter Sunday. The guests were Mr. and Mrs. C. J. Chelson and two sons, Private Lawrence Norlan. Mr. and Mrs. E. H. Hibbard and family. Mr. Norlan was of course the guest of honor, having recently arrived from active service in France. All enjoyed the stories of Mr. Cochran's and Lawrence's army experiences.

RETURNING BOYS

Sunday night, La Rue Pritchett, Will Heise, and John Kozina, each of whom had seen active service in France, returned home. The editor listened to the incidents the boys gave of warfare as they saw it, and hopes at an early date to give some of these striking things to our readers red hot. It is certainly thrilling to hear the boys talk.

Gus Faust also returned this week. This following week's issue will contain an article from Gus, which we believe will portray some of his experiences vividly, to the intense interest of our readers.

Glen Stewart also arrived in the early part of the week. Our readers

will remember that Glen had the distinction of having the best shooting machine gun squad in his battalion.

Ray Tozer has been back a little over a week, and feels that he is beginning to get acquainted again.

Hugh Kelley returned yesterday, and if he isn't too bashful, he can tell some tales that will make your hair stand upon end, for he was some fighter.

And Jack Kennelly is home again, after a year's service with the 91st. He has a grin from ear to ear; we hope it's because he's glad to see us. We're glad to see him.

Enoch Folsom arrived this week. Enoch kept a diary, from which we hope to have the privilege of giving

our readers some extracts.

Boys, we're proud of you. If the editor of this paper doesn't say his appreciation right,—if it fails to properly carry conviction—it is only because we seldom come up to even our own expectations. But the Chronicle will do its best. The Delta boys were in the thick of it, and saw the bloody work at its worst; some Millard boys remain over there to sanctify with their life's blood the noble cause they fought for; some were wounded, but thankfully, we believe, escaped the more serious mutilations; and some, luckily, went thru the thickest and worst, without even a scratch or mark.

UTAH CASUALTIES IN THE WORLD WAR

GALLANT FIGHTERS WHO MADE SUPREME SACRIFICE IN THE STRUGGLE FOR FREEDOM.

Of the 23,000 Men Who Made Up the Army Sent from Utah, Many Laid Down Their Lives in Defense of Their Country.

Salt Lake City.—The state council of defense has issued the following list of fatalities among Utah men who were called to the colors. A total of 23,000 men were assigned to the various branches of the army and navy, and of these 535 made the supreme sacrifice. The total list, it is estimated, will include 700 names. The state council is compiling a service record of the 23,000 Utahns engaged in the world war. This work is being done by Secretary Arch M. Thurman and Mrs. Mary Gilmer Rankin. The honor role to January of this year is as follows:

William H. Adams, Cass City.
Reni C. Ahlquist, Salt Lake City.
Yoncengom Albo, Helper.
Guy B. Alexander, Heber City.
Clarence E. Allen, Jr., Salt Lake City.
Oria W. Allen, Logan.
James L. Altop, Tooele.
James Anagnost, Bingham.
Alexander Anderson, Salt Lake City.
Clarence Anderson, Aurora.
Darrell Anderson, American Fork.
Edward C. Anderson, Clear Creek.
George E. Anderson, Lake Shore.
George E. Anderson, Richfield.
Junius M. Anderson, Monroe.

Fred Elder, Fountain Green.
Ernest Horatio Ellerman (Lieut.), S. L. City.
Walter B. Elliott (Capt.), Fort Douglas.
Melvin A. Elwood, Ogden.
Emmett Erickson, Salt Lake City.
Harry D. Estes, Salt Lake City.
H. L. Evans (Lieutenant), Nephi.
Kenneth Evans, Salt Lake City.
Leonard Guy Farley, Ogden.
G. E. Farnow, Salt Lake City.
George Felton, St. George.
Harold M. Ferguson, Ogden.
Alonzo Finch, Linwood.
Robert A. Finnical, University of Utah.
Evangeles Fintrilakis, Salt Lake City.
The Rev. Edward H. Fitzgerald (Major.)
Garfield Deford Fletcher, Salt Lake City.
Marion J. Fletcher, Kaysville.
John Thomas Forman, Bluff Dale.
Fauntleroy Fosgren, Brigham City.
Ray Clyde Foster, Salt Lake City.
Raymond H. Foster, American Fork.
Herbert Fowles, Hooper.
William B. Fowles, Hooper.
Lucin E. Frazier, Ogden.
Lorenzo Frederickson, Salt Lake City.
Andrew J. Fredson, Ogden.
Frank S. Fuller, Springville.
William O. Funk, Smithfield.
Anthony Furmanski, Bessemer.
Melvin W. Galbraith, Blanding.
James H. Gardley, Beaver.
Charles Elwood Garvin, Park City.
George Gidney, Brigham City.
Elmo Gillen, Murray.
John W. Gillespie, Salt Lake City.
Morris Ginsburg, Salt Lake City.
Herman Glassmeier, Salt Lake City.
William T. Gleason (Lieut.)
Herbert Glethill, Sigurd.
Frank Lewis Glick, Garfield.
Theodore E. Gourgiotis, Garfield.
Willard G. Gowans, Tooele.
Ray N. Gowers, Nephi.
Fred J. Grant, Ruth, Nev.
Edwin M. Gray, Elsinore.
Wallace Gray, Santa Clara.
Armistead A. Green, Jr., Salt Lake City.
Arthur R. Green, Murray.
Lawrence Green, Salt Lake City.
George A. Greenlee, Tooele.
Clayton B. Griswold, Ogden.
Normal J. Haeckel, Salt Lake City.
Jacob Hafen, Jr., Mount Pleasant.
Jay H. Hague (Lieut.)
Lloyd Burt Haight, Trenton.
Howard J. Hales, Spanish Fork.
Fleming Hall, Midvale.
Henry F. Hall, Midvale.
Ralph Hall, Ogden.
Fred Halverson, Oakley, Idaho.
Walter B. Hanks, Grover.
Milton G. Hansen, Providence.
Hass Hanson, Spanish Fork.
Paul O. Hanson, Levan.
Ben A. Harding, Helper.

George L. Moore, Spanish Fork.
Lester E. Moreton (Major), Salt Lake City.
Adrian L. Morin (Lieut.), Salt Lake City.
William C. Morris, Greeley, Idaho.
Ross Moore, Heber City.
Clyde W. Morse, Salt Lake City.
C. W. Morse, Millcreek.
Clyde Muir, Clinton.
Russell Wagoner Muir, Heber City.
John Moulder, Ogden.
James H. Murphy, Park City.
Francis Vere Naylor, Salt Lake City.
Charles E. Nelson, Salt Lake City.
George R. Nelson, Manila, Utah.
Roy P. Nelson, Randolph.
William Netcher, Trenton.
Arthur S. Nielsen, Logan.
Boyd Nielson.
Clarence Nielson, Richfield.
Harry D. Jones, Salt Lake City.
Bert Oakley, American Fork.
Raymond B. Oldham, Logan.
Alfred M. Olsen, Brigham City.
Andrew M. Olsen, Fountain Green.
Charles F. Olsen.
Delbert F. Olsen, Brigham City.
Oran Openshaw, Santaquin.
John H. Osborne, Salt Lake City.
Weeden E. Osborne, Salt Lake City.
Frank R. Ostler, Nephi.
Thomas Weeks Ostler, Nephi.
Carl J. Ostlund, Salt Lake City.
Carl J. Ostlund, Murray.
Henries Dewey Otteson, Manti.
Harvey A. Parker, Bennion.
George D. Parkinson, Whitney.
James A. Parnell (Lieut.)   Salt Lake City.
Eugene Pasini, Salt Lake City.
Melvin C. Patten, Payson.
That Delos L. Peay, Provo.
Hyrum E. Perry, Springville.
Ralph Perry, Vernal.
Edward McClure Peters (Lieut.)
George E. Peters, Vernal.
Alvin George Peterson, Gunnison.
Arthur L. Peterson, Salt Lake City.
Frank Howard Peterson, Snyderville.
John O. Peterson (Corporal), Welby.
Leonard H. Peterson, Salt Lake City.
Vern A. Peterson, Salt Lake City.
Peter D. Pitts, Marysville.
William Raymond Platt, Salt Lake City.
Dan Potovich, Bingham.
John Henry Polson, Mammoth.
Thomas J. Powell, Lehi.
Clayton D. Preston (Sergeant), Logan.
William Price, Ogden.
Arthur Leon Pritchard, Garfield.
Marlin Proctor, Panguitch.
Reuben W. Radmall, Pleasant Grove.
Albert L. Ralph, Rockland, Idaho.
Cleyon J. Reber, Santa Clara.
Jerry V. Reece, Payson.
O. D. Reeder, Brigham City.
Ornamon Remington (Serg.), Salt Lake City.
Abraham Reush, Manti.

Otto A. Anderson, Salt Lake City.
Wilford W. Anderson, Logan.
Lester Andrus, Spanish Fork.
George N. Ansley, Salt Lake City.
Clarence Mann Argyle, Salt Lake City.
Horace R. Argyle, Spanish Fork.
Winston Arnett, Salt Lake City.
Wallace Asher, Lehi.
Earl Ashton, Lehi.
James B. Austin (Captain), Salt Lake City.
Lear E. Austin, Salt Lake City.
Spot Austin, Salt Lake City.
Axelson Sheldon, Elmo.
Charles A. Bacon, Magna.
James C. Gagan, Grantsville.
Herman Baker, Ogden.
Evan Banes, Sunnyside.
Joel O. Barlow.
John Barnes Jr., Heber City.
Charles Barrett, Provo.
Edward H. Barrus, Grantsville.
Cliff Barton, Ogden.
Milfur Almond Bates, Ogden.
Arthur Tennyson Bates, Grantsville.
Joseph N. Bates, Wanship.
Joshua A. Bates, Wanship.
James Clinton Bawden, Salt Lake City.
Louis G. Beauman, Jr., Ogden.
Otto Beeba, Circleville.
LeRoy E. Benson, Coalville.
Christian Best, Panguitch.
Ralph Biddle, Salt Lake City.
Elmer E. Bishop, Hinckley, Utah.
Allen M. Blain, Spring City.
John Blundell, Salt Lake City.
Rufus G. Bolton, Salt Lake City.
Phillip E. Booth, Salt Lake City.
Fred E. Booth, Salduro.
John David Boyd, Jr., Provo.
Ralph Brandy, Mt. Pleasant.
Ross J. Bracken, St. John.
George Walter Brandley, Salt Lake City.
Alexander Leland Brewer, Ogden.
James Roy Brighton, Salt Lake City.
Caleb Bolwar Brinton, Big Cottonwood.
Early P. Brown, Salt Lake City.
Eugene Allen Brown, Duchesne.
Ira Brown, Lehi.
William A. Brown, Hoytsville.
Carl Brunson, South Bountiful.
Logan H. Bryant, Cedar City.
George Elwood Bunker, Hinckley.
Herbert H. Burns, Vernal.
Harold H. Burrows, Salt Lake City.
Hubert G. Bush, Salt Lake City.
Arthur L. Cahoon, Deseret.
Joseph A. Cain, Salt Lake City.
Alton Calder, Vernal.
Harold Cameron, Salt Lake City.
R. O. Campbell, Ogden.
Philip V. Campbell, Ogden.
Fred T. Cannon, Ogden.
George W. Carlisle, Heber City.
Gurney F. Carlson, Murray.
Charles T. Carrol, Blanding.
Maurice R. Carter, Salt Lake City.

Earl S. Harper, Smithfield.
Marion Hatch, Spanish Fork.
Golden Hatfield, Springville.
Jefferson Hayes, Loa.
Manford Hayes, Manila.
Leon Haws, Salt Lake City.
Orion Helm, Murray.
George A. Hendrickson, Salt Lake City.
Lavon N. Hickman, Logan.
Robert F. Hildebrand, Salt Lake City.
Stanford Hinckley, Salt Lake City.
Vivian H. Hobson, Richmond.
Thaddeus Hodges, Mount Carmel.
Amos Hoeft, Vernal.
Henry Hofele, Salt Lake City.
John Arthur Hogan, Tooele.
John W. Hogan, Salt Lake City.
Raymond Holmes, Ogden.
Fred Perry Holton.
Cecil J. Horton.
Ira Hentz, Springville.
Hadley Howard (Lieut).
Samuel E. Howard, Riverton.
Seymour Oswald Howell, Nephi.
James P. Howell, Tooele.
William H. Huffman, Lockerby.
Russell Hughes, Garfield.
L. A. Humphrey, Ogden.
Harry D. Humphries, Murray.
Basil Hunsaker, Brigham City.
Thomas Hunt, Monroe.
Russell Ingersoll, American Fork.
Wallace Ipson, Beaver.
Frank Isakson, Ogden.
Arthur Ivie, Heber City.
Rau Ivie, Salina.
William L. Jacobs, Heber City.
William G. Jakos, Garfield.
Arthur Janney, Salt Lake City.
Leo M. Jensen, Richfield.
Wilbert Johnson, Heber City.
Niels Oliver Jensen, Centerville.
Roy Jensen, Mapleton.
Waldemar Jensen, Salt Lake City.
Elmer V. Jesperson, Cedar City.
David Jesperson, Ogden.
Ernest F. Johnson, Randolph.
Raymond R. Johnson, Salt Lake City.
Charles Clayton Jones, Salt Lake City.
David Lane Jones, Clearfield.
Henry M. Jones, Enoch.
John Jones, Willard.
Joseph Jones, Randolph.
Joseph Leo Jones (Captain), Hooper.
Joy V. Jones, Provo.
Marvin L. Jones, Wellsville.
Guy J. Judgensen, Salt Lake City.
Bill Kallis, Bingham.
Daniel Lester Keate, St. George.
Theras Kechepalos, Garfield.
Harry D. Keith, Nada.
Vea Kelley, Murray.
Michael J. Kelly, Eureka.
George Kerr, Salt Lake City.
Peter L. Keyes, Ogden.
Scott P. Kimbal, Salt Lake City.

Lowell F. Richardson, Salt Lake City.
Harold Richie, Eureka.
Earl R. Ridd, Salt Lake City.
Brutus H. Rideout (Corp.), Salt Lake City.
Elmo Ridges, Salt Lake City.
James R. Riggs, Panguitch.
Cleon J. Robert, Santa Clara.
William R. Robbins, Provo.
John Roberts, Jr., Wellington.
Alexander G. Roberts, Jr., Sandy.
Joseph Robertson, Salt Lake City.
Lewis S. Robison, Pleasant Grove.
Grant Romney, Salt Lake City.
William L. Rook, Salt Lake City.
Louis Rowe (Lieut.), Salt Lake City.
Thorvald Y. Rowley, Logan.
Orville Wallace Ruby (Lieut.), Ogden.
Ernest R. Russell, Salt Lake City.
Sterling Russell, Grafton.
Albert Stanley Sadler, Payson.
Herbert Charles Sadler, Spring Lake.
Frank George Sainsbury, Fielding.
Elmer John Sandberg, Salt Lake City.
Martin Sanders, Richmond.
Santarelli, Tooele.
Charles E. Scannell (Lieut.), Orangeville.
Vernie L. Scott, Springville.
Fred L. Schmaltze, Ogden.
Albert E. Schneider, Salt Lake City.
William A. Seler, Sandy.
James Shaw, Ogden.
Scott M. Sheets, Salt Lake City.
Leslie O. Shilder, Salt Lake City.
George M. Silver, Salt Lake City.
Kiwan Sinia, Salt Lake City.
Niels Skeen, Nephi.
Ardie Smith, Salt Lake City.
Gilbert L. Smith, Randolph.
Henry Smith, Park City.
Lehi Larsen Smith, Salt Lake City.
William Smith, Salt Lake City.
Elmer S. Snyder, Salt Lake City.
Grover V. Sorenson, Vineyard.
Hyrum Sorenson, Salt Lake City.
Joseph Sorenson, Salt Lake City.
Walter J. Sorenson, Brigham City.
Sidney A. Sorenson, Salt Lake City.
Bert Spakman, Richmond.
Sparginnino, Salt Lake City.
Harry Speight, Salt Lake City.
Ross W. Spencer.
James Keene Sprunt.
Edwin Ellis Squires, Salt Lake City.
William Squires, Salt Lake City.
William R. Steglich, Salt Lake City.
George Stevenson, Price.
Charles J. Stewart, Spanish Fork.
Nels Stewart, Salt Lake City.
William G. Stonebreaker, Ogden.
Hyrum Stusnegger, Manti.
Arthur G. Sullivan, Eureka.
Osborne Sutton, Nephi.
William Moir Swan, Salt Lake City.
Alfred Swens, Eureka.
Horace R. Tanner, South Cottonwood.
Gilbert Tardley, Beaver.

Stefano Casciano, Murray.
Albert Casera, Bingham.
James Wesley Chipman, Salt Lake City.
Eddie Christensen, Lehi.
Jesse M. Christensen, Gunnison.
Parley B. Christensen, Salt Lake City.
Royal C. Christensen, Redmond.
Parley P. Christensen (Captain), Ephraim.
Roger Harvey Clapp (Lieut.), Salt Lake City.
John G. Clark, Cedar City.
Earl L. Cobb, Ogden.
Eldridge S. Coffin, Salt Lake City.
William Colby, Duchesne.
Virgil Cole, Salt Lake City.
Vernell W. Coleman, Midway.
Umberto Conedera, Bingham.
George B. Cook, Willard.
George Cottam, Salt Lake City.
Herald Cox, Fairview.
James Abraham Crawford, Salt Lake City.
Abraham Crawford, Helper.
Teddy Crawford, Castlegate.
James W. Crawland, Holden.
George Howland Croft, Centerville.
Earl F. Crow, Salt Lake City.
Raymond Francis Crow, Salt Lake City.
Elmer J. Criddle, Kaysville.
James Cuff, Salt Lake City.

Thomas Kirkland, Salt Lake City.
Moroni Kleinman, Toquerville.
Alexian E. Koshaba, Salt Lake City.
Henry R. Kramer, Spanish Fork.
Edward A. Kupfer, Salt Lake City.
Vahram Kurkilan, Salt Lake City.
George C. Lambourne, Salt Lake City.
Isaac H. Langston, Springdale.
Jesse L. Larrabee, Salt Lake City.
Alfred L. Larsen, Provo.
Cleveland C. Larsen, Salt Lake City.
Lawrence E. Larsen, Spanish Fork.
Orville H. Larson, Brigham City.
Diamond L. Larson, Sterling.
Herbert Layton, Kaysville.
John H. Lee, Salt Lake City.
William Hunter, Leon.
Henry J. Lefevre, Spry.
Carl H. Leishman, Wellsville.
William Leitz, Castlegate.
Frank Leland, Salt Lake City.
Harold Lewis (Capt.), Salt Lake City.
Daniel J. Limb, Alamsville.
Edward L. Lister, Tooele.
George Lloyd, Salt Lake City.
Dan L. Lockhart, Wellsburg.
William Lofthouse, Willard.
Arthur F. Longshaw, Salt Lake City.

August G. Turghetta, Salt Lake City.
Lynn Taylor, Ouray.
Robert B. Taylor.
Hadley H. Teter (Lieut.), Salt Lake City.
Frank W. Thomas, Salt Lake City.
H. H. Thomas, Jr., Salt Lake City.
Guy Thomas, Price.
Alonzo P. Thomas, Spanish Fork.
William O. Thompson, Sterling.
Heber Parris Thomas, Jr.
Ransford T. Torgerson, Monroe.
Vernon W. Tozer, Delta.
Thomas Tragastia, Bingham.
Charles Lee Tucker, Myton.
Parley C. Turner, Holden.
Roland Twelves, Provo.
J. Edwin Taylor, Salt Lake City.
Albert Valvleet, Eureka.
Harlow H. Vincent, Salt Lake City.
Don Crandall Wade, Ogden.
Charles A. Wagner, Magna.
Blaine J. Wall, Salt Lake City.
Wilford R. Wansberg, Murray.
Ben Wagstaff, Provo.
Stuart Walcott, Provo.
William Walkington, Helper.
E. H. Walters (Captain), Logan.
Edward H. Walters (Lieut.), Logan.

LeRoy Curtis, Payson.
James Dacollar, Salt Lake City.
Jams Dacoles, Salt Lake City.
Joseph Ladd Damron, Salt Lake City.
Jesse Daley, Salt Lake City.
Edwin Dahlquist, Sandy.
George F. Darrow, Salt Lake City.
Gilford Davidson (Lieut.) San Francisco.
Russell W. Davies, Salt Lake City.
Bryce E. Davis, Salt Lake City.
George R. Day, Bountiful.
David Day, West Layton.
Albert Dean, Beaver City.
David LeRoy Dean, Woodruff.
Fletcher G. Defors, Salt Lake City.
Charles Densley, Bluffdale.
Peter Detomo Jr., Silver City.
Roy DeWitt, Logan.
Jared Dikison, Morgan.
Thomas W. Dimond, Salt Lake City.
James M. Dodds, Price.
John Dole, Ogden.
Rural King Dorrity, Beaver City.
Ora J. Douglas, Bingham.
Charles Lionel Dover, Cedar City.
Austin Draper, Redmond.
Jabez Draper, Clearfield.
J. R. Draper, Morgan.
Earl J. Drown, Midvale.
Oliver R. Drysdale, Ogden.
C. L. Duffi, Ogden.
Arthur Duffin, Ogden.
Frederick J. Duncan, Centerville.
Edward Duhnt, Spanish Fork.
Robert Durat.
George E. Earl, Centerville.
Fred Elder, Fountain Green.
Frank J. Edwards, Beaver City.
John Abel Elen, Provo.

Charles R. Longson, Salt Lake City.
George Lord, Salt Lake City.
Wayne Loveless, Huntington.
Grant H. Lyman.
Arthur McCord, Provo.
William Jones McComb, Helper.
Seth McConkie, Vernal.
Harold McConnell, Cedar City.
Charles Snead McDonald.
Monroe McDonald, Heber City.
Douglas McFarlane, Stockton.
Alvin McKean, Salt Lake City.
Angus R. McKellar, Salt Lake City.
Robert McLoughlin, Salt Lake City.
Melvin B. McMillan, Murray.
George D. McMillan, Cleveland.
David L. McNeil, St. George.
John W. Martin, Tooele.
Samuel Martinez, Beaver City.
William Earl Mace, Bingham.
Ray Van Cott Madsen, Blackfoot, Idaho.
Harry Malone, Ogden.
Harold Manwaring.
David Arvill Margetts, Salt Lake City.
William Martin, American Fork.
William G. Marvin.
Clarence James Mason, Brigham City.
Frank Walter Medell, Huntsville.
Arrol H. Merrill, Richmond.
Joseph Hyde Merrill, Salt Lake City.
Alfred Meyer, Salt Lake City.
Daniel R. Michelsen, Salt Lake City.
Maurice K. Miles, Smithfield.
Bert R. Miller, Ogden.
Glen S. Miller, Panguitch.
W. E. Millerberg.
Charles Mills, Salt Lake City.
Francis O. Monk, Benson.
Walter A. Monson, Ogden.

Keith Warby, Manila, Utah.
Ernest H. Watkins, Salt Lake City.
Devere Watkins, Tremonton.
Ellis L. Weeter (Lieut.), Salt Lake City.
Harley Weir, Salt Lake City.
Wilford Wells, Salt Lake City.
Richard C. Werner, Salt Lake City.
Russell J. West, Pleasant Grove.
George H. Western, Deseret.
James Hughes Weston, Logan.
Mearl Wheelwright, Ogden.
Ira Bartlette Whitaker, Willard.
Charles L. White, Jr., Kanesville.
Fred T. Whitehouse, Salt Lake City.
W. A. Whiteley, Salt Lake City.
Mason Whitmore, Salt Lake City.
Clifford Williams, Greenfield.
Alden Whitbeck, Vernal.
Joseph S. Wilkes, Salt Lake City.
John E. Wilbeck, Vernal.
Raymond O. Williams, Tooele.
Joseph C. Willmore, Logan.
Herbert L. Wilson, Eureka.
Orson P. Wilson, Duchesne.
Welton Woodland, Willard.
George Woodward, Panguitch.
Joseph R. Woolley, Grantsville.
Neldon F. Worley, Wellington.
Jack P. Wright, Salt Lake City.
George L. Young, Salt Lake City.
Homer S. Young (Capt.), Ogden.
Henry M. Zabriskie, Mount Pleasant.
Walter Zabriskle, Provo.
Henry R. Zobell, Castlegate.

Millard County Progress
May 2, 1919

DESERET

The A. C. Nelson school year came to a successful close Friday, after a short and broken term. Of the eight months school was in session but four months, making it impossible to complete the work usually outlined. But all schools were equally affected by the influenza, so that new outlines were made.

Thursday night the school gave a unique and appreciated program of songs, plays and tableaux. It is generally acknowledged that the program, like the school was the best in years. There was not a hitch during the entire evening and the parents left loud in their praise of the school.

Following the plan thruout the District most of he pupils were promoted with the proviso that the work be finished next year. This will place the pupils of the county on a uniform basis with all schools in the state.

There will be several changes in the teaching force next year. Mr Gull will go to Idaho, Miss Cottom to Fillmore, Mr Western and Miss Damron to the University of Utah; Miss Philips and Miss Prisbrey will return

The Misses Cottom and Prisbrey have returned to Saint George and Miss Philips to Provo.

Mr D. J. Black has returned from Salt Lake where he went with Mr. Leon Jackson. He reports Mr. Jackson in a precarious condition yet full of courage and hope. An iron constitution and a will to live are his greatest assets.

Mr John Dawsnip has opened a new cabaret, combining this with his picture show.

The late storms and the warm weather have made the crops grow beyond belief. The trees are all in full leaf and bloom. The farmers look forward to a most prosperous season.

Friday night the Walton Stock Co. presented Rube and his Ma to a crowded and enthusiastic house. This rural comedy chuck ful of the richest humor. The audience was convulsed with laughter at the antics of Rube and Zeke. The Company handled the plot with professional care. The players go to Delta and Hinckley next week then will play in Holden, Fillmore and other towns of the county.

Saturday night the Holden Orchestra gave a dance that was largely attended. They will give another night in the same hall. The A. C. Nelson is becoming famous for its dancing, having one of the best floors in the county.

HATTON

Miss Josie Bird who has been teaching school on the WestSide returned home on Monday.

Mr and Mrs Alfred Robison arrived home from the north on Monday.

Mr and Mrs Leslie Robison of Fillmore have spent the last week here visiting with their parents, Mr and Mrs. Hyrum P ,Robison. They left for their home on Monday last.

Mr and Mrs Ennis Robison are receiving congratulations over the arrival of a fine baby boy.

Mr Spencer Lee left for Salt Lake City last Monday on business.

Word has just been received by Mrs Ellen Bird that her son Fred, who has been in the service of his Country has arrived in Salt Lake and is expected to be home soon.

Miss Sarah Bowers of Orderville arrived here from Nephi on Monday

Mr and Mrs Elmer Robison have moved down on their land north of Fillmore, which Mr Robison has recently purchased .

A large number of our town people were in attendance at the funeral of Sister Emma Watts ,which was held in Kanosh, on Tuesday last.

MRS. CROCKSWELL IS LAID AT FINAL REST.

The body of Mrs. Alice Crockswell who died at Baker Nevada on Wednesday April 23rd. 1919 from dropsy, arrived in Fillmore, on Saturday and was laid at its final resting place in our ellient city. Mrs Crockswell was born in Fillmore, in the year of 1870, she was the daughter of Mr and Mrs Marcellus Webb, the family moved to Deseret wher she spent her girlhood days and was married to Mr. Will Crockswell of that place to this union 3 daughters and a son were born, they are Mr. Leland Crockswell of California. Miss Vera Crockswell of Pocatello Idaho., Mrs. Wm. T. Brow of Brigham City, and Miss Anna Crockswell who being

(Concluded On Page 8.)

MRS CROCKSWELL IS LAID AT FINAL REST.

her youngest child was with her mother at the time of her death.

Besides her children Mrs Crockswell is survived by the following brothers and sisters, Mr Chester Webb, Mr. Clyde Webb of Brigham City. Utah, Mr. Lyman Webb of Salt Lake City, Utah, and Mrs Alfred Bellander of Baker Nevada, who were all here to attend the funeral excepting her son Leland who could be located in time to attend the funeral.. Mrs Anna Bellander and Mrs Chester Webb were also here to attend the funeral.

The funeral services here were held at the graveside Mr John Cooper pronounced the Dedication, large services were held in Baker in honor of Mrs. Crockswell before the body was shipped here for burial.

May her spirit rest in peace.

Millard County Chronicle
May 8, 1919

SUTHERLAND SEARCHLIGHTS.

The Sutherland Sunday School will observe Mother's Day with a fitting program. Everyone is invited, especially the mothers.

* * *

Miss Gertrude McCheyne and Miss White were in Sutherland last Thursday. They visited the poultry and gardens in the morning and held a meeting of the ladies in the afternoon. Everyone who came out felt well paid.

* * *

The infant son of Alvin Jensen has been very sick the past week.

* * *

W. R. Walker made a business trip to Gunnison last week, returning Monday evening.

WOODROW WRITINGS.

Still our boys are coming home! La Rue Pritchett, William Heiso and John Kozina arrived Sunday night from overseas, hale, hearty, and happy to return to a primitive community after a visit to the other side, bcause here their loves and hopes are centered, and here is home. We are proud of our boys and still prouder when they return and show their eagerness to take up the old life. "Therein true virtue lies."

* * *

Sunday next is Mother's Day all over America. The Woodrow Sunday school will have some special services commemorating the love and sacrifice of parents for their children, and all are requested to attend.

* * *

Dr. Louise Richter, who spent a summer here sveral years ago, is now traveling through Oregon under the direction of the United States Health Service, lecturing to women and girls exclusively on the social evils which Uncle Sam is at last aroused to view in their proper light, and to try to eradicate.

* * *

BIZZIE BIRD

Woodrow has a stork who is sure some enterprising bird. Last Monday morning he dropped three beautiful healthy boys at the home of Mr. Joseph Brinkerhoff. Mother and boys are doing well, and the whole community is as proud of our triplets as are the fond parents.

* * *

Mrs. Isaac Jacob was called to Salt Lake City, because of the advent of the stork who called at the home of her daughter, Mrs. Ella Dean, and left twin babies.

* * *

A cablegram from India announces the sudden death of Professor Ralph Cahoon Whitenack, who was Economic Adviser to the Maharajah Gaeknar of Baroda. Prof. Whitenack was a nephew of Dr. Tracy and the eldest son of Mrs. A. D. Whitenack, who spent the winter with the Tracys two years ago. Mr. Whitenack visited Woodrow in 1914 while en route to Japan where he occupied the chair of Economics in Tokio University for two years, leaving there to return to his work in India, (from which he had resigned) at the urgent call of the Maharajah Gaeknar, who is recognized as the most progressive ruler in the Far East, and who was earnestly striving with Mr. Whitenack's assistance to incorporate the best of our Western civilization with the effete East.

SOLDIER DAY AT HINCKLEY

On Friday, May 9th, a fine program will be held at Hinckley on Soldier Day, beginning with a parade at 10:30 combining a Soldiers' Drill. After these numbers, there will be a Basket luncheon, to which all are invited to attend; bringing your own baskets with you, and let's be sociable together. After luncheon, the early afternoon will be spent in entertainment, and at 3:30 there will be a Mass Meeting of citizens with a program of seventeen interesting and live numbers. The day will fittingly close with a grand ball at the Academy Gym. Let everybody turn out. All go. Make this celebration at Hinckley a rousing success. We owe it to the boys, and The Chronicle asks all Deltans to join with our sister town to make this affair theirs jointly with the proud parents of the Hinckley boys who saw service "over there." Go one, go all.

WEDDING BELLS

Mr. J. W. Walker, of Woodrow, announces the marriage of his daughter Phyllis to Mr. Ted Johnson, of California. The ceremony was solemnized at the home of Mr. W. J. Heinlein, at Woodrow, Monday, April 28th. The young couple are now on their honeymoon, and later will make their home in Stockton, California.

Miss Phyllis is one of the most highly esteemed young ladies of the North Tract, and made a very sweet bride. Mr. Johnson is a young man of sterling worth, and has just recently been discharged from the service; he was in the Aviation.

We are very sorry to have these young folks leave Delta, but we wish them many years of wedded bliss.

DESERET DOINGS

One more school year has come to a successful close. Never before has the A. C. Nelson labored under more adverse conditions yet terminated more successfully. Out of the year of eight months school ran but 83 days, and many of them with but few pupils.

Adjustments were made to meet these handicaps and most of the courses outlined were finished as planned by the District Superintendent.

Thursday night a rousing program was rendered. The auditorium was filled to overflowing and many were the merited words of praise given the pupils and teachers. The teachers put forth every effort to make the closing day so pleasant that the pupils will anxiously greet the first school day in the fall.

General promotions were given, which are conditional however. The pupil will begin where he leaves off and finish next year before taking up the next grade. This will prevent any serious breaks in the education of the boy or girl.

It is rumored that there will be several changes in the teaching force next year. Mr. Gull, the principal this year, has accepted a position in Idaho for the coming year, Miss Damron and Mr. Western will return to the University; Miss Cottam will go to Fillmore, while Miss Phillips and Miss Prisbey will return. It is not yet given out who the other teachers will be. The teachers of this year have done splendid work and leave an enviable record.

DELTA NEWS NOTES.

Mrs. R. R. Betz made a short visit in Delta this week.

—)(—

Ben Douglas went to Salt Lake on a business trip the first part of the week, returning Wednesday.

—)(—

Jack Kennelly and his wife arrived in Delta the first part of this week to visit with Jack's folks, Mr. and Mrs. I. V. Many, of the South Tract.

—)(—

A. L. Broderick and his family motored over to Gunnison last week for a visit with relative. They were accompanied by Miss Stella Peterson.

—)(—

'La Rue Pritchtt, who has the honor of being asked by King George if there were many more soldiers at home like him, left for Boise last Wednesday, for a visit with his folks. He will return later for Mrs. Pritchett, who was Miss Cora Heise before their marriage.

—)(—

The Florence and Perfection oil cook stoves, cheap for cash, at the Delta Furn. Store.   m1-8

The O. Z. O. Club met this week with Mrs. Sweet, and the meeting was an especially pleasant one.

—)(—

A. S. Rogers has just returned from a trip through Cache Valley and around Logan. Mr. Rogers was much impressed with the beauty of that country and especially their schools and splendid educational system.

—)(—

The O. Z. O. Club met at Mrs. T. R. Sprunt's home on Wednesday, April 30th. Mrs. Frank Beckwith was the guest of honor at this meeting, and the club gave a party for her that evening, in honor of her birthday, May 1st. The party was still going strong when the clock struck the first hour on May 1st.

—)(—

Leslie D. Pace has resigned as our Rural Mail Carrier, to be effective June 1st. In this connection, altho his duties cease June 1st., yet he receives salary to the 15th in recognition of the good service he has rendered in that position; he began July 24th, three years ago, and has not missed a trip in that time. His work has been so satisfactory that

this little bonus is given in appreciation.

—)(—

Mr. and Mrs. Isaac Jacob of Woodrow have moved into town, having bought the W. L. Allred property.

—)(—

Hugh Hilton was a Delta visitor Tuesday and gave the Chronicle a pleasant call.

—)(—

Born to Mr. and Mrs. John H. Jensen a baby girl on Wednesday morning early. John wears a smile that looks much like a million dollars.

—)(—

Mrs. Kelley of Deseret, mother of Virge Kelley, had a serious fall this Wednesday, dislocating her shoulder and her hip. Dr. Hamilton was called in.

—)(—

J. W. Rocklidge, receiver of the Alpha Farms, and D. F. Drayton, of Gustin, Gillette & Drayton, attorneys of Salt Lake, were in Delta this week on business.

—)(—

Mrs. Bertha N. Wells sold her Delta home to Mrs. Beckwith, and

has gone to Salt Lake City to prepare for taking a position with Westminster College. Mrs. Wells was accompanied by her two sons.

—)(—

Mrs. Will Killpack came to Delta Sunday, her father bringing her over from Manti as far as Scipio, at which point Will met them and brought Mrs. Killpack to Delta. They are building a new house in the Lyman addition.

—)(—

The Board of Education met in

Delta Tuesday on important business connected with the Consolidated A. C. Nelson school. Also at that meeting matters pertaining to the use of the Hinckley grade school were discussed and decided upon.

—)(—

Will Killpack has added a skilled mechanic to his force at the garage, namely, M. O. Porter. Mr. Porter has seen experience in Kansas, and is competent to render the very best of service.

—)(—

The Brass Band was out in full force to meet Mr. and Mrs. Jerome

Cook, when they returned from Salt Lake Tuesday evening. Then there was a parade up and down the main streets, the band playing at playing, followed by a string of Fords, and at the very end, seated in a trailer, rode the young couple, while big signs on the sides of their handsome equipage proclaimed to the world that they were "Just Married."

—)(—

Big May Dance given by the "5 O'clock Boys", Saturday night, May 10th, Woodrow Hall. Latest music; Superba Syncopated Orchestra.

Millard County Chronicle
May 15, 1919

WEDDING BELLS

Le Grande Law and Miss Viola Turner left for Salt Lake City Tuesday evening to be married in the Salt Lake Temple May 15th.

Le Grande is the son of Mr. and Mrs R. J. Law, a young man of sterling worth, bound to rise in business to a foremost place in our community. The bride is the daughter of Mr. and Mrs. Lorenzo Turner, one of our most popular and well-esteemed young ladies. We congratulate Le Grande, and we wish the young bride much hapiness.

WOODROW WRITINGS.

John Kozina, who arrived from "Overseas", is now basking in the sunlight of California, whither he has gone to visit with his relatives.

* * *

Mr. Crowl has moved his family from Delta to Woodrow for the summer.

* * *

Mrs. Wells of California is visiting with her daughter, Mrs. Irvin Greathouse.

* * *

SUGARVILLE SIFTINGS.

Mr. and Mrs. J. B. Seams and daughter Pauline, and Mrs. O. W. Anderson and Mr. Abbott motored to Salt Lake City last week where they spent the week end on business and pleasure. They reported a very enjoyable trip. While there Pauline had an operation performed for the removal of her tonsils, which the specialist said was the cause for her poor health the last few months.

* * *

Mrs. J. S. Barker will entertain the F. T. Club at her home next Wednesday afternoon.

STORK ARRIVES

Born to Mr. and Mrs. John Alvey on May 7th, a fine baby girl. Our congratulations and best wishes go to John and Mrs. Alvey.

OAK CITY NEWS ITEMS

It is a general rule that you will find in the Millard County Chronicle the "Sugarville Siftings", the "Hinckley Happenings", or the "Delta Doings", and nothing from Oak City. We wish to break the silence and have a put in from Oak City occasionally, since there is something in our town once in a while besides an eclipse of the sun or a change of the moon.

* * *

The biggest events of the season have been the return of some of our overseas soldiers; Clinton Dutson, who belonged to an artillery unit, and Jack Allredge and Willard Christenson of the ninety-first division, infantry. Dutson was in the battles of Chateau Thierry, St. Mihiel, Verdun, and the Argonne. Allredge and Christenson fought in the Argonne and gave the Hun a final kick out of Belgium. Jack thinks he could have brought home a few medals if the war had lasted a few minutes longer, as he was sharpening his bayonet in preparation to make a trip over the top at 11:20 the day the armistice was signed. The boys were all given a rousing welcome and dance the following night after their arrival. After the dance the younger set indulged in an early breakfast. Our little town was fortunate in not losing a single man in the big scrap altho six of them were in actual battle. They are all home now but three who are still with the A. E. F.

* * *

Clare Walker, who has been teaching school the past winter in Blanding, is here visiting with friends and relatives.

Gus Faust, Willis Lyman and Marvin Lyman, who recently arrived from overseas. The Lyman boys were residents of Oak City at one time, as was Gus, also, in a way, so we were glad of a chance to do them honor.

* * *

This week there is a number of people making the trip to Manti on the Deseret stake temple excursion.

* * *

We easily went over the top with the Victory Loan, and could have reported so before now but thru some mistake the blanks did not reach here until the last week of the drive. Our allotment was five thousand five hundred.

* * *

Mother's Day was duly observed, and especially by the Sunday school, where a very appropriate program was given.

* * *

Last week the corrals and sheds on Lewis Somers' farm were completely destroyed by fire. The fire also consumed all of his harnesses and two setting hens. It originated from the usual cause; a small boy and some matches.

* * *

The infant son of Mrs. Mamie Wells is reported to be very ill. His mother is in Hawaii where she went to meet her son Dick, who expects to return with her from his mission. Mrs. Wells reports that they have to "line up" and wait their turn to get passage back to the U. S.

* * *

Lawrence Anderson, the son of Franklin Anderson, died on the eleventh of this month from what was thought to be an abcess in one of his lungs.

* * *

* * *

Mrs. Fred S. Lyman is leaving for her home in San Juan County this week. She and her husband spent the winter here; he having returned home some time ago.

* * *

Clinton Dutson has gone to St. George in quest of his wife who has been living there with her mother during his sojourn in the army. Lem Roper also made the trip to St. George last week with a bridal party from Leamington. Lem and his big Paige are an ideal combination for such a party; a trial will convince anyone.

* * *

There was an enjoyable social last Saturday, given in honor of

The stork made two visits here recently. One was to the home of Mr. and Mrs. Ray Finlinson and the other to Mr. and Mrs. Jos. L. Anderson. All concerned are doing well and appear to be happy also in spite of the fact that both the new arrivals are girls.

* * *

The crops in Oak City and vicinity are fairly promising with the exception of the alfalfa, which was damaged slightly by the frost and is being held back by the weevil, but in view of the fact that we have promise of a plentiful supply of water, the next crop should be better than the average. Our fruit prospects are very favorable as are also the garden crops. Spraying of apple trees for the codling moth will begin this week.

BADLY BURNED

Miss Irma Cropper was quite badly burned by gasoline Wednesday afternoon while washing clothes. She had the boiler of clothes on the stove, at about a boil, and attempted to pour some gasoline in, when the heat vaporized it instantly, and the direct fire from the stove set it ablaze. The bottle of gasoline dropped to the floor, setting fire to her stockings and clothes. Her cries for help brought people out of the Kelley Hotel to her aid, and the flames were extinguished, but not until she was badly burned about the feet, leg and arms. That she escaped even at that is miraculous.

Her parents were informed of the accident and came in and took her home Wednesday afternoon. Miss Cropper has been employed at the Kelley Hotel for some time.

DELTA NEWS NOTES.

Cyril Cluff will succeed Leslie D. Pace as rural mail carrier.

—)(—

Mr. and Mrs. Carl Steele arrived in Delta Wednesday from Escalante.

—)(—

You can always buy something good to eat at Baker's Bakery.

—)(—

O. L. Crawford, of Deseret paid this office a pleasant visit last week.

—)(—

J. H. Jenkins was a Salt Lake visitor this wek.

—)(—

Old papers for sale at the Chronicle. 25 cents for 100.

—)(—

Mr. Leonard Sprowl stopped off in Delta Wednesday, en route to Washington, D. C.

—)(—

Miss Lucins Jimpson went to Salt Lake this week to continue her music studies.

—)(—

W. L. Jones of Fillmore was in town Wednesday, a guest of P. H. Robison.

—)(—

Dan Kelly has succeeded Ernest Goddard as salesman on the road for Scowcroft & Sons of Ogden.

—)(—

Do you want a good bright light? Get a Coleman Gasoline, or Rayo coal oil and common lamps at the Delta Furniture Store.   m-15-22

—)(—

Dr. Charles' office in Hinckley has been moved to first door west of Frank Wright's residence. Hours as usual, Tuesdays and Fridays, 3 to 6.

—)(—

If you want to buy a Diamond Ring, remember that you get that square deal at Landow's, as he guarantees quality and price.   m-15

Miss Maud Heise left for Salt Lake Monday to finish her business course. She will graduate in June and will take a position in Salt Lake or Delta.

—)(—

A lot of small house furnishing conveniences will soon be in place. Call and see them at the Delta Furniture Store.   m15-22

—)(—

Everybody get ready for our big SOLDIER'S NUMBER of the Chronicle. We expect to put out a number devoted entirely to the boys from Millard county.

—)(—

Miller Hall of the South Tract made a hurried business call to Rupert, Idaho. Our readers will remember that his brother, Jim, is now living there.

—)(—

Dr. J. J. Buswell, Ophthalmic Specialist of Salt Lake, will be at the Hotel Ward, Delta, Monday, May 21. No charge for testing eyes. References. Glasses are worn for health as well as vision.   m-15

—)(—

Wallace M. Scott, from the National Copper Bank, in Salt Lake City, is now employed in the Delta State Bank. Mr. Scott will take the place of Mr. Fernly, who has returned to Salt Lake.

—)(—

It is of interest to our local readers that the Literary Digest under date of May 3 on page 79 gives a large photo view of the beautiful home of Capt. J. R. De Lamar, owner of the Delta Sugar Factory.

—)(—

Mrs. May Berger has returned from spending a few months at Placentia, California, and will work her farm again this year. Mrs. Berger is a good manager and has made an enviable success on her farm, getting large crops and good returns.

—)(—

Mrs. Walter Moffit has returned to Delta. Walter and his younger brought George Moffit home Wednesday evening from Salt Lake, where he has been very ill with rheumatism. They intend to stay in Delta now. We hope George will regain his health soon.

—)(—

Work has commenced on a new house for Marion Killpack in the same block with J. E. Works. When built in, according to plan, this unit will be the most beautiful in town, with winding paths, shrubbery, and buildings laid out in a well designed display, in perfect accord with Delta when it grows to 3,000.

—)(—

Mr. W. F. Rimington from the North Tract came into Delta Tuesday on his way north to Tooele, where his father is quite sick, necessitating his presence. The editor became well acquainted with Mr. Rimington's brother-in-law at Oakley, Idaho, Wm. N. Garvin.

—)(—

J. A. Townsend gives us an idea of what building is going on at the present moment by the following contract he has under way for homes: J. E. Works, Will Killpack, Mr. Gifford, Marion Killpack, J. A. Townsend, and A. S. Rose.

This represents only the contracts held by one contractor—in all there are about two score of buildings on which the work is already under way, or the contract let, work to follow.

DEATH OF MRS. SIEVERT.

Mrs. Dorothy Sievert, the wife of station agent J. C. Sievert, passed away after a prolonged sickness, on last Sunday morning. Mrs. Sievert had long been suffering with pulmonary tuberculosis, and her death was not unexpected.

Mrs. Sievert was born in Cissina Park, Illinios, and is survived by her mother and sister, now in that State, and by a sister in Iowa, and also by Will Sievert, the son, who was called from San Diego to the bedside of his dying mother. The son will go to the Philippines as an aviator for the Government.

The remains were taken to Denver, accompanied by Mr. Sievert, for cremation.

Mr. Sievert has the sympathy of all in his hour of sorrow.

OAK CITY NEWS ITEMS

Last Friday Thomas Talbot's little seven year-old girl was playing with an old twenty two calibre rifle, when it went off, the bullet entering the face of the little four year old girl, who was standing nearby, just below the cheek bone. Dr. Hamilton was called but could not determine just how serious it was. She was taken to Salt Lake Sunday morning by her mother and brother Clifford, who just returned the day before from a two years mission to the northwestern states.

* * *

Conference visitors to Salt Lake are back with the exception of Emma Anderson, who has gone for a visit to Idaho and Oregon.

Oak City has had a number of visitors the last week. Mr. Harris of Beaver stopped off on his way home from France, being entertained by Miss Silva Lovell.

* * *

Lafe Olson has had a visit from two of his sisters from Idaho.

* * *

Joseph Dutson, wife, mother and sister of Idaho are here visiting with friends and relatives. He expects to go on a mission to California next month.

* * *

Mrs. Gus Faust is visiting her mother a few days.

* * *

Hilda Christenson and Norma Anderson are home from a trip to Levan.

* * *

Mandy Roper and Margaret Nielson have gone to Provo to attend summer school at the Brigham Young University.

* * *

The ball team met with a severe reverse at Hinckley last Saturday. They claim that the wind and a poor diamond did not make them feel very much at home.

DELTA NEWS NOTES.

Rosell's Jazz Kings will furnish the music at the dance in Delta Friday night. Come early and stay late.

—)(—

Wallace Jones bought out the vulcanizing plant of N. R. Greenwood, and is now equipped and ready for all kinds of vulcanizing. In the building opposite the Cooper Block.

—)(—

K. D. Hardy, representative of the Home Investment Co. of Salt Lake was a Delta visitor on business last week, appraising a mortgage loan for his company.

—)(—

Mr. Bowers, who has been in Delta the past few months doing carpenter work and contracting, has returned to his home in San Diego.

—)(—

Wm. J. Strickley bought the S. C. McCormick farm due east of the Woodrow store last week. Mr. Strickley will move from his present farm to this new purchase. The deal was consummated by Fred Rock and Frank Beckwith.

—)(—

The friends of Joe Sampson will be glad to know that he is advertising manager of the Denver Rock Drill Co., in Denver, a very big and successful firm. Joe writes us that he is doing well, likes his work immensely, and is very well content.

—)(—

W. G. Emmett is back in Delta, having disposed of his Mills holdings as well as of his farm on the North Tract. Mr. Emmett has in mind the erection of a hotel on the corner west of the Bluebird, and will make announcement of his plans as soon as matured.

—)(—

Ben Douglas took Mrs. Douglas to the Holy Cross Hospital in Salt Lake Sunday, where she was found to be in a very serious condition, too o' ... en to be operated on. Her ... ere ... still precarious. Just as ... we have word that ... improvement.

... that the ... came into Delta ... evening, on one of his returns trips back up to the city from an excursion south on business connected with his government work. As he travels much, he has many opportunities for observation, but no where does he see as much building activity as at Delta.

—)(—

Is it generally known that Juab County has the second largest mine production in the state. In 1915 Salt Lake County lead with over $65,000,000, and Juab followed next with $8,933,104. The Park City district came next, closely followed by Tooele.

—)(—

Reserved seats for "THE HEART OF HUMANITY", June 24 and 25, will be placed on sale Sunday, June 15. Telephone, write, or call at the ticket office for reservations. Tickets will be held on request until 8:30 on night of the performance.

—)(—

Mrs. T. R. Sprunt returned from Salt Lake Sunday, with her two little children.

—)(—

L. E. Perrin has received a car load of shorts and bran. Call early and leave your orders.

DESERET DOINGS

The Misses Ora and Hulda Hales are home from Provo where they have been in attendance at the Brigham Young University.

* * *

Dudley Crafts, a student at the A. C. college, Logan, is home for the summer vacation.

* * *

L. R. Cropper, who recently visited his son Edgar at his home in Midvale, extended his visit to Salt Lake City and returned this week accompanied by his grandson, who will spend some time with his grandparents on the farm.

* * *

Miss Angie Harmon, one of Holden's most popular belles, and an esteemed teacher of the Hinckley schools last year, and George Cahoon of this place, were married in Salt Lake City this week. The young couple were escorted to an early train Tuesday morning by a few very concerned friends who, along with their blessings, "much joy", and advice, freely showered with the time-honored rice in quantities requisite to the future happiness of the pair.

* * *

Mrs. Edna Johnson of Gridley, California, formerly Miss Justinson of this place, was the guest of Miss Norma Moody for a week. Mrs. Johnson will visit in other Utah towns before returning home.

Miss Nova Cropper will also attend summer school at the same institution, leaving late in the week for the city.

* * *

Mr. and Mrs. A. D. Ryan, son Kelly, and baby Florence, left for their home in Salt Lake City Monday night. Mrs. Ryan has been visiting the past month with her sister, Mrs. Jos. W. Damron, while Mr. Ryan was on a business trip which took him to some remote but interesting points thru the southern part of the state and Arizona.

BIG FAMILY REUNION

The Abbott Family Reunion held at Sutherland last week was probably the greatest social event in the history of that village. It was scheduled for the 26th, 27th and 28th of June and was staged at the home of M. A. Abbott. One hundred cards were sent out, most of them double invitations.

The guests began to arrive on the 22nd from distant parts and each day after until the 26th when more than 100 were present. Tables were built under the trees with a seating capacity of more than fifty persons. Three settings were necessary to accommodate the crowd; 134 people were fed (not counting infants). The banquet was at once substantial, sumptous and delicious, consisting of meats, bread, pastry, new potatoes, fruits, cheese, butter and other things that go with them, lemonade and ice cream.

In the afternoon a program was held at the school-house, consisting of congregational singing (led by David Abbott of Mes??, Nevada, a young giant weighing ?? pounds), a speech of welcome by La??nce Abbott, a speech and historical sketch of the family by M. A. Abbott, songs and solos by several female members of the family, creditably rendered. The program as a whole was very entertaining and much appreciated, but probably the most interesting talk was made by Israel Abbott, a young "devil dog marine" just returned from France," spending his honeymoon with his beautiful bride at the homes of his brothers in Sutherland and Delta. He related his experiences in the war where he fought at Chateau Thierry, Soisons, St. Mihiel, Belleu Wood and Champaigne. He bears a large ragged scar on the shoulder and neck where he was struck by a piece of shrapnel.

Many of the company visited the theatre and dance at Delta in the evening.

Friday the 27th the whole party took an excursion over the North Tract, returning for luncheon served in picnic style in the afternoon. Nearly all went to the flume and disported themselves in bathing suits. The visitors were surprised and pleased and pronounced the bathing excellent. In the evening again many visited the show and Dance in Delta.

On Saturday the guests assembled and partook of a another picnic luncheon, and in the afternoon went on an excursion to Hinckley and on west where the drainage machines were working and listened to M. A. Abbott explaining drainage matters in Millard county. Returning, the party went to Delta and visited the sugar factory. They were much pleased with what they saw and with the courtesy and interesting talks of their guide, Mr. Stokes. Returning to the home of Mr. John Steele, they had a lawn frolic, ate a delicious lunch, listened to a program of songs and music, said their goodbyes and separated about 10 o'clock, tired but happy, some taking trains for their homes, others waiting until morning taking autos; all claimed to have had a very enjoyable time.

At a meeting of the heads of families held on Friday a family organization was formed to promote fraternal acquaintance and good will and to expedite work along certain lines in which the whole family is interested.

Several were interested and impressed with the possibilities in the Delta country and expressed a determination to come and cast their lots with us.

Another family gathering will be held two years from now at some place to be selected by the executive committe.

LYNNDYL LINES

The marriage of Mr. Reeve Richardson of Lynndyl and Miss Thresa Brough of Nephi occurred last week. Mr. Richardson is employed by the land company here. They are at home in the Walker building.

* * *

Mr. and Mrs. Charley Gunn are receiving congratulations on the arrival of a daughter, who came to their home last Monday.

* * *

Mr. and Mrs. R. E. Robinson of Hinckley visited with their daughter, Mrs. G. L. Kelly, last Saturday and Sunday.

* * *

Mr. G. W. Sudbury has returned from a trip to St. George and southern points.

* * *

Mr. Ernest Scannell has returned home after spending eight months overseas. His brother Carl is expected home soon.

* * *

The Kemp Jass orchestra of Eureka furnished music for the last two Wednesday night dances. Everybody reported a pleasant time.

The Princess Theatre has been taken over by Mr. Geo. L. Kelly and Fred Burrows. They have installed a new Simplex motion picture machine. They assure good shows for the future.

* * *

The bazaar given by the Relief Society here last week proved to be a huge success. Refreshments and dancing finished the day.

* * *

Mrs. William Trimble has her sister, Mrs. Brunson of Fillmore, visiting with her.

* * *

Mrs. P. T. Hall and daughter Ethel have gone to Michigan to spend the summer.

* * *

Mrs. B. H. Ogden is visiting relatives and friends in Nephi.

* * *

The Bishopric was again reorganized here last Sunday evening. Albert Hurst was appointed Bishop to succeed Mr. E. A. Jacobs who with his family are making their home in Provo.

The Lynndyl baseball team will play in Nephi on July 4. We wish them success.

* * *

Mr. and Mrs. Paul Shaeffer have returned home after a pleasant visit in the East.

* * *

Mrs. Frank Belliston has gone to Nephi to spend a few weeks.

* * *

Mr. and Mrs. Frank C. Johnson left July 1st to make their home in California. They will be accompanied by Mrs. Johnson's parents, Mr. and Mrs. Alfred Johnson.

* * *

Mr. Thos. Reed is spending a short vacation in California.

* * *

A number of Lynndyl people attended conference at Deseret last Sunday.

* * *

Mrs. M. J. Penrose has left for Los Angeles, Cal., to join her husband, who is working there.

* * *

Dr. W. P. Murray left this week for a short vacation to the Pacific Coast.

WOODROW WRITINGS.

Preaching service Sunday morning at 11 a. m. All invited.

* * *

Miss Bracewell is home from school in California.

* * *

Mrs. Heffelman and her daughter, Ethel, accompanied by William Heise motored to Provo for the 4th of July celebration.

* * *

Messrs. Hugo Thompson, Burton and Joseph Alward, and Lawrence Titus spent the Fourth of July in Salt Lake City.

* * *

The Webster family and Dr. Tracy motored to Tayloraville, Utah, for a reunion of the Webster family over the Fourth, returning Sunday p. m., and report a fine time.

* * *

Much sympathy is expressed for Mr. and Mrs. Jensen of Sugarville for the loss of their infant son last Monday morning.

* * *

Messrs. Brown Sanford and Harold Steele met with an accident which caused their car to overturn Sunday p. m. Mr. Sanford escaped a very serious injury by the forethought and agility of Mr. Steele, who altho being thrown from the car himself, sprang to his feet and caught the car with his hands in such a way as to prevent pressure upon Brown's leg, which was pinned down by the car, thus preventing the severing of the Popliteal artery and allowing him to escape with a few minor cuts.

* * *

The Church meeting at the Spillway was well attended by Woodrow representatives Wednesday.

* * *

We advise all persons to paint any insect bites with iodine immediately, as the Pahvant Plague is still prevalent, and bids fair to give more trouble this year than any previous season.

* * *

The Jolly Stitchers will be entertained at the Hall next Friday by Mrs. Kinn and Dr. Tracy.

DIED

Mrs. Christine Eickler of Abraham died Sunday and was buried from the Presbyterian Church on Monday at 3 p. m. Mrs. Eickler was born in Russia and came here recently from Idaho with her husband and children and has been living on the Lewis and Schroeppel place. She had been a victim of tuberculosis for years, but was only seriously ill for a few days before her death. She was 63 years of age.

SUTHERLAND SEARCHLIGHTS.

Sutherland is going to celebrate the 24th of July with a program in the morning and sports in the afternoon. Everyone bring their lunch and have a good time with us. Program to be at 10:30 a. m.

Songs by congregation.
Prayer by Chaplain M. A. Abbott.
Quartette by Mrs. Jensen and Co.
Oration by M. M. Steele Jr.
Violin Solo by Jos. J. Miller.
Reading by Margaret Simons.
Speech by "Utah".
Song by Mrs. Frank Hunt and Co.
Short Talk on Pioneers by Simeon Walker.

W. R. Walker and family with a crowd of young people went to Oak City canyon for the 4th.

* * *

Most of our citizens spent the 4th at Hinckley enjoying the shade.

* * *

Any Sutherland Farm Bureau members wishing fruit this year please leave orders with H. G. Ottley.

* * *

Miss Louisa Jones of Sutherland and Stanley Lovell of Oak City are to be married at the Manti temple Wednesday, July 9th. Stanley returned home from France, June 29th. The young couple expect to locate in Oak City. We all wish them a long and happy life.

LYNNDYL LINES

Mr. and Mrs. D. E. Carter and Mrs. J. Lunn came down from Provo and spent a few days with friends.

* * *

Mr. and Mrs. J. J. McCarty have returned home after spending two months in New Jersey and Pennsylvania.

* * *

Guy C. Campbell has returned home after spending some months overseas.

* * *

The Imperial Jazz orchestra of Nephi furnished music for last Wednesday night dance. The music was great. Each member of the orchestra was a real musician, and everybody had the time of their life.

* * *

Mrs. Roy Love has returned home after spending a few days visiting her parents in Murray.

* * *

Mr. and Mrs. Robert Robinson Jr. and Mr. and Mrs. Marion L. Bishop of Hinckley motored to Lynndyl and spent the week-end with Mr. and Mrs. George L. Kelly.

DELTA NEWS NOTES.

Vennis Mickelsen had her hand caught in a gas engine, mashing the tips of her fingers. Dr. Charles, the physician in attendance, dressed the hand, but may find it necessary later to amputate the fingers.

—) (—

Mr. George Bishop, of Garrison, Utah, writes us that if we will visit his valley, he will show us the traces of a people who lived there thousands of years ago. That would be very interesting, and in as much as we can't go over there, we invite Mr. Bishop to write us items of interest about his community.

Milton R. Noble of Springville has bought property in the Abraham district, having purchased the forty of Mr. Hale there south of Hickman's, of which there is a crop of beets. Mr. Noble sold his ranch at Paul, Idaho, and comes to this section, where the outlook for beets is very attractive and the future promising.

—) (—

George M. Frank, with his wife and little daughter, is visiting in Delta with his sister, Mrs. Lena Faust. Mr. Frank has just returned from France where he has been in the service. Returning on the same boat with him

was an American soldier with his French wife, and a brand new baby, which arrived on the voyage home, so they named it after the big boat, Zeppelin, Zeppelin Louise.

—) (—

W. H. Pace and his two sons, Carlos and Frank, left Delta Monday last for a trip into and through the Yellowstone National Park. This will be a trip of interest, and gives them all a fine experience to be well remembered. George Palmer of Cedar City is helping in the garage during their absence.

F. L. Copening was in Delta this week, on one of his frequent business trips.

—) (—

A good choice in bed springs, mattresses and cots of all sizes and prices at the Delta Furniture store. j17-24

—) (—

Ben Eldredge, State Inspector, is in town, with Dean Peterson, inspecting the dairies.

—) (—

Dr. Charles, Mrs. Charles and Miss Crystal Crane made a flying trip to Salt Lake City Wednesday morning, returning Wednesday evening.

—) (—

The Misses Vida Anderson and Lorena Law, and Mesdames Harry Aller and J. W. Thurston, left Delta Saturday for a sojourn in California.

—) (—

Pvt. Ed Pearson, of the 66th Engineers, has arrived at Camp Mills, Long Island, from duties overseas. Ed will visit in Nebraska before returning to Delta.

J. A. Melville, Sr. came down from Salt Lake City to attend the annual meeting of the Delta State Bank.

—) (—

Rent a vacuum cleaner from the Delta Lumber & Hardware Co. ju10tf

—) (—

Mr. and Mrs. Lorenzo Christensen are the proud parents of a baby boy, who arrived July 10th.

—) (—

Dr. H. L. Charles has successfully fitted the editor with a pair of eye glasses, relieving an eye strain of long standing.

—) (—

A new china closet, kitchen cabinet, library table, center table, rocker and almost anything that will help to please the housewife, at the Delta Furniture Co. jy17-24

—) (—

C. A. Vorwaller of Abraham was a Delta visitor Monday. Charlie reports good returns from his dairying business.

—) (—

Drink your soda from sterilized glasses. The first fountain in Utah to adopt this new long looked for innovation. Delta Blue Bird. ju10

—) (—

In Sunday's Tribune was a picture of the Shelley Gun club, and among these far-famed crack shots was the mug of our erstwhile citizen Norman Lambert.

Mr. Ted Olson has moved his wife and family here from Richfield, and they will make their home in the Eccles house. Mr. Olson comes here to take a position with the Consolidated Wagon & Machine Co.

—) (—

Mrs. A. C. Harned of Lompoc, California, is here visiting with her son, L. C. Harned, of the North Tract. The prospects for big beet and alfalfa crops look first rate to Mrs. Harned, and already she has become a booster for this country.

—) (—

Take our advice, and take along a sack when you go shopping. Then you can stow your victuals in that, carry it home in one hand and have your other hand free in case of accident. For accidents will happen. (Phil Purdy take notice.)

—) (—

The Lincoln Theater has arranged to have Paramount Artcraft Pictures every Sunday evening beginning August 3rd. This is a high class production, giving the Sunday evening theater goer just what is exactly suitable to every taste for that night. These pictures always please—art of the highest order, with subject matter of equally high standard.

—) (—

Buy your coal now. Next winter when delivery can't be made, and when coal is several dollars higher in price—but that's not the time to buy. Buy now. Summer prices. Buy now and store. Bonneville Lumber Co. j26tf

---

Millard County Chronicle
August 7, 1919

WEDDING BELLS

John A. Miller and Miss Olive Cook left this forenoon for Fillmore to be married. Congratulations! We wish the young couple all happiness.

WOODROW WRITINGS.

Mr. and Mrs. Jerome Tracy left last week in their car for Philadelphia and New York where they will visit relatives for a few months. Mrs. John DeLapp and children accompanied them as far as Evanston, where they took the train for Iowa, where Mrs. DeLapp will visit her sister for a few weeks.

Word from Fred and Mrs. Rock, who left last month in their car for California, indicates that cheap land in the Golden State has some undesirable characteristics as regards soil, water or climate, and that land desirable from every point of view is too high-priced for ordinary mortals. Rocks are now looking over the country around Los Angeles and may go on to Arizona. If you can't find anything you like better, we will try and hunt you up a garden spot in Millard.

LYNNDYL LINES

Misses Veda and Cora Vest of Provo spent the week here as guests of relatives and friends.

Mr. and Mrs. Dan Rogerson and children have gone to Beaver for a visit.

Miss Erma Romney of Alberta, Canada, visited her sister, Mrs. Albert Hurst, then continued on to Dixie for a visit there.

Mrs. G. A. Neerman and children have returned home after a two-month visit in California.

Mrs. Clarence Mortensen has gone to Hinckley to visit with her mother.

Wedding bells have chimed the past week relieving the midsummer dullness in social circles.

Miss Bessie Greathouse and Spencer Nelson of Leamington were quietly married last week. A wedding dance was given them in Leamington the other Wednesday night.

Mr. Roy Love and Miss Ruth Roberts of Mona were married Monday at Salt Lake. A reception was given them at the home of his mother in Salt Lake.

Mr. Otto Stewart of Deseret and Miss Ruby Neilson were quietly married in Nephi Saturday.

The latter two couples will make make their homes in Lynndyl. We join in wishing them all a long and happy life.

The new post office building is nearing completion.

Mr. Geo. L. Kelly is home suffering from injuries in the left side received in a baseball game here a week ago.

Mrs. William Trimble is a Salt Lake visitor this week.

Mrs. Myron Vest, who has been very ill the past month, left for Nephi this morning to visit with her mother and also receive further medical aid.

Mr. and Mrs. Lloyd Hubbard and children returned home a few days ago after a month's visit with relatives in Oregon.

Mrs. Janet Lynn and children, who have been making their home in Provo the past eight months have returned again to Lynndyl.

NORMAN I. BLISS DIES

Norman I. Bliss of Hinckley, Utah, died in the L. D. S. Hospital last Monday, following injuries received on his farm. A few days previous Norman was moving his hay derrick to a new location, and in doing so, left the hay fork sticking in the stack. When the derrick had gone forward to the end of the rope, as it was pulled taut, the fork came out of the stack, and swinging forward on an arc, hit him. One of the sharp tines entered his side, and punctured his intestines, what was known at the time as a serious accident. He was sent to the hospital in Salt Lake, but death followed the accident.

Norman Bliss, or "Norm" as he was always called, was one of our best and most respected men. Liked by all, he had a character and ways that won him firm and lasting friendship. He could always be entrusted with business or responsibility. He was a man whose business honor was unquestioned—his word was binding, and always lived up to. His loss will be severely felt in his comunity. He was the kind of man whose influence for the best was so pronounced that he should have been spared for a long life. The community sympathizes deeply with the stricken family.

Norman I. Bliss was born in southern Utah, and early came to Hinckley. He lost his first wife. Later he married Hattie Theobald. He leaves a large family, being survived by his children by his former wife, and as well, by the children of his widow. For years he ran the Woodruff Ranch near Abraham, for the owners of it then, who were Cincinnati people. His own farm, or rather, two farms, lies in Hinckley. He was a man in comfortable circumstances, with an excellent future before him.

We extend our fullest sympathy to to the family.

SUGARVILLE SIFTINGS

Miss Tora Jäderholm is down from Salt Lake visiting her parents.

Iver Iverson and wife and little girl drove down from Ephraim and visited with his mother a few days last week. On their return trip they were accompanied by Mrs. Iverson and daughter Ethel and Alvin Iverson who will visit with friends and relatives at Ephraim for a week or ten days.

Mr. Chelson purchased a new Ford car last week.

Miss Blanche Rimington is visiting with friends and relatives at Salt Lake City. From there she will go on to Idaho for a visit.

The Friendship Club held its annual business meeting and election of officers at the hall last Wednesday. The following officers were elected: Mrs. Fred Ashby, President; Mrs. Fred Barben, Vice-President; Mrs. Pearl Baker, Secretary; Miss Victoria Miller, Treasurer; Mrs. J. B. Seams and Mrs. Hibbard as two of the directors.

The next meeting of the Thimble Club will be next Wednesday with Mrs. Miller and daughter Victoria as hostesses.

Mr. Sturnum, brother-in-law of Claire Dale is very sick with the Pahvant Valley Plague.

SUTHERLAND SEARCHLIGHTS.

Miss Florence Moore of Provo is here visiting her sister Mrs. R. E. Wolfe.

A bundle shower was given Mr. and Mrs. A. P. Austin by neighbors and friends last Wednesday eve. A very enjoyable time was had by all.

M. M. Steele, Jr., and W. R. Walker held meetings in Oak City and Leamington, Sunday, discussing the road bond issue.

Mrs. M. A. Abbott was very ill Sunday, but seems to slowly improve.

The ladies of our community regret that Miss White, our home demonstrator, is leaving us. Those who were working with her and following her instructions, were receiving great benefits. Miss White's friends all know that she does not think the things published in that article, much less say them. We wish her all success in whatever place she chooses to go.

The Relief Society met with Mrs. Della Lloyd on Tuesday, holding meeting and serving refreshments afterward.

The Keelers are building a new home.

OASIS ODDITIES

Peter Peterson has arrived home from duty overseas.

* * *

Mrs. Ada Williams has returned to her home in Salt Lake after an extended visit with her parents.

* * *

Born, to Mr. and Mrs. Cecil Cahoon, a ten pound boy.

* * *

J. E. Hawly and son Rollo have gone to Salt Lake. There Rollo has undergone a serious operation.

* * *

Mr. and Mrs. Betenger have moved to Milford.

* * *

G. L. Huff is expected home Sunday from Pioche, Nevada.

* * *

Mr. and Mrs. J. E. Blackburn entertained as their guests, Sunday 'eve., Mr. and Mrs. Theodore Christensen of Delta.

* * *

Ward Moody of Hinckley was an Oasis visitor Monday.

OAK CITY NEWS ITEMS

Perhaps the biggest event of the season in Oak City was the Soldiers' Day celebration held on Tuesday, the 19th, in honor of the boys who had returned. Martin Snerriff wears a gold chevron, having been gassed in service. Eldon Anderson made the responses for the boys and gave some very interesting experiences.

* * *

The Rawlinson family gave a reunion in the Amusement Hall on the 20th, with attendance of three generations.

* * *

Don Anderson made the trip to Beaver last week to take down his brother Eldon and wife.

* * *

Miss Eva Lovell is home from summer school at the B. Y. U.

* * *

A baby was born to Mrs. Lewis Somers on the 22nd.

SUTHERLAND SEARCHLIGHTS.

Mr. and Mrs. J. E. Reed and daughters Catherine and Lucile of Salt Lake visited with H. J. Reed and family of Sutherland last week. They made the trip in their car.

* * *

The new officers of the "Jolly Stitchers" are: President, Mrs. W. R. Walker; 1st vice pres., Mary E. Iles; 2nd vice pres., Mrs. Geo. Webster; secretary, Mrs. Irvin Greathouse; treas., Mrs John Wind.

* * *

Beth, the 10-year old child of V. C. Waddoups of Milford, fell from a horse Tuesday, dislocating her elbow. She is stopping at the home of H. J. Reed this summer, and is a ... Mrs. Reed.

* * *

The Jolly Stitchers met with Mrs. Walker last Friday afternoon with a good attendance and a pleasant time was spent. A party will be given for Mrs. S. H. Thompson Friday afternoon, Aug. 29, at the home of Mrs. Norris.

DELTA NEWS NOTES.

ALL SCHOOLS of Millard County will open SEPTEMBER the 8TH.

—)(—

Max Pace came in Tuesday morning after a year in the service.

—)(—

The plate glass for the Delta Merc. came Tuesday and is being installed.

—)(—

The Misses Mildred and Pearl Forrest went to Clar Lake last week for a few days' outing.

—)(—

Went Lewis went up to Salt Lake City last week to re-enlist. We congratulate this young man on his choice of determination.

—)(—

Miss Rose Fielding went to Salt Lake City last Saturday, where she will visit for a week before going on to her home in New York City.

—)(—

Now is the time to get your orders in for stove castings and repairs. Don't wait till you need them. A. Miller.   au21-sf

—)(—

Owing to unforeseen events, R. T. Patterson may be compelled to remain until he straightens out matters connected with his recent sale.

—)(—

One of Charlie Ashby's boys had his arm broken the other day while driving a team. The injury was attended by Dr. Charles.

—)(—

WE GROW!

Born, to Allen Searle, a baby girl; to Norman Gardner, a boy. The stork also left a bundle at the home of Lewis Webb.

—)(—

Geo. C. Clemens has a new Ford auto, with new axles, new differential, new gears and new parts throughout, for sale for $325. A bargain.   (adv.)

—)(—

Harman & Edwards will get their building ready for occupancy in a short time now, and order in their stock of groceries. They will conduct a strictly cash business, with prices to attract.

—)(—

Dr. J. J. Busnell, ophthalmic specialist of Salt Lake City, will be at the Ward Hotel Wednesday, Sept. 3rd. No charge for testing eyes. References. Glasses are worn for health as well as vision.   a28

—)(—

Dr. Francis lectured before the ladies of the Delta Relief Society last Wednesday on the subject of preventing the spread of disease and resisting disease. His lecture was very interesting and beneficial.

—)(—

Sneak thieves are busy at work around town. The other day a couple hundred pounds of ice were stolen right out from under Broderick's nose. If this goes on we may expect to see ...i ...urdy's red hot range go toteing off up the pike. Cass Lewis please take notice.

—)(—

A. M. Cornwall sold the Murray place of 120 acres, located just across the river on the main road, to Andrew Jones for $150 an acre. We welcome Mr. Jones to the country. Mr. Cornwall does not yet know what his plans will be, though he will probably go elsewhere for the winter.

—)(—

Frank Lanhan is still down with the "Pahvant plague." A peculiarity of this malady is that the subject has intermittent high fevers, coming on suddenly, with sever headache and followed by extreme weakness. He has been sick for about two weeks, at times apparently improving, and then coming down again.

—)(—

Alfalfa seed is being contracted for at 20 cents per pound, the buyer to furnish the sacks. This is a good figure and will net a nice sum to the grower. Later, when crops are up, we wish to give space to several of the choicest yields, and so will ask our seed raising friends to kindly see that the information gets to us.

—)(—

The ladies of the Delta Relief Society wish to announce that at their next meeting this following Wednesday they will begin the first of the work for the next season, and they ask a goodly attendance.

—)(—

For sale: Steel range, heater, dining table, parlor stand, wooden bed, dresser, wash stand, 6 dining chairs, iron bed, springs, mattress, sectional book case, large rocker, 9x12 rug (Crex), electric vacuum cleaner, 3 wash tubs and basket, Mason jars, wash bowl, wash boards, copper wash boiler. A. S. Rogers.   a28

—)(—

A piano recital was given by Mrs. S. L. Wright at her home Wednesday evening, under the auspices of the MacDowell Music Club. This club is organized to enable its members to become acquainted with the best music—operas and selections—, and the study is helped by the use of victrolas in addition to piano lessons.

—)(—

Dr. Francis, the Government expert who has been conducting investigations as to the Pahvant Plague, has taken his Guinea pigs and other animals used in his experiments back to Washington, D. C. to give them a thorough examination in a fully equipped laboratory. He will probably continue his work here again later.

WEDDING BELLS.

Our genial friend, Proctor H. Robinson and Miss Nina Hoyt were married at Nephi on the 14th and are now living in one of the Copening houses. The many friends of this well liked couple wish them happiness.

Millard County Chronicle
September 11, 1919

DELTA NEWS NOTES.

A very clever series of names for the Winebrenner-Works-Thurston addition are; Brentworth, Arborea, and Arbordale Park.

The Delta Studio is now open for business. Call and get finished photos and proofs.   s11-25

Mrs. Ada Works wishes to announce to the ladies that this week and next she has a fall opening of Millinery.

Delta played Lynndyl last Sunday, 14 to 13 in favor of Delta. As the editor was up Oak Creek canyon that day, and has been given no "dope" on the game, nothing is published.

Tuesday night, at the play "It Pays To Advertise", our readers will remember a short address was given about a moving picture coming soon, being made by a young man in uniform. His name is Forrest Cornish, a former member of the Northwest Mounted Police of Canada, who resigned from that to enter the "Princess Pat" regiment. This Princess Pat regiment has received world-wide notice in the press, for valor, hard fighting and pluck. 1200 men formed the regiment, of whom only 32 came out at the end, of the original number.

Ruby Bunker, the little daughter of Arthur Bunker, came near to what might have been a serious injury. She was riding horseback along Clark Street, when her horse stumbled, and fell with his weight upon her foot and lower leg; but fortunately, the pressure was so applied as not to break a bone or crush any part. How she escaped so luckily is a wonder to all who saw the accident. Bert Johnson took her home in his machine.

We saw a very artistic specimen of the handicraft of picture mounting, done by Farrel K. Pack, 1840 Lincoln Street, Salt Lake City, reflecting credit for taste and workmanship. We have no hesitancy in recommending our readers to place their orders there for similar work.

Quite a number of people are going to St. George to visit during the Fair to be held there this week. Among those to go are Oscar Anderson and wife, Irvin Jeffery, and Wm. E. Bunker, besides a number of the younger people. We have many residents at Delta who formerly lived in Dixie and the St. George region, so that it will be a homecoming event for them.

LYNNDYL LINES

The celebration of Labor Day at Lynndyl was most successful. Many hundreds of people were present including many visitors from surrounding towns. The main events of the day were horse racing, foot races, boxing, broncho busting and a fast game of base ball between Lynndyl and Nephi with a score of 5 to 7 in favor of the visiting team. An enjoyable feature of the day was the excellent music furnished by the Fillmore Band. A moving picture show and dance in the Princess Theatre ended the day's enjoyment.

School will begin Sept. 8 in our new modern school house, erected last year, with the following teachers: Mr. Jacobson, Prin. Miss Margaret Neilson and Miss Amanda Roper.

The old school building has been purchased by the Land Company and being remodeled into and up-to-date garage.

Little Miss Evelyn Lundall was taken to Salt Lake to a hospital to be treated for a very severe case of tonsilitis.

Mr. and Mrs. D. E. Carter of Provo are visiting with Mrs. Carter's mother, Mrs. Janet Lunn.

Miss Rose Evans of Provo is visiting with her sister, Mrs. Alfred Anderson.

Mr. and Mrs. F. G. Eyre have returned to Hinckley after a week's visit with Mr. and Mrs. G. L. Kelly. Mr. Eyre has accepted a position in the Millard Academy this winter.

Miss Celia Browne, who has been the guest of Mrs. Sarah Campbell the past two weeks, will return Wednesday to her home in Zion City, Ill.

OASIS ODDITIES

George Jensen has arrived from duties overseas.

Mr. and Mrs. Callister of Oak City spent a few days with Mr. and Mrs. A. J. Christensen.

Mr. G. L. Huff is a Salt Lake visitor this week.

A large number of our young people went to Fillmore to the big celebration.

Mrs. Belenger has returned to her home in Milford after spending a few weeks with her mother Mrs. Howells.

Mrs. A. J. Henry expects to leave Thursday for Salt Lake.

Found—A cure for watermelons. Inquire of Joe Fidel.

CHILD PASSES AWAY

Helen, the year old daughter of Mr. and Mrs. O. A. Anderson, passed away last Thursday from peritonitis, induced by stomach trouble. The child had been ailing about two weeks, and despite the best care and medical skill her life could not be saved.

Interment took place at Delta Friday last.

The community joins with the sorrowing parents in their loss.

WEDDING BELLS.

Richard Lyman and Miss Ruby Jacobson were married at the Manti temple last week. "Rich", as he is known familiarly, is the son of Mrs. Mary M. Lyman, a respected and well liked young man of this community. The bride is a popular young lady from Oak City.

The Chronicle joins with the many friends of this happy young couple in wishing them a long married life and much happiness.

Millard County Chronicle
September 18, 1919

DELTA NEWS NOTES.

A nice rain came Monday, which should lay the roads now for all fall.

—)(—

Three forgeries of checks occurred in Delta last week. We are asked to withhold names and data.

—)(—

J. C. Sievert returned to his duties at the station after a pleasant visit in Los Angeles and Denver.

—)(—

Alma J. Greenwood, of American Fork, is visiting with his brother-in-law, A. C. Sorenson.

—)(—

The stork called at the home of R. J. Law last week, leaving a girl baby.

—)(—

O. M. Tillotson's son, Bell, met with a slight accident the other day in which his hand got somewhat cut, though not seriously.

—)(—

Mrs. H. L. Sherer, of the North Tract, has her mother, Mrs. Matthews, and her niece, Mrs. Pocock, visiting with her.

—)(—

The M. I. A. Convention will be held at Delta September 21 in the schoolhouse. All officers and members are requested to be present at the 9:00 o'clock meeting.   s11-18

—)(—

R. J. Law's little daughter Elsie had her hand injured by being partly crushed in a wringer. It is not expected to leave any permanent effects.

—)(—

Mrs. Julia Eardenschn came to Delta to visit with her parents, Mr. and Mrs. Albert Rose prior to their departure to southeastern Iowa to better Mr. Rose's health.

—)(—

J. W. Cropper, who used formerly to live on the North Tract, is now at Pomona, Cal., and wishing to keep informed about Delta doings, subscribes to the Chronicle.

—)(—

While playing with a lawn mower, the young Rice boy got his finger in the knives. Dr. Charles dressed the finger, and it is hoped it will not be necessary to amputate it.

—)(—

Mr. Jerome O'Neill has taken a position with the sugar factory, as traffic manager, his experience with the railroad well fiting him for this work.

—)(—

James P. Sprunt, promoter of the sugar factory, is in Delta visiting with his son Russell. Mr. Sprunt has just promoted and built four alfalfa mills, and is here for the same purpose.

DIED

Mrs. Henry Hickok, of Hinckley, Utah, aged 52 years, died in a Salt Lake City hospital Friday last.

HINCKLEY HAPPENINGS

The Hinckley District School started Sept. 8th, with an enrollment of 270 students, with John A. Watts as principal. Other teachers are Keith Robins, Miss Isabelle Whatcott, Miss Delma Scott, Mrs. May Ann Watt, Miss Damron, and Miss Gergerson.

* * *

The Millard County Academy will start the 22nd, with what points to be a very successful year.

Mrs. Celestial Knight returned from Cary, Idaho, where she has been spending a few months with her son, Vernon Knight. Her grandson, Eldred Knight, returned with her to attend the academy this winter.

* * *

The Hinckley town board has decided to light the streets. And they are also talking of building a jail—

too many of our boys are much too frisky in melon patches nights, and too many cars are driven off in joy rides. So the city fathers will provide a place for them.

* * *

The highest price paid in Hinckley as yet for seed this year is $27.80, (this written Monday).

SUGARVILLE SIFTINGS

A little lassie arrived at the home of Mr. and Mrs. Elmer Golden last Thursday, and will now share honors with Master Julian Golden.

* * *

The Friendship Thimble Club will be entertained next Wednesday by Mesdames Pearl Baker and Grace Watts, at the home of the former.

* * *

There will be a Community Shadow Social at Sugarville next Saturday night for the benefit of E. R McCoy and his mother, who had the misfortune to lose three horses, which they depended on to do the work. The ladies to bring pie, cake, or sandwiches. Everybody come and buy a shadow and have a good time.

COUNTY OFFICERS' REGISTER.

County Commissioners:
O. C. Warnick, Oasis.
Carl Brown, Scipio.
Christian Christensen, Kanosh.

Carl H. Day, County Clerk.
Harrison Anderson, Treasurer.
Grover A. Giles, Attorney.
Mrs. Bertha Warner, Recorder.
G. W. Cropper, Sheriff.
A. T. Rappleye, Assessor.
George T. Theobald, Surveyor.

State Legislators:
Senator Eighth District—Danie' Stevens, Fillmore.
Representative—Joseph Finlinson Leamington.

Millard County Chronicle
October 9, 1919

HINCKLEY HAPPENINGS

On what is known as the Humphrey Farm, now owned by David Sanderson, was found a pocket of flint, evidently buried by the American Indians years ago. The cache consisted of bones, flint, stones and pieces of pottery. The fire marks were in evidence, showing that the use of fire was then in vogue.

* * *

An up-to-date cement garage is in course of construction by two of Hinckley's progressive young men,

Hilton and Moody. The enterprise is a boost to the business section of the town.

* * *

Sept. 27th and 28th, the Deseret Stake Conference was held at Hinckley. Apostle James E. Talmage and Presiding Patriarch Hyrum G. Smith were the principal speakers. The sessions were well attended and a very profitable gathering was expressed by all who attended.

* * *

Some of the Conference and Fair

visitors are: Prin. Thomas L. Martin, Pres. A. A. Hinckley, Heber Bishop and family, James M. Rigby and Milton Moody.

* * *

Ward Moody left Oct. 4th for a short visit in Salt Lake, after which he will attend the B. Y. U. at Provo.

* * *

Wednesday Millard Academy Student Body held an election of class presidents and officers for the ensuing year. A burst of enthusiasm bespoke the genuine spirit of the students who have registered at the institution this season.

DELTA NEWS NOTES.

Frank Beckwith sold Job Riding forty acres near Abraham last week.

—)(—

Eph Blackburn will have pretty near $3,000 worth of seed off his farm this year.

—)(—

J. V. Many has bought a thresher, ot use on the South Tract, not only for his own use, but as well, for use of others thereabouts.

—)(—

Delta was well represented at the Salt Lake Fair this year. The editor tried to take in everything in one day, and saw many other Deltans trying to do the same thing.

—)(—

R. F. Crum has given possession of his farm to Ernest Blackburn, and Mrs. Crum and the children have gone to Ogden to visit with her parents. "Dick" is living in bachelordom with George Dhyse.

Cyrus Gifford and Miss Ina Bundy were married in Manti last week and returned to Delta to make their home. Mr. Gifford is the brother of Mrs. George Day. The Chronicle joins with their friends in wishing them much success and happiness.

—)(—

Clark Street is receiving a surfacing of cinders, nicely smoothed up rounded over, and packed down. With the first fall storm this will pack into a fine road bed. We thank the city dads and the sugar company.

—)(—

Clyde Maxfield has taken a contract to do all the cement work required in the drainage work to be done in District No. 3 (the Melville Tract), which will run to nearly $20,000. Quite a feather in Clyde's cap.

—)(—

The Salt Lake City banks enforce strictly the clearing house rule that should an acount drop below $100 on deposit at any time in the month, the customer is charged 50c. Why do we know? Well, if we ever had a hundred plunks at once we wouldn't speak to darned subscriber we've got.

The erection of the alfalfa meal, syrup and ice plant at Delta, is one of the largest and most profitable enterprises yet launched in Millard Co. Local people are urged to subscribe for as much of the treasury stock as possible as it means big profits and safe investment.

—)(—

A. E. Bloomquist and Miss Nellie Irene Geary were married in Ogden Oct. 6th. The young couple will make their home in Delta. Mr. Bloomquist being manager of the Thornton Drug Co. here. We welcome Mr. Bloomquist and his bride, and wish them many long years of happy married life.

—)(—

Charlie Friberg of the North Tract was in the office Saturday. He got an average of about 30 bu. of wheat, and his beets are a fair crop, ranking along with the average around him. Mrs. Friberg has returned to Nebraska to live. Charlie may sell out and join her.

—)(—

J. P. Sprunt returned from Salt Lake City, Tuesday, with articles of incorporation for the new alfalfa meal and syrup plant to be erected at Delta. He also brought prices on machinery to be submitted to the board of directors. The board of directors will be composed of local men of their own

PERSONAL PARAGRAPHS

H. B. Prout was in Delta Sunday.

—)(—

Born, to Mr. and Mrs. A. C. Sorenson, a fine baby boy.

—)(—

Miss Hattie Ward is back from her school work in Salt Lake City.

—)(—

Wanted, an experienced lady clerk. Golden Rule Store.   09

—)(—

Some good mirrors at the Delta Furniture Co.   10|2 9

—)(—

Mrs. George Stratton, of Hinckley, has been seriously ill for several days.

—)(—

Wanted, a good woman cook, unencumbered, at Ward Hotel.   (adv)

—)(—

Teams are at work on the Emmett hotel, excavating for the basement.

—)(—

Ernest Theobald, who was operated on just recently by Dr. Charles for hernia, is recovering rapidly.

—)(—

Mrs. H. F. Aller arrived in Delta Tuesday night, for a visit with her daughter, Mrs. J. M. Baker.

—)(—

Mrs. Wolf and Mrs. Hickman will entertain the Jolly Stitchers' Club on Oct. 17 at Mrs. Hickman's home.

—)(—

J. H. Kinshella, contractor under District No. 2, from Wisconsin, was a visitor in the Chronicle office last week.

—)(—

Miss Bobbie Robinson, from Salt Lake City, was in Hinckley nursing a case for Dr. Charles. After her work there was finished, she spent several days at the home of Dr. and Mrs. Charles, visiting with them and Miss Hummel, the doctor's assistant. Miss Hummel and Miss Robinson had been associated together before, in the hospital in Salt Lake.

—)(—

Mr. and Mrs. A. L. Harman left for Salt Lake City Saturday, where they were called on account of sickness.

—)(—

Norman K. Riddle is making a short visit with Mr. and Mrs. Hewlett. Mr. Riddle is connected with the Western Weighing Association.

—)(—

William B. Shaw was a Fillmore visitor again this week. This is getting to be a regular thing with Bill. Gasoline must have taken a big drop.

—)(—

John Nutsch is living with Mr. and Mrs. C. M. Cochran on the North tract, where he will continue to stay for the remaining time he is with us.

—)(—

The friends of Mrs. Julia B. Giegley an Arsdale will be glad to learn that she is coming out to Delta from Galesburg, Ill., sometime in the latter part of this month.

—)(—

J. A. Jackson, of Hinckley, left for Salt Lake City this week to have an x-ray examination made of his arm, which had been broken and set, but was not mending as it should.

—)(—

Will Heise celebrated a birthday last week. We always enjoy celebrating our thirty-seventh—have, in fact, every time it comes around, for the past five years.

—)(—

Mr. and Mrs. La Rue Pritchett are visiting with the latter's mother, Mrs. Frank Heise, on the North tract, having come here from Meridian, Idaho.

—)(—

Ed Pearson of the South Tract is now in Bertrand, Nebraska, visiting with his father. The fatted calf has been potted, boiled, stewed, fricasseed, and baked, and when the last mouthful has been stowed away in the inner man, Ed may break loose and hie him to Utah. His dad must not get to thinking he's going to hold Ed, for he aint; we'll have him in Utah before snow flies.

—)(—

As we go to press we hear this—Charles Jacobson, from Mt. Pleasant, has bought 120 acres at Sugarville from L. Anderson. More data on this will be forthcoming later.

—)(—

Dr. and Mrs. De Garmo are back from a sojourn in southeastern Iowa, where they went overland to visit his natives. He will open up an office and continue his practice as a chiropractor.

—)(—

Mrs. James Robinson, Jr., and her two little daughters are preparing to join Mr. Robinson in Delta, where he wired for them Monday. He is employed at the Sugar Factory and will reside there.   —Beaver Press.

—)(—

Mrs. W. L. Lackyard is back from an extended visit with Mr. Lackyard's natives. Bert Lackyard, a younger brother of Mr. Lackyard, returned with her to stay the winter in Delta and attend school here.

—)(—

Mrs. Harry Aller leaves Wednesday for an extended visit with friends and natives. She will go first to Longmont, Colo., to visit her sister, Mrs. Ben Da Shiell, formerly Miss Louise Aller, of this city. From there she will go to Denver, and thence to her home in Oregon.

—)(—

Carl Elmer has about the niftiest "ujigger" for backfilling we have yet seen, which does the work for him on his contract on District No. 2 better than any machine or man or he has seen tried out. It certainly handles the work fast, and at a low cost. We hope it makes him a nice clean up.

—)(—

The friends of Dr. and Mrs. C. A. Broaddus will be interested to know that Dr. Broaddus has left for Chicago, Philadelphia and New York for his further post-graduate work in his specialty, Eye, Ear, Nose and Throat. Mrs. Broaddus and the two children will remain in Salt Lake for the present. Dr. and Mrs. Broaddus have been in Las Cruces, N. M., and have returned just recently, coming the entire way in their car, camping part of the time.

Millard County Chronicle
October 16, 1919

NELSON S. BISHOP

Nelson S. Bishop died suddenly at his home in Delta, Thursday morning Oct. the 9th, just a little before noon, from heart failure.

Mr. Bishop had been up to Salt Lake City accompanied by relatives, and there had complained a little about his stomach. But by taking care in his eating, and skipping a meal or two at times, he had escaped any bad consequences. On Thursday morning he planned taking Mrs. Bishop to her daughter's, Mrs. Bassett, and to take his brother-in-law over to Hinckley. He did not feel exactly well. On cranking up his Ford in the garage, he was seized with a very sudden and very severe pain in the stomach, and was taken to the house, where he lay down. The pain was intensely severe. Bishop Maxfield and Mr. Steele were in the house at the time, and Mr. Bishop becoming better and easier, they talked for a few moments, and the two visitors left.

Almost immediately thereafter, Mr. Bishop was taken again, more severely, and died. It seems that acute gastritis affected the heart, and by the time medical aid came, Mr. Bishop had passed away.

Nelson Spicer Bishop was born in Fillmore, Utah, November 1st, 1855, his next birthday to have been his sixty-fourth. He was prominent in the public life of Fillmore, and served as a city councilman, and also as Mayor of Fillmore. In 1886 he left Fillmore for a mission to New Zealand, and was there three years. He was so impressed with his experience that he named his third daughter "Waiora". He was one of the Bishop's Councilors under Thos. C. Callister in the town of his birth.

On February 23rd, 1878, he was married to Annie Elizabeth Melville, three children gracing that union, namely, Mrs. Ella Bassett of Delta, Mrs. Nora Ingersoll, American Fork, and Mrs. Waiora Wallace, of Delta. He is survived by his widow and the three children, and besides by Artemis Bishop, a brother, and Mrs. Julia Law, a sister, both living in California; Mrs. Susan Meeks, a sister in California; Mrs. Bessie Twitchell, a sister in Escalante; Heber Bishop, a brother, in Hinckley, Utah, and Mrs. Brigham Melville, of Fillmore.

In 1907 he came to Delta, and built the first home to be erected here. Many times in ward meetings and reunions, he has given his experiences of early pioneer life in Delta. He took a prominent part in public affairs, being at the time of his death a member of the Board of Education.

Nelson Bishop was a man of sterling worth, well respected for his strong opinions, which he fearlessly upheld. His loss will be keenly felt in the community.

The sympathy of his many friends is extended to his widow and children in their hour of bereavement.

The funeral held at the Ward Hall on Sunday afternoon was possibly one of the largest ever held in Delta. Friends of the deceased thronged to the bier of sorrow to pay their last tribute of respect. Prominent speakers spoke earnestly of the character and life of their departed friend, in the warmest terms. In honor of Mr. Bishop as our local board of education member, the pupils were lined up in open file before the meeting house, through whose ranks the funeral concourse passed. The floral tribute from the teachers and pupils was beautiful, and Clark Allred, principal of the Delta school gave a fiting and ardent tribute to him whose memory was then being honored. Among the other speakers were Apostle Richard R. Lyman, from Salt Lake City, President A. A. Hinckley, Patriarch M. M. Steele, Bishop Rufus Day of Fillmore, E. W. Jeffery, James Kelly of Fillmore, and Bishop H. E. Maxfield.

The community loses an ardent worker, a strong character, and man whose loss makes a gap in our community life unfilled. As Apostle Lyman fittingly said, "His life was gentle, and the elements so mixed in him that Nature might say to all the world, 'Here was a man'."

DELTA NEWS NOTES

Born: To Mrs. Hyrum E. Tanner, a baby girl.

—)(—

Mrs. Sadie Pace is in Delta, visiting her parents, Mr. and Mrs. Walter Gardner, Sr.

—)(—

Orin Clark is back again in Delta, now working with the sugar factory. We are glad to see Orin back again.

—)(—

FOUND—A bundle of new motor cycle spokes. Owner can have by calling at Chronicle and paying 50c.

—)(—

Tom Cropper of Deseret raised 290 bu. of alfalfa seed off 18 acres, which he sold for 25 cents. This is better than 16 bu. to the acre.

—)(—

O. A. Anderson has been chosen as the Delta member of the Board of Education, in the place of our late respected citizen, Nelson S. Bishop.

—)(—

Mrs. Jetta Cavanaugh, formerly of Abraham, is back again after a lengthy visit in the East. Mrs. Cavanaugh's health is much improved.

—)(—

Theo. F. Warmboldt is in town, looking after his two farms, both of which are in the Melville district. He will stay with us a couple of weeks or so.

—)(—

C. A. Glazier, former Bank Commissioner of the State of Utah, is visiting his son-in-law, Archie O. Gardner, on the South Tract.

—)(—

Afred I. Bliss of Hinckley raised 85 bu. of alfalfa seed off 6½ acres, which brought him the snug little sum of $1065! Alfred is quite elated over his success.

—)(—

Mrs. R. F. Van Arsdale came to Delta Tuesday, from Galesburg, Ill. Mrs. Van Arsdale owns property just on the edge of town south, another piece at Abraham, and two parcels near Kanosh. She will remain several days.

—)(—

Geo. S. Forest reports two sales made this week, one being 120 acres for J. D. Miller, and the other 40 acres of Wm. A. Miller. Mr. Forest is receiving many listings and is quite successful in getting sales.

—)(—

Lost, a jointed telescope, about three inches diameter, length closed about sixteen inches; length open about five feet. $5.00 reward will be paid for the return of this instrument at the Chronicle office and no questions asked.

—)(—

John Talbot, of Hinckley, got his foot badly crushed at the Erwin Beet dump, in an accident in moving some cars. He was sent up to the L. D. S. Hospital Wednesday night last, accompanied by Miss Hummell, with the hope that possibly his foot might be saved. The injuries were attended to here by Dr. Charles.

—)(—

THE BLUEBIRD LUNCHEONETTE
Soups   Tamales   Tomato Flip
FOUNTAIN DRINKS
The best in the city.

Mr. L. C. Neeley of Hinckley got 550 bushels off his 50 acres of seed land, an even average throughout of 11 bu. to the acre. Mr. Neeley got the going price at the time of his sale.

—)(—

We note that several of our northern neighbor towns are having a closing of schools to permit the youth to work in the beet fields. As yet, Delta has not thought of resorting to that step. But, be it said, the labor situation is not exactly easy.

—)(—

Marion Pace and wife are back in Delta to settle and live with us again. Marion has been in Glenwood Springs for the past several years. We welcome them back and wish them success in getting lined up here profitably.

—)(—

At the next meeting of the Commercial Club, the matter will be taken up of having a big, well advertised Harvest Dance next month, either along about Tuesday the 18th, or Wednesday the 26th. The latter date will be Thanksgiving Eve. Outside music will be got, and a rip snorting humdinger of a time had. Let's do it.

—)(—

Geo. S. Forest, investment broker and realty dealer, has bought for himself the former Eccles home just across the track, into which he will move in a short time. Mr. Forest is meeting with much success in selling land, and says that this year will surpass all others in land transfers.

Dr. J. J. Busnell, ophthalmic specialist of Salt Lake, will be at the Ward hotel Wednesday, Oct. 29th. No charge for testing eyes. References. Glasses are worn for health as well as for vision.   (adv)

—)(—

An idea of how the town is crowded with people may be gotten from the fact that the Ward hotel turned away fourteen persons one day last week; the Delta hotel is providing cots in the halls, so crowded are they; the Kelley hotel is full up; private persons are taking visiting friends in, so scarce and so overcrowded are hotel accommodations. Surely, this campaign, Delta is humming.

—)(—

Mrs. C. E. Lewis, and little daughter Anna May, are registered at the Ward Hotel, on a visit from Ft. Collins, Colo. Mrs. Lewis will be remembered as teaching in the schools at Abraham. Mr. Lewis and Mrs. Lewis' father, Mr. Chas. Schroeppel, rented their land here and moved. Mr. Lewis is among the Colorado sugar factories and is now operating a dry cleaning establishment.

—)(—

John S. Wind, of the North Tract, brought in four large handsome sugar beets, and placed them on display in the Delta State Bank. These beets are some of the largest and best shaped ones we have seen. Mr. Wind expects to get 18 tons on the best of these, and 13 tons on about 7 acres of others. For the benefit of our out of town readers, we will say that he

has just sold his farm for $130 per acre to Leo Johnson. This farm is just south of Woodrow, so that this selling price serves as an indication of values thereabouts for similar property.

—)(—

C. L. Webster, on the edge of the reservoir, cut four crops of hay on his farm this year. He did not let but a very small portion go to seed, from which he got one wagon-load of seed that netted him $150.00. Of his 55 acres he has 40 acres in to alfalfa for a hay crop, and got a trifle over 205 tons, so that he ran a little better than five tons to the acre. As and indication of what he and several others along the edge of the river bank hold their farms at, Clarence says he will take no less than $250 an acre for his, and even at that he is not particularly anxious to sell out.

OASIS ODDITIES

The M. I. A. gave a party Friday evening. A program was rendered, after which refreshments were served and dancing enjoyed by the young people.

* * *

Mrs. Maude S. Nelson is home on a short visit with her parents, Mr. and Mrs. John Styler.

* * *

One of our townsmen just told us that J. P. Fidel was inquiring for a city lot. Joe said he was tired of batching and besides all the buttons are off his clothes.

* * *

Mr. Edmund Jr. just returned from Douglas, Arizona, where he was serving in the United States Cavalry. We don't expect to have June with us very long, as he expects to return to Arizona for his bride.

* * *

Mrs. David Rutherford has taken her daughter Leona to Salt Lake City for medical treatment.

* * *

Misses Tecla and Inga Christensen just returned from Salt Lake City where they spent the last six months.

* * *

Mrs. J. C. Hawley and family have gone to Provo to spend the winter, where the children will attend the B. Y. U.

SUTHERLAND SEARCHLIGHTS.

Hagan Brothers have purchased Mrs. Flora Davis' ranch at Sutherland.

* * *

Bishop Roberts and wife went to Annabell last week to attend the funeral of Mrs. Roberts' father, Mr. Nebeker, who was killed in the Elsinore sugar factory. Mr. Nebeker and wife were here visiting last spring.

* * *

Mrs. A. P. Austin's brother from Kansas City is visiting at the Austin home.

* * *

George M. Abbott and Miss Doris Aldridge made a trip to Fillmore last week and surprised all their friends by getting married. We wish them much happiness.

* * *

We understand that Mr. Titus has sold his farm and expects to leave us. Mr. John Wind has sold his place but still thinks this is a good place to live.

* * *

The Jolly Stitchers met with Mrs. Hickman and Mrs. Wolfe last Friday. A very pleasant afternoon was spent. The ladies decided to give a bazaar the early part of December. The next meeting to be Oct. 31st, at the home of Mrs. H. G. Ottley, Mrs. Jensen and Mrs. Ottley entertaining.

Delta Makes Favorable Comparison With Twin Falls

The Salt Lake Tribune contains a special item, publishing a red clover crop got by an Idaho man, in which 18 acres brought 210 bus. of seed, which sold for $6,000; besides this, there was a crop of hay got off the land, valued at $450, making a total of $6,450 off 18 acres, or $358.36 per acre.

We compare favorably with this yield. Will Reuben Black got $289 an acre for his alfalfa seed alone, and Jos. E. Blake for a total in all of better than $375. When the writer was in Idaho, he visited Twin Falls several times, and saw their land and noted their prices; it takes $350 to $450 to buy it, and the whole countryside is rich, marvelously rich. As soon as you hit the suburbs of Twin Falls you know you've got among 'em—among the arrivees, not the goin'toos, nor the somedays.

Now Delta has got to reach that same class. Push our crops; push our lands; publish our water; make us prosper with new blood, ginger and pep.

Invite it in.

Personal Items

John Kelley is over from Mills, visiting with his father and sisters at Delta.

—)(—

Mr. and Mrs. Fred Cottrell are the proud parents of a baby girl, born Nov. 10th.

—)(—

A baby girl arrived at the home of Mr. and Mrs. O. M. Sprague, Nov. the 10th.

—)(—

Don't wait until the last minute. Buy your Christmas present right now and save money. Remember $1500.000 worth of presents just arrived. Come and look over the stock and be convinced. D. Landows, Expert Watchmaker and Jeweler.

Lafayette Sigler and family are visiting with N. H. Folsom. Mr. Sigler is from Trementon, though he used to farm on the North Tract.

—)(—

L. Anderson of the North Tract was in town Monday. He and family will leave some time in December for California to live.

—)(—

M. J. McCurdy sold 500 bu. of alfalfa seed grown by him at Hinckley, selling at 25 cents. Figuring this out at 60 pounds to the bushel and Mack gets a nice snug sum. Congrats.

—)(—

H. L. Sherer of the North Tract got 16½ tons of beets to the acre off 11 acres. Hi usually exceeds this tonnage, as his returns heretofore have been 18, 19, and 21 tons to the acre off the same ground.

Seats for "Mickey" will be placed on sale Sunday, Nov. 16.

—)(—

A young man in Oasis had a narrow escape last week. He was looking down the barrel of a gun he thought was empty and it went off. The bullet took off a corner of his ear. We don't know how the bullet was deflected in its course, unless good old solid bone kept it from going right through his head.

—)(—

Ed Pearson is helping out at the Delta State Bank during the sugar campaign. Ed brings back some very interesting pieces of French paper money, of the small 50 cent size, which Americans used to call "shin plasters" when we had them, just after the Civil War. One piece that Ed has is printed in bright red and green, a florid thing like a circus bill done in little; but the hunk of paper is only good on the Mediterranean—in central and northern France they are not accepted.

DELTA NEWS NOTES

Jim McCardell brought in a deer Monday which brought quite a crowd around his auto.

—)(—

Eugene Hilton, a teacher in the schools at Lehi, and brother-in-law to Ray Bishop, was operated on Monday last for appendicitis.

—)(—

Manager N. G. Peterson of the Lincoln got a deer while on a hunting trip out of Fillmore just after the opening of the shooting season.

—)(—

The Y. M. C. A. has turned over all of its huts, buildings, and other permanent improvements to the Government. But even at that, the "Y" still continues to serve the service men through its permanent organizations.

—)(—

Don't wait until the last minute. Buy your Christmas present right now and save money. Remember $1500,000 worth of presents just arrived. Come and look over the stock and be convinced. D. Landows, Expert Watchmaker and Jeweler.

—)(—

We would call the attention of our merchants to space on the curtain at the Lincoln Theatre; the following ads appear on it that can be sold to others—W. L. Lackyard; Geo. E. Billings; City Drug Store; B. E. Cooper; M. F. Goble. There is a chance to get effective space for a nifty ad which the people really read.

—)(—

W. R. Walker, salesman for the firm of Walker & Jensen, agents for the Oldsmobile, sold Messrs. Wadleigh and Battson a brand new Olds Six to be used by that firm in its realty dealings. Walker & Jensen will soon occupy the former Eccles Building, and garage and auto sales room.

—)(—

Mr. John D. Spencer, of Salt Lake City, is in town, representing the New York Life Insurance Co. Mr. Spencer is an expert salesman, and has conducted classes on that subject in the Salt Lake Commercial Club; when the editor was working in Salt Lake City he attended many lectures by Mr. Spencer, who is a forceful and pointed speaker. We can highly recommend both Mr. Spencer and his company. He has associated with him on this trip into our region Mr. M. H. Horton. We feel that these gentlemen will meet with the success in their line that they merit.

—)(—

The Salt Lake Tribune contained an article under date of the 9th that the Burley sugar factory had fallen below 35,000 tons, and that the factory at Paul will finish the full season's run within about two weeks. Certainly Delta has reason to congratulate itself, for our tonnage and run will continue to nearly the full season.

On acount of Nov. 27 being a legal holiday, the Chronicle will be printed one day earlier; that is, the inside sheets will be printed Monday and the outside sheets Tuesday, and the paper in the mail Wednesday. We will ask our correspondents and also our advertisers to kindly be one day earlier for that issue.

—)(—

"Mickey" is a human story, well told, rich in incident—a simple, familiar story so delightfully narrated that the very familiarity of every scene and episode makes the picture doubly fascinating. Mabel Normand reveals her versatility as its irrepressible heroine in a way that would make the film a monument to her ability. Never, in one picture, did any actress have such opportunities to display her gifts to the utmost. And Mabel does everything her admirers thought she could do—besides a lot of things no one believed she could. She's our cleverest comedienne. At the Lincoln Theater Nov. 19th and 20th.

—)(—

THE BLUEBIRD LUNCHEONETTE
Soups   Tamales   Tomato Flip
FOUNTAIN DRINKS
The best in the city.

SUGARVILLE SIFTINGS

The Friendship Thimble Club will hold its next meeting at the hall next Wednesday p. m.

* * *

Mr. G. Meeker, from Delta, Colorado, is visiting at the home of Claire Dale. He reports harvesting a beet crop at Delta, Colo., of 20 tons per acre.

Last Saturday night a crowd of young folks surprised Clifford Ashby and Ovie Emrick at the Fred Ashby home. Mr. Emrick had been invited to Ashby's for supper and while visiting, a crowd came in and surprised them. The evening was spent in playing games and listening to music on the Victrola, after which refreshments, brought by the uninvited guests, were served. Mr. Ashby and Mr. Emrick expect to leave for California next week.

ATTORNEY MELVILLE WINS IMPORTANT CASE

At the District Court held in Fillmore last week, Attorney J. A. Melville, Jr., representing the estate of Alman Robison, deceased, presented his case before the jury in a three-day trial of an action on a claim presented by Lewis Brunson involving $95,300; the Court instructed the jury to return a verdict in favor of the Estate and against the claimant, Mr. Brunson.

Millard County Chronicle
November 20, 1919

WEDDING BELLS

Married at Fillmore, on November 17th, 1919, Alphonzo Gronning and Miss Edna Theobald. Mr. Gronning is one of our young men, popular, respected, and well-known to all, son of Mr. and Mrs. T. C. Gronning. For several years he worked with his father in the blacksmith business, and then later, both became employees of the sugar factory.

The bride is one of the popular young ladies of Hinckley, daughter of Mr. and Mrs. T. George Theobald. The young couple will make Delta their home. The best wishes of their many friends go with them.

Married, in Salt Lake City, Mr. Ray Emery Wadleigh and Miss Alice Kimball, daughter of Frank D. Kimball of the Sevier River Land & Water Co. Mr. and Mrs. Wadleigh will make their future home in Delta, after their honeymoon to the coast.

CELEBRATES BIRTHDAY

W. W. Baker of the North Tract celebrated his thirty-ninth birthday at his home last Friday evening, when about twenty-five of his friends gave him a very pleasant surprise, the evening being spent in music and games, and light refreshments being served. About midnight all departed for their homes, wishing Mr. Baker many happy returns of his birthday.

STORK OVERWORKED

. The bird of increase paid a visit to Robert E. Robinson's home, leaving a baby girl.

Bishop Roberts, at Sutherland, received a girl.

Mrs. Dillenbeck was next on the list, and a little girl was left at her house.

Another call was made to the home of W. L. Allred, likewise a girl.

And as there's good luck in odd numbers, he flew over the home of Andy Clark, making Mrs. Eliza Hook grandmother to a fine young lad, the first arrival to give her that appellation.

The stork made a visit to the home of J. Alfred Jacobson, leaving an eight pound lad.

SUTHERLAND SEARCHLIGHTS.

Mrs. W. R. Walker is visiting with relatives in Dixie.

* * *

The Jolly Stitchers met with Mrs. Tinsley last Friday p. m. A very pleasant afternoon was spent. It was decided to hold the bazaar on Saturday Dec. 13 instead of on Thursday. The next meeting to be Friday Nov. 28, at the home of Mrs. Evan Evans.

* * *

Ed Henrie and family have gone to Panguitch to visit relatives. They went overland.

* * *

A farewell party was held in Sutherland Friday evening in honor of Elders Dewey Sanford and Fullmer. A nice purse was collected to help them on their way. They both go to the southern states.

SOUTH TRACT ITEMS

. We had quite a nice little visit with Frank B. Johnson the other night; in fact, at the Armistice dance. Frank this year got better returns than heretofore. He attributes that partly to the benefit of drainage and partly due, of course, to participating in the good year so favorable to hay and seed.

* * *

Joe Fidel got a good crop off his place, which ran thoroughly satisfactorily.

* * *

Harry Pearson got a good quantity of seed; Bert Whitmore got good returns; Geo. E. Beach reports a better year than usual.

* * *

J. W. Thurston reports that he took off $2,000 in seed from his farm,

with that much also to the renter—a pretty slick little item in itself both ways.

* * *

I. W. Many got a good crop hay and seed, details of which we hope to have later.

* * *

Irvin Jeffery has the usual bunch of big fine looking hay stacks on his place, attesting to a good crop.

* * *

J. W. Underhill got pretty close to $3,000 off his forty acres. It is reported to us, so that Brer James feels quite pleased with the year.

* * *

Angus Allred got some of the nicest spuds he has ever grown; his hay and seed were also good.

* * *

Jake Hawley has six big stacks on his place this year. In the Commer-

cial Club folders the hay picture of four stacks is taken from his place.

* * *

Wm. E. Bunker got 13 tons of beets off part of his home place; Edward H. Bunker did as well.

DELTA NEWS NOTES

Louis Schoenberger is back at Deseret from a sojourn at Jerome, Idaho.

—)(—

F. C. Kenney got an average of eight tons to the acre on twenty acres of sugar beets.

—)(—

Owen Bunker got 19 tons of beets per acre on his beet patch; this is exceptionally good for this year, and brings the young man $190 an acre.

—)(—

Jenson & Walker sold an Oldsmobile truck to M. Roper of Oak City, for his use on delivery of produce to Delta.

—)(—

Mrs. Battson arrived in Delta last Friday, to join Mr. Battson, of the Wadleigh-Battson Realty Co. They will make their home here.

—)(—

Mr. and Mrs. John Mess of Milford are guests at the Ward Hotel. Mr. Mess is connected with the Delta Land & Water Co. at Milford.

—)(—

I have everything good for the Thanksgiving Dinner; all kinds of fruits, oranges, fresh nuts, fancy fruit baskets; choicest California viands off all kinds. Open every day but Sunday. Mrs. F. N. Davis. adv.

—)(—

I solicit the listing of your lands for sale, or exchange; farms a specialty. I have bargains in Hinckley and North Tract lands. Write or see Wm. Blake, Hinckley, Utah.

n20d11p   (adv)

—)(—

The display advertisement for the COSMOPOLITAN appears elsewhere in this issue, being placed in the supplement; the magazine is for sale at Delta Drug Co. and Thornton Drug Co.

—)(—

I have associated with me now, Mr. A. Q. Robinson, an expert watchmaker, known throughout the southern part of Utah; don't send your watches away to be fixed, but bring them to me. D. Landows, Delta, Utah.

I solicit the listing of your lands for sale, or exchange; farms a specialty. I have bargains in Hinckley and North Tract lands. Write or see Wm. Blake, Hinckley, Utah.

n20d11p   (adv)

—)(—

The display advertisement for the COSMOPOLITAN appears elsewhere in this issue, being placed in the supplement; the magazine is for sale at Delta Drug Co. and Thornton Drug Co.

—)(—

I have associated with me now, Mr. A. Q. Robinson, an expert watchmaker, known throughout the southern part of Utah; don't send your watches away to be fixed, but bring them to me. D. Landows, Delta, Utah. n20-2   (adv.)

—)(—

Mr. N. G. Peterson turned over the Lincoln Theatre to his friend and former room-mate, Mr. Cory Hanks, on Monday night last for a lecture on the World War and the League of Nations. Mr. Hanks gave an interesting lecture, which was well attended.

LYNNDYL LINES

Mr. and Mrs. J. H. Davis and two small sons of Nebraska are the guests of Mr. and Mrs. C. W. Sudbury this week.

* * *

Mrs. Wm. Kinross and son Robert have returned home after visiting for some time with her daughter in Des Moines, Iowa.

* * *

Mrs. J. F. Belliston was called to Nephi on account of the serious illness and death of her aunt.

Mrs. Ray Love has returned to her home after being absent the past two months on account of sickness.

* * *

Mr. and Mrs. Clarence Mortensen leave this week for an extended trip to El Paso, Texas to visit his relatives. They expect to return via San Francisco to meet his sister and husband who are returning from a four-year's mission in Japan.

Mr. Vernon Trimble, who has been serving Uncle Sam in the U. S. Navy the past two years returned home in time to spend Thanksgiving with his parents. He brings with him a bride from New York City.

* * *

Mr. Lawrence Hinckley and Miss Nola Greathouse were married recently in Salt Lake. Both are much respected people of Lynndyl and they will make their home on his farm near Lynndyl.

* * *

Mrs. Jessie Stott has gone to Salt Lake to remain indefinitely.

* * *

Mr. Wm. Jarret bought Austin Hunter's farm house and has moved it into town. Also Lon Davis has moved his farmhouse in to help decrease one of the h. c. of l. (high rent).

* * *

School in the lower grades was not resumed at the beginning of this week on account of the serious illness of Miss Amanda Roper's brother in Oak City.

* * *

The Post Office was moved to its new quarters last week under the direction of Miss Cora E. Paxton, postmistress.

* * *

A very appropriate program was rendered Sunday evening under the direction of the Y. L. M. I. A. in honor of its Jubilee Year.

OAK CITY NEWS ITEMS

Among the newest arrivals in town is a baby boy, born at the home of George Anderson.

Many of our High School students who are attending the Millard Academy at Hinckley, returned home for Thanksgiving Day and helped eat the national bird.

The Thanksgiving Dance given at Oak City last Thursday night was a well attended and enjoyable affair.

The Wood Dance and Supper given by the Oak City Relief Society at the Amusement Hall was very elaborate, given for the men and boys who responded so generously in hauling wood for the poor and Ward Hall.

Our enterprising townsman, Mr. Jess Peterson, has recently purchased a large automobile truck car.

DELTA NEWS NOTES

SAY! Come in and have wide tires put on your wagon at Bunker's Delta.

—)(—

Evans Bros. got an average of 9½ tons off 60 acres, from their farm just across the river.

—)(—

It used to be, "Have you a little Fairy in your home?" Times have changed since then; now it's "Have you a little still in your cellar?"

—)(—

L. Turner on the North Tract, got 10 to 14 tons to the acre off his seven acres adjoining his son, Reuben Turner, next to Sanford's.

—)(—

Senator Reed Smoot is a subscriber to The Chronicle, finding it gives him the news of Millard County, and the Delta district in particular.

—)(—

Watch for the bill of fare the Bank Cafe will publish in our issues of Dec. 18th and 25th. Phil promises no hollow spot after that meal.

—)(—

"I know a man who thinks he's poor,
But he is rich indeed;
He has a chair, a friend who's sure,
And three good books to read."

—)(—

The party who took a pair of gloves from the counter of the bakery was seen and is known. He will please return them and greatly oblige John M. Baker. adv.

—)(—

As the world comes to an end Dec. 17th, how lonesome heaven will be with only editors there; but how durned crowded t'other place will be with all you uns in it.

—)(—

Delbert Searle got 100 tons of good alfalfa hay off his forty this season, average 5 tons to the acre on production. Beets suffered from excess heat.

C. C. Lauck got between 13 and 14 tons of beets on 21 acres.. In hay he got 100 tons of choice alfalfa, of which he wishes to sell part or all; so buyers looking for that product will do well to correspond with him. Christie is well satisfied with this year's returns to him.

—)(—

Manager Peterson, of the Lincoln Theater, has installed a brand new projector, so that now he can give continuous performances without the necessity of waiting while one reel is placed on the single machine. This places the Lincoln with full complement of machinery, the foremost movie show in Millard County.

—)(—

News print paper has taken another advance in price. The papers have been full, lately, of scarcity in supply betokening a threatened rise, and now comes the information to all newspapers that their ready print advances; the present advance is 60 to 75 per cent above cost in 1916, and over more than 150 per cent more than prices in 1914.

DELTA, UTAH

Delta, Utah, in this year of Grace, nineteen hundred nineteen, is a town only twelve years old, the first two years of which were calamitous, making it practically ten years old. As far as growth is concerned, it may be classed conveniently as a ten year old town. In fact, the Delta Ward, of the L. D. S. Church, celebrated its tenth universary this fall.

Delta is now a thriving town of 1200 or a little better, brisk, business like, and moving with a spirit of vim and vigor. It supports two banks, the Delta State Bank, established in February, 1913, and the First National Bank, which expected to be opened and ready for business by the 13th of this month, but the cold weather and delivery delay in materials will prevent this for some time yet.

In 1908 Delta was called Aiken, and was a box car. Old residents of that period are growing scarce. The late Nelson S. Bishop, and Walter M. Gardner were among the very earliest pioneers here, when Delta was merely a log hut and a few tents.

Preceeding the period of Delta, there was the then old-established town of Deseret, a close follower after the settlement of Fillmore; then came Hinckley, and later Oasis. In fact, the first Irrigation works on the flat was the Deseret Irrigation Co. with a diversion dam just west of a continuation of Clark Street. Then followed the Abraham Irrigation Co., a project put on the map quickly and with ample financial success by the Fitzgerald Bros. This success stirred another company to make a similar profit, and the Melville Irrigation Co. was started.

Then followed the Oasis Land & Irrigation Co., which was started on Carey Act, before Delta was much of anything. This company met with two bad years, one when the diversion dam went out, and the other when the canal broke, so that the company saw fit to retire and it was superceded by the Delta Land & Water Co.

Properly speaking, the growth of Delta begins with the Delta Land & Water Co. That company put on a campaign of selling, advertised extensively, and got the people in. Farms were quickly dotted on the North and South Tracts, and the farming community was really made by their selling efforts.

Then came the Midland Irrigation Co., an offspring of the Abraham Company.

And lastly came the Sevier River Land & Water Co.

In all the acreage as at present runs beyond 123,000 acres, with other lands yet to be brought in, so that the acreage is usually classed as being 150,000.

Perfect Water System.

Delta gets its water from the big Sevier Bridge Reservoir, at Mills, Utah, about fifty-five miles from Delta. This is a huge earthern dam, with sheet metal and cement cores, long slope upstream, and of generous dimensions. With the cores and the slope of construction, this dam is perfectly safe. It s usually filled anywhere from the 93 foot level up, according to the precipitation. with the cores and the slope of con-

struction, this dam is perfectly safe. It is usually filled anywhere from the 93 foot level up, acording to the precipitation.

The Deseret and Abraham Companies get the primary or normal river flow in the proportion of three fifths and two fifths respectively; beside this primary right, they both own impounded water. (Impounded water is water caught in the big reservoir from high water periods and at any times other than the irrigating season.)

All the other companies own impounded water in this reservoir. At the 93 foot level, the capacity of the reservoir is 252,000 acre feet, which with primary rights, is sufficient to water 125,000 to 150,000 acres of land, after losing what seeps and evaporates away. With a year under normal precipitation, water masters exercise care in water delivery; the greatest good will prevails among all the companies, so that should one's outlook be rather limited. the others come to its relief, as was experienced in 1919. when the upper and lower Sevier companies donated twenty-four hours rights to one company, saving 1200 acres of crops, valued at at estimate of about $55,000.

It is a fact of note that even in the year 1919, when many companies in Utah and Idaho were absolutely without water, or at least running on scant measure, we of Delta were not cut down a bit. There was no drought in Delta in 1919.

Our water system, we think, is perfect, adequate, and the basis of our community.

Water Companies

The lands under the Deseret, Abraham, Melville, Midland, and Sevier Companies are all patented lands; The Delta Land & Water Co.'s holdings are Carey Act.

The Deseret Irrigation Co. supplies Oasis, Deseret, Hinckley, and some portions of Abraham, and a little on the South Tract. This company is the oldest in the field. Its lands were consequently the first to show retention of water, and Drainage Districts Nos. 1 and 2 are within its boundaries.

Oasis built a lumber yard, a creamery, a flour mill, a nice neat substantial brick bank building, and is the largest alfalfa seed shipping center of the county—all built up from the basis furnished by the Deseret Irriga-

tion Co. The bank and the irrigation company office together. Under this system, the lands are old and bear well in alfalfa. The credit of growing the record crops of Millard County fall under the water distribution given by this company, namely, Will Reuben Block of Deseret, who raised 19 bushels of alfalfa seed in 1919, and Jos. E. Blake, who raised 19½ bushels per acre.

The Hinckley district supports a thriving bunch of business houses and the Millard Academy. The school situation is thus taken care of by a High School at Fillmore and the Academy at Hinckley, with a grade and Junior High at Delta.

WEDDING BELLS

Cards are out announcing the marriage on December 24 of Miss Clara Dean McBride to William B. Shaw.

Miss McBride is the charming daughter of Mr. and Mrs. William N. McBride of Fillmore, a popular young lady of talent. Mr. Shaw is well known on this side, and has a host of friends wishing him a happy married life.

The Chronicle joins in well wishing. The young married people will make their home at Delta, after February, 28th, 1920.

MRS HASKETT DIES.

Mrs. Milton Haskett died in Salt Lake at the L. D. S. Hospital on Dec. 20th. She was 39 years of age, and leaves a family of nine children, the youngest six weeks old. The body was taken to Nephi for burial. Three children have preceded her in death. The family came from Indiana 13 years ago. They have lived at Sigurd, Nephi and Mammoth before coming to Delta.

Mr. Peay of Nephi came to speak at the funeral, he having baptized Mr. and Mrs. Haskett when they were converted to the L. D. S. gospel. Another speaker was Mr. Hall of Sugarville. Bishop Maxfeld conducted the services.

DELTA NEWS NOTES

The stores will remain open every night until 7 o'clock from now until Xmas.

—)(—

The new barber shop will be ready for business this week, in the First National Bank Building.

—)(—

"DADDY LONG LEGS" on New Year's Eve, at the Lincoln Theater—Mary Pickford's greatest play.

—)(—

Bruce Anderson, bookkeeper for the Delta Lumber Co., was called to Salt Lake City on account of the illness of his mother.

—)(—

All the teachers left Friday and Saturday to attend Teachers' Institute, and from there to go to their respective homes, for Xmas cheer with Paw and Maw.

—)(—

Must sell at once—a high grade, upright Gabler piano, in good condition. Very reasonable price An unusual bargain. Inquire of Mrs. Chidester, or 'phone 10-2.   d25

—)(—

The little child of Mr. Dotson got a severe burn a few days ago by falling on a hot stove. Help to the family, work of which falls upon a young girl of thirteen, will be a kindness which will be deeply appreciated.

Among the young persons back from school, to visit over Christmas with their parents are the Misses Harriet Ward, Flora Steele, Wealthy Beckwith, Dycia Law, Mildred Clark, Ida and Ada Underhill, Cecil Seerer, Wanda Boyack, and Fred Clark.

—)(—

N. B. Dresser left for Salt Lake City last Friday, to spend three months in full enjoyment of his earnings made at the factory during the campaign just ended. Were he an editor instead of an ex-editor, he could spend all his summer's earnings in three days, not three months.

—)(—

Undoubtedly it will be of interest to the people of this locality to know that Mrs. Minnie Iverson Hodapp, a sister of Mrs. Wm. N. Gardner, was awarded the prize for the Christmas poem published in the Deseret Christmas News. Mrs. Hodapp is well known here, having taught school for two years in Deseret.

—)(—

That Delta is a good business point and that our farmers are doing well

is seen in the report of the Con. Wagon, who had cash sales amounting to $2200 on Tuesday the 16th, which was pay day at the factory. Their total deposit the next day, cash and credit sales paid up, was over $4,000.

—)(—

Jeff. H. Howell, the Utah bandit who was recently shot in the leg while robbing a bank in California, was a buddy in the Spanish-American War, serving on duty in the Philippines with Marion Grundy, Geo. H. Morrison, and Arthur Dennis, all Delta men.

—)(—

An interesting letter was received by the editor from Captain H. E. Soule, who owns land on the north bench, under the Sevier system. The Captain had just returned to Boston, from a trip to Athens Greece, taking a ship load of flour from Montreal, and stopped at Malta, Gibralter, Spain and the Azores. He remarks that he expects to start on another voyage soon.

—)(—

If you want to make a very nifty, and yet extremely practical gift this Xmas, make it a Thrift Stamp. The utility of this is easily apparent, and the gift will prove a most worthy one.

Personal Items

James A. Melville is a Delta visitor this week.

—)(—

Messrs. William and Louis Wetzel are visitors at the home of their cousin, James Faust.

—)(—

Miss Verna Nelson arrived home Sunday from Salt Lake, to spend the holidays at home.

—)(—

Mr. and Mrs. R. A. Nelson left for California on the 18th, for a visit of several months.

—)(—

George Searle is in town, visiting with his relatives on the South Tract, Mr. and Mrs. J. H. Peterson.

—)(—

Albert Robison and Bert Trimble of Fillmore were Delta visitors last week.

—)(—

Wm. Titus of the North Tract left for California to visit with his father and other kin folks.

—)(—

Miss Battson arrived in Delta Sunday night to spend some time here visiting with her brother, Mr. Battson, of Wadleigh-Battson Co.,

—)(—

Mr. C. G. Hoyt left Sunday for Wayne, Ill., to join Mrs. Hoyt in a visit to his and her folks. Commodore will remain there several weeks.

For used cars, see P. H. Robison.

—)(—

Mrs. Ethel Lambert and her small daughter Vay will arrive in Delta the day after Xmas, to spend New Year with her parents, Mr. and Mrs. A. B. Ward.

—)(—

I expect a car of corn in this week; those who will leave their orders now, and go to the car and get their stuff, will get a cheaper price.
L. E. Perrin, Delta.

—)(—

Mrs. L. Anderson went to California Saturday to remain. She has been much troubled by rheumatism which it is hoped will be relieved by this change.

—)(—

Miss Reva Gardner left Delta for her home in Salem to spend the holidays. Miss Gardner expects to be back with us again in the very near future.

—)(—

Miss Rama Rowley, the accomplished young "devil" of The Progress print shop at Fillmore was a Delta visitor Sunday, en route to Milford and from there to Salt Lake City.

—)(—

Mrs. F. N. Davis has received plenty of Holly and Mistletoe. Fresh fruits, nuts, figs, and California products will be received Monday and another shipment Wednesday, so that everything will be strictly fresh. Her shop will be open Xmas day to 10:30 o'clock.   adv.

We want every discharged Soldier, Sailor and Marine to join us, as there are benefits to be derived by sticking together. Hang together, Buddies.
GEO. A. FAUST, Chairman,
Delta Post No. 91, American Legion.

—)(—

Dr. and Mrs. I. W. Waite, from Salt Lake City are Delta visitors. They are en route to St. George for the winter, but will spend the holidays in Delta as guests of Mr. and Mrs. Walter M. Gardner.

JURY LIST FOR 1920

IN THE DISTRICT COURT OF THE FIFTH JUDICIAL DISTRICT OF THE STATE OF UTAH IN AND FOR THE COUNTY OF MILLARD. List of Names from which the grand and petit jurors shall be drawn to serve in the District Court, in and for the County of Millard, State of Utah, during the next succeeding calendar year, to-wit.

ABRAHAM
No. 1, John W. Fullmer, Abraham, Utah, No. 2, Charles M. Hickman, Abraham, Utah.

BLACK ROCK
No. 3, Walter James, Black Rock, Utah.

BURBANK
No. 4. E. W. Clay, Burbank, Utah.

CLEAR LAKE
No. 5. Barclay John, Clear Lake, Utah

DELTA
No. 6 J. Avery Bishop, Delta, Utah.
No 7 Ervin Jeffery, Delta, Utah.
No. 8. Abner Johnson, Delta, Utah.
No. 9 Burt F. Johnson, Delta, Utah.
No. 10. W. L Allred, Delta, Utah.
No 11 J. E. Works, Delta, Utah.
No 12. Charles A Ashby, Delta, Utah
No. 13. Morton Kilpack, Delta, Utah.

DESERET
No. 14. Earl Cropper, Deseret, Utah
No. 15. John Rogers, Deseret, Utah
No 16. Peter Erickson, Deseret, Utah.

No. 17 Thomas B. Allred, Deseret, Utah.
No 18. Warren W. Moody, Deseret, Ut.
No. 19 John M. Cahoon, Deseret, Ut.
No. 20. John H. Wesetrn, Deseret, Ut.

FILLMORE
No. 21. William Frampton, Fillmore, Utah.
No. 22. Alonzo Beauregard, Fillmore, Utah.
No 23 Albert Dearden, Fillmore, Ut.
No. 24. Parker Smith, Fillmore, Utah
No. 25. O. L Robinson, Fillmore, Ut.
No 26 J W Swallow, Fillmore, Utah
No. 27. Miah Day, Fillmore, Utah.
No. 28. P L. Brunson, Sen., Fillmore Utah
No 29 P L Brunson, Jr., Fillmore, Ut.
No. 30. Jos. S. Smith, Fillmore, Utah
No 31 Charles Iverson, Fillmore, Utah
No. 32. Parker P. Robison, Fillmore, Ut.
No. 33. Verne Bartholomew, Fillmore, Utah.
No. 34 Lorenzo Hanson, Fillmore, Ut.
No. 35. Milo D. Warner, Fillmore, Ut
No 36 Wayne Robison, Fillmore, Ut
No. 37 William Critchley, Fillmore, Utah
No. 38. Antone Sorenson, Fillmore, Utah,
No. 39. Don C. Wixom, Fillmore, Ut.
No. 40 Rufus Day, Fillmore, Utah.
No. 41. Willard Rogers, Fillmore, Ut.
No. 42. George W. Black, Fillmore, Utah
No. 43 James W. Payne, Fillmore, Ut.
No. 44 James Mitchell, Fillmore, Ut.
No. 45. Wm. N. McBride, Fillmore, Ut

GARRISON
No. 46. Thomas Dearden, Fillmore, Utah.

HINCKLEY
No. 47. William Stapley, Hinckley, Utah.
No. 48. Don Bishop, Hinckley, Utah
No. 49. Peter G. Peterson, Hinckley, Utah.
No. 50. John H. Hilton, Hinckley, Ut.
No. 51. T. Geo. Theobald, Hinckley, Utah.
No. 52. William Webb, Hinckley, Ut.
No. 53. R. F Robinson, Hinckley, Ut

HOLDEN
No. 54. Bruce Johnson, Holden, Utah.
No. 55. Ambrose Hunter, Holden, Ut.
No. 56. Bruce S. Stephenseon, Holden Utah.
No. 57 Jas. T. Stephenson, Holden, Ut
No 58 Mark Johnson, Holden, Utah
No. 59. Lloyd Porter, Holden, Utah
No. 60. Austin G. Ashby, Holden, Ut.
No 61 Edgar Turner, Holden, Utah

KANOSH
No. 62. Weldo George, Kanosh, Utah.
No. 63. Henry Whitcott, Kanosh, Ut.
No. 64 Guy Bement, Kanosh, Utah
No 65 D. S. Dorrity, Kanosh, Utah
No. 66. Ahinadi Abraham, Kanosh, Ut
No. 67. Collie Charlesworth, Kanosh, Utah.
No 68 E. T. Rappleye, Kanosh, Utah
No 69 Harvey Cummings, Kanosh, Ut
No 70 William Watts, Kanosh, Utah
No. 71. Henry Paxton, Kanosh, Utah
No 72 Roy Rollins, Kanosh, Utah
No 73 Lewis Barney, Kanosh, Utah

LEAMINGTON
No. 74. Rodney B. Ashby, Leamington, Utah
No 75 William Bradfield, Leamington, Uath
No 76 Heber Sorenson, Leamington, Utah.
No 77 Lewis Stout, Leamington, Ut.

LYNNDYL
No. 78 Alfred Johnson, Lynndyl, Ut.
No. 79 John Greathouse, Lynndyl, Ut

MEADOW
No 80 Emil Pearson, Meadow, Utah
No 81. Elias Edwards, Meadow, Uath
No 82. Rodney Stott, Meadow, Uath
No 83. Heber Beckstrand, Meadow, Utah.
No 84. Joseph Fisher, Meadow, Utah
No. 85. Daniel Bushnell, Jr., Meadow, Utah.
No 86. Joseph L. Stott, Meadow, Ut.
No 87 Howard Bushnell, Meadow, Ut

MALONE
No. 88. H. E. Adam, Malone, Utah

OAK CITY
No 89, Charles Roper, Oak City, Ut.
No. 90 Soren Christensen, Oak City,
No 91 J. R. Peterson, Oak City Uath
No 92 William Lovell, Oak City, Uath
No 93 Wm. G. Finlinson, Oak City, Utah.
No 94 Eddie Dutson, Oak City, Uath
No 95 John Lovell, Oak City, Uath

OASIS
No. 96. Sims M. Hawley, Oasis, Uath
No. 97 Nephi Peterson, Oasis, Uath
No. 98 John V. Styler, Oasis, Uath
No. 99 Henry Jackson, Oasis, Utah.

SCIPIO
No 100 Ourila E. Johnson, Scipio, Ut
No 101 Wm. Hailstone, Scipio, Utah
No 102 Wm. R. Thompson, Scipio, Utah.
No. 103 Con D. Robins, Scipio, Utah
No 104 Lester Walch, Scipio, Uath
No 105 L areJenson, Scipio, Utah
No 106 George Monroe, Scipio, Utah

No 107 Leonard Robins, Scipio, Utah
No 108 John Hanseen, Scipio, Uath
No 109 James A. Memmott, Scipio, Utah.
No No 110 Samuel Memmott, Scipio, Utah.
No 111 James C Olson, Scipio, Utah

SUTHERLAND
No 112 G. I. Smith, Sutherland, Uath
No 113 Walter Roberts, Sutherland, Utah.
No 114 George A. Johnson, Sutherland, Utah

No 115 Simeon Walker, Sutherland, Utah.
No 116 Byron Jacobs, Sutherland, Utah.

WOODROW
No 117 H. F. Fredericks, Woodrow, Utah.
No 118 Albert Watts, Woodrow, Ut.
No 119 Mary D. Simmons, Woodrow, Utah.

SMITHVILLE
No 120 Isaac P. Robison, Smithville, Utah.

Made in the USA
San Bernardino, CA
14 January 2019